Moving and Learning

The Elementary School Physical Education Experience

Moving and Learning

The Elementary School Physical Education Experience

BEVERLY NICHOLS, Ph.D.

Associate Professor
University of Vermont
Burlington, Vermont

THIRD EDITION

with 634 *illustrations including* 20 *in color*

St. Louis Baltimore Boston Chicago London Madrid Philadelphia Sydney Toronto

Editor-in-Chief: James M. Smith
Acquisitions Editor: Victoria E. Malinee
Developmental Editor: Wendy Schiff
Project Manager: Patricia Tannian
Production Editors: John P. Casey, Suzanne C. Fannin
Designer: Rokusek Design
Manufacturing Supervisor: John Babrick
Cover Illustration: University of Vermont Media Photography Service

THIRD EDITION

Printed in the United States of America

Composition by Graphic World, Inc.
Printing/binding by Von Hoffmann Press, Inc.

Mosby–Year Book, Inc.
11830 Westline Industrial Drive
St. Louis, Missouri 63146

Library of Congress Cataloging in Publication Data

Nichols, Beverly.
Moving and learning: the elementary school physical education experience / Beverly Nichols.—3rd ed.
p. cm.
Includes bibliographical references and index.
ISBN 0-8016-7770-X
1. Physical education for children—Study and teaching. I. Title.
GV363.N53 1994
372.86—dc20 93-47616
CIP

94 95 96 97 98 / 9 8 7 6 5 4 3 2 1

To the Metcalf girls

Ev, Jo, Edna, and Do

and

My Mother

Lucille Nichols

Preface

Elementary school physical education has undergone considerable change in the past two and a half decades. Slowly we see emerging curriculum philosophies that put movement, skill learning, social skills, and fitness as primary objectives of physical education. This is in contrast to programs where learning activities was the primary goal.

Physical education's goal is to change one's life—to fill it with purposeful, meaningful, and enjoyable physical activity. The elementary school physical education program has a significant role to play in this endeavor. An important ingredient in a healthy life-style is regular, active participation. The elementary school physical education program fosters participation as it begins to build the foundation on which lifetime participation will depend. This foundation includes developing an understanding of the capacity for movement, skillful movers, and the social skills needed to interact with others in movement activities, as well as maintaining a body capable of enjoyable movement.

Knowledge about human movement is an important aspect of the physical education experience. Since one cannot be totally prepared in physical education for every possible movement activity in which one might participate in a lifetime, movement is essential to future learning. Learning to use the body and space in moving efficiently and to control force, balance, and time are important in moving effectively in any situation and essential to becoming physically educated. Higher order thinking skills are involved in this process as children explore, analyze, and problem solve, using critical thinking skills in responding to movement challenges posed by the teacher or the activity itself.

The elementary school years are important for motor skill development. During this time children master fundamental motor skills and are introduced to beginning dance and sport skills to encourage their continuing participation. Activities to practice skills include not only those for improvement of technique but also those that lead to greater understanding of how the body is used and how skills are adapted under varying conditions.

Although there is recognition of the need for physical activity throughout life, studies continue to report a relatively inactive life-style among children and adolescents. A significant number of physicians involved in sports medicine are beginning to focus concern on the activity habits of children. Since activity habits are established early in life, physical education has an important role in teaching children about fitness and the effects of exercise on the human body, as well as providing vigorous activity and teaching children motor skills for use outside of school. The development and maintenance of health-related physical fitness are integral aspects of physical education, as presented in this text. Activities that maximize participation for children in vigorous activity to ensure the development of all aspects of health-related physical fitness are found throughout the text. Emphasis is given to developing fitness activities within each unit of instruction to help children learn how fitness may be developed and maintained in activities that are challenging and fun rather than through repetitive, boring exercises.

All teachers have the responsibility for developing children's social skills so important to participation in a democratic society. Physical education offers a unique opportunity within its more informal structure to enhance interpersonal skills, especially individual and group goals. Children first must learn to assume responsibility for their own behavior as well as to develop cooperative learning skills that enable them to interact successfully and appropriately with others.

As children are exposed to individuals of different cultures within the United States, as well as those of people from other lands, they will need to develop an understanding and appreciation of world cultures as well as their own cultural heritage. In addition, children will learn to work with the opposite gender as well as with children of varying ability. Physical education can provide an important laboratory that enriches children's understanding of others and themselves.

Sports and dance are important elements in our culture. The integrated movement curriculum developed in this text is unique in its approach to establishing the relationship between knowledge, motor skills, and movement activities. This is accomplished by first suggesting movement activities to develop understanding of human movement, an essential aspect of beginning physical education experiences. This understanding is then applied to the learning of fundamental movement skills and later to the development of dance and sports skills for use in and out of school.

This text blends the teaching of knowledge, motor skills, social skills, and fitness with the hope that greater understanding of human movement, movement efficiency, and the importance of physical activity to a healthy life might result.

WHO IS THE BOOK WRITTEN FOR?

This book is written as a text for elementary education and physical education majors studying elementary school physical education. Depending on the needs of students, it may be considered as a text of elementary school physical education content, a text for curriculum planning and teaching physical education, or a combination of the two.

In addition, the book serves as a valuable resource for teachers in the field, with its extensive coverage of activity content for use in physical education classes at the elementary school level.

SPECIAL CONTENT FEATURES

Several areas set *Moving and Learning* apart from other elementary school physical education textbooks.

Integrated Movement Curriculum

The content and development of *Moving and Learning* is consistent with an educational philosophy that recognizes the relationship between knowledge and skillful movement. Chapter 12, Understanding Human Movement, is devoted to activities to be used in introducing the movement concepts to children. In each activity chapter, movement concepts important for success are identified, and activities to enhance development are suggested. Throughout the book, movement concepts are mapped to show progression in learning and specific outcomes to be achieved. Activities are included for each outcome identified. Emphasis on increasing awareness of one's movement potential and the use of other movement concepts are stressed in all activities included in the text. Activities are used as the means for furthering understanding of human movement rather than as ends in themselves.

Concept mapping is used to identify the movement content important in the development and use of motor skills and in successful play in various activities. These maps enable teachers to identify concepts common to a variety of activities in planning for the transfer of learning.

Developmental Approach and Levels

The developmental approach emphasizes progression in learning as a result of maturation and experience rather than age alone. Since the movement experiences of children differ considerably from one school setting to another, expectations for performance vary for children in any particular class from school to school. This approach also recognizes the great variability within any one particular group of children. It assists the teacher in identifying developmental needs of the particular group. Throughout the book, selection of activities is based on four developmental levels rather than grade levels, which tend to overlook the individual needs of children. Each developmental level includes expectations for motor, cognitive, and social development as well as health-related physical fitness.

Learning Process

Children move through several learning processes as they develop motor skills and knowledge. In planning and conducting physical education experiences, teachers need to identify the level of learning achieved in order to select learning experiences that challenge children at different stages of development. Five learning processes are identified. At the beginning level, children first perceive the task and then move on to refine it. As skill and knowledge improve, children learn to vary their responses as the situation requires and to apply what they have learned to a variety of movement activities. The highest level of learning results in the creation of new movements. Chapter 3, The Elementary School Physical Education Program, introduces the learning processes that are further developed in the activity chapters of the book.

The concept maps included in Chapter 12 assist the teacher in identifying the movement content associated with each learning process.

Social Skills

Although most elementary school physical education texts cite social skills as an objective of physical education, few devote much space to its development. If appropriate social skills are to result, physical education experiences must be carefully planned and conducted. Children need not only skills to help them fully participate in the family and society but also those social skills important for successful participation in motor activities. The Hellison model for developing social skills is introduced and developed under the appropriate chapter headings. As a first step children must learn to assume responsibility for their own behavior. This includes interacting in ways that are safe and not interfering with the learning of others. It is only when they have achieved this goal that they can learn to interact appropriately with others in learning cooperatively, resolving conflicts, and respecting others' gender, culture, and abilities.

They also learn skills important for successful participation, including sportlike behavior, playing fairly, and handling winning and losing appropriately. Unique to *Moving and Learning*, Chapter 14, Developing Social Skills, explores how to teach this important part of physical education experiences at the elementary school level. Activities that encourage cooperative learning skills are identified in Chapter 14 as well as in the activity chapters of the text.

Health-Related Physical Fitness

Chapter 15, Fitness, Stress Reduction, and Movement Efficiency, is devoted to health-related physical fitness, which is introduced as an important objective of physical education in Chapter 1. It includes each of the components of fitness and their importance to health, as well as activities to assess and improve each component. Emphasis is placed on making fitness fun while enhancing the health-related physical fitness of children.

Health-related physical fitness has an important knowledge component that needs to be identified and presented at the appropriate level during the elementary school years. Children's understanding of fitness should grow with their ability to grasp more complex concepts and relate them to their own activity. Children learn to analyze their use and development of the fitness components in a particular activity as well as the basic principles involved in improving fitness and the means of assessing fitness. This chapter stresses the value of maximizing the vigorous activity of all children in the physical education class. The knowledge to be developed for levels I through IV is identified in this chapter. Furthermore, the new Healthy People 2000 objectives are discussed with implications for physical education.

Variety of Activities

Moving and Learning includes a variety of activities for selection in developing goals at all developmental levels in the elementary school. Numerous activities are included to introduce and apply movement concepts and to practice motor skills. Additionally, a large selection of rhythmic activities, dance, games, and team sports lead-ups, gymnastics, and other individual activities are provided to enhance development.

Teaching Styles

A variety of teaching styles are introduced in Chapter 7, Teaching Strategies in Physical Education, with a special emphasis placed on those that permit greater decision making on the part of the student. Throughout the text, examples of exploration, problem solving, and guided discovery are found in movement challenges designed to enhance individual learning. The use of practice, reciprocal, and task teaching styles is also suggested.

In addition to selecting an appropriate teaching style teachers must learn to focus student learning on the lesson objectives. Steps in effective teaching are discussed to assist the teacher in planning and conducting the lesson from beginning to end to maximize learning for each child.

Evaluative Criteria and Teaching Points

A requirement of effective teaching of motor skills is the analysis of movement to determine individual needs. *Moving and Learning* develops a model for analysis and evaluation through the development of evaluative criteria or teaching points for each of the fundamental movement and sports skills presented. These teaching points also serve as points of reference for children as they move and analyze their own performance.

Games Analysis

In selecting games for children, it is necessary to examine motor skills, movement knowledge needed, and social interactions required for successful participation. Introduced in Chapter 23, Teaching Children's Games, the games analysis approach is designed to help teachers match games to the needs of the children in the class and to recognize the motor, social, and movement knowledge components for which they might be selected. This is accomplished through the use of helpful games analysis charts in Chapters 24 to 31.

Safety

Chapter 8, Safety, Organizational Strategies, and Class Management, helps establish the importance of a safe environment in physical education. In addition to concern for legal liability, the teacher strives to establish an environment in which children are encouraged to try new skills and to feel safe. Some activities require special considerations in planning to provide for the safety of all participants. Concerns for safety are identified in each of the activity chapters to help teachers in providing a safe movement environment.

Curriculum Integration in the Elementary School

All school subjects are enhanced by integrating learning across the curriculum. Physical education can contribute to learning in other areas. Other subjects can also enhance learning in physical education. Chapter 4, Teaching

Across the Elementary School Curriculum, examines how teachers in other subjects can enhance learning of physical education content (unique to this text), as well as how the physical education class can integrate material from other elementary school subject areas.

NEW TO THE THIRD EDITION

Many important features have been added to this edition. For example, a new emphasis on cooperative learning and activities that enhance cooperation are incorporated into the text. Chapter 14, Developing Social Skills, introduces cooperative learning, including the learning environment necessary and the skills needed to work cooperatively with others, the steps in developing cooperative learning, as well as how cooperative learning can be enhanced in the physical education setting. A few activities are suggested for developing cooperative skills including group interdependence for each of the four developmental levels. Additional cooperative activities that may be used to further develop these important skills are identified throughout the text by a "holding hands" symbol.

Conflict Resolution

Additional new content in Chapter 14 includes conflict resolution strategies. The section discusses the importance of developing these skills, how conflicts are generally resolved, the outcomes of conflicts, and the steps children need to learn in resolving conflicts with others.

Multicultural Education

Developing understanding of people of other cultures within our own society as well as throughout the world is vital to education today. Chapter 14 also includes a section on teaching about diversity. The chapter discusses the importance of a positive self-esteem in accepting others, developing an awareness and acceptance of diversity in school, and how stereotyping behaviors promote discrimination of persons who are perceived as being different. Goals for teaching about diversity are included as are some suggestions for helping children develop an understanding of others. Multicultural activities have been added throughout the text to further children's interest in people of different cultures. These can be easily identified by the "globe" symbol.

Critical Thinking

Marzano's dimensions of learning are introduced in Chapter 6, Learning and Motor Learning, with some guiding principles for encouraging thinking in physical education.

Chapter 7, Teaching Strategies in Physical Education, further develops this important aspect of physical education. Teaching strategies that encourage analysis and problem solving by the children are emphasized. In addition, the section on creative learning has been rewritten to include critical thinking. This section also introduces the steps involved in the process, the relationship between the integrated movement curriculum and thinking, and basic principles for the development of critical thinking skills in physical education.

Integration of Subjects in the Elementary School

New Chapter 4, Teaching Across the Elementary School Curriculum, has been added. This chapter discusses the new thrust in education in integrating subject matter and offers some suggestions for (1) integration of the physical education content in other subjects, (2) integration of other subjects into the physical education program, and (3) development of school themes to which each subject area contributes. Several models for integrating subject matter are suggested.

ORGANIZATION

The book is divided into eight parts. Part One discusses the importance of physical education in the elementary school, its goals and objectives, brief history, recent laws that affect physical education, the changing needs of elementary school children, and the implications of age characteristics in planning and conducting movement experiences.

Part Two focuses on curriculum development. The relationship between knowledge of human movement and motor skills is established as the basis for curriculum planning. The developmental approach is introduced and the progression in learning processes examined. The integration of subject matter across the curriculum is presented. Suggestions for curriculum and annual, unit, and daily planning are developed.

Part Three provides suggestions for conducting physical education experiences. Learning principles and a variety of teaching styles are introduced. The dimensions of learning are presented with some guiding principles for encouraging critical thinking in physical education. Safety, liability, strategies for effective class management, effective communication, and measures for class control are discussed. The special needs of children and considerations for enhancing independence in learning are developed. Evaluation techniques for assessing student needs, teaching effectiveness, and the success of the physical education program are also included.

Part Four introduces the content for the four objectives of physical education—the study of human movement, the development of motor skills and social skills, and the enhancement of health-related physical fitness. Movement concepts of body awareness, space, and quality of movement are defined and a series of objectives developed through a variety of movement challenges. Fundamental movement skills are analyzed, evaluative criteria suggested, and a variety of activities presented to develop skillful movers. The development of social skills includes a progression for levels I through IV and strategies to enhance appropriate social behavior in general and in activity participation. Cooperative learning and conflict resolution strategies are discussed. The teaching about diversity is also included. The development of health-related physical fitness includes a discussion of each component, as well as important knowledge, tools for assessment, and suggested activities for their development.

Parts Five, Six, and Seven develop what might at first glance be referred to as the traditional content of physical education—gymnastics and other individual activities, dance, games, and team sports lead-ups. However, coverage goes well beyond that found in other books. Skills are presented with evaluative criteria, suggestions for teaching, common errors, and activities to use for their development. Activities are presented in order of difficulty. In addition, in a presentation unique to *Moving and Learning*, the important movement concepts are identified and activities suggested to further their development within the context of the activity itself. Concept maps in each chapter identify the movement content, and activities are matched with the concepts, as well as learning process, to help teachers select appropriate activities for their classes. Complete summary tables in Chapter 21 help teachers select dances based on developmental level, dance steps, formations used, and nationality. Games analysis in Chapters 24 through 31 help teachers match games to the developmental level of the children in the class.

Part Eight concludes the text with a discussion of extracurricular activities—intramurals, special events, open gym, and special interest groups. Guidelines for extraclass and youth sports are included with special concerns raised that must be addressed if these activities are to be used in the best interests of children.

LEARNING AIDS IN THE TEXT

A number of learning aids are included to assist the teacher and student is using the material contained in each chapter.

Part Openers

Each of the eight parts of the text begins with an overview about the material covered in that part, the relationship between its topics, and the importance to elementary school physical education.

Chapter Objectives

Objectives are listed at the beginning of each chapter to assist the student in identifying the chapter's key topics.

Second Color

A second color is used throughout *Moving and Learning* to highlight and identify important aspects of each chapter and facilitate student use.

Photographs

To enhance the presentation, numerous photographs including some in four-color are used throughout the text. Additionally, photographs are used to depict the movement sequence for many of the skills. These assist the teacher in analyzing movement and in helping children to develop the most efficient form.

Line Drawings

Illustrations throughout the text demonstrate and clarify various concepts and activities and are also used to show movement sequences for a variety of skills.

Boxed Material

Boxed material, including guidelines and examples, aids the students in organizing information discussed in the chapters and provides practical tools for future reference.

Chapter Summaries

Summaries at the close of each chapter carefully reiterate the main points and reinforce the chapter objectives.

References and Resources

Each chapter includes the most complete and up-to-date references for further study of the material covered.

Annotated Readings

Unique to this text, selected annotated resources are provided to enhance the learning process.

Glossary

Important terms are defined in the comprehensive glossary and are printed in boldface throughout the text. The glossary contains the page number where each term first appears.

Appendices

Equipment and other materials are needed to teach physical education. To aid schools in the selection process the following material is included:

1. Equipment for use in elementary school physical education with suggestions for care and storage
2. Vendors for elementary school physical education equipment, including a list of records and record companies for dance and rhythmic activities
3. Plans for homemade equipment
4. Computer software for use in physical education
5. Screening devices, sources, and IEP forms for determining student needs
6. Medical and accident forms
7. Tools to assess teacher effectiveness

SUPPLEMENTARY MATERIALS

An Instructor's Manual and Test Bank, A Lesson Plans Manual, overhead transparency acetates, Computerized Test Banks, and a videocassette complete the package of educational materials. This comprehensive package has been carefully planned and developed to assist instructors in using and getting the most benefit out of the text.

Instructor's Manual and Test Bank

Robert Hautala, Ph.D., of the University of Vermont has prepared the instructor's manual and test bank for this edition. Each chapter includes a chapter overview, behavioral objectives, the identification of important terms and concepts, a chapter outline with suggested notes and activities, suggested learning experiences and projects, annotated sources such as films, software, and additional readings for further understanding of the material and a test bank. Also included are more than 60 transparency masters of important charts and drawings to help in presenting material. The manual is perforated and three-hole punched for convenience of use. It is available to those who adopt the text.

Lesson Plans Manual

The Lesson Plans Manual is designed to give examples of lessons for elementary school children in a variety of activities and at varying developmental levels. Each lesson includes a statement of the day's objectives and the development of fitness, motor skills, and movement concept activities. Where appropriate, a culminating activity for the lesson is included to bring together the various parts of the lesson. Material is referenced to the pages in the text where the information needed by the teacher may be found. While a variety of teaching strategies are suggested, each lesson maximizes the activity time for each child in the class. Selected lessons are provided for various stages of each activity, enabling the student to see a progression in learning for each developmental level. The manual is perforated and three-hole punched for convenience of use. It is available to those who adopt the text and to their students.

Computerized Test Bank

Qualified adopters of this text may request a Computerized Test Bank package available in IBM and Macintosh formats. This software is a unique combination of user-friendly computerized instructional aids such as a test generator, record-keeper for grades, and date book for class management.

Overhead Transparency Acetates

Thirty of the most important tables, diagrams, and charts including twelve in two-color are available as transparency acetates. These useful tools facilitate learning and classroom discussion and were chosen specifically to help explain difficult concepts. This package is also available to adopters of the text.

Videocassette

New to this edition is a videocassette designed to illustrate learning processes and movement concepts relating to motor skill development. Children demonstrate the correct technique and common errors in the refining process as well as modifications of the technique when varying the skills. This unique educational tool is available to qualified adopters of the text.

ACKNOWLEDGMENTS

I would like to thank the following persons who helped in the preparation of the manuscript: Janice Lange for library research, and preparation of the index: Richard Farnham and Jon MacDonald for reviewing chapters in the book; Charlotte Leary, Betty Moody, and Eunice Aloise for typing and retyping tables and concept maps.

I would also like to thank the following reviewers who offered valuable feedback to me in preparation and refinement of the manuscript. Their considerable contributions are present on every page.

Sherry L. Folsom-Meek, Ph.D.
Mankato State (formerly at the University of Missouri)

Leon Green, Ph.D.
University of Kansas

Steven Grineski, Ed.D.
Moorhead State University

Kathryn Hilgenkamp, Ed.D.
Creighton University

Grace Goc Karp, Ph.D.
Washington State University

Amy A. Pettigrew, M.A.
Kent State University

Lynette Silvestri, Ed.D.
University of New Orleans

Thomas B. Steen, Ph.D.
University of North Dakota

Jacqueline A. Williams, Ed.D.
University of Illinois-Chicago

Rolayne Wilson, Ph.D.
Utah State University

A special thanks to my photographers, Arthur Huse, Joan Knight, Sally McCay, and Bill DiLillo, and to those administrators and teachers who let us interrupt their programs to photograph their children in action: Brian Hunt, Marie Froeschl, Anita Davie, Joe Johnston, and Cathy Anger of the Colchester Schools; John Concannon, Spencer Noble, and Chris Sears of South Burlington Schools; Robin Woodley and Claire Wilcox of Essex Junction Schools; Win Goodrich of Montpelier Schools; Chris Souliere and Cinder Thrane of Burlington Schools; Robin Markey, Janice Lange, and Pam Childs of UVM for their assistance with arranging photographs and reviewing the text, and Susan Schwager for sharing her writing in critical thinking.

A special thanks to my students for the inspiration they provided in the undertaking of this project and especially to Mary Jane Schmidt, who suggested the term *movement challenge*.

This book would not have been possible without the enthusiasm of those involved at Mosby. Thanks to Vicki Malinee and James Smith for their support in this project and Michelle Turenne for her help in the first two editions. A very special thanks to Wendy Schiff, my Developmental Editor, for her enthusiastic guidance in the revisions for the third edition.

Beverly Nichols

Contents in Brief

PART SEVEN
GAMES FOR ELEMENTARY SCHOOL CHILDREN

PART EIGHT
EXTRACURRICULAR OPPORTUNITIES

Contents

PART TWO
PLANNING THE PHYSICAL EDUCATION EXPERIENCE

PART THREE
CONDUCTING THE PHYSICAL EDUCATION PROGRAM

PART FIVE
INDIVIDUAL ACTIVITIES

PART SIX

DANCE AND RHYTHMIC ACTIVITIES

PART SEVEN
GAMES FOR ELEMENTARY SCHOOL CHILDREN

PART ONE

Overview and Value of Physical Education

Physical education is an important part of the elementary school program. It contributes to the overall goals of the elementary school as well as making its unique contribution to the study of human movement and the development of motor skills. It is concerned with the total development of children—their physical, motor, cognitive, social, and emotional development.

Each child comes to the physical education experience with a unique genetic and experiential background. Teachers carefully examine the age characteristics of individual children in their charge to plan and to conduct meaningful movement experiences.

OUTLINE

CHAPTER 1

Physical Education in the Elementary School

OBJECTIVES

After completing this chapter the student will be able to:

1. Describe the relationship of physical education to other aspects of the elementary school curriculum
2. Describe physical education as a developmental process
3. Explain the role of the teacher in establishing an environment for learning and fostering positive attitudes toward active participation
4. Explain the importance of physical education in the development of children
5. Describe the goal of physical education in the elementary school: preparation for a lifetime of physical activity
6. Explain the four objectives essential to meeting the goal of physical education: development of an understanding of human movement, effective and efficient motor skills, health-related fitness, and appropriate social skills

The challenge of American education is to optimize the learning opportunity for all children—boys and girls of varying cognitive and physical abilities and from diverse socioeconomic, ethnic, and cultural backgrounds. In doing so, the school strives to build a foundation of skills and knowledge for lifelong learning. While this is an important outcome in itself, skills and knowledge are not enough. The school must provide a model and setting that foster the desire and disposition to use the skills and knowledge outside of school, as well as beyond the formal school years.

ELEMENTARY SCHOOL EDUCATION

Physical education is an important part of the school's instructional program. It is the only area of the curriculum that presents motor skills and the study of human movement and provides the opportunity to facilitate their development.

All areas of the school curriculum, including physical education, strive to enhance the development of positive feelings toward lifelong learning by:

1. Helping children set realistic goals of achievement regardless of their ability and encouraging each child's self-appraisal of accomplishments
2. Providing for the needs of children at varying levels of skill and social development through a series of progressively more challenging tasks
3. Developing knowledge and a variety of skills that form the foundation for future learning
4. Fostering **critical thinking** and creative decision making through the use of **problem solving,** analysis, and the seeking of solutions in a variety of settings
5. Supporting learning across the curriculum
6. Fostering the understanding of other cultures, including Native Americans, and their contributions to society and the world
7. Teaching democratic ideals as children develop skills in working together, respecting, supporting, and listening to the contributions of others; and developing adequate communication skills

Although no significant relationship between the opportunity for physical activity and academic achievement has been found, a positive physical education experience may support learning in the classroom by enhancing individual attributes important to a favorable learning environment. In the Vannes experience in France, nearly one third of the school day during the elementary school years was devoted to physical education (Bailey). The experimental group (physical education) did better academically, were less susceptible to stress, were more independent, had good social skills, were more mature for their age, and had an outlet for controlling aggression as compared with the control group. Upon entering the secondary schools, these students were academically comparable with other students; in better health, stronger, keener, and happier; tired less easily; had better attitudes about school; experienced fewer discipline problems; adapted to the new school more easily; and suffered less stress. As a result of this study, the Ministries of Education and Youth and Sports in France concluded that physical education had positive effects on learning and should be regarded as an important part of the elementary and secondary school curriculum.

The move to restructure schools has raised questions about school curriculum. A more concerted effort is under way to integrate learning across the curriculum. Science and health classes provide background information regarding human anatomy, physiology, and nutrition, all of which are important to study in physical education. Physical education, on the other hand, can support work in math and social studies—for example, through taking various measurements in assessing fitness and keeping score and in learning about the cultures of other lands in a folk dance or international games unit. All teachers assist in language arts development as they help children develop vocabulary and communication skills. Restructuring has taken the form of organizing the curriculum around movement or adventure skills in some schools. Objectives for an elementary school can be found above.

In addition, classroom teachers may use movement activities in the classroom to provide variety in the learning activities for children and to help meet the young child's need to be more physically active. In these activities children learn and practice concepts important to reading, math, and other classroom subjects (Cratty). (Chapter 4 provides a further examination of integration activities.) Movement in the classroom is not a substitute for physical education, which has its own set of movement objectives.

ELEMENTARY SCHOOL GOALS

PROGRAM

This program places strong emphasis on the teaching and learning of basic skills while offering students opportunities to learn from firsthand experiences in the natural environment. The program educates the whole child through academics, physical activity, and other challenges and mind-stretching tasks that motivate students to learn and enhance their self-esteem.

LEARNING GOALS

1. To increase the student's sense of personal confidence
2. To increase mutual support within a group
3. To develop abilities that contribute to group decision making and leadership
4. To foster appreciation and respect for differences within the group
5. To develop an appreciation of the interdisciplinary nature of problem solving
6. To develop an increased familiarity and identification with the natural world
7. To increase ability, physical coordination, and joy in one's physical self

PHYSICAL EDUCATION IN THE ELEMENTARY SCHOOL

What Is Physical Education?

Physical education may be defined as the aspect of education in the schools designed to develop skillful, fit, and knowledgeable movers through a series of carefully planned and conducted motor activities. This definition assumes that physical education takes place in a special learning environment characterized by planned conditions that foster the overall development of children—cognitive, physical, and social. These experiences may take place in the gymnasium or multipurpose room, on the playground, playing fields, or other specialized playing areas. The experiences develop understanding of how humans move and how to execute movements that are safe, efficient, and effective. These activities are conducted in a way that encourages appropriate social interactions of children. The National Association for Sport and Physical Education (NASPE) definition of a physically educated person may be found on p. 5.

Intramural and recreation activities that evolve from physical education provide extended opportunity for all children to participate voluntarily in motor activities conducted before, during, or after school hours. These activities are generally, but not necessarily, taught in physical education. The development of after-class programs is discussed further in Chapter 32.

Developmental Physical Education

Physical education in the schools is developmental. Experiences at the elementary school level are designed especially for elementary school–aged children and are designed to match the cognitive, physical, and social needs of children at this level.

The physical education experiences are based on what we know about the needs of youngsters. It recognizes that children may be at different stages in their cognitive, physical, and social development. It focuses on the uniqueness of individual children and their needs. It emphasizes individual goal setting and assistance in meeting these goals.

These physical education experiences make no assumptions about what children have learned at any particular grade level. It allows children to begin learning at an appropriate level of difficulty based on their development and moves them to higher levels of skill and understanding.

History of Elementary School Physical Education

The earliest attempt to introduce physical education into the school curriculum was made by Catherine Beecher, at the Hartford Female Seminary. In 1824 she introduced an exercise program, which was conducted for 30 minutes twice a day. Although her efforts to establish physical education failed, another American, Dio Lewis, added beanbag, dumbbell, clubs, and wand activities, calling the program "light gymnastics." His system was adopted in Boston in the mid 1800s.

While organized physical education was being established in the late 1800s, the play movement was also gaining popularity. Play spaces for children became a part of the landscape as states began to pass legislation recognizing the needs of children for a place and opportunity to play. This interest continued after World War I and the Great Depression years as government programs sponsored the construction of parks and recreational facilities.

In the early 1900s emphasis shifted from calisthenics, gymnastics, and dance to games and sports. Jesse Bancroft in New York published modified rules of games and sports to meet the needs of elementary school children.

The change in elementary school physical education in the 1920s to a movement-centered program designed to develop an understanding of the way in which humans move has been dramatic. Although many consider the movement approach a relatively new development of the past three decades, Margaret H'Doubler proposed that the study of basic movement was the foundation of all physical education in the 1930s. Movement fundamentals programs for women appeared shortly thereafter on college and university campuses, especially in the Midwest and East. These programs were often required for all female students as a foundation for future physical education experiences.

In the years preceding World War II, research in many areas of child growth increased our understanding of the needs of children. Ruth Murray, Dorothy LaSalle, Gladys Andrews, and others suggested a new elementary physical education curriculum with greater concern for the individual child's needs, the enhancement of creativity, and the development of an understanding of movement.

After World War II and the Korean conflict, there were periods of concern for our nation's fitness. In 1953 the Kraus-Weber Minimal Fitness Test published results indicating the low fitness level of American children in comparison with children in Europe. As a result, President Eisenhower convened a White House Conference, which resulted in the formation of the President's Council on Youth Fitness, renamed in 1968 the President's Council on Fitness and Sport. Since the Kraus-Weber test measured only flexibility and abdominal strength, a test of overall fitness was developed. In 1956 the American Association for Health, Physical Education, and Recreation (AAHPER) published its first motor fitness test of seven items with norms for girls and boys between 10 and 18 years old. Physical education programs reflected this concern; however, the emphasis on basic movement was never really lost.

Before World War II, Rudolph Laban, an Austrian dancer, went to England. Although his theory of movement was known to the dance community throughout much of the world, it was new to physical education. Known as **movement education,** this theory of move-

NASPE DEFINITION OF A PHYSICALLY EDUCATED PERSON

A Physically Educated Person:

HAS learned skills necessary to perform a variety of physical activities

1. The learner will develop body, spatial, and temporal awareness.
2. The learner will develop locomotor, manipulative, and nonlocomotor skills.
3. The learner will combine locomotor, nonlocomotor, and manipulative skills in movement, dance, games, and sports.

IS physically fit

PARTICIPATES regularly in physical activity

4. The learner will understand the benefits of regular physical activity and will enhance personal fitness.

KNOWS the implications and benefits of involvement in physical activities

5. The learner will be a knowledgeable consumer in the areas of health and fitness.
6. The learner will develop listening skills and safety awareness.
7. The learner will understand the general function and structure of the body.
8. The learner will understand, appreciate, and apply rules, regulations, strategies, and etiquette for movement, dance, games, and sports.
9. The learner will appreciate the aesthetic and creative qualities of movement.

VALUES physical activity and its contributions to a healthful life-style

10. The learner will develop self-confidence and interpersonal skills.

SENATE RESOLUTION 43/HOUSE RESOLUTION 97

To encourage State and local governments and local educational agencies to provide quality daily physical education programs for all children from kindergarten through grade 12.

Whereas physical education is essential to the physical development of the growing child;

Whereas physical education helps improve the overall health of children by increasing cardiovascular endurance, muscular strength and power, flexibility, weight regulation, improved bone development, improved posture, skillful moving, increased mental alertness, active life-style habits, and constructive use of leisure time;

Whereas physical education helps improve the mental alertness, academic performance, readiness to learn, and enthusiasm for learning of children;

Whereas physical education helps improve the self-esteem, interpersonal relationships, responsible behavior, and independence of children;

Whereas children who participate in quality daily physical education programs tend to be more healthy and physically fit;

Whereas physically fit adults have significantly reduced risk factors for heart attacks and strokes;

Whereas the Surgeon General, in *Objectives for the Nation,* recommends increasing the number of school-mandated physical education programs that focus on health-related physical fitness;

Whereas the Secretary of Education, in *First Lessons—A Report on Elementary Education in America,* recognized that elementary schools have a special mandate to provide elementary school children with the knowledge, habits, and attitudes that will equip the children for a fit and healthy life; and

Whereas a quality daily physical education program for all children from kindergarten through grade 12 is an essential part of a comprehensive education: Now, therefore, be it

Resolved by the Senate (the House of Representatives concurring), That the Congress encourages state and local governments and local educational agencies to provide quality daily physical education programs for all children from kindergarten through grade 12.

ment soon replaced the physical training syllabus as the basis for physical education in England.

In the late 1950s an enthusiastic group of Americans went to England for the First Anglo-American Workshop on Physical Education. At this conference and a second conference held in the 1960s, American physical educators were introduced to Laban's movement education approach.

In the 1960s and 1970s programs of movement education in the United States were developed and sometimes replaced traditional programs of games and sports. Other programs included the movement content in their course of study. Federal grants were awarded for the development of movement education programs in several areas of the country. In Plattsburgh, New York, Joan Tillotsin and others developed a model elementary school physical education program. Further discussion of the movement approach to elementary school physical education is found in Chapter 3.

Today the movement approach takes many different forms, all of which are based on Laban's model or some modification of it. Some programs emphasize movement content throughout the elementary school years. Others emphasize the development of motor skills, using the movement content to help children develop more skillful movement.

The Status of Physical Education in the Schools

In 1984 and 1985 the National Children and Youth Fitness Studies I and II were undertaken to study the fitness and physical activity habits of children ages 6 through 18. One aspect of the study examined physical education time allotment. Although 97% of the children surveyed were scheduled for some form of physical education weekly, only 36.4% of first through fourth graders, 18.7% of fifth graders, and 27.4% of sixth graders had daily classes in physical education. The average for all children was approximately three classes per week. Another 37.2% of the first through fourth graders had physical education only one or two days per week, compared with 48.4% of the fifth and 42% of the sixth graders. The average class period was 33.4 minutes for first through fourth graders. Fifth and sixth grade children averaged about 90 minutes per week of physical activity time (Ross, 1985, 1987). One of the objectives of Healthy People 2000, a statement addressing the health needs for the nation published by the U.S. Department of Health and Human Services, is to increase to at least 50% the proportion of children and adolescents in the first through twelfth grade who participate in daily physical education (Public Health Service).

Most states today have some mandate regarding physical education instruction in the schools. Many, however, are stated in very general terms, and interpretation is left up to individual school districts. On the national level several laws passed in the past two decades have had serious implications for physical education.

One of the most famous laws passed was Title IX of the Educational Amendments of 1972, which states:

> No person in the United States shall, on the basis of sex, be excluded from participation in or be denied the benefits of, or be subjected to discrimination under any educational program or activity receiving federal financial assistance.

Reviewing with children fosters learning.

The passage of this act provided greater equity of opportunity for girls and women in interscholastic and intercollegiate sports, as well as in physical education classes, with the result that physical education is often conducted in a coeducational setting.

Law 94-142, the Education of All Handicapped Children Act, commonly known as the mainstreaming law, was passed in 1976. This law specifically required that instruction in physical education, the only subject named in the law, be provided in an appropriate setting for all children with disabilities and that it be provided in the least restrictive environment based on their verified disability. As a result, disabled children who were previously excluded from physical education instruction have the opportunity for participation in physical education. Many of these children are in classes with their nondisabled classmates.

In 1987 Congress passed resolutions encouraging states to require daily physical education for all children in grades K through 12 (see the box on p. 6). These resolutions resulted from concern for the health and fitness of American children. Although the resolution does not require daily physical education, it raises the level of concern for the importance of physical education in the education of all children.

At the national and state levels, professional physical education associations are actively promoting quality daily physical education. The President's Council on Physical Fitness and Sport and the various state governors' councils support physical education in the schools through recognition of outstanding programs of physical education and other projects. The American Academy of Pediatrics urges parents and school officials to work together to maintain or increase physical education in the schools.

The Physical Education Teacher in the Elementary School

The elementary school years are an important time in the development of attitudes toward active participation for life. Although children enjoy moving and participate enthusiastically in physical education activities, these feelings may be enhanced or discouraged during the elementary school physical education experiences. The teacher is an important model in recognizing the importance of an active life-style. The teacher assists in the maintenance of positive feelings about moving. Positive attitudes are strengthened through the careful planning and conduct of the physical education activities. Positive attitudes result when children find success and the support of classmates and teacher. Further discussion regarding the establishment of a positive learning environment is found in Chapter 9.

The teacher sees the children in a more informal setting in physical education than in the classroom. Because each child has the opportunity to interact with all other children more frequently, social behaviors such as sharing and working with others may be observed more easily in the gymnasium than in the classroom. The health status of children may also be readily observed. Problems of posture, the feet, obesity, low fitness, and low motor ability may be first recognized during physical education activities.

When special needs are identified, teachers must make every effort to communicate their observations and share their concerns about individual children with other school professionals such as the psychologist, nurse, or social worker. The planning together of all those involved is essential if children are to get the most from their school experience.

GOAL AND OBJECTIVES OF PHYSICAL EDUCATION

Physical education encompasses a variety of individual and group movement experiences designed to meet the cognitive, social, and physical needs of elementary school children. The scope and sequence of these activities allows children of all abilities to be challenged as they move from simple to more complex movement experiences. Because a responsibility of schooling is to prepare students to live in a changing world, the program attempts to provide a foundation on which future learning can take place.

The Goal of Physical Education

The goal of physical education in the schools is to assist each child to develop attitudes, skills, and knowledge of human movement that will result in a lifetime of participation in physical activity. Physical activity has important implications for health. Physical inactivity is perhaps the greatest risk factor for chronic disease. Regular physical activity reduces the risk of all-cause mortality by more than 25% (Paffenbarger) and to increase life expectancy by more than 2 years over the population average (Pekkanen) as well as help to prevent and manage diseases such as osteoporosis and diabetes (Siscovick) and reduce the rates of stroke (Salonon). In spite of the evidence, physical activity of Americans has shown little if any increase in recent years.

The goal of physical education can be achieved only in an environment in which the natural enjoyment of moving is enhanced for all children—the poorly skilled, the "average," as well as the gifted. It is an atmosphere in which each child feels the thrill of achievement and where **self-esteem** is enhanced. These experiences promote attitudes that value physical activity as an essential part of one's life-style. Although most elementary school children enjoy being physically active, this interest is not necessarily maintained throughout life. The best physical education experience promotes lifelong habits of physical activity, thus reducing the risks of acquiring debilitating diseases and premature death.

Regarding the goal of physical education, Bain suggests the following:

1. Student enjoyment of movement participation is the central purpose of the physical education program.
2. Specific program decisions should be based on the contribution to student enjoyment of movement participation.
3. Programs should be evaluated by examining the degree to which they increase students' voluntary participation in movement activities.

Bain's conclusions do not imply that fun is the only concern in physical education. Children enjoy being physically active. They are challenged by progressively more difficult movement experiences. Carefully designed and implemented physical education experiences developed at an appropriate level of difficulty result in continued interest and enjoyment of participation in physical activity.

Only when we have achieved this goal will the impact on the lives of those we serve be realized and the value of physical education in our schools be fully recognized.

Objectives of Physical Education

The elementary school years are a time of continual change for the developing child. As part of the elementary school curriculum, physical education contributes uniquely to human development in the areas of physical growth, fitness, and the development of motor skills. It also contributes to social and **affective** development, as well as the cognitive component in the study of human movement. To meet our goal of preparation for a lifetime of activity, instruction in physical education must result in the following:

1. The development of understanding in the study of human movement
2. The acquisition of **fundamental motor skills**—locomotor, nonlocomotor, and manipulative—and higher level sports and dance skills and provision for their use now and in the future in a variety of activities
3. The development of an understanding of the importance of health-related physical fitness and the tools to assess, acquire, and maintain fitness throughout one's lifetime
4. The development of appropriate attitudes and social skills essential to successful participation.

Although some programs may emphasize one or more of these objectives, this text develops a model for developing all four.

The Study of Human Movement

Physical education is both a cognitive and movement experience. Through carefully planned physical education experiences, children develop knowledge about their movement that can be applied to a variety of movement activities during the school years and beyond.

The study of human movement includes knowledge

about one's movement potential, movement in space, and movement efficiency. **Body awareness** concepts include knowledge of body parts, joint actions, the relationship of body parts while moving, body shape, and the use of the body in communication. **Space concepts** include use of available space, moving in different **pathways, directions, levels,** and **ranges.** Movement efficiency referred to as **qualities of movement** concepts include the study of principles regarding the application and absorption of force and balance and the study of time and **flow.** These **movement concepts** are an important outcome of the physical education experience.

A child-centered approach to teaching these concepts provides children with the critical thinking and creative problem-solving skills they need to be successful movers throughout life. Children are provided with many opportunities to explore the meaning of these concepts as they respond to the **movement challenges** posed and develop a variety of possible movement responses.

Students will later use these same skills in the application of movement concepts to specific activities and in the analysis and subsequent decision making and strategy development of more advanced games. Their use is also encouraged in the development of dance and gymnastics, in which children learn to express their ideas in routines and original dances. Developing a flowing movement sequence and remembering it so that it may be repeated again and again are other outcomes of dance and gymnastics.

Other knowledge is also important in physical education. Information necessary to move safely is important as children learn to respond safely to a variety of movement situations and to modify conditions to ensure their safety at play.

Mastery of rules and knowledge important to success in activities is also included. As activities increase in complexity, the individual must learn to judge the conditions under which specific rules and knowledge apply.

Teaching this knowledge does not imply that children are seated in a classroom. Knowledge should be a part of the gymnasium experience taught at the appropriate time through activity. *The Basic Stuff,* educational materials developed by NASPE Council on Physical Education for Children of the AAHPERD, is designed to help teach the knowledge basic to our understanding of human movement and human behavior. Developing a better understanding of human movement and the movement potential of the body provides a sound basis for children to understand and learn to perform a variety of motor skills and to adapt them as the situation requires.

Verbalization of ideas, movement analysis, or a new strategy is as important to learning and sharing in physical education as it is in the classroom. Verbally identifying important elements leads to greater understanding. It also provides information essential to the teacher in determining individual needs. Although physical educators seek to maximize activity for all, they must also give children the opportunity of time to think, to develop their ideas, and to communicate these ideas to others.

Early correction of errors is essential in learning motor skills.

Chapter 12 develops the curricular materials for beginning instruction in the movement content. Activity chapters that follow suggest activities to further their development in an activity context.

Motor Skills

Early motor experiences of children vary considerably. Some children begin their school years with a wealth of motor experiences behind them, including the opportunity to attempt many locomotor, climbing, and manipulative skills. For others, motor experiences have been limited. Opportunity for activity alone does not necessarily result in effectively and efficiently executed skills. Instruction early in life is essential. The longer children perform skills incorrectly, the more difficult it becomes to unlearn faulty patterns and to use more efficient movements. Although many of the fundamental motor patterns, including locomotor and manipulative skills, are established before the child enters school, an instructional program early in the school experience, beginning preferably in kindergarten, is needed to ensure the refinement of these basic skills and the acquisition of more difficult locomotor and manipulative skills used in dance and sports activities.

The teaching of motor skills has been an important part of the physical education experience since its beginning. Elementary school children need exposure to many skills and a variety of situations in which to use them. Fundamental motor skills should be mastered first, before a child is taught more advanced skills such as higher-level gymnastics and sports skills. Many performers are limited by their own inadequacy of the fundamentals when they have moved too rapidly to higher-level skills. The physical educator's role is to challenge children to greater achievements by individualizing the tasks to be accomplished according to the child's current physical abilities. In developing a motor skill, a series of progressively more difficult tasks are developed, with each child beginning at an appropriate level of difficulty. Children may be given the opportunity to choose the equipment as well as the specific task to perform.

In learning skills, children should be able to verbalize the key points to success and to analyze their performance based on these key elements. To be successful, one must be able to diagnose one's efforts. For example, children who are not able to get the ball into the target might recognize they are not following through in the direction of the target. Chapter 13 begins the development of the content in this area of study, including suggestions for providing a variety of experiences for practice and integrating skill learning with the study of human movement.

Physical education provides the opportunity for all children to learn and practice motor skills. These practices must be well planned and organized for maximum participation at an appropriate level of difficulty and with appropriate feedback given to the learners to enhance their performance. Although game activities provide for some use of skills, they do not individualize the practice needed to ensure optimum skill development. The physical education classes broaden the child's repertoire of skills and the opportunities to use them. No other area of the curriculum concerns itself with the development of these important movement skills.

Physical Growth and Health-Related Physical Fitness

The relationship between human growth and physical activity is well documented. Physical exercise is an important component in the growth of healty tissues, organs, and bones. Muscles increase in size **(hypertrophy)** and strength with use, but **atrophy** with decreased activity; muscle atrophy occurs at an alarming rate with disuse during illness or injury.

Bones show evidence of increased mineralization as a result of activity. During long periods of inactivity, such as when broken bones are set in casts, decalcification of bone occurs; about one half of the calcium is lost from a bone in 1 week (Bailey). Activity throughout life is important to maintain healthy bones (Bailey, Smith).

Because exercise requires an increased oxygen supply to working muscles, the acceleration of breathing and heart action to meet this demand results in an increased lung capacity, a better exchange of gases, and a more efficient heart muscle capable of pumping more blood. Unfortunately, this is not a permanent condition; cardiovascular efficiency is reduced when exercise levels are lowered.

The human body was built for movement. Vigorous physical activity is required to develop a healthy body. With the increase in school busing and a more sedentary life-style, the only place where many children are encouraged to be physically active is in physical education classes. Although daily vigorous physical education is recommended, physical education classes may be available only two or three times a week in some schools. The physical education teacher must strive to teach the skills and knowledge important to active participation in an atmosphere that encourages their use in out-of-school play.

Health-related physical fitness is defined as the ability to perform strenuous activity without excessive fatigue and to show evidence of the traits and capacities that limit the risks of developing diseases or disorders that limit a person's functional capacity (Pate, 1983). Components of health-related physical fitness are identified as **cardiorespiratory endurance, body composition, flexibility,** and **muscular strength** and **endurance.**

Fitness is considered an important factor in delaying cardiovascular problems in later life as well as in the recovery from heart attacks (Powell, Sallis). An increasing body of evidence appears to link many adult health problems to inactivity during childhood. Autopsies of children show the beginnings of clogged blood vessels, a serious problem in adults with cardiovascular disease. Documenting the progress of arteriosclerosis in men, Rose states that the first signs may appear as early as age 2 years. As the disease progresses, it becomes a serious health problem by the early forties. High levels of cholesterol and triglycerides, two substances found in the blood, are commonly associated with risks in coronary heart disease. Blood levels of both have been shown to be reduced as a result of exercise (Bryant).

Childhood obesity, usually the result of poor nutrition and lack of activity, is another problem believed to be linked to adult health problems. The increase in childhood obesity in recent years is a cause of concern (Gortmater, Pate [1985], Ross [1987]). Obese children have special needs in physical education. Because added weight tires these children more quickly and makes vigorous activity uncomfortable, they tend to be relatively inactive, which impedes normal physical development. Physical educators must be sensitive to the needs of overweight children in planning experiences that are nonthreatening and that encourage them to move actively. They must help children to recognize their weight problems and to provide the support and guidance needed to overcome them.

Muscular strength and endurance are important in-

Children need the opportunity to explore movement possibilities.

gredients in performing daily motor tasks. Strong muscles protect the joints from injury and assist in good posture, endurance, and resistance to fatigue. Low abdominal strength is often the cause of back problems that plague many adults today. Weak abdominal muscles and inflexible posterior thigh muscles allow the pelvis to tip forward, resulting in an abnormal arch in the lower back, which is often accompanied by low back pain. Muscular endurance permits the individual to sustain activity over time without strain and fatigue.

Flexibility is an important component of good posture and sports skill performance. It is also important in carrying out daily tasks by preventing muscle strain and back injuries. Flexibility is relative to each joint. Individuals may be flexible in some joints and not in others. Differences in flexibility may be associated with the types of activities in which one participates. For instance, a successful gymnast or diver possesses greater flexibility in the spine than performers in team sports. Adequate stretching of muscles before activity is important to enhance flexibility and should be initiated in the upper elementary school grades.

Health People 2000 recognizes the importance of regular physical activity to health through the establishment of objectives focusing on an increased percentage of people of all ages developing a healthy life-style through regular physical activity. Physical education plays a vital role in the development and maintenance of fitness and health. Daily physical activity is a must. A program of progressively more demanding activities is provided until the level of fitness desired is achieved, at which time a maintenance program is incorporated. Physical education programs in the elementary school should promote attitudes favorable to an active life through fun-filled vigorous activity. Recent surveys confirm the low fitness levels of many of our school children (Pate, 1985).

It is important for children to develop an understanding of the body's need for activity and fitness. Studying the effects of physical activity on the body, including the muscular, cardiovascular, and respiratory systems, is a valuable part of the physical education movement experience. In an activity in which the children have been running hard and respiration is increased, the teacher might take a little time to talk about what is happening internally as children take a short rest. In an address to the Vermont Association for Health, Physical Education, Recreation and Dance, Dr. Norma Carr of Cortland State University suggested that it would be great if in a science lesson in which children were studying the human body, the children could say, "We already learned that in physical education." Knowing what fitness is, why it is important to healthful living, what the relationship is between activity and diet, how the various components may be tested, what their fitness assessment is, and how to improve and maintain an appropriate level of fitness are important to a healthy life. Chapter 15 further develops the components of health-related fitness and suggests activities for use in developing them.

Self-Concept and Social Development

Each person controls the development of his or her **self-concept** through action or some conceptual reorganization; each of us has an inner drive for self-fulfillment (Goldhaber). Children enter school with a self-concept that has been developed over their short lives through the fulfillment of needs and feeling of worth derived from their relationship with their family. During childhood significant others will influence children's feelings about themselves as the environment expands. Teachers and peers play a part in developing the children's positive or negative estimates of themselves.

Research into the relationship between self-concept and motor success is inconclusive. We do know children's self-concepts include feelings about their physical being. A pleasant physical appearance is valued in our society, as is physical skill. One might also observe that elementary school children with good physical skills are not only looked up to by their peers, but also are often the children assuming leadership roles at an early age. Perhaps their valued skill level gives them the self-assurance or confidence needed to lead their less able classmates.

Physical education can play an important role in the development of a positive self-concept. The physical education class is conducted in an atmosphere that emphasizes new learning rather than accentuates incompetency and values the progress of each child. When children come to school, they create a social position for themselves. The physical education teacher must set the stage so that the physical education experience is a positive one in which honest effort is valued by both peers and teachers, each child engaging in physical activity is successful, and children perceive physical education as pleasant and encouraging. Further discussion regarding the development of a positive self-concept may be found in Chapter 14. The perceptions children have about themselves are reflected in the way that they interact with others and therefore become an important aspect of their social development.

The social development of children undergoes dramatic changes during the elementary school years. During this 7-year period an egocentric five-year-old is transformed into a group-centered 12-year-old. Beginning social skills as well as the more advanced skills required for working cooperatively with others are learned.

Social systems outside the school also affect social development. The family, community recreation, and the media are important in this regard. Through the interaction with and the modeling of significant others, children learn to accept certain behaviors for themselves, which may or may not be the behaviors the school wishes to encourage. For instance, the aggressive behavior of certain professional baseball players toward their opponents or the win-at-all-cost attitude of some Little League coaches is not to be valued. The school can affect only those attributes that are reinforced outside the school setting. If the child encounters different opinions outside the school, little change will probably occur.

Children come to the physical education experience with varied backgrounds in social development. Some have had little experience in playing with other children, whereas others have had much experience in playing with brothers, sisters, or other children in the neighborhood. Some have learned to share, to take turns, and to play with other children of similar ages; for others this experience will be almost entirely new.

The informality of physical education classes provides a natural environment for the development of social skills and emotional control. Group cooperation, leadership, followership, and group problem-solving skills are an important part of the physical education experience. Good sportsmanship and emotional control are valued outcomes of programs in which competition is carefully controlled and winning and losing are kept in perspective.

Physical education is a laboratory for social interaction. In the early years, sharing equipment, taking turns, learning to listen to the ideas of others, following directions, developing independence in learning, and learning courtesy, cooperation, and responsibility are important in an environment in which individual skill development and movement exploration are achieved. Later years provide opportunities to interact in small and large groups in cooperative play. Group acceptance of everyone and group planning and decision making in increasingly complex social environments become important outcomes of the physical education experience. Cooperative learning activities focus children's learning on those skills needed to work with others in accomplishing a task. Controlled competitive activities in which opponents are equal in skill and emphasis is placed on performance rather than score should result in appropriate social behavior and favorable attitudes toward participation, since success and failure are kept in balance.

A recent focus in physical education is multicultural education. Games and dance activities provide children with an interesting environment to explore people of other lands and the many cultures and ethnic groups that make up American society. A number of activities are identified throughout the book that can be used to foster multicultural understanding.

Physical education has come under some attack regarding its claims of enhancing positive social attributes because there is little research to back up these claims. Merely participating in an activity does not necessarily produce positive social results. Too often the opposite may be the result. Sportsmanship and fair play are learned only through identification with and imitation of admired persons who demonstrate these behaviors. Havighurst suggests that character values and attitudes are well defined by age 10 and change very little thereafter. If this is true, then early physical education experiences may have more of an impact on the development of favorable attitudes and resultant behaviors than upper elementary school years. Chapter 14 suggests strategies and activities that encourage appropriate social behaviors and understanding.

SUMMARY

Physical education is an important part of the elementary school instructional program. Not only does it contribute to the overall goals of education, but it focuses on the development of the skills and knowledge needed to be a lifelong participant. To achieve this goal, it provides for the study of human movement, the development and maintenance of fitness, and the development of motor skills and appropriate social behaviors and understanding. Physical activity is the medium in which this learning takes place. Goals and objectives are not necessarily the automatic outcomes of the program for which they have been stated. Careful planning is needed if objectives are to be realized.

REFERENCES AND RESOURCES

Bailey D: The growing child and the need for physical activity. In Albinson J and Andrews G, editors: *Child in sport and physical activity,* Baltimore, 1976, University Park Press.

Bain L: Socialization into the role of participant: physical education's ultimate goal, *JOPER* 51(7):48, 1980.

Bryant J and others: The effects of an exercise program on selected risk factors to coronary heart disease, *J Arkansas Medical Society* 81(1):69, 1984.

Cratty B: *Active learning games to enhance academic learning,* ed 2, Englewood Cliffs, NJ, 1985, Prentice-Hall.

Dotson C and Ross J: Relationship between activity patterns and fitness, *JOPERD* 56(1):86, 1985.

Goldhaber D: *Life-span human development,* New York, 1986, Harcourt Brace Jovanovich.

Gortmater SL and others: Increasing pediatric obesity in the United States, *American Journal of Diseases of Children* 141(5):535, 1987.

Havighurst R: *Developmental tasks and education,* ed 3, New York, 1979, Longman.

NASPE: *Basic stuff,* Reston, Va, 1987, AAHPERD.

NASPE: *Definition of a physically educated person,* Reston, Va, 1990, AAHPERD.

Paffenbarger RS, Hyde RT, and Wing AL: Physical activity and physical fitness as determinants of health and longevity, In Bouchard C and others, editors: *Exercise, fitness, and health,* Champaign, Ill, 1990, Human Kinetics Books.

Pate R: A new definition of youth fitness, *The Physician and Sports Medicine* 11(4):80, 1983.

Pate R and others: The new norms: a comparison with the 1980 AAHPERD norms, *JOPERD* 56(1):28, 1985.

Pekkanen JB and others: Reduction of premature mortality by high physical activity: a 20-year follow-up of middle-aged Finnish men, *Lancet* 1:1473, 1987.

Powell K and others: Physical activity and the incidence of coronary heart disease, *Annu Rev Public Health* 8:253, 1987.

Prentice WE and Bucher CA: *Fitness for college and life,* ed 2, St Louis, 1988, Mosby–Year Book.

Public Health Service: *Healthy people 2000: national health promotion and disease prevention objectives,* Washington, DC, 1990, US Department of Health and Human Services.

Rose K: To keep the people in health, *JACHA* 22:80, 1973.

Ross J and others: What are kids doing in school physical education, *JOPERD* 56(1):73, 1985.

Ross J and others: What is going on in the elementary physical education program? *JOPERD* 58(9):78, 1987.

Ross J and others: Changes in the body composition of children, *JOPERD* 58(9):74, 1987.

Sallis J and others: Relation of cardiovascular fitness and physical activity to cardiovascular disease risk factors in children and adults, *American Journal of Epidemiology* 127(5):933, 1988.

Salonon JT, Puska P, and Tuomilento J: Physical activity and rise of myocardial infarction, cerebral stroke and death in eastern Finland, *American Journal Epidemiology* 115:526, 1982.

Siscovick DS, LaPorte RE, and Newman JM: The disease-specific benefits and risks of physical activity and exercise, *Public Health Rep* 100:180, 1985.

Smith E and Gilligan C: Effects of inactivity and exercise on bone, *The Physician and Sports Medicine* 15(11):91, 1987.

ANNOTATED READINGS

Croce R and Lavay B: Now more than ever: physical education for the elementary school-aged child, *The Physical Educator* 42(2):52, 1985.

Examines the findings of an active life-style for children and the benefits of activity to growth and development, physiological development, cognitive and academic learning, and psychosocial development.

Espiritu J: Quality physical education programs—cognitive emphasis, *JOPERD* 58(6):38, 1987.

Cognitive learning in physical education is more than learning rules, terminology, and court dimensions. It is integral in the development of a physically educated person. Emphasizes that teachers need to focus on cognitive aspects of movement, skill performance, and fitness.

Grineski S: What is a truly developmentally appropriate physical education program for children? *JOPERD* 63(6):33, 1992.

Discusses developmentally appropriate physical education and suggests some principles for program planning.

Osness W: Lifetime fitness—outcomes of an exemplary school physical education program, *JOPERD* 58(7):55, 1987.

Examines the potential outcomes of a well-designed physical education program based on research findings. Motor performance, metabolic performance, body structure, and psychosocial and cognitive outcomes are discussed.

Ross J and others: Are kids getting appropriate activity? *JOPERD* 56(1):82, 1985.

Report of the National Child and Youth Fitness Study to determine the degree to which children are participating in physical activity that will maintain functional cardiorespiratory fitness.

Seefeldt V and Vogel P: The value of physical activity, Reston, Va, 1986, *AAHPERD.*

A summary and interpretation of the content of physical activity and well-being. Reflects a review of literature concerning physical activity and its relationship to health, and implications for the planning and conduct of physical education experiences.

Stein L, Keeler B, Carpenter PJ: Helping children enjoy physical activity experiences, *JOPERD* 62(8):17, 1991.

Applications of research to help teachers understand outcomes desired by students in physical education.

Stroot SA, Carpenter M, Eisenaugle K: Focus on physical education—academic and physical excellence at Westgate alternative school, *JOPERD* 62(7):49, 1991.

A discription of a school where the curriculum focus is on physical education.

CHAPTER 2

The Elementary School Child

OBJECTIVES

After completing this chapter the student will be able to:

1. Discuss the changes in the physical, perceptual, motor, cognitive, social, and affective development of children during the elementary school years
2. Explain the implications for the selection and conduct of activities in the elementary school physical education program based on growth and developmental changes

To be effective in initiating changes in the behavior of students, whether cognitive, motor, physical, social, or affective change, teachers must have an understanding of the developmental status of the girls and boys in their classes. All aspects of human development undergo dramatic change over the 6 or 7 years children spend in the elementary school. During this time a period of steady physical growth ends in a growth spurt for most children. Motor skills become refined, and children begin to integrate skills into smooth, flowing movements. It is a time for active learning and cognitive development as children begin and complete up to one half of their formal education. While many children spend considerable time before the school years outside the home in some kind of day care, it is also a time in which the social environment for children expands as they move more independently outside the family, interact with other children more fully, and are more influenced by teachers and peers.

The terms **growth** and **development** are often used interchangeably in discussing the changes in the human organism from birth to death. This chapter refers to growth as a change in size and development as the process of maturation in which changes lead to more advanced use of particular mechanisms. For example, the enlargement of muscle is considered a process of growth, whereas the increased ability to use the muscle in performing tasks requiring finer control is a process of development.

As one looks at the various aspects of human development and traces their emergence through the elementary school years, one recognizes that although all humans follow a similar sequential process, each is a unique individual. Not all children mature at the same rate. There is a great variation in individual development, and these differences increase with age and experience throughout the school years. Many factors contribute to these growth patterns including, heredity, substance abuse, nutrition, and environment.

Although the topics in this chapter may suggest separate components of human development, in fact the child develops as a whole. A teacher who looks at children developmentally may find a child to be more mature in some areas than in others. For instance, individual children may have mature physical and motor development for their age and yet be functioning socially at a less advanced level. In planning experiences appropriate for children, the teacher must not make decisions based on only one aspect of human development but rather must look at the total child. In the past teachers have often used chronological age as the sole factor in selecting activities for children. A developmental approach will allow the teacher to better meet the needs of the children in the class through an examination of their developmental status rather than age alone.

PHYSICAL GROWTH

In tracing the growth changes in children during the elementary school years, one notes a variation in rate of growth of various parts and systems of the body over the years. At certain periods the growth rate is accelerated; at other times it is relatively steady. These patterns are predictable and are important to teachers in planning appropriate experiences for children. As one looks at these various changes, one discovers greater variation within each sex than between the sexes.

Height and Weight

Rapid increases in height and weight occur during infancy and again at the onset of adolescence. As children

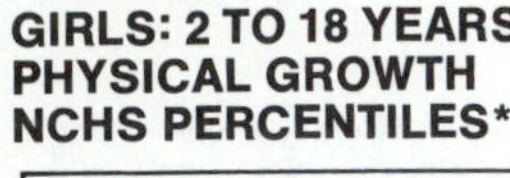

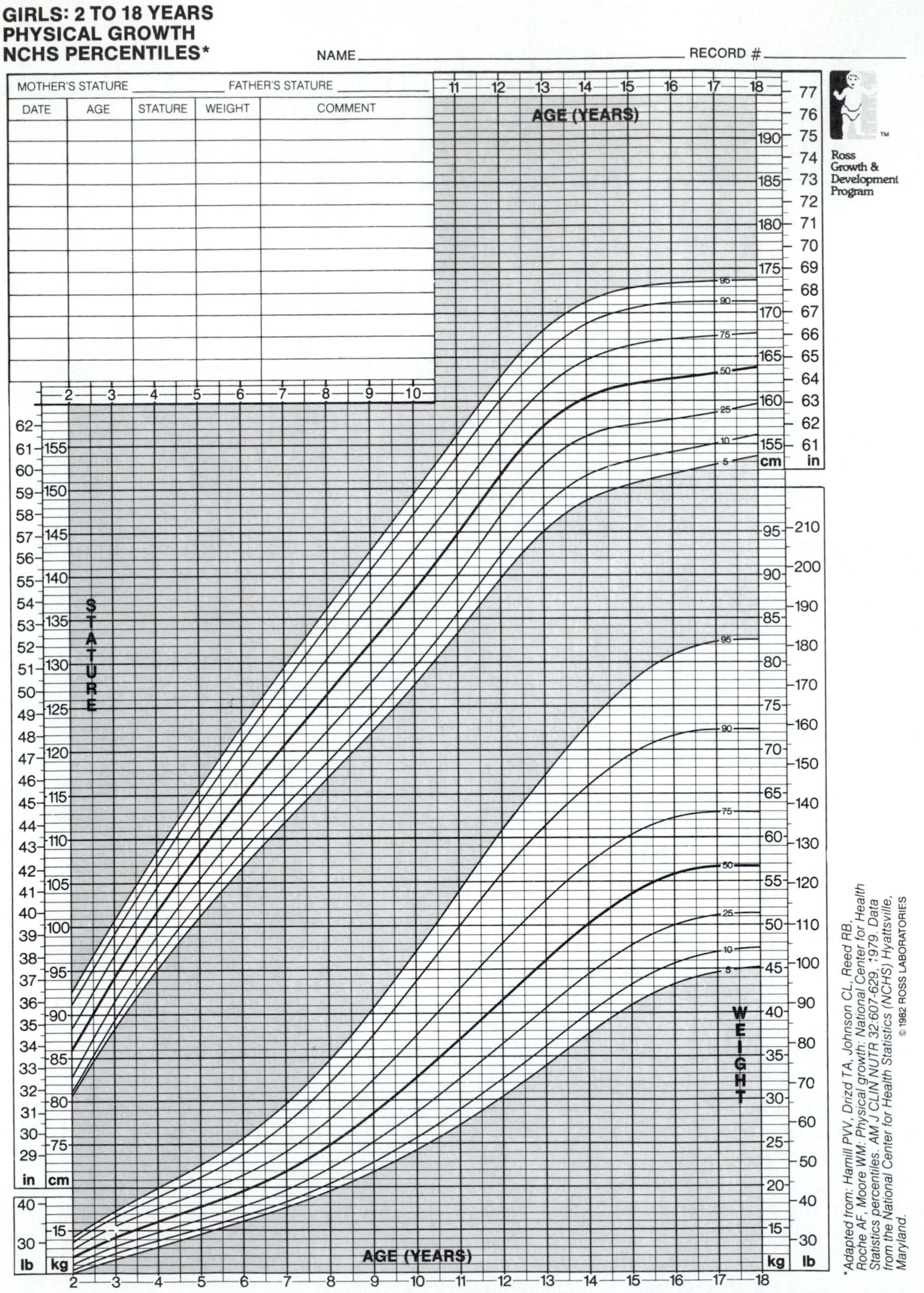

GIRLS: 2 TO 18 YEARS
PHYSICAL GROWTH
NCHS PERCENTILES*

NAME ____________________ RECORD # ____________

MOTHER'S STATURE ____________ FATHER'S STATURE ____________

DATE	AGE	STATURE	WEIGHT	COMMENT

AGE (YEARS)

STATURE

WEIGHT

AGE (YEARS)

Ross Growth & Development Program

*Adapted from: Hamill PVV, Drizd TA, Johnson CL, Reed RB, Roche AF, Moore WM: Physical growth: National Center for Health Statistics percentiles. AM J CLIN NUTR 32:607-629, 1979. Data from the National Center for Health Statistics (NCHS) Hyattsville, Maryland.

FIGURE 2-1 Percentiles for stature and age.

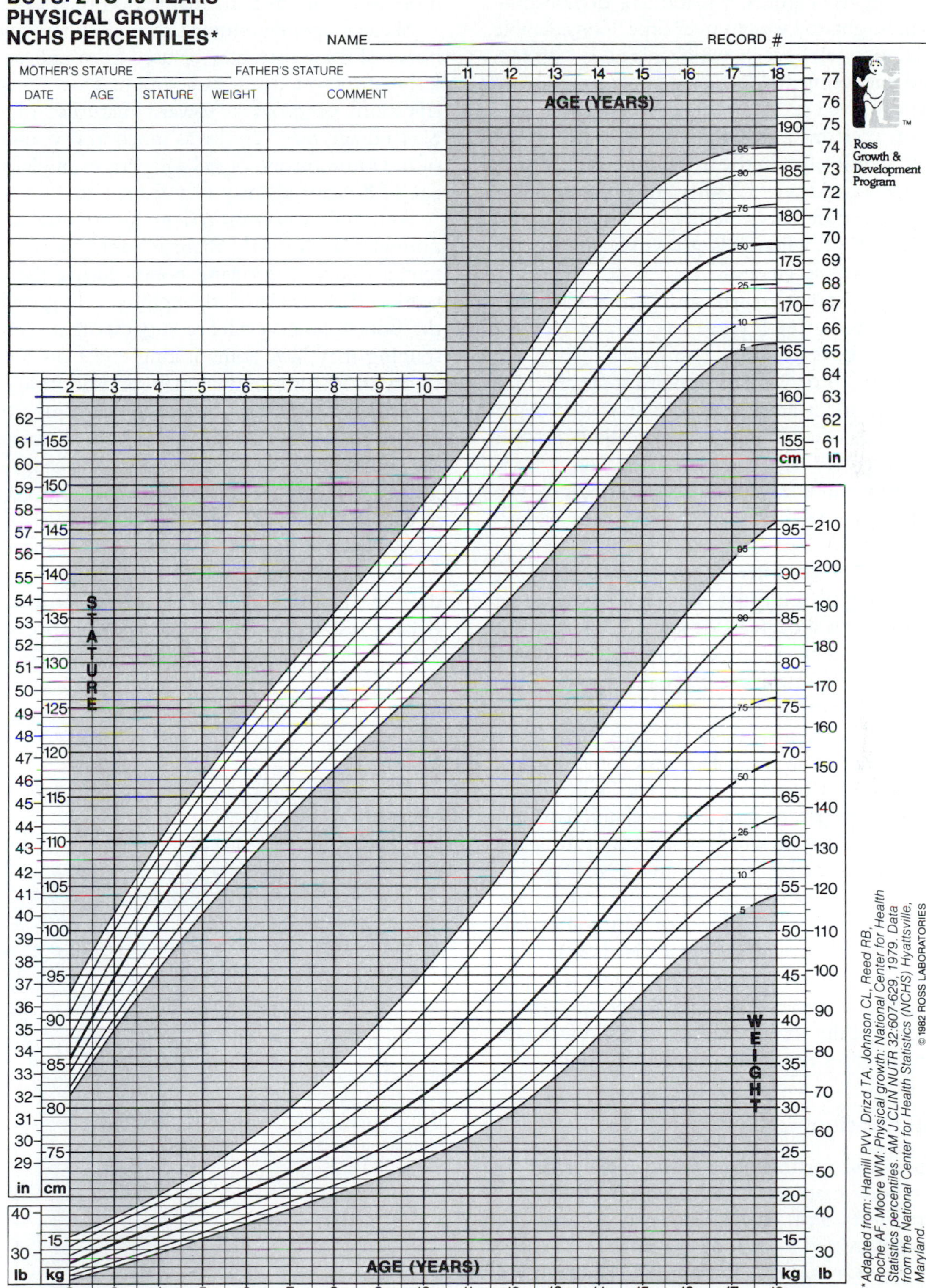

FIGURE 2-2 Percentiles for stature and age.

enter school they are in a period of steady growth that continues to around 9 years of age for girls and approximately 11 years of age for boys, when the adolescent growth spurt begins. Figures 2-1 and 2-2 demonstrate the changes in height and weight over time. Considerable individual variation can be seen, which increases with age. Heredity and environmental factors interact to influence these differences. Even greater variation can be seen during periods of accelerated growth.

There is little difference in the height of boys and girls until about age 11. At age 12 girls are generally taller than boys. These differences in height continue until around 13 years of age, when girls' growth begins to level off and boys' growth accelerates.

Onset of the adolescent growth spurt varies. Girls may begin the accelerated growth period as early as age 9 or as late as age 12; boys experience this period from age 11 to as late as age 13 or 14. This growth spurt also may last a relatively short or long time. Children who begin the growth spurt early tend to complete their growth sooner than those who begin at a later age. The result is that late-maturing children tend to be taller because they have had a longer period of growth than their earlier-maturing classmates.

There is relatively little difference in weight until about age 11, when the girls are often heavier. The girls' rate of weight gain shows a decrease at age 15, whereas the boys' rate of weight gain continues at an accelerated rate because of an increase in muscle mass. After age 15 the boys again outweigh the girls.

The period of steady growth in the early elementary school years makes this an important time for steady improvement in the performance of motor skills. Later, taller children will begin to gain the mechanical advantages of their longer limbs, which will account for some of the increased variability seen in motor skill performance. Awkwardness observed during the adolescent growth spurt is more psychological than physical as children adjust to the changes taking place in their bodies. Beginning in adolescence, the light individual will gain some advantage in activities requiring the body to move through space, and the somewhat heavier child will gain advantage in activities requiring object projection.

Skeletal Maturation

Bones begin as soft cartilaginous tissue and harden, or ossify, as the body matures. **Ossification** begins before birth and continues until late adolescence. At birth ossification has progressed to include the entire shaft of the long bones. At each end of the bone is a cartilaginous growth center called the **epiphysis** (Figure 2-3). Secondary ossification centers appear in the epiphyseal area. Between the secondary growth center and the shaft of the bone lies the epiphyseal plate, the growth plate, where the bone continues to grow until maturation. The appearance of the secondary ossification centers and the closure of the growth plate at maturation vary with the bone and sex. During these developing years, girls are more advanced in bone maturation than boys.

Skeletal age, determined through x-ray studies of the bones of the wrists, may be used as an indicator of physical maturation. These radiographs show the stage of ossification, or progress toward maturity, of the bones. Skeletal age may vary by as much as 6 years in children of the same chronological age. For example, the skeletal age of 8-year-olds may vary from 5 to 11 years.

Although vigorous activity is essential to stimulate normal bone growth, there is some concern about potential injury to growing bones during the developing years and especially to the epiphysis or growing part of the bones. Some evidence suggests that stress of overtraining may have some lasting effect on bone growth. Injury to mature children may result in little disturbance in the growth of bones, but epiphyseal injury to the young athlete may result in greater growth disturbance, since the younger child has many more years of growth before maturity. This potential problem is discussed more fully in Chapter 32.

Evidence indicates that boys more advanced in skeletal age tend to be more successful in motor activities than their less mature counterparts. However, this advantage is later lost when their later-maturing peers reach ma-

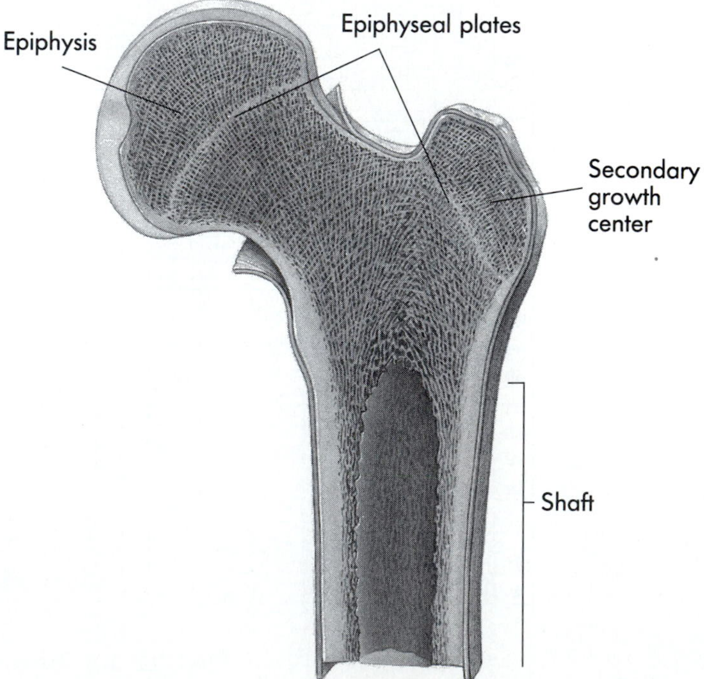

FIGURE 2-3 Bone growth.
Cross-section of bone showing growth centers.

turity. For girls the opposite may be true. In some activities such as gymnastics, delayed biological maturation seems to put late-maturing girls to some advantage over their earlier maturing classmates. One theory supporting this view is that performance for girls appears to peak at the onset of the menstrual cycle; thus the late-maturing girls have maintained more interest in participation in motor activities for a longer period than earlier-maturing girls (Payne). This loss of interest is probably due to social and psychological influences in our society regarding the participation of girls in physical activity.

Body Proportions

During the period of physical growth from birth to maturity, the proportions of body segments to total body size change dramatically. The head, which at birth represents one fourth of the body length, doubles in size but makes up only about one eighth the body length at maturity. The legs increase five times their length at birth to become about one half the body length at maturity. The arms increase in length four times their length at birth. The trunk triples in length. Body segments have accelerated growth rates of their own at various stages during the growing years. For example, the 4- or 5-year-old's short, stubby fingers will accelerate in growth, making object handling easier for the 6- and 7-year-old. Another example of varying growth rate occurs at the onset of the adolescent spurt in growth, when the legs increase in length at a more rapid rate than other body segments. This longer leg length affects sprint speed.

Another aspect of changing body proportions can be seen in the changing relationship of shoulder width to hip width, known as the biacromial/bicristal ratio. Differences between the sexes before adolescence are minimal, but during adolescence, a noticeable difference in this relationship is observed. Boys experience a widening of the shoulders, and girls grow wider in the hips in relation to their shoulder width. This ratio is relatively constant in boys between 9 and 18, but steadily declines in girls whose hips grow relatively wider in relation to their shoulders. The wider shoulder width in boys will give them some advantage in throwing skills. The girls' shorter legs and wider pelvis will give them an advantage in balancing activities because they have a lower center of gravity, but will be a disadvantage in both running and jumping activities.

Changes in body proportions also affect the location of the center of gravity, or weight center, of the body. The center of gravity is higher in children than in adults because children carry a higher proportion of their weight in the upper body. Boys have a slightly higher center of gravity than girls. As children enter school, the location of their center of gravity is in the vicinity of the umbilicus. During the school years it descends at a uniform rate to the pelvic area as changes in stature occur.

Because young children tend to be more top heavy with their higher center of gravity, controlling the body when coming to a quick stop, for example, may be difficult. Ball-handling skills, especially with large balls, may also be affected by this easy loss of balance. When an object is received its weight shifts the location of the center of gravity forward and upward, depending on the level the ball is received. This movement of the center of gravity may result in a loss of balance in the direction of the object, which causes the child to drop the ball after momentary possession.

Fat and Muscle Tissue

The rate at which fatty tissue is deposited in the body increases for a brief period from birth to the age of 6 months. It then decreases until 6 to 8 years of age; the decrease is more marked in boys. An increase in the rate of fat deposition occurs again just before the adolescent growth spurt. Another decrease occurs during the growth spurt for boys but not for girls. There are also sex differences and great variation within each sex in the location of fatty tissue. This difference accounts for the variation in contours between boys and girls and the variability of shape within each sex.

During the growing years, muscles increase in length, breadth, and width. The number of muscle fibers is determined primarily by heredity and will not increase much during life. Muscle weight increases about 40 times from birth to maturity. At birth muscle weight makes up from one fifth to one fourth of the body weight; by early adolescence it constitutes one third of the body weight and increases to two fifths of the body weight by early maturity.

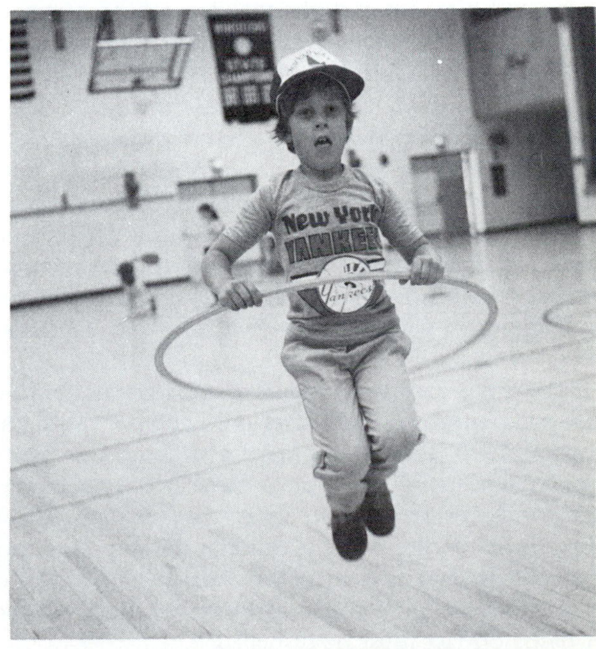

Vigorous activity is needed to stimulate bone growth.

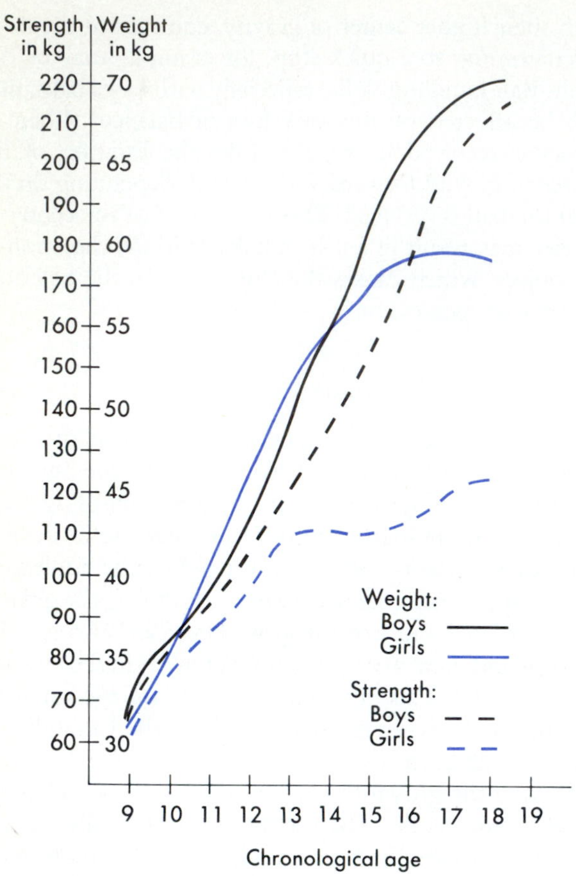

FIGURE 2-4 Weight and strength of school-aged children.

Muscle growth lags behind changes in height, so it is not possible to determine children's strength by their size (Figure 2-4). Children grow taller and heavier before they grow stronger. There is little difference in the strength of girls and boys before puberty, although boys may be slightly stronger. Both sexes increase in strength at the same rate before adolescence. Boys begin their spurt at around age 14. Girls begin approximately 1 year before menarche and slow down once again at about age 13. At age 13 boys have acquired about half of their adult strength, whereas girls have three fourths or more of adult strength, depending on the strength measurements used. At puberty, increase in the production of the male sex hormones influences muscle development. Early-maturing children are stronger than their later-maturing classmates.

During the early and middle elementary grades, because of the similarity in strength, girls and boys are about equal in physical activity, when the difference in size is considered. Girls often perceive themselves as being less strong and boys see themselves as stronger than girls. It is up to the teacher to help children develop a realistic view of their own movement potential to allow them to develop to their fullest potential. Perceived sex differences not based on fact must be dispelled.

Cardiovascular Changes

The heart rate, the number of heart beats per minute, undergoes much change during the life of the individual. At rest, children's heart rates are consistently higher than those of adults; the heart rate of a child under 6 years averages greater than 100 beats per minute. Girls tend to have a slightly higher heart rate than boys. By early adulthood, the heart rate has decreased to about 70 for men and 79 for women.

In preadolescent children the heart rate response to submaximum efforts declines with age. The higher heart rate of younger children is probably due to their smaller **stroke volume,** the amount of blood ejected into circulation with each contraction of the heart. Stroke volume is affected by heart size, contractile force of the heart, vascular resistance to blood flow, and the venous return of blood. **Cardiac output,** the amount of blood that can be pumped out of the heart each minute, is also less for children than for adults both at rest and while exercising.

Exercising and the ability to sustain physical activity over time create demands for more oxygen being carried by the blood to active muscles. **Maximal oxygen consumption (max VO_2)** is the greatest amount of oxygen a human can consume at the tissue level. This represents the working capacity of the individual. It is difficult to measure max VO_2 in young children because it is difficult to get them to perform at a maximum effort. When body weight is held constant, young girls have a working capacity almost as high as boys. Apparently, however, the rate declines with age, probably because of increased body fat, lower hemoglobin concentrations at puberty, and lesser degree of muscle development in the lower extremities (Payne).

Most children are highly motivated in physical education. They tend to work hard, so they tire easily; however, they seem able to regulate their own activity by slowing down until they recover and then going back again to full activity. Currently, there is little data about the effects of training on the cardiorespiratory system of children, although there is some concern about long-distance training for elementary school–aged children (see Chapter 32).

PERCEPTUAL DEVELOPMENT

Sensory **perception** refers to the ability to use input received through the sense organs to make judgments about one's environment. Most sensory perceptual experts agree that there are three major developmental trends in sensory perceptual maturation: (1) a shift in dominance of the sensory systems; (2) an increase in **intrasensory discrimination,** the ability to use various sensory input from a single sense organ; and (3) an improvement in **intersensory integration,** the ability to use input from several sensory organs at the same time.

As children respond to their environment, dominance

in the use of sensory input shifts from **tactile-kinesthetic** to visual. This shift not only expands the sensory input beyond the child's reach, but also utilizes a sensory system with greater facility for discrimination and increased speed in processing. At maturity there is greater dependence on vision than on other sensory systems. Although children do process visual information more slowly than adults, marked improvement in this ability occurs between the ages of 6 and 10 (Williams).

Visual perception plays an important role in motor skill learning and performance for young children. Williams has demonstrated that visual perceptual ability such as depth and figure-ground perceptions of 6-year-olds is important in learning gross motor tasks such as hopping and ball bouncing. Children with greater development of these perceptions began and maintained a higher level of performance throughout learning. The rate of improvement was steadier than for children with less advanced perceptual capacities. No differences were observed in 8-year-olds regardless of visual perceptual development. Thus it appears that these abilities may become less important as the child matures.

With age there is also a refinement in the sensory systems, which permits greater discrimination of sensory input. The child is capable of using more sensory data at any one time, can select the most relevant information, and can make more precise judgments about the input received.

In addition, children are able to use the information received from several sensory systems simultaneously. This process occurs concomitantly with improvements in intrasensory discrimination. In any situation they can use tactile, visual, auditory, or olfactory input in the perceptual process. In this way children have more information at their disposal to use in making decisions.

The perception of movement is important to success in physical education. The ability to make accurate judgments and to respond to projectiles depends on this ability. A number of factors influence an individual's ability to accurately track objects, including the object's speed, predictability, and trajectory. Balls moving slowly or very fast cause greater error. Wiffle balls or Frisbees offer challenge as the flight path is more difficult to predict, whereas balls directly thrown to a person rather than in an arc are more easily caught (Payne). Tracking ability can be improved with training. This perceptual skill undergoes marked improvement during the elementary school years. Decisions about the movement of objects cannot be made quickly and accurately until the age of 11 or 12 (Williams).

Body awareness and kinesthetic perception of the position of body parts and the body's orientation in space undergo varying rates of development during the elementary school years. Young children develop a concept of the whole body before they are aware of its parts. Children entering school often have some difficulty in responding in activities calling for the movement of various body parts. At age 5, accuracy in verbally identifying the major body parts is about 55%, whereas a 12-year-old can accomplish the task with 100% accuracy (Williams).

Physical education experiences that develop children's understanding of their own body parts and their potential movement are essential because body awareness is so important in motor skill development. Teachers can also help children focus on particular sensory cues as they move.

MOTOR SKILL DEVELOPMENT

The elementary school child is capable of controlled purposeful movement. These motor skills are generally referred to as **psychomotor skills** because they are voluntary actions initiated by impulses from higher brain centers in the motor cortex of the brain. This is in contrast to those reflex actions, which are initiated in lower brain centers or the central nervous system. Many locomotor skills are well established by the time the child enters school. Walking, running, jumping, and hopping, which are executed in an even rhythm, may be accomplished with perhaps only a few mechanical errors such as foot placement or use of the arms. Some children entering school may not have yet mastered skipping or galloping, which are more complex patterns of movement in which two locomotor movements are combined and performed in an uneven rhythm. Girls tend to skip earlier than boys, but boys may show greater ability in the gallop.

Throwing and striking skills vary more during the elementary school years, with boys demonstrating some-

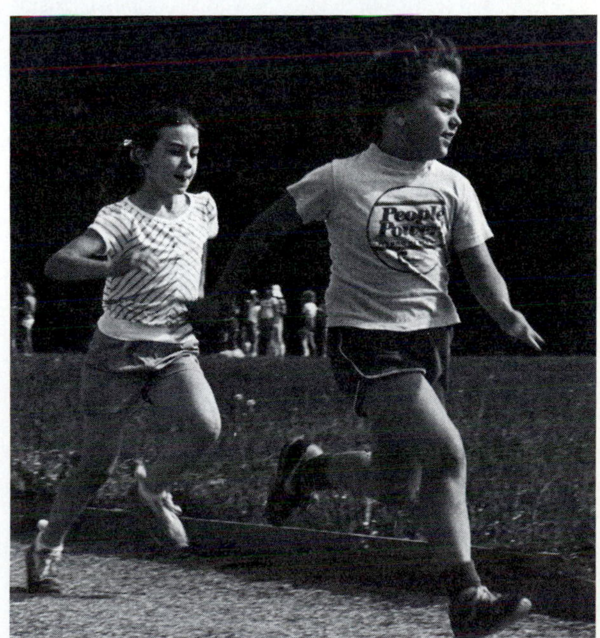

Running is well established by the time the child enters school.

DEVELOPMENTAL SEQUENCES FOR RUNNING

LEG ACTION COMPONENT

Step 1. The run is flat-footed with minimum flight. The swing leg is slightly abducted as it comes forward. When seen from overhead, the path of the swing leg curves out to the side during its movement forward. Foot eversion gives a toeing-out appearance to the swinging leg. The angle of the knee of the swing leg is greater than 90 degrees during forward motion.

Step 2. The swing thigh moves forward with greater acceleration, causing 90 degrees of maximum flexion in the knee. From the rear, the foot is no longer toed-out nor is the thigh abducted. The sideward swing of the thigh continues, however, causing the foot to cross the body midline when viewed from the rear. Flight time increases. After contact, which may still be flat-footed, the support knee flexes more as the child's weight rides over the foot.

Step 3. Foot contact is with the heel or the ball of the foot. The forward movement of the swing leg is primarily in the sagittal plane. Flexion of the thigh at the hip carries the knee higher at the end of the forward swing. The support leg moves from flexion to complete extension by takeoff.

ARM ACTION COMPONENT

Step 1. The arms do not participate in the running action. They are sometimes held in high guard or, more frequently, middle guard position. In high guard, the hands are held about shoulder high. Sometimes they ride even higher if the laterally rotated arms are abducted at the shoulder and the elbows flexed. In middle guard, the lateral rotation decreases, allowing the hands to be held waist high. They remain motionless, except in reaction to shifts in equilibrium.

Step 2. Spinal rotation swings the arms bilaterally to counterbalance rotation of the pelvis and swing leg. The frequently oblique plane of motion plus continual balancing adjustments give a flailing appearance to the arm action.

Step 3. Spinal rotation continues to be the prime mover of the arms. Now the elbow of the arm swinging forward begins to flex, then extend during the backward swing. The combination of rotation and elbow flexion causes the arm rotating forward to cross the body midline and the arm rotating back to abduct, swinging obliquely outward from the body.

Step 4. The humerus (upper arm) begins to drive forward and back in the sagittal plane independent of spinal rotation. The movement is in opposition to the other arm and to the leg on the same side. Elbow flexion is maintained, oscillating about a 90-degree angle during the forward and backward arm swings.

From Roberton M. and Halverson L: *Developing children: their changing movement,* Philadelphia 1984, Lea & Febiger.

what more mature skills. In our culture the equipment and opportunities to develop these skills have generally been more accessible to boys than girls.

The development of locomotor and manipulative skills may be examined by looking at the changes that take place in the movements of various body segments from the beginning attempts of children to the emergence of the mature pattern of movement. These changes do not necessarily take place in all body segments at the same time. Some children's skills may show more mature movement in some body segments than in others. Robertson and Halverson of Wisconsin have contributed much to the study of these developing motor skills (see the box on the left).

Sex differences in skill performance before the onset of puberty are more a matter of opportunity and cultural expectations than a result of any physical differences between the sexes. Girls do better in skills that are expected of girls, and boys do better in skills considered to be more masculine. At adolescence the greater strength and size of boys gives them an advantage in the execution of many motor skills. In the elementary school grades, it is important for the teacher to help each child develop an optimum level in a variety of skills and avoid sexist stereotyping.

Through quality instruction, including early correction of errors, three changes in motor development occur during the elementary school years: mastery and refinement of fundamental motor skills, adaptation of these skills under varying conditions, and the combining of motor skills with greater ease. In beginning physical education experiences, motor patterns are established for those who have not established them before. These skills are then refined during the period of steady growth. Once mastered, these skills undergo adaptation to new movement situations as children learn to execute skills with more or less force, with bigger or smaller equipment, alone or with others, and in a variety of movement activities. Finally, children's movement patterns become more fluid as they move through space combining movements and changing level, direction, pathway, and speed. Chapter 13 and the activity chapters in this book explore more fully the development of motor skills in elementary school children.

In the upper elementary school grades there is great variability in motor skill performance for children of any one age and sex. Through the elementary school years, girls tend to stay in their relative position in the group regarding skill development, but boys do not. A boy who is outstanding at the elementary school level may or may not become a star in high school (Rarick, 1973).

COGNITIVE DEVELOPMENT

According to Piaget's theory, which suggests there are four distinct stages in cognitive development from early

PIAGET: STAGES OF COGNITIVE DEVELOPMENT

Stage	Age	Characteristic
Sensorimotor	Birth to 2 years	Motor interaction with environment Motor activity coordinates with perception Increasing experimentation, trial-and-error exploration Beginning of intellectual reasoning
Preoperational	2 to 5 years	Expresses self with language rather than moving Imaginative play uses motor and cognitive processes Uses past experience and beginning use of symbols to represent objects in the environment Focus on one aspect in problem-solving situations Uses elementary logic and reasoning
Concrete operational	7 to 12 years	Can deal with multiple aspects of the environment Can mentally organize or modify thought processes Beginning to develop strategies based on what others do
Formal operational	12 years	Abstract ideas possible Relate multiple aspects of the situation to problem solving Chooses the best solutions to problems through rational and abstract reasoning Deductions reached by hypothesis

childhood to adolescence, movement plays an important role in cognitive development (see the box above). In the early years, the sensorimotor stage, cognitive development is enhanced by the child's physical interaction with the environment. At this level, motor activity coordinates with perception. As children gain more control over their movement capabilities, there is increased experimentation and trial-and-error exploration. Infants learn to anticipate situations that are likely to occur in their environment. They discover new ways to produce the results they desire. According to Piaget, this is the beginning of intellectual reasoning. Children begin to see objects as independent from themselves and as possessing their own qualities. They begin to see themselves and objects in past, present, and future situations. Children can now ponder alternatives and make predictions of outcomes without having to physically perform the task itself.

In the preoperational stage (2 to 5 years) the child uses elementary logic and reasoning as they learn to use past experiences and the beginning use of symbols to represent objects in their environment. This process leads the way to oral communication. Now they can express themselves in language rather than movement. Language development is believed to be enhanced by the child's ability to walk unassisted, which provides the opportunity to explore an ever expanding environment. Imaginative play uses both motor and cognitive processes. At the beginning of this stage, children see the world only from their own perspective. This egocentrism results in little sensitivity for others. As the child reaches the close of this stage, egocentrism has decreased and there is considerable improvement in the use of symbols. Children at this stage are limited to the amount of stimuli to which they can attend. They tend to focus on one aspect in problem-solving situations. This limitation may be seen as children play games. Because they are unable to attend to multiple aspects that must be considered in problem solving, they may be unable to determine the best solution for the problem. For instance they may be more focused on getting across the end line or to score than to respond to the movements of taggers or to work with another to achieve the game goal.

Between the ages of 7 and 12 years, children move to Piaget's third stage, concrete operational. Children reach this stage when they have learned to deal with multiple aspects in the environment at once. At this stage children develop the capacity to mentally organize or modify their thought processes. They can now mentally represent objects or a series of probable events. Children can now begin to develop strategies in activities based on what the other team might do.

The next level of cognitive development developed by Piaget is known as the formal operational stage. This stage may begin as early as age 11 or 12. At this age abstract ideas are possible. The enhanced level of cognitive processing allows children to relate one or more parts of a situation to another in the problem-solving process. The individual is able to systematically look at possible solutions to a problem and, through rational and abstract reasoning, choose the best solutions for the problem. At this stage deductions are reached by hypothesis.

Piaget advocated learning by doing. Language and communication skills, reasoning, memory, and attending (attention) skills are some of the cognitive skills developed during the elementary school years. All have meaning for the physical educator.

Attending behavior changes dramatically over the first 6 or 7 years of school. Kindergarten and first grade students usually attend for only a short time, although they occasionally attend longer in those activities where their personal interest is high. Upper grade children are able to stay with a task for much longer periods. Young children are easily distracted by other children or other environmental conditions, whereas older children can block out irrelevant stimuli as they work to accomplish their goals.

Elementary school children are intellectually curious, wanting to learn about themselves and the many activities that make up the physical education program. They have vivid imaginations and can be creative in solving movement challenges. The development of imagination and creativity appears to be decreased in later years, as the peer group gains in control over children's behavior.

The physical education experience should encourage children not only to move but also to think as they move. Problem solving and **guided discovery** stimulate their cognitive development. Young children in school are able to deal with limited bits of information at any one time, whereas upper grade children are able to handle more complicated rules and other knowledge. Therefore activities should be kept simple for young children and gradually increase in complexity for upper grade youngsters to challenge them intellectually. Feedback should focus young children's attention on one or two critical elements or teaching points, whereas older chidren can deal with a little more information at a time. The physical education experience should also encourage verbal communication between the teacher and the students and should foster reasoning skills and decision making as new strategies are discovered. Classroom and physical education teachers should work together to help children apply what they have learned in one setting to other settings in the school. Changes in cognitive processing result in changes in motor performance as well.

SOCIAL DEVELOPMENT

Socialization, the process of learning behavior acceptable to life in society, is a lifelong process. Motor behavior provides some of the first socializing experiences as children reach out into their environment, interacting with parents and siblings and later others outside the home. During the preschool and elementary school years, children move from the social context of the home to the school, peer group, and other social groups such as scouting or church groups. In these settings they will learn to interact with others and grow to understand the behavior expected in each setting. During these developing years, children learn the specific roles of family member, student, friend, and activity participant. Much of the learning will be through the modeling of behavior of adults and other children.

As a result of these early social experiences, the child will develop self-esteem, that is, feelings of self-worth. The early social interactions shape feelings of self-worth as a reflection of the value others demonstrate regarding the individual. Successful participation in physical activities increases a person's self-esteem. These increased feelings of worth may be a factor in the observation of more highly skilled children assuming leadership roles inside and outside the school setting.

During these years four major developmental trends appear:

1. Movement from egocentric to group behavior
2. Recognition of sex roles and preferences in play
3. Movement from dependence on the family and other adults to dependence on the peer group as behavior models
4. Increased competitive behavior

These trends have far-reaching implications for education and physical education.

Kindergarten and first grade children tend to be egocentric in their behavior. They may come to school with few group behavior skills. They work best alone or alongside other children where they do not depend on another child to reach the play goal. Although today many children have been placed in day-care settings at an early age, some have not had the opportunity for much experience with a peer group, so they need to learn to share and to take turns. As they advance through the elementary school years, they begin to focus their attention on group activity. They learn to work together, to share in decision making, and to cooperate with teammates. By the fifth grade, many prefer group activities to working alone. Sensitivity to the feelings of others begins to emerge in the later elementary school years.

Children learn sex role expectations early in life. Parents and family members model behavior expectations, so by the time children enter school they have some idea of appropriate behavior for each role. There is little place for stereotyping of behavior in today's society, and teachers must be careful not to reinforce stereotypes. Often girls have the perception that physical activity or particular activities are for boys only, or that they can never be as good as boys in motor skills performance. Boys may believe that activities such as dance are for girls alone and that they have physical superiority over girls. These perceptions can be dispelled by thoughtful teachers who help each child become the best they can be regardless of sex or activity interest and who present activity models of both sexes. Children at all elementary school ages tend to select members of their own sex as partners. The teacher should design activities so that children work with all children in the group. During the third or fourth grade, some children may demonstrate antagonism toward the opposite sex by avoiding close contact or exhibiting aggressive behavior. Teachers need to deal with these behaviors by avoiding awkward social situations that intensify boy-girl relationships. Chapter 14 discusses strategies to use in dealing with these problems.

Dependence on adults decreases during the elementary school years. By the fifth or sixth grade, most children begin to become more dependent on their peers to determine acceptable behavior. Conflicts between adults rules and children's desires are not uncommon. Even though the peer group is increasing in importance in the life of the child, upper elementary school children still look up to adults. Young children may seek approval openly, whereas older children are more subtle in their approach. All seek encouragement and recognition. Although children become group oriented, they often seek the help of adults to assist them in organizing their activities. Some sport sociologists believe there has been a decrease in spontaneous play of American children as the children become more involved in organized sports activities.

Children show an increase in competitive behavior during the elementary school years. This characteristic appears to be a cultural phenomenon because children in some other cultures tend to develop more cooperative behaviors. Although competition is important to our American society, teachers should strive to emphasize the cooperative aspects of play. Group physical education experiences play an important role in helping upper elementary school age children to learn to work with others to achieve activity goals as well as teaching children about the division of labor.

IMPLICATIONS FOR PHYSICAL EDUCATION

The characteristics and needs of children and the implications for physical education are summarized in Table 2-1. Some specific implications for motor activity have already been cited in each of the previous sections.

Children require vigorous physical activity to stimulate normal growth and development. Because many children today do not have adequate opportunity for sustained vigorous activity, it is an important aspect of the elementary school physical education program. Maximum activity should be provided for all children and activities selected that stimulate the development of the cardiorespiratory and neuromuscular systems (see Chapter 15).

The period of steady growth is an important time for the refinement of motor skills and the development of confidence in one's movement ability. The physical education program should provide a variety of activities to enhance the mastery of fundamental motor skills. The higher center of gravity of young children should be considered both in selecting equipment and activities for physical education. As children approach adolescence,

Great variability in height may be seen in upper elementary school children.

they are forced to cope with rapid changes in size and shape. These changes may result in a change in their perceptions of themselves as movers. Teachers must develop sensitivity to the needs of children adjusting to their new bodies. Because there is little difference between the size of boys and girls during the preadolescent period, there is no reason to separate boys and girls in physical education. The growth changes during the adolescent period suggest some special considerations, as the increased size and weight of the boys puts the girls at a physical disadvantage.

Children's perceptual development has significance for physical education. Children process sensory information much more slowly than adults. Manipulative skills, especially those of receiving an object, may be difficult for some children due to the underdeveloped system of tracking. Size and perhaps color of objects (against the background) will need to be considered if children are to be successful.

Young children have little awareness of the body and its function. Five- and 6-year-olds may be aware of most large body parts but few small ones. Seven- to 12-year-olds are capable of greater body awareness, with increasing ability to analyze their own movements as they progress through the elementary school years. Perceptual mechanisms have progressed to the point that the 11- and 12-year-old can make accurate judgments about moving objects and can accurately move to intercept them.

Physical education activities should be designed to improve the children's perception of themselves and the use of body parts to perform a variety of motor movements. In presenting skills the teacher explains how body parts are used and then helps the children to use this knowledge to anlayze their own performance. The evaluative criteria included in the skills and activity chapters of this text describe the use of body parts in the performance of each skill. The elementary school years are important for the development of a variety of motor skills. In the early years

TABLE 2-1 AGE CHARACTERISTICS, STUDENT NEEDS, AND IMPLICATIONS FOR THE PHYSICAL EDUCATION PROGRAM

	5-6 YEARS	7-8 YEARS	9-10 YEARS	11 YEARS
GROWTH				
Characteristics	Steady increases in height and weight	→	Growth spurt begins for girls	Girls generally taller and heavier than boys
	Steady growth in strength for boys and girls	→	Increase in strength for girls	→
	High center of gravity	→	Center of gravity lowering	→
	Flexibility good		Loss in flexibility	→
The student needs	Vigorous physical activity to enhance fitness, growth and development	→	→	→
			Flexibility activities	→
	Equal expectations for strength of boys and girls	→	→	→
The teacher provides	Running, climbing, supportive activities	→	→	→
	Equal strengthening activities for boys and girls	→	→	→
			Stretching activities to enhance increased understanding of fitness	→
PERCEPTUAL SKILLS				
Characteristics	Aware of large body parts	Increasing awareness of body parts and their position in space	→	→
	Inaccurate judgments of moving objects	→	→	Accurate judgments in intercepting moving objects
	Process sensory information slowly	→	Improvement in speed of processing sensory information	→
	Focus on one aspect of the environment →	Focuses on an increasing number of aspects in the environment	→	→
The student needs	Increased use of all body parts	→	Awareness and development of all body parts and systems	→
	Opportunity to manipulate objects in simple individual tasks	→	Opportunity for more complex activities in using the body and manipulating objects alone and with others	→
The teacher provides	Movement challenges to explore location and possible movements of body parts	→		
	Knowledge of how body parts are used to perform motor skills	→	→	→
	Activities for total body development	→	→	→
	Simple activities involving equipment varying in size, color, shape and weight	→	Increasingly complex activities requiring the use of balls, paddles, etc.	→

TABLE 2-1 AGE CHARACTERISTICS, STUDENT NEEDS, AND IMPLICATIONS FOR THE PHYSICAL EDUCATION PROGRAM—cont'd

	5-6 YEARS	7-8 YEARS	9-10 YEARS	11 YEARS
PSYCHOMOTOR SKILLS				
Characteristics	Gross motor skills improving →	Gross motor skills refined		
		Fine motor skills improving	→	→
		Increasing variability in motor skill performance	→	→
	Perform motor skills singly	→	Combine motor skills more fluidly	→
			Balance improved	
The student needs	Opportunity to refine and use gross motor skills	To use gross motor skills in a variety of situations	→	→
		Opportunity to refine manipulative and other fine motor skills	→	→
	Opportunity to work with medium-sized objects	To work with equipment varying in size and weight	→	→
			To use motor skills in a variety of sports and dance activities	→
			To develop combinations of skills into movement sequences or routines	→
The teacher provides	A variety of experiences in using skills	A variety of experiences to challenge each child and requiring greater body and object control	→	→
	Experiences to explore the use of equipment such as ropes, hoops, balls, and wands	→	→	→
		Activities to further develop skills in ball handling	Activities requiring greater accuracy	→
			Activities combining motor skills and beginning sports and dance skills	→
COGNITIVE SKILLS				
Characteristics	Short attention span	Attention span short but increasing	Attention span increasing	→
	Very creative	→	→	→
	Deals with small bits of information at a time	→	Deals with increasing bits of information	→
	Uses past experiences and symbols in representing the environment →	Can mentally represent a series of probable events	→	Systematically looks at possible solutions to a problem and chooses the best
	Imaginative play uses motor and cognitive processes	→	→	Abstract ideas possible
The student needs	Short-duration activities	→	Activities increasing in length of time and complexity	→
	Opportunity to develop own ideas	→	→	→
	Simple rules	→	Rules increasing in complexity	→

Continued.

TABLE 2-1 AGE CHARACTERISTICS, STUDENT NEEDS, AND IMPLICATIONS FOR THE PHYSICAL EDUCATION PROGRAM—cont'd

	5-6 YEARS	7-8 YEARS	9-10 YEARS	11 YEARS
COGNITIVE SKILLS—cont'd				
The teacher provides	Movement into activity quickly	→	→	→
	Simple instructions	→	More complex instructions	→
	Many different activities within the lesson	→	Increasing time spent on activities in the lesson	→
	Activities with little information to remember (few game rules, simple dances)	→	Activities increasing in complexity	→
	Activities that challenge their imagination and creativity	→	Activities requiring higher levels of problem solving	→
	Work with one movement concept	Combinations of movement concepts increasing in difficulty	→	→
SOCIAL SKILLS				
Characteristics	Egocentric	Able to work where a little cooperation with partner or small group is needed	Interest in group activities increasing	→
	Aware of sex role expectations; prefers same-sex partners	→	Some sex antagonism	Sex antagonism decreasing
	Depends on adults for guidance	→	Looking more to peers for direction	→
			Competitive, team spirit high	→
			Capable of working cooperatively to achieve group activity goals	→
			Insensitive to others' feelings	Increasing sensitivity to others
The student needs	Activities to work alone or alongside others	Work with partners	Work with 3-5 persons in a group	→
	Opportunity to work with both sexes	→	→	→
	Direction from teacher on expectations for behavior	To assume increasing responsibility for own behavior	→	→
	To learn skills of sharing, taking turns	→	Work on developing cooperation and joint decision making	→
	To recognize individual worth of all children	→	→	→
The teacher provides	Activities in which children work independently of others	Activities working with partners	Activities requiring group decisions	→
	Games with little cooperation needed	→	Games that require more cooperation and delegation of responsibilities	→

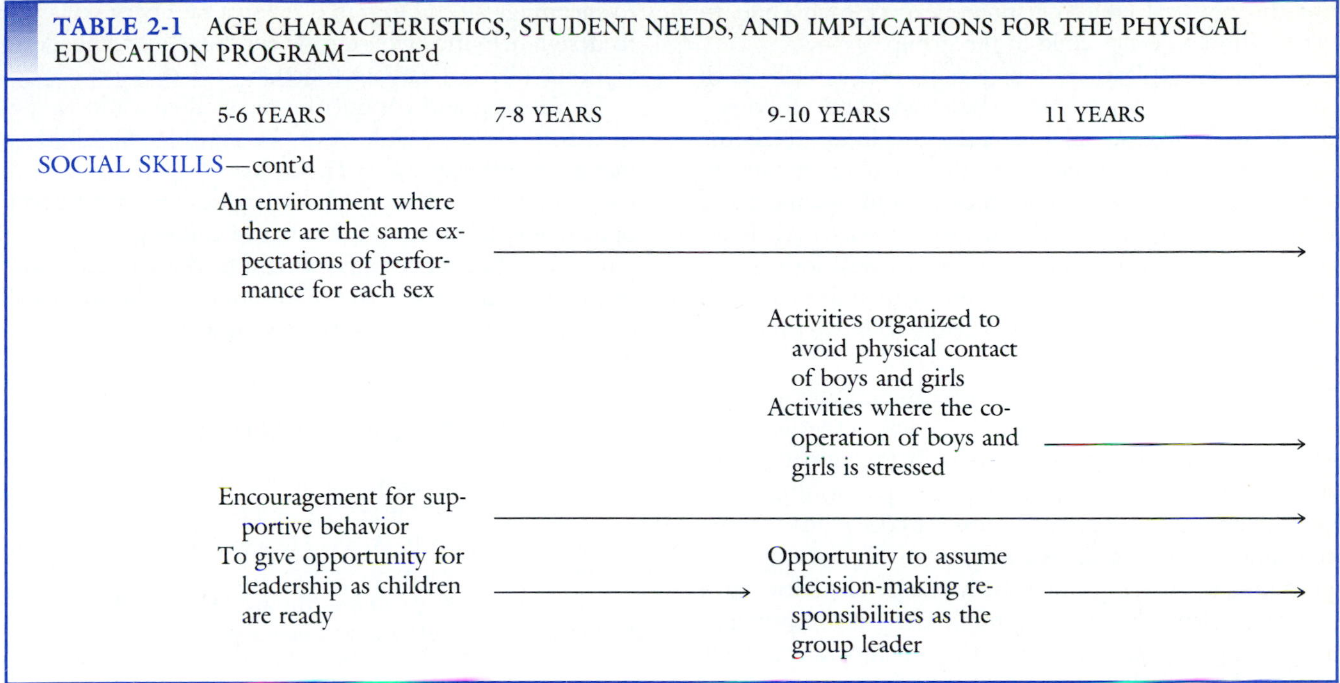

TABLE 2-1 AGE CHARACTERISTICS, STUDENT NEEDS, AND IMPLICATIONS FOR THE PHYSICAL EDUCATION PROGRAM—cont'd

5-6 YEARS	7-8 YEARS	9-10 YEARS	11 YEARS
SOCIAL SKILLS—cont'd			
An environment where there are the same expectations of performance for each sex	→	→	→
		Activities organized to avoid physical contact of boys and girls	
		Activities where the cooperation of boys and girls is stressed	→
Encouragement for supportive behavior	→	→	→
To give opportunity for leadership as children are ready	→	Opportunity to assume decision-making responsibilities as the group leader	→

the children concentrate on one skill at a time, whereas in the later elementary school years activities may require the combination of skills. It is important for the teacher to plan a variety of experiences in which the children will use each skill. These activities may vary in the level of proficiency expected, such as varying the distance to or the size of targets. Within the lesson children should be given some choice in activity based on their own perceived ability. When given these choices, children usually choose activities at their perceived level of competency because they offer more of a challenge. These varied experiences provide opportunities for children not only to perfect their skills but to adapt them for use in new activities. This ability to successfully adapt learned skills to new situations is essential to using motor skills throughout one's lifetime.

Children begin elementary school with a relatively short attention span, which requires the teacher to plan a variety of activities of short duration for each lesson. Instruction should be short and to the point because cognitive development enables the children to deal with only small bits of information at any given time. Games are of short duration with few rules. Children are very creative and enjoy activities in which they can use their imagination. Children respond spontaneously to movement challenges that call for simple movement responses.

As the children progress through the elementary school grades, their more advanced cognitive development and lengthening attention span permit them to deal with increasing amounts of information and more complex movement challenges and other activities. With some teacher direction, they will be able to deal with several movement concepts at one time and can understand some of the finer points of skill execution. The complexity of games increases with more rules, the designation of different responsibilities to participants, and more advanced use of skills. The activities increase in duration as they increase in complexity.

Physical education activities for young children tend to be individual or parallel play. Activities may require children to work independently or alongside other children but with little dependence on one another. The interaction of players in games may require a one-on-one confrontation, such as in a tag game in which each child, while moving in a group, is really interacting with the child who is "it." Although young children generally select a partner of the same sex, they are willing to work with all children in the group.

Group behavior emerges during the elementary school years. The physical education experiences gradually move to activities in which there is more demand for working with others. This process begins with activities in which partners work together to accomplish a task; gradually the size of groups increases so that by grades five and six there is some decision making in groups of four or five. The progression in games and team sports lead-ups demonstrates the increased social interaction and group dependency of children. The structure of folk and square dancing also depends on group cooperation. In the middle grades, some children may be more adamant about having same-sex partners. It may be advisable not to insist that children hold hands while performing folk dances, but the physical educator should expect each child to work with any other child in the group.

Children will learn various group roles as well. Each should have the opportunity to be a leader and a follower. In the beginning, squad leaders may begin as merely the first person in line or the one to distribute equipment to the group. As they are able they should assume more responsibility. In later years the group leader may determine the rotation of players to various positions in the activity, help children in the group with skill execution, or determine when the group is ready to move on to the next activity.

As team spirit increases, so does the competitive behavior of children. In the early grades, activities often have no declared winner, whereas in the upper grades there may be competition between teams resulting in a team score. The teacher must stress the cooperative efforts of teams rather than the winning score. Equalizing competition and avoiding emotionally charged activities such as relays will go a long way in minimizing the importance of winning. Children need to learn to compete in socially acceptable ways. Sportspersonship and strategies to aid its development are discussed in Chapter 14.

SUMMARY

During the elementary school years a number of growth and developmental changes take place that have implications for the physical education program. The steady growth in height and weight of the early years makes it an important time for skill refinement. This period of steady growth is followed by an adolescent growth spurt for girls at about 10 or 11 years of age and for boys 1 year later. Vigorous physical activity is important at all ages if normal growth and development are to occur.

The perceptual mechanisms mature during this time, with increased body awareness and the ability to use sensory input to make movement decisions. Increased body awareness aids the child in the refinement and adaptation of skills to new movement situations. As the neuromuscular system matures, children move more smoothly as they combine motor skills to accomplish the tasks required in a variety of individual and group activities.

Understanding of their own potential for movement is an important aspect of cognitive development in elementary school children. As children progress through the elementary school grades, they become increasingly able to use more information in analyzing movement situations.

An egocentric kindergarten child is transformed socially into a group-centered participant by the fifth or sixth grade. Dependence on adults is replaced by a growing importance of the peer group for establishing patterns of behavior. Girls and boys may have developed some perceptions of expectations regarding the suitability of some activities for each sex. The teacher must continue to encourage all children to develop a variety of skills and to design activities where girls and boys may engage in vigorous physical activity together.

In planning and conducting physical education experiences, the whole child must be considered. Children mature at different rates. Their physical, perceptual, motor, cognitive, and social characteristics may vary developmentally. In meeting the needs of children the teacher must plan experiences appropriate to the characteristics of the individuals and the class. Physical education will only be successful if the activities meet the total needs of children.

REFERENCES AND RESOURCES

Albinson J and Andrew G: *Child in sport and physical activity,* Baltimore, 1976, University Park Press.

Baumgartner R, Roche A, and Himes J: Incremental growth tables: supplementary to previously published charts, *American Journal of Clinical Nursing* 43:711, 1986.

Branta C: Physical growth and motor performance, *JOHPERD* 53(5):38, 1982.

Corbin C: *A textbook of motor development,* ed 2, Dubuque, Ia, 1980, Wm C Brown Group.

Cratty B: *Perceptual and motor development in infants and children,* ed 3, Englewood Cliffs, NJ, 1986, Prentice-Hall.

Gabbarad, C: *Lifelong motor development,* Madison, Wis, 1991, Wm C Brown and Benchmark Publishing.

Gallahue D: *Understanding motor development in children, preschool through the elementary grades,* Madison, Wis, 1989, Wm C Brown and Benchmark Publishing.

Goldhaber D: *Life-span human development,* Atlanta, 1986, Harcourt Brace Jovanovich.

Haywood K: *Life-span motor development,* Champaign, Ill, 1986, Human Kinetics.

Kaluger G and Kaluger M: *Human development the span of life,* ed 3, New York, 1989, MacMillan.

Karp GG and DePauw K: Neurodevelopment bases of human movement, *Physical Educator* 46(2):77, 1989.

Lowrey G: *Growth and development of children,* ed 8, Chicago, 1986, Mosby–Year Book.

Malina RM and Bouchard C: *Growth, maturation and physical activity,* Champaign, Ill, 1991, Human Kinetics.

Payne VG and Issacs L: *Human motor development: a life-span approach,* ed 2, 1991, Palo Alto, Calif, Mayfield Publishing.

Rarick G: *Physical activity: human growth and development,* New York, 1973, Academic Press.

Rarick G: Motor development: its growing knowledge base, *JOPERD* 51(7):26, 1980.

Ridenour M and others: *Motor development: issues and applications,* Princeton, NJ, 1978, Princeton Book Co.

Roberton M and Halverson L: *Developing children—their changing movement,* Philadelphia, 1984, Lea & Febiger.

Strom RD, Bernard HW and Strom SK: *Human development and learning,* New York, 1987, Human Sciences Press.

Thomas J: *Motor development during childhood and adolescence,* Minneapolis, 1984, Burgess.

Tudderham R and Snyder M: *Physical growth of California boys and girls from birth to eighteen,* Berkeley, Calif, 1954, University of California Press.

Wickstrom R: *Fundamental motor patterns,* ed 3, Philadelphia, 1983, Lea & Febiger.

Williams H: *Perceptual and motor development,* Englewood Cliffs, NJ, 1983, Prentice-Hall.

ANNOTATED READINGS

Andres F and others: Actual and perceived strength differences, *JOHPERD* 52(5):20, 1981.
The authors discuss that preadolescent boys and girls, although physiologically similar in strength, perceive that there is a difference in favor of boys.

Broekhoff J: The effect of physical activity on physical growth and development. In Stull G and Eckert H, editors: Effects of physical activity on children, *The Academy Papers* 19:75, 1986, Human Kinetics.
Looks at studies of the effects of activity on body dimensions and proportions, body composition, and maturation.

Chausow S and others: Metabolic and cardiovascular responses of children during prolonged physical activity, *Research Quarterly for Exercise and Sport* 55(1):1, 1984.
Evidence that children's response to prolonged exercise is much like that of adults, but their short attention span results in their drop out from activity.

Kraft RE: Misconceptions of children's physical abilities, *ACHPER National Journal* September 1988, p 10.
This article looks at research findings that dispel some of the myths of children's physical abilities.

Moen S: Visual skills: watch the ball? *Strategies* 2(6):20, 1989.
In paddle and racquet activities, watching the ball doesn't guarantee success. Teachers must help participants integrate available visual, spatial, and kinesthetic information.

Taylor W and Baranowski T: Physical activity, cardiovascular fitness, and adiposity in children, *Research Quarterly* 62(2):157, 1991.
A study of the relationships between level of physical activity, age, gender and body mass in children 8 to 13.

Thomas J and French K: Gender differences across age in motor performance: a meta-analysis, *Psychological Bulletin* 98:260, 1985.
Presents an analysis of 64 studies of gender differences from age 3 to 20. Small differences found seem to be accounted for by the encouragement boys receive. Large differences, such as distance and throw velocity, might have a biologic basis favoring boys.

Whiting H: *Acquiring ball skill,* Philadelphia, 1970, Lea & Febiger.
Presents a systems analysis of perceptual motor skill performance and discussion of factors that affect the development of ball skills, including information processing, judgments needed, reaction time, and visual factors.

Wlliams H: Perceptual-motor development in children: information and processing capacities of the young child. In *NASPE: echoes of influence,* Washington, DC, 1977, AAHPERD.
Changes in perception during the developing years, and some of the differences between slowly and normally developing children.

PART TWO

Planning the Physical Education Experience

The movement approach to physical education in the elementary school emphasizes the understanding of human movement and a child-centered approach to learning. A variety of activities are planned to help children develop motor skills and to increase understanding of their own movement potential and human movement in general. A developmental approach enables teachers to identify cognitive, motor, and social/affective needs of children in selecting curriculum content and process for learning.

Today's schools are beginning to focus on the common content across the many curriculum areas found in the elementary school. Physical education has the potential for enhancing the content in language arts, math, social studies, science, and music. These subjects also can contribute to learning in physical education.

Adequate curriculum that provides annual, unit, and daily planning is the first step to good teaching. The elementary school teacher of physical education must carefully set objectives and select the content and processes to challenge children cognitively as well as in the use of motor skills.

OUTLINE

CHAPTER 3

The Elementary School Physical Education Program

OBJECTIVES

After completing this chapter the student will be able to:

1. Describe several curriculum implementation models that have evolved over the years as curriculum focus has changed
2. Describe the content of the integrated movement curriculum, including the development of an understanding of body awareness, space, and quality of movement concepts, and their application to a variety of motor skills and movement activities
3. Explain the processes of learning in the integrated movement curriculum, which include perceiving, refining, varying, applying, and creating
4. Explain the developmental approach to teaching in physical education, recognizing that all children do not learn at the same rate and that experiences must be carefully planned to enhance individual development
5. Describe a number of instructional outcomes that can be identified for each developmental level of the integrated movement curriculum

The focus for a meaningful curriculum in physical education must be for grades K through 12, with each level building on the previous level and advancing the student one step closer to developing the skills and knowledge for lifetime participation. The elementary school years are a time for children to explore their bodies' potential for movement, to refine fundamental motor skills, to become acquainted with the mechanical principles that govern efficient movement, and to learn about the use of space. It is a time when activity habits are forming and children learn about the importance of exercise in being physically fit. Beginning social skills of sharing, respecting others, and playing cooperatively are also learned. As children advance through the school years, skills and knowledge are expanded through experiences in a variety of movement activities.

If the elementary school program is successful, children moving on to secondary school programs have the knowledge and skills to make decisions about their future movement activities. At the junior high or middle school level children need exposure to a variety of dance and sports activities to further develop the skills and knowledge they began to acquire at the elementary school level. At the high school level students should be given the opportunity to choose those activities that they would like to pursue at a much higher level of skill.

Significant changes in school physical education programs have taken place in the United States in the twentieth century. One of the most significant is the evolution of the movement approach to learning.

MOVEMENT APPROACH IN ELEMENTARY SCHOOL PHYSICAL EDUCATION

Chapter 1 traced the evolution of the movement approach in elementary school physical education. Movement education has been defined by Tillotsin as "that phase of the total education program which has as its contribution the development of effective, efficient and expressive movement responses in a thinking, feeling and sharing human being." The aim of movement education is to develop "an awareness of the self in the physical environment, the body and its capacities, and the components of movement which, in turn, contribute to the understandings, knowledge and movement responses of each

TABLE 3-1 MOVEMENT

ASPECTS	DIMENSIONS
Body (what body does)	Actions of the body Actions of body parts Activities of body Shapes of body
Effort (how body moves)	Time Weight Space Flow
Space (where body moves)	Areas Directions Levels Pathways Planes Extensions
Relationship (what relationships occur)	Body parts Individuals and groups Apparatus and equipment Other types

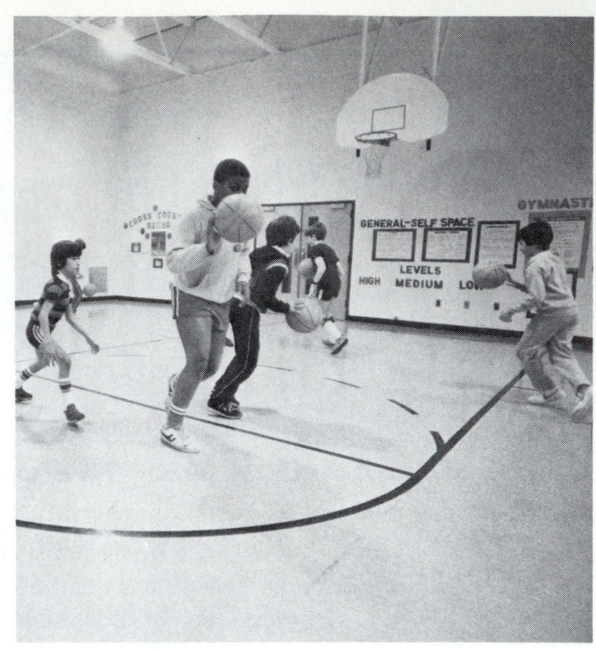

Moving in general space with a ball.

child in every class" (Tillotson). Table 3-1 is a basic framework of Laban's classification system as outlined by Logsdon. In the body aspect the teacher helps the children to understand the actions of the body—curl, stretch, and twist; the actions of body parts in supporting body weight, leading the movement, and applying force; the types of body movement—locomotor, nonlocomotor, and manipulative; and the shape the body may assume in performing various movements. In space the child explores self (personal) and general space, direction, level, pathway, planes, and extensions (range). In studying effort, the child learns about time, sudden or sustained; weight, firm or fine; space, direct or indirect; and flow, free or bound. The relationships of body parts in performing various movements, the relationship of individuals or groups as they move in space, and the relationship of individuals or groups as they move with equipment or apparatus are explored.

With the introduction of movement education came not only a change in physical education philosophy, but also a significant change in the methodology and content of elementary school physical education experiences. Content shifted from the teaching of specific skills, games, and other activities to the development of a broader understanding of the body as a tool for initiating movement and an understanding of the environment in which movement takes place. The goal was the development of a process for understanding movement that an individual could apply to any motor activity. Methodology shifted from a direct approach to problem solving and **exploration.** Today, however, a variety of teaching styles from direct to indirect are used in presenting the content.

In both England and the United States movement education theory has been readily applied to what has become known as educational dance and educational gymnastics. The integration with sports skills has been slow in coming. The application to games is being seen today not only in elementary school physical education but in high schools and in higher education and athletics. Coaches, primarily in the field sports, have been developing small group games and practices in which an understanding of movement concepts and especially space is developed.

Much has been written about movement education, and Laban's theory of movement has undergone many interpretations and modifications; however, the idea of a physical education program based on the development of an understanding of human movement is here to stay.

CURRICULUM MODELS

The content of elementary school physical education programs has been organized into several curriculum models that depict the relationship of the important elements. These models are discussed in relationship to the inclusion of the movement content.

The **activity curriculum model** is an activity-centered curriculum composed of those activities long associated with elementary school physical education: games and sports, dance, and individual activities. Relative emphasis in each area is based on age characteristics, with the greatest emphasis on individual activities throughout the early years and games and sports in the upper grades. Units of instruction are planned for each activity area and include games, folk dance, stunts and tumbling, and so forth. Units focusing on the movement content may be included in some programs. Each unit is viewed as a unique experience. The major disadvantage of this model is that the movement content, if included, is treated as a separate experience from games, dance, and individual activities. Therefore, children are not taught to see the relationship between the movement content and the other content areas. Although a variety of teaching strategies may be utilized in this curriculum, teacher-centered approaches tend to be used most often.

The **motor skills model** emphasizes the development of motor skills and the use of these skills in a variety of contexts. Activities are developed around skill themes such as traveling, balancing, striking, etc. Several levels of mastery may be recognized in developing progressions for learning. The movement content may be utilized in the development of activities centered around each theme.

In the **fitness model** the focus of the program is on the acquisition and maintenance of physical fitness. Activities are selected for their contribution to the health and wellness of children. The curriculum may be restricted to the health-related physical fitness components of body composition, cardiorespiratory endurance, flexibility, and muscular strength and endurance. Emphasis is on individual prescription and improvement. Knowledge about the importance of fitness to a healthy life is a key component of the program. The movement content is not addressed in programs emphasizing fitness. Many programs do not have adequate time to develop fitness components during the school day and must rely on children working on their own outside of school to achieve fitness goals. This model is most often introduced in the upper elementary school grades.

The **movement model** stresses the movement content as the only legitimate content of the elementary school physical education program. Emphasis is placed on the development of an understanding of the components of Laban's movement framework. Table 3-2 includes a repeat of the three content areas during the school year. In the beginning of the year children work with the concepts using only body movements. They work later with balls, hoops, or other small equipment and finally with large apparatus to further their understanding of the movement content. Other approaches may also be used. Exploration, problem solving, and other child-centered teaching strategies are usually used, but other teaching styles may also be included. In this model, motor skill development is believed to occur as a result of the movement experiences. In some programs they are taught as a part of the movement experience; in others they happen only by chance. Traditional physical education activities, such as games, track and field, gymnastics, and folk dance, are usually not included. This model is used more frequently in the lower elementary school grades.

An **adventure model** has emerged in recent years. In this model program goals are based on several components including self-esteem, cooperation, risk taking, trust, challenge and problem solving. These components are developed through carefully selected and planned experiences in a variety of physical activities and in a learning environment that may be more complex and less predictable than the usual physical education setting. The program may focus on monthly or seasonal themes as seen in Table 3-2. Students are encouraged to interact in positive ways, assuming responsibility for their actions and demonstrating concern for others as they develop their skills in problem solving and working with others. Children in adventure programs are encouraged to be actively involved in the process and are given choices that challenge their physical, social, and cognitive capacities. The movement content and methodology may be included as one area in which the goals might be achieved, but is generally not a primary focus of the activities.

INTEGRATED MOVEMENT CURRICULUM

As knowledge in all areas continues to increase rapidly education has shifted its emphasis in curriculum planning from the accumulation of facts to the development of learning skills that enable the individual to continue to learn throughout life. The **integrated movement curriculum model** developed in this book combines the content of physical education with the development of a process that enhances lifelong learning. It provides children with knowledge about their movement as they learn to move efficiently and effectively. These skills and knowledge are presented in a way that encourages thinking and self-discovery.

The goal of physical education is to provide movement experiences that enhance the involvement of individuals in physical activity throughout their lifetime. Many of the activities in which learning begins during the elementary school years will not be the activities in which future adults will participate. Therefore activities of the elementary school physical education program are designed to meet present needs and also to facilitate future learning. The goal of physical education thus becomes one of providing experiences that will aid the individual in selecting and successfully participating in activities appropriate at various stages of life.

The integrated movement curriculum model is perhaps the most appropriate model for elementary school physical education today. In this model the relationships of the movement content to the development of motor skills

TABLE 3-2 ORGANIZATION OF CONTENT FOR CURRICULUM MODELS FOR LEVEL II (GRADE 3)

MODEL I	MODEL II	MODEL III	MODEL IV	MODEL V	MODEL VI
Activity	**Motor Skill**	**Fitness**	**Movement**	**Adventure**	**Integrated***
FALL					
Movement concepts Basic skills Soccer lead-ups	Traveling Chasing, fleeing Dodging Kicking	Jogging Rope jumping Outdoor apparatus Stunts	Body awareness Space Qualities of movement (use of the body)	All about "Me" Developing cooperation	Develop concepts: Space, force Apply concepts: Motor skills Running and tag games Soccer lead-ups
WINTER					
Creative dance Folk dance Rhythmic activities Stunts and tumbling Large apparatus Net games	Time Traveling Balance Weight transfer Volleying Dribbling Throwing, catching	Cross-country skiing Folk dance Endurance games Relaxation Tumbling	Body awareness Space Qualities of movement (with small equipment)	Building community Problem solving	Develop concepts: Time, space Apply concepts: Creative dance Folk dance Rhythmic activities Develop concepts: Balance, body awareness Apply concepts: Stunts and tumbling Large apparatus Develop concepts: Space, force Apply concepts: Net games
SPRING					
Running games Ball games Small equipment Track and field	Traveling Throwing, catching Striking Jumping	Endurance games Track and field Stunts	Body awareness Space Qualities of movement (with large apparatus)	Environment Choice	Develop concepts: Space, force Apply concepts: Running games Ball games Develop concepts: Body awareness, space Apply concepts: Small equipment Track and field

*All concepts integrated, special emphasis listed.

and their combined use in a variety of activities are clearly established. Learning begins with the study of human movement (body awareness), their environment (space), and movement efficiency (qualities of movement) in the early years. As children's understanding of the movement content increases, they are taught to see the relationship between these movement concepts and the motor skills they are developing. They also begin to apply these concepts to their performance in a variety of physical education activities. In the upper grades the curriculum appears to shift to more traditional physical education activities. However, the teacher uses these activities to further teach the movement content by identifying and teaching the movement concepts most important to success at each level in the progression of learning these activities. The activity unit is then built around the concepts identified.

Movement Content

The content of the elementary school physical education curriculum in this text goes beyond Laban's movement theory. Figure 3-1 outlines the curriculum within the scope of this book. An attempt has been made to include experiences that broaden children's understanding of themselves as movers as well as develop an understanding of principles of effective and efficient movement.

Body Awareness

Body awareness activities enhance children's understanding of themselves as movers and help develop a sensitivity to their physical being. Learning begins with the identification of body parts and knowledge about the body's capacity for movement. Developing an understanding of how the human body moves includes becoming aware of how the body works, that is, muscles and joints, respiration, and the cardiovascular system. Moving safely with control is emphasized. Awareness of body tension and the development of conscious relaxation techniques should begin at the elementary school level. Communication through the use of the body should be explored and should include purposeful and unintentional body language. As children develop motor skills, body awareness is encouraged as they learn to use body parts efficiently and effectively in performing motor tasks.

Space

An understanding of space concepts is essential if children are to move effectively. In a program emphasizing individual movement and problem solving, an understanding of **self** and **general space** is crucial. Children must first recognize their own space and the space of others if they are to move independently. This concept is also important for success in the classroom, where children must learn to share space with each other, whether at a table or sitting with a group in a reading lesson. Effective use of space also includes the ability to move in different directions and at all levels: high, medium, and low. Pathways, the line of movement in space, and range, the relationship of the body parts to each other or the body to objectives in space, are other concepts to explore.

Qualities of Movement

The study of the qualities of movement enhances children's understanding of movement and the laws that apply to movement efficiency. Children learn to use body parts to create an appropriate amount of force for a task, as well as to absorb the force of the body as in landing or stopping or to absorb the force of objects in catching. Time is another aspect of the qualities of movement. Children learn the importance of timing movements under various activity conditions, as well as speed and the rhythm of movement, either imposed by the self or by an outside source such as musical accompaniment. Children also learn about gravity and the efficient use of the body in losing and regaining balance in a variety of movements. The study of flow, the smooth combination of body actions, is also included.

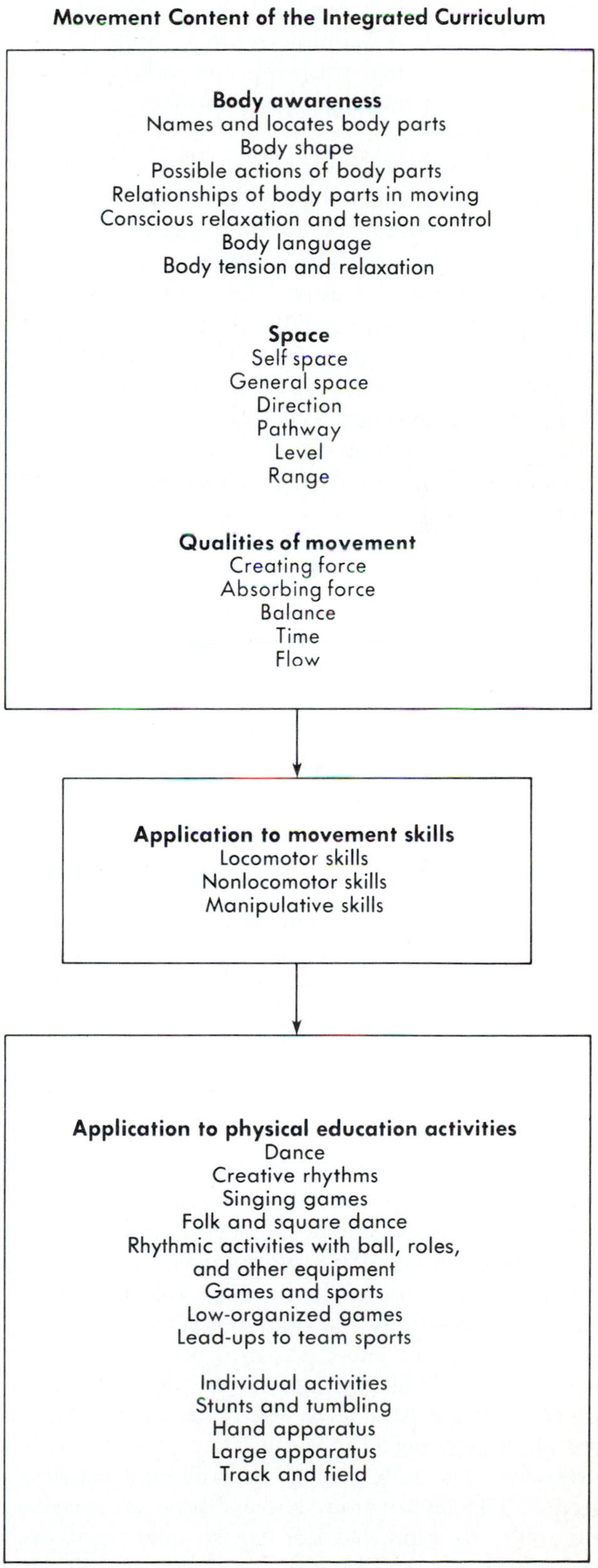

Movement Content of the Integrated Curriculum

Body awareness
Names and locates body parts
Body shape
Possible actions of body parts
Relationships of body parts in moving
Conscious relaxation and tension control
Body language
Body tension and relaxation

Space
Self space
General space
Direction
Pathway
Level
Range

Qualities of movement
Creating force
Absorbing force
Balance
Time
Flow

↓

Application to movement skills
Locomotor skills
Nonlocomotor skills
Manipulative skills

↓

Application to physical education activities
Dance
Creative rhythms
Singing games
Folk and square dance
Rhythmic activities with ball, roles, and other equipment
Games and sports
Low-organized games
Lead-ups to team sports

Individual activities
Stunts and tumbling
Hand apparatus
Large apparatus
Track and field

FIGURE 3-1 Movement content of the integrated curriculum.

Application to Movement Skills

As children begin to understand the three areas of movement concepts, they are helped to apply them to other learning in physical education. One of the first applications is made in the development and use of fundamental motor skills, such as skipping, running, hopping, pushing, pulling, catching, throwing and striking—an important aspect of the elementary school physical education curriculum.

Because children have varied motor backgrounds, it is essential for the teacher to help children reach their movement potential through a carefully planned and conducted program of activities. A variety of interesting activities that encourage mastery of these important motor skills is presented. These skills become more meaningful to children as they gain understanding through the application of movement concepts. This link between knowledge and skill enables children to plan and use their skills more effectively in solving movement challenges. This understanding of movement concepts and the ability to apply them to motor skills make it possible for children to move on to the application of the movement concepts in dance, games, and individual activities. For instance, as children learn to vary force to successfully complete a task involving variations in distance thrown, they can use this knowledge in a variety of games where moving teammates change the force needed to succcessfully get the ball to them. Another example is the application of pathways in finding the open path so that a ball may be moved past an opponent to the goal.

Application to Physical Education Activities

The application of movement concepts to the more traditional activities of an elementary school program becomes increasingly important as the child moves through the elementary school years. As the activities increase in complexity, children's success depends on their ability to solve more advanced movement challenges. Activities become more complex in the nature and use of the skills required. Children learn to combine skills in interesting and functional ways in activities such as gymnastics or basketball. Children combine movements creatively in dance and rhythmic activities. The interaction of individuals requires children to relate to an increasingly larger group. Each participant plays a unique role in the activity, such as the positions and changing player relationships in a soccer game. These activities provide an exciting experience for children in the movement challenges they impose. It is not possible to teach each child all the skills and knowledge needed for a lifetime of motor activity. Exposure to a wide variety of skills and activities is needed. The key to future success, however, may lie in the ability to apply old learning to new situations. A process for accomplishing this goal must begin during the elementary school physical education experience.

PROCESS FOR LEARNING

Much learning in physical education is achieved through the imitation of skills presented by the teacher, with little understanding of why the skills are executed in a particular way. The integrated movement curriculum attempts to bring to a conscious level the understanding of efficient movement. If we are to emphasize understanding the environment, movement, and people, as Allenbaugh suggests, then the physical education program must reflect this thinking.

In the past the physical education curriculum has included a set of broad goals and a list of the activity content. Today the curriculum has a much broader scope that includes all the planning that takes place before teaching begins (Jewett). If we accept this broader definition, then the physical education curriculum must include not only the content but also the process involved in learning. Teaching the motor content is relatively easy. Developing the understanding is more difficult but very important. In this conceptual framework, the physical educator becomes the facilitator in helping each child learn how to learn.

Physical education is concerned with the education of the "whole" person. Learning is focused not only on the development of motor skills but also on the cognitive, social, and affective development of children. Contemporary trends in physical education pay closer attention to each learner. If physical education is to really educate the whole person, then the whole child must be involved. The study of the behavioral domains summarized in Table

An important aspect of motor development is developing awareness of what the body does in performing various activities.

3-3 is helpful in our attempt to organize and analyze educational objectives in physical education.

The cognitive domain is concerned with the child's intellectual skills. In the 1950s Bloom and his associates published a taxonomy of educational objectives for the cognitive domain. Cognitive behaviors in physical education often stop with the knowledge of rules and terminology, which falls at the lower end of Bloom's taxonomy. Problem solving, creative endeavors, and decision-making abilities, which involve higher-level processes, are more difficult to measure and are often neglected in the evaluation of the physical education curriculum. Corbin suggests that the loss of interest in physical education as children progress through the educational system may well be the result of our unwillingness to move students beyond these lower-level objectives.

After studying the works of Bloom and others, Jewett and Mullan formulated the taxonomy of integrated movement process categories. These processes trace motor skill development from early perception of what a skill is to creative movement and the emergence of new forms of movement unique to the individual.

The learning processes of the integrated movement curriculum are a blending of the taxonomies of Bloom and Jewett and Mullen. Because cognition plays an important part in learning to move efficiently and effectively, these processes are used in both the development of the movement content and motor skills.

Knowledge associated with the movement content forms the foundation for motor skill learning. It is through the application of this knowledge that children learn to move effectively under varying environmental conditions.

Physical education experiences in the past have primarily dealt with the learning and refinement of a variety of motor skills with the assumption that students who have mastered them will automatically use them effectively as circumstances demand. In the integrated movement curriculum, more attention is given to the process of **perceiving** by attending to the need for better self-awareness. In these experiences the child is introduced to the concept or motor skill. In motor skill learning, the child develops a general understanding of how body parts are used, with identification of two to three **critical ele-**

TABLE 3-3 BEHAVIORAL DOMAINS

COGNITIVE (Bloom)	MOVEMENT PROCESSES (Jewett)
1. Knowledge: knowing facts and other specifics 2. Comprehension: ability to interpret, translate, and extrapolate 3. Application: ability to apply what is known to a variety of situations 4. Analysis: ability to identify key elements, to see relationships 5. Synthesis: ability to arrange an entire structure 6. Evaluation: ability to make judgments	1. Generic: operations of data collection; awareness of body parts, relationships, positions, and their use in performing motor skills 2. Ordinative: organizing, refining, and performing motor skills 3. Creative movement: inventing or creating movement to serve individual purposes
INTEGRATED MOVEMENT PROCESSES	**SOCIAL (Hellison)**
1. Perceiving: beginning awareness of a concept or skill 2. Refining: expanded knowledge of a concept or skill to include finer points of understanding and performance 3. Varying: modification in the use of a skill or concept under externally imposed conditions 4. Applying: awareness of the importance and the use of a skill or concept for successful performance 5. Creating: development of new movements or use of movements	1. Self-control: without interfering with others 2. Involvement: willing to stay on task and work hard 3. Self-responsibility: take responsibility for own actions 4. Caring: reaching beyond themselves to others
AFFECTIVE (Krathwohl, Singer)	
1. Receiving: willing to receive or attend to certain cues or situations 2. Responding: motivated to actively attend, willingness 3. Valuing: determining worth in a behavior, from accepting to commitment	4. Organization: structuring values in a system 5. Characterization: stabilization, consistency in value organization

ments that the child must master for success. For example, in introducing catching the teacher might identify reaching out and pulling the ball in as the first important aspects of a successful catch. In concept learning the first experiences help the child define what the concept is and is not. This definition is expressed verbally as well as through movement. For instance, children learn to define self-space as the space they take up within their normal body extensions and explore through movement the size of their self-space. They also recognize that everyone has a self-space.

Once the task has been accurately perceived, attention is focused on **refining** the skill or concept. During this phase, children learn to use body parts more consistently to accomplish the task. Teacher assistance is important during this phase to help children learn the correct movement patterns. As the children master elements of the skill, finer points in the technique are identified. Mastery of skills takes time and practice, so this phase may last for extended periods of time depending on the difficulty of the skill. In refining catching children learn to move to line up with the oncoming ball and to more accurately track balls into their hands. In concept learning, children expand their understanding of the concept being studied. In refining self-space, children learn to respect the self-space of others as well as learn that their self-space goes with them as they move in space.

During the **varying** learning process the teacher imposes different conditions in the learning environment, such as changing the size of space or the type of equipment used. In these experiences children learn to adapt their movement response to the conditions imposed. In varying, children learn to catch objects varying in size, shape, and weight and throw to various levels and pathways. In varying self-space children explore moving in different ways in self-space as well as recognizing an enlarged self-space as they move with balls, hoops or other equipment.

In the **applying** learning process children must analyze more complex, perhaps even continuously changing movement environments and make decisions regarding the application and use of concepts and motor skills. These changing conditions are not under the direct control of the teacher, but are the result of movements of others in the group or other factors. Catching skills are applied in a number of games where students have to make decisions appropriate to the game conditions. In applying what they have learned about self-space in games children may have to adjust their self-space in working alone or with others to close space to balls or opponents. This important aspect of learning in physical education assists children in using the knowledge and skill acquired in other lessons for some direct purpose. It is the beginning of transfer of learning so important for continued success in moving throughout life.

Chapters 12 and 13 and the activities chapters found in the last half of this book suggest objectives and activities for perceiving, refining, varying, and applying.

The **creating** learning process takes the children one step further in creating or inventing their own movement responses unique to the individual. Emphasis is on individualizing the movements to meet the performer's purpose. These movements may be the result of improvising in some movement situation or the careful creation of some movements such as those developed in creative dance. This creative aspect of movement has led to new moves in gymnastics or new techniques such as the Fosbury flop in high jumping. Children may also discover new ways to receive an object or to use their self-space in a unique way.

Social and Affective Domains

Hellison has formulated a social domain moving from a level of controlling one's behavior, to assuming more responsibility for one's actions, and finally to a level of caring for others. The physical education class provides more opportunity for social interaction than any other subject taught in the elementary school. It is a natural environment in which to develop social skills; however, acceptable social behaviors do not happen by chance. Physical educators must be careful to plan and conduct motor activities in such a way that appropriate social behaviors are the result. Before children can learn to control their behavior the teacher must be in control of the learning environment. A program that promotes feelings of self-worth, personal responsibility for one's actions, acceptance of others in a helping atmosphere, fair play, and a cooperative spirit will do much to develop the social behaviors we prize highly. This domain is further developed in Chapter 14.

The affective domain formulated by Krathwohl includes emotions, interests, attitudes, motivation, and values. Because the building of attitudes conducive to lifelong physical activity is an important outcome of the physical education program, attention to the affective domain is essential. Attitudes toward participation will most likely be the result of the conduct of the elementary school physical education program rather than the activities themselves. Elementary school children enjoy physical activity. College students interviewed about their likes and dislikes regarding their past participation in physical education most often cite class organization and other problems of conduct as their reasons for disliking physical education. Too often these problems may be traced to their early physical education experiences in the elementary school.

Because behaviors of the affective domain are not concrete, they are difficult to assess. Successful performance in motor activities may be the result of such behaviors because interest and motivation affect a person's achievement. The values we hold for participation will also be reflected in our movement behavior. For instance, an individual who values physical fitness behaves in a way that improves or maintains an adequate fitness level.

Looking at behavior in terms of these domains does not assume that the child can be divided into parts. Each domain is strongly linked to the others. By looking at all domains, teachers begin to develop objectives in physical education that go beyond the development of motor skills. Examples of objectives may be found later in this chapter.

Education is a process that changes the learner. Physical educators must ask themselves which changes they seek. Physical education is an active learning experience in which the learner uses motor skills in solving movement challenges while interacting with others. If the goal for the learner is to develop processing skills, then the physical education program must be process oriented. One who understands not only will move more efficiently but also will solve movement challenges more effectively.

DEVELOPMENTAL APPROACH TO CURRICULUM EMPHASIS

A grade level approach to the organization of content assumes similar experiences for all children at a particular grade level. Because physical education may be scheduled from 1 to 5 days per week during the elementary school years, the level of achievement of children from program to program varies dramatically. Therefore a grade level approach is inappropriate in helping teachers select suitable experiences for the children in their classes.

The activity content in this text utilizes a developmental approach, which was first introduced by Schurr. Four levels have been identified: level I represents the beginning stages of learning, and level IV the most advanced level that may be achieved during the elementary school years. Each level represents a distinct period in the development of the physically educated child. In this approach teachers select activities based on the behavioral needs of children—psychomotor, cognitive, and affective/social. In selecting appropriate activities the teacher uses information about each child to determine the kind of experience needed. Depending on their movement background, children may be ready for experiences at one level in some activities and at another level in others.

Program objectives for the four developmental levels follow. Programs for levels III and IV may vary considerably from school to school depending on the equipment and facilities available. For this reason specific motor skills are not listed for levels III and IV. The program objectives listed may be met in experiences unique to each physical education setting. Some children with daily instruction in physical education may achieve the objectives by the end of the following years: level I, first grade; level II, third grade; level III, fifth grade; and level IV, sixth grade. Obviously, children with limited physical education will not reach the objectives for level IV by the sixth grade. Program objectives for each level may be found beginning on p. 44.

Level I

Level I comprises the first physical education experiences. It is a time for beginning the study of human movement and an important time for the development of fundamental motor skills. Children begin to define the movement concepts verbally and in movement responses. The majority of time in physical education should be devoted to these outcomes. In addition to these important areas, children should be given the opportunity to use their skills and begin to apply the movement concepts in a variety of activities. It is a time for learning to share equipment, to take turns, to control one's behavior, and to play with others. It is also a time to establish values about the importance of physical activity in their lives. Games provide the opportunity to use the motor skills they are learning, and rules and the structure of games are easily understood. Games require very little interaction of players. Singing games, folk dances, and simply rhythmic activities with balls and other hand apparatus challenge the children to respond to an imposed rhythm. Creative dance, stunts and tumbling, and activities with large apparatus, beanbags, balls, wands, and other equip-

Dance provides an opportunity to develop interpersonal skills.

PROGRAM OBJECTIVES FOR ELEMENTARY SCHOOL PHYSICAL EDUCATION

LEVEL I

Psychomotor Domain

The child:

Performs the following locomotor skills—walk, run, jump, hop, gallop, slide, leap, skip
Starts and stops efficiently
Jumps and lands in a balanced position from a low bench
Jumps over a series of low obstacles
Jumps the long rope in rhythmical fashion beginning in the rope
Rolls ball from side of body to partner
Throws a medium-sized playground ball with a two-hand underhand throw
Catches a rolling ball with two hands
Catches an accurately thrown playground ball
Throws a small ball overhand for distance
Bounces a medium-sized playground ball with either hand
Kicks a stationary ball with inside of foot
Moves on and off apparatus with control
Moves in a variety of ways while the body is in various spacial orientations (i.e., inverted)
Controls force when executing locomotor or manipulative skills
Absorbs force appropriately while stopping, jumping, hopping, and other locomotor skills
Responds to signal to start/stop movement
Moves within the boundaries or within the immediate area of a circle
Overtakes and gently tags another child
Avoids being tagged by changing direction, pathway, or speed
Assumes a balanced position on one or more body parts
Maintains balance while walking on a line or low balance beam
Balances objects on various body parts
Adjusts speed from very fast to very slow
Moves to the underlying beat of the accompaniment
Recognizes and responds to tempo changes
Performs locomotor and nonlocomotor movements in time to music
Performs simple singing games and children's dances
Responds appropriately to movement stimuli such as stories, poems, and songs

Cognitive Domain

The child:

Locates and names all body parts
Matches own body parts with those of others
Is aware of possible movements of body parts
Understands how body parts are used in the execution of fundamental motor skills
Knows the difference between tension and relaxation
Understands the importance of physical activity in maintaining physical fitness
Knows four components of health-related physical fitness
Knows some activities to develop each component
Is aware of the dimensions of self space
Knows a variety of ways to move in self space
Finds own space in general space
Is aware of the dimensions of general space
Selects a variety of ways to move in general space
Is aware of others' self space while moving in general space
Is aware of possible directions in space
Selects a variety of ways to move in all directions
Is aware of levels in space
Is aware of a variety of movements in the high, medium, or low levels
Is aware of possible pathways in space
Selects a variety of ways to move in different pathways
Is aware of range in space
Varies range
Understands how body parts are used to create and absorb force
Creates force with various body parts
Applies understanding of balance to simple movement challenges
Solves simple movement challenges on apparatus
Recognizes even and uneven rhythm
Responds to phrasing

Social Domain

The child:

Listens to the teacher and classmates
Follows simple directions
Shares equipment with other children
Takes turns
Plays cooperatively with children in small and large groups in simple group activities
Respects others' space by moving with control, avoiding personal contact
Adheres to safety rules while at play
Takes care of equipment and helps to put it away

Affective Domain

The child:

Willingly participates in all activities
Stays at the task at hand (for a short time)
Respects the feelings of others

LEVEL II

The child demonstrates the objectives of level I.

Psychomotor Domain

The child:

Changes locomotor movements with little hesitation
Dodges effectively
Enters and exits the long jumping rope
Performs simple stunts while jumping the long rope
Jumps the short rope rhythmically
Performs beginning-level running and field events in track and field
Executes a two-hand underhand throw with increasing accuracy
Executes a shoulder pass
Dribbles a playground ball with either hand while moving
Adjusts body position to receive a ball thrown to either side
Dribbles ball with the feet with some control
Strikes ball with hand in an underhand motion
Hits a moving target with a ball with increasing accuracy

PROGRAM OBJECTIVES FOR ELEMENTARY SCHOOL PHYSICAL EDUCATION—cont'd

Absorbs force with various body parts
Absorbs force appropriately in ball skills
Performs simple dance steps to musical accompaniment
Moves to accompaniment in various meters: 2/4, 3/4, 4/4, 6/8
Performs simple folk dances
Performs simple ball rhythms
Performs beginning skills on apparatus
Performs simple combinations of stunts on the mat or on apparatus

Cognitive Domain

The child:

Understands the use of body parts in the execution of skills
Assumes a variety of body shapes while moving through space supported or nonsupported
Has a beginning understanding of conscious relaxation
Has adequate body awareness to perform simple fitness activities
Relates performance in some activities to personal physical fitness
Has increased understanding of the four components of health-related fitness
Has a repertoire of activities to develop each of the four components of fitness
Recognizes empty spaces without hesitation
Sees the empty spaces to put objects in
Recognizes and moves to available pathways while moving in general space
Anticipates the pathway of other children and objects
Uses space wisely while moving with partners
Controls objects while moving in space
Adjusts movement as space increases or decreases
Selects a variety of ways to move in one, two, or all three levels
Controls force in performing ball skills by selecting the appropriate amount of force for the task
Assumes a balanced position in more complex balance problems
Adjusts speed without hesitation as the task requires
Distinguishes changes in rhythm or tempo

Social Domain

The child:

Willingly works with a partner designated by the teacher
Begins to recognize the need to delegate responsibilities in games
Works with others to achieve game goals

Affective Domain

Works independently of direct adult supervision
Assumes responsibility for own actions

LEVEL III

The child demonstrates the objectives of level II.

Psychomotor Domain

The child:

Throws balls varying in size with increasing accuracy to stationary and moving targets
Moves a ball through space with control by striking it with a body part or an implement
Receives objects varying in size with the hands, feet, other body parts, or an implement
Performs beginning skills required in the team sports progression
Throws balls varying in size with increasing accuracy to stationary and moving targets
Moves a ball through space with control by striking it with a body part or an implement
Receives objects varying in size with the hands, feet, other body parts, or an implement
Uses game skills without hesitation
Combines movement skills efficiently
Performs simple square dance moves such as allemande right and left, grande right and left
Matches steps with those of a partner's so they move together in performing dances
Performs a movement sequence alone, with a partner, or with equipment
Performs more advanced skills on the mats and apparatus
Combines a number of skills in a logical progression and performs them smoothly
Performs more advanced movement sequences with balls, hoops, or other small equipment

Cognitive Domain

The child:

Uses space more effectively in game play
Selects the appropriate amount of force to control an object while working with objects of varying size, shape, and weight
Judges with accuracy the flight of an object
Maintains relationships with partners and others in the group while performing dances and other rhythmic activities in a variety of formations
Recognizes the fitness benefits of activities
Measures own level of health-related physical fitness
Creates and repeats a movement sequence

Social Domain

The child:

Works with others in small groups to solve more complex game goals
Shares in the decision making in developing simple strategies
Accepts the judgment and decisions of others
Is helpful to children who are less skilled

Affective Domain

The child:

Recognizes the need for and follows game rules
Works independently to achieve personal goals
Assumes responsibility for organizing activities in a group

LEVEL IV

The child demonstrates the objectives of level III.

Psychomotor Domain

The child:

Is more accurate in the use of skills
Combines skills as needed

Continued.

PROGRAM OBJECTIVES FOR ELEMENTARY SCHOOL PHYSICAL EDUCATION—cont'd

LEVEL IV—cont'd

Psychomotor Domain—cont'd

Creates and performs a movement sequence with or without equipment in a small group
Performs a variety of folk and square dance movements in time to the music
Smoothly combines skills into a routine on the mats and apparatus

Cognitive Domain

The child:

Relates to an increasing number of individuals in games and other group activities
Understands the delegation of responsibilities for various positions in the game
Selects and uses skills effectively during game play
Participates in group problem solving in developing strategy for more advanced games
Creates spaces for self, others, or objects
Can close spaces to opponents or objects in games
Varies the force used in performing skills
Can set up a program to improve or maintain own fitness level
Creates and repeats a movement sequence using a ball, rope, or other equipment alone or with others
Creates gymnastics routines increasing in length and complexity

Social Domain

The child:

Solves more complex movement problems as a member of a group
Works well with all levels of ability in the group
Supports each member of the group emotionally

Affective Domain

The child:

Assumes more responsibility for the organization and conduct of group activities
Assumes responsibility for leading a group in various capacities
Officiates an activity impartially

ment provide an opportunity for the development of new uses of the body.

Level II

Level II is also an important time for the development of an understanding of human movement and fundamental motor skills. At this level concepts should be well defined, and children are able to work with increasingly more complex movement challenges. In fundamental motor skills children work on control and accuracy. Games may require more group cooperation, and there may be some delegation of responsibilities. During this time simple dance steps may be introduced. Children's dances not only include a variety of steps but also are less imitative and use fewer nonlocomotor movements. Children use problem solving to apply what they know about movement and their ability to move in the many different activities in which they engage. For example, the teacher structures movement challenges to close and open pathways, which is then used later in the lesson in a game or other culminating activity. At this level children are actively involved in learning and are willing to practice skills and concepts with the teacher's continued encouragement.

Level III

Level III marks a transition in curriculum content. At this level, concept education and skill development continue through traditional physical education activities. Children are now able to grasp the more complex relationships between what they know about movement and the new activities in which they are engaging. Motor skill development enables the development of more advanced movement patterns. Children's ability to combine skills more easily is demonstrated as they move smoothly from one skill to the next. Lead-ups to team sports all but replace other forms of games. Learning in this area progresses through increasingly more complex movement activities through levels III and IV. Dance activities include folk and square dance and rhythmic activities with not only balls but also ropes and other equipment. Individual activities require increasingly more advanced skills and application of the movement content. Students learn to assume more responsibility for their actions, analyze their own needs, problem solving with others, and work to achieve goals with indirect teacher supervision. At this level we begin to see more individual goal setting and willingness to work independently to achieve personal goals.

Level IV

Level IV continues the study of human movement through traditional physical education activities. At this level lead-ups to team sports require the interaction of more persons, higher-level sports skills, and more complex rules and strategy. Dance activities include folk and square dance in which more advanced dance steps are needed and more complex relationships of individuals within the group are required. Individual activities require more complex application of the movement content as children learn more advanced techniques. Children at this level are able to go beyond themselves in giving support and helping others.

SUMMARY

The elementary school physical education content has been influenced by several different curriculum implementation models. The activity unit model uses an activity-centered approach and treats each unit as a separate entity. It usually does not include the movement content. The motor skills model emphasizes the development of motor skills as its primary focus. The movement model presents only the movement content throughout the school year. The fitness model and adventure model develop fitness and social skills.

The integrated movement approach focuses on the learning of the movement concepts as the basis for all learning, with application to a wide variety of motor skills and activities. The curriculum includes the study of the body's potential for movement, the use of space, and the qualities that affect efficient movement—namely balance, force, time, and flow. These movement concepts are integrated into the learning of motor skills and sports and dance activities.

The integrated movement curriculum takes in all aspects of human development. Taxonomies of cognitive, motor, affective, and social learning are considered in developing the curriculum content for elementary school-aged children. Physical education has received some criticism for its adherence to only low-level objectives. The integrated movement curriculum focuses its attention on moving the children from perceiving, refining, and varying to higher-level objectives in the learning process, including application and creative movement as well as higher levels of interpersonal relations and self-fulfillment.

The developmental approach to selecting curriculum content enables teachers from varying educational settings to identify the motor, cognitive, affective, and social needs of the children in their classes. Teachers then select program objectives with these needs in mind.

REFERENCES AND RESOURCES

Allenbaugh N: Learning about movement. In Sweeney R, editor: *Selected readings in movement education,* Reading, Pa, 1970, Addison-Wesley.

Bloom B: *Taxonomy of educational objectives the classification of educational goals,* New York, 1984, Longman.

Corbin C: First things first, but don't stop there, *JOPERD* 52(6):12, 1981.

Graham G and others: *Children moving: a teacher's guide to developing a successful physical education program,* ed 2, Palo Alto, Calif, 1987, Mayfield Publishing.

Hellison D: *Goals and strategies for teaching physical education,* Champaign, Ill, 1985, Human Kinetics.

Jewett A and Bain L: *The curriculum process in physical education,* Dubuque, Ia, 1985, Wm C Brown.

Jewett A and Mullan M: *Curriculum design: purposes and processes in physical education teaching-learning,* Washington, DC, 1977, AAHPER.

Krathwohl D: *Taxonomy of educational objectives: the classification of educational goals,* New York, 1984, Longman.

Logsdon B and others: *Physical education for children: a focus on the teaching process,* Philadelphia, 1984, Lea & Febiger.

McAleese WJ: Are you asking the right questions? *Strategies* 3(5):5, 1990.

McIntosh P: The recent history of physical education in England with particular reference to the development of movement education. In Bennett B, editor: *The history of physical education and sport,* Chicago, 1971, The Athletic Institute.

Melograno V: The balanced curriculum, where is it, what is it? *JOPERD* 55(6):21, 1984.

Mozzini L and Pangrazi B: *Child/youth physical fitness program management system,* Reston, Va, 1985, AAHPERD.

Rink J: *Teaching physical education for learning,* ed 2, St Louis, 1992, Mosby–Year Book.

Schurr E: *Movement experiences for children,* ed 3, Englewood Cliffs, NJ, 1980, Prentice-Hall.

Seefeldt V and Vogel P: What can we do about physical education? *Principal* 70(2):12, 1990.

Singer R and Dick W: *Teaching physical education,* ed 2, Boston, 1980, Houghton Mifflin.

Tillotsin J: A brief theory of movement education. In Sweeney R, editor: *Selected readings in movement education,* Reading, Mass, 1970, Addison-Wesley.

ANNOTATED READINGS

Broer M: Movement education: wherein the disagreement? *Quest,* Monograph II:19, 1964.

Discusses the meaning of "movement" and looks at the teaching of efficient movement as an aim of physical education.

Espiritu J: Quality physical education programs—cognitive emphasis, *JOPERD* 58(6):38, 1987.

Two areas of cognitive learning are an important aspect of physical education programs today—wellness concepts and physical fitness, and the disciplinary knowledge of our field. Cognition is important in the development of a physically educated person and essential to motor skill learning. Concepts must be carefully planned for and taught.

Hammersley CH: If we win, I win—adventure education in physical education and recreation, *JOPERD* 63(9):63, 1992.

This article reviews the status of adventure education with some suggestion of activities that might be incorporated into the physical education class.

Hellison D: The affective domain in physical education—let's do some housekeeping, *JOPERD* 58(6):41, 1987.

Program goals need to be established and strategies planned to clarify and develop results in the affective as well as the other domains.

Howard S: The movement education approach to teaching in English elementary schools, *JOPERD* 37(6):30, 1967.

Describes observations of movement education in England and its effects on participants—proficiency in body management skills, interest and active participation, success for all, and a high level of physical fitness.

Lawson H: Teaching the body of knowledge—the neglected part of physical education, *JOPERD* 58(7):70, 1987.
Physical education is a learning as well as a doing experience. It is time to give our students a scientific and scholarly understanding of their participation in a variety of movement activities.

Melograno V: Quality physical education—setting the standards step by step, *Strategies* 5(6):15, 1992.
The presentation of potential standards for curriculum, instruction, students, teachers and teacher evaluation and administration for examining a physical education program.

Silverman S and others: Academic learning time in elementary school physical education (alt-pe) for student subgroups and instructional activity units, *Research Quarterly for Exercise and Sport* 55(4):365, 1984.
Discusses a study of the time on task (alt-pe) in cognitive or motor activity, motor practice, and level of difficulty of practice in a movement and a traditional setting. A variety of activity units and student characteristics such as sex, skill level, and special needs were studied.

CHAPTER 4

Teaching Across the Elementary School Curriculum

OBJECTIVES

After completing this chapter the student will be able to:

1. Recognize the importance of integrating subject matter across the curriculum
2. Discuss several models for implementing integration in the schools
3. Suggest ideas for the integration of physical education content across the elementary school curriculum and offer suggestions for physical education's contribution to broad curricular themes as well as the integration of other subjects in physical education

Schools have traditionally organized subject matter as distinct and separate units. In examining a school schedule in the past, one found that each subject was allotted specific bocks of time and planned as isolated parts of the elementary school day. Time was set aside for language arts, science, math, etc. as well as art, music, and physical education. Although an assumption about education was that individuals needed to integrate what they had learned in these isolated settings to give meaning to their lives, the school did little to foster this integration.

THE INTEGRATED CURRICULUM

A major thrust in curriculum development in schools today is the integration of subject content across the curriculum. **Integration** refers to the mutual relationship between subject matter. Whereas this text in general strives to build relationships between various aspects of physical education in the integrated movement curriculum model, this particular chapter develops a broader view of integration, that of building relationships between all areas of study that make up the school curriculum. Subject integration enhances learning in several ways:

1. It promotes understanding by reinforcing curriculum content in a variety of educational settings.
2. It encourages students to transfer what is learned in one setting to new settings.
3. It increases meaning of what has been learned by giving students the opportunity to see information in new relationships and to apply it in new situations.
4. It reinforces curriculum content by more in-depth exposure to the material.

In addition, subject integration provides an opportunity for teachers to work together to achieve common goals and to appreciate the objectives and activities of each area of the curriculum.

Integration in schools may take on different forms, including the sequenced, shared, and webbed models referred to by Fogarty. In the **sequenced model** each subject is taught separately but scheduled so that similar units coincide in several subject areas. An example for the integration of social studies and physical education might include scheduling a physical education folk dance unit, which includes dances from a country being studied in social studies at the same time. Each subject carries out its unit activities separately, but each contributes to an increased understanding of the common content.

In the **shared model** two distinct disciplines may be brought together into a single focus using overlapping concepts. In this model teachers of different subject areas might plan a unit of study together focused on the shared concepts. Physical education and science teachers might plan a unit together focusing on principles of force used in activities in both disciplines. This model requires shared teaching as well as planning. The unit may be conducted within the scheduled time for each subject or in some special block of time set aside for the project.

In the **webbed model** a theme is developed that encompasses a variety of subject areas. A cross-disciplinary team chooses a theme and then each subject area uses the theme in planning activities within its area of study. This model might be used in schools periodically throughout the year or as an organizer in schools planning their curriculum around a theme such as the physical education and project adventure schools in Columbus, Ohio (Stroot). Examples of schoolwide themes might be the Olympics (Canadian Olympic Association), Fitness for Life, Together We Can (social skills) (Stroot), etc. The web planning form may take two different approaches. In one, each subject area is identified, with the teachers of each subject listing the activities to be included in developing the theme. In the other approach broader school objectives are identified, with the teachers listing the activities to be developed in each subject under the appropriate school objective. Examples of these two webbed planning forms may be found in Figures 4-1 and 4-2.

In considering integration projects, objectives from each subject matter should be strengthened rather than compromised. For integration to succeed, a feeling of mutual respect for each teacher and the subject matter must be present. The major focus should be the enrichment of learning in the integrated subjects.

Integration is not busy work. The appropriateness of activities should be based on their ability to move the students closer to meeting important educational goals.

Some examples of integration possibilities follow. They are organized for integration of subject matter in three ways: the content from physical education to be integrated across the curriculum, the content from other school subjects to be integrated in physical education, and some general topics that might be included in all subjects in the elementary school. Some of the activities included for other subjects suggest physical activity as a part of the learning experience. Other activities that have integration potential are found in the activity chapters throughout this book.

PHYSICAL EDUCATION CONTENT

Teachers have many opportunities to support what is being learned in physical education across the curriculum. Because children are interested in movement, these relationships may spark the interest of children as they work in math, language arts, science, social studies, health, art, music, and other subjects. In addition to the activities suggested in Table 4-1 and Table 4-2, teachers may establish physical education learning centers in the library or other classrooms where books, magazines, other reading material and original games and other activities may be available for children to further develop the content being taught in physical education.

The Movement Content

Body awareness, space, and quality of movement concepts have a great deal of potential for integration across the curriculum. The terminology used in this important content area in physical education has broad use throughout the school curriculum. Many of the concepts have additional meaning in science, math, and other subject areas. Body awareness and quality of movement concepts are closely related to areas of study in science. Body structure, function, and joint actions are important areas of study in science as well as principles of balance and force.

The space concepts of self and general space also have important meaning as children learn to share space in the classroom and to use various spaces in the school appropriately. For instance children may need to share space at tables as they work on various class assignments as well as know what movement is safe in the halls or other school spaces.

Fitness

Fitness is another area that has common knowledge in a variety of school subjects. By increasing an understanding of fitness, children may study the functions of the cardiorespiratory, skeletal, and muscular systems in science as well as study nutrition and the effects of diet on the body. In math children may learn to take different types of measurements and to graph numerical data.

Other Physical Education Content Areas

Other physical education activity content such as the use of small equipment, games, and dance may also be studied across the curriculum. In studying other cultures children are interested in types of play activities. Here children can begin to appreciate many activities popular in the United States that originated in other parts of the world as well as gain an understanding of their own family heritage. Language arts skills are improved as children read and write about what they are learning in studying the play activities of children of other lands. Principles that affect movement efficiency are further studied in science.

CONTENT FROM OTHER SUBJECT AREAS

Physical education can contribute to learning in other content areas as well. It not only provides a fun-filled laboratory to reinforce content that has mainly been considered the realm of other teachers in the school, but also stimulates interest in physical activities and learning more about them through recreational reading and other activities. Enhancement of overall learning can take many foms including the development of interesting bulletin boards and other written materials as well as activities within the physical education class.

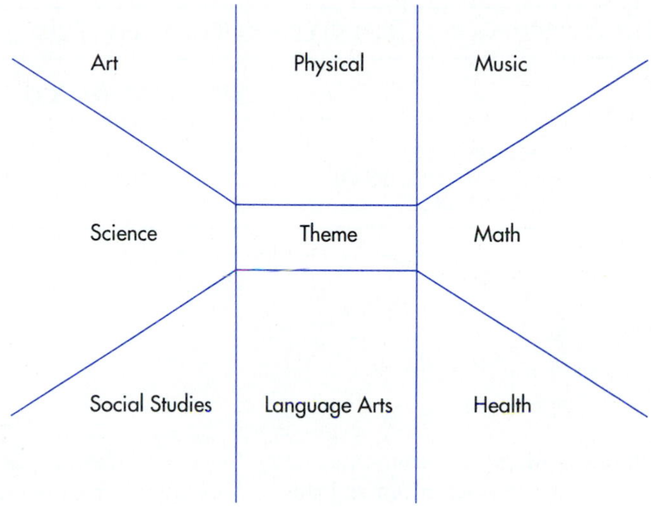

FIGURE 4-1 Cross-curricular web planning form.

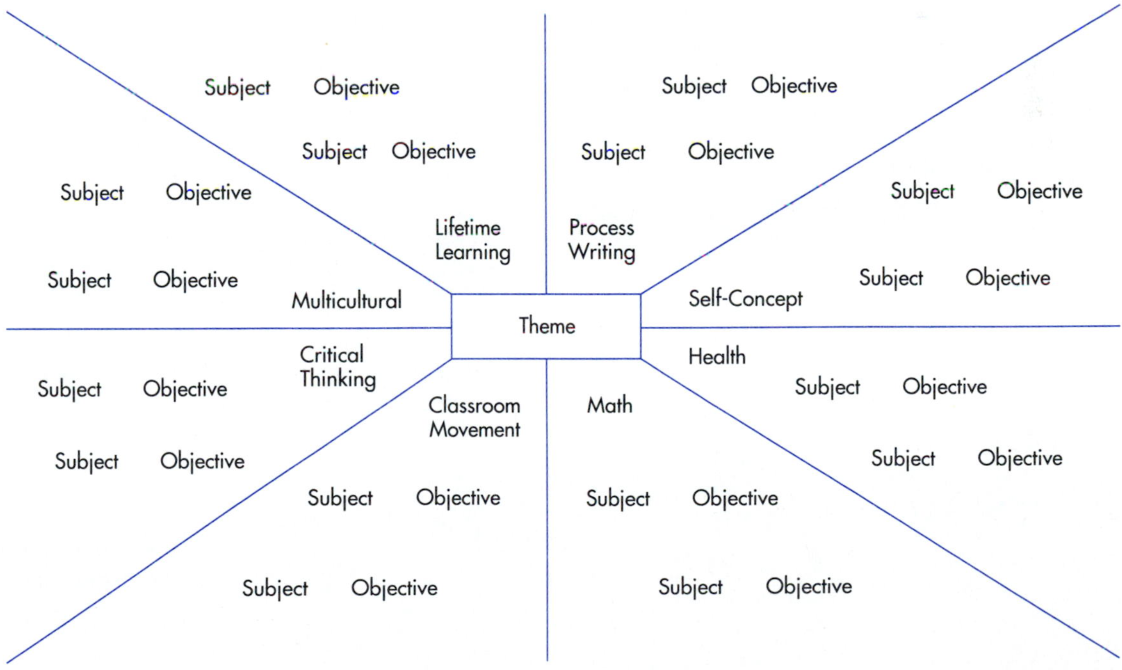

FIGURE 4-2 School goal web planning form.

TABLE 4-1 PHYSICAL EDUCATION CONTENT INTEGRATION ACTIVITIES

	BODY AWARENESS CONCEPTS			
SUBJECT	BODY PARTS	MOVEMENTS/ RELATIONSHIPS OF BODY PARTS	SHAPES	TENSION/RELAXATION
Language arts	← Develop terminology →			
			Identify letter shapes	Words that suggest relaxation or tension Poetry that creates images of relaxation
Math	Measure length of body parts or segments Ratios of parts to the whole	Measure circumference of muscles at rest and contracted	Identify number shapes Measure or weigh shapes	
Art	Draw human forms labeling body parts	Make clay forms of the body in motion Draw pictures of the body in motion	Identify shapes in the classroom Make patterns of shapes	
Science	Study body parts and their function			Learn how muscles work
Social studies			Examine shapes of houses in different parts of the world	Research Oriental cultures
Music				Select music for its relaxing or tensing effects

SPACE CONCEPTS			QUALITIES OF MOVEMENT		
SELF/GENERAL	DIRECTION/ PATHWAY	RANGE	BALANCE	FORCE	TIME
← Develop terminology →			← Develop terminology →		
← Use terminology in sentences and stories →			← Write stories of poetry using terminology →		
	Write instructions for someone to get to some place Write a story of a trip taken	Contrast ranges in poetry or stories			
Measure size of spaces or self-space Compare self-space and that of others			Balance objects on a scale or balance board		
Make a mural of neighborhood in correct relationship	Use pathways to create a design or other art form		Examine balance in pictures Mold sculptures with different bases of support Study principles Study gravity and its effect of balance	Draw pictures depicting forces of nature (wind, gravity, etc.) or effects of forces Study principles of creating and absorbing force Study force in nature Examine potential force of body parts	
	Study maps		Study balance of power in government (legislative, executive judicial branches)		Sequence historical events
		Build long and short sounds into rhythmic patterns			Study meter, tempo, rhythmic pattern, phrasing

TABLE 4-2 INTEGRATION OF PHYSICAL EDUCATION ACTIVITY CONTENT

SUBJECT	DANCE	FITNESS	GAMES	GYMNASTICS	SMALL EQUIPMENT	TRACK
Language arts	Read or write stories or poetry to use as themes for dances	Define terms Write sentences using terms	Write rules, modifications of an original game Learn terminology in a foreign language Write stories about games	Write out routines	Develop vocabulary in a foreign language	
Math	Create rhythmic patterns	Measure fitness components Solve math problems regarding changes in scores Graph changes in performance	Keep score Keep game statistics		Keep score Count repetitions	Measure distances Convert inches and feet to meters Measure time with a stopwatch
Social studies	Research cultures and dance origins	Look at cultural norms for different events	Research game origins, famous participants	Research origins of stunts or famous athletes	Research origins or equipment	Research records and famous athletes Study ancient Olympics
Art	Draw costumes and art of other cultures		Draw native dress and pictures of children playing games		Design and construct new equipment	Create sculptures of participants
Music	Study musical instruments Study underlying beat, tempo, and phrasing					
Science	Explore value of dance to health	Study fitness value of activities Study skeletal, muscular, and cardiorespiratory systems Relates activity to nutrition		Apply movement principles		Study requirements of different events (endurance, etc.)

Development of the movement content offers a number of opportunities to integrate learning as well as activities in dance, games, or other activities. A few of the many possibilities are included in the following section. Additional activities may be found in the activity content chapters throughout the book.

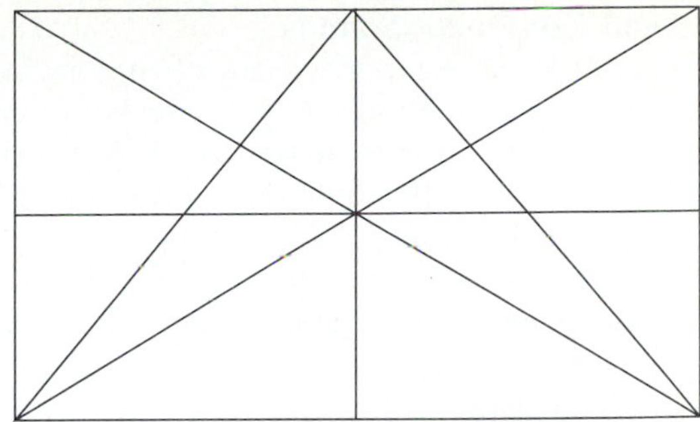

FIGURE 4-3 Line grid.

Language Arts

A number of areas in language arts may be reinforced in physical education. They include the alphabet, vowel and consonant sounds, spelling, sentence structure, reflective writing, writing research reports, and reading and writing stories or poetry. Some suggested activities follow.

Alphabet

In conjunction with studying shape and pathway, a child may:

1. Make the shape of letters of the alphabet with their bodies
2. Make the first letter of their names
3. Make a letter with straight lines, curved lines, or a combination of straight and curved lines
4. Make a letter standing up or lying down
5. Make a letter with a partner
6. Make a letter with a rope and trace its pathway in space

Using a grid of lines, one child suggests a letter while the other traces the letter by walking on the lines (Figure 4-3). Using a grid of letters, one child suggests a word which the other child spells by hopping or performing some other movement from one letter to the next (Figure 4-4).

H	E	P	C	L
O	S	W	T	N
K	X	A	U	J
B	U	Y	D	Q
M	I	F	R	G

FIGURE 4-4 Letter grid.

Spelling

As individuals move in general space:

1. A word is given and the children stop to make the first letter of the word with their bodies and then on the next signal move to act out the word.
2. With individual letters, on the signal they find others to make up a three-letter word

Children may also:

1. Create words, with three or four children making the letters with their bodies.
2. With a parachute, spell words in groups of three or four, with children moving on the signal and one at a time under the parachute to find letters, one per person, scattered there or create words by finding letters for different word endings, for example, *-at, -ank,* and *-ill.*
3. Practice spelling words by adding a letter each time the child hits the ball in a game of four square
4. Use the correct spelling of a word as a way to be released from prison in a game of capture the flag.

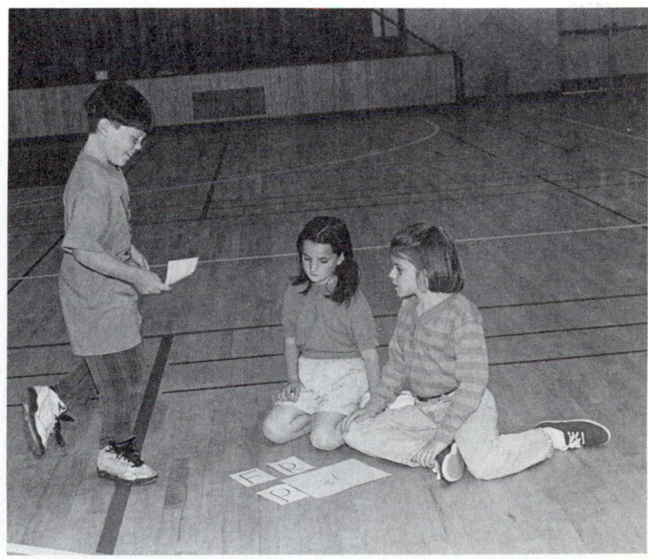

Children may develop locomotor skills as they practice spelling.

Vowel and Consonant Sounds

1. In partners one makes the shape of an object with a short vowel sound given by the teacher or drawn from a box; the partner makes the shape of another object with the same short vowel sound—cat, hat; snake, rake.
2. Use long or short vowel sounds as the signal to run in a game of crows and cranes or other games.

Sentence Structure

1. The teacher calls out a word. If it is a noun the children make a shape, if it is a verb they act it out.
2. Listening to a story, the children act it out, with special attention given to the adjectives explaining the nouns (large tree, small mouse, round belly, etc.) or adverbs explaining the verbs (dodge quickly, jump high, run fast).
3. Children are given a noun or verb. Working in groups of two or three, on the signal they move under the parachute one at a time, picking up words placed there to complete a sentence.
4. In games the signal to go is given when an individual child or a group of children complete a sentence using a word given by the leader.

Reading and Writing

1. Act out a series of instructions written on a task card.
2. Keep a journal in physical education writing about what you did, how you liked it, and how you felt about it.
3. Read about a famous athlete or an activity and write a report to be put up on the bulletin board.
4. Write a sports story or report of a physical education or intramural activity for the school newspaper.
5. Write a task analysis or a description of a motor skill or fitness test describing the movements of the body to help someone understand the task.
6. Write a set of personal goals for improving or maintaining fitness or level of achievement to be attained in an activity unit.
7. Write up the strategy developed for use in a game and the level of success it achieved.

Math

A number of areas of math can be incorporated easily into physical education lessons. Math readiness activities such as range, shapes, and numbers lend themselves to the development of the movement content, and other math concepts such as counting, sets, computation, and measurement can be enhanced in many other physical education activities.

Math Readiness Activities

In developing the concept of body shape children can:

1. Make shapes varying in size—large and small, tall and short, wide and narrow.
2. Make numbers with body parts or their whole bodies, alone or with a partner. Street numbers, telephone numbers, or the date may also be used in making numbers with the body.
3. Make a number with a rope and trace its path on the floor.
4. Trace the pathways of numbers in the air and then on the floor moving in different ways or in different directions.

Journal writing strengthens both writing and physical education comprehension.

Counting

1. The children respond by taking the number of steps, skips, hops, etc. called by the leader in a game of Simon Says.
2. The teacher holds up a number of objects or claps a number of times. The children count the objects or claps and then make the shape of the number with their bodies.
3. In rhythmic activities the teacher performs a series of claps, hits with sticks, ball bounces, etc; the children count the number and repeat the sequence.
4. In the game of Midnight, the fox calls the number of steps to be taken before the children can ask for the time.
5. The children make up a combination of rope jumps or ball skills to a number given by the teacher.

Sets

1. In a group of three, each makes a low shape, another group of three make shapes in the medium level, while a third group makes shapes in the high level; each group forms a set.
2. With a partner or in a group of three, children create a set and describe it to the class.
3. After the children form sets, several different sets stand up and the quantity of the sets is compared. Is the middle set greater or less than the set to its right? How does it compare with the one to its left?
4. Have children create sets of two people—rounded, straight, and bent shapes; describe the sets; rearrange the groups so that each contains a round, straight, and bent shape. New sets are thus formed that have the same number of shapes and the same shapes.

Computation

1. The children make a number which is the answer to a math problem given by the teacher. If the answer requires two or more numbers children may use a partner or form groups.
2. While moving in general space, on the signal the children group themselves to create math problems to an answer given by the teacher by having an appropriate number of people and selecting the correct math signs (for example, answer 4; possible solutions $2 + 2$, 2×2, $3 + 1$, $5 - 1$, etc.).
3. Make up a sequence of three different movements and perform it with one or more repetitions.
4. In some tag or ball games, one can count the number tagged and determine the number left, the percentage out, etc.
5. In a game of Crows and Cranes, the signal to go is an odd or even number called by the leader, or the odd or even answer to an addition, subtraction, multiplication or division math problem.
6. A similar application may be made in games such as Steal the Bacon, Toss-up Basketball, Sideline Hockey, etc. A math problem is given and the persons with the number of the answer begin active play.
7. With ropes, balls, or other small equipment one child performs a number of jumps, bounces, etc. The second child adds another set of skills, the third then performs the sum of the two.
8. In working with bean bags that have numbers marked on them, groups of children throw at targets on the floor. Their score is represented by the total of the numbers on the beanbags hitting the target. Children repeat the exercise, trying to better their scores.
9. In working with rhythmic activities, beats are broken down into whole, half, quarter, and eighth notes as children move with sticks or balls to the music.
10. Mapping and graphing may be included in plotting changes in fitness scores, heart rate before and after performing different activities, number of succcessful attempts on each set of trials in performing a skill.
11. Compute game statistics such as batting averages, percentage of shots made, etc.
12. Develop math skills in computing bowling scores.
13. In self-testing activities children compute the percentage of successful attempts out of ten, repeating the activity to try to improve their score.

Measurement

1. Children make a number by moving in its pathway in general space; they repeat the activity but now make their number twice as large, half as big, one quarter the size.
2. In studying time and using clocks as a time reference, children move as the hour hand, minute hand, second hand. Then repeat the activity, with some moving in a circle as seconds on the outside, minutes on the inside, and hours in the center.
3. Moving in general space between two points, children count the number of steps (giant steps, skips, etc.) it takes to cover the space.
4. Children measure the distance jumped in the standing or long jump, the distance a ball has been thrown, or measure time on a stop watch for a 50-yard dash.
5. Children convert meters to yards for a distance run.
6. Children estimate the distance to be jumped or ball thrown and then compare with actual performance.

Arts

Physical education represents the human aspect of the arts. Through physical education children begin to understand the body, its capacity for movement, and the use of movement to convey ideas. Physical education provides an opportunity to develop the aesthetic nature of movement in dance and rhythmic activities. In addition some body awareness concept activities enhance an understanding of the arts.

Study of the arts in physical education can begin with a study of the common elements: space, balance and symmetry, rhythm and time, mood and interpretation, and shape and form. Children need the opportunity to explore these elements and their relationships in compositions using locomotor and nonlocomotor movements.

In studying body awareness, children can create symmetrical and asymmetrical shapes with their bodies or objects, such as ribbons or ropes. From ideas suggested by the teacher or the students, the children may also create human sculptures that depict the body in motion. In a similar activity, one child may move the body parts of another child to create a human sculpture. In exploring the potential of the body in communicating ideas, children may move and interact with imaginary objects varying in texture—smooth, rough, tacky, etc.

The dance chapters (Chapters 19 through 22) provide many activities to enhance the arts.

Science

Much of the material studied in science has a close relationship to the content in physical education. The movement content provides an opportunity for children to explore their bodies as well as many of the principles taught in science, such as the creation and absorption of force, stability, trajectory, spin, and rebound. In addition children learn about gravity, air, and water resistance. The movement content provides the opportunity to explore these concepts as children develop greater control of their moving bodies and in manipulating objects. Chapter 12 includes a number of activities relating movement to scientific principles.

Social Studies

Many of the activities in physical education can be used to integrate with units in social studies. Children can easily relate the history of sports, games, and dance to social studies units. In addition children may study world competitions—Olympics, World Cup, etc.—learning about competing countries as well as famous athletes from around the world. Children can learn about activities popular in different cultures. The teacher can also relate the type of activities popular in various parts of the world with the climate and terrain. In studying our own country, physical education can include activities popular at various times in our history or in different parts of the country. Another possibility is to explore sports in pictures, the media, literature, poetry, song, etc.

GENERAL THEMES

Integration may be achieved through an all-school activity on a particular theme. These themes may focus on some school goal, an event taking place, or some other idea. A few examples follow.

Theme: The First Americans

Many people have contributed to our way of life in America. Native Americans lived in our country long before European settlers arrived. Activities in a number of school subjects can help children learn about these early Americans and their national heritage.

Physical Education: Study the origins of games and activities (lacrosse, lummi sticks, etc.) and learn Native American games and dances.

Social Studies: Research the various tribes and nations and the area of the United States where they lived

Language Arts: Study storytelling and legends

Art: Learn about the art of various tribes, their costumes, jewelry, signs, face painting, etc.

Music: Listen to Native American music and instruments

Science: Examine the relationship of Native Americans to their environment

Theme: Together We Can (cooperation and concern for others)

Children need to learn the value of working with others and assuming responsibility in cooperative settings. Activities can be planned that help develop a cooperative learning setting in the school and that demonstrate some concern for their fellow human begins.

Physical Education: Structure activities so that children must work together to accomplish a task. For example, in partners or small groups, complete a task with one idea from each person; play games where children must work together to develop offensive and defensive strategy; use the **reciprocal teaching style** where children work together to develop a motor skill; have children work in pairs to distribute and collect equipment; have children work in a small group on a new task that is completed when everyone can do it; have children restructure games so that scoring depends on cooperation such as number of passes completed, etc., rather than on points scored; have children share in making rules for the class or a game.

Other subjects: Work on projects requiring children to work together, share equipment in working on an in-class project, work with another child reading, doing math problems, completing an art project etc; work on an assignment alone and then with a partner, then discuss the difference in what was learned; involve children in a class project to aid others in the community—collecting food or clothing for a shelter, putting on a holiday meal, planning a party for preschool children in a shelter, etc.

Theme: The Olympics

The Olympics is a popular theme every 4 years to foster understanding of people in other lands. The Canadian Olympic Committee developed materials to study the Olympics across the curriculum in preparation for the winter and summer games in 1992.

Physical Education: Research and learn the Olympic events by actually performing them or exploring the movements through movement challenges. Discuss the training required to be a successful competitor.

Social Studies: Choose a country to study. Learn about the people, history, climate, geography, etc. Learn about the importance of sport in the country and identify the sports in which the country will compete. Learn about some of the country's top athletes. Report on the events as they are taking place and record on a large bulletin board display the placement of each country's competitors.

Art: Make the flag of the country, study the clothing of the country, and represent that country in a Olympic pageant. Draw event logos in preparation for an all-school Olympic event.

Music: Study music from the country.

Math: Practice the techniques of scoring the events. Study the currency of the country and its equivalent in U.S. dollars. Discuss expenses of the host country—hotel costs, food, and transportation.

Language Arts: Write stories about the Olympics. Write a newspaper story about one of the athletes or the results of an event. Learn to pronounce the French names of countries as they will be introduced in the Olympic opening ceremonies.

Theme: Building Community

An important part of the educational process is understanding and contributing to one's own community. School activities can help children feel a part of their community and learn more about it.

Physical Education: Look at the community resources for an active life-style and learn some of the activities. Learn some games or dances that may be part of the national heritage of the people who live in the community. Plan an event in which children participate with their families, such as a games or square dance party. Plan an intergenerational event with senior citizens or grandparents. In learning about the disabled in the community, the children participate in activities as if they were blind, physically handicappted, or deaf.

Social Studies: Survey the resources, services, businesses, and town government of a community. Identify needs that are being met and those that are not. Study the people of the community—their nationalities, socioeconomic background, disabilities, etc. Plan an event to help meet one of the needs, for example, bringing food for the homeless or planning a party for children at a shelter.

Language Arts: Write a letter to someone in town government or an invitation to a school event. Research and write a report of the town government. Write a history of the community.

SUMMARY

The integration of content across the curriculum is an important part of education today. This integration may take several forms. It may involve teachers conducting separate units during the same time period in the sequenced model, teachers working together to plan and teach units in the shared model, or a group of teachers developing content around a common theme in their own subject areas in the webbed model.

The objectives of the integrated subject matter are strengthened in the integration process. Understanding is increased as students have more opportunity to study the content, see its relationship across the curriculum, and transfer what they have learned in one setting to other settings.

The integration process should include strengthening the physical education content in other subject areas as well as enhancing the content of other subject areas in physical education. In some settings teachers plan and conduct activities focused on a central theme.

REFERENCES AND RESOURCES

Anderson M and Krambeer J: Writing to learn, *Strategies* 4(1):16, 1990.

Brophy J and Alleman J: A caveat: curriculum integration isn't always a good idea, *Educational Leadership* 49(2):66, 1991.

Burton EC and Lane C: Using computers to facilitate the integration of art, music and movement, *JOPERD* 60(7):58, 1989.

Canadian Olympic Association: *The Olympic collection 1992,* Ottawa, Canada, 1991, Canadian Olympic Association.

Cratty B: *Intelligence in action,* Englewood Cliffs, NJ, 1973, Prentice-Hall.

Cratty B: *Academic learning: games to enhance academic abilities,* ed 2, Englewood Cliffs, NJ, 1985, Prentice-Hall.

Drake SM: How our team dissolved the boundaries, *Educational Leadership* 49(2):20, 1991.

Fogarty R: Ten ways to integrate curriculum, *Educational Leadership* 49(2):61, 1991.

Frey R and Alan M: Alaskan native games—a cross-cultural addition to the physical education curriculum, *JOPERD* 60(9):21, 1989.

Gilbert A: *Teaching the three r's through movement experiences,* New York, 1977, Macmillan.

Grubaugh S and Virgilio SJ: Strategies for the development of reading skills through physical education, *Reading Improvement* 22(2):138, 1985.

Kern K: Teaching circulation in elementary PE classes, a circulatory system model, *JOPERD* 58(1):62, 1987.

McSwegin P, Pemberton C, Petray C, Going S: *Physical best: the AAHPERD guide to physical fitness education and assessment,* Reston, Va, 1988, AAHPERD Publications.

Parcel GS and others: School promotion of healthful diet and exercise behavior: an integration of organizational change: social learning theory interventions, *Journal of School Health* 57(4):150, 1987.

Parrish B: Reading practices and possibilities in physical education, *JOPERD* 55(3):73, 1984.

Perkins DN: Educating for insight, *Educational Leadership* 49,2:4, 1991.

Petray CK: Classroom teachers as partners—teaching health related physical fitness, *JOPERD* 60(7):69, 1989.

Ricklin L Perfect and Perfect-Miller S: Come to the fair, *Teaching K-8* November/December 1991, p 57.

Rubinstein B: A sports history: motivation for reluctant readers, *Elementary English* 30:591, 1975.

Stroot S, Carpenter M, Eisnaugle K: Focus on physical education: academic and physical excellence at Westgate Alternative School, *JOPERD* 62(7):49, 1991.

Wentzell SR: Beyond the physical—expressive writing in physical education, *JOPERD,* 60(9):18, 1989.

Werner P and Burton E: *Learing through movement,* St Louis, 1975, Mosby–Year Book.

Werner P, Simmons M, Bowling T: Combining the arts and academics, *JOPERD* 60(7):55, 1989.

Yeager S: Tuning in to the Olympics, *JOPERD* 59(3):59, 1988.

ANNOTATED READINGS

Beach L: World class geography, *Instructor* 100(6):27, 1991.
Identifying countries, continents, analyzing cost of air-fare, meals and accommodations, determining distances, keeping travel logs, writing reports, doing research, map reading, comparing currency, etc.

Bowyer G: Getting the classroom teacher involved, *Strategies* 6(3):28, 1992.
Suggests several strategies to get classroom teachers involved in the physical education program.

Crawford SAGM: Unusual applications of sports studies in the elementary school, *Physical Educator* 44(2):296, 1987.
Suggests several integrated studies of sport including literature, cinema, video, geography, the media, stamps, art, cartoons, memorabilia, and the animal kingdom.

Markle S: Hands-on whole science, *Instructor* 100(6):89, 1991.
The fitness challenge—combining science of fitness with social studies, language arts, math and more—giving students a jump on getting and staying in shape.

Novelli J: Culture meets curriculum, *Instructor* 99(8):31, 1990.
Integrating Native American (Ojibwe) culture, arts, and traditions.

O'Doud K and Franz M: Immersed in math, *Instructor* 100(8):30, 1991.
Suggestions for math in measuring heights and objects, weighing, balancing, making estimates, and calendar math.

CHAPTER 5

Program Planning

OBJECTIVES

After completing this chapter the student will be able to:

1. List factors that affect the elementary school physical education program
2. State several guiding principles that must be considered in planning the instructional program
3. Describe sound curriculum planning—program, annual, unit, and daily lessons—which requires looking at factors affecting the school's curriculum, goal setting, selecting content, and planning for evaluation

Successful implementation of the program begins with careful planning of all aspects of the elementary school physical education experience. Each school setting is unique because it is affected by the interaction of factors such as environment, budget, staffing, and the learners themselves. Regardless of these individual characteristics, physical education experiences are an integral part of the school curriculum. Each elementary school physical education program is developed on the following premises:

- All children shall have an equal opportunity for participation in physical education.
- Physical education provides an opportunity for all children to develop their unique qualities. The rights of the individual and the nature and needs of a democratic society are reflected in the physical education experiences.
- Physical education promotes favorable attitudes about personal worth and activity for life.

The physical education program incorporates several levels of planning. Initially the curriculum content must be determined. Once we have determined what we want to include in our physical education program, the annual plan is developed to fit the curriculum content to the school calendar and to ensure the relative emphasis of each part of the program. Next, the units of instruction are developed for each activity based on the time available and the age and experience of the students. Finally, we are ready to plan the individual lessons through which the unit content will be presented to the students.

CURRICULUM PLANNING

Curriculum planning is the first step in the improvement of instruction and a means to better teaching. It does not guarantee effective teaching, but it gives good teachers direction in the planning and carrying out of appropriate learning experiences for children.

Physical education curriculum planning is a district-wide responsibility. All teachers at all levels should share in the decision making for the kindergarten through twelfth grade program of study. Although curriculum planning is often directed by local or district beliefs about physical education, it may also respond to state or professional guidelines for curriculum content.

Curriculum planning is a long-range task, as a sound curriculum is developed over time. Curriculum change is a continuous endeavor. Those responsible for the curriculum must be willing to make the necessary modifications to keep it viable as conditions in education and society change. In today's society curriculum must consider more than the activity content of physical education. The process for acquiring skills and knowledge about human movement must also be a concern if individuals are to acquire the tools for continuous learning in the future.

The physical education curriculum must have as its foundation of common core of learning experiences beginning in the early years and culminating at high school graduation. This core content should be centered around the understanding of movement and body management skills. Each level of the curriculum should include appropriate learning activities geared to meet the developmental needs of children. A wide variety of activities are used to enable children to use their skills and understanding in many different situations. The physical education curriculum must provide maximum opportunity for youngsters' involvement in learning situations that require cognitive, social, affective, and motor responses and that result in favorable attitudes, skills, and knowledge.

The curriculum provides sequential, progressive learning experiences that allow not only for the acquisition of skills and knowledge but also for the ability to process information in more sophisticated ways. The curriculum takes children beyond the accumulation of information and develops in them the ability to vary, apply, and create as the movement situation requires.

Program planning involves an analysis of factors that affect the curriculum, the development of program goals, the selection of content and processes as discussed in Chapter 3, and a plan to evaluate the program.

Step 1: Analyzing Factors That Affect the Curriculum

A number of factors must be considered in planning the curriculum; some are outlined in Figure 5-1.

Status of the Learners

The needs, interests, and experiences of the learners are important considerations in curriculum planning. Previous physical education experiences, as well as the informal play experiences of the children, are important. If children have long bus rides to and from school, their leisure-time activities may be limited to activities, usually sedentary in nature, that they engage in after dark during short winter days. Their attitudes about activity and their concept of physical education will reflect their previous experiences in physical education. The children's experience at home and in school also will affect their ability to be self-directed, which has implications for curricular decisions. These factors will not only affect what is offered but at what level of difficulty the experiences begin and the expectations for learning for each aspect of the program. The structure for the learning experiences must also reflect students' social maturity and willingness to assume responsibility for their behavior and learning.

The Community

The value and importance parents and the school board place on physical education are reflected in the curriculum. The family influences children's attitudes toward school in general and physical education in particular. Some communities may value a positive physical education experience for all children. Others may value only the successful high school athletic teams. Community interest in age group sports activities may influence expectations for physical education. It is important for the school to interpret the program to the public so that they can understand the goals and the activities to achieve them.

Geographic Location

The location of the school system will affect the physical education curriculum. Climate, length of seasons, and natural surroundings are important factors in curricular decisions. Obviously the curriculum for a community in the Southwest, with its heat and wind, will differ considerably from a physical education program in much cooler New England. Whereas programs in northern states will plan many activities for indoors, some southern states will rely almost totally on outdoor facilities.

Facilities and Equipment

The facilities and equipment available in the school may place some limitations on curricular options. However, facilities in the community, both private and public, may be used to supplement those available at the school. The budget for equipment must be adequate to provide maximum activity for all children. Ball skills cannot be developed with one ball, just as reading cannot be taught with one book. Physical educators must set priorities regarding equipment purchases to provide the best possible learning environment for all. An array of equipment is important in providing an adequate variety of activities. Often, industrial art classes at the high school or interested parent groups can provide equipment for the playground and for physical education use at a minimum cost. In some communities it may be necessary to share equipment among the schools. This approach requires careful planning so that all schools have access to the equipment sometime during the school year. A plan for the maintenance, repair, and storage of equipment is required if each piece of equipment is to last as long as possible.

Staffing

The teacher responsible for the physical education program may be a trained professional in physical education or the classroom teacher. Obviously the trained specialist has the background to provide the best possible program.

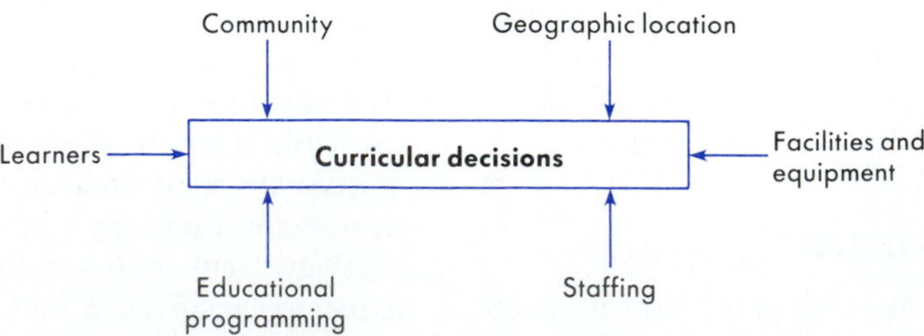

FIGURE 5-1 Factors affecting curriculum planning.

Professional physical educators may be hired to teach all the classes, or the physical education specialist may be responsible for the program development, with the classroom teachers carrying out the implementation. In other situations the physical educator may work with the children 1 or 2 days each week while the classroom teacher continues the program for the remaining days. When the responsibility for instruction is shared by physical educators and classroom teachers, much effort is required to coordinate the efforts of both. **Inservice training** for classroom and physical education teachers must be provided on a regular basis.

Educational Programming

Educational programming in the school has several implications for physical education. Where possible, physical education classes should be held daily for periods of approximately 30 minutes for young children and 40 to 45 minutes for children in the upper elementary school grades. Unfortunately, 2- and 3-day-a-week programs are more often the rule. Although time is not the only factor affecting the quality of the program, much more can be gained from a program that meets every day than from one that meets only twice a week.

Another factor in educational programming is the organization of classrooms and children. In some elementary schools, children of several ages may be grouped together in the class. This approach has serious implications for physical education classes because the needs that resulted in the arrangement may not be the same needs considered for grouping in physical education.

Step 2: Establishing Program Goals

The second step in curriculum planning is the establishment of overall goals for each child who participates in the physical education program. These goals must be in tune with the overall goals of the educational system in which the physical education program is a part, as well as state guidelines. Although these goals tend to be broad, they should not be so broad as to be meaningless. Each goal should be able to be translated into specific outcomes for each age level.

The whole person must be considered in determining these important goals. Physical education programs have traditionally included goals in physical development and fitness; the development of motor skills, social skills, and affective behaviors; and cognitive development. One should answer the following questions in determining program goals:

1. What motor skills should children be able to perform?
2. What knowledge should children have?
3. What is the level of fitness to which each child should aspire?
4. How should children behave as they work alone or with others?

These questions are all closely related as goals are established and later translated into meaningful learning experiences for children.

The physical experience in physical education is unique to education. As participants in motor activities, children not only enhance their physical development but also acquire the foundational motor patterns necessary for successful participation throughout life. Some programs of physical education choose to stress the development of motor skills, some stress physical fitness, and others combine the two. With the introduction of the movement content into American physical education, more emphasis has been placed on the knowledge base in physical education. Understanding body awareness, space, and movement qualities and applying this information to a variety of activities have been added to our knowledge base. Physical educators now seek to impart knowledge beyond the rules, the execution of skills, and set strategies. Movement situations are designed to help children solve movement challenges that require varying skills, as well as improvising and creating new movements.

Social and affective goals are commonly included in the physical education curriculum; however, they are not automatic outcomes of a physical education program. Experiences must be carefully planned and conducted to realize appropriate behaviors. Examples of school and National Association of School Physical Education goals may be found in Chapter 1.

Step 3: Determining Content and Process

The third step in curriculum planning is to determine content and the processes through which children will become movement educated. We must now answer the following question: "What kinds of experiences should children have to meet the stated goals?" To respond to this question, we must consider the activities in which the children will engage and the nature of the experiences that will facilitate understanding and application of what we know about human movement while they also enhance the motor skills, physical fitness, social skills, and attitudes for which we strive. The selection of content may go beyond the scope of this text. Physical educators may choose additional activities characteristic of the leisure interests of those in their geographical area, such as cross-country skiing and aquatics. Including activities popular in the area is important in preparing students for lifetime participation.

Guiding Principles for Selecting Content

The following statements are guiding principles in selecting content for the elementary school physical education program.

The movement content is the core of the physical education program. Physical education has as a primary responsibility the study of human movement, including the understanding of the human body's movement potential and the external factors that affect the efficiency and effectiveness of the movement in which we engage. The concepts of body awareness, space, and the qualities of movement enrich children's understanding of movement. Application of such knowledge now and in future physical activities increases movement possibilities and enhances success as children and adults engage in new motor activities.

Activities should be selected on the basis of their contribution to the goals of the physical education program. Activities that contribute to more of the educational goals should have priority over those that contribute to fewer goals. Some activities contribute to all or most of the goals of physical education. Other activities contribute to only a few. For instance, softball and volleyball do not contribute to fitness goals. They do, however, contribute to other goals by providing group activity and involving striking skills. Gymnastics provides unique experiences in body awareness, and folk dance provides the need to move to an imposed rhythm. In settings in which time is limited for physical education, planners must make careful choices when selecting content to ensure that goals will be met.

Content should be selected to address the needs and interests of children. The content should be developmentally appropriate. The selection of content should be based on what we know about children at each developmental level. It should be content for children, not adult activities and games. Activities that children enjoy doing and in which they can find success with regard to motor, cognitive, and social skills required are important to achieve positive attitudes about participation. Input from children can help the teacher see the activities from the children's perspective.

The content should be planned with continuity in mind. Sufficient time should be allocated to master the skills and knowledge. In a program that meets 1 or 2 days per week, the number of possible units of instruction are limited. Most units require a minimum of eight 30-minute lessons to provide adequate time for meaningful learning. Where more time is allowed for physical education, longer units should be planned.

Relationships between activities, motor skills, and the application of movement concepts are important if learning is to be continuous. The integrated movement curriculum depends on continuity from one activity to the next.

The content should provide for progressions from year to year, with each experience becoming increasingly complex. Many activities in the curriculum are offered annually. It is important to offer children a progression of experiences that challenge them at each level and meet their changing needs. Progression in the complexity and use of skills, learning process required, social interactions required, and complexity of activities to challenge children cognitively are important if physical education is to remain interesting and enjoyable.

Content should consider the development of the whole child. Each activity should be selected with the total development of children in mind. Physical fitness, motor skills, cognitive development, and social skills must all be considered in the selection of the content areas.

The content should recognize individual differences in the rate of learning. Within each content area a range of activities should be considered to meet the needs of all the children, those who are able and those whose skills and understandings are below our expectations. The teacher provides a variety of skills and activities for each level of ability within the group. New skills and activities are introduced as children are ready to try them or when something new is needed to maintain interest.

The program should include a variety of activities. Sometimes the physical education program is limited to the activities that the teacher chooses to teach rather than a variety of activities that will meet the needs and interests of all children. If the students are to be well served, each teacher must continue to grow as a professional by updating skills and knowledge and developing new activity areas. At beginning levels emphasis is on the development of an understanding of the movement content and fundamental movement skills. At each level the variety of experiences offered should include dance, individual activities, and games. These activities should enable children to use the skills and concepts in many different movement situations. Figure 5-2 defines the content areas of the elementary school physical education program with relative emphasis by level developed in this book. Obviously, many other activities could be included under each of the headings. A program that does not include a variety of games, dances, and individual activities in addition to the movement content is not a complete physical education experience.

The physical education content should be integrated with other areas of the elementary school curriculum. If carefully planned, physical education may contribute to reading, math, and other school subjects. A coordinated effort by teachers in various areas of the school curriculum results in favorable outcomes for all areas of the curriculum. For example, movement challenges in the primary grades contribute to math and reading readiness as children explore shape, size, and pathway. Other subject areas also may contribute substantially to the goals of physical education.

The content should be selected with practical limitations in mind. Although physical education experiences should be offered on a daily basis, often they are not. Every program has its limitations. A program that meets only 2 days per week will not accomplish the breadth and depth of experiences that could result from daily physical education. It is better to do fewer things well than to try to give the children a little of everything.

Facilities and equipment may also limit the content of the program. Programs operating with limited financial resources will need to plan carefully to maximize the use

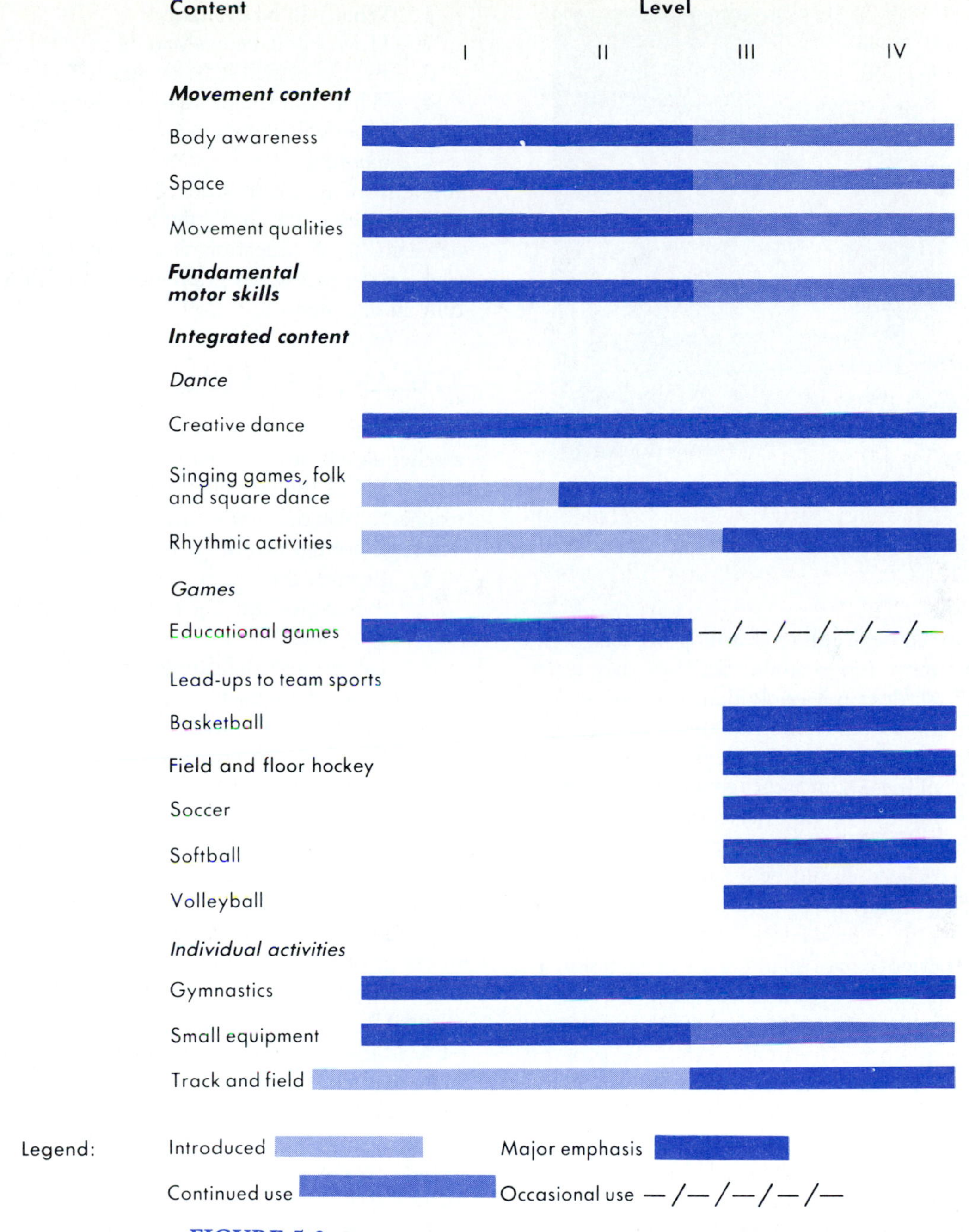

FIGURE 5-2 Content of elementary school physical education.

of available equipment and facilities. Teachers will need to be resourceful in extending the program with the use of community resources.

Geographical location affects the length of seasons and the availability of some activities. Each setting provides unique opportunities for children to learn skills that they can use throughout life.

The curriculum should meet or surpass the state and professional guidelines. Most states have some regulation regarding the minimum physical education requirement. In addition the state board of education or the state physical education society may develop guidelines that go beyond the state regulations in providing guidance for curriculum development.

Planning for Learning

One of our primary concerns in the integrated movement curriculum is teaching children to be independent learners, to think, and to analyze ever-changing movement situations. If this goal is to be realized, physical education experiences must be carefully planned and conducted and must incorporate experiences that require higher and higher levels of thought processing.

Emphasis in physical education today is on child-cen-

Sharing ideas is an important part of concept development.

tered rather than teacher-centered learning. In these styles children assume more responsibility for their own learning. This approach does not imply that teachers put out the equipment and leave children to their own devices. Nor does it mean that children decide fully what is to be learned. The use of these approaches requires careful planning in considering the varying needs of children in the class and in clarifying teacher expectations for working and learning. Teachers should be a valuable resource in the process of learning, but not necessarily the only resource.

Learning experiences are planned in progression to meet the learning process goals discussed in Chapter 3. Experiences in physical education begin with the perception of the task, move to refinement of the task, progress to varying and applying, and finally to creative movement. One should not assume that application and creative movement occur only in the upper grades. Each process should occur at each level. At each level there will be perceiving and refining as children are introduced to new motor skills and work to master them. Varying and applying follow as they learn to use the skills under imposed or spontaneously changing conditions. Finally, creative responses provide children with the challenge that will keep them moving all their lives.

Step 4: Planning the Evaluation of the Program

Evaluation is an important aspect of physical education program planning. It enables us to look objectively at the curriculum content with regard to the program goals and student achievement. It is an ongoing process that results in changes that sharpen the program focus in meeting the needs of the children. Planning requires determination of the following:

1. What will be evaluated?
2. How will it be evaluated?
3. By whom will it be evaluated?
4. When will the evaluation take place?
5. How will changes in curriculum be implemented?

Input from teachers, students, parents, administrators, other professionals in the field, and members of the state department of education is an important aspect of the evaluation process. Program evaluation is discussed more fully in Chapter 11.

THE ANNUAL PLAN

Once the goals, content, and processes have been defined, a schedule of units of activity, the **annual plan,** is developed. The annual plan enables the physical education teacher to plan the year's experience in physical education. Through annual planning the teacher:

1. Ensures the relative emphasis for each aspect of the curriculum—games, dance, individual activities, and the movement content.
2. Determines the number of lessons to be planned for each activity area.
3. Blocks out the daily units of instruction.
4. Schedules activities based on the availability of equipment and facilities.
5. Schedules activities with the seasons in mind.
6. Schedules activities so that overall body development is assured.
7. Schedules activities with prerequisites in mind.

At each level in the curriculum, emphasis depends on the needs of children as defined by their age characteristics. In the beginning experiences in physical education (levels I and II), the movement content should receive about 40% of the time alloted for physical education. Another 30% of the time should be devoted to the development of fundamental movement skills, the use of small equipment, and gymnastics. Dance and rhythmic activities should receive at least 20% of the remaining time and games 10%.

Once the children have mastered the movement concepts they are ready to apply them (levels III and IV) in a variety of sports and dance activities. Early experiences in the development of fundamental movement skills provide the background for the development of beginning sports or dance skills incorporated into each unit of instruction. At this time lead-ups to team sports receive increasing emphasis ranging from 40% to 45% of the available time. Dance and rhythmic activities make up another 25% with individual and dual activities constituting 30% to 35% of the time allotted for physical education.

Using the school calendar as a guide, the teacher determines the number of lessons for each unit and writes them into the year's schedule. A sufficient number of lessons is essential if there is to be time for adequate

Folk dancing may be a vigorous wintertime activity.

COMPARISON OF SOLID AND MULTIPLE UNIT PLANS

SOLID UNIT PLAN (FOR A PRIMARY GRADE)

Week	Monday	Tuesday	Wednesday	Thursday	Friday
1	Space concepts		Space concepts		Space concepts
2	Space concepts		Space concepts		Space concepts
3	Space concepts		Space concepts		Space concepts
4	Fundamental motor skills		Fundamental motor skills		Fundamental motor skills
5	Fundamental motor skills		Fundamental motor skills		Fundamental motor skills
6	Fundamental motor skills		Fundamental motor skills		Fundamental motor skills

MULTIPLE UNIT PLAN (FOR AN UPPER ELEMENTARY GRADE)

Week	Monday	Tuesday	Wednesday	Thursday	Friday
1	Softball	Track	Softball	Track	Softball
2	Track	Softball	Track	Softball	Track
3	Softball	Track	Softball	Track	Softball
4	Track	Softball	Track	Softball	Track
5	Softball	Tract	Softball	Track	Softball

learning. Units generally vary from 8 to 12 or 15 lessons, depending on the activity and age level.

In settings where more than one teacher will be responsible for the physical education classes, it is helpful if teachers plan the activity schedule together. It may save class preparation time to involve classes in the same activities. The preparation of areas for use, such as lining fields, or the arranging of equipment, as in gymnastics, can be accomplished more easily when teachers work together. This approach may not be possible, however, if equipment is limited and different activities must be scheduled at the same time to maximize the use of available equipment.

Some activities may be considered prerequisites for others. Creative dance activities in which body parts are moved to musical accompaniment are lead-ups to rhythmic activities or folk dance. If stunts and tumbling are taught separately from apparatus activities, the conditioning and body positioning used in tumbling may be considered a prerequisite for later work on apparatus.

Overall body development should be considered in planning. Few units of activity provide the development of all physical fitness components. Activity scheduling should enhance the development and maintenance of overall health-related physical fitness. For example, a unit in soccer that develops cardiorespiratory and muscular endurance might be followed by a unit in stunts and tumbling to develop flexibility.

Two basic methods, the solid unit approach and the multiple unit approach, are used to schedule units of activity to fit within the school calendar. In the solid unit approach, one unit is introduced at a time. This approach is best when the physical education class is scheduled 3 or fewer days per week. It provides more continuity because allots sufficient time for the unit each week. In the multiple unit approach more than one unit is taught per week. This approach is best for a 5-day-a-week program because it allows for more variety within the week. Two units per week are perhaps the maximum to maintain continuity. When multiple units are taught, one unit may complement another. For example, a unit in softball combined with a unit in track provides for the maintenance of fitness better than a softball unit taught alone. An example of each of these approaches is found in the box on p. 67.

THE UNIT PLAN

The final preparation for teaching involves the development of units of instruction from which the daily lessons will later be devised. A unit of instruction is a series of related learning experiences based on a common theme. The **unit plan** enables the teacher to organize a series of related learnings into lessons that follow a logical progression. Unit planning involves the following steps:

1. Establishing the educational outcomes
2. Determining equipment and facility needs
3. Determining the number of lessons
4. Selecting the content and learning processes
5. Considering the health and safety of the participants
6. Organizing learning materials
7. Organizing the class
8. Creating the block plan, which places the content and processes within the number of lessons to be developed
9. Planning the evaluation of the students and the unit

Establishing the Educational Outcomes

Objectives are developed on the basis of past experience, future needs, and the present status of the students. The first step in this process is to develop the general outcomes of the unit. Why have we chosen to present this unit? How does this unit contribute to the overall objectives of our elementary school physical education program? What is unique about this experience in the development of children? These educational outcomes are followed by a set of objectives that address the more specific outcomes of the unit. Each of the general goals is broken down into a series of specific learning outcomes. Examples of general goals and their specific objectives are found in the box below. The number of specific outcomes is determined by the age and experience of the students and the amount of time available for developing the unit.

These objectives may reflect a progression in development throughout the unit. For example, a beginning skill objective may be concerned with the technique, whereas the **terminal objective** (the statement of the intended final outcome of the unit) may deal with its use in different situations.

Objectives may be stated qualitatively or quantitatively. **Qualitative objectives** help the teacher identify

UNIT OBJECTIVES

General:
To develop the understanding and use of the concept of general space
Specific:
1. To move within the boundaries of general space
2. To move in general space avoiding others
3. To move in a variety of ways while moving in general space
4. To use all the space as the general space increases and decreases

General:
To develop the basic skills of fielding in softball
Specific:
1. To field a grounder by getting in line with the ball, lowering the hips, reaching out with the glove, fingers pointing downward, watching the ball into the glove, and covering the ball with the other hand
2. To field a fly ball by getting in line with the ball, reaching upward with the fingers of the glove pointing upward, watching the ball into the hands, and covering the ball with the other hand
3. To move into position and field ground balls and flies coming to the right, left, in front of, or behind the player

General:
To develop appropriate social skills for participation in basketball
Specific:
1. To verbally encourage teammate's efforts during practice and play
2. To make positive statements to others when they make errors
3. To pass the ball to others during play

the behavior necessary for success by describing the form of the movement desired. These objectives reflect the points to be emphasized in the teaching and evaluative processes. **Quantitative objectives** measure the result of the behavior. These objectives reflect the behavior or skill, the conditions underwhich the skill is performed, and the criteria, usually some numerical reference. For example, a qualitative objective in catching might be stated as follows: To catch a playground ball by getting in line with the ball, reaching out for it, and pulling the ball in toward the body with both hands. A quantitative objective might be stated as follows: To catch the playground ball, thrown at chest height, 8 out of 10 times. Some objectives lend themselves more easily to a quantitative statement, whereas others may be better suited to a qualitative statement. Qualitative objectives may be more important in initial learning, whereas quantitative objectives may be more helpful in advanced stages of learning in which the effectiveness of the performance may be a more appropriate measure.

Objectives should be written with the age and experience of the youngsters in mind. A catching objective for level I should vary from that for level II, just as an objective at the beginning of a unit should differ from one at the end of the unit. At level I the teacher may emphasize the use of body parts, as is suggested in the previous paragraph. At level II emphasis may be on the ability to adjust catching to varying conditions, such as balls thrown to the side, in front, or behind the receiver or catching balls of different sizes. In writing meaningful objectives the teacher should:

1. Assess the children's status with the objective to be developed. Is the objective totally new to the children? If not, how much experience have they had with it?
2. Determine the needs or points of emphasis for the present experiences. What do the children need to know to be successful as they begin the unit?
3. Determine where the children should be at the end of the unit. In other words, what is the terminal objective?

A series of objectives may be written to describe the development of a particular skill or knowledge in the unit, as described in the evaluative criteria in Table 5-1.

Determining Equipment and Facility Needs

The next step in unit planning is to determine the equipment and facility needs. In doing so the teacher must answer the following questions: What is the minimum amount of equipment necessary for maximum learning? Will additional equipment need to be acquired through purchasing or borrowing from another school? What are the space needs? Are particular field or court markings required?

Setting the Number of Lessons

Based on the objectives of the unit and the relative importance given this activity in the annual plan, the number of lessons required for sufficient experience to accomplish the objectives is determined. Units shorter than eight to ten lessons probably will not provide ample time to accomplish the unit objectives. When physical education time is limited, fewer units of study will be presented. Children need time to develop the skills and understanding and to apply them.

Selecting Content and Learning Processes

Once the unit objectives and the number of lessons have been determined, a list of the activities to be included is devised. This list includes the skills to be taught, the

TABLE 5-1 UNIT PLANNING OF CONTENT AND PROCESS FOR FIFTH GRADE BASKETBALL

SKILL	CONCEPT DEVELOPED	TASK ANALYSIS	PROCESS BEHAVIOR	EVALUATIVE CRITERIA (POINTS OF EMPHASIS AND SPECIFIC OBJECTIVES)
Terminal objective: to dribble while moving against an opponent, protecting the ball, changing hands and speed as needed.				
Dribbling	Uses body parts appropriately Controls force and level; moves in general space	Dribbles comfortably with either hand	Refining	Pushes ball with fingertips, head up (not looking at ball), ball low
	Avoids others or objects	Dribbles around stationary objects, changing hands	Varying	Keeps body between object and ball
	Changes speed	Changes speed while dribbling	Varying	Pushes ball a little more ahead as he or she accelerates
	Changes direction and pathway	Dribbles while moving against an opponent	Applying	Keeps body between ball and opponent, opposite hand up

TABLE 5-2 UNIT PLANNING FOR FIRST GRADE GENERAL SPACE CONCEPTS

CONCEPT OBJECTIVES	TASK ANALYSIS	PROCESS BEHAVIOR	QUESTIONS (POINTS OF EMPHASIS)	EVALUATIVE CRITERIA
Terminal objective: to move in a variety of ways in general space controlling objects and avoiding others.				
Moves within boundaries of designated space	Explores general space without touching others	Perceiving	"Can you move within the black lines?"	Moves within designated boundaries
Uses all the space available	Explores general space using all space available	Refining	"Have you been to all parts of the space? Corners? Center? Sides?"	Moves to all parts of the space
Moves in a variety of ways	Moves in a variety of ways in general space alone	Varying	"What were some of the ways you moved? (locomotor movements, speed, directions, etc.)"	Uses several different locomotor movements; changes the body parts used to move, speed, direction, etc.
Adjusts movements as the size of space changes	Increases and decreases available space	Varying	"How did your movements change as space increased? Decreased?"	Adjusts movements to the increase and decrease in size of general space
Moves with others in the space	Moves with a partner in general space	Varying	"What ways did you move? Were some the same as when you moved alone? Different? Which ways?"	Adjusts movements to those of partner; cooperates in deciding how to move
Controls objects within the space	Moves in a variety of ways with a ball	Varying	"Which ways were you able to move keeping the ball under control? Which ways were easiest to avoid others? Hardest? Why?"	Keeps ball under control while moving

concepts to be developed, and any special learning experiences in which the children will engage in meeting unit objectives. Examples are given in Tables 5-1 and 5-2.

A task analysis is developed that describes how the children will progress from their present status to the terminal objective. This task analysis gives direction about how each skill or concept will be practiced or developed.

Process behavior, as discussed in Chapter 3, is included for each step in the progression, depending on children's previous experience with the skill or concept. If the skill or concept is new, they begin at the perceiving level. If they have learned the skill or concept previously, they may begin at the refining or varying levels. Time available and difficulty of the skill or concept determine the processes that may be achieved.

Evaluative criteria are included for each stage in the learning process. These criteria reflect our specific outcomes and become the points of emphasis as children learn the skill. In developing concepts, questions to be used as points of emphasis may also be included. These questions challenge the children to develop a variety of responses as well as help to keep the children on task.

The number of different activities included in the unit varies with the type of unit and the difficulty of the tasks. In developing the content and processes, one must consider whether it is better to expose the children to a wide variety of activities or to develop a few more fully. For example, in a unit in basketball for the fifth grade, the development of certain game aspects may require more time to be spent on one or two different lead-up games so that the children may go beyond learning basic rules and have the necessary time to learn the game concepts.

Health and Safety

Some units of instruction require special consideration for the health and safety of the participants. For example, in gymnastics, care must be taken to provide the safest possible learning environment for all children. A set of safety rules may need to be written and communicated to the students. In other activities safe use of equipment,

BLOCK PLAN FOR FIFTH GRADE FOLK AND SQUARE DANCE

Day 1	Day 2	Day 3
Move in time to music R.*7 Jumps Christ Church Bells	Move in time to music Do-si-do R. Christ Church Bells Virginia Reel	R. Do-si-do Ladies chain Right and left through R. Virginia Reel Sicilian Circle
Day 4	**Day 5**	**Day 6**
R. Ladies chain R. Right and left through Sicilian circle Free choice	Move to ¾ time Tinikling	R. Move to ¾ time R. Tinikling
Day 7	**Day 8**	**Day 9**
Grand right and left Bingo Oh Susanna	R. Grand right and left R. Oh Susanna Free choice	Corner/partner relationship Solomon Levi Oh Johnny
Day 10	**Day 11**	**Day 12**
R. Corner/partner relationship Visiting couple R. Oh Johnny R. Solomon Levi Birdie in the Cage	R. Visiting couple R. Birdie in the Cage R. Oh Johnny	Dance party Free choice

**R indicates review.*

such as keeping balls low or keeping equipment in designated areas, may be of concern.

Children should be dressed appropriately for the activity to avoid unnecessary loss of control. To avoid injuries, appropriate warm-up activities are important. In the upper elementary school grades, stretching before most activities and warm-ups for the fingers in volleyball are examples of care taken to provide a safe environment. Further discussion of considerations for the safe conduct of physical education activities may be found in Chapter 8 and in activity Chapters 16 to 31.

Organizing Learning Materials

The use of visual aids, demonstrations, or special class projects helps to create and maintain interest in the unit of activity. Additional materials may be needed to enhance the children's learning. Posters, bulletin board displays, rules digests, periodical articles, filmstrips, videotapes, and other materials may provide additional motivation for students.

Demonstrations and visits by athletes or dancers often help children realize the potential for movement that the unit provides. The children look up to local high school or college athletes, and their visits may have positive effects on unit outcomes. A culminating learning experience such as participation in a demonstration for other classes, a special event, or a tournament gives additional opportunities to use the new skills and knowledge acquired in the unit.

Class Organization

General procedures for class organization need to be developed. Some activities lend themselves to individual work, others to work with partners or in small or large groups. Station work may be used, or the entire group may participate in the same activity. Plans for establishing partners and groups must be considered. Standard procedures to begin and end the class must also be determined. Further discussion of organizational strategies may be found in Chapter 8.

Block Planning

The **block plan** is the tentative calendar of events that provides for all the material to be included in the period of time designated for the unit. Each block in the plan represents one lesson. Activities are arranged in logical progression, with continuity planned within each lesson. The block plan includes the introduction of new material and its subsequent review. It includes the skills, concepts, and activities for the day. In determining the amount of time to be devoted to any particular aspect of the unit, the teacher must consider the process level to be achieved and the teaching methods to be used.

However, one must remember that the block plan is only tentative. Changes will need to be made in the plan as the unit progresses. Even teachers with a great deal of teaching experience find it necessary to make changes in the block plan. Each group of children differs. Some groups will need more time to develop certain skills and understanding than others. The success of the unit is not determined by the amount of material covered but by the quality of the learning experience. An example of a block plan may be found in the box on p. 71.

Evaluation of the Results

Planning for the evaluation of the unit outcomes is a part of the preplanning. Teachers must determine the most significant outcomes of the unit and devise a method to evaluate their success. It is assumed the teacher has an accurate assessment of student needs before instruction begins. Evaluation is an ongoing process that extends beyond the need to assess students for the school's reporting system. Evaluation happens daily as the teacher helps each child work toward the accomplishment of unit objectives.

A second phase of evaluation involves review of the unit at its close. The teacher determines the extent to which the objectives were accomplished, changes that would make the unit more effective another time, and which activities might be eliminated or which new activities might be added. Evaluation procedures are discussed further in Chapter 11.

DAILY PLANNING

With the unit plan completed, the final preparations for teaching are made with the development of the daily **lesson plans.** These plans each represent one day of the block plan. Often the difference between effective and ineffective teaching is a matter of working out the details of the individual lesson. Careful planning is required if teachers are to help students accomplish worthwhile objectives. Continuity is achieved when teachers carefully construct a lesson so that each part leads smoothly to the next. Physical education time is limited. Successful planning can maximize the participation of all through careful organization of the class and smooth transitions from activity to activity. Lesson planning includes the development of:

1. The objective for the day
2. The lesson activities
3. The points to be emphasized
4. The procedures to be used in organizing and moving the group
5. The equipment and materials needed
6. The evaluation at the close of the lesson

A number of models for lesson planning have been developed. A sample lesson plan is shown in the box on p. 73.

Lesson Objectives

The first task in preparing the lesson is to determine the objectives to be developed. These objectives should include the skills and movement concepts to be introduced or reviewed and, when appropriate, the social behaviors to be stressed. In writing objectives the teacher determines individual and group needs. In developing objectives the teacher considers the process behavior at which the class is functioning regarding each skill or concept to be attained.

Objectives are selected from the unit and describe what is to be worked on for the day. Because they are written in behavioral terms that describe the outcome of the performance, these objectives may describe the execution of a skill (how body parts are used) or the use of a skill in a variety of movement situations. The objectives are a valuable tool to determine the needs of children in future lessons. At the close of the lesson, the teacher determines how well the objectives were met and makes plans for the next lesson, with further emphasis on some objectives and the introduction of new objectives as needed.

Planning the Lesson Activities

Once the day's objectives have been determined, the teacher then selects from the unit plan those learning experiences that help each child master the objectives. Activity selection is partially based on the process behavior achieved by the children. Activities for children at the perceiving level differ from those at the applying level. Sometimes children may progress through several process levels within a lesson. Activities are arranged in order of difficulty, with each activity leading smoothly into the next.

The opening of the lesson (set, **anticipatory set**) is an important time for preparing the class for the material to be learned and for developing their interest in the lesson material. The teacher may begin with a discussion of the relationship of the lesson material to the unit of study and past lessons, how it fits in, and why it is important. The teacher may ask questions regarding the students' perceptions of needs based on previous lesson experiences. The use of visual aids—posters, loop films, videos—or a guest presentation also may be used. The opening gives a purpose to the lesson, helping the students to see what is needed to develop the skills and understanding required to accomplish the lesson objectives. Following this introduction, activities are selected to meet the objectives for the day.

Lesson closure is another planned experience. At the conclusion of the lesson, the teacher takes some time to review the material, eliciting student feedback about what was learned and perhaps a preview of what might be expected in future lessons. It is helpful to tie the parts of the lesson together so that the students see the relationship of the parts to the whole. The verbal responses of students to questions posed assist the teacher in deter-

SAMPLE LESSON PLAN

Date: *September 15* Day: *2* Unit: *Educational Games* Grade: *1* Equipment: *None*

OBJECTIVES

1. To create force in starting by beginning with the feet in a forward stride position and knees bent, leaning forward, with the arms bent at the sides to drive on the start, and pushing off on the balls of the feet.
2. To absorb force in stopping by assuming a forward stride position, bending the knees, and bringing the body weight back over the base.

THE LESSON

Procedure	Activity	Points of emphasis
Children enter and immediately begin moving in general space	Warm-up/fitness Teacher calls out locomotor movements: "Skip, run, gallop."	Keep space between self and others. Use all the space available inside the black lines. Can you set a pace at which you can keep moving?
"Stop and sit where you are. On the signal if you are close to someone else move to a new space and sit down before I count to 3."	Set: "Today we will be doing some activities in which we will need to start and stop quickly. Let us begin by practicing stopping."	
	Practice stopping: "On the signal we will move in general space. When I say 'Stop,' I want to see how quickly you can stop on your feet. Then we will begin again. Try different ways of stopping and absorbing the force"	Think about what you do with your feet, legs, arms, and body as you try different ways to stop.
	"Did you try to stop with your feet close together? Far apart: Knees bent? Legs straight? Leaning forward? Body over your legs? What position seemed to be the best?"	
Now move to the line and do a good stop. (Children line up in one line at the end of the gym.) Children practice starts moving in line. As they return to starting line, the class begins Jet Pilot.	Practice starting: "Pretend you are in a race and you want to get a fast start. What would be a good position? Take a position you think would be good and be ready to start when I give the signal. Ready, go. Now stop. Was it a good starting position? Did you create force quickly? Try another. Ready, go. Stop. (Repeat several times having the children try different positions.)	Forward stride, knees bent, weight over base
	Which position seemed to be the best?"	Feet in a forward stride, knees bent, arms bent to drive, lean forward
	Jet Pilot: "You must have a good stop to be the first one back."	"Are you ready for a fast start? Can you stop very quickly in a balanced position?"
	Red Light:	"You must stop quickly and be still."
As the children stand in line, the teacher divides them into groups of 3 with the 2 outside children holding hands and the third child in the center; 3-4 children do not have a tree.	Squirrels and Trees:	"Is everyone ready to start? Can you stop quickly in a new tree?"
Children sit down where they are	Closure: "Who can tell me what we learned today about stopping? Starting?"	Stop: feet in a stride position, knees bent, weight over base Start: feet in a stride position, knees bent, leaning forward, arms bent to drive

EVALUATION

The children need to be reminded to use their arms to help them get off to a good start.

In stopping, some are not bringing their weight back over the base and also have their feet too close together.

mining the students' grasp of the material in planning the lessons that follow.

Points of Emphasis

Points to be emphasized should be noted for each activity. Learning is not necessarily the result of participation. It is the result of effective teaching. Sometimes these teaching points are toward the execution of skills, as in giving demonstrations or feedback as the children work in the activity. In other activities the understanding and application of movement concepts or the use of motor skills is stressed. One must always keep in mind that the activity is the means, not the end, to learning about human movement.

Procedures

Once the activities have been selected, the teacher determines how the class will be organized. Safety is a primary concern in structuring the activity and in organizing for maximum participation. Children should be grouped for maximum learning and participation in each activity. Children may work as individuals or in small or large groups, depending on which grouping will maximize movement for all. A smooth transition from one activity to the next must also be carefully planned. Inexperienced teachers often take class organization for granted. They believe that anyone can organize a group of children into a circle of four groups. However, valuable time and attention are often lost when teachers do not carefully consider the moves required for a successful lesson. Suggestions for classroom management are found in Chapter 8.

Equipment and Materials

The amount of equipment used should maximize learning for each child. As many children as possible should be actively engaged in skill practice, concept development, or activity participation. When the amount of equipment is limited, a variety of kinds of equipment may need to be used so that all children have an equal opportunity for practice. Chapter 8 suggests several methods of maximizing learning opportunities for children. In addition, special materials may be needed. Task cards, posters, pictures, and the like may make the learning more interesting.

Evaluation

As soon as possible after the lesson, the teacher should evaluate the learning experience. The teacher must determine the extent to which the objectives were met, which objectives need additional emphasis in the next lesson, and needs for future lessons. Because teachers often have many classes a day that immediately follow one another, it may be necessary to make a few meaningful notes between classes and follow up with a more detailed evaluation later in the day. Further discussion of evaluation is found in Chapter 11.

SUMMARY

The successful implementation of the physical education program depends on careful planning. Each school provides a unique setting for learning because the environment, the school, and learners themselves influence curriculum development.

Steps in curriculum planning include an analysis of the factors affecting the curriculum, development of program goals, selection of the content and processes to meet these goals, and evaluation of the curriculum. An annual plan is developed to fit the curriculum to the school calendar. Units of instruction and then daily lesson plans are developed. Each organizes learning experiences into a logical progression, carefully considering the needs of individual children and the class.

Planning does not ensure effective teaching, but it is the first step in providing for the needs of children. Teachers must then carry out the plans using their teaching skills to help children become the best they can be.

REFERENCES AND RESOURCES

Austin D and Miller M: A curriculum development study school/community collaboration, *JOPERD* 57(9):50, 1986.

Ennis C and Zhu W: Value orientations: a description of teachers' goals for student learning, *Research Quarterly* 62(1):33, 1991.

Harrison J: *Instructional strategies for physical education,* ed 3, Dubuque, Ia, 1992, Wm C Brown.

Jewett A and Bain L: *The curriculum process in physical education,* Dubuque, Ia, 1985, Wm C Brown.

Jewett A and Mullan M: *Curriculum design: purposes and processes in physical education teaching-learning,* Washington, DC, 1977, AAHPERD.

Lawson H: A model for the development of innovative physical education programs, *Physical Educator* 39(2):59, 1982.

Mager R: *Preparing instructional objectives,* ed 2, Belmont, Calif, 1984, DS Lake Publishers.

Rink J: *Teaching physical education for learning,* ed 2, St Louis, 1992, Mosby–Year Book.

ANNOTATED READINGS

Cooper J and others: *Classroom teaching skills: a handbook,* ed 4, Lexington, 1990, DC Heath.

Discusses instructional planning from writing objectives to teaching skills and concepts, classroom management, observational skills, and evaluation.

Ennis C and Weimo Z: Value orientations: a description of teachers' goals for student learning, *RQ* 62(1):33, 1991.
A study to determine the extent to which physical education teachers were consistent regarding student learning goals within various value orientations.

Metzler M and Young J: The relationship between teachers' preactive planning and student process measures, *Research Quarterly for Exercise and Sport* 55(4):356, 1984.
A study of two teachers and the fourth-grade student process behavior differences resulting from different lesson-planning patterns.

Moyer SW: Professional practice: the three part theme lesson, *Strategies* 3(3):21, 1990.
Using a three-pronged approach to developing successful skill lessons.

Stroot S and Morton P: Blueprints for learning, *JOTPE* 8(3):213, 1989.
A study of the planning of teachers at various stages of their careers that looks at the type, extent, and dependence on plans in teaching lessons.

Vogel P and Seefeldt V: Redesign of physical education programs: a procedural model that leads to defensible programs, *JOPERD* 58(7):65, 1987.
A twelve-step procedural model to redirect ineffective physical education programs.

Weiller KH: Successful learning = clear objectives, *Strategies* 5(5):5, 1992.
Using a four-stage process in creating successful lessons.

PART THREE

Conducting the Physical Education Program

Selecting the content and processes is the first step to a successful physical education program. Implementation of the program involves planning the teacher's interactions with the students—selecting methodology, planning the class management, establishing an environment conducive to learning, and evaluating the outcomes of the program.

OUTLINE

CHAPTER 6

Learning and Motor Learning

OBJECTIVES

After completing this chapter the student will be able to:

1. Identify several principles of learning and motor learning
2. Explain the dimensions of learning and their application to learning in physical education
3. Explain how children learn motor skills
4. Describe the implications of learning principles for the teaching of physical education

Learning may be defined as a relatively permanent change in behavior brought about as a result of practice or experience. Children need a stimulating environment for learning if they are to meet their optimum movement potential. Children are totally involved in the learning process, and although the emphasis is on the cognitive process and the motor response, in physical education children are involved as total social and emotional beings.

Learning and performance are not synonymous. **Performance,** a temporary occurrence or action, is a function of learning and other variables. Motor skill performance is related to physical characteristics, motor ability, perceptual ability, cognition, and emotional state. The physical education teacher contributes substantially to the development of children by providing a variety of experiences in which the thinking, moving, and feeling child develops. Motor learning and performance are both handicapped if the physical qualities needed for skilled movement are not present.

An important aspect of learning in physical education is the development of skills that will enhance lifelong learning. These skills are not the automatic outcome of the physical education experience, but the result of carefully planned activities that encourage thinking and analysis.

Learning theory and principles involve maturation, leadership, learning set, motivation, whole-part learning, practice, knowledge of results, transfer, reinforcement, and retention. These factors require attention in setting the stage for learning. This chapter discusses learning theory and learning principles of concern to teachers in all areas of the school curriculum.

LEARNING AND MOTOR LEARNING

Developmental theories are pertinent to the study of motor learning. The stage theory suggests that individuals proceed through a series of events or stages that follow in a logical sequence. One aspect of the stage theory involves the development of motor movements. Motor development may be traced fom early involuntary movements to purposeful motor activities. This theory suggests that children should be able to perform certain motor skills within various age ranges. The emergence of these skills may be also studied as a series of events from primitive attempts of the skill to mature motor patterns. A developmental sequence for running may be found in the box on p. 22.

The critical periods theory of child development suggests that certain times in the developmental process are important for the learning of particular skills. If these skills are not developed at the appropriate time, future success in the performance of these skills is affected. Deprivation of opportunities in the elementary school may have a lasting effect on a person's ability to move successfully throughout life. During these early years, children need the opportunity to not only master the fundamental motor skills that are the foundation for future dance and sports skills but also to develop the understanding of their own movement important in the transfer of learning. Future success depends on these early experiences.

Learning is often depicted in educational psychology as a performance curve (Figure 6-1). Steep vertical rises show active learning, whereas horizontal lines depict a slower rate of learning. The initial horizontal line rep-

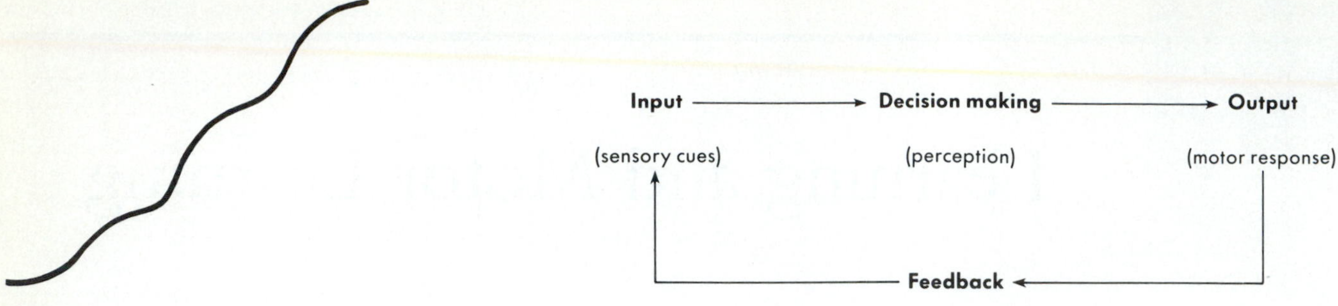

FIGURE 6-1 Performance curve.

FIGURE 6-2 Motor learning model.

resents beginning understanding of the task and body actions. As the child gains insight into the task, performance improves and the curve rises vertically. This rise may represent mastery of parts of the task and enthusiasm for learning. Transfer of learning, motivation, and success all account for this steep rise. Horizontal lines throughout the curve indicate plateaus in learning. They represent declines in the rate of learning. Plateaus may be the result of conditions within the learner or within the learning environment. The student may have lost interest, may need time to integrate the skill, or may have reached a high degree of skill after which improvement will take greater effort. The teacher may be moving too slowly or too rapidly or may need to change method or practice to make learning more appealing to students. Environmental factors such as the climate, facilities, or equipment may be a factor. To minimize plateaus the teacher must recognize individual needs, give encouragement and appropriate feedback, avoid excessive anxiety in the learners, and provide interesting experiences to practice the skills.

Figure 6-2 presents a learning model. In the first step the learner receives certain stimuli or input through the senses. This input may be visual, auditory, or tactile-kinesthetic. Individual differences in the sensory mechanisms' ability to receive stimuli vary the input from child to child. The second step involves some decision making, which may be labeled perception. This process involves analyzing the sensory data based on present conditions and past experience, which has been stored in the brain. This process is highly individual. Judgments are made and decisions for action considered and selected. A motor response is the result. As the action is taken, the child receives feedback about the effects or result of the response through the sensory modalities, and the process is repeated. For example, in catching a fly ball a fielder receives the sensory data—the sound of the bat making contact with the ball and the ball in flight coming toward the fielder. Past experience helps the fielder make judgments about the ball's flight, how fast it is moving, where it is headed, and where in the field it might be caught. In response the fielder moves in the line of flight to receive the ball.

As we have seen in Chapter 3, children generally pass through several processes of learning in developing motor skills. Once they have grasped an understanding of the sequence of the task, they are ready to practice the pattern, correcting errors as needed. During these early processes the teacher provides explanation and demonstration, focusing on important aspects of the skill and giving suggestions to help the children achieve a correct movement response. The opportunity for a great deal of practice is very important. Once a relatively automatic performance is attained the children are ready to concentrate on the use of the skill in different situations under varying conditions, with different size or shaped objects, moving in different directions and pathways, adjusting force for different situations, and the like in very carefully structured practice situations and in the application of the skill in a variety of activities where they will need to adjust the skill as the situation requires. During this time, practice activities need to be developed and questions posed to help children analyze the situation and problem solve the possible solutions. Children may also be encouraged to go beyond these varying and applying processes to create movements unique to themselves and/or activity. These learning processes are further developed in Chapters 12 and 13 and in the activity chapters.

Maturation and practice play important roles in the development of motor skills. Maturation provides the capability for learning. Early motor development depends on the neuromuscular maturation of the child. Once sufficient neuromuscular maturity has been attained, practice plays an increasingly important role in the development of motor skills. Motor skills improve with age, but the effect of maturation on motor skill acquisition during the elementary school years is not clearly understood.

There is considerable variation in motor development among individuals at any one age level. The range in individual differences increases with age. Girls mature faster than boys, but not necessarily with regard to motor skills because our society still encourages their development more often in boys than in girls. Differences also occur due to variation in physical attributes and body proportions. In providing for the needs of each child the teacher should focus on an analysis of why skills are inefficient, determining whether inexperience, lack of understanding, or the absence of some physical quality such as flexibility or strength may be the cause. Finally, it is important to remember that children progress at their own rate; early success is not necessarily an indicator of future accomplishment.

Children exhibit different styles of learning. According to Strom, children may learn through different sensory modalities. Some may be visual learners; others may learn more by listening, doing, touching, or manipulating. Some children may learn more effectively from their peers by being leaders, participants, or observers within the group. Some will learn best from adults, and others will learn best alone as experimenters, reflective thinkers, readers, or observers. Differences in thinking also occur. Some children accumulate knowledge and organize it into patterns; others get an overall picture and then study the details. Learning styles also parallel life-styles. For some children, learning stems from structure, rules, authority, and established values. Others prefer independence, freedom, and self-direction. Still others take cues from peers, parents, and teachers. Some children are deliberate and reflective; others are impulsive, energetic, and intuitive. Some are field-dependent learners, relying on the situation, peers, and teachers to choose activities and find answers; others are field-independent, preferring to make their own choices and drawing their own conclusions.

Teachers need to offer instruction in a variety of ways to capitalize on these various learning styles. They also need to be careful observers of children and their learning to maximize learning for each child.

DIMENSIONS OF LEARNING

Motor learning should encourage thinking. Physical education should teach the child to think as well as to move. The teacher must attempt to make the learning purposeful and meaningful, not just a conditioned response in which little or no thinking is involved. The teacher must teach for understanding and skill. Motor skill learning is more than trial and error, with the teacher helping the children to develop the thinking needed for continued success by attending to relevant stimuli. This process should include understanding how the body is used and how movements need to be changed under various conditions. Planning for the movement processes of perceiving, refining, varying, applying, and creating discussed in Chapter 3 is essential to encourage higher levels of cognition.

In translating research on the learning process, Marzano has developed a model of instruction called the dimensions of learning. This framework for learning focuses on the interaction of five dimensions of thinking.

Learning will be affected by the learner's perceptions about the learning situation. The first dimension is a positive attitude and perception about learning. The learner's perceptions about their ability to succeed play a major role in their success. Fear of failure or other feelings of inadequacy in a group often affect a student's success. These tensions affect learning. The emotional setting must be considered. The emotional state of the learner may facilitate or inhibit performance. Although an optimum level of tension is conducive to learning, the best environment is one in which the level of anxiety is not too high. Too much tension lowers the level of learning because energy is wasted handling the tension. The teacher attempts to arouse students without causing too much anxiety. Stressful settings are more disruptive to learning complex tasks than simple tasks. Through the learning of progressively more difficult skills, children are challenged and their confidence level raised. Competition is controlled so that too much anxiety does not result.

Teaching is more than a process of dispensing knowledge. The second dimension addresses the thinking involved in acquiring and integrating knowledge. According to Marzano, it is "a highly interactive process of constructing personal meaning from the information available in a learning situation and then integrating that information with what we already know to create new knowledge." It involves a "subjective process of interaction between what we already know and what we want to learn." Learning becomes more difficult when the new material cannot be related to something already known, when knowledge gained in one situation cannot be transferred to a new situation. This dimension strongly supports the conceptual approach developed in this book—developing a common core of knowledge—the movement content, and applying it in a variety of learning situations. "Effective learning requires a more in-depth analysis of the new information to organize and shape it in ways that highlight what's important and to weed out errors" (Marzano). The final aspect of this process is internalizing the information so that it can be readily used. It must be overlearned so that it can be retrieved and used with little effort.

Students need to learn to use knowledge in different ways. In the third dimension the thinking involved in extending and refining knowledge, we help students use the knowledge in different ways. In this book, it is the point at which children are taught to use what they've learned in different situations. Students learn to observe similarities and differences and classify learning into definable categories and to use inductive and deductive reasoning to infer principles and generalizations and their possible consequences. Obviously the use of questioning is an important part of this process.

Students need to be engaged with learning over time. The fourth dimension involves thinking and using knowledge meaningfully. This process goes beyond dimension 3. It requires a long-term involvement with the material, engaging the learner in more complex tasks. It requires the learner to take ownership of the task, to be fully involved.

Decision making, investigation, experimentation, and problem solving may become a part of dimension 4.

Students need to work at the edge of their competence. The final dimension, productive habits of mind, involves a persistence for learning when the going gets tough. This persistence allows the student to become the expert. According to Amabile, it requires being sensitive to feedback, seeking accuracy and precision, persisting when answers and solutions aren't apparent, viewing situations in unconventional ways, and avoiding impulsiveness. This dimension requires the student to persist and to risk working at the edge of their competence.

These dimensions do not represent a sequenced series of steps but rather the interaction of these variables in all learning situations. They are an integrated part of the learning in physical education as can be seen in the following discussion of motor learning variables as well as in Chapter 7.

Leadership is important in learning. The physical educator plays an important role in the learning of children. The teacher presents a clear picture of the lesson objectives, uses demonstration and verbal explanation to translate the objective to the class, poses questions that stimulate student thinking, plans interesting practice, is alert in detecting and correcting errors, and is responsive to the individual needs in the group. The teacher exhibits a sincere interest in children and their efforts.

MOTIVATION

Motivation is the process of instilling in an individual the desire to behave or perform in a way that satisfies a need. The teacher does not give students motivation but rather alters the variables that affect motivation.

In the process of motivating students, the teacher alters several variables that affect motivation, namely, interest in learning, level of aspiration, feeling tone, rewards, success, and knowledge of results. Students react differently to the manipulation of these variables. Some students may be more motivated by certain variables than by others. To be successful the teacher must discover which variables individual students respond to best.

If there are pleasant feelings associated with the learning, motivation is enhanced. Motivation is related to students' feelings about learning. Feeling tone is important. Pleasant feelings about learning motivate, whereas negative feelings reduce motivation. Feelings are affected by the learning environment. If children like and respect the teacher and believe that the teacher views them in the same way, motivation is enhanced. Assisting students in achieving the correct response when using questioning activities by providing more time for them to respond, restating the question, giving credit for correct portions of an incorrect response, or giving hints all help students maintain a sense of acceptance. Variety in the way skills are practiced or in the methods of presentation and the selection of activities themselves can help children find physical education challenging and fun.

Children must also have positive feelings about their relationship with their classmates. These feelings are more likely to develop in an atmosphere that fosters mutual respect and support.

Students must be interested in the goal toward which they are working. Interest in learning a particular skill or motor activity may be influenced by several factors. Children need to feel that participation in the activity is worthwhile. Athletic ability is valued by many in American culture. Adequate skill may be important to group membership. An individual may wish to develop skills for leisure-time pursuits. There may be interest in improving one's appearance or in improving or maintaining health. These factors and others may influence children's interest in learning.

The student's level of aspiration is an important factor in motivation. Level of aspiration varies with the individual. Some children seek the highest level of accomplishment, focusing most of their energies into the pursuit of one or a few activities. Others are content with a recreational level of skill. A higher level of intended achievement usually yields a higher level of performance. Success results in a rise in the aspiration level, whereas continued failure may lower the desired goal. At times the teacher's view of what a child should accomplish and the child's personal goal for achievement may differ.

Students must understand the goal to which they are working to maintain motivation. Task clarity is essential. Students need to understand what is to be learned and why it is important. Children must be given appropriate reasons for engaging in any activity. The relationship of what is being learned in physical education to other school subjects or use in school, home, or community activities must be understood. Students are motivated to learn when they see meaning and relationship in what they are learning. When they are assigned tasks within their ability, they can easily see what they do each day to bring them closer to meeting goals. Motivation for practice increases as practice more closely assimilates the use of the skills or concepts in the activity in which they will be used.

Success enhances an interest in continued learning. Success enhances success. The teacher must be aware of student needs and goals. Activities are selected with the age and maturity of the students in mind. Children enjoy moving, and the teacher assists them in finding ways to move that have meaning for them. The teacher begins at the students' level of interests and abilities and proceeds to help children in setting goals. Student involvement in goal setting increases motivation. A progression of increasingly difficult tasks is provided to meet the needs of the individuals and to guarantee continued success in learning. Feedback about the degree of success affects motivation and is discussed more fully later in the chapter.

Variety in practice may increase motivation.

Confidence is gained and progress is much more rapid as children engage in successful learning.

Rewards and recognition are powerful motivators. Successful performance yields recognition from both peers and teacher. Social reinforcement is a powerful motivator. Although material rewards are not usually recommended, verbal praise and recognition in the group, if given with sincerity and appropriately for improvements in performance, may encourage some students. Rewards in physical education should be within the activity itself, as children see the effects of their participation and contribution to the activity.

WHOLE-PART LEARNING

A question that must be addressed in planning learning experiences for children is whether to present the new material as a whole or to divide and present it in parts. A whole may be defined as the largest whole that the learner can grasp. It may be considered the activity itself, for example, soccer, or a particular skill involved in a game, such as the serve in tennis. Skills may also be considered wholes, and some may be practiced in parts. Several factors concerning the task and the learner must be considered when deciding whether to use the whole or part method.

The nature of the task and condition of the learner must be considered in selecting the whole or part method. If the task is simple, if it is made up of integrated parts, if the parts are not meaningful to the learner, or if the parts are performed simultaneously, the whole method is probably best. On the other hand, if the task is complex, if it has independent parts, and if work on segments is necessary, the part method is preferable. For example, in teaching the backward roll, the hand placement on the mat is extremely important for success. It may be helpful to practice the roll back to the placement of the hands on the mat below the shoulders before attempting the "whole" backward roll.

If the learner is capable of remembering long sequences, is highly skilled, and is able to concentrate over a long period of time, the whole method may be used successfully. When the learner has a limited memory, has a short concentration span, and is having difficulty with one part, the part method may be used to an advantage. A combination of whole and part methods usually works best.

As a general rule, children learn motor skills better and faster when they are taught as a whole. It may be more feasible to break games down into specific parts for practice. The teacher begins with the general concept and then breaks it into meaningful parts. Observing a soccer game may give meaning to the learning of particular skills. In developing parts, immediate feedback is essential to help the learner focus on the part being learned.

The parts may have meaning only if the learner sees them

as a part of the bigger whole. Seeing a skill used in an activity may give meaning to practicing it alone. The teacher must be careful not to dwell too long on developing parts without putting them back into the whole. Interest in learning may be lost if the children lose sight of the meaning of the practice because too much time is spent on one or more parts. If the children spend most of the unit working on skills, with little opportunity to use them in the game, the skill practices may lose their meaning for the group.

TRANSFER

Speed in learning depends somewhat on the abiiity to adapt and apply previous learning, a process called **transfer.** Although each motor skill is specific, general, perceptual, motor, and maturational factors may be the same and can enhance learning from one skill to another. Transfer is a critical factor in problem solving, decision making, creativity, insight, and reasoning. Transfer of learning is an important component of dimensions of learning 2 through 4 discussed earlier in this chapter.

Transfer may facilitate or interfere with learning, and it may be both positive and negative. In positive transfer, old learning facilitates new learning, such as in transferring passing ahead of the receiver in basketball to soccer. In negative transfer, old learning interferes with the learning of new material, such as in learning tennis skills, which require a firm wrist, after learning badminton skills, which require a flexible wrist, or in passing above the receiver in volleyball rather than at chest height in basketball. Positive transfer provides economy in the use of time and energy in learning, whereas negative transfer increases the time and energy spent for new learning.

The teacher must identify the factors that generate positive or negative transfer and structure the setting to maximize the former and minimize the latter. Four factors affect transfer: similarities between the two learning situations, degree of original learning, association of the old and new learning, and perception of essential and unvarying elements between the old and new learning (Hunter).

The identification of similar elements in the old and new learning situations can enhance transfer. The identification of similar elements signals the relevance of previous learning to new learning. These critical elements or points of emphasis in physical education might be the use of particular body parts, similar functions with different implements, or the use of force, balance, and other movement principles. The critical elements that receive attention must be important to the new task; focusing on nonessential elements may result in negative transfer. The elements identified must be within the understanding and experience of the learner. Identifying these key points helps to focus the learner's attention on critical aspects of the new skill or concept and increases conscious recognition of these elements in the new situation. Identifying these elements is an essential aspect of teaching for transfer.

The better something is learned, the more appropriately it may be transferred. The more meaningful and purposeful the original learning experience, the greater the likelihood that transfer will take place. On the other hand, poorly learned material is transferred inappropriately. With adequate learning of the first task, the second task may be learned more efficiently in less time. It is probably better to spend time learning a few things well than to spend time learning too many things. Research indicates that time spent on successful learning of an easy task yields better transfer to more difficult tasks than spending the same time on difficult tasks (Hunter). Material partially learned will probably not be applied to new situations.

The greater the similarities between the old and new learning situations, the more likely transfer is to occur. To encourage transfer, the two learning situations should be as alike as possible. The learning conditions as well as the similarities of the activities must be considered. The feelings, motivation, and set to perform are important factors. Conditions that bring about anxiety, such as the threat of a test or a highly competitive activity, may actually interfere with learning. The "set to perform," the way a student is thinking, results in the student perceiving the new situation as similar or different from the previous situation. If the previous situation interferes with learning, the teacher should attempt to structure it as differently as possible to avoid the effects of negative transfer. The teacher must decide what conditions will enhance positive transfer. The similarity of the methodology, the sensory mode, and the approach to the new learning must be considered. The integrated movement approach encourages perceptions of similarity through discovery teaching and problem solving. In planning for skill practice, the closer the practice simulates the use of the skills in the activity, the more likely that transfer will occur.

When two learning situations are associated, transfer is more likely to occur. Attitudes, feelings, and beliefs affect transfer. If the association is pleasant, such as having fun in the gymnasium, positive transfer is more likely to occur. If motivation to transfer is high, there is a greater chance that transfer will occur. However, an anxiety-producing situation or failure negatively affects transfer. The teacher can associate past successful experiences with the new material by focusing children's attention on a previous experience in which they applied the skills successfully. In planning for transfer the teacher determines how the students' past experience can be used successfully in the new context.

If transfer is to occur, the teacher must teach for transfer. Transfer of learning is not automatic; it occurs only with careful planning. The teacher is in control of the information to be transferred. In presenting new material the teacher stresses the concept or key points to be learned, facilitates transfer by pointing out the relationships or similar elements with previous learning, and plans practice building on these essential elements. Whether learning basic principles facilitates learning specific skills is not clear. Gestalt theorists support teaching basic movement principles and generalizations. The integrated movement approach is based on the premise that learning principles will transfer from one situation to another. Teaching for transfer should encourage thinking and problem solving. The age, maturity, and experience of children affect their ability to transfer learning. Young children require more assistance to achieve effective transfer. The teacher must enhance the chance for transfer by pointing out the similarities in the old and new learning and by helping children apply movement principles.

Teaching for transfer is the ultimate goal. Because it is not possible to prepare children for every movement situation that will occur, one must teach for transfer with the hope that the reasoning and thinking skills developed will enhance transfer of learning outside the school.

PRACTICE

Student learning is the number one priority. We learn by doing. Practice provides the opportunity to repeat an action numerous times and to develop smooth-flowing movement in the best form.

Motor skills are taught, not caught. Moving does not necessarily imply learning. Teachers at times may assume that learning is taking place in an activity because the children are active. An effective practice involves purposeful activity in which students' attention is focused on what is to be learned. The teacher identifies the key points for successful performance, and the students develop these important aspects through conscious effort.

Practice makes perfect only if practice is perfect. The quality of the practice is important in developing proficiency of performance. The practice must be interesting to maintain high motivation. Early analysis and correction of errors are essential to prevent fixation on incorrect form. The students must develop understanding of the task to respond to the teacher's feedback and to analyze their own performances based on the resulting action. Practice situations should be arranged so that a good performance is required for success. For instance, in working on throwing accuracy, the student should be placed far enough from the target so that only a throw in good form will carry the distance to the target, rather than being placed so that success can be achieved with only a simple toss.

Variety in the way the practice is conducted is important to maintain interest and motivation. Different formations, relationships with partners and opponents, and equipment are used to broaden the understanding and use of the skills being practiced. Problem solving adds to the interest as children attempt to use the skills effectively under varying conditions. As soon as students have developed an adequate level of skill and understanding, skills and concepts should be practiced as they will be used. The practices should be organized to maximize learning by providing each student the opportunity to attempt the skill as many times as possible in the practice period.

Academic learning time in physical education (ALT-PE), or the time a student is engaged with lesson content at an appropriate level of difficulty, is an important consideration in planning the practice of motor skills. If the practice is too easy or too difficult, the desired motor response will not be achieved.

Practice beyond the first correct response yields **overlearning,** which is important for retention. The object of practice is to increase understanding and perfect performance. Once the skill has been performed correctly, additional practice helps to retain the skill in the correct form. Although errors still may be made after the first correct response, errors should be gradually eliminated in subsequent attempts. Overlearning results in better retention, and long-term retention requires more overlearning; there is, however, a point of diminishing returns. Too much practice of any one skill can result in boredom and detract from further learning.

The length of practice is governed by the nature of the skill and the age and level of ability of the participants. Short, frequent practice periods are best during the early stages of learning. Because frustration and fatigue may result from early attempts in learning a motor skill, short practice periods may be advantageous; however, the practice should be long enough to have meaning. Student maturity determines optimum practice times, since young children have a shorter attention span than older children. With young elementary school-aged children, periods of 5 to 7 minutes are appropriate for the practice of one skill. The length of practice for activities requiring strength and endurance is determined by the physical condition of the participants. As children in the upper grades recognize the importance of being well skilled, their interest in practice increases. Once a certain level of skill has been achieved, interest in practice may also increase because there is satisfaction in practicing the skill. Skills requiring a high degree of accuracy or vigorous activity require more frequent rest periods, so short practices may be preferable.

The practice schedule is planned according to the learner's capacity and stage of learning and the difficulty of the skill. **Massed practice** refers to practice periods scheduled close together or when the amount of time between attempts is short or nonexistent. **Distributed practice** refers to practices in which time between practices may vary or when rest time between attempts is longer. If exploration is needed or if remembering is important to success, such as in the learning of folk and square dance sequences, massed practice may be best. On the other hand, if the skills are difficult, distributed practice may be best to give

Maximizing practice opportunities is important to skill development.

the children a longer time to develop the skill and understanding necessary for success. For young children during the development of gross motor skills, distributed practice appears to be best. Skills learned in massed practice may be retained by distributed practice once a particular level of skill has been achieved. Distributed practice offers young children more variety in programming, which is important in maintaining interest.

Practice should usually proceed at as nearly normal a tempo as possible for the skill. Speed and accuracy must both be considered in the practice activities. Motor learning specialists disagree about whether one should practice for speed or accuracy first. Skills that require both speed and accuracy should be practiced at the required speed when possible. In some cases, however, it may be necessary to gradually work up to the desired speed in the skill performance. Some evidence suggests that in developing skills that require a variety of speeds, the practice should include working at different speeds for best results (Sage).

KNOWLEDGE OF RESULTS

As an individual performs a motor task, information, or **feedback,** about the success or failure of the performance may be readily available. For example, if the performer is able to get the ball to the receiver, the effectiveness of the task may be readily seen. On the other hand, if the throw was short or was intercepted by an opponent, the performer receives information about the task's ineffectiveness. Many times the feedback available tells students that they were not successful but not why the performance failed. The teacher provides the information to help improve the performance another time. Perhaps the technique was incorrect or the timing too early or too late. This information supplied by the teacher or other observer of the performance is called **augmented feedback,** or teacher feedback. Augmented feedback, commonly referred to in the literature as *knowledge of results (KR)* or *knowledge of performance (KP)*, is important when the available information is inadequate. KR is associated with the extent to which a goal was achieved, whereas KP refers to the quality of the performance.

Improvement in performance is related to the amount and nature of the feedback received. Augmented feedback is important to correct errors in the early learning period and to continue learning once the basic form has been attained. This feedback should go beyond a judgment of success or failure, such as comments like "good job" or "nice try." It should be given in an encouraging way, reinforcing the correctness of the performance and in suggesting changes needed for improvement. Comments such as "I like the way you moved to line up with the ball" (in fielding a softball), or "this time concentrate on a level swing" (in the forehand stroke with a paddle) go a long way in helping students focus on the important aspects of motor skills. Appropriate feedback will not only help in improving performance but also may motivate students to learn more.

The knowledge of performance should provide students with the information needed at their individual level of skill. The teacher must decide what information is necessary to improve the performance depending on the age and ma-

Giving feedback early in the learning process is essential to successful performance.

turity of the students and the performance level at which they are working. Young children can handle limited bits of information at one time. Beginners need information basic to the performance of the task, whereas more advanced performers may need information on some of the finer points of the technique. Verbal cues should be short and to the point.

Augmented feedback assists the learner in attending to relevant cues. The teacher identifies the most important cues for the student's attention when helping children perfect their technique or improve their use of a skill. If a child is not accurate in throwing to a target, emphasis on the follow-through may be needed to improve the accuracy of the performance. If a child cannot guard another student effectively, perhaps watching the opponent's waist may improve the guarding technique. Relevant cues vary with the needs of the individual students and their level of understanding.

Feedback should match the student's learning style. To be most effective, feedback should be given using an appropriate sensory modality for the student's learning style. Although in general visual cues such as a demonstration may be more effective in helping students during early learning, some students may learn best by verbal cues or by having the teacher physically move the body parts to get a feel for the movement.

REINFORCEMENT

Reinforcement is any event that increases the probability of the occurrence of a behavior or that maintains the strength of a behavior. It provides satisfaction or recognition for behaving in a certain way or for doing something.

Reinforcers differ with each individual. Children respond differently to reinforcers. What is a reinforcer for one child may have little effect on another. It is important for the teacher to get to know the students well enough to know what reinforcers work best with each one. Reinforcers may also change in different situations. What is a reinforcer for a child in one situation may not be in another.

The best reinforcers build feelings of self-worth and enhance the children's self-concept. Positive reinforcers are desired. They may give recognition, opportunities, or special privileges. For example, the teacher may say "That was well done, Mary," "Now that you have completed the assignment, I will help you with a new skill," or "You have done so well that you may have free time now to choose your next activity."

To strengthen behaviors, the teacher should respond with sincere praise, recognizing effort, progress toward goals, and success in learning new skills or activities, as well as with praise for a task successfully mastered.

Immediate reinforcement is more effective than delayed reinforcement. Reinforcement after a task is successfully completed is most effective. Delaying reinforcement may lead to confusion over which response is being rewarded. The teacher should carefully select a reinforcement that will assist the child on the next trial.

Intermittent reinforcement is generally more effective than reinforcement given on each trial. It is not necessary to give reinforcement on each trial. After the initial reinforcement is given, a schedule for reinforcing future accomplishments may need to be established. Ratio, interval, variable, or fixed schedules may be used. Reinforcement is given after a set of appropriate responses in the ratio schedule, after a set period of time in the interval schedule, on an irregular schedule in the variable schedule, and on a regular basis in the fixed schedule. Some evidence suggests that students given intermittent reinforcement perform better than those who receive reinforcement on each trial (Sage, Schmidt). This evidence is important to consider in physical education because the teacher often gives a lot of reinforcement during practice, but is often unable to give much reinforcement in the game situation where the student must continue to perform as taught.

Reinforcers may strengthen appropriate and inappropriate behaviors. The inappropriate behavior of children is often reinforced by the teacher's response to it. If the negative response of the teacher gives children the attention they desire or permits them to avoid a situation for which they have anxiety, they may continue the behavior. The teacher must work hard to reinforce only desirable behaviors. It may be necessary sometimes to plan strategies not only to strengthen appropriate behavior but also to reduce inappropriate behavior.

A behavior may be weakened or extinguished when the behavior is not followed by a reinforcer. Inappropriate behavior may be extinguished by ignoring the behavior. If a child seeks the teacher's attention through behavior, the teacher's response strengthens that behavior. Ignoring the behavior and carefully rewarding appropriate behavior may encourage the child to seek more acceptable ways of performing. During the teacher's attempts to extinguish a behavior, the behavior may in fact increase momentarily, as the child continues to seek attention, before it decreases and finally stops.

RETENTION

Retention refers to the degree to which learning is remembered over time.

That which has meaning is retained longer than information and skills that do not. The more meaningful the original learning, the more likely it will be retained. Learning that has personal importance, in which the goal is important to the learner and the learner can see a use, is retained longer than other learning. Providing children with a variety of activities in which to use a motor skill increases its meaning, as does relating its importance to success in an activity the children enjoy.

The degree of success in original learning affects retention. Longer retention is the result of developing a degree of proficiency in a skill. Retention is favored when a skill is not only performed well but is understood. Both motor skills and knowledge are retained if the degree of original learning was good. The teacher's use of review and practice aids retention. Summarizing the main points, helping students use the material in new ways, transferring old to new learning, and practicing help students retain skills and knowledge longer.

Motor skills that are well learned are retained longer than other learning. Each repetition of a skill wears a deeper neuromuscular pathway within the organism. These connections appear to be retained longer than in other forms of learning over a period of time of disuse. Skills in which there is a high degree of sequential and temporal patterning or proficiency will be retained (Singer, 1986). Timing may be lost with disuse, whereas sequence is more easily retained.

Motivation and feeling tone influence retention. Learning that is associated with a felt need and that is related to pleasant experiences is retained longer than learning that creates feelings of anxiety or other unpleasantness. The goals for learning in physical education are a quality performance, variety in the use of skills, and the ability to transfer learning from one situation to another. The teacher must help children think about their actions and to focus attention on the day's objectives. Thinking while doing is important to learning and retention.

SUMMARY

In addition to understanding children and knowing their subject matter, teachers must understand and apply what they know about learning and motor learning. Motor skill performance is related to physical characteristics, motor and perceptual abilities, cognition, and emotional state of the learner. Early motor learning depends on the learner achieving the neuromuscular maturation required for the task. Once achieved, learning is affected by factors over which the teacher may have some control. The teacher plays an important part in the learning process by clearly presenting the material to be learned, providing interesting activities in which learning will take place, giving appropriate feedback to help correct errors, and encouraging children to do their best.

Motor learning should encourage thinking. Teaching to encourage thinking involves complex processes. Teachers must attend to the environmental conditions that affect students' perceptions about the learning situation and help students find meaning in the learning experience. In addition teachers help students use what they've learned in different ways over time, building on previous learning and challenging students to work at the edge of their competence.

Learning is marked by rapid and slow changes in behavior. Motivation, whole-part learning, transfer, practice, knowledge of results, and reinforcement all affect learning and retention. Rate of learning varies with the individual and the material. Thinking is as important a factor in learning in the gymnasium as it is in the classroom.

Level of aspiration, interest in and understanding of the goals, a pleasant learning atmosphere, rewards, recognition, success, and failure all affect motivation for learning. The teacher cannot motivate students but may alter the variables that affect motivation. Motor learning may involve whole or part learning. Generally a combination of the two is most effective. Relatively simple skills are best taught as a whole, whereas more complicated skills may be broken down into parts and then put together.

Transfer is the ability to apply what was learned in one situation to other situations. Pointing out the similarities of previous learning to new learning may aid in the learning process. Transfer is not automatic. The teacher must teach for transfer by helping students see the relationships between old and new learning.

Motor skills are learned through meaningful practices that encourage a correct response. The practice of skills should be as similar as possible to their use in the activity. Practice should be planned with the age, maturity, experience, and stage of the learner in mind.

Feedback is important in learning. Although the student receives some feedback as a result of the performance, this information may be lacking in helping a student analyze the performance in depth. The teacher provides valuable information, augmented feedback, to assist children in correcting errors and improving the quality of the performance. The information given varies with the learner's age, maturity, and stage of learning. A beginner may need help with the basic technique, whereas a more advanced performer may need assistance in adapting the skill to a new situation.

Positive reinforcement increases the probability of the recurrence of a behavior. Reinforcement should build confidence and feelings of self-worth. With attention to these factors, teachers can effectively assist children in meeting class goals. Failure in this regard inhibits learning and may even discourage children from active participation in physical education activities.

REFERENCES AND RESOURCES

Amabile TM: *The social psychology of creativity,* New York, 1983, Springer-Verlag.

Bruner J: *In search of mind,* New York, 1983, Harper & Row.

Cole J: Feedback: a one to one strategy, *Strategies* 4(3):5, 1991.

Dochoff DM: The feedback sandwich, *JOPERD* 61(9):17, 1990.

Dodds P, editor: *Basic stuff: motor learning,* Reston, Va, 1987, American Alliance for Health, Physical Education, Recreation, and Dance.

Fox K: Motivating children for physical activity, towards a healthier future, *JOPERD* 62(7):34, 1991.

Harrison JM and Blakemore CL: *Instructional strategies for secondary school physical education,* ed 3, Dubuque, Ia, 1992, Wm C Brown.

Hunter M: *Motivation theory for teachers,* El Segundo, Calif, 1983, Tip Publications.

Hunter M: *Retention theory for teachers,* El Segundo, Calif, 1983, Tip Publications.

Hunter M: *Teach for transfer,* El Segundo, Calif, 1983, Tip Publications.

Marzano, RJ: *A different kind of classroom.* Alexandria, Va, 1992, Association for Supervision and Curriculum Development.

Oxendine J: *Psychology of motor learning,* Englewood Cliffs, NJ, 1984, Prentice-Hall.

Rikard GL: The short-term relationship of teacher feedback and student practice, *JTPE* 10(3):275, 1991.

Robb M: *The dynamics of motor-skill acquisition,* Englewood Cliffs, NJ, 1972, Prentice-Hall.

Sage GH: *Motor learning and control,* Dubuque, Ia, 1984, Wm C Brown.

Schmidt RA: *Motor learning and performance,* Champaign, Ill, 1991, Human Kinetics Books.

Singer R: *Motor learning and human performance,* ed 3, New York, 1980, Macmillan Publishing.

Singer R: Children in physical activity: motor learning considerations. In American Academy of Physical Education: *Effects of physical activity on children,* Champaign, Ill, 1986, Human Kinetics Publishers.

Strom RD, Bernard HW, Strom SK: *Human development and learning,* New York, 1987, Human Sciences Press.

ANNOTATED READINGS

Ashy M and Lee A: Applying the mastery learning model to motor skill instruction for children, *Physical Educator* 41(2):60, 1984.

The mastery learning model matches children's needs to the quality and quantity of teaching. A summary of findings from mastery learning research in the cognitive domain and suggestions for the application of mastery learning in physical education are included.

Boyce BA: The effects of an instructional strategy with two schedules of augmented kp feedback upon skill acquisition of a selected shooting task, *JTPE* 11(1):47, 1991.

The results of a study looking at instructional strategy and two KP feedback schedules verses no feedback.

Cardinal B: Motivation: strategies for success, *Strategies* 4(6):27 June 1991.

Offers a strategy for teachers to create a less threatening and more productive environment for student learning.

Kovar S, Matthews H, Ermler K, Mehrhof J: Feedback: how to teach how, *Strategies* 5(7):21, 1992.

Examples of inappropriate feedback and suggestions for appropriate feedback focusing on the application of movement principles.

Martin CL: Enhancing children's satisfaction and participation using a predictive regression model of bowling performance norms, *Physical Educator* 45(4):196, 1988.

Prior expectations play an important role in satisfaction with physical activity. Managing these expectations can go far in motivating children.

Melville S: Process feedback made simple, *Physical Educator* 40(2):95, 1983.

Discusses the use of videotape and checklists with drawings to give meaningful feedback regarding skill performance.

Rarick G: Concepts of motor learning: implications for skill development in children. In Albinson J and Andrew G: *Child in sport and physical activity,* Baltimore, 1976, University Park Press.

Presents a recap of what is known about motor learning regarding age, maturity, motor ability, practice, retention, transfer, learning specificity, individual differences, and knowledge of results.

Shultz B: Making practice more effective, *Physical Educator,* 40(3):127, 1983.

Presents a look at the importance of practice and considerations for improving its effectiveness—setting the stage for learning, planning and sequencing the activities, information needed by the students, how long and how frequently to practice, and the quality of the practice itself.

Tobey C: The best kind of feedback, *Strategies* 6(2):19, 1992.

Discusses three elements of augmented feedback and provides suggestions for giving appropriate feedback to students.

Weiss M: Developmental modeling: enhancing children's motor skill acquisition, *JOPERD* 53(9):49, 1982.

Examines strategies to enhance learning in children who process visual information more slowly than older children and adults.

CHAPTER 7

Teaching Strategies in Physical Education

OBJECTIVES

After completing this chapter the student will be able to:

1. Describe teaching strategies available to the teacher of physical education that involve varying degrees of teacher and student decision making
2. List the advantages and disadvantages of each teaching strategy
3. Describe the conditions under which each strategy can be best used
4. Describe the development of a lesson to deliver effective instruction
5. Describe thinking in physical education and offer suggestions about how thinking skills can be enhanced in physical education lessons

Effective teaching results from the combination of carefully planned and organized learning experiences and the teacher's ability to carry out the lesson successfully. The teacher must be able to determine the needs of the children in class and select appropriate learning activities. These activities are then organized in a logical sequence into units of instruction and then into daily lessons. After this careful planning, the teacher must be able to conduct these activities in a way that is meaningful to children, efficiently uses time, and achieves the stated objectives.

In planning for learning in the physical education lesson the teacher must answer a number of questions:

- What are the past experiences of the children with the content, and what are they ready to learn?
- What teaching style can be used to best meet the objectives of the lesson?
- How will the material be presented and the lesson planned for continuity from beginning to end?
- What potential adjustments might need to be made during the lesson to maximize learning for each child?
- What motor learning principles will be applied to maximize the learning opportunities for each child?

DETERMINING THE LESSON OBJECTIVES

The first step in instruction is choosing appropriate objectives for the group. These objectives are not what we as teachers want to achieve, but rather are goals the children are capable of achieving. These objectives begin where the children are at the beginning of the lesson and not the end point. Whatever the objectives, they should facilitate individual development of the lesson material. The cognitive, psychomotor, social, and affective development of the child should be considered in planning and presenting the lesson material. The objectives should plan for progression in learning. The model for developing these progressions developed in Chapter 3 will help the teacher in this endeavor.

Once the content and process are known, the teacher then selects the teaching strategies to be used to accomplish the lesson objectives.

TEACHING STYLES

In conducting learning experiences for children, the teacher may select from a variety of **teaching styles** or teaching methods. These styles are actually strategies for organizing and presenting learning experiences to children. Teaching styles range from direct, teacher-centered

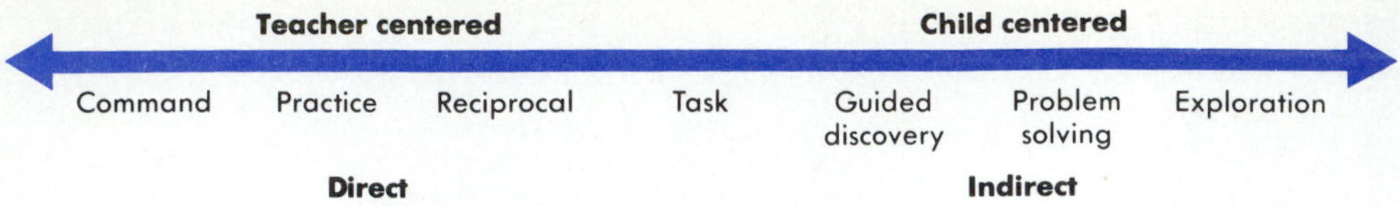

FIGURE 7-1 Continuum of teaching styles.

approaches to those that are indirect and more student centered. Figure 7-1 places the methods included here on a continuum from teacher centered to child centered. At one end of the continuum is a style in which the teacher makes decisions exclusively. At the other end is a style in which the children are the prime decision makers; between the two is a gradual shift in decision making from the teacher to the children.

Generally speaking, child-centered teaching styles take more time to develop, but the benefit of these methods in developing understanding far outweighs the time spent. Planning, in which the teacher must anticipate the children's possible responses, must be carefully thought out beforehand. Skill in the use of these approaches takes considerable practice by the teacher. Children also need time to develop skills in solving movement challenges and to gain confidence in their own ideas.

Command

The **command** style is the most teacher-directed style of teaching (Mosston, 1986). Although the word *command* connotes a dictatorial approach to learning, this is not necessarily the case. The teacher's manner in this approach depends on the teacher's personality more than on the style itself. In the command style the teacher is the sole decision maker. The teacher decides what to do, how to do it, and the quality of the performance that is acceptable.

In the command style the teacher first demonstrates the movement to be performed with an explanation of the important points to be emphasized. After the demonstration and explanation, the teacher leads the class en masse through the various steps in performing the task. The task is repeated several times as the students put the movements together in proper sequence and/or timing, with added clarifying statements made by the teacher to the group or individuals as needed.

Some examples in the use of the command style include teaching a dance step, with the students following the verbal commands of the teacher such as "Step, step, step, hop," for the schottische step, teaching an aerobics routine, or leading a group of young children through the movements for an overhand throw.

The command style has several advantages. It provides the most direct route to the objective. If time is short, it may be the most efficient and effective means to present motor skills. Because the teacher decides what will be taught and structures the practice so that all perform together, there is little time lost in organizing the group. Maximum practice for all can be easily accomplished.

The command style enables the students to see the objectives directly and therefore clarifies the expectations for performance. If the explanation and demonstration are well executed, there can be little doubt by the students about the aspects of the performance upon which they should focus their attention. If a uniform response is desired, this method may be most effective. This style is also effective with large groups because the class may be organized quickly and all the children are doing the same thing. The command style requires a less thorough knowledge of the material because the teacher alone controls the flow of information.

The command style also has several disadvantages. First, this style is insensitive to individual differences and needs. One way is presented, and only one response is appropriate. Usually the presentation is geared to the so-called average students, so those who are well skilled or not yet ready for the material are given little consideration. In addition, the command style does not encourage a creative or innovative response by the students because the teacher tells them how to respond. If understanding and concept development are the goals of the lesson, the

A good demonstration is important.

command style is a poor choice because it does not encourage thinking by the students.

Practice

The **practice** style is one of the most frequently used methods of teaching in physical education (Mosston, 1986). As in the command style, the teacher is the principal decision maker, determining what information is needed by the learner to perform the task and setting up the practice session to provide optimum practice.

The practice style is divided into several steps. As in the command style, the teacher begins with an explanation and demonstration of the task to be accomplished. This demonstration provides students with a correct example of the skill and identifies the critical elements. The demonstration may include the use of audiovisual aids or a demonstration by the teacher or a selected student. Questions about the task are answered. The students then practice the task with the teacher moving among the group, correcting errors and offering encouragement. The teacher may suggest modifications of the activity to fit the more specific needs of students in the group. During the practice students may be allowed some minor decision making, such as where to practice, or if practice includes working with a partner the desirable distance between partners in practicing the skill. At the close of the practice there may be a review or discussion, with the teacher again reinforcing the main points of emphasis before moving on to the next part of the lesson.

An example of the use of the practice style follows. The teacher is introducing the chest pass. The group is seated as the teacher explains the chest pass, its use, and the points of emphasis. A demonstration follows, with the teacher executing the pass a few times and again emphasizing the major points in the execution of the skill. The children are then divided into partners and begin practice. The teacher moves among the group, giving feedback as needed. At the close of the practice the teacher asks the group to verbalize the major points once again. The teacher then moves on to the next part of the lesson.

This style has many of the same advantages and disadvantages as the command style. The opening demonstration and explanation enable the students to see the objective clearly. It enables a relatively simple organization of the class for practice, with each student or group of students, as the case may be, doing exactly the same thing as the rest of the class. Although the style has the potential to be a little more sensitive to individual differences because the practice conditions can be varied, it usually requires all students to practice the skill at the same level of performance. Because it requires a given response by all students, it does not lend itself to developing creativity or innovative responses. It may be used most effectively in introducing a skill that is new to all students in the class.

Reciprocal

In the reciprocal style we begin to see a greater shift in decision making from teacher to students (Mosston, 1986). Students assume more responsibility for observing the performance of their peers and providing immediate feedback on each attempt.

In this style the teacher prepares a reciprocal task sheet that describes the task to be performed with evaluative criteria (what the observer will look for) in determining when the doer has performed each aspect of the task correctly. It may include pictures as well as a description to assist the observer in the task analysis. In addition, the task sheet describes the role of the observer and the doer as well as the amount of time or number of trials to be given each in the practice session. An example of a task sheet may be found in the box on p. 94.

Generally the session begins with a teacher demonstration, an explanation of the skill, and clarification of the reciprocal skill sheet. Practice follows, with the doer performing the task and the observer checking each aspect of the task, recording when it has met the criteria and giving feedback to the doer to improve performance or to indicate when it is completed. Children should be encouraged to give positive feedback to their partners as well as to assist them in the correction of errors. After the designated number of trials the two change roles. In this style the teacher moves among the children, helping to clarify the task for both doer and observer and giving additional assistance as necessary.

This style has several advantages. First, the task and criteria are clear to all. It allows for feedback on each trial, which is not possible if only the teacher is giving feedback. It adds to the learner's understanding of the task as he or she observes and applies the criteria to another's performance. It also aids in developing a learning

Using a task sheet.

DRIBBLING—RECIPROCAL SKILL SHEET

Doer ______________________________

Observer ______________________________

Instructions to observer:

1. Tell the doer about how he or she is doing on the dribble, using the points of emphasis below.
2. Be positive. Begin with those aspects the doer is doing well. Example: "You are pushing the ball with your fingerpads as the sheet suggests." "Good, you can dribble without looking at the ball."
3. Suggestions for improvement might be stated: "Can you dribble and look at me? Can you change hands? Can you push the ball more ahead of you as you move?"

Task: The doer will dribble the ball in the space you have chosen, first with one hand and then the other. After you have practiced a while using each hand the observer will ask you to change hands on command, "Right, left."

	Right Hand		*Left Hand*	
Things to Look for on the Dribble	***Yes***	***Needs Practice***	***Yes***	***Needs Practice***
Pushes ball with fingerpads Pushes ball slightly ahead while moving Looks up to see where he or she is going Keeps ball moving by controlling ball with appropriate force Dribbles with ball at waist height or slightly below				

	Yes	***Needs Practice***
While changing hands, keeps the ball moving While changing hands, continues to look up		

Reciprocal teaching enhances understanding and skill performance.

environment where all, children and teacher, assume responsibility for the learning of others. As a result of experience in this style, children should improve their communication skills, develop patience and tolerance, and develop analytical skills.

This style also has some disadvantages. Although it may be simplified, the reciprocal skill sheet may require a reading level beyond some of the students. The value of the feedback is based on the understanding of the observer. Children with little experience with a task may not be able to analyze another's performance or match it with the pictures and description on the reciprocal skill sheet. The ability to analyze performance is difficult for young children who have limited body awareness. This style requires the careful pairing up of students, since not all students can work well together and accept the suggestions of their peers. This style takes more time to develop because in the early experiences, children may feel uncomfortable in their new role as observer. Obviously, only tasks that have concrete criteria are appropriate for use with this style.

Task

In the **task** style the teacher determines the content, but the children are allowed some decision making as well as the opportunity to work at their own pace (Mosston, 1986). The teacher designs a series of tasks leading up to the unit outcomes. These tasks are broken down into a series of activities through which the children progress to achieve the final task. These activities should begin at a level below the most poorly skilled and progress to a level above the most highly skilled children. The task style may be used at three different levels, each requiring more decision making by the student. At the lowest level the teacher presents a task that is broken down into several levels of achievement. All the children work on the same task, but each begins at a comfortable stage in the progression of the activity.

At the second level the teacher may assign individual children tasks on which to work, depending on their level of ability. This technique may be most effective in gymnastics, where individual differences in ability vary greatly. Each child may be given a task card with several tasks designed individually for that student.

At the third level more independence of action is required. The student receives a task booklet that describes all the tasks to be completed in the unit. The children choose the tasks and assume responsibility for working on each task within the unit time. At this level students take more responsibility for determining their needs and work accordingly to meet unit objectives.

In the task style the teacher must provide resources to aid individual learning. The teacher is a valuable resource, but the children also should have posters, books, loop films, and other aids available to assist them in the learning process. The children must be encouraged to use a variety of resources; otherwise they often depend on the

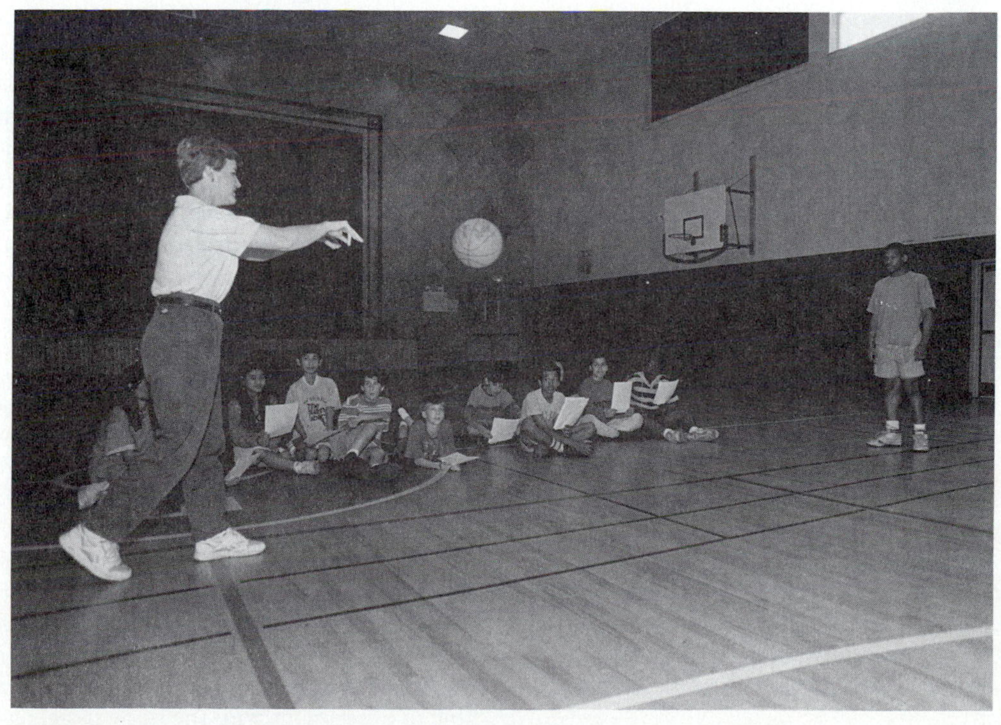

Demonstrating tasks is an important aspect of task teaching.

teacher as the most direct path to the information they need. Often, the station approach to organizing the group is used, with practice of different tasks at each station.

As tasks are developed for the children, the terminal objective or evaluative criterion must be carefully spelled out. The children must be able to determine when they have accomplished the task. This criterion may be qualitative or quantitative. It may be something that the child or a partner may evaluate, or it may require the teacher's evaluation. It is a good idea to include several means of signing off on tasks. Having the teacher check each task is inefficient use of the teacher's time. Children need the opportunity to be responsible for their own evaluation as well as to assist in the evaluation of others.

The organization of the class and the time must be carefully developed. Children need to know how they can proceed in completing the tasks. If there are any expectations regarding the number of tasks to be worked on, time spent in certain areas or with different equipment, etc. within the period, they must be clearly understood. The teacher will need to monitor the class carefully to be sure each child is working at an appropriate level of difficulty and accomplishing the work as needed. This style also requires independent learning. Some children will be able to accomplish a lot in this type of learning environment, with little teacher supervision; other children will need more guidance in the process. While the children are working, the teacher circulates among the class, providing feedback to help the children achieve the task goals.

Safety concerns or prerequisite skills should be clearly stated in the description of the task. If spotting is required, a spotter (either student or teacher, depending on the activity) should be designated.

An example of a task developed as a part of a gymnastics unit for first-grade children follows:

1. Mount the low beam. With a spotter, who walks in front of and along the side of the beam with an arm up to offer assistance if needed, walk forward to the end of the beam. Dismount.
2. Mount the low beam. With a spotter, as in No. 1, walk backward to the end of the beam. Dismount.
3. Mount the low beam. With a spotter, as in No. 1, walk sideways to the end of the beam. Dismount.
4. Mount the low beam. With a spotter, as in No. 1, walk forward to the center of the beam. Walk through the hoop and continue to the end of the beam. Dismount.
5. Mount the low beam. With a spotter, as in No. 1, walk to the center of the beam. Stand and turn. Continue walking forward to the end. Dismount.
6. Mount the low beam. With a spotter, walk to the center of the beam. Turn and walk backward to the end of the beam. Dismount.
7. Mount the low beam. With a spotter, walk to the center of the beam. Make a one quarter turn and walk sideways to the end of the beam. Dismount.

A series of pictures may be included on the task sheet to provide a visual description of the tasks as well. Similar tasks would be developed for other pieces of equipment used in the unit.

Tasks may also involve some problem solving. This may be accomplished by asking the children to experiment with different uses of the body or body parts in the execution of skills. In this manner they must find the most efficient way of moving on an individual basis.

The task style allows for individual differences in skill level and recognizes individual needs in working on particular skills. Children select not only the task they begin to work on but also the level at which they begin to work. In this style the teacher's ability to assist is maximized because the teacher is free to circulate among the group, helping individuals as they work on various tasks. Because children are working on their own, success and failure are known only to the individual. All children, however, should experience success as they work at a level of performance at which they are comfortable.

The task style also permits maximum use of facilities and equipment. This style is extremely helpful for situations in which the amount of any particular piece of equipment is limited, because it does not require each child to use the same type of equipment at the same time.

The advantage of allowing children to choose the task and to work on their own may also be this style's greatest disadvantage. It requires increasing independence of action and assumption of personal responsibility for accomplishing the tasks, which may be difficult for some children. The teacher must be alert to the progress the children are making in achieving the tasks and help those who are not self-directed to select and complete tasks along the way. Improved self-direction, however, is clearly a desirable objective for this style of teaching.

Guided Discovery

The guided discovery approach uses teacher-designed movement tasks, but in a manner that allows the children to make individual decisions about how to move (Mosston, 1986). Their attention, however, is focused toward a specific movement response, so that the nature of the responses produces similar movements from the entire class. This approach is used effectively in situations in which the teacher is interested in children discovering the most suitable movement response for a given task or in the development of a new skill. In this way children are able to experiment with the body to achieve the objective

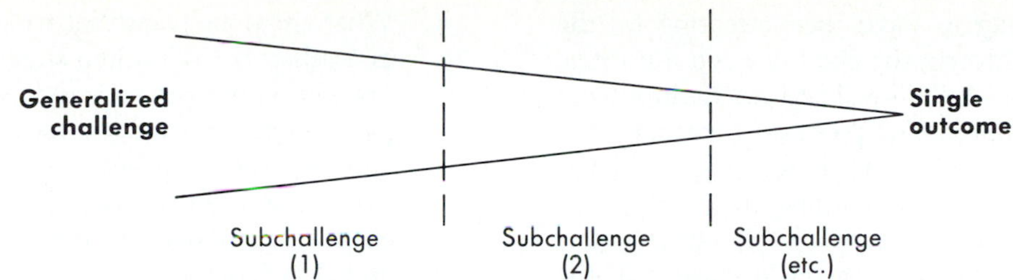

FIGURE 7-2 Guided discovery.

and develop greater understanding about why particular movements are more efficient and effective than others. Motor activity begins with a general response to a movement challenge and proceeds through a series of steps, each of which narrows the focus of the response until the ultimate movement goal is achieved. Figure 7-2 demonstrates the nature of responses that result from this style.

As the children move, limitations are imposed that indicate the content being developed and that limit the range of movement responses. The teacher guides the student in the discovery of how to perform the movement task. The students make decisions about how they will respond.

This style is the first on the continuum that requires higher-level thought processes. Whereas in the previously described styles the teacher determined not only the content but also how it was to be achieved, in guided discovery the teacher only defines the intended outcome of the movement response. This approach then gives the children the opportunity to experiment with the movement, to make comparisons with other movement responses in their repertoire, and to analyze the possible motor responses.

An example of guided discovery follows. The teacher states the challenge: "Begin in a standing position and jump for distance on the mat." The children experiment with the task. Subchallenge 1 focuses their attention on the landing position: "Try landing in different positions. Land so that all body parts are as far from the starting line as possible. What position seems to be the best?" Subchallenge 2 focuses on the take-off: "How can your feet be positioned to get the best possible take-off?" Subchallenge 3 focuses on the use of the arms in aiding the take-off: "Try using your arms in different ways. Which ways help you jump the farthest?" Subchallenge 4 focuses on the body position: "Try jumping from an upright position. Now try bending your knees and leaning forward. Which position helped your jump the most?" During each subchallenge, children experiment with the use of the body parts mentioned. Additional questions may need to be asked at each step to help the children focus on the most efficient movement. As the subchallenges are developed, the skill becomes more and more like the standing long jump. It is important for the teacher not to show the response desired but to guide the children in the discovery process.

In a lesson the teacher may wish to introduce a skill using this style to help children internalize how body parts are used to perform the skill with maximum efficiency. Once this is accomplished, the teacher provides a series of challenging practice activities in which the children further their personal skill performance. In the example just given, the practice might include jumping various distances or over some low obstacles.

Using guided discovery in a basketball unit the teacher may wish the students to discover how to protect the ball while dribbling.

1. After warming up by dribbling in general space changing hands on the signal, the teacher positions several students in the general space, who remain stationary as the rest of the class dribble in the space. The stationary players attempt to hit the ball away as the dribblers come within range. What did you do to avoid the stationary players? The children may respond by saying, changing pathway, direction, speed, etc.
2. Now all the children are moving in the space, with several children without balls trying to gain possession of the ball by pushing it away from those who are dribbling. Again ask the question: What did you do as the player without a ball came near? If no one has discovered that they must keep their body between the person trying to take it away and the ball, repeat the activity again reducing the space. Additional questions may then need to be introduced to get them to see that many of them did in fact position themselves between the ball and the other player.

Success with this style depends on the teacher's ability to respond to the children's experimentation with movement while continuing to focus their attention on the task. This style should help the child develop a positive self-concept because each child will find success in solving the movement challenges. The process of learning that takes place gives students the tools to apply what has been learned to other movement situations.

A disadvantage to this style is that it takes time—time for the children to be guided to the discovery of the movement solution and time for the teacher to think through the steps the children will need to take to get there. This style requires a great deal of patience by the teacher, as do all child-centered methods. Children often take more time than we expect to reach the solution. Teachers must allow children the time they need and not be too eager to give them the answers before they discover them. This is learning in its truest form.

Problem Solving

Problem solving is similar to guided discovery in approach, but whereas one similar solution to the movement problem was the goal in guided discovery, many different solutions are the outcomes of problem solving. Figure 7-3 focuses on the motor responses obtained using this method.

In problem solving the teacher poses a movement challenge that has some parameters, such as the use of space, pathways, or locomotor movements to be used, and the children try to find as many solutions to the problem as they can. Any movement response that meets the criteria of the task is acceptable. The teacher is again a resource in bringing the focus of the activity to their attention as needed and in helping individuals work toward possible solutions.

An example of the development of a movement challenge using this style follows. The problem is to explore moving in a variety of ways in general space with a change of direction. The teacher poses the following questions. Each question follows a period of experimentation with the previous question. As each step is added, a new focus to the movement challenge is added, which broadens the range of possible movement responses.

1. What are some ways that we could move in general space? (Children suggest a few options.) Staying within the area and avoiding other people's self-space, choose a movement to begin and each time you hear the signal "change" move in a different way. Other than the ways already mentioned, what were some of the ways you chose to move?
2. What are some ways we can move other body parts as we move in space?
3. Can you move on different body parts other than your feet?
4. What are some of the directions we can move in general space? (Children suggest different directions.) On the signal move in one direction, changing direction each time the signal "change" is given.
5. Now let us try moving in some of the ways we have already explored, changing direction as well. Pick a way of moving and change direction each time you hear the signal.
6. Can you change movement and direction at the same time? Let's try it. Pick a direction and movement, changing on the signal.

Additional questions may need to be asked to help the children as they experiment with movement in response to the questions stated here. In developing questions to aid the children, the teacher must be careful not to let personal expectations for possible solutions interfere with the children's own solutions to the task. The teacher must be patient in using this style as children need time to think, to interpret the challenge, and to explore possible solutions.

As in guided discovery this style requires a great deal of time for the children to develop the lesson objectives. This style is exceptionally well suited for activities in which conceptualization is important. It permits children to work at their own level of understanding. If the challenges are well designed, there is greater cognitive involvement than in guided discovery and greater individualization of responses as children work to solve the movement challenges on their own. It requires careful planning on the part of the teacher, and its success is

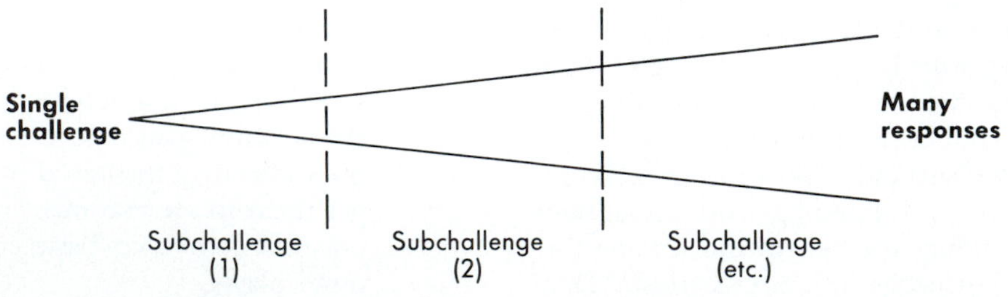

FIGURE 7-3 Problem solving.

based on the teacher's anticipation of possible solutions and the ability to respond on the spot to aid children in broadening their repertoire of movement possibilities.

Movement challenges may vary in complexity with the ability of the group. With younger children the challenge may be relatively simple, with only one or two elements involved. As the children develop skill in these child-centered approaches, challenges become more complex and include subchallenges to solve as well. The outcomes of these movement challenges might be the development of skills, the understanding of concepts and relationships, or variations in skills and strategies. Suggestions for the development of movement challenges may be found in Chapter 12.

In planning the lesson one may begin with one idea, developing its possibilities over the entire lesson or plan a series of ideas, each of which will be developed as parts of the lesson. For instance, in creative dance we may wish to explore one objective such as variations in locomotor movements in the lesson. Or, we might develop several aspects, such as possible movements, the use of general space, and level, which might be required in a culminating activity at the close of the lesson. The children would use each to develop their own individual dances.

Exploration

Exploration is the most child-centered style on the continuum. In this style the movement task is designed to enable the children to move freely as they desire, within the limits of safety. This style is similar to problem solving, but the children explore movement in a more general way with minimum teacher direction. This style may be used to introduce concepts, ideas, new equipment, and the like or to elicit original responses and ideas from the children.

Exploration gives children the opportunity to move in unique ways.

This style is most effective with young children who are involved in their first physical education experience. It enables the children to work on their own and explore their own capabilities. This style is geared for everyone's immediate success and should result in greater confidence in students' ability to move and in moving.

This style does not imply that the teacher puts out the equipment and allows the children to have free play. Tasks used in this style are directed by the teacher in some way. For example, the teacher may ask "How many different ways can you move on the balance beam on two feet?" or "Pick a piece of equipment and see how many ways you can use it." It is important for the teacher to be responsive to the children's needs by suggesting new challenges when it is time to move on. It is of value to have the children share some of their movement experiences with others to increase the movement possibilities for everyone.

CHOOSING A STYLE

The style of teaching depends on the particular learning situation and the purpose of the lesson. Table 7-1 summarizes the use of each of the previously discussed styles. An illustration of the use of each style in teaching a ball skill is given in the box on p. 100. Factors that influence the style chosen include age and experience of the children, stage of learning, content, level of the task, resources available including the amount of equipment and space, number of students, time available, and personality of the teacher.

EFFECTIVE TEACHING

For effective teaching, regardless of the strategy to be selected in a particular learning situation, the teacher must consider each of the following:

1. The preparation of the students for the learning experience
2. The presentation of the lesson material
3. The activities to develop the lesson objectives
4. The feedback and adjustments made in the activities to meet the varying needs of the students
5. The summary at the end of the lesson to bring the lesson to closure

Each of these aspects must be carefully planned before beginning the lesson.

Preparing the Students for Learning

All lessons require a good introduction to enhance student learning. In the Hunter model for effective teaching (Batesky) the introduction is referred to as anticipatory set.

TABLE 7-1 TEACHING STRATEGIES

STRATEGY	DECISION MAKING TEACHER	DECISION MAKING STUDENTS	ADVANTAGES	DISADVANTAGES
Command	Exclusively	None	Uniformity of response; most direct method to task, saves time; needs minimal preplanning and knowledge of activity	Does not individualize instruction; little thinking involved
Practice	Almost exclusively	Selects where to practice	Uniformity of response; saves time in organizing group for activity	Does not recognize individual differences; little thinking required
Reciprocal	Develops content	Determines when accomplished	Develops understanding and analytical skills; students share responsibility for learning; internalizes points of emphasis; provides maximum feedback; students see objective clearly	Feedback based on beginner perceptions; takes time to develop skill sheets
Task Level 1 Level 2 Level 3	Develops content Individualizes tasks for children Develops task content for the unit	Selects entry level Selects tasks on which to work Selects tasks based on individual needs	Individualizes instruction; children determine needs; maximizes use of equipment and facilities; performance goals defined and communicated; children move on to new material when ready	Tasks all planned prior to beginning of unit; takes time to develop tasks; requires independent learning skills
Guided discovery	Determines terminal goal	Decides movement solutions toward goal	Involves thinking; develops understanding of efficient movement	Takes time; requires careful planning; difficult with groups in which there is great variability in skill
Problem solving	Sets parameters of movement challenges and safety; raises questions to stimulate a multitude of responses	Decides how to move within parameter of movement challenge	Very good for conceptual development; cognitive development enhanced; develops skills in problem-solving technique; enhances creativity	Does not teach specific outcome
Exploration	Sets parameters of movement challenges and safety	Free movement responses	Allows children more freedom in moving; enhances creativity in movement	Is inappropriate if specific outcomes are desired

DEVELOPING THE BALL SKILL OF BOUNCING (DRIBBLING) WITH A VARIETY OF TEACHING STYLES

Objective: To dribble a ball in general space under control by pushing the ball slightly ahead with the fingerpads, below waist height, looking up to avoid others, and protecting the ball by keeping the body between the ball and an opponent.

COMMAND

1. The teacher gives an explanation and demonstration of the dribble, emphasizing the points above. The children are seated.
2. Each child gets a ball and practices dribbling. As the children move in general space the teacher calls out the change of hands, "Right hand, Left hand," etc.
3. As the children practice, the teacher offers suggestions for improvement and reinforcement of good dribbling.
4. At the close of the practice session the teacher leads a summation of the important points to remember about dribbling.

PRACTICE

1. The teacher explains and demonstrates the dribble, emphasizing the points listed above.
2. The students go to the designated space and practice dribbling.
3. The teacher circulates among the class, giving feedback as needed.
4. At the close of the session the teacher reviews the skill and summarizes the points of emphasis.

DEVELOPING THE BALL SKILL OF BOUNCING (DRIBBLING) WITH A VARIETY OF TEACHING STYLES—cont'd

RECIPROCAL

1. The teacher goes over the reciprocal skill sheet, clarifying important points and demonstrating and explaining the skill as needed. (See p. 94)
2. The class is divided into partners. Pick up equipment and pencils and find a space for practice.
3. Students perform roles as doer and observer as teacher circulates among the group, giving feedback.

TASK

Dribbling: When you complete the unit you should be able to:

1. Execute a dribble with good control with either hand.
2. Protect the ball while dribbling.
3. Dribble into an open space.
4. Dribble around an opponent.
5. Use the dribble to draw an opponent to create space for teammates.

Execution of the skill:

1. Include a reference for them to check.
2. A description of the skill, with common errors cited.
3. Suggest the use of a loop film.

Task 1: Practice dribbling the ball with the preferred hand in the space designated.

- a. Pushes the ball with the fingerpads.
- b. Controls the ball just below waist height.
- c. Dribbles the ball without watching it.

Task 2: Practice dribbling the ball with the nonpreferred hand in the space designated.

- a. Pushes the ball with the fingerpads.
- b. Controls the ball just below waist height.
- c. Dribbles the ball without watching it.

Task 3: Dribble around the cones 5 feet apart, changing hands so the hand farthest from the object is used for dribbling as you pass the object.

- a. Keeps the ball moving.
- b. Keeps the body between the object and the ball.

Task 4: Working with a partner, try to dribble the ball around your partner as your partner attempts to get the ball.

- a. Keeps the body between the ball and the opponent.
- b. Keeps the ball moving.
- c. Dribbles at a level that is easy to control and keeps the ball from the opponent.

Task 5: In a group of eight, in the space provided, each dribbles the ball, avoiding contact with the others.

- a. Dribbles without watching the ball.
- b. Keeps the ball moving.
- c. Protects the ball.

Task 6: In groups of four to six (three per team), dribble, drawing an opponent to create spaces for teammates.

- a. Keeps the ball moving.
- b. Dribbles without looking at the ball.
- c. Protects the ball against opponents.

GUIDED DISCOVERY

1. Establish a signal for listening.
2. Children are scattered in self-space within the assigned boundaries.
3. Each child has a ball.
4. Problems:
   - a. Let's see how many different ways you can bounce the ball in your self-space. What body parts can you use? Which parts enabled you to have the most control? (Hands) At what level was it easiest? (Medium)
   - b. Now let's bounce the ball in general space. Try using different body parts, including different parts of the hand. Which enabled you to have the best control? (Fingers) Now let's try to find the level at which to bounce the ball for greatest control. Try it high, low, and in the middle. At which level could you move the easiest? (Low)
   - c. Move in general space, dribbling the ball. As you move in general space while dribbling, what do you have to do to avoid bumping into others? (Look up)
   - d. Now we are going to alternately increase and decrease the amount of space we have. How did your dribbling change as the space changed? (Bounced closer to the body, took smaller steps, controlled the height of the dribble, etc.)
5. Summarize the findings of the children regarding an effective dribble.

PROBLEM SOLVING*

1-3. As above.

4. Problems:
   - a. How many ways can you move the ball in your self-space? Another way? Now move the ball in general space. Can you move it in the same ways? In different ways?
   - b. Can you change the body parts used to control the ball in self-space? In general space? Did you keep the ball under control?
   - c. At what levels can you control the ball in self-space? In general space?

EXPLORATION

This method would not be used to develop the dribbling objective.

*This method may not result in meeting the dribbling objective, since the children are not directed toward a specific response, but will develop prerequisite skills and vocabulary.

In the opening of the lesson the teacher prepares the students by developing their interest in the lesson material. In preparing the students the teacher states what is to be learned and its relationship to previous lessons and present or future activities. It is important to actively involve the learners. Questioning, visual aids, and class discussion are some of the activities used as openers. It is important to develop openers that require students to think. Because children are eager to get started, the opening should be short and to the point.

Presenting the Lesson Material

The teacher must focus the children's attention on the objectives to be developed in the lesson. At the beginning of the lesson the teacher describes the material either directly or with questions or discussion to involve the learner more actively in the process. Once this is accomplished, the teacher continues to focus on the objective through one of the teaching styles discussed earlier. Activities used develop the content, with the teacher giving feedback, raising questions, and helping children in the analysis of their own performance. All children should be actively involved in each aspect of the lesson, both in movement or in discussion at the beginning and close of the lesson.

A good demonstration is important to present or review motor skills by using the command, practice, reciprocal and task teaching styles. The demonstration is a model of the motor skill to be practiced. Along with a concise verbal description of the skill, it enables students to see how body parts are used, relationships of body parts and objects, the sequence of body actions, and the desired result. The demonstration may need to be repeated several times for the students to get a concise picture of what is to be done. If the teacher is unable to perform the skill, a student may give the demonstration with the assistance of the teacher, or a loop film or other visual aids may be used. The teacher should provide time for questions to check for student understanding before moving the group to the practice activity.

In presenting new material the teacher should avoid giving too much information, which may cause confusion for learners who are attempting to grasp too much information too quickly. Attention should be focused on a few critical elements at a time, no more than two or three. Young children may be able to focus on only one or two. The teacher must be able to analyze the task and to determine what information the children need initially and at what stage they need further information. Presentations should take no more than 1 to 3 minutes.

Guiding the Lesson Activities to Meet the Objectives

The teacher must be concerned with (1) the quality of the performance, (2) variety in the use of skills and knowledge, and (3) the transfer of skills and knowledge to new learning situations. Teacher expectations play a significant role in the motor performance of children. Students of teachers with high expectations achieve more than students of teachers with low expectations (Harrison, 1987). Teacher expectations should be high for all children. Research indicates that children judged to have less ability receive less praise, assistance, and encouragement from their teachers than those perceived to be more capable. The best efforts of all children should be enthusiastically encouraged. Learning is the primary focus of the physical education experience. The teacher must study why a student's movement is not effective and be able to take action that will result in a more successful performance. Early correction of errors is important.

This approach does not imply that all children's responses should be the same. In the skills lesson students may be working on motor skills at different levels of mastery. In the movement lesson many different responses may meet the objectives. Furthermore, the teacher should provide a wide variety of experiences to enhance a broader understanding and use of skills and concepts. Finally, the teacher must help children see the relationship between new learning and previous learning experiences (in other words, teach for transfer).

The teacher must communicate an expectation for learning—improving performance and knowledge—to all the students in the class. Research indicates that instructor-stated goals positively affect motor skill acquisition and retention. Although each student may not accomplish the lesson objectives at the same level of mastery, all children should strive to improve what they can do and what they know about human performance. This expectation is communicated not only in the grading process, but in the attention and encouragement given to each child in the class.

The teacher must provide sufficient time for learning to allow the children to grasp the material before moving on to the next part of the lesson. The teacher must develop a sensitivity about when it is time to move on, allowing adequate time for learning and maintaining the children's interest.

The practice of skills and concepts should be closely related to the use of skills and concepts in the specific unit and should stimulate children's thinking. Children may not see the relationship between the use of skills in the practice situation and the use of skills and concepts in the activity. Practice of skills and concepts should prepare children for their use in an activity. Interest in practice is difficult to maintain when practice is dissimilar to activity use of skills and concepts.

Regardless of the teaching style, the children should be involved intellectually in the learning process. Although the child-centered styles involve children more in searching for answers on their own, each style should encourage verbalization by the students and an understanding of why we do things a certain way. This approach helps students connect their feeling state to the movement, environment, and outcomes.

Giving Feedback and Adjusting the Activity

The feedback given students should continue to focus their attention on the lesson objectives. The teacher continues to focus on the lesson material by providing feedback about the points emphasized in the presentation of the lesson objectives. Feedback should be given to the least as well as the more advanced student, to girls as well as boys. Unfortunately, some research evidence suggests that this is not always the case (MacDonald, Markland). Comments about what students are doing well, as well as what they need to improve, should be included. Feedback on aspects of the skill performance other than those cited in the beginning of the lesson (other than when individualizing the activity for more advanced learners) are often confusing.

Individual differences must be recognized. Variability in skills, understanding, past experience, learning style, and rate of learning must be considered in the selection of teaching styles. The teacher should strive to become skillful in the use of a variety of styles because no one style is best for all children and in all situations. Several different styles may be used effectively within a single lesson. Studies indicate that learning is at a higher level when a variety of teaching strategies are used (Pettigrew).

The teacher must be responsive to the changing needs of children as the lesson proceeds. The teacher must recognize when a change of pace is needed, when further clarification is necessary, and when a change in the practice procedures would be beneficial. In monitoring the activity the teacher must anticipate what changes are needed. Perhaps the class needs a reminder of some of the teaching points that have been presented to refocus their attention on the task, or perhaps they are ready for some additional cues. Maybe the children are losing interest in the activity or need to have the activity adjusted to their developing skills and knowledge. Perhaps they are ready to move to the next part of the lesson. Whatever the cause, the teacher must determine the needs to be met and adjust the lesson accordingly.

Summarizing the Lesson for Closure

Closure at the end of the lesson ties the parts of the lesson together for the students and reemphasizes the important points developed in the lesson. Statements or questions at the close of the lesson help students see the relationship of the parts of the lesson, their importance in the unit, and the important points that will be carried forward to the next lesson. In a vigorous lesson it also gives the children a chance to catch their breath as they reflect on the lesson and prepare for the next activity in the day's schedule. Lesson closure should also recognize the effort of the group and areas of improved skill and concept development. In reflecting on the lesson, children can be given an opportunity to identify areas where further work is needed. Closure may also be used to help children think about the lesson and its possible carry-over to activities outside school.

Lesson Evaluation

As soon as possible the teacher needs to reflect on the lesson evaluating the extent to which the objectives were met, plans for future lessons, and the effectiveness of the teaching. The evaluation of teaching is discussed in Chapter 11.

In addition to the requirements for effective teaching, one must remember that *the most effective teachers teach learners how to learn.* The results of effective teaching should be a desire in children to continue learning and the development of skills needed to be independent learners. Teachers who help children find success and make learning fun through a variety of interesting and challenging activities enhance future learning.

ENCOURAGING CRITICAL AND CREATIVE THINKING

Because there is a lack of clarity in the literature regarding critical thinking, a number of different definitions have been proposed. For our discussion we will use the definition by Schwager and Labate, "an array of thinking processes or skills that all of us use to help us make decisions everyday." In considering this definition one thing is clear: the critical thinking skills taught should help students meaningfully solve the problems they face in everyday life, and the ultimate goal is for students to be thinkers and to use their thinking skills as they move in a variety of situations in and out of school.

A focus on the development of thinking skills does not mean that we must sacrifice the content of physical education. Thinking and program content are compatible. We have a wonderful medium for thinking. Children are enthusiastic about physical education. The activities are stimulating for children cognitively as well as in moving. According to Adler, teachers should require all students to think about what is being taught in the way they teach: "Learning without thinking is only memorization of facts, not understanding resulting in the formation of mere opinions, not the position of genuine knowledge and understanding." In motor skill learning it is relatively easy to develop skills with little understanding of how the skill is performed. This lack of understanding may limit the child's ability to use the skill effectively in a variety of movement situations. We want the children to reflect on their thinking about the content of physical education. The learning environment must be structured so that students are more aware of their own thinking and how to use that thinking to be more effective and efficient in a variety of movement situations.

As the children develop thinking skills through interaction with the physical education content, we must determine the important aspects of physical education that are worth serious thought. How will they use the content to solve movement challenges as they move throughout their lives? Each of the objectives of physical education has potential for critical thinking. In the development of the study of human movement we want children to think about what their bodies can do, how to improve their efficiency of movement, and how to move in space. We also want to think about how this knowledge of movement concepts is important in moving successfully in games, sports, dance, individual, and dual activities. In the development of motor skills we want them to think about how the body is used and, once they have acquired sufficient skill, what changes they must make to use the skill as the movement situation requires. With regard to social skills, the children can think about ways to interact more effectively with others. In fitness they learn to think about the fitness components, principles applied to improve them, and what they can do to enhance their own fitness level.

Several models have been suggested for developing thinking skills. The following steps are important in the thinking process:

1. Determining the goal
2. Identifying the problem
3. Devising possible solutions to the problem
4. Predicting the results of possible solutions
5. Selecting and trying out a solution
6. Evaluating the results

Once the goal of the task has been determined, the students are ready to examine the problem and to find possible solutions. One of the important and sometimes difficult tasks is identifying the problem and all its parameters. Students may not readily see the problem and may need help from the teacher. At times teachers may structure the activity so that certain problems arise. For example, a game requiring the delegation of several different responsibilities may be organized. After a few minutes of unsuccessful play, the activity is stopped and a class or small group problem-solving activity performed to determine what changes are necessary for success. Students should be encouraged to define the problem through questioning and other strategies rather than having the teacher define the problem. Students may identify aspects that have little relevance or are extremely important in defining the problem. Teachers need to help them distinguish between the two. One way the teacher may help students define the problem is by having them recall earlier similar experiences.

After the problem is identified students are ready to focus their thinking on possible solutions. As they develop possible solutions, they should be encouraged to think about the probable outcomes of selecting each one. Step five involves selecting a solution, or in some cases several solutions, to try. The students then try the solution(s) and evaluate their outcomes. As the students work, more possibilities may be discovered that require more opportunity for experimentation, More than one solution may be successful in completing the task.

A solution may also create more problems. For instance, a successful offensive strategy may require new thinking for the opposing team's defense. Thus the thinking processes are repeated, with each group moving to higher levels of analysis and problem solving.

The movement processes model introduced in Chapter 3 and developed in Chapters 12 and 13 and in the activity chapters throughout this book, as well as the dimensions of learning introduced in Chapter 6, help define further the thinking that will be needed. To begin, a learning environment must be established that enhances thinking.

The teacher creates an environment where thinking is encouraged. If children are to be comfortable using their own thinking, they must feel safe in developing their own ideas and in recognizing that it is okay to make a mistake. The teacher must help the children not to take their mistakes too seriously and also to encourage them to seek a more appropriate answer if necessary. In communicating with children, the teacher encourages them to take risks, emphasizing their ability to solve problems.

The teacher links tasks to student goals. Children are more motivated to work on tasks that meet personal goals. While the teacher sets high expectations for learning and thinking for the class, the teacher must also help children set high expectations (within their ability) for themselves. The teacher should encourage the children's self-reliance in taking responsibility for accomplishing the goals. Through a variety of activities at different levels of difficulty and the use of many different kinds of equipment, the teacher creates an exciting learning environment where children are eager to learn. The learning environment is discussed further in Chapter 9.

The teacher plans for depth of understanding and skill mastery. In selecting content the teacher must decide what content is the most important for future physical activity use. We cannot teach everything. Units of instruction should be planned to provide sufficient time for the children to acquire some depth of understanding and proficiency in those aspects that are important to future learning.

In the limited physical education time, it is best to plan fewer units than to spend only 3 or 4 days each on a greater variety of activities. Effective thinking requires depth of study through time with the subject matter. This depth of understanding will enable children to use the information in a meaningful way in a variety of movement situations now and in the future.

Unit and lesson content should provide ample time

for the children to learn and feel comfortable with the content. Within a unit of instruction, some aspects are more important than others. The teacher needs to focus the thinking of the learner on those aspects and plan for more time to be devoted to mastering a few important skills and knowledge. For instance, in teaching soccer, the time devoted to kicking skills should be maximized, with very little time spent on aspects such as the throw-in.

The children will not develop any depth of thinking if they are always trying to learn new material. For example, it is impossible for children to be able to develop game strategy if they are learning new games every day, with new sets of rules, organization, and so on. Physical education is more about teaching important ideas than a lot of different activities.

Thinking begins in the earliest physical education experiences. At the perceiving level children's thinking centers around getting a general idea about what the motor skill is or the definition of a particular movement concept. At the refining level their thinking helps them acquire greater understanding of how to use body parts in performing the motor skill, or in developing the idea of the movement concept more fully.

The teacher assists students in gaining meaning from new material by helping them to think about what they already know that relates to the new learning situation. For instance, in teaching striking with a paddle, the children might recall the similarities of previous experiences in striking with the hand. Or, in teaching the use of space in basketball, the teacher might have the children recall how they used space in an earlier soccer unit. Content, as well as the processes for thinking about content, must be taught. This process of teaching for transfer becomes extremely important not only in defining the problem but also in devising possible solutions, predicting their outcomes, and selecting solutions to try.

Children need ample time to learn the content if they are to perform with relative ease. An important phase of learning a skill involves internalization or habituation. This process occurs ideally when the refining process has been completed. Children need ample time to acquire mastery of skills and concepts through a series of gradually more complex activities in which increased information focuses the thinking of the learner on finer points of the technique or in understanding the concept. Examples of activities to use in developing skill and concept use can be found in Chapters 12 and 13 and the activity chapters.

As skills and concepts are mastered children are ready for higher levels of thinking and problem solving. Physical education is more than mastering motor skills and knowing movement concepts. Once the children have achieved an adequate level of motor skill mastery or understanding of a concept, they are ready to focus their thinking on adjusting the technique or using the concept in different ways. These explorations become the basis for further analysis and thinking in applying what they have learned through problem solving in games, dance, and other activities. The varying and applying activities found throughout the book encourage children to use their skills and knowledge in many new ways.

The teacher uses questions to enhance thinking. The teacher asks questions that require more than a yes or no response or simple recall. Appropriately placed questions develop a sense of inquiry. A technique to check for understanding may involve the children generating their own questions or backing up their answers with evidence. These types of questions and answers focus on the process as well as the content.

Questions cue different kinds of analytical thinking, comparing one situation to another, one activity to another, one skill to another. In varying and applying, children translate general information and previous experiences and apply them to new situations.

To enhance thinking the teacher acts as a facilitator or coach rather than the expert with all the answers. In varying and applying the teacher uses a process orientation by encouraging a much broader look at what the children have learned. During the varying and applying processes, the teachers will help the children see what they have learned in many different ways, thus changing the nature of the information.

"The most effective learning occurs when we continually cycle through information, challenging it, refining it . . . Once information is acquired and stored it can be changed, and in the most effective learning situations, it is changed" (Marzano). In this phase, conceptual learning in physical education reaches a high point. As the movement situations increase in complexity and as we apply what has been learned to many different situations, the children's understanding of their own movement increases. Each application encourages the children to think about the content in different ways.

Every physical education experience should encourage some original thinking. Creativity is often thought to be a part of only the dance experience. Dance does provide the opportunity for the child to express ideas through movement. However, all physical education should require creative thinking, whether it be creating a gymnastic routine, determining a group strategy in a game, or deciding how to outwit an opponent in soccer.

The creative thinking process parallels that of critical thinking. In developing creative ideas, a person moves through several steps. First, an idea is developed. During this phase the children seek as much information as possible. What are the facts? What are the parameters? Once the information is gathered, the children experiemnt with possible solutions until they find one they especially like. This solution may then be developed further. The children have then reached the stage in which they share their creation with others. At this point some evaluation by the group may take place, with the teacher encouraging the children to tell what they liked about the ideas expressed.

Creativity can happen only in an environment conducive to creative thinking. Ample time must be provided if creative thinking is to take place. To provide a model for such behavior, the teacher must do the following:

1. Encourage the children to develop their own ideas
2. Demonstrate a value for new ideas
3. Give reassurance to children engaging in the creative process
4. Make resources available that encourage the children's search for ideas
5. Encourage risk taking in problem solving
6. Encourage nontraditional use of the body and objects
7. Ask questions that require thinking
8. Do not leave creativity to chance

SUMMARY

A number of different teaching styles may be used in the teaching of physical education. These styles involve varying degrees of teacher and child decision making. The command style is the most teacher centered, with the teacher making the decisions of what, how, and when certain skills or concepts are learned. The practice style is also very teacher directed. The teacher gives a demonstration and explanation and sends the students off to practice while the teacher circulates among the group, giving feedback as needed. In the reciprocal style children take some responsibility for the learning of their peers by working with partners, giving each other feedback as they perform the task. In the task style the teacher decides how and what will be learned, but the children also have some decision making in selecting the task or the level at which they work on the learning task. In guided discovery the teacher guides the students through a series of activities leading to their discovery of the correct solution to the movement task. Problem solving and exploration are much more child centered, as the learning allows the children to make more decisions about their movement response. In problem solving the teacher imposes certain parameters such as the locomotor movements, space, and qualities of movement concepts to be used. Movement challenges in the exploration method are general, with a minimum of guidance by the teacher.

Each style has value for learning in physical education. Not all children learn best by the same style. Some material may be taught better by one style than another. The time available for learning and the desired outcomes also affect the selection of teaching style. The teacher must determine the relationship between what is to be learned and the process of learning in selecting the best teaching style for the situation.

If teaching is to be effective the teacher must:

1. Prepare the students for learning
2. Present the lesson material in a clear and concise manner
3. Provide feedback and encouragement to all the students in the class
4. Adjust activities to meet the individual needs of the students
5. Summarize the lesson material at the close of the lesson

The development of thinking skills is an important part of the physical education experience. Children need to develop their thinking skills as they explore the content of physical education. The class setting should make children feel comfortable in developing their own ideas. To encourage thinking the teacher focuses the content around student goals and plans for the depth of understanding needed for students to be able to use the knowledge and skills meaningfully in future activities. The movement process provides a model for the development of thinking in physical education. The teacher is a coach, using questioning and other strategies to help the children think about the activities. The teacher assists children in recalling previous experiences, which may help them analyze the situation and decide on possible solutions to the problem.

Creativity, the highest level of learning, should be encouraged in all aspects of physical education. Creative responses will result in an environment that encourages thinking and the development of one's own movement ideas.

REFERENCES AND RESOURCES

Adler, MJ: Critical thinking programs: why they don't work, *Education Digest* 52(7):9, 1987.

Alvino, J: Nurturing children's creativity and critical thinking skills, *PTA Today* 49(9):48, 1984.

Batesky J: Inservice education increasing teacher effectiveness using the Hunter lesson design, *JOPERD* 58(7):87, 1987.

Brophy J: Probing the subtleties of subject-matter teaching, *Educational Leadership* 49(7):4, 1992.

Cooper J and others: *Classroom teaching skills: a handbook,* ed 4, Lexington, Mass, 1990, DC Heath.

Dougherty N and Bonanno D: *Contemporary approaches to the teaching of physical education,* Scottsdale, Ariz, 1987, Gorsuch Scarisbrick.

Ennis C: Discrete thinking skills in two teachers' physical education classes, *The Elementary School Journal* 91(5):473, 1991.

Gabbard C: Developing an understanding of exploration, *Physical Educator* 43(3):118, 1986.

Harrison J: A review of research on teacher effectiveness and its implications for current practice, *Quest* 39(1):36, 1987.

Harrison J: *Instructional strategies for physical education,* ed 3, Dubuque, Ia, 1992, Wm C Brown.

Lee A and Poto C: Instructional time research in physical education: contributions and current issues, *Quest* 40(1):63, 1988.

MacDonald D: The relationship between the sex composition of physical education classes and teacher/pupil verbal interaction, *JTPE* 9(2):152, 1990.

Markland R and Martinek T: Descriptive analysis of coach augmented feedback given to high school varsity female volleyball players, *JTPE* 7(4):289, 1988.

Marzano RJ: *A different kind of classroom,* Alexandria, Va, 1992, Association for Supervision and Curriculum Development.

McBride R: Critical thinking-an overview with implications for physical education, *JTPE* 11(2):112, 1992.

Miller D: Energizing the thinking dimensions of physical education, *JOPERD* 58(8):76, 1987.

Mosston M: Tug-o-war, not more: meeting teaching learning objectives using the spectrum of teaching styles, *JOPERD* 63(1):27, 1992.

Mosston M and Arnsworth S: *Teaching physical education,* ed 3, Columbus, 1986, Charles E Merrill.

Moyer S: Teaching tips: a reciprocal criteria sheet and a nontraditional batting style, *JOPERD* 59(7):8, 1988.

O'Neil J: Rx for better thinkers: problem-based learning, *Update* 34(6):1, 1992.

Onosko JJ: Exploring the thinking of thoughtful teachers, *Educational Leadership* 49(7):40, 1992.

Pettigrew F and Heikkinen M: Increased psychomotor skill through eclectic teaching, *Physical Educator* 42(3):140, 1985.

Rink J: *Teaching physical education for learning,* ed 2, St Louis, 1992, Mosby–Year Book.

Schwager S: Using critical thinking to teach sport skills, Presentation Regional Games Conference, Hofstra University, Hempstead, NY, May 1992.

Schwager S and Labate C: Teaching for critical thinking in physical education *JOPERD* 64(5):24, 1993.

ANNOTATED READINGS

Annarino A: The teaching-learning process: a systematic instructional strategy, *JOPERD* 54(3):51, 1983.
Discusses a plan for achieving instructional goals, including behavioral objectives, content, teaching style, teacher interventions, and evaluation.

Gerney P and Dort A: The spectrum applied: letters from the teachers, *JOPERD* 63(1):36, 1992.
Two teachers talk about using the spectrum of teaching styles.

Lambdin D: Winning battles, losing the war, *JOPERD* 57(4):34, 1986.
Describes a successful teacher at work.

McAleese W and Scantling E: Are you asking the right questions, *Strategies* 3(5):5, 1990.
Offers suggestions for asking questions using Bloom's taxonomy.

Metzler M: Analysis of a mastery learning/personalized system of instruction for teaching tennis. In Peiron M and Graham G, editors: *Sport pedagogy,* Champaign, Ill, 1986, Human Kinetics Publishers.
Describes the use of ML/PSI to teach tennis (similar to the task method).

Rink J: The teacher wants us to learn, *JOPERD* 52(2):17, 1981.
Describes ways teachers communicate expectations to children during teaching.

Ritson R: Psychomotor skill teaching: beyond the command style, *JOPERD* 58(6):36, 1987.
Explains the importance of using teaching styles that enhance children's creativity.

Schwager S: Thinking about thinking in physical education, Inquiry: *Critical Thinking Across the Disciplines,* 8(2):12, 1991.
Discusses the use of critical thinking skills in the development of learning skills.

Weiller H: Successful learning = clear objectives, *Strategies* 5(5):5, 1992.
Introduces a four-stage process for developing meaningful lessons.

Weiss M: Modeling and motor performance: a developmental perspective, *Research Quarterly* 54(2):190, 1983.
Indicates modeling affects to be dependent on the age of the observer in comparing 4- to 8-year olds.

CHAPTER 8

Safety, Organizational Strategies, and Class Management

OBJECTIVES

After completing this chapter the student will be able to:

1. Describe policies and procedures necessary for a physical education program founded on sound health practices
2. Identify guidelines for establishing a safe environment for physical education experiences necessary to protect the safety of all children
3. Describe class organization and management techniques used to ensure maximum participation for all children in every class

Successful experiences in physical education require not only careful planning of content and activities in the daily lessons but also the establishment of policies that guarantee the safe and healthful participation of all children. These policies must be concerned with the degree to which the childen may participate in physical education, the nature of the experiences deemed appropriate for each child on a temporary or permanent basis, and the safe conduct of the physical education program.

POLICIES FOR HEALTHFUL PARTICIPATION

Medical Examinations

Each child should be required to have a physical examination and medical history by a physician before participating in physical education. It is the school administrator's responsibility to see that this information is available. In locations where this request puts an undue financial burden on the families of schoolchildren, the school should arrange to have these important examinations completed by a local physician or medical society. The examinations are important not only for participation in physical education but also to guarantee the child's well-being in all aspects of school life.

Results of the school examinations should be kept on file, and periodic examinations should be required throughout the school years. Changes in the health status of children may require even more frequent examinations. Teachers should be given the opportunity to review medical records so that they are aware of existing or potential health problems. It may be helpful for the physical education teacher to devise a form for the school nurse to use to notify the teacher of any changes in health status, medical restrictions, medications, allergies to insect bites, etc.

Regarding physical education, physicians should be required to state in writing the extent to which each child may participate. In cases in which a health problem requires some special considerations in physical education, all restrictions must be carefully defined. In dealing with these restrictions, it is often best to have the school nurse or the physical educator communicate directly with the physician because the physician may have little understanding of the activity requirements of various physical education activities. In this way the best possible program can be prescribed for each individual student. An example form for medical clearance for physical education may be found in Appendix 6. A list of the physical education activities to be included in the physical education program may be added to assist the physician in determining the level of participation for a child who will have some restrictions. Although no medical examinations are required or are required only on entrance to school, parents should be surveyed annually for any medical restrictions or changes in health status.

Identification of Health Problems

Physical educators or classroom teachers often note changes in individual children that may signal potential health problems. Problems in vision or hearing and changes in behavior or reaction to activities may be observed first by school personnel. In addition the teacher may also find indications of child abuse or poor nutrition. These observations should be made known to the school nurse or other authority so that appropriate action may be taken. Early detection of potential health problems is essential. Early care often results in better health as well as considerable savings in medical costs for remedial services.

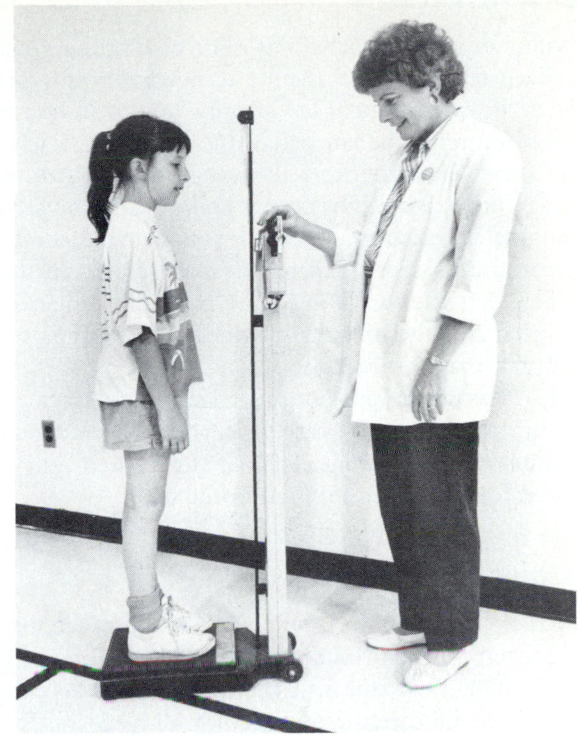

Weighing and measuring are a part of the periodic health examination.

Excuses from Participation in Physical Education

It is advisable to select a person, preferably the school nurse, as the only one who may excuse a child temporarily from participation in physical education. In responding to requests by family physicians or parents, the school nurse in consultation with the physical education teacher determines the extent to which children may safely participate. This procedure also permits adequate health records to be maintained and potential health problems to be brought to the attention of the appropriate personnel. When children's participation in physical education has been restricted, their return to full participation should require the authorization of the school nurse or designated authority.

If a school nurse is not available, excuses or restrictions from activity should be directed to the teacher of physical education, either the physical education specialist or the classroom teacher. Teachers need to communicate the nature of the physical education experiences to help parents make appropriate requests regarding any restrictions in participation of their children. It is generally a good policy to honor parents' requests for students to be excused or participation to be limited in some activities, as liability could become an issue regarding who has the right to make such decisions. A possible guideline to handle such requests may be that a student may be excused from physical education for 3 days at the parents' request, after which a physician's or school nurse's request is necessary.

Attire

Children should be attired for safe participation in physical education activities. In many elementary schools boys and girls do not change their clothes but are required to wear sneakers. Appropriate footwear is essential to safe participation. In some activities and where health policies allow, moving barefoot may be beneficial. If proper footwear is not available, going barefoot is much safer than participating in stocking feet. If all children cannot provide their own footwear, parents' groups may be enlisted to initiate a fund to provide shoes for those in need. In other situations the teacher may provide a box for shoes, clean and washed, that children have outgrown. These shoes may be given to those who need shoes temporarily or permanently.

Children should remove all jewelry and objects from their pockets before participating in physical education. Failure to do so may cause injury if a child falls or bumps into equipment or other children. For safe participation in most activities, long hair should be pulled back and secured to provide unrestricted vision of the environment.

Heavy clothing that restricts movement or results in overheating should be removed. Whenever possible, at least in the upper elementary grades, children should change clothes for participation in physical education activities. Changing clothes is important in establishing sound personal hygiene habits. Clothes worn for physical education should be laundered regularly, and clean socks should be worn each day. In classes in which children do change clothes, adequate supervision must be provided for both boys and girls in the changing areas. A sweater or jacket and long pants or warm-up suits should be available for outdoor play during the fall or spring.

SCHOOL SAFETY

The safety of children at school must be a primary concern. Each teacher must assume responsibility for providing a safe environment for learning and must be consistent in enforcing the safe behavior of children. Teachers should know the activities well enough to recognize the type of injuries that might occur. They must be aware of potential safety hazards and take appropriate measures to minimize the risks to the safety of the children in their care. Few activities are considered naturally dangerous. Most often it is the manner in which an activity is conducted that makes it hazardous.

Regardless of the precautions taken, minor accidents do occur occasionally. In case of an accident, emergency procedures should provide care of the injured and supervision for the other children in the class.

Emergency Procedures

All teachers should have training in first aid procedures, including current cardiopulmonary resuscitation certification (CPR). Procedures to follow in case of an emergency should be carefully defined for all teachers. Adequate procedures include:

1. Notification of designated school officials (the school nurse or school administrator) of the injury or other emergency
2. The first aid treatment to be administered
3. Who has decision-making authority if local medical emergency services are required
4. How and when to notify parents

Responsibility for the child's care should be delegated to the parents as soon as possible.

For the teacher working with young children, notifying local school personnel may be a problem because the injured child should not be left alone, and the other children in the group may be too young to transmit the information to others. Procedures may need to be worked out with a teacher close by so that adequate supervision is provided.

A written report of the accident should include a statement of what happened, the circumstances surrounding the incident, the treatment given, the time of the injury, the witnesses if any, the activity in which the accident took place, and to whom the child was released. This report should be completed as soon as possible after appropriate care has been given to the injured child. A sample accident report form may be found in Appendix 6. A copy of the teacher's lesson plan for the day should also be filed.

Follow-up measures should be taken immediately to eliminate the cause of the injury and to prevent further accidents. Responsibility for follow-up action should be designated to someone on the school staff. This information might include repairs to equipment or facilities if needed.

Most school districts offer low-cost accident insurance for children, which covers most school accidents. This insurance is especially important for children who are not covered by any other family medical insurance. Lack of adequate medical coverage is often cited as the reason for suits against school districts as a result of school accidents.

LEGAL LIABILITY

All teachers share the responsibility for the well-being of all students. Although physical education activities are not inherently dangerous in themselves, they require the careful planning and conducting of activities to ensure the safety of all.

Legal liability refers to a responsibility that can be enforced by a court of law in an action brought by one person against another, or by one person against a group, such as a school board. In the schools, failure to meet one's responsibility in providing for the safety of students is considered negligence. A **tort** is an injury, physical or psychological, that results when someone fails to meet their legal responsibilities. To be considered negligent the law requires that the following elements be present:

1. That the individual in charge had the *responsibility* to ensure the safety of the participant
2. That the individual in charge *violated this responsibility*
3. That an *injury did occur*
4. That the *injury was the result of the violation of the responsibility* for the safety of the individual

Teachers have a responsibility to provide a safe environment for learning for all students in the class. This responsibility includes providing appropriate instruction, adequately supervising the activity, and conducting the activity in a safe manner. The teacher's behavior may be viewed as negligent when he or she fails to do what is required, such as providing instruction in the safe use of a piece of equipment; acts incorrectly, as in spotting incorrectly; or intentionally acts in a way that is illegal, as in using corporal punishment. Clear evidence must be provided that injuries did occur and that the injuries were the direct result of the teacher's negligent behavior.

In cases of serious injury, the injured person or the parents (the plaintiffs) may initiate a legal action against the teacher, the school board, and other involved persons such as equipment manufacturers (the defendants). Because accidents are bound to happen, all teachers should have liability insurance. Insurance provided by the school district most often provides some liability coverage for teachers. Teachers should fully understand their liability, the insurance coverage the school system provides, and the laws concerning liability in their state.

Defenses against negligence may include the following:

1. *Contributory negligence:* The injured person directly contributed to the injury by behaving in a negligent manner. For instance, after being re-

minded several times about where to stay, a student is hit by a foul ball after moving from behind the back stop. Individuals must assume some responsibility to act safely.

2. *Comparative negligence:* The injured person and the defendant are both responsible for the accident.
3. *Assumption of risks:* When a student understands and accepts that participation in an activity involves certain possibilities of injury that may not be able to be prevented, the student, in participating, then assumes the risks involved. Gymnastics is one activity believed to be potentially dangerous. This assumption of risk is only for the individual's behavior and not for the negligence of another person.
4. *Act Of God:* An unavoidable accident due to the forces of nature, for example, being struck by lightning while playing outdoors on an apparently clear day.
5. *Legal precedents:* Court decisions made in similar situations may serve as a precedent in other court cases.

In fulfilling the teacher's duty for the safe participation of all children, three major responsibilities must be addressed: (1) The activity must be appropriately supervised, (2) the activity should be suitable for the participants and carefully conducted, and (3) the environment in which the activity takes place must be one in which safety is controlled. In fulfilling liability responsibilities, it is important that policies for healthful participation be followed closely. The following discussion establishes guidelines for each of these important concerns.

Supervision

All persons conducting physical education classes should be appropriately trained. In providing adequate supervision of physical education activities, one must first consider the qualifications required for the assigned personnel. The teacher of physical education should have an understanding of human anatomy and physiology as well as the age characteristics of elementary school children. The teacher should know the general physiological responses to specific motor experiences. For example, knowing the specific effects of exercise on body segments, muscles, and other body systems should enable physical educators to select appropriate experiences for the children in their classes. Teachers should be competent in all the activities they will teach. This should include knowledge of the progressions in moving from one level of competency to the next, the prerequisites needed for particular skills, and the awareness of risks that will minimize potential dangers. Teachers must also recognize the special needs of students with disabilities and be able to provide appropriate placement as well as modification of activities for their safe participation. Appropriate supervision also assumes that the teacher has the ability to administer first aid and to react immediately in case of injury. Aides or volunteers involved in the program must also be adequately trained to assume their responsibilities and to be aware of any potentially dangerous situations that might arise.

The supervision provided may be either general or specific. **General supervision** is provided by the teacher's overall observation of the area and the activities in which the children are engaged. **Specific supervision** assumes the teacher is working directly with the students, interacting with them as they participate in the physical education activities.

Specific supervision is important in the introduction of a new activity. Teachers stay with the participants until they are familiar with the activity, understand their own capacity to accomplish the task, and understand and adhere to the safety rules. The more inexperienced the participants, the greater the responsibility of the teacher. Safety is a primary concern in the conduct of activities. Students must be well aware of the safety factors and understand any risks; it is not enough merely to inform them of risks.

Young elementary school children as well as some disabled children may require more specific supervision because they are not always mature or capable of fully appreciating the safety concerns of the teacher. For example, when introducing a new piece of apparatus, such as the horizontal ladder, the teacher should stay with the children until each has had the opportunity to mount, to move, and to land safely.

Activities in which there is greater risk of injury, such as some moves in gymnastics, require specific supervision. In teaching skills in gymnastics, children need to be instructed about prerequisite skills for the new skill, as well as which skills they may try on their own and which require the specific supervision of the teacher.

Both general and specific supervision are important in maximizing the participation for all children. As the teaching methods become more child centered, the teacher may be giving some specific supervision to some children while generally supervising the remaining children. General and specific supervision shifts from some individuals or groups to other individuals or groups as the teacher moves through the activity area. Station work and use of the task style of teaching involve general supervision for at least part of the class.

Any failure by the participants to adhere to safety rules or any change in the condition of participants requires more specific supervision until the condition can be reversed. General supervision assumes that the supervisor is located in the immediate area and is accessible to anyone who needs assistance. Teachers must position themselves where they can oversee the entire group. In providing general supervision the individual must be alert to any unsafe conditions that may arise. Safety rules should be taught, reviewed regularly, and reinforced at all times. Horseplay should always be discouraged. The teacher should quickly address inappropriate behaviors, giving feedback to the students on more appropriate courses of action. Highly emotionally charged situations should be avoided, and the class should be brought under control quickly when such situations arise. Equipment should always be used safely, and participants should only work within their ability.

Adequate supervision must be provided for all school experiences. Supervision of the playground activities may be the responsibility of the physical education or classroom teacher. If the children change clothes for physical education activities, supervision must also be provided in locker room areas. Physical education facilities should be locked when supervision is not available, especially when large apparatus or other equipment is being used. Intramurals and other after school activities require the same concern for supervision as physical education classes.

Selection and Conduct of Activities

Activities should be appropriate to the age, size, physical condition, and ability of those participating. Individual differences must be considered in the selection of activities for any group. Children should be encouraged to work to their level of ability but should not be pressured into attempting activities that they do not feel ready to try. Lack of confidence in performing a particular motor activity may result in an injury because of increased anxiety.

Instruction should be carefully planned to meet the needs of all students. Progressions for the development of skills to meet individual needs are important in providing appropriate instruction for all students. Evidence of the careful planning that has gone on in preparation for the physical education classes should be available to demonstrate the professional manner in which instruction has been provided. The means of assessing student performance should be noted and records kept on individual student skill development. Instructions on safety should be included in each lesson.

Activity organization should ensure the safety of all.

No child should attempt an activity without careful instruction. Safety is of utmost importance during the instruction phase, and children should not be asked to take unreasonable risks. Instruction must be geared to the maturity of the students because lack of maturity may jeopardize the children's safety. Children should never be forced to try new activities before they feel they are ready.

Potential risks to safety must be anticipated. Thorough planning is important not only in the selection of activities but also in the manner in which they are conducted. Activities should be organized with special consideration for special needs. Children should be able to move freely. They should not interfere with one another and should be able to move away from obstacles and equipment. In situations in which safety hazards cannot be avoided, activities must be modified. If this modification does not reduce the risks, then the activity should be discontinued. The names of games that suggest overly aggressive behavior, such as "killer ball" or "suicide ball" should be renamed and modified if necessary. Special concerns for safety are included in each of the activity chapters that follow.

In case of an emergency or when a potentially dangerous situation arises, the teacher must remain calm. The teacher's display of confidence should be reassuring to the children and may even eliminate behavior that can lead to potentially dangerous situations.

A list of additional safety tips for teachers may be found in the box on p. 113.

The Environment

Rules of safety should be established for all areas of the school, including classroom, gymnasium, and playground. These rules should be posted and must be enforced consistently by all school personnel. The activities of one child should not endanger others.

The atmosphere in the physical education class should be one in which children not only participate safely but also feel safe. Children who are comfortable in a situation are more willing to participate freely and to behave safely. It must be an environment where children assume responsibility for their own safety and the safety of others.

Protective equipment and other safety devices should be provided and kept in good working condition. Protective equipment should fit the participants using them. When safety equipment is needed, children should be taught how to use it effectively.

Floors and other surfaces should be inspected regularly for safety. Unsafe conditions should be reported immediately.

Repairs should be made promptly and all areas well maintained. Teachers should use good judgment in using facilities and equipment until appropriate repairs are made.

Outdoor surfaces should be appropriate to guarantee the safety of the children. More than 60% of playground accidents are the result of inappropriate surfaces (Thompson). Lack of surfacing, inappropriate surfacing, and an inadequate depth of surfacing are the primary causes of playground injuries. Grass surfaces provide the best surface for game activities. Wood chips, mulch, and shredded bark appear to be the best surface under playground equipment up to 12 feet tall.

Heat and ventilation should be controlled, with activities moderated where environmental conditions warrant. In some areas monitoring air quality, temperature, or high humidity may necessitate changes in the activities for the day.

Rainy day activities should be related to the units of instruction being taught because children are developing skills and awareness of safety that reduces the risks of injury. Modifications in activities or equipment may be needed, however, where space is reduced dramatically to ensure the safe participation of all. Moving activities indoors may also require some changes in the equipment used. For example, using soft or foam balls for indoor soccer and hocky or covered fleece or rag balls for softball activities is important in ensuring the safety of all children.

SAFETY TIPS FOR TEACHERS

1. Know your class and the capabilities of individuals.
2. Develop a set of safety rules with the children; remind them regularly and post them where all can see them.
3. Be consistent in reinforcing safety.
4. Establish activity boundary lines a safe distance from walls, fences, and other obstructions (a minimum of 10 feet).
5. Clearly mark boundaries with cones or other objects.
6. Use soft balls when space is limited and there is the possibility of children being hit with a ball.
7. Stress control of balls and other objects and assuming personal responsibility for one's actions.
8. Plan for and build safety into each lesson plan.
9. Emphasize safety for self and others, reinforcing appropriate behavior.
10. Be in charge. If an activity seems to be getting out of control, stop it immediately and take appropriate action.
11. Carefully match children for activities based on their motor, cognitive, and social abilities, and physical condition to ensure their safe participation.
12. Deal with emotionally charged situations promptly and be sure that any conflicts are resolved before the children are dismissed from your class.

If the concerns for adequate supervision, appropriate selection and conduct of activities, and a safe environment are met, we are well on the way to providing a safe physical education experience for all children.

CLASS MANAGEMENT AND ORGANIZATIONAL STRATEGIES

Successful teaching is the result of careful planning of both instruction and management. **Instruction** is composed of all the activities that the teacher uses to meet the lesson objectives. **Management** includes the operations that are required to move the class smoothly from one activity to the next, from the beginning of the lesson to its conclusion.

Many times a lesson is unsuccessful because the teacher fails to manage the class effectively. Regardless of how well the instructional phase is planned, failure to be concerned with management operations leads to disaster.

The teacher must distinguish between instructional and management activities. Instructional activities include (1) diagnosing class needs, (2) planning and presenting information, (3) asking questions, and (4) evaluating progress. Management activities (1) create and maintain the instructional conditions, (2) reward appropriate behavior, and (3) develop teacher-student rapport (Cooper).

Problems that arise during the lesson must also be diagnosed. Some may be the result of inadequate planning, whereas other problems may be difficult to anticipate. Instructional problems require instructional solutions, and management problems require management solutions. Table 8-1 differentiates some typical instructional and management problems that may occur in physical education.

Classroom management skills are essential to good teaching. Good classroom management practices introduced by the teacher result in the development of good self-management skills by the students. Once students learn to be more self-managed, it is easier for the teacher to concentrate on effective teaching. Children must learn to assume responsibility for their own actions and to share responsibility for classroom management. For example, children can learn to be responsible for getting out equipment, taking care of it, and putting it away. They can also learn to work in a group and not distract others. However, these skills are learned not by chance but through the management activities of the teacher.

In planning the lesson the teacher should identify each part of the lesson in which management skills will be used. These parts should be worked out ahead of time to minimize the management time and maximize the learning time. Beginning teachers are often so worried about lesson content that they overlook the necessary management operations. Yet it is in this area that the lesson most often breaks down.

TABLE 8-1 INSTRUCTIONAL AND MANAGEMENT PROBLEMS IN PHYSICAL EDUCATION

PROBLEM	PROBABLE CAUSE	SOLUTION
INSTRUCTIONAL PROBLEMS		
Several children in the class are unable to do the skills needed in the unit.	Great variation in ability in group	Plan activities to develop skills in progression for all levels of ability in the group.
In a gymnastics lesson not all children are working.	Loss of interest because skills are too difficult or too easy	Provide a variety of activities to challenge all ability levels.
The class is having some difficulty using a concept.	Not ready for the application	Determine level of understanding. Provide activities at a lower level to prepare students for the movement challenge.
The children do not appear to understand how to perform a skill.	Lack of understanding of what is to be done.	Provide another demonstration and explanation of the task and ask questions to determine understanding.
MANAGEMENT PROBLEMS		
Two children are fighting during a game.	Not enough activity	Restructure activity to maximize active participation for all.
A child is not chosen by anyone in the group as a partner.	Child may be unliked by others	Arrange children into partners.
Two children in the rear of the group are not listening.	Not within eye contact or hearing of teacher	Arrange children in close so all can hear explanations and see demonstration.
Several children are unable to follow the instructions given.	Instructions unclear	Repeat instructions; ask questions for clarification.
The class is noisy and not responsive to the signal for listening.	Signal not clear	Clarify signal for listening; practice response to signal.
The class is unable to reorganize for the new activity within the lesson.	Directions unclear; children not listening	Get group's attention. Go over steps in reorganization. Move group.

As the teacher and students move through the lesson, the teacher uses verbal and nonverbal cues in organizing the class in moving them from one activity to another and from one formation to the next. These cues are also used in securing, using, and putting away equipment as well as in reacting to the behavior of students on and off task.

The time taken to manage the class or to perform these functions should be minimal. As children learn to become more self-managed, time is further reduced. If the teacher takes too long for management tasks, the chance for disruptive behavior by the students increases. To maximize learning time the teacher must carefully plan management activities. For example, anyone can organize a group into a circle, but it may take one teacher a few seconds and another a few minutes. The less time available to children while they wait for the next part of the lesson to happen, the greater the chance the move will go smoothly.

Class management techniques should be as unobtrusive as possible so as not to detract from the instructional aspects of the lesson. If well planned, they will move the group quickly into activity and smoothly from one activity to the next. Rather than merely reacting to problems as they occur, management operations should prevent problems from occurring. Several factors affect the selection of appropriate management strategies:

1. The maturity of the students and their relationships to one another must be considered. Are the students self-directed, or do they need more structure within which to learn? Are they well disciplined? Can they follow directions and stay on task with little direct supervision? What has been the nature of their previous learning experiences?
2. The number of students, the amount of space, the equipment, the time constraints, and the goals for the lesson are all considerations in selecting appropriate management procedures.
3. The teacher's personality is also an important factor. What is the teacher's preferred teaching style? What rapport has been established with the group?

The first task in effective management is to develop a cohesive group. The teacher must strive to develop an atmosphere that promotes good teacher-student and student-student relationships where mutual support is the

All children should be listening during class instruction.

rule. In this atmosphere children can feel comfortable in striving to do their best.

Management problems may be individual or group. Individual problems may often be intertwined with group problems, which may cloud the issue in determining strategies to overcome them. In Table 8-2 group management problems and their descriptions, first identified by Cooper and associates, have been modified to fit the physical education setting, with some solutions suggested to improve group interactions. Individual behavior problems and strategies to deal with them are discussed in greater detail in Chapter 9.

The following sections offer suggestions for developing effective class management techniques.

Establishment of a Class Routine

One important concern in classroom management is the establishment of a class routine. Children are creatures of habit. The routine should include how the class begins, what signal is to be used to get the group's attention, and what is expected in listening and following directions, in working with others, in the use of space for particular activities, and in special routines for the use of playground, gymnasium, and other spaces.

These routine behaviors are best taught in the early physical education experiences or when several teachers are involved in the physical education instruction at the beginning of the school year. The earlier these behaviors are established, the sooner maximum activity can be achieved. Time spent early to establish the class organization and procedures results in better attitudes toward physical education and greater student achievement throughout the year (Fink). If routines are to be established painlessly, teachers must be consistent in defining the specific behaviors appropriate in these different situations.

If the children change clothes for physical education, there may be free time at the beginning of the period. This time should be used constructively. Posting a list of activities to work on before the beginning of class is helpful. In this way children may use the time beneficially to further their own development.

Getting Started

Establish a signal for listening. A signal for listening must be established if the class is to begin quickly. A great deal of time can be lost if this routine is not set. Signals for starting an activity should not be confused with the signal for listening. Often a voice command is all that is needed for beginning, but a louder signal such as a whistle may be more effective for getting the group's attention in some situations, such as when playing games or when the class is out of doors. Using the word "freeze," raising a hand, and dimming the lights are examples of signals used to get the attention of the class. Positive feedback is important in establishing the signal for listening. The teacher should encourage the children to respond quickly and praise their efforts when they do. Such comments as "Good listening, Mary," and "I like the way John is listening" go a long way in establishing good listening skills. It may be helpful to have the children practice the signal through some activity at the beginning of the lesson. For

TABLE 8-2 GROUP CLASSROOM MANAGEMENT PROBLEMS AND THEIR BEHAVIORAL DESCRIPTIONS

PROBLEM	BEHAVIORAL DESCRIPTION	SOLUTIONS
1. Lack of unity	The class lacks unity, and conflicts occur between individuals and subgroups, as: (a) When groups split, become argumentative over competitive situations such as games, or boys side against girls (b) When groups split by cliques or minority groups (c) When group takes sides on issues or breaks into subgroups; when hostility and conflict constantly arise among members and create an unpleasant atmosphere	Use a sociogram to determine groupings; assign students to predetermined groups; structure activities to foster working together with a partner and eventually small groups to solve problems.
2. Nonadherence to behavioral standards and work procedures	The class responds with noisy, talkative, disorderly behavior to situations that have established standards for behaving, as: (a) When group is entering or leaving room or changing activities, lining up, or getting out or putting away equipment (b) When group is working in ability groups or engaging in committee work (c) When group is completing assignments, receiving assignments, or handling equipment (d) When group is engaged in discussion, sharing, or planning	Work with students to establish rules for class in listening to instructions and their peers and working in groups; practice responding to signal; reinforce students who behave appropriately; stand between potentially disruptive students when giving instructions.
3. Negative reactions to individual members	The class becomes vocal or actively hostile toward one or more class members, as: (a) When group does not accept individuals and derides, ignores, or ridicules members who are different (b) When group reacts negatively to members who deviate from group code or who thwart group's progress; when a member's behavior upsets or puzzles members of the class	Use a sociogram to determine groupings; establish expectation that everyone works with everyone else in the class; change groupings often so that children work only a short time with any one person; model the acceptance and worth of each child; establish strategies to help unaccepted students gain acceptance by using appropriate behavior.
4. Class approval of misbehavior	The class approves and supports individuals, as: (a) When they talk out of turn, act in ways which disrupt the normal work procedures, or engage in clowning or rebellious activities	Work with students to establish needed rules of behavior; reinforce appropriate behavior.
5. Being prone to distraction, work stoppage, and imitative behavior	The group reacts with upset, excited, or disorderly behavior to interruptions, distractions, or constant grievances, as: (a) When group is interrupted by monitors, visitors, or a change in weather (b) When members constantly have grievances relating to others, lessons, rules, policies, or practices they believe are unfair and when settlements are demanded before work proceeds	Encourage and reinforce individual efforts; prepare class for visitors ahead of time and discuss expectations for behavior.

TABLE 8-2 GROUP CLASSROOM MANAGEMENT PROBLEMS AND THEIR BEHAVIORAL DESCRIPTIONS—cont'd

PROBLEM	BEHAVIORAL DESCRIPTION	SOLUTIONS
6. Low morale and hostile, resistant, or aggressive reactions	The class members engage in subtle, hostile, aggressive behavior, creating slowdowns and work stoppages, as: (a) When they don't get the piece of equipment they want (b) When there are constant requests for assignments to be repeated and explained (c) When students constantly complain about behavior of others with no apparent loss of friendship (d) When children accuse authority figures of unfair practices and delay classwork with their claims	Focus on positive aspects; be consistent in reinforcing procedures and rules; organize group for maximum participation; provide for exchange of equipment if necessary to ensure all get equal opportunity; avoid emotionally charged situations such as those brought on by overly competitive relays and games.
7. Inability to adjust to environmental change	The class reacts inappropriately to such situations, as: (a) When a substitute takes over (b) When normal routines are changed (c) When new members transfer into the class (d) When stressful situations such as fitness testing cause inappropriate reactions	Prepare students for changes ahead of time and the expectations of behavior; explain reasons for changes in routine or other needed adjustments; introduce new class members; emphasize personal best rather than best in the class in testing situations.

Modified from Cooper and associates.

example, when working on individual ball activities the teacher may have the children work with the equipment to see how quickly they can hold the balls when the signal is given.

Get off to a good start. To begin the lesson promptly, it is important to have all materials ready that will be used in the class before the class begins. Sometimes children may help organize the materials for the lesson. As children gain experience in helping, they will require less time to get out the equipment and other materials, allowing more time for the instructional phase of the lesson.

In beginning the lesson it is important that the children be arranged in a manner conducive to good listening. The class should be seated where all are able to see and hear. When meeting outdoors the class should assemble away from distracting noises. If it is windy, the class should face the incoming wind so that the teacher's voice is projected toward the class. On sunny days the teacher should face the sun so that the children do not have to strain or shield their eyes to see the teacher and the demonstrations.

Get the class into activity quickly. In order for the lesson to be most effective, it is important to get the class into activity quickly. Often a lesson never really gets its momentum because too much time is taken for management at the beginning of the lesson. The class should begin on time. When the children enter the gymnasium, the lesson should begin immediately. Once the daily routine is established, children should be able to enter the area and immediately begin the warm-up activities or to receive the instructions for the first activity. Children are eager to get started. Teachers must channel this enthusiasm by getting the children moving quickly in the lesson.

A time-saving method should be used to take the roll if necessary. Often this can be done while the children are engaged in the warm-up activities or the first activity of the lesson.

Instructions should be short and to the point. Minimum time should be used for giving instructions. Momentum is often lost because teachers dwell too long on points of emphasis or other instructions. This is an important time in which attention can be lost if instruction takes too long.

In moving the group into activity, it is important that the children listen to all the instructions before moving. Children are eager to get moving and often begin before the instructions are actually completed. When giving instructions it is often a good idea to:

First, tell the children when they will move ("When I give you the signal").

Second, tell them where and how they will move ("I want you to find your own space inside the black boundary lines").

Third, tell them what they will do when they get there ("and sit down").

When giving instructions to help children, for example to move to a new formation, it often helps to establish a time reference. For example, to help children move quickly one might say "When I say 'go' I want to see if everyone can line up on the black line before I count to three. Go. One, two, three."

Children need encouragement to follow the new instructions quickly. Positive feedback is always helpful in establishing good management habits. At times a group may need to be rewarded for responding quickly to instructions, especially when the group is just beginning to develop self-management skills. The reward might be a free choice of individual or group activities during the last part of the period.

Managing the Lesson

Establish momentum and keep the lesson moving. In an effective lesson, momentum is established and the lesson parts flow smoothly from one to another without breaks. Disruptions often occur when there is a break in the activity flow or an unnecessary slowdown. These disruptions may be the result of a child's change in behavior, the occurrence of some unplanned event, stopping an activity before its conclusion, prolonging an activity beyond its usefulness, or failure to maximize activity, resulting in the loss of interest of the group. They may also result when the teacher takes too much time for an explanation or does not sense when it is time to move on.

Occasionally, teachers must deal with several events taking place simultaneously. For example, a teacher giving a demonstration of a new skill to the class notices that two children are inattentive. The successful teacher must be able to deal with these two events at the same time if momentum is not to be lost. A question posed to either of the two children or a remark or an instruction given to the children as the explanation and demonstration continue will help keep the lesson moving.

Teachers should be careful to stay on task and not become distracted by random events. There are occasions when circumstances lend themselves to the "teachable moment," but teachers should most often avoid situations that get them off track.

Teachers must also develop an awareness of when it is time to move on in the lesson. It is important to permit adequate time for children to develop the skill or concept and to move on to the next activity before the children lose interest.

Maximize the opportunities for each child to participate. It is important to maximize the amount of activity for each child during the lesson. Time studies often disclose that individual children have spent far too little time being physically active in the lesson. Teachers must maximize use of equipment and organize the group so that as many children as possible are actively engaged in moving throughout the lesson. Whenever possible teachers should attempt to have all children active at one time. Mass teaching involves organizing the class so that all children are working in their own space individually on a particular skill or concept, with the teacher circulating among the children and giving help where needed. Because skills or concepts are best learned over repeated practice, this approach maximizes individual development. This mass teaching approach is perhaps a little unnerving for beginning teachers because the children may be spread over a large area, and the teacher may feel some lack of control over the group. With experience teachers will feel comfortable in using this technique of organizing the group for individual work.

We often do not have an adequate supply of any one kind of equipment to allow each child to work alone. Opportunities for practice may be improved by gathering all the balls available rather than insisting on the use of only one type of ball. The children should share the equipment so that all have the opportunity to use balls of a variety of sizes and types while practicing the skill. When school resources are limited, parents' groups are often interested in providing equipment for physical education.

Another method for maximizing learning opportunities when limited pieces of equipment are available is to use the station approach. The children are divided into several groups, with each group practicing different skills; the available equipment is used to its maximum. After a period of practice, each group moves on to a new station, to a new skill, and to new equipment. In this manner all the children are actively practicing their skills with little waiting, if any, for a turn. In using this approach it is very important to explain carefully at the beginning of the lesson what is to be accomplished at each of the stations and when the groups will move on to a new station and activity. The teacher must watch the time carefully so that all have an opportunity to work at each station. Children readily display their disappointment at not having an opportunity to try each activity.

Activity modification is another means to maximize opportunities for all children. In developing group learning experiences the teacher must determine what is the smallest group necessary to fulfill the activity objectives. A suggested minimum number of participants for each activity is included in the games analyses in Chapters 24 through 31. Reducing the number of participants per group, however, results in maximum participation only when the teacher substitutes several small group games participating at the same time for one large group activity.

Increasing the amount of equipment used or the number of active participants in an activity is another way to maximize the opportunities for each child. In this way children will have many opportunities to use their skills in a minimum amount of time. The games analyses in Chapters 24 through 31 suggest the amount of equipment needed to maximize the activity.

Plan the transitions from one activity to the next. Transitions from one activity to the next must be carefully planned. The teacher should avoid any moves that are not essential to the success of the activity. The children should be moved from one activity and formation to the next as smoothly as possible. The most efficient method of moving the group with as few moves as possible must be determined. The teacher should avoid bringing the children together between each new formation. For example, if the children are arranged in a circle, it is not necessary to bring them in close and then organize them into partners in two lines for the next activity. Dividing the circle in half and putting each half in position facing the other half, or assigning partners in the circle and putting them into position, would be much more efficient. Carefully preplanning the order of activities may avoid needless reorganization of children.

Grouping Students

Plan the technique for grouping students. In a physical education class the teacher divides the group into partners or small groups. These groupings may be for the entire unit, for a part of the unit, for the day, or for an activity within the lesson. Many times individual work lends itself to a group activity, in which the children work individually on a particular skill but within a small group setting.

Small group work has considerable value in the learning experiences of children. These experiences give children the opportunity to work with less direct teacher supervision. They also provide an opportunity to develop leadership skills. Children may be given responsibility to secure, take care of, and put away the equipment they will be using. It also provides an environment for sharing, planning, and working together. Children may be asked at various times to assume leadership and followership roles.

Several methods may be used to divide children into groups. At no time should any method be used that emphasizes the inadequacy of any child, such as putting the children in a line and having the captains alternately pick their groups. This method is often cited by individuals of all ages as a reason for disliking physical education.

Teachers should not relinquish their responsibility in dividing the class into partners or groups. Saying "Find a partner" does not always have the result the teacher would like. There undoubtedly will be some children who will not readily seek a partner and others who are unwilling to be someone's partner. Often the least secure children end up being together. In many situations this is not the best possible pairing because the insecure children lack confidence, which will limit their success. The teacher may also need to develop strategies for grouping that will separate children who tend to misbehave when put together.

Within the class, grouping can be attained by numbering off (1, 2, 3, 4, 1, 2, 3, 4 . . .). The names of animals, cars, toys, or other objects may be substituted for numbers. Children may also be grouped by their birth month, height, weight, or size. Children may also be grouped according to their ability in an activity or by their social behavior. Groups may also be formed by having the children draw colors or numbers out of a box. The teacher may also pick groups randomly by dividing parts of a circle or some other formation into groups.

In assisting children to be more self-directed, the teacher might ask children to find a friend they can work with for a partner. If the result is that some do not have a partner, the teacher might repeat the process and continue to repeat the process until all have a partner. This technique takes more time at first, but it helps children assume more responsibility for the group action, in this case everyone having a partner.

The teacher often groups the children before a class by matching them heterogeneously or homogeneously depending on the activity. Some activities may call for matching children according to ability to equalize individual as well as team competition. Homogeneous grouping may be effective in gymnastics or when practicing special events such as the high jump, when raising and lowering the bar for different abilities within the group cuts down on individual practice time. A disadvantage to homogeneous grouping may be that poorly skilled children do not have the opportunity to observe a good performance. In using heterogeneous grouping, the more able youngsters not only become models for performance, but may also be called on to help their less able classmates.

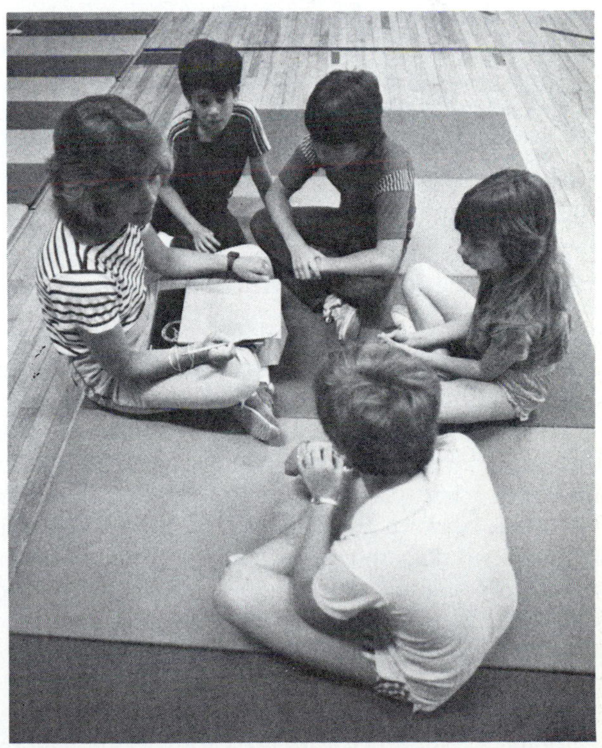

Children may meet with the leader outside of class to determine class grouping.

The use of a sociogram to determine groups may also be effective. Children may be instructed, "List three persons you would like on your soccer team." The children respond in writing and the teacher, before the next class, groups them into equal teams, ensuring that the children will be with at least one person of their choice. To begin the process of grouping, the teacher begins with the children who were not picked by anyone or who were chosen by only a few. The response of the children in selecting those with whom they would like to be grouped varies somewhat with the activity, but this method enables the teacher to have a clear look at what is going on in the class. The teacher can use the information to affect the social interactions of the group.

Another grouping method that actively involves the children is one in which the teacher or the class elects captains. The captains then meet privately with the teacher and group selection takes place. In this way the teacher can help the children make individual choices that will benefit the group and yet give them more opportunity in the grouping process. In this manner only the captains and the teacher know who is chosen last. Whatever method of grouping children is used, children do need to work with lots of different persons, so partners and groups should be changed frequently.

When grouping children into squads or teams that will be used for more than 1 day in the unit, it may be helpful to assign, or better yet, give the children an opportunity to select a name for their group. This helps especially young children to remember their groups from day to day. A game to play to aid children in remembering their groups is to call quickly the name of a group and ask them to do something. ("Elephants, stand up. Zebras, turn around.") Calling the names quickly and having the children respond to some instruction several times furthers their listening skills and helps them to remember their groups.

Using Space and Equipment

Organize the skills practice for optimum learning. The skills practice is an important part of the lesson. Games lessons should be balanced between skill practice and game play. The practice of skills allows children to repeat the skills, which is important in mastery and may not always be achieved in game play. Children often do not see the relationship between the skill and the game. Therefore the practice of skills should be similar to their use in the activity. This practice should allow time to work in increasingly challenging activities. In determining the practice of skills, a task analysis that defines the progression in skill development is essential.

A variety of formations may be used to enhance skill development. Once they learn these formations, children may move quickly into place to begin the activity, saving valuable time for the practice of skills. In using any formation for skills practice, the teacher should organize the group within the available space, minimizing safety hazards so that each group has sufficient space, and the activity of one group does not interfere with the activity of another. Teachers should circulate among the individuals and groups as they work and position themselves in such a way so that all children can see them if there is a need for further clarification. In choosing a formation the teacher should make every attempt to maximize the opportunities for each child by providing the greatest number of practice trials in the time devoted to the task. Each practice grouping should be made up of the minimum number of children required for the task.

Plan the care and efficient use of available equipment and space. The equipment to be used in the lesson should be collected in advance and be ready for distribution at the appropriate time. If several teachers will be using the same equipment, it may be possible for the first group to get it out and the last group to put it away. Teachers may also use student or adult aides or paraprofessionals to help prepare the area for the physical education class.

The distribution, care, and collecting of the equipment for the physical education lesson must be carefully planned. If instructions are vague or incomplete, children may use the equipment in an unsatisfactory way. This stage is often when a lesson breaks down. The instructions should always include how the equipment will be obtained and especially what to do with it when it is received.

Children must be taught to assume responsibility for taking care of the equipment. Children not only should learn the routines for obtaining and putting away equipment, but also should be taught how to use it in a way to promote long-term service. Children need to learn to respect the school's equipment and value its care.

If elementary school children are to use equipment effectively, it should be of appropriate size and weight. Today, a variety of elementary school–sized equipment is available. Apparatus should also be proportional to the size of the children. The use of foam balls increases the safety for children in many activities. When possible a variety of types of equipment should be available so that children have the opportunity to handle them and to learn their properties.

Methods used in securing and putting away equipment include the following:

1. Having the equipment arranged in the area to be used; each child goes to a piece of equipment. In this way children are arranged in their own spaces.
2. Organizing the class into groups or formations; one member of each group secures and distributes the equipment to the group.
3. Arranging the equipment at various stations; children are assigned to each station, where they go to pick up equipment.

These arrangements may be reversed for collecting the equipment at the end of the activity.

In maximizing use of space, using the walls often increases the space and keeps equipment contained in the area. The use of walls also maximizes individual activity and permits variation according to ability because individual children control their own skill work. Using walls often allows for a better practice situation than would be found when working with a partner. Children can also concentrate on the pattern of movement rather than being concerned about where the object goes.

Ending the Lesson

Plan a good ending for the lesson. The lesson should always have a strong finish. As the class period comes to a close, the teacher should plan for good closure. Time is usually taken to put away equipment and to summarize the major points of emphasis in the lesson. The teacher also may wish to prepare the class briefly for the next lesson's activities. The group should leave the physical education area in order. If the children do not change clothes, they should move in an orderly way to their classroom. Any issues raised during the physical education class should be addressed and resolved before the children return to the classroom. Physical educators must take the time to be sure children are ready for the remainder of the school day. The physical education class often is very stimulating. Children need to be brought down to a level of excitement that enables them to begin calmly the next activity. Often the time taken to summarize the lesson is all that they need. In other cases, time spent in relaxation training may be important.

Special Concerns When Using Child-Centered Methods

Child-centered methods require children to assume more responsibility for their own learning, with less direction and seemingly less structure provided by the teacher. It is important to establish a good working relationship with the class before attempting child-centered methods. Children need to have some expectation of acceptable behavior before developing more independent learning.

Obviously, these methods rely heavily on a good signal for listening. The signal used with the group must be established. One way to practice responding to the signal might be to instruct the children to move in a variety of ways in general space and to see how quickly they can stop and be ready to listen when the music stops or some other signal is given.

The use of imagery when establishing the boundaries or when finding one's own space adds to the fun of the lesson. For example, "Inside the black lines is a big piece of bread. You are all peanut butter. Spread out." One must always present instructions in a way that challenges the children to follow them. They do it because it is challenging, not because the teacher tells them they must.

The teacher must develop a sensitivity for the children as they are working. It is important to know when to pose questions or to move on to the next activity. This should be done when they have had enough time to explore possible solutions but not so much time as to lose interest. The teacher should use a variety of challenges to maintain interest.

One certainly must be aware of previous learning experiences in using this approach. Children who have had only teacher-centered learning experiences have some difficulty at first in using this approach. A teacher must gradually introduce the approach and use it for short periods at first, until the class begins to feel more comfortable in exploring movement and solving problems on their own.

The teacher should encourage but not force performance in front of the group. The teacher must be sensitive to the children's feeling about their performance and organize it in such a way as to prevent the children from feeling overly self-conscious. In the lower grades children may enjoy performing in front of the group. In the middle and upper grades they may be more hesitant. At this level the teacher may organize the class so that several children or a group of children perform at the same time, although they are working independently of one another. Once they gain confidence in group presentations, individuals may find performing alone a challenge.

USE OF VOLUNTEERS AND PARAPROFESSIONALS

In recent years the use of volunteers and paraprofessionals in the school setting has increased dramatically. Physical education is one area that can benefit greatly by using aides. Parents, interested adults, high school students, or upper elementary school children may be willing to volunteer in physical education classes.

These aides may serve in a variety of ways. They may help set up the physical education site by getting out apparatus and other equipment, putting up nets, marking boundaries, and other tasks. They may work with individuals or small groups under the direction of the teacher, which results in greater individual help in skill development. If these volunteers are adequately trained, they can be of considerable benefit to the teachers and children alike.

The use of peer teaching in the elementary school has proven to be effective in enhancing learning. Children enjoy helping others. Upper grade children may be used to work with specific children to help them improve their motor skills. Buidling relationships between older and younger children is important in creating a school environment where all children feel safe and are encouraged to learn.

SUMMARY

All teachers share in the responsibility for providing a safe learning environment. Safe behavior must be consistently encouraged. If an accident occurs, the injured child should receive prompt attention and first aid. Emergency procedures should be carefully developed and communicated to all school personnel. Teachers must be aware of their responsibility in providing adequate supervision of all activities, selecting and conducting activities with safety in mind, and providing a safe environment for learning to take place.

Effective classroom management is essential if learning is to be maximized. Management and instructional problems must be diagnosed and appropriate management or instructional solutions implemented. Effective management includes procedures for getting the class started, giving meaningful instructions, grouping students, securing and putting away equipment, organizing and moving the class throughout the lesson, and planning lesson closure. There is no substitute for careful planning of management techniques if class activities are to move smoothly from beginning to end.

REFERENCES AND RESOURCES

Boyce BA and Walker P: Establishing structure in the elementary school, *Strategies* 5(2):20, 1991.

Clement A: Educational malpractice: physical educators should be concerned, *Physical Educator* 44(1):226, 1986.

Clements R: Let your students know: "I care!", *Strategies* 4(6):8, 1991.

Cooper J and others: *Classroom teaching skills: a handbook,* ed 4, Lexington, Mass, 1990, DC Heath & Co.

Dougherty N: Liability, *JOPERD* 54(6):52, 1983.

Dougherty N and Bonanno D: *Contemporary approaches to the teaching of physical education,* ed 2, Scottsdale, Ariz, 1987, Gorsuch Scarisbrick.

Dreikers R and Cassel P: *Discipline without tears,* ed 2, New York, 1991, Hawthorn Books.Fink J and Siedentop D: The development of routines, rules, and expectations at the start of the school year, *JTPE* 8(3):198, 1989.

Harrison J and Blakemore C: Instructional strategies for secondary school physical education, ed 3, Dubuque, Ia, 1992, Wm C Brown.

Henderson D: Physical education teachers how do I sue thee? Let me count the ways, *JOPERD* 56(2):44, 1985.

Lambdin D: Shuffling the deck a flexible system for class organization, *JOPERD* 60(3):25, 1989.

Luke M: Research on class management and organization: review with implications for current practice, *Quest* 41(1):55, 1989.

Morris G and Stiehl J: *Physical education from intent to action,* Columbus, Ohio, 1985, Charles E Merrill.

Rink J: *Teaching physical education for learning,* ed 2, St Louis, 1992, Mosby–Year Book.

Schurr E: *Movement experiences for children,* ed 3, Englewood Cliffs, NJ, 1980, Prentice-Hall.

Siedentop D: *Developing teaching skills in physical education,* ed 2, Palo Alto, Calif, 1983, Mayfield Publishing.

Thompson D: Safe playground surfaces: what should be used under playground equipment, *JOPERD* 62(9):74, 1991.

Vandermars H: Effects of specific verbal praise on off-task behavior of second grade students in physical education, *JTPE* 8(2):162, 1989.

Van der Smissen B: Legal aspects of adult fitness programs, *JOPERD* 45(2):54, 1974.

ANNOTATED READINGS

Belka DE: Let's manage to have some order, *JOPERD* 62(9):21, 1991.

Poor management increases the likelihood of inappropriate behavior and reduced learning time. Two scenarios are presented, with suggested solutions to improve the learning situation.

Carpenter L and Acousta R: Negligence: What is it? How can it be avoided? *JOPERD* 53(2):51, 1982.

Discusses physical educators' responsibilities for safe participation by providing supervision, good judgment, proper instruction, and measures to avoid negligence.

Dougherty N: Intramural liability, *JOPERD* 56(6):45, 1985.

Provides a checklist for safety in conducting intramural programs.

Gray GR: Written lesson plans minimize the risk of injury, *JOPERD* 62(7):31, 1990.

Ten principles of preparing lesson plans to avoid needless injuries.

Hart J: Locker room liability, *Strategies* 3(3):19, 1990.

Discusses liability in the locker room and the need for adequate supervision and planning.

Kneer M: Ability grouping in physical education, *JOPERD* 53(9):10, 1982.

Provides considerations for determining ability groups and how to accommodate them in the curriculum.

Lehr C: Test your liability quotient, *Strategies* 1(5):26, 1988.

A questionnaire to test knowledge of liability in physical education.

Metzler M and Young J: The relationship between teachers' preactive planning and student process measures. *Research Quarterly for Exercise and Sport* 55(4):356, 1984.

Provides a comparison by two teachers using divergent lesson planning patterns, resulting in management procedures that varied the academic learning times for the fourth grade students in their classes.

Phillips J and Carter J: Tired of being chosen last? Humanistic alternatives to group division, *JOPERD* 56(1):96, 1985.

Offers guidelines and methods to divide a class for activity.

Sanders A: Class management skills, *Strategies* 2(3):14, 1989.

Provides suggestions for developing attention, appropriate behavior, and organizational techniques.

Schwager S and Mante M: Three simple rules: the key to cooperation, *JOPERD* 57(6):85, 1986.

Examines communicating behavior expectations to children in physical education.

CHAPTER 9

Establishment of an Environment for Learning, Communication, and Class Control

OBJECTIVES

After completing this chapter the student will be able to:

1. Describe the aspects important in creating a class environment conducive to learning
2. Explain the importance of good communication between teacher and students for all students to get the most from the physical education experience
3. Describe several strategies used to enhance appropriate behavior
4. Suggest several strategies to use in dealing with behavior problems
5. Describe how the learning environment must be structured for children to become independent learners

If lifetime participation is to become an outcome of physical education children must have pleasant feelings regarding their physical education experiences. While the careful selection of activities is an important part of creating a favorable atmosphere, it is not the only consideration. Teachers must plan carefully to provide a learning environment that encourages children to be active participants, that recognizes and meets the needs of individual children, and that enables them to work toward the completion of tasks independent of direct interaction with the teacher. The physical setting and general atmosphere of the classroom as well as the communication that develops between the teacher and students are important factors in assisting children in the development of positive dispositions toward physical activity.

CREATION OF AN ENVIRONMENT CONDUCIVE TO LEARNING

The physical appearance of the space should convey that it is a learning setting or classroom. Colorful bulletin board displays and other materials placed throughout the room create an environment where learning is the theme. These displays may be created by the teacher or with the help of the children bringing in materials. These displays should convey important information at an appropriate level for elementary school children. They should be changed frequently to interest children in seasonal activities and new units to be introduced. Putting up slogans or developing school physical education logos adds focus to the purpose of activities presented there.

Posted materials might include terminology important to activities or vocabulary words that reinforce appropriate behavior, such as cooperation, responsibility, caring, etc., which are introduced, emphasized, and then referred to as needed during the class. For instance, a teacher might interrupt children who were working at stations and displaying off-task behavior by pointing to the appropriate word, *responsibility,* and asking the children what it means and what they need to do to be able to continue to work at their stations independent of direct teacher supervision.

The physical space should be an area where children will want to move and be comfortable in doing so. The

Good communication is essential.

areas used should be clean and well maintained for safety, with equipment stored out of the way of the moving children. In addition the heat and ventilation should be controlled to enable children to move comfortably.

Background music of interest to children often adds to the enjoyment of the experience.

Children should feel comfortable in the physical education setting. It should be one where all can feel the support of teacher and classmates. It should be apparent that the emphasis in the class is on teaching *individuals* not *activities*.

The teacher should work to establish a group spirit within the class, where all share in the success of individuals. If carefully planned, activities that require children to work together can also foster feelings of acceptance in the group. The atmosphere should not be overly competitive.

COMMUNICATION WITH CHILDREN

The learning environment must foster adequate communication between teacher and learners. The teacher plays an important role in setting the tone for the class. Adequate communication is essential in establishing good teacher-pupil relationships.

Communication may be verbal or nonverbal. We communicate verbally by the words we use, by the tone of voice, or perhaps by silence—by not answering at all. We communicate nonverbally by our appearance, posture, facial expression, lack of attention, the distance between ourselves and those to whom we are communicating, and in the way we model the behavior we value.

Nonverbal behavior is important. Teachers must be conscious of their own feelings and attitudes as they respond to children. The teacher's posture and facial expressions may communicate to the child an interest or disinterest in what is being communicated and positive or negative feelings about what is being said. Nonverbal behavior is an important aspect of class control. Through our nonverbal actions we often demonstrate our assertiveness in dealing with children's inappropriate behavior. Eye contact, assuming a position close to the child, giving them a thumbs-up or thumbs-down signal in response to their behavior, or expressing our resolve in how we approach children are some of the ways we communicate nonverbally. Once children learn to respond to these behaviors, teachers need to use them only intermittently to reinforce desired behavior. As a result of good communication, the teacher gains a better understanding of children and their needs, and children recognize the value of physical activity to healthful living.

To enhance communication the teacher must be attentive and a good listener. When listening the teacher must try to distinguish between what was actually said and what was really meant. If a child says, "This isn't any fun," the actual meaning may be "I am frustrated because this is too difficult." If the teacher is not sure of the meaning, students may be asked questions to help clarify what they are trying to say. The teacher should acknowledge the child's feelings and alter the situation to bring about the desired change if appropriate. These adjustments might include changing the grouping of students or the activity itself.

Physical education teachers communicate the importance of physical activity, its meaning for students, the nature of the physical education class, expectations for behavior, and the value they place on the accomplishments of each child. Teachers, directly or indirectly, communicate feelings about the importance of physical activity in a person's life through their physical appearance, good health, and vitality and through their enthusiasm for the activities in the physical education classes. Teachers must help their students see physical activities as a means to meeting student goals.

In communicating about the nature of the learning environment in the physical education class, the distinction between recess and physical education may need to be clarified. Recess is a time for children to determine which activities, if any, they will pursue. In physical education teachers have the responsibility first for what students learn. Teachers set the standard for listening and other expected behaviors (see Chapter 8) as well as the standard for performance. They communicate what is to be learned and how it is to be learned. Teachers help children set goals and assess their progress toward these goals. They give encouragement as improvement occurs and help each child reset personal goals for achievement.

The teacher communicates feelings about the children. Turner and Purkey outline teacher behaviors that invite or disinvite child participation in physical education. Children respond positively to physical education if they feel they are invited to participate by a teacher who they believe views them as able and responsible. Some children may feel disinvited if they perceive the physical educator as one who values only those children who are gifted movers. The teacher must be careful to communicate a sincere interest in all children and their success in physical education.

Children need to feel accepted. Teachers need to demonstrate their interest in children as individuals and to support behaviors that recognize individual worth. The teacher should make every effort to learn the children's names and to address them by name in and outside of class. Making eye contact with all children during the lesson and moving around in the space to be close to learners are other ways that teachers express a concern for each child.

Welcoming children back after vacation, illness, or other absences is another way that teachers demonstrate their interest in children. Recognizing children for their accomplishments in physical education or in other settings, as well as remembering birthdays and other special days, is also important. Giving new students an invitation to share something about themselves with the class is another way teachers invite the active participation of children.

Not only must the teacher demonstrate feelings of acceptance of all children but class acceptance of each child must also be encouraged. Teachers need to communicate their support for the behaviors that support their classmates' efforts.

Students communicate their interest in physical education. They communicate their interest in learning particular skills and knowledge, their understanding of what is to be learned and how it is to be learned, their assessment of their progress toward the objectives, and their satisfaction or frustration toward the learning experience. To other students they communicate their likes and dislikes, their feelings toward specific others, and their willingness to work with individual children and to help each other. In a good learning environment, the relationship between teacher and students encourages students to express their ideas and feelings positively.

Journal writing is another approach to improve the communication between students and teachers. Children may be asked, perhaps once a week as a homework assignment, to write about their physical education experiences: what they've learned, how they feel about the activity or a particular class, etc. Young children may draw pictures to communicate their feelings before they have the writing skills to portray them. The teacher may then respond in writing or verbally to individual children about the messages they've conveyed.

The learning environment must be free of conflict between the desires of teacher and students, and the needs of individual children must be recognized and met. Children need an opportunity to express their thoughts and feelings openly. They may need help to understand their feelings in a nonthreatening way. When interacting with students the teacher describes rather than judges. The teacher must look at a situation from the students' point of view by being sensitive to their feelings. The teacher should respond in a way that helps the children understand when the teacher's point of view is in conflict with theirs and should do so in a nonthreatening manner. Teachers must be careful to send to desired messages to children by being alert to their own feelings and nonverbal cues.

POSITIVE APPROACH TO CLASS CONTROL

An important result of adequate communication is a learning environment in which there is order—in which certain standards of behavior are practiced. Class control is a planned strategy rather than a response to a situation that arises. It is action rather than reaction. The best strategy is to structure the situation so that inappropriate behaviors are avoided. In other words, the teacher acts in a manner that prevents discipline problems.

If the lesson is conducted with maximum participation and effective transition from one activity to another, and if the lesson objectives and subsequent activities are meaningful to the individual students, behavior problems are minimized. Good management and effective instruction are important ingredients of an effective learning environment.

The school attempts to prepare children to participate in our democratic society. Democracy ensures each individual certain freedoms. Children must learn to accept the obligations and responsibilities associated with freedom and to respect the freedom of others. All societies must have order, with some restrictions placed on their members. Schools develop standards of behavior for the benefit of all children to ensure their rights and optimum development. The physical education class has its rules of behavior also, written or unwritten. Rules should be minimal in number and general enough to apply to many different situations. They should be concisely written and positive in nature, describing the behavior desired. Some examples of rules are the following:

- Play safely
- Work hard
- Listen and follow instructions
- Be helpful to others
- Take care of the equipment

It is helpful to post them in the gymnasium where all can see them and where they can be referred to quickly. A discussion early in the year to go over the rules and why they are important is essential to getting everyone off to a good start. It may be valuable to have the children help to determine the rules they need for successful participation in the physical education class because they are more apt to follow rules they had a part in determining than those imposed by an adult.

Consistency in reinforcing rules is essential. In the

beginning of the school year when children are getting acquainted or reacquainted with the rules, the teacher gives more direction in the conduct of the class. As children learn to function appropriately in the class setting, the class becomes more student directed. One must be firm regarding adherence to the rules, especially when introducing new rules at the beginning of the school year. Cracking down later in enforcing rules is much more difficult because it is frustrating for children who interpret the actions as changing the rules. The importance for certain standards of behavior becomes apparent as children respond to the teacher's enforcement of the rules.

The teacher should also communicate consequences of inappropriate behavior, but in doing so must be willing to follow up with the consequences if inappropriate behavior occurs. Telling children you will respond in a particular way and then not doing it will only confuse children into thinking it is either not very important to behave in a particular way or you don't really mean what you say.

Students share in the responsibility for the physical education class. Children are given an opportunity to assist in taking care of equipment, establishing class routines, organizing themselves for activity, and setting the standards for behavior. It should be an environment where the children recognize the importance and are challenged and helped to behave appropriately. In helping children choose appropriate behavior, the teacher explains the effects of the behavior on the class, for instance, "When we listen quietly we can get to the activity sooner."

Teacher Strategies to Avoid Behavior Problems

The teacher may use several strategies to enhance positive behavior. Whenever possible the teacher should respond to positive behavior and ignore negative but nondestructive behavior; however, one must respond to the misbehavior when it causes concern for the safety of an individual. Rewarding appropriate behavior often goes a long way in eliminating negative behavior. Responding to desired behavior may help many children learn to be responsible for their behavior.

The atmosphere should be nonthreatening and as positive as possible. It is better to say "I like the way Mary is listening" than "Susan, will you please pay attention," which focuses on the nonlistening behavior of another child. Where an inappropriate behavior is to be corrected, one should focus on the behavior and not the child. Saying "I'm disappointed with your not listening" is better than saying "I'm disappointed in you, Bill." When behavior improves recognition is also important. "I appreciate how you really worked today" helps to reinforce the desired behavior. Recognizing positive aspects by telling other teachers is also a good way to reinforce and give recognition to individuals or classes of children.

Often, potential problems may be prevented by anticipating them and taking action before they occur. For example, standing between two potential talkers when giving instructions may discourage the behavior and help children to listen. Organizing the class into partners or small groups in ways that separate potential problems is another prevention strategy. If a child is unable to hold a piece of equipment still while the teacher is talking, the teacher may simply choose to use that equipment when demonstrating for the class. Teachers may help a child remain on task when they spot inattentiveness by calling the child's name and by asking a question about the task at hand. These strategies are not only preventive but establish a positive learning environment where lapses in appropriate behavior are treated in a nonthreatening way.

Another part of the teaching strategy that can have positive effects involves the giving of feedback and time spent with each child. It may be beneficial to spend a little more time with children who tend to more easily get off task or to time the feedback given at intervals where off-task behavior might occur. For instance children with attention deficits may require the teacher to work a little more closely with them after a minute or two into the task to help them continue to work. As teachers circulate among the class giving feedback to all the children, they are mindful of those who require more guidance and move to them at appropriate times during the lesson. In many cases using this approach during the first days of class may help children become socialized to the expectations, and the approach may be needed only occasionally later on.

The teacher may also set up a reward system for children or classes which behave appropriately. Recognizing "Super Kids" who work faithfully and cooperatively by awarding stickers, T-shirts, extra physical education time, and so on is a way to encourage appropriate participation. The use of "happy grams," notes with smiling faces, for exceptional work of a class is another way to recognize the efforts of children.

Another reward system might involve some free time or free choice of an activity at the end of the class if the class works well on the lesson objectives. The teacher might use a stopwatch and suggest a particular amount of time that all need to be working if the reward is to be given. The watch is started. If children get off task, the watch is stopped until all are working again. Any remaining time at the end of the designated work period will be allocated for the reward. A gentle reminder is often all that is needed to get the class or individuals back on task and the watch started again.

CORRECTION OF INAPPROPRIATE BEHAVIORS

A situation occasionally arises in which the teacher needs to reestablish order or alter the behavior of an individual, a group, or the entire class. Harrison defined **discipline** as "a process of assisting youngsters to adjust to their environment and develop acceptable inner controls." Teachers must be consistent in their interactions with the students. They also should know what behavior they wish to approve, ignore, or disapprove so that they respond consistently to a specific behavior. The teacher must strive to respond most often to significant student behaviors. All children should be treated fairly. The teacher must respond to a behavior regardless of who the child is; there can be no favorites. If for some reason the teacher responds differently, then the children must understand why.

The first step in dealing with inappropriate behavior is to restore order. Then the cause of the behavior must be determined by responding to the following questions:

Is the cause anything the teacher did or did not do?
Are the expectations clear to the students?
Are the activities challenging the students?
Do the planned activities provide maximum activity for all?
Are there distractions in the environment that have resulted in the behavior?
Is the behavior a problem of an individual, a group, or the entire class?
Is the child capable of the behavior desired?
Is the expected behavior important to the child?
What are the child's goals?

Dreikurs and Goldman suggest there are four possible goals of a child's misbehavior: attention getting, power, revenge, and a display of inadequacy. Children may seek the attention of an adult in many ways. If the reward for misbehaving provides the needed attention, even though the adult response is negative, children may continue to seek attention through misbehavior. Children seeking power want to be the boss, to demand their way in a particular situation. Children seeking revenge wish to hurt the teacher, and children displaying inadequacy usually want to be left alone, with no demands put on them. Dreikurs and Goldman also suggest that the teacher's natural reaction to the behavior may be the key to determining the cause. If the teacher is inclined to react with annoyance, reminding and coaxing the child to behave in a particular way, it is probably a response to attention-getting behavior. If children provoke the teacher, they seek power over the teacher. If the teacher feels hurt or wants to "get even," the goal is probably revenge. If the teacher feels despair and helplessness in assisting the child, he or she is probably responding to a display of inadequacy.

Several different strategies may be used to deal with behavior problems once the cause is determined. The solution should be based on the cause. Sometimes a change in organization, a clarification of information, or a modification in activity or teaching method may be all that is needed to correct the situation. In other situations the teacher may need to deal with an individual or group of students to initiate a change in behavior.

The teacher should respond promptly to the situation but avoid responding on first impulse, which may intensify the behavior rather than correct it. The teacher should view the behavior from the child's point of view, anticipate what response the child expects, and then not respond in the expected way. The teacher must then take responsibility for the action.

It is important to match the reaction to a behavior with the seriousness of the transgression. The teacher should convey recognition that all make mistakes. In dealing with behavior problems the teacher should express concern, warmth, and caring. Knowing the children helps to establish priorities for positive responses. Responses should be directed to specific behavior. It is important to communicate why a behavior is inappropriate at a particular time.

It may be just as important to deal with the child's feelings as the inappropriate behavior. In observing the child the teacher may discover that the child is bored, frustrated, etc. The teacher might then pose a question: "Are you bored with this activity, John?" Children are more likely to respond positively to this type of question than to a statement about their inappropriate behavior. This might lead to a more positive response and perhaps a change of activity, resulting in a happier child and teacher as well.

In correcting children the teacher shows disapproval for the behavior, not for the child. Discipline must not lower a child's self-esteem. Negatively singling out a child in front of the group can have serious social implications. Children perceived by their peers as being disliked by the teacher are not liked by their classmates. The teacher should react to the present behavior and not past transgressions and must be careful to determine which child is at fault rather than merely singling out the child who is usually disruptive.

Johnson identified the following teacher behaviors as roadblocks to communication:

1. Ordering, commanding, and directing: "You quit complaining and just pay attention!"
2. Threatening: "If you guys don't stop messing around, I'm going to have to put you on report!"
3. Preaching or moralizing: "You girls know better than to behave that way!" "Is that any way to behave?"
4. Offering advice or solutions prematurely: "You'll just have to have your mother help you to get your gym clothes ready on time."
5. Judging, criticizing, and blaming: "You are just lazy." "You two are always causing trouble in this class."
6. Stereotyping or labeling: "Don't act like a fourth grader." "You are acting like a baby!"
7. Interrogating or cross-examining: "Why in the world did you do that?" "How come you didn't ask me first?"
8. Distracting or diverting: "Why don't we talk about it some other time?" "Now isn't the time to discuss it!"

Hoffman and associates suggest that the way the teacher addresses students about their behavior has certain implications. The "you" messages cited here can only be interpreted negatively. An "I" message, such as "I like the way Jane is working," is a statement communicating positive feelings about the student's behavior.

It is important for the teacher to remain under control when correcting children. One must speak calmly and not respond emotionally to the children. There should be no ridicule or sarcasm. Teachers should not allow themselves to get involved in arguments with children. If a child attempts to confront the teacher in a power struggle, the teacher should withdraw from the situation by moving away or ignoring the behavior, which has the effect of dissipating the child's power. The teacher should avoid coercion, forced apologies, detaining children after school, imposing extra work, such as a written report or additional exercise, and corporal punishment.

Modeling can have a positive effect on behavior. The teacher targets the desired behavior without mentioning the inappropriate behavior. A teacher might say, "I like the way Mary is listening," or "I like the way John is sharing the ball with Mike." In this way positive behavior is reinforced, and the undesired behavior is ignored.

Reality therapy is another technique that may be used successfully. This approach puts the responsibility for behavior on the child. It avoids putting the teacher in the position of judging the appropriateness of the behavior. The teacher assists the child in identifying the inappropriate behavior and the consequences of that behavior. The child then can judge whether the behavior is appropriate and develops a plan to attain the desired goals. For example, as a result of poor listening skills, a child does not know what is to be done and is distracting others. The child meets with the teacher and together they develop a plan to help the child change the behavior. The child will sit next to the teacher when instructions are being given and away from a classmate to whom the child likes to talk. Reality therapy is concerned with what the behavior is rather than why the child behaved that way.

Reality therapy may also be applied when a change in behavior is needed by a group of children or an entire class. This is called **norm setting** (Harrison). In this approach the teacher and students share in the goal setting for the class, stating the goals so that they are easily understood. The next step is to determine what both the teacher and the students will do to meet the goals and the consequences if the goals are not met. It may be necessary to use reality therapy with individuals as well. Success in working toward the goals should be rewarded along the way. The group should evaluate progress toward the goals and suggest any changes that may be needed.

Time-out is another strategy for dealing with inappropriate behavior. The misbehaving child is removed from the activity momentarily until he or she is ready to participate within the established rules. The teacher might put a child out of the activity by saying, "Bill, time-out for 2 minutes for not following instructions" or "Time-out, Jim, for not listening. When you are ready to listen you may rejoin the group." Time-out gives children the opportunity to regain self-control. Return to the activity depends on children assuming responsibility for their behavior. Time-out is one of the most widely used strategies for dealing with inappropriate behavior; however, it is only effective in activities the child enjoys. Time-out should be given for short periods of time not to exceed 5 minutes and preferably only a minute or two. If the child who returns to the activity does not assume responsibility for appropriate behavior, time-out may be repeated or some other strategy used. Time-out will not work with all children.

Loss of privileges is another approach. Children learn to view the consequences of their behavior as the loss of some opportunity in the class. The teacher might set aside some time in the class period for those children who have been on task and demonstrated appropriate behavior to participate in an activity of their choice. At the same time those who were off task or behaving inappropriately engage in an activity the teacher chooses.

Another approach is the **contingency contract** (Harrison). This approach also helps children assume responsibility for their own behavior. Children are given a reward for appropriate behavior. This approach may work with a group as well as individual children. In essence the teacher directs the children by saying, "If you do this, then you may do that." This approach gives the children a sense of accomplishment in achieving the goal and in receiving the reward.

The teacher may also enter into a written contract with a student regarding expectations for behavior and the rewards to be provided if the behavior improves.

Punishment has been used to initiate changes in behavior. Although it may stop a behavior, it will not eliminate the cause or reduce the factors that prompted it. Punishment creates a negative relationship between the transgressor and the person administering the punishment and increases anxiety for all. It should be avoided if possible. If it is to be used, punishment should be administered firmly and consistently. There should be no threats of punishment, especially if the teacher does not wish to make good on the threats. Mass punishment should be avoided. Exercise or running laps should never be used as punishment.

Occasionally, children experience behavior problems that do not seem to respond to these strategies. The teacher should seek help from other professionals. A staff meeting may be called for all teachers working with the child and other school personnel, such as the school nurse, psychologist, and social workers, to establish the probable cause of the misbehavior and to plan a strategy to help the child become a more productive member of the class. By working together, the staff may achieve a more consistent effort to help the child overcome difficulties.

DEVELOPMENT OF INDEPENDENT LEARNERS

One goal of education is to produce independent, lifelong learners. The school strives to enhance the children's love for learning by assisting in developing skills of inquiry and investigation. The physical education program plays an important part in the development of independent learning through individualized goal setting, the children's assumption of responsibility for their own learning, and discovery teaching.

Independent learning takes place in a setting that promotes a good teacher-student relationship. There is mutual trust, mutual support, and a respect for the rights of the individual. The environment provides freedom for learning but also structure. The rules of conduct are defined, and the expectations for listening, following directions, and working are understood. Safety is carefully considered, with the children understanding safety rules and why they are needed. The children work at their own level of ability in a nonthreatening, friendly, and helping atmosphere.

The child is the focus in the learning experience. There must be flexibility in goal setting and expectations. The students are assisted in setting realistic performance goals. Although they are not given choices in what they are to learn, they may choose how they will work toward the goal, how long they will work, how well they will achieve the goal, and through what activities they will practice. In making these decisions children generally make safe choices. They do not choose to do something for which they do not believe they are ready. In most instances they make a selection that pushes them to greater achievement.

Children come to the school setting varying in self-confidence. Past success and failure affect the children's self-esteem and consequently their confidence to try new things. It is up to the teacher to structure learning in the physical education classroom so that all children can be successful through careful selection and conduct of activities.

The movement curriculum provides opportunities for children to solve problems within their own skill and understanding. This approach to learning uses problem solving to enable children to process information, to make choices, to act, and to evaluate the results of their action. Sequential learning experiences develop confidence as children are successful at each step in the progression.

The learning environment provides opportunities for children to relate to each other in many ways. Assuming responsibilities as an individual or in a small group for staying on task, taking care of equipment, and the like is an important aspect of the learning experience. When they are ready, children may assume different roles in the group as follower, shared decision maker, or leader; the responsibilities vary with the maturity of the child. These responsibilities may range from being at the head of the group when moving to a new station to organizing the other children in the group for activity.

The learning environment provides a wide variety of experiences geared to the interests and needs of each child to challenge their abilities, to arouse their imagination, and to develop creative ideas. It is an atmosphere in which questions are raised by both student and teacher and answers are sought rather than given. Emphasis is on personal inquiry and investigation. The teacher does not do for the students what they can do for themselves. Several resources should be available to facilitate learning, including the teacher, other students, books, posters, and the like. These enable the children to seek appropriate help as needed. Children need assistance to evaluate their progress in meeting goals and to reset goals and change the activity for practice as needed.

The teacher helps to direct the inquiry through further questioning. Questions may be raised to help the children establish relationships between old and new learning, to make judgments about structure, appearance or function, or to suggest experimentation, such as "Is it better to . . . or. . . .?"

Children need time to explore and to discover their answers. The teacher must exercise patience by not helping too soon. At times the teacher may need to assist in alleviating children's frustration at not finding an easy answer, or they may need to help children get back on track if they stray.

Questioning is an important skill. Questioning should seek verbal responses that suggest understanding or the lack of understanding rather than yes-or-no answers. Once the question has been posed, the teacher must give the child sufficient time to respond. Questions should be open ended to provide for a variety of responses within the child's level of understanding.

The class ideally provides indirectly supervised activity to give children freedom to work on their own. There may be several choices for practice to meet the day's objectives, and the children may work alone or with other children.

Several techniques may be used to help children select appropriate activities. One is the use of a checklist, either a grand list for the class or an individual list for each child. An individual list designed to meet the needs of each child is most effective. Children are highly motivated when the activities are challenging and yet within their ability to achieve. When using checklists, activities should be categorized into those that the children may check for

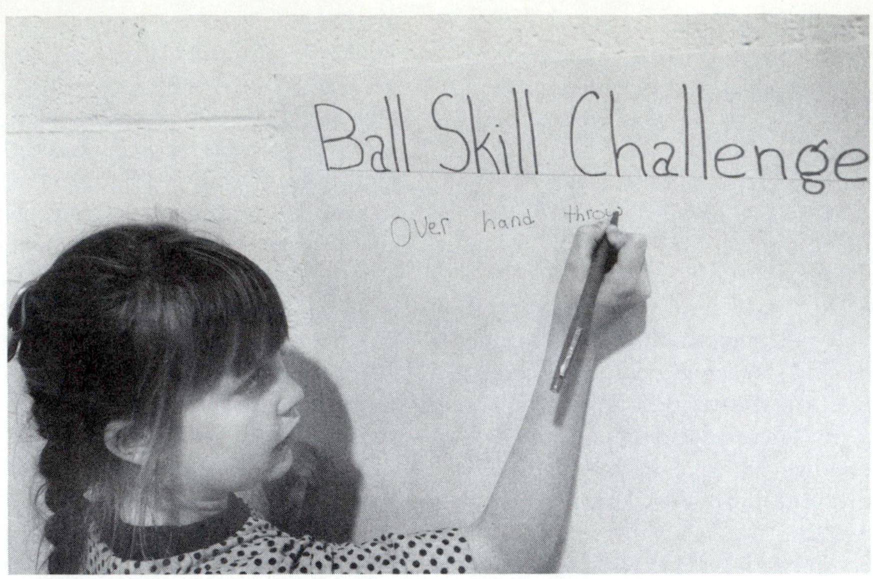

Writing challenges.

themselves and those that must be monitored by the teacher. As the children accomplish all the activities in their individual lists, a new list is provided. The inclusion of stick figures or drawings may clarify the tasks for young children with limited reading skills.

Another approach to the checklist is to organize the activities into separate categories based on difficulty. The first category would include those activities that all children should be able to accomplish by the end of the unit. These might be called the red activities. The next category, the white activities, would include the activities that the majority of the children would accomplish. The last category, the blue activities, would include that those only the top students in the class might master.

Challenge cards are another approach. A list of challenges may be placed at each station for the children to try. Children add new challenges to the list as they develop their own ideas. The box below provides an example of a challenge card. The teacher may need to assist some children in writing new challenges. In addition the new challenges may be announced or demonstrated to the class periodically as another way of communicating to all the children in the class.

BALL SKILLS CHALLENGES

1. Standing behind the line and using the underhand throw, throw the ball into the basket. How many times can you get the ball in the basket?
2. Move back three steps and try it again.
3. Throw the ball overhand into the basket.
4. Throw the ball between your legs into the basket.

Student-teacher contracts are another approach to get students to be more responsible for their learning. The contract specifies what will be learned and the level of mastery to be achieved. The contract begins with a statement of behavioral objectives, a definition of objective components, the manner in which the objectives will be assessed, and a time frame in which the objective will be completed. The teacher and student work together to develop the contract, with the teacher offering advice as needed.

The task style of teaching described in Chapter 7 offers a similar approach to individualizing learning, but whereas the contract is developed between an individual student and the teacher, the tasks are developed for a group of students, who decide individually the level of achievement they hope to attain and the order in which the tasks will be completed.

The teacher gradually relinquishes responsibility for individual learning as children are able to take more responsibility for the learning process. This is not a laissez-faire approach but rather a plan carefully conducted to bring about independence in children. In the beginning children may learn to work in indirectly supervised settings, with the teacher assuming responsibility for what is to be learned and practiced. As children develop their ability to set goals and plan a course of action, more freedom is gradually introduced to accommodate this development. The teacher still remains an active part of the process, providing a variety of experiences and equipment

DEVELOPING INDEPENDENCE IN LEARNING

THE LEARNING ENVIRONMENT

Communication between teacher and students
Children and teacher supportive of one another
Safety rules understood and followed
Expectations for listening, following directions, taking care of equipment, and general behavior understood

ACTIVITIES

A variety of activities planned for each lesson
Progression from simple to complex

TEACHER AND STUDENT ROLES

Teacher	Student
Determines goals	Chooses activity
	Determines how long to practice
	Determines level of skill to achieve
Provides resources	Chooses resource: teacher, book, poster, video
Evaluates progress to goal	Seeks help in assessing progress
Organizes the group for activity	Assumes responsibility to stay on task
	Assumes role as group member
	Assumes role as group leader
	Assumes role as shared decision maker

for the students to make choices and to help students when needed.

As children develop independent learning skills, they respond to each new situation by examining the alternatives, risks, and consequences and by choosing a course of action. An evaluation of the result of this action results in new responses. The wide range of skills and activities in which they are interested challenges the children to take risks in learning, to try new skills, and to relate to others. The box above summarizes the changes that take place as the children assume more responsibility for their own learning.

SUMMARY

To enhance a love for learning, schools and teachers attempt to establish a learning environment in which there is adequate communication and order, and in which individual needs are of primary concern in planning and conducting the physical education activities.

The teacher must establish a good working relationship with children that fosters adequate communication between teacher and students. Teachers and students communicate both verbally in what they say and how they say it and also nonverbally in their facial expression and posture. The teacher must be a good listener, distinguishing between what was said and what was meant. Teachers communicate the value they place on physical education and each child in the class. Students communicate their likes and dislikes in the physical education class.

Class control is a planned strategy to avoid the need for discipline. With the help of the students, the teacher establishes the expected behavior and consistently rewards those children who behave appropriately. Careful planning involves strategies that encourage appropriate behavior. Several strategies may be required to deal with inappropriate behavior. All focus on helping children assume responsibility for their own behavior. Reality therapy or norm setting in which children develop a plan to change their behavior, time-out, loss of privileges, and contingency contracts all help children to function in more socially acceptable ways.

The overall goal of education is learning for a lifetime. If this goal is to be reached, children need to be encouraged to pursue learning on their own, independent of direct teacher intervention. Building confidence, encouraging inquiry, making available alternate resources, and providing for children as they are ready for more complex social interactions must be carefully built into the physical education experience.

REFERENCES AND RESOURCES

Charles CM: *Building classroom discipline from models to practice,* New York, 1985, Longman.

Cooper J and others: *Classroom teaching skills: a handbook,* ed 4, Lexington, Mass, 1990, DC Heath.

Dougherty N and Bonanno D: *Contemporary approaches to the teaching of physical education,* ed 2, Scottsdale, Ariz, 1987, Gorsuch Scarisbrick.

Dreikurs R: *Psychology in the classroom,* ed 2, New York, 1968, Harper & Row.

Dreikurs R and Goldman M: *The ABC's of guiding the child,* Chicago, 1967, North Side Unit of Family Education Association.

Dreikurs R and Soltz V: *Children: the challenge,* New York, 1990, Plume.

Estvan F: Teaching the very young: procedures for developing inquiry skills. In Anderson R and Shane H, editors: *As the twig is bent,* Boston, 1971, Houghton-Mifflin.

Fernandez-Balboa JM: Helping novice teachers handle discipline problems, *JOPERD* 62(7):50, 1990.

French R and others: Take a lap, *Physical Educator* 42(2):180, 1985.

French R, Silliman L, Henderson H: Too much time in time out! *Strategies* 3(3):5, 1990.

Harrison J: *Instructional strategies for physical education,* ed 3, Dubuque, Ia, 1992, Wm C Brown.

Hellison D and others: *Personalized learning in physical education,* Reston, Va, 1976, American Alliance for Health, Physical Education, and Recreation.

Hoffman H and others: *Meaningful movement for children: a developmental theme approach to physical education,* ed 2, Dubuque, Ia, 1985, Kendall/Hunt.

Jansma P and others: Behavioral engineering in physical education, *JOPERD* 55(6):80, 1984.

Johnson D: Reaching out: interpersonal effectiveness and self-actualization, ed 5, Boston, 1993, Allyn Bacon.

Jones F: The gentle art of classroom discipline, *National Elementary Principal* 58(4):26, 1979.

Karlin S and Berger R: *Discipline and the disruptive child,* Englewood Cliffs, NJ, 1992, Parker.

Seeman H: *Preventing classroom discipline problems,* Lancaster, Pa, 1988, Technomic.

Siedentop D: *Developing teaching skills in physical education,* ed 3, Palo Alto, Calif, 1991, Mayfield.

Turner R and Purkey W: Teaching physical education: an invitational approach, *JOPERD* 54(7):13, 1983.

ANNOTATED READINGS

Fink J and Siedentop D: The development of routines, rules and expectations at the start of the school year, *JTPE* 8(3):198, 1989.

A look at the establishment of routines, rules, and expectations at the beginning of the school year by teachers varying in teaching experience and how they were taught.

Gallahue D: Toward positive discipline in the gymnasium, *Physical Educator* 42(1):14, 1985.

Discusses the requirements for positive behavior: a positive role model, efficient planning, effective communication, self-assessment, and consistency.

Jones C and Nelson B: Helping students with problems, *JOPERD* 56(2):50, 1985.

Provides suggestions for helping students with problems to get the most from their physical education experience.

Kirch R and McBride R: Physical discipline problems in the gymnasium, *Physical Educator* 44(3):355, 1987.

Reviews writers' suggestions to deal with discipline in physical education.

Seeman H: Are you preventing or promoting disruptions? *Strategies* 1(2):16, 1987.

Presents a checklist for determining what causes disruptions in physical education.

Tenoschok M: Handling problems in discipline, *JOPERD* 56(2):29,1985.

Discusses discipline and offers six steps in dealing with discipline problems.

Wurzer D and McKenzie T: Constructive alternatives to punishment, *Strategies* 1(1):6, 1987.

Discusses the use of constructive discipline in physical education.

CHAPTER 10

Meeting the Special Needs of Children

OBJECTIVES

After completing this chapter the student will be able to:

1. Explain legislation that has been enacted on the state and federal levels to ensure equal educational opportunity for all children
2. Describe the conditions that require special consideration in planning physical education experiences for all children
3. List the steps that must be taken to determine the special needs of each child in the class before planning physical education experiences
4. Explain the conduct of activities that enable all children to benefit from their physical education experiences
5. Describe strategies to provide for needs of gifted children in physical education

Children come to the physical education class at varying stages of development, from many different backgrounds, and with various physical abilities and disabilities. Not all children can meet physical education lesson objectives without some special consideration. Whereas some children may have had limited opportunity in a variety of motor experiences, others may not find the objectives challenging to their advanced abilities. Still others may not be able to meet lesson objectives because of a disabling condition. This group includes children who are overweight or malnourished, those with a low level of fitness, children with temporary or permanent physical disabilities, those with social maladjustments or developmental disabilities, and children with learning disabilities. Because the goal of education is to help all children reach their full potential, it is the responsibility of the physical educator to plan experiences that will address the special needs of all children in their charge.

LEGISLATION

With the introduction of Public Law 94-142, the Education of All Handicapped Children Act of 1975, many physical education programs took on a new responsibility of extending physical education to all students, including those with disabilities. In many communities this previously had been the responsibility of special educators rather than physical educators. This law provides the opportunity for children to receive special help in physical education when they need it.

Public Law 94-142 requires an **individual education plan (IEP)** for the child with a disability and the opportunity for learning in the **least restrictive environment.** Physical education is the only school subject named in the law. It is important for the physical educator to be involved in establishing the IEP. The least restrictive environment in physical education is one in which the child can participate successfully and safely in as near normal a setting as possible. **Mainstreaming,** not addressed in the law but a desirable outcome, provides an opportunity for children with disabilities to enhance their social, cognitive, motor, and emotional development in a setting with nondisabled children. It offers the normal child a chance to get to perceive children with disabilities as capable and contributing members of society. Although not all children can benefit totally from the mainstream setting, every attempt should be made to provide at least some experiences with their peers.

PL94-142 emphasized educational opportunities for students aged 5 to 21 years. A similar need for services

Mainstreaming in physical education.

for children below the age of 5 was quickly recognized. Public Law 99-457, the Education for the Handicapped Act, passed in 1986, authorized services to children from birth to age 2 on a discretionary, not mandated, basis. Developmental delays that make an infant or toddler eligible for services include cognitive, physical, language and speech, and psychosocial development as well as self-help skills. As children needing special services begin to receive them at an earlier age, school programs must adjust services they are now providing to accommodate these students. Important aspects of these regulations are the role of the family in determining the services needed and a preference for services being offered in a setting with nondisabled children.

Instead of an IEP, this law requires that services for infants and toddlers and their families be guided by an **Individualized Family Service Plan** (IFSP). The IFSP is developed by a multidisciplinary team that includes the child's parent or guardian. It includes an assessment of the child's status, family strengths and needs, outcomes to be achieved, services to be given, dates and duration of services, a case manager named to monitor the services, and a transition plan for 3-year-olds.

An addition amendment to the law, PL101-476 in 1990, renamed The Education for the Handicapped Act to the Individuals with Disabilities Education Act. This amendment is commonly referred to as IDEA and encompasses the legislation contained in PL99-457.

Individual states have enacted additional legislation regarding the education of individuals with disabilities. Teachers should familiarize themselves with these laws to be sure they are in compliance.

CHILDREN REQUIRING SPECIAL CONSIDERATION

A number of physical and mental conditions require special consideration in physical education. Some of the conditions described here are associated with children who have always participated in the regular physical education class but whose individual needs have rarely been considered. Others describe children who are now in the public schools as a result of the legislation described in the previous section. The descriptions here are brief. More detailed information may be found in the references at the end of the chapter.

Asthma

Asthma is a chronic lung disease that involves an obstruction or blockage of the airways, which is often managed through medication. Most children outgrow asthma as they mature, but there is some evidence of exercise-induced asthma that occurs at all ages. Asthma attacks result in wheezing, breathing difficulties, coughing, and a feeling of obstruction in the chest. Because physical activity often brings on attacks, children with asthma have often been restricted in their physical activity by their parents and may have anxiety about participating in such activities. However, with proper medication and knowledgeable supervision children can safely participate in physical education activities.

The Blind and Visually Impaired

Children who are blind or who have other visual disabilities benefit from the mainstreamed setting. These children often lag in physical development because of their lack of physical activity. Special equipment including balls with bells or other sound devices to help children track objects may be needed to provide children the optimum physical education experiences.

Cerebral Palsy

Cerebral palsy is a neuromuscular condition caused by some injury to the motor areas of the brain. Most cerebral palsy is caused by conditions before or during birth. Many of these children are multiply disabled because the conditions that resulted in motor dysfunction often also affect other areas of the brain. Many suffer throughout their lives from abnormal retention of reflexes that their peers lose at an early age. Some children are ambulatory; others are more seriously affected, requiring the use of a wheelchair and other devices to control movements. Adaptations of activities and equipment will be needed as children are mainstreamed in physical education.

Diabetes Mellitus

Diabetes mellitus is the result of the body's inability to produce sufficient insulin. Although insulin injections may be given to provide adequate insulin, diabetes mellitus is one of the six leading causes of blindness and often leads to circulatory problems. Management of diabetes mellitus is based on proper diet, exercise, and insulin injections. Insulin amounts must be adjusted to activity level so daily activity of a consistent intensity is important.

Hearing Impairments

Children who are deaf or hearing impaired have a communication disorder. Unable to hear sound undistorted, they have difficulty receiving sound messages and in developing speech to communicate with others. The inability to communicate is frustrating for the child with a hearing impairment and for their classmates as well; thus socialization is a problem in mainstreaming these children into the school setting. Today, translators often accompany these children to class to assist them in understanding verbal instructions. In addition more effective transmitters are available that expand the hearing capacity of these children.

Hyperactivity (Attention Deficit Disorder)

Children who are hyperactive have difficulty listening, thinking, following instructions, and staying on task in physical education. The physical education environment often overstimulates these children. They often act impulsively, bother other children, and in general may be unable to control their own behavior. They function best in a highly structured environment, in a limited space, and with the elimination of irrelevant auditory and visual

Signers can help the hearing impaired learn in physical education.

stimuli, conditions often difficult to attain in the physical education setting. They usually work better alone or in small groups and should be grouped with children who do not exhibit these hyperactive behaviors. Consistency in the environment, routines, and behavior expectations are important in helping these children gain from their educational experiences. Many of these children are on medication to control their behavior so that they can function in school.

Learning Disabilities

Children with learning disabilities may exhibit any of the following behaviors: hyperactivity, distractibility, dissociation, perseverance, social imperception, immature body image, poor spatial orientation, and nonspecific awkwardness. All have implications for physical education. A well-structured learning environment is important for these children.

Low Fitness

Low fitness is often associated with other factors such as obesity, poor nutrition, asthma and other chronic respiratory conditions, or an inactive life-style. The cause for low fitness must be determined before a plan to improve fitness can be successful.

Low Motor Ability

Some children in physical education class will appear considerably less skillful than their classmates. Some may fit the definition for clumsiness, lacking in good coordination, balance, or agility. Some may have neurological deficits that are compounded by environmental factors or a poor self-concept. Other children simply may have not had the opportunity to develop some motor skills, especially manipulative skills usually associated with the early school years.

Mental Retardation

Mental retardation is one of the most prevalent of disabling conditions in the United States. Generally, two classifications of mental retardation are identified: mild and severe. These classifications are based on the child's functional capacity with regard to skills in communication, self-care, functional academics, health and safety, home and community living, work, social skills, and leisure. Some believe there is a need to distinguish between severe mental retardation and profound, which is used to classify individuals with very limited awareness and response capacities. Whereas in the past, only higher functioning mentally retarded youngsters were placed in the public schools, in the past decade many states have mainstreamed these children. Most of these individuals are developmentally behind their peers in physical, social, motor, and cognitive development.

Obesity

Obesity affects 15% to 25% of the school-aged population in the United States. Although the cause of obesity could be endocrine in nature, the majority of cases are related to diet, familial or genetic patterns, and environmental influences including an inactive life-style and psychological factors. Parents who are overweight or obese tend to have children with weight problems. Because overweight children may perspire excessively after minimal physical activity, have less mobility due to excess layers of fat, experience chafing between the legs and other rubbing body parts while moving, have difficulty breathing due to excessive pressure on the diaphragm from the excessive abdominal fat, and may move with a broader base in locomotor skills, physical activity may be an unpleasant experience. The sensitive teacher needs to encourage their physical activity and to suggest adaptations in activities to develop their self-esteem and desire to be an active participant.

Orthopedic Disabilities

Children with orthopedic disabilities may be included in the public schools today. Some may have suffered congenital or traumatic amputations or central nervous system injuries. Others may have temporary or permanent growth disorders. Some of these children may be ambulatory, whereas others are confined to wheelchairs or leg braces. Some may use prosthetic devices to improve their motor function. Adaptations to equipment and activities may be needed to help them get the most from their physical education experiences.

Seizure Disorders

Epilepsy, seizure disorders, or convulsive disorders are terms commonly used to denote a condition of the central nervous system characterized by seizures. These seizures range from a momentary loss of consciousness of as little as a few seconds, to grand mal seizures in which there is more violent, uncontrolled contraction of muscles. Many individuals suffering from these events are able to control them with medication so that seizures rarely occur. As a precaution, activities in which falling might occur should be performed with a partner, in a group, or with the teacher spotting.

Other Conditions

In addition to the conditions already discussed in this section, some children may have other disabling conditions such as muscular dystrophy, arthritis, or cardiac

TABLE 10-1 COMMUNICATING WITH AND ABOUT PERSONS WITH DISABILITIES

ALTERNATIVE PHRASE	NEGATIVE PHRASES
People with disabilities	Disabled
Person who is blind	The blind
Person who is visually impaired	
Person who is deaf	The deaf
Person who is hearing impaired	
Person who has cerebral palsy	CP victim
Person who has muscular dystrophy	Stricken by MD
Person with mental retardation	Retarded: mentally defective
Person with epilepsy	Epileptic
Person who uses a wheelchair	Confined or restricted to a wheelchair; wheelchair bound
Person without disabilities	Normal person (implies person with a disability is not normal)
Physically disabled	Cripple; lame; deformed
Unable to speak, nonverbal	Dumb; mute
Seizure	Fit
Successful; productive	Courageous (implies the person is a hero or martyr)
No alternative for these	Drain; burden; unfortunate

conditions. These require special considerations in physical education.

Communication With and About People With Disabilities

Persons with disabilities seek acceptance in society. They wish to be treated with dignity. Words we use to describe these individuals portray the value we place on them as individuals. Words used to describe anyone should focus on abilities rather than disabilities. Developed by United Cerebral Palsy of Vermont, Table 10-1 identifies phrases commonly used that have positive and negative connotations.

DETERMINATION OF NEEDS AND SPECIAL SERVICES NEEDED

The first step in providing for the education of children is to gather the information to determine each child's status and needs. This information is usually obtained upon entry into school through a medical examination (see Chapter 8) and a series of screening tests covering all school subjects. The physical education teacher usually administers the motor assessment test. As a result of these screening tests, the special needs of each child are identified.

Children identified as having special educational needs may undergo further testing to determine their eligibility for special services. To undertake these additional assessments, parents must be informed and give their consent for additional testing. Further motor assessments are administered by the physical education teacher.

After this comprehensive evaluation determines that special services are needed, the IEP process is begun with a meeting of a multidisciplinary team, including the person who will administer the plan in physical education. At this meeting the team members agree on the level of functioning and decisions are made regarding the goal and objectives to be achieved, services needed, time line, and evaluation plan. These variables are written into the IEP and each member of the team signs the IEP form.

In planning the physical education phase of the IEP, the assessment should be based on the objectives of the physical education program and should include an evaluation of the child's fitness, motor skill development, understanding of movement, and social development. It may include standardized tests as well as assessment tools based on observational data. Chapter 11 suggests techniques that may be used in undertaking this evaluation. When the testing is completed the physical education teacher determines the needs of each child and how they will be met (Figure 10-1). Many needs may be met in the physical education class by planning and conducting activities that:

1. Provide a wide range of activities to fit the varied abilities of the children
2. Use a progression in learning to guarantee the success of each child
3. Present information in a multisensory approach (visual, auditory, verbal, and tactile) to enhance all possible channels for learning
4. Use a variety of teaching styles
5. Use a variety of equipment to meet the individual needs of the child

In addition to the regular physical education class, two additional programs may be needed: the resource room and the adapted physical education class. In the resource room, children receive additional help from the teacher on a one-to-one basis. A child might come regularly to a resource class, usually in addition to regular physical education, or may come only for help in certain activities. A child who has had limited experiences in gymnastics may come for extra help during that unit. The resource room may also be used to help children improve their health-related physical fitness. The adapted physical education class is for those children who cannot safely or

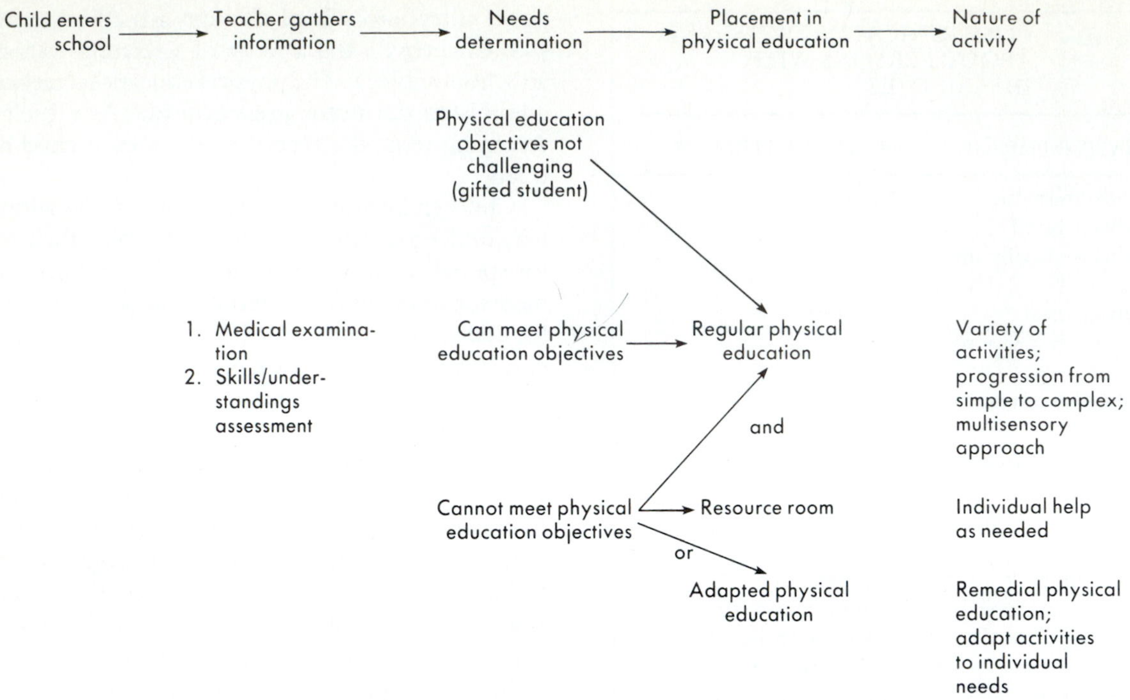

FIGURE 10-1 Meeting individual needs in physical education.

successfully meet the objectives of the regular physical education class. Children may be assigned to the adapted class on a permanent basis or only during the activities in which their participation is not possible. For instance, a child who is blind may participate in many of the activities in the regular physical education program but be assigned to the adapted class during some of the volleyball unit because safe participation in the game is impossible. A child temporarily disabled by an accident may be assigned to the resource room or to adapted physical education during rehabilitation.

In determining the best possible setting to achieve the educational goals, the teacher must consider all aspects of human development—fitness as well as motor, cognitive, and social development. Children and teacher work together to establish short-term and long-term strategies to meet these goals. Through a planned progression of motor activities and knowledge and through opportunities to work in increasingly complex social situations, children move successfully to meet these goals.

An aide or upper class student may be required to assist individual students in the regular or adapted physical education class. Assistance in working directly with the student or being close by to help keep the child on task will be essential in keeping the lesson moving smoothly and providing the individual attention needed to help the child get the most from the physical education experience.

CONSIDERATIONS FOR PLANNING INSTRUCTION

The social integration of children with disabilities into physical education classes with their normal peers is not automatic. The teacher may need to prepare the other children before a child with a disability appears. Helping children understand the disabling condition and the special assistance that will be required can help the children accept the child with a disability.

The goals for successful integration of children with disabilities are the following:

1. To develop life skills that enable them to be as independent as possible. In physical education children develop motor skills and improve fitness for a productive, active life.
2. To develop a positive self-concept. This is not an easy task in a discriminating world. Children develop motor skills for a lifetime of activity with emphasis on what they can do. Physical education helps children accept limitations by developing their skill potential and modifying activities to meet their needs.
3. To learn socially acceptable behavior. Children learn appropriate social behavior relating to play and recreational activities.
4. To develop personal grooming habits. Children learn personal grooming habits relating to active participation and personal hygiene.

Meeting Motor and Fitness Goals

Youngsters with disabilities often have difficulty in physical education because of past inactivity. Delayed motor development and low levels of physical fitness are common. Some children have not been encouraged to be physically active. Sometimes the natural drive of children to be physically active may appear to be subdued. Parental concern may also be a cause of inactivity. Because physical activity may cause discomfort in some conditions, such as asthma, parents may discourage activity in their anxiety for the child's well-being. Some parents may not encourage their child to play with other children to avoid awkward social situations for the child. Many of these fears are imagined rather than real. Because of restrictions and parental attitudes, children may not have a self-concept that includes seeing themselves as movers. Their body awareness may be poor. Inactivity has the result of keeping children developmentally behind their peers.

Poor motor skill development or low fitness level may require placement in adapted physical education or the resource class. In many activities variations in skill may be accommodated within the activity in the regular physical education class. Some children are intolerant of their less able peers. Modifications within group activities are possible to increase the total success for everyone. The teacher, in the IEP process, must decide if placement in regular physical education with or without the resource room help will enable the child to be successful in meeting the goals set for the child, or whether temporary or permanent placement in adapted physical education would be better.

Meeting Cognitive Needs

In placing disabled children in physical education, the teacher must also consider the cognitive level of functioning. Children function best in the mainstream setting if they can function on the same intellectual level as their peers. Administrators fail at times to consider this aspect of human development when placing children in physical education. Many children with disabilities have difficulty with abstract ideas that are a part of the physical education experience. Exploring movement and developing creative solutions to movement challenges are extremely difficult for the deaf because of their limited language development and difficulty in thinking abstractly. Developmentally disabled youngsters may also have difficulty in these activities because of their lack of understanding of terminology and inadequate body awareness.

Many group activities in the upper grades require an ability to understand complex rules and changing relationships of participants. Sometimes a large group activity may be too distracting for satisfactory performance for some children.

Building vocabulary is important in developing the movement curriculum. Teachers should use a variety of ways to present material to help children. Pictures and written words, as well as verbal explanations, provide a variety of approaches to help in developing understanding of concepts and other knowledge.

Developing Social Goals

Social skills are of concern for both normal and disabled children in the mainstream setting. Through modeling and other techniques, the teacher must establish an environment that discourages discriminatory behavior and encourages supportive behavior. Physical appearance is a factor in social integration. The more "normal" an individual appears or the more physically attractive, the greater the chance for social acceptance in the group.

Communication skills are also important for social integration. Children who are deaf or who have hearing impairments are not easily socially mainstreamed. Communication skills are often limited, and the other children may feel awkward in trying to talk or to understand the speech of a child with a hearing impairment.

The more contact children with disabilities have with their peers, the greater the chance for social integration. Some children with disabilities are only mainstreamed in the physical education setting, whereas others may attend classes with their peers for most of the school day. The more exposure children have to one another, the greater the chance for social acceptance. Adolescence may be a time of greater anxiety for children with disabilities as they seek the peer relationships so important at this stage.

Some children with disabilities have had little experience with children the same age. These children may not have acquired the social skills needed for successful group activity. The teacher has to carefully structure the situation so that appropriate social skills are learned and reinforced.

The teacher should strive to develop independence and avoid being overprotective. The teacher must be well aware of the disabling condition and activities that might be contraindicated. On the other hand, knowledge about a child's disabilities should not be allowed to limit the opportunity for development of the child's full potential.

Social integration is much more easily accomplished in the class setting than in recess or other periods of free play. In the recreational setting, children often ignore or avoid classmates with disabilities. The physical education teacher must be aware of these potential problems when structuring intramural activities so that all children wishing to participate are included.

Making Mainstreaming Work

Physical education is required by law for all children with disabilities. Children should not be indiscriminantly placed in regular physical education with little regard for their needs. Through the development of the IEP, the teacher must decide which goals can and cannot be met in the mainstream setting.

It is important that the child get a good start. A screening device is included in Appendix 5. Some children require special services in addition to those provided in the physical education program. Some may benefit from physical therapy. Others may require psychological or nutrition counseling to help them overcome some difficulties. If adequate services are provided at an early age, some children may move completely to regular physical education programming during their school years.

An example of an IEP, which is required by law for all children with disabilities, is found in Appendix 5. It should include both long-term and short-term goals for the child and the plan for meeting these goals. A review should be conducted periodically to determine progress toward meeting these goals. Goals should reflect the overall goals of the physical education program.

In placing the child with a disability in regular physical education, the teacher must plan experiences that will not compromise the educational goals for other children in the class. Teacher aides, adult volunteers, and peer tutors may be used to provide additional individual help in the physical education setting. Older elementary, middle school, or high school students often provide assistance. Using school-aged assistants is valuable in creating better understanding between the child with a disability and their schoolmates. These assistants may be used to assess movement potential, in giving individual help in motor skill development, in classroom management, or in controlling behavior.

Since implementation of Public Law 94-142, children with profound disabilities have been placed in some public schools. These children usually are not successfully mainstreamed; their special needs require placement in adapted physical education, where in some large school systems an adapted physical education specialist works with the children. These individuals need extensive work in the acquisition of motor skills for everyday living, such as going up and down stairs and stepping over objects. Their ability to concentrate is limited, and the activity period should end before boredom and frustration occur. Retention is limited. Skills need to be repeated frequently with a planned reinforcement schedule for skills previously learned. The children benefit from encouragement, praise, and material rewards. Punishment or withdrawal of privileges may be beyond their understanding. Rewards must be given immediately after each successful performance if they are to be valuable.

THE GIFTED CHILD

In addition to having exceptional intellectual ability, gifted children tend to be well coordinated, healthier, and better adjusted than their classmates. Because they often are channeled into some other area, such as math or science, they do not meet their own movement potential. The physical education program must strive to challenge these children by providing movement activities that maintain interest in physical activity.

The movement medium provides an important experience for gifted children. Expressive and creative movement experiences offer these children a chance to use their creative abilities in expressing their ideas. Movement exploration and creative opportunities in a variety of activities offer another dimension to their learning. Creative physical activities provide a rich environment for sensing, reasoning, and expressing as they use their problem-solving skills to find new ways of moving alone, with others, or with equipment.

The program for gifted children also is one of enrichment. Within each unit of activity, the teacher plans to introduce more advanced skills and knowledge as the children indicate a readiness for more advanced work by:

1. Providing more technical information to the student during the learning phase
2. Using questioning to stimulate higher-order thinking skills in the analysis of skills and their use in activities
3. Encouraging gifted children to find out more about the activity through reading in the school or public library, which they can share with their classmates
4. Challenging them in analyzing movement situations, devising and implementing new strategies, and evaluating the results
5. Providing opportunities to learn more advanced skills

Cooperative learning is also important for gifted children. Because cognitive growth requires social interaction and the exchange of varied opinions, cooperative learning situations benefit all children. Research evidence (Johnson) indicates that when gifted children work in heterogeneous groups, all benefit from the exchange of ideas. In addition, mastery and retention are better in cooperative groups than competitive or individual learning situations. The quality of the reasoning tends to be at a higher level, and in explaining the material to others, gifted children increase the level of their own achievement as well as their cognitive reasoning.

Gifted children may need some assistance in accepting the mistakes and lack of understanding of classmates. They may at times be called on to help other children with motor skills and movement concepts, but assisting others may not always meet their own needs for physical activity and should not be used to the detriment of their own development.

Gifted children excel not only in the physical education class but in the intramural or special interest club opportunities. At these levels of participation, their needs may be more fully met as they engage in activities with children of similar abilities outside their own class.

SUMMARY

In recent years federal and state legislation has been enacted to ensure the opportunity for all children to have equal educational opportunity in our schools. Public Law 94-142, the Education of All Handicapped Children Act of 1975, particularly calls on schools to provide physical education experiences for all children in the least restricted environment. By law each child designated as needing special services must have a written IEP (individual education plan), which includes any special concerns for physical education.

Many children with disabling conditions such as visual disabilities, deafness or hearing impairment, cerebral palsy, obesity, low fitness or motor ability, orthopedic disabilities, seizure disorders, asthma, or diabetes, have special needs in physical education.

Since the needs of children vary in any group, the teacher must individualize instruction by matching instruction with the needs of each child in the class. Some children find the physical education objectives too difficult, whereas other children of advanced ability find the objectives too easy. Children may be placed in regular physical education classes where a variety of experiences are provided to meet their needs. Other children may be placed part-time in the regular physical education class and may go to the resource room for additional help in areas of special need. Adapted physical education may be scheduled for some children to help them during a period of rehabilitation or to adapt activities to meet their special needs. The goal is to place all children in a physical education experience as close to normal as possible, but one in which growth in skill and understanding is assured.

The gifted child also has special needs that must be met in physical education. These children need to be challenged if they are to continue to be active participants.

REFERENCES AND RESOURCES

Auxter D and Pyfer J: *Principles and methods of adapted physical education and recreation,* ed 7, St Louis, 1992, Mosby–Year Book.

Baumgartner T and Horvat M: Problems in measuring the physical and motor performance of the handicapped, *JOPERD* 59(1):18, 1988.

Blackett P: Child and adolescent athletes with diabetes, *Physician and Sports Medicine* 16(3):133, 1988.

Brown A: The integration of children with movement problems into the mainstream games curriculum, *British Journal of Physical Education* 18(5):230, 1987.

Cowden E: Critical components of the individualized family service plan, *JOPERD* 62(6):38, 1991.

Cratty B: *Adapted physical education in the mainstream,* ed 2, Denver, 1989, Love Publishing.

Davis R and others: Reverse mainstreaming, *Physical Educator* 43(1):247, 1986.

Decker JT and Jansma P: Identifying least restrictive environment options in physical education, *Physical Educator* 48(4):192, 1992.

Ellison L: Using multiple intelligences to set goals, *Educational Leadership* 50(2):69, 1992.

Fait H: Teaching and evaluating physical education for severely and profoundly retarded. In NASPE: *Echoes of influence for elementary school physical education,* Washington, DC, 1977, AAHPERD.

Jambor T and Gargiuolo R: The playground: a social entity for mainstreaming, *JOPERD* 58(8):18, 1987.

Johnson DW and Johnson RT: What to say to advocates for the gifted, *Educational Leadership* 50(2):44, 1992.

Katims DS and Yin Z: Ten questions about mainstreaming, *Strategies* 6(4):12, 1993.

McCubbin J and Zittel L: PL 99-457: what the law is about, *JOPERD* 62(6):35, 1991.

Rimmer JH: A vigorous physical education program for children with exercise-induced asthma, *JOPERD* 60(6):90, 1989.

Samples B: Using learning modalities to celebrate intelligence, *Educational Leadership* 50(2):62, 1992.

Schloss PJ: Mainstreaming revisited, *The Elementary School Journal* 92(2):233, 1992.

Sherrill C: *Adapted physical education,* ed 4, Dubuque, Ia, 1993, Wm C Brown.

ANNOTATED READINGS

DeBenedette V: Exercise for hyperactive kids, *Physician and Sports Medicine* 15(4):39, 1987.
Discusses the use of exercise and low sodium diet before considering drug therapy for hyperactive kids.

Forest M and Pearpoint JC: Putting all kids on the map, *Educational Leadership* 50(2):26, 1992.
Describes a process for collaborative planning to meet the needs of children.

Gavron S: Surviving the least restrictive alternative, *Strategies* 2(3):5, 1989.
Offers suggestions for accommodating students with disabilities in physical education.

Grosse SJ: How safe are your mainstreamed students? *Strategies* 4(2):11, 1990.
A checklist for evaluating physical education settings that include mainstreamed activities.

Grosse SJ: The need to know: information sharing and the mainstreaming process, *Strategies* 5(6):5, 1992.
Physical education teachers are often not included in the IEP process. Information sharing is an important aspect of planning to meet the needs of children with disabilities.

Holland B: Fundamental motor skill performance for nonhandicapped and educable mentally impaired students, *Education and Training in Mental Retardation* 22(3):197, 1987.
Presents a study of motor performance of nonhandicapped and mentally handicapped students, suggesting that evaluation is needed before mainstreaming.

Parks S: PL99-457: Impact on one school district, *JOPERD* 62(6):46, 1991.

Use of a motor development team to address physical and motor needs of children identified for services under PL 99-457, including direct services, consultation and monitoring of services offered.

Pyfer J: Teachers don't let your students grow up to be clumsy adults, *JOPERD* 59(1):38, 1988.

Examines the clumsy child and a suggested mainstreaming device for assessing developmental delays.

Schack FK, Cranfield P, Marsallo M: Physical education, mainstreaming, and you! *Strategies* 4(3):14, 1991.

The use of peer teaching and identification on the social needs of children with disabilities and strategies to encourage their development.

Schleien S: Leisure education for the learning disabled student, *Learning Disabilities: An Interdisciplinary Journal* 1(9):105, 1982.

Discusses a study to demonstrate and evaluate instructional procedures for teaching cooperative skill activities to children with severe learning disabilities.

Ulrich D: Children with special needs–assessing the quality of movement competence, *JOPERD* 59(1):43, 1988.

Develops a checklist to identify level of performance.

Weber RC: Motivating and teaching disabled students using task variation in adapted PE, *JOPERD* 60(2):85, 1989.

Discusses two components of task variation to enhance student motivation: presenting different types of instructions rather than the same task repeatedly and ensuring competency by presenting tasks that have been mastered previously by interspersing them among the new tasks.

CHAPTER 11

Essentials of Evaluation

OBJECTIVES

After completing this chapter the student will be able to:

1. Describe the importance of evaluation in the educational plan in physical education
2. Identify strategies for evaluating student status in physical education objectives
3. Describe techniques for evaluating teacher effectiveness
4. Apply guidelines for evaluation to the physical education program

Evaluation is an important part of the educational process. It is the act of making judgments around which educational decisions will be made—decisions about meeting the needs of children, the effectiveness of teaching, and the value of the physical education program itself. It is the means to more effective teaching and learning.

Some think of the evaluation process as the end or final act or judgment. Actually, it is an ongoing process that begins the first moment of the first day and is not completed until the end of the lesson, the end of the unit, or the final moments of the school year. Along the way it helps teachers keep abreast of individual and group needs and provides valuable information needed to plan the next steps in learning. This **formative evaluation** also helps children to see what they have accomplished and to determine the direction for future work. The final or **summative evaluation** at the end of the unit or program gives us an indication of the total achievements of individuals and the group.

Evaluation also improves learning. It helps children focus on important objectives and the expectations the teacher has for their learning. When the evaluation of important objectives becomes the basis for grading in physical education, students' level of achievement and retention increases (Boyce).

PLANNING FOR EVALUATION

Evaluation is an important factor in validating the importance of physical education in the school program for children. It is essential to curriculum, unit, and daily planning. A plan to evaluate the outcomes of the program as a whole needs to be developed. Techniques to measure the extent to which unit and daily objectives are being met should be in place before the curriculum is implemented or the unit or daily lessons begun. The planning process includes the development of objectives, the selection of activities and methodologies to be used to meet the objectives, and planning of the process for the evaluation to determine the extent to which the objectives are met. This process of developing objectives, teaching, and evaluating is repeated time and time again as the unit of instruction is under way. Figure 11-1 schematically depicts this process. On the basis of the evaluation process, if it is judged that the objectives have been met, the process is repeated with a new set of objectives. These new objectives may be of a higher order based on the same skills, knowledge, or behaviors, or they may be a totally new set of motor skills, knowledge, or social behaviors. If the objectives require more work, a new course of action may be required. Perhaps the objectives are too difficult or require additional time for mastery. Therefore the objectives may need to be restated or modified so that achievement is possible. Additional activities or new teaching strategies may need to be incorporated as well. For example, an objective for refining a motor skill may be identified with a series of activities to use in attaining the objective. At the conclusion of the activities, the evaluation may indicate that the children are ready to move on to a new set of objectives, perhaps at the level of varying, such as varying distance thrown or throwing to a space in front of the moving receiver. On the other hand, the evaluation may indicate that the children need

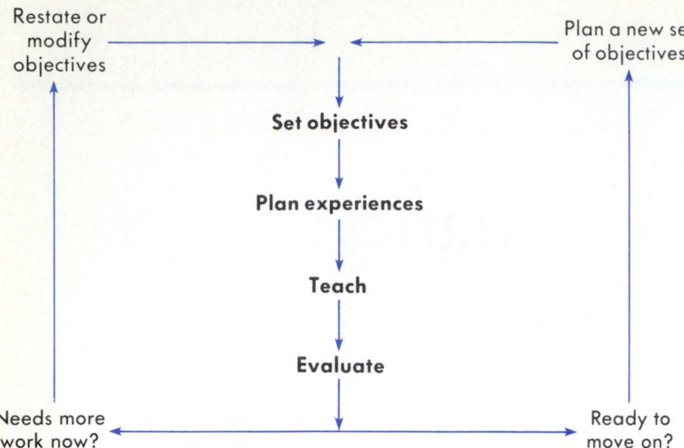

FIGURE 11-1 Curriculum implementation plan.

more time to refine the skill. Some of the activities may be repeated or new activities devised to continue efforts to refine the skill.

The evaluation plan includes the determination of what is to be evaluated, selection of the measures to be used, the organization of the testing situation, administration of the measures, analysis of the results, educational decision making based on the judgments made, and record keeping.

Determining What Is to Be Evaluated

Evaluation is driven by the goal and objectives of the program and each instructional unit and lesson plan. All purposes for the evaluation must be determined. Is it to be used to evaluate the effectiveness of the program or the teaching? Is it to measure student achievement? The information gathered may be used to determine the extent to which program goals are being met, to initiate changes in the curriculum, to improve teaching effectiveness, to establish or reestablish individual performance goals, or to communicate to parents, teachers, and administrators the present status of the children's efforts.

Outcomes of the curricular effort or the effects of the use of a particular teaching technique or an assignment given may be studied. It may be a look at the skills, understanding, and/or social behavior of children. The teacher may want a preassessment before beginning a unit, a determination of status at the end of a unit, an assessment of improvement made during a particular unit of activity, or some prediction of future success.

Because time in physical education is limited, evaluation should focus on important outcomes and those where adequate time has been provided for learning and improvement of performance.

Selecting Measurement Techniques

Once the purposes of the evaluation have been clearly defined, measurement techniques are selected. The teacher may choose observational techniques or more formal skill and written tests.

The instruments may be **norm referenced** or **criterion referenced.** In norm-referenced measures, the scores may be compared with the scores of other children of similar age and sex. Some fitness tests such as the AAHPERD Youth Fitness Test are examples of norm-referenced tests. Information from such tests is quantitative; it is a numerical score of what the children did, for example, how fast they ran or how far they threw. From these test results, percentiles or other standard test norms are computed. Criterion-referenced measures may be quantitative or qualitative. In quantitative measures the teacher establishes some criterion for the class to reach. Perhaps it is 30 sit-ups, a standing jump of 5 feet, or some other quantitative performance standard. The Physical Best fitness test is an example of a test that uses quantitative measures as criteria. A qualitative criterion measures how a person performed rather than the result of the effort. Qualitative criterion-referenced information is helpful in determining errors in performance important to improving the effectiveness of skill and also in looking at behaviors that do not lend themselves to a norm, such as certain social behaviors. The evaluative criteria found throughout this book in the analysis of motor skills are examples of qualitative criterion-referenced measures.

Another consideration in selecting measures is to determine the conditions under which the testing will take place. Is a maximum effort or a typical performance required? Will the skills be measured within the activity, in combination with other skills, or in isolation? The number of trials or observations to provide an accurate measure must also be determined.

Organizing the Class for Evaluation

Each lesson should provide maximum learning for each student. The teacher must plan carefully if testing is to be done effectively and efficiently and maximum learning and activity are to be provided for the entire class. The testing in most cases will be conducted within the regular class period. Most tests, especially those at the primary grade level, require the teacher to administer the test to one student at a time. At the same time, the other students should be engaged in meaningful activity. A number of approaches may be used.

The teacher may conduct the evaluation of skills while the children are engaged in practice or game activities, depending on the objective to be tested. This approach may take several lessons, since the children are engaged in any one activity for relatively short periods of time within the lesson. It can be accomplished relatively easily, with the children unaware that they are being evaluated.

The teacher may organize the class into station activities and conduct the evaluation at one of the stations. At the testing station, the children not being evaluated are engaged in an activity while the teacher takes the students one at a time to be tested. In this way the student being tested is not asked to perform under the watchful eye of other students waiting to be tested and children are actively participating in a meaningful way rather than sitting and waiting for their turn to be tested.

In another approach the teacher removes one child at a time from a large or small group activity. This approach requires student self-direction, perhaps more so in a large group activity to keep the activity going with only general supervision of the teacher. With some groups of children, it may be necessary to have an upper grade student, aide, parent, or other volunteer to work with the group while the teacher conducts the testing. These assistants require training if they are to contribute to the learning of the children in the activities planned.

The teacher may also train aides or volunteers to conduct the tests while the teacher conducts the other learning activities in the class. Quantitative measures are more objective and may be conducted by trained assistants. Qualitative measures require greater judgment and are best left to trained specialists.

Administering Measurements

The teacher should be knowledgeable about the techniques used. All materials should be ready and the organization and conduct of the testing session well planned. Practice with the instrument before use in a class may sometimes help improve the efficiency and effectiveness of the measure being used.

The testing should be as unobtrusive as possible. Student anxiety in the testing situation will hinder the performance of many children. Some of the organizational strategies suggested in the previous section should help alleviate some of the anxiety children may feel when being asked to perform motor skills in the testing situation.

Scoring should be fair and consistent among students. The teacher must also be aware of individual conditions that might affect the test results, such as illness, inattentiveness, distractions, cheating, or the teacher's personal feelings about a student.

Because the goal is to provide maximum participation in each class period, students who are not being tested should be channeled into some meaningful activity during the class period.

The test should be appropriately timed. If the test is to be used for preassessment to determine the needs at the beginning of a unit, the teacher must know what information students need to yield appropriate results. For example, if the skill is new to many of the students, they will need sufficient information about the skill to perform the skill for the test. If it is a test of achievement, students need sufficient time to develop their skills before testing. If it is to be used to help both teacher and student determine needs, it should be placed appropriately in the unit. For instance, giving a written test on the rules of basketball after a few lessons may determine areas of confusion that could be clarified early in the unit to enable the children to use the rules more effectively as they play the game. Testing at the end of the unit tells the teacher and student what has been achieved but does not give direction for future action, since the unit has concluded. It may not be as motivating for students to be tested at the end of a unit because there is not time for further improvement.

Analyzing Information

It is important to analyze the test results after the data have been collected. The information should discriminate between the varying levels of ability of the students. Test

Performance testing is an important aspect of the evaluation process.

results often identify the top and bottom students but do not differentiate the needs of the majority of students who fall between. In all probability the teacher already knows which students are outstanding and which need the most help. If "average" children are to be helped to achieve their movement potential, measures must be used that determine their needs as well.

Another concern in the analysis is whether the results provide important information. Do they tell us what we need to know? Do they serve the purpose for which the test was intended? For example, do they give us an insight into the needs of the children or the degree of improvement during the unit?

Making Decisions

Once the results have been analyzed, the teacher makes decisions about what course of action to take. The teacher must decide what the results of the measurements actually indicate. To what extent are the goals and objectives being met? What changes are suggested to improve teaching? What are the possibilities for curricular change? The teacher looks at the alternatives. Should more time be spent on the items measured? What needs must be addressed? Do the results indicate that the children are ready to move on to new material? Is a change in activity or method needed to enhance future learning? The teacher looks at the consequences of each possible alternative. For instance, if more time is spent on a skill, what effect will this have on other unit material? Weighing the consequences of each alternative, the teacher chooses the best solution for the particular situation.

Record Keeping

The teacher must plan for the record keeping of evaluation results. Computer programs have been established for many of the fitness tests including the Physical Best and the Fitnessgram, which also include printouts for students and parents. Other test scores may be recorded using computer-generated spread sheets. Because the physical education teacher is responsible for so many students, it might be useful to have a volunteer who assists the teacher in recording evaluation information. Appendix 4 lists some available computer programs.

ASSESSING PUPIL ACHIEVEMENT

The primary goal of evaluation is to diagnose student needs so that more effective instruction may be planned. An evaluation of pupil status regarding program goals is essential for determining program direction, setting individual achievement goals, and communicating to both students and parents the progress being made. A sample screening device for entry into physical education may be found in Appendix 5. Evaluation of student performance is an ongoing process from the beginning to the end of each unit of instruction. It may be used to establish baseline levels of competency at the beginning of a unit, to group children homogeneously or heterogeneously, to diagnose needs throughout a unit, and to determine the total accomplishments at the end of a unit. Because activity time is generally limited, the teacher must minimize the time taken in evaluation. Sufficient time must be set aside to complete the job, but the time allotted should not take away from other aspects of the lessons.

BEHAVIORAL OBJECTIVES IN PHYSICAL EDUCATION

QUANTITATIVE

The student will put 8 out of 10 balls into the target area.

The student will jump a minimum of 5 feet.

The student will catch 4 out of 6 medium-sized playground balls thrown in the medium level from 10 feet away.

QUALITATIVE

The child will throw underhand, holding the ball in the fingers, stepping forward on the opposite foot, swinging the arm in an underhand motion, and ending with the fingers pointing to the intended target.

The child will jump from a standing position, bending the legs at the knees, hips, and ankles, taking off on two feet, swinging the arms forward as the jump is taken, and landing softly with the body forward of the feet.

The student will catch the ball by getting in a direct line with the oncoming ball, reaching out with both hands toward the ball, grasping it in the fingers, and pulling it in toward the body.

The evaluation process begins with the development of meaningful, measurable objectives written in behavioral terms. These objectives may be quantitative or qualitative. Quantitative objectives give students a goal to aim for in performance and an opportunity to self-test their achievement along the way. Qualitative objectives often require the assistance of someone else to help children describe their performance, at least until they have developed adequate body awareness to analyze their own movement. Behavioral objectives are discussed in Chapter 5. Several examples are given in the box above.

Qualitative objectives may be developed at different levels of ability to recognize individual differences in performance level. Some objectives may focus on refining the technique, whereas others may be directed toward varying or applying the technique under different conditions. For example, the following objectives demonstrate progression in learning underhand striking skills.

The student will:

1. Strike the ball after a bounce in an underhand manner with the finger pads, ending with fingers pointing in the desired path of the ball (refining)

EVALUATING MOTOR SKILLS

CRITERION REFERENCED OR NORM REFERENCED

Criterion Referenced

Qualitative/quantitative

Easily identifies errors in performance

Self-testing for children (may require maturity to analyze own performance)

Looks at skills that do not lend themselves to norms (such as forward roll) or those measured in time, distance, number, etc.

Requires several performances

May be observed in an activity

Norm Referenced

Quantitative

Measures all-out performance

Compares performance with norms of children of same age and sex

Self-testing for children (score easily interpreted)

Looks at skills in which performance is easily measured in time, number, or distance

May require several trials

Requires a special testing situation

Isolates skill, perhaps in context of activity

CHOOSING THE TECHNIQUE

Teacher Observation (does not require a specific testing situation)

Checklist

Identifies specific aspects to be observed

Helpful in diagnosing specific errors in performance

Helps children see what specifically they need to work on

Subjective (some objectivity)

Requires several observations

Rating scale

Establishes a numerical or word description of performance

Does not identify specific reasons for rating

Subjective (lacks objectivity)

Takes time and several observations

Skill Tests

May be teacher made or standardized

Performance easily interpreted by students

Motivating for students

Require a specific testing situation

May remove skills from the context of the activity

Standardized tests not readily available for elementary school children, especially those in primary grades

Student Self-Evaluation

Teacher develops list of skills and criteria

Qualitative or quantitative

Motivating for students

Helps students assess own performance

Helpful in helping students set their own performance goals

Lends itself to individualizing instruction

Requires maturity in analyzing own performance

Requires feedback from teacher

Takes time to develop lists of skills and criteria

2. Vary the force of the hit, alternately hitting softly and hard, keeping the ball in the opponent's court area (varying)
3. Alternately hit the ball to the opponent's right and left (varying)
4. Vary the force and/or path of the ball in a game of four square in relation to the opponent's position on the court (applying)

Objectives to be measured should be those most important in the unit of instruction and whose importance has been communicated to the children.

Several techniques may be used to obtain the information necessary to plan appropriate experiences for children (see the box above).

Teacher observation is one method commonly used to assess pupil performance. A well-trained observer can easily pinpoint the strengths and difficulties by observing the children in activity. Observations in this context offer a way to compare the performance of children of the same age and experience. For observations to be useful, several should be made within a lesson and in several lessons because elementary school children's performance may not be consistent. Observations focusing on the lesson objectives help the teacher determine what feedback

Student name	Uses an overhand pattern	Grips ball in fingers	Side to target	Transfers weight back and then forward	Points fingers where ball is to go	Throws ball to chest level of receiver	Adjusts force for distance so ball is easily received
R. Cummings							
K. Flynn							
P. Hald							
M. Newton							

FIGURE 11-2 Motor skill checklist: overhand throw.

Rating	Criteria
5	(a) Uses an overhand pattern, (b) grips ball in fingers, (c) side to target, (d) transfers weight to back foot and then forward, (e) ends pointing fingers in direction of the throw
4	Performs the skill with 4 of the above criteria
3	Performs the skill with 3 of the above criteria
2	Performs the skill with 2 of the above criteria
1	Performs the skill with 1 of the above criteria

Name	Rating	Criteria needing more work
P. Piscopo	5	
A. Huntington	3	c, e
A. Hill	4	e
H. Gifford	1	b, c, d, e
B. Baker	2	b, c, d

FIGURE 11-3 Sample rating scale: refining the overhand throw.

is necessary and what further emphasis is needed. Because observations are subjective, they are susceptible to being influenced by personal feelings toward particular children. To make observations meaningful, it is helpful to use a checklist or scorecard that identifies important aspects to be observed. Evaluative criteria to be used in checklists have been identified for motor skills and are included in the activity chapters of this book. Observations then diagnose specific errors in execution that clearly identify student needs. An example of a motor skill checklist may be found in Figure 11-2.

The use of **rating scales** is another observational technique. The teacher determines a rating scale for each skill, ranging from an excellent performance to one needing more work. In using a rating scale the teacher must carefully define each rating. Rating scales are usually of limited value because they do not identify the specific reasons the children receive a particular rating. A rating scale combined with a space for comments may be more valuable in helping to identify and communicate student needs. When using rating scales, the observer must plan sufficient time to observe each child and should use the entire scale of ratings to differentiate performance. When using a rating scale with five categories—for example *consistently excellent, generally good, average, fair,* and *needs more work*—some children should be classified into each category to truly discriminate between the performances of the children. If only the top three categories are used, average becomes the lowest observed performance. An example of a rating scale is given in Figure 11-3.

Teacher observation and rating scales may be used for assessment by observing a live performance in class or by watching a videotape later of children engaged in the appropriate activity during the class.

Skill tests, either standardized tests in the literature or teacher-made tests, may also be used. Examples of teacher-made skill tests include measuring the distance of a long jump, the time of a 50-yard dash, or the distance of a softball throw. They should be used only when they can provide information not available by other means. Formal skill testing is motivating, and if the scores are easily understood, they do provide valuable information on performance for the children. Fitness tests fall into this category. In developing or selecting skill tests, the following criteria should be considered:

1. The test accurately tests what the teacher wants it to test.
2. It isolates the skill being tested.
3. The test is appropriately difficult for the group being tested.
4. It tests one student at a time.
5. The test may be administered easily and efficiently.
6. The scoring is simple and the scores are easily interpreted.
7. Norms or criteria are available for the age and sex being tested.

In administration of skill tests every effort should be made to maximize the activity for all children and to organize the testing so that a minimum amount of time is needed. Often other techniques are more efficient and permit the children more activity than formal skill testing.

Another technique is the **child self-evaluation.** All children are given an individualized checklist of skills. When they feel they have met the criteria, the children check them off or seek the teacher to assist them in determining whether the criteria have been met. Positive teacher feedback is important in using this technique. The teacher encourages the children to identify those skills needing more work. A combination of teacher and student checks may be used. Students may check off some skills on their own, whereas a teacher may be required to check off other skills. This technique works best after the children have developed sufficient body awareness and the maturity to look at themselves objectively. Primary school-aged children are more successful recording quantitative measures, whereas upper elementary school-children may be able to make some qualitative assessments.

Knowledge in physical education should be evaluated in such a way as to minimize periods of inactivity, for example, by observing children's responses to movement problems, questioning, or written tests.

The movement content lends itself more easily to qualitative evaluation. In assessing the children's movement responses, the teacher must define specifically what he or she is looking for as the children move. The teacher may seek several different responses or a particular type of response. This does not mean the teacher looks for the same response from each child. Examples of evaluative criteria in observing movement knowledge might include the following: stays within the boundaries of the general space; leads with appropriate body parts when moving forward, backward, left and right; or moves in a variety of ways (at least five) while moving in general space.

Questioning may also be used to seek information about knowledge. Throughout the lesson the teacher raises questions that require the children to organize their thoughts and respond verbally. Responses should call for more than a "yes" or "no". These responses may be recorded in some way as a record of who responded correctly. These questions need to be planned in advance so that the teacher has a record of what information was sought.

Written tests may be given in the upper elementary grades. Tests should be carefully constructed to test important knowledge in a minimum amount of time. Tests of rules and other important knowledge about games may be given early in the unit to determine those that need clarification to be used effectively. Written tests at the elementary level are short, usually 10 to 15 questions, and require short answers (simple recall), fill-in, or response to true/false, multiple-choice, matching, or alternative response items. In designing questions one should

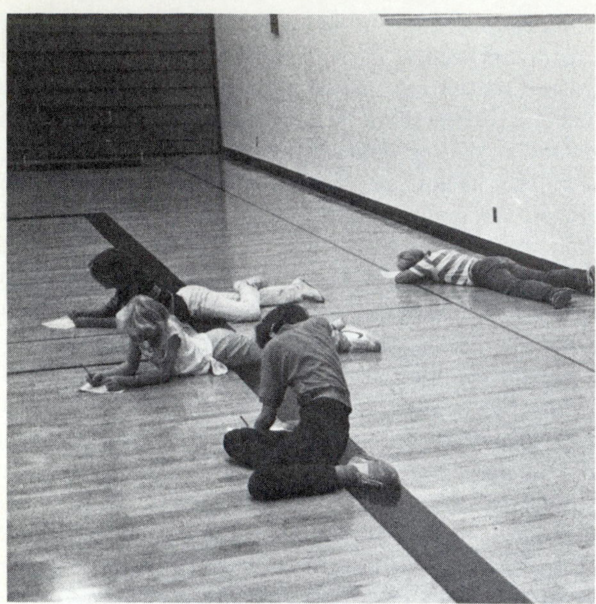

Written tests should be short.

keep in mind the following: (1) fill-ins should include only one or two blanks per question; (2) credit should be given for any correct response in fill-in or short-answer questions; (3) true-false should include only one main idea; (4) multiple-choice questions should include only plausible foils; and (5) matching should be homogeneous. There should be no trick questions. All items should test important information and be stated clearly and simply.

Short written tests (up to 5 minutes) may be given at the beginning or end of the lesson to the entire group. Or, the teacher might take the last few minutes of several classes to have the children write out answers about material covered in the day's lesson, such as the definition of terminology, explanations of rules, important teaching points to remember regarding skills, or the application of movement concepts.

Another approach to knowledge testing in physical education is through journal writing, which may be given as homework.

Evaluating social behavior in physical education does not lend itself to formal testing. These skills often include the children's work habits in listening, staying on task, as well as their ability to interact with the teacher and classmates. Many of the observational techniques previously mentioned serve the teacher well in obtaining the necessary information. It is important to identify specific social skills being taught and reinforced within different units of instruction in making these assessments. For instance, some units such as gymnastics focus more on assuming individual responsibility for working safely, whereas a folk dance experience may focus more on the child's ability to work with others. Sociometric forms, described in Chapter 8, may be used to determine what is going on in the group and which children need help in developing better social relationships. Anecdotal records are another technique that uses observation of performance. The teacher records incidents or certain events. This method may be of considerable help in evaluating social behavior as the teacher tallies the occurrence of certain social behaviors.

Regardless of the tools of assessment used, the teacher must make every attempt to communicate the meaning of the assessment results to students so that they can assume more responsibility for their own learning. Through these efforts children can be assisted in developing realistic personal goals for further learning.

Evaluation data are used throughout the unit to determine the next steps in planning for learning as well as to report pupil progress to the school administration, to teachers who will be working with the students at the next grade level, and to parents.

Developing Student Portfolios

A recent trend in assessing student learning is the development of the student **portfolio.** The portfolio includes samples of the student's work including the results of evaluation. This process may be developed in specific subject areas, such as math, writing, and physical education or may encompass all the learning experiences of the child in the school environment.

The development of the student portfolio is a very important educational process and reflects the philosophy of learning advocated in this book:

1. It recognizes learning as a developmental process, allowing for individual differences in learning.
2. It considers the whole child when it is used to assess all the learning experiences the child has in the elementary school. It recognizes the multiple dimensions of the child's school experience.
3. It supports the integrated approach to the elementary school curriculum.
4. It motivates children's learning in helping them set goals and seeing the result of their efforts.
5. It helps children take more responsibility for their own learning through self-assessment of the progress they are making.
6. It encourages teacher's reflections on program, unit, lesson, and children's goals.

In planning portfolios, Herbert suggests that teachers must ask the following questions:

1. How is learning to be defined?
2. Where does learning take place?
3. How does one recognize learning?
4. How should instances of learning be reported?
5. How should the teacher communicate children's learning to parents in a way that cor-

rectly describes the child, speaks of accountability while maintaining integrity of our beliefs about children and how they learn, reflects the different ways that teachers structure learning, and provides concrete information compatible with parent expectations?

The portfolio process is an active process for both the teacher and student; each assumes important responsibility for its development. Both teachers and students set goals and objectives for learning. Both assume responsibility in meeting those goals, the teacher in planning and carrying out the learning activities and the child through full participation in those activities. Both assume responsibility for assessing the learning that has taken place. In some situations both share in communicating the portfolio to parents. For instance, a parent/child meeting might be held in which the teacher explains the portfolio and the child helps to interpret it to the parents.

Although this approach to learning assessment is just beginning in the schools, it holds bright promise for physical education. We have lots of tools of assessment at our disposal. By answering the preceding questions and developing a system that includes both teacher and child reflection on what is being learned in physical education, we can be responsive to both our program goals and objectives, and the developmental needs of children in the elementary school.

REPORTING PUPIL PROGRESS

Report forms are the most important instrument of communication between the school and parents. They give tangible evidence of student achievement and areas needing more work, as well as communicating program expectations for developing motor skills knowledge, fitness, and appropriate social skills. They may be used in conjunction with parent conferences to discuss the individual child's progress.

The form of the report card for physical education should conform with what is used in other curricular areas. Marking needs to be interpreted so that both pupil and parent understand the methods of arriving at the marks. It should reflect the program goals and the progress the child has made in achieving those goals. All areas considered in arriving at a mark and the weighting for each should be reported.

In reporting fitness test results, schools often develop a fitness profile in which each year's test scores are recorded, giving parents a picture of how the test scores have changed from one year to the next. It is also important to develop a cover letter that explains the fitness testing and what the scores mean to help parents interpret their child's fitness scores.

Letter grades are usually not given in the elementary school, but they may be given in the upper elementary grades in some schools. They are not as individualized as other reporting forms. Although many teachers view letter grading as not in the best interest of children, the system still exists, and parents find such grades easy to interpret. Unfortunately, grades may discourage the child who needs most activity. If letter grades are given in all subjects including physical education, physical education is on a par with the other school subjects. On the other hand, if other subjects receive grades and physical education does not, it may appear that physical education is of less value than other school subjects.

Rating scales may be used in place of letter grades. They have some of the same limitations as letter grading in that they are not individualized and may discourage the poor performer. Parents may also interpret a five-category rating scale as letter grades.

A descriptive statement of written comments on performance is probably most meaningful. The teacher can communicate the child's strengths and also the areas in which more work is needed. They require more time to prepare, but they actually tell the parent more than other forms of reporting. Fitness test scores or other performance measures may be included in the written report.

MEASURING TEACHER EFFECTIVENESS

Evaluation to improve teaching effectiveness is essential for all teachers. Systematic evaluation of teaching too often ends with graduation and an undergraduate teaching degree. Throughout teachers' professional careers they may periodically be observed by an administrator, but these sporadic evaluations of teaching usually create momentary anxiety and have little effect on future teaching performances. Although it often seems to have negative connotations, evaluation should be a positive experience.

All teachers must be dedicated to a systematic plan of evaluation if they are to continue to grow as professionals. In planning the evaluation, teachers must first determine what they would like to know about their teaching. Student achievement, time spent in the various parts of the lesson, types of interactions with students, student time on task, effectiveness of management techniques, teacher flexibility in responding to changing needs of the students, teacher focus on the objectives from opening to closure, effective use of space, and movements of the teacher are some of the information of interest to teachers. The collection of data regarding one's teaching is not meant to be judgmental in any way, but merely a recording of what occurred. The teacher alone determines the significance of the events and responds accordingly. Several techniques are possible for collecting data about teaching. Some use self-analysis that is completed by the teacher, whereas others require the help of a trained observer or assistant.

One form of **self-analysis** is the written daily lesson evaluation. Shortly after the lesson has been completed, the teacher jots down notes about what took place. The focus of the lesson evaluation is the degree to which the lesson objectives were met. It may include comments about particular students and their needs, management problems, or group problems with the lesson objectives. In a short time the teacher may note trends in teacher behavior by analyzing these daily evaluations. The evaluation of beginning teachers often focuses on their own behavior, but not necessarily on its effects on children's learning. If teaching is to improve, teachers must be good observers of their own behavior in relation to student achievement. Effective use of this form of evaluation is developed over time as the teacher focuses attention on various aspects of teaching.

In another self-evaluation technique the teacher records the lesson on an audiotape recorder for later playback. A portable microphone is helpful in hearing what has been said a distance from the recorder. A great deal of information can be gathered in the playback regarding the teacher's verbal presentation, students' questions, and teacher feedback during the lesson activities. In this way one can evaluate the flow of the lesson from beginning to end. Questions to be answered include the following: Were the verbal explanations clear? Did the teacher talk too long? Was the class listening? Which students received attention and what was the nature of the attention? How did the teacher respond to class questions? Was the feedback to children related to the lesson objectives, pupil behavior, or other aspects of the lesson? Was the feedback of a general nature or specific to the points emphasized in the presentation of the lesson material or the behavior desired?

With the help of another teacher or older student, the teacher can use several additional techniques. A videorecording of the lesson may be obtained and analyzed in much the same way as with the audiotape recording. This recording can focus on a number of different teacher behaviors as well as the result of the interaction of the teacher and students.

The teacher may also use an observer who records information systematically. A **duration** study may be conducted by recording the amount of time spent on various aspects of the lesson. For example, the teacher may wish to know how much time was spent on management—getting the class started, giving the beginning directions, or moving the class from one activity to the next; how much time was used in presenting the lesson objectives (instruction); and how much time was given to student practice of the objectives (activity time).

Event recording is another observational approach. A list of possible events is made, and the observer tallies the number of times each event occurs. Interactions with students, both positive and negative, correcting or encouraging, may be recorded.

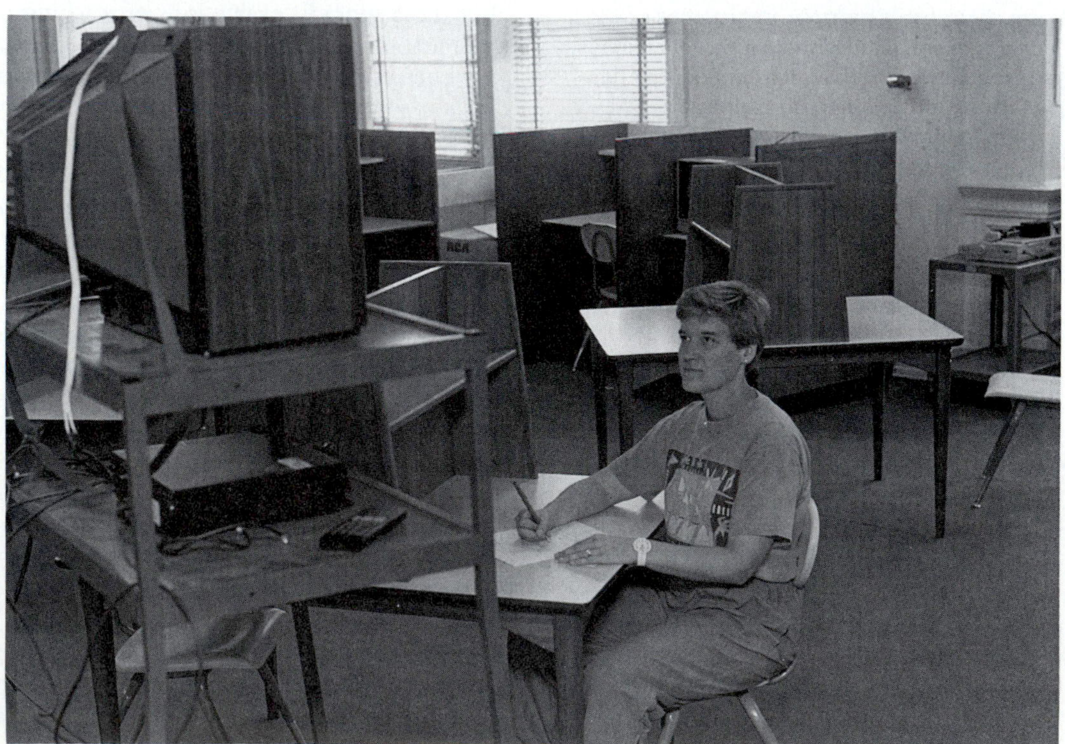

Using a videotaped lesson to systematically observe one's teaching provides important information for the teachers.

An example of event recording might include a record of the teacher's movements throughout the lesson. A map of the space used is divided into sections like a grid. The recorder traces the movement of the teacher by drawing connecting lines from one part of the grid to another as the teacher moves throughout the area, numbering the sequence of each move. The time spent in each part of the room might also be recorded.

Another example of event recording is a record of feedback given by the teacher. This record should include (1) the type of behavior receiving feedback—skill, knowledge, or social behavior; (2) the nature of the feedback, whether general or specific; (3) whether the feedback was positive or corrective; (4) whether it related to the lesson objectives or some other points of emphasis; and (5) to whom the feedback is given.

Event recording might occur at certain time **intervals** throughout the lesson. These recordings characterize what was taking place over the given time period. For instance the observer may record three times for 3 minutes at the beginning, middle, and end of the lesson. A typical recording might give information regarding whether a child was on task, off task, waiting, or assisting another child.

Another recording technique is **group sampling.** At particular intervals throughout the lesson, the observer scans the group and records the number of children engaging in a particular activity, such as waiting for a turn, listening to an explanation, watching a demonstration, practicing a skill, working on a concept, or moving from one activity to another. Several examples of teaching evaluation tools may be found in Appendix 7.

If periodic observation by administrators is to result in improved teaching effectiveness, teachers and administrators must develop a good working relationship. This relationship must be supportive and nonthreatening. All school personnel have the same ultimate goal—the maximum learning of all children. Personal growth in teaching should be valued highly. The observation of teaching should take place on a regular basis, not just at the annual review. Observers may begin the discussion by asking the teacher to provide a personal account of how the lesson progressed. The observer must be careful to begin with discussion of the aspects of the lesson that were accomplished well, reinforcing the good teaching observed in addition to offering suggestions for improving the effectiveness of other parts of the lesson. The result of effective administrator-teacher relationships will be more effective learning for children in an atmosphere that assures the continued growth of teachers.

PROGRAM EVALUATION

The purpose of program evaluation is program improvement. Program evaluation provides valuable information for determining the appropriateness of the goals of the physical education program and to what extent the goals are being met. It provides information regarding the relative importance of program goals, program implementation, and the effects of the program on the participants. It should encompass all aspects of the program, including the instructional program, intramurals, special interest groups, and special events. A program review should be undertaken regularly, usually ever 3 to 5 years.

The program evaluation may be conducted within the school by teachers and administrators or with the assistance of consultants from other schools, neighboring colleges of education, or the state department of education. Local, state, or professional criteria may be used. The AAHPERD has published a program appraisal checklist for elementary physical education. If evaluation is conducted with outside help, approval of the administration and board of education should be sought.

Program evaluation includes an examination of the written products of the program, the statement of philosophy, goals and objectives, unit and lesson plans and student assessment.

In preparation for the evaluation, a program statement is developed that includes all necessary information about the program, including the philosophy of the program, its relationship to school goals and other school curricula, scheduling, equipment and facilities, personnel, activity content, teacher/pupil ratio, and cost. Program goals are listed, and any particular concerns about the program are raised. These concerns may be the reasons the program is being reviewed.

Program goals are broken down into a series of measurable objectives that identify the questions to be asked and the criteria for evaluation. Social skills and knowledge as well as motor skills and fitness should be included.

The evaluation process should provide information regarding the impact of the program on students, the total school curriculum, and the community. As we analyze the results of the program and its impact, an attempt might be made to answer the following questions:

1. What changes have occurred in the child's knowledge of human movement? Motor skill performance? Fitness? Social skills?
2. What level of mastery has been achieved in knowledge and motor skills?
3. Do students of varying abilities find success and encouragement?
4. Do students voluntarily participate in physical activities at recess? During after-school hours? After graduation?

Information may be gathered from various sources. Teacher-constructed tests or standardized tests may be used to determine students' comprehension of the objectives. Frequency charts in which the number of times children participate in extracurricular activities may be used. Student interviews and questionnaires can be administered. Parents and administrators may be interviewed. Teachers who work with the children at the next educational level (middle, junior high, or high school) may be asked for information regarding their perceptions about strengths and weaknesses. Observations of how children use free time at school may be a reflection on the effectiveness of the physical education program.

After attaining the data to help answer these questions, the teacher should seek information regarding program factors that have caused the results, such as frequency and time for physical education, facilities and equipment available, budget resources, teacher effectiveness, and teaching styles used, as well as support of administration, school board, and community.

Once the information is received, an analysis is undertaken to determine the extent to which the objectives are being met and the implications for program revision. Recommendations should be forwarded to administrators and the board of education.

SUMMARY

Evaluation is an essential part of effective teaching. It is a process that begins the first day of teaching and is not concluded until the school year has come to a close. Evaluation is important to curriculum, unit, and daily planning, helping teachers to plan challenging learning experiences for children.

Curricular implementation involves setting objectives, planning learning experiences, teaching, and evaluating the outcomes. If the evaluation indicates that the objectives have been met, the process is repeated with a new set of objectives and learning experiences. If the evaluation determines that more work is needed on the objectives, the objectives are restated or modified to meet the needs of the children.

The assessment of student progress is important if appropriate learning experiences are to be planned. Motor skills, knowledge, fitness, and social behaviors should be included as important aspects of the physical education program. Several techniques may be used, including observations, written tests, and motor performance tests. Children's progress is recorded and reported in written form to administrators, other teachers, and parents. New processes for children's assessment are emerging through the development of student portfolios, which have great promise for physical education.

Another goal of the evaluation program in the schools is the improvement of instruction. Teachers may use a variety of techniques, including self-analysis or peer observations, to help them identify areas in which they could be more effective.

Program evaluation is another aspect of evaluation. Periodic evaluation of the program is conducted by the physical education teachers themselves, with the assistance of administrators, personnel from neighboring schools or colleges of education, or the state department of education. This review provides valuable information for the continued improvement of the program in meeting the needs of children.

Well-planned evaluation in education results in keeping the curriculum up to date, improving teacher effectiveness, and identifying student needs. As a result, student learning is enhanced as the physical education program prepares children for a lifetime of physical activity.

REFERENCES AND RESOURCES

Boyce BA: Grading practices—how do they influence student skill performance? *JOPERD* 61(6):46, 1990.

Cooper J et al: *Classroom teaching skills: a handbook,* ed 4, Lexington, Mass, 1990, DC Heath.

Dougherty N and Bonanno D: *Contemporary approaches to the teaching of physical education,* ed 2, Scottsdale, Ariz, 1987, Gorsuch Scarisbrick Publishers.

Griffin L and Oslin J: Got a minute? A quick and easy strategy for knowledge testing in physical education, *Strategies* 4(2):6, 1990.

Gronlund N: *Measurement and evaluation in teaching,* ed 6, New York, 1990, Macmillan.

Harrison J: *Instructional strategies for physical education,* ed 3, Dubuque, Ia, 1992, Wm C Brown.

Hensley LD, Aten R, Baumgartner T et al: A survey of grading practices in public school physical education, *Journal of Research and Development in Education* 22(4):37, 1989.

Herbert A: Portfolios invite reflection—from students and staff, *Educational Leadership* 49(8):58, 1992.

Jewett A and Bain L: *The curriculum process in physical education,* Dubuque, IA, 1985, Wm C Brown.

Johnson B and Nelson J: *Practical measurements for evaluation in physical education,* ed 4, Minneapolis, 1986, Burgess Publishing.

Loughrey T: Evaluating program effectiveness, *JOPERD* 58(6):63, 1987.

Melograno V: Quality physical education setting the standards step by step, *Strategies* 5(6):15, 1992.

Metzler M: Using systematic analysis to promote teaching skills in physical education, *Journal of Teacher Education* 37(4):29, 1986.

Metzler M: A review of research on time in sport pedagogy, *Journal of Teaching Physical Education* 8:86, 1989.

Safrit M: *An introduction to tests and measurement in physical education and exercise science,* ed 2, St Louis, 1990, Mosby–Year Book.

Siedentop D: *Developing teaching skills in physical education,* ed 3, Palo Alto, Calif, 1991, Mayfield Publishing.

Veal M: Pupil assessment issues: a teacher educator's perspective, *Quest* 40(2):151, 1988.

Vogel P and Seefeldt V: *Program design in physical education,* Indianapolis, 1988, Benchmark Press.

ANNOTATED READINGS

Batesky J: Teacher performance self-appraisal for physical education, *Strategies* 1(4):19, 1988.
Features a self-appraisal form for planning, teaching, lesson evaluation, data-based goals, and personal qualifications.

Brown E: Visual evaluation techniques for skill analysis, *JOPERD* 53:(1):21, 1982.
Develops techniques for observing motor skills, including vantage point, movement simplification, balance and stability, movement relationships, and range of movement.

Byra M: Measuring qualitative aspects of teaching in physical education, *JOPERD* 63(3):83, 1992.
Explains a systematic observation tool to measure teaching effectiveness.

Carlisle C and Phillips A: The physical education teacher assessment instrument, *Journal of Teaching in Physical Education* 2:62, 1983.
Discusses a technique for evaluating the physical education teacher's performance.

Colten D: How do your tests stack up? *Physical Educator* 44(2):311, 1987.
Discusses 15 principles of written test construction.

Gustafson J: Observing two important teaching variables to evaluate teaching, *Physical Educator* 43(3):146, 1986.
Looks at teacher expectations and teacher flexibility in evaluating teaching.

Johnson RE and LaVay B: Fitness testing for children with special needs—an alternative approach, *JOPERD* 60(6):50, August 1989.
Suggestions for adapting physical fitness tests for children with disabilities.

King H and Aufsesser K: Criterion-referenced testing—an ongoing process, *JOPERD* 59(1):58, 1988.
Describes the use of criterion-referenced testing in physical education to determine the extent to which individual students have achieved objectives.

Lambdin D: Keeping track, *JOPERD* 55(6):40, 1984.
Describes recording techniques to help students and teachers assess physical education outcomes.

Laughlin N and Laughlin S: The myth of measurement in physical education, *JOPERD* 63(4):83, 1992.
Discusses several plans for grading in physical education and the reality of student motor skill achievement and motivation.

Melville S: Teaching and evaluating cognitive skills, *JOPERD* 56(2):26, 1985.
Provides suggestions for teaching and developing written tests to measure cognitive skills.

Petray C, Blazer S, LaVay B, Leeds M: Designing the fitness testing environment, *JOPERD* 60(1):35, 1989.
Discusses Physical Best testing and steps in setting up the testing situation.

PART FOUR

Foundations of Physical Education

Several foundational areas of understanding and skills underlie all movement experiences. To move effectively and efficiently an individual must have an understanding of human movement, a repertoire of basic motor skills, appropriate social skills to interact with others, and sufficient health-related fitness to sustain the activity. The goal of the elementary school physical education program is to develop these fundamentals essential to a lifetime of enjoyable physical activity through a variety of meaningful, fun-filled motor experiences.

OUTLINE

CHAPTER 12

Understanding Human Movement

OBJECTIVES

After completing this chapter the student will be able to:

1. Explain the importance of concept teaching in physical education
2. Describe specific procedures for the planning and conduct of movement-centered experiences for children
3. Develop movement challenges to enhance the understanding and application of body awareness, space, and qualities of movement concepts
4. Explain the four learning processes—perceiving, refining, varying, and applying—important in concept learning

The teaching of concepts is an important aspect of learning in physical education. A movement concept is an understanding basic to the development of efficient, effective movement. It is a generalization transferable to many different movements. Concepts enable students to think about the structure of the content of physical education and to develop the language of the field. Concepts help organize our world. They provide categories in which we can organize our knowledge and experience. They enable us to simplify learning tasks. Concepts not only organize our experience but affect how we reflect on the experience. Once formed they eliminate the need to treat each new piece of knowledge or experience as a separate category, which can be a hindrance to learning. Cooper describes concepts as "hooks on which we can hang new experience." If the new information matches that already on one of the hooks, it is hung there; otherwise it is hung on a new hook of its own, to which no doubt additional information will be added later.

Concepts speed communication. When we share concepts with our students, we do not need great detail to communicate because we have shared meanings of the terminology. For instance a child who understands self-space can easily find a space away from others when asked to do so. The teacher's use of the movement vocabulary is an essential part of learning in physical education.

The concepts discussed in this chapter are inherent in any movement, from the simplest locomotor task to complex sports skills; from the movements of the unskilled laborer to those of a surgeon. These concepts are important in early learning in physical education and are later integrated into the learning of all the physical activities in which one participates throughout life. They provide a foundation on which future analysis of physical activities will be based.

The information is meaningful to children because they are curious about themselves and the movement tasks in which they engage in physical education. These experiences teach children to understand and appreciate their own movement potential. It provides an opportunity for them to develop their own ideas in challenging and enjoyable ways as they attempt to solve movement tasks.

Although the concepts have been divided into three distinct areas—body awareness, space, and qualities of movement—it must be remembered that all are interrelated and are involved in any movement. The activities included here represent only a few suggestions for developing the basic understanding of each concept.

LEARNING MOVEMENT CONCEPTS

Concept development in physical education includes the four learning processes discussed in Chapter 3. The development of concepts through these processes is further defined in the box on p. 160. In the earliest experiences—

LEARNING PROCESSES AND CONCEPT DEVELOPMENT

PERCEIVING

The first step in concept development
Defines the concept
Introduces all terminology associated with the concept

REFINING

Examines the concept more fully
Develops parameters of the concept—what it is and what it is not
Identifies safety concerns and personal responsibility
Defines basic movement principles

VARYING

Teacher-controlled altered conditions under which concept is used
Varies movements used
Varies equipment used
Varies use of concept with partners and groups
Combines concept with other concepts

APPLYING

An ever-changing movement environment alters the conditions under which the concept is used
Movement challenges prepare students for use of concepts in activities
Concepts applied in games, dance, and individual activities
Concept application relies heavily on activity coaching
Motor skill learning and concept application rely heavily on activity coaching

perceiving—children explore the definition of the concepts and terminology associated with the concept. For instance, in studying direction children develop a definition for direction and become familiar with the various directions one might move—namely forward, backward, right, left, up, and down. In refining, children increase their depth of understanding of each concept through a variety of experiences. For example, in furthering the understanding of direction, children may explore the body parts that lead the movement in each of the directions. During these refining activities, children should be introduced to safety precautions such as bending forward at the hips when moving backward, as well as any movement principles important to the concept. Children should be exposed to these concepts in their early physical education experiences.

Varying includes further development of the concepts through a variety of movements, the use of equipment, working in different relationships with others, or in combination with other concepts. For example in varying direction, children might use a variety of locomotor movements, move with balls or hoops in each direction, or move with another child in directions that are called. They might also explore movements that require a combination of level and direction. The use of other concepts depends on the children's understanding of these concepts. Obviously, they must know the concepts well if they are to be successful in combining one concept with others. After the varying activities, children are ready to begin applying the concepts in a variety of increasingly complex activities.

Applying includes the use of concepts for successful participation in a variety of more traditional physical education activities. Simple application may begin in the early physical education experiences but becomes a more important aspect of physical education in the upper elementary grades and beyond as children are taught the use of concepts through more traditional physical education activities. Discovering the best position to move in any direction may be important to success in a number of different game activities. Seeing the similar use of concepts in a variety of activities is an important aspect of learning. The application of concepts is developed in the activity chapters of this book.

These processes may be easily translated into developmental levels. Success at each level requires proficiency at the preceding level. At level I the child is developing a beginning understanding of the concepts (perceiving). At level II (refining) greater understanding is achieved. At level III the children are ready to expand their use of the concept in varying activities and simple applications. At level IV they are ready to use the concept in more complex applications.

It is important that the children's earliest experiences in physical education be centered around the movement content. This approach extends the time devoted to developing an understanding of human movement, but often is more difficult to initiate in the upper grades. As children begin to become more group oriented, they may not respond well to individual problem solving unless they have had previous experience with this method. If their orientation to physical education has been the traditional activity-centered approach, then the concepts may more easily be grasped through more activity-related experiences because this approach provides a familiar framework. Problem solving continues to be a viable method in teaching traditional physical education activities.

PLANNING AND CONDUCTING MOVEMENT EXPERIENCES

The initial step in teaching concepts is to determine the students' level of understanding and the mastery level desired. The teacher might seek answers to the following questions:

Is the concept new to the children?
Are they familiar with the concept and related terminology?
Is there a clear understanding of the concept?
Are the children ready to use the concept under varying conditions?
Are they ready to use the concept and see its relationship to successful participation in selected physical education activities?

The answers to these questions determine the objectives and the movement challenges required to develop greater understanding and use of concepts.

Concept Mapping

Concept mapping may be of some help in determining objectives and subsequent activities for concept development. A concept development map is provided in Figure 12-1. Sample concept maps are developed in the sections that follow. These are by no means the only objectives to be developed for each concept. The teacher may develop additional objectives for each of the learning processes. If the teacher determines that the concept is new to the children, the focus may be on perceiving activities. Thus the perceiving part of the map is further developed to include the concept definition as well as that of all related terminology. If the children are ready to refine the concept, the teacher develops a set of objectives leading to greater understanding of the concept, safety and personal responsibility, and identification and understanding of any movement principles involved. If the concept has been well developed, the children may be ready for varying activities in which the teacher controls the new conditions, such as through the use of a variety of movements or equipment, partner and small group work, or perhaps in combination with other concepts. If applying is the process to be developed, the teacher carefully analyzes the activity to be used, determines the way the concept is used, and structures movement challenges that prepare the children for use of the concept in the activity. Then the children participate in the activity with further coaching from the teacher during play.

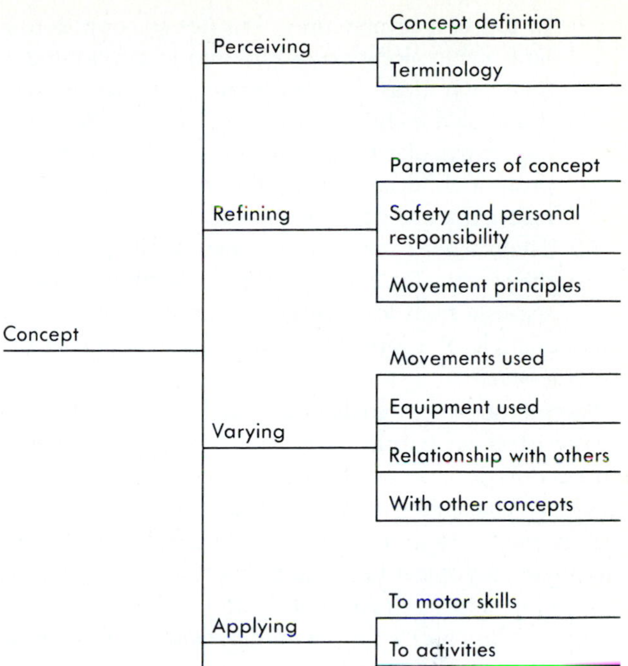

FIGURE 12-1 Concept development map.

Developing Movement Challenges

The success of indirect or child-centered styles of teaching lies in the teacher's ability to develop movement challenges with the children. Many times these challenges are unsuccessful because the teachers have not formulated in their own minds the expected outcomes of the experience. This approach does not suggest that the teacher should look for a specific or single outcome, but rather that careful planning must be used to enable the children to meet the purpose of the activity.

Once the objectives have been determined, the teacher designs the movement challenges through which the outcomes will be achieved. In planning for children, teachers should keep the challenges simple but specific to the outcome they wish to achieve. At this stage the teacher must establish the framework in which the children will work. Children often are unable to meet the outcomes because the teacher states the challenge too vaguely. The following steps provide a logical progression in the development of these movement challenges:

1. Generally, one begins with the introduction or review of terminology related to the concept as needed.
2. Next, the teacher states the challenge.
3. An example or two is given to clarify the challenge and to get the children started.
4. As the children work the teacher circulates among the group, raising questions or offering assistance as needed to help the children develop their solutions to the challenge. The teacher may ask the children for ideas as they develop their solutions. For example, the teacher may ask the children what other body parts they could use in a movement challenge exploring the use of different body parts.
5. As the children work further, they may share examples, which helps to broaden the repertoire of possibilities for all the children. Timing of this sharing is crucial. It must occur when children have explored their ideas and are ready for

an infusion of new ones, but not so soon as to limit the exploration of children in developing their own ideas. Inappropriate time sharing may signal to the children that the teacher is looking for a particular type of response, which will prompt children to copy the movements shared rather than to develop their own ideas.

6. The teacher moves on to a new challenge when the teacher feels development is accomplished or senses a need for change from the children.

An example of a movement challenge is found in the box below.

Several movement challenges may be used to develop any one objective within the lesson. A variety of activities is needed to develop greater understanding. Exposure to a series of challenges that relate the concept to a variety of movement situations is crucial. Generally, in the beginning phases of learning, themes of three to five lessons are developed for each concept. In this way children have a longer time to develop an understanding of a single concept before moving on to the next.

It is not enough to put the children into the activity and assume that they will achieve the objective. The children may enjoy the activity and never really understand its purpose. An important part of the planning process involves anticipating the responses of the children and developing questions that will respond to their movements and keep them on task. This technique is the most crucial part of planning movement challenges. Questions should encourage creative or innovative solutions to the challenge. They should encourage all to have the courage to try something new. They should be questions in which a yes or no answer would be inappropriate. Children should be encouraged to verbalize their responses to partners, to small groups, to the teacher, or to the entire class. Students should be able to verbalize about something they really know. Beginning teachers may find this task difficult; however, as they gain experience in working with children and the movement concepts, they will be able to draw on past experiences in anticipating the responses children might make. One cannot deny that "If you become the teacher, by your pupils you'll be taught," as suggested in *The King and I.*

When working with and responding to children during the movement activities, the teacher must encourage individual children to find their own ways of moving and their own solutions to the movement tasks presented. This is not to say that whatever movement response a child makes is appropriate. As the teacher circulates among the group, additional questions and suggestions to help keep children on task should be stated in a way that encourages the individual responses of children.

As children are encouraged to think and to develop their own ideas, their success is closely related to their self-concept. Children with greater self-confidence will be more comfortable in developing their own solutions to movement challenges. Much effort must be made to sincerely recognize the efforts of those lacking confidence to help them feel successful.

Emphasis should be on the quality of movement. Chil-

SAMPLE MOVEMENT CHALLENGE FROM A LESSON ON GENERAL SPACE

Lesson objective: To move in a variety of ways in general space.

(The children are seated in front of the teacher).

"In our last lesson we worked on the concept general space. Who can tell me what general space is? (Student response: the space we have to move in within the black lines.) We have already learned about self space. What is our self space? (Student response: The space I take up and space I can reach.) How is self space important as we move in general space? (Student response: We try to stay in our self space and not touch anyone.) On the signal I want you to find a self space within the black lines. Ready? Go!" (Children find a space.)

"Today we are going to explore some different ways we can move in general space. Some of the ways we moved last time were walking and running. On the signal let's walk in general space, being careful to stay in the boundaries and to avoid others. Ready? Go!

(Children move.) "Now let's try running, trying to cover as much of the general space as possible." (Children move. On the signal to stop the teacher continues.)

"That was very good. What is another locomotor movement we can use to move?" (As other ways are identified the children try them out.)

(Taking the challenge another step, the teacher gives the children some choices.) "On the signal I want you to select some way of moving you liked best. On each signal to change, change the way you move." (Several signals are given with the children changing their movements on each one. The teacher might ask a few children which ways they liked best. As the children move the teacher circulates among the group giving feedback and offering suggestions to those who may be having difficulty remembering the various ways they moved previously.)

The teacher may then ask the children what would be some other ways of moving, which they try as each is suggested. The children may suggest moving in various directions, pathways, or in varying the movements used, such as moving on hands and feet, taking large or small steps, etc.

At the close of the lesson, the teacher reviews with the children the various ways they moved by asking the children some of the following questions. "What ways of moving did you like best? What ways were the easiest to control? Which were more difficult? Which enabled you to cover the most space more quickly?"

dren should be helped to evaluate their own responses to the movement challenges in a nonthreatening way that emphasizes the positive aspects of their performance. The teacher must foster a supportive attitude by asking the children what they liked about the performance.

Organizational Concerns

It is important to establish rapport with the group before attempting a movement approach to learning. Children need a framework within which to work, so it is important for the teacher to have an established relationship with the children before proceeding. When beginning the school year with a new group of children, it is best to plan a few lessons to help establish the rules for expected behavior and the class routine before moving to the less structured movement approach.

The teacher should define with the children the space to be used. Other areas, such as the cafeteria or multipurpose room, may also be used for physical education so furniture or other equipment may occupy some of the space. If the teacher wishes the children to avoid some areas, the teacher must define the space by setting the movement boundaries to exclude those places.

A signal for listening and changing activities needs to be established before the children begin moving. It need not be the same signal each day. Practice in responding to the signal may be helpful for young children, such as giving them a chance to move around in the space and stop on the signal a few times. Some teachers refer to the signal as the signal to "freeze."

Developing Social Skills

The development of movement challenges offers several opportunities to enhance social skills. During the early years children are more successful working alone in solving movement challenges, and they learn to share their ideas with the group as well as listen to the ideas of others. Gradually, they learn to work with a partner and later a small group of three or four where they will need to work together to accomplish the challenge. It may be helpful in this early experience to state the challenge so that the children must use at least one idea from each member of the group to solve it. Some activities may also require more confident youngsters to help their less sure classmates in formulating ideas for the partners or group to use. Others might require children to share with the class ideas they received from a friend.

Developing Physical Fitness

Although the development of the movement content requires some verbal exchange between student and teacher, vigorous activity should be provided whenever possible. Many of the activities are very stimulating for young children and most move vigorously. Sustaining a movement activity a little longer or until the children are breathing a little harder is often all that is necessary to provide some cardiorespiratory workout for everyone. In developing strength and flexibility as children move in different ways, they may be asked to hold positions that require supporting body weight or maintaining body segments in a stretched position.

Integration of the Movement Content Across the Curriculum

Once the objectives for concept development have been written, the teacher looks at the many ways they can be developed and used in the elementary school by integrating learning of the movement content across the curriculum. Teachers can further the understanding of these concepts in a number of different classroom settings, with some activities involving movement, others in quieter activities. Chapter 4 includes a number of activities that may be used outside the physical education setting to enhance the understanding of the movement content. Additional activities for integration also may be found in this chapter.

The following sections develop the movement content identified in this book. It is only a beginning to help teachers get started in developing the movement content. Teachers may develop other objectives in place of or in addition to the ones described here. Each of the objectives may be developed in one or over a series of lessons. Additional activities will also need to be developed.

BODY AWARENESS

The primary purpose of body awareness activities is to acquaint children with themselves as movers—to gain understanding of what the body can do and to increase awareness of the body through movement. Although research in this area is limited, one might expect that the more children understand about the body and its actions, the more effective they might be in solving movement tasks. Moving children may have little conscious awareness of their body parts and their potential for movement. These activities focus the children's attention on themselves and their moving body parts. Beginning activities focus on a general awareness of the body and the concept followed by movements that develop the terminology. The application of these concepts is an important aspect of motor skill development. The program content to be achieved in the study of body awareness includes the following:

1. Naming and locating body parts of self and others
2. Awareness of possible body shapes
3. Recognizing possible movements of body parts

4. Awareness of the relationship of body parts while moving
5. Understanding the use of the body in communication (body language)
6. Awareness of body tension and relaxation

Objectives should be stated for each of the content areas and a series of movement challenges planned to meet each objective. It is assumed that appropriate vocabulary and understanding of one's anatomy and physiology are also the result of these experiences. Beginning activities focus on developing a general awareness of the body and its movement potential. These activities are followed by those that develop the movement terminology and further understanding of the concept.

The application of these concepts is important as the children learn various motor skills. In addition some children's dances as well as creative dance, gymnastics, and working with small equipment require good body awareness for success.

Naming and Locating Body Parts of Self and Others

The naming and locating of body parts are often taken for granted. Yet it is not uncommon for elementary school children as late as second grade to be unsure of where certain body parts are, such as their shins and thighs. Children learn body parts that they use at an early age to manipulate their environment—arms, legs, and fingers. They also learn those that may be frequently bumped or banged, such as knees or elbows. They may be unfamiliar with some parts of the arms and legs. The key concepts are found in Figure 12-2. In perceiving, children will begin to identify that the body is made up of many parts and that each has a name. In refining, children take a closer look at the concept, recognizing large and small body parts, the articulations where body parts come together, and the personal responsibility of controlling one's movements. In varying, children recognize individual differences in body parts. Application of this concept enables children to respond to instructions regarding the use of body parts in performing various motor skills and their specific use in nonlocomotor and locomotor movements, games, dance, and individual activities.

Matching body parts with others.

Key Concepts and Activities

Perceiving—Level I

Recognizes body parts.
Names body parts.

1. Move a body part while in self space. Try another. Another. (Often when children get beyond identifying five or six parts, they begin to experience some difficulty in identifying others. This activity demonstrates the degree of awareness they have of their own bodies.)
2. Balance a beanbag on a body part. On how many different parts can you balance a beanbag?
3. The teacher calls the name of a body part and the children point to it or move it.
4. Students move a body part and name the body part moved as the teacher calls on them.
5. Toss a beanbag. Catch a beanbag on the body part that a partner names.
6. The teacher names a body part and moves a body part, but not necessarily the body part named.The children respond by moving the body part named.
7. The teacher calls out instructions and the students execute the movements required, e.g., touch your elbow to your knee, touch your ear to your shoulder, etc. After a few examples the children might suggest possible matches. Which parts were easiest to touch? Which were more difficult?
8. Name and move body parts that begin with A, B, and so on.
9. Body tracings: Children work in partners with each child in turn lying on a large piece of paper and the other tracing the outline of the body with a marking pen. What body parts can you identify from the tracing? How do your body parts compare with your partner's?

Refining—Level II

Identifies large body parts.
Identifies small body parts.
Recognizes that small body parts are part of larger body parts.
Identifies body parts with the eyes closed.
Names the articulations of the body.
Assumes responsibility for controlling body parts.

1. The leg is considered to be a large body part. Move your leg. Move another large body part. What is it called? What other large body parts can you move?
2. The fingers are considered to be small body parts. What are some other small body parts you can move? Move

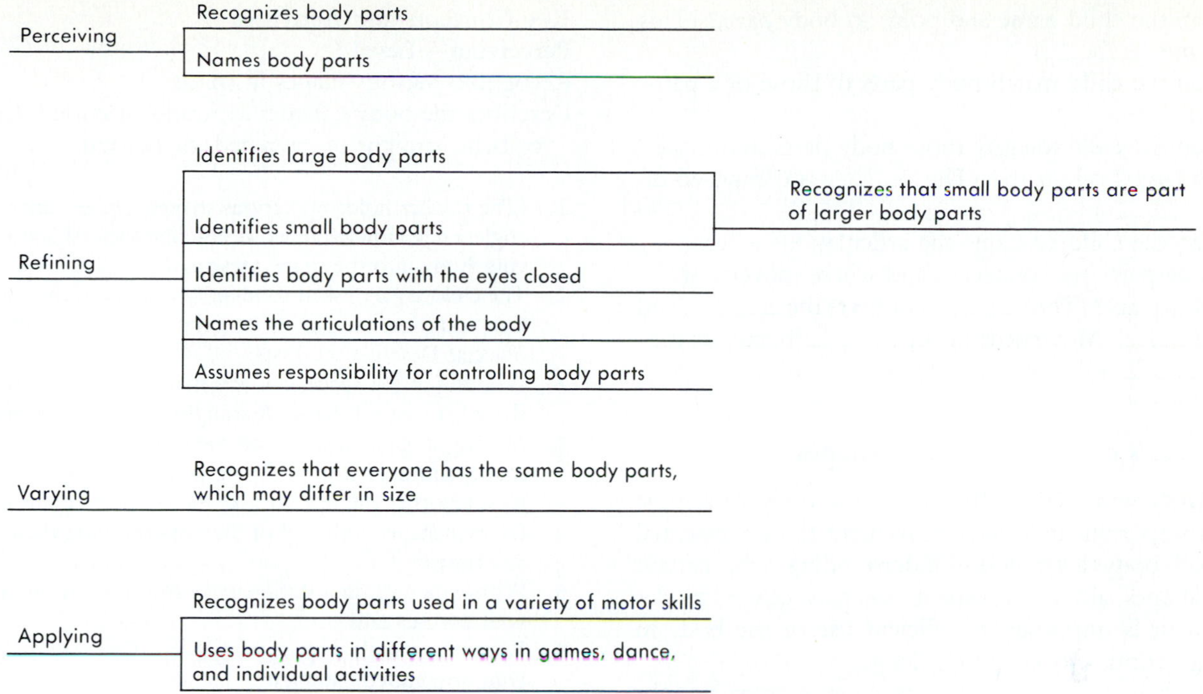

FIGURE 12-2 Key concepts for naming and locating body parts on self and others.

some small body parts. What small body parts did you move? (Teacher calls on some individual children. Children then move the small parts identified.)

3. Call out the names of body parts—forearm, thigh, shin, wrist, etc. What are they parts of?
4. Begin moving a body part. On the signal move a body part that is smaller than the one moved. On each signal move another part smaller than the previous part moved. Ask some children the parts moved.
5. Repeat *No. 4* but begin with a small part and move a larger part on each signal.
6. Explore the large body parts and their small parts. Look at your arm. What are the names of the parts that make up the arm?
7. Select a large body part. Move each of the small body parts that make up the large part, moving one at a time. What are the small parts called?
8. Can you begin moving one small part and gradually move the connecting body parts until the entire large body part is moving?
9. With eyes closed point to the body part your teacher names.
10. From various positions, such as kneeling, on hands and feet, lying on your back, etc., touch body parts called by the teacher.
11. With eyes closed move a body part your partner names.
12. In partners, one calls the name of a body part. The other indicates where the body part begins and ends by running the fingers along the entire length of the part. For example: How long is your shin?
13. Where your forearm and hand meet is called the wrist. Move your wrist. Name the connections (articulations) to which the teacher points.
14. With a partner, name the articulations that your partner moves.
15. Move a body part. Where did the movement begin? Try another.
16. In a large space move a body part. Try another. Now decrease the amount of space. How did your movements change so that you could control them to avoid contact with your classmates?

Varying—Level III

Recognizes that everyone has the same body parts, which may vary in size.

1. Working with a partner, one is the leader. Move the same body parts the leader moves.
2. With a partner, match your body parts called by the teacher by touching them together.
3. Repeat *No. 2* adding: What differences are there between your partner and your body parts matched?
4. Working with a partner, move your partner's body part as he or she names it.
5. Working with a partner, compare the length of large body parts, now small body parts. What differences did you discover?

Related Knowledge

Names and spelling of body parts.

Evaluative Criteria

1. Can the child move or point to body parts named by the teacher? (How quickly can you touch your _______ ?)

2. Can the child name and point to body parts? (This is my ______ .)
3. Can the child match body parts to those of a partner?
4. Can the child identify those body parts that make up large body parts? (The ______ is composed of ______ .)
5. Can the children name the articulations where body parts are connected and where movement takes place? (The ______ connects the ______ and ______ . Movement of my ______ begins at the ______ .)

Awareness of Possible Body Shapes

Familiarity with actions that allow the body to assume shapes important in specific movement tasks is essential to good body awareness. Understanding why certain body shapes aid a movement whereas others hinder movement is important to efficient use of the body in solving various movement challenges.

The body may assume shapes ranging from straight to rounded or twisted. Key concepts are mapped in Figure 12-3. In perceiving, children identify the shapes that the body may assume. As they refine the concept, they explore making and changing shapes. In varying, children explore the size of shapes, the relationship of shape to space available, and making shapes with equipment and classmates. The application of the concept will be important in assuming and changing shapes to meet movement requirements in the execution and use of motor skills.

Key Concepts and Activities

Perceiving—Level I

Recognizes various shapes in space.

Describes the body's shapes as round or curled, flexed or bent, straight or stretched, or twisted.

1. (The teacher holds up various shapes: circle, square, triangle, etc.) How would you describe these shapes? Make your body into the shape presented.
2. The children are asked to identify objects in the room. Can you make your body into the shape of one of the objects? Describe the shape.
3. Working in self space, can you make a round (curled) shape? A twisted shape? A straight (stretched) shape?
4. Moving in general space, on the signal, freeze, assume a shape, and hold it until the signal to move is given. (After a few tries the teacher asks the children to show their favorite shape, with half of the class showing their shapes at a time.)
5. With a partner, in a stationary position, make the shape your partner calls.
6. Experiment with shaping body parts. Can you make your arm curled? Straight?

Refining—Level II

Assumes a variety of shapes.

Changes body shape smoothly.

1. Repeat *No. 5* in perceiving but call the same shape several times to see how many different kinds of bent, curled, etc. shapes they can make.
2. Have the children make shapes from various positions on the floor such as sitting, kneeling, on three body parts, etc.

Perceiving	Recognizes various shapes in space
	Describes body shapes as round or curled, flexed or bent, straight or stretched, or twisted
Refining	Assumes a variety of shapes
	Changes shape smoothly
Varying	Assumes shapes varying in size
	Changes shape to fit the available space
	Makes shapes with equipment, with a partner, or with a group of people
Applying	Makes shapes that aid movement

FIGURE 12-3 Key concepts for body shape.

Exploring body shape.

3. Can you make your upper body round while you bend your lower body? Experiment shaping different body segments.
4. Use your body to make the shape of a letter of the alphabet. What letter did you make? How would you describe its shape? Try another.
5. Same as *No. 4* but make animal or other object shapes.
6. Make a *(round)* body shape. As I count to 3, change to another *round* shape (or a different shape, i.e., change from a round shape to a straight shape).

Varying—Level III

Assumes shapes varying in size.

Changes shape to fit an available space.

Makes shapes with equipment, with a partner, or with a group of people.

1. Working in self space, make a very large shape with your body. Can you slowly change your shape from large to small? Can you change your small shape to a large one?
2. Working in self space, make a shape that is narrow, wide, tall, short, etc.
3. Repeat *No. 6* in refining but change from small to large, wide to narrow, etc.
4. Using one or two elastic ropes held by two persons, vary the height of the ropes and try different ways of going over and under the ropes. What body shapes could you assume when you went over the ropes? Under? How did your body shape change as the space got smaller? Larger?
5. With a partner who holds a hoop, move through the hoop in a round shape. What other shapes can you use to get through the hoop?
6. With a partner, make a shape your partner can go under, now one to go over. Repeat, changing roles. Repeat again having half the class make shapes and the other moving over, under, etc.
7. (Have the children make a shape with a piece of equipment—hoop, wand, rope, etc.) Did the piece of equipment change the size of the shape you could make?
8. (With a partner, have the children make a shape and join it to their partner's shape.) How would you describe the shape you made?
9. Working with a partner, can the two of you make a curled shape? A straight shape? A twisted shape? Can you make a shape with one of you curled, the other straight? What other combinations of shapes could you try?
10. Repeat *No. 9* but change the shape with a partner on the count of 5.

Related Knowledge

Terminology: round, curled, straight, stretched, twisted, flexed, bent

Evaluative Criteria

1. Can the child recognize various shapes of objects and the body?
2. Can the child vary the body shape in solving the movement challenges?
3. Can the child vary the shapes of body parts or the size of the shape?
4. Can the child adjust the body shape to fit into the available space?
5. Can the child change shapes smoothly without hesitation?
6. Can the child make shapes with equipment or other children?
7. Can the child recognize what shapes aid or hinder movements?

Recognizes Possible Movements of Body Parts

Before children can successfully learn and use motor skills, they must have an understanding of how their body parts function. The possible movements of body parts include **flexion, extension, rotation, supination, pronation, adduction,** and **abduction.** These activities attempt to help children realize their movement potential. Figure 12-4 includes a map of the key concepts. In perceiving, children explore the many ways individual body parts may be moved. During refining activities children continue to explore movements of body parts and to identify where the movements begin at the articulations of body segments. Varying activities include moving objects with different movements and varying direction and range of movement. The application of this concept is important in identifying the type of movements necessary to efficiently perform motor skills and the use of these movements in creating and absorbing force.

Key Concepts and Activities

Perceiving—Level I

Recognizes that body parts may move in a variety of ways. Moves body parts in the following ways: flex, extend, rotate, supinate, pronate, abduct, and adduct.

1. Select a body part. Move it in any way you choose. Try another part. Another. Show someone close by some of the ways you moved.
2. Can you move your legs without touching them to the floor? How many different ways could you move them?
3. Move one body part. Now add another as you keep the first moving, now a third. How many body parts can you move at the same time?
4. In partners, one moves a body part, the other does the same and then moves the part in a different way. Keep going until you run out of ways to move. Repeat with another part.
5. Bend one body part. Try another. When we bend body parts, we call that flexion. Straighten a body part. When we straighten body parts, we call that extension. When we bend a body part, the muscles we use to bend it are flexed. Some muscles are also relaxed. Can you feel the flexed muscles?

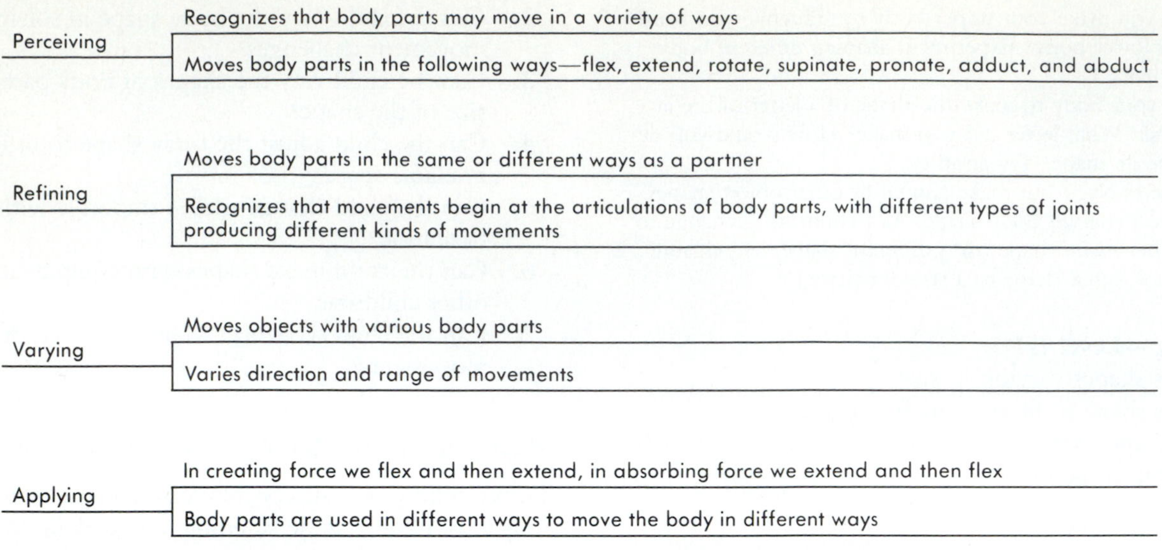
Perceiving
Recognizes that body parts may move in a variety of ways
Moves body parts in the following ways—flex, extend, rotate, supinate, pronate, adduct, and abduct
Refining
Moves body parts in the same or different ways as a partner
Recognizes that movements begin at the articulations of body parts, with different types of joints producing different kinds of movements
Varying
Moves objects with various body parts
Varies direction and range of movements
Applying
In creating force we flex and then extend, in absorbing force we extend and then flex
Body parts are used in different ways to move the body in different ways

FIGURE 12-4 Key concepts for possible movements of body parts.

6. In self-space, which parts could you bend (flex)? Extend?
7. Turn (rotate) a body part. Try another. Which body parts do not turn? Why? Some of the joints of the body allow for rotation but others do not. See how many parts you can rotate. What are their names?
8. Repeat with supinate and pronate and also adduct and abduct.
9. Working with a partner, one is the leader. The leader tells the partner to bend, extend, or rotate specific body parts. The partner responds with eyes closed. Take turns being the leader. Were you able to respond to your partner without looking at the body parts you were asked to move?

Refining—Level II

Moves body parts in the same or different ways as a partner.

Recognizes that movements begin at the articulations of body parts, with different types of joints producing different kinds of movements.

1. In partners, one moves a body part and the other copies the movement, calling out the type of movement made.
2. In partners, one moves a body part (such as flex at the elbow and each in turn adds another flexed part). How many parts did you flex? Repeat with other movements.
3. In partners, one moves a body part and the other must move it in a different way.
4. Explore different movements of body parts from various positions: sitting, lying down, standing on one foot, etc.
5. Can you move the parts of your arm (or leg) in different ways?
6. Can you move through general space keeping one leg extended and the other flexing and extending? What other ways can you move parts in different ways at the same time?
7. Human sculpture: One person is the artist, the other the lump of clay. The artist moves his or her partner's body parts to form the sculpture. In what ways were you able to move various body parts? Describe them to your partner.
8. Review activities in *No. 2* and locate the articulations (joints) where the movements take place.
9. In partners, one moves a body part and the other describes where the movement took place. What movements were possible in the joints used?
10. Explore the movements in various joints, and if possible use a skeleton or pictures to show the various joints and how they work.
11. Hold up some stick figures of humans in various positions. Can you move your body parts to match these drawings?
12. Draw a stick figure. Assume the position of the figure. How did you have to move your body parts to assume the position of the stick figure? Share your drawing with another child. How did they move to assume the correct position?

Varying—Level III

Moves objects with various body parts.

Varies direction and range of movements.

1. Explore moving various objects (ball, beanbags, etc.) with different parts of the body. How did you move the body parts to move the object?
2. Working with a partner, one is the leader who suggests ways of moving a ball for the other to attempt. What kind of movements were necessary to move the ball? What body parts and movements seemed to work the best?
3. What body parts can you bend forward? Backward? To the side?
4. When you move sideways how does your leg move? Try other directions.

5. Flex your arm as much as possible. Slowly extend it until it has just the smallest amount of flexion. Try other parts and other movements.
6. Try various locomotor or ball skills using varying degrees of movement. What happened when you used little flexion? A lot? Try other movements also.

Related Knowledge

Terminology of the types of movement possible: bend, flex, stretch, extend, rotate, pronate (rotate forward and toward midline), supinate (rotate away from midline), adduct (toward the median axis of the body or together), abduct (away from the median axis or apart).

Types of joints: ball and socket, hinge, pivot, condyloid. When a body part moves, some muscles contract and others relax. Movements through space are called locomotor movements; those in which one remains stationary are nonlocomotor or axial movements.

Evaluative Criteria

1. Can the child move body parts in the correct movement on command? (Flex your wrist.)
2. Can the child verbalize and move body parts in all ways? (My wrist can flex, extend, and rotate.)
3. Can the child describe the type of movements possible in the various types of joints?

Awareness of the Relationship of Body Parts while Moving

The content in this area develops an understanding of the relationship of body parts in three areas: that some body parts may be used for support and nonsupport functions; that in any action some body parts move while others remain still; and that in any action body parts may move in unison, sequence, or opposition. Figure 12-5 maps the key concepts. In perceiving, children learn the possible relationships—support/nonsupport, moving/still, and unison, opposition, and sequence. Refining takes the children a step further in exploring the use of the body in each of these functions. Varying activities include changing supporting body parts and working with others. These relationships are further developed as children apply them in the learning and execution of motor skills.

Key Concepts and Activities

Perceiving—Level I

Recognizes that body parts support the body.

Recognizes that some body parts move while others remain still.

Recognizes that body parts may move in unison, opposition, or in sequence.

1. Moving in general space, on the signal become a statue. What body parts are your support? Move again. When I say "freeze" become a new statue supported on some other body parts.

Level	Key concept
Perceiving	Recognizes that body parts support the body
	Recognizes that some body parts move while others remain still
	Recognizes that body parts may move in unison, opposition, or in sequence
Refining	Uses varying numbers of body parts for support
	Changes stationary and moving body parts with the movement
	Move body parts in unison, opposition, or in sequence in different ways
Varying	Changes support from one body part to another
	Moves in unison, opposition, or in sequence with a partner
Applying	Motor skills may require the maintenance or change of supporting body parts
	Motor skill effectiveness is dependent on the movement of some body parts while others remain stationary
	Motor skill performance requires body parts to move in unison, opposition, and in sequence

FIGURE 12-5 Key concepts for relationship of body parts.

2. Think of movement you can do with your arms. Try it while standing. What body parts support the movement? Now try it while sitting. What body parts support the movement now? In what other positions can you perform the movement? What body parts did you use for support? Repeat with other movements.
3. With one body part stationary, move in your self space. Try moving again with another body part stationary. Increase the stationary parts to two or three. Try it again.
4. Move your body from the waist up. Waist down. Were you able to keep half of your body still as you moved the other half?
5. Begin moving one body part. Now add another part and move them in unison. What other two parts can you move together?
6. Can you move one body part one way and another in an opposite way? Which other body parts can you move in opposition?
7. Can you begin a movement with one body part and continue it with another, so that one part moves and then the other? This is called moving parts sequentially. Which other parts can you move sequentially?

Refining—Level II

Uses varying numbers of body parts for support.

Changes stationary and moving body parts with the movement.

Moves body parts in unison, opposition, or in sequence in different ways.

1. Support your body on four body parts. Can you use three parts for support? Try again. Which two body parts can you use for support? Which other two? Now try supporting the body on one part. What other parts could you use?
2. Try a movement keeping one body part stationary. Can you repeat the movement, keeping another part of the body still? Try it again.
3. Working with a partner, move and tell your partner which parts are moving and which are stationary. Repeat with a new activity with your eyes closed. Were you able to tell your partner which parts were moving and which were still without looking at them?
4. Balance a beanbag on some body part and keep it still. How many different ways can you move other body parts and still keep the beanbag on that part? Try another part for supporting the beanbag and move again.
5. Can you touch two body parts together? Three?
6. Can you make two body parts move away from each other and then meet? Three?
7. Can you flex a body part and extend another part nearby?
8. Begin a movement with one body part. Continue the movement with another.
9. Can you move one body part in one direction? Can you move another in the opposite direction at the same time?

Varying—Level III

Changes support from one body part to another.

Moves in unison, opposition, and in sequence with a partner.

1. On the signal, make a statue with your body parts. On the count of three, slowly change your supporting body parts. Hold. Repeat. Which body parts did you use? Which provided the best support?
2. With a partner, make a statue. On the count of 5, slowly change your supporting body parts. With what parts did you begin? To what parts did you change?
3. With a partner make a statue, with each person using different body parts for support. On the count of 5, gradually change supporting parts so that each person moves to the supporting parts of the other.
4. Move on three body parts. As you move, gradually change the body parts used for support. Which body parts did you begin with? Move to (varying)?
5. Working with a partner in self space, move body parts in unison. Try some others.
6. Now move in general space moving with your partner in unison. Repeat using movements in opposition and finally in sequence. What were some of the movements you did in unison? In opposition? In sequence?

Related Knowledge

Terminology: support, nonsupport, unison, sequence, opposition.

Evaluative Criteria

1. Can the child accurately respond to challenges that call for keeping some body parts still while others are moving?
2. Is the child comfortable using various body parts for support?
3. Can the child change supporting body parts smoothly?
4. Can the child respond to problems that call for body parts to move in unison, sequence, and opposition?
5. Can the child respond to movements of others by moving in unison, sequence, and opposition?

Understands the Use of the Body in Communication (Body Language)

This section is designed to help children learn to use their bodies to communicate ideas and to become aware of how we unconsciously communicate to others through posture, facial expression, body movements, and gestures. Figure 12-6 maps the important concepts to be developed. Perceiving involves recognition that we do communicate with our body actions. Refining looks at the different ways we communicate with others. Varying explores the different ways we can communicate. Application is an important aspect of creative movement as well as recognition of how body language communicates to others.

Key Concepts and Activities

Perceiving—Level I

Recognizes that one communicates to others through body movement.

1. Show us how you would feel if you were invited to a birthday party. If it were Halloween. If you heard a strange noise. If you had hurt your knee.
2. Pretend you are your favorite animal. How can you show it to others without making a sound?
3. With a partner, choose an emotion. Act it out. What did you do to show the feelings you had?
4. With a partner act out an emotion as your partner acts out the opposite. If one is happy, then the other is sad. What did you do to act out the emotion? How were actions different?
5. Show us how you sit in a chair, without a chair being there. What body movements conveyed the ideas?

Refining—Level II

Identifies ways we communicate to others—body posture, gestures, facial expression, and movement.

1. Moving in general space, can you move like a person who is happy? Sad? Tired? Energetic? Disgusted? Pleased? How did your movements change as you changed the idea you were communicating?
2. Repeat *No. 1* but use only facial expression to communicate. What did you do to communicate with your face?
3. Repeat again using only body posture. Describe the posture that communicated the idea.
4. Repeat again using gestures or other body movements. What movements conveyed the idea?
5. Working with a partner, act out an emotion as your partner acts out the same emotion with each acting it out in a different way?
6. Repeat *No. 5*, but one uses facial expressions, the other body movements.

Varying—Level III

Uses different kinds of movements to communicate to others.

1. Pretend you are a clown. What would you do to make others laugh? What kind of movements did you use?
2. Think of something you would like to share with your partner. How could you tell him or her without using words? What kind of movements did you use? Could you do it again with different movements?
3. Facing a partner, one is standing stationary, the other is trying to move past to the partner's left or right. Use body language. Try to fool them into thinking you will go to one side and then go to the other. Your partner will put up the arm of the side they think you will go to. What body language did you use to be successful?
4. With a partner, act out something you would like to share with the group with only facial expressions. Repeat using other body movements.
5. Act out a story using facial expression, gestures, and body movement. What movements best communicated the story?

Related Knowledge

The body may be used as an instrument for communicating ideas.

Sometimes we communicate feelings to other people that we do not really mean and that hurt their feelings. We must be more aware of how we use our body language.

Evaluative Criteria

1. Can the child use the body successfully to communicate ideas?
2. Is there a growing awareness of what we communicate to others through our actions?

Awareness of Muscle Tension and Relaxation

Perhaps the greatest contribution physical education can make is to develop an awareness of tension and the ability to perform conscious relaxation. This is an important aspect of movement, not only for the highly skilled but for everyone. The activities that follow are prerequisites for the application of the concept through the development of conscious relaxation found in Chapter 15. The key concepts are mapped in Figure 12-7. Perceiving activities develop an awareness and distinction between tension and relaxation. Refining activities develop understanding of how tension and relaxation play a role in skill performance and further develop awareness of tension and relaxation of body parts. Varying explores ways of moving that increase relaxation.

Perceiving	Recognizes that one communicates through body movement
Refining	Identifies ways we communicate to others—body posture, gestures, facial expression, and movement are used to communicate to others
Varying	Uses different kinds of movements to communicate to others
Applying	Through body actions we communicate moods and feelings, ideas and interpretations

FIGURE 12-6 Key concepts for understanding the use of the body in communication.

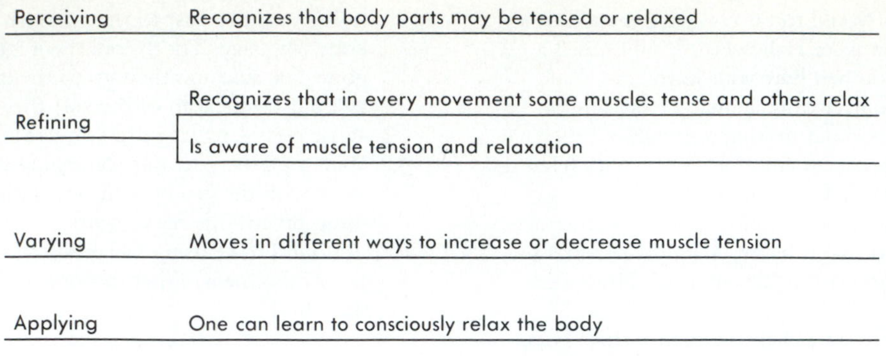
Perceiving
Recognizes that body parts may be tensed or relaxed
Refining
Recognizes that in every movement some muscles tense and others relax
Is aware of muscle tension and relaxation
Varying
Moves in different ways to increase or decrease muscle tension
Applying
One can learn to consciously relax the body

FIGURE 12-7 Key concepts for awareness of muscle tension and relaxation.

Key Concepts and Activities

Perceiving—Level I

Recognizes that body parts may be tensed or relaxed.

1. Alternately tense and relax the body parts called by the teacher. Could you feel the tension leaving the body part as you relaxed it?
2. Working with a partner, tell your partner which body parts to tense. Check to see that they are tense by touching. Touch other parts. Are they tense, too?
3. Stand on one leg. Can you feel tension in the muscles of your leg that is supporting you? What other body parts feel tense? relaxed?

Refining—Level II

Recognizes that in every movement some muscles tense and others relax.

Is aware of muscle tension and relaxation.

1. Balance on various body parts. Touch those parts where you feel tension.
2. (Use imagery.) Pretend you are floating on a cloud. Can you be a snowflake?
3. Pretend you are throwing a beanbag. What muscles are relaxed? Tense?

Varying—Level III

Moves in different ways to increase or decrease muscle tension.

1. Perform slow, relaxed movements. For example, how slowly can you move your arm?
2. Working with a partner, match the slow movement your partner makes.
3. Move in general space with as many muscles as tense as possible. Now with as many relaxed as possible. What muscles remained tense throughout your movements?

Related Knowledge

Terminology: relaxation, tension

Evaluative Criteria

1. Can the child identify body parts that are tense and relaxed?
2. Is the child able to tense those body parts called for by the leader while keeping all others relaxed?

SPACE

The understanding of space is another essential element in the study of human movement. Success in moving depends in part on the individual's ability to use space successfully, whether the task is creating a dance or out maneuvering one's opponent on the soccer field. Program content includes the study of:

Self space
General space
Level
Direction
Pathways
Range

Each of these areas of study is broken down into several key concepts in the following material.

Self Space

Self space, or personal space, is the immediate area surrounding a person, including the space within the natural body extensions. Children must have an understanding of their own space if they are to work effectively with others in their spaces. Beginning learning experiences help the child define the concept and recognize that each has a self space. Refinement includes recognition and respect for the self space of others, gaining an understanding that self space moves with us wherever we go, and that personal responsibility involves finding one's own self space in general space when working in physical education. In varying, children explore moving in a variety of ways as well as recognition that working with objects increases the space needed. In addition children learn that the available space they can have as their self space is limited by the general space available. In applying self space, children will learn to move in relation to others and adjust self space to the space available and the task requirements. Figure 12-8 maps the key concepts for the study of self space.

Perceiving	Defines self space as the space one occupies within one's normal extensions
	Recognizes that each person has a self space
Refining	Understands that a person's self space varies with the individual's size and length of limbs
	Recognizes that a person's self space moves wherever the individual moves
	Respects the self space of others
Varying	Moves in a variety of ways in self space
	Recognizes that the space a person may have for self space decreases as the space available decreases and increases as the space available increases
	Recognizes that moving with an object increases one's self space
Applying	Works independently in self space and in general space
	Moves in relation to others' and own self space
	Adjusts self space for the space available and the task requirements

FIGURE 12-8 Key concepts for self space.

Exploring the size of self space.

Key Concepts and Activities

The children each have their own space in the physical education area.

Perceiving—Level I

Defines self space or personal space as the space one occupies within one's normal body extensions.

Recognizes that each person has a self, or personal, space.

1. Reach out with your arms. How far can you reach while you are standing in one spot? As far as you can reach, that is your self space.
2. How wide is the space? How high does it go? How low does it go? Can you touch all parts of your self space? In front of you? Behind you? To the sides?
3. Take one body part and trace the outline of your self space in the air. How wide was it? How high? Can you touch all parts of your self space with a body part other

than your hand? Which ones did you use? Did you use your feet? Your elbow? Your knee?

4. How can you move your body parts to take up as much space as possible? As little space as possible?
5. In partners, take turns showing each other your self space. How high does it extend? How wide?
6. On the signal we will move in general space. Move with your partner, but without touching. Stop. Define your self space. Is it within your partner's self space? Repeat the activity. Can you move with your partner and yet remain outside your partner's self space?
7. With a partner, each move in general space, but away from each other. On each signal, move a little closer to your partner but not in your partner's self space. Could you maintain your self space and stay out of your partner's self space?

Refining—Level II

Understands that a person's self space varies with the size and length of limbs.

Recognizes that a person's self space moves wherever the individual moves.

Respects the self space of others.

Works independently in own self space in general space.

1. Working with a partner, define your self space while your partner outlines it with a rope. Repeat this process, changing roles and using another rope. What was the size of your self space? Was it the same size as your partner's? Others in the class?
2. Standing in a hoop, show me the size of your self space. Move out of the hoop and show me your self space. Do it again in the hoop and then out in a new space. Did you notice how your self space goes wherever you go?
3. Moving in general space, on the signal stop and show me your self space. Move again in a different way. Stop. Where is your self space?
4. Move your self space as close as possible to the child near you. How close can you get without touching (or getting into another person's self space)? How do you feel when you are very close? How did your self space change?
5. How close can you get your self space to everyone in the class without touching? Move your self space away. Now close again. Did you like getting your self space close? Why? Why not? (This could lead to a discussion of individual space needs. Sometimes we don't mind others close; sometimes we need more space.) When do you need more space? Less?
6. Moving in a circle, one behind the other, make your self space as large as possible. Now as small as possible. Be sure you do not touch one another. Keep moving in the circle. How does the circle change as your self space increases and decreases?
7. Working in partners, one moves around the other, but outside the partner's self space. How close could you move and not be in your partner's self space?

Varying—Level III

Moves in a variety of ways in self space.

Recognizes that the space a person may have for self space decreases as the space available decreases and increases as the space available increases.

Recognizes that moving with an object under control increases one's self space.

1. Move one body part. How many ways can you move it around you in your self space? Try another part. Can it move in the same way? Why? Why not?
2. Can you move more than one body part in your self space? Can you move two body parts in the same way? In different ways? How many can you move at the same time in your self space?
3. On the signal move in general space, staying in front of me and making your self space as large as possible. As I move, the space will either increase or decrease. As you move be sure you do not touch anyone. What happened to your self space as the general space increased? Decreased?
4. Move in general space with a hoop. Be sure you do not touch anyone. Stop. Can you touch anyone or their hoop? If so move away. Repeat. Did you need more space as you moved with the hoop? Move again, keeping the hoop under control and staying out of others' self space.
5. What are some things we can do with a ball? (Take a few suggestions.) Try as you move in general space. As long as the object is in control we will consider it to be in self space. If the ball gets away from you, it is no longer in your self space. Working with the ball can increase our self space. How did your self space increase? How much did it increase?
6. Moving in general space, make your self space as large as possible. How much space can you take up? Now move with as small a self space as possible. What movements were possible when we had a large self space? A small self space?
7. Mouse tails: children hold a rope behind them and move in the general space in ways called by the teacher or suggested by the children. As they move they must watch that their mouse tail does not touch the mouse tails of others. How did you move to avoid others' tails? What did you do to keep your tail from touching others?

Related Knowledge

Terminology: self space

Evaluative Criteria

1. Can the child demonstrate the dimensions of self space?
2. Can the child move in a variety of ways in self space?
3. Does the child demonstrate that the self space moves as he or she moves in general space?
4. Can the child demonstrate the potential changes in self space as general space decreases or increases?

General Space

General space is the space available for movement, which varies with the physical dimensions of the space and the number of individuals and/or objects sharing it. An understanding of general space is important in any movement situation, especially when the movement environment contains obstacles, equipment, and other individuals. Concepts are mapped in Figure 12-9. In perceiving activities, children explore the available space or designated space. In refining, children work to define general space more specifically, to use all the available space and to move in relation to others in the space. While varying, children work to develop a variety of possible movements as well as to work with others and objects. In applying, they learn to adjust their movements to a changing space and further develop the relationship of self space and general space.

Key Concepts and Activities

Perceiving—Level I

Defines general space as all the space available for movement.

Recognizes that general space may be defined by natural or prescribed boundaries.

1. After defining the area to be used, ask the children to move around the area just inside the boundary lines. As you move look at the space we have inside the boundaries. All of this space is our general space.
2. After defining the area to be used, ask the children to move to all parts of the available space without getting into another's self space. Have you been to the corners? Middle? Sides? How quickly can you stop on the signal (a good activity for establishing the signal for listening)? Be sure to move to all parts of the space. Did you move to empty spaces?

Moving in a variety of ways.

Perceiving	Defines general space as the space available for movement
	Recognizes that general space may be defined by natural or prescribed boundaries
Refining	Moves within the boundaries of general space
	Uses all the space available
	Avoids others and objects while moving in general space
Varying	Moves with others in general space
	Moves with objects in general space
	Moves in a variety of ways in general space
	Varies movements in general space as the space changes size and shape
	Moves in varying relationships with others and objects as one moves in general space
Applying	Moves to an open space in general space
	Opens and closes spaces as the situation demands

FIGURE 12-9 Key concepts for general space.

3. Imagine you are a paintbrush. Paint the general space your favorite color. Did you miss any places?
4. (Mark small, medium, and large circles on the playing surface, one for each child. Have the children choose a circle and move within its general space.) How many different ways can you move? Now move to a new circle of a different size. Repeat the activity. Change circles again. Repeat the activity. Did you move the same ways in each space? Why? Why not? Which ways did you like best in each size circle?
5. Moving with a partner, one leads, the other follows. Move to all parts of the general space. Change leaders. To what parts of the general space do you have yet to move to cover all the space?

Refining—Level II

Moves within the boundaries of general space.
Uses all the space available.
Avoids others and objects while moving in general space.

1. Using a general space of different shapes such as a square, rectangle, circle, or triangle, move within the confines of the shape. Which shapes were the most restrictive? Which shape did you like best? Why?
2. In partners, the children define their general spaces with ropes, cones, etc. They then move in the general spaces they have created. Repeat changing the boundaries of your general space. Did you cover all of the general space? Which spaces offered the most challenge for moving?
3. Moving in general space, on the signal stop. Point to a part of general space where you haven't been. Move to that place and keep moving. Stop. Repeat the activity a few more times. Have you been to all of the space?
4. (Holding the outside edges of a parachute, the children are numbered off by threes. As their number is called, the children move under the chute, covering as much space as possible before it comes down.) Which ways did you move? Which worked best to cover as much space as possible and avoid the self space of others?
5. (Half the children or hoops or other objects are scattered throughout the area as obstacles. The remaining children move in the space available.) How did you move in general space? How did your movements change as you moved around the obstacles? Did you look for the empty spaces? Were you able to move without touching the other children and the obstacles? (Increase the number of obstacles or decrease the available space and repeat.)

Varying—Level III

Moves with others in general space.
Moves with objects in general space.
Moves in a variety of ways in general space.
Varies movements as the space increases or decreases.
Recognizes that when we move in general space our self space goes with us.
Moves in varying relationships with others and objects as one moves in general space.

1. We are going to move in general space in as many different ways as we can. Each time I give the signal, change the way you move. What were some of the ways you chose to move? Can you move on one foot? Two feet? Hands and feet? Which ways of moving did you like best? Why?
2. Execute a movement as you remain in your own space. Now, do the same movement while moving in general space. Repeat. What were some of the movements you tried? Which movements were you able to do exactly the same while standing and while moving? What kind of movements required you to add other movements so you could move in general space? Which movements did you like best? Why?
3. (Alternately increase and decrease available space as children continuously move in general space.) Were you able to continue moving and keep within the boundaries of the general space? How did you change you movements as the space got smaller? Larger? Did your self space change? How? Were empty spaces harder or easier to find as the space got smaller? Larger?
4. (Mark a grid on the floor. Have the children explore the space available in each area marked off in the grid.) How did you move? How did the space available affect the way you moved?
5. Pass a ball around a circle of four to five persons. Increase and decrease the diameter of the circle. What did you have to do to get the ball to the others in the circle as the general space of the circle became larger? Smaller?
6. Working with a partner, follow the leader as you move in general space. Use as much space as you can. Did you move to the corners? Middle? Sides? The leader must always look for the empty spaces. Were you able to follow your leader and keep your self space away from the self space of others?
7. Change the size of your self space as you move through general space. What happens to the general space when we all make our self space as large as possible? Small? Tall? Short? Wide? Narrow?
8. (Make a circle on the floor with a 10- to 12-foot rope for each eight to ten children. All the children put one body part inside the circle, then two parts, three parts, their whole bodies, without touching the rope or each other.) How many parts could you all get in the circle? Make the circle smaller and repeat. Which parts did you choose that enabled the group to get as many parts in the general space of the circle as possible?
9. (Repeat any of the activities described under general space with the children using hand apparatus, such as a ball or hoop.) What did you do to keep the hoop or ball under control? (Emphasize control and a variety of ways of using the piece of equipment while moving in general space.)

Related Knowledge

Terminology: general space, boundaries, empty space

Evaluative Criteria

1. Does the child stay within the designated area (demonstrates the dimensions of general space)?

2. Can the child move with control in a variety of ways in general space alone or with others and/or objects?
3. Can the child demonstrate an understanding of how movements change as general space increases or decreases?
4. Does the child move to an open space when moving in general space with others and obstacles?

Level

Level is height in space: low, medium, and high. The high level may be defined as above the shoulders, the medium level between the shoulders and hips, and the low level below the hips. Level may also be defined at the articulations of body segments. For instance, raising the arm above the shoulder puts it in its high level, whereas lowering it to the side puts it in its low level. The key concepts for level are mapped in Figure 12-10. In perceiving activities children define where the levels begin and end. Refining activities include moving in space or body parts at each of the three levels. Varying enables the children to explore moving in a variety of ways at each level, moving objects at each level, moving body parts at more than one level, and moving the body from one level to another. In applying the concept, children learn to change level as the task requires and to move objects at an appropriate level.

Key Concepts and Activities

Perceiving—Level I

Recognizes level as height in space.
Identifies the three levels—high, medium, and low.

1. Body parts above your shoulders are in your high level. What body parts are in that level? Move a body part in the high level. Try another.
2. Body parts between your shoulders and hips are in the

Leading with different body parts.

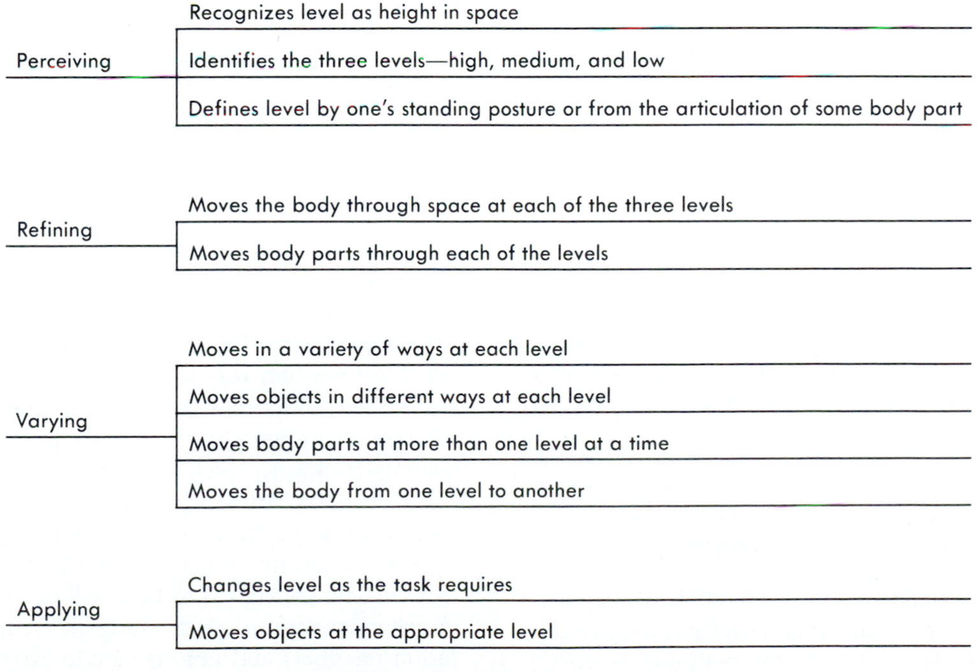
Perceiving
Recognizes level as height in space
Identifies the three levels—high, medium, and low
Defines level by one's standing posture or from the articulation of some body part
Refining
Moves the body through space at each of the three levels
Moves body parts through each of the levels
Varying
Moves in a variety of ways at each level
Moves objects in different ways at each level
Moves body parts at more than one level at a time
Moves the body from one level to another
Applying
Changes level as the task requires
Moves objects at the appropriate level

FIGURE 12-10 Key concepts for level.

medium level. On the signal move a body part in the medium level. What parts did you move?

3. Body parts below your hips are in the low level. Move a body part at the low level. Which one did you move? Can you move another?
4. Explore all the high level of your self space with your hand or another body part. Now the medium level. Now the low level. How far out did the levels extend?
5. Level can also be defined by where body parts are attached. If we move a part above its attachment it is in its high level; if we move it below its attachment it is in its low level. Where is the high level for your arm? The low level? Try another body part. Show me its high level, its low level, its medium level.
6. Move around the gymnasium in general space. On the signal, assume a shape with as many parts in the ______ level as possible. Repeat with other levels.

Refining—Level II

Moves body parts in each of the levels.

Moves the body through space at each of the three levels.

1. Move a body part at the ______ level. Name it as it moves. What other body parts can you move at that level? Move another body part at that level. Try another level and repeat several times.
2. Move a body part at the ______ level. Add another part moving. Keep adding parts until all parts at that level are moving.
3. Put all body parts in the low level. Now move one part to the medium level. Another. Can you put one in the high level as well?
4. Moving in self space, alternately move one body part from one level to another (arm medium to high, leg low to medium, etc.) Which levels were more challenging in moving body parts?
5. Repeat *No. 4*, moving in general space. What movements did you use to move body parts from one level to another?

Varying—Level III

Moves in a variety of ways at each level.

Moves objects in different ways at each level.

Moves body parts at more than one level at a time.

Moves the body from one level to another.

1. Move a body part at the ______ level. What other ways can you move it at that level? How many different ways can you move it at that level? Repeat with another body part.
2. Move a body part at the ______ level. On the signal move it to another level. Repeat with several other body parts. Were you able to move it in the same way at each of the other levels? If you changed movements why did you change?
3. Can you move a body part at one level? Add another at a different level. Now add a third part at the last level at the same time. Repeat moving two body parts at each level. What different ways did you move at each level?
4. Moving in general space, continue moving on the signal but changing level. What ways can you move at each level? Can you move the same way at two or all three levels?
5. Working with a partner and a ball, what skills can you display at each level? Can you move the ball as you move through general space at the high level? The medium level? The low level?
6. Working with a partner and a ball, what do you do to make the ball change levels? Can you move the ball from the high to the medium to the low level? Medium to high to low? Low to high to medium?
7. With the apparatus, how many ways can you move at the low level? Medium level? High level?
8. With a partner move in general space. On the signal stop and make a shape in two different levels. Move again, but moving in the levels chosen. Repeat several times changing level each time. What levels challenged you the most in thinking of shapes to make or ways to move?

Related Knowledge

Terminology: level

Evaluative Criteria

1. Does the child understand that there are three levels in space and know where each begins and ends?
2. Can the child move in a variety of ways at one, two, or all three levels at a time?
3. Can the child change level smoothly and efficiently?

Direction

There are six directions: forward, backward, right, left, up, and down. Direction is defined by which body surface is leading in the movement. Important concepts are outlined in Figure 12-11. In perceiving activities children become aware of the six directions in which one might move in space. Young children may have some difficulties with left and right. The term sideways may be substituted for these directions. Putting a left and right hand print on the wall may help children distinguish left from right. Having children hold their hands up with the thumb perpendicular to the fingers so that the left hand forms an "L" is another way to help children determine which hand is left. In refining, they explore leading the direction of movement with various body parts, conditions for moving backward safely, and the directional movements of body parts. In varying activities children develop a variety of movements in each direction, moving with objects in various directions, and moving in relation to others. The concept direction will be applied in any directional change in performing skills, in moving in relation to others and objects, and in responding to directional changes determined by phrasing in dance.

Level	Key concept
Perceiving	Recognizes the six directions in space—forward, backward, right, left, up, and, down
Refining	Identifies body surfaces that naturally lead as one moves in each direction
	Identifies other body parts that could lead in each direction
	Moves body parts in any direction
	Changes direction smoothly
	Moves backward by bending slightly forward at the hips to maintain balance
Varying	Moves in a variety of ways in each direction
	Moves with objects in each direction
	Moves in the same or in opposite directions while moving with others
Applying	Changes direction in performing skills
	Changes direction in relation to others or objects
	Responds to directional changes to musical phrasing in dance

FIGURE 12-11 Key concepts for direction.

Key Concepts and Activities

Perceiving—Level I

Recognizes the six directions in space—forward, backward, right, left, up, and down.

1. Move forward in the general space. In what other directions could we move? Let's all move in the ________ direction.
2. Begin moving in general space, in a forward direction. On the signal change directions. What directions did you choose? Which did you like best? Why?
3. In partners, one is the leader who tells the other in what direction to move. Repeat with mover's eyes closed.
4. While sitting in self space, move your fingers in a forward direction on the floor. Can you move them backward? What other directions can you move them? Repeat with another body part.

Refining—Level II

Identifies body surfaces that naturally lead as one moves in each direction.
Identifies other body parts that could lead movement in each direction.
Moves body parts in any direction.
Changes directions smoothly.
Moves backward by bending slightly forward at the hips to maintain balance.

1. Scattered in general space, let's see how many different directions you can move. Pretend there is a string attached to your nose and let it pull you through space. In what direction did you move? What part of your body usually leads when you move forward? Repeat with the children selecting body parts to attach the string to. What body parts lead when you move backward? Right? Left? Up? Down? Move the string and lead the movement with a different body part. How do you adjust your body position for the new lead?
2. Standing in a space away from others, move one body part in any direction. Move it in another direction. Can you move more than one part in the same direction?
3. Select three points in the room. Move to each, changing direction as you move from one to the next. Repeat. This time move in a different direction to each point. Which body parts led? Can you change leads and not direction as you move from one point to the next?
4. Move in general space to the right. On the signal stop. Move a body part in the same direction. What body part did you move? What other direction might we try to move in general space and then with a different body part? (Try some of their suggestions.)
5. Move one body part in a forward direction. Can you move one part in one direction while you move another in another direction? Keep adding body parts, each moving in a different direction.
6. In partners, one is the leader and suggests which body parts to move and in what direction to move.
7. Move in any direction in general space. On the signal "change" change direction. How did you get ready for the change of direction?
8. When we move backward sometimes we do not feel balanced. Moving in control how can we adjust our body position to feel comfortable? Move backward. Stop. What did you do to move in a more controlled manner? Move backward again, bending slightly forward at the waist.

Varying—Level III

Moves in a variety of ways in each direction.
Moves with objects in each direction.
Moves in the same or in opposite directions while moving with others.

1. Select a direction in which you will move. On the signal continue in that direction but change the way you move. What changes did you make? Which did you like best? Now try a new direction. Which ways of moving were easiest? Most difficult? In which direction(s) could you move in the most ways? Why?
2. Moving in general space, change the direction and movement on the signal. Which did you like best? Least? Why?
3. Stand on a line on the floor. Can you move down the line and change direction without losing your balance? Remember, do not look at your feet but at a spot out in front of you. Which directions were easiest and most difficult in staying on the line? Now try it on the balance beam.
4. Moving on lines painted on the floor, change directions and movements each time you move to a new line. Were you able to stay on the lines as you moved from line to line and changed direction?
5. With a partner, follow the leader, changing direction as you move through space. Was it easy to follow your partner's direction and avoid others? What adjustments did you have to make?
6. Working with a partner, change movement and direction while following your partner. Which movements were most difficult in following your partner and watching out for others?
7. Facing your partner, move in the same direction he or she moves. Were you able to do it? Which directions were most difficult? Now move in the opposite direction. Were any directions easier?
8. Use any of these challenges and change direction as you move through space while controlling a hoop, ball, or other object. In which directions did you have the best control? How did you move with the object in each direction? What did you need to do to change direction with the object?

Related Knowledge

Terminology: direction, forward, backward, right, left, up, down

Evaluative Criteria

1. Can the student move in all six directions with appropriate body parts leading?
2. Does the child move in a variety of ways in all directions alone, with others, and/or with objects?
3. Can the child control movement while changing direction alone or in relation to others or objects?

Pathways

Pathways are the lines of movement in space: straight, curved, or combinations of both. Key concepts are mapped in Figure 12-12. In perceiving the children define the possible pathways they might move in space. In refining, the children gain an understanding that the available pathways are determined by the placement of objects and other persons in space. They also learn to recognize pathways in the air as well as on the floor. In varying, children explore moving in a variety of ways alone, with others, or with objects. The application of the concept involves creating and closing pathways as needed and moving in the desired path in games and other activities.

Key Concepts and Activities

Perceiving—Level I

Defines pathway as the line of movement in space.
Identifies straight, curved, and combinations of straight and/or curved pathways in space.

1. Find a spot in the room. Move to that spot in a straight line. You have just moved in a straight pathway. Now move back to your starting place in a curved line. You have moved in a curved pathway.
2. Move in general space in a long straight line. Now on the signal move in a straight line but change your straight line each time I say "change." Did you move in a zigzag or some other combination of straight lines? Repeat moving in a large curved line and then in smaller curved lines.
3. Working in partners, one partner tells the other which type of pathway to move in. In what pathways were you directed to move?
4. Think of letters of the alphabet. Can you write the first letter of your name on the floor as you walk in general space? What pathways did you use? Make a letter that is made up of straight lines only. Which did you do? Now try a letter with only curved lines. Try a letter that is made up of curved and straight lines.
5. Working with a partner, place three cones in their own general space. Move in your space in as many different pathways as you can. What pathways did you use? Move the cones, and repeat. How did the placement of the cones affect the pathways you traveled? One of the partners moves to the self space of another group. Did you move in different pathways than the original partners? Which pathways did you find?

Refining—Level II

Recognizes that objects and other persons affect the pathways that are available in space.
Moves body parts as well as the whole body in various pathways.
Creates pathways with objects that may be followed.
Changes pathways smoothly.

1. Find two points in the room. Begin at one and move to the next. How many different pathways could you use? Can you move from one to the other in straight lines only? Combinations of straight lines? Curved lines only? Combinations of curved lines? Combinations of curved and straight lines?
2. (Place many objects as obstacles scattered on the floor.

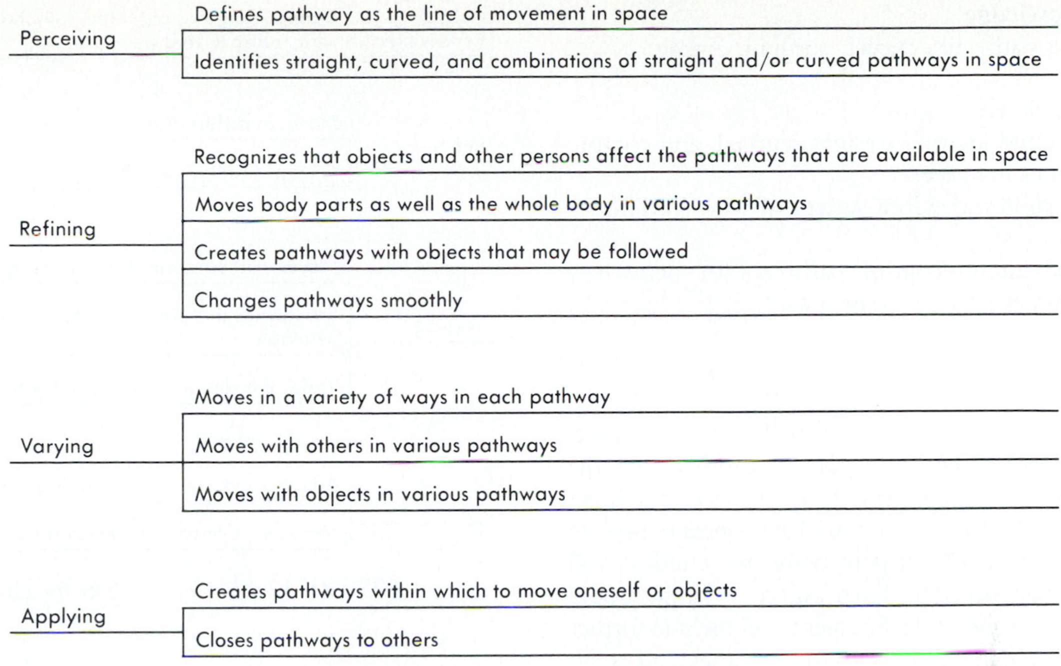
Perceiving
Defines pathway as the line of movement in space
Identifies straight, curved, and combinations of straight and/or curved pathways in space
Refining
Recognizes that objects and other persons affect the pathways that are available in space
Moves body parts as well as the whole body in various pathways
Creates pathways with objects that may be followed
Changes pathways smoothly
Varying
Moves in a variety of ways in each pathway
Moves with others in various pathways
Moves with objects in various pathways
Applying
Creates pathways within which to move oneself or objects
Closes pathways to others

FIGURE 12-12 Key concepts for pathways.

Children move throughout the space, finding available pathways.) Describe the pathways you followed. Were they straight lines? Curved lines? Combinations?

3. Trace a pathway in the air with your hand. Now follow that same pathway on the floor. Did you use straight lines? Curved? Combinations?
4. (Each individual has a long rope with which to create a design on the floor and then traces the design by moving along its path.) How many different ways can you move along the pathway you have created? Can you change your movement when you come to a change in the pathway? Move around the room to the pathways your classmates have made. Trace them, moving in a different way along each path. Were any ways of moving more difficult than others? Did you have any favorite paths?
5. (Each child has a piece of paper and a pencil or crayon. Each draws an interesting design on the paper with a continuous line. After drawing the design, each draws it on the floor by walking in general space.) How large can you make your design on the floor? How small? Trade designs with someone near you. Draw that design on the floor. How would you describe the design you just made (for example, a combination of curved lines)?

Varying—Level III

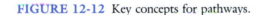

Moves in a variety of ways in each pathway.
Moves with others in various pathways.
Moves with objects in various pathways.

1. Follow the leader with a partner who is moving through space in various pathways. Call out the pathway in which you are moving as you follow your partner.
2. Repeat No. 1 but this time move in a different way as you follow your partner's path.
3. With a partner select two points in the room to which you will move. One moves in one path, the other in another. What paths did you choose? Where did they take you as you moved from one spot to the other?
4. Working with a partner, decide who is the writer and who is the pencil; the writer stands behind the pencil with hands on the pencil's hips or shoulders. The eyes of the pencil are closed. The writer moves the pencil to make a letter on the floor. The pencil attempts to guess the letter.
5. Working with a partner, each draw a design on a piece of paper. Take turns telling each other how to move as you trace the design on the floor. Did your partner suggest some ways of moving that were difficult to do? Why?
6. In partners, follow the leader. On the signal, break to an open space, moving in a new pathway. Find someone who is moving in the same types of path and follow them.
7. In groups of three, one rolls a hoop. When it stops each follows its path but moves in a different way. Describe the path. What way did you move?
8. (With the children in groups of four or five, one is a plane, one a control tower operator, and the others obstacles. With eyes closed, the plane attempts to follow the control tower operator's instructions in moving through the open paths.) Which instructions were helpful? Which were not?
9. (With the children in groups of three or four, one person is given a piece of paper with a design on it. That person must communicate the design to the group without showing it to them.) Did everyone have the same idea about what was being said? How could the design be explained more simply?

Related Knowledge
Terminology: pathways, curves, straight, zigzag

Evaluative Criteria
1. Can the child identify straight, curved, and combination lines in space?
2. Can the child move in a variety of ways in different pathways?
3. Do the children recognize pathways for themselves and others as they move in space?

Range

Range includes the relationship of the body to self-space, the relationship of one body part to another, and the relationship of body parts to objects in space: big/little, tall/short, wide/narrow, near/far. Key concepts may be found in Figure 12-13. In perceiving, the children will define the ranges possible. Each aspect of range should be developed separately. Refinement will include further development of their understanding of range and activities requiring a smooth change in the range of movement. Varying includes moving in a variety of ways with others and objects, and the relationship of range to space available. Application will involve adjusting movements to range in performing skills and in moving in relation to others.

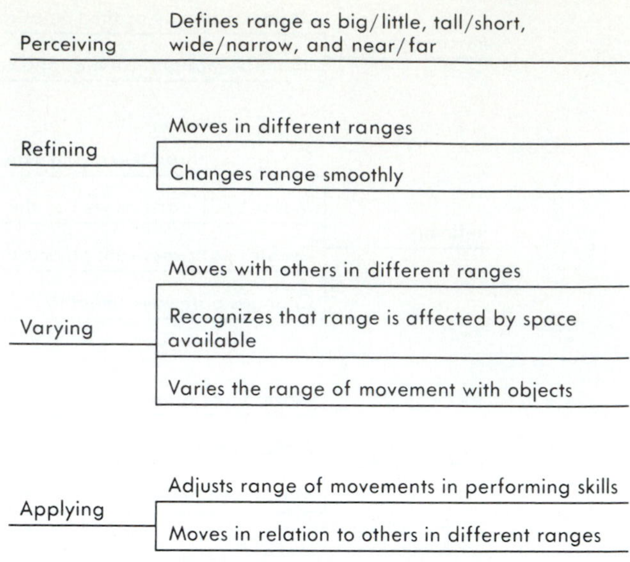

Perceiving
Defines range as big/little, tall/short, wide/narrow, and near/far
Refining
Moves in different ranges
Changes range smoothly
Varying
Moves with others in different ranges
Recognizes that range is affected by space available
Varies the range of movement with objects
Applying
Adjusts range of movements in performing skills
Moves in relation to others in different ranges

FIGURE 12-13 Key concepts for range.

Key Concepts and Activities
Perceiving—Level I
Defines range as near/far, large/small, tall/short, wide/narrow.

1. In your own space, make the largest body shape you can. Now the smallest. Repeat. This time see if you can smoothly change your large shape to the smallest possible.
2. Make a wide shape. Now a narrow one.
3. Make a tall shape. Now a short one.
4. Find a point in the room. Move as close to it as possible. Now as far away as possible.
5. Move two body parts as close together as possible. Now far away. Can you move them any farther?
6. Working in partners one performs a nonlocomotor movement, the partner calls out the range. What ranges did your partner use? Can you think of any others?

Refining—Level II
Move in different ranges.
Changes range smoothly.

1. Make a large shape. As I count to 5 gradually change it to a small shape. Repeat.
2. On the count of 3, move your hand as far away from your body as possible. Now near. Move any two body parts far away from each other as I count to 3. Now close together. What parts did you use? How far away could you get them?
3. Repeat No. *1* again with tall/short and wide/narrow.
4. The teacher calls a range; the children move in the opposite range. Repeat with other dimensions of range.
5. Move on a line on the floor (narrow range). Can you make wide movements with other parts of the body as you move on the line?

Varying—Level III
Moves with others in different ranges.
Recognizes that range is affected by space available.
Recognizes how movements change as range changes.
Varies the range of movement with objects.

1. Working with a partner and a ball, stand as close to your partner as you can without touching. Throw the ball so that your partner can catch it. Now gradually move farther apart, going only as far as you and your partner can still throw and catch the ball successfully. How did your movements change as you moved farther apart?
2. Moving in general space, make a body shape as wide as possible. Keep moving as the space gets smaller. How close together could you be and still keep the wide shape? As the space gets smaller and smaller, adjust your shape so you can continue to move without touching. What happens to your possible range as the space gets smaller?
3. Working with a partner, get as near to each other as possible. Now as far away as possible. Increase the size of the groups, adding one person at a time until you have everyone in the class in one group. Why was it easier to work with one partner as opposed to the larger group? How did the possible range change as the group got bigger?
4. Working with a partner, execute a movement while your partner copies it but changes the range of movement. Which types of movements were most difficult to change the range? Which were easiest? Why?

5. Working in groups of three or four, pretend you are cheerleaders. Make up a cheer. After doing it successfully, change its range. Do it with moves as big as possible. With moves as small as possible.
6. Working with a partner make a shape within a particular range (large). On the count of 5, change it to the opposite range (small). Repeat changing range each time.

Related Knowledge

Terminology: range, near, far, wide, narrow, tall, short, large, small

Evaluative Criteria

1. Can the child demonstrate the dimensions of range?
2. Can the child understand the relationship of range to the amount of space available?
3. Does the child control the range of movement of body parts?

QUALITIES OF MOVEMENT

Along with developing an understanding of the body and its movement potential and moving in space, children need to experience other factors that affect movement. Many of these qualities of movement require the application of mechanical principles. In the objectives that follow—for balance, force, time, and flow—important mechanical principles are included in the related knowledge.

Balance

All movement through space is the result of moving off balance and then regaining balance again. Because body parts may be used in various ways in shifting from balance to off balance and back again, it is important for children to experience many different kinds of balance challenges that enhance their understanding of principles concerned with this important movement quality. **Dynamic balance** (balance while moving) and **static balance** (stationary balance) should both be studied. Figure 12-14 maps the key concepts for balance. In perceiving, children learn that moving in space requires alternately losing and regaining balance and the difference between static and dynamic balance. In refining, children explore different balance positions on one or more body parts, learning to adjust the base of support to improve balance. In varying they explore balancing objects and balancing with objects and others. The application of this concept is important in the performance of motor skills as well as in adjusting body position in performing various individual or partner balance activities.

Key Concepts and Activities

Perceiving—Level I

Recognizes that movements in space require alternately moving off and on balance.

Differentiates between dynamic and static balance.

1. Standing in general space, gradually lean forward. Do you feel you are losing your balance? Keep leaning and as you continue to lose your balance take a step forward to regain your balance. Repeat several times. What did you do to regain your balance?
2. Move on hands and feet in general space. As you begin to move feel your body losing balance. Can you regain your balance by stepping forward with a hand or foot? Maintaining your balance while moving is called dynamic balance.

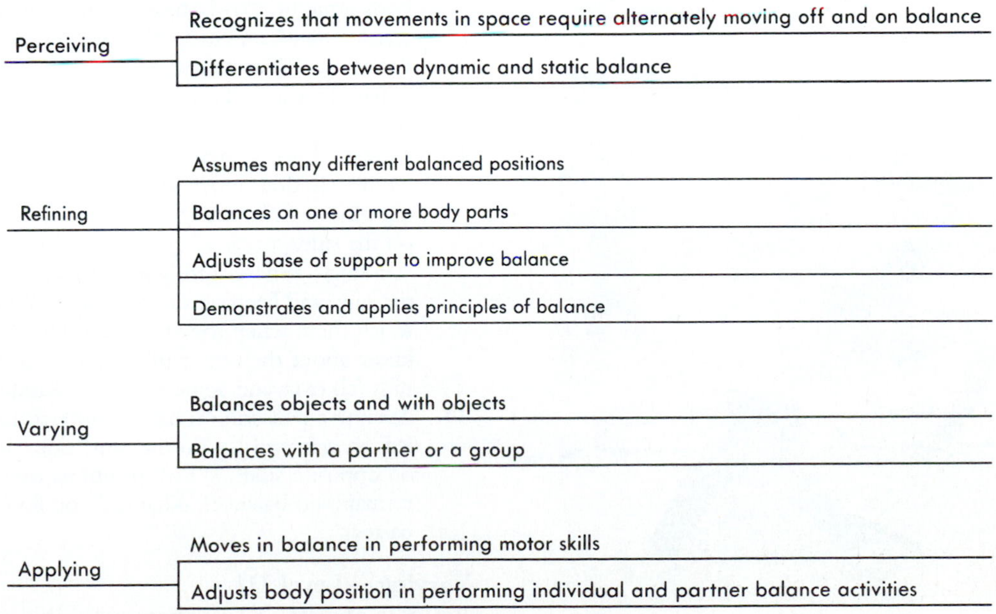

Perceiving	Recognizes that movements in space require alternately moving off and on balance
	Differentiates between dynamic and static balance
Refining	Assumes many different balanced positions
	Balances on one or more body parts
	Adjusts base of support to improve balance
	Demonstrates and applies principles of balance
Varying	Balances objects and with objects
	Balances with a partner or a group
Applying	Moves in balance in performing motor skills
	Adjusts body position in performing individual and partner balance activities

FIGURE 12-14 Key concepts for balance.

3. Moving in space, on the signal assume a balanced shape and hold it. Balance while we are still is called static balance. Now slowly move your body parts off balance and move again. Try another balanced position this time. Repeat. What position of body parts enabled you to keep your balance easily?
4. Moving in general space, on the signal stop in a balanced position. Slowly change the position of movable body parts but maintain balance. What body parts did you use? How did you move them to keep balanced?
5. Move on a line. Try moving in different ways, keeping your balance. Stop and assume a balanced position. Move again. Stop and balance in a new way. How did you keep your balance when you were moving (your dynamic balance)? When you were still (your static balance)?
6. Move in general space and stop in different positions. Hold for a count of 10. Which could you hold? Which were most difficult? Why? Describe your position when you were balanced. Off balance.

Refining—Level II

Assumes many different balanced positions.
Balances on one or more body parts.
Adjusts base of support to improve balance.
Demonstrates and applies principles of balance.

1. Balance on two (three, four) different body parts. Can you lose your balance and then regain balance on the same two (three, four) body parts? On different parts?
2. Balance on four body parts. Find a new balance position on three body parts. Now two, now one. What positions enabled you to balance most easily? Why? The body parts we balance on form our **base of support.**

Balance on three body parts.

3. Find a balanced shape on several body parts. Now decrease it by one. Now add two other body parts. What happened to your balance? What was the most stable base of support? Why?
4. Working with a partner, have the partner tell you on which body parts to balance; i.e., can you balance on one foot and one hand? Which body parts were most difficult to use in balancing?
5. (Have the children use different locomotor movements and move in general space.) On the signal stop in a balanced position. Vary the speed of movement. What positions helped you maintain your balance best on stopping? Try different ways of stopping. What did you do with your legs and feet? Your arms?
6. Put a number of objects scattered in the general space, such as bowling pins, cones, beanbags, etc. The children move in general space trying to touch as many objects as possible without knocking them down. Those that fall over remain down. What objects were more easily knocked over? Why? The part of the object resting on the floor is called the base of support. Describe the base of support for those objects which were harder to touch and keep standing. What positions should help us to keep our balance?
7. Stand with your feet close together. Lean forward. Keep leaning until you lose your balance but do not fall down. Repeat the activity but this time put your feet apart with one foot in front of the other. Repeat trying several other positions. In which position was it more difficult to lose your balance? What does this tell you about your base of support?
8. On the signal make a shape. Describe it. Are you on or off balance? What is your base of support? How does your balance change as you make your base bigger? Smaller?
9. The lower abdominal region of the body is the location of the weight center of the body or the **center of gravity.** While standing in self space, keeping your upper body straight, slowly move your center of gravity forward. What happened? Now move it to the side. Now backward. What happened as you moved your center of gravity forward? To the side? Behind your base of support?
10. (Scatter bowling pins in the general area.) On the signal the children move in the space touching the bowling pins at different spots—on top, low to the floor, on the sides, neck, etc.—while trying to keep them standing.) Where were you most successful in touching the pins and keeping them upright? Where did you touch them when they fell over? Think about what you know about the center of gravity. Explain why some pins fell over and some remained standing.
11. Assume a position on hands and feet. Lift an arm, a leg, an arm and leg on the same side, an arm and leg on opposite sides. Which positions were most difficult to maintain balance? What did you do to maintain your balance?

Varying—Level III

Balances objects and balances with objects.
Balances with a partner or a group.

1. (Make available a variety of equipment such as beanbags, balls of various sizes and composition, hoops, and wands. The children select a piece of equipment and balance it on various body parts.) What did you do to balance the object on big body parts? Small body parts? Take a different piece of equipment and repeat. What objects were easiest to balance? Why? What body parts offered the best balance points?
2. With a partner, balance an object between you. How did you work together to accomplish the task?
3. Move and stop with your feet close together. Were you balanced? Have the children explore different stopping positions—side stride, forward stride, legs straight, legs flexed, arms at side, arms out to side, etc. What positions helped you balance? Which did not?
4. Working in partners, one assumes a balanced position on one, two, or three body parts; and the partners gently try to push them off balance. What positions or bases of support enabled you to maintain your balance as your partner gently pushed you?
5. In groups of three make a balanced shape with all three touching. What is your base of support? Repeat making a shape with only three body parts forming the base of support. What other balanced shapes can you make on the number of body parts you choose?
6. With a partner on opposite ends of a line or low balance beam, move toward each other. When you meet see if you can pass one another without stepping off the line or beam? What did you do to work together to keep both of you on the line or beam?
7. Walk on a line holding an object such as a weighted jug. How did you adjust your position to stay on the line? What does that tell you about carrying objects and your center of gravity?

Related Knowledge*

1. Every object has a center of gravity about which the body weight in all directions is balanced.
2. A body is balanced when its center of gravity is over its base of support.
3. The nearer to the center of the base the **line of gravity** falls, the more stable the body.
4. The larger the base, the more stable the body.
5. The lower the center of gravity, the more stable the body.
6. The base should be enlarged in the direction of the moving or opposing force to allow for a decided shift of the center of gravity without the line of gravity falling outside the base.
7. Whenever one body part moves away from the line of gravity in one direction, the center of gravity shifts in that direction. If this shift puts the center of gravity beyond the base, another body part must move in the opposite direction to bring the center of gravity back over the base or balance is lost.
8. External weights added to the body become part of the total body weight and affect the location of the center of gravity, displacing it in the direction of the added weight.
9. In supporting an object, to keep the center of gravity over the base, the person's body shifts away from the object.
10. The closer to the center of gravity the weight is held, the less it changes the location of the center of gravity and the less effort is needed to hold it.

*From Broer M and Zernicke R: *Efficiency of human movement,* ed 4, New York, 1973, Holt, Rinehart & Winston.

Evaluative Criteria

Can the child adjust body positions to maintain balance in a variety of balance situations?

Force

Force is the energy required to move an object or individual. As the body or an object is moved, it is acted on by a force initiated through muscle contraction. To stop the movement, the force must be absorbed by the same body parts or others. As children master movement skills, their ability to use them effectively in various situations depends partially on their ability to control the force created and to absorb the force appropriately. Figure 12-15 maps the key concepts for force. In perceiving children

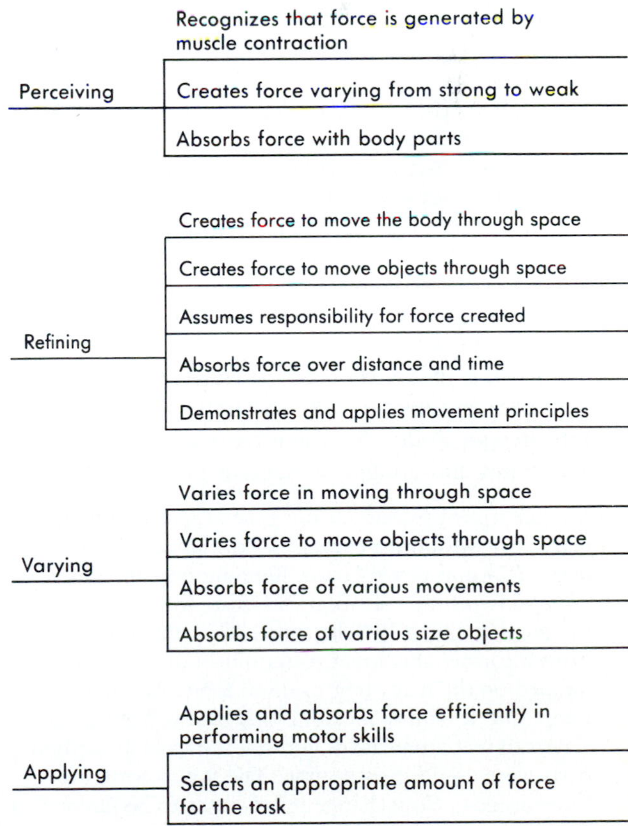
Recognizes that force is generated by muscle contraction
Perceiving
Creates force varying from strong to weak
Absorbs force with body parts
Creates force to move the body through space
Creates force to move objects through space
Assumes responsibility for force created
Refining
Absorbs force over distance and time
Demonstrates and applies movement principles
Varies force in moving through space
Varies force to move objects through space
Varying
Absorbs force of various movements
Absorbs force of various size objects
Applies and absorbs force efficiently in performing motor skills
Applying
Selects an appropriate amount of force for the task

FIGURE 12-15 Key concepts for force.

learn that muscle contraction creates force and that force may vary from very strong to very weak. In addition they learn about the use of the body to absorb the force of body movement or objects. In refining, children further develop the concept in creating force to move the body and objects and to assume responsibility for the force they create. Absorption of force is further developed as children learn to use body parts to absorb varying degrees of force. In varying, children explore creating force and absorbing force in different movements of the body and with objects. The application of this concept will be used in efficient skill performance and the selection of an appropriate amount of force for the task at hand.

Key Concepts and Activities: Creating Force

Perceiving—Level I

Recognizes that force is generated by muscle contraction. Creates force varying from strong to weak.

1. Use a little force, just enough to get you moving. Now increase the force so that you move strongly. Reduce the amount of force again until you are barely moving. Describe your movements to someone close to you. How did the movements change as you became stronger? Weaker? What did your muscles do that enabled you to move?
2. Move strongly and make a loud noise. Can you move strongly and yet be quiet?
3. Explore moving strongly as you move in general space. How many ways can you move? Now try moving weakly. What were the differences? How did it feel?
4. Move a body part strongly. Can you move another part strongly?
5. Move a body part strongly. Can you move another body part weakly at the same time?
6. Move a body part strongly. Now can you move the same body part weakly? How did the movements differ?
7. Repeat activities Nos. *4, 5,* and *6* with a partner watching. What did you see? Describe what the body parts looked like as they moved strongly and weakly.

Refining—Level II

Creates force to move the body through space.
Creates force to move objects through space.
Assumes responsibility for force created.
Demonstrates and applies movement principles.

1. (Scatter some obstacles in the general space, varying in height but within the capacity of the students to jump over.) Move in general space jumping over the obstacles. How did you use your body to create the force needed to complete the task? What body parts did you use?
2. With a partner and a mat, determine a distance to be jumped on the mat using medium force. Attempt the jump. Did it require medium force? How many different ways can you jump the designated distance? What body parts were used for each jump? Did you control the force needed? Now change the distance to be jumped, either farther or nearer. How did you change your jump to land within the designated target?
3. Creating force with balls: Working with a partner, practice throwing to one another. Use the fewest number of body parts for the task. Increase the distance. Change the size and/or the weight of the ball used. How did you change the throw as the distance (size or weight) of the object changed? Did you change the skill? Did you use more or fewer body parts? How did you consistently throw the ball with just enough force so that your partner could receive it easily?
4. Keeping your leg as straight as possible, kick the ball toward a wall. Now bend your leg as you kick the ball. Which resulted in the most force? Why?
5. Standing in self space, lift your arms up in front so that they are parallel to the floor. Hold the position. Why do your arms feel tired? What is the force that is making us want to put our arms down again?
6. Standing on a line throw the ball to targets at various heights on the wall, some low, medium, and high. Could you hit each of the targets? Why were some harder to hit?
7. Now try to throw as far as possible. Think about the targets on the wall. Try several throws. Throw high, medium, and low. Which throws went the farthest? What does this tell us about the release point?

Varying—Level III

Varies force in moving through space.
Varies force to move objects through space.

1. Explore creating force for starting. Use your feet in different ways. How did you use your legs to get a good start? Add the use of your arms. What do you do if you want to get a very fast start? Try starting using as few body parts as possible.
2. Explore the use of the body in creating force to move the body through space, executing various locomotor and nonlocomotor movements such as running or jumping. Which body parts did you use to create force when running? How did you use them differently when jumping?
3. Think of a task that someone in your household performs. Can you pretend to do it? How much force does it take to perform the task? Where did the force come from?
4. Throw the ball to a wall with just enough force for it to come back to you. Can you throw the ball so that it rebounds very close to the wall? To a line on the floor? How did you adjust your movements to accomplish the task?
5. Using some cardboard boxes, move the empty boxes across the floor. Can you do it with one hand? What muscles did you use? Gradually add objects to the boxes to make them heavier to move. How did you move the box as the box became heavier? Now imagine you have a refrigerator in the box. What muscles will you need to use to push it more easily?
6. With a paddle or the hand, hit the ball to the wall by dropping it and hitting it. Where did the ball go? Where did you apply the force to the ball? Repeat several times. Now see what happens when we apply force to the un-

derside of the ball. Where did it go? Now apply force to the right or left of the center of the ball. Closer to the top side of the ball. What was the result of applying force to different parts of the ball?

7. Throw a ball so that it bounces on the floor and rebounds to hit targets at different heights on the wall. Where did you bounce the ball to hit each target? Why?

Key Concepts and Activities: Absorbing Force

Perceiving—Level I

Absorbs force with body parts.

1. Moving in general space where a number of hoops have been placed on the floor, move quickly into a hoop on the signal, absorbing force a different way each time. What different ways did you absorb the force in stopping? Which ways seemed to work best? Why?
2. Working with a partner, throw a ball so that it lands on various body parts of your partner. Can you absorb the force so that the ball drops close to your body? What did you have to do as the ball made contact with your body? Which body parts were easiest to absorb the force? Why?
3. Throw a ball against various surfaces (wall, curtain, mat, etc.). Which surfaces absorbed the object more easily? What does that tell you about the use of your own body surfaces in absorbing a force?

Refining—Level II

Absorbs force over distance and time.
Demonstrates and applies movement principles.

1. Moving on mats, on the signal stop as quickly as you can. How did you absorb the force? What other body parts could you use to absorb the force?
2. Children practice throwing and catching balloons and balls varying in size and weight. What did you do to absorb the force of the lightest objects? The heavier balls? The largest? The smallest? How did you move to make the force easier to absorb?
3. Toss a ball up in the air. Position the hands for catching it at waist height, shoulder level, below the waist, above the head, close to the body, far away from the body, etc. Which positions were the most difficult for absorbing the force of the ball? The easiest?
4. Play catch with a partner. Catch the ball in different ways, such as with arms straight and stiff, relaxed, arms away from the body, close to the body. Which positions helped you more easily absorb the force of the ball?

Varying—Level III

Absorbs force of various movements.
Absorbs force of various sized objects.

1. Run as fast as you can in general space. On the signal, stop as quickly as you can. What did you do with your legs as you stopped? What was the position of your body?
2. Practice jumping from or over objects of varying heights. How did your landing change as the distance jumped became greater? Did you land softly?
3. Falling. (See the activities in Chapter 17.)
4. Practice catching a ball, pretending it is a fresh egg or a balloon filled with water. How did you catch it to prevent the egg or balloon from breaking?
5. While practicing catching, vary the distance between individuals and/or the size and weight of objects. How did your catching change in these different situations? How did you use your body to soften the force received?
6. Catch a Nerf ball on a paddle. What did you do to keep the ball from bouncing away? Try a tennis ball. Which was easier? Why?

Related Knowledge*

1. The greater the distance, and therefore the time over which momentum can be developed, the greater the momentum possible.
2. The longer the force applied to an object, the greater the force imparted.
3. The more contributing the muscles, the more force attainable.
4. The stronger the muscles called into play for a task demanding a good deal of force, the more efficient the action and the less the muscular strain.
5. The more fully a muscle is extended (lengthened), the greater the force it can exert.
6. Force should be applied as nearly as possible in the direction of the desired movement to use minimum energy.
7. If linear motion is desired, the more nearly through the center of gravity the force is applied, the less force required to move a given object.
8. The farther from the center of gravity the force is applied, the less energy necessary to rotate an object.
9. Spin is caused by an off-center application of force.
10. A ball with backspin stays in the air longer, or rises, its roll is shortened, and its bounce is higher and shorter than normal.
11. A ball with forward spin drops more quickly, its roll is lengthened, and its bounce is longer and lower than normal.
12. Ordinarily a ball will rebound at an angle equal to that at which it strikes a surface.
13. Three forces act on a projectile: gravity, air resistance, and the initial force that put it in motion.
14 The distance an object travels depends on its initial speed and the angle of release.
15. When air resistance is not a factor, the optimum angle of release for maximum distance is 45 degrees.
16. If the purpose of the projection is speed rather than distance, the angle should be as low as possible to carry the required distance.
17. Injury or rebound can be avoided by reducing the shock of the impact.
18. The force of impact depends on the weight of the moving object and the speed of the object.
19. The more gradual the reduction of this force, the less likely an injury or rebound.
20. Force should be absorbed gradually by increasing the distance and the time over which the force is absorbed.

*From Broer M and Zernicke R: *Efficiency of human movement,* ed 4, New York, 1973, Holt, Rinehart & Winston.

21. The nearer to the center of gravity the force is received and the more nearly the center of gravity is kept over the center of the base, the more readily balance will be maintained.

Evaluative Criteria

1. Can the child select an appropriate amount of force for the task?
2. Can the child adjust the body position to absorb the force of the body or object appropriately?

Time

In exploring time, children become aware of time in space as a measure of speed and in moving rhythmically to their own rhythm or an imposed rhythm. Key concepts may be found in Figure 12-16. In perceiving, children explore time from very fast to very slow and begin to develop an understanding of moving to an imposed rhythm. In refining, children move with control at varying speeds, changing speed smoothly and moving to an imposed rhythm. In varying, children move in a variety of ways with others and with equipment. The application of the concept of time is important in adjusting speed as a task requires, moving to an imposed rhythm; changing direction, pathway, or movements in dance or rhythmic gymnastics; or in timing movements in games and sports as the situation demands.

Key Concepts and Activities

Perceiving—Level I

Recognizes that speed varies from very fast to very slow. Recognizes that movement has a rhythm of its own or we move to an imposed rhythm.

1. Move a body part in self-space. Now change the speed that you move that part. Move it slowly. Now very slowly. Move it once again at a moderate speed. Now very fast. Repeat with other body parts. Were you able to control the movements? Could you move very slowly? Quickly?
2. Moving in general space, respond to the instructions of the teacher. Move very fast. Now slow down. Speed up to a medium speed. Now move very slowly. Speed up just a little. Now move faster. How did you adjust your speed to the instructions?
3. Move in general space as slowly as you can. Try moving another way but moving even more slowly. Another. Which was your favorite slow movement? Why?
4. Move a body part at the speed of your choice in self space. Now move in general space at that same speed. Change speed. Now stop. Move the body part at the new speed in self space. Repeat with moving different body parts and different movements in general space. How did you control your movement? What did you do to match the speed of the body parts and the locomotor movements?

Refining—Level II

Controls speed of movement.
Moves to an imposed rhythm.
Changes speed smoothly.

1. We are going to move in general space, changing speed. Select two points in the room. How quickly can you move from one to the other? How slowly? Can you pick a speed between? How did your movements change as you went faster? Slower? What determined how fast you could go as you moved in general space? Try it again, but this time move in a different way.
2. Begin moving slowly in general space. Each time I say "speed up," move a little faster. I will repeat this several times but I do not want you to achieve your top speed

Perceiving	Recognizes that speed varies from very fast to very slow
	Recognizes that movement has a rhythm of its own or we move to an imposed rhythm
Refining	Controls speed of movement
	Moves to an imposed rhythm
	Changes speed smoothly
Varying	Moves in a variety of ways varying speeds or to an imposed rhythm
	Moves with others varying speed or to an imposed rhythm
	Moves with equipment varying speed or to an imposed rhythm
Applying	Adjusts speed as the task requires
	Moves to an imposed rhythm changing direction, pathways, or movements in dance or rhythmic gymnastics

FIGURE 12-16 Key concepts for time.

until I tell you. How did you gradually increase your speed?

3. Reverse *No. 2.* Begin at full speed and gradually reduce speed until you are barely moving. Remember to control the change so you don't move the slowest speed until I give the signal. How did you gradually reduce your speed? Which was easier for you, increasing or decreasing speed? Why?
4. On the signal, move in general space at the speed of your choice. Watch me as I gradually reduce the space. Can you maintain your speed and avoid others as the space gets smaller? If not, find a speed that works in the new space. What did you discover as the space got smaller?
5. Responding to clapping, a drum beat, or recorded music, move in time to the beat. Begin clapping in time and then begin moving and clapping. Were you able to move in time to the clap? Faster? Slower?
6. Repeat *No. 5* but instead of clapping, match the beat with some other body movement. Then add moving in space.

Varying—Level III

Moves in a variety of ways at varying speeds or to an imposed rhythm.

Moves with others varying speed or to an imposed rhythm.

Moves with equipment varying speed or to an imposed rhythm.

1. Think of a skill that you know. How slowly can you do it? Move in slow motion. Think of another. Can you move even slower?
2. Moving to a count, can you make a balanced shape on three body parts within the count for four? Take all four counts to get there. Try another. Can you curl in four counts? Stretch? Roll?
3. Think up a shape you can make or a movement you can do to your own count. Plan how you will change on each beat. Do it as I count for you. Did it work out? How did you stay with your count.
4. Move in general space as quickly as you can. Can you move quickly with big steps? Small? Medium? Move slowly changing the size of your steps from very small to very big. Move at a speed in between. How did you control your movements?
5. With a partner, one moves in general space while the other claps the beat of the movement. Now move with your partner, matching their movement but without touching them. Repeat changing roles and movements several times. Which movements were easy to match? More difficult? Why?
6. As I beat out a rhythm, i.e., slow, slow, quick, quick, slow, etc., move to the rhythm, with locomotor or nonlocomotor movements. How did you change your movements to keep the rhythm?
7. Repeat *No. 6* but working with a partner. Each moves in a different way to the rhythm. Repeat several times. What movements did you choose? Which did you like best? Why?
8. Select a piece of equipment (e.g., a ball or hoop). On the signal move in general space keeping your piece of equipment under control. Now change the speed at which you move. Change speed several times on the signal. How did you maintain control of the ball or hoop as you moved faster or slower?
9. Move in general space tossing a ball up in the air and catching it. Change your speed. How did you change the toss to maintain control as you moved faster? Slower?
10. Repeat *No. 9,* but dribble with the hand or feet. How did the dribble change as you changed speed?
11. Move in general space in various pathways. Change speed. Repeat several times changing pathways. Which pathways were easiest to move in quickly? More slowly? Why?
12. Select a direction to move in general space. Change speed on the signal moving in the same direction. Remember to lean forward if you are moving backward. Change speed a few times. Repeat moving in another direction. In which direction could you most easily change and maintain various speeds? Why?

Related Knowledge

Speed is a measure of time. Speed varies from slow to fast. It is important to select a speed appropriate for the task—one that is not too fast or too slow.

One must always control speed while moving.

Rapid acceleration or deceleration may be important in some movement tasks.

Evaluative Criteria

1. Can the child move at varying speeds, ranging from very slow to very fast? (Young children often do not have a slow speed.)
2. Does the child control speed when moving in general space?
3. Can the child move to an imposed rhythm?
4. Can the child adjust movements to move with objects at various speeds?

Flow

Flow is the ability to combine movements smoothly. Flow may be **free,** in which there is a continuity of movement, or **bound,** characterized by the control or momentary restraint of movement in which the body may be stopped. In the early years, children have difficulty combining movements without a break in the action. As they mature in their motor development, children are able to combine movements in a flowing manner. Key concepts are mapped in Figure 12-17. In perceiving, children begin to move in simple combinations of movement. In refining, they will develop an ability to combine movements smoothly. During varying activities, they will explore combining movements with changes in direction, level, or pathway and also with a change of balance, force, or time. Application involves the smooth combining of movements under varying activity conditions.

Perceiving	Moves in simple combinations of skills
Refining	Combines movements smoothly
Varying	Combines movement with a change in level, direction, or pathway
	Combines movements with a change in balance, force, or time
Applying	Smoothly combines skills under varying activity conditions

FIGURE 12-17 Key concepts for flow.

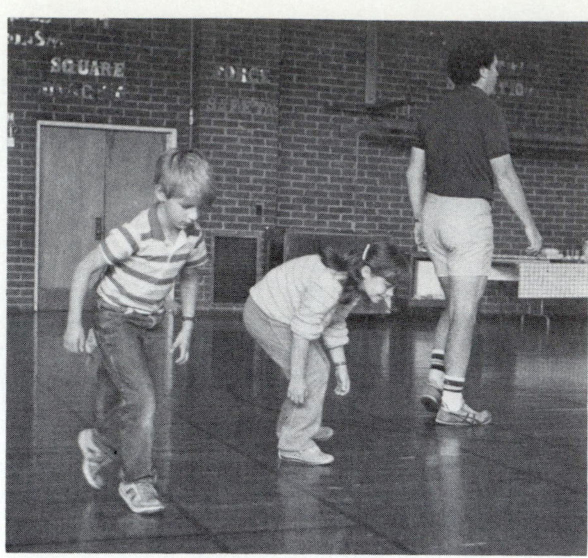

Moving softly.

Key Concepts and Activities

Perceiving—Level I

Moves in simple combinations of skills.

1. Move in general space performing locomotor or nonlocomotor movements on command from the teacher. As I tell you how to move, think about it first and gradually change your movement to the new movement. Which movements were easy to change? More difficult?

Refining—Level II

Combines movements smoothly.

1. Can you combine locomotor and nonlocomotor movements as you move in space? Begin from a stationary position, doing nonlocomotor movements. Now begin moving in general space, adding locomotor movements. If you wish, you may continue the nonlocomotor movements as you move, or you may stop them.
2. Combine two different movements into a movement sequence. Can you perform them smoothly? When the children are ready, increase the number of movements to be included or add changes in level, direction, force, or time.
3. Pretend you are water in the ocean. Gradually move toward the shore as a wave. Land on the shore and then move back to sea. Think about how you moved, how one movement led smoothly into the next.
4. Moving in general space, transfer body weight from one foot to the other thinking about how you are moving. Now move on hands and feet or other body parts. Keep a smooth, steady transfer of weight from one part to the next.

Varying—Level III

Combines movements with a change in level, direction, or pathway.

Combines movements with a change in balance, force, or time.

1. Move in general space. Can you keep moving as you change direction or pathway to avoid others? Can you change locomotor movements on the signal without stopping? How did you plan so that you could keep moving? Continue moving, changing speed, level, etc.
2. Move in general space to a drum. Gradually change the tempo so that the children speed up and slow down. Did you gradually adjust your movements for the change in time?
3. Assume a balanced shape. On the count of 3, gradually move to a new balanced position. Keep the movement going until you assume the new position.
4. Objects are scattered in the general space (e.g., beanbags, cones, hoops). The children move in the space among and over the objects without hesitation. How did you plan your movements as you approached the object to keep moving smoothly? What did you have to think about?
5. Move along a rope placed on the floor. Begin at one end and move to the other. Change movements along the way but keep the movement going. Have someone nearby watch you. Were you able to change movements smoothly without hesitation, keeping it going from one end to the other? Change roles.
6. Make up a movement sequence using three different movements. Repeat it several times, thinking about the smooth transition from one movement to the next.

Related Knowledge

Terminology: flow, free flow, bound flow, movement sequence

Evaluative Criteria

1. Can the child smoothly combine movements?
2. Can the child create a movement sequence?

SUMMARY

The movement content provides the basis for understanding human movement. Three general areas are explored: body awareness, space, and qualities of movement. Each represents a progression in learning from the first perceiving experiences to refining, varying, and finally to applying the concept in different movement situations.

Body awareness enhances the children's understanding of themselves as movers. Activities enrich their understanding of body parts, the movement potential of these body parts, and how the body parts move together to perform a variety of movement tasks. Other areas of study include the body as an instrument of communication and tension and conscious relaxation.

Space concepts are important to successful movement. In many individual and group activities in which there is competition between two or more individuals, success is most often achieved through the manipulation of available space. Topics of study include self space and general space, level, direction, pathway, and range of movement.

Qualities of movement include the creation, application, and absorption of force, balance, time, and flow. These elements are controlled by the individual, resulting in effective, efficient movements.

Because these concepts are important to all movement, study begins early in the elementary school experience. Once understood, they may be further developed through a variety of physical education activities.

REFERENCES AND RESOURCES

Auxter D and Pyfer J: *Principles and methods of adapted physical education and recreation,* ed 6, St Louis, 1989, Mosby–Year Book.

Broer M and Zernicke R: *Efficiency of human movement,* ed 4, New York, 1973, Holt, Rinehart & Winston.

Carr N, editor: *Basic stuff, series I and II,* Reston, Va, 1987, AAHPERD.

Cooper J et al: *Classroom & teaching skills: a handbook,* ed 4, Lexington, Mass, 1990, DC Heath.

Gilliom B: *Basic movement education for children: rationale and teaching units,* Reading, Mass, 1970, Addison-Wesley.

Laban R: *Mastery of movement,* ed 3 (revised by L Ullman), London, 1971, MacDonald & Evans.

Logsdon B et al: *Physical education for children: a focus on the teaching process,* ed 2, Philadelphia, 1984, Lea & Febiger.

Rasmus C and Fowler J, editors: *Movement activities for places and spaces,* Reston, Va, 1983, AAHPERD.

Riggs M, editor: *Movement education for preschool children,* Reston, Va, 1980, AAHPERD.

ANNOTATED READINGS

Barrett K: Phys ed is movement ed. In NASPE: *Echoes of influence for elementary school physical education,* Reston, Va, 1977, AAHPERD.

Discusses the movement content in elementary school physical education and provides examples of how the content is implemented.

Cunningham C: How we teach it: balance challenges. In NASPE: *Echoes of influence,* Reston, Va, 1977, AAHPERD.

Describes balance challenges on skates, stilts, and unicycles.

DeSorbe B.: How do you get the ball from here to there? *JOPER* 48(6):35, 1977.

Discusses using exploration and problem-solving techniques to teach children about angles and trajectories.

Elliot ME: Concept learning in elementary physical education, *Strategies* 3(3):8, 1990.

Discusses the teaching of concepts with an example for teaching the angle of release.

Kovar SK, Mathews HM, Ermler KL, Mehrhof JH: Feedback: how to teach how, *Strategies* 5(7):21, 1992.

Offers hints on teaching movement principles and giving appropriate learning cues.

McAleese WJ and Scantling E: Are you asking the right questions? *Strategies* 3(5):5, 1990.

Offers suggestions for asking questions using Bloom's taxonomy.

Ratliffe T: Using worksheets in physical education, *JOPERD* 53(7):47, 1982.

Looks at developing worksheets that reinforce classroom learning in reading and writing and that enhance understanding in physical education.

Sakola S: A K-6 progression built on organizing concepts, *JOPERD* 53(7):38, 1982.

Looks at developing skills through progressions that encourage transfer of learning and application of movement concepts.

CHAPTER 13

Fundamental Movement Skills

OBJECTIVES

After completing this chapter the student will be able to:

1. Explain the learning processes used in the development of fundamental movement skills
2. Describe concerns for the planning and conduct of activities to develop fundamental movements
3. Analyze the fundamental movements and identify mechanical principles involved in their execution
4. Describe the use of the movement content in the development and use of motor skills
5. Suggest activities for the development of fundamental movement

The development of motor skills is an important aspect of the elementary school physical education program. Beginning learning in physical education includes the further development of **locomotor movements** such as walk, run, **jump, hop,** and **leap;** body control skills of stopping, starting, dodging, and landing; and **nonlocomotor movements** of bend/stretch, push/pull, **swing/sway,** and **twist** and **turn.** Combinations of locomotor movements such as the **skip, gallop,** and **slide** are also taught. In addition, children learn manipulative skills including throwing, catching, bouncing, and striking with the hands and feet. Mastery of these fundamental movement skills included in this chapter is essential to future success in the development of sports or dance skills that may be used throughout one's lifetime.

MOTOR SKILL LEARNING

Motor skill learning results from careful consideration in the planning and conduct of learning experiences that challenge children at all levels of skill development. To meet the goal of physical education, we must develop skillful movers with the desire to use the motor skills learned and to develop new skills as they participate in physical activities throughout their lives. Motor skill practice should be purposeful. As a result of motor skill learning, students should accomplish the following:

1. Understand how the body is used to perform the skills.
2. Perform motor skills with good technique.
3. Adjust skills to changing activity conditions as they use the skills effectively in a variety of games, dance, and individual activities.

In these beginning experiences, the quality of performance is emphasized rather than the result, for example, how body parts are used in catching rather than whether the ball was consistently caught. A consistently successful performance will result once the technique has been mastered.

The physical education experience must challenge students at varying stages of learning, involving the students cognitively as well as in their motor performance. Children should be able to verbalize about their skill performance as well as perform well. In addition, movers must be able to adjust skill performance as activity conditions demand. In planning appropriate skill progressions, the teacher must look carefully at the movement content as it relates to motor skills development and their use and the processes of learning in which the children should be engaged.

Application of the Movement Content

The application of movement concepts is an important part of motor skill learning. In the beginning experiences, body awareness concepts are important as children begin to understand how body parts are used in the performance of skills. Identifying the body parts used, the movements they perform, and their relationships is important during these early experiences. Some quality of movement concepts, especially those of creating and absorbing force as well as balance, may also be incorporated in the beginning phases of learning. Tension/relaxation concepts also are important in skill performance, as children analyze the muscle groups used to create force while others are relaxed.

Once the children have developed some control of their movements in performing the skill, they are ready to use space and other quality of movement concepts. These concepts are essential to success in using skills efficiently and effectively in any number of different movement situations. For instance, children will be required to change speed, direction, range, and pathway as they move through general space. They also will need to create and absorb varying amounts of force as they perform locomotor, nonlocomotor, body control, and manipulative skills in different movement situations. The movement content important in motor skill development is found in each of the skill sections that follow in this chapter.

Learning Processes

The learning processes described in Chapter 3 are important in the development of motor skill progressions in physical education. As children learn to use motor skills, they move through learning processes that take them to higher levels of understanding and skill performance. It is important to match learning process with individual level of ability to maintain interest in learning motor skills. Children lose interest in working on motor skills when objectives and learning processes are not at an appropriate level of difficulty. The processes used in motor skill development are outlined in the box on pp. 194 and 195. In each of the processes:

- The students are given the important information and are challenged by the teacher, who raises questions during the practice.
- Cognitive understanding of motor skills and their use is developed.
- A greater level of understanding is achieved than in the previous process.
- More skillful movement results.
- The movement vocabulary is further developed and used by both the teacher and students to describe movements performed.
- Higher levels of analysis and problem solving are required than during the previous process.

In the initial phase of learning, perceiving, students learn generally what the skill is. The teacher introduces the skill, giving beginning information about the task. The teacher identifies the first one or two critical elements or teaching points important to skill performance. These are points introduced and emphasized during the activities that follow. Feedback is given exclusively on these points of emphasis. Experiences planned at the perceiving level may be characterized by exploration or guided discovery as well as direct teaching. The movement vocabulary is used as teachers relate the movements of body parts to body awareness and quality of movement concepts.

Examples of critical elements in perceiving activities include identifying and concentrating on the grip and overarm motion in an overarm throw, focusing on pushing the ball with the finger pads in dribbling, and running with the toes pointing straight ahead. Once the students have the rudimentary knowledge and skill, they are ready to move on to more information about the skill being learned.

In refining, the children are ready to receive more information about the technique, so more and finer critical elements or teaching points are identified. The refining process may take several lessons or even years to accomplish, depending on the complexity of the skill. The teacher gradually introduces additional points of emphasis as the children become ready and plans activities designed to emphasize these points of performance. Feedback is again directed to those points identified as the children practice the skill. The experiences conducted result in greater understanding of the technique as well as improved skill performance. This understanding should be apparent in the verbal responses of the children as well as in their skilled performance. In addition this knowledge should help children as they problem solve in the error analysis of their own or a peer's performance. The reciprocal style of teaching can be very valuable at this phase of learning. Examples of refining critical elements include emphasis on the side orientation and follow-through for the overhand throw, dribbling while keeping the ball low and eyes looking ahead, and swinging the arms in a forward/backward motion when running. Once the skill has been refined, the skill is habituated, resulting in a relatively smooth performance in which the child no longer must think about the critical elements in performing the skill.

In varying, the children are ready to modify skill performance to be successful under different conditions. The teacher identifies the movement concepts important for successful use of the skill. The teacher then structures the learning environment so that certain changes in performance are necessary. These conditions are carefully controlled by the teacher, who might, for example, alter the amount of space used, time, or size of equipment. The teacher should encourage thinking and discussion of the adjustments needed in performance in each variation included. Examples include changing the distance or height of targets in throwing overhand; changing hands, direction, or pathway when dribbling; and changing direction, speed, or pathway when running.

This phase of learning may be used before refining is

LEARNING PROCESSES AND MOTOR SKILL DEVELOPMENT

PERCEIVING

Description: Skill introduction
Beginning knowledge of the task
Identification of one to three critical elements

Student: Develops general understanding of skill
Verbalizes points of performance emphasized
Uses body awareness concepts
Performs skill at a beginning level

Teacher: Introduces the skill
Identifies the first points of emphasis
Conducts a variety of activities to develop beginning skill
Gives feedback stressing points of emphasis
Uses the movement vocabulary

Move on: Student is ready for more information about the skill

REFINING

Description: Greater understanding and more skillful movement
Identification of finer points of technique
Error analysis
Skill mastery and habituation

Student: Gradually receives finer points of emphasis
Uses body awareness and quality of movement concepts
Demonstrates verbally points of emphasis
Demonstrates improved skill performance
Analyzes own errors and offers suggestions for improvement

Teacher: Gradually adds finer points of emphasis as students are ready
Conducts a variety of activities designed to develop points of emphasis
Gives feedback exclusively on points of emphasis
Uses the movement vocabulary

Move on: Skill is refined
Students at a plateau

complete in complex skills. This approach may be needed to maintain interest in learning the skill, which is especially important when students have reached a plateau in learning and need more variety to maintain their interest in working on the skill.

In applying, the student is ready to use the skill effectively in an activity during which the situation may be continually changing, requiring any number or type of adjustments to successfully use the skill. While the same concepts may be used in the activity as those practiced in varying, the major difference is in decision making.

In varying, the teacher carefully controls the environmental conditions under which adjustment in skill performance is necessary. In applying, the student makes the decisions during active participation. The adjustments needed will not be under the direct control of the teacher. Before the students use the skill in the activity, however, the teacher analyzes the activity in which the skill will be used and determines how the concepts will be applied to the skill. The teacher breaks it down into its simplest components for practice before its use in the activity.

For instance, in the game, Barnyard Upset, which requires one-on-one competition in moving in general space against the farmer, the activity calls for moving while changing direction, pathway, and/or speed. In varying, the teacher might have the students move in general space changing direction, pathway, or speed on the signal. In applying, the teacher may structure a practice of one on one, similar to its use in the game, in which the child must change pathway, direction, or speed in moving in a space around an opponent. The practice at this simple level requires the student to decide which actions will be effective. As the students practice, the teacher focuses their attention on the changes they made to be successful, giving feedback about the use of the movement skill, raising questions, and providing further exploration of the movement possibilities.

Applying is a very important aspect of skill learning and especially in the effective use of skills. Through this process students should be encouraged to further develop their analytical skills. These skills are essential for a movement-educated person. Successful lifetime participation depends on these abilities.

LEARNING PROCESSES AND MOTOR SKILL DEVELOPMENT—cont'd

VARYING

Description: Modification in skill performance brought about by changes in the environment under the direct control of the teacher

Student: Ready to modify skill performance
Adjusts skill to conditions imposed by the teacher
Uses space concepts in adjusting skills
Uses quality of movement concepts in adjusting skills

Teacher: Identifies movement content important in using the skill
Structures learning activities to require use of movement concepts
Raises questions regarding use of movement concepts
Uses movement vocabulary

Move on: Students ready to use skills in activities

APPLYING

Description: Modifications in skills needed for success in a variety of physical education activities
Modifications occur in a changing environment not under direct control of teacher

Student: Practices use of movement concepts
Analyzes activity in reference to use of skill and concepts
Appropriately uses skills in the activity
Describes skill use using movement vocabulary

Teacher: Analyzes use of skills in specific activity
Plans and conducts practice activities to develop their use
Coaches students regarding use of skills and concepts in the activity
Uses movement vocabulary

Move on: Students ready to develop new skills

CREATING

Description: New skills or techniques needed to meet individual needs

Student: Understands and uses body awareness and quality of movement concepts
Develops new skills or techniques to meet individual needs in the activity

Teacher: Encourages individual variation in technique or development of new skills
Structures learning environment to enhance creativity

Creating is the highest learning process. Through this process skills new to physical education or unique to the individual emerge. Not all children or perhaps only a few will experience the actual creation of a new skill. Children need to be encouraged to develop new ways of doing things in physical education. Body movement tasks, the use of equipment, and new moves or transitional moves in gymnastics are some of the areas where new skills may be developed.

PLANNING AND CONDUCTING FUNDAMENTAL MOVEMENT EXPERIENCES

In planning learning experiences for children, the teacher responds to the following questions:

- What is the children's present skill level?
- What is the purpose of the skill practice?
- What level of mastery is desired?
- What kinds of activities move the student from present to desired levels of performance?

Mapping Skill Progressions

A concept map outlines the possibilities for developing the motor skill. The three general areas of the movement content are identified in the first headings. Each is then broken down into more specific concepts to be developed. This general map may be modified as the teacher selects those concepts that are most appropriate for the motor skill being developed. If the skill is new to the children, perhaps only the body awareness concepts will be developed. Concept maps also show progression in learning. Figure 13-1 is an example of a concept map for running.

The concept map might be further developed to identify specific outcomes desired for each concept. For instance, in Figure 13-1 the concept map develops a progression leading up to the use of running in games for a primary age class. In the perceiving and refining levels, the body awareness concepts of the use of body parts and the relationships of body parts might be developed with emphasis on looking up, for example, along with creating and absorbing force such as landing softly, under qualities of movement. At the varying level, children might work on changing speed, combining running with other move-

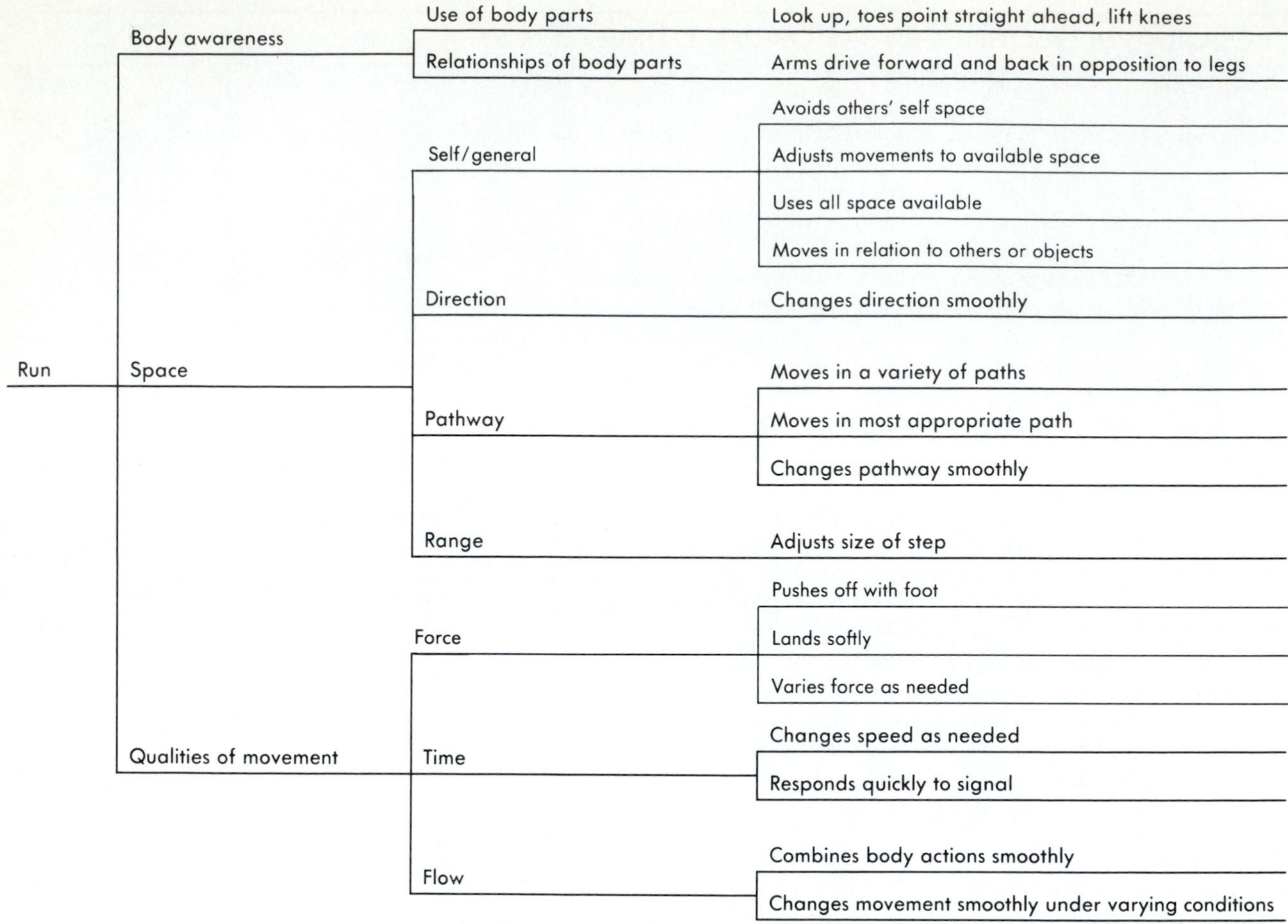

FIGURE 13-1 Concept map for running.

ments (flow) such as stopping and starting and moving in different directions and pathways. At the applying level we might add self space/general space concepts as well as changing pathways smoothly, moving in the most appropriate paths, or changing movements smoothly under various conditions. Activities would be developed to emphasize each of the points identified.

Conducting Learning Experiences

Learning motor skills requires carefully planned instruction, practice, and the early correction of errors. Children should understand the important aspects of each skill and the consequences of executing skills incorrectly. This approach will help them begin to analyze their own performance and adjust their body movements to perform various motor tasks. A part of the learning experience should involve the verbalization of the major aspects of the skill—how the body is used to accomplish the task. Without the basic understanding of how the skill should be executed, children who perform a skill well may have more difficulty in adjusting the skill to meet the new demands of various movement tasks and applying what they know about one skill to a similar skill. Children also learn the mechanical principles that apply in the execution of the movement skills. Once these principles are understood, the teacher should assist the children in applying them to new situations.

Beginning learning experiences should provide the children with an opportunity to explore the use of their bodies and various pieces of equipment. If guided properly, the children acquire a better understanding of the use of the body in performing skills and also the properties of the equipment they are using. As the children are working, the leader should use the movement vocabulary in raising questions. Learning experiences should encourage the children to use what they know about their potential body movement, space, and movement qualities.

Equipment used should be of an appropriate size and weight for elementary school children. As a part of the learning experience, children should be exposed to a variety of equipment to enable them to adjust their body movements as the equipment demands. A list of equipment for elementary school children is found in Appendix 1.

Activities for practicing skills should be arranged to encourage the use of the best possible techniques. For example, targets used for ball skills should be large enough and far enough away so that the children must execute the skill correctly to be successful.

To develop fundamental movements, children need the opportunity for maximum participation. In many activities all the children may be working simultaneously to perfect their skills. If equipment is being used, it may be necessary to use a station approach to learning, where a variety of activities and equipment is used, especially if there is not sufficient equipment for all to be engaged in the same activity at the same time.

In helping children correct errors in performance, the teacher should focus on one error at a time. The teacher must determine which error is most important to tackle first. Sometimes, correcting one error also corrects others. For example, getting a child to assume a side orientation to the target in throwing overhand will probably help correct problems of weight transfer and trunk rotation as well as throwing with the opposite foot forward.

Where possible the teacher should teach for transfer, relating the new skill to similarities in skills previously learned. Use of imagery also helps in motor skill learning. For instance having the children pretend that the ball is a water-filled balloon or an egg may help them absorb the force of the throw in catching.

Controlling one's movements for the safety of oneself and others is an important part of the learning experience. Taking responsibility for one's movement should always be encouraged.

The following sections include an analysis of a variety of movement skills that should be mastered during the elementary school years. Teaching suggestions and activities to aid in the development of these skills are included. Learning processes are identified. Some activities may be used for more than one process, depending on the emphasis of the teacher. For example, an activity may be used for refining in exploring the technique or varying in modifying the use of body parts to move in a variety of ways.

Developing Social Skills

The development of motor skills offers many opportunities for children to interact with one another socially. While many of the activities included in this chapter suggest individual exploration of various movements and their variations, the discussion and sharing of children's responses provide opportunities for children to contribute their ideas as well as listen to the ideas of others. Individual recognition and support of classmates are important parts of the socialization process in physical education. Some of the activities also call for working directly with a partner in different relationships, requiring the children to communicate what they are going to do and to modify their own movements to move with their partner. These activities elicit beginning cooperative efforts. In addition, the use of the reciprocal teaching style has the potential to help children assume responsibility for helping others and to develop communication and interpersonal skills.

Developing Health-Related Physical Fitness

Cardiorespiratory fitness blends well with the activities to develop motor skills, as maximum participation is provided and the children move vigorously to the challenges posed by the teacher. Flexibility is enhanced in many of the activities, especially the nonlocomotor movements, as children move in a variety of ways. Muscular strength and endurance may be developed as children explore locomotor movements—especially hopping, jumping, and leaping—and work with objects varying in size and weight while developing manipulative skills.

LOCOMOTOR SKILLS

The concept map in Figure 13-2 outlines possible concepts used in developing locomotor skills.

Walk

Although the walk is the locomotor movement attempted first by children and generally mastered by the time the children reach the elementary school, the technique continues to undergo refinement through the adolescent years.

The walk in a forward direction is executed by transferring the body weight from one foot to the other as the legs swing alternately in front of the body in an even rhythm. As the leg moves forward, balance is temporarily lost but is regained by the placement of the forward foot on the floor. Body weight is transferred from two feet to one foot, back to two feet, and then to the other foot. The foot placement begins with contact on the heel, moving to the outer edges of the foot, and finally toward the toes. One foot remains in contact with the floor at all times. As the forward heel touches the ground, the rear heel is lifted to begin the next leg swing. The toes point straight ahead, and placement of the feet forward is on either side of an imaginary line on the ground that bisects the body. The body is erect with the head up. The arms swing freely at the sides in a forward and backward direction in opposition to the leg movements. The walk may also be executed in a backward or sideways direction (Figure 13-3).

Mechanical Analysis

Balance

Walking is a matter of moving the body weight beyond the base of support and the line of gravity and regaining

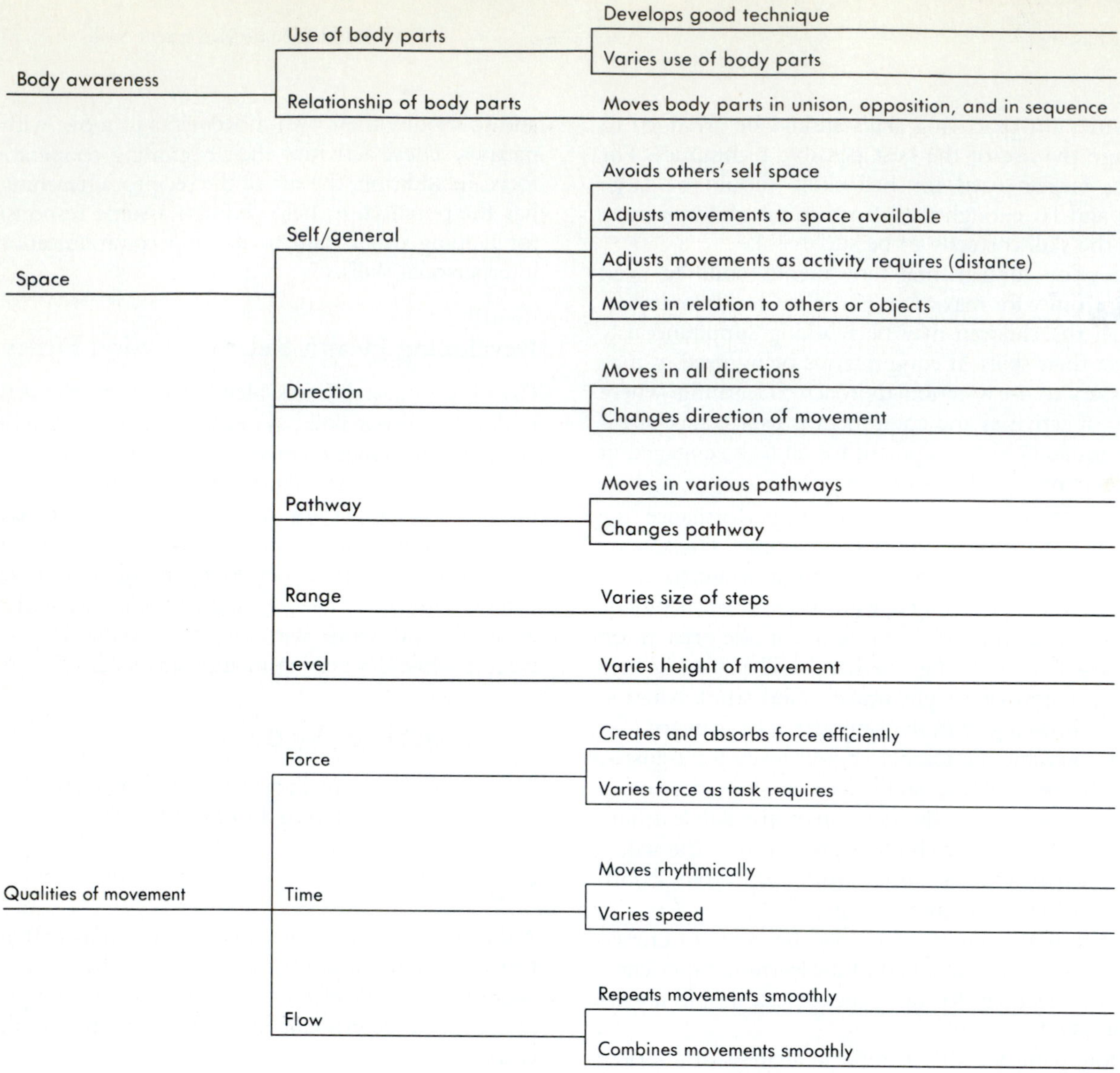

- Body awareness
  - Use of body parts
    - Develops good technique
    - Varies use of body parts
  - Relationship of body parts
    - Moves body parts in unison, opposition, and in sequence
- Space
  - Self/general
    - Avoids others' self space
    - Adjusts movements to space available
    - Adjusts movements as activity requires (distance)
    - Moves in relation to others or objects
  - Direction
    - Moves in all directions
    - Changes direction of movement
  - Pathway
    - Moves in various pathways
    - Changes pathway
  - Range
    - Varies size of steps
  - Level
    - Varies height of movement
- Qualities of movement
  - Force
    - Creates and absorbs force efficiently
    - Varies force as task requires
  - Time
    - Moves rhythmically
    - Varies speed
  - Flow
    - Repeats movements smoothly
    - Combines movements smoothly

FIGURE 13-2 Concept map for locomotor skills.

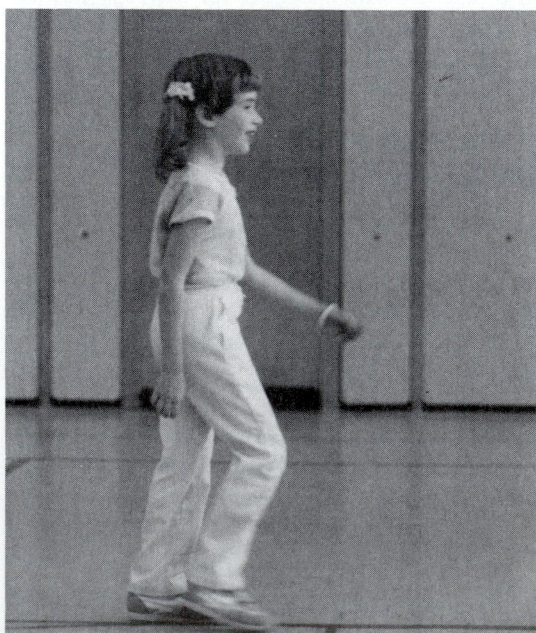

FIGURE 13-3 Evaluative criteria for the walk.
- Head is up, body erect.
- Leg swings forward.
- Arms swing in opposition to legs.
- Heel-to-toe placement of foot.
- Toes point straight ahead.

balance by stepping on the forward foot to bring the center of gravity back over the base of support. Because both feet are in contact with the ground for some time, stability is easily maintained.

Force

The action is begun with a diagonal push-off backward against the ground with the ball of one foot.

The push of the foot directs the force forward and upward through the center of the body weight.

The force is absorbed gradually as the weight is taken first on the heel, then on the outer edges of the foot, and finally on the toes.

Teaching Points

1. Keep the body erect, with the head up and the eyes facing forward.
2. Point the toes straight ahead.
3. Place the feet a comfortable distance apart.

Movement Concepts

Children should experience walking:

1. In general space, avoiding others and recognizing how walking changes with space available.
2. Forward, backward, and to the side and changing direction without hesitation.
3. In various pathways.
4. Changing the range of step.
5. At various speeds.
6. Varying the force used.
7. Changing the use of body parts to walk in different ways.
8. In relation to others or objects.

Activities

Because the walk is well established, activities in the elementary school focus on refining some aspects of the skill, but most of the activities involve varying.

1. Walk leaning forward. Toeing in. Toeing out. With wide steps. With narrow steps. (refining/varying)
2. Walk on your heels. On your toes. Flatfooted. (refining/varying)
3. Walk in general space controlling your movements to avoid contact with others. (varying)
4. Walk changing direction. In which directions is it easiest to walk? Hardest? Why? (varying)
5. Walk in a curved pathway. Straight lines. Or combinations of curves, straight lines, or both. (varying)
6. Walk changing the length of stride. Take big steps. Little steps. (varying)
7. Walk changing the speed of your walk. Can you walk faster? Slower? (varying)
8. Walk taking heavy steps. Soft steps. (varying)
9. Change the amount of space available. How does your walk change as the space gets larger? Smaller? (varying)
10. Walk like a clown. A happy person. A soldier. A sad person. An old person. A tired person. As if in a parade. (varying)
11. Walk as if you were walking on ice. In mud. On glue. (varying)
12. Walk with a partner. Now hold hands and walk again. Can you stay together? (varying)
13. Walk with a partner, standing behind one another. Face to face. (varying)
14. Walk with a partner, moving in step with that person. (varying)

Run

The mechanics of the run are similar to those of the walk. In the run, however, the speed of movement is faster, the stride is longer, the arms are used more purposefully to add power to the movement, and there is a time when the individual is air-borne.

The run is executed with the head up and the body leaning slightly forward. The support foot contacts the ground close to the body's center of gravity. At slow speeds initial contact is with the heel or the whole foot. At faster speeds the lateral border of the ball of the foot touches first. The foot placement is with the toes pointing straight ahead. On contact the bending of the knee and consequently the increased flexion in the ankle permit a greater thrust of the push-off foot. As the foot is placed on the ground, the push-off sends the body momentarily into the air as the opposite leg swings forward. As the leg reaches forward, the knee swings forward and upward as the lower leg flexes, bringing the heel close to the buttocks. The arms are bent at the elbows and move in opposition to the leg movements, helping to drive the body forward. The arm swing is in a forward/backward direction (Figure 13-4).

Mechanical Analysis

Force

Flexion of the knee and ankle on contact allows the leg muscles to extend more forcefully, thus creating greater force, which results in greater speed. The action of the arms adds to the movement by increasing the contributing muscles involved.

As the body moves forward on contact, the location of the center of gravity forward of the supporting foot permits a greater horizontal component and thus more thrust forward (horizontal) and less force upward (vertical). There is more of a vertical component than in the walk.

Teaching Points

1. Keep the head up and the eyes looking forward.
2. Swing the arms in a forward/backward direction.
3. Push-off with full leg extension to get the body into the air.
4. The foot lands softly on the running surface.
5. The length of stride is a comfortable distance.
6. Bring up the heel near the buttocks during the recovery phase.

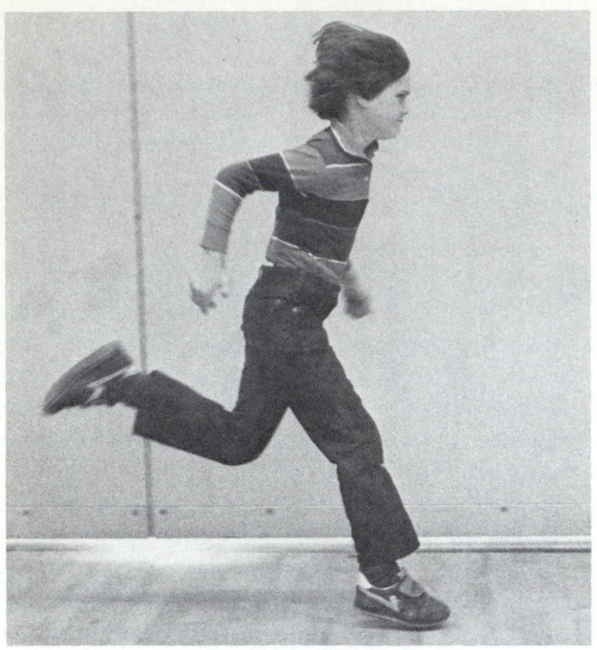

FIGURE 13-4 Evaluative criteria for the run.
- Head is up, body leans forward.
- Knee swings forward and upward with lower leg flexed.
- Arms drive in opposition to legs.
- Nonsupport phase with both feet off the ground.
- Foot contact under the center of gravity; toes point forward.

Movement Concepts

Children should experience running:

1. In general space avoiding contact with others and recognizing how running changes with the space available.
2. Forward, backward, and to the side and changing direction without hesitation.
3. In various pathways.
4. Changing the range of stride.
5. At various speeds.
6. Varying the force of the run.
7. Changing the use of body parts to run in different ways.
8. In relation to others or objects.
9. For time and distance.
10. Noticing how running changes for sprints and distance running.

Activities

1. Explore running leaning forward. Toeing in. Toeing out. With wide steps. With narrow steps. (refining/varying)
2. Explore running on your heels. On your toes. Flat footed. (refining/varying)
3. Run in place. Then run in general space controlling movements to avoid contact with others. (varying)
4. Run changing directions. Can you run forward? Backward? To the right? To the left? (varying)
5. Run in a straight line. Now a curved pathway. Can you combine a straight line and a curve as you run? (varying)
6. Run changing the length of stride. Take small steps. Take long steps. (varying)
7. Change the amount of space available. How does your running change as the space becomes smaller? Larger? (varying)
8. Run changing speed as you go. Can you run slower? Faster? (varying)
9. Run changing the speed of the arm movement. How does that affect your run? (varying)
10. Run with a partner. Hold hands and run again. Can you stay together? (varying)
11. Run with a partner, moving in step with that person. (varying)
12. Run with a partner, standing one behind the other. Now face to face (varying)
13. Run in a group, following one another. Can you set a pace where all can stay together? (varying)
14. Run in a group of four or five persons, one behind the other. As you run, the last person sprints to the head of the line. Repeat. (varying)
15. Run around obstacles in an obstacle course. (varying)
16. Run for a specified distance, such as a 30-yard dash. (applying)
17. Run for a long distance, such as once around the field. (applying)
18. Run a shuttle run. (applying)
19. Run for time. How far can you run in 10 seconds? (applying)
20. Run for a long time. Can you set a pace and continue to run for 3 minutes? (applying)

Jump

The jump has many variations, depending on the task to be accomplished. The take-off may be from one or both feet with the landing on two feet. The action may begin from a stationary position, or it may be preceded by a run or walk. The vertical jump and the horizontal jump for distance are described in this section. The standing and running long jump and the high jump are described in Chapter 18.

In preparation for the vertical jump, a deep crouch is taken by flexing the hips, knees, and ankles. As the jumping action begins, there is a forceful extension of the legs, and the arms move forward and upward to aid in the lift of the body. The body remains fully extended until the feet are ready to touch the floor on the landing. At that time flexion in the ankles, knees, and hips helps absorb the force for a soft landing.

If the purpose of the jump is to reach or touch an object high above the head, the reaching arm is extended well above the body and the other arm at the height of the jump (Figure 13-5). In the horizontal jump for distance, the jump is usually preceded by several running

- Flexion in hips, knees and ankles.

- Forceful extension of legs.
- Arms reach forward and upward.
- Body fully extended.

- Soft landing with flexion in ankles, knees, and hips.

FIGURE 13-5 Evaluative criteria for the vertical jump.

FIGURE 13-6 Evaluative criteria for the horizontal jump.
- Take off from one foot.
- Head is up.
- Knees, hips, and ankles flexed in flight.
- Arms at the sides and swing in direction of flight
- Knees, ankles, and hips flexed to absorb force in landing; arms bent at sides.

steps. The take-off is from one foot, with the landing on two feet.

Before the take-off, flexion in the hip, knee, and ankle allows for greater thrust to propel the body off the ground. The arms move in opposition to the legs during the approach and swing in the direction of the jump during the take-off. The head is up and the body is extended during the take-off and flight. On landing, both legs reach forward and the ankles, knees, and hips flex for a soft landing. The arms are bent and may be held out to the sides to aid in balance on landing. The feet are a comfortable width apart (Figure 13-6).

Mechanical Analysis

Force

Flexion in the hip, knee, and ankle permit the force to be applied over a greater distance.

The force is applied downward and backward and results in the body being propelled upward and forward in flight.

Through the flexion of ankles, knees, and hips, the force is absorbed in landing over a greater distance.

The arm action aids the jump in that more muscles are contributing to the effort.

Each force is applied at the optimum time when the preceding one has made its greatest contribution to the task.

Balance

In jumping for distance, the child's arms are positioned out to the sides of the body to add stability to the flight and landing.

Teaching Points

Vertical Jump

1. Drop to a deep crouch before the take-off.
2. Use the arms, timing them with the leg action, to aid the jump.
3. Reach to full body extension at the height of the jump.
4. Land softly by bending the knees.

Horizontal Jump for Distance

1. Take off from one foot.
2. Perform the approach and the take-off as one continuous action.
3. Swing the arms forward to aid in the jump and slightly to the side for balance.
4. Land softly by bending the knees.
5. Reach forward on landing.

Movement Concepts

Children should experience jumping:

1. In all directions.
2. Various heights.
3. Various distances.
4. Over objects.
5. Changing the use of body parts to jump in different ways.
6. Varying the approach used.
7. In various pathways.

Activities

1. Explore jumping from one foot or two feet and landing on one or two feet. (refining)
2. Explore jumping using the arms in different ways. (refining)
3. Vary the landings used: Land on one foot, make a four-point landing, land and roll, land with feet apart, land with feet close together, etc. (refining)
4. Jump varying the approach used. (refining)
5. Jump forward, backward, and to the side. (varying)
6. Jump varying the height jumped. (For jumping over objects a bamboo pole or jump rope may be held loosely by supports or children so that it falls if the jumper makes contact with it.) (varying)
7. Jump in and out of a hoop placed on the floor. (varying)
8. Jump over objects such as beanbags, benches, or boxes. (varying)
9. Jump a specified distance such as 3 feet. (varying)
10. Jump and vary the distance jumped. (varying)
11. Jump with a partner. Now hold hands and jump again. (varying)
12. Jump and turn in place. (varying)
13. Jump moving forward and turning while in flight. (varying)
14. Jump over a moving object. (varying)
15. Execute a series of jumps maintaining momentum. (varying)
16. Execute a series of jumps moving in a straight line. A zig-zag. A curved line. A circle. (varying)
17. Jump off an object such as a box or bench. (varying)
18. Jump onto an object such as a box or bench. (varying)
19. Jump and touch an object high overhead, or make a chalk mark on the wall at the height of the jump. (applying)

Hop

The hop requires good balance and sufficient leg strength to propel the body upward and forward from one leg. It is a push-off from one foot and a landing on the same foot. The nonsupporting leg is held up with the knee bent and usually with the foot held back. The body is erect. As the hop is initiated, flexion in the hip, knee, and ankle increases to permit greater force to overcome the body's inertia and project the body into the air. The arms are bent at the elbow and are out slightly from the body to aid in balance. The arms may be moved upward to help increase the height of the hop. The landing should be soft, with flexion in the ankle, knee, and hip to absorb the force. Contact with the ground begins with the forward part of the foot, shifting gradually to the ball of the foot and finally to the heel (Figure 13-7).

Children should be encouraged to develop hopping skills on both the right and left feet.

FIGURE 13-7 Evaluative criteria for the leap.
- Body is erect.
- Push-off with one foot.
- Use arms for balance.
- Land bending at the hip, knee and ankle.

Mechanical Analysis

Projectiles

The laws governing projectiles apply to the hop.

To increase vertical distance the angle of take-off should be as close to vertical as possible.

Balance

Because the support is on one leg only, holding the arms out to the sides improves balance.

Force

Flexion in the hip, knee, and ankle allows the leg muscles to extend more forcefully on the push-off.

Flexion at the hip, knee, and ankle on the landing permits the force to be absorbed more gradually.

Teaching Points

1. Bend knee, hip, and ankle to get a good push-off.
2. Use the arms to help propel the body upward.
3. Land softly by bending the knees.
4. Use the arms to the sides to maintain balance.
5. Establish a rhythm for hopping to hop several times in succession.

Movement Concepts

Children should experience hopping:

1. In general space avoiding contact with others.
2. In all directions.
3. In various pathways.
4. Changing the range of step.
5. Varying the height of the hop.
6. At various speeds.
7. Maintaining a steady rhythm to enable them to hop repeatedly on one foot.
8. Changing the use of body parts to hop in different ways.
9. In relation to others or objects.

Activities

1. Hop on one foot several times; then hop on the other foot the same number. Repeat several times. (refining)
2. Hop changing the position of your arms as you hop. Out to the sides. One forward and one backward. Close to your sides. Over your head. (refining/varying)
3. Hop landing softly. Land heavily. (refining/varying)
4. Hop in general space controlling movements to avoid contact with others. (varying)
5. Hop changing direction. In which direction was it easiest to hop? Most difficult? (varying)
6. Hop in a straight line. Now a curved line. Can you combine straight lines, curves, or both as you hop? (varying)
7. Hop changing the length of your hop. Take a short hop. Now a long hop. (varying)
8. Change the amount of space available. How does your hopping change as the space gets smaller? Larger? (varying)
9. Hop changing speed as you hop. Can you hop slower? Faster? (varying)
10. Hop over obstacles such as a rope or low balance beam. (varying)
11. Hop around obstacles scattered in the area. (varying)
12. Hop in place several times, and then hop in general space the same number of times. (varying)
13. Hop and turn in place. (varying)
14. Hop in and out of a hoop placed on the floor. (varying)
15. Execute a high hop. A low hop. (varying)
16. Perform a series of hops with each progressively higher than the hop before. (varying)
17. Hop with a partner. Now hold hands and hop again. Can you stay together? (varying)
18. Hop in step with a partner. (varying)
19. Hop with a partner, standing one behind the other. Now face to face. (varying)
20. Alternate soft and heavy landings. (varying)
21. Hop low. Hop high. Hop somewhere in between. (varying)
22. Combine a series of high, low, and medium hops. (varying)

Leap

The leap is similar to the run; however, there is a greater vertical component as the body moves through the air in the nonsupported phase of the skill. In the leap the body remains airborne much longer than in the run, with the objective being to cover a greater distance while moving through the air. The body is more fully extended than in the run as the performer reaches forward in the air.

• Head is up, body forward.
• Flexion in hip, knee and ankle to thrust on take-off.

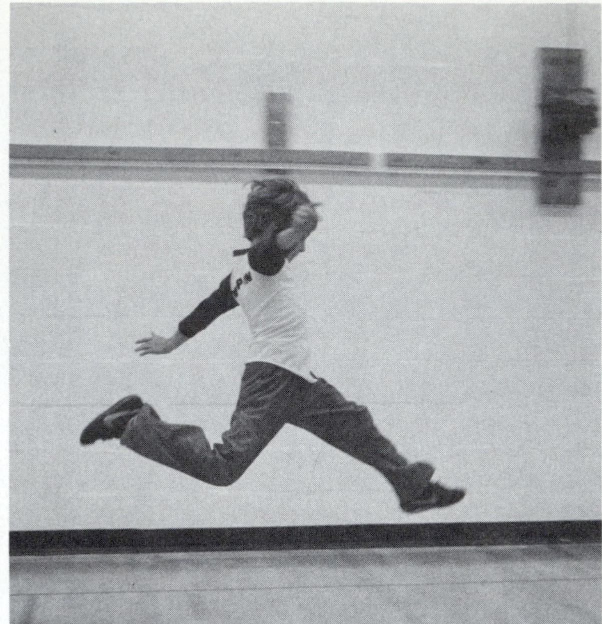

• Arms drive in opposition to legs and upward.
• Legs extended.
• On landing, there is flexion in the hip, knee, and ankle for soft landing.

FIGURE 13-8 Evaluative criteria for the leap.

The take-off is from one foot with the landing on the other foot. The arms move in opposition to the legs as in the run but move upward as well to increase the height of the leap. During flight the take-off leg is fully extended, with the forward leg reaching forward for maximum distance. To absorb force the landing should be soft with flexion in the ankle, knee, and hip of the contacting leg. The arms aid in balance.

The leap is usually preceded by a series of running steps (Figure 13-8).

Mechanical Analysis
The mechanical analysis is similar to the run, with increased thrust from the take-off leg to increase the time of the nonsupported phase.

Projectiles
To increase the vertical component the angle of take-off should be closer to the vertical than in the run.

Teaching Points
1. The take-off projects the body upward to get maximum height.
2. Use the arm swing to aid getting the body upward.
3. Get full extension of the legs during flight.
4. Land softly by bending the knee.
5. Use the arms to maintain balance on landing.

Movement Concepts
Children should experience leaping:
1. In general space avoiding contact with others.
2. In all directions.
3. Changing the range of the step.
4. Varying the height of the step.
5. Changing the use of body parts to leap in different ways.
6. Varying the approach.
7. Varying distances.

Activities
1. Take small leaps. Wide leaps. (refining)
2. Take low leaps. High leaps. (refining)
3. Leap landing softly. Landing heavily. (refining)
4. Leap without using your arms. Using your arms. Using your arms forcefully. (refining)
5. Leap over a low obstacle. (varying)
6. Leap over two ropes placed on the floor some distance apart. (varying)
7. Combine the leap with a series of runs and repeat. For example, run, run, leap; run, run, leap. (varying)
8. Leap over a series of obstacles while maintaining momentum throughout. (varying)
9. Holding hands with a partner, leap together. (varying)
10. Leap over a series of obstacles that require varying distances to cover. (varying)
11. Combine a series of high and low leaps. (varying)

- Body is erect; head is up.
- Step (leap) to the side (long).
- Draw, transfer weight (short).

- Step (leap) again with the same foot leading (long)

FIGURE 13-9 Evaluative criteria for the slide.

COMBINATIONS OF LOCOMOTOR SKILLS

The gallop, slide, and skip are combinations of the locomotor skills previously described that are performed in an uneven rhythm. These skills are often used in children's dance and rhythmic activities (see Chapters 19 through 22), as well as in some sports. The concepts outlined in Figure 13-2 are also appropriate for these skills.

Slide (Gallop)

The slide is initiated with a step to the side. This maneuver is followed by a drawing or closing step with the other foot, bringing it to the side of the leading foot. As the weight is transferred to the trailing foot, the lead leg reaches to the side again. The same foot leads each step. The slide is in uneven rhythm, with the step being a longer step than the draw phase of the slide (Figure 13-9).

A slide performed in a forward direction is known as a gallop. A step is taken in a forward direction. After the weight is taken on the forward foot the rear foot closes to a position next to the heel of the lead foot. The sequence is repeated with the same foot leading. Children should practice the gallop with both the right and left foot leading. The rhythmic analysis for the slide and gallop follows:

Step	Draw	Step	Draw
1	and	2	and
Long	Short	Long	Short

Mechanical Analysis

Many of the principles that apply to the walk and the leap also apply to the slide. In addition the application of the following principles are important:

Force

The leaping action generates the force either sideways or forward.

Balance

It is important to keep the center of gravity over the base, especially as the base decreases in size with the drawing foot.

Teaching Points

1. Keep the legs relaxed.
2. Keep an uneven rhythm.

In the slide, the children, scattered in general space, move sideways after the teacher's command, "step, close," with the children responding to a gradually quickening tempo and a change to an uneven rhythm. To practice the gallop, the step is taken in a forward direction. Activities for the slide and gallop follow the discussion of the skip.

Skip

The skip combines a walk and a hop in an uneven rhythm. Commonly executed moving forward, it may also be performed while moving backward (Figure 13-10).

The step is initiated by taking a step forward on one

- Body erect, head up.
- Step (long)
- Hop on same foot (short)
- Lead leg lifts.
- Arm swing forward and upward.

The skip is repeated with a step on the opposite foot.

FIGURE 13-10 Evaluative criteria for the skip.

foot. This maneuver is followed by a hop on the same foot, during which time the opposite foot is brought forward to begin the next step. The step forward is performed on the first beat in the rhythm, and the hop is actually taken on the upbeat to the next beat. The rhythm is analyzed as follows:

Step	Hop	Step	Hop
1	and	2	and
Long	Short	Long	Short

As the skip is taken, the arms move in opposition to the legs and may be brought upward as well as forward, especially when height is desired in the skipping motion.

For children having difficulty establishing the rhythm of skipping, it may be helpful to have them skip with another child or the teacher. Children often gallop before they can skip and should be allowed to substitute the gallop for the skip until they are developmentally ready to learn the skip.

Mechanical Analysis

The mechanical principles of the walk and hop also apply in the skip. The following also apply:

Balance

The arms held out to the sides add stability to the narrow base of support.

Force

The upward swing of the arms aids in propelling the body up into the air as does the lifting of the nonsupporting leg on the hop.

Teaching Points

1. Swing the opposite leg forward on the hop.
2. Swing the arms to add height and distance on each skip.
3. Lift the lead leg for height on the hop.
4. Keep the uneven rhythm going.

Movement Concepts for the Skip, Gallop, or Slide

When skipping, galloping, or sliding, children should experience moving:

1. With control in general space while recognizing how the skip, gallop, or slide changes with space available.
2. Forward, backward, and to the side, changing direction without hesitation.
3. In various pathways.
4. Changing the range of the step.
5. At various speeds.
6. Varying the height of the step.
7. Changing the use of the body parts to skip, gallop, or slide in different ways.
8. In relation to others and objects.

Activities for the Skip, Gallop, or Slide

1. Move getting as much height in flight as possible. (refining)
2. Move in general space, controlling movements to avoid contact with others. (refining)
3. Move with your arms still at your side. Move swinging your arms. Which position helped you the most? (refining)
4. Move changing the length of stride. Take large steps. Small steps. (varying)
5. Move in general space changing direction. (varying)
6. Move in a curved, a straight, or a combination of pathways. (varying)
7. (Change the amount of space available as the children are moving.) How does your movement change as the space becomes smaller? Larger? (varying)
8. Move changing speed as you skip, gallop, or slide (varying)
9. Move covering as much distance as possible. (varying)
10. Move with a partner without holding hands. Now move again holding hands. (varying)
11. Move lightly. Heavily. (varying)
12. Move around obstacles placed on the floor. (varying)
13. Move in step with a partner. (varying)
14. Move with a partner, standing one behind the other. Face to face (varying)
15. Perform a series of steps, alternating large and small steps. (varying)
16. Perform a series of steps, alternating high and low steps. (varying)

CONTROLLING ONE'S MOVEMENT

The movement content important in body control skills is identified in Figure 13-11.

Start

In starting, the feet are in a comfortable forward/backward stride position with flexion in the ankles, knees, and hips. The body leans slightly forward; the head is up. The arms are bent at the elbow and ready to drive in opposition to the leg action. At the start there is a forceful extension of the legs and a driving action of the arms in the direction of the start.

Mechanical Analysis

Balance

The body lean aids in getting the body off balance and quickly into motion.

Force

The flexion in the ankles, knees, and hips permits a forceful extension of the legs to get the body moving quickly.

The arm action adds momentum to the start.

Movement Concepts

Children should experience starting:

1. Using body parts in different ways to affect the start.
2. To move in various directions.
3. To achieve various speeds (varying force).
4. To various signals.
5. Various locomotor movements.
6. In relation to others or objects.

Teaching Points

1. Bend your knees and lean forward.
2. Push-off.
3. Use your arms to drive the body forward.

Activities

1. Practice starting with feet close together. Wide apart. A comfortable distance. Which seems best? (refining)
2. Practice starting with the body leaning forward. Standing straight. Leaning slightly backward. Which did you like best? (refining)
3. Practice starting with the arms in various positions, such as at your sides, bent and driving at the start, behind

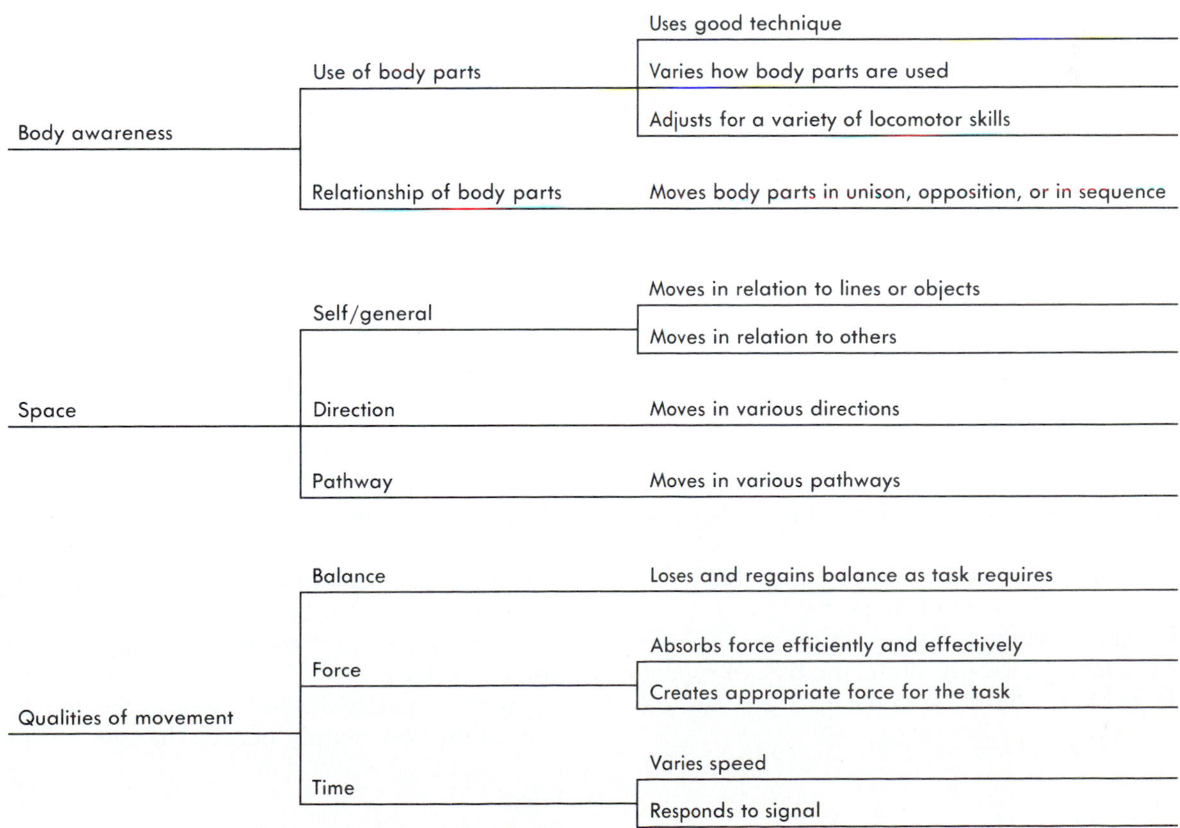
Body awareness
Use of body parts
Uses good technique
Varies how body parts are used
Adjusts for a variety of locomotor skills
Relationship of body parts
Moves body parts in unison, opposition, or in sequence
Space
Self/general
Moves in relation to lines or objects
Moves in relation to others
Direction
Moves in various directions
Pathway
Moves in various pathways
Qualities of movement
Balance
Loses and regains balance as task requires
Force
Absorbs force efficiently and effectively
Creates appropriate force for the task
Time
Varies speed
Responds to signal

FIGURE 13-11 Concept map for body control skills.

Getting ready for a good start.

your back, or over your head. Which helped best to get you off to a good start? (refining)

4. Practice starting moving forward. Backward. To the side. (varying)
5. Try starting for a walk. A run. A skip. A hop. A gallop. (varying)
6. Try to get off to a fast start. A moderate one. A slow start. (varying)
7. Holding hands with a partner, start together. (varying)
8. Start on the signal: Ready, go. (varying)
9. Start from behind a line. (varying)

Stop

In stopping, the initial action places one foot out in front of the other in a forward/backward-stride position. To absorb force on contact with the floor, there is flexion in the ankle, knee, and hip. The arms may be extended slightly to the side to aid in balance. The body weight is brought back and down over the base of support.

Mechanical Analysis

Balance

The flexion in the ankles, knees, and hips lowers the center of gravity for greater stability.

The body weight is pulled back so that the line of gravity falls within the base of support.

The forward/backward stride position used in stopping, while moving forward, allows the base of support to be enlarged in the direction of the force and thus aids stability.

Force

The flexion in the ankles, knees, and hips permits the force to be absorbed more gradually.

Movement Concepts

Children should experience stopping:

1. Using their body parts in different ways to absorb the force.
2. From various speeds.
3. From various locomotor movements.
4. While moving in various directions.
5. In relation to others and objects.

Teaching Points

1. Step forward with one foot.
2. Bend knees, hips, and ankles to absorb the force.
3. Use arms to the sides for balance.

Activities

1. Stop with your feet together. Wide apart. A comfortable distance. A forward/backward stride. A side stride. Which position helped you for a controlled stop? (refining)
2. Stop leaning forward. Standing upright. Leaning back slightly. (refining)
3. Stop with your arms at your sides. Over your head. Behind your back. Out in front of you. (refining)
4. Stop while moving slowly. From a moderate speed. Fast. (varying)
5. Stop while skipping. Walking. Running. Hopping. Galloping. (varying)
6. Stop while moving forward. Backward. Sideways. (varying)
7. Moving with a partner, stop together. (varying)
8. Stop on the signal. (varying)
9. Stop at a line. (varying)

Dodge

Dodging involves the quick shifting of the body or body parts away from an object or a person. The direction of movement and/or the pathway of movement may be changed.

When dodging, the individual hesitates in moving, bends the knees, and shifts the body weight over the base of support and then in the new direction of movement. This maneuver is followed by a push-off with one or both feet to get moving in the new direction of movement.

Mechanical Analysis

Balance

The bending of the knees lowers the center of gravity and increases stability before the change of direction.

To increase stability the base is enlarged in the direction of the force.

To move quickly the body leans in the new direction, moving the body weight outside the base of support.

Force

The bending of the knees allows a more forceful extension of the legs in pushing off to move in the new direction.

Dodging.

Movement Concepts

Children should experience dodging:

1. Around stationary objects in space.
2. Around moving objects in space.
3. Using body parts in different ways to dodge.
4. While moving at various speeds.
5. In different directions.
6. While moving in various pathways.
7. While moving with various locomotor movements.

Teaching Points

1. Shift body weight in the direction you want to go.
2. Bend knees, push-off and move in the new direction.

Activities

1. Move in general space. Dodge the stationary objects placed throughout the room. (refining)
2. Move in general space. Dodge anyone you meet. (refining)
3. Moving in a reduced general space, dodge anyone you meet. (varying)
4. Move with different locomotor movements while dodging individuals or objects. (varying)
5. Dodge the balls that half of the class roll toward you. (varying)
6. Move with a ball in general space. Can you dodge others and the balls they are controlling? (varying)

Landing

Landing after a period of flight requires the controlled and gradual absorption of force as body parts contact a surface. In landing on the feet, contact is made first with the balls of the feet and rolls down the foot to the heels. The force is absorbed by flexion beginning in the ankles, moving to the knees, and finally reaching the hips. The head is up and the upper body is straight. The arms may be extended out to the sides for balance.

Mechanical Analysis

Force

Force is gradually absorbed by flexion, beginning in the joints closest to the point of contact and spreading to joints farther away.

Balance

Flexion in the ankles, knees, and hips lowers the center of gravity, which aids in stability.

Keeping the head up and upper body straight maintains the center of gravity over the base of support.

Movement Concepts

Children should experience:

1. The use of different body parts to land.
2. The controlled relaxation of body parts.
3. The use of body parts in different ways to land.

Teaching Points

1. Bend knees, ankles, and hips (or other body parts) as you contact the landing surface.
2. Keep body weight over your base of support.
3. Extend arms to sides for balance when landing on your feet.

Activities

1. Land in various positions, such as on one foot, two feet, or hands and feet. (refining)
2. Working with a partner, jump and land together. Can you land differently? (varying)
3. Land in various ways while jumping for distance. (varying)
4. Land in various ways while jumping over an object. (varying)
5. Land in various ways while jumping from a bench or box. (varying)

NONLOCOMOTOR MOVEMENTS

Nonlocomotor, or axial, movements are generally performed from a stationary base. However, they may be accomplished in combination with locomotor movements as well as in a standing, kneeling, sitting, or lying position. The movement content important in the development of nonlocomotor movements is found in Figure 13-12.

Bend/Stretch

Bending is a movement around a joint where two body parts meet. It is also called flexion. Stretching is an ex-

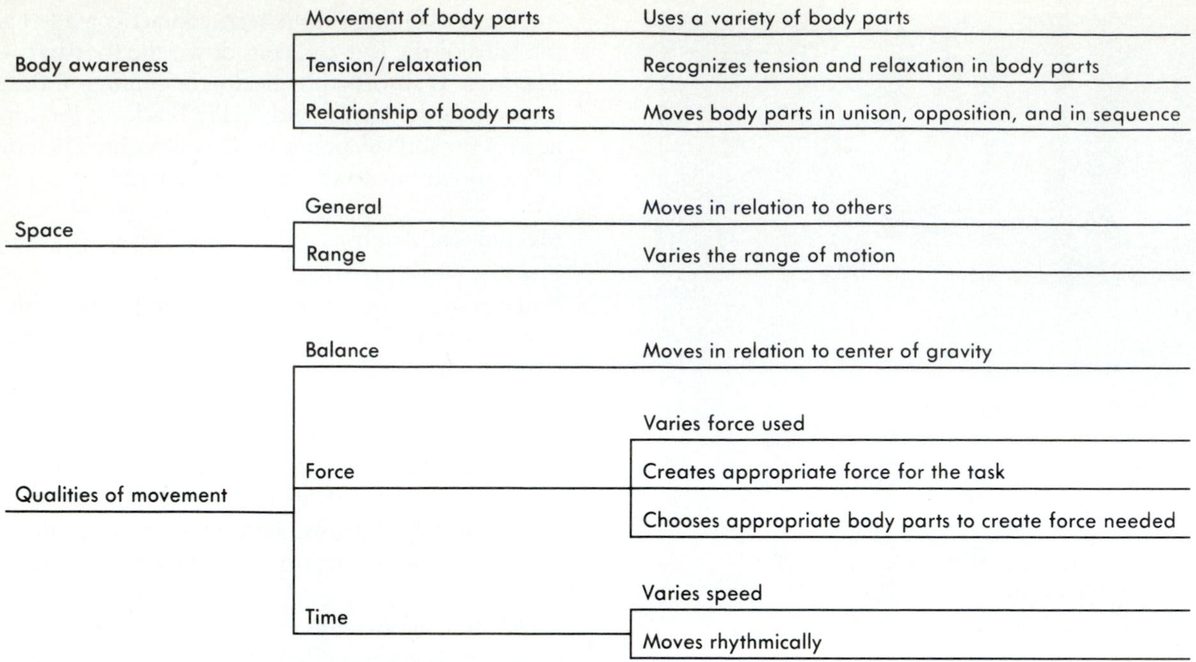
Body awareness
Movement of body parts
Uses a variety of body parts
Tension/relaxation
Recognizes tension and relaxation in body parts
Relationship of body parts
Moves body parts in unison, opposition, and in sequence
Space
General
Moves in relation to others
Range
Varies the range of motion
Qualities of movement
Balance
Moves in relation to center of gravity
Force
Varies force used
Creates appropriate force for the task
Chooses appropriate body parts to create force needed
Time
Varies speed
Moves rhythmically

FIGURE 13-12 Concept map for nonlocomotor skills.

tension at the joints. Stretching becomes increasingly important as children mature in maintaining flexibility and in warming up for physical activity to prevent muscle soreness. Static stretching is the safest and most effective. After force is exerted in the stretched position, it should be held for a period of time (5 to 30 seconds).

Movement Concepts

Children should experience bending and stretching:

1. Various body parts leading to a beginning understanding of the movement potential of each body part.
2. To feel the tension and relaxation in muscles involved in stretching and bending.
3. In varying ranges of movement.

Activities

1. Bend one body part. Now stretch it. Try another. Another. (refining)
2. Bend two body parts at the same time. Does one bend more than another? Why? Try two more. (refining)
3. Bend several body parts at the same time. Now stretch them. Try it again. (varying)
4. Stretch your body as tall as you can. Now bend (curl) to become as small as possible. Try it again, but this time do it while lying on the floor. (varying)
5. Jump and stretch. Land and bend. (varying)
6. Working with a partner, one is the leader. The leader bends one body part. Can you bend another? Continue. How may different body parts bend? Now repeat the activity, stretching body parts one at a time. (varying)

Push/Pull

The push is a forceful movement that moves an object away from the body or the body away from an object. The pull is a forceful movement of an object closer to the body or the body closer to an object.

Movement Concepts

Children should experience:

1. The effects of pushing close to and far from the object's center of gravity.
2. The use of various muscle groups to perform pushing and pulling movements.
3. Pushing and pulling with differing amounts of force.

Activities

1. Try pushing an object using different body parts, such as arms only, trunk, or legs. (refining)
2. Pull an object using various body parts. (refining)
3. Push an object through its center of gravity. Above it. Below it. To the side of it. (refining)
4. Push or pull light objects. Moderate objects. Heavy objects. (Real or imaginary.) (varying)
5. Try pushing an object while standing. Sitting. Kneeling. Lying down. Try to pull the object from these positions. (varying)
6. Push or pull a partner over the line using various body parts. (varying)
7. Push or pull an object quickly. Forcefully. Slowly. Gradually. (varying)

Swing/Sway

The swing is a circular or pendular movement around a fixed center with the axis above the moving part.

The sway is a pendular movement with the axis below the moving part.

Movement Concepts

Children should experience:

1. Tension and relaxation in body parts.
2. Awareness of which body parts swing and sway.
3. Swinging and swaying at various speeds.
4. Swinging and swaying using body parts in unison, in opposition, or in sequence.
5. Swinging and swaying in various ranges of movement.

Activities

1. Swing or sway different body parts. Swing or sway one body part. Now try another. Another. (refining)
2. Swing or sway at different speeds. Can you move slowly? Now increase speed until you move as fast as you can. Now slowly again. (varying)
3. Swing and sway in various ranges of movement. Swing one body part with a big swing. Can you swing that same part in a small swing? (varying)
4. Swing two body parts in opposition. In unison. In sequence. (varying)
5. Swing two or more body parts at the same time. (varying)
6. Swing or sway to a beat or musical accompaniment. (varying)

Twist/Turn

The twist is a rotation of the body or body parts around a stationary base.

The turn is partial or full rotation of the body while shifting its base of support.

Movement Concepts

Children should experience twisting and turning:

1. Various body parts.
2. In various ranges of motion.
3. At various speeds.
4. Using the body in different ways to maintain balance.

Activities

1. Move one body part in large circles. Small circles. (refining)
2. Turn a one-quarter turn. A half turn. A three-quarters turn. A full turn. (refining)
3. Twist a body part. Now try another. Another. (refining)
4. Twist or turn as you move through space with various locomotor movements. (varying)
5. Turn with a partner. Can you twist as well? (varying)
6. Twist body parts while standing, sitting, kneeling, and lying down. (varying)
7. Try supporting yourself on different body parts. Which parts can you twist or turn on? (varying)

MANIPULATIVE SKILLS

Manipulative skills involve the use of body parts to propel an object. A few selected skills are included here. Additional skills may be found in Chapters 16 and 25 through 31. The movement content for the skills included here is identified in Figure 13-13.

Vertical Throw

The vertical throw is used by children in their exploration with balls and in a select number of games played at level I.

The ball is held in front of the body in the fingers of two hands, with one hand on either side of the ball. As the throw begins, the ball is lowered and the hips and knees bend to lower the ball further. The arms are raised and the legs are extended. The arm action is up, with the ball released above shoulder height. The arms continue to follow through straight up, following the flight of the ball (Figure 13-14).

Mechanical Analysis

Force

Flexion of the hips and knees permits greater force production for the throw.

The follow-through determines the direction of the flight.

Teaching Points

1. Keep the body straight, bending only in the legs.
2. Follow through straight upward.
3. Watch the ball into flight.

Movement Concepts

Children should experience:

1. Varying the height of the throw.
2. Using body parts in different ways to perform the skill.
3. Varying the force used to propel the ball.
4. Varying the speed used to propel the ball.
5. Throwing balls that vary in size and weight.
6. Controlling the throw so someone else can catch it.

Activities

1. Throw the ball pointing your fingers up overhead. Out in front of you. Behind you. Where did the ball go? (refining)
2. Throw the ball while keeping your legs straight. Now throw the ball keeping your legs bent. Now throw, bending and then extending your legs. (refining)

Body awareness	Use of body parts	Uses good technique
		Uses body parts in a variety of ways
		Adjusts movements for different objects
Space	Self/general	Controls object in self and general space
	Direction	Varies direction
		Changes direction to move to an object
	Pathway	Uses appropriate path to get object to the target
	Level	Varies height of the object
		Moves object through two or more levels
Qualities of movement	Force	Applies force in relation to object's center of gravity
		Applies force to objects with body parts or implements
		Creates appropriate force for object's size and weight
		Creates appropriate force for task
		Varies force
	Time	Varies speed of objects

FIGURE 13-13 Concept map for manipulative skills.

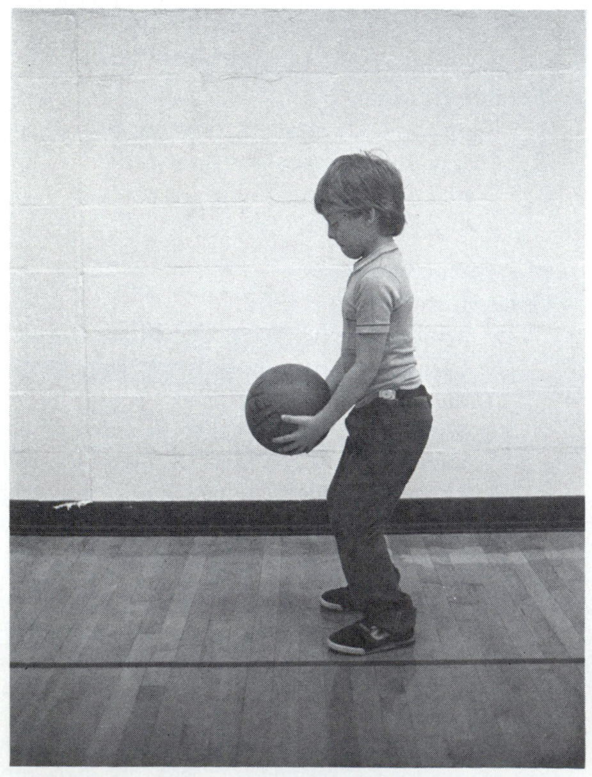

- Ball held with fingers in two hands.
- Hip and knee flexion as ball is brought down.

- Legs extend.
- Arms are raised.
- Ball released; arms continue to follow flight.

FIGURE 13-14 Evaluative criteria for the vertical throw.

3. How high can you throw the ball and keep it under control so you can catch it without taking more than one step? (refining)
4. Begin the throw with the ball at different levels. (varying)
5. Can you throw the ball so it goes just above your head? Five feet above you? Close to the ceiling? (varying)
6. Can you throw the ball forcefully? Softly? (varying)
7. Can you throw the ball fast? Slowly? (varying)
8. Working with a partner, can you throw the ball up so your partner can run under it and catch it? (varying)
9. Can you throw the ball over the rope strung across the gym? (varying)
10. Can you throw the ball so that the flight is up and in front of you? Back over your head? (varying)

Underhand Throw

The underhand throw may be performed using one or two hands to support the ball. In levels I and II many of the children throw a medium-sized ball underhand with two hands because their hands are not yet large enough to control the ball with one hand.

Two-Hand Underhand Throw

The ball is held in the fingers at one side of the body. As the ball is brought back to begin the throw, the body weight shifts to the foot on that side as a step is taken backward. As the ball is brought forward the body weight shifts to the opposite foot, which is forward. The ball is released and the arms follow through in the direction of the throw (Figure 13-15).

One-Hand Underhand Throw

The one-hand throw is similar to the two-hand throw but the ball is held in the fingers of one hand only (Figure 13-16).

Mechanical Analysis

Force

The backswing and follow-through ensure maximum time to develop force for the throw.

The transfer of weight to the rear foot and then to the forward foot permits a greater distance over which to develop force for the throw.

The transfer of weight increases force for the throw because more mass is applied to the throw.

- Held in the fingers of two hands
- Arms swing back; weight shifts back.

- Arms swing forward; step on opposite foot.

- Follow through in direction of the throw.

FIGURE 13-15 Evaluative criteria for the two-hand underhand throw.

- Ball held in fingers.
- Ball brought back; weight shifts back.

- Arm swings forward; step on opposite foot.

- Follow through in direction of the throw.

FIGURE 13-16 Evaluative criteria for the one-hand underhand throw.

The angle of release of the ball and the velocity of the ball at release determine the distance the ball will travel.

Teaching Points

1. Transfer the body weight to the supporting foot on the backswing.
2. Step forward on the opposite foot on the throw.
3. Watch the target throughout the action.
4. The body should face the target on release.
5. Follow through in the direction of the throw.

Movement Concepts

Children should experience throwing:

1. At different levels.
2. Various distances.
3. At various speeds.
4. Using body parts in different ways to perform the throw.
5. Varying the force of the throw.
6. Balls of various size and weight.
7. With accuracy and control to targets and to partners.

Activities

1. Roll the ball using the body in different ways. Examples: Roll without the step forward. Hold the ball on the top and bottom. Roll without a follow-through. What happened? (refining)
2. Throw using the body in different ways. Examples: Throw without the step forward. Hold the ball on top and bottom. Throw without a follow-through. What happened? (refining)
3. Throw the ball so that it hits the wall 5 feet away. Now take a step back and throw again. Continue to move back until you can no longer hit the wall. How did you change your throw to get the ball to the wall? (varying)
4. Throw the ball as hard as you can. Now softly. (varying)
5. Throw the ball to the high level. The medium level. The low level. (varying)
6. Throw the ball as fast as you can. At a moderate speed. Slowly. (varying)
7. Throw the ball to the target on the wall or into a basket. (varying)
8. Throw the ball to a partner. Was your partner able to catch it at the chest level? Try it again. If you are successful, take a step back and throw again. (varying)

Overhand Throw

The overhand throw is difficult to execute for some elementary school children. Its success depends on the ability to coordinate the body actions sequentially. In addition the object thrown is relatively small, which requires a great deal of control for accuracy.

Practice should begin at level I, but the children do not begin to use the skill effectively in most games until levels III and IV.

The ball is held in the fingers of the throwing hand. As the ball is brought back, initiating the throwing action, the body rotates so that the opposite side is presented toward the target and the weight shifts back to the foot on the same side as the throwing hand. The arm is bent at the elbow, and the elbow leads slightly as the arm is brought forward for the throw. As the arm comes forward, there is a step forward on the opposite foot and the hips rotate forward. The arm extends and the ball is released; the arm follows through in the direction of the throw and finally down across the body. The body is erect and the eyes continue to face in the direction of the throw throughout the throwing action.

It may be helpful to begin young children in a side orientation to the target and straddling a line. In this manner they are already in position for the arm action, the trunk rotation, and the final weight transfer to the opposite foot. Because children throw with their side toward the target, it is natural for them to turn to face the target as they release the ball (Figure 13-17).

Mechanical Analysis

Force

Weight transfer and body rotation increase the distance over which the force is developed.

Projectiles

The angle of release and velocity of the ball at release determine the flight and, therefore, the distance the ball travels. For maximum distance the ball is released at approximately a 45-degree angle.

Balance

Stability is maintained because the step forward increases the base of support in the direction of the force.

Teaching Points

1. Grip the ball with the fingers.
2. Turn the side of the body toward the target.
3. Step forward on the opposite foot.
4. The elbow leads as the arm moves forward.
5. Release the ball as the arm extends.
6. Follow through in the direction of the throw.

Movement Concepts

Children should experience throwing:

1. At different levels.
2. Various distances.
3. Varying the force of the throw.
4. The ball at various speeds.
5. Using body parts in different ways to perform the throw.
6. Balls of various sizes and weights.

- Fingers grip the ball.
- Side to target, weight back.
- Elbow leads.
- Ball release; opposite foot forward.
- Follow through in direction of throw.

FIGURE 13-17 Evaluative criteria for the overhand throw.

Activities

1. Throw the ball using the body in different ways. Throw with feet parallel. With arms straight. (refining)
2. (Begin at a distance for which the children will need a complete arm swing.) Throw the ball to hit the wall. If you are successful, move farther from the wall. Continue to move back until you can no longer hit the wall. (varying)
3. Practice throwing so that the ball lands on the high part of the wall. The medium level. The low level. (varying)
4. Throw the ball as hard as you can to the wall. Now softly. Can you throw the ball so that it rebounds to you? So that it hits the wall and remains close to the wall? (varying)
5. Throw the ball as fast as you can. Slowly. (varying)
6. Throw the ball to a target. (varying)
7. Throw the ball to a partner. Can you throw it so that your partner can catch it at chest level? If successful, take a step back and throw again. (varying)

Catching

Catching is difficult for elementary school children to execute, especially catching a small object. Until children can make accurate judgments about the flight of an object, their catching skills are inconsistent. They might have more success in catching, however, if the balls they were attempting to catch were from short, vertical throws. Obviously, the speed and accuracy of the throws affect the difficulty in catching. Children have more success catching medium-sized balls in the beginning stages of learning. Not until later development of catching skills can they catch small balls consistently. Using foam balls may help build confidence in catching, especially in activities in which children vary the force and level of the throws.

As the object approaches, the child judges where it may be intercepted and moves to a position directly in line with the object at that spot. Eyes are fixed on the object, and the child prepares for the catch by reaching out with both arms toward it. It may be necessary to take one or two steps forward or back to correct for the speed of the object.

As contact is made, the hands are brought in toward the body to absorb the force. The ball should be contacted with the fingers (Figure 13-18).

Mechanical Analysis

Force

Extension of the arms followed by flexion at the elbows as the ball is contacted increases the distance and time over which the force is absorbed.

If the object received is coming forcefully, stepping back with one foot and bringing the arms back to one side of the body allow for a more gradual absorption of force.

Balance

A forward/backward stride position increases stability as the force is received.

Teaching Points

1. Move to line up with the ball.
2. Palms face the direction of the oncoming ball, with the fingers pointing down for low balls and up for high balls.
3. The fingers are curved and relaxed.
4. The finger pads receive the ball, not the palms.
5. Watch the ball into the hands.
6. Gradually absorb the force by pulling the hands in toward the body.

Movement Concepts

Children should experience catching objects:

1. Of various sizes and weights.

- In line with the ball.
- Reaches toward the ball with both hands.
- Watches ball into hands.

- Contacts ball and pulls it in toward the body.

FIGURE 13-18 Evaluative criteria for catching.

2. Thrown directly to them, to their left, to their right, in front of, and behind them.
3. Thrown at different levels.
4. Thrown at various speeds.
5. Thrown with varying force.
6. Thrown from close range and from farther away.
7. Using the body in different ways to catch the ball.

Activities

1. As you catch a ball, take a step forward. Backward. Assume a side stride position before catching the ball. (refining)
2. Catch a ball keeping it as far from your body as possible. Now bring it in close. (refining)
3. Select several different kinds of objects for the children to catch. Which objects were easiest to catch? What did you have to do to catch the largest? The smallest? The heaviest? The lightest? (varying)
4. Working with a partner, throw a ball back and forth. Throw the ball directly to your partner. Now have your partner move to one side or the other. Back or forward. (varying)
5. Practice catching balls at various levels. How did your catching change as you caught a ball coming from the high level? The low level? In which level was it easiest to receive the ball? (varying)
6. Working with a partner, begin close together and practice catching. Now move farther apart but only as far as you can be successful in catching. (varying)
7. Catch a ball thrown vertically. An underhand throw. An overhand throw. A sidearm throw. Catch a ball that has been struck with the hand. With a paddle. (varying)
8. Can you catch the ball with body parts other than your hands? (varying)

STRIKING SKILLS

Striking is a form of manipulative movement directed toward an object. A variety of body parts as well as implements held in the hand may be used. The object to be struck may be stationary or moving. Hand-eye and foot-eye coordination are important to success in striking. This section includes activities for beginning striking skills—bouncing and dribbling, striking with the hand and small implements, and kicking.

Additional striking skills for games and sport lead-ups may be found in the following chapters: striking with the hand, Chapters 25, 28, and 31; with the feet, Chapters 27 and 29; and with an implement, Chapters 26, 28, and 30.

Bouncing (Dribbling)

Bouncing is one of the earliest striking skills perfected by children. It is performed by striking (actually pushing) the ball with the finger pads. The wrist is flexed and the fingers are spread and cupped. The body leans slightly forward and the knees are slightly bent. As the ball is pushed, the arm and hand extend downward. As the ball rebounds from the floor, the arm, wrist, and hand retract to push the ball once again after it has reached hip or waist height. Children may bounce the ball with one or two hands while stationary and with one hand while moving (dribbling). Figure 13-19 describes the evaluative criteria for bouncing and dribbling. Children should practice bouncing and dribbling with the right and the left hands.

Mechanical Analysis

Force

The force applied to an object must be great enough to overcome its inertia and the external forces such as gravity, wind, or friction.

The force produced by the body must be transferred to the object.

The force in bouncing is directed downward so that the object rebounds under the hand that pushed it.

In dribbling, the force is directed downward and forward so that the ball rebounds at an angle which enables the dribbler to continue moving as the dribble continues.

Teaching Points

1. Push the ball with the finger pads.
2. Push the ball slightly ahead when moving forward.
3. Look up to see where you are going.
4. Keep the ball under control at waist or hip height while dribbling.

Movements Concepts

Children should experience bouncing and dribbling:

1. With various body parts.
2. In self space and in general space.
3. Varying force.
4. Varying level.
5. Varying direction and pathway.
6. Varying speed.
7. With objects varying in size and weight.
8. In relation to objects and others.
9. With implements varying in size, length, and shape.

Activities

1. Bounce a ball with different body parts? Which parts gave you the most control? Why? (perceiving)
2. Bounce a ball in self space. (refining)
3. Bounce (dribble) a ball in general space. (refining)
4. Bounce a ball from the right hand to the left hand. From the left hand to the right hand. (refining)
5. Bounce or dribble a ball alternating hands. (refining)
6. Bounce or dribble a medium-sized ball. A small ball. A large ball. (varying)
7. Dribble a ball around obstacles. (varying)
8. Dribble a ball in a hoop. Around a hoop. In and out of a hoop. (varying)
9. Dribble a ball along a line. (varying)
10. Bounce a ball around your body. Under a leg. (varying)
11. Bounce or dribble a ball at different levels. (varying)

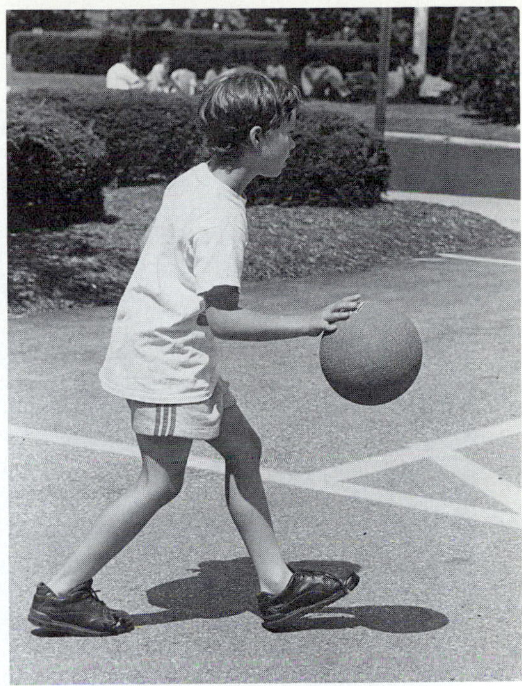

FIGURE 13-19 Evaluative criteria for bouncing.
- Ball pushed slightly ahead with fingerpads.
- Knees slightly bent.
- Ball controlled at hip or waist level.

12. Dribble while moving in various directions. (varying)
13. Dribble while moving in different pathways. (varying)
14. Dribble while performing various locomotor movements. (varying)
15. Dribble and increase speed. Decrease speed. (varying)
16. Dribble over and under obstacles. (varying)
17. Bounce or dribble, contacting the ball with a paddle. (varying)

Striking with the Hand

As in throwing, successful striking with the hand requires a backswing, contact when optimum speed in the swing has been achieved, and a follow-through in the direction of flight. Usually, a forward/backward stride position is assumed, with a weight transfer from the rear foot to the forward foot as contact is made with the object. The orientation of the body to the object and the degree of body rotation depend on the specific striking action. If an implement is used, it must be gripped firmly to maintain control when contact is made. Practice in striking should begin with the use of the hand. Paddles, bats, sticks, and racquets should be introduced in progression as soon as the children gain control of the action.

In striking the ball in an underhand motion, the ball is dropped to bounce slightly ahead and to the side of the forward foot. The arms swing forward. As the ball rebounds it is contacted with the fingers. The weight is transferred to the forward foot, and the arms and fingers continue forward to follow through in the direction of hit (Figure 13-20).

FIGURE 13-20 Evaluative criteria for underhand striking.
- One foot is forward.
- The ball is dropped to bounce slightly ahead of and to the side of the forward foot.
- The weight is transferred to the forward foot.
- Ball is contacted with the fingers.
- Hands and arms continue forward to follow through in intended path of the ball.

The ball also may be contacted in an overhead fashion. In this movement the body assumes a position with the forehead under the ball to be contacted. Legs are flexed, with one foot slightly ahead of the other. The arms are up, with elbows bent and fingers spread, with thumbs pointing to one another. On contact the fingers, arms, and legs extend to add force to the hit. Hands and arms follow through upward and toward the target (Figure 13-21).

FIGURE 13-21 Evaluative criteria for overhand striking with two hands.
- Object above the forehead.
- Arms up and flexed, thumbs pointing toward each other.
- Arms, hands, and legs extend as ball is contacted.
- Body, arms, and hands extend up and in direction of the target.

Mechanical Analysis

Force

The force applied to an object must be great enough to overcome its inertia and external forces such as wind or friction.

The force produced by the body must be transferred to the object.

The direction of the force applied determines the pathway the object will move.

The greater the speed of the arm and hand or implement at contact with the object, the greater the speed of the object struck. The greater the striking mass at contact, the greater the speed of the object struck. Striking mass is increased by a firm grip on the implement, so that the body and the implement become the striking mass.

A force applied to an object above or below its center of gravity results in spin.

The transfer of weight to the rear foot and then to the forward foot increases the length of the arm swing and, therefore, the amount of force that may be transferred to the object.

The transfer of weight also moves the whole body mass in the direction of the force applied.

The forward/backward stride adds stability to the action.

Teaching Points

1. It is important to have an adequate base of support in striking an object. A forward/backward stride position is taken.
2. The arms and legs are bent in preparation for contact with the ball.
3. Contact the object close to its center of gravity unless spin is desired.
4. The ball is contacted with the fingers.
5. The arms and hands extend on contact with the ball.
6. Follow through in the desired direction of flight.

Movement Concepts

Children should experience striking objects:

1. With various body parts.
2. With implements varying in size, length, and shape.
3. Varying force.
4. In various pathways.
5. In various levels.
6. At various speeds.
7. That are stationary and moving.
8. Varying in size and weight.
9. At different points on the object (to learn about spin).
10. From various positions, such as in front of, on top of, to the side of, and behind the object or varying the stance.

Activities

1. Strike a ball using one body part. Strike it again with another body part. Another. With more than one body part. What did you have to do to control the object with different body parts? (perceiving)
2. Strike an object so that it goes to a partner who catches it. (refining)
3. Strike balls or balloons varying in size and weight with your hand, sticks, table tennis paddles, or racquetball or paddle tennis racquets. (varying)
4. Strike an object with your hand(s) or an implement so that you can strike it again and again. How many times can you hit it with control? (varying)
5. Strike an object suspended from a string. Off a tee. (Varying)

6. Strike an object that you drop so that it goes into the air. Bounces. (varying)
7. Strike an object so that it goes to the wall and rebounds to you. (varying)
8. Strike an object as hard as you can. Now softly. (varying)
9. Strike an object with just enough force to reach the wall and not rebound. (varying)
10. Strike a ball so that it goes just over your head. Higher up, but only as high as you are able to control it. (varying)
11. Strike an object so that it goes over a net or suspended rope. (varying)
12. Strike a ball so that it goes up. Down. (varying)
13. Strike a ball so that it bounces to a partner. (varying)
14. Strike a ball so that it hits a wall target. (varying)
15. Strike a ball coming toward you that is bouncing. In the air. (varying)
16. Strike a ball so that it can be easily returned with a hit by a partner. How long can you two keep it going? (varying)
17. Strike an object so that it goes directly to your partner. Now to the side of your partner. (varying)
18. Strike a ball with paddles and racquets increasing in length. (varying)

Striking with the Feet

Children may strike a stationary or moving ball with the inside of the foot or the instep. In kicking for distance or to a partner, the nonkicking foot is placed next to the ball. The body leans slightly forward and the head is up. The kicking foot is drawn back and then downward and forward to contact the ball. On contact the leg is straight and the foot then follows through in the direction of the target (Figure 13-22).

Children may also dribble with the feet by alternately kicking the ball with the inside of the foot. The body leans slightly forward and the head is over the ball. The ball is kicked with a soft controlled kicking motion, keeping the ball relatively close to the moving kicker.

Mechanical Analysis

The principles included for striking with the hand also apply to striking the ball with the foot.

Teaching Points

1. Bring nonkicking foot next to the ball.
2. Lift kicking leg backward and upward.
3. Contact ball with the inside of the foot or instep.
4. Contact the ball below its center.
5. Follow through to target.
6. Control force of the kick to keep ball close. (Dribbling)

Movement Concepts

Children should experience striking with the foot:

1. In self and general space.
2. With stationary and moving objects.
3. Varying force.
4. Varying level.
5. Contacting different points of the object.
6. Balls varying in size and weight.
7. In various pathways.
8. As you move in different directions.
9. At varying speeds.

FIGURE 13-22 Evaluative criteria for kicking.
- Non-kicking foot placed next to ball
- Kicking leg drawn back
- Kicking leg swings forward and downward
- Contact ball with inside of the foot
- Kicking leg follows through in intended path of the kick.

Activities

1. Kick a ball with different parts of the foot—inside of the foot, outside of the foot, instep, heel. With which parts did you have the greatest control? (varying)
2. Move and kick the ball, keeping it under control. (refining)
3. Kick a ball to the wall. (refining)
4. Kick a stationary ball. A moving ball. How was it different? (varying)
5. Kick a ball so that it rebounds to you from the wall. (varying)
6. Kick a ball as hard as you can. Softly. (varying)
7. Kick a ball to a wall so that there is no rebound. (varying)
8. Kick (dribble) a ball in different pathways. (varying)
9. Kick a ball as you move in different directions. (varying)
10. Dribble a ball slowly. At a medium speed. As fast as you can and still keep it under control. (varying)
11. Kick a ball to a stationary partner. A moving partner. (varying)
12. Kick a ball so that it can be easily received by a partner. (varying)
13. Kick a ball in a goal.
14. Dribble a ball along a line.

SUMMARY

The development of motor skills is a unique aspect of the elementary school physical education program.

Learning begins with the perception, refinement, and mastery of motor skills believed to be the basis for many sports and dance skills used in later years. These skills include locomotor, nonlocomotor, and manipulative skills, as well as those used in controlling the body's movement, such as starting, stopping, dodging, and falling.

As children refine these fundamental movements, they learn how the body parts are used to produce efficient and effective movement. In addition they learn to vary the movements and apply the movement concepts of body awareness, space, and qualities of movement as they engage in a variety of motor activities designed to enhance their skills and understanding.

REFERENCES AND RESOURCES

Ainsworth J and Fox C: Learning to learn: a cognitive processes approach to movement skill acquisition, *Strategies* 3(1):20, 1989.

Anshel M H: An information processing approach to teaching motor skills, *JOPERD* 61(5):70, 1990.

Broer M and Zernicke R: *Efficiency of human movement,* ed 4, Philadelphia, 1979, WB Saunders.

Corbin C: *A textbook of motor development,* ed 2, Dubuque, Ia, 1980, Wm C Brown.

Gallahue D: *Understanding motor development: Infants, children, adolescents,* ed 2, Indianapolis, 1989, Benchmark Press.

Graham G: Motor skill acquisition—an essential goal of physical education programs, *JOPERD* 58(7):44, 1987.

Jones-Morton, P: Skills analysis series: part 3: analysis of running, *Strategies* 4(1):22, 1990.

Jones-Morton P: Skills analysis series: part 5: striking, *Strategies* 4(3):28, 1991.

Melville D: Thinking and moving, *Strategies* 2(1):18, 1988.

Roberton M and Halverson L: *Developing children: their changing movement,* ed 2, Philadelphia, 1984, Lea & Febiger.

Thomas J: *Motor development during childhood and adolescence,* Minneapolis, 1984, Burgess Publishing

Wickstrom R: *Fundamental motor patterns,* ed 3, Philadelphia, 1983, Lea & Febiger.

ANNOTATED READINGS

Barnett B and Merriman WJ: Misconceptions in motor development, *Strategies* 5(3):5, 1991.
Identifies some misconceptions regarding the development of motor skills in school-aged children.

Heitmann H: Integrating concepts into curricular models, *JOPER* 52(2):42, 1981.
Discusses a curriculum in which knowledge about human movement is integrated into motor skill learning.

Jones-Morton P: Skills analysis series: part 2: analysis of the overarm throw, *Strategies* 3(6):22, 1990.
Identifies critical elements in teaching the overarm throw.

Kraft RE and Smith JA: Throwing and catching: how to do it right, *Strategies* 6(5):24, 1993.
Suggests a progression of activities for developing throwing and catching skills in the elementary school grades.

Lewandowski D: Shoestrings and shoeboxes, *JOPERD* 55(6):34, 1984.
Presents homemade equipment to enhance motor skill development.

McClenaghan B and Gallahue D: *Fundamental movement: a developmental and remedial approach,* Philadelphia, 1978, WB Saunders.
Discusses the development in children of fundamental movement skills, program design, and experiences to enhance their development.

Mielke D and Morrison C: Motor development and skill analysis, *JOPERD,* 56(9):48, 1985.
Linking biomechanical theory with the teaching of motor skills enables teachers to improve children's motor behavior.

Weiss M: Developmental modeling: enhancing children's motor skill acquisition, *JOPERD* 53(9):49, 1982.
Suggests strategies for helping children get the most out of demonstrations of motor skills.

Weiss M et al: Show and tell, *Research Quarterly for Exercise and Sport* 58(3):234, 1987.
Report of a study that indicates verbal rehearsal strategies may be needed along with a visual model to help children attend to relevant task components.

Whiting H: *Acquiring ball skill,* Philadelphia, 1971, Lea & Febiger.
Features a systems analysis of mechanisms involved in ball skill performance.

CHAPTER 14

Developing Social Skills

OBJECTIVES

After completing this chapter the student will be able to:

1. Discuss social development as an important objective of physical education in the elementary school
2. Identify social skills important to success in our society and to successful participation in sports and dance
3. Identify social skills that may be taught in physical education and select strategies for planned social learning during the elementary school years
4. Describe the importance of play in the social development of children
5. Identify stereotyping and discriminatory behavior and strategies to promote understanding and appreciation of diversity
6. Suggest strategies in using physical education activities to enhance social skill learning in physical education
7. Describe activities to build group cohesiveness and caring

The elementary school years are an important period in the emergence of social skills in children. The developmental nature of the acquisition of social skills in elementary-aged children was traced in Chapter 2. The development of social skills occurs in many different social environments, as identified in Figure 14-1. Each social setting dictates its values and norms for behavior. Through the reinforcement of appropriate behavior and the punishment of inappropriate behavior, children learn how to behave. In each setting, the role that individuals play, with whom they interact, and how they interact will be clearly determined by significant persons. During childhood these standards of behavior are almost exclusively prescribed by adults.

The children's experiences in school add to their social development. One objective of education in any society is to teach children cultural social values. The social development of children is the responsibility of all teachers in the school and in this regard physical education has the opportunity to play an important role. In the United States these social skills are required for participation in a democracy. Today many children have early social experiences outside the home in day-care centers. There they learn to function without their parents and to engage in simple social interactions with adults and children of their own age. During the elementary school years children develop many skills important to successful participation in our society.

Because sport and play involve role playing, there is a belief that both are basic contributors to the socialization of children. Piaget believed that games gave children practice with societal rules (McPherson). Whereas many school subjects have devoted little effort to the development of appropriate social skills, physical education has included the social development of children as an important goal. Although social development was thought to be the obvious and automatic result of the physical education group experience, we now recognize that these skills must be taught. They must be carefully defined; activities must be carefully selected, planned, and conducted for their achievement; and an evaluation process must be in place to determine the extent to which success has been achieved. Social skills to be developed during the elementary school years are listed in Figure 14-2. Physical education experiences that are not carefully planned and conducted not only may result in undesirable behavior but also may be a detriment to continued participation throughout life.

The social objectives of the physical education program focus in two directions. First, the physical education experience should contribute to the development of skills needed to function as a productive member of groups in

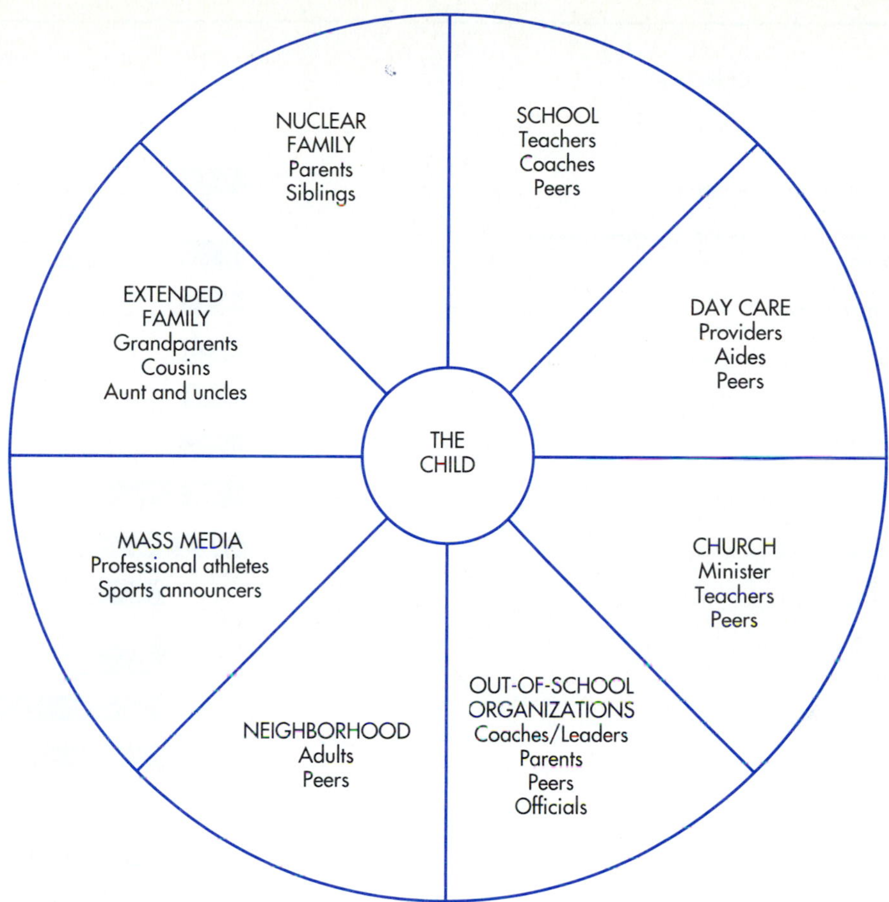

FIGURE 14-1 Significant others. Significant others in the social world in which a child may interact.

school and society in general, which all teachers help to develop. This objective focuses on the development of skills including controlling one's behavior, assuming responsibility for one's actions, and working alone, alongside, and with others. Accepting individual differences and the ideas of others, supporting others, sharing in decision making, and assuming group roles (such as taking on leadership responsibilities) should also be promoted. Understanding and accepting diversity are becoming more and more important as our society changes from a society dominated by white middle-class values to one that recognizes many cultures and varied value systems.

Second, the physical education experience should provide for the learning of social skills important for participation in physical activities. These skills include learning how to compete through cooperation and how to control aggression. **Sportslike behavior** such as respect for authority, playing fairly, accepting losing, and being a gracious winner are also important.

Teachers play an important role in the development of social skills:

1. They direct the learning by directly or indirectly interacting with the students, helping them to interact with each other, and reinforcing values and behaviors that occur in the class.
2. Teachers structure the learning environment to foster the positive interaction of children.
3. Teachers serve as models for the behavior they desire in children and recognize and reward the appropriate behavior of the children.

SELF-CONCEPT AND SELF-ESTEEM

Before individuals can function effectively as a part of a group or with another person, they must have a good feeling about themselves. Self-concept refers to the perceptions an individual has of himself or herself; self-esteem refers to the value one places on those perceptions. These feelings result from experiences with others. Success and failure and the impressions we have about how significant persons in our lives feel toward us help to shape our feelings about ourselves. Relationships with parents, siblings, and others in the home before day care and school years begin and the relationships outside the home that develop beginning in the preschool years are important in establishing the self-concept.

The children's physical being helps to shape their

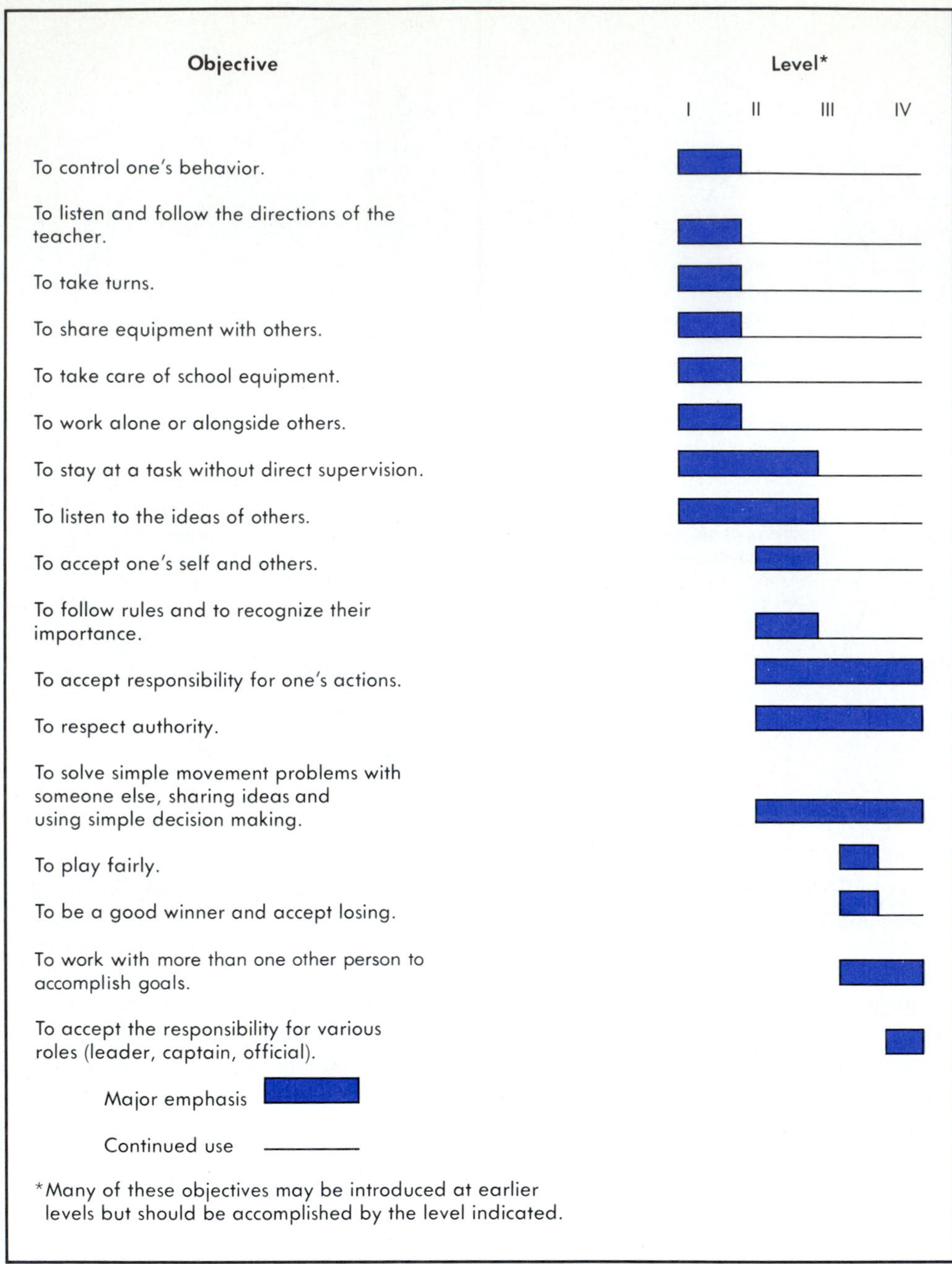

FIGURE 14-2 Social objectives of the elementary school.

impressions of themselves. Their world is filled with physical activity. Much of the early learning of children is accomplished through physical contact with the environment. Success and failure in these physical or motor pursuits is important in shaping the feelings about the self. Therefore children entering school have some feelings about their own physical potential before beginning formal physical education. Early success is important in viewing oneself as a mover. Competence builds confidence. Successful children want to move and will probably make physical activity an important part of their lives if success continues.

All experiences make their contributions to children's concepts of themselves. Learning to deal with disappointment or failure is a part of the maturing process. Individuals must have an accurate concept of self. They must be able to accept both their negative and positive characteristics, and they must like themselves as they really are. Self-advocacy is important. Children must see themselves as persons who can do things—persons who have skills. Children who like themselves are willing to make positive statements about themselves, to undertake new tasks with the expectation for success, to be active participants in the group, to take risks, and to become doers.

The self-concept develops in a group setting. Children attempt to validate their feelings of self-worth by seeking experiences with others. It is important that these group encounters be planned and conducted carefully to ensure that they result in helping all children feel good about themselves.

The teacher facilitates the formulation of the feelings of self-worth. Encouragement and positive feedback are important in helping children view themselves as a success. Physical educators often take success for granted. In our eagerness to help children, we often look for mistakes or errors in performance to correct rather than to give praise for a job well done. Children need our help to correct errors, but they also need our encouragement when they are successful. In helping children the teacher should emphasize the positive while giving assistance in correcting motor patterns. For instance in helping a child who is having difficulty in catching, the teacher might say, "I like the way you pulled the ball in, John. Lining up with the ball will also help you in catching. Give that a try next time." Competence in motor skill performance or concept development takes time and practice. Children with confidence will persist in the practice of skills and concepts, thus yielding competence in skill performance and concept understanding. Teachers must be patient and help children see their success in the steps along the way.

Teacher expectations reinforce both positive and negative behavior. If children perceive that the teacher expects them to act in a particular way, they will act that way. For example, children who perceive that the teacher does not expect them to listen and follow directions probably will not do so. Children who think the teacher expects them to do well at a particular skill will probably do so. Not only is the teacher's perception of a child's worth communicated to that child by the teacher, but also it is eventually communicated to the child by other children, who model the teacher's behavior. Teachers should praise a child's efforts in front of other children, provide equal opportunities for the participation of all children, provide for the organization of teams so that children are not publicly chosen, and organize the class so that all have equal opportunity to assume the various roles and responsibilities during the class activities. The teacher's behavior results in similar child behavior as children interact.

To enhance the development of a positive self-concept the teacher must:

1. Treat each child as an individual, helping all to reach their movement potential by providing for the needs of each through a series of experiences designed for different levels of ability that result in success for each child.
2. Communicate feelings of worth to each child by being supportive and encouraging supportive behavior by and toward all children.
3. Help children set realistic goals for themselves and communicate these goals to parents.
4. Provide children with choices and decision-making opportunities such as in deciding which activity to try or which size ball to use.
5. Use a variety of teaching methods, emphasizing those that allow for individual differences in performance.
6. Help all children develop skills that they can use in participation with other children by providing interesting practice activities and adequate practice time to develop a skillful performance.

As the children mature, progressing through the elementary school grades, they gradually become socialized as a member of the school and society and as a participant in a variety of physical activities.

SOCIAL SKILLS FOR PARTICIPATION IN A DEMOCRATIC SOCIETY

As stated earlier, the physical education experience provides an environment for learning social skills important to life in our democracy. While democracy offers many individual freedoms, it requires all individuals to assume responsibilities for their actions and to respect the rights and freedoms of others. The social climate of the class can interfere or enhance the skill and knowledge development that will take place. Life in a democracy depends on the individual assumption of responsibility and adequate social skill in interacting with others. Teachers of physical education must help children develop their potential in an environment where these skills are learned and where discriminatory and gender stereotyping does not exist.

According to Hellison, controlling one's behavior is the first step in the socialization process. Without this ability no other objective for social behavior can be met. Control of one's behavior requires children to take charge of their behavior, not because the teacher says they must, but because they are willing to do so. Controlling one's behavior implies we act in responsible ways and respect the rights of others.

In the Hellison model (Figure 14-3), five levels of social behavior are recognized. Level O, irresponsibility, is the level we try to avoid. At this level students display behavior that is nonfunctional in the class setting. They may be off task or disruptive or fail to assume responsibility for their actions by complaining about others and making excuses. At level I, self-control, students control their own behavior, accepting responsibility for what they say and do and are willing to cooperate to the extent that they do not interfere with the learning of others in the class. At this level, a child may choose not to participate but will do so in a manner that is not disruptive to the class. At level II, involvement, students not only willingly participate in the physical education class but participate enthusiastically in the class activities including skill and concept practice, fitness, games, dance, and other activities with appropriate supervision. At level III, self-re-

LEVEL 0: IRRESPONSIBILITY

Unwilling to participate in a responsible way and to respect the rights of others

LEVEL I: SELF-CONTROL

Willing to be in control of one's behavior without interfering with other children

LEVEL II: INVOLVEMENT

Willing to engage in class activities, including skill and concept practice activities and fitness activities

LEVEL III: SELF-RESPONSIBILITY

Willing to work on tasks without direct supervision, to identify own needs and interests, and to plan and execute own physical activity program

LEVEL IV: CARING

Willing to cooperate, help, support, and show concern for others

FIGURE 14-3 Hellison's Goals for Social Development.

sponsibility, students take more responsibility for their own learning, making choices and working independently of specific teacher supervision. At this level they may set their own goals, plan, and work to achieve their personal physical activity objectives. Level IV, caring, moves the students beyond themselves to concern for others. At this level, they willingly cooperate with others in achieving activity goals and help others in the movement tasks.

The implications for these levels are discussed further in the following sections. Success in this model depends on the direct teaching of the levels and the reinforcement and modeling of appropriate social behaviors.

Working Responsibly

In the process of becoming socialized, children must adjust to various environments. In physical education certain procedures are established in the best interests of all. The first social interactions involve the children with the teacher as the authority figure. During these first experiences children learn the behavior appropriate for the physical education setting through discussion, teacher modeling, and reinforcement. Teachers must be consistent in their expectations if appropriate social behavior is to be learned quickly. Inconsistency in expectations results in confusion and frustration for both the students and the teacher. In summarizing the lesson, the teacher should also address the social behavior that occurred in the lesson and how well the expectations for social behavior were achieved. Some children respond quickly to the expected behavior, whereas others need more help and understanding.

Appropriate social behavior involves developing responsibility in three areas: responsibility for one's own actions, responsibility for acting safely, and responsibility in caring for school equipment and facilities. Assuming responsibility in these areas includes the knowledge of why certain behavior is appropriate and the consequences of actions that are not. The first steps in being responsible for one's own actions include responding to the signal for listening and following directions, staying on task for a reasonable amount of time, and learning to work independently of specific adult supervision. It also includes assuming responsibility for one's actions without making excuses or blaming others for what one did or did not do. As was noted in Chapter 8, good management skills help children develop responsibility in these areas. One rule in helping children assume responsibility is never to do for them what they can do for themselves.

Behaving safely is also important. Children should learn to assume responsibility for their own safety and for the safety of others. As children begin to assume responsibility for the safe conduct of the physical education class, the learning environment becomes safe and less threatening for everyone.

As children develop social skills during the elementary school years, they may assume more responsibility and decision making. They may organize themselves for practice and small group work. They may decide the level of task on which they will work and make other decisions affecting their performance in physical education. Caring for school equipment and facilities is another responsibility that children must assume. Children must learn to respect the property of others and take pride in maintaining the environment. They must be taught the consequences of equipment and facility abuse—its impact on themselves, the community, and the economy in general. Children enjoy helping with equipment and should learn to assume responsibility for its distribution, care, and storage.

The teacher and students must take an active role in the development of these social skills. Discussion, modeling, and reinforcing appropriate social skills are a must. In addition, specific activities should be planned to enhance the development of these important skills. They include:

1. Allowing the children to assist in getting out, caring for, organizing, and putting away the equipment
2. Giving children the opportunity to assume responsibility for their own activity by working as individuals or in a small group with general supervision from the teacher
3. Allowing children to define specific goals and to judge their accomplishment
4. Organizing small groups of children to work on

Working together to achieve a goal.

a task, taking responsibility to see that all have an equal opportunity for participation

5. Giving children the responsibility to help in formulating rules of behavior for the safe participation of all

As the children learn to work responsibly, they also begin to develop group skills that will help them in working with others. As a result of these early experiences, children should develop a sense of belonging to a group and a feeling of cohesiveness.

Interacting with Others

Once children have accepted themselves, they are ready to accept others. Persons who accept their own strengths and weaknesses can realistically accept the strengths and weaknesses of others. An important aspect of the acceptance of others is the recognition that all have certain rights in the social environment. Each child has an equal opportunity for participation, for use of equipment, and for assistance and support of the teacher and others in the group.

The physical education experience should be one in which caring (level IV) for others is paramount. In their first activities, children learn to take turns and to share equipment. Helping and supporting others should be encouraged. These early opportunities prepare children for future group activities in which support for one another in the team effort is necessary.

In the learning environment children are competing for the attention and approval of the teacher. This is not conducive to a supportive environment. The teacher must be an effective model in assisting and supporting each child to create a supportive environment. Demonstrating the importance of each child in the group is essential.

In the upper elementary school years, much attention must be given to developing sensitivity to others' needs and feelings. Children often unknowingly hurt one another by their remarks and body language. Hoffman suggests that children need to have the opportunity to work out feelings by answering the following questions:

1. How do I feel when I make a mistake?
2. How do I like people to correct my errors?
3. Would I like someone to help me learn a new skill?
4. What happens when I don't take care of my things?
5. How do I feel when I don't get a turn to do something?
6. Do others feel the same way as I do?

The teacher must reinforce the observed behaviors in which children show sensitivity and support of others. Responding to supportive behavior by saying "I like the way Jim recognizes Joe's effort" will help children value this type of behavior. Conducting activities in which helping and supporting each other are important to success will go a long way in developing these social skills.

An important part of learning in schools is to develop skill in working with others. In many facets of education today, a great deal of emphasis is placed on meeting individual needs, with little regard for the child as a member of a group. Society has seen the result of this emphasis for the past decade. A strong democratic society requires group effort. Our progress as a nation will likely depend in the future on our ability to work in groups using the expertise of each of the members to solve problems. Education has a vital role in developing citizens willing and able to assume responsibility for undertaking the process of and accepting group decisions.

Cooperative Learning

Cooperative learning, the process in which a group of individuals works together to achieve one product or one solution to a problem, is seen today as an important aspect of the learning process in schools. Merely arranging children into groups and giving them a task to do does not often result in cooperative learning. Some children prefer to work alone rather than with others, some have difficulty getting along with others in the group, some are unmotivated by the task, and still others may be unable to keep up with the other children in the group. In achieving the task, children often rely on one or two individuals to do most of the work while the others watch. Sometimes they are unable to accomplish the task because they cannot decide on what to do, how to do it, or who will do what aspects of the task. If the skills needed in cooperative learning are to be acquired by children, they must be carefully planned and taught. These skills must become a priority, with the teacher structuring the class environment to enhance student cooperation. This environment fosters interdependence that results in the children working together, with all contributing to the final product. It goes beyond sharing equipment or helping one another.

Emphasis in the physical education class setting has often been seen as one in which individualistic or competitive goals are achieved. Although children may be operating in groups, little effort is often being made to help them really work together. That is not to say that there is no place for individualistic and competitive goals, but they should be balanced with cooperative goals.

As a result of cooperative grouping, children learn to like one another, to work with children who are different from themselves in ability and cultural and ethnic backgrounds.

According to Moorman and Dishon, a number of concerns must be addressed in planning the cooperative learning experience. They include grouping, organization of the space, the lesson content, positive interaction, the social skills to be taught, monitoring, and providing feedback in the process and processing student work.

The size of the groups and the group composition must be carefully considered. At the primary school level, children may begin work in partners and then perhaps groups of three. At the upper elementary school level, children may work in larger groups of three to five members. If the groups are to function with a minimum of problems, the group composition must be carefully considered. Each group requires a membership of individuals who are compatible. A range in all aspects of ability, gender, race, and interest is also important in each group. In some cases it may be important that each group includes one child who is highly skilled in physical education or who has a high degree of social competence. These groups may be formed beforehand or randomly at the beginning of the activity. The children might be involved in the process, for example, by selecting a partner and the teacher then matching two sets of partners for a group of four.

The space needs to be carefully arranged to ensure that each group has adequate space and is far enough away from other groups to function independently and safely.

Beginning experiences should include class material that is well within the ability of the class and simple to achieve. Only after considerable experience and the development of appropriate skills will groups be able to tackle successfully more challenging material. The beginning tasks should also be those that can be accomplished in a relatively short time. Tasks requiring more time to achieve may end in frustration rather than successful completion of the task. Both the tasks themselves and the process for achieving them should be carefully described, both in written and oral form.

The task should include the expectations for what each member will contribute to the end product fostering positive interdependence. Accountability for each member of the group achieving the goal is one way to foster positive interdependence. Each member of the group assumes some responsibility to help each of the other members in accomplishing the task (i.e., learning a particular skill). Another strategy involves sharing resources in which each member adds some resource to the task at hand. In physical education it could include each child selecting a different piece of equipment to be used in the final product of assigning different roles for each member of the group. In another strategy, goal interdependence, the group shares a common goal to produce a product, for example developing a rhythmic ball routine, or for the group to achieve a particular goal such as all jumping a total of 15 feet or getting 12 balls to hit a target.

A number of social skills are important in achieving the cooperative learning objectives (Moorman and Dishon). Some are task related, including providing information or ideas, staying on task, asking questions, paraphrasing what has been said, and checking others' understanding of the task. These skills are important in keeping the group focused on the task at hand. Other skills involve sharing feelings, encouraging the participation of each member of the group, responding to the ideas of others in a positive way, appreciating the contributions of others in the group, and making group decisions about the ideas to be used. These skills directly affect whether the task is achieved and whether the children still like each other after it is completed. These skills need to be carefully taught, as they are not the automatic outcome of the group experience. As teachers assess the needs of the group, they discuss with the children the skills that are the focus of the experience. Questioning may be used to help children think of ways to achieve the skills needed, for instance, asking "How can we encourage each member of the group to share an idea?" or "How will we find a solution which helps each member of the group feel good?"

Once these decisions have been made, the children are ready to begin the group experience. The teacher now has the important task of helping the groups achieve the objective, the social skill, and/or the end product. Feedback is extremely important. Monitoring group interactions is one way to help children in the group process. The teacher may simply record the nature of the interaction, such as sharing ideas, encouraging others, etc. Asking questions about the ideas they have shared to ensure that the ideas of each member have been included is another approach. The class should know ahead of time what the teacher will be doing. Individual feedback on the process is also important so the children can get a sense of their own contributions to the activity.

At the conclusion of the activity, the teacher processes the group work. Getting the children to respond orally or in journal writing to a question or two will be helpful in getting their response to the group work. They might respond to questions about what they learned, whether the experience was pleasant or unpleasant, or make other comments about the experience. This processing is important if the teacher is to continue to identify and meet individual and group needs.

In physical education the requirements for cooperation begin with sharing an idea with a partner. Working with one other person to solve a simple movement challenge is the next step in learning to work with others. Finally, children become ready to work with others in increasingly larger groups in more complex shared decision making. The development of these skills occurs as the socialized child emerges during the elementary school years. Along the way, opportunities for working with others must be planned carefully for each child at each level of social maturity. As children develop group skills, they improve their ability to communicate with others in sharing their ideas. They learn to accept differences of opinion and to disagree without blaming. They learn to value the ideas of others in planning for group action to solve a variety of movement challenges. The solutions for some movement challenges may call for a division of labor or the delegation of different responsibilities in the group.

Elementary school children enjoy and need the opportunity to assume responsibility and leadership within the class. Group or squad leaders can share in the management responsibilities for the class as well as develop leadership skills. In the early grades these leadership experiences may include distributing and collecting equipment, getting the group ready to move on to the next activity, or organizing a small group into activity. In later years children may be involved in checking off skills the group has accomplished, leading a warm-up activity, or assuming responsibility for the rotation of players in a game.

As the social structure of solving movement challenges becomes more complex, specific roles in the group emerge. Some children become group leaders, and others are content to follow. Roles vary as children participate in different groups. Motor skill development appears to be a component of leadership in physical education because often children who emerge as leaders are those who are well skilled. Perhaps the confidence they gain from being well skilled and the value placed on it by other children enable these children to assume leadership roles more easily.

Children model the behavior of significant adults and peers. They become the kind of leaders and followers they have observed. If they observe the democratic process in action, they become democratic leaders. If they view leaders as the ultimate authority, they become more autocratic. As they are ready, children need to assume responsibility in the leadership roles of group leader, team captain, umpire, and/or coach.

A number of activities have been included in this chapter as well as suggestions and activities included in the activity chapters of this book to enhance a cooperative and caring spirit in the physical education class.

Conflict Resolution

Conflicts occur everyday in homes, the neighborhood, and at school. In far too many cases children observe aggression and even violence as the means for resolving these disputes. If we want a better world for children, we must help them develop skills in resolving conflicts more peacefully.

Regardless of how much we stress caring and cooperation, conflicts will erupt periodically in the physical education class and children need to learn how to deal with these disputes without calling on an adult to do so. **Conflict resolution** is an important outcome of informal play but often a very painful one. In physical education we have an opportunity to structure the environment where all children can learn these valuable skills and resolve conflicts in a manner where there are no losers.

According to McFarland, conflicts are generally resolved with three styles of behavior: dominating, appeasing, or cooperating. All three of these behaviors are used by each person depending on the conflict situation.

When there is a felt need for control, the dominating style is used. Children using this style may not only fear not getting their way, but also having their ideas, feelings, or contributions rejected by the other person or group. Children may want their ideas accepted by the group in working on a group task and when rejected, they try harder to get their way.

Children use appeasement to resolve conflicts when they lack confidence in the situation. They may feel in-

Having children work together to resolve conflicts can be an effective strategy.

adequate in the skill or knowledge required and, wanting to avoid an unpleasant situation, may not attempt to communicate their true feelings. Because they lack confidence in their own ability and want to be accepted, they compromise by quietly going along with the group.

In the cooperating style, all share in finding a solution to the dispute. Children are not threatened by differences of opinion and consider disagreement a part of life. They work willingly with each other to find ways to resolve the problem to everyone's liking.

According to Johnson and Johnson, conflicts have some positive outcomes. Conflicts heighten our awareness of problems and the variety of possible solutions available to us. They encourage change, forcing us to learn new skills or to change old habits. Conflicts can be a source of new resolve in meeting personal goals. They give us insight into our lives and surroundings. They encourage our creativity in examining possible solutions as well as improving the quality of the decisions we make. They can also deepen or improve relationships between individuals and groups as mutual benefits are recognized and negotiated.

In solving conflicts children need to learn to:

1. Be a willing and good listener and to open communication with the other person or group
2. See both sides of the problem separating the people from the problem
3. Use self-control skills in not blaming others for the problem
4. See the problem as both sides perceive it and be willing to discuss these perceptions honestly
5. Explore possible solutions that are in the mutual interest of all parties, so that everyone wins
6. Agree on a solution and stick with it

Several strategies may be used to resolve disputes. In one approach the children go off to one corner of the space where they follow a procedure described in the preceding steps. First one talks and then the other, clarifying the problem and their own feelings about it. After listening to each other they may need to ask some questions to further clarify perceptions about what the other is saying about the problem. After this clarification, they examine some possible solutions and how each child would feel about each one. (The teacher may ask them to develop at least three possible solutions from which to choose.) A solution is then mutually agreed on, they shake hands, report to the teacher what has been decided, and follow the plan chosen.

If the children cannot resolve the dispute, they may need a mediator, who can be the teacher or a trained student. This person, who remains neutral, helps the children talk through the problem and find solutions.

In extreme cases when children are unwilling to sincerely enter into negotiations, the teacher may have to decide who was right and who was wrong and offer the plan to be followed. Developing conflict resolution skills takes time, but the effort is well worth it.

Avoiding Discriminatory Behavior by Teaching About Diversity

Prejudice and discrimination occur in every facet of society, including sports and dance. Individuals who look, speak, or act differently from the expected norm are treated differently by individuals and groups. Those receiving differential treatment include minority racial groups, ethnic groups, sexual preference minorities, those with disabilities ranging from obesity and other physical disabilities to mental retardation, those from some socioeconomic groups, as well as those whose physical skills are not well developed and females. An important part of the educational experience is the recognition and acceptance of individual differences. Positive self-esteem is important in accepting others. Often, the child with poor self-esteem acts out the most against others who are different.

Teaching about diversity is an important aspect of learning in today's schools. The United States is increasing its awareness of diversity as it recognizes the needs of an increasing diverse population and the rights of minority groups. Loridas has formulated questions that teachers should ask themselves regarding their teaching about diversity (see the box below).

TEACHER'S CHECKLIST

1. Am I knowledgeable of and sensitive to the cultural backgrounds, values, and traditions of the children?
2. Am I able to respect the children, their cultures and backgrounds, even if they are different from mine?
3. Have I provided the children with a classroom atmosphere and decor that recognizes and respects their cultures?
4. Am I cognizant of differences in learning styles, and do I try to present lessons accordingly?
5. Do I provide support by focusing on "good" behaviors rather than on "bad" behaviors?
6. Do I do my best to supplement the often inadequate and inappropriate curricular materials with culturally appropriate materials?
7. Have I been honest with the children and let them know when I don't understand something about their culture? Have I let the learning and teaching work both ways?
8. Do I invite the children to share their culture with others if they so choose?
9. Have I discarded stereotypes and supported each child's growth as an individual?
10. Have I made myself visible and available to the children, the parents, and the community, and have I made them welcome in the classroom?
11. Have I made an effort to relate to the children in a culturally acceptable manner?

From Loridas *Culture in the classroom, a cultural enlightenment manual for educators,* Lansing, Mich, 1988, Michigan State Department of Education.

Children need to be made aware of diversity, experience diversity, and develop empathy for all others. School experiences should stress the value of each individual and should be a celebration of the uniqueness of each child in the class. Children also need to have an opportunity to work collaboratively with each of their classmates. In addition experiences should be planned in which understanding and empathy, not sympathy, are developed as children recognize the challenges that life poses for many persons in our society.

Children often learn discriminating behavior from adults. Teachers must act in ways that demonstrate the value they place on all members of the class. More role modeling of individuals working together is needed. Teachers must provide the best models if children are to respond positively to all other children. Teachers must avoid giving children labels such as disadvantaged or handicapped. They should respond to stereotyping statements such as "All _______ are good basketball players" or "_______ are all lazy" by correcting such misconceptions. There is no place in the school for ethnic jokes or comments that highlight differences in dress, physical appearance, etc. Statements that criticize, judge, or devalue people of various cultures must be avoided.

The teacher must help children learn about each other. When children who are different are introduced to a group, children seek information about their differences. Adults are often embarrassed by the questions children ask. Teachers need to learn to deal with these questions. Many times a simple explanation is all that is needed to begin to develop new understanding, and often the child who is different can handle the questions better than an adult.

Our goals for teaching about diversity should include the following:

1. Instilling respect for all people regardless of race, gender, cultural, and ethnic background and ability
2. Helping children recognize that people of a culture share similar values, customs, views of the environment, socialization processes, games, and other activities
3. Helping children to recognize the similarities and differences among cultures
4. Enabling children to experience the contributions that races, genders, cultures, etc. have made to physical activity and to America
5. Helping children increase their awareness of prejudicial language and acts of discrimination and to develop strategies to deal with inequities and prejudice
6. Preparing children to work effectively with others
7. Taking pride in one's own cultural heritage

Teachers must also increase their understanding of cultural differences, because cultural socialization affects the responses of individuals in the school setting. In some cultures, calling attention to one's self is frowned on. Therefore being called on in class may lead to an uncomfortable social situation. In another culture one does not make eye contact with other persons. These differences may lead a teacher to interpret this behavior as being inattentive. Cultures may view the role of each gender in different ways and in male dominated societies children may have difficulty relating to the female teacher. Table 14-1 briefly summarizes some of the characteristics of some cultures represented in the United States today and special concerns for education (Loridas).

Schools should assume responsibility to teach children about other races, cultures, or disabling conditions. As understanding is increased, prejudice, which is based on ignorance, is decreased. Children should be taught the interdependence of cultures, the histories of minorities, and the causes and treatment of disabling conditions. Children need to become aware of stereotyping and prejudice in our society. They must become aware of social issues from the point of view of the disabled and the various racial or cultural groups. They need to learn how the dominant culture holds down and penalizes groups and individuals. While much of the teaching of different cultures in the elementary schools is a part of social studies, it has implications across the curriculum.

Physical education has an important role in helping children learn about people and their uniqueness. What can be more interesting for children than to learn activities that are played in other parts of the world? Whereas the multicultural experience in physical education traditionally has been limited to teaching folk dances of different countries, today recognition of the origins of many of the traditional physical education activities and the introduction of new activities popular in Native American and other cultures is an important part of the physical education activity experience. Examples of multicultural activities are identified in the activity chapters of this book.

Some additional suggestions for enhancing the understanding of others include the following:

1. Keeping score or counting in a foreign language
2. Providing the history of activities presented and learning the terminology in the originating country's language
3. Learning supportive statements in another language
4. Having children of different cultures share activities with the class or including activities the teacher knows are representative of activities of the cultural heritage of children in the class
5. Simulating disabling conditions to get an idea about the challenges to learning
6. Pairing non–English-speaking children with those who speak English

Sport elitism is another form of discrimination, referring to the preferential treatment of skillful students over those displaying less skill. This form of discrimi-

TABLE 14-1 UNDERSTANDING CULTURAL DIFFERENCES

NATIVE AMERICANS	
Family Life	Extended family includes all relatives Look to elders for advice In disciplining children many parents believe in talking quietly to the child rather than scolding, helping children understand the consequences of the behavior, after which the child decides whether or not to do it
Education	Education is based on observation of the environment Listening and observing are expected skills of children Hurrying is disharmonious with nature, so clock time isn't important
Social/Culture	Taught not to invade other's privacy so may not like teachers or others touching them Bravery is expected, and one is responsible for supporting friends Patience is important, as is sharing with others Sees an important connection between humans and their environment Have a rich oral history and enjoy storytelling
ARABIC–LEBANESE	
Family Life	Obedient to parents, especially the father and extended family, Parents use strict discipline A person's behavior must be above reproach of persons outside the family Consider a child's inappropriate behavior in school as a shame on the entire family
Education	College education is the goal for each child (especially sons) Taught to respect teachers
Social/Culture	Boys and girls are separated in school in Lebanon, which may cause some problems in American schools Seating in the classroom might reflect custom for sexes not to mingle Objects are not handed to another person as this might imply servant status
HISPANIC	
Family Life	Large extended families with strong family unity Family responsibilities have precedence over other responsibilities Try to solve problems within the family first before seeking outside help Father is the central figure with first son next in line of authority, while mother runs household and assumes responsibility for children's education Sons have more independence and freedom than daughters, and assume more responsibility for taking care of the girls and family
Education	Teachers are held in high esteem A high school education the goal for all, with a college education revered among the people Barriers, such as transportation, work, child care, etc, often keep parents from involvement at school Parents trust teachers to make proper educational decisions regarding their children Time less important than individuals
Social/Culture	Cooperation, pride, and cultural solidarity important Don't ask Hispanic children to look you in the eye when you are speaking to them May have some difficulty in relating to female authority (teacher) Like to work in small groups May find "OK" gesture offensive
CHINESE	
Family Life	Parents and grandparents the authority in the family; when a parent speaks the child listens Parents willing to sacrifice in providing for children Family more of a clan or kinship group Family demands unquestioning obedience to parents Disobedience, aggression, and failure to fulfill responsibilities punished
Education	Teachers held in high esteem Parents support school as a place for learning and expect appropriate academic achievement Responsibility for child's education on the teacher and the school Chinese symbol is visual rather than the American symbol, sound
Social/Culture	Taught to suppress behavior, expression of negative emotions, etc. and exert self-control Known for good manners, hospitality, and reserve Do not like to be touched by people they do not know

TABLE 14-1 UNDERSTANDING CULTURAL DIFFERENCES—cont'd

JAPANESE	
Family Life	Family the foundation, bound by obligation and duty Moving away from large multigenerational families Father greatly respected for his role in taking care of the family Motherhood a profession, education of children the primary responsibility
Education	Interested and supportive of education, with education reinforced in the family Achievement in school often rewarded
Social/Culture	Sense of personal privacy in Japanese culture Tend to be formal with strangers Touching may not be acceptable so handshakes should not be forced Cherish custom and identify with history
VIETNAMESE	
Family Life	Large and extended family with strong sense of unity Children respect parents, with strict obedience to them Father makes most of the family decisions with wife's consent Wife second in command, followed by eldest son, then daughter
Education	Education a primary concern of parents Expect children to learn as much as possible Concept of education is of the whole person Teachers highly respected, parents usually not involved with schools unless there is some problem Parents expect homework, and that children come home immediately after school Work slowly and thoroughly, unlike our rapid pace
Social/Culture	Students often exhibit little self-confidence, as they are taught not to show off what they know

nation is often the reason given for disliking physical education. The old form of picking teams—where the captains alternately choose players publicly for their teams—is an example of discriminatory behavior. Research indicates that teachers tend to give more encouragement and feedback to children who are well skilled than to those who are not. Planning a lesson in which all children participate in the same activity may be another form of sport elitism because it tends not to meet the needs of all in the group. Giving skillful children more responsibility for organizing groups, as team captains, helping with equipment, verbally praising or making comments about some children's lack of ability, etc. are other forms of sport elitism.

The physical education class should be structured so that all children have the opportunity to work with all other children in the group, not just those of equal ability or special friends. The teacher often needs to assume responsibility for pairing up children as partners or determining small group composition to provide each child the opportunity to work with all others in the group.

Gender Stereotyping

Parents and other significant persons are important influences in the development of gender roles in children. Through the observation of their parents as they interact with each other, children learn the expected behavior for their gender. The roles each gender assumes are determined more by society than biology. Women have been viewed as homemakers, as obedient and subservient wives and mothers, as attractive sex symbols, as dependent and emotional beings. Although this image of women still persists somewhat today, the roles of women in the past decade have expanded rapidly. The roles acceptable for males as aggressive, domineering, self-confident, tough-minded, willing to take risks, and unemotional also have not necessarily been in men's best interest.

In our society, sport has long been regarded as a male domain. The girl athlete has experienced role conflicts between the expectations for being a woman and the expectations for being an athlete. Title IX in 1972 was intended to eliminate gender discrimination and segregation in schools, but it did not necessarily result in gender equity.

Society's assumption that being male is best has not had a positive influence on sport in general. Girls' programs have been set up to imitate boys' programs, many of which have not always been conducted in the best interests of the participants. Today there are many opportunities for the female athlete. At the elementary school level, there may be experiences in equal but separate teams for girls or in activities conducted on a coeducational basis.

The value of play in the socialization of children, especially boys, has long been recognized in the writings of such observers as Margaret Mead and Jean Piaget (Lever). During play we observe the development of those gender roles that have been thought to be crucial to success in society. The play deemed appropriate for girls and for boys has socialized both genders into their perceived roles in society. In a study of elementary school children's play, Lever and associates found the following:

1. Boys played outdoors more than girls (85% of the boys and 60% of the girls spent more than one quarter of their play time outdoors). Indoor play is more restrictive and also more private. Boys appeared to gain in independence from the outdoor play experience.
2. Boys played in larger groups (72% of the boys and 52% of girls played in groups of four or more). The games boys chose required larger numbers of participants.
3. Boys played in more heterogeneous groups: 8- to 12-year-olds seemed to prefer sex-segregated, age-homogeneous groups; but because boys' activities required larger numbers of participants, they tended to play in more heterogeneous groups than girls. Girls playing in mixed groups tended to play down to the level of the youngest members. Boys, on the other hand, required the younger players to play up to the level of the older children.
4. Girls were more apt to play in predominantly male games than were boys to participate in girls' games. (Many believe that girls are probably not punished early or as severely for inappropriate behavior and, therefore, feel freer to participate in boys' activities.) Girls played the boys' games seriously, whereas the boys who participated in girls' games tended to play the part of a tease and not a serious competitor.
5. Boys played competitive games more often than girls (65% of the boys as opposed to only 35% of the girls). These games had a set of rules and a specific aim to be achieved, such as scoring a goal. They were games in which a winner was declared.
6. Boys' games lasted longer than girls' games. During recess the boys' games often lasted the entire 25-minute recess period. The girls' games never lasted longer than 15 minutes.
7. Boys' games required higher skill levels that could be developed only over a long time. Girls' activities tended to be those such as rope jumping in which skill mastery was acquired in a short time.
8. Boys' activities had more opportunity for surprise and risk taking. Girls' games required taking turns, and in many of the activities no strategy or rules were left up to interpretation.
9. The boys appeared better able to handle disputes that came up as they played the games. This ability may have been the result of modeling of the older boys as they played in heterogeneous-aged groups. When disputes arose in the girls' activities, the activities often came to an end.

In summary, Lever and associates concluded that the play of children probably does prepare them to assume different sex roles. The boys' play activities seem to prepare them for a wider range of work settings than does the play of the girls, which is more private and more in the sphere of the home and roles as wives and mothers. Boys' play seems to further independence and encourage the development of organizational skills through the greater complexity of the play and the need to delegate responsibility in various games. The boys learn to play in larger and more diverse groups. They learn to function in a rule-bound environment and to deal with disputes. They learn to take risks in an environment where the payoff is high and the risks are not a life-and-death matter. They receive immediate feedback on the success or failure of their efforts. There may be greater opportunities to develop leadership skills, and they learn how to compete. Both skills may help them in future encounters in the business world.

Girls, on the other hand, seem to develop more delicate socioemotional skills. They work in small, intimate groups in more private play. The age-heterogeneous play develops nurturing skills. Their play is more spontaneous and free from structure and rules. The organization of their play tends to be cooperative rather than competitive. The play of girls may be training for future heterosexual courtship; they play more in pairs than in larger groups and tend to have a single best friend. They develop sensitivity and empathy toward each other.

The findings of this study may suggest that perhaps the play of children before entering school gives boys the edge in the skills needed to be a successful participant. As a result boys often dominate in many of the activities included in the physical education program.

In addition research on teaching physical education indicates that teachers treat girls and boys differently (Harrison). Expectations for skilled performance tend to be higher for boys than for girls. Teachers generally give more attention and feedback to boys. Although boys receive more negative feedback on their conduct in class, they also receive more positive feedback regarding their skills, especially highly skilled boys. The manner in which teachers talk to children also reflects the gender relations of the larger society (Wright and King).

Although evidence suggests that gender differences before puberty in most motor skills are the result of cultural expectation and resultant opportunity, we have continued to perpetuate the myth that boys should be better skilled than girls, even to the extent of developing gender-related norms for fitness tests. These tests give girls the impression at an early age that they are less capable than the boys in their class.

The physical education experience should provide opportunities to develop greater understanding between the sexes and to develop their biological potential. To avoid gender stereotyping teachers must:

1. Provide opportunities for boys and girls to work together
2. Control activities so that all children have an equal opportunity to practice and participate

through activity organization that maximizes the learning opportunity for all
3. Positively reinforce the performance of all children
4. React to stereotypical remarks, such as "Tom throws like a girl"
5. Control activities so that children who are better skilled and more aggressive do not dominate in games for example by having children change roles frequently during the activity
6. Provide nonsexist role models, such as boys dancing or girls playing basketball
7. Provide opportunities for all children to learn the skills of cooperation and competition
8. Provide developmentally appropriate activities to enhance the ability of both girls and boys

SOCIALIZATION FOR PARTICIPATION

Sports and dance are well established as important aspects of our American culture. Television and radio coverage, newspapers, and magazines report the excellence achieved by individuals and teams. Individuals vary in their activity habits, ranging from spectator to occasional participant to dedicated athlete or dancer. Team sports, once thought to be the pastime of high school or college persons or professional athletes, are a growing part of adult recreational pursuits. Lifetime activities such as racquetball, tennis, golf, running, walking, or jogging continue to be popular leisure activities. Many forms of dance are also pursued by the adult population through local dance companies, in folk and square dance groups, or as evening entertainment. The variety of recreational sports and dance activities available continues to expand rapidly for all age groups.

Successful and satisfying participation in many motor activities depends on acquiring some proficiency in the motor skills required and also learning the appropriate social behaviors needed to interact with others. Because the overall goal of physical education is to prepare the individual for a lifetime of physical activity, socialization for participation is extremely important.

In the broader context, sports roles are learned through modeling and imitating significant others, such as older children, parents, coaches, and professional athletes. Childhood and adolescence are important years in learning sports roles. Children may assume the role of spectator or participant. Participation is valued if parents, teachers, peers, and others demonstrate that it is important. Children appear to be socialized toward participation by the age of 8 or 9, boys generally earlier than girls. Each sex seems to be influenced most significantly by different groups. Boys seem to be influenced more by peers, followed by family and school. Girls are influenced more by family, followed by peers and community (McPherson et al).

Working to achieve personal goals is important.

Good Sportlike Behavior

Today the term *sportlike behavior* has replaced the somewhat sexist term sportsmanship. Even so the meaning of the term is vague, and behavior considered to be appropriate at one level of competition might be unacceptable at another. In this text the good sport is one who respects the rules and authority, plays fair, knows how to cooperate to compete, and in winning and losing keeps the game in perspective.

Respecting Rules and Authority

Learning to respect rules and authority is a part of the socializing experience. Throughout life individuals need to adjust to the written (laws) and unwritten rules in dealing with others and persons of authority. All groups need rules to indicate the behavior expectations for members of the group. They permit groups to operate with a minimum of disruption and nonproductive behavior.

Teachers must communicate their rules to the group. Children need to understand the nature and basis for the rules they must follow. Rules that are understood are more apt to be followed than those that are imposed indiscriminantly. Within the group there should be a process for formulating and modifying rules. Children should participate in this process. They need to learn that people make rules and people can change them.

Young schoolchildren view rules as being absolute. As they mature during the elementary school years, their experiences with rules help them to understand that rules may be relative as the situation changes. Children learn that rules are made in the best interests of the group and help to balance individual and group needs. When rules are formulated, they should be as few as possible and broad enough to cover many different situations.

Many of the rules in the physical education class relate to safety, equal opportunity for all, and fair competition. Children learn that rules may be modified to serve the players. For instance, we do not need to play by the "official" rules of the game. Children need to be provided with opportunities to formulate rules and to suggest modifications for the activities in which they are to participate.

Playing Fairly

Playing fairly begins with respect for others. Each participant plays within the spirit of the rules. All participants should always give their best effort without humiliating the opponents. Playing fair includes working with teammates. It also includes playing without distracting or interfering with participants on the opposite team.

Winning and Losing

Someone said, "There is no such thing as a good loser"; everyone wants to be a winner. Winning is a legitimate goal, but it may prevent children from keeping the game in perspective. To children the game at times may seem to be a life-and-death matter. The value of playing the game must be broadened to mean something more than winning. Putting more emphasis on the process of accomplishing the goal than on the score may make the game experience fun for all. Discussion of the outcomes of games at their conclusion—focusing on how well the team worked together, used skills appropriately, or developed strategy—helps children view the outcome as more than winning or losing. Children often have no desire to keep score, but just to enjoy the game play.

To maximize the sportlike behavior of all, the teacher should equalize competition so that all have an opportunity to win and no one is able to humiliate the others. Goals other than scoring should be stressed, such as working together or supporting teammates. Scoring may be modified by giving points for completion of a specific number of passes or for each team player handling the ball. With these methods the team score represents the team's efforts, not the mistakes of the other team. In some games players may be rotated from one team to the other so that each player is a part of the winning and losing effort.

Participation in motor activities has its rewards. It is fun, and many find pure joy in moving. There are also the feelings of good health and being "in shape," the pride in accomplishment and the satisfaction of approval of friends and family, and the camaraderie in working with others to achieve a goal. These rewards should be a part of the physical education experience.

Aggression

Aggression, the act of vigorously pursuing a goal, usually in a manner in which one attempts to dominate or master others (Coakley), is a learned behavior. It may have positive or negative results. If persons work to achieve the goal in a socially acceptable manner by doing their best and within the rules of fair play and sportlike behavior, aggression is thought of as a positive act. If individuals do not play fairly or attempt to harm their opponents, aggression is thought to be negative.

Society differentially reinforces the aggressive behavior of individuals or groups. In the United States, men are reinforced more for aggressive behavior than are women. Lower socioeconomic groups reinforce aggressive behavior more than middle or upper socioeconomic groups. Boys learn that sports are a means of recognition at an early age. The desire to win and the reinforcement of aggressive behavior may push some children into psychologically untenable situations.

Children tend to imitate the behavior they observe. If sports heroes such as professional athletes display aggressive behavior, it may influence the behavior of children, especially when they participate in games and other motor activities. Although most sports personalities display the type of aggressive behavior we value for young athletes, some do not. At times children may need assistance in determining which behavior they should emulate.

Many times aggressive behavior is the result of frustration. Teachers must watch for the conditions that would result in negatively aggressive behavior and make the appropriate adjustments in the environment to bring about the needed changes in behavior. The rotation of players in positions or on teams and the equalization of competition can go far in promoting desirable behavior.

Competition Through Cooperation

Competition refers to a contest between individuals or groups or between individuals or groups and a standard. It may be (1) an individual or group against another individual or group, (2) an individual or group against an object, or (3) an individual or group against a standard or their own record. Competition is a learned aspect of behavior and probably culturally determined. In sport it is the product of an individual's experiences. There is considerable variation in competitiveness among persons, and an individual's competitiveness may vary in different situations. Competitive behavior is reinforced by others. If it is reinforced, it will persist. A higher level of reinforcement for competitive behavior may result in an individual seeking out experiences in which individuals or teams compete with one another such as tennis, soccer, or basketball. Those with a lower level of reinforcement for competitive behavior may tend to select activities in which competitive behavior is minimized, such as hiking or rock climbing.

Schools use competition as a motivational device. Grading, being first, striving for the teacher's attention, and the like may stress competition and may not be in the best interest of educational goals. Education has put greater emphasis on being an individual than on functioning as a member of a group. A person may have difficulty in our society without group skills. Children need to learn to share, to work cooperatively with one another, to delegate responsibility, and to contribute to and accept group decisions. Children may benefit from competition in some situations, but it may be detrimental in others. In some situations competition in which children try to beat time, distance, or numbers may be preferable to beating people.

Cooperation is the working together of individuals to achieve a goal. The degree of cooperation required varies with the situation. In early cooperative experiences, simple delegation and assumption of certain roles in activities may be all that is needed. Later activities may require a higher level of cooperation as children share in the decision making in the development of strategy in a game or in the design and creation of a movement sequence in dance or gymnastics.

Cooperation is also a learned behavior. As children interact with others and become more socialized during the elementary school years, their ability to work with others increases. Play with others places external controls on the behavior of individuals. It reduces freedom of action of the individual and increases the possibilities for interaction of the group. In group activities individual and group behavior is reinforced. Actions not conducive to the group effort are not reinforced and actually may be punished by the group. Teachers, parents, and others are important in helping children to develop group skills that enable them to work cooperatively.

In physical education competitive situations that involve more than one person on a team require cooperation among individuals or group members to achieve success. Learning to compete through cooperation is an important educational goal because our culture is based on both. Learning experiences should foster the development of both, not one at the expense of the other.

The misuse of competition (such as valuing the score more than the people or the way the goal was achieved) does not favor educational results. Too much competition may inhibit learning and personal development. Children may lose interest in a worthwhile activity because of an overly competitive environment. In actuality more might be accomplished in a cooperative setting.

Learning how to compete involves more than winning and losing. Children need to be taught how to compete in an environment in which the focus is on the process of competition rather than the outcome. Having a single winner and the best performance as criteria may interfere with children's perception of success. We need to foster sharing and involving others in accomplishing group goals, such as passing to teammates. Children may become negative about an activity in which the element of fun is lost in the eagerness to have the best score. Competitive gaming and interest in rule governed play appears to peak at about the fourth or fifth grade (Ellis). For children to maintain a high level of interest in competition, the outcome of the activity must be unpredictable, as when there is an equal probability of winning.

Group decision making is an important aspect of game play.

Children may need help in defining goals that go beyond a winning score. Examples of alternate goals include committing no more than five errors, completing ten passes, or predicting the point spread. With these types of goals, the children's attention is focused on a specific outcome rather than the score.

Activities to develop cooperative behavior include working together to achieve some task such as moving a large object from one place to another, keeping an object balanced, helping organize an area for activity by getting out and placing the equipment where needed, including activities where there is a delegation of responsibilities or different positions to be played, developing original games, and using peer teaching. The idea of New Games Curriculum (Fluegelman) promotes the notion of group cooperation in activities in which there is no team score.

ACTIVITIES TO ENHANCE THE DEVELOPMENT OF SOCIAL SKILLS IN PHYSICAL EDUCATION

The following activities are suggested for enhancing the appropriate development of cooperative social skills in physical education. Additional activities and suggestions may be found throughout the text in the activity chapters. These activities may be used in conjunction with the development of other units of activity physical education or may be used in the development of an activity unit in which the primary focus is the development of social skills, perhaps at the beginning of the school year to build group cohesion.

ISLANDS

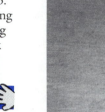

Level: I
Purpose: Sharing space
Children move in the general space in which a number of hoops (islands) have been placed. On some signal, such as stopping the music, children move to occupy a vacant hoop. On each turn some hoops are removed, with children sharing space in the remaining hoops. Keep removing hoops adding to the challenge of getting everyone in. How did you work together to get everyone touching some space in the hoop?

HELPING HOOPS

Level: I
Purpose: Helping others
Children form a circle holding hands. (Small groups of five to six maximize the activity for all the children.) A large hoop is placed over the arms and between two children. The children attempt to move the hoop around the circle without letting go of hands. How can you help the person next to you to pass the hoop?

TOE TAG

Level: I
Purpose: Caring for others
Children move in the space gently tagging the toes of the other children. Each gentle tag is answered by a "thank you." How many thank yous did you get? Try it again to see if you can beat your record.

GREETINGS

Level: I
Purpose: Awareness of diversity
The children learn to say hello in the nationalities represented in the class (Spanish—hola; French—bonjour; Vietnamese—chao; German—guten tag; Swahili—jambo; Hebrew—shalom, etc.). The children choose a nationality or use their own and move in the general space saying hello in that language, trying to greet as many of their classmates as possible.
Variation: Have the children say hello in the language of the person they meet.

BALLOON BALANCE

Level: I
Purpose: Working with a partner
The children are in groups of two with one balloon. They attempt to move in the general space while they balance the balloon between them in some way. How many different ways can you hold the balloon between you? How did you adjust to keep it there?
Variation: Gradually enlarge the group by adding a third person and another balloon, etc.

Islands—a cooperative game.

PARTNER TRUST

Level: II
Purpose: Developing trust
One child is blindfolded or has eyes closed and hands held up in front of chest. The other child stays close by as the blindfolded partner moves in the space, giving them instructions as they move through a maze to keep them on course.
Variation: Instead of moving through a maze, have the children moving in the general space.

COVER UP

Level: II
Purpose: Group interdependence
Groups of children are given a number of beanbags and a small area marked off on the floor, a box, or some other space. One at a time they attempt to toss the beanbags into the space so that the entire space is covered with no part of the space remaining uncovered. How did you work together to cover the space?

WAGON WHEEL

Level: II
Purpose: Group interdependence
Children in groups of four to six sit on the floor with legs extended and feet touching and hands on the floor next to their hips. They push with their hands to lift their buttocks off the floor and move one step to their right, moving their wheel to the right. They continue moving one step at a time. Repeat moving to the left.

The blanket toss is a cooperative activity from the Native American Eskimo culture.

ON THE MOVE

Level: II

Purpose: Group interdependence

Children are scattered in an area with lots of tennis or small fleece balls on the floor. The challenge is to keep all the balls moving at all times. How can you work together to keep all the balls moving and in the area?

BLANKET TOSS

Level: II

Purpose: Group interdependence

This activity is an adaptation of the Eskimo seal skin blanket toss in which a person was tossed high in the air by a group holding a seal skin blanket in an attempt to look out over the water to look for whale spouts.

Children hold a blanket on which a large stuffed toy has been placed. Working together they move the blanket up and down to toss the toy into the air controlling the movement to catch the toy on the blanket as it comes down.

CIRCLE SIT

Level: III

Purpose: Group trust

Children form a tight circle all facing clockwise. On the signal they sit back to sit on the knees of the person behind them. Repeat facing counterclockwise.

THROW-UP

Level: III

Purpose: Group interdependence

Children toss a ball up at least 10 feet into the air and catch as many balls as they can (not their own) as they come down. The object is to catch all the balls. How many were caught? What strategy can we use to catch more of the balls another time? Have children suggest strategies and try them out. Or, set targets for number of balls to be caught.

Variation: Have children throw balls up, one from each hand.

TARGET IT

Level: III

Purpose: Group interdependence

The object is to get a ball into a target area. In partners one is blindfolded. The other person gives their partner instructions about how to get the ball to the target from a designated line on the floor. After several tries have the partners change roles as the target or distance are changed.

KNEE TAP

Level: III

Purpose: Group interdependence and caring

Children stand in a circle with their hands on the knees of the persons on either side of them. On the signal to begin, one begins by tapping the knee of the person on the right once, who in turn taps the knee of the person on their right, etc. until the tap comes back to the starting player. Check the

time taken. Try it again going to the left. Which was faster? Try it again trying to beat the time either to the right or left. Or have someone suggest a time to beat.
Variation: Beginning on opposite sides of the circle have one tap begin to the right and the other to the left. Which finishes first?

BALLOONS ALOFT

Level: III
Purpose: Group interdependence
In groups of three with one balloon per group, the children hold hands forming a circle. Working together they strike the balloon with joined hands only to keep it aloft. How long can they keep it up? Repeat to beat your record.
Variation: Try other body parts such as: hands and head, head, knees, shoulders and hands, toes and nose, or blowing (not touching any body parts), etc.

CONNECTIONS

Level: IV
Purpose: Group interdependence
Children in groups of four or five solve the following challenge. Everyone must be connected in some way with only your hands on the floor.

ROPE SIT

Level: IV
Purpose: Group trust
Children form a tight circle facing the center and holding a rope on the inside of the circle. On the signal 1-2-3-sit, they sit down, low but not touching the ground. On the signal 1-2-3-up, they come back up to a standing position.
Variation: Repeat with eyes closed.

Balloons aloft—a cooperative activity.

THROUGH THE WEB

Level: IV
Purpose: Group interdependence and trust
A web is created by tying strings between two 4-foot portable standards. The object is to get each person through the web. The children in groups of three to five must work to get each person through holes in the web. Once a hole has been used, it may not be used again.

DANDELIONS

Level: IV
Purpose: Group interdependence
The group is scattered in a space that is not too large. The idea is to keep the dandelion seeds (balloons) from touching the ground. A large number of balloons are distributed, many more than the number of children. They attempt to keep the balloons up in the air as long as possible. Balloons touching the ground are counted and when six or more or some other number are down, they begin again. Can you keep them up for a longer time? What can we do to work together?

ON TRACK

Level: IV
Purpose: Group interdependence
Children in groups of three to five form a line with a beach ball between each of them, which is supported between them without the use of their hands. On the signal they move in the space or from one line to another, keeping the beach balls firmly held in place. Change positions and repeat. How can you work together to keep the beach balls from falling and move in space?
Variation: Have them move with different kinds of movements, in different directions or pathways or at different levels.

SUMMARY

The development of social behavior appropriate for life in a democracy is an important goal of education. Physical education has the added responsibility of teaching those social behaviors important for the participant. Appropriate social behavior does not necessarily result from active participation with others. Careful planning and conduct of physical education experiences is essential to develop appropriate social skills. The maturity of the children and the nature of the activities themselves guide the teacher in planning for appropriate social development.

The children's feeling and behavior toward others are influenced by their own feelings of self-worth. The first step in planning for appropriate social behavior is to help each child feel like an important part of the class. The teacher must model the appropriate behavior, valuing each child and reinforcing supportive behavior.

The physical education class should enhance those social behaviors taught in other settings in the school. These social skills are important for success in school and in society. They include assuming responsibility for one's own actions; effectively interacting with peers, other children, and adults; and recognizing the worth of each individual in teaching about diversity and avoiding discriminatory and gender-stereotyping behavior.

Cooperative learning and conflict resolution skills are an important part of the educational experience in the elementary school, and physical education provides an important laboratory for their enhancement.

In addition the physical educator helps each child develop those skills important to participation as a sports participant, namely playing fair, accepting winning and losing, controlling aggression toward others, and learning to compete through cooperation with others in socially acceptable and effective ways. Activities must be carefully planned and conducted in physical education if these important skills are to result.

REFERENCES AND RESOURCES

Calhoun D: *Sports culture and personality,* ed 2, 1987, Champaign, Ill, Human Kinetics Publishers.

Coakley J: *Sport in society,* ed 4, St Louis, 1990, Mosby–Year Book.

Dodds P: Stamp out the ugly "isms" in your gym. In Pieron M and Graham G, editors: *Sport pedagogy,* Champaign, Ill, 1986, Human Kinetics Publishers.

Ellis M: *Why people play,* Englewood Cliffs, NJ, 1973, Prentice-Hall.

Ellis SS and Whalen S: Keys to cooperative learning, *Instructor* 101(6):34, 1992.

Evans J and Roberts G: Physical competence and the development of children's peer relations, *Quest* 39(1):23, 1987.

Fluegelman A, editor: *The new games book,* Garden City, NY, 1976, Dolphin Books/Doubleday.

Hallersley BJ: If we win, I win—adventure education in physical education and recreation, *JOPERD* 63(9):63, 1992.

Harrison J: A review of the research on teacher effectiveness and its implications for current practice, *Quest* 39(1):36, 1987.

Hellison D: *Goals and strategies for teaching physical education,* Champaign, Ill, 1985, Human Kinetics Publishers.

Hoffman H et al: *Meaningful movement for children,* Dubuque, Ia, 1985, Kendall/Hunt Publishing.

Instructional Services Department: *Multicultural nonsexist education in the Omaha public schools,* Omaha, 1988, Omaha Public Schools.

Johnson D and Johnson F: *Joining together and group theory and group skills,* ed 4, Englewood Cliffs, 1991, Prentice-Hall.

Johnson D, Johnson R, Dudley B, Burnett R: Teaching students to be peer mediators, *Educational Leadership* 50(1):10, 1992.

Leonard W: *A sociological perspective of sport,* ed 4, New York, 1993, Marwell Macmillan.

Lever J: Sex differences in the games children play. In Yiannakis A et al: *Sport sociology: contemporary themes,* ed 4, Dubuque, Ia, 1993, Kendall/Hunt.

Loridas L: *Culture in the classroom, a cultural enlightenment manual for educators,* Lansing, Mich, 1988, Michigan State Department of Education.

Mastro J et al: Cultural and attitudinal similarities—female and disabled individuals in sports and athletics, *JOPERD* 59(9):80, 1988.

McFarland WP: Meeting of the minds recognizing styles of conflict management helps students develop "people skills," *Vocational Education Journal* 76(5):26, 1992.

McPherson B et al: The social structure of the game and sport milieu. In Albinson J and Andrew G, editors: *Child in sport and physical activity,* Baltimore, 1976, University Park Press.

Moorman C and Dishon D: *Our classroom we can learn together,* Englewood Cliffs, NJ, 1983, Prentice-Hall.

Orlick T: *The second cooperative sports and games book,* New York, 1982, Pantheon Books.

Rohnke K: *Cowstails and cobras II,* Dubuque, Ia, 1989, Kendall-Hunt.

Rohnke K: *Silver bullets,* Dubuque, Ia, 1984, Kendall-Hunt.

Romance T: Observing for confidence, *JOPERD* 56(6):47, 1985.

Seidentop D: *Developing teaching skills in physical education,* ed 3, Palo Alto, Calif, 1991, Mayfield.

Swisher K and Swisher C: A multicultural physical education approach—an attitude, *JOPERD* 57(7):35, 1986.

Synder E and Spreitzer E: *Social aspects of sport,* ed 3, Englewood Cliffs, NJ, 1989, Prentice-Hall.

Wright J and King RC: "I say what I mean," said Alice: an analysis of gendered discourse in physical education, *JTPE* 10(2):210, 1991.

ANNOTATED READINGS

Connelly D: The shy child in physical education, *Strategies* 1(4):5, 1988.

Discusses strategies to help the shy child in physical education.

Entzion BJ: A child's view of fairplay, *Strategies* 52(2):16, 1991.

Children's comments on what they perceive means fair play.

Fox H: Helping students to be more responsible, *Learning* 74, 1986.

Provides suggestions for helping children assume more responsibility.

Griffin P: Girls' and boys' participation styles in middle school physical education team sports classes: a description and practical application: *Physical Educator* 42(1):3, 1985.

Looks at the different roles girls and boys play in the physical education class.

Hellison D and Georgiadis N: Teaching values through basketball, *Strategies* 5(4):5, 1992.

Use of the Hellison model for developing appropriate social skills in a basketball unit.

Romance T: Promoting character development in physical education, *Strategies* 1(5):16, 1988.

Suggests strategies that consider the rights of others.

Thomas J and Thomas K: Development of gender differences in physical activity, *Quest* 40(3):219, 1988.

Discusses sex differences in the motor skills and fitness test scores of children.

CHAPTER 15

Fitness, Stress Reduction, and Movement Efficiency

OBJECTIVES

After completing this chapter the student will be able to:

1. Explain stress reduction and health-related physical fitness as an integral part of the physical education program
2. Describe techniques to teach stress reduction
3. Define the components of health-related physical fitness
4. Identify the tools for assessment and the activities for development of fitness based on sound health practices
5. Identify the important movement principles in performing daily tasks efficiently
6. Identify good posture and common postural deviations

Wellness has been defined as "a way of life which you design to enjoy the highest level of health and well-being possible during the years you have in this life" (Ardell).

Aspects of a healthy life-style include good nutrition, weight control, taking care of oneself by avoiding substance abuse, being physically fit and leading an active life, controlling stress, developing good relationships with others, living by high values and ethics, and giving some thought to spirituality. Physical education plays an important role in wellness through the development of stress control and health-related physical fitness in addition to its cognitive, motor, and social objectives.

Learning to control stress involves the realization of tension and developing the means to keep it under control through physical activity and conscious relaxation. Health-related physical fitness is (1) "the ability to perform strenuous physical activity with vigor without excessive fatigue, and (2) demonstration of physical activity traits and capacities that are consistent with minimal risk or developing hypokinetic disease" (Pate). (Hypokinetic disease refers to those diseases or disorders, generally of the muscular, skeletal, or cardiorespiratory system, that limit the capability for movement.) An understanding of **body mechanics,** the efficient use of the body in maintaining good alignment and in performing daily tasks, is important in knowing how to use the body in lifting, carrying, pushing, and pulling without creating undue stress on body segments.

STRESS REDUCTION AND CONSCIOUS RELAXATION

Life experiences are filled with potentially stressful situations. Stress may be positive when it results in improved performance or negative when as a result of too much stress performance is disrupted. There are many types of stressors. Some are psychological, resulting in fear or anxiety. Too much caffeine, sugar, or salt may result in physiological stress. Family problems may result in social stress. Noise, heat or cold, boredom, loneliness, or illness may be other causes of stress.

Uncontrolled stress may be a serious matter for elementary schoolchildren as well as adults. Events in our lives that do not cause anxiety in adults may be stressful for children because they have a limited perspective of the challenges life has to offer and the probable outcomes of stressful situations.

Warning signs of stress include the inability to concentrate, muscle tension, anxiety, impulsive behavior, crying, depression, nervous laughter, stuttering or other speech problems, headache, nausea or stomachaches, loss of appetite, perspiring, frequent urination, or neck or back pains. Overeating may also be the result of stress, which over time can lead to obesity.

The cardiovascular system is affected by stress. Increased heart rate and blood pressure are often the body's attempts to deal with stress. These conditions can be a serious threat to health if stress remains uncontrolled over a long time.

Because stress is an ever present part of daily life, children need to learn to deal with it in a positive and realistic manner. The individual must take control of emotions and make adjustments to control stress. While it is not an easy task, children need to be helped to keep stressors in proper perspective. Teachers play an important role in helping children keep anxiety of performance in perspective by treating potentially stressful situations for children with relative calm and by not building up individual anxiety by overemphasizing the importance of an event, whether it be taking a test or playing in a soccer game.

The exact effect that participation in physical activity has on reducing stress is not yet fully understood. It can be very important in controlling stress, but only if it does not add to the anxiety and stress already present. Seeking unrealistic performance goals can only add stress. Teachers can help children set realistic goals for themselves that are challenging and rewarding, yet reduce stress. In addition teachers can help children develop an awareness of muscle tension as a sign of stress and techniques to reduce the tension. Chapter 11 suggests some activities to use in helping children improve their awareness of tension and relaxation. In addition the following techniques may be used:

1. Explore the emotions through movement, helping children to recognize the total body response (physical, mental, emotional) to various situations. Children explore how they look and feel in different emotional responses. A mirror may also be used to help children see how they look, adding a visual dimension to the exploration.
2. Use role playing to explore emotions.
3. Use imagery as children lie on mats to get them to reduce tension by relaxation, by describing relaxing environments.
4. Use slow stretching as a reducer of tension.
5. Incorporate slow deep breathing in situations that have or may result in some tension.
6. Conscious relaxation is another technique that can be used to reduce muscle tension.

Conscious Relaxation

Learning to control muscle tension through conscious relaxation begins with the body awareness activities suggested in Chapter 12. Activities in which children explore tensing and relaxing muscles through the use of movement challenges and imagery prepare them for the development of the conscious relaxation techniques that follow.

The environment for conscious relaxation must be comfortable, with little distraction. Generally, it is helpful to begin lying on a mat rather than on the hard floor. Once learned, conscious relaxation may be practiced under many different conditions, but initially it is helpful to be in an environment that is comfortable, sufficiently warm, not brightly lit, and relatively quiet. The leader should have a pleasant, relaxing voice.

Conscious relaxation should not result in sleeping because the goal is to remain conscious. When working on conscious relaxation, children should be encouraged to tighten only those body parts called for in the exercise. The leader should move around the room, touching the children to help them become increasingly aware of tension in body parts other than those with which they are working.

Conscious relaxation technique (Auxter and Pyfer):

1. Lying on your back on the mat, slowly take a series of deep breaths. Slowly breathe in and out.
2. Make a fist as you bend your arm at the elbow and hold. Feel the tension in the muscles in the front of your upper arm. Relax the fist slowly, until the arm feels limp and relaxed. Try it again. (If they have difficulty, begin with one arm at a time.)
3. Point your toes away from the rest of your body. Hold. Feel the tension in the back of your legs. Now slowly let it go. Repeat.
4. Now flex your ankles so that your toes try to point toward your head. Feel the tension in the front of your legs. Hold. Now let it go until your feet fall limply onto the mat. Try it again.
5. Turn your knees out forcefully. Hold that position. Feel tension in the outer thigh area. Now let it go so your knees turn back into their original position. Repeat.
6. Rotate your knees inward. Hold. Now relax. Repeat. Do you feel tension in your inner thighs?
7. Tighten your abdominal muscles, pressing your back into the mat. Hold. Slowly let it go back to your starting position. Try it again.
8. Press your head back, lifting your upper back off the mat. Hold. Feel the tension in your upper back and neck. Slowly lower your back to the mat and your head to its resting position. Repeat.
9. Pinch your shoulder blades together, feeling tension in the back of your shoulders. Hold. Slowly relax and sink into the mat. Repeat.
10. Roll your shoulders forward and upward, keeping your arms on the mat. Hold. Feel the tension in the front of your shoulders. Slowly relax and bring your shoulders back to their resting position. Try it again.
11. Spread your fingers. Hold. Feel the tension in your fingers. Slowly relax and let your fingers fall limply to the mat. Do it once more.
12. Make a fist with both hands. Hold. Feel the tension in your fingers and hands. Let it go and allow your hands to lie limply on the mat. Repeat.
13. Touch your chin to your chest. Hold. Feel the tension in the front of your neck. Slowly return your head to the mat. Repeat.

14. Wrinkle your forehead by raising your eyebrows. Hold. Feel the tension in your forehead. Now slowly relax. Repeat.
15. Close your eyelids as tightly as you can. Hold. Now slowly let it go. Repeat.
16. Open your mouth as wide as you can. Do you feel like yawning? Now slowly close your mouth. Repeat.
17. Pucker your lips as hard as you can. Feel the tension at the edge of your mouth. Now slowly let your lips relax. Repeat.
18. Make a forced smile as you bite down hard. Hold. Feel the tension in your jaw and lips. Now slowly relax. Repeat.

FITNESS

Fitness has been an important aspect of physical education in the United States since physicians, the first physical educators, recognized the importance of physical activity for healthful living. In 1956 the American Association for Health, Physical Education and Recreation established a series of tests to assess the motor fitness of youths 10 to 18 years old. The components tested were believed to be important to a person's overall motor ability. The tests included items to measure agility, power, cardiorespiratory endurance, muscular strength and endurance, and speed. The test items included a 50-yard dash, a shuttle run, a 600-yard run, sit-ups, the standing jump, a softball throw for distance, pull-ups for boys, and a flexed arm hang for girls. National norms were established and revised periodically between 1958 and 1976.

During this time, discussion focused on the test items and their relationship to health. Speed and power were found to be heavily dependent on genetic factors and not particularly responsive to training. Agility, although an important component of some motor activities, has little relationship to health (Pate). Some questioned whether the tests actually measured the motor components they were supposed to measure; for example, whether the standing jump measured leg power or the ability to jump from a standing position. Table 15-1 compares the components of motor and health-related physical fitness.

Because all the components in motor fitness were not believed to be important to health, a new term, ***health-related physical fitness,*** emerged with a redefinition of fitness. Health-related physical fitness includes those components that can prevent disease and/or promote health, namely cardiorespiratory endurance, body composition, muscular strength and endurance, and flexibility. In 1988, the AAHPERD introduced its second health-related physical fitness test, The Physical Best. The test items were designed to assess these components, and similar test items are suggested in this chapter.

Cardiorespiratory endurance has been conclusively linked to coronary heart disease. The relationship of body composition and activity level has been clearly established. With the establishment of the relationship of inactivity to health problems involving the bones, musculature, cardiorespiratory system, and weight control, fitness has become an important concern for individuals of all ages. The activity habits developed as part of the physical education experiences have lasting effects on an individual's health now and in the future. Those who exercise regularly have a much brighter prospect for a healthy life. Those who choose not to exercise have to assume the consequences.

Goals for the Nation and Elementary School Physical Education

The health of our nation is of vital concern today in assisting people to live healthy lives and reduce the cost of health care, much of which is the result of lifestyle. Much evidence suggests that lifelong activity patterns begin in childhood. The sedentary lifestyle begins at an early age. For example studies of television viewing have found that children 6 to 11 years of age watched 24 hours of

TABLE 15-1 PHYSICAL FITNESS COMPONENTS

COMPONENT	DEFINITION	MOTOR FITNESS	HEALTH-RELATED FITNESS
Agility	Ability to change direction quickly, easily, and with control	X	
Body composition	Percentage of body fat		X
Cardiorespiratory endurance	Maximum functional capacity of the cardiorespiratory system to continue activity over a period of time	X	X
Flexibility	Range of movement in a joint	X	X
Muscular endurance	Ability to continue muscular effort over a period of time	X	X
Muscular strength	Amount of force that can be exerted by a muscle	X	X
Power	Use of strength to apply force in a particular task	X	
Speed	Ability to move the body quickly	X	

television per week in 1982, 13 year olds watched an average of 23 hours per week in 1988, and 72% of all seniors in high school watched television every day in 1990 (Office of Educational Research and Improvement). Children also have significantly more body fat today than children in the 1960s, with a 50% increase in obesity and a 100% increase in superobesity (95th percentile) (Gortmaker). Although these trends are of utmost concern, the strategies for intervention are uncertain. What role do social and environmental factors play? What activities seem to produce the best results? These important factors must be studied to develop a plan to correct these serious threats to good health.

In 1990 the US Department of Health and Human Services published its document, *Healthy People 2000: The National Health Promotion and Disease Prevention Objectives,* to be accomplished by the year 2000. Included in the document are 12 objectives related to physical activity and fitness. The major health emphasis in this group of objectives is the reduction of coronary heart disease deaths and obesity. Risk reduction objectives include increasing daily moderate activity, vigorous activity at least 3 days a week for 20 minutes, activities to enhance muscular strength and endurance and flexibility, and increasing leisure time physical activity. Several of the objectives of services needed to reduce the health risks and meet the health objectives are important to physical education and youth fitness. These objectives are as follows:

1. To increase daily physical education for children of all school ages
2. To increase the physical education class time spent being physically active, preferably in activities that prepare them for a lifetime of physical activity
3. To increase each community's availability and accessibility of hiking, biking and fitness trails, swimming pools, and park and recreational facilities

Obviously the first two objectives have a direct relationship to programs in physical education and the third an indirect relationship in preparing and encouraging children to be physically active outside of school.

What impact can physical education have on the health and fitness of today's boys and girls? Most physical education programs are inadequate to meet the need. Many meet for only one or two days a week. The time is short. There are many demands in these programs for meeting objectives other than fitness, including those of other subject areas. What can we hope to achieve? We must first recognize that children are not going to improve their physical fitness in physical education class alone. Improvement requires efforts outside the school environment and a personal commitment to health and wellbeing. What then is the role of physical education in achieving this objective?

1. Physical education should provide an environment that fosters a love for physical activity.
2. Physical education should help children develop physical skills and knowledge necessary for successful lifelong participation.
3. Physical education classes should help children recognize the fitness value of activities in which they engage and help them test and plan for their own fitness development.
4. Physical education teachers should demonstrate an interest in what children do outside school, encouraging them to be physically active.

In achieving these goals fitness must be an important consideration in planning and conducting the physical education program.

IMPLEMENTING THE HEALTH-RELATED PHYSICAL FITNESS PROGRAM

Pate defines the fitness goals for the child's total physical activity/physical education/health education experience as:

1. Maintenance of good functional capacities in the health-related physical fitness components during childhood
2. Exhibition of a level of habitual physical activity sufficient to stimulate normal growth and development
3. Demonstration of a level of health-related physical fitness that minimizes the risks of later development of hypokinetic diseases
4. Acquisition of the skills, knowledge, and attitudes that optimize the chances of maintaining good health-related physical fitness throughout life

In structuring the physical education experiences to meet the goals for health-related physical fitness the following must be considered:

Fitness is an integral part of the physical education experience. Fitness is not a unit of activity, but a part of every activity included in the physical education curriculum.

The development of fitness includes the presentation of fitness knowledge as well as physical activity. Children need to become knowledgeable about fitness at their own level of understanding. This includes knowledge about why fitness is important, the risks of not being fit, how to evaluate fitness, and activities to use to enhance one's fitness.

Fitness is concerned with total body development. Motor activities included in physical education have the potential of developing specific components of health-related physical fitness but not necessarily all. Units of instruction must often be supplemented with additional activities to ensure total body development. Table 15-2 looks at the fitness components that may be developed in various

TABLE 15-2 POTENTIAL CONTRIBUTION OF PHYSICAL ACTIVITIES TO HEALTH-RELATED FITNESS*

	FITNESS COMPONENTS			
ACTIVITY	CARDIORESPIRATORY ENDURANCE	MUSCULAR STRENGTH AND ENDURANCE	FLEXIBILITY	BODY COMPOSITION†
Movement content	X	X	X	X
Fundamental skills		X		
Educational games	X			
Basketball	X	X		X
Field hockey	X	X		X
Softball		X		
Soccer	X	X		X
Volleyball		X		
Track and field	X	X		X
Gymnastics		X	X	
Creative dance		X	X	
Folk and square dance	X	X		X
Rhythmic activities with balls, sticks, and ropes	X	X		X

*Assumes maximum participation for all.
†Body composition is related to the amount of activity. Activities that require sustained vigorous activity would contribute the most.

physical activities. It must be remembered that the actual contribution an activity makes to fitness depends on the manner in which the activity is conducted. Because activities are designed to work on specific fitness components, a variety of activities are required to ensure total body development.

Fitness should be fun. Fitness activities often have been characterized as a series of boring and tedious exercises and calisthenics or as punishment for minor infractions. Fitness is developed through a variety of physical activities selected to meet the needs and interests of children.

Fitness should be motivated by a desire for self-improvement. All children strive to do their best in an environment in which positive efforts are reinforced and improvement noted.

Fitness should be nonthreatening. The environment should foster support between children and teacher. Each child should be valued. There must be no possibility for ridicule or public judgment of anyone's performance. Testing should emphasize individual improvement rather than rank in class.

Fitness must be vigorous. Each lesson should include vigorous activity in which the children's heart rates are increased and a maximum amount of movement for each child is ensured.

Fitness is achieved only when activities are executed in a manner that enhances fitness. When children perform fitness activities incorrectly, such as failing to keep the body straight when doing push-ups, the result is not improved fitness. Activities should be selected within the children's ability and body awareness to be performed correctly.

Fitness should be individualized. Children should (1) know their fitness status, (2) be helped to set realistic goals for improvement, and (3) be assisted in establishing a program of activity to achieve their goals. The activity prescription should be based on each individual's initial level of fitness. Those with lower fitness levels should begin with a program of exercise of lower intensity. A fit individual will have to begin at a much higher intensity program if fitness is to be improved further.

Fitness must be progressive. The goal must be to increase the work capacity of each child through a series of progressively more demanding physical activities. An increase in muscle strength requires that the muscle be exercised at higher levels of activity than normal. The heart increases its efficiency as a result of demands to work harder than usual. Flexibility is improved by increasing the range of movement in the various articulations (joints) of the body.

Fitness requires frequent activity. A minimum of three 45-minute periods of vigorous physical activity are recommended for acquiring and maintaining health-related fitness. Because the 45 minutes are in excess of an optimum period for learning in the early school years, a daily 30-minute period for kindergarten through the third grade is suggested. Because the physical education period is devoted to skill and knowledge development as well as fitness activities, children must be encouraged to be physically active outside school, especially if physical education is not offered on a daily basis. Activities such as walking for fitness and distance runs in which distance is accumulated over weeks may be sponsored. Some events may encourage family participation. Giving suggestions or having children discuss their vacation activities is another effort to encourage outside of school participation.

Fitness should include periods of warm-up and cooling down. Most activities are performed best when the body temperature has been raised slightly, which is the result of warm-up activities. Although young children apparently do not need warm-up activities, in the upper levels children may benefit from warm-ups to prevent muscle and joint injury and soreness as a result of strenuous exercise and to establish the importance and habit of warming up and cooling down. Stretching activities are important in the warm-up and cool-down periods. A series of stretches is found in the flexibility activities in this chapter.

Fitness requires a maintenance program once the desired fitness is reached. If a person stops exercising, the level of fitness achieved is lost in a short time. Therefore, an exercise program must be continuous. Because it is easier to maintain fitness than to acquire it, a lower intensity program usually suffices.

Fitness improvement and maintenance require a conscientious effort by the individual. Fitness will not be improved unless individuals value fitness for themselves. All persons must take the responsibility for carrying out their fitness programs. Setting realistic goals that include short- and long-term objectives is important. The school can assist by providing programs that encourage fitness activities in and out of school, for instance, a run to the state capital organized by classroom with individuals running laps that are totaled for a group record. Keeping a log of activities and achievements along the way should help children remain sufficiently motivated and interested to continue working.

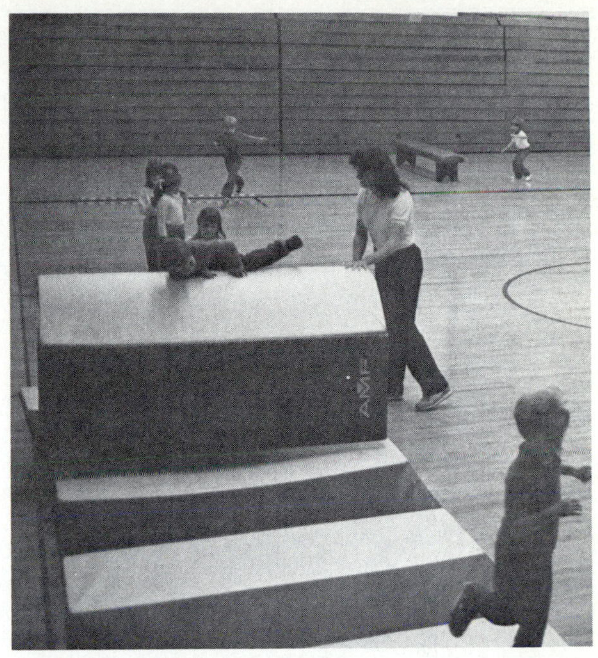

An obstacle course provides a fun way to work on fitness components.

Understanding Fitness

As children learn about fitness in physical education, they should be exposed to knowledge that increases their understanding about themselves and the effects of exercise on the body. Much of the knowledge may be included in the elementary school curriculum in other subject areas as well as in physical education. The study of fitness is an example of how the integration of the areas of physical education, health, science, and math may result in greater understanding. Written reports may help internalize and reinforce the value of health-related fitness. The content to be developed in the study of health-related fitness in the elementary school is illustrated in Table 15-3.

In the beginning years in physical education, the teacher develops an understanding of the fitness terminology. At levels I and II the children develop simple understandings of the vocabulary, which they define in their own words. For instance, the definition of fitness may simply be that one can play hard for a long time without getting out of breath or tired. At levels III and IV, more scientific definitions of the terms are appropriate as children have greater understanding about the body and its functions.

The importance of fitness and an active life-style needs to be established early. At levels I and II, children need to learn how exercise can help one maintain a healthy body and the relationship between diet and exercise. At levels III and IV, with their increased knowledge of the human body through their study in health and science, children should have a more advanced understanding of nutrition and the effects of exercise on body tissues. They should also begin to recognize and understand how stress affects their lives and how physical activity and conscious relaxation can be used to help individuals control stress. It is important for children at this age to develop good activity habits and to begin to use a warm-up and cool-down as a part of the activity experience.

Another important area of content is studying the effects of health-related fitness on motor performance. Children are interested in performing well, and they often have little understanding about why they do or do not perform as well as they would like. Beginning to recognize the fitness components important in various activities helps to focus their attention on their own fitness needs as they pursue activities of their own interest.

One of the most difficult areas to teach is the health risks of being unfit and their long-term effects on the body. These effects can be readily seen, even with adults who know what they should do and do not do it. Human beings have a hard time realizing our own mortality. The attitude that heart disease or other debilitating conditions

TABLE 15-3 HEALTH-RELATED FITNESS KNOWLEDGES AND SKILLS

	LEVELS I AND II	LEVELS III AND IV
Terminology	Defines terminology in own words: Fitness Strength Endurance Body leanness Flexibility	Defines terminology more scientifically: Health-related fitness Muscular strength Flexibility Cardiorespiratory endurance Muscular endurance Body composition
Recognizes the effects of exercise on the body	Describes that the body needs regular vigorous activity to (1) develop and maintain a healthy heart and lungs, (2) keep the body lean, and (3) control stress. Recognizes that diet and exercise are both important in being fit Identifies persons they know who have a healthy life style	Explains the effects of exercise on muscle tissue, bones, and the cardiorespiratory system (See Chapter 1) Describes the relationship of diet and exercise, generally how the body uses and stores excess food, and the potential value of the various food groups in the diet to the body Explains stress as a factor in everyone's life, how activity can be used to reduce stress, and suggests several activities they can use to reduce stress Describes how warming up and cooling down help the body prepare and recover from exercise and aid in avoiding injury and muscle soreness
Recognizes the effects of health-related fitness on motor performance	Describes how fitness helps motor performance by (1) enabling us to do skills with better form and less strain, (2) enabling us to do the activity longer without fatigue, and (3) enabling us not to get out of breath so easily	Identifies health-related fitness components important to activities in which they participate in and outside of school
Recognizes health risks	Explains how a low activity level affects health now by (1) too much weight for one's body type, (2) poor heart and lung function, and (3) uncontrolled stress	Explains some of the long-term effects of low fitness on the heart Explains how low activity level may affect weight control Explains that low fitness may result in body injury
Testing fitness	Can informally test own fitness: 1. How far can I jog before getting out of breath? 2. Can I touch my toes without bending my knees? 3. Can I pull myself up to the bar? 4. Do I tire easily? 5. Can I pinch an inch? 6. Can I tense and then relax a muscle (group)? 7. Do I stand and sit with good posture?	Can administer and record (with the help of others where needed) their own fitness test results Has developed the following testing skills: 1. Can read a stopwatch or second hand on a watch 2. Can take their own pulse at the wrist or neck 3. Can read a meter stick 4. Can use a caliper Interprets test results in terms of own fitness

TABLE 15-3 HEALTH-RELATED FITNESS KNOWLEDGES AND SKILLS—cont'd

	LEVELS I AND II	LEVELS III AND IV
Recognizes fitness as a personal responsibility	Explains that everyone needs daily activity in which the heart beats faster and there is a feeling of being slightly out of breath Describes how activities may be changed to enhance fitness by increasing the time or speed of the activity, adding arm movements, etc. Can name two activities to develop each component of health-related fitness Can perform beginning conscious relaxation techniques	Identifies several activities they can do to develop each health-related fitness component Recognizes factors in own lives that influence fitness Explains basic principles for improving each component of health-related fitness Develops short- and long-term goals for improving own fitness Demonstrates a series of stretches to warm up each body segment Performs conscious relaxation techniques Designs an activity program for improving personal fitness

only happen to others is prevalent. The closer we can bring the health risks to the children's own age level, the more likely we are to be successful in helping children begin to take responsibility for themselves.

Fitness testing is another important area for learning. As a result of their physical education experience, children should be able to test their own fitness level and be able to interpret the results. In the early years in addition to any formal testing in the schools, children should be able to test themselves informally during the school year on each of the components of health-related fitness. In the upper grades these informal tests may become more sophisticated as children develop the skills for more accurate measurement of the fitness components.

Knowledge about the importance of fitness and fitness testing is not enough. Children need to learn to take charge of their own fitness needs. They need to recognize their fitness level as their own responsibility. They need to learn to set realistic personal fitness goals, short- and long-term, and to identify activities they can do to improve their fitness as well as control stress. In levels I and II, they will need lots of help in this area. In levels III and IV, they should begin, with our help, to set their own individualized fitness programs and to carry out the program they have designed.

The physical education class should be designed to help children meet both their fitness and motor skill needs.

Planning and Conducting Fitness Activities

Where possible fitness activities should be built into the development of the unit and related daily activities. Sustaining an activity for longer periods of time, increasing the vigor (speed) of movement, or holding a position for a time is all that is needed to improve fitness. For example, in a basketball lesson, the children may be dribbling en masse in general space, responding to the teacher's instructions to change hands, speed up, change direction, or change pathway. The activity is sustained long enough to increase the children's heart rates. In a movement lesson, the children may be asked to hold a particular shape, which may require stretching or muscle endurance. In this way children work on fitness as they develop skills and knowledge in other areas.

In addition supplementary fitness activities may be organized in several different ways. They may be performed en masse, with the children working in unison. The teacher or a student calls out the activity and the students perform the activity to a count.

Activities may also be organized to provide group activity, but with each individual working on their own fitness goals. For instance, the activities may be organized so that the children perform a series of individual activities alternated with running or jumping rope. In this way activities to develop various aspects of fitness and using various body parts are alternated with cardiorespiratory exercise. Flexibility, muscle strength, and muscular endurance may be developed as the children move with little break in the activity. An example exercise might consist of running in place, arm circles, running in place, sit-ups, running in place, etc. Activities might also include running in place or rope jumping alternated with some activity performed on the floor, such as alternately curling and extending the body.

Circuit training is another method of organizing for fitness activities. In this technique a series of stations is arranged in the playing area. Stations may focus on different aspects of fitness, with the children selecting the activities they will do at each station. The children are divided into groups and evenly distributed at the stations. Time intervals of 20 seconds to 1 minute are used, depending on the fitness level and age of the children. On the signal to begin, the children perform the exercises to be completed at their particular station. They continue to repeat the exercise until time is called. They move on to the next station and begin again on the signal. Activities should be chosen that allow the children to work alone. Individual scorecards may be used on which the children enter their scores before moving on to the next station. Each day the children should make an effort to equal or slightly improve their previous day's performances. More than one activity exercising a particular body segment may be used, but these activities should not be placed too close together. An example of a circuit is found in the box on p. 251.

Aerobic Exercise

Aerobic exercise performed to music is another way to develop fitness. A simple combination of activities is used, including locomotor movements, stretching, and the like. Children enjoy these routines, especially when a catchy tune is used or the music is brought to the class by the students. Exercises should be performed to the beat and the phrasing of the music.

Aerobic exercise should be preceded by a warm-up period in preparation for the workout. The warm-up prepares the muscles for activity as well as preparing the cardiorespiratory system for vigorous activity. Many different movements may be used. Examples of warm-up activities include arm swings and circles, crossing the arms over head and then bringing them to the sides, extending the arms to the side at shoulder level and moving them in front of the body or overhead one at a time, imitating picking apples by alternately raising the arms up overhead in front of the body or shaking the arms overhead. Walking and other locomotor movements such as skipping, sliding, or even a grapevine step may be used with the children changing directions, length of stride, gradually changing speed, moving on the toes or heels, or using a high knee action. Deep breathing may also be incorporated into the warm-up. Easy stretching might be added to the warm-up, such as slapping one hand to the upper opposite side of the back, knee hugging by raising one knee and hugging it with both hands, or crossing one foot in front of the other and touching the foot to the floor.

After the warm-up the children are ready for the aerobic exercise. Locomotor movements, rope jumping, dance steps, or exercises such as jumping jacks may be performed if the activity keeps going. Adding arm movements or raising the knees generally increases the heart rate. The activity may begin slowly with stretching to music, gradually increasing in aerobic activity and then gradually decreasing once again in effort required. Movements are usually performed in a series of eights to fit the music. Cueing is helpful to assist the children in anticipating the changes in movement and staying with the music. Upper grade children enjoy making up their own combinations of movements. Young children enjoy an aerobic train trip as they follow the leader, performing a different aerobic exercise at each station.

Many of the activities included in the following section of this chapter may be used in developing an aerobic exercise. Some of the movements that might be selected for aerobic exercise are included in the box. A simple combination might include a step to which a leg movement is added followed by the addition of an arm movement. An example might be: Step in place (8), add a touch to the side (step, touch) (8), add an arm swing to the side (8), repeat. Another example would be to select a movement and alternate it with a turn to face another direction in four jumps. When building exercises the teacher should remember that arm and leg movements added to the steps increase the demands placed on the body. Suggestions for a simple routine are found in the box on p. 251.

However they are organized, the activities should be specific to developing total body fitness. Exercises to develop cardiorespiratory endurance, flexibility, and muscular strength of the upper body, abdomen, back, and lower body should be included.

A cool-down follows the workout in which the pulse returns to a near preexercise level and flexibility exercises are used to prevent muscle soreness in upper elementary schoolchildren. Conscious relaxation may also be added as a part of the cool-down.

Step aerobics is a more recent development in aerobic training. Elementary school children may use folded panel mats for their step benches adjusting the height by the number of folds used for the various levels of ability present. The steps may be performed while standing facing the mat, with the side facing the mat, on the mat or from the end of the mat. The sequences are usually combinations of 4 or 8 counts. The following steps may be used:

1. *Basic step:* Facing mat or from the end of the mat: step up with the right foot, then up with the left, down right, down left. Cue: Up, up, down, down.
2. *Tap step:* From the front, side, end or on top of the mat: Step up with the right, tap left up, left foot down, right foot down. Cue: Up, tap, down, tap.
3. *Knee lift:* Right up, lift left knee, down left, right down, left up, lift right knee up, right down, left down. Cue: Up, lift, down, down, up, lift, down, down.
4. *Alternate tap:* Right foot up, left foot up, right down, left tap down, left foot up, right foot up,

CIRCUIT TRAINING: AN EXAMPLE

Time interval: 20 seconds per station for primary age children (increase to 60 seconds for older children)

Run in place (number of steps)

Sit-ups (number)
or
Crab walk in all directions*

Rope jumping (number of jumps)

Agility run (number of trips) between two points

Pull-ups on low horizontal bar or parallel bars
or
Seal crawl*

Inch worm*

*Sustain activity for the entire time.

POSSIBLE MOVEMENTS FOR AEROBIC EXERCISE

STEPS

Step/run in place
Step, together, step
Hop, skip
Step-hop
Bleking
Schottische
Rocking step, front to back
Jumping jacks
Rope jumping

LEG MOVEMENTS

Knee lifts
Toe touches to side, front, or back
Kick to side, front, or back
Leg kicks (chorus line)
Shaking movements

ARM MOVEMENTS

Circles
Swings
Alternate flexion and extension
Raising above head and lowering
Punching-shaking movements
Swimming movements

STRETCHING

Overhead, to the sides, forward, back (standing or sitting)

SAMPLE AEROBIC EXERCISE

	Count	Number	Activity
Part I			
	16	8	2 count: jumping jacks
	16	8	2 count: step in place (1), kick in front, alternating legs (2)
	16	16	1 count: alternating kicks to the side
	16	16	1 count: alternating kicks to the rear
Part II			
	Repeat part I		
Part III			
	8	8	1 count: hop in a circle to the right
	8	8	1 count: hop in a circle to the left
Part IV			
	Repeat Part I ending in a side straddle position with arms raised and spread overhead.		
	Music: Anchors Aweigh.		

left foot down, right foot down. Cue: Up, up, down, tap, up, up, down, down.

Steps 3 and 4 are more advanced and should not be introduced until there has been considerable experience with the first two steps. The children may develop many other steps, based on their own level of ability and should be encouraged to develop their own routines.

Arm swings and other movements of the arms may be added as the children develop proficiency in performing the steps.

DEVELOPING HEALTH-RELATED PHYSICAL FITNESS

Developing health-related fitness requires a knowledge of body function, an understanding of how each aspect of fitness may be improved, and a means for assessing the degree to which fitness has been attained. The following sections provide this information. The assessment instruments in this text include the following items from the AAHPERD Physical Best Fitness Test: the 1-mile run, skinfold measures of body composition, the sit and reach test of flexibility, and a sit-ups test and a pull-up test for muscular endurance. The criteria listed have been derived from other sources. A more detailed test booklet with Physical Best criteria is available through the AAHPERD. In addition the quarter- and half-mile run and the Vermont modified pull-ups tests are included as alternatives to the mile-run and pull-up tests. A standard is included for each test by age to help the teacher establish a baseline for acceptable performance. This text suggests one standard for girls and boys to encourage all children to achieve the best performance they can.

Testing should be used to help children set fitness goals to improve or maintain fitness. It is a starting point. All persons have difficulty dealing with a poor test score. The Physical Best philosophy is one of recognizing each individual as a valued member of the class with the potential for improvement. The standards suggested are *to help the teacher* establish a base score from which to help children set realistic personal goals.

An important consideration in planning fitness activities includes the **frequency, intensity,** and **time** devoted to the activity. Frequency refers to the number of days per week needed to improve fitness. In most cases 3 days is the minimum time recommended, with 4 or 5 days yielding better results. In beginning fitness activities it may be best to begin with 3 days and gradually work up to 5 to minimize muscle injury and resulting soreness. In the beginning a day of rest between workouts is definitely beneficial.

Intensity refers to the degree of vigor or the amount of effort expended during the activity. The intensity of the activity should gradually increase during the workout, be sustained at the desired level for a period of time, and then gradually decrease once more. Intensity is measured by the heart rate in a cardiorespiratory exercise, the number of sit-ups or pull-ups for muscular endurance, and the degree beyond normal stretching that is achieved in flexibility exercises.

Time or duration refers to the length of the activity periods and is closely related to intensity. If the exercise is very intense, the workout will be short. If the activity is of low intensity, the workout will be longer.

A number of different activities may be used for developing components of health-related fitness. Many can

Working on cardiorespiratory fitness.

be built into the regular unit activities. Other activities may be used, and children should be given some choice in the activities they choose to work on each component.

Cardiorespiratory Endurance

Cardiorespiratory endurance is the ability to sustain physical exercise and to recover from vigorous physical activity in a reasonable time with no lasting side effects. It is concerned with the **aerobic efficiency** of the body, which is the ability of the body to supply fuel and oxygen to the muscles being used. The heart's capacity for pumping blood is a major factor in cardiorespiratory endurance. A conditioned heart is able to exert greater force with each heartbeat, and as a result a greater volume of blood is released into the arteries to be carried through the body.

The efficiency of the lungs to take in sufficient air and to expel carbon dioxide is also an important factor in cardiorespiratory endurance. In order for the body at work to use food supplied by the blood, oxygen is needed. The lungs inhale air, and oxygen from the air is transported to the heart in the blood and then ejected from the heart to be carried to the organs needing oxygen. From the organs the blood carrying carbon dioxide is returned to the heart and finally to the lungs, where the carbon dioxide is released in exhalation.

Improving Cardiorespiratory Endurance

Frequency: Three to five sessions a week are required to improve and maintain cardiorespiratory endurance. Exercise on a regular basis may be helpful in establishing an exercise habit.

Intensity: The activity should result in raising the heart rate 60% to 75% of the maximum for a sustained period of time. The **maximum heart rate** of elementary school-aged children is approximately 210 to 220 beats per minute. The heart rate should be raised to approximately 160 beats per minute during exercise to improve cardiorespiratory endurance.

Table 15-4 provides some estimates for elementary school children. The desired heart rate may be found by subtracting the resting heart rate from the maximum heart rate (210 or 220), then multiplying this number by the desired percent (60% or 75%). The resting heart rate is then added to this number to yield the target heart rate.

Children in the intermediate and upper elementary school grades can learn to take their own pulse at the wrist or at the neck. To find the pulse rate at the wrist, the index and second fingertips are placed on the radial artery, located on the thumb side of the wrist. To take the pulse at the neck, the index and second fingers are placed just under the jaw and slightly above and to the side of the Adam's apple on the carotid artery. The fingers should press easily until the pulse is found. The pulse is counted for 10 seconds and then multiplied by six to find the rate per minute, or a target rate for 10 seconds can be set and compared to the actual rate counted.

TABLE 15-4 TARGET HEART RATE ESTIMATES FOR ELEMENTARY SCHOOL CHILDREN

RESTING HEART RATE	60% OF MAXIMUM	75% OF MAXIMUM
60 and below	150	173
60-64	151	173
65-69	153	173
70-74	155	175
75-79	157	177
80-84	159	178
85-89	161	179
90 or above	162	180

Taking one's pulse after running.

Shortly after exercise, in approximately 3 minutes, the pulse rate should drop dramatically back to a near normal level. If it does not, a physician should be consulted.

Duration: Activity sessions should last for 15 to 20 minutes at the elementary school level. The duration of the activity is related to the intensity of the workout. If the workout is of **low intensity,** such as walking, the activity period needs to be longer. Activity generally begins at a low intensity, with the intensity raised as the children show improvement in cardiorespiratory endurance.

Warm-ups: Walking or other locomotor movements followed by stretching exercises of the upper and lower legs.

Activities: Activities in which there is a continuous energy output or those in which high- and low-intensity activities are alternated are used. Many of the skill and concept activities found in the activity chapters may be turned into fitness activities by increasing the intensity and/or time of the practice. Examples include:

- Fast walking. Walking is becoming recognized as an appropriate cardiorespiratory fitness activity. A walk at a brisk pace can increase the heart rate and is easier on the legs and joints than running or jogging.
- Jogging.
- Alternating sprinting and jogging.
- A steeplechase course in which the perimeter of the gymnasium or the playing area is set up with imaginary water hazards, obstacles to cross or go around, and areas for sprinting. The children may repeat the course several times, timing each attempt.
- Sustained locomotor skills in which the teacher or a student calls out the skills, which may be an extension of the day's unit activities, as the children keep moving: "Skip . . . ; now run . . . ; try hopping."
- In soccer, hockey, or basketball, continuous dribbling with the teacher calling the variations used, including changing direction, pathway, and speed.
- Dribbling in intervals, alternating dribbling for speed (fastest speed at which they can control the ball), and dribbling while walking or in place.
- Folk dances performed to vigorous music also help raise the heart rate.
- Mass running and tag games.
- Follow the leader who must keep moving. Imitate whatever movements the leader does.
- Running a number of laps around the playing area, attempting to maintain a steady speed: "Run 5 laps."
- Running laps for time: "How many laps can you complete in 2 minutes?"
- Running in place and then, on the signal, running a lap, repeating several times.
- Rope jumping forward or backward: "How many consecutive jumps can you do? How many jumps can you complete in 30 seconds?"
- Marching.
- Bench step on stairs or a 10- to 14-inch high bench. The individual steps up on the bench with one foot (count 1); brings the other foot next to the first (count 2); steps down with one foot (count 3); brings the second foot next to the first (count 4); and repeats.
- Obstacle course including a number of events such as rope jumping and moving over or under obstacles.
- Jumping jacks. From a standing position with arms down at the sides, the arms are brought up from the sides with hands touching overhead as the legs jump to a side stride position (count 1). The arms are brought back down to the sides as the legs return to the starting position (count 2).
- Aerobic routines to music.
- Step aerobic routines to music.

Assessing Cardiorespiratory Fitness (AAHPERD, 1988; AAU)

Distance Run (quarter-mile, one-half, and one-mile runs)

Purpose: To measure maximum functional capacity and cardiorespiratory endurance.

The test may be administered on a 440-yard or 400-meter track or any other flat measured surface, such as around a measured outdoor play area.

The students are organized in partners. On the signal "Ready, start," one of each set of partners runs one-half or one mile in the fastest time. As the runners cross the finish line, the timer calls out the running time. The individuals not running listen for their partner's running time and record it on a piece of paper. Walking is permitted, but the individual should attempt to cover the distance as fast as possible. (The youngest children will need assistance in getting their partner's score.)

An alternative is to have a person call the times as runners cross the finish line which another person records. Another assistant passes out popsicle sticks which are numbered consecutively representing the order of finish to the children as they cross the finish line. After the run is complete, the children turn in their sticks and their name is recorded next to the time of finish. The distance is recorded in minutes and seconds.

Standard for the quarter-mile, half-mile, and mile runs (minutes and seconds) (AAHPERD, 1988; Auxter and Pyfer; Ross)

Quarter mile	Half mile	One mile
Age 6: 2:23	Age 8: 4:31	Age 10: 9:50
Age 7: 2:13	Age 9: 4:20	Age 11: 9:00
		Age 12: 8:45

Substituting shorter runs for young children is advisable because of their shorter attention span. If distances shorter than the quarter mile are used, criteria may be established by the school or school district from scores collected for 1 or more years and updated as the children's performance improves.

Body Composition

Body composition refers to the amounts of specific body tissues in the human body. Generally, regarding fitness we consider the **lean body weight** and body fat. The lean body weight is made up of the bones, muscles, and internal organs. The body fat is the fat stored in and around the muscles and body organs.

Body composition, although partially due to heredity, is primarily the result of activity and nutrition. The food we consume contains carbohydrates, fats, and proteins. Each of these substances is important to the vital processes that take place in the body.

Carbohydrates provide an energy source for the cells. Carbohydrates in excess of what is needed are converted to fat and stored as adipose tissue beneath the skin and in the hips, thighs and abdominal area.

Fats provide more than twice the amount of energy as an equal proportion of carbohydrates. The fatty layer surrounding the vital organs protects them from trauma, and fat is also a source of insulation protecting the body from cold temperatures. In high temperatures, however, excess fat may cause overweight or obese individuals to feel distress sooner than normal weight individuals. Like carbohydrates, excess fats are stored in the body for future use. Although by-products of fats (cholesterol and triglycerides) have been associated with heart disease, fats should not be eliminated entirely from the diet.

Although proteins are not a major energy source, they are important in the growth and repair of cells. They are found in cell walls and the cell nucleus.

The process of breaking down energy sources into glucose to be used by the cells is called metabolism. The metabolic rate varies with the individual. Some persons appear able to consume large quantities of food without gaining weight. Others tend to gain weight consuming small quantities of food. One might assume that the overweight individual has a more efficient system, requiring little food to provide for its energy needs.

Activity level is also a factor in weight control. Generally, overweight children exercise less than children of normal weight. Increasing the activity level is necessary for weight reduction. Sufficient exercise and an appropriate diet bring about the best results in weight control.

Childhood obesity is a serious health problem in the United States. Excessive weight has ramifications for the developing child physically, socially, and psychologically. Society values a lean body. As children enter school, they quickly become aware of how others react to them. Overweight children are often ridiculed or excluded from group membership. Failure to be accepted influences children's feelings about themselves.

Obese children require some special consideration in physical education. Vigorous activity is more tiring for them. Obese children heat up more rapidly than their normal-weight peers, and chafing of the legs may make some activities painful. The added weight may interfere with skill development. Ill-fitting clothing may restrict movement.

Screening preschool children may identify early weight problems. A number of growth tables are available similar to the one found in Chapter 2 to aid the teacher in assessing weight. Children with weight problems need understanding and counseling. The child and the family may need help in nutrition and diet planning as well as in recognizing the importance of daily exercise. A child's overeating may be a reaction to problems at home. Often when children are upset, eating becomes a way of coping with their problems. Before a child's weight problem can be dealt with, the cause must be determined. Is it the availability of desserts or other foods with a high sugar content? Is overeating a way of dealing with problems at home? Is poor nutrition the cause of the weight problem? How physically active is the child? What are the child's favorite leisure pursuits?

Overcoming weight problems is difficult for children. It requires maturity, dedication, and often sacrifice. This is only possible if the entire family supports the efforts. Unfortunately, it is easier to begin with good habits than to change them.

Improving Body Composition

Frequency/intensity: Regular daily exercise is required to improve body composition by lowering the percentage of body fat. In working with overweight children, it is best to begin with low-intensity exercise, which gets them moving but does not result in overheating and other discomforts associated with physical activity. Once an activity habit is established, the intensity of the activity may be increased to moderate intensity. Children with low self-esteem and a body concept in which they see themselves as inept in physical activity may not be willing participants. Beginning with activities in which fun is stressed and they can feel successful is important. Activities that provide successful social experiences with other children and little pressure to perform at a high level of skill result in greater interest in being physically active. The activity level may then be increased gradually to accommodate weight loss.

Duration: Activity sessions of 30 to 45 minutes suffice. Sessions may increase in duration as the children's condition improves.

Warm-ups: Warm-up activities include stretching for all body segments following light exercise such as walking or jogging.

Activities: Generally, all the activities included for cardiorespiratory endurance may be used. Vigorous activity is necessary if children are to metabolize a sufficient number of calories.

Assessing Body Composition

Skinfold measures in which the thickness of a section of skin is determined with a **skinfold caliper** are used to measure the percentage of body fat. Several sites on the body are used. The following procedure is used to measure a skinfold (AAHPERD, 1980).

1. Grasp the skinfold between the thumb and forefinger and lift up.
2. Place the contact surface of the caliper 1 cm (1 inch) above or below the fingers.
3. Slowly release the grip on the calipers, enabling them to exert their full tension on the skinfold.
4. Read the skinfold to the nearest 0.5 mm after the needle stops (1 to 2 seconds after releasing the grip on the caliper).

Children should wear short-sleeve shirts and shorts for the test.

There are several calipers on the market. The AAHPERD recommends the Harpenden (Quinton Instrument Co., Seattle, Washington) or the Lange (Cambridge Scientific Industries, Maryland) calipers for measuring skinfolds. Whatever caliper is used, it should be carefully calibrated and should register zero when in the closed position. The Adipometer (Ross Products, Division Abbott Laboratories, Columbus, Ohio) is a less expensive caliper that is affordable for all schools.

Using the calipers accurately takes practice. It may be necessary to test the accuracy of the measurements by repeating them on several individuals. By repeating the measurements, the tester should develop skill using the calipers so that there is little discrepancy between the repeated readings.

Table 15-5 indicates the percentage of body fat considered to be obesity for white elementary school children at various ages.

TABLE 15-5 OBESITY STANDARDS FOR WHITE AMERICANS

AGE	THICKNESS (MM)*	
	MALE	FEMALE
5	12	14
6	12	15
7	13	16
8	14	17
9	15	18
10	16	20
11	17	21
12	18	22
13	18	23
14	17	23

*Minimum triceps skinfold thickness (millimeters) indicating obesity.

Triceps and Sum of Triceps and Calf Skinfolds

Purpose: To determine the level of fatness.

Two skinfold sites are used for the test: the triceps and calf (Figure 15-1). The triceps skinfold is measured over the triceps muscle of the right arm at the midpoint between the acromion process of the scapula and the elbow (Ross, 1985; Ross, 1987). The skinfold is parallel to the longitudinal axis of the upper arm. The students should have the arm hanging relaxed at their side. The calf skinfold is taken on the inside (medial side) of the right lower leg at the largest part of the calf girth (AAHPERD, 1988). Before grasping the calf skinfold, the student should place the right foot on a bench with the knee slightly flexed.

Each skinfold should be measured three consecutive times, with the median (middle) score being recorded.

Standard for the sum of the skinfolds (mm) (Ross et al.)

Age: 6 to 9
Score: 16 to 19 (boys); 21 to 26 (girls)

Triceps skinfold (mm) (Kendall, 1965; Kendall et al. 1985)

Age: 6 to 12
Score: 8 to 10 (boys); 11 to 13 (girls)

In determining individual needs based on test scores, children with scores higher than the criteria should probably engage in a program to reduce body weight to bring their leanness to a more acceptable level.

Flexibility

Flexibility refers to the range of motion in the joints, which varies with age and physical condition. Figure 15-2 shows the difference in flexibility with age and changing body proportions. Because there is great variability, children must be helped to establish realistic goals for themselves and not have the same expectations for performance as other children in the group. Flexibility should not be stressed in the beginning because children vary considerably in this condition and may be discouraged if they are extremely inflexible. They may also notice a difference in their ability to stretch the two sides of the body.

Flexibility is specific to the particular articulations of the body. A person may have good flexibility in some areas and not in others. Those articulations where the full range of movement is used retain their flexibility; those joints not used in the full range of motion become less flexible.

Adequate flexibility is important to everyday living. It enables one to more successfully complete daily routine tasks. Individuals with good flexibility also may be less susceptible to joint injury.

Improving Flexibility

Frequency: Three to five times per week is recommended.

Intensity: Static stretching is used following the procedures indicated on p. 258. The stretch should be repeated several times.

Duration: Stretches should be held for 10 to 30 seconds.

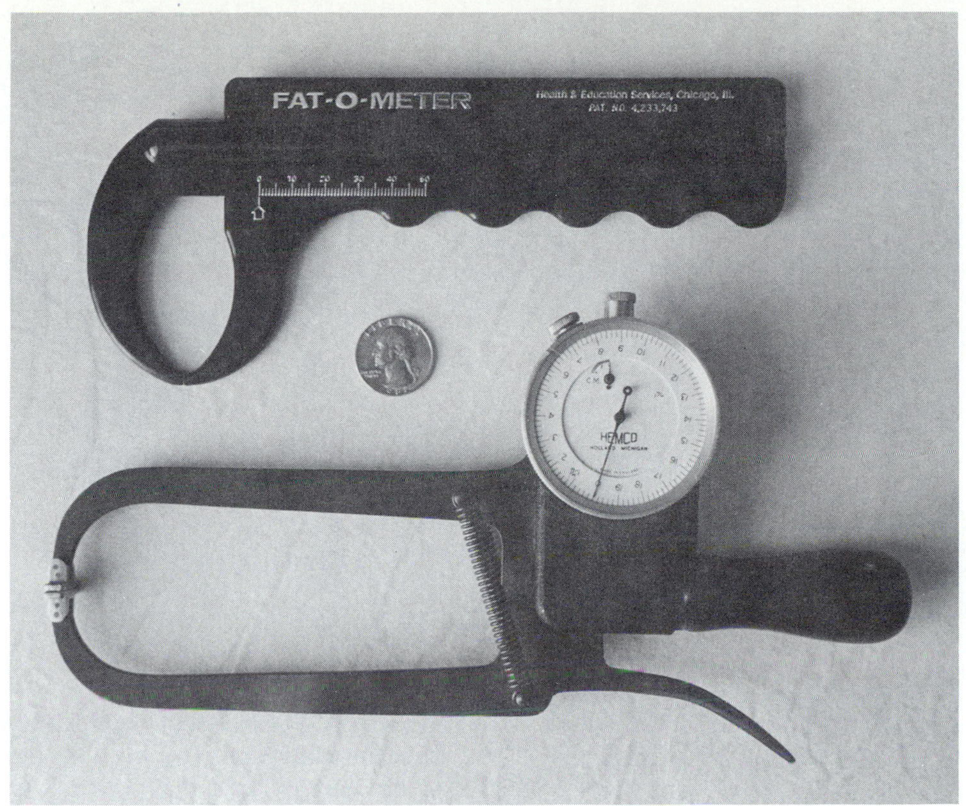

Skinfold calipers.

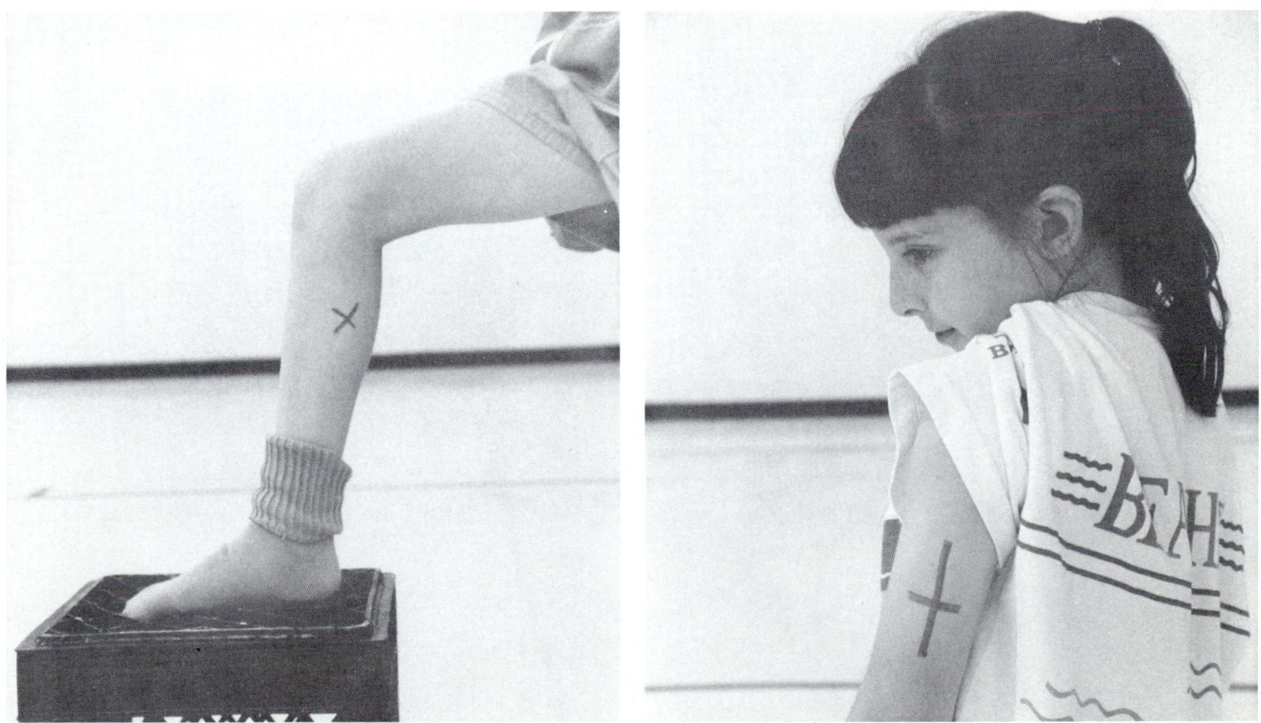

FIGURE 15-1 Leg and arm skinfold sites.

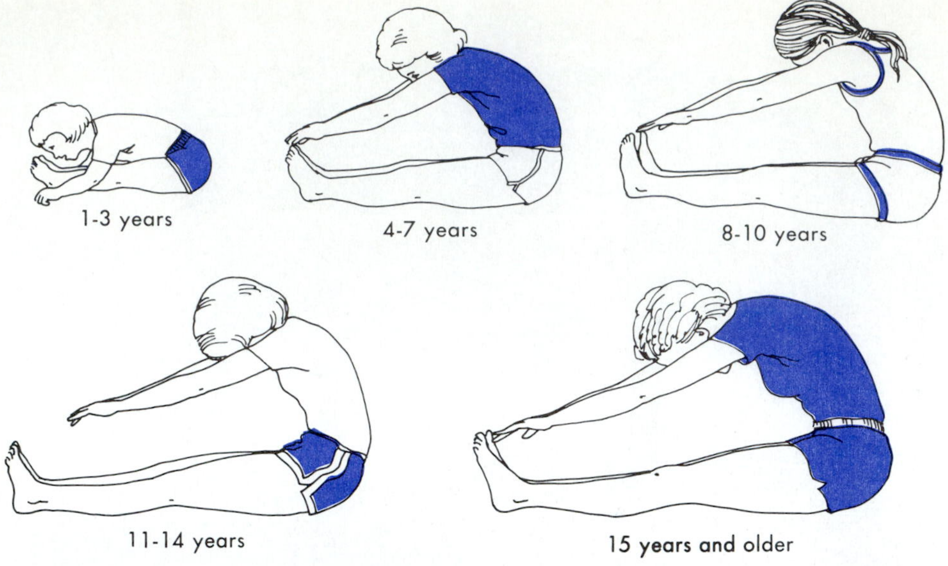

FIGURE 15-2 Normal flexibility at various ages.

Warm-ups: Easy stretches following some easy locomotor activities should be used.

Activities:

Stretching: Stretching is an important activity for warming up and cooling down the body. Slow, static stretches are more effective than ballistic or bouncing stretches for increasing mobility in the joints and preventing soft tissue injury. It is vital to stretch the body segments that are important to the specific activity of instruction. The individual begins the stretch to a point of feeling a little tension in the body part being stretched. As the body relaxes, the stretch is extended and held again. Individuals should stretch within their own limits. The stretch should not be strained or painful. Breathing is rhythmical during the stretch, and relaxation is important. On recovery from a bending stretch while standing, the child's legs should be bent slightly to lessen the strain on the lower back.

Side stretches as a group warm-up.

Stretching becomes an increasingly important aspect of warming up for activity.

Leg kicks.

Stunts: Stunts described in Chapter 17 may be used, including inch worm, bear walk, gorilla walk, ostrich walk, snail, thread the needle, bridge, and back bend.

Movement activities: Many movement activities include potential flexibility activities. Holding freezes in various body positions is fun and at the same time may include stretching.

Miscellaneous activities such as arm circling or the bear hug may also be used.

Assessing Flexibility

Sit and Reach (AAHPERD, 1988)

Purpose: To evaluate flexibility of the lower back and posterior thighs (hamstrings).

The test apparatus consists of a specially constructed box with a measuring scale on which 23 cm is at the level of the feet. See Figure 15-3 for construction specifications. The measuring stick reads 23 cm at the level of the feet.

The starting position is assumed by sitting at the apparatus in bare or stocking feet with the knees fully extended and the feet a shoulder width apart. The feet are placed so they are flat against the board. The arms are extended forward with the hands placed on top of each other. The pupil reaches forward with palms down along the measuring scale four times and holds the position on maximum reach on the fourth trial for at least 1 second. The hands must reach evenly. The score is the most distant point reached on the fourth trial measured to the nearest centimeter.

Standard for the sit and reach test (cm) (AAHPERD, 1980)

Age: 6 through 12
Score: 25 to 26

Muscular Strength and Endurance

Muscular strength refers to the ability of the muscles to do work; muscular endurance is the ability to sustain work over time. Muscular strength and endurance are specific to each set of muscles. Muscles that are used more are stronger and have greater endurance than those that are not used as much. If the muscles continue to be used, the level of strength and endurance is maintained. Reduced use decreases strength and endurance.

The legs, which are used daily to move from place to place, have the strongest muscles. The upper body, especially the muscles of the shoulder girdle, tends to be weaker, and except for a few occupations, it does not have the demands placed on it to improve and maintain muscular strength and endurance. The abdominal muscles may also be weak. Weak abdominals may be a cause of low back problems. A program should include activities that strengthen and maintain all the muscles of the body.

Much debate has focused on strength testing and the development of tests that isolate the desired muscle groups and provide an adequate distribution of scores. In addition some tests are difficult to control as children compensate in performing the test items. For instance in the sit-ups test, children may attempt to bounce up rather than pull themselves up with their abdominal muscles. Positioning is important in the tests to be sure the appropriate muscle group is actually being tested. Some tests may be so difficult that many of the children cannot achieve a test score. In the pull-ups test, for example, many children are unable to do even one pull-up. With these difficulties in mind a variety of tests are described.

Improving Muscular Strength and Endurance

Frequency: Three to five sessions a week is recommended.

Intensity: The workload, or demands on the muscle groups, should be increased gradually but not too fast.

Duration: The number of repetitions is gradually increased.

Warm-ups: Light activity such as fast walking or jogging.

Activities: For specific body segments the following activities may be used:

For the upper body:

- Crab walk, seal crawl, coffee grinder, seal slap, bridge, lame puppy walk, bear walk, inch worm, wheelbar row, mule kick, bridge, or other stunts in which the body weight is taken on the arms (see Chapter 17)
- Chinning or bent arm hang on a horizontal ladder, jungle gym, or other climbing apparatus
- Traveling on a horizontal ladder or straight arm traveling on parallel bars
- Throwing objects and gradually increasing the size and/or weight (a basketball is a heavy object for an elementary school child), from standing, sitting, and lying positions
- Climbing ropes: climbing, pull-ups, or bent arm hang
- Push-ups if performed correctly or wall push-aways
- Inverted hangs on ropes or horizontal or parallel bars

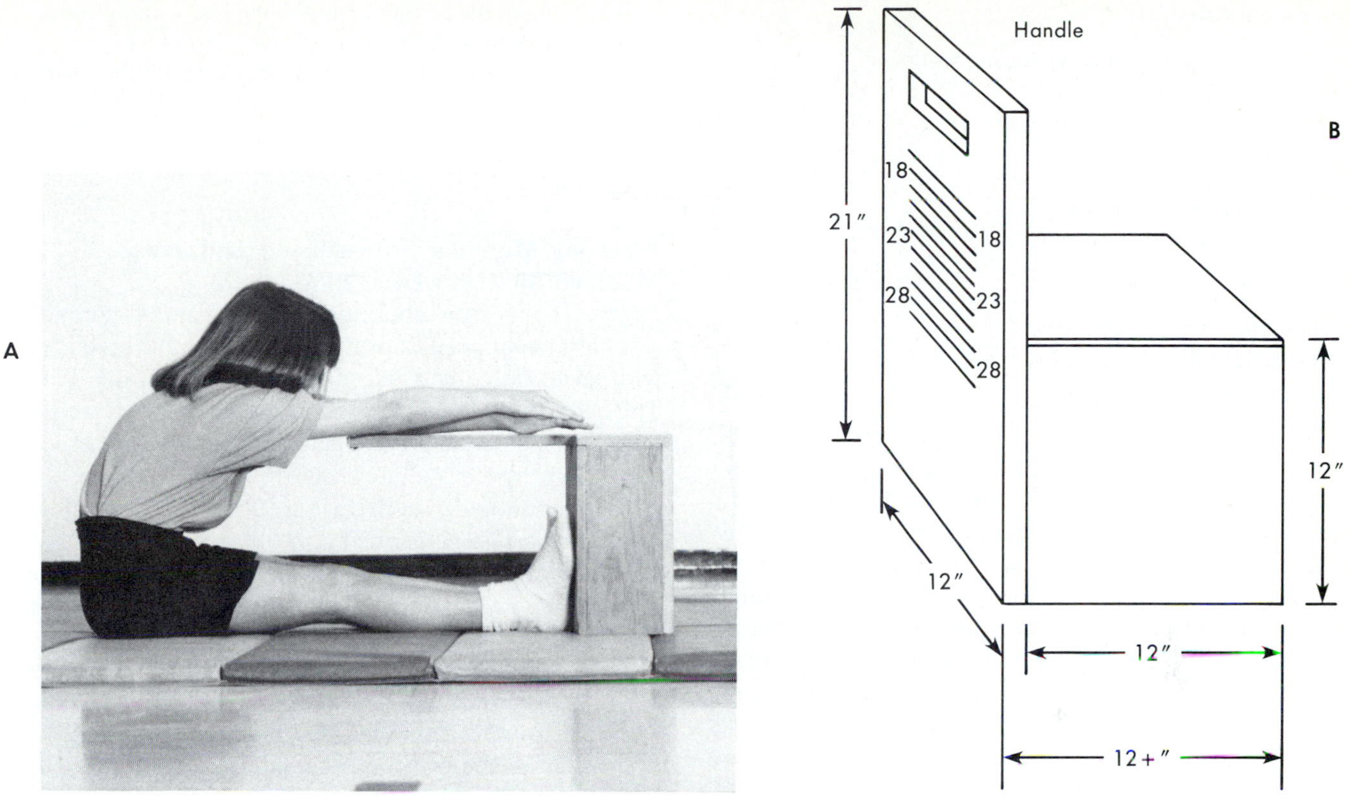

FIGURE 15-3 Flexibility. **A,** Sit and reach test. **B,** Apparatus for flexibility testing.

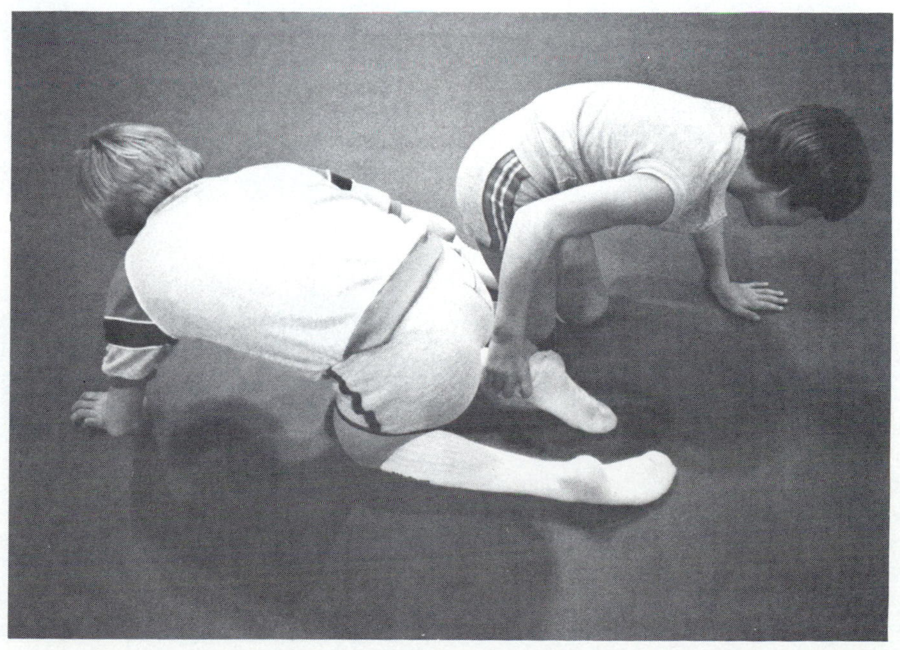

Ankle pull.

For abdominals:

- Modified sit-ups with an increasing workload
- Crab walk, V-sit
- Alternate knee raisers or knee circles

For the back:

- Upper back lift, lower back lift
- Straight back raise

For the legs:

- Jumping for height or distance
- Running in place, jogging, running
- Rope jumping

Combatives provide an opportunity for children to apply mechanical principles and to engage in friendly competition with others as they work on muscle strength and endurance. Children of equal size and weight should be paired. At times they may wish to challenge children with a size advantage, but this should be allowed only within a reasonable range. For safety combatives should be performed on a mat. The following combatives may be performed in the middle and upper elementary school grades when children have acquired the necessary body awareness and control for success.

Ankle pull: Partners are on hands and knees, next to each other and facing in opposite directions. Each picks up the other's nearest ankle and tries to crawl forward, dragging the partner along.

Backward goat: Partners are on hands and feet, back to back with hips touching. On the signal and using only their hips they each try to push the partner over a line ahead of them. (The hands should be kept well in front of the body to guard against the child bumping the chin against the mat.)

Bottoms up: Partners begin sitting, facing each other with hands joined, legs spread, and feet touching. Each tries to pull the other so that the hips are raised up off the mat.

Chest push: Partners place both hands on each other's chest near the shoulders and attempt to push each other backward over a line.

Foot wrestle: Partners stand facing each other with hands on hips and one foot off the floor; using the free foot, each tries to make the other touch the raised foot on the floor.

Indian hand wrestle: Partners stand facing each other with right hands grasped at the level of the head. With the outer edges of the right feet together and touching and the left foot back for balance, they attempt to push each other, trying to upset the other's stance. If the right foot moves or any part of the body other than the feet touches the mat, the player loses.

Indian leg wrestle: Partners begin lying on the mat on their backs, side by side, and facing in opposite directions. On the signal, they raise the inside legs perpendicular to the floor, and each attempts to hook the other's leg at the knee to cause the partner to roll over.

Lumberjack wrestle: Partners lie down facing each other with legs spread apart, right hands held together with the elbows touching, and left hands behind the backs. Each tries to force the partner's hand to the mat without moving the elbow off the mat.

Stork wrestle: Partners stand facing each other with their left feet raised in back and held with the left hands. With right hands joined, they attempt to pull each other off balance and force the partner to put the left foot down to the mat.

Assessing Muscular Strength and Endurance

Modified Sit-Ups (AAHPERD, 1988)

Purpose: To measure abdominal strength and endurance.

The starting position is assumed by lying on the back with knees flexed and the soles of the feet on the floor. The heels should be between 12 and 18 inches from the buttocks. The arms are crossed, with the right hand at the top of the left shoulder and the left hand at the top of the right shoulder. A partner holds the feet to the floor as the sit-ups are performed. On the signal "ready, go," the individual curls to the sitting position. The arms maintain contact with the chest throughout the sit-up. The sit-up is completed as the elbows touch the thighs. The student then returns to the down position until the midback makes contact with the floor. Students may rest between sit-ups but should be encouraged to do as many as possible in the 60 seconds. The score is the number of sit-ups that can be completed in 60 seconds.

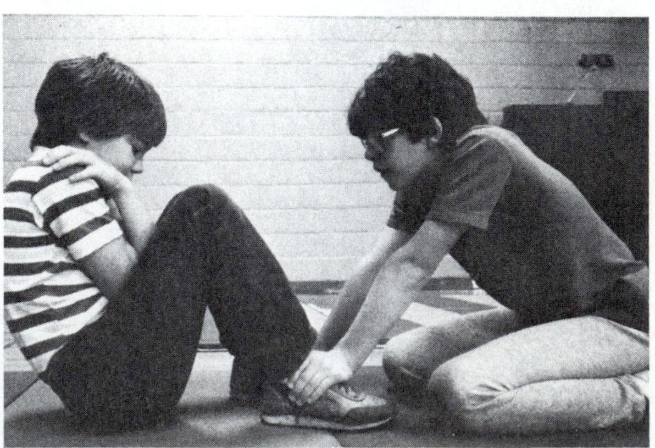

Sit-ups.

Standard for the modified sit-up test (number of sit-ups completed) (Ross et al., 1985, 1987)

Age:	6	7	8	9	10	11	12
Score:	19	23	26	28	34	36	38

Note: There is some evidence that holding the feet obscures weakness in the abdominals, enabling the student with weak abdominals to perform the sit-up (Kendall).

Pull-ups (AAHPERD, 1988)
Purpose: To measure arm and shoulder girdle strength and endurance.

A bar is used that is high enough to permit the individual to hang with arms and legs extended and the feet off the floor.

The individual begins in a position hanging from the bar with body fully extended. The individual holds the bar with the palms facing away from the performer and raises the body with the arms until the chin can be placed over the bar and then lowers once again to the hanging position. The pull-up is repeated as many times as possible.

One trial is permitted. The body should not swing during the execution of the pull-up. The legs are kept straight and no kicking is allowed. The score is the total number of pull-ups completed.

Standard for the pull-up test (number of pull-ups completed) (Hunsicker and Reiff)

Age:	6	7	8	9	10	11	12
Score:	1	1	1	1	1	2	2

Vermont Modified Pull-ups Test (Vermont Governor's Council on Physical Fitness and Sport)
Purpose: To measure arm and shoulder girdle strength and endurance.

The test is performed on an apparatus that consists of two 3-foot upright 2 × 4 posts notched or drilled every 2 inches, beginning at a height of 14″ above the floor, to support a crossbar at various heights. An elastic band is stretched between the two posts two thirds of the height of the bar (Figure 15-4).

The bar is positioned so that the student can reach the bar from a back-lying position with arms straight from the shoulders and the back off the floor about 2 to 3 inches. The body is straight, and only the heels are in contact with the floor. The arms are in front of the elastic band, with the hands gripping the bar so that the palms face the feet. On the signal "go" the student raises the body, keeping the heels on the floor and the body straight until the chin is above the elastic band, and then returns to the starting position. Only the arms may be used for the pull-up, and they must be fully extended when returning to the starting position. The legs and body must remain straight throughout the exercise. When the student can no longer complete a pull-up, the test is over. There is no resting between pull-ups.

Criteria for the Vermont modified pull-up test (number of pull-ups completed)

Age:	6	7	8	9	10	11	12
Score:	9	10	13	16	18	18	18

Modified Push-up Test (Nelson)
Purpose: To test upper body strength and endurance.

The test is performed in partners. Students being tested stand with feet shoulder-width apart. Bending at the hips, they place their hands on the floor a shoulder width apart. The arms are extended and knees straight. This is the "up" position. The partner places one hand on one of their partner's arms at the elbow and the other on the floor between the arms of the child being tested.

To begin the test, the children bend the elbows back toward their feet and lower their forehead so that it touches their partner's hand. They then return to the "up" position. The knees are kept straight throughout the test.

The modified push-ups are performed to a 2-second cadence of "up, down" called by the tester. The partners count out loud each push-up completed. The test is over when the performer fails to do a push-up within the 2

Pull-ups.

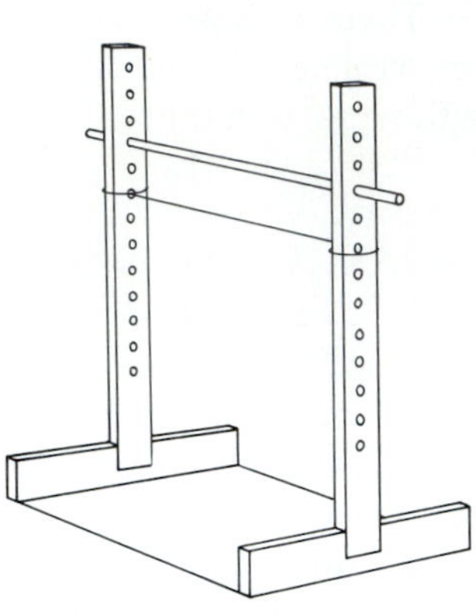

FIGURE 15-4 Modified pull-ups test.

count sequence. Using a 2 to 3 minute tape of the cadence helps in administering the test. The score is the number of modified push-ups completed on one trial.

Standards for the modified push-up test (Nelson)

Age 6:	12	*Age 9:*	17
Age 7:	16	*Age 10:*	20
Age 8:	18	*Age 11:*	22

POSTURE

Posture may be defined as the alignment of body parts to maintain an upright position. Posture is dynamic. The skeletal system is comprised of many bones joined and bound together by ligaments, muscles, and their tendons. Movement is possible in a variety of ways, which allows the body parts to be aligned in different ways. In addition, even when it appears to be motionless, the body is constantly adjusting to the pull of gravity. Good posture or body alignment requires each body part to be aligned with the one directly below it so that the center of gravity of each part is directly above the one below. In this alignment gravitational stresses are minimized. In good alignment the three major body segments—the hips, trunk, and head—are directly over one another (Figure 15-5).

A plumb line dropped to the side of a standing person should pass through the lobe of the ear, the tip of the shoulder, the center of the trunk, the center of the hips, slightly behind the kneecap, and slightly in front of the ankle bone.

When viewed from the front, the feet are slightly apart (2 to 3 inches), the body weight is carried over the middle of the feet, the knees are straight but not hyperextended, the pelvic girdle is aligned with the feet, the chest is balanced over the pelvis, the shoulder girdle is relaxed with the arms hanging loosely at the sides, and the head is balanced over the upper end of the spine.

When the person is sitting in a chair, the head is aligned directly over the shoulders, the hips are well back into the chair so that the thighs are supported, the back is straight and resting comfortably against the back of the chair, the knees are flexed at right angles, and the feet are flat on the floor.

If the chair does not fit, the child's back and thighs may not be supported and/or the feet may not touch the floor. When a child is working at a desk, the top of the desk should be at the level of the elbows. It should be close enough so that the child does not have to lean too far forward or sit on the edge of the chair.

Often in physical education, students sit on the floor, on mats, or on bleachers, which have insufficient back support. Having children sit next to walls for back support may help. Because children sit for very little time in physical education classes, the chance for poor sitting posture is minimized.

The posture of children differs slightly from the standard recognized as good alignment for adults. Children undergo a series of growth changes from birth to maturity that affect posture. Different segments of the body grow at different rates. As bones grow, the body proportions change. Children have greater mobility and flexibility than adults. The children's range of movement in the joints permits greater momentary deviations in posture than would be considered healthy for adults. This mobility protects children from fixed postural faults to some degree. As children approach adulthood, ligaments and fascia tighten gradually, which begins to limit the range of movement in the joints and consequently increases stability.

In growing children there is an imbalance in the muscle strength of the back and front sides of the body, with the muscles of the back being stronger. As children mature, this imbalance decreases, although generally the muscles of the back of the body remain slightly stronger throughout life. Weak abdominals may contribute to poor postural habits.

Another factor that cannot be overlooked in a discussion of the posture of children is nutrition. Proper nutrition is essential to the healthy development of body tissues. Poor diet has lasting effects on children's posture. Although good diet is important throughout life, it is perhaps of greater significance during the developmental years.

Back problems in adulthood are more often the result of abuse through poor posture and poor body mechanics than the result of an accident. Poor posture may also result in muscle spasms and tension.

Good posture is aesthetically pleasing. It conveys the impression of confidence. It is often a characteristic that gives a favorable first impression. A person's postural habits may be difficult to change. A person may know what good alignment is and yet fail to achieve it for many reasons. Children who are taller than their classmates may slouch to appear shorter. Adolescents may choose postures common to their group. Small children may walk on tiptoes to appear taller. Good alignment must be valued for good posture to develop.

The physical education teacher is often one of the first to notice deviations in posture. Common faults include the following:

The head held forward of its normal alignment
An increased pelvic tilt, which results in an exaggerated curve in the lower back
Protruding abdomen
Round shoulders
Protruding scapula
One shoulder higher than the other
One hip higher than the other
The feet turned in or out with the weight carried on the inner ankles
Knees turned toward each other

Some postural deviations such as a protruding abdomen or scapula are developmental in nature, appearing at a particular age and developmental period and disappearing without correction. Others may lead to serious problems if not treated.

The largest number of postural deviations occur between the ages of 10 and 15 years. Postural screening is important during this period. The physical education teacher is often responsible for conducting the initial posture screening. Children with postural deviation from the normal standard are referred to the school nurse or their own physician. The physician makes the exercise prescription to be carried out by the physical education teacher. During the adolescent growth spurt, spinal deviations may occur. These deviations may be serious and should receive appropriate medical attention promptly to prevent serious and costly medical problems later. Figures 15-6 and 15-7 show normal spinal curves and three common deviations: **scoliosis,** one or more lateral curvatures of the spine; **lordosis,** characterized by an increased lumbar curve; and **kyphosis,** an increased thoracic curve. These conditions should receive immediate medical attention.

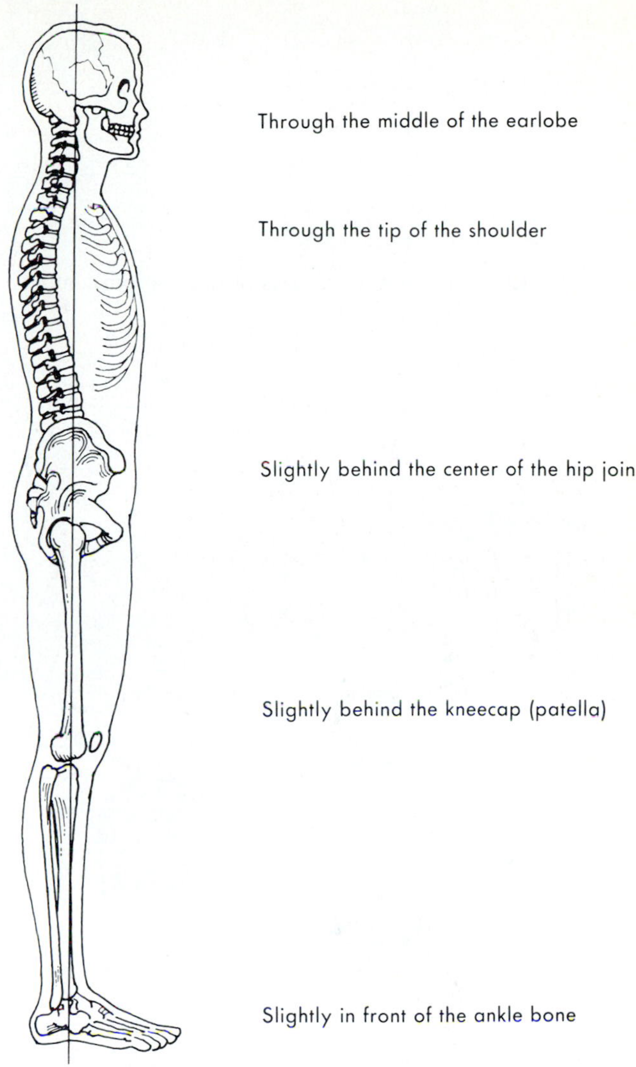

FIGURE 15-5 Alignment of body parts in standing position.

Postural Screening

Postural screening should include both the static (stationary) and dynamic (moving) posture. Several observations should be made before an orthopedic referral is

FIGURE 15-6 Side and back views of normal spinal curves.

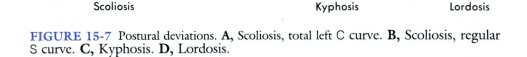

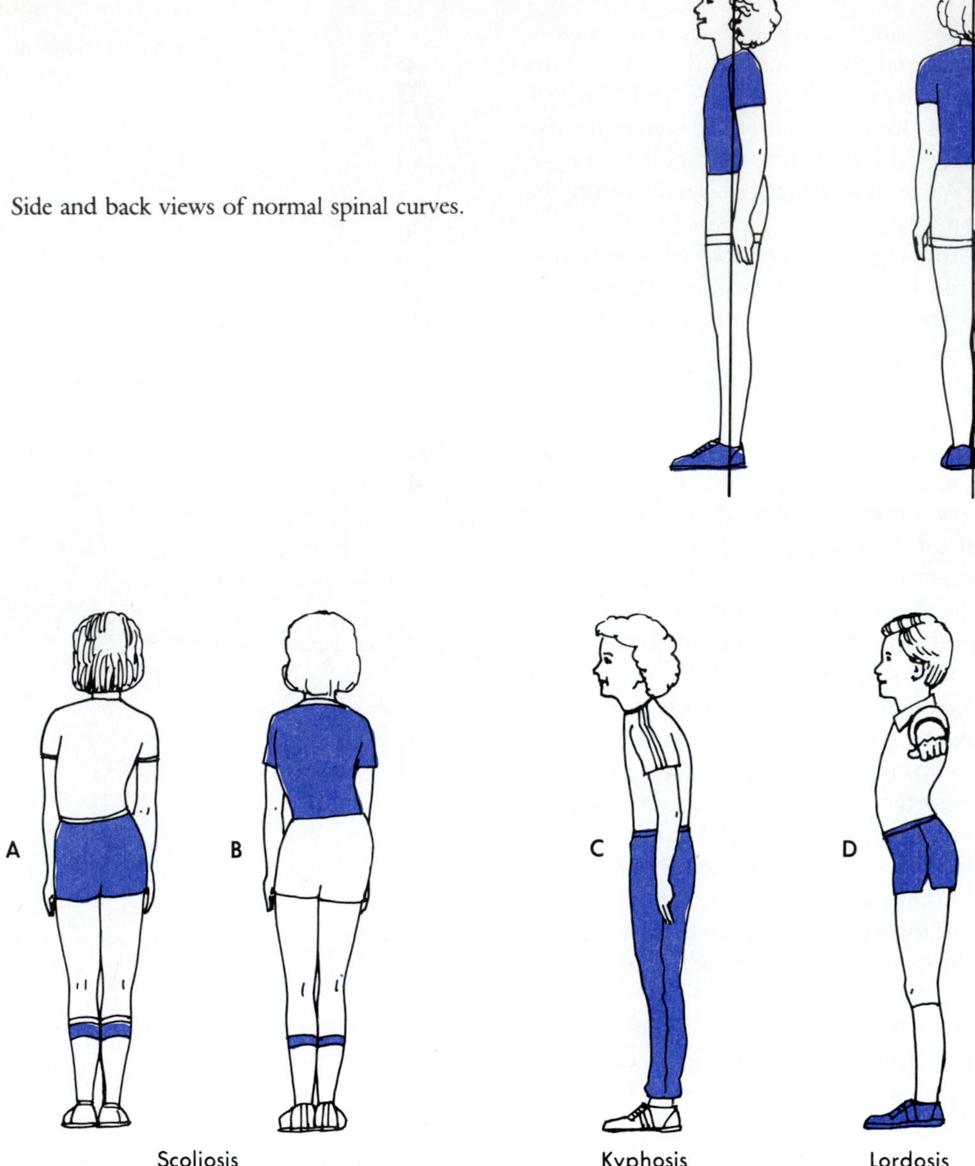

FIGURE 15-7 Postural deviations. **A,** Scoliosis, total left C curve. **B,** Scoliosis, regular S curve. **C,** Kyphosis. **D,** Lordosis.

recommended. In screening posture, the following questions should be answered. If the answer to any of the questions is yes after repeated observations, the child should be referred to the school nurse.

Is the head tilted to one side or forward when walking?

Is one shoulder closer to the ear than the other?

Do the shoulders appear to be tight or positioned forward?

Is one hip higher than the other or appear to be more prominent?

Do the knees turn toward one another? Do they appear to be locked or turned away from each other?

Do one or both feet usually point in or out?

Do the hips protrude in a side view?

The spinal curves in lordosis or kyphosis may be easily seen in the side view of the body. Scoliosis, on the other hand, may be suspected if the shoulders or hips are uneven or if one scapula is prominent and the other does not show. In screening for scoliosis, the child bends forward at the waist. The lateral curvature may then be observed in following the spine from the neck to the hips. One side of the body may appear to be higher than the other as well. Girls should wear halter tops for the screening.

BODY MECHANICS

Exercising good body mechanics as we perform daily tasks can aid in preventing strains of muscles and sprains of ligaments. Whenever possible, loads should be kept to a reasonable level. For example, putting groceries in two bags rather than overloading one may not only prevent the items from spilling from a torn bag but also avoid undue strain on the body. Careful examination of mechanical principles and their application to daily tasks should result in more efficient use of the body.

Lifting

Principle 1: *The heavier the object, the stronger the muscles required to lift the object.*

Principle 2: *An object to be lifted becomes a part of the body weight as it is held.*

Principle 3: *To avoid strain in lifting objects one should attempt to apply all forces vertically through the line of gravity of the body.*

Lifting light objects may require the use of only one body part. Heavier objects require the use of more and stronger body parts. As heavy objects are lifted, the strongest muscles, those of the legs, should be used. This is only possible when the legs are flexed, assuming a stooping position and then straightening as the load is lifted. When the body bends to lift an object, the weaker and smaller muscles of the lower back exert the force for lifting.

Because the object becomes a part of the body weight, it should be held as close as possible to the body.

As the body assumes a stooping posture, the force generated should be applied vertically through the center of the weight. Bending over to lift an object applies the force diagonally upward and backward, which is a mechanical disadvantage for the body.

To lift heavy objects one should stand as close to the object as possible. The feet should be kept in contact with the floor. The legs are flexed and then extended, with the legs doing most of the lifting. The back is kept relatively straight and the object is lifted close to the body.

Carrying Objects

Principle 1: *An object being carried becomes a part of the individual's weight and causes the center of gravity to shift slightly in the direction of the added weight.*

The object should be carried as near the individual's line of gravity as possible. The body leans slightly away from the load to counteract the pull of the load and help to maintain balance.

The head and trunk should be kept erect and the abdominal muscles should be tight. When a heavy load is carried on one side of the body, the opposite arm may swing to help relieve the strain of the load.

The object being carried must be controlled to avoid unnecessary swinging or swaying.

Pushing

Principle 1: *In pushing an object, the application of force must be continuous, because force must be used to overcome the object's inertia and keep it moving.*

Principle 2: *The force should be applied as near the object's center of gravity as possible and in the desired direction.*

Principle 3: *The heavier the object to be pushed, the stronger the muscles that must be used to move the object.*

Principle 4: *Friction may make it difficult to push objects that are soft or have a large surface area in contact with the ground or floor.*

Some objects are too heavy or too large to carry and must be pushed. Other objects are designed to be pushed, such as grocery carts and lawn mowers. In pushing an object, the person's back should be kept fairly straight, with the body lean beginning at the ankles. The trunk and head are aligned. The feet are in a forward-stride position and pointing in the direction of the force. The hips are kept low, the forward knee is bent, and the back knee is straight. The foot pushes against the supporting surface.

Pulling

The principles for pushing apply also to pulling.

Pulling is used for objects too heavy, large, or awkward to lift and when pushing is not desirable or possible. In pulling an object, it may be necessary to pull it down from above the shoulders, pull it over ground from above, or pull it horizontally. In pulling, the vertical component of force is increased. Friction is reduced because the vertical component of the force provides a lifting action.

The back should be kept as straight as possible. The knees are bent to add power, the body is inclined slightly forward to allow the body weight to do the work, and the object is grasped firmly.

SUMMARY

An active life-style and control of stress are important factors in wellness today. Elementary school children need to learn to recognize stress and to use activity and conscious relaxation techniques to help control it.

The development and maintenance of health-related physical fitness are important aspects of physical education. Children at the elementary school level not only need to be fit but also need to understand why fitness is important and how to test and improve fitness levels.

Many physical fitness tests are available for use during the elementary school years. The Physical Best health-related physical fitness test of the AAHPERD measures cardiorespiratory endurance, body composition, flexibility, and muscular strength and endurance. Test standards should encourage all children to their best efforts. The tests are only a beginning. After the assessment is complete, children need to be guided in developing their personal fitness goals and an activity program to pursue them.

The improvement and maintenance of fitness are ongoing concerns throughout the school year. Many times activities may be built into the daily lesson by modifying the activity, such as sustaining the activity or holding positions for longer periods. Because many physical education activities do not provide for optimum fitness development, the teacher must often supplement the daily activities with activities that meet the fitness objectives.

Understanding the principles of good posture and the efficient use of the body in lifting, carrying, pushing, and pulling are also concerns for physical education. The physical education teacher is often responsible for postural screening during the early adolescent years to identify postural deviations, which if untreated may become chronic or permanent conditions of adulthood. Many adult back problems are the result of abuse rather than accident. Children need to be made aware of the importance of good alignment and the appropriate use of the body in performing daily tasks.

REFERENCES AND RESOURCES

AAHPERD: *Health-related physical fitness test manual,* Reston, Va, 1980, AAHPERD.

AAHPERD: *Physical best,* Reston, Va, 1988, AAHPERD.

AAU: *Physical fitness program,* 1990, Bloomington, Ind, The Chrysler Fund-Amateur Athlete Union.

Anderson B: *Stretching,* London, 1981, Pelham Books.

Ardell D: *The history and future of wellness,* Dubuque, Ia, 1985, Kendall Hunt.

Auxter D and Pyfer J: *Principles and methods of adapted physical education,* ed 6, St Louis, 1989, Mosby–Year Book.

Edwards V and Hofmeir J: A stress management program for elementary and special-population children, *JOPERD* 62(2):61, 1991.

Fox K: Motivating children for physical activity: toward a healthier future, *JOPERD* 62(7):34, 1991.

Fox K and Biddle S: The use of fitness tests: educational and psychological considerations, *JOPERD* 59(2):47, 1988.

Francis LL: Teaching step training, *JOPERD* 64(3):26, 1993.

Gortmaker S, Dietz W, Sobol A, Wehler C: Increasing pediatric obesity in the United States, *American Journal of Diseases in Children* 141:535, 1987.

Hockey R: *Physical fitness: the pathway to healthful living,* ed 7, St Louis, 1993, Mosby–Year Book.

Hunsicker P and Reiff G: *AAHPERD youth fitness test manual,* rev ed, Reston, Va, 1976, AAHPERD.

Katch F and McArdle W: *Nutrition, weight control and exercise,* ed 4, Philadelphia, 1992, Lea & Febiger.

Kendall F: A criticism of current tests and exercises for physical fitness, *Journal of the American Physical Therapy Association* 45(3):193, 1965.

Kendall H et al: *Posture and pain,* Malaber, Fl, 1985, Robert E Krieger Publishing.

Kuntzleman C, Kuntzleman B, McGlynn M, McGlynn G: *Aerobics with fun,* Reston, Va, 1991, AAHPERD.

Lowenstein J: A is for apple, p is for pressure—preschool stress management, *JOPERD* 62(2):55, 1991.

Lubell A: Potentially dangerous exercises: are they harmful to all? *The Physician and Sports Medicine* 17(1):187, 1989.

McGinnis J: The public health burden of a sedentary lifestyle, *Medicine and Science in Sports and Exercise* 24:196, 1992.

Nelson J, Yoon K, Seung K, Nelson K: A field test, for upper body strength and endurance, *Research Quarterly for Exercise and Sport* 62(4): 360, 1991.

Office of Educational Research and Improvement: *Youth indicators 1991,* Washington, DC, US Department of Education.

Pate R: A new definition of youth fitness, *The Physician and Sports Medicine* 11(4):80, 1983.

Pemberton C and McSwegin P: Sedentary living: a health hazard, *JOPERD* 64(5):27, 1993.

Prentice W and Bucher C: *Fitness for college and life,* ed 3, St Louis, 1991, Mosby–Year Book.

Ross J et al: New standards for fitness measurement, *JOPERD* 56(1):62, 1985.

Ross J et al: New health-related fitness norms, *JOPERD* 58(9):70, 1987.

Seltzer C and Mayer J: A simple criterion of obesity, *Postgraduate Medicine* 38:101, 1965.

United States Department of Health and Human Services: *Healthy people 2000 national health promotion and disease prevention objectives,* Washington, DC, 1990, US Department of Health and Human Services.

Vermont Governor's Council on Physical Fitness and Sport: *School fitness manual,* Montpelier, VT, 1982, State Department of Education.

ANNOTATED READINGS

Ballinger D and Heine P: Relaxation training for children—a script, *JOPERD* 62(2):67, 1991.

Presents a script for developing conscious relaxation in young children.

Claxton D and Lacy A: Pedagogy: the missing link in aerobic dance, *JOPERD* 62(6):49, 1991.

Makes recommendations for the training of aerobics instructors including appropriate teaching techniques.

Corbin C et al: Youth physical fitness awards, *Quest* 40(3):200, 1988.

Looks at the various fitness awards and the effects of awards on motivating youth to improve fitness.

Davis R: Teaching stress management in an elementary classroom, *JOPERD* 62(2):65, 1991.

Suggestions for helping children learn to control stress.

Groves D: Is childhood obesity related to TV addiction? *The Physician and Sports Medicine* 16(11):117, 1988.

Discusses a report of physicians on the probability of television viewing as a cause of obesity.

Hopper C et al: A family fitness program, *JOPERD* 63(7):23, 1992.
Describes a program to encourage families for improving their fitness together.

Hutchinson G, Freedson P, Ward A, Rippe J: Ideal to real—implementing a youth fitness program, *JOPERD* 61(6):52, 1990.
Describes a plan for the integration of fitness teaching across the school curriculum.

Johnson R and Lavay B: Fitness testing for children with special needs—an alternative approach, *JOPERD* 60(6):50, August 1989.
Suggests modifications for testing children with disabilities.

Karp GG, DePauw K, Langendorfer S: Using play structures to enhance health and skill-related fitness, *JOPERD* 64(4):83, 1993.
Describes three different pedagogical approaches to using play structures to enhance fitness.

Pemberton C and McSwegin P: Goal setting and motivation, *JOPERD* 60(1):39, 1989.
Describes motivational techniques to help children improve personal fitness.

Petray C et al: Designing the fitness testing environment, *JOPERD* 60(1):35, 1989.
Provides suggestions for fitness testing.

Rupnow A: Upper body strength, helping kids win the battle, *JOPERD* 56(8):60, 1985.
Provides suggestions for developing upper body strength.

Sander A and Burton E: Learning aids—enhancing fitness knowledge in elementary physical education, *JOPERD* 60(1):56, 1989.
Suggests aids for teaching fitness.

Sharpe G et al: Exercise prescription and the low back—kinesiological factors, *JOPERD* 59(9):74, 1988.
Describes the correct use of exercises to improve fitness.

PART FIVE

Individual Activities

Individual activities are an important aspect of the elementary school physical education program. Children are challenged through the use of small equipment and large apparatus. These activities promote individual skill development as well as creative use of the body as the children move with or without equipment. The understanding of the body's movement potential is enhanced as children move in space in relation to equipment and apparatus, controlling force, balance, time, and flow.

OUTLINE

CHAPTER 16

Moving with Small Equipment

OBJECTIVES

After completing this chapter the student will be able to:

1. Provide suggestions for effective teaching and conducting of experiences using small equipment
2. Suggest ways of using small equipment to teach and to apply movement concepts
3. Identify a variety of activities using small equipment

Children enjoy working with small equipment. They derive much pleasure from manipulating balls, beanbags, discs (Frisbees), hoops, wands, and other small equipment. Scooters, stilts, and balance boards provide challenging play opportunities for children of all ages. Children should be encouraged to develop creative ways to use small equipment as well as skill in using the equipment in more traditional ways.

The application of movement concepts is an important part of the experience with small equipment. Body awareness is enhanced as children develop interesting ways of using body parts in manipulating objects. The use of space provides the additional challenge of moving with a piece of equipment. Controlling force is important in the use of any equipment. New challenges for balance are provided using stilts and balance boards.

Goals that may be developed in the use of small equipment include the following:

1. Develop the use of the body in unique ways to manipulate and control objects
2. Learn the properties of objects and special considerations for their use
3. Apply movement concepts in using small equipment
4. Use equipment as an extension of the body's movement, such as in using paddles, bats, or stilts

Activities From Other Lands

The play of children all over the world is characterized by the use of small equipment. Many of the activities commonly played by children in the United States are also played by children across the globe. Hopscotch, rope jumping, and juggling are examples of international activities. The addition of equipment such as rings (quoits) and Eskimo yoyos adds to the understanding of Native American culture. The use of a variety of shuttlecocks and paddles also contributes to understanding of Asian cultures.

Social Skills

The use of small equipment offers children an opportunity to work alone in a variety of challenging activities. In these experiences children need to be encouraged to assume responsibility for their own actions by keeping the object under control in the space provided and to cooperate with others in sharing the space.

In addition these experiences provide an opportunity for children to develop their own ideas and to work with others, sharing ideas in finding solutions to movement challenges. In developing partner or small group sharing the teacher must determine the groups carefully, and it may be necessary to require the use of at least one idea from each partner or group member in the solution to ensure that all have an opportunity to contribute to the final product.

Health-Related Physical Fitness

Health-related fitness can be enhanced in the small equipment experiences of children, but only if the opportunity for activity is maximized for all. The teacher must determine the fitness potential of the activities to be included in the lesson and to include activities that will contribute to the overall fitness of children. For example rope jumping can be a good cardiorespiratory activity if the class is organized for maximum participation, i.e., each child with a short rope or groups of three to four for each long rope. Panelchutes and the parachute offer opportunities for upper body strength and endurance. Other activities may require some stretching for flexibility. If a variety of activities are planned for each lesson, a number of different fitness components may be realized.

SUGGESTIONS FOR TEACHING

The following suggestions for conducting experiences with small equipment should be considered. Additional suggestions may be found in Chapter 8.

When establishing a signal for listening, the teacher should tell the children what to do with the equipment during the period of explanation or clarification. It is difficult for children to hold equipment quietly when instructions are being given. At the beginning of the lesson, instructions should be given before the equipment is assigned to the children. During the lesson it may be helpful to have the children put the equipment on the floor in front of them to avoid constant reminders about holding the equipment still. Children might also be challenged to hold the equipment quietly and praised when they do it well. If the task of holding the equipment quietly while the teacher or others are talking is presented as a challenge, most children will do well.

It is important to define the area to be used. Some equipment, especially that in which control is easily lost, such as balls and discs, requires more individual space. In station work each station area should be clearly defined. In individual, partner, or small group work, children should be arranged with adequate space within which to work without interfering with the activity of others. The teacher should stress keeping the equipment under control and recognize individual efforts in accepting this responsibility. The teacher should make moving with control a challenge for everyone.

Some equipment or activities require considerable space for the safety of all. In addition younger children may require more space than older children because they tend to lose control of the objects more frequently. The teacher must be sure children are aware of these space needs before equipment is distributed. Children should be taught to use equipment safely. Special safety concerns are identified in the activity descriptions that follow. It may be necessary to discuss uses that are unsafe and why they pose a danger to the group. Children must be taught to assume responsibility for the safety of themselves and all other children in the group.

Children should also be taught appropriate use and care of the equipment. They should understand for instance that volleyballs are not made to be kicked or that sitting on inflated balls will damage the valves. Teaching care of equipment goes a long way in helping children take responsibility for the school's property so that it may be in use for a long time.

Spreading out the equipment before its distribution will decrease the time needed for each child to secure a piece of equipment and be ready to begin the activity.

Many pieces of small equipment may be furnished by the group. Empty bleach or soda bottles make adequate area boundary markers and objects to hit or maneuver around. Wands may be made from dowel rods. Tin can stilts for outdoor use can be made from large canned food containers. Suggestions for homemade equipment may be found in Appendix Three.

In developing the activity progression, the learning processes must be kept in mind. Experiences totally new to the children begin at the perceiving level, with each child developing a general idea of the task. As the children work to develop their skill, they move toward refining the task. Later, they will be asked to vary the task as they explore additional movement concepts, such as level, pathway, force, etc. Finally, they may apply what they have learned to new tasks, which will involve a number of different movement decisions.

MOVEMENT CONCEPTS

The use of small equipment requires the use of a number of movement concepts in each of the activities. Figure 16-1 outlines the movement content to be applied in the use of small equipment. Beginning movement challenges involve the use of one skill and/or one concept. As the children gain in experience with the equipment, its use, and the movement content, the movement challenges posed become more complex. They may call for the combination of skills and/or the purposeful use of more than one movement concept. In the beginning children may work individually; in later experiences they share in the decision making with partners and small groups of three or four. In this way the possibilities for solutions to movement challenges are expanded beyond the ideas of individual children.

Activities may be organized around a theme—for instance, having the children explore one concept using a variety of equipment. For example, the children might be using balls, hoops, scooters, and ribbons around a theme of pathways. At each station the children would explore moving the objects in various pathways and then moving with the object in the same or different pathways. Discussion would be centered around how they controlled the objects to have them move in the desired paths, the levels used, and pathways explored.

Another approach would be to develop a number of different concepts, one at each station. A variety of equipment could be provided at each station, with the children choosing one or more pieces of equipment to use to explore the concept. At one station the children might be exploring creating force, at another controlling objects at different levels, at another balancing objects, and at a fourth absorbing force.

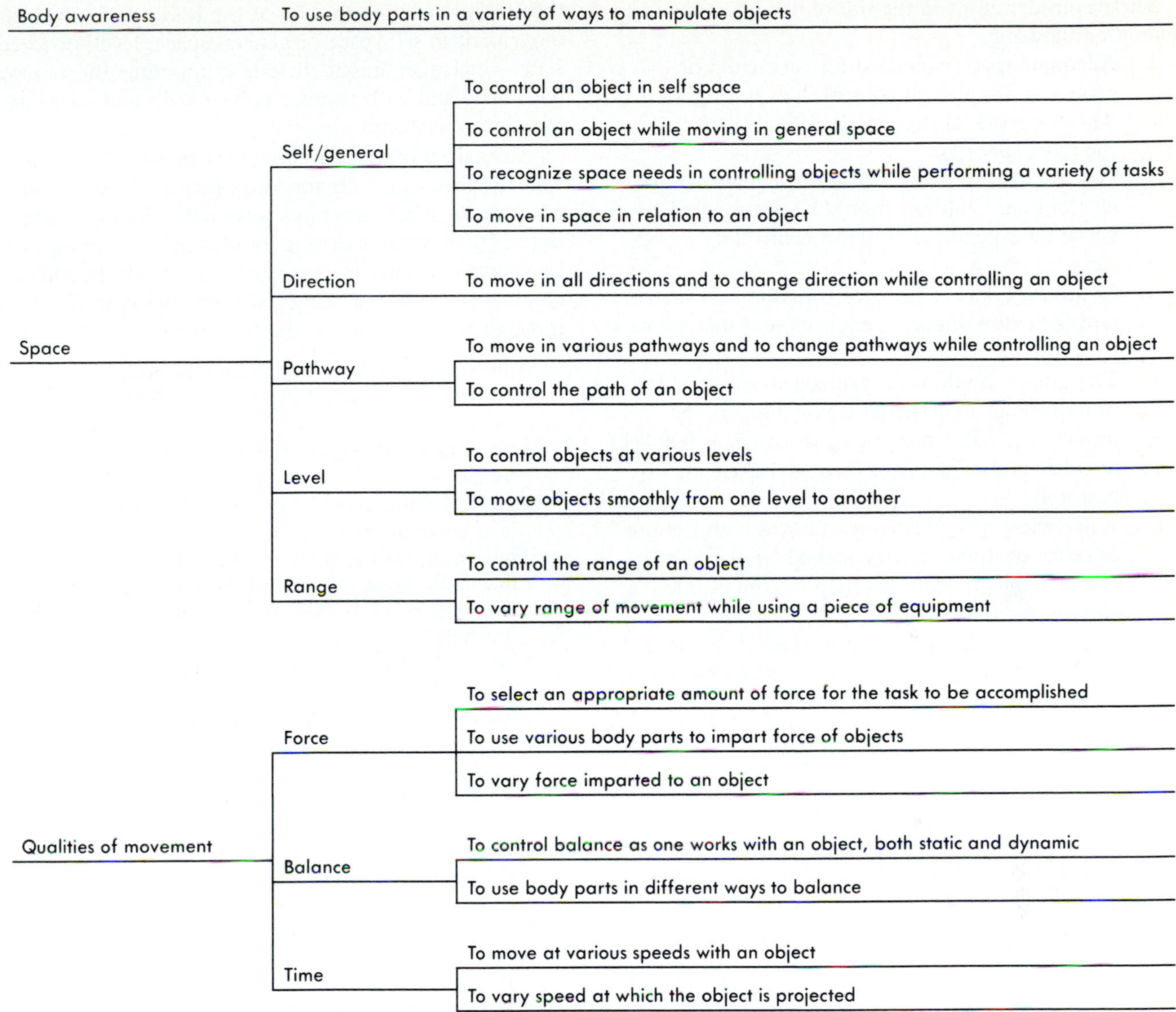

FIGURE 16-1 Movement concepts to be developed with small equipment.

The following sections of this chapter suggest activities for use with a variety of equipment. Some include the movement terminology. As the children explore their own movement in all the activities, the teacher should develop a series of questions to ask to continue to focus the children's attention on the movement concepts. These activities are but a few of the possibilities for use with small equipment. They are listed in order of difficulty.

BALLS, BEANBAGS, BALLOONS AND BEACHBALLS, DISCS, AND RINGS

Balls, beanbags, balloons and beachballs, discs, and rings are popular equipment for elementary schoolchildren. This equipment comes in a variety of sizes, compositions, shapes, and weights. Children should experience working with as wide a variety as available. The solutions to movement challenges and the execution of skills often vary with the specific piece of equipment being used.

In many schools maximizing the activity for children requires the use of a variety of equipment, such as several types of balls. The teacher should take this opportunity to develop further understanding of the self, the properties of the equipment, and other movement concepts as the children work with many different pieces of equipment. Children may also learn that specific types of equipment may be more suited for use in some activities than in others. For instance, a foam ball is best in dodge ball games, a football is not designed for rolling, or a beanbag might be best in a target toss, where scoring depends on the object remaining in a limited area of the target. The versatility in the use of balls, beanbags, and balloons challenges both the youngest and the oldest child.

Safety considerations in the use of this equipment include the following:

1. Adequate space is needed for each child or group so that loss of control does not interfere with the work of others. (Balls and discs require the most space.)
2. Control of the object should be a challenge for all children. Children should be encouraged to know their personal limits in controlling an object.
3. Controlling level and force is particularly important for maintaining an environment that is safe for everyone.
4. The group should be organized so that the flow of movement in activities involving partners moving the ball from one to the other is parallel to other groups and not through other sets of partners.
5. When these activities are combined with the use of other equipment, they should be placed to one side where walls can help to contain the equipment in an area.

Although each of the following sections includes specific activities for each type of equipment, many of the activities could be used with all three.

Balls

The box on p. 277 outlines some of the possible skills and movement content that might be developed with the use of balls. In the beginning the teacher may select one skill, for instance, the bounce with one hand, and have the children explore the use of the body parts involved, movement in self space or general space, level, or force. Later challenges might include combining the bounce with one hand with another skill or skills and/or a combination of concepts.

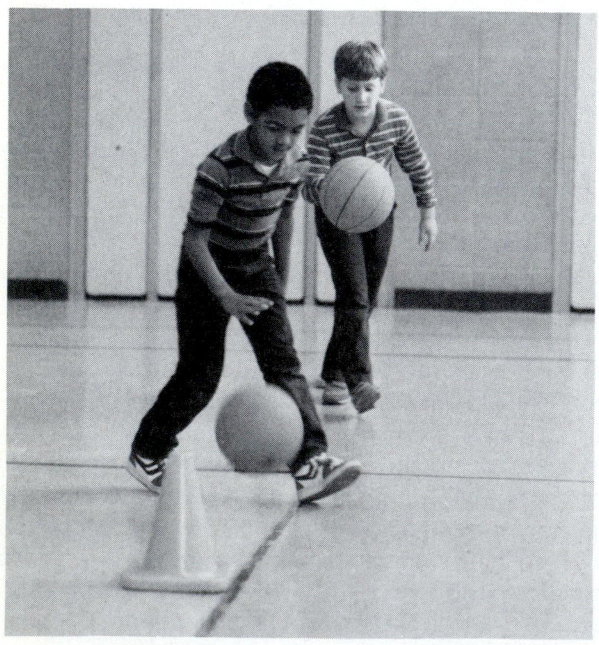

Moving with balls around obstacles.

An analysis of the skills used may be found in Chapter 13. The following activities supplement those found in Chapter 13, where emphasis was on developing the technique of throwing, catching, bouncing and striking, and body awareness in the execution of the skills. In addition children may explore using balls in relation to the body through activities such as the following:

While standing, roll the ball around the body.

While standing, roll the ball around the body and in between the legs.

While sitting with legs crossed, roll the ball around the body.

While in a sitting position, roll the ball around the body and under the legs.

While on the floor, roll the ball down the legs.

While on the floor, roll the ball down the legs, lifting the legs, tossing the ball off the toes into the air, and then catching it.

While on the floor or standing, rolling the ball down the tops of the arms.

While on the floor, roll the ball down the tops of the arms, down the body, down the legs, tossing it off the toes and catching it.

From a standing position, roll the ball over the hands to a position overhead.

While standing, toss the ball and catch it on the back of the hands with palm down and then toss and catch it in the palms of the hands.

Holding the ball with a straight arm out to one side, toss the ball high overhead and catch it in the opposite hand.

Throwing the ball under and over the arm, catch it with the opposite hand.

Holding the ball with a straight arm out to the side, carry the ball horizontally forward under a flexed elbow as the palm turns inward and upward, then toss the ball straight upward, uncurling the hand to catch the ball.

Using ball skills described here or in Chapter 13 and the use of the body in creative ways to manipulate balls, children may:

Execute skills with balls varying in composition, size, and weight.

Execute skills while stationary or moving through space with various locomotor skills or dance steps.

Execute skills from various positions such as standing, kneeling, sitting, or lying on the floor.

Project balls:

- For distance into space.
- To partners.
- To walls.
- To targets varying in level and/or size, distance, the accuracy required (bowling at one or more pins), and rebounding to the target from the floor or wall.

Execute skills while moving in space, avoiding others and/or obstacles.

BALL SKILLS AND MOVEMENT CONCEPTS

Roll:
- With 2 hands
- With 1 hand

Bounce:
- With 2 hands
- With 1 hand
- Alternating hands
- To another person

Throw:
- Underhand
  - With 2 hands
  - With 1 hand
- Overhand
  - With 1 hand
  - With 2 hands (shoulder)
  - Overhead
- Vertically

Catch:
- A rolling ball
- A bouncing ball
- A ball in the air
- A falling ball

Kick:
- With the inside of the foot
- With the instep
- Repeatedly (dribbling)
- Punt
- Dropkick

Strike:
- With the hand
  - Underhand
  - Overhand
  - A ball suspended from a rope

Body awareness:
- Use body parts to control a ball

Space:
- Control a ball in self space.
- Control a ball in general space.
- Control a ball while moving in different directions.
- Vary the path of the ball.
- Control a ball at different levels.

Qualities of movement:
- Control and vary the force used.
- Absorb force with different body parts.
- Vary the speed of the ball.
- Execute skills while moving at various speeds.

Combine skills to accomplish a task. (Example: Starting from this line, move the ball to the target area and hit the target using three different skills.)

Make up a ball game for three or four people to play using (name) skills.

Combine ball skills with locomotor skills. (Example: Throw the ball in the air, move under it, turn around, and then catch it; or skip as you dribble the ball with your hands.)

Move the ball through space, to a partner, or to a target using body parts other than hands or feet.

Cage Ball

Using a cage ball children may:

Work with a partner to push the ball to a line or around obstacles.

Carry it as a group.

Lift or hit it over a rope or net.

Lie on the floor in two lines with feet facing, one line attempting to kick the ball over the heads of the other.

Play reverse tug-of-war.

Beanbags

With beanbags children may:

Explore the use of the beanbag while sitting. Standing. Lying down on the back. Lying in a prone position. Kneeling.

Place the beanbag on the floor and move around it. Over it.

Balance the beanbag on different body parts while stationary. While moving in general space.

Balance the beanbag on a body part and move that part, keeping the beanbag balanced.

Balance the beanbag on a body part while performing various skills, such as a crab walk or frog jump, keeping it balanced.

Throw the beanbag from one hand and catch it in the other.

Move the beanbag around the body in the medium level. The high level. The low level.

Throw the beanbag in the air. Do something with the body. Catch the beanbag.

Exchange beanbags with a partner. See how many ways children can exchange beanbags while keeping the beanbag on the floor. In the air. At different levels. While moving.

Move the beanbag with different body parts in general space. To a partner. To a target.

Toss the beanbag from behind the back and catch it.

Toss the beanbag between the legs to a partner. To a target. Catch it in front of the body.

Toss the beanbag as high as possible and catch it.

Catch the beanbag with two hands. One hand. Other body parts.

Pick up a beanbag with various body parts and put it in the hand.

Put it in a basket.

Juggle two or three beanbags.

Balloons and Beachballs

With a balloon a child may:

Strike it with various body parts.
Control a balloon or beachball in self space while standing or sitting.
Control it at different levels.
Control a balloon while moving in general space.
Hit it to a partner.

Hit it over a net.
Vary the force in hitting it different distances.
In a small group keep the balloon in the air by hitting it. Add another balloon.
Create a game for three players with a balloon.

Discs

Discs, commonly called Frisbees, are a relatively new piece of equipment that have become popular in the past three decades. Beginning as a toy used primarily for throwing between individuals, it has evolved as a piece of equipment that may be used in several games, one of which is ultimate Frisbee (see Chapter 24). It is also used in competitions in which a variety of skills and routines are tested and creative use of the disc in "free style" activities is judged. The International Frisbee Disc Association (IFA) has identified three levels of proficiency: expert, master, and world class master. The discs come in a number of different styles and sizes, with some meeting the specifications of the IFA.

Discs are difficult for elementary schoolchildren to control. They require more space than balls require. The safety considerations listed earlier in this section are very important. Because they are difficult to control, disc activities may be more appropriate as levels III and IV activities.

Cross-body backhand.

Sidearm throw.

Throwing

CROSS-BODY BACKHAND THROW

Grip: Grasp disc as if to fan yourself, with the thumb on the top side and the index finger on the rim.

Execution: Turn the throwing side in the direction of the throw. The weight is transferred to the rear foot. As the backswing is taken by bringing the disc in front of the body and then back, the upper body turns toward the throwing arm. As the forward motion begins, the weight is transferred to the forward foot and the upper body rotates. On the release, the index finger points in the direction of the flight. The flight of the disc is parallel to the floor.

Suggestion: Practice the motion without releasing the disc at first.

SIDEARM OR FOREHAND THROW

Grip: Grasp the disc with the thumb on top and the middle and index fingers extended on the bottom, the middle finger against the rim.

Execution: The nonthrowing side of the body is facing the direction of the throw. The disc is brought back to the side. As the disc is moved forward, the weight is transferred to the forward foot. The hips lead the body motion followed by the shoulders and the throwing arm. The wrist snaps as the disc is released, adding force to the throw.

Suggestion: Practice the motion without releasing the disc for a few times.

UNDERHAND THROW

Grip: Grasp the disc as in the cross-body backhand.

Execution: The throwing side faces the direction of flight. The disc is brought down and back behind the thrower. The knees are bent. The upper body is slightly rotated in the direction of the throw. As the arm is brought forward, the lead foot steps in the direction of the throw. The swinging and forward motions are primarily from the arm, with a snap of the wrist as the disc is released out in front of the body.

Suggestion: This is a difficult throw. It may help to practice the motion slowly to get a feeling for it.

Flights

Several flights are possible with each type of throw. The angle of the disc on release affects the flight. The children should be encouraged to experiment with the angle of the disc as they work on the various skills. The skip flight is the most difficult for elementary school children (Figure 16-2). Note that a skip curve curves to the left for a right-handed backhand, a roll curve to the right.

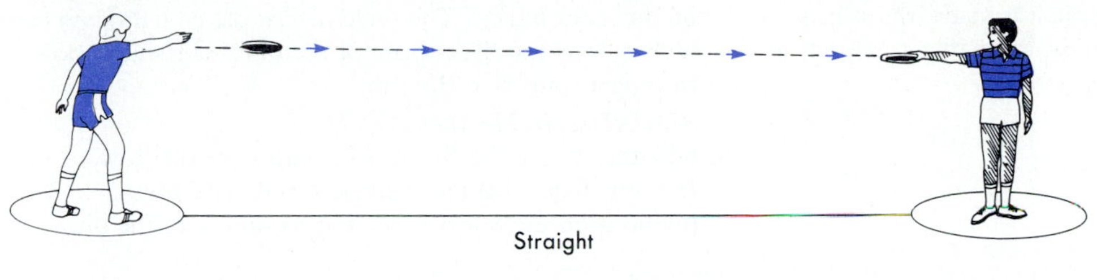

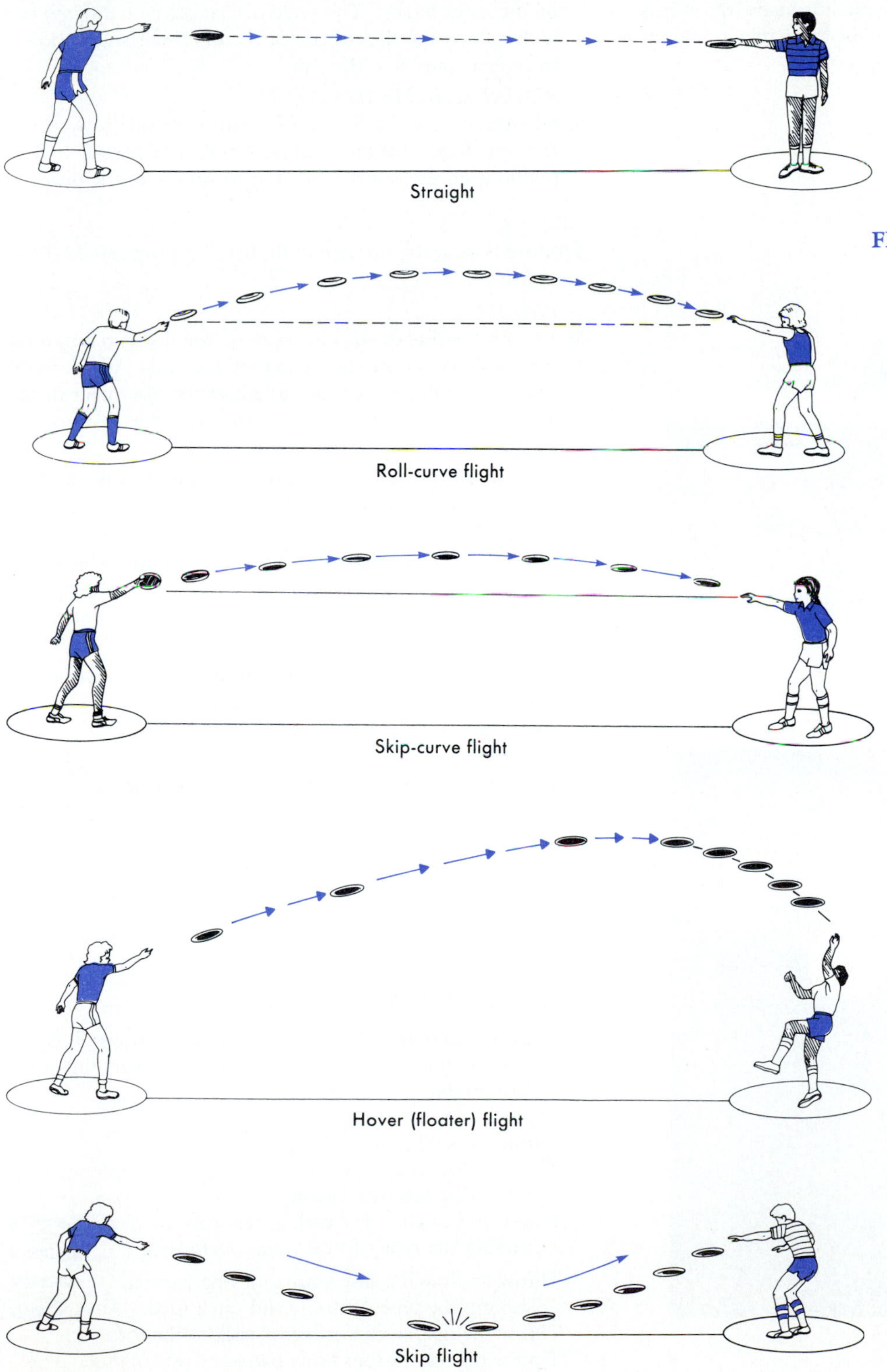

FIGURE 16-2 Possible disc flights.

Roll-curve flight

Skip-curve flight

Hover (floater) flight

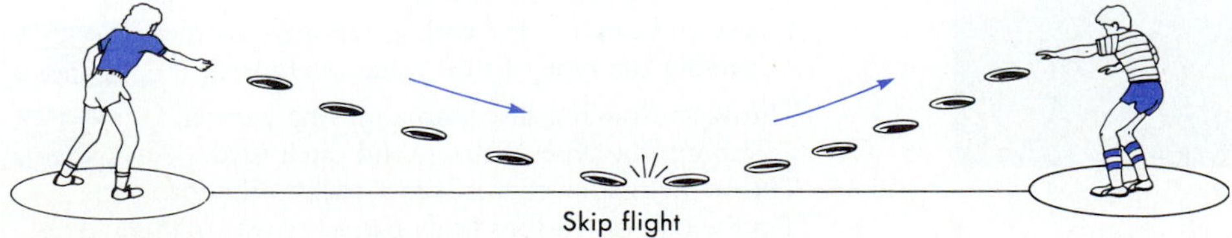

Catches

TWO-HAND CATCH (PANCAKE)

Line up with the disc. Reach out and pull in the disc with two hands, one hand on top, the other on the bottom of the disc.

ONE-HAND CATCH

Line up with the disc. Reach out and pull it in with one hand.

BETWEEN-THE-LEGS CATCH

Used to catch low flights. Face the thrower. Line up with the intended flight of the disc. As the catch is made, the side is facing the throw; there is a jump in the air so that at impact, both feet are off the ground, the closest leg is up, and the disc is watched into the hand as it is caught under the leg. The thumb is on top of the disc.

Two-hand catch.

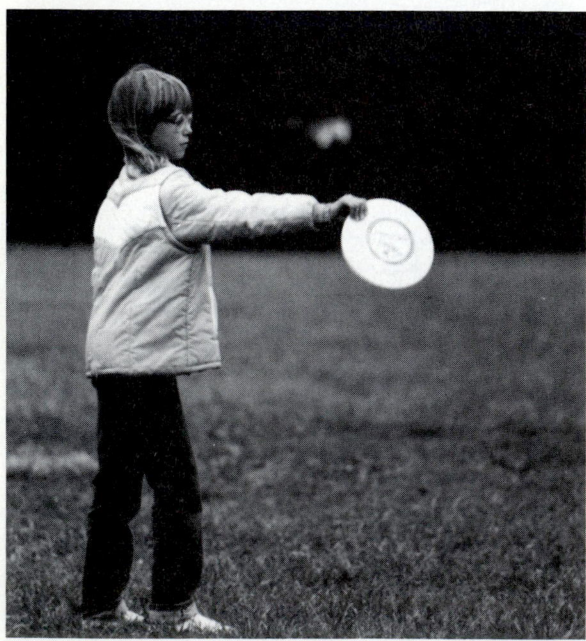

One-hand catch.

BEHIND-THE-BACK CATCH

Place the feet in line with the flight. Watch the disc as long as possible into the hand. The thumb is on top of the disc.

FINGERTIP CATCH

Good for catching high floaters. Match the speed of the disc with the hand or the whole body. Give as the disc is contacted on the index fingers. The finger is first placed lightly on the underside of the flight plate of the disc. As the disc slows, the finger spins it to the rim.

BEHIND-THE-HEAD CATCH

Stand either facing the thrower or with your side toward the thrower. Reach behind your neck and make the catch. The thumb is on the bottom, the fingers on top of the disc.

Tipping

Tipping is easiest from hover flights. Tipping can be done as follows:

FINGER

Move with the disc or stop its motion. The disc is received on the index finger in the center of the disc. After several contacts it will be necessary to adjust the placement of the finger slightly off center to keep the disc under control.

KNEE

Lean back and raise the knee high enough to make a clean contact with the disc.

HEAD

Tilt the head back to make contact at the hairline. The action of the legs from flexion to extension produces the tipping action.

TOE

This is easiest with a disc dropping from a tip. The action is a kick to the disc with the toe. With this tip one should be able to get the disc high in the air.

ELBOW

Lean the upper body to get the elbow straight up.

HEEL

Executed to the side of the kicking leg or behind the opposite leg. Timing is important to get a clean tip.

Suggestion: Mark the center of the disc with a felt pen to help in finding the initial striking point.

Activities

With a disc children may:

Execute a straight flight using each of the throws. Roll-curve flight. Skip-curve flight. Hover (floater) flight. Skip flight.
Throw a disc for distance.
Throw a disc through a hoop.
Throw a disc to a target.
Throw a disc into the basket.
Throw and catch a disc with a stationary partner, varying the type of throw and catch used.
Throw and catch a disc with a moving partner, varying the type of throw and catch used.
Throw the disc so that it comes back to the thrower.
Tip the disc on various body parts.

Throw a disc into the wind.
Throw a disc with the wind.
Play the following games:
Frisbee golf: Set up a course with the holes marked by discs or natural boundaries agreed on ahead of time by the teams. Players travel the course throwing and moving the disc until they get the disc to the hole. The number of throws taken on each hole constitutes the score.
Ultimate Frisbee: See Chapter 24.
Frisbee horseshoes: In groups of three, decide on the area to be used. The first player throws the Frisbee to land in the general area, establishing the target for the other two players. Each of the other players throws in turn trying to touch the Frisbee of the Frisbee target. The closer is awarded 1 point. If a Frisbee lands on or touches the target, 2 points are awarded. Play continues with player two throwing the Frisbee target and the other two trying to hit it. Repeat once more with player three throwing first. Continue until someone has scored 10 points.
Disc croquet: A series of hoops are scattered in the playing area as wickets in croquet. Each player in turn tries to throw their disc so that it passes through the wicket. Whenever players are playing for the same wicket or at the beginning of the game, two players throw at the same time, attempting to hit the other player's disc. If a player is successful, the hit player must begin again at wicket one. The first player to complete the course is the winner.

Rings (Quoits)

Rings are available in several different materials. The most common are made of molded rubber, rubber tubing, or a heavy hemp rope.

Rings may be thrown so that the ring travels parallel to or perpendicular to the floor or so that the ring travels end over end in flight. The grip most commonly used is to shake hands with the ring as it is held perpendicular to the floor.

Many of the activities previously listed in this chapter may be modified for the use of rings. In addition children may:

Twirl one or more rings on various body parts. Throw the ring onto dowels on a target board.
Pass the ring from different body parts to others in a small group.
Toss rings onto the legs of a chair turned upside down.
Throw rings into several target areas on the floor, using a different type of throw each time.
Toss the ring to a partner who must catch it on a different body part each time.
Make up a game for two or more players with the ring.

Quoits varying from small solid spruce discs to wooden rings were used in a variety of games by northern Alaskans, i.e., the Aleuts, Tlingits, Eskimos, and Athapaskans. The two activities described were favorite pastimes of these groups.

1. This game was played in twos or in small groups. A green mat of seal skin with a colored stripe across the center was used by the Aleuts. The participants, sitting on the ground or squatting, in turn throw two rings each, trying to land them as close as possible to the stripe. The ring closest scores 1 point.
2. An orange mat made of caribou hide with two squares (one 1 inch per side, the inner square ½ inch per side) in the center was used as the target area. Players tried to toss small wooden discs, 2½ inches in diameter, to cover the inner most square. Athapaskans marked their discs with cross marks and slashes, whereas the Eskimos used one or three dots on one side of the disc. Scoring was as follows:
   1 point—closest disc to the square, with none covering the square
   1 point—part of the outer square covered but none of the inner square with the marked side of the disc up
   2 points—both squares covered and the marked side of the disc down
   3 points—part of the outer square covered but none of the inner square and the marked side of the disc down
   4 points—both squares covered and the marked side of the disc down

   This game could be modified using a larger target area and using beanbags marked on one side or shuffleboard discs or other round objects as throwing pieces.

ESKIMO YOYO

An Eskimo yoyo consists of two small balls or other shapes made originally from seal skin, which are fastened to the ends of a string. A knot is placed in the string

Getting started with an Eskimo yoyo.

somewhat off-center so that the string is longer on one side than on the other. The goal is to get the two balls moving in circles in opposite pathways in a vertical plane. A source for purchasing Eskimo yoyos may be found in Appendix 2. There are two ways to get the yoyo in motion:

1. Lay the yoyo on the floor in a straight line. Grasp the knot and lift the knot up off the floor while moving the wrist up and down in a slow rhythmic motion.
2. Holding the knot in one hand, gently start the shorter end moving in a clockwise pathway while moving the wrist up and down. Then begin the second ball in the opposite path.

Working the yoyo is not an easy task; it takes some practice. The skill is probably best suited for children at level III or IV.

FOOTBAGS

The origin of the footbag may be traced back to ancient China, where a small leather oblong object filled with hair was used in a kicking game. In other cultures, such as China, Japan, and Korea, shuttlecocks varying in size and construction, but generally made of chicken feathers anchored in cork or some other material, have been used for a number of different kicking activities. In Malaysian countries, the national sport, sepak takraw, involves a takraw ball, 6 inches in diameter and made of woven rattan. The game combines soccer and volleyball, with participants kicking the ball across a 5-foot high net. The ball may be spiked with the head or foot, which the opposite team attempts to block with a foot, leg, or back.

A variety of objects may be used as footbags, including the HackeySack, a small leather footbag, small compact beanbags, or various kinds of large shuttlecocks.

In developing skills with the footbag the child should attempt to become proficient with either foot. Controlling the small object is a challenge, with children at levels III and IV having greater success in controlling the force and coordinating the actions needed. A number of kicks may be developed.

The *inside kick* involves bending the leg so that the kicking surface, the inside of the foot, is almost parallel to the ground and in front of the body. The supporting leg is slightly bent, and the hips point straight ahead. Contact is made low and around knee level. Curling the toes under rotates the ankle up to help create a flat surface on which to contact the footbag.

The *outside kick* is a little more difficult to execute. It is used when the footbag is dropping to a point outside the width of the shoulders. The foot is rotated outward with the toes up. To maintain balance, the supporting leg is slightly bent and the arm on the opposite side of the kicking leg is up above the shoulders. Lift the kicking foot so that the outside of the foot, the kicking surface, is parallel to the floor. The footbag is contacted in the middle of the outside of the foot at about knee level with a smooth lifting motion. A common error in the outside kick is to contact the footbag too close to the body. The kicker should move slightly away (laterally) from the footbag to allow a more fluid motion when contacting the footbag.

Although the *toe kick* may appear to be an easy kick, it is somewhat harder because the surface used is relatively small. As the footbag drops to the floor, the weight should be balanced on the supporting foot, with the body in an upright position. The toes are flicked upward and contact is made just before the footbag touches the floor. The supporting leg is slightly bent, and contact is made at the base of the toes. On contact the leg extends first at the ankle and then at the toes.

The *knee kick* is similar to the knee control in soccer. It is used to control the footbag, or slow it down, setting the footbag up for one of the other kicks. The contact is made on the mid thigh, which is lifted until it is parallel to the floor. The weight is balanced over the supporting foot, the leg slightly bent. The kick is taken at waist level. This kick is successful when the footbag is coming directly toward the kicker rather than moving across in front of the body.

A good progression in learning the skills includes:

1. Practice the action without the footbag, by lifting the leg into position and then touching the hand to the foot.
2. Drop the footbag and attempt to kick the footbag straight up into the air, catching it in the hand each time.
3. Repeat #2 but try to kick the footbag twice in a row before catching.
4. Perform the kick with a partner who tosses the ball to the kicker to practice each kick (World Footbag Association).

Activities for Use of the Footbag or Buka (Woven Ball)

1. Individual kicking—see how many consecutive kicks you can do using one of the four kicks.
2. Repeated kicks using all the kicks, but not the same one twice in a row.
3. Establish a pattern for kicking using each of the kicks, i.e., four inside kicks, two outside kicks, two foot kicks, four knee kicks.
4. See how long you can keep the footbag in the air with a partner or in a small group.
5. Follow the leader, in partners, repeat the kick of your leader.
6. Move with the footbag, kicking back and forth with a partner.
7. Pass the footbag to a partner, who kicks the footbag into a target (hoop).

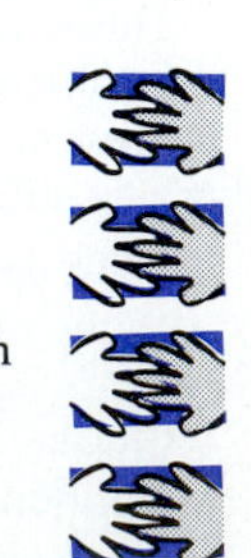

8. Footbag golf—set up targets as holes, either on

the ground or up off the ground. Count a stroke each time the footbag touches the ground on the way to the hole.

9. Buka: A group of three or more children arranged in a circle work together to keep the ball in the air as long as possible. 

Twirling a hoop.

HOOPS

Hoops varying in size are available in wood and plastic. Plastic hoops may often be purchased at discount stores. Hoops may be made from ½-inch black plastic water pipe. A piece 7 feet 10 inches long will make a 30-inch hoop. The plastic may be joined together with plastic pipe fitting or with a 3-inch piece of a ½-inch dowel glued inside the two ends.

Working with a hoop requires adequate space. Children should explore how the hoop increases their self space and then find a space that does not interfere with the work of other children.

With hoops placed on the floor, children may:

In response to a partner, place different body parts in each hoop.

Move through a maze with the hoops placed at different angles.

Hop or jump into hoops placed on the floor in different patterns.

Jump or leap over a hoop placed on the floor.

Hop in and out of a hoop, following its curved path.

See how many children fit inside the hoop without touching.

Hold hands with a partner, one standing in a hoop placed on the floor, the other outside the hoop. The children jump together, one jumping backward out of the hoop while the other jumps in the hoop. Repeat.

Twirling a hoop at various levels.

Moving a hoop in general space, children may:

Roll the hoop in general space.
Roll the hoop while moving in different directions.
Roll the hoop in various pathways.
Roll the hoop at varying speeds.
Roll the hoop and have it come back.
Roll the hoop up and over the body.
Roll the hoop up and down the arms.
Roll a small hoop through a larger hoop.
Roll the hoop around objects, using one hand to control it. Repeat using other hand.

Children may:

Swing the hoop across the body.
Swing the hoop across the body changing hands.
Swing the hoop behind the body changing hands.
Swing the hoop up to overhead, change hands, and swing down.
Swing the hoop forward and backward at one side of the body.
Swing the hoop overhead.
Swing the hoop parallel to the floor, around the body.
Jump it as a rope.
Twirl a hoop around the waist (Hula-Hoop).
Twirl a hoop on the thumb and first finger in front of the body.
Twirl a hoop on the arm held in front of or to the side of the body.
Twirl a hoop around the neck.
Twirl a hoop on the leg or ankle.
Move while twirling the hoop on various body parts.
Balance a hoop on different body parts.
Throw the hoop in the air and catch it from a swing at the side of the body.
Throw the hoop with an overhead throw in the frontal plane.
Throw the hoop horizontally overhead.
Bounce a ball through a hoop.
Spin a hoop as it rests vertically on the floor.
Spin a hoop and as it turns do various movements in a circle moving around the hoop.
Spin a hoop and lift a leg over it as it spins.

With a partner children may:

Roll the hoop alternately controlling the hoop.
Roll the hoop to a partner.
Throw a hoop to a partner.
Roll two hoops back and forth.
Roll three hoops back and forth.

Moving through a hoop children may:

Move through a stationary or moving hoop with various body parts leading.
Move through a stationary or moving hoop in different ways.
Pass the hoop in a small group while holding hands.

JUGGLING

Juggling is another popular activity worldwide. Evidence of juggling dates back to ancient Rome and to wall paintings on the Nile dating back to 4000 BC. Juggling is a challenging activity for all ages. It involves keeping three or more objects moving at the same time. A wide variety of objects may be juggled, including balls varying in size, blocks, scarves, duck pins, or rings.

Suggestions for juggling:

1. The first steps in juggling require using the same kind of object and controlling its flight in height and distance from the body. Scarves work very well since they more or less float in the air, giving the beginning juggler more time to toss and catch.
2. The toss should begin at a level slightly above the waist.
3. Practice each trick with both the dominant and nondominant hand.
4. Decide on the number of repetitions you will work for and end at that number, rather than ending on an error. Set a realistic goal of repetitions and gradually increase as skill increases.

Four types of juggling with three objects will be described here: cascade juggling, column juggling, shower juggling, and partner juggling.

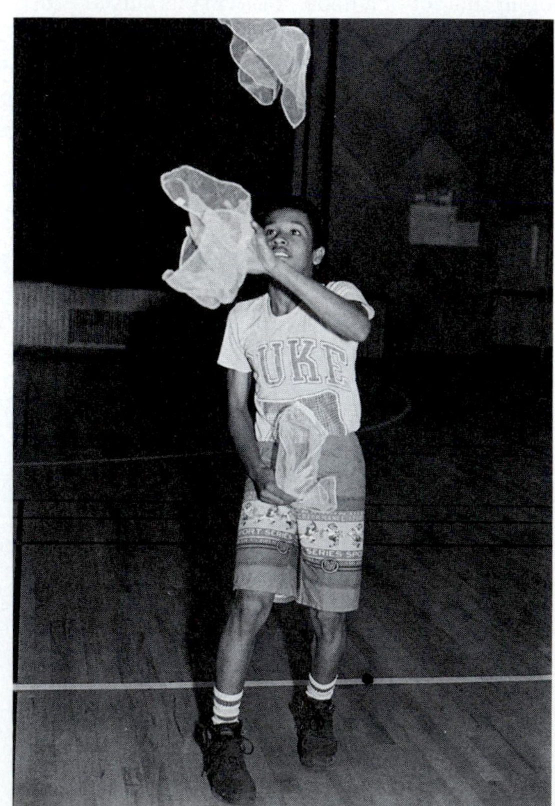

Juggling.

Cascade Juggling (Figure 16-3)

1. Begin with one scarf, held in the center with the remainder of the scarf hanging down.
   a. Raise the scarf up across in front of the chest and toss it.
   b. Reach high with the other hand and catch it with a downward motion in the fingers.
   c. Raise the other arm across the chest in the other direction, tossing the scarf. Catch it with the other hand.

   THINK: Toss, catch, toss, catch.
2. Juggle with two scarves holding one in each hand as described above.
   a. Begin raising one scarf as you did in *1a*.
   b. When the first scarf reaches the height of its flight, toss the second scarf across in the opposite direction.
   c. Catch the first scarf with a downward motion with the hand not throwing it.
   d. Catch the second scarf with the nonthrowing hand.

   THINK: Toss, toss, catch, catch.
3. Add a third scarf, holding one in the fingers of one hand, a second between the thumb and index fingers of the other hand, and a third between the last two fingers and the palm of the same hand. The scarf held with the thumb and index finger will be the first one thrown.
   a. Throw the first with an upward motion across the chest as when throwing one or two scarves.
   b. When the first scarf reaches the top of its flight, throw the second scarf from the opposite hand.
   c. When the second scarf reaches the top of its flight, throw scarf three in the same path as the first scarf.
   d. As the second hand comes down from throwing, it catches the first scarf.
   e. The hand throwing the third scarf now catches scarf two as it comes down, and the number one scarf is thrown again with the other hand, beginning the sequence of throwing and catching again.
   f. Continue alternating tosses and catches.

   THINK: Toss, toss, toss, catch, catch, toss, catch.

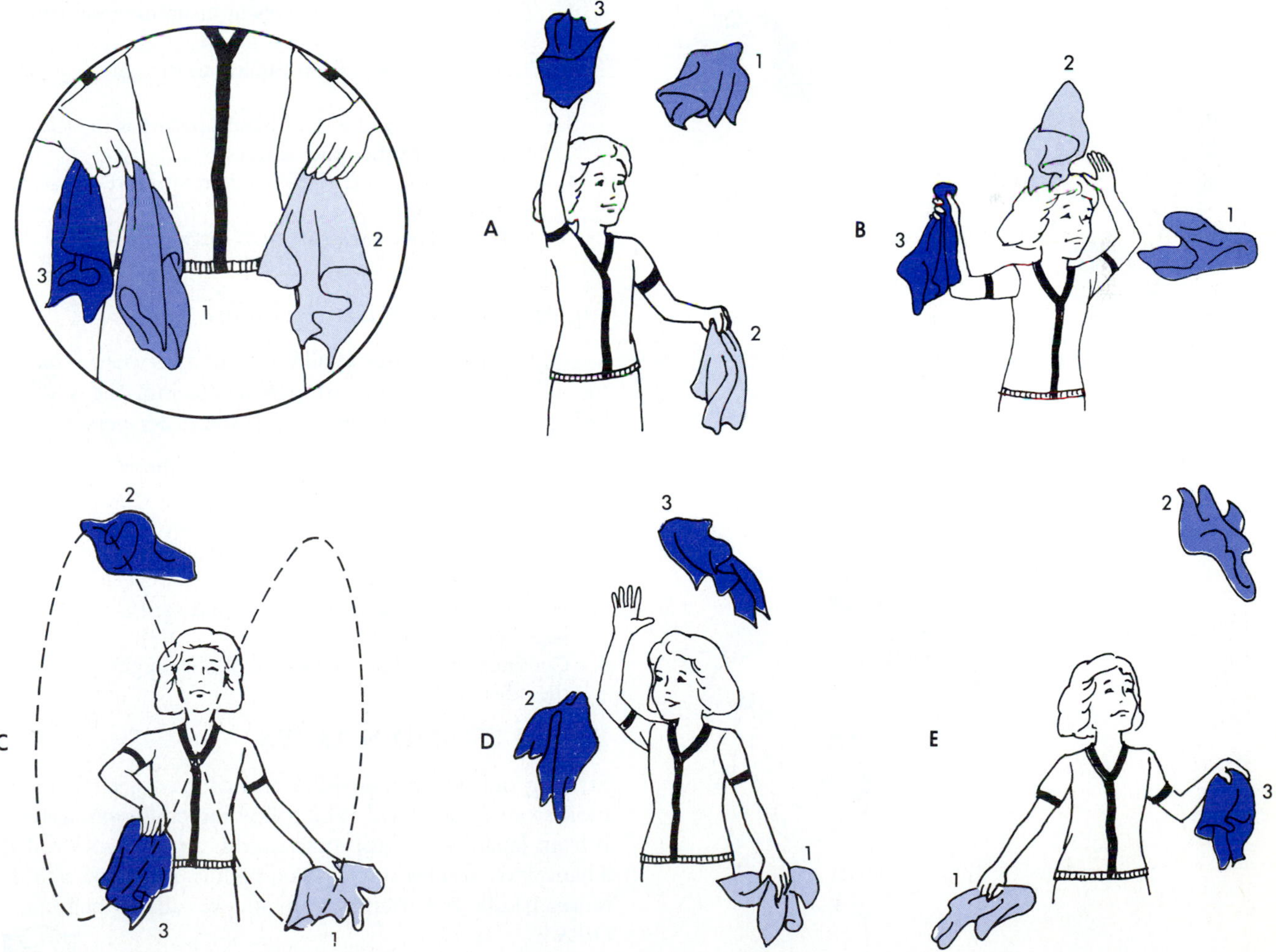

FIGURE 16-3 Cascade juggling.

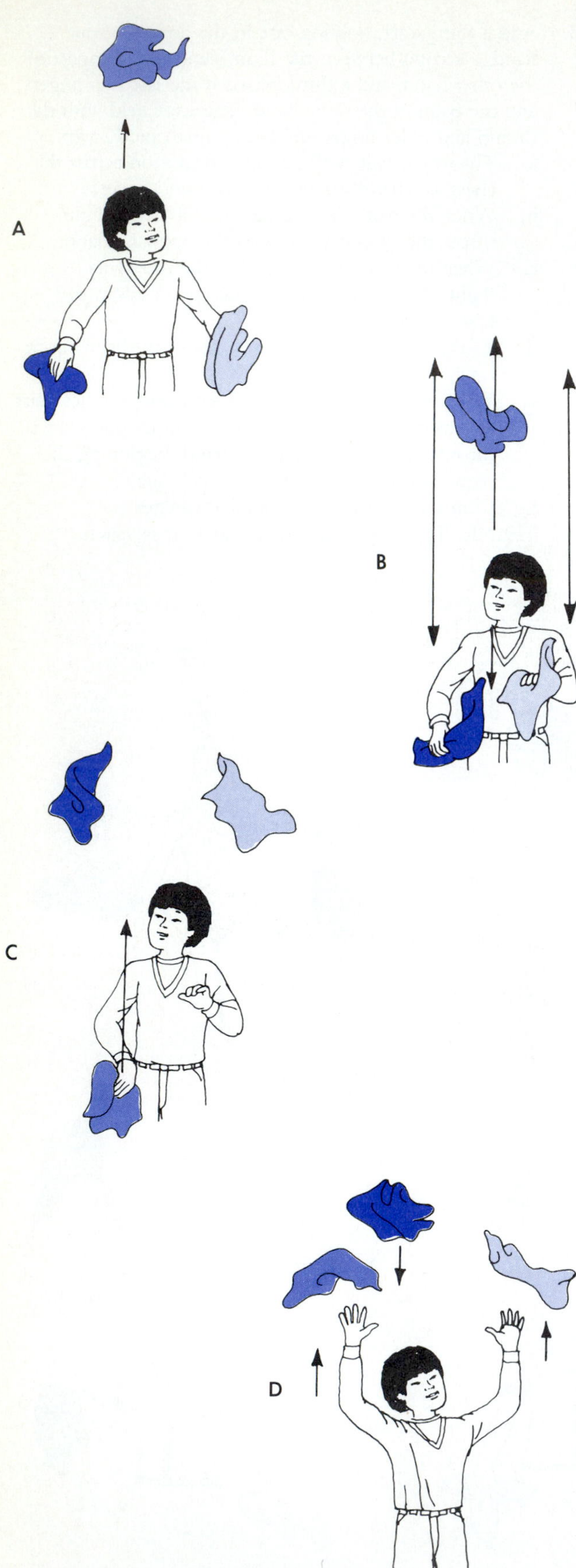

FIGURE 16-4 Column juggling.

Column Juggling (Figure 16-4)

In column juggling the three scarves are tossed upward in their own path or column.

1. Hold the three scarves as in cascade juggling.
   a. Throw one scarf (from the hand that is holding two) straight up.
   b. When the scarf gets to the top of its flight, throw the other two scarves up at the same time straight up on either side.
   c. Reach down with either hand to catch the first scarf.
   d. Throw the scarf back up in the air and catch the remaining two scarves, one in each hand.

   THINK: Toss, toss 2, catch, toss, catch 2.

Shower Juggling (Figure 16-5)

Shower juggling involves moving the three scarves in a clockwise circle, with the right hand doing all the throwing and the left hand doing all the catching. Once the clockwise path is controlled, try it moving the scarves in a counterclockwise fashion.

1. To begin, throw two scarves up from the right hand, one after the other.
2. Pass the third scarf from the left to the right hand at waist level.
3. Toss the scarf in the right hand upward as the left catches one of the other scarves.
4. Pass the scarf to the right hand and prepare to catch the third scarf.

   THINK: Toss, toss, pass, toss-catch, pass, catch.

Juggling With a Partner (Figure 16-6)

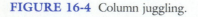

A figure-eight pattern will be formed between the two jugglers. Begin with partners facing, one holding two scarves in one hand, the other person one.

1. The person with two scarves begins by throwing one scarf up toward the partner.
2. When the throw is halfway there, the second person throws the second scarf in an underhand action so that it passes under the first scarf.
3. When the second scarf is up, the third scarf is thrown under the second.
4. Continue alternating the throws of one juggler and then the other.

PADDLES AND SCOOPS

Striking objects with paddles and other objects is common around the world. The following children's activity is from Japan. The equipment used is a shuttlecock called a hane and a solid short-handled paddle, much like a table tennis paddle but triangular in shape, called a hagoita.

OIBANA

Two players face each other about 20 feet apart. One begins by hitting the hane to the other. The receiver attempts to

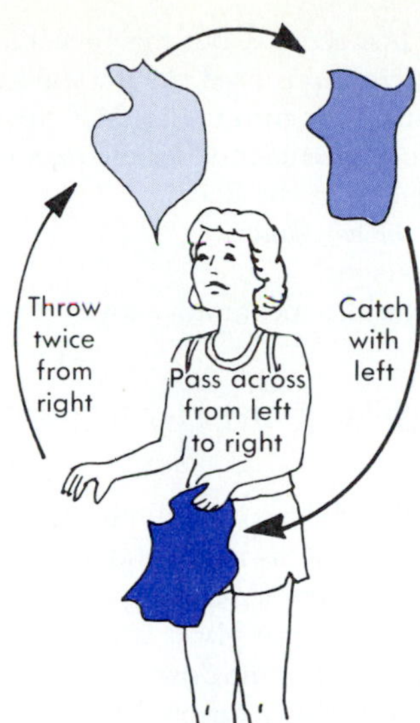

FIGURE 16-5 Shower juggling.

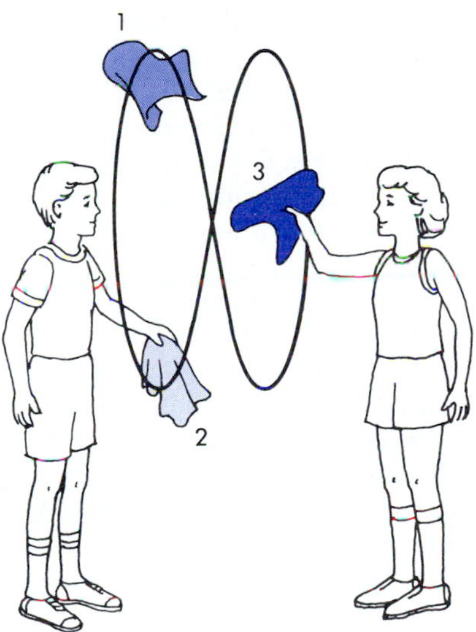

FIGURE 16-6 Partner juggling.

hit it back and they continue to hit it back and forth until someone misses or the hane touches the ground. Only one side of the hagoita may be used to strike the hane; the other side is brightly decorated with a portrait of Kabuki actors. Play begins again with the player who failed to hit the hane putting it in play. In the original game the player who kept the hane in play the longest was the winner. A better scoring method, which encourages cooperative play, is to count the consecutive hits, trying to improve the number in each game. A short paddle and a badminton shuttlecock could be substituted for the hane and hagoita.

Activities for paddles may be found in Chapter 28.

Scoops

Scoops are commercially made of plastic or may be improvised by cutting large plastic jugs. Directions for making scoops may be found in Appendix 3.

Many of the activities with balls and paddles may be modified for use with the scoop. In addition children may:

Throw a ball using an underhand, forehand (sidearm), or overhead stroke for distance.
Throw to a target varying in size, distance, and level.
Throw to a partner.
Throw and catch a ball under the leg.
Catch a ball behind the back.
Throw and catch a ball while moving in general space.

PARACHUTES AND PANELCHUTES

The use of parachutes and panelchutes in physical education has become popular in the past decade. Parachute activities are excellent for upper body development, especially for the shoulders, arms, wrists, and fingers. Parachute activities further social development because the cooperation of the children is required to accomplish the tasks.

Parachutes

Parachutes made of silk, nylon, or other lightweight fabrics are available in various sizes and colors through physical education equipment companies. They may also often be obtained from US Air Force installations for a minimum fee. A parachute about 24 feet in diameter is easy for a group of young children to handle. Using a parachute is exciting for children. Care of the parachute should be stressed; the children should be taught how to spread it out and to fold it. When the parachute is used outdoors, areas where it can raise dirt should be avoided.

FIGURE 16-7 Holding a parachute.

Forming a bubble.

In using the parachute, the children form a circle around the parachute, which is spread out on the floor. The children lift the parachute from the floor, holding it with both hands. The parachute may be held with an overhand, underhand, or mixed grip (Figure 16-7). Most of the activities involve lifting the parachute overhead on a signal. Some activities involve the children outside the parachute. Other activities are performed under the raised parachute. The children may perform the following activities:

Move the parachute up and down:

Making waves by holding the parachute and raising it up and down with large arm movements.

Making small ripples by moving the arms up and down in opposition, with one hand going up while the other goes down.

Reaching up as far as possible with the parachute and then bringing the edges down to the floor.

Beginning with the parachute close to the floor, lift the parachute up, take two to three walking steps into the center, filling the parachute with air to form a bubble. Walk back out.

Raising the parachute as in the bubble, but releasing it on a signal so that it floats away overhead.

Make an igloo:

Beginning with the parachute close to the floor, lift it up, reaching high in the air with the arms. Quickly pull the parachute down so that the edges are on the floor, trapping as much air inside as possible to form an igloo.

Similar to the previous activity, but this time the children lie down as they bring the parachute down with their heads inside the parachute and their bodies on the outside.

Similar to the first activity, but this time a mixed grip with hands crossed is used. As the children bring down the parachute, they turn under their crossed hands to face outside and remain under the parachute as it is brought quickly to the floor.

Rapidly rotate the parachute:

Held at waist height.

Moving with various locomotor movements or dance steps.

In addition children may play the following games:

Numbers In: The children are numbered off by fours or fives. The parachute is raised and a number is called. Those with the number called go into the center and come out at their own places when the center of the parachute starts to come down.

Variation: Performing various locomotor or rope-jumping skills determined by the leader.

Variation: Performing various stunts or tumbling skills while under the parachute.

Variation: Performing various ball skills while under the parachute.

Jaws: One person is the shark and moves under the parachute with one hand up just above the head to form the fin. The shark recruits other sharks by touching those holding the parachute.

Numbers Change: The children are numbered off by fours or fives. The children whose number is called move under the parachute, changing places with someone as they come out as the parachute comes down.

Steal the Bacon: The children are divided into two teams and each team is given numbers. Objects, the bacon, are under the parachute for each team. As a number is called, the children from each team with that number move under the parachute and attempt to retrieve the "bacon" before the parachute comes down.

The children are divided into groups. A number of objects are placed under the parachute. When a team is called, they attempt to go under the parachute and pick up as many objects as possible before the parachute comes down. A variation is to give point values to different objects and adding up the total points the groups score or designating a specific color of objects to be retrieved.

The group is divided into two teams; one team holds the parachute while the other is positioned under the parachute. As the parachute is rapidly pulled down, the team inside attempts to get out.

The group is divided into two teams, one holding the parachute and the other running around the outside of the parachute. On a signal the group on the outside runs into the middle and then out again, trying not to get caught as the group holding the parachute attempts to catch them inside as they bring the parachute down.

Circle Tug of War: A line is marked under the parachute. Each team tries to pull the other half of the parachute over the designated line. (What body position helps to keep you from being pulled?)

Horse Pull: Similar to the circle tug of war but with the children standing with their backs to the parachute gripping the parachute with both hands, palms down.

Inside the parachute.

With balls and the parachute the children may:

Holding the parachute at waist height, kick several balls underneath back and forth, trying to keep the balls under the parachute.

With several balls placed on the parachute, bounce the balls on the parachute by raising their arms up and down, trying to keep the balls on the parachute. (How high can you bounce the balls? How long can you keep all balls on the parachute?)

Keep two balls moving on the parachute without touching each other.

Divided into two teams, each holding one half of the parachute, each team attempts to roll a ball so it goes off the parachute on the opposite team's side.

Dodge Ball: Similar to the previous activity, but each team attempts to roll the ball so that it touches a player on the opposite team.

Roll one or more balls around the edge of the parachute.

Recite a rhyme as the ball is rolled along the edge of the parachute. When the rhyme is completed, the child closest to the ball suggests a new rhyme. (How quickly can you roll the ball so that it does not stop with you?)

Try to roll a small ball through the hole in the center of the parachute.

With an odd number of balls on the parachute and the group divided into two teams, one team on each side of the parachute, bounce the balls on the parachute. On a signal to stop, the team with the fewest number of balls on their side of the parachute wins.

Similar to the previous activity, but this time the children try to bounce the balls off the parachute on the opponent's side. The team with the fewest number of balls bouncing off the parachute on their side wins.

With one or more balls placed on the parachute, count off by twos alternately around the parachute. The ones attempt to keep the ball(s) on the parachute while the twos attempt to bounce it off.

With the group divided into two teams, one team holds the parachute while the other stands outside the parachute. The team holding the parachute attempts to bounce the balls off while the children outside the parachute attempt to keep them on by catching the balls and throwing them back on the parachute.

Kick It Back: The class is divided into two teams, with each team numbered consecutively. When a number is called, the opposing players with the number called go under the parachute and attempt to kick a ball back to their teammates before the parachute comes down.

With the group divided into two teams, as the parachute goes up, each team kicks a ball under the parachute to the other team. When the parachute comes down, the team without a ball receives a point.

Panelchutes

Panelchutes are made from 100% cotton fabric 18 to 28 inches wide and 6 to 10 feet long. The ends are hemmed to form a casing through which a piece of PCV pipe, small in diameter, is placed to provide a handle for gripping the cloth.

Beach towels may be substituted for panelchutes.

Activities

Some of the activities described for the parachute may also be performed with the panelchute. In addition children may:

Move with the panelchute in various pathways and directions.

Move with the panelchute while performing partner dances.

Roll objects on the panelchute.

Bounce and catch balls on the panelchute.

Move with a partner turning under the chute to wring the dishrag.
Alternately, move under the panelchute twisting and untwisting it.
Catch a ball thrown from a third person on the panelchute and toss it back to them.
Toss a ball to targets varying in distance and level.
Perform various stretches while holding the panelchute.
Make up combinations of skills into a routine to share with the class.
In groups of four, hold the panelchutes parallel with each other or cross the panelchutes in the middle. Repeat the activities above in unison, opposition, or in sequence.
Move an object from one panelchute to the other.
Make up combinations of movements to perform as a group.

RIBBONS

Ribbons are made of heavy satin from 1⅝ to 2⅔ inches wide and 12 to 21 feet long. They may be hand held or attached to a ⅜ inch dowel from 12 to 24 inches long. The ribbon is attached to the dowel, with fish line passing through a hole in the stick or through a ring normally used at the end of a fishing rod. Crepe paper ribbons may be used, which are glued to dowels.

If ribbons attached to sticks are used, they should be held in one or both hands, with the stick resting between the thumb and middle fingers. The index finger is extended, and the other fingers merely rest on the stick.

The movements of ribbons are generally categorized as swings, circles, figure eights, serpentines, spirals, and throws.

Swings:

Swing the ribbon back and forth at one side of the body.
Swing the ribbon in front of the body.
Swing the ribbon overhead from side to side.
Swing the ribbon forward and backward overhead.
Swing the ribbon in front and snap it back to catch the end in the other hand.
Holding both ends, swing the ribbon around the body.

Circles:

Circle the ribbon to one side of the body.
Circle the ribbon in front of the body.
Circle the ribbon horizontally overhead.
Circle the ribbon low and under the body, jumping over it as it comes around.

Figure eights:

Perform a figure eight from one side of the body, in front, and from the other side.
Perform a figure eight in front of the body.
Perform a figure eight horizontally overhead.
Jump over the rope as you perform a figure eight from one side of the body to the other.

Serpentine movements (up and down, zig-zag patterns):

Perform movements to one side of the body.
Perform movements in front of or behind the body.
Perform movements overhead.
Perform movements as the ribbon is brought around the body.
Turn and simultaneously serpentine the ribbon around the body.

Spiral movements (small circles):

Spiral in front of the body.
Spiral to one side of the body.
Spiral in back of the body.
Spiral small circles, gradually increasing the size of the circles.

Tossing:

Toss the ribbon while moving and catch it.
Toss the ribbon, perform a forward roll, and catch it.

Ribbon activities may be performed while standing or moving in space with various locomotor movements or dance steps. In addition children may work together performing various movements and exchanging ribbons in some fashion.

ROPES

Ropes have many uses in physical education. Many activities with ropes provide excellent activity for developing cardiorespiratory fitness, leg strength, and endurance. Many of the activities may be used to enhance children's skill in jumping as well as timing their jumps to a moving rope.

Ropes provide application and practice of movement concepts in individual and group activities. For example, the child's self space is extended in using a jump rope, controlled creation and absorption of force are important in jumping, and timing is essential in coordinating body movements to a moving rope. Creativity should be encouraged by giving the children opportunities to invent new movements for rope jumping.

Safety is a concern in using ropes. Children need to be reminded about the space needed in various activities and should be discouraged from swinging the ropes randomly. In activities in which children move a rope for others to jump, they should be taught to release the rope at the first feeling of increased tension caused by a rope touching a child's legs. This technique should avoid tripping on the rope or having the rope wrap around one's legs. In all jumping activities, children should be encouraged to land softly.

Ropes may be inexpensively made from No. 8 or 9 sash cord available at hardware stores or from sheeting available at marine supply companies. Ropes are needed in various lengths for individual and group activities. Lengths may be color coded by dipping the rope in paint or marking them with colored tape. Children and the teacher may then quickly identify the length needed for a particular activity. Ropes may be easily stored in boxes or baskets individually folded and tied in large knots to prevent tangling. Elastic ropes of various lengths are also available for individual and group activity.

Activities with Stationary and Moving Ropes

HELICOPTER

One person stands in the center with a long rope. The rope is swung in a circle by the center person to make the action of the helicopter blade. The end of the rope should circle low and close to the floor. Children move into the helicopter by watching the rope and moving when it goes by; then they squat next to the turner. When all are in, they attempt to move back out in a similar fashion.

JUMP THE SHOT

A long rope is used with a beanbag attached at one end. One child turns the rope in a circle parallel to the floor while the other children attempt to jump it as it comes by. The turner may vary the height and/or the speed with which the rope is turned.

JUMP THE BROOK

Two ropes are placed parallel to each other on the floor with the ropes closer together at one end and farther apart at the other. The children begin jumping at the narrow end and continue jumping as the distance between the ropes increases until they can no longer jump the space required.

JUMP THE SNAKE

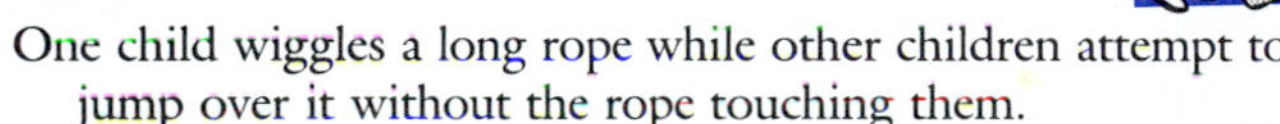

One child wiggles a long rope while other children attempt to jump over it without the rope touching them.

ELECTRIC FENCE

Similar to jump the snake, but the rope moves up and down in quick movements. The rope should not come above the knees of the jumpers.

TIDAL WAVE

The rope is always on the floor. Two children move the rope forward in long slow movements and then back a few steps like waves on a beach. The other children move with the rope as it moves away and then jump the rope as the wave recedes.

HIGH WATER

Two children loosely hold a long rope between them, higher on one end than the other. The other children attempt to go over the rope without touching it as it is gradually raised.

THE BULLDOG

Four children hold a rope to form the four corners of a square. On a signal each tries to pull the other three corners in his or her direction.

Activities with an Elastic Rope

Elastic ropes of various lengths may be purchased from equipment dealers. With a long elastic rope the children may:

Walk on the rope placed on the floor as a tightrope.

Move over and under the rope held at various heights in as many ways as possible without touching it.

Move with another person over or under the rope.

Perform a stunt while moving over or under the rope, such as an animal walk, cartwheel, etc.

Using two ropes, one held high and the other low and varying the distance between the two ropes, children attempt different ways to go over one and under the other without touching the ropes.

Rope Jumping

Rope jumping, dating back to ancient Greece, is a favorite activity of children around the world. In Native American cultures, the ropes children used were made of braided strips of rawhide or grasses. In China the words for rope jumping are *tsyana tobi;* in Japanese *tobi-koshi* means jumping over, which is the term used for rope jumping.

Jumping the Long Rope

Long ropes should be from 10 to 14 feet long. Shorter ropes are easier for young children to turn.

Children should turn the rope with the lower arm, rotating at the elbow and keeping the wrist firm. Children tend to increase speed when turning the rope and need help in maintaining a steady rhythm.

Long rope jumping is easier than jumping the short rope because a child needs only to establish the timing for jumping and does not have to coordinate the turn and the jump. Children who have difficulty establishing the rhythms for jumping may be helped by holding hands with the teacher or another child and jumping together. A **double-beat** or **single-beat** jump may be used.

The first step in jumping is establishing the rhythm and relationship to the rope. Repeatedly saying "Jump, jump, jump, jump" may help the children develop a steady, even rhythm. If a double-beat jump is used, the first and then every other beat are accented.

Activities to Teach Long Rope Jumping

LINE OR STATIONARY ROPE JUMPING

The children stand with their sides to the line or rope. On the signal and in the rhythm established by the teacher, the children jump back and forth over the rope. On a single-beat jump, they pass over the rope on each jump. With a two-beat jump, they jump over the rope on the first beat, jump to the side of the rope on the second beat, and jump over the rope on the next beat to begin the two-beat sequence on the other side of the rope.

CRADLE

With their side to the rope, the children jump the rope, which is gently swung back and forth.

CRADLE TO A TURN

The child begins with the cradle; after the rope is swung several times and the jumping rhythm established, the rope is brought up and overhead to turn as in long rope jumping.

STANDING IN

A child begins standing with one side to the rope; on the count of three, the rope is brought up and around to begin turning.

RUN THROUGH THE FRONT DOOR

The rope is turned so it is moving down and toward the jumper. As the rope passes in front of the jumper, the jumper runs through as the rope moves up and away. The jumper should stand close to the rope to correctly time the move. It may be easier to move through at an angle to the rope rather than straight on.

RUN IN THE FRONT DOOR

This time the jumper moves in, but rather than running through, stops in the center and jumps the rope one or more times.

RUN THROUGH THE BACK DOOR

The rope is moving up and toward the jumper. The jumper moves as the rope comes up and passes the jumper's eyes, waits briefly for the rope, jumps the rope, then moves out away from the rope.

RUN IN THE BACK DOOR

Similar to run through the back door, but the jumper stays in to jump the rope several times.

To jump out of the rope the child jumps out of the rope if it is moving down. If the rope is moving upward and away from the jumper, the child jumps the rope and follows the rope out.

Many stunts may be performed while jumping the long rope. The children may:

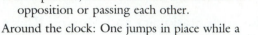

Move in to the rope and jump a specified number of times before moving out of the rope. (Example: first jump once, then twice, then three times, and so on.)
Touch a heel in front while jumping.
Touch a toe behind while jumping.
The child turns while jumping: quarter turn, half turn, three-quarter turn, a whole turn.
Touch a hand to the floor while jumping.
Travel forward and backward while jumping.
Pepper: The rope is turned rapidly.
With a partner, travel backward and forward in opposition or passing each other.
Around the clock: One jumps in place while a partner jumps, moving around the stationary jumper.
Use some of the steps suggested in short rope jumping.
Jump to rhymes.
Jump a short rope while jumping the long rope.
Bucking bronco: On all fours, jump so the rope passes under the hands and then the feet simulating the action of a bucking bronco.
Make up some new movements for long rope jumping, alone, with a partner, or for a small group.
Several long ropes may be positioned as the spokes of a wheel, in a zigzag formation or in a long line, with jumpers moving from rope to rope performing the same or different stunts at each one.

Ball skills may also be used. The rhythm of jumping should be established before the ball skill is begun. The children may:

Play catch with a partner standing outside the rope. 
Bounce or toss a ball to self while jumping.
Play catch with a partner who is jumping with you. 

INUIT SKIPPING

A seal skin or caribou hide rope was used. Tied to the center of the rope was a seal skin bundle, about 1 foot in diameter, stuffed with grass, moss, or other material. The rope was threaded through the bundle. A blanket or rolled sleeping bag may be substituted for the seal skin. The children will

Using three turners in learning to get into double dutch.

need some practice in turning the rope with this weighted center. The children are then ready to try jumping the rope and its bulky bundle. In the Inuit version the rope is turned first in a pendulum motion first to the right then back to the left, under the jumper's feet and then continuing to turn over the jumper's head. The rope then moves in a pendulum fashion on the left, moving then to the right and all the way over the jumper's head. The path of the rope is reversed each time. The jumper always faces the rope, so jumps and half-turns are necessary as the rope's path is reversed.

Activities with Two Long Ropes of Equal Length

EGG BEATER

Two ropes are held perpendicular to one another with four turners. The ropes are turned so that both touch the floor at the same time. Of the four corners from which to move into the rope, one is a front door, one is a back door, and two are mixed. The front door and back door corners are used to move into the center to jump, moving in as the rope passes in front of the eyes.

DOUBLE DUTCH

Some 300 years ago, Dutch settlers brought this activity to what is now New York City. In 1973, two New York policemen watched some girls jumping and decided to set up some rules and develop a tournament for double Dutch jumping. The first tournament was held in New York City in 1974, with over 900 children participating.

Two turners hold the ends of two ropes. The ropes are turned toward each other so that as one rope is up the other is touching the floor. Each time the children jump, a rope is passing under their feet, requiring a single-beat jump. It is easier to move into the rope at an angle, standing with their shoulder next to the turner and the foot away from the turner slightly forward. Children should watch the "front door" rope but be prepared to jump the "back door" rope as they move in.

It may be easier for jumpers to enter the rope by using three turners. One turner holds both ropes while the other two each hold one rope. The turner with both ropes initiates the turning, turning the two ropes in double Dutch fashion. The ropes form a V, with the jumper standing in the open end close to one of the turners. The jumper jumps into one of the ropes, establishes the rhythm for jumping, and then the second rope while in motion is brought over to the rope the jumper is now jumping.

Once the children have gotten the rhythm of jumping, they are ready to begin some tricks such as turning to the right or left while jumping, crossing, and uncrossing the feet or any other long or short rope jumping tricks. They may jump with one or more jumpers in the rope as well.

DOUBLE IRISH

Similar to double Dutch, but the ropes are turned away from each other. The child moves in at an angle following the "front door" rope and jumping over the "back door" rope. This style of jumping also requires a single-beat jump.

Rhymes for Jumping

Teddy bear, Teddy bear, turn around.
Teddy bear, Teddy bear, touch the ground.
Teddy bear, Teddy bear, show your shoe.
Teddy bear, Teddy bear, you'd better skidoo.

Brick house, glass house, stone house, tin.
I move out and (name person) moves in.

All in together, very fine weather.
In (out) goes one, in (out) goes two.
In (out) goes three, and in (out) goes you!

(This may be performed with one jumper in on one, two moving in on two, etc.)

Come, come the kids are calling, calling (name B) to my door. (Name B) is the one who's going to have fun, so we don't need (name A) any more.

The rhyme starts with *A* jumping. As *B* is called he or she comes into the rope. *A* moves out of the rope on the last line. It is repeated until all have had a turn to jump.

Hippity, hippity hop. How many times before I stop?
One, two, three, four, etc.

I like coffee, I like tea.
I'd like (name) to jump with me.

Oh in I run and around I go.
Clap my hand and nod just so.
I lift my knee, and slap my shin.
When I go out, let (name) come in.

(Name, name) set the table.
And don't forget the salt and pepper. (On the word *pepper* the rope is turned rapidly.)

I have a little duck, his name is Tiny Tim.
I put him in the bathtub to teach him how to swim.
He drank up the water, and ate up all the soap.
He woke up in the morning with a bubble in his throat.
In came the doctor, in came the nurse.
In came the lady with the alligator purse. (Add people here.)
"Sorry" said the doctor. "Sorry" said the nurse.
"Sorry" said the lady with the alligator purse.
Out walked the doctor. Out walked the nurse.
Out walked the lady with the alligator purse. (People go out.)

I'm a little tea pot, short and stout.
Here is my handle, here is my spout.
When I get all steamed up, then I shout.
Just tip me over and pour me out.

Sick in the head, called for the doctor
And this is what he said.
Take two steps forward, turn yourself around.
Do the hokey-pokey and get out of town.

Oh the funniest thing I've ever seen
Was a tomcat sewing on a sewing machine.
Oh, the sewing machine got running so slow. (Slow the rope.)
And it took seven stitches in the tomcat's toe.

Donald duck was a one-legged, one-legged, one-legged duck.
Donald duck was a two-legged, two-legged, two-legged duck.
Donald duck was a three-legged, three-legged, three-legged duck.
Donald duck was a four-legged, four-legged, four-legged duck.

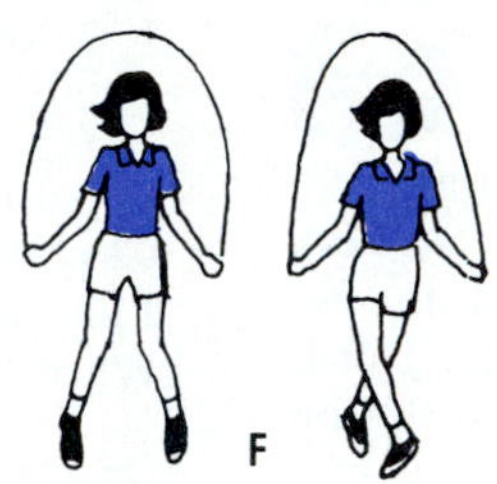

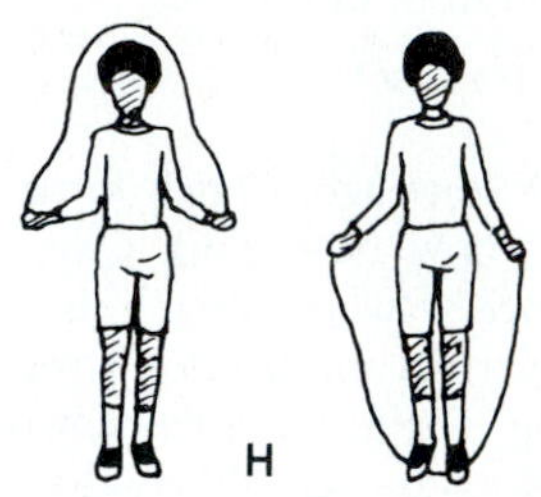

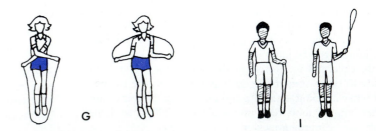

Basic stunts. **A,** Skier (side-to-side). **B,** Bell (forward and backward). **C,** Straddle (feet shoulder-width apart). **D,** Scissors (reverse feet). **E,** Heel-toe (alternate heel-toe touch). **F,** Straddle cross (feet shoulder-width apart). **G,** Crossover (cross arms). **H,** Double under (two rotations of rope with one jump). **I,** One-handed sideswing left (rope parallel to left side).

Jumping the Short Rope

Short ropes for elementary schoolchildren should be cut into 6-, 7-, and 8-foot lengths. Some of the taller youngsters in the upper grades may need a 9-foot rope. To select the proper length for jumping, the child takes an end of the rope in each hand and steps on the rope. The ends should then reach the armpit for a proper fit. If the rope is too long, it may be wound on the hand.

Once the children have mastered the rhythm of long rope jumping, they are ready to try the short rope. Jumping while turning the rope backward may be easier for some children because it eliminates the tendency to throw the rope with too much force to the floor. Another approach to helping children jump the short rope is to have them hold the rope in both hands and out in front of them so that it forms a U. They then try to jump over the rope without moving it or without it touching their feet.

The rope is held in the fingers. When turning the short rope, the hands should be close to the side, with the wrists and hands doing most of the work. It is not necessary to jump high but merely high enough to clear the rope as it hits the floor. The feet should land softly. The body should be erect, with the head up.

A single-beat jump, in which the jumper jumps only when the rope passes under the feet, or a double-beat jump, in which the child jumps when the rope passes under the feet and again as the rope is overhead, may be used.

Short Rope Activities

Short rope activities are performed by swinging the rope back and forth like a pendulum and jumping over it. While turning the rope forward or backward, the children may:

Jump the rope with two feet together.
Jump the rope on one foot.
Jump on first the right and then the left foot alternately.
Move forward or backward while jumping.
Jump while moving both feet from one side to the other (skier).
Jump while moving both feet forward and then backward (bell).
Move the feet to the side and apart and then together while jumping (side straddles).
Move the feet in a forward/backward stride position, alternating the lead leg (forward/backward straddles).
Point a toe to the side while jumping.
Alternately point a toe in front and then behind while jumping.
Touch a heel in front and then to the side while jumping.
Touch a heel in front and then a toe behind while jumping.
Rock back and forth from the left to the right foot while jumping.
Skip while jumping.
Cross the feet while jumping.
Twist from side to side while jumping.
Do a dance step while jumping, such as the step-hop, bleking, schottische, fling, step-swing, or grapevine.
Turn while jumping: quarter, half, three-quarter, or full turns.
Criss-cross: As the rope is jumped, the arms are crossed so that the rope is crossed as it passes under the body and then uncrossed as it passes overhead.
Double under: The rope passes twice under the feet on a single jump.
Triple under: The rope passes three times under the feet on a single jump.

Rope Twirling

In addition to rope jumping skills, the rope may be twirled before or during a jumping sequence. The rope may be swung to make a three-quarter circle or a full circle.

Single-side swing: The rope is held in both hands and twirled either forward or backward, vertically on one side of the body.
Double-side swing: Similar to the single-side swing, but the rope is twirled alternately on the right and left sides of the body.
Front swing: The rope is twirled in front of the body.
Horizontal swing: The rope is swung horizontally and jumped as it comes around.
Figure eights: The rope is twirled in a figure eight in front of the body.

TWIRL AND TOSS

Begin with single-side swing or front swing. Toss the rope and catch it.
Twirl and toss the rope, perform some locomotor movement or dance step, and catch.
Twirl and toss the rope, perform a forward roll, and catch.

Partner Jumping

With one child turning children may:

Jump facing one another, both facing the same direction, or back to back.
One partner jumps and turns 360 degrees while the turner turns and jumps.
Both jumpers turn while jumping.

With two or more short ropes and holding one end of another's rope, children may:

Jump side by side.
Jump while moving in different directions.

In addition, children may:

Hold the rope ends in one hand. Swing the rope beginning overhead and gradually lower the rope to jump over it.
Hold the rope ends in each hand, circling the rope around the body.
Wrap the rope around the body or an arm or leg with a full-length or folded rope.

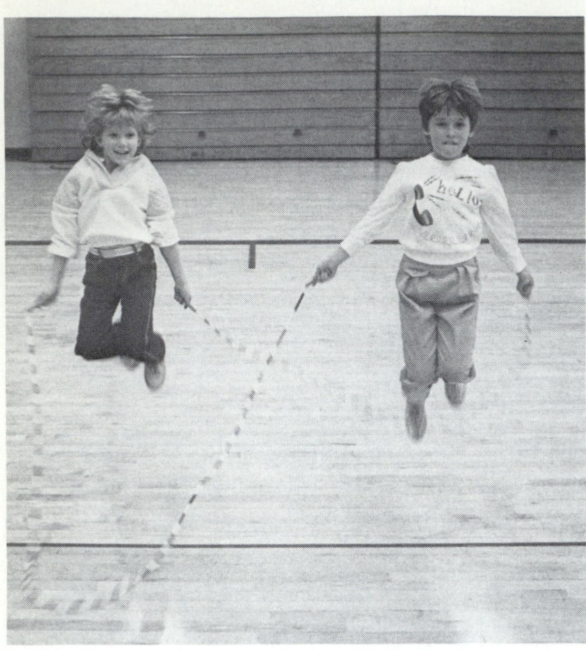

Partner jumping—two ropes.

Hold the ends of the rope in one hand, the other hand sliding down the rope about three-quarters of the way up the rope.
Perform figure eights or circles with the shortened rope.
Holding one end of the rope on the hip, wrap the rope around the body with the other hand. Unwrap.
With the rope extended behind, snap it up and catch in either hand. Continue with a side swing to a toss.

SCOOTERS

Scooters are popular with children. They provide opportunities for children to control a wheeled object and to explore movements from various positions.

Scooters are available from several manufacturers. They are made of wood or plastic with heavy-duty caster wheels. They can be made relatively inexpensively of plywood. Suggestions for the construction of scooters may be found in Appendix Three.

Because scooters may be a hazard to both the user and the observer, special care must be taken to ensure their safe use. Children should be taught to keep their clothing and fingers away from the wheels and to propel or push the scooter so that it remains under control. The children should not stand on the scooters.

With a scooter children may:

Assume the following positions to propel the scooter: sitting, kneeling, and prone with hips on the scooter.
Move forward, backward, or to the side.
Move with control, varying speed.
Move around objects, through an obstacle course, following lines on the floor, and in various pathways, such as tracing letters on the floor.
Move with a partner in any of the above activities.
Play follow the leader with a partner.
Link several scooters together and move with others.
Explore various ways of stopping and starting.
With a partner make a wheelbarrow.
Throw to targets while moving on the scooter.
Throw to partners while moving on the scooter.
Play games with scooters, such as Steal the Bacon.

STILTS AND BALANCE BOARDS

Balance activities are challenging for children. Balance boards and stilts involve both static and dynamic balance and balancing at various heights.

When using both stilts and balance boards, it may be helpful to have the children work in partners so that they can obtain a balanced position on the equipment with help before attempting to balance alone.

A good surface on which to use the equipment is important. The surface must not be too slippery. Indoor tile surfaces are generally better than varnished wooden surfaces. A mat may be advisable for use with some balance boards.

Stilts

Stilts provide an opportunity to develop dynamic balance while balancing varying heights from the floor. Stilts may be made of wood or of tin cans to which ropes have been attached. Appendix 3 includes specifications for constructing stilts.

While balancing on stilts children may:

Move in various directions: forward, backward, or to the right or left.
Move in various pathways.
Follow lines on the floor.
Move over lines or ropes placed on the floor.
Move around objects.
Follow an obstacle course.
Vary the size of the step taken.
Walk, straddling one or two lines.
Walk over objects varying in height (tin can stilts).
With three stilts (one a double stilt with a foot rest on each side) move with a partner performing any of the above activities.

Balance Boards

Balance boards provide an opportunity to develop static balance from an unstable base. Several types of balance boards are available. Specifications for constructing balance boards may be found in Appendix 3.

On a balance board children may:

Hold hands with a partner, who is standing on the floor, and assume a balanced position.
Balance unassisted.

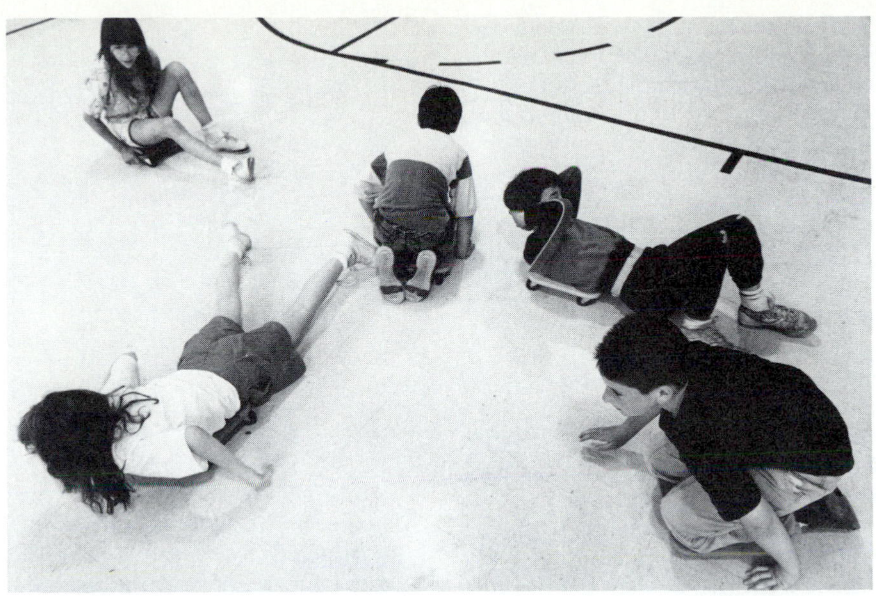

Moving in a variety of ways on scooters.

Balance with arms held in various positions.
Balance while assuming various body shapes.
Balance while holding objects of varying weights in each hand.
Balance while balancing beanbags on different body parts.
Balance while performing various ball skills alone or with a partner who is also balancing on a balance board.

WANDS

Wands may be made from 1- to 2-inch dowels 3 feet long, which may be purchased in hardware stores or building supply centers. Golf tubes purchased through golf supply companies may also be used. They are easily stored in long boxes or baskets, which can be brought into the gymnasium for easy distribution.

Safety may be of some concern as the children move with wands. They should be encouraged to keep the wands low when getting them out and putting them away, to be sure they have adequate space with the wand, and to avoid swinging the wands at any level.

With a wand children may:

Balance the wand vertically on various body parts, in various positions—standing, kneeling, and lying down.
Balance the wand with a partner.
Balance the wand horizontally on various body parts.
Balance the wand while moving in general space.
Balance the wand on one body part and transfer it to another.
Balance the wand on one body part and transfer it to a body part of a partner.
Toss it vertically from hand to hand.
Step over the wand while holding the wand in both hands and then bring it around the body.
Grasp an upright standing wand with one hand and duck under the wand without letting go of it.
March with a wand, moving it in various ways.
Imitate a partner's movements with a wand.
Do pull-ups with a partner. One child holds the wand with two hands in front of the body and faces and straddles the second child lying on the floor at about shoulder level. The child on the floor grasps the wand with an overhand grip and executes as many pull-ups as possible, bringing his or her chin up to the bar.
Wring the dishrag with a wand. (See gymnastics.)
Support a wand on two boxes and move under the wand in as many ways as possible without touching it.
Balance a wand on its end on the floor, let it go, and turn around and catch it before it falls.
Pick up objects.
Bring the legs alternately over and under the wand while sitting on the floor, holding the wand in both hands. (Can you do it without touching the wand with your legs?)
Sitting on the floor holding the wand in two hands, raise the legs bending at the knees, and then put the legs between the wand and the body; bring the wand down toward the floor. Reverse, raising the wand, bending the knees, etc.
Step over a wand held by another at various heights.
While moving in a forward direction attempt to pass under the wand held by two children. The wand is gradually lowered (limbo).
While facing and holding the wand with a partner, stand up and sit down alternately with this person.

Similar to the previous activity, but both sitting and then standing together.

Twirl a wand like a baton.
Jump over it while holding the wand in both hands.

Place the wand vertically on the floor, holding it with one hand. Raise one leg so that it passes over the wand, releasing the wand and then regrasping it with the other hand. Repeat with the same leg to return to the starting position. Then, move the other leg over the wand.

Place the wand on the floor. See how many ways you can move over it without touching it.

With a partner, one holds the wand horizontally at about chest height. The other places the hands with palms down just above the wand. Without warning the child holding the wand lets go, and the other child tries to catch the wand before it touches the floor.

In a small group, each child has a wand, one end of which is on the floor. Each child balances the wand vertically with one finger. On the signal the children let go of their wands and try to catch the wand of another child before it touches the floor. This activity requires the children to work together to determine how they will go about catching all the wands before they fall.

Similar to the previous activity, but with a partner. Each time they take a step back and then on the signal try to catch the wands before they fall to the floor.

PLAYGROUND GAMES

Many games using small equipment are ideal for use on the playground during recess and other periods of free play. These games are best suited for small group or partner play. The rules permit some modification, and the selection of skills to be used are well within the ability of the children to organize and conduct.

FOUR SQUARE

Four square is a very popular playground game. It is described in Chapter 28.

HOPSCOTCH

Hopscotch is another children's activity played around the world. Human beings found a way to represent perfection through geometry, with order and balance in nature represented in artistic drawings. There are many forms of these representations in various cultures, from the designs on Indian blankets to the motifs of Persian blankets. Symbolic drawings may have lost their significance but remain today in children's games, such as hopscotch. Beliefs and superstitions may also be restated in the games of children. Being unlucky to step on cracks in the sidewalk somehow became a part of the rules for hopscotch (Russell).

One of the oldest forms of the game is a Latin version called hop-round. Several versions of the game follow. These games may all be played by children at level II. To maximize the activity, three or four children should play each game. All require underhand throwing and hopping.

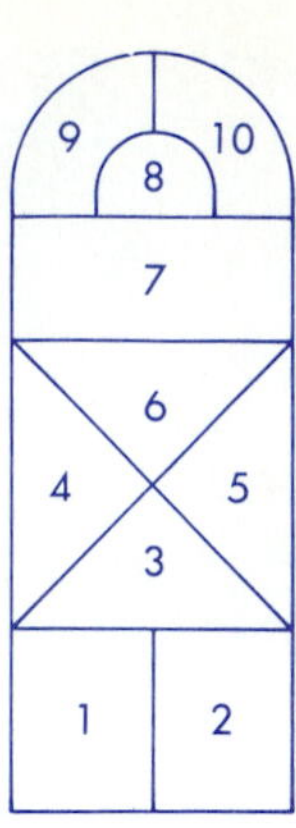

American hopscotch.

AMERICAN HOPSCOTCH

Equipment: A small stone or other flat object to use as the "scotch."

Area: An area of pavement marked out as shown.

Description:

Version I: Play begins with the scotch being thrown into square no. 1. The first player then hops into that square, turns without putting down the foot being held up, and kicks the scotch out over the starting line. Play continues, tossing the scotch into each successive numbered square, kicking the scotch over the starting line, and then hopping in each square back to the starting line. When the first player commits a foul, the turn is over and the next player begins the process from square 1. On the second turn for each player, play is resumed at the square in which the previous error took place. As play continues farther from the starting line, several kicks may be needed to get the scotch back to the starting line. As the children progress to squares 4 and 5 and 9 and 10, both feet are placed simultaneously in the squares. In these squares the turn is performed by jumping and turning so that both feet land simultaneously in the squares.

Version II: Play begins as in version I with a toss of the scotch into square 1. The player hops through the grid skipping square 1, jumping simultaneously in squares 4 and 5 and again in 9 and 10 as in version I. On the return the player picks up the scotch while standing on one foot in square 2 and then hops into square 1 and out of the grid. The player continues throwing the scotch in each square until a foul is committed. On the second round of turns, each player begins with a toss into the square in which he or she lost the turn in the previous round.

Fouls: (Version I and II)

1. Stepping on a line when hopping in and out of the squares.
2. The scotch stopping on a line as it is kicked back to the starting line.
3. Tossing the scotch into the wrong square.
4. Tossing the scotch so that it lands on a line.
5. Touching the nonhopping foot to the ground during the turn.
6. Tossing the scotch without assuming the hopping position.

Penalty: Loss of turn.

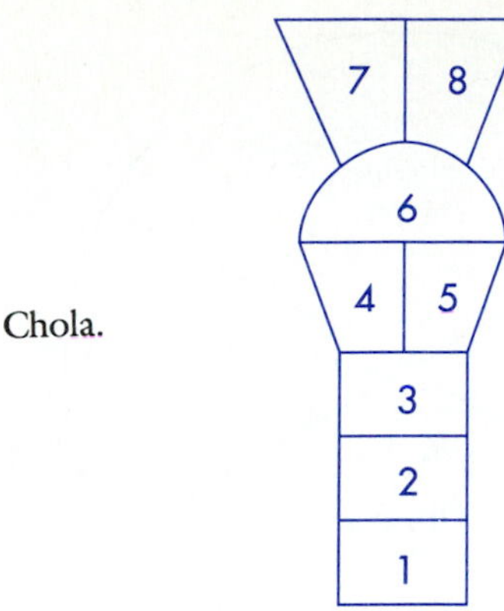

Chola.

CHOLA

(Chaldean—rulers of ancient Babylon)

Equipment: A flat object or puck 3 inches in diameter with one side smooth enough to slide over the surface.

Area: As drawn above.

Description: Play as version II of American hopscotch, except the puck is slid across the playing surface rather than thrown.

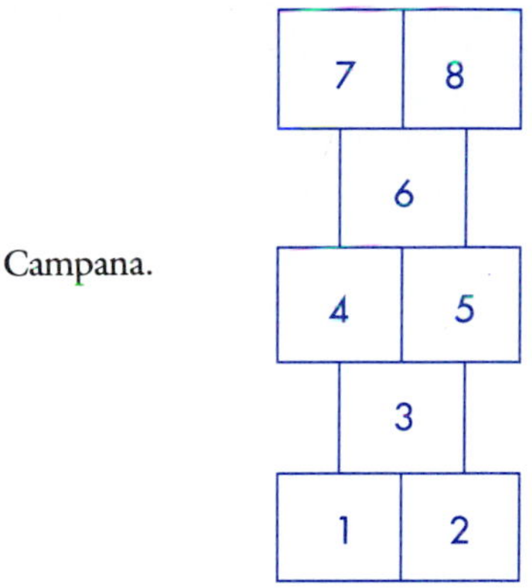

Campana.

CAMPANA

(Italian meaning the bell)

Equipment: Two pebbles per player.

Areas: As shown.

Description: Part I: Beginning with square 1 the player throws his/her pebble in each square. On each throw he/she hops up to 8 and back picking up the pebble on the return trip. In squares 1 and 2, 4 and 5, and 7 and 8, the player lands simultaneously with one foot in each square. Having completed part one, i.e., throwing the pebble from 1 to 8 and 8 to 1, the player is ready for Part II. Part II: Repeat the process but this time balancing one pebble on his/her shoulder as they throw the other and hop to each square. The first player to complete Part I and II is the winner. Any time that a player steps on a line, throws the pebble in the incorrect square or on a line, or drops the second pebble from the shoulder, his/her turn is lost and another child begins play.

Hinkelbaan.

HINKELBAAN

(Dutch meaning court)

Equipment: One stone for each player.

Area: As drawn above.

Description: The first player tosses the stone into one of the squares. Beginning at square one, the player then hops on one foot only as far as the square where the stone has landed, picking it up and then returning to the starting area. When they reach 6-7, players may land with both feet simultaneously in the two squares. When the diagram has been completed, players turn their back to the diagram and throw the stone over the shoulder. If it lands in a square players take the square as one of their "houses." During the game other players must avoid hopping in the houses of other players, but the owner may land with two feet in that square. At the end of the game, the child with the most houses wins. This version of hopscotch is known as Hinkelspiel in German.

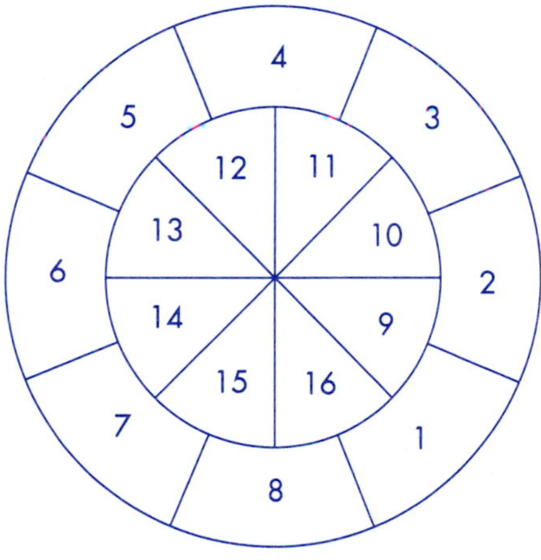

Hop-Round.

HOP-ROUND

(Latin)

Equipment: Each child has five pebbles.

Area: As drawn, with a starting line 10 feet away from the diagram.

Description: The numbers on each square represent the number of points for that particular square. The first player begins behind the starting line and throws the five pebbles, one at a time into the playing area. When all are thrown the child hops on one foot from 1 to 16 and back, picking up the pebbles on the way without stepping on the lines or missing any square. The child must hop on the same foot for the 16 squares, but may change to the other foot for the trip back. If successful, players score the total number of points of the squares where the pebbles landed. If a child fails to retrieve any of the pebbles, it means a loss of points for that particular square. The next player then repeats the process.

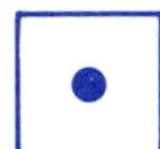

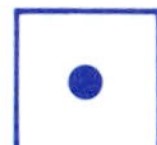

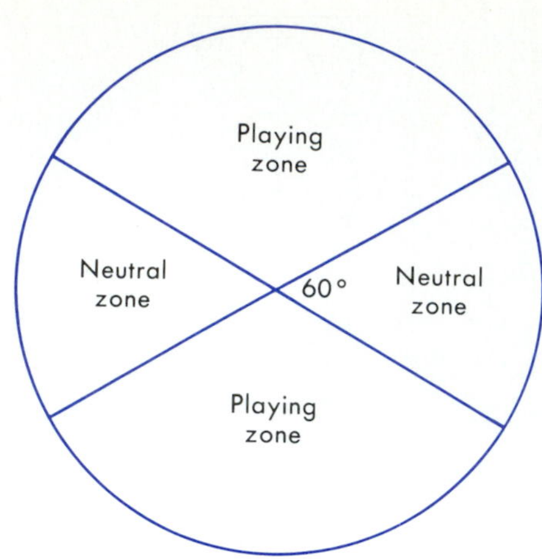

HORSESHOES

Level: III.

Equipment: A set of junior horseshoes for each player, two stakes secured into the ground.

Area: An area off to the side of the playground 10 feet wide and 25 feet between stakes.

Participants: Two to four players.

Skills: Tossing the shoes.

Description: To begin play, the first participant stands to the side and behind an imaginary line drawn from the stake. Tossing the horseshoe with an underhand motion toward the opposite side, the first player attempts to ring the stake with the horseshoe. The next player tosses a horseshoe. Then each player in turn tosses a second horseshoe. Points are awarded after all players have thrown their two horseshoes. A ringer is declared when the horseshoe circles the stake so that a straight-edge touching the open ends of the shoe would not touch the stake. Three points are scored for each ringer. If there are four ringers, no score is awarded. The horseshoe closest to the stake wins 1 point if there are no ringers or one ringer for each player. If all horseshoes are an equal distance away, no points are given. A leaning horseshoe does not count more than another horseshoe touching the stake. An official game is 50 points. The number of points should be determined before the game begins if fewer than 50 are played.

Scoring is as follows:

Closest to the stake: 1 point
Two shoes closer than the opponents: 2 points
One ringer: 3 points
Two ringers: 6 points
One ringer and one closest to the stake: 4 points
One player with two ringers, against one for the opponents: 3 points
If each player has one ringer the next closest shoe, if it is within 6 inches: 1 point
Ties: 0 points

Fouls: Tossing the horseshoe from a position in front of the stake.

Penalty: No score on the shoe.

Suggestions: Be sure that horseshoe areas are placed near the perimeters of the playing area so that children in other activities do not move through the area.

TETHERBALL

Level: III.

Equipment: A tether ball attached to a pole.

Area: A circle 20 feet in diameter.

Participants: Two to four players.

Skills: Striking with the hand.

Description: The ball is put in play by the first server hitting the ball around the pole. After the ball makes one complete revolution of the pole, the opposing player hits the ball in the opposite direction. Play continues with each player attempting to wind the ball completely around the pole. If teams are composed of more than one player, teammates alternately hit the ball.

Fouls:

1. Hitting the ball with any part of the body other than the hands.
2. Holding, throwing, or catching the ball during play.
3. Touching the pole or rope during play.
4. Playing the ball while outside the court limits or while in the neutral zone.

Penalty: Loss of game.

Other games for playground use may be found in Chapter 28.

SUMMARY

Children find work with small equipment challenging. Many activities are self-testing in nature; that is, children have the opportunity to test their own ability and to set goals for improvement and challenges for themselves.

These activities provide valuable experiences for elementary school children to apply the movement concepts they have learned; to explore the use of body parts in performing various tasks; to use space concepts; and to experiment with time, force, balance, and flow. They also provide a multicultural experience for children as they learn activities played in various parts of the world. In addition to the activities suggested in this chapter, many of the activities in Chapter 13 may be adapted for use with small equipment.

REFERENCES AND RESOURCES

Adams P, Parham J, Taylor M: Jumping rope—tsyana tobi, tobi-koshi, and el reloj, *JOPERD* 61(6):27, 1990.

Alaska State Museum: *Alaska games,* Juneau, Alaska, 1977, Alaska Department of Education.

Alaska State Museum: *Some Alaskan games . . . how to play them,* Juneau, Alaska, 1977, Alaska State Museum.

American Double Dutch League: *Here is your official double Dutch rule book,* United Technologies Corporation.

American Heart Association and AAHPERD: *Jump for the health of it,* Dallas, American Heart Association.

Blackwell D: *So you want to jump rope,* Riverton, 1982, The Riverton Ranger Printing Dept.

Carleton N: Chute the works: motivating for fitness and movement, *JOPERD* 60(1):73, 1989.

Casten C: Rhythmic sportive gymnastics, Boston, 1989, Paper presented at the American Alliance for Health, Physical Education, Recreation and Dance Convention.

Corbin D and Corbin C: Homemade play equipment for use in physical education classes, *JOPERD* 54(6):35, 1983.

Danna M and Poynter D: Frisbee player's handbook, ed 3, Santa Barbara, Calif, 1980, Parachuting Publications.

Finnigan D: *The complete juggler,* Edmunds, Washington, 1992, Jugglebug.

IFDA: The discourse: *Frisbee flying disc manual for students and teachers,* ed 3, San Gabriel, Calif, 1989, International Frisbee Disc Association.

Jernigan SS and Vendien CL: *Playtime: a world recreation handbook,* New York, 1972, McGraw-Hill.

Kalbfleisch S and Bailey L: *Double Dutch handbook,* 1987, Ancaster, Canada, 1987, Ceta Publishing.

Maguire J: *Hopscotch, hangman, hot potato, and ha ha ha,* New York, 1990, Simon and Schuster.

Oriam Sports: *Buka,* Venice, Calif, Oriam Sports, Inc.

Orlick T: *The second cooperative sports and games book,* New York, 1982, Pantheon Books.

Oxendine JB: *American Indian Sports Heritage,* Champaign, Ill, 1988, Human Kinetics Publishers.

Rasmus C and Fowler J, editors: *Movement activities for places and spaces,* Reston, Va, 1983, AAHPERD.

Russell AR: *Game for anything: multi-cultural games and activities for children,* Edmonton, 1981, Alberta Association for Young Children.

Seker J and Jones G: *Parachute play,* Deal, NJ, 1969, Kimbo Educational Records and Educational Activities, KBH Productions.

Tips C: *Frisbee by the masters,* Millbrae, Calif, 1977, Celestial Arts.

Tips C: *Frisbee disc sports and games,* Millbrae, Calif, 1979, Celestial Arts.

Valbuena F et al: *Multicultural awareness for the classroom: The Chaldeans,* Detroit, 1978, Detroit Public Schools Department of Bilingual Education.

World Footbag Association: *Footbag: an instructional manual,* Golden, Colo, 1987, World Footbag Association.

ANNOTATED READINGS

Bryant T and Doss T: Tire activities, *JOPER* 50(7):75, 1979.
Provides ideas for using automobile tires to enhance motor skill and fitness in physical education classes.

Clark E and others: Ultimate Frisbee, *JOPERD* 52(9):56, 1981.
Provides rules for ultimate Frisbee.

Corbin D: Inexpensive equipment for learning kicking and striking skills, *JOPER* 51(5):57, 1980.
Suggests how to use materials found around the home to improve kicking and striking skills.

Hardy R: Two broomsticks and a ball, *JOPER* 50(2):60, 1979.
Presents a variety of activities for wands and balls.

Kraft RE and Smith JA: Throwing and catching: how to do it right, *Strategies* 6(5):24, 1993.
Suggests activities for developing throwing and catching skills in the elementary schools.

Lavay B and Horvat M: Jump rope for heart for special populations, *JOPERD 63(2):74, 1991.*
Outcomes to be achieved in incorporating rope jumping for children with special needs.

Margo R and Davis K: The versatile geodesic ball, *JOPERD* 56(2):33, 1985.
Suggests activities to develop eye-hand tracking skills with a geodesic ball.

Plimpton C: Hanging hoop maze, *JOPER* 50(2):60, 1979.
Hanging hoops from varying heights to have children move through and around them in a variety of ways.

CHAPTER 17

Gymnastics

OBJECTIVES

After completing this chapter the student will be able to:

1. Describe the content of gymnastics, including stunts, tumbling, rhythmic gymnastics, and apparatus activities
2. Offer suggestions for teaching gymnastics to maximize the activity for all and provide a safe environment for learning
3. Identify the movement concepts important to successful participation in gymnastics activities and suggest activities for their further development

Children enjoy climbing, swinging from, and performing skills on large apparatus as well as rolling, balancing, and performing a variety of stunts. Many playgrounds and gymnasiums are equipped with some types of apparatus to provide for the developmental needs and interests of children. Mats, balance beams varying in width and height, horses and vaulting benches, climbing ropes, and parallel, uneven, and horizontal bars are some of the equipment often provided. Children need to be taught how to enjoy this equipment to its fullest while participating safely. Rhythmic gymnastics provides the additional opportunity to work with small equipment in the gymnastics setting.

The program of gymnastics in the schools is designed to meet the needs of each individual child in the class, enabling each to perform activities at the individual's level of ability. Because the goal is educational rather than competitive, emphasis is placed on developing greater awareness of the body's potential for movements through the development of movement challenges and a wide variety of individual, partner, and group skills rather than competitive skills and events.

Gymnastic activities promote a better understanding of body awareness, including how body parts may be used and the relationship of body parts in various spatial orientations and to equipment. Children with little experience in inverted positions often become disoriented when assuming positions other than upright. Balance in different body positions is explored, and the use of body parts to create and absorb force while maintaining body control is enhanced. Using the available space to the fullest and moving in different directions and pathways are required in the use of both mats and apparatus.

Creativity should be encouraged in each lesson as children make up their own stunts or transitional moves from one stunt to the next. Individual development is enhanced as children develop their own ways to solve the movement challenges with which they are confronted. Because many solutions are possible, all children can find ways of moving that are comfortable for them.

Social Skills

Gymnastics provides an opportunity for children to work alone while sharing mats and equipment with others as well as to work with partners and small groups in stunts and pyramids. If maximum participation is to be realized in a safe environment, each child must assume responsibility for their own safety and to a degree for the safety of others. Children also share responsibility with others in developing partner and group routines. Because gymnastics is an area where individual achievements vary, it should be one where all share in the accomplishments of others, from the simplest stunts to the most advanced routines. Children need an opportunity to share their accomplishments and to have them recognized by their teacher and peers.

Health-Related Physical Fitness

Gymnastic activities also contribute to some aspects of physical fitness. Participation should lead to improved flexibility, agility, coordination, explosive power, and upper body and leg strength. Stunts and skills need to be selected carefully if each child is to receive these fitness benefits.

Gymnastics Goals

The following goals should be realized in the gymnastics program in the elementary school:

1. To develop body awareness in various shapes and spacial orientations.
2. To explore the use of the body to balance; move on and off balance; move from one place to another; move on, along, over, and off a piece of equipment; and become airborne and land with control.
3. To discover ways to move on the floor, on mats, and in relation to apparatus.
4. To put a series of stunts together into a simple combination (routine) with flow from beginning to end.
5. To work with others to organize and perform gymnastic activities.

GYMNASTIC CONCEPTS

The movement concepts important to success in educational gymnastics are outlined in Figure 17-1. These concepts should be stressed in each lesson as children explore movement challenges, are introduced to new skills, and practice in individual, partner, or group activities.

Movement challenges to aid in the understanding and development of these movement concepts are included in the activities that follow.

TEACHING GYMNASTICS

The gymnastics program poses some special concerns for the teacher. The health and safety of the children must be considered in the conduct of the activities. To meet individual needs the teacher must use a far greater number of different skills than in many other units of instruction. The nature of the activity lends itself to individualized instruction. The following suggestions for teaching address each of these concerns.

Health and Safety

Setting Up the Equipment

Many activities require the use of mats. Mats should be placed where needed so that children avoid injury in landing while dismounting from a piece of equipment. Metal supports or other projections on apparatus should be padded in case of accidental falls or uncontrolled landings. Several thicknesses of mats may be needed where children will dismount from a considerable height. Mats should be butted together rather than overlapped or left to gap. Mats should be cleaned on a regular basis. Mats, however, are not the sole protector of the participant. Sound instruction, sequential progression of skills, and spotting complement the use of mats. Additional mats may be piled to lessen the height of equipment for children.

Any large apparatus should be checked periodically to ensure that it is safe for use. When the apparatus is set up, all knobs should be tight to avoid movement during use, and it should be properly secured to avoid sliding on the floor. Children should not be allowed under any circumstance to adjust the equipment. Only those versed in the procedure should be permitted to adjust the equipment. Equipment must be placed carefully and should not be too close together, close to walls or other stationary objects, or where there is a poor flow of traffic.

Chalk (carbonate of magnesia) may be used on the palms of the hands to prevent slipping when gripping the apparatus, especially when children are perspiring.

Selecting the Content

The selection of stunts should be based on anatomical capabilities. Stunts that put a strain on the ligaments surrounding the knee and hip joint, such as the duck walk, should be avoided. Stunts that involve hyperextension of the spine should not be used excessively. Examples of these activities are bridges and back bends. Partner stunts requiring heavy lifting should also be avoided. In addition stunts that might result in even momentary weight bearing on the head and neck such as rolls or inverted balances such as headstands, tripods, etc are contraindicated for children who are overweight.

Conduct and Supervision

The rules for the safe conduct of the activity should be clearly defined. It may be helpful to have them posted where they can easily be reviewed periodically. No horseplay can be tolerated. Children need to know the consequences of not adhering to the safety rules. Children need to assume responsibility for their own safety and the safety of their classmates.

In circulating among the children the teacher should always be in a position where the entire group is in view. In this way all activities may be adequately supervised and comments made to children who are far away as well as those who are close by. If maximum participation is provided, supervision is easier because the children are all busy working on something constructive. Many injuries occur when children are waiting for turns and looking for something to do.

The teacher may supervise in a general way by moving among the various groups of children as they are working or combine general supervision with specific supervision by staying with a group of children as they work on a new skill or one requiring the teacher's assistance. When working with a particular child or group of children, the

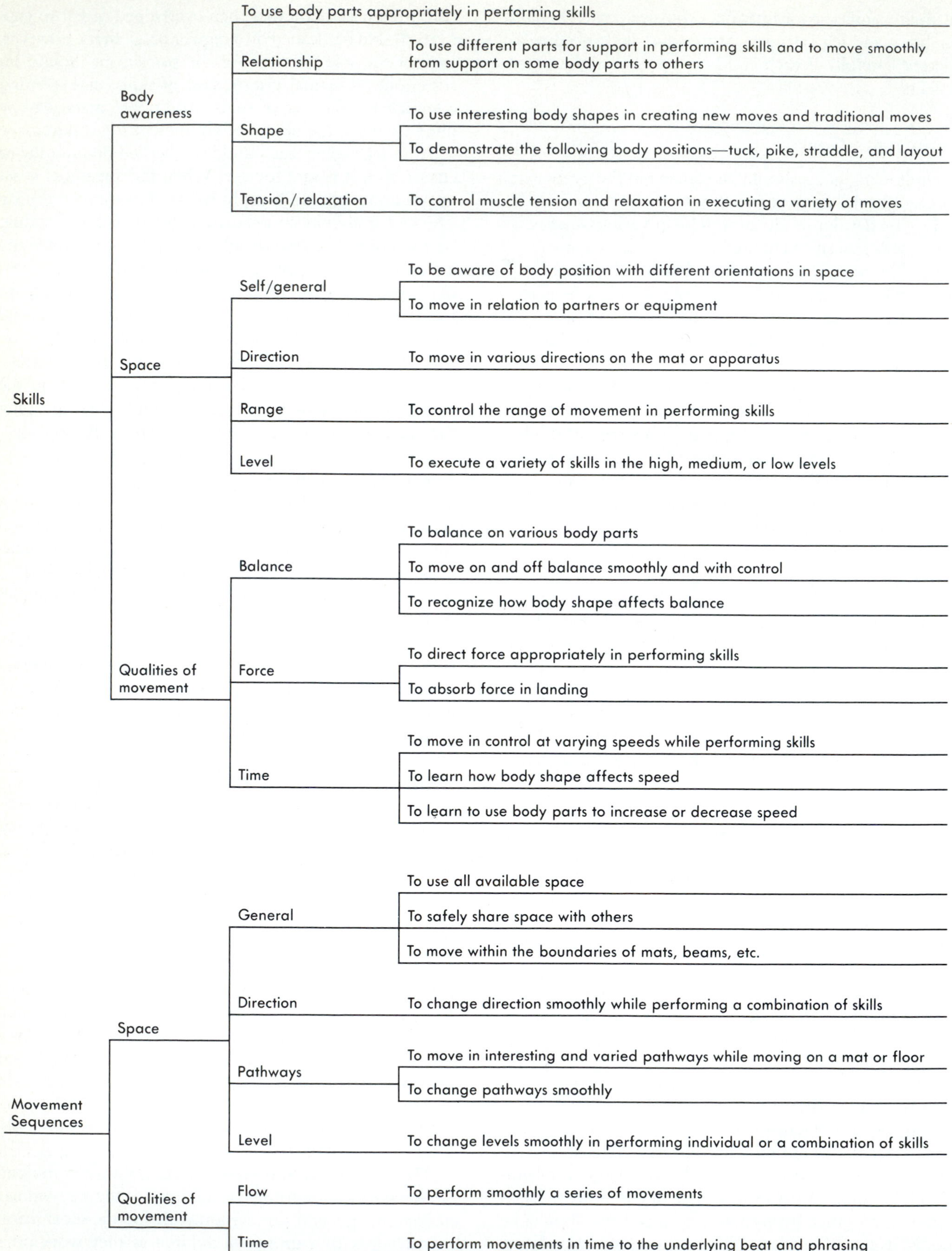
To use body parts appropriately in performing skills
Relationship
To use different parts for support in performing skills and to move smoothly from support on some body parts to others
Body awareness
Shape
To use interesting body shapes in creating new moves and traditional moves
To demonstrate the following body positions—tuck, pike, straddle, and layout
Tension/relaxation
To control muscle tension and relaxation in executing a variety of moves
Self/general
To be aware of body position with different orientations in space
To move in relation to partners or equipment
Space
Direction
To move in various directions on the mat or apparatus
Skills
Range
To control the range of movement in performing skills
Level
To execute a variety of skills in the high, medium, or low levels
Balance
To balance on various body parts
To move on and off balance smoothly and with control
To recognize how body shape affects balance
Qualities of movement
Force
To direct force appropriately in performing skills
To absorb force in landing
Time
To move in control at varying speeds while performing skills
To learn how body shape affects speed
To learn to use body parts to increase or decrease speed
General
To use all available space
To safely share space with others
To move within the boundaries of mats, beams, etc.
Space
Direction
To change direction smoothly while performing a combination of skills
Pathways
To move in interesting and varied pathways while moving on a mat or floor
To change pathways smoothly
Movement Sequences
Level
To change levels smoothly in performing individual or a combination of skills
Qualities of movement
Flow
To perform smoothly a series of movements
Time
To perform movements in time to the underlying beat and phrasing

FIGURE 17-1 Concepts for gymnastics.

teacher must continue to observe and comment on what is happening in others parts of the area. One rule of safety to be stressed in stunts, tumbling, and large apparatus is that no practice periods are permitted unless the teacher is present.

Many activities require **spotting** during the learning stages. Activities in which there is danger of falling, especially where the body is inverted or is moving through the air unsupported, require spotting. At the elementary school level, the teacher must assume responsibility for spotting because the children lack the maturity and understanding to be effective spotters. However, elementary school children may spot headstands or simple balance beam stunts, and spotting techniques for these skills should be taught as they are introduced to the class. This assistance may develop an attitude of concern for the safety of others. For safe participation the number of children assigned to work at a piece of equipment or mat should be limited to an appropriate number to maximize participation.

Children should be taught how to land and to fall when they lose control to avoid injury. A roll often may be used to absorb force when losing one's balance. Partner stunts are often included in the gymnastic program. In stunts performed with a partner, partners should be of equal size and weight. In activities in which one child supports another, the weight should be carried on those body parts capable of supporting the additional weight. For instance, in simple pyramids the weight should be carried on the hips and shoulders.

Organizing the Class

A concern in gymnastics as well as in other activity areas is organizing the activity for maximum participation for all children. Ample equipment should be provided so that the children can use the time in practice rather than in waiting for a turn. If equipment or mats are limited, it may be necessary to combine gymnastics activities with activities using small equipment to maximize the activity time for each child. If there are not enough mats for use with the apparatus and tumbling activities, it may be advantageous to separate tumbling and apparatus work into two separate units of instruction.

Some pieces of large apparatus are traditionally used by one sex only; for example, boys compete on the parallel and horizontal bars, whereas girls compete on the beam and uneven bars. However, at the elementary school level all children should have the opportunity to develop skills on all available equipment. Although children may not use some equipment in later years, it is developmentally sound to learn the skills needed, and it teaches them appreciation for the attributes that make participation successful.

In activities using mats, it may be possible for all children to work at once. This approach is especially useful when they are learning simple stunts or during movement exploration or problem-solving activities.

Station work is also used in the teaching of gymnastics. Several pieces of equipment are set up in the gymnasium area, and the children rotate from station to station as they accomplish tasks or most often on a signal from the teacher. Children may be assigned to work on specific skills at each station or to solve a particular movement challenge on the various pieces of equipment being used. Children may be ability or mixed ability grouped for these activities. Sometimes it may be helpful to organize the groups by the size of the student to avoid excessive adjustment of the equipment during the lesson to accommodate each child. Station work may also best serve the short attention span of the primary age child.

Children should learn to take responsibility for helping to set up and put away some equipment. They should be taught to fold mats correctly and to carry them rather than drag them on the floor. Children need to work together to help with the mats and apparatus.

Setting up the equipment is time consuming. Classroom teachers, especially those teaching young children, may wish to work together to set up the equipment before school, with each class using it throughout the school day, and then to put it away as the school day ends. It may also be possible to get aides or upper-grade children to assist with equipment.

Children should assume responsibility for their personal preparation for activity, including appropriate dress. Clothing that is loose or too tight may inhibit children's movements. Long hair ought to be pulled back so that it does not hinder vision during participation. Sneakers, gymnastic slippers, or bare feet are appropriate for various individual activities. Pockets should be empty and jewelry removed before participation. In classes in which children do not change clothing for activity, girls may wish to wear shorts if they are wearing skirts or dresses.

Effective Teaching

Because the ability of children varies greatly in gymnastics, many different activities must be included to provide for the needs of individual children. Some children do not develop their potential because they are forced to work continuously on skills that are beyond their abilities. In their frustration they often quit working and merely watch their more able classmates. Others may not be challenged by the level or variety of skills offered. Gymnastics requires the teacher to look closely at the needs of individuals and to plan accordingly. For students whose ability is well beyond that of the class and teacher, it may be necessary to work with them on combinations of skills or transitional moves rather than on developing many new skills that require the direct assistance of the teacher.

Opportunity for creative movement is essential. Children should be encouraged to solve movement challenges in gymnastics and to discover new skills. It is fun to name new creations after the child who developed them, adding them to the gymnastic curriculum. This approach not only develops a sense of pride in accomplishment but rewards the creative efforts of children.

Warm-up activities that prepare the children for the day's activities are an important part of the lesson. Because there is little vigorous activity in gymnastics, a few activities that increase the heart rate should be included.

The teacher should avoid lifting children onto apparatus. Mats stacked under the equipment have the effect of lowering the apparatus. Children should be helped to find their own ways to mount apparatus. Their attempts may result in the development of some new and interesting moves.

The selection of activities should provide for all-around development. Activities requiring flexibility, agility, balance, and strength should be included in each lesson. Excessive time spent in any one type of activity should be avoided. Too much time performing rolls, inverted balances, and some stunts is fatiguing and also may result in dizziness or headaches. Sufficient time should be provided for practice, but the teacher should be ready to move on to a new activity before the children become fatigued or other discomforts result.

When introducing new activities, time should be taken to carefully emphasize the technique, critical points, and safety considerations. The skill should be demonstrated if possible. If a demonstration is not possible, talking an able child through the skill will help the group to see how it should be performed. It should be clearly stated that the new activity should be attempted only with the teacher on hand.

New activities should be related to similar activities that have been taught previously. Before children attempt a new skill, they should review the stunts that are prerequisites for the new activity.

Stunts that are basic or are lead-ups to other stunts should be considered before more difficult activities are taught. Prerequisites should be mastered before children attempt more advanced activities. A stunt should be taught, not at a particular grade level, but rather when the child is ready to attempt it.

Children need the opportunity to set their own goals rather than the teacher determining what each child will do. In this way all achieve success, and the needs of children with diverse abilities and interests are met. Children should be encouraged to work at their own level of ability. They may need encouragement to do some activities of which they are capable. The selection of new activities should be the joint effort of the children and the teacher. When both the teacher and student feel the time is appropriate, new skills are introduced. New skills should be encouraged but not insisted on.

Two ways to organize the class for maximum learning are the use of task cards and mass sign-up sheets. In using task cards, the teacher designs a task card for each child within their level of ability, which includes a variety of five to six different stunts and skills. The student in consultation with the teacher may add two to three more skills to the list. When the list is completed (all tasks accomplished satisfactorily), a new task card is provided and the process is repeated. In the mass sign-ups individual skills are listed separately on sheets of paper, which are posted on the gymnasium walls. These skills might be coded by level of difficulty such as red for the easiest, white for the next in difficulty and blue for skills of highest difficulty. They could also be coded by the type of skill—animal walks, tumbling, stunts, individual balances, partner balances, and mounts, moves and dismounts on apparatus. Children work at their own level of ability. As they complete tasks they sign their names to the appropriate sheet. This is different from the class sign-up chart, which has everyone's name and all the stunts listed. It is a more positive approach as children sign anywhere on the sheet (it looks more like graffiti than a check list) when they have accomplished the skill. This form provides some idea about who has accomplished what skills but does not single out the children who have not yet achieved the task. The teacher can periodically check the lists to help monitor the children's work, encouraging those with few sign-ups and checking some of the skills that the children have signed as accomplished.

Good form should be emphasized in the performance of all activities. Each stunt or routine should have a controlled beginning and ending. The teacher should help the children toward pride in their accomplishments with the principle that only through proper practice can one reach a high level of perfection. Stunts should be put into simple combinations early in learning to give children practice in moving smoothly from one skill to another. This approach also provides opportunities to develop transitional moves between stunts.

STUNTS AND TUMBLING

Stunts and tumbling provide children with the opportunity to use their body parts in a variety of ways. As the children progress through the elementary school grades, an increase in body awareness enables them to perform more difficult skills and to analyze their own movements. Children in the beginning years are not discriminating in their own performances, whereas in later elementary school grades they can better assess their own performance and take action to improve their skill.

Movement challenges contribute substantially to an increased understanding of the body's potential for movement. A few examples of challenges that may be used follow.

Developing the Movement Content

The use of movement challenges should constitute much of the time spent in gymnastics, especially at the beginning levels of learning. Children should be given the opportunity to develop their own ideas as they learn to manipulate their body parts and control their body actions. These activities provide challenging opportunities for all because the children individually use the movements they have acquired and no specific gymnastics skills are required. The following are examples of challenges for the use of the body without equipment:

1. Assume a curled shape. In what ways can you move?
2. Make a stretched shape. Can you make a stretched shape with both sides of the body alike? Different?
3. Start with a stretched shape as you move? Gradually move to a curled shape as you continue to move. Did your way of moving change?
4. Can you combine a locomotor movement with a body shape? For example, can you combine a jump and a curl?
5. Vary direction and shape as you move.
6. Can you move in general space and on the signal assume a balanced position? Repeat, moving and balancing. Now move again and balance in a new way. What body parts can you use for support as you balance? What levels?
7. Move and, on the signal, assume a balanced position. Try it again with a new balanced position. Once more. Repeat several more times. Select one of your favorite ways of balancing. We will try moving in a variety of ways; on the signal balance in your favorite position. Move another way and balance. Now try a new balance position on the signal. Repeat several times, moving and assuming the new position. Repeat once more with a new balanced position and new ways of moving. Now we will combine the three balances. Select a way of moving and balance with the first position on the signal. Move again and balance in the second position. Finally, move and then balance in the third position and hold.
8. Can you balance on one body part? Another one? Another? Repeat, balancing on two parts. Three. Can you make up a sequence of balances and moves balancing on one body part, then two, then three?
9. Balance on two body parts. Move the supporting body parts close together and balance once more. Now as close as possible. Now move them far apart. What was the best position to balance easily?
10. Balance on three body parts. Move the supporting body parts in a straight line. Move them as close together as possible. Now apart. How else might you place the three body parts to balance? What positions made balancing more difficult? Easier?
11. Working on a mat, assume a balanced position. Now lose your balance, curling your body to roll to a new balanced position.
12. Can you find different ways to balance with a partner? 

Exploring balance.

Balancing on three body parts.

13. Can you balance with a partner so that three body parts are in contact with each other? Two? One? Does reducing the number of contact points increase or decrease the difficulty in balancing?
14. With a partner, balance, lose your balance, and then balance once again.
15. As you move in general space, can you change the body parts you use as you travel? Begin moving on your feet. Now change and move on some other body parts. Move once again on your feet. Now other parts.
16. Using different body parts as you move in each direction, can you travel forward? Backward? Sideways?

17. Move on a mat. How many ways can you move from one end to the other with control? Move on different body parts. Vary your body shape, direction, pathway, or speed.
18. Move on the mat, changing levels as you go.
19. Make a curled shape with a partner and move in that shape.
20. Make a stretched shape with a partner and move in that shape.
21. Combine a curl and a stretch with a partner. How did you move to get from the curl to the stretch?
22. Using stunts and tumbling skills you have learned, can you do a forward roll with the head leading? A cartwheel, hands leading in a sideward direction? What body parts lead as you perform various skills? In what directions did you move?

Falling

Falling is a safety skill that should be taught. As children develop skills in gymnastics, they should learn how to control the body when losing balance and landing from apparatus by applying principles of force described in Chapter 12.

1. Early problems might involve rolling as the children purposely lose their balance from a variety of balance positions. For example, balance on three body parts. Lean until you lose your balance. Curl your body and roll.
2. The children should move in general space. For example, on the signal make a shape and hold. Now fall from the shape to a relaxed position on the floor. Try it again with a new shape and fall. What shapes made falling easier? More difficult?
3. Falling can be combined with locomotor movements. For example, walk and fall. Run and fall. Skip and fall.
4. Children should explore landing with control from varying heights and then finishing with a roll.
5. Children should learn to fall from a kneeling position.
   Position: Kneeling on a mat, back straight and head up.
   Action: Keeping the back straight, the child falls forward, reaching out with the arms. As the hands touch the mat, the arms bend at the elbows, gradually absorbing the force as the body continues to fall to the mat.
   Suggestion: A soft landing should be encouraged.
6. Children should learn to fall from a standing position.
   Position: On a mat, standing with legs straight.
   Action: The child falls forward as in No. 5, absorbing the force with the arms.
   Suggestion: Arms should be fully extended as contact is made to permit absorption of force over the greatest distance.
7. Children should learn to fall from a height or from apparatus.
   Position: Standing on two or more stacked mats.
   *Action:*The child falls so the feet land first, absorbing the force by flexing at the knees, ankles, and hips.
   Suggestion: If the landing is off balance, the child should fall forward as in No. 6 or roll.

Animal Walks

Animal walks are simple stunts in which everyone can find success. They are excellent body awareness activities because body parts are used in different relationships as well as for developing flexibility and muscular strength. In some animal walks, body parts are moved in unison. In others, body parts on one side of the body may move at the same time. In still others, some parts may be stationary while other parts are moving. They are listed in order of difficulty. Although specific actions are suggested, the children should be encouraged to make up their own interpretations of how various animals move. Emphasis in teaching should be in helping the children see the relationships as well as how the body parts are used.

LAME DOG

Position: On hands and feet.
Action: One foot is lifted off the floor, and the child moves on one foot and two hands or on one hand and two feet.
Suggestion: The child can alternate which hand or foot is held up.

OSTRICH WALK

Position: Standing, bending at the hips.
Action: Grasping the ankles, the child moves in this position, keeping the legs fully extended.

SNAIL

Position: Lying on the back with hands at the sides, palms down on the mat.
Action: The body is curled up, bringing the hips and legs up over the head so that the toes touch the mat behind the head.

BEAR WALK

Position: On hands and feet.
Action: The child moves with the hand and foot on the same side moving forward at the same time, that is, right foot and right hand, then left foot and left hand.

SEAL CRAWL

Position: On the floor in a prone position.
Action: Keeping the body straight and relaxed and using the hands and arms to move forward, the body is dragged along the floor.

INCHWORM

Position: On hands and feet with legs straight.
Action: The child walks the hands out as far forward as possible. Keeping the hands stationary, the feet are walked up to hands, keeping the legs straight.

GORILLA WALK

Position: Standing with the feet spread shoulder width apart. Bend at the waist, grasping ankles.
Action: With knees straight, walk forward while holding ankles.

CRAB WALK

Position: On hands and feet with the front of the body facing upward.
Action: Keeping the hips up and back straight, the child walks with the feet leading, head leading, or moving to the right or left.

Inchworm.

Crab walk.

Turk stand.

SEAL SLAP

Position: Body straight and on the floor with the upper body supported on the straight arms and hands.

Action: The child pushes off with the hands and claps the hands together before returning the hands to the floor.

MULE KICK

Position: Standing.

Action: With the hands on the mat the child springs from the feet, taking the weight on the hands with arms straight and shoulders shrugged. The head is up. When the hips are above the head, the legs are extended forcibly upward. In the handstand position, the hips are flexed, and the child pushes from the floor with the hands and the shoulders and snaps the legs down. The hands come off the floor for a brief period before the feet touch the mat.

Suggestion: Younger children may perform this stunt without an airborne phase. Control of the upward leg movement is important to avoid throwing the legs over the head, causing the child to fall.

Individual Stunts

The following stunts may be used in addition to the animal walks. They enhance body awareness, balance, and body control. Most may be accomplished easily by everyone. They are listed in order of difficulty.

HEEL SLAP

Position: Standing.

Action: The child jumps into the air, bending the knees and raising the heels behind. The heels are slapped with the hands at the height of the jump. The landing should be soft.

ELEVATOR

Position: Sitting with legs crossed and hands folded at chest level.

Action: The child leans forward and comes up to a stand, then lowers the body to sit once again.

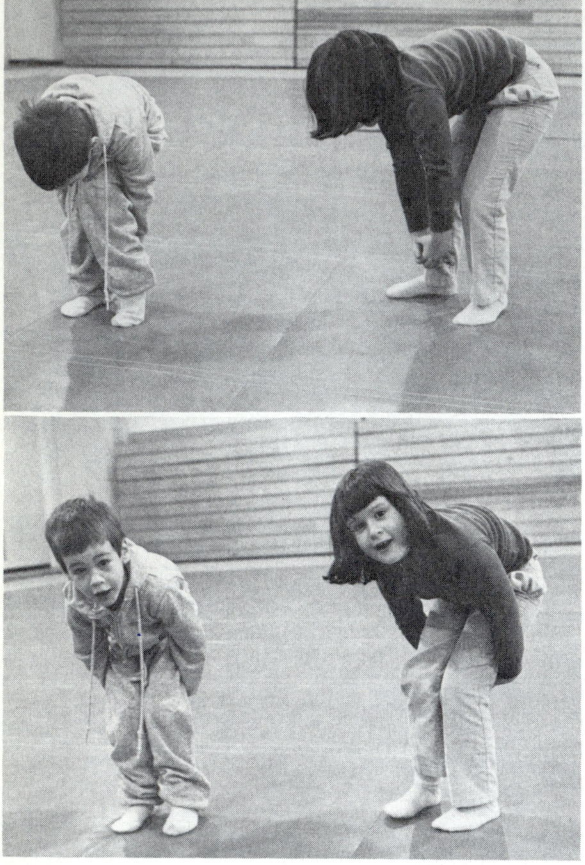

Thread the needle.

THREAD THE NEEDLE

Position: Standing, grasping the hands in front of the body.

Action: The child steps through the arms with one foot and then the other so that the hands are behind the back. The action is reversed, coming back to the starting position.

JUMP AND TURN

Position: Standing.

Action: The child jumps into the air, completes a half turn, and lands softly in a balanced position, then jumps, completes a full turn, and lands softly in a balanced position.

HEEL CLICK

Position: Standing.

Action: The child jumps, moving the legs to one side and clicking the heels together at the height of the jump. The child may try to click the heels twice or even three times.

HUMAN ROCKER

Position: In a prone position.

Action: Arching the back, with head up and the hands grasping the ankles, the child rocks forward and back.

COFFEE GRINDER

Position: With the body supported on one hand and extended to the side and the feet touching the floor.

Action: The feet are walked in a circle, pivoting on the supporting hand.

SWAGGER WALK

Position: Standing.

Action: The child walks by alternately stepping forward by bringing each foot behind and to the outside of the supporting foot.

KNEE SPRING

Position: In a kneeling position, with the head up and the back straight.

Action: The arms are forcefully swung forward to jump from the knees to land on the feet in a squat position.

SINGLE LEG CIRCLES

Position: In a squat position with both hands on the mat. One leg is between the arms, the other extended to the side.

Action: The extended leg swings forward. As it reaches the closest arm, the arm is raised to touch the floor again outside the leg. Shifting the weight to that arm, the leg continues to circle under the other leg and hand and back to the starting position. The back is kept straight and the inside leg bent.

Partner and Group Stunts

Partner and group stunts add the challenge of coordinating efforts with others. They are listed in order of difficulty.

WRING THE DISHRAG

Position: Partners facing and holding hands.

Action: Partners lift one arm; both turn toward and under the lifted arm. They continue to turn and end facing each other.

PARTNER GET-UP

Position: Two children of equal size sit back to back with the knees bent and the arms interlocked at the elbows.

Action: The two stand up by pushing equally on each other's back, then sit down again.

ROCKER

Position: Partners of equal size facing and sitting on each other's feet with knees bent and the hands holding each other's upper arms.

Action: The children rock forward and back alternately lifting the hips of one and then the other off the floor.

Coffee grinder.

WHEELBARROW

Position: Partners both facing the same direction; one is on the floor on hands and feet and the other is standing.

Action: The standing child holds the legs of the other. The first child walks forward on the hands, while the standing child walks behind.

Suggestion: The standing child must not push the wheelbarrow but merely supports the legs as the wheelbarrow moves. It may be helpful to hold the legs at the knees to give more support.

TANDEM WALK

Position: Two children of equal size, facing the same direction; one is down on hands and feet, while the other squats in front.

Action: Taking the body weight on the hands, the child in front places raised legs on the back of the other child. The upper legs are at the supporting child's shoulders. The children walk forward, the first on hands, the second on hands and feet.

MONKEY WALK

Position: One child stands with feet apart, the other lies on the back between the legs of the standing child with the feet in front and the head behind.

Action: The standing child bends forward, putting the hands on the mat. The second child wraps legs around the partner's waist, then reaches upward to support the body off the mat by holding on the partner's back. The child in the hands/feet position walks forward supporting the other child beneath.

Suggestions: Moving slowly and keeping the legs wrapped at the waist should be stressed.

ELEPHANT WALK

Position: Two children facing one another. One, with hands on the other child's shoulders, jumps up, puts the legs around the partner's waist, and holds the legs in position by wrapping ankles.

Action: The supported child lowers the upper body and with the hands walks the upper body and head between the legs of the supporting child. The standing child bends forward, taking the body weight on the hands and feet. The other child grasps the top of the supporting child's ankles, lifts the head, and extends the arms. The child in the hands/feet position walks forward supporting the other child.

Elephant walk.

Suggestion: Walking slowly and keeping the legs wrapped at the waist should be stressed.

CAMEL WALK

Position: Two children stand facing the same direction, one in front of the other. The person in back is holding the other person's waist. With the support of the rear person, the person in front jumps up and wraps the legs around the waist of the rear child.

Action: With ankles crossed to keep the legs in position, the child drops down and between the legs of the supporting child. The standing child bends forward and takes weight on the hands and feet. The child on the bottom raises up and grasps the top of the ankles of the other child with arms held straight. The two move forward as the child on top moves on hands and feet supporting the other child.

PARTNER HANDSTAND

Position: Two persons stand facing each other.

Action: One person bends down and places the hands on top of the feet of the other child. The bending child then kicks up into a handstand. The partner supports the handstanding child approximately at the knees and slowly walks forward.

Suggestion: The legs should be straight to avoid kicking the supporting child.

PARTNER WHEEL

Position: One person is lying on the mat with the legs bent at the hips and lifted into the air. The other is standing straddling the down child at the neck and holding the ankles of the down child. The child on the floor grasps the standing child's ankles.

Action: The standing child bends forward and brings the other child's legs and feet to the mat. The child then springs easily and does a forward roll between the legs of the down child. By this action, the positions of the two children are reversed. The child who was on top is now on the bottom, and the child who began on the mat is standing. The action is repeated several times as the two progress down the mat.

Suggestion: Each child should be able to perform a good forward roll before attempting this partner stunt.

SKIN THE SNAKE

Position: A group of children stand one in front of the other in a long line with their left hand extended between their legs to hold the right hand of the person directly behind.

Action: On the signal the last person in line lies down on the floor without releasing the hand and the line moves backward, straddling the child lying down. The line continues to move back with each person lying down in turn. When all are down, the last person in the line stands up and begins moving forward, straddling the other persons. Each in turn stands up until all are standing once again.

MONKEY ROLL

Position: Three persons lying parallel on a mat with their heads in a line. They are numbered one, two, and three.

Action: Number one begins the action by raising up slightly and moving over number two to roll on the opposite side of two. One and two continue to roll. Number three moves over one in a similar fashion. Then two over three. They continue to move in this fashion.

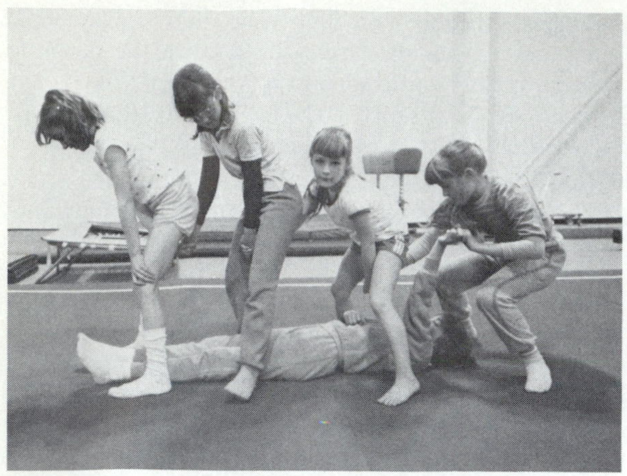

Skin the snake.

Centipede.

DOUBLE WHEELBARROW

Position: Two children assume the wheelbarrow position, with a third child in position behind the first two and facing in the opposite direction. The third takes the body weight on the hands, lifting the legs and placing them between the hands and ankles of the wheelbarrow couple.

Action: As the wheelbarrow moves forward, the child behind moves backward.

WALKING CHAIR

Position: A group of from four to eight children line up one behind the other facing the same direction.

Action: With their hands on the hips of the person in front of them, all assume a sitting position by bending at the hips and knees and keeping the back straight. They move forward, each stepping first with the right foot and then the left.

CENTIPEDE

Position: In groups of three in a line one behind the other.

Action: The last person in line bends forward and takes weight on the hands and feet. The second person takes weight on the hands and lifts the legs, bending the knees and turning the knees out to each side so they rest on the hips of the person behind. The person in front repeats the action of the one behind, resulting in three persons in line with their weight on all hands and the feet of the last person in line. They walk forward in this position, moving first the limbs on one side and then the other.

MERRY-GO-ROUND

Position: A group of eight or ten children form a circle and hold the wrists of the persons on either side. They number off consecutively. The odd numbers sit on the floor with their legs straight and their feet touching.

Action: On a signal, the even-numbered children take a step backward as the odd numbers raise their hips off the floor, leaning back with their bodies and keeping the legs straight. The even numbers then move around in a circle with the others turning with them by pivoting on their heels. Roles are reversed and the activity repeated.

THIGH MOUNT

Position: Three persons stand side by side facing the same direction. The outside persons with their inside hands hold the center person at the waist; the inside person puts the hands on the shoulders of those on either side.

Action: On the signal, the two outside persons bend their inside legs to form a flat surface parallel with the floor. The inside person steps up putting one foot on the inside thigh of the outside persons. When balanced the inside person extends the arms up and out to the side. Hold the position.

Individual Tumbling Skills

Individual tumbling skills form the basics for beginning combinations in **floor exercise.** Many combinations and variations are possible. With the help of the teacher, children select skills and make up combinations to fit their abilities. The skills are listed in order of difficulty.

LOG ROLL

Position: Lying on the mat with arms at the sides.

Action: The child rolls over to the side in as straight a line as possible.

Suggestion: This stunt may be performed from a lying position with arms extended overhead.

EGG ROLL

Position: In a tuck position, grasping the legs with the hands.

Action: The child rolls on the mat, moving sideways.

SHOULDER ROLL

Position: Standing with the side to the mat.

Action: The performer drops to the knee closest to the mat, taking the body weight momentarily on the hand and arm on the same side. The elbow turns in and the individual lands on back of the shoulder blades. The child continues to roll, coming up on the opposite knee and finally to a stand.

Common error: Rolling on the entire back.

Suggestions:

1. To learn the skill, begin in the knee position and execute the roll.
2. The child should practice slowly at first to get the body position.
3. Emphasize the continuous action of the roll so that the body's force is absorbed over a larger area.

FORWARD ROLL

Position: In a standing position facing the mat.

Action: To begin the roll, the performer assumes a squat po-

Merry-go-round.

Shoulder roll.

sition with hands on the mat and the head tucked to the chest and between the legs. With a gentle push with the feet, the roll begins with a lift of the hips overhead, the weight shifting from the feet to the hands. As balance is lost, the roll continues with the head well under and the weight taken on the upper back and shoulders. The momentum of the roll should carry the individual back to the standing position. The arms reach upward or are extended forward from the shoulders as the individual comes to a stand.

Common errors:

1. Failure to tuck the head to the chest, resulting in rolling on the head.
2. Failure to maintain a tuck position throughout the roll.
3. Pushing with the hands a second time at the end of the roll to aid in standing.

Suggestions:

1. To spot the roll, one should kneel next to the tumbler, placing one hand where the neck and back meet and the other on the back of the thighs. In this position, the spotter can help in keeping the tumbler in the tucked position and also support the neck if necessary on the roll. Under no circumstances should the spotter push the tumbler into the roll.
2. Most children have little difficulty with the forward roll. Some large children need more assistance in learning to do the roll safely.
3. Beginners should start the roll from the squat position.

Variations:

Continuous forward rolls: A series of rolls is combined by maintaining the tuck position from one roll to the next.

Forward roll.

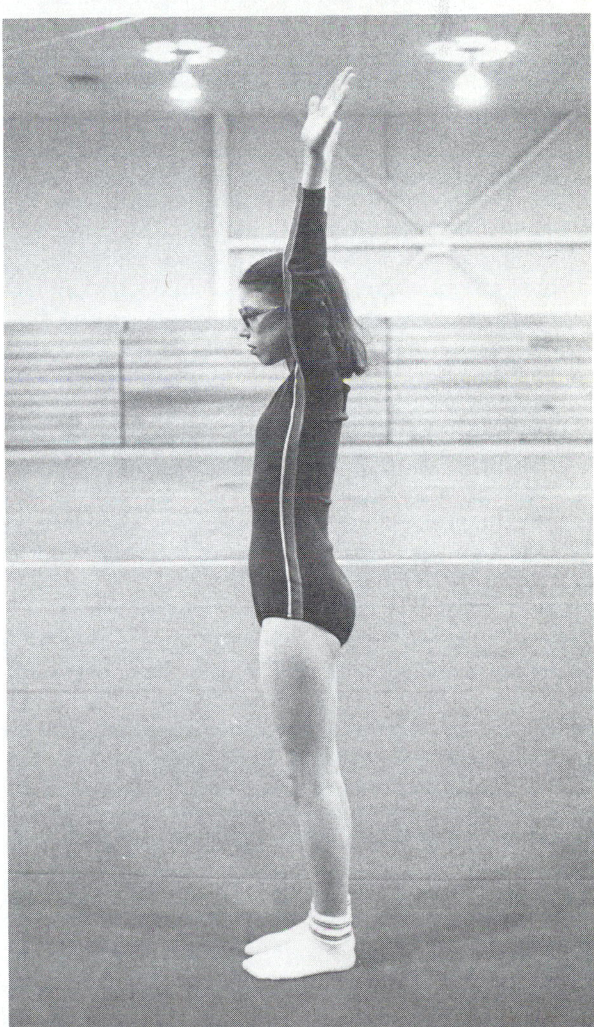

Backward roll.

Straddle: The roll is begun with the legs wide apart and continues in this position, coming up to a stand.

Feet crossed: From the standing position with the feet crossed, this position is continued throughout the roll.

Forward roll step out: One leg is tucked in and the other extended as the roll is taken.

BACKWARD ROLL

Position: Standing with the back facing the mat.

Action: The body is lowered as in sitting down and the arms are bent with the hands at the shoulders, palms up, and fingers pointing in the line of direction of movement. As the hips make contact with the mat, the head is tucked to the chest and the body begins the roll from the hips to the upper back. As the weight is taken on the upper back, the hands push to lift the body slightly to get the head under. The roll ends in a standing position.

Common errors:

1. Failure to place the hands in the correct position for the push.
2. Failure to keep tucked as one rolls back.
3. Failure to push or to push evenly with both hands.
4. Turning the head to one side while rolling.

Suggestions:

1. Teaching the backward roll should begin from the squat position.
2. In getting the idea for the roll, the children can do the snail but put the hands in the correct position for pushing.
3. The roll is spotted by kneeling next to the individual and holding the tumbler's hips on either side and lifting the hips as the tumbler rolls to the shoulders.
4. Another method of spotting may be used in which the spotter places one hand at the spot where the neck and back meet and the other on the back of the thighs. The spotter lifts the tumbler, supporting the neck in the hand. Under no circumstances should the tumbler be pushed over so that the body weight is taken on the neck.
5. The backward roll is much more difficult for children to master. Larger children in the class will need special help.
6. The shoulder roll may be preferable for less skilled children or used as a prerequisite for the backward roll.

Variations:

Continuous backward rolls: A series of backward rolls is completed, maintaining the tuck position from one roll to the next.

Straddle: The roll is begun from a standing position with the legs spread apart and the hands between the legs.

Pike: From a standing position, the body is lowered as in a backward roll but bending at the hips and keeping the legs straight. The roll begins from a long sitting position on the mat, with the legs swinging overhead as the hands move to the shoulders. The roll continues with straight legs to the standing position.

Back extension: The roll is begun as for a tucked or pike backward roll. As the legs are brought overhead, the hands push and the body extends to a handstand, which is held for a moment. The body then bends at the hips with straight legs to finish in a standing position. This is spotted as a backward roll, with hands at the hips helping the lift and handstand position.

Fish flop: Similar to the back extension, but after the body extension the arms bend, lowering the body so that it finishes with the back arched and contact on the mat moving from the chest to the lower body.

CARTWHEEL

Position: Standing facing the direction of movement.

Action: The performer faces forward, extending the arms upward and out toward the side. The weight is transferred to the foot away from the line of movement and the other foot lifted. A step is now taken on the lifted foot and the hand on that side of the body is placed on the floor with the fingers pointing to the side of the body. There is a push from the stepping foot as the other leg is swung upward. The legs are in a straddle position throughout the stunt. As the body turns 90 degrees to a side orientation, the second hand is placed on the mat in a line with the first hand. As the movement continues, the weight is carried to the second hand and the body begins to drop to the side. The weight is then transferred to one foot and then the other. The cartwheel ends in the standing position with legs and arms spread, the body finishing facing the line of movement.

Common errors:

1. Touching both hands to the mat at the same time.
2. Improper hand placement on the mat, either too near or too far from the front foot.
3. Failure to get the hips over the head.
4. Kicking the leg to the side instead of behind.
5. Landing with feet together or on knees.
6. Inability to keep the arms straight as they take the body weight.
7. Bending the legs as they come up over head.

Suggestions:

1. The sequence is hand, hand, foot, foot.
2. To spot the cartwheel and to help children get the feeling of having the hips overhead, one can stand behind the individual with the arms crossed and the hands at the hips. As the child attempts the cartwheel the body is supported at the hips, keeping them up and overhead.

Variation:

One-handed cartwheel: Similar to the two-handed cartwheel, but touching only the first hand to the mat. The body momentum carries the body weight back to the standing position. The sequence is hand, foot, foot.

ROUND-OFF

Position: Standing facing the direction of movement.

Action: The round-off is similar to a cartwheel in that the body weight is shifted to the hands and then the feet. In the round-off, however, the sequence is hand, hand, and then both feet. A running approach is used in the round-off with a hop step or hurdle step preceding the execution of the skill. As the first hand is brought rapidly to the mat, the opposite leg is straight and raised up overhead. As the body weight is taken on the two hands, the legs are extended overhead, with the feet coming together. There is a slight twist in the body, and the hips forcibly flex to bring both feet down to the mat in a snapping action. As the legs snap the hands push from the mat as in the mule kick. In the landing the arms are overhead and the body is facing the starting position.

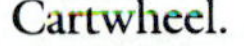

Cartwheel.

Common errors:

1. Beginning from a standing position with insufficient momentum to perform the skill correctly.
2. Placing the hands too close or too far from the front foot.
3. Failure to bend the front leg.
4. Failure to get the hips overhead.
5. Not pushing with hands from mat so that there is no phase when feet and hands are in the air before landing.
6. Failure to flex hips forcibly.
7. Not bringing legs together overhead.
8. Failure to keep arms straight throughout.

Suggestions:

1. Children can begin learning the skill from a standing position and add a moving approach when ready.
2. The teacher should insist on a moving approach before beginning the skill to develop sufficient momentum.
3. The teacher should emphasize the push with the hands as the hips flex.
4. The cartwheel and mule kick should be practiced before trying this skill.
5. The teacher may draw a line on the mat and have the students practice the round-off by following the line.

SNAP-UP (KIP)

Position: Sitting on the mat with legs straight and toes pointed, hands at the sides.

Action: The body rocks back, bringing the piked legs overhead, and the hands move to a position at the shoulders as if attempting a backward roll. The legs are quickly snapped forward and downward. The back is arched and the hands push forcibly as the leg action is taken. The feet are brought under the body and the upper body is snapped forward. The skill ends in a standing position with the arms extended upward and slightly to the side.

Common errors:

1. Hesitating between the rock back and snap, losing momentum.
2. Failure to push with hands, head, and shoulders as the legs are snapped.
3. Snapping the legs upward and forward rather than forward and downward.

Suggestions:

1. To spot the snap-up, the spotter kneels at the tumbler's shoulders, grasping the underside of the upper arm with one hand and the lower back with the other. As tumbler snaps, the spotter lifts until the feet are under the body. A spotter on each side may be used.
2. Another spotting technique involves kneeling at the performer's side and spotting the lower back by the waist with two hands after the tumbler has rocked back. As the tumbler snaps, the spotter lifts until both feet are under the performer.
3. The child may begin with a snail to get the proper positioning.
4. A squat position for landing is a simpler variation for beginners.

BRIDGE

Position: Lying on the back on the mat with hands at shoulders, fingers pointing toward feet.

Action: Pushing with hands and feet, the body is lifted into a back bend and held.

Common error: Not pushing simultaneously with feet and hands.

Suggestions: This is a prerequisite skill for the front limber, forward walkover, front handspring, and headspring.

FORWARD LIMBER

Position: Standing, facing the direction of movement.

Action: The skill begins with a kick up into a handstand. Keeping the legs together and straight, the back is overarched and the legs lowered to the mat with the toes turned out. The arms are straight. As the feet touch the mat, the hands push off and the body rocks forward to rise to a stand. The arms remain overhead, the head is back, and the back is arched as the performer comes to a standing position.

Common errors:

1. Failure to keep the arms straight.
2. Failure to keep the back arched.
3. Failure to time the push with the rocking forward of the body.

Suggestions:

1. The bridge is a prerequisite skill.
2. One may spot from the side, placing one hand at the upper back and the other ready to support at the waist as the tumbler comes up to a stand.

FORWARD WALKOVER

Position: Standing facing the direction of movement.

Action: The movement begins with a kick up into a handstand, with the legs split, one forward and the other back. The legs are lowered with the forward leg leading. It is placed on the mat as close to the hands as possible. There is a slight bend at the knee. To come up to a stand, there is a push with the hands and the trailing leg is raised. Starting with reaching, the hands continue to reach overhead as the performer stands.

Common errors:

1. Failure to keep the arms straight throughout the performance.
2. Throwing the body over rather than lowering the legs with control.
3. Failure to keep the legs split throughout the move.
4. Not placing the foot close to the hands.
5. Failure to push with the hands and to thrust the body forward.
6. Failure to arch the lower back.

Suggestions:

1. The tumbler may think about stepping over an obstacle as the second leg is brought forward and down to maintain an erect position.
2. The spotter places one hand at the base of the neck and top of the shoulders and the other ready to support the lower back as the performer begins to lower the legs.

BACK BEND

Position: Standing on a mat with arms raised overhead, and head back.

Action: The body is lowered backward, pushing the hips forward and slightly bending the knees. The hands are placed on the mat as close as possible to the feet. The arch is held and the child stands up by thrusting hips forward.

Common error: Not thrusting the hips forward to stand.

Forward walkover.

Suggestion: A spotter should have one hand on each side of the hips to help to control the downward descent.

BACK WALKOVER

Position: Standing with the arms raised over head and the back facing the mat. One foot is slightly forward and the weight is on the rear foot.

Action: Reaching back for the mat, the hands are placed on the mat as close as possible to the feet. One leg is raised. Pushing off with the other foot vigorously, the individual assumes a handstand position with one leg forward and the other back. The forward leg is lowered to the mat, the legs remaining in the split position. A push with the hands and a lowering of the trailing leg brings the tumbler back to the standing position.

Common errors:

1. Failure to keep the arms straight throughout the stunt.
2. Placing the hands too far from the feet.
3. Throwing the body over rather than moving with control.

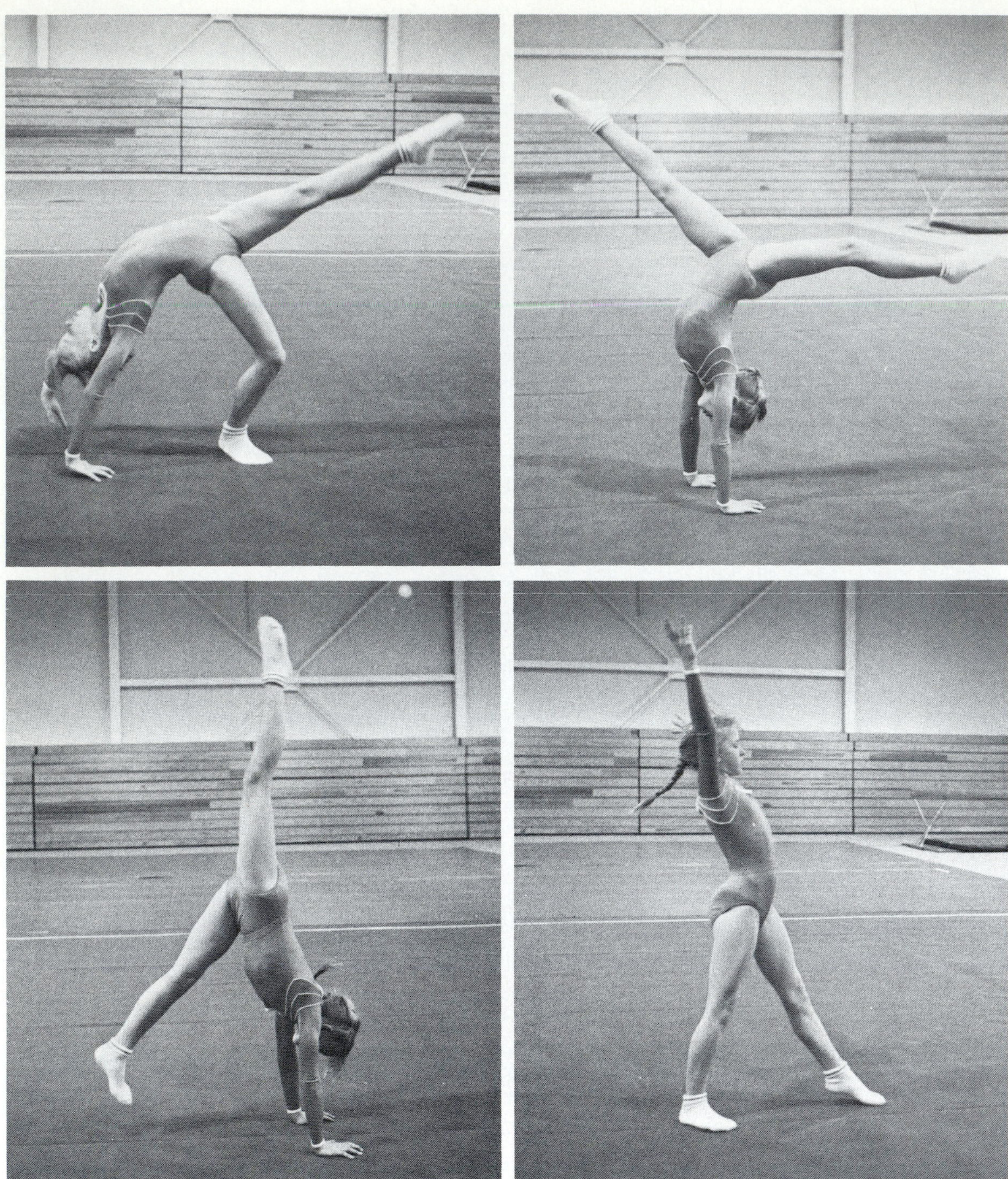

Back walkover.

4. Scissoring legs or failure to keep them split throughout the stunt.
5. Failure to swing the leg vigorously as the hands are placed on the mat.

Suggestion: To spot one stands next to the performer, placing the inside hand on the lower back and the outside hand on the back of the upper thigh of the front leg. In this manner one may support the lower back and also help the leg swing forward by lifting the leg.

HEADSPRING

Position: Standing facing the direction of movement.

Action: The headspring may be performed from a straddle or pike position. The hands are placed on the mat with the head on the mat between the hands. The legs are lifted in the pike or straddle position. The body leans forward, and as it does the legs are kicked up and over. As the body continues to move off balance there is a forceful push of the hands to bring the body to its feet. The landing is on the balls of the feet, the knees are slightly bent, and the arms are overhead.

Common errors:

1. Failure to use a two-foot take-off.
2. Failure to get hips beyond head before thrusting legs.
3. Failure to maintain the pike or straddle position.
4. Failure to push with the hands.

Suggestions:

1. To spot one kneels beside performer, grasping the upper arm with the inside hand and supporting the lower back with the outside hand.
2. This skill is often taught from a rolled mat, which makes it easier for the performer to get the feet under and close to the hands.

FRONT HANDSPRING

Position: Stand, facing the direction of movement.

Action: A moving approach is taken with a final push-off on one foot and a lift of the opposite knee and leg to increase the height of the jump. As the body moves forward and downward, the hands are placed on the mat shoulder width apart, and the free leg is raised in an extended position. The body is moved quickly through a handstand position, the legs coming together as they move beyond the head and shoulders. As balance is lost the toes reach for the mat and the hands push the body away from the mat. As the feet touch the mat, the upper body is raised, ending in a standing position with knees slightly bent and arms overhead.

Common errors:

1. Failure to keep the arms straight throughout the stunt.
2. Failure to push with the shoulders and hands.
3. Failure to keep the back arched.
4. Failure to keep the body in an extended position throughout the stunt.

Suggestions:

1. To spot the front handspring one stands next to the performer, placing the outside arm at the top of the shoulders as the inside arm supports the lower back.
2. This skill may be practiced over a rolled mat for support.

BALANCE STUNTS

Balance activities are an important part of the gymnastic experience. Beginning work on the mats and large apparatus includes balancing in various body positions. Both individual and partner or group balancing activities should be included.

Individual Balances

Skill combinations or gymnastic routines include balance activities. Although they may be held only momentarily, they demonstrate the child's control over the body's movement.

KNEE SCALE

Position: Kneeling on one knee, with the opposite hand on the floor.

Knee scale.

Action: The other leg is raised upward and backward, pointing the toes. The opposite arm is extended and the hand forward with the fingers pointing ahead. The head is up.

ARABESQUE

Position: Standing.

Action: The weight is kept on one foot as the other is lifted back as high as possible. The trunk is bent forward slightly and the back is arched. The hands may assume a variety of positions. The most common position is to have the arm on the same side as the lifted leg extending forward and the other back. Both arms form a straight line from the shoulders.

V-SIT

Position: Sitting on the floor or a mat.

Action: Both legs are lifted to a V or pike position while pointing the toes. As the legs are lifted the arms swing forward and upward to grasp the ankles. The hands may also be extended to the sides or to the rear.

ONE-LEG BALANCE

Position: Standing with the hands at the sides.

Action: Keeping the weight on one foot, the other leg is raised sideward and upward as high as possible, the heel held with the hand.

NEEDLE

Position: In an arabesque.

Action: The child bends forward, touching hands to the floor and simultaneously raising one leg backward and upward toward the ceiling. A variation in hand position commonly used is to grasp the ankle of the supporting foot with one hand while the other touches the floor.

L-SUPPORT

Position: In a long sitting position on the mat with hands touching the mat at the sides of the body and fingers pointing forward.

Action: The body is raised upward and supported on the hands. The legs should be extended forward with the toes pointed and off the mat.

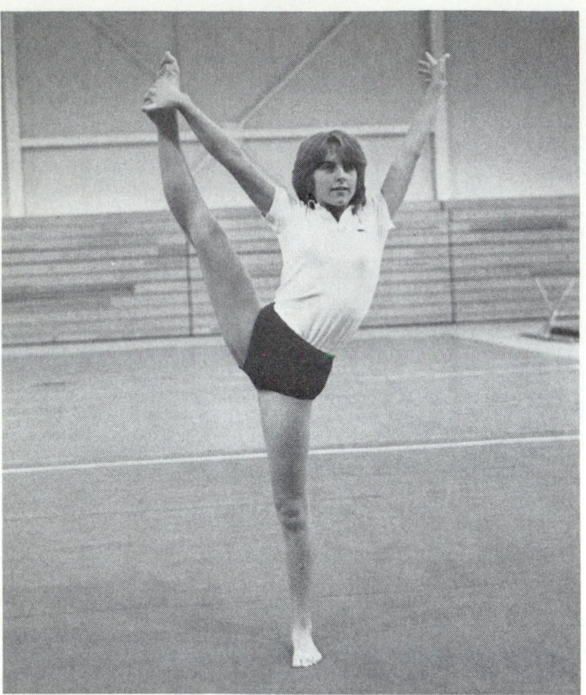

One-leg balance.

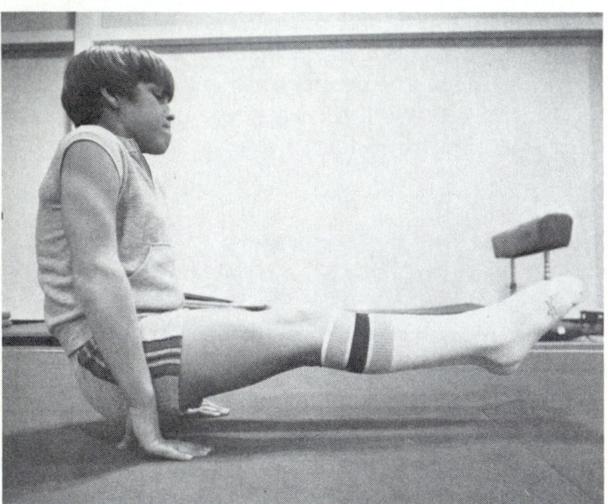

L-support.

Tripod.

Inverted Individual Balances

Some activities that involve balancing in the inverted position should be included in the gymnastic experience. These challenge the child to control the body while balancing on the head and hands or hands alone.

SHOULDER REST

Position: In a long sitting position.

Action: The individual rocks back until the hips are over the shoulders. The legs are extended overhead. The hands support the hips with the elbows on the mat.

TRIPOD

Position: In a squat position with the hands placed on the mat in front of the feet.

Action: The forehead is placed on the mat out in front of the hands to form a triangle with the hands. The performer rocks forward taking the body weight on the hands and head. The legs are raised and the knees are placed on the bent elbows.

Suggestions:

1. This stunt is a prerequisite to the headstand.
2. The weight should be equally balanced on the hands and forehead. Keep the neck firm.

HEADSTAND

Position: In a squat position.

Action: The headstand begins as the tripod, but instead of placing the knees on the elbows the legs are extended overhead. The back is slightly arched, the legs together, and the weight evenly distributed on the forehead and hands.

Suggestions:

1. Children may assist in spotting the headstand. As the performer raises the legs, the spotter either extends an

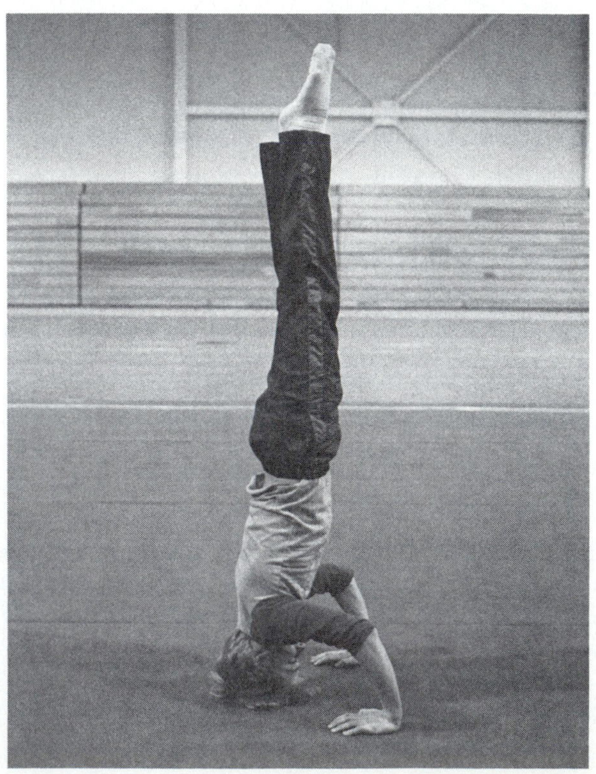

Headstand.

arm behind the legs or holds the legs until a balanced position is assumed. The spotter should not lift the legs but merely support them until balance is gained.

2. When balance is lost in the headstand, it is easy to curl the body and perform a forward roll.

Variations:

Headstand splits: Once balance is gained in the headstand, the performer moves the legs apart either to the sides or forward and backward.

Headstand turn: Once balance is gained, the performer slowly turns the head and hands to turn 360 degrees in place.

TIP-UP

Position: In a squat position.

Action: The hands are placed on the mat in front of the feet. Keeping the elbows bent and the head up, the performer rocks forward, supporting the knees on the outside of the elbows and balancing with the two hands for support.

TIGER STAND

Position: In a kneeling position.

Action: The hands and forearms are placed on the mat in front of the knees and parallel to each other. One leg at a time is kicked to an inverted balance position. The back should be arched and head up.

HANDSTAND

Position: Standing.

Action: The performer bends forward, placing the hands on the mat shoulder width apart. One leg swings up and then the other, ending in a position with both legs extended overhead. The arms should be kept straight throughout the stunt.

Handstand.

Suggestions:

1. Children may work in partners, with the spotter standing to the side to take the ankles as they are raised upward. The spotter should not lift the legs but should keep them from continuing to move forward from the overhead position.
2. Once the balance position is attained, the performer may attempt to take a few steps by walking on the hands.

Variations: Handstand splits: The legs are split in a forward/backward direction.

Handstand straddle: The legs are split in a sideward position.

Stag handstand: The forward leg is bent at the knee and the back leg extended back.

Double stag: Both legs are bent at the knee, one forward, the other back.

Partner Balances

Partner balances are a challenging activity for children to work together. The partners who are the base should have sufficient strength to support their classmates. A third person may assist the child balancing on top during the learning phase.

KNEE STAND

Position: The base person kneels on one knee, with the thigh of the other leg parallel to the mat.

Action: The top person steps up and puts one foot on the knee of the base. The base person supports the top person by grasping the upper leg. The top person extends the arms out to the side and the free leg is raised back.

KNEE-SHOULDER BALANCE

Position: The base person lies on the mat with the knees bent and the feet close to the buttocks. The top person stands facing the base and at the base's feet.

Straddle handstand.

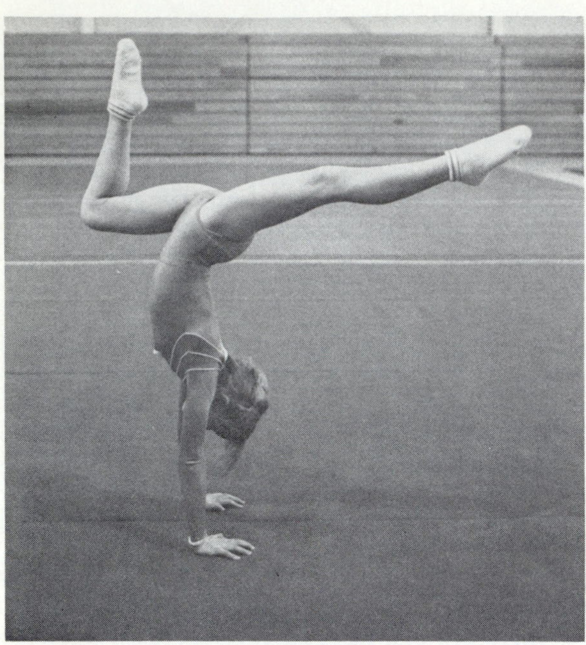

Stag handstand.

Double-stag handstand.

Action: The top person leans forward, placing the hands on the knees of the base person and the shoulders on the outstretched hands of the base person. The top person then kicks up both feet overhead, arching the back slightly and lifting the head to face the base person.

SWAN BALANCE

Position: The base person lies on the mat with the knees bent; the legs are raised and the hands are reaching upward. The top person stands at the base person's feet facing the base.

Swan balance.

Action: The top person leans forward, taking the hands of the base person and placing the front of the hips on the feet of the base person. Straightening the legs, the base person lifts the top person into the air. The top person assumes a balanced position parallel to the mat and when secure releases the hands and extends the arms out to the side.

CHEST STAND

Position: The base person assumes a hands and knees position on the mat with the top person standing to one side facing the side of the base.

Action: The top person bends forward, placing the chest across the back of the base person, the chin on the other side of the back, and the hands grasping the partner's lower chest and abdomen. Both feet are kicked upward to assume a balanced position with the legs over head.

TABLE STAND

Position: The base person assumes a position on the mat with the legs extended upward at right angles at the mat. The hands are at the shoulders with the palms up. The top person stands at the base person's head, with the feet in the partner's hands.

Action: The top person places hands on the feet of the base person and, pushing downward as the base person extends the arms upward, is raised into the air. Both should keep the arms and legs straight as they balance.

SITTING ON FEET

Position: The base person lies on the mat with the hands next to the ears and the palms up. The top person stands on the hands of the base person, but facing away.

Action: The base person lifts the legs, placing the heels on the partner's buttocks and the feet along the back of the thighs. The top person sits on the partner's feet as the base person extends the legs, keeping them at right angles to the mat. The hands of the top person are placed at the hips.

THIGH STAND (ANGEL)

Position: The base person stands behind and close to the top person. The base person squats, places the head between the

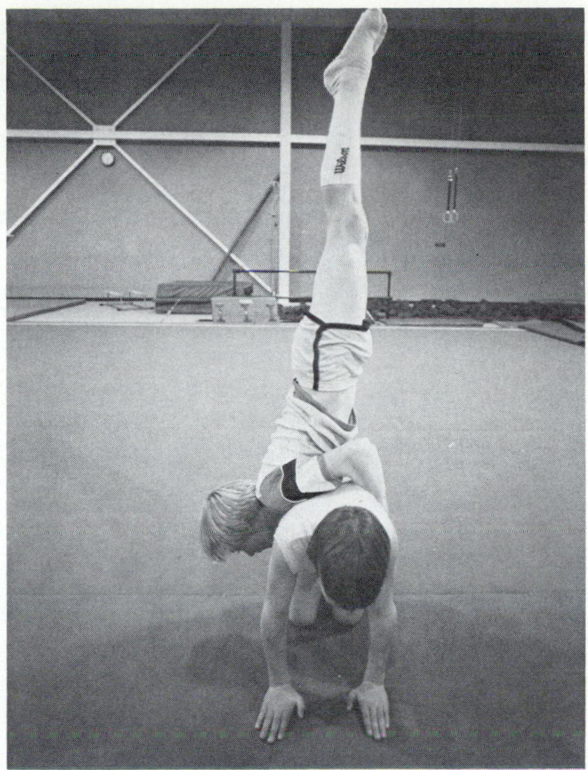

Chest stand.

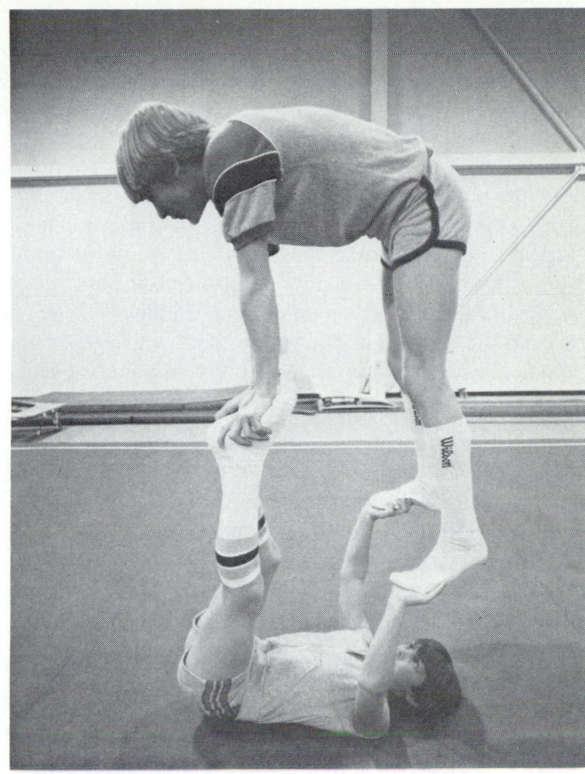

Table stand.

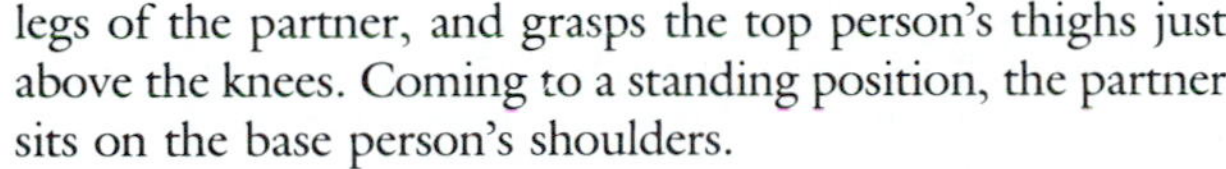

legs of the partner, and grasps the top person's thighs just above the knees. Coming to a standing position, the partner sits on the base person's shoulders.

Action: The base person bends at the knees and hips, and the top person places the feet on the base person's thighs. The base person holds the other's thighs just above the knees as the top person extends the legs to stand. At the same time, the base person tucks the head out from between the legs of the top person. The base person leans back slightly to straighten the arms. The top person arches the back slightly and extends the arms out to the sides.

DOUBLE CRAB

Position: The base person assumes a hands and feet position on the mat with the abdomen facing upward.

Action: The top person assumes a similar position on the base person with feet on the partner's thighs and the hands on the shoulders. The arms and legs of both should be kept straight and perpendicular to the mat.

BACK SWAN BALANCE

Position: The base person lies on the mat with arms out to the side and the legs extended upward. The top person stands with heels next to the base person's buttocks and facing away from the base.

Action: The base person places heels on the top person's buttocks and the toes at the lower back. The knees are slightly bent. The base person extends the legs as the top person leans backward. The base person grasps the partner's upper arms. As the top person assumes a balanced position with the head down and the back arched, the base person releases the arms, which are extended out to the sides. The base person should keep the legs straight and perpendicular to the mat.

Sitting balance.

SITTING BALANCE

Position: The base person lies on the mat with the legs extended upward and the arms at the sides. The knees are bent and the top person stands close to the extended legs facing away from the base.

Action: The base person places heels diagonally across the buttocks of the partner and the toes well down on the thighs. The top person extends the arms backward to grasp the base person's extended arms. With a general push-off from the mat, the top person assumes a sitting position on the feet of the base person. The base person straightens the legs and releases the hands. The top person keeps the legs as straight as possible and extends the arms out to the sides at shoulder level.

Pyramids

Pyramid building offers a group activity in problem solving. Pyramids are built by combining individual, partner, and group stunts into an interesting shape. The children work together to choose the overall design and the stunts to be used in putting it together. Pyramids may be made with as few as two persons or as many as are in the group. Although balance stunts are primarily used, various tumbling skills may be included in the making or dismantling of the design.

Pyramids are usually symmetrical in shape, but children may combine stunts into asymmetrical designs as

Four-person pyramid.

Eight-person pyramid.

well. They may be of uniform height, high in the middle, high to one side, high on the sides and low in the middle, or whatever the children prefer. They may start by drawing a design on paper and then planning the stunts they will use to create it.

An interesting floor pattern may also be used. Although many pyramids may be created in a straight line, the stunts may also be formed in squares, circles, triangles, the spokes of a wheel, or other formations.

Pyramids may be formed with moving as well as stationary parts. For example, the merry-go-round, human rocker, coffee grinder, or other moving parts may be added to a pyramid of individual or partner balances.

The parts should be practiced first before the children attempt to put the design together. Once the children are fairly certain of the part they will play, it is time to put the pyramid together.

A good beginning and ending should be encouraged. Once the design and stunts have been decided, the children need to work on the organization for building the pyramid. A planned sequence for adding the stunts is needed. If it entails more than two persons, the design is usually built in stages. On a signal, usually counting (1001, 1002), each part is added. After it is completed, the pyramid is usually dismantled to a count.

Whenever children construct pyramids in which they support one another, care should be taken to be sure those in the base are strong enough for the task. Weight bearing should only be on body parts that are firmly supported. For instance, in the simple pyramid of three persons, two as base on hands and knees and the third on top in the same position, the top person should place the hands at the shoulders of the bases and the knees at their hips. At no time should the back be used for weight bearing.

The problem-solving approach may be used in building pyramids. For example, the following challenges might be posed.

1. Make a design with one other person. Two. Three.
2. Make a pyramid that is high in the middle. Uniform in height. High to one side.
3. Make a pyramid that is in a straight line. In a square. In a triangle. In a circle. Shaped like the spokes of a wheel.

DEVELOPING A MOVEMENT SEQUENCE

One of the goals of educational gymnastics is to build a combination of movements into a gymnastics routine. In stunts and tumbling this approach is often referred to as a floor exercise. In this exercise the performer moves on a square mat, using as much of the space as possible to perform various skills while moving in different pathways across the mat.

Because the movement sequences are the combination of several skills, children should be encouraged to combine skills throughout the learning process. These combinations may include moving directly from one skill to another or using transitional movements between skills.

Creativity is an important aspect in the development of an exercise. In developing gymnastic routines or floor exercises, children should be encouraged to:

1. Choose two or more *stunts and tumbling skills,* including at least one of the most difficult skills the child can perform.
2. Select individual *balances* to provide variation in tempo and level to make the exercise interesting.
3. Use *locomotor sills, nonlocomotor skills, dance steps,* and other movements to creatively form smooth transitions from one skill to the next.
4. Plan for a variation in *level,* performing some skills on the mat and others in the air (jumps or leaps).
5. Plan for smooth and interesting changes of *direction.*
6. Incorporate a change in *tempo* by performing movements at slow, medium, and fast speeds (in time to musical accompaniment if used).
7. Use an interesting *floor pattern or pathway* in covering all of the space.
8. Plan a *dynamic beginning,* which sets the stage for the routine and a definite and *interesting ending.*

In developing a floor exercise, the problem-solving approach may be used. This approach permits the children to develop their own creativity, as well as to work within their own ability. Challenges may be posed to stimulate simple combinations of skills that later may be put together into a longer movement sequence. Creating long movement sequences is difficult for many children. Remembering them also poses a problem for some. Figure 17-2 includes a form that may help children plan a floor exercise. The combinations of young children may vary from two to four or five to seven moves. The sequences will not include all of the preceding components. Some children at levels III and IV have the experience to develop somewhat more complex sequences. Older children may develop an exercise by combining several shorter sequences of skills they have developed over the unit.

Young children are not able to deal with too many components at one time. Keeping the problems simple gives the children confidence in their ability to combine skills and works to improve the flow of their movements. The children may explore several challenges within the period and at the end of the lesson put a couple of their solutions together. A few movement challenges and some possible solutions follow.

1. Combine a moving stunt with a balance. Examples: Forward roll to a V seat. Backward roll to a knee scale. Headstand to a forward roll.

Floor Exercise

Name________________________ Music_______________________

Skills

1.________________________

2.________________________

3.________________________

4.________________________

5.________________________

6.________________________

7.________________________

8.________________________

9.________________________

10.________________________

FIGURE 17-2 Form for recording floor exercises.

2. Combine two skills in the low level. Examples: Forward roll with crossed legs to a backward roll. Seal walk to a forward roll. Crab walk, turn over, bear walk.
3. Begin with a skill in the high level and move to a skill in another level. Examples: Cartwheel to a forward roll. Hand stand to a chest roll.
4. Move from a low level to a high level. Examples: Backward roll to a back extension roll. Backward roll to a head stand.
5. Move in one direction and then change direction. Examples: Cartwheel to a forward roll. Roundoff to a backward roll.

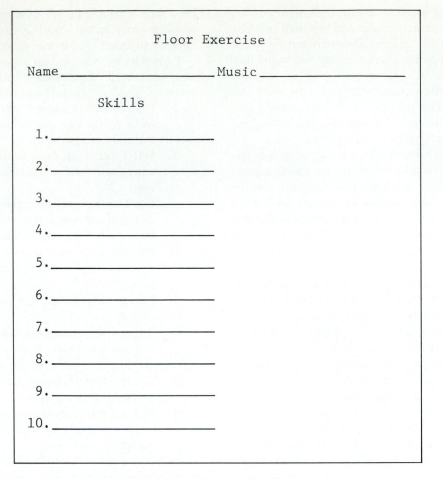

Another approach to floor exercise is to develop a movement sequence that all the children are able to do. Once they learn the sequence, the children may make substitutions in the routine.

Additional Skills for Building Movement Sequences

Tumbling and balance skills included earlier in this chapter are an important part of the floor exercise routine. The following dance skills and transitional movements add to the flow of the movement sequence. These skills may be developed in levels III and IV.

ATTITUDE

Position: In an erect position with the weight on both feet.

Action: The body weight is shifted to one foot, the other leg raised backward and upward, and the knee turned outward. The arm on the supporting side of the body is extended out from the shoulder, with a bend of the elbow bringing the forearm around in front of the body. The other arm is extended upward, with a slight bend at the elbow to bring the hand over the head.

TURNS

The children should experiment with developing some interesting ways to perform one or a series of turns between the stunts, tumbling skills, and balances they have chosen.

TOUR JETÉ

Position: Standing with the arms down at the sides.

Action: Begin with a step on the right foot, kicking the left leg forward and upward. The body quickly turns 180 degrees with a landing on the left foot as the right leg swings upward and to the rear. The body should be kept erect throughout the movement. The arms move to a position overhead as the left leg swings upward. The head is up with the eyes focusing on a stationary object.

DANCE STEPS

A variety of dance steps may be used to add variety to the movements, such as the schottische, two-step, and polka. A description of possible dance steps to use is found in Chapter 21.

BODY WAVE

Position: Standing with the feet together or one foot in front of the other. The arms are down at the sides.

Action: The arms are lifted forward and upward as the hips and knees bend. The arms swing backward and upward. The arms then continue to move to a position overhead as the body assumes an erect position. The knees are forced forward and the legs straighten by pushing the hips forward. The back is arched, but the shoulders remain back. The shoulders then hunch slightly forward as the legs are completely straightened.

SCISSORS KICK

Position: Standing.

Action: A step forward is taken on one foot and then the other leg is kicked forward as high as possible. As the kicking leg drops, the stepping leg is forced upward so that the legs switch positions in the air. The landing is on the kicking leg. The arms are held out to the sides from the shoulders. The body should be kept erect throughout.

JUMP WITH THE LEGS BENT TO THE REAR

Position: Standing with the body weight on both feet.

Action: The knees and hips are bent and the child springs into the air, bringing the heels up to the buttocks. The arms begin at the sides and are raised forward to shoulder height. The landing is soft. The trunk should be kept erect.

CAT JUMP

Position: Standing.

Action: The performer springs into the air from both feet, raising the knees to the side and touching the soles of the feet under the body. One arm is raised overhead; the other is extended to the side at shoulder height.

SPLIT LEAP

Position: Standing.

Action: After a couple of running steps, the child leaps into the air with the legs split, one forward and the other back. The arms move in opposition to the legs, one extended upward and backward, the other forward and upward. The head is up and the back is arched.

STAG LEAP

Position: Standing.

Action: The performer leaps upward and, while in the air, extends the back leg and bends the forward leg back at the knee so that the sole of the foot is close to the back knee. The forward arm is straight up overhead; the other is extended diagonally upward and backward. The head is up and the body erect.

DOUBLE STAG LEAP

Position: Standing.

Action: Similar to the stag leap, but both legs are bent at the knee. The forward leg is angled downward, the rear leg upward. The head is up and the back straight.

SIDE LEAP

Position: Standing.

Action: The movement begins as a split leap, but as the forward leg is raised, the hips are rotated 90 degrees so that the body faces to the side of the direction of movement.

Split leap.

Stag leap.

Double-stag leap.

Side leap.

RHYTHMIC SPORTIVE GYMNASTICS

Although rhythmic gymnastics activities were performed in Greek, Scandinavian, and German cultures for many years and were introduced into the United States by immigrants 130 years ago, rhythmic sportive gymnastics is a relatively new sport. Recognized in 1962 as a world event by the International Gymnastics Federation, it has been gaining in popularity in the United States. In 1984 it was introduced as an Olympic event.

The rhythmic gymnast performs a sequence of skills with a ball, club, hoop, ribbon, or rope to music, combining the skills with body movements very much like the gymnast develops a floor exercise routine combining gymnastic skills with body movements. Leaps, body waves, turns, and dance steps are some of the types of movements used. Rolls and splits may also be used in moderation. The body movements are described in the previous section of this chapter; the dance steps are described in Chapter 21. Activities for balls, hoops, ropes, and ribbons are described in Chapters 16 and 22.

In combining the skills with the hand-held apparatus and the body movements, emphasis is on making the movements flow from one to the next, and the use of the equipment becomes an extension of the body's movement. The skills may be performed while the person is standing, kneeling, or lying down. Individual and group routines should be explored.

LARGE APPARATUS

Playground equipment and large apparatus used indoors are enjoyed by children of all ages. Climbing, hanging from various body parts, swinging, and other movements are challenging for children as they engage in activities that they perceive as risk taking within individual limits of controlled movement.

Many playgrounds are equipped with climbing equipment. Much of the playground equipment constructed today is made of wood. Not only is it constructed to be appealing to the imagination of children and conducive to creative use of the body, but it provides a safer environment than the steel used in swings, slides, and teeter-totters, which have been standard playground equipment over the years. Several considerations must be made in planning or constructing playground apparatus. It should be located where it can be easily supervised and does not interfere with other forms of activity taking place on the playground. The surface beneath apparatus should be well drained and provide for a soft landing as children dismount from the equipment. The base should be anchored to the ground to provide the necessary stability with cement or other material used below the ground surface. The height of apparatus should be appropriate for the size of the children using it. The material used should provide a safe, splinter-free, and nonslippery surface for hand and footholds. A program of preventive maintenance is important for anticipating and removing potential hazards before they arise.

Many of the activities suggested for use with a horizontal bar or parallel bars may be adapted for use on jungle gyms and other playground apparatus. The physical education program should include movement challenges and traditional activities for the use of this equipment. Emphasis should be placed on the safe use of the equipment so that children will have the knowledge and skill to play on the equipment without direct supervision. It is important to take some time at the beginning of each school year to go over the safety considerations and some of the skills children might need to prepare them to use the apparatus responsibly.

Indoor apparatus may be equally challenging for children. In the sections that follow, specific movement challenges and other activities are suggested for use on a variety of apparatus available for use by elementary school children. When possible, equipment should be purchased to fit the size and ability of the children who will be using it. It should also be checked regularly to be certain that it is in safe working condition. Mats should be placed to protect the children from landing on apparatus supports and should extend out from the equipment to provide a safe landing area in all directions.

Creative movement is an important aspect in using large apparatus, whether indoors or outdoors. Early experiences should focus on exploration in the use of the body and the movements possible on each piece of equipment. As they learn more traditional activities, children should experiment with new variations and also new ways to move from one skill to the next.

Simple combinations of skills should be attempted in the early phases of learning as in stunts and tumbling. The routine or combination should be built around the essential elements. Each routine should include a mount, moves on the particular piece of equipment, balances or poses, and a dismount. Children should practice the moves in combination. For instance, when they practice a mount, the next move should also be included. In this way children begin to develop movement sequences that have flow from the beginning to the end. As always, a good beginning and ending should be encouraged.

Balance Beam

Balance beams are constructed in both 2- and 4-inch widths and vary in height from a couple of inches to 4 feet from the floor. The height of the beam is usually adjustable, with elementary school age children working no higher than 36 to 40 inches. The narrow beam is adequate for young children, but makes many of the skills performed in later grades difficult because a wider beam offers more support.

When working on the beam, the children should focus on the end of the beam rather than looking down at their feet. The hands may be out to the sides for balance, especially if the beam is narrow.

Many of the activities on a low beam do not require spotting by the teacher, but it is desirable to have the children spot for each other to establish the habit of assuming responsibility for each other. Obviously, children may spot simple locomotor skills and balances. More complex moves and rolls require spotting by the teacher. When spotting, the child should be positioned next to the beam with the closer arm extended across the beam in front of the performer for the low beam and extended upward for the high beam. In this manner the arm is readily available to grasp if balance is lost. Both spotter and performer move in the same direction, with the spotter picking a tempo to stay within an arm's reach of the performer but not so close as to hinder the performer's movements.

Many of the skills on the balance beam can be taught first using a line on the floor or by using a low beam, 6 to 12 inches in height, with mats stacked to an equal height on both sides of the apparatus and making contact with it. This step should be taken before the skill is attempted on a higher beam. It allows the student to try the skill and alleviates the risk factor and the element of fear.

Moving with equipment may add an additional challenge in the early phases of learning when children are experimenting with balance. Filling bleach bottles or other jugs with varying amounts of sand and then balancing while stationary (static) or while moving (dynamic) should help children learn about balance and what happens when weight is added. Moving and picking up or stepping through or over objects adds to the fun.

Movement Challenges

Movement challenges are an important part of learning to use the balance beam. They should be incorporated at all levels of learning to encourage the children's creativity in developing individually designed movements. The examples that follow are but a few of the possibilities.

1. How many different ways can you mount the beam?
2. While on the beam can you make a shape using two body parts for balance? Two others? One foot? Another part?
3. Can you balance on a large body part? A small body part?
4. How many different ways can you travel along the beam?
5. What different ways can you use your arms as you travel along the beam?
6. Can you change direction as you move along the beam?
7. Can you change level as you move along the beam?
8. Carrying one or two jugs varying in weight, what shapes can you make as you balance on the beam?
9. Carrying one or more jugs varying in weight, how many different ways can you move along the beam?
10. Can you pick up a beanbag as you walk along the beam?
11. On what body parts can you balance a beanbag while balancing on the beam? While moving?
12. Can you step over a wand held by a partner as you move?
13. Can you move through a hoop held by a partner?
14. While moving on the beam, can you create enough force to become airborne and then land back on the beam, absorbing the force?
15. How many different ways can you dismount from the beam?
16. Can you make a shape in the air as you dismount and still land with control?
17. Can you dismount and land with your back to the beam? Your side? The front of the body?

Skills

Many skills for use on the balance beam follow. They include ways of mounting the beam; movements, turns, and tumbling skills to travel along the beam; poses or balances; and dismounts.

Mounts

Mounting the high beam and mounts in which all body parts are raised require the use of a beat board.

STEP-UP MOUNT

Position: Standing on the floor or on a low bench at one end of the beam.

Action: The performer steps up on the beam with one foot swinging the free foot forward and upward onto the beam in front of the stepping foot.

Spotting: The spotter should stand next to the beam with an arm extended to offer support if needed.

FRONT SUPPORT MOUNT

Position: Standing facing the side of the beam with both hands grasping the top of the beam about shoulder width apart.

Action: With a spring from both legs and a push with the hands, the body is brought to a front support with the hips resting on the beam. The hands may remain on the beam or may be momentarily extended to the sides.

ONE-KNEE MOUNT

Position: Standing facing the side of the beam. The hands are on top of the beam with fingers pointing away from the body.

Action: With a spring from both feet the performer jumps to a straight arm support with one knee on the beam between the hands and the other leg extended behind. The head is up and the back is arched.

Spotting: The spotter should stand on the opposite side of the beam facing the performer and be ready to give support at the shoulders if the spring carries the performer too far forward.

SQUAT MOUNT

Position: Stand facing the beam.

Action: A jump is taken from both feet, placing the hands on the beam shoulder width apart and fingers pointing away from the body. Both feet are placed on the beam between the hands as the body assumes a squat position on the beam. The head is up and the back is parallel with the floor.

Spotting: The spotter should stand on the opposite side of the beam and support the shoulders as in the one-knee mount.

Moving on the Beam

A good posture, with the body poised and extended and the head up, is important for moving along the balance beam. Using the arms in interesting ways adds to the movements on the beam.

WALK

Forward, backward, sideward.

HOP

Forward, backward, sideward.

SKIP

Forward, backward.

Dip walk.

DIP WALK

As the performer moves on the beam, each leg is dipped to the side as it swings forward by bending the supporting leg and dropping the free leg as it swings forward with the toe pointed.

CHASÉ

As the performer moves forward, the lead foot slides forward, the rear foot closes to the front foot, and the front foot slides forward once again.

TOE-TOUCH

As the performer walks forward, the toe of the moving foot is extended and touched briefly on the beam in front before taking weight forward on the foot. This maneuver may be performed backward by touching the toe backward before stepping on the foot.

STEP-HOP

A step is taken forward on one foot, followed by a hop on the same foot, lifting the opposite knee upward. It is repeated, stepping forward on the other foot.

GRAPEVINE

A step is taken sideward with the right foot. The left is crossed over in front of the right. One more step is taken sideward to the right, finishing by crossing the left behind the right.

The following movements described in the skills for movement sequences may also be performed on the balance beam:

Scissors kick
Jump with legs bent to the rear
Split leap
Stag leap
Body wave

Turns

SQUAT TURN

Position: On the beam facing one end.

Action: The child assumes a squat position on the beam and pivots on the balls of the feet to turn to face the opposite way. The arms are extended to the sides for balance.

PIVOT TURN

Position: On the beam facing one end.

Action: The performer rises up onto the balls of the feet and pivots to face in the opposite direction. The head is up and the body is extended. The arms may be extended to the sides or one arm may be forward, the other extended to the side.

ONE-LEG TURN

Position: On the beam facing one end.

Action: Taking the weight on one foot, the performer turns 180 degrees with the free leg extended forward of the body. The arms are extended out to the sides, the body is erect, and the head is up. As the turn is made, the forward foot is extended behind.

TOUR JETÉ

Described in skills for floor exercise.

Tumbling Movements

The following tumbling skills may be easily adapted for use on the balance beam.

FORWARD SHOULDER ROLL

Position: From a kneeling position, gripping the underside of the beam with one hand on each side of the beam.

Action: One shoulder is placed to one side of the beam. The hips are pulled up in a pike position; then the child slowly rolls forward to finish straddling the beam with the legs straight and toes pointed. The hands regrip the beam in front of the body.

Spotting: Spotters may be used on both sides of the beam, spotting the hips as they come over until the body is balanced over the beam once again. This skill may be adequately spotted by one person as well.

BACK SHOULDER ROLL

Position: Supine on the beam with the hands gripping the underside of the beam over the head. The arms are bent and the elbows are close together. The head is on one side of the beam.

Action: The legs are pulled up over the head in a pike position. As the legs come over, one knee is placed on the beam. (If the head is on the right side of the beam, the left knee touches first.) As the legs come down, the hands shift to a position grasping the top of the beam. The second leg may be raised behind as in a knee scale.

Spotting: A spotter on each side of the beam supports the hips as they come over until the body is balanced once again. One person can adequately spot this skill.

Balances

The following balances included in balance stunts may be performed on the balance beam:

Knee scale (with two hands on the beam in front of the body)
Arabesque

Forward shoulder roll.

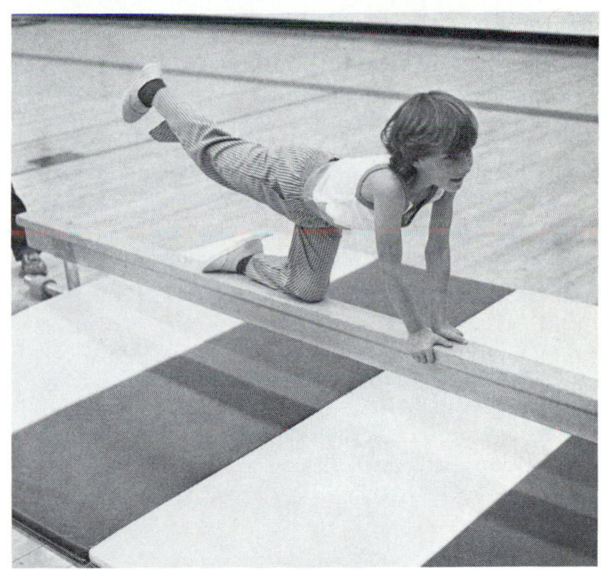

Knee scale.

V-sit
One-leg balance
Needle

Dismounts

Some assistance may be needed for dismounts from the balance beam. The spotter should stand ready to assist on landing but out of the way of moving body parts such as the legs. The teacher should emphasize landing on two feet by slightly flexing the hips and knees to absorb the force.

JUMP

Position: Standing anywhere on the beam.

Action: The performer jumps from the beam to the floor (1) with a turn to end with the back, side, or front facing the beam or (2) assuming a pike, tuck, or straddle position in the air.

KNEE SCALE DISMOUNT

Position: Knee scale position with two hands on the beam in front of the body.

Action: The body leans slightly forward as the free leg swings down and then backward and upward. The hands push and the body is lifted off the beam. The landing is with the side to the beam, the knees bent, the near hand on the beam, and the other arm extended to the side.

FRONT VAULT

Position: A front resting position on the beam with the body supported on the feet and hands. The arms are extended so that the upper body is off the beam.

Action: The leg on the side of the landing is kicked upward, followed by the other leg; then the legs swing off one side of the beam to land with the side facing the beam and the near hand on top.

Skill Combinations

Beginning combinations include a mount, movement on the beam, and a dismount:

Step-up mount, walk forward, jump dismount.
Squat mount, grapevine step, jump dismount, ending with the side to the beam.

Add a balance:

Step-up mount, dip walk, arabesque, jump dismount.
Front support mount, knee scale, chasé jump dismount.

Add a turn:

Front support, knee scale, dip walk, pivot turn, toe-touch walk, V-sit, side seat dismount.

Add an aerial move:

Front support, knee scale, dip walk, squat turn, step-hop, pivot turn, arabesque, knee scale, front vault dismount.

Horizontal Bar

The horizontal bar is often both a piece of playground apparatus and a piece of indoor equipment. For outdoor use there may be several bars set at varying heights for elementary school children. The indoor bar is most often adjustable for use as a low or high bar.

For most of the skills suggested in this text, a bar about shoulder height is desirable. It may be helpful to organize the children according to height when doing station work to avoid the need to constantly adjust the bar to the height of each child. For safety the children should grip the bar with the thumb and fingers on opposite sides of the bar. In the **regular grip** the fingers are on top of the bar and the thumb underneath. In the **reverse grip** the thumbs are closer to the performer and the fingers behind the bar (Figure 17-3). In the **mixed grip** one hand assumes a regular grip, the other a reverse grip. To determine the grip to be used, it is helpful to remember that the individual usually moves around the bar in the direction in which the thumbs point.

Mats should be used under the bar and should extend far enough in front and behind to provide a safe landing area for a drop from a swing. The bars should be kept clean of chalk and rust. Special care is required for outdoor bars because corrosion may make the surface of the bars rough and, therefore, hazardous.

Prolonged practice of skills in which the performer circles the bar may cause blisters on the hands. Carbonate of magnesium chalk or hand guards should be used to protect the hands. Spotting the skills is usually at the nearer wrist or over the hand and at the hips. If the bar has been raised, the spotter can stand on one or two folded mats placed to the side of the performer to bring the spotter up to a level suitable to assist the child in performing the skill. Placement of mats should not obstruct the performer in any way.

Movement Challenges

Movement challenges encourage the children to discover unique ways of working on the horizontal bar.

1. How many ways can you find to get on the bar?
2. Can you hang from two body parts? Two different parts? Three? One?
3. How many ways can you balance on the bar?
4. How many ways can you move under the bar?
5. How many ways can you dismount to land on your feet? To face the bar? To face away from the bar? With your side to the bar?
6. Can you move from under the bar to the top of the bar?
7. How many ways can you use a curled shape on the bar?
8. How many ways can you use a straight shape on the bar?
9. Can you move from a straight to a curled shape on the bar? A curl to a straight shape?
10. How many ways can you change direction on or under the bar?

Skills

The following skills may be performed by elementary school children on the horizontal bar.

Mounts

FRONT SUPPORT MOUNT

Similar to the front support mount described in balance beam activities. A regular grip is used.

BACK HIP PULL-OVER

Position: Standing close to the bar with a regular grip, hands shoulder width apart.

FIGURE 17-3 Gripping the horizontal bar. *Left,* overhand grip; *middle,* mixed grip; *right,* reverse grip.

Action: One leg is kicked up and over the bar; keeping the arms bent, the body is lifted under and over the bar to end in a front support position.

Spotting: Spotting should be at the shoulders and hips to keep the body close to the bar.

Suggestions: It is important to keep the body close to the bar. There is a tendency to straighten the arms, dropping the body away from the bar, which then requires pulling the body back to the bar before the pull-over can be completed.

Stunts

SINGLE KNEE HANG

Position: Hanging under the bar with a regular grip.

Action: One leg is swung up over the bar. The child hangs from one leg and two hands.

Spotting: The spotter stands at the side, spotting at the near hand and the hips.

DOUBLE KNEE HANG

Position: Hanging under the bar with a regular grip.

Action: Both legs are brought up between the arms and then over the bar to hang from two legs and two hands.

Spotting: Spotting is from the side, at the near hand and hips.

INVERTED HANG: TUCK

Position: Hanging under the bar with a regular grip.

Action: Both legs are pulled up between the arms in a tuck position and held.

Spotting: Spotting is from the side, at the near hand and hips.

INVERTED HANG: PIKE

Position: Hanging under the bar with a regular grip.

Action: Both legs are brought up between the arms in a pike position and held.

Spotting: Spotting is from the side, at the near hand and hips.

INVERTED HANG: LAYOUT

Position: Hanging under the bar with a regular grip.

Pike inverted hang.

Action: Both legs are brought up and between the arms in a tuck position. As the legs pass under the bar, they are extended to a layout position perpendicular to the mat.

Spotting: Spotting is from the side, at the near hand and hips. As the body extends upward, the hand at the hips shifts to the front side of the body to assist in keeping the body close to the bar.

SKIN THE CAT

Position: Hanging under the bar with a regular grip.

Action: Both legs are swung up and between the arms. The child stays tucked and touches the feet to the mat over the head, then springs lightly with both feet from the mat, tucks the chin, and returns to the starting position.

Spotting: Spotting is from the side, at the near arm and hip. To assist in coming back to the starting position one hand is at the hips, the other at the back of the neck.

FRONT SUPPORT

Similar to the front support described in balance beam activities. This move may be used as a pose on the bar as well as a mount. The arms may be extended to the sides once the balance position has been attained.

Spotting: The spotter stands in front of the performer and spots at the shoulders.

STRIDE SEAT

Position: A front support.

Action: One leg swings over the bar to finish extended in front, the other behind. The hand regrasps the bar on the outside of the leg. The body is up off the bar supported on the hands.

Spotting: The spotter stands in front and slightly to the side of the performer, spotting at the wrist and shoulder.

BALANCE SEAT

Position: From a stride position on top of the bar with a regular grip.

Action: The rear leg is swung over the bar to end in a sitting position on top of the bar with both legs extended in front, hands gripping the bar. The hands may be extended to the sides once balance is attained.

Spotting: The spotter stands to the side with one hand in front and the other behind the performer.

BIRD'S NEST

Position: Hanging under the bar with a regular grip.

Action: Both legs are kicked up into a tuck position between the arms. As the legs come through, the insteps of both feet stay touching the back side of the bar. The body continues through, ending in a position hanging from the hands and the feet.

Spotting: Spotting is from the side at the near wrist and hips, then shifts from the hips to the front of the body to finish.

Suggestion: As children's body proportions change, this skill may become more difficult on the horizontal bar for children with long legs.

MILL CIRCLE (PINWHEEL)

Position: A stride position on the bar with a reverse grip.

Action: As the circle begins, the arms lift the body up off the bar and the front leg reaches out as if taking a giant step. As the circle continues, the arms pull and the body flexes slightly to bring the body back up to a sitting position.

Spotting: The spotter stands to the side with one hand on the arm and the other at the back of the leg. Spotting is moved to the back during the second half of the stunt.

Dismounts

ROLLOVER DISMOUNT

Position: Front support position with a regular grip.

Action: The body leans forward, beginning to circle the bar. As the legs come around, they come off the bar, the hands release their grip, and the performer lands on the mat in a standing position.

Spotting: The spotter stands at the side and spots at the shoulder and near wrist.

BACK DISMOUNT

Position: Front support.

Action: The legs swing forward under the bar, then backward with the hands pushing away from the bar and releasing their grip. The body remains in a vertical position as the performer moves back from the bar and then to the mat. The knees flex on landing and the arms may be out to the sides for balance.

Spotting: Spotting is from the side at the near wrist.

SWING AND DROP

Position: Standing slightly away from the bar, which is slightly above the extended arms and hands.

Action: The performer springs up from both feet to take the bar with a regular grip. The hips flex to begin the swinging action of the body. Just before the maximum forward movement, the performer drops from the bar to land on the mat in a balanced position, with the knees, ankles, and hips flexing and the arms out to the side for balance.

Suggestion: The performer may choose to drop at the height of the backswing rather than on the end of the forward swing.

Spotting: Spotting is from the side at the waist and midback. If the performer chooses to drop on the backswing, the spotter moves back to assist if necessary with one hand on either side of the body.

PENNY DROP

Position: Double knee hang with a regular grip.

Action: At the end of the backward swing, the hands are released, swinging the arms forward. At the end of the forward swing, with the body parallel to the mat, the knees are brought off the bar and the performer lands on the feet.

Spotting: The spotter stands next to the performer, extending one arm across the chest to assist if more spin is needed. The other hand is across the legs to keep them from straightening.

Skill Combinations

A few combinations of skills for the horizontal bar follow.

Front support mount, rollover dismount.

Back hip pull-over mount, front support balance, balance seat, double knee hang, penny drop.

Back hip pull-over mount, straddle seat, balance seat, double knee hang, one-half skin the cat dismount.

Front support mount, stride seat, skin the cat, double knee hang, penny drop.

Front support mount, mill circle, balance seat, double knee hang, tuck inverted hang, single knee circle mount, front support, back dismount.

Parallel Bars

Parallel bars may be part of the playground equipment and set at a fixed height of about 30 inches or may be an adjustable piece of the indoor apparatus. In the elementary school the bars often are a standard set of bars passed down from the high school. It is important to adjust the height and width of the bars for elementary school children. It may be necessary to use a bench at the end for mounting and several mats piled under the bars to adjust the height for elementary school children.

These suggestions should enable the children to mount the bars on their own.

Teachers should avoid lifting children up to the bars. Many of the stunts on the parallel bars require upper body strength, which is often not well developed in elementary school children. For traveling above the bars, the spotter needs to help support the upper and lower arm to prevent collapsing of the arm. Skills under the bar are generally spotted by holding one of the child's hands to the bars and helping to lift at the thighs with the other hand.

Pike inverted hang.

Movement Challenges

Movement challenges encourage children to find interesting ways of moving. A few of the possibilities follow.

1. Can you mount the bar at one end? From the side of the bars? From underneath?
2. What shapes can you make under the bars as you support yourself with four body parts? Three? Two?
3. What shapes can you make on top of the bars?
4. Can you make a shape as you dismount the bars to end facing the bars? With your side to the bars? With your back to the bars?
5. How many ways can you travel on top of two bars? One? Underneath two bars? One?
6. How many ways can you move from under the bars to on top of the bars?
7. How many ways can you move from the top of the bars to underneath the bars?
8. How many ways can you change direction on the bars? Under the bars?

Skills

The following skills included for horizontal bars may also be performed on the parallel bars. Many of these skills may be performed between the two bars as well as on one bar.

Front support mount
Back hip pull-over mount
Front support
Single knee hang
Double knee hang
Inverted hang: tuck, pike, layout
Skin the cat
Bird's nest
Stride seat
Balance seat
Rollover dismount
Back dismount

Mounts

JUMP TO A STRAIGHT ARM SUPPORT

Position: Standing at one end of the bars, with hands gripping the top of the bars.

Action: The performer springs from both feet, pushing with the hands to finish with the body extended above and between the bars supported by straight arms.

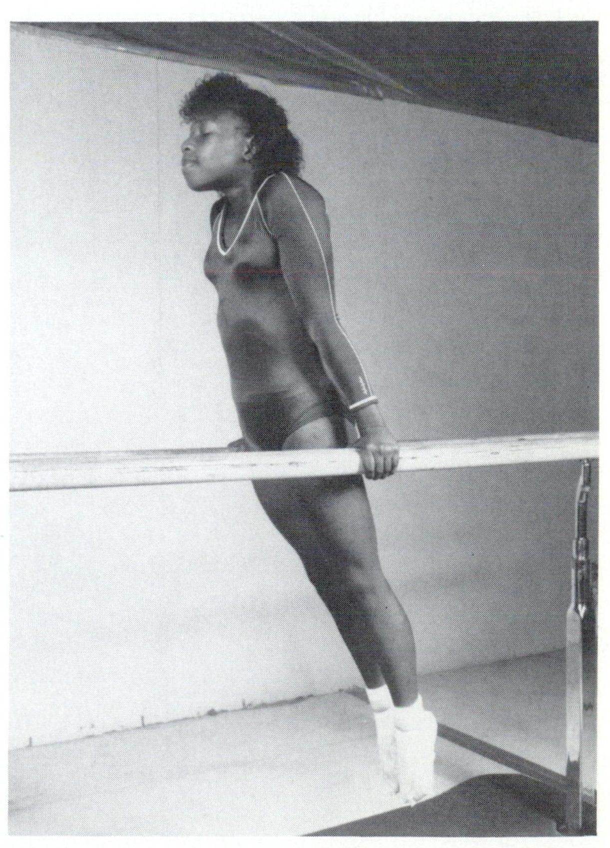

Straight arm support.

Spotting: The spotter stands to one side and supports the near upper and lower arm. Another spotting technique is to assist the student from behind by having one hand on each side of the performer's waist.

SWING UP FROM UNDER THE BARS

Position: At one end of the bars, hands gripping the bars from underneath.

Action: The legs are kicked up between the bars, ending with one leg over each bar, gripping the bars behind the knees. The arms are brought up inside the bars and the hands regrasp on top, pulling the body up between the bars to finish in a straddle seat position with one leg over each bar.

Spotting: The spotter stands to one side, holding one of the child's hands to the bar and assisting at the thigh with the other hand.

SLOTH WALK

Position: Under the bars with the hands grasping one bar.

Action: The feet swing up to grasp the bar in front of the body. By pulling or pushing with the legs and walking the hands on the bar, the performer moves either head or foot first. This stunt may also be performed using both bars with a hand and foot on each bar.

Spotting: The spotter stands at the side with one hand on the child's hand and the other at the thighs to assist in lifting the legs.

Balances

ANGEL (KNEE SCALE)

Position: A front rest position.

Action: The legs are drawn up onto the bar to a position where the knees are on one bar and the straight arms on the other. One leg is lifted behind, the back slightly arched, and the head raised. One arm may extend forward.

Spotting: The spotter stands between the bars with one hand at the wrist.

STRADDLE SEAT

Position: A straight arm support.

Action: Both legs are swung up over the bars to finish straddling both bars with the legs extended and the toes pointed to the sides. The hands may grip the bars behind the hips or may be extended to the sides.

Spotting: Spotting is from the side with one arm at the upper and lower arm.

BACK FOOT LEANING REST

Position: A straight arm support.

Action: Both legs are swung forward and up onto the bar, finishing in a position with the legs extended in front and the upper body supported on straight arms. The head is up and the back is straight.

Spotting: The spotter stands at the side and spots the near upper and lower arm.

FRONT FOOT LEANING REST

Position: A straight arm support.

Action: The legs are lifted to the bars behind the body, finishing with the legs extended behind and the body supported on the straight arms and feet. The head is up and the back slightly arched.

Spotting: From the side the spotter holds the arm and the front of the thigh to assist in keeping the legs from hitting the bar too hard.

SIDE REST

Position: A straddle seat position on the bars.

Action: The body is rotated to face one side. The forward leg is flexed at the knee to point back under the bar. The rear leg is extended. The hand on the same side as the forward foot grasps the forward bar; the other arm is extended to the side.

Spotting: The spotter stands to the side and slightly behind the performer and holds the arm on the forward side.

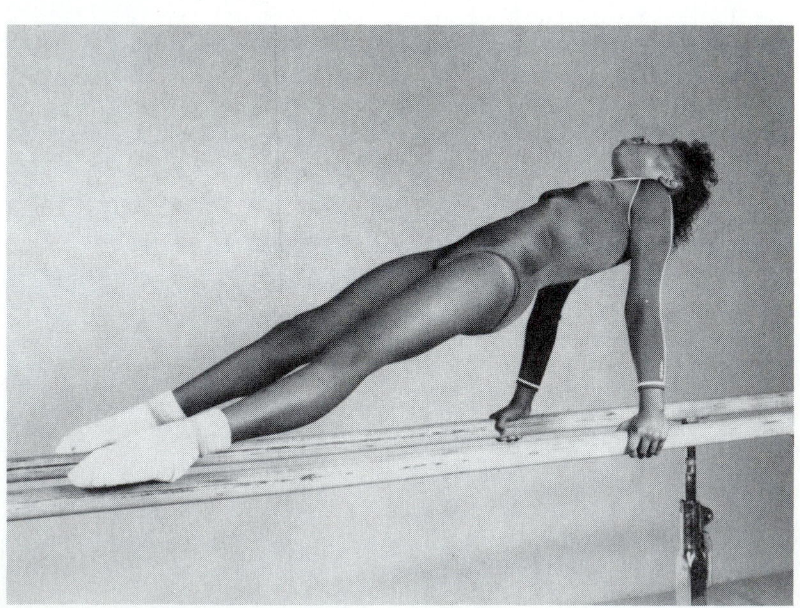

Back foot leaning rest.

CHEST STAND

Position: A front support position with the hands grasping the bars underneath.

Action: The upper body drops forward to the far bar with the head on the outside of the bar and the shoulders on the inside. The legs kick up over head to balance with the back slightly arched.

Spotting: The spotter stands in front of the performer with one hand on each side of the hips.

Chest stand.

Travel/Swing

STRAIGHT ARM SUPPORT SWING

Position: A straight arm support.

Action: The body swings forward and back to a comfortable and controlled height, the legs coming above the bars on both the forward and backward swings.

Spotting: Spotting is from the side at the near upper and lower arm.

STRAIGHT ARM WALK

Position: A straight arm support.

Action: The hands walk forward or backward on the bars while the body remains straight and the head is up.

Spotting: The spotter stands at the side and holds the near upper and lower arm.

STRADDLE TRAVEL FORWARD

Position: A straight arm support.

Action: The body swings forward, lifting the legs up above the bar. The legs separate to come down in a straddle position over the bars. The hands regrasp the bars in front of the body, with the body leaning forward and the legs swinging backward and free of the bars to repeat the action.

Spotting: Spotting is from the side at the near upper and lower arm.

STRADDLE TRAVEL BACKWARD

Same as the straddle travel forward, except the legs move from front to back and straddle behind the hands.

INVERTED WALK

Position: Under the bars with one hand under and on the outside of each bar.

Action: The performer kicks up into a pike inverted hang. Moving the hands one at a time under the bar, the body is propelled forward.

Spotting: From the side the spotter holds the near hand and assists at the hips if needed.

CRAB WALK

Position: A straight arm support.

Action: The legs are swung forward and up onto the bars in front of the body. From the crab position the hands and feet are walked forward or backward on top of the bars.

Spotting: From the side the spotter supports the near arm and hips.

HAND WALK ON ONE BAR

Position: A straight arm support.

Action: Rotate the body to one side and regrasp so both hands are on the top of one bar. Walk the hands along the bar, keeping the body straight and the head up.

Spotting: Spotting is from a position behind the performer at the hips.

FORWARD ROLL TO A STRADDLE SEAT

Position: In a straddle seat position grasping the bars in front of the body.

Forward roll to a straddle seat.

Action: Leaning forward, the upper arms are placed on the bars with the elbows on the outside. Keeping the body in a pike position, the hips are raised and brought over the head. The hands are released and regrasped behind the back. The roll is continued to a straddle position.

Spotting: The spotter stands to the side to support the upper back and the thighs.

Suggestions: The bar width must allow shoulder support for each performer.

Dismounts

SWING AND JUMP

Position: Between the bars, facing the end, in a straight arm support position.

Action: On a swing forward the body reaches out from the bars and the hands push and release to land with knees slightly bent and the body erect on the mat. The head is up and the hands may be extended to the sides or forward.

Spotting: From the side the spotter supports the near arm.

SIDE SEAT DISMOUNT

Position: Sitting on the outside of one bar with a hand on each bar, the forward leg bent at the knee, the rear leg extended back, and the toes pointed.

Action: The arms and hips are pushed against the bar to force the body away from the bars. The performer lands with the side to the bars. The near hand may be on the nearest bar.

Spotting: The spotter stands at the side and slightly behind the performer and supports at the hips.

FRONT VAULT DISMOUNT

Position: From a straight arm support.

Action: The legs are swung well up above the bar behind the body. When the legs are at the height of the swing, the left hand pushes hard and the legs swing over the right bar. After passing over the bars, the left hand moves to grasp the right bar as the right moves off the side and is extended to the side. The performer lands with the side to the bars.

Spotting: From the side and in front of the performer the spotter supports the near upper and lower arm.

REAR VAULT DISMOUNT

Position: From a straight arm support.

Action: The legs are swung forward well above the bar. As the legs reach the height of the swing forward, the child pushes with the left hand and swings the legs over the right bar. As the legs cross the bars, the left hand moves to grasp the right bar and the right hand is extended to the side. The performer lands with the side to the bars.

Spotting: From the side and behind the performer the spotter supports the near upper and lower arm.

Skill Combinations

Combinations include a mount, movements on the bars, and a dismount.

Jump to a straight arm support, swing forward and back, swing to a sitting position on the outside of one bar, side dismount.

Jump to a straight arm support, swing to a straddle seat, straddle travel, jump dismount.

Jump to a straight arm support, straight arm walk, swing to a straddle seat, drop below the bars, pike inverted hand, one-half skin the cat dismount.

Pike inverted hand, layout inverted hand, pull-up to a straddle seat, straddle travel, front vault dismount.

Front support mount, angel, chest balance, straddle seat, straight arm support, straight arm travel, rear vault dismount.

Ropes

Rope activities contribute to upper body strength and coordination of the arms and legs. Children may begin with activities requiring upper body strength before attempting climbing activities. Climbing, if executed properly, uses the muscles of the back and legs to support the body weight; great arm strength is not required.

Ropes are usually of hemp and if not used properly can result in rope burns and splinters. Children should learn to come down the rope with control by using a hand-under-hand method of grasping the rope rather than sliding down. It is helpful to have a rope that extends at least to the floor. The ropes should not be knotted because children tend to use the knots for weight bearing and the ropes become frayed and weakened from this use. Mats should be positioned under the ropes.

Movement Challenges

1. How many ways can you support yourself on the rope?
2. What shapes can you make as you hang from the rope?
3. What can you do on one rope? Two ropes?
4. Can you do something on one rope and then repeat it using two ropes?

Activities with One Rope

PULL-UPS

Position: Lying on the mat next to the rope with the hands reaching up and gripping the rope.

Action: Keeping the body straight, the body is lifted to a stand by pulling with the arms and regrasping in a hand-over-hand style.

Suggestions: Children should be encouraged to keep the body as straight as possible.

BENT-ARM HANG

Position: Standing next to the rope with the hands reaching and grasping the rope overhead.

Action: With a spring from the feet the body is lifted and held up off the mat, pulling with the arms, which are bent at the elbows. The position is held as long as possible.

CLIMB

Position: Standing next to the rope, grasping the rope overhead with both hands. The elbows are straight. The rope is positioned to the outside of the ankle, over the foot, and to the inside of the knee of the rear foot. The toe is raised slightly.

Action: The body is pulled up and the body weight is supported by the upper body. The front foot crosses over the rear foot and secures the rope between the outer ankles and inner surfaces of the knees. The legs are extended foreward from the hips. The body is raised by extending the legs, resulting in the arms bending at the elbows. The body weight is then alternately supported in the legs and then the hands. As the body weight is once again supported in the legs, the arms reach upward in a hand-over-hand manner until the body is again extended. The arms take the body weight, and the legs are pulled up and regrasp the rope. The climb is continued in this manner to the desired height. To descend the rope the arms climb down the rope in a controlled hand-under-hand manner, as the legs alternately release and regrasp until the climber is once again on the mat.

Common errors:

1. Attempting to use the arms only to support the body weight.

2. Improper foot position, which is unstable in supporting the body weight.

Spotting: The spotter stands next to the performer as the climb is begun.

Suggestions:

1. The manner of descent should be introduced before the children attempt to climb.
2. Colored tape on the rope at various heights gives the children visual goals and sets limits for children during the learning phase when fatigue could be a concern for some.

ROPE SWING AND DROP

Position: Standing holding the rope in one hand, bringing the rope several steps back from the vertical position.

Action: As the individual moves forward the hand slides up the rope and the other hand grasps above the first. As the vertical position is reached, there is a spring from one foot, jumping upward with the hands reaching up as high on the rope as possible, ending in a bent arm hang. The knees are drawn up and the body leans slightly backward with the back arched and the legs extended forward. As the height of the swing is reached, the body is turned to face downward. The rope is released. On landing the body is carried forward, the knees and ankles bending to land softly.

Common error:

1. Failure to get a high enough grasp on the rope.

Suggestions:

1. Children love to swing on the ropes. At times it may be necessary to limit this activity to get the children to work on other rope skills.
2. Children may drop at the end of the backswing just before the rope begins to move forward.

INVERTED HANG

Position: Standing next to the rope grasping the rope in both hands high overhead.

Action: The child springs up with both feet to a bent-arm position and draws the legs up, bending at first and then extending them overhead.

Spotting: From the side the spotter assists at the hips to help lift the legs and to hold them overhead.

Pull-up.

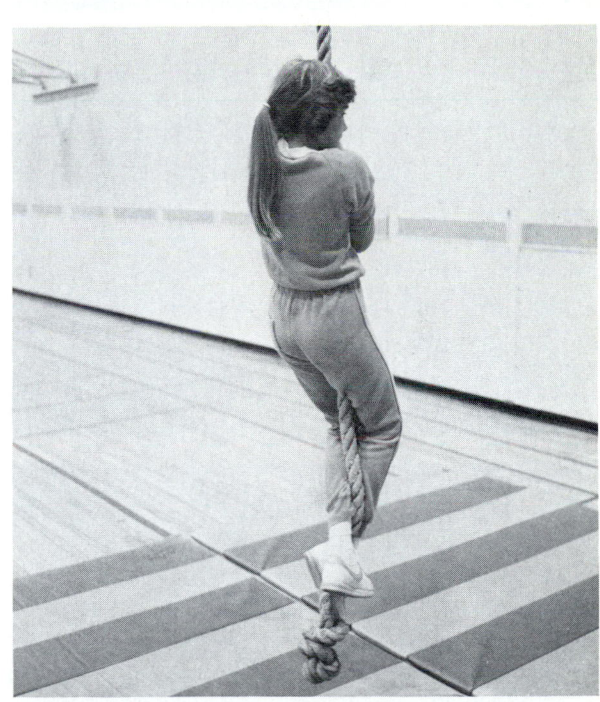

Rope climb.

Activities with Two Ropes

Several stunts included in the activities for the horizontal and parallel bars also may be performed with two ropes. Examples include inverted hangs, skin the cat, and the bird's nest. These stunts are spotted as they would be on the horizontal or parallel bars.

TWO ROPE SWING

Positions: Holding the ropes back from the vertical position.

Action: This skill is similar to the bird's nest, but preparatory steps are taken, so that as the bird's nest position is assumed, the individual is swinging back and forth on the two ropes.

Uneven Parallel Bars

Uneven parallel bars combine the challenge of working on a low and high bar and moving from one to the other. Like work on the parallel bars, work on the uneven bars contributes to upper body strength. In the beginning some children may be hesitant to work on the high bar because of its height from the mat. Many of the skills may be practiced on the horizontal bar, with the bar gradually raised as the children adjust to the new height.

Movement Challenges

Exploring movement challenges results in the development of new moves on the bars.

Back hip pull-over mount.

1. How many ways can you get on the low bar? The high bar?
2. What stunts can you do under the low bar? The high bar?
3. How many ways can you balance on one bar?
4. How many ways can you move from the low bar to the high bar? The high bar to the low bar?
5. What stunts can you do between the two bars?
6. Can you go over one bar and then under the next? Under the first bar to over the second bar?
7. Can you change direction while moving on one bar? On two bars?
8. How many ways can you dismount from the low bar? The high bar?

Skills

Many of the skills performed on the horizontal bar and parallel bars may also be executed on the uneven bars. A few are named in the skills that follow.

Mounts

FRONT SUPPORT

Included in the skills for the horizontal bar.

BACK HIP PULL-OVER MOUNT

Included in the skills for horizontal bar.

SHOOT OVER THE LOW BAR

Position: Standing facing the high bar.

Action: The performer jumps to a hanging position on the high bar and swings the legs up and over the low bar to end with the hips resting on the low bar and hands grasping the high bar.

Spotting: The spotter stands behind the performer and lifts at the hips.

Back pull away.

CROSS SEAT MOUNT

Position: Standing between the bars facing one end of the bars.

Action: The performer jumps, grasping the high bar with one hand and the low bar with the other. The arm on the low bar is straightened to support the body weight and swing the legs up and over the low bar. The performer ends in a cross seat position, the rear leg extended downward and the forward leg bent back at the knee.

Spotting: Facing the low bar, the spotter supports the arm on the low bar as the legs swing over.

Balances

Balances are no longer used in bar routines, but they are appropriate activities for elementary school children.

SEAT BALANCE

Position: Sitting on the low bar with one hand grasping the high bar, facing one end of the bars.

Action: One leg is extended downward to the outside of the low bar and the other foot is drawn close to the hips, bending at the knee. The free hand grasps the low bar behind the hips.

Spotting: The spotter stands to the outside of the low bar and grasps the arm.

V-SIT

Similar to the V-sit described in floor exercise. This stunt is performed on the low bar, facing one end of the bars. One hand is on the high bar, the other on the low bar.

BACK PULL AWAY

Position: Standing on the low bar facing the high bar, both hands grasping the high bar.

Action: The performer pushes away from the high bar by extending the arms and lifts one leg behind to end in a position with the head up, the back slightly arched, the hands on the high bar, and one foot on the low bar.

THIGH REST

Position: A front support on the high bar, facing the low bar.

Action: The performer bends forward and grasps the low bar in a regular grip. With the arms straight and the head up, the legs slide forward to finish with the thighs resting on the front of the bar. The back is slightly arched.

Spotting: The spotter stands in front of the performer and spots at the elbow.

ARCH BACK

Position: A double knee hang from the high bar facing the low bar.

Action: The low bar is grasped in a regular grip. The arms straighten as the performer arches the body to finish in a position gripping the low bars, with the back of the thighs close to the knee resting against the high bar.

LUNGE

Position: Standing on the low bar, grasping the high bar in one hand and facing one end of the bars.

Action: One leg is bent at the knee so that the upper leg is parallel to the bars. The other leg is extended back so that the top of the foot rests on the low bar. The free hand is extended to the side, the head is up, and the back is straight.

STRADDLE SEAT

Position: Hanging from the high bar facing the low bar.

Action: The legs are swung up over the low bar in a straddle position, so that the thighs are on the low bar. One hand is released from the high bar and placed between the legs onto the low bar. A balanced position is assumed, and the second hand is shifted to the low bar between the legs. The body is lifted off the bars to balance on the hands.

SWAN BALANCE

Position: A front support position on either the high or low bar.

Action: The performer assumes a balanced position, lifts the hands off the bar, and extends them to the side. The head is up and the back arched.

Swinging/Moving

SKIN THE CAT

Described in skills for the horizontal bar.

SKIN THE CAT TO A ONE-LEG SQUAT (BASKET)

Position: Hanging from the high bar with the back to the low bar.

Action: The legs are lifted up and through the hands for a skin the cat. As the legs come over, one foot is placed on the low bar and the other with the top of the foot touching the bar. The performer pivots on the low bar to a one-leg squat with the free leg extended in front.

Spotting: The spotter stands behind the low bar and helps with the foot placement onto the low bar.

SIDE CIRCLE

Position: Straddling the bar facing the end of the bars, with the hands gripping the bars in front of the body in a mixed grip.

Action: The body is lifted slightly off the bar by pushing with the hands. The body is kept stiff while circling sideward around the bar.

Spotting: The spotter stands behind the performer in front of the low bar, ready to assist as the performer comes back up to the bar by spotting at the shoulder.

Suggestions: It is important to move rapidly around the bar to have sufficient momentum to return to the upright position.

PULL-OVER TO HIGH BAR

Position: Hanging from the high bar facing the low bar.

Action: One leg is lifted to the low bar and the other straight up between the bars. The foot pushes on the bars and kicks the straight leg up to the high bar. At the same time the arms pull the body up to the high bar. The pull is completed over the high bar, ending in a straight arm support on the high bar facing the low bar.

Spotting: The spotter stands between the bars and pushes the hips up over the bar.

Suggestions: It is important to pull the upper body up close to the high bar as the legs are brought up.

Dismounts

SINGLE-LEG FLANK VAULT

Position: Straddling the low bar, facing one end of the bars with one hand grasping the high bar, the other on the low bar behind the hips in a reverse grip. The inside leg is extended downward and the outside leg is bent back at the knee with the toes pointed.

Action: The inside leg swings up over the low bar as the body weight is taken on the hand on the low bar. The landing is with the side to the low bar, one hand on the low bar and the other extended to the side.

Spotting: The spotter stands between the bars and spots the wrist on the low bar.

PIKE POSITION SHOOT-OFF DISMOUNT

Position: Sitting on the low bar facing away from the bars with the legs extended in front of the body in a pike position and the hands gripping the bars next to the hips.

Action: The performer pushes with the hands and momentarily lifts the legs in front before extending the body to land in front of the bars.

Spotting: The spotter stands in front of and to one side of the performer, spotting the performer at the near wrist.

Skill Combinations

Back pull over on low bar, front support, back pull away, forward roll over high bar.

Front support mount, side circle, back pull away, skin the cat to a basket, V sit, single-leg flank vault dismount.

Jump to hang on high bar, pull over to high bar, swan balance, roll forward over high bar to hang, shoot over low bar, pike position shoot-off dismount.

Shoot over the low bar mount, straddle seat, swan balance on low bar, straddle seat, single-leg flank vault dismount.

Vaulting

At the elementary level, a variety of equipment is used for **vaulting,** such as benches, Swedish boxes, and horses. This equipment should be of varying heights and adjustable from relatively low for young children to greater heights for older students. A springboard, either commercially produced or a homemade inclined plane, is used to gain lift to get over the equipment.

Spotting is very important in vaulting, and adult spotting is necessary, with the exception of a few movement challenges in which the children are always in contact with the equipment. The spotter should stand on the landing side of the equipment and to the side, being ready to assist at the wrist of the performer. For vaults in which one or both legs are extended to one side, the spotter is positioned on the side away from the legs.

A 2-foot take-off is used in vaulting.

Movement Challenges

1. How many ways can you get on the bench?
2. What shapes can you make on top of the bench?
3. How many ways can you find to go over the bench?
4. What body parts touch the bench as you go over?
5. What directions can you move over the horse?
6. How many ways can you move from the bench?
7. What shapes can you make in the air as a dismount?
8. What directions can you face as you land from the horse?
9. Can you change supporting body parts as you move over the horse?

Skills

KNEE MOUNT

From the 2-foot take-off both hands are placed on the horse with fingers pointing toward the landing area. The performer lands on the knees on the horse.

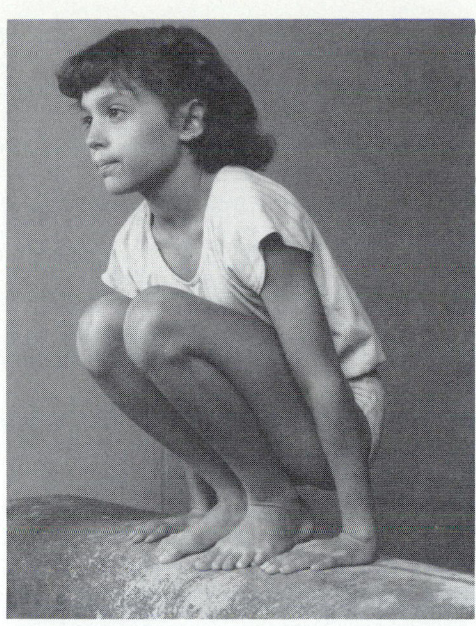

Squat mount.

COURAGE DISMOUNT

From a knee mount, the performer forcefully swings both arms forward and upward, lifting the body up off the horse and landing on the feet in front of the horse. Children may be hesitant at first to try this skill. The teacher may assist by taking one wrist and helping to swing it forward, lifting the performer off the horse.

SQUAT MOUNT

From a 2-foot take-off with both hands on the horse, fingers facing away, the child pushes with the hands to help lift the body, ending in a squat position on top of the horse.

The spotter should be ready to assist the children should they fail to get both feet up.

Long-legged children may have more difficulty with this skill.

JUMP DISMOUNT

The performer stands from a squat mount and jumps to the mat. In jumping to the mat the individual may assume a tuck, pike, or straddle position in the air or may execute a turn varying from a quarter to a full turn before landing.

SQUAT VAULT

The child assumes the squat position as in the squat mount, but continues over the horse to land in a balanced position on the other side.

FRONT VAULT

From a 2-foot take-off the hands are placed parallel and positioned on both sides of the horse; the legs are lifted to the rear. The front of the body passes over the horse. The back is arched and the head is up. The landing is with the side to the horse.

FLANK VAULT

From a 2-foot take-off the hands are placed on the horse as in the squat vault. The legs are lifted up to the side and over the horse so the side of the body passes over the horse. As the body passes over the horse the upper arm is lifted, taking the weight on the one arm momentarily. The finishing position is facing away from the horse.

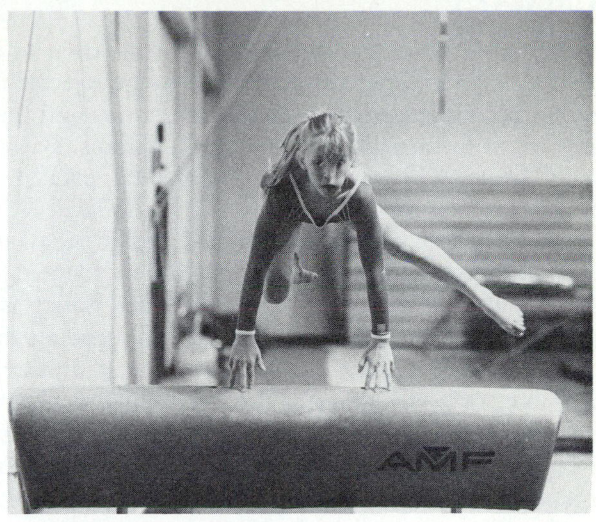

Wolf vault.

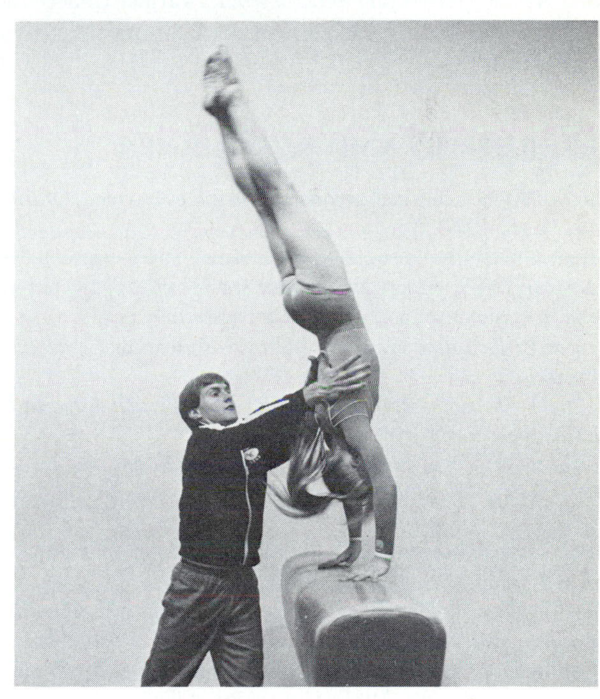

Handspring vault.

REAR VAULT

From a 2-foot take-off both hands are placed on the horse as in the squat vault. The legs are raised up to the side and then over the horse in a pike position. One hand and then the other is lifted as the legs come around and over the horse. The landing is with the side to the horse.

WOLF VAULT

In the vault the body assumes a squat position with one leg and a straddle with the other.

HANDSPRING

From a 2-foot take-off the hands are placed on the horse with the body passing over the horse in a handspring position. See stunts and tumbling for a description of this skill.

SUMMARY

Gymnastic activities are challenging for children of all abilities. A wide variety of activities may be selected including individual, partner, and group stunts and tumbling or work on different kinds of apparatus. Balance beams; vaulting boxes or horses; horizontal, parallel, or uneven bars; and ropes are some of the possibilities. Many schools also have outdoor apparatus, and many of the skills taught on the indoor apparatus may be adapted for use on jungle gyms or horizontal ladders. Safety is a primary concern and the teacher must take the time that is needed to emphasize the safe use of mats and large apparatus. In a few activities the children may assist as spotters; in others adult spotters are needed.

Exploring the use of the body in relation to mats and large apparatus is an important aspect of early experiences in gymnastics. Creativity in making up new movements should be encouraged throughout the elementary school years. At the elementary school level a variety of activities should be provided in each lesson to maximize the activity for all children.

REFERENCES AND RESOURCES

Boucher A: Educational gymnastics is for everyone, *JOPER* 49(7):48, 1978.

Caspen C: Rhythmic sportive gymnastics, Paper presented in Boston, 1989, American Alliance for Health, Physical Education Recreation and Dance Convention.

Cooper P: *Feminine gymnastics,* ed 3, Minneapolis, 1980, Burgess.

Cooper P: *Teaching basic gymnastics: a coeducational approach,* ed 3, New York, 1993, Macmillan.

Educational Committee: *Sequential gymnastics for grades 3 to 6,* Tucson, Ariz, 1989, United States Gymnastics Federation.

Hicks S: Basic movement: building a foundation for educational gymnastics, *JOPER* 50(6):26, 1979.

Logsdon B et al: *Physical education for children: a focus on the teaching process,* ed 2, Philadelphia, 1984, Lea & Febiger.

O'Quinn G: *Developmental gymnastics: building physical skills for children,* Austin, 1985, University of Texas Press.

Reiken G: Women's gymnastics: teaching and learning progressions, *JOPERD* 56(3):33, 1985.

Rovgno I: The art of gymnastics: creating sequences, *JOPERD* 58(3):66, 1988.

Szypula J and Szypula G: *Contemporary gymnastics,* Chicago, 1979, Contemporary Books.

Wiseman E: The process of learning in gymnastics, *JOPER* 49(7):44, 1978.

ANNOTATED READINGS

Kruger H: A focus on body management, *JOPER* 49(7):39, 1978

Describes three levels of program objectives for gymnastics to meet the needs of all children.

Mulvihill L: Vaulting, *JOPER* 51(1):64, 1980.

Describes physical prerequisites for success in vaulting, safety in teaching falling, drills, and progressions for teaching vaulting skills.

Parent S: To rouse an interest, *JOPER* 49(7):32, 1978.

Discusses developing themes in educational gymnastics.

Sander A and Griffin M: Skill, fitness, and critical thinking through gymnastics, *Strategies* 4(3):10, 1991.

Discusses the organization of a gymnastics lesson that incorporates fitness, skill, and work and culminates in activities that encourage critical thinking in solving movement challenges.

Sim L: Teaching your gymnasts to swing: biomechanics in plain talk for the novice coach, *JOPERD* 56(3):39, 1985.

Discusses the application of mechanical principles to swinging in gymnastic activities.

Standeven J: More than simply movement experience, *JOPER* 49(7):35, 1978.

Describes the process of learning in educational gymnastics.

Underwood M: Teaching strategies and pupil social development in physical education, *Research Papers in Education* 2(3):200, 1987.

Focuses on teaching methods in gymnastics where students take more responsibility for their own and other's learning; emphasis on individual and social development.

Warrell E: Safety in using gymnastics equipment, *JOPER* 49(7):35, 1978.

Discusses teaching concerns for establishing and maintaining a safe gymnastics environment.

CHAPTER 18

Track and Field

OBJECTIVES

After completing this chapter the student will be able to:

1. Explain events included in track and field in the elementary school
2. Identify movement concepts important to track and field events
3. Describe a progression for introducing track and field activities at the elementary school level
4. Offer suggestions for the teaching and organizing of track and field activities

Track and field activities are an extension of the accomplishments of children in the development of the fundamental skills of running, jumping, and throwing and their understanding of human movement. In the elementary physical education program, emphasis in developing competency in fundamental motor skills begins in the earliest experiences. These skills are further refined as children learn the running and field events in track and field. In addition the children learn to control body movements and to use balance, the creation and absorption of force, and speed. Space concepts are also important to a successful performance.

Running and field events are highly motivating because they are self-testing. Because performance is easily measured children are able to get a clear picture of their level of achievement. Emphasis in these activities should be on improving one's personal performance, with children setting goals for their own achievement.

Native American Sport Traditions

Running, especially long distance running, has been recognized as an important tradition in Native American life. Although running was important for a number of reasons other than sport, such as hunting, carrying messages, and transportation, it was also important in the informal play of children and the ceremonial life of adults. The Zuni and other Southwestern Native American tribes often painted their bodies for identification and artistic and spiritual purposes before races. Running accounts are included in much of the oral history and folklore of most tribes where it was used to explain differences between people and animals, distinctions within the animal kingdom (tortoise and hare), and the importance of perseverance in achieving goals. Several running activities of Native Americans are included in the running events described later in this chapter.

Forms of jumping also have a tradition in Native American life in Alaska and Canada. Today, the 1- and 2-foot high kicks are included as events for men and women in the Eskimo Indian Olympics and the Arctic Winter Games. These two events are described in the jumping events section of this chapter.

MOVEMENT CONCEPTS

Quality of movement and body awareness concepts are important in track and field. Application of space concepts is a factor in some events. Figure 18-1 outlines the movement concepts important in track and field at the elementary school level. Because the use of concepts is important for success in the events, they should be stressed throughout the learning period. Movement challenges to explore the use of body parts in taking-off, running, jumping, moving through space, landing, and projecting objects should be used in the early phases of learning as suggested in Chapter 13.

SUGGESTIONS FOR TEACHING

The following are suggestions for teaching track and field.

1. Instruction in track and field in the early grades should include an exploration of the use of the body in performing various tasks, such as starting, going over low obstacles, etc. Short distance runs, the standing jump, and activities

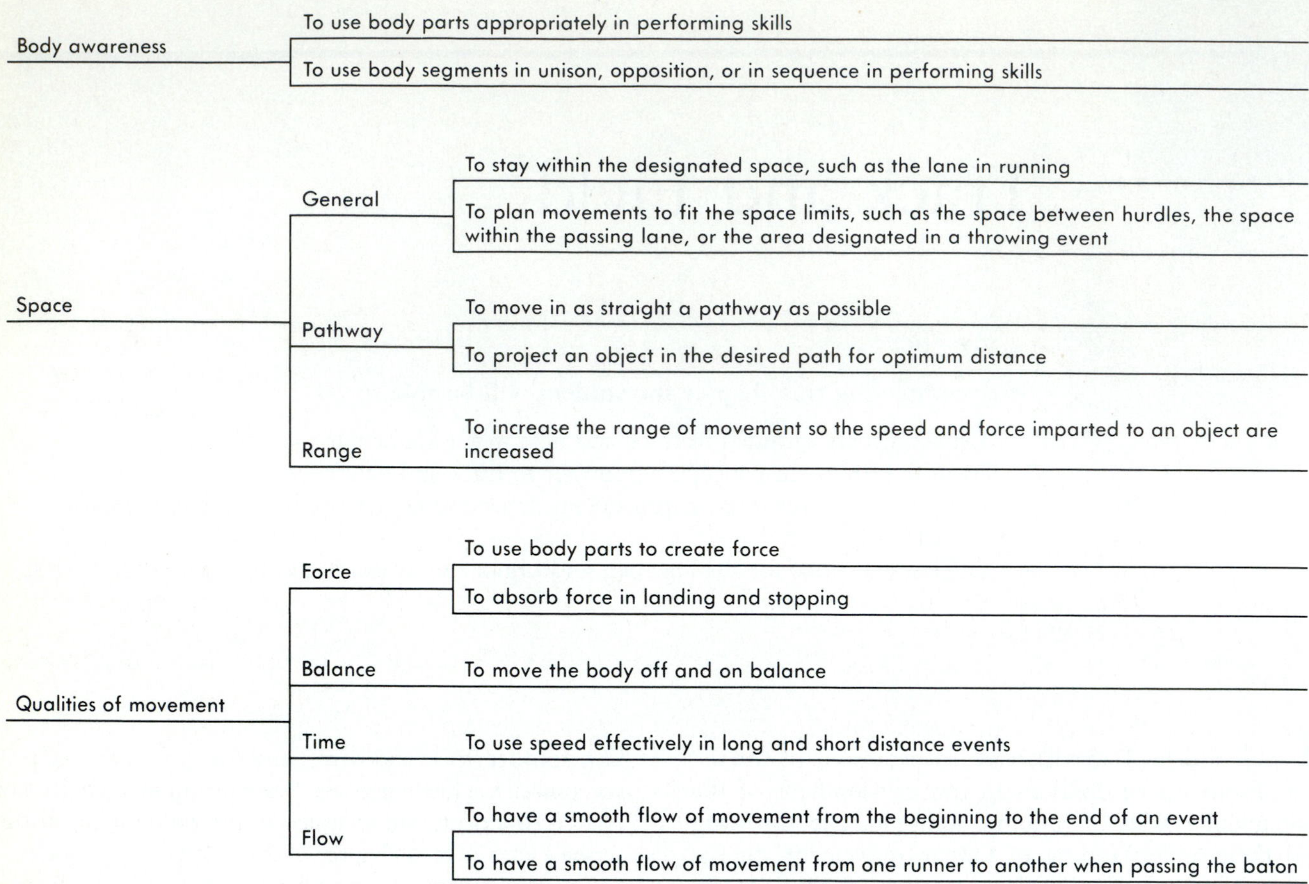

FIGURE 18-1 Key concepts for track and field.

TABLE 18-1 TRACK AND FIELD FOR ELEMENTARY SCHOOL CHILDREN

	DEVELOPMENTAL LEVEL			
EVENT	I	II	III	IV
WALKING/RUNNING EVENTS				
Walk	One time around the area	Walk for distance/ time	Walk for distance/ time	Walk for distance/ time
Sprints	Short distances	20-30 meters	30-40 meters	40-50 meters
Starts	Standing	Standing	bunch, medium	bunch, medium
Distance runs	One time around the area	One time around the area	100-200 meters	200-400 meters, mile
Relays		Shuttle 10-15 meters	Shuttle 20-25 meters	Pursuit 100-220 meters
Hurdles		10 inches, 30 meters	15 inches, 30-50 meters	18-21 inches, 40-50 meters
FIELD EVENTS				
Standing jump	All levels			
Long jump	Jump the brook	Long jump	Long jump	Long jump
High jump	High water	High water	High jump	High jump
Throw for distance	Softball	Softball	Softball, soccer ball	Softball, soccer ball
Shot		Tennis ball	4-pound shot	4-pound shot

such as jump the brook and high water/low water may be used as preliminaries to learning the track and field events of the later years. Table 18-1 lists the suggested activities for elementary school track and field. In addition Native American events can be included to provide a multicultural experience.

2. Warm-ups of easy jogging and stretching must be encouraged if muscle soreness from a strenuous effort is to be avoided.
3. Variation in ability among the children is common. In organizing events, ability or mixed ability groups may be used. In running events, it is important to have the children run with at least one child of equal ability to maximize their effort. In the high jump, ability grouping may be beneficial because opportunity for practice becomes limited to those children who can clear the set height. The advantage of mixed ability grouping is that all children are exposed to a good performance.
4. Personal improvement in each event is the goal. It is advisable to have numerous opportunities for children to record their performances on individual record cards. An individual record permits the children to chart their own progress in performing their personal best. In addition it is challenging for children to set personal, class, and school records that become the school standards. Measuring, recording, and graphing personal achievements may become a part of learning in math as well.
5. Station work may be used to provide maximum activity for all within the constraints of limited equipment and facilities.
6. Track and field facilities often must be improvised. Specific suggestions for each event may be found in the material that follows.
7. It is important to organize events for maximum safety. Safety concerns may be found in the discussion for each event.

Social Development

Although track and field activities are individually oriented, they provide an opportunity for children to share in each other's personal achievements. The competitive aspects such as who is the fastest or who can jump the farthest should be minimized. Emphasis should be on personal achievement and improving one's own performance. Each child's personal best should be celebrated. Children should be encouraged to coach one another as well as to encourage the best performance of each participant. Activities should include some choices for children in selecting running distances or in objects for throwing events.

Health-Related Physical Fitness

Track and field activities can contribute to fitness if maximum activity is provided in organizing events for elementary school children. Daily warm-up activities include stretching, which increases flexibility. Cardiorespiratory endurance is improved as children work to develop running events. Strength of various body segments is enhanced through practice of the field events.

WALKING AND RUNNING EVENTS

Walking as well as running can be a good aerobic activity. It can be built into a track and field unit as an event. Children can walk for time or distance. Children should begin with a distance that they can walk comfortably at a brisk pace. As their endurance improves the distance should be increased. To develop walking within the class and provide time to practice other events, distance walked within a particular time might be recorded. Children should be encouraged to walk vigorously, with one foot always in contact with the ground surface. An arm swing should be incorporated to enhance their walking and to raise the heart rate. The form in walking is described in Chapter 13.

Running events may be categorized into individual and team events. Individual running events include the short distance races, called **sprints** or dashes, and the middle and long distance runs. The team events are the shuttle and pursuit relays. Running events require an unobstructed path. Adequate space must also be provided beyond the finish line to allow children to run at full speed past the line and to slow down and stop safely. The width of the running area should permit each runner to use full body movements without interfering with others. The running surface should be smooth, dry, and free from loose gravel or stones. Grass often provides an adequate surface for running events. Children should be taught to run in a straight path for sprints, avoiding the paths of other runners. In distance events children should watch space carefully to avoid being tripped or tripping others in starting or passing.

All running events require an efficient running pattern in which the runner moves with a comfortable, even stride, and all body actions propel the body forward. An analysis of the run may be found in Chapter 13.

Sprints

Sprinting requires the runner to cover a short distance in the least amount of time. Because the distance is short, a good start is important, and the runner must accelerate quickly and maintain a maximum effort throughout the race. The race may require extra effort at the end to outdistance an opponent. Maximum speed should be maintained well past the finish line. One common error in running events is slowing down as the finish line draws near.

- Thumb and fingers parallel to the line, hands below shoulders, knee down next to forward foot.
- Hips up, head and neck in line with trunk, weight forward, eyes looking ahead.
- Legs extend, body rising, arms drive.

FIGURE 18-2 Evaluative criteria and teaching points for the bunch or crouch start.

FIGURE 18-3 Comparison of bunch and medium starts.

Placing markers 5 yards beyond the actual finish line will be of some help in getting children to run through the finish when measuring their times.

Elementary school children generally run sprints from 20 to 50 meters long, with the younger children running dashes of 20 to 30 meters and the upper elementary school grades running 30 to 50 meters. A 100-meter dash is actually a long distance run for young elementary school-aged children and a middle distance run for children in the upper elementary grades.

Three types of starting positions are usually taught in the elementary school grades. The standing start described in Chapter 13 is used in the lower grades. It may also be taught in the upper grades, when the starting surface does not make other types of starts advantageous, and for long distance running. The **bunch** or crouch **start** is usually used in sprinting events.

On the signal, "Runners, take your mark," the runner assumes a position behind the starting line as described in Figure 18-2. On the next signal, "Get set," the hips are raised slightly above the shoulders and the feet are close together with one foot slightly ahead of the other. On the signal, "Go," there is an explosive push as the legs extend to drive the body forward and gradually upward. The arms move quickly to a position with the elbows bent and drive forward in opposition to the action of the legs. As the runner assumes a more upright position the length of stride increases.

The **medium start,** which is also used in sprinting, is similar to the bunch start, but the feet are a comfortable step apart. The medium start sacrifices power for a more comfortable stance.

Common errors:

1. The head is facing downward, which may result in loss of balance at the start.
2. The distance between the hands and feet is too great, so power is lost.
3. The legs are straight and the hips too high on the signal, "Get set."
4. The hands are positioned too far forward in front of the body rather than directly under the shoulders.
5. Putting too much weight on the hands, resulting in stumbling out of position.
6. Failure to respond quickly to the signal, "Go."

Teaching suggestion: To help correct error No. 3, a string or rope may be strung across the starting area. A runner who comes up too high too soon will hit the string.

Distance Runs

Distance races require the runner to accelerate and to find a speed that can be maintained over the longer distance. A common error in distance running is beginning at too fast a speed and tiring before the distance can be covered.

The stride is longer in distance running than in sprinting races and the body is held more erect. Because endurance is a primary factor in long distance running, a standing start is generally used rather than a crouch or medium start. The runner assumes a forward/backward stride position with the knees bent, the body leaning forward, and the arms ready to drive on the signal, "Go." The crouch or medium start may be used in middle distance runs. The runner attempts to set a pace that can be maintained throughout the race. As children improve their endurance, the pace increases.

Whereas sprinting is performed in a straight line, distance runs involve running in curved paths as well. In running a curved path, the body leans toward the inside of the curve and the outside foot pushes a little harder. The outside arm may also swing slightly across the body as the curve is taken.

Although many schools do not have a track on which to run, a running area may be measured on the playground, with flags or stakes marking the corners. Performance targets for the unique distances may be established over a few years of keeping scores for the various distances used.

Relays

Relays offer a team activity to running events. Four runners comprise a team. In **shuttle relays** the runners, two positioned at each end of the running area, run back and forth between two lines with each runner completing the distance between the lines. In the **pursuit relay** the racers run an oval course, with each runner covering a part of the distance.

The shuttle relay requires less space, with the distance between the lines varying with the age of the runners. Young children may run a shuttle with as little as 20 feet between the lines, and upper grade children may each run 25 meters. In shuttle relays the next runner begins as a baton is passed or after a tag on the shoulder.

When passing the baton the runner holds the baton vertically in the right hand, thrusting it out in front of the body. The receiver grasps the baton in the right hand above the runner's hand and then quickly proceeds to the opposite line.

In pursuit relays passing the baton involves the two runners moving in the same direction in a passing zone, approximately 22 yards long. The receivers may look over their shoulders to see the coming runner or may receive the baton while facing the direction of the run. Although a **visual pass** is slower, it is easier for elementary school children. The **blind pass** is faster, but there is a greater chance for error because the receiver is not looking in the direction of the pass.

Passing the baton in pursuit relays involves a left-to-right or right-to-left hand exchange. Because it is best

- Runner in ready position with hand out to the side to grasp baton.
- Runner thrusts baton forward in right hand.
- Right hand exchange.

FIGURE 18-4 Evaluative criteria and teaching points for baton passing for the shuttle run.

- Receiver waits at edge of passing zone, hand back ready to move.
- Runner approaches receiver.
- Both run, receiver accelerating.
- Arm swings upward and into receiver's hand between thumb and index finger; both arms extended.

Or,

- Arm swings downward, baton received in open palm, both arms extended.
- Receiver leaves passing zone.

FIGURE 18-5 Evaluative criteria and teaching points for blind pass in pursuit relays.

- Arm swings upward and into receiver's hand between thumb and index finger, both arms extended.

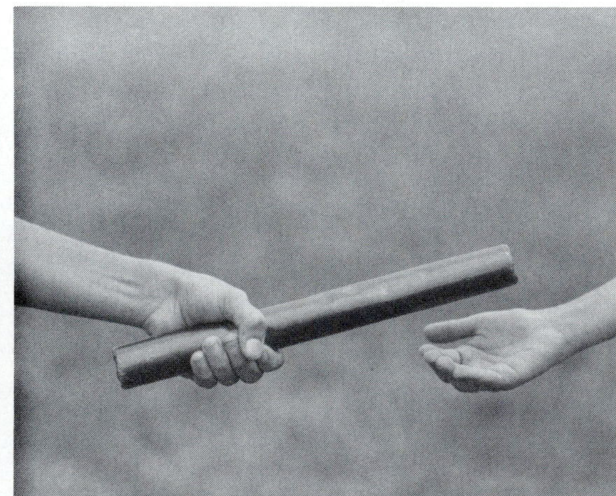

- Or arm swings downward, baton received in open palm, both arms extended.

FIGURE 18-6 Baton passing in pursuit relays.

not to change hands for the pass, the passer uses the hand in which the baton was received and passes it to the opposite hand of the next runner.

Note that the baton may be passed in an upward or downward motion. In preparing for the pass, the receiver waits in the passing lane close to the oncoming runner. As the runner approaches, the receiver begins to move forward with the receiving hand extended back and in position with the palm up or turned down. Both runners move in the passing lane with the receiver accelerating.

The pass is completed with the arms of both runners fully extended. The pass requires perfect timing, and practice is necessary to get a smooth, efficient pass. The passing lane is 22 yards long for the 220-meter relay. The distance to be run is divided into four equal parts, with the passing lane overlapping each of the four distances. The distance will vary with the distance of the race for elementary school-aged children.

Activities to Practice Individual or Team Walking or Running Events

1. Have the children practice the event with at least one other child of equal ability.
2. Have the children form lines of about four, one behind the other, walking or jogging. As the line moves, a signal is given in which the person at the end of the line sprints up to become the new leader.
3. Have the children practice the events using locomotor movements other than running or changing movements on a signal.
4. Have the children practice the events changing the direction of movement from forward to either moving right or left (not backward for safety reasons).

Hurdling

Hurdling is a running event with the added challenge of moving over obstacles. Hurdles for elementary school children range in height from 10 to 21 inches. The fear of falling or hitting the hurdles presents a psychological barrier for children. Hurdles must be constructed so that they fall forward if contacted by the jumper. Heavy canvas fastened with Velcro strips to the side supports make excellent cross pieces that "tear away" at impact and reduce the fear of hitting the hurdles. Hurdles may also be improvised using cones across which weighted ropes or string weighted with fishing weights are placed. The hurdle height should be adjusted to the height of the hurdler, about mid thigh height, as the child stands next to the hurdle.

Hurdling events may vary from 30 to 50 meters long, with the number of hurdles varying with the distance—a maximum of four for the 50-meter event. The hurdles should be evenly spaced over the distance with a sufficient distance to establish a good stride before encountering the first hurdle, approximately 8 to 10 meters.

In hurdling, the stride should be even between the hurdles so that the same leg leads over the hurdle each time. The action is a leap as hurdlers project themselves forward and upward. The take-off is on the ball of the foot, with the landing on the opposite foot. The action should be smooth, with no loss of stride in landing. The trailing leg is up and abducted as it clears the hurdle. The center of gravity is ahead of the driving leg during the lift, which results in the upper body and head well out in front. The hurdler must determine the number of strides to the first hurdle and the number of strides between hurdles to determine the lead foot at the start.

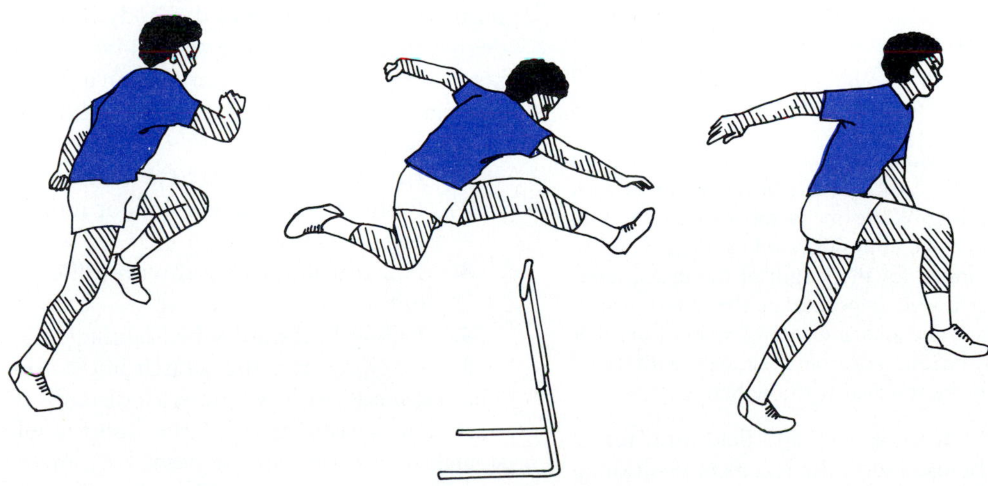

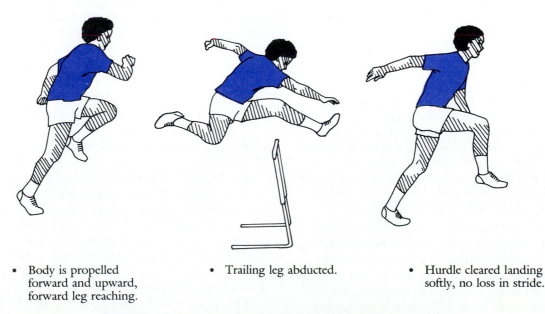

- Body is propelled forward and upward, forward leg reaching.
- Trailing leg abducted.
- Hurdle cleared landing softly, no loss in stride.

FIGURE 18-7 Evaluative criteria and teaching points for hurdling.

Common errors:

1. Failure to lead with the same leg in going over the hurdles.
2. Breaking stride when approaching the hurdle.
3. Breaking stride when landing from a hurdle.
4. Failure to abduct the trailing leg so that it hits the hurdle.

Teaching suggestions: In developing the technique the runner should first practice the start and run, stopping after the first hurdle has been cleared.

To get the feeling of the stride before and between hurdles, the runner should move along the side of the course a few times.

Native American Events

KIWI TRAIL OR TWISTED TRAIL

In this child's running activity, children ran to a designated spot and back to the starting line after running around several trees. This path caused the children to become dizzy as they moved, much to the pleasure of the adults who watched. This activity can be modified by placing a number of cones along the course, which the children must run around on their way to a designated line and then back to the start/finish line.

BALL RACE

This event, at one time a very popular sacred custom in the southwestern United States with Zuni, Pima, and Papago tribes and the foremost sporting event in Mexico with the Tarahumare, involved kicking a small wooden ball or stick along as the runner moved from the start to the finish line. The foot was placed under the object, which was lifted into the air, moving it as far as possible in the direction of the finish line. The race course distance varied from relatively short distances to distances up to about 25 miles. This event was popular among men and women, with the women often using a stick to toss a hoop or ring ahead rather than kicking a ball.

As the race began, the lead runner was positioned at the starting line with team members dispersed several yards away to kick the ball again on landing. While one member kicked the ball, the others ran ahead to be in position to kick the ball again. This approach continued for the length of the race course. Accuracy in kicking was as important as the ability to run and kick because the ball could land among rocks or in other areas and could only be retrieved from these areas with sticks, as the ball could not be touched with the hands.

To modify this event for a track and field unit, teams of two to four may be used with the receivers positioned ahead of the beginning runner. A medium-sized foam or rubber ball can be kicked along the ground or lofted into the air. An additional requirement might be that each member of the team must kick the ball in moving it toward the finish line. It may be necessary to limit the number of teams competing at a time to two due to the space required. Another event to help prepare for the ball race may include kicking for distance or accuracy.

FIELD EVENTS

Field events include jumping and throwing skills. At the elementary school level, jumping events may include the standing jump, the long jump, and the high jump. Throwing events are the softball and soccer ball throws for distance and the shot put.

Jumping

Jumping events need ample space for approaches that do not interfere with other events. Landing surfaces should be loose and raked to provide an evenly smooth surface. Dry sand or wood shavings may be used for the standing and long jumps. (Wet surfaces do not provide as much force absorption as dry surfaces.) Net bags filled with pieces of foam, crash pads, or tire tubes tied together and covered with a mat may be used to pad the landing areas for high jumping. High jump standards may be improvised using a bamboo pole or a long rope supported by two adjustable standards. The rope or pole should always be placed so that it falls away from the standards and the jumper if it is accidentally touched by the jumper.

The *standing jump* is the first jumping event to be taught. The jumper attempts to cover as much horizontal distance as possible. The jump is measured from the scratch line to the closest point of contact of any body part in the landing area.

The jumper begins with both feet parallel and just behind the starting, or scratch line, and follows the procedure described in Figure 18-8. As the arms swing forward, an explosive extension of the legs and body and a push with the feet propel the body into the air at a 45-degree angle. The landing should be controlled with the body weight forward, the arms moving forward for balance, and the legs flexing to absorb the force.

Common errors:

1. Failure to coordinate the arm and leg actions.
2. Pushing with the whole foot rather than the ball of the foot.
3. Not reaching forward with full extension on the jump.
4. Falling backward when landing.
5. Stepping over the scratch line before take-off.

The *long jump* involves a jump for distance after a running start. The measurement of the jump is taken from the scratch line to the nearest point of contact of any body part in the landing area. The take-off surface is a board measuring 4 feet long, 8 inches wide, and 8 inches thick that is flush with the ground.

The approach in the long jump is a run with increasing speed on each step, until a maximum and yet controlled

- Toes behind the line; body bent at hips, knees, and ankles; arms bent at side.

- Arms swing back, weight shifts to balls of the feet.

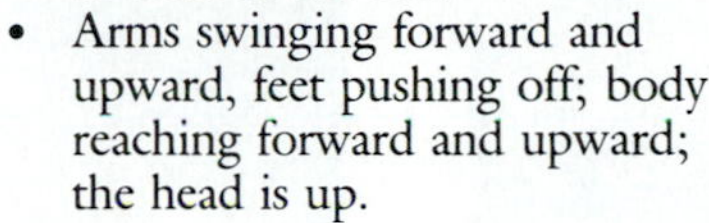

- Arms swinging forward and upward, feet pushing off; body reaching forward and upward; the head is up.

- Land with arms movıng forward, heel touch first, legs flexed, body weight forward.

FIGURE 18-8 Evaluative criteria and teaching points for standing jump.

speed is attained. The last stride before take-off is slightly shorter to allow the jumper to prepare for the jump. The take-off is from one foot, and the free leg moves forward and upward to help propel the body into the air. The center of gravity is directly over the board as the take-off foot touches. The forceful extension of the take-off leg completes the upward motion. The angle of take-off is somewhat less than 45 degrees as the body is propelled upward and forward. During the airborne flight both arms and legs reach for maximum distance. The arms and upper body should be kept high, with the head up. Maintaining balance and keeping the body weight forward are important in landing.

Common errors:

1. A break in stride in the approach.
2. Failure to achieve a maximum controlled run in the approach.
3. Stepping over the take-off board on the jump.
4. Failure to stretch on the take-off.
5. Head down and failure to lift the chest.
6. Propelling the body forward rather than upward and forward.
7. Loss of balance on landing.

Teaching suggestions:

1. The number of strides for the approach must be determined individually. It should be long enough to attain the desired speed but not long enough to be tiring. Each person should determine the number of strides and should mark the point from which to begin the approach.
2. Emphasize running through the board rather than placing too much emphasis on the take-off.

The *high jump* combines a short run with a jump over an obstacle, which is raised in height after each successful jump. The jump is measured from the ground upward, perpendicular to the top of the crossbar where the crossbar is closest to the ground.

A scissors jump is described here as a possible lead-up to the flop, a style of jumping used in competition (Figure 18-10). In the scissors jump, the body passes in a vertical position over the bar. Success in clearing the bar depends on a forceful thrust of the take-off leg and upward swing of the arms. The landing should be on the feet and controlled.

Common errors:

1. Failure to coordinate the extension of the leg and upward swing of the arms.
2. Taking off too close to the bar, so that the free leg hits the bar as it is brought upward.
3. Taking off on two feet.

Alaskan Native Games

Two additional events taken from Eskimo Indian competition might be introduced in the track and field unit, namely the 1- and 2-foot high kicks. In each event the jumper has three attempts to successfully jump the new height. The jumper may begin from a running or standing position, but both feet must be together on the take-off.

ONE-FOOT HIGH KICK

The jumper attempts to kick a small seal-skin object suspended above the floor by taking off on two feet, kicking the object with one foot and then landing in a balanced position on the foot that was used to kick the object. The event is measured as the height that the object is suspended from the floor. The world records for this event is 9 feet 2 inches for men and 6 feet 9 inches for women.

- Approaching the board with controlled acceleration.
- Foot plant on board, free leg bent and moving forward, head up.
- Extension of take-off leg, movement forward and upward, chest lifted.

- Both legs reach forward, arms reaching forward; head erect, chest up.

- Balanced landing, heels touch first; body flexed, weight moving forward.

FIGURE 18-9 Evaluative criteria and teaching points for long jump.

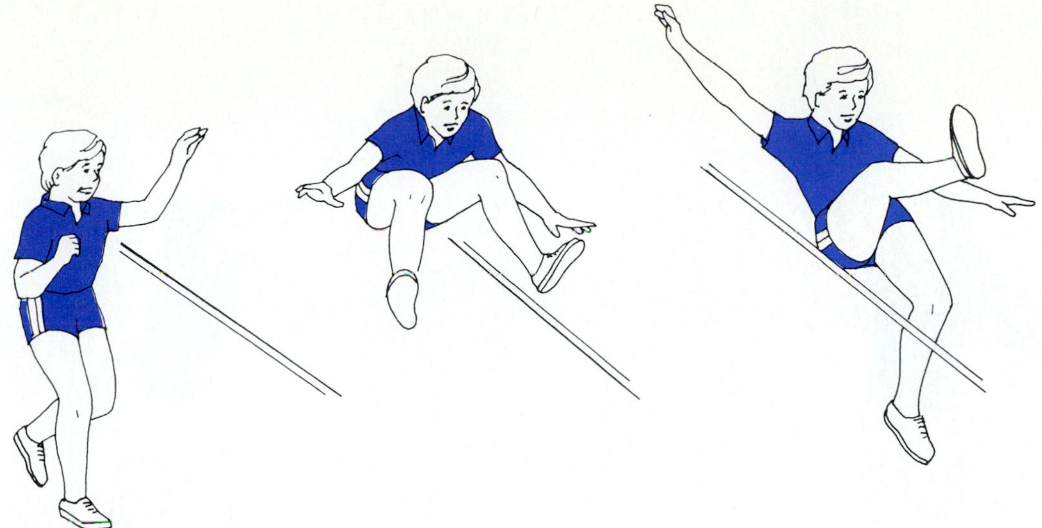
• Bar approached at slight angle; foot planted away from bar, flexing ankle and knee.
• Leg forcefully extended while free leg swings up to clear bar and arms swing upward; trailing leg is lifted up over bar.
• Legs flex on landing to absorb force, arms out for balance.

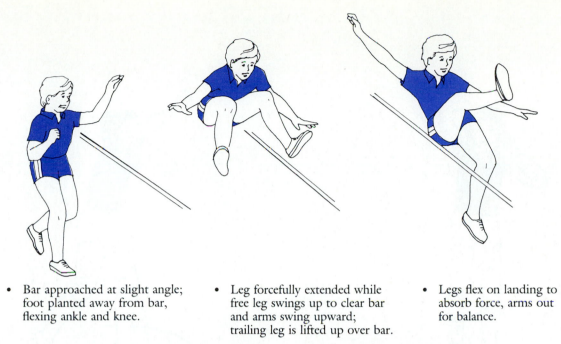

FIGURE 18-10 Evaluative criteria and teaching points for scissors jump.

TWO-FOOT HIGH KICK

The jumper tries to kick an object suspended above the floor taking off with two feet, kicking the object with two feet, and then landing on both feet. The feet remain together throughout, and if balance is lost on landing, the kick is disallowed. The world record for men in the two-foot high kick is 8 feet 8 inches and the women's record is 6 feet 4 inches. This event is believed to have its origin in whale and caribou hunting. When an animal was sighted or caught, a young runner was sent back to the village to alert the people. When in sight of the village, he would jump high in the air with both feet in front of him, signaling the villagers to make the necessary preparations.

Both of these events can be modified for use in physical education. A small Nerf ball, beanbag, or other object can be suspended from a basketball hoop beginning about 18 inches from the floor and raised as the children gain control of their jumps. Mats should be used for jumping. Although they do not aid the take-off for the jump, they do provide a safer surface for landing.

Throwing Events

The throwing events in track and field meets include the javelin, discus, and shot put. At the elementary school level, throws for distance often include a softball and a soccer ball throw. The javelin and discus are seldom included. A 4- and 6-pound shot is used in the shot put.

Safety is an important consideration in throwing events. The throwing area and the direction in which the throws will be made should be away from the other events. The area should be clearly defined to permit children to see the restricted area. When more than one person is throwing at a time, a signal for retrieving the objects is used so that the children only retrieve after all objects have been thrown.

The *throw for distance* may be thought of as an event itself or as a lead-up to throwing the javelin. Analysis of the overhand throwing pattern used in this event may be found in Chapter 13 along with common errors and teaching suggestions. In the early grades a standing throw is used. In the upper grades the throw is combined with a moving approach to maximize the force produced. In all throws a release angle of slightly less than 45 degrees is desired for maximum distance. Measurement is taken from a point on the starting line to the point of first contact with the ground.

The softball (fleece ball for younger children) throw is included in all elementary school grades, and a soccer ball throw is introduced in the upper grades only. While the soccer ball throw is not really a field event, it provides children the opportunity to handle a heavier object, which should enhance upper body development. When using a soccer ball, children may need to use two hands to control the larger ball.

The *shot put* may be introduced in the upper elementary school grades. In the first experiences a softball may be used, gradually working up to a 4- or 6-pound shot. In the elementary school the shot should be put from a standing position. Although the shot put is included as a throwing event, it is actually pushed rather than thrown.

Measurement is taken from the standing line or the edge of the circle to the first point of contact with the ground in the landing area.

- Held at base of four fingers, thumb and little finger supporting.

- Back of hand at clavicle, shot close to neck.

- Semi-squat position, weight over supporting foot, side facing direction of put.

- Forceful extension of knees and arm as shot is pushed outward and upward.

FIGURE 18-11 Evaluative criteria and teaching points for shot put.

The shot putter stands in a comfortable position, with the feet about shoulder width apart, behind the scratch line, and the side of the body facing the landing area. The shot put is held high in the palm of the hand and supported against the base of the middle two fingers of the hand farthest away from the throwing area. The fingers may be spread slightly for children with small hands. To place the shot in the ready position, the arm is straightened overhead and then lowered so that the back of the hand is on the clavicle and the shot is near the neck. Beginning with flexion in the knees, hips, and ankles and the weight over the throwing leg, the shot is released with a forceful extension of the legs and arm in an outward and upward direction and a transfer of weight to the forward foot. The angle of projection should be about 45 degrees. The putter should be careful not to step over the scratch line or out of the circle as the shot is released.

Common errors:

1. Attempting to throw the shot rather than push it.
2. Letting the shot rest in the palm of the hand.
3. Failure to coordinate leg and arm extension into a smooth, continuous movement.
4. Stepping over the scratch line or out of the circle.

Teaching suggestions:

1. Because the shot is usually put from a circle 7 feet in diameter, this area may be used rather than a straight line.
2. Emphasize the pushing action and the extension of both the leg and the arm to propel the shot.

SUMMARY

Track and field activities involve the adaptation of the fundamental motor skills of running, jumping, and throwing to specialized events. As the children progress through the elementary school years, new techniques are introduced as they are ready. These activities involve the application of the movement concepts as the new skills require their use. Track and field events are self-testing because performance is easily measured and children can readily see improvements made. Native American events may be included to add a multicultural experience.

REFERENCES AND RESOURCES

American Academy of Pediatrics: Risks in long-distance running for children, *The Physician and Sports Medicine* 10(2):82, 1982.

Frey RD and Allen M: Alaskan native games—a cross cultural addition to the physical education curriculum, *JOPERD* 60(10):21, 1989.

NASPE and Hershey Corporation: *Track and field resource book for upper elementary and middle school children,* Hershey Pa, 1993, Hershey.

Oxendine JB: *American Indian sports heritage,* Champaign, Ill, 1988, Human Kinetics Publishers.

Powell J: *Track and field: fundamentals for teacher and coach,* ed 4, Champaign, Ill, 1987, Stipes Publishing.

Schot PK: Effective sprint starts, *Strategies* 6(1):9, 1992.

Seidel B et al: *Sports skills: a conceptual approach to meaningful movement,* ed 2, Dubuque, Ia, 1980, Wm C Brown.

Simons H, editors: *Heartbeat World Eskimo Indian Olympics,* Juneau, Alaska, 1986, Fairweather Press.

ANNOTATED READINGS

Connolly O: Shot put and discus, *JOPER* 51(1):65, 1980.
Presents an analysis of the shot and discus events and a training program for beginning athletes.

Cook T: Games of a Greek Olympiad, *JOHPER* 45(2):59, 1974.
Looks at teaching students about the Olympics by reenacting an Olympiad from 468 BC.

Dufek JS: Jump high . . . then what? making landings safe, *Strategies* 5(7):9, 1992.
Discusses safe landings from surfaces to footwear and their effects on the absorption of force.

Jones-Morton P: Skills analysis series, part 3, analysis of running, *Strategies* 4(1):22, 1990.
Analyzes the running pattern identifying five critical elements to running efficiency.

Jones-Morton P: Skills analysis series: part 4 the standing long jump, *Strategies* 4(2):26, 1990.
Analyses of the standing jump identifying five critical elements to efficient jumping.

Nelson J: Achieving horizontal velocity in the long jump and the triple jump hop, *Strategies* 1(5):19, 1988.
Examines the approach in the long jump to gain velocity for the jump.

Siegel J: Distance running, a game for primary age children, *JOPERD* 58(1):56, 1987.
A game introducing long distance running that maximizes competition.

Tenoschok M: Jogging geography, *JOPER* 49(6):68, 1978.
Discusses geography as part of a jogging program.

Wilkerson J: Shot put, glide and spin technique, *Strategies* 1(2):25, 1987.
Presents an analysis of the glide and spin technique in shot putting.

PART SIX

Dance and Rhythmic Activities

Dance and rhythmic activities are an essential part of the elementary school physical education program. Several kinds of dance and rhythmic experiences are developed in the following chapters. Creative dance gives children the opportunity to explore the use of the body in communicating ideas. Singing games and American and international folk dance provide group experiences in moving to the beat and phrasing of the accompaniment. Rhythmic activities present children the opportunity to move with a piece of small equipment to the musical accompaniment. Each experience contributes in a unique way to the goals and objectives of the physical education program.

OUTLINE

CHAPTER 19

Children's Dance and Rhythmic Activities

OBJECTIVES

After completing this chapter the student will be able to:

1. Describe the importance of dance and rhythmic activities in the elementary school physical education program
2. Define the content of the elementary school dance program based on the development of movement skills and the application of movement concepts with special emphasis on rhythmic elements
3. Provide suggestions that will enable the teacher to plan and conduct appropriate dance and rhythmic activities for elementary school children

Human beings have danced throughout the ages. They have danced to acknowledge the seasons, such as the planting and reaping of the harvest. They have danced in the celebration of their gods as well as before battle, and dance has often been the medium for demonstrating athletic prowess.

Today in many states, we are seeing a new curriculum emphasis in the arts and dance being recognized as an important part of arts education. In the schools, dance is often shared by physical education and music, with physical education assuming the major responsibility for the development of dance and other rhythmic skills. Dance and rhythmic activities have remained unchanged by the introduction of movement content into the elementary school physical education curriculum, because both have always used the movement content and the methodology associated with the movement approach.

THE VALUE OF DANCE AND RHYTHMIC ACTIVITIES IN THE ELEMENTARY SCHOOL PHYSICAL EDUCATION PROGRAM

Dance as an art and as the expressive entity of creative movement is vital to the development of the total individual. All of the arts provide ways in which human beings can bring shape and order to a fragmented and rapidly changing world. But dance provides a primary medium for expression involving the total self, rather than just a part, like the voice, or expression that is totally separated from the physical self, like painting or sculpture. Dance and the movement that produces it is "me" and, as such, is the most intimate of expressive media. A child's self-concept, identity, and self-esteem are improved in relation to such use of the body's movement. If we believe that movement plays a crucial role in the developing life of the child and that all education should foster creativity, then body movement as a creative medium in early childhood education has great significance (Murray).

Dance and rhythmic activities contribute significantly to the objectives of the elementary school physical education program. Dance and rhythmic activities are well known for their contribution, not only to an individual's skill development but also to the further development of the child's creative and rhythmic abilities. Dance is the only area of the physical education curriculum that deals with the arts and aesthetic education. In dance and other rhythmic activities, children have the opportunity to use movement to express their ideas and to develop aesthetically.

Children's body awareness is greatly enhanced by the opportunity to create their own movement sequences as they communicate their ideas to others. This body awareness is further developed as children use locomotor and nonlocomotor movements in their own or more traditional dances.

Other movement concepts become important as children learn the effective use of space and experiment with the movement qualities of force, balance, time, and flow. The development of rhythmic skills is an important part of the dance and rhythmic activities experience. Children may use their own natural rhythm or move to the imposed rhythm of the accompaniment. This imposed time adds another dimension to their understanding of themselves as movers.

Dance and rhythmic activities give children the opportunity to work alone or with others in small groups to solve movement challenges. Sharing in the decision making becomes increasingly important as children move through the elementary school years.

Dance and rhythmic activities are also important contributors to physical fitness. Through these activities, agility and flexibility are greatly enhanced, as is cardiorespiratory fitness. Moving to the imposed rhythm of an accompaniment may be one of the more invigorating and physically demanding experiences of the physical education program.

Dance as a Multicultural Experience

Dance is an embodiment of culture: a living, breathing culture-creating activity. It is a way of knowing, a way of communicating traditions, a kinetic human history (Frosch-Shroder).

Children's education is incomplete without the development of understanding beyond their own personal world. Dance is an important aspect of the multicultural experience of children. Through rhythmic activities, creative dance, and folk and ethnic dance children have the opportunity to gain a vital perspective of the human experience, past and present, of people around the globe. These experiences enable children to develop a new understanding of dance as a shared human heritage with an impact on American culture, the relationship of dance with the other arts, as well as the use of dance in religion, healing, recreation and entertainment, and in the transmission of history, stories, and legend.

DANCE AND RHYTHMIC ACTIVITIES IN THE ELEMENTARY SCHOOL

The Task Force on Children's Dance in Education formulated the following objectives as desirable outcomes of children's dance. These objectives also apply to rhythmic activities.

1. To assist the children through movement-centered dance activities and other movement experiences they may have to:
   - Realize their biological urges to experience primal patterns of movement
   - Develop an adequate degree of satisfaction in and mastery of their body movements for their own pleasure, confidence, and self-esteem
   - Greatly expand their movement resources by offering them many opportunities to explore, discover, invent, and develop different ways of moving and to structure sequences
   - Increase their aesthetic sensitivity by emphasizing the expressive and imaginative potential of their movements, as well as the physical and athletic aspects
   - Develop their appreciation of dance as art, by relating it to appropriate experiences in music, literature, painting, and sculpture
   - Relate their movements effectively to accompanying sounds and to music
   - Participate with others in recreational folk and ethnic dances by helping them learn traditional dance steps and understand the different ways they have been used through centuries of people dancing together
   - Make dances for themselves and others and, when they seem ready for the experience, perform them for peer audiences
2. To assist the children through audience-centered activities to:
   - Understand the ancient and honorable tradition of dance as art and ritual
   - Develop sensitivity to the essence of movement as communication as they observe the performances of their peers
   - Appreciate the many forms of dance that have evolved in different cultures, all based on common movement resources from which human beings have drawn for expressive purposes
   - Understand, as they grow older, something of the demanding discipline and training of the body necessary for a professional dancer
   - Enjoy viewing concert and theatre dance and develop a discriminating awareness of movement as an artistic medium (Murray)

Content of the Elementary School Dance and Rhythmic Activities Program

The elementary school dance and rhythmic activity program is composed of several different kinds of experiences. Dance activities include creative dance, singing games, dances of American origin, and international folk dance. Rhythmic activities include movement experiences with balls, ropes, hoops, sticks and other equipment to musical accompaniment. Besides the activities that are developed in the following chapters, ballet, jazz, tap, and other forms of dance may be included in the dance program. Teachers may not always feel qualified to deal with these varied forms of dance. Usually help may be found from local dance groups, dance companies, or dance studios. Intergenerational experiences in which adult groups teach and dance with children or the reverse in which children teach dances to their families can be an important part of the dance experiences in the elementary school.

Teachers in various subject areas may work together to provide an integrated dance experience. This integration goes beyond a teacher asking that children be taught some folk dances from a particular country they are studying in social studies. It includes an in depth study of the cultural aspects relating to the dance experience, its relationship to cultural life and art forms, etc. Combining creative dance, art, and music enhances the aesthetic development of children. Many forms of dance and rhythmic activities including folk and square dance are often taught with appropriate units in social studies. These experiences give new meaning to children's dance as they discover the relationship of their dance movement to other areas of study.

Dance and rhythmic activities depend on the use of locomotor and/or nonlocomotor skills and movement concepts. It includes an extension of the movement vocabulary into the study of dance.

Locomotor Skills

Locomotor skills involve the body moving through space from one place to another. They are defined as even and uneven movements. The even locomotor movements include the walk, run, hop, jump, and leap. The uneven movements are the skip, gallop, and slide.

The use of locomotor skills depends on the type of dance or rhythmic activity in which one is engaged. Locomotor skills may be used singly or in simple combinations as composed by the student. They may also be used in combinations imposed by the teacher or by the execution of dance steps as in the polka, step-hop, two-step, schottische, or waltz. Locomotor skills may be combined with other elements such as nonlocomotor movements, space concepts, rhythmic elements, or other movement qualities. Possibilities for combinations increase with the age and experience of the children. Locomotor movements are analyzed in Chapter 13. An analysis of dance steps may be found in Chapter 21.

Nonlocomotor Movements

Nonlocomotor or axial movements used in dance and rhythmic activities include bending, stretching, pushing, pulling, swinging, swaying, twisting, and turning. These movements may be executed individually or in combinations with other nonlocomotor movements and/or locomotor movements. Nonlocomotor skills may be varied in their use with the movement concepts. Younger children use them frequently in singing games as well as in creative dance.

Movement Concepts

All movement concepts are used in dance activities. Creative dance has traditionally made use of these concepts as the dancer attempts to communicate with the audience. The use of movement concepts has been on a more conscious level in dance than in other movement activities. The dancer must pay close attention to these concepts in expressing ideas in a meaningful way.

Body awareness is essential in the skillful use of the body in dance and rhythmic activities. The dancer must have full control of the body and its parts in making maximum use of the body in conveying ideas or performing intricate dance steps. Space concepts are important in using space in an interesting manner and in maintaining relationships with other dancers and/or equipment. Movement qualities are important in all dance and rhythmic activities. Force, balance, and time must all be used effectively. The following rhythmic elements are unique to these kinds of experiences:

Underlying beat or pulse beat: The underlying beat is the steady even beat found in any piece of music or rhythmic sequence.

Swing your partner in square dance.

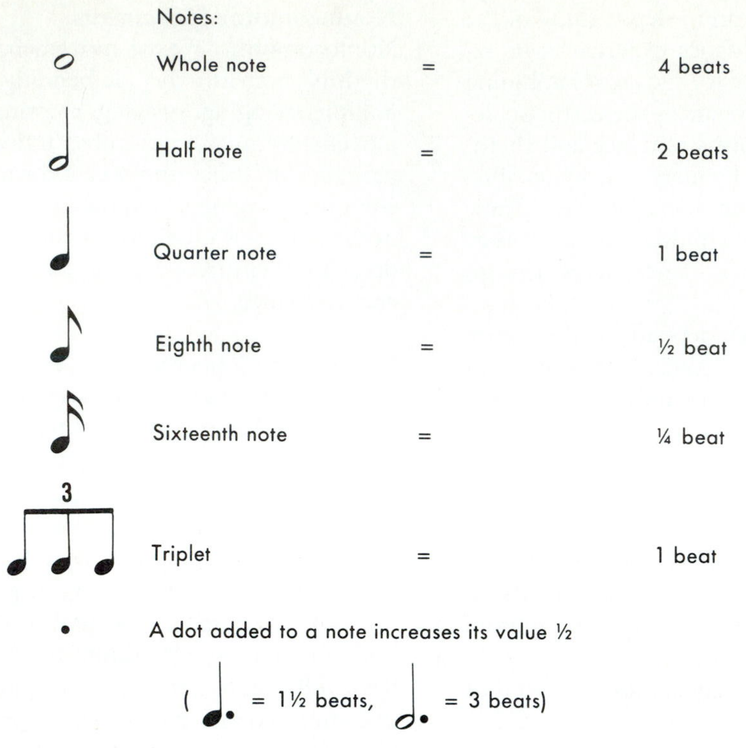

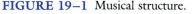

FIGURE 19–1 Musical structure.

Measure: A measure is a number of underlying beats grouped together into a unit, the number of which depends on the meter.

Meter: Meter indicates the number of beats in a measure such as 2/4, 3/4, 4/4, or 6/8. The upper number represents the number of beats per measure, the lower number the type of note getting the beat. For example, in 2/4 time there are two beats to the measure, with a quarter note getting one beat.

Phrase: A phrase is a group of measures that constitute a musical thought.

Rhythmic pattern: The rhythmic pattern is a combination of notes, even and/or uneven, that constitute a measure or a phrase.

Tempo: Tempo is the rate of speed—fast, moderate, or slow.

Accent: An accent is emphasis put on a beat. It is usually on the first beat of a measure, but it may occur on any beat.

Mood: Mood is the character of an accompaniment, which depicts a sadness, gaiety, seriousness, or other feelings.

Intensity: Intensity denotes the loudness or softness of an accompaniment.

Suggestions for teaching and using these rhythmic elements may be found in other chapters in the text.

Understanding and using these rhythmic elements are an important part of the dance and rhythmic activity experience. Many are concerned with the structure of

TABLE 19-1 PROGRAM EMPHASIS IN DANCE

LEVEL	CREATIVE	SINGING GAMES FOLK/SQUARE DANCE	RHYTHMIC ACTIVITIES
I	Use of locomotor/nonlocomotor movements and their variations Body awareness, space and quality of movement concepts Use of concrete ideas using imagination and fantasy Individual work Individual sharing of ideas	Use of locomotor/nonlocomotor movements Singing games and simple folk dances Move to beat and musical phrasing Moving with a partner in simple formations	Introduce balls, hoops, and sticks when adequate control is possible Explore possible movements Use music with clear beat Simple sequences of 2-3 skills with long repetitions of each skill Move to beat and musical phrasing
II	Simple combinations of locomotor/nonlocomotor movements of 2-3 motor skills Challenges increasing in complexity Body awareness, space and quality of movement concepts used in dance challenges Concrete ideas within their experience Individual and partner work	Simple folk and American dances Mixers Locomotor skills Simple dance steps Improved ability to work with partners and maintain formations	Object control improved Change skills more smoothly Shorter repetitions before changing skills Add rope jumping to skills used
III	Use motor skills and concepts at the same time Explore movement possibilities of each aspect before combining Challenges require more time to complete Want to develop their own unique ways of moving Need time to experiment with own movements Individual, partner and small group work Dances may require repetition Beginning to work with more abstract ideas	Square dance, international folk dance, line dance A variety of dance formations and partner relationships Use dance steps—polka, schottische step-hop etc. Learn background of dances also	Create simple sequences for partner and small group work Enjoy sharing ideas with others and trying new ways of moving with equipment
IV	Continued development in all areas Special interest in group work, but work as individuals and partners as well Continued growth in expressing ideas through dance Dances of longer development and duration	Increasingly difficult steps, figures, formations and partner relationships Two-step and waltz introduced	Utilize more advanced skills and more complex movement sequences May work several lessons to develop sequences Add space and quality of movement concepts in developing final sequences

music. A piece of music is made up of a series of notes arranged in measures. Measures in turn are arranged in phrases, and the combining of phrases completes the piece of music. These rhythmic elements form relationships in time, relationships of notes to notes, notes to measures, measures to measures, and eventually measures to phrases and phrases to phrases. If students are to fully use accompaniment as they move, they must understand these relationships and use them as they dance or create rhythmic sequences. They must, for example, understand how a movement sequence fits in time to the notes, measures, and phrases. They must learn to use phrasing in sequencing dance and rhythmic movements, to complete a movement thought, or to change formation and/or movement in a folk dance. An example of the structure of music is provided in Figure 19-1.

Program Emphasis

The developmental approach to dance and rhythmic activities enables the teacher to plan appropriate experiences for children based on experience rather than grade level.

Emphasis on each level assumes mastery of the previous level; however, the teacher must carefully select activities that appeal to the maturity of the students. The content is summarized in Table 19-1.

Level I

During these beginning experiences, children master the locomotor skills and begin exploring their variations through imaginative activities that challenge their body awareness and space concept understanding. Nonlocomotor movements are explored as well. Space, body awareness, and quality of movement concepts learned in previous units are integrated into the dance and rhythmic activities. In exploring time rhythmic elements are introduced as children move in space to a variety of accompaniments.

Creative dance is an important part of these beginning dance experiences. The movement challenges introduced deal with concrete ideas within the children's experience. Children enjoy using their imaginations and fantasy as they develop movements unique to themselves in solving the challenges posed. Most of the problem solving occurs on an individual basis, but occasionally the children may work with partners. Most enjoy sharing their ideas with others in the class.

Singing games and simple folk dances allow children to develop locomotor and nonlocomotor skills in time to music and to develop an awareness of musical phrasing. Many of the dances require moving with a partner and maintaining a relatively simple formation.

Rhythmic activities with hoops, sticks, and balls may be introduced when children gain some control in the use of such equipment. Children enjoy exploration in the use of the equipment as they move to music with a clear beat. They enjoy simple sequences of two or three skills, repeating each skill many times before changing to the next.

Due to the relatively short attention span of children at this level, the challenges and activities should be able to be accomplished in a short time.

Level II

During this developmental period, children explore simple combinations of locomotor and/or nonlocomotor movements moving at first in sequence and then simultaneously. Combinations developed may use variations of one skill as well as combinations of several locomotor and/or nonlocomotor movements. Combinations generally involve only two or three different motor skills.

The use of body awareness, space, and quality of movement concepts play an important role in the creative dance experiences. Individual and partner problem-solving activities continue with occasional work in small groups. Children generally continue to work with concrete ideas within their experience.

Simple folk and American dances are used at this level and include easy mixers in which the children change partners throughout the dance. Improvement is seen in their ability to move with a partner as well as in maintaining relationships with others in the formation. Some simple dance steps may be introduced toward the end of this level.

Ball control has improved substantially, enabling the children to be more successful in ball rhythms. Although repetition of each skill is important in developing movement sequences, children are able to change skills more smoothly after shorter repetitions of the preceding skill. Work with hoops and sticks continues, and the children may begin to jump rope to accompaniment.

Level III

Creative dance at this level includes challenges in which children are able to use several skills and concepts at the same time. As each new element is added, movement

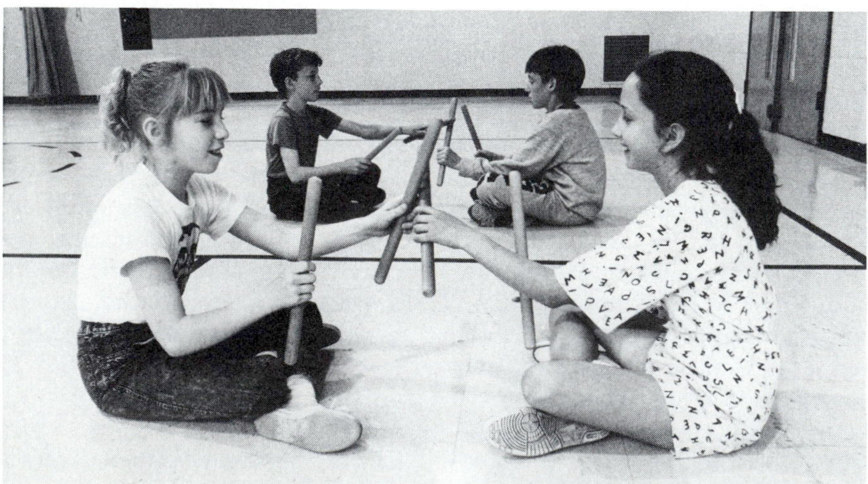

Lummi sticks

possibilities are explored before combinations with previously learned material are attempted. Movement challenges presented require a longer time to develop than those at level I or II. Children at this level are interested in developing their own unique ways of moving and need to be provided with sufficient time to experiment with the various movement possibilities for each challenge. The children may now work in small groups as well as individually or with a partner. Children are able to create dance sequences that may be repeated, and the creative dance activities begin to deal with more abstract ideas.

Square dance is introduced, and international folk dance and other American dances are continued. A variety of dance formations are used with various partner relationships. Dance figures such as the grand right and left are introduced. The dances are more demanding in that specific dance steps are used rather than the simple locomotor skills such as the walk, run, or skip, which were used in levels I and II. The polka, schottische, and step-hop are commonly used dance steps. Line and circle dances without partners also may be included. Children are interested in learning more about the background of dances and the people who created each dance.

Children at this level enjoy rhythmic activities with sticks, ball, hoops, and ropes. They can make up simple combinations of skills, which they may perform with a partner or in a small group. Many enjoy sharing their ideas as well as trying the ideas of others.

Level IV

Level IV is characterized by further development in all areas. Children are especially interested in group work at this level, but there should be time for individual and partner work as well.

Creative dance allows children to use their improved body awareness and other concepts and skills in communicating ideas. Dances may be developed over a series of lessons, with each lesson adding ideas to explore for the final product.

Combining nonlocomotor and locomotor movements.

Folk and square dances include increasingly difficult dance steps and figures, formations, and partner relationships. The two-step and waltz may be introduced at this level.

Rhythmic activities include more advanced skills and more complex movement sequences created by the children. Movement sequences may be developed over several lessons as children explore and share movement possibilities with others. They may begin developing a sequence of movements and then add a variety of space and quality of movement concepts in creating the final product.

PLANNING AND CONDUCTING DANCE AND RHYTHMIC ACTIVITY EXPERIENCES

Dance instruction requires creative teaching. Success depends on the teacher's ability to use problem solving as well as guided and free exploration. Many beginning teachers will feel inadequate in using these approaches. Experience is needed to master these techniques; the beginning teacher must plan and evaluate carefully the outcomes of the lessons.

Elementary school children need vigorous activity. Dance experiences should be planned with a maximum of activity. The lesson should move smoothly from one activity to the next, with some change of pace provided between activities that are vigorous. Generally, the activities should be short, although in the upper elementary grades children will remain interested in activities for longer periods of time. Instructions should be simple and to the point so that the activity can begin quickly.

Individual skills and the understanding and use of the movement concepts should be encouraged. Creativity in finding many different solutions to movement challenges should be promoted. Adequate space must be provided to give children the freedom of movement required to develop their own movement potential. When small equipment is used, there must be an adequate supply to maximize the activity of all children, and it must be of appropriate size and weight so that the children can control it easily. Adequate space is essential if the children are to use the equipment safely.

The dance experiences should include individual, partner, and small group work. Sharing ideas is an important part of the dance and rhythmic activity experience. Children should have the opportunity to work with all their classmates at one time or another. They should be encouraged to participate with different children as the lesson develops.

Movement challenges within the lesson or unit should move from the simple to the more complex. This process should be accomplished by working with single elements and gradually combining elements as children are able to deal with more than one element at a time.

In developing movement challenges in dance and other rhythmic activities, the teacher must give the children a framework within which to move. The teacher must think through carefully the objectives to be developed and the kinds of outcomes that will indicate mastery of the objectives. Children must be given sufficient information to successfully meet the objectives of the dance experience. This process does not limit creativity. Without a framework within which to work, there is little creativity. Playing a record and telling the children to move to the music will not result in creative movement responses. Not only will children become frustrated by having to make too many decisions, but also teachers will become frustrated by students who do not respond appropriately. In the younger grades, elementary school children work best with concrete ideas. As children progress through the elementary school grades they become increasingly able to deal with more abstract ideas.

Movement challenges should be structured around the content of the day's lesson solely or with previously learned material. Within a lesson, subchallenges are developed that lead into a culminating activity in which several ideas are used. The lesson usually begins with simple movement challenges in which the children work with a single concept or a movement idea. As the lesson progresses, the children add to their solutions by using additional concepts and movements.

Additional concerns for planning and conducting dance and rhythmic activity experiences may be found in subsequent chapters.

SUMMARY

Dance and rhythmic activities contribute substantially to the objectives of the physical education program in the elementary school. They expand the children's understanding of their own movement potential, contribute to their aesthetic development, and provide challenging activities in which human movement is further expanded. They also can be used to foster multicultural understanding. Many forms of dance and rhythmic activities may be included. Creative dance, rhythmic activities, folk and square dance, as well as ballet, tap, or jazz, may be a part of the dance experience, as children further develop their use of locomotor and nonlocomotor movements and use of the movement concepts.

REFERENCES AND RESOURCES

Bucek LE: Constructing a child-centered dance curriculum, *JOPERD* 63(9):39, 1992.

Carr D: Dance education, skill, and behavioral objectives, *Journal of Aesthetic Education* 18(4):67, 1984.

Dimondstein G: *Children dance in the classroom,* New York, 1971, Macmillan Publishing Co.

Dimondstein G: Moving in the real and feeling worlds, *JOPERD* 54(7):42, 1983.

Frosch-Schroder J: A global view dance appreciation for the 21st century, *JOPERD* 62(3):61, 1991.

Hanstein P: Educating for the future—a post-modern paradigm for dance education, *JOPERD* 61(5):56, 1990.

Joyce M: *First steps in teaching creative dance,* ed 3, Mountain View, Calif, 1993, Mayfield Publishing.

Murray R: A statement of belief. In Fleming G, editor: *Children's dance,* Reston, Va, 1981, AAHPERD.

Stinson S: Aesthetic experience in children's dance, *JOPERD* 53(4):72, 1982.

ANNOTATED READINGS

Allen B: Teaching training and discipline based dance education, *JOPERD* 59(9):65, 1988.
Examines dance as a discipline to be studied in the schools.

Baloche L and Blosko J: Learning together a new twist, *JOPERD* 63(3):26, 1992.
A multigrade approach to teaching dance at the elementary school level.

Barker JH: Body language, *Alaska Magazine* January 1992, p 23.
Discusses the use of dance to tell Yupik stories.

Brown C: Elementary school dance teaching rhythms and educational forms, *JOPERD* 57(2):39, 1986.
Provides suggestions for building dance lessons and a progression in learning from preschool through the sixth grade.

Gingrasso S and Stinson S: An update on states' dance curricula, *JOPERD* 60(5):31, 1989.
Looks at a report from 13 states regarding dance in the schools.

Hanson M: The right of children to experiences in dance/movement/arts, *JOPER* 50(7):42, 1979.
Discusses the value of dance/movement in the education of elementary school children.

Kerr KA: Analysis of folk dance with LMA-based tools, *JOPERD* 64(2):38, 1993.
Discusses the importance of folk dance as a part of dance education.

Mehrhof J, Ermler K, Kovar S: Set the stage for dance, *Strategies* 6(7):5, 1993.
Suggestions for preparing children for and conducting dance experiences.

Minton S and Beckwith B: Dance and sport—the elusive connection, *JOPERD* 57(5):26, 1986.
Discusses techniques used in the teaching of dance that can be applied to teaching sport.

Wallen LA: *The face of dance Yup'ik Eskimo masks for Alaska,* Calgary, 1990, Glenbow Museum.
Discusses dance as a part of Alaskan Yup'ik culture with pictures of dance masks.

Woodruff J: Improvisation for the inhibited, *JOPERD* 56(1):36, 1985.
Explains how to use improvisation to expand the dance experience and build confidence using contact with others and props.

Wyckoff W: Movement programs and aesthetic education, *JOPER* 51(4):65, 1980.
Discusses the goals of aesthetic education and the nature of movement programs in meeting these goals.

CHAPTER 20

Creative Dance

OBJECTIVES

After completing this chapter the student will be able to:

1. State the goals of creative dance in the elementary school
2. Give suggestions for planning and conducting creative dance experiences
3. Describe the content of creative dance at the elementary school level and suggest ways to develop it

The dancer is the communicator of ideas, the creator of moods, the entertainer, and the storyteller. To dance requires movements more purposefully executed than in any other movement activity. The dancer is perhaps the most controlled athlete of all. Besides being a skillful mover, the dancer must also understand how to use body parts to accomplish the goals of the dance. In no other movement form are the movements solely the result of the creative genius of the individual, because the dancer uses the body in unique ways controlling space, force, and time to create the dance.

CREATIVE DANCE IN THE ELEMENTARY SCHOOL PHYSICAL EDUCATION PROGRAM

Creative dance is the most neglected area of instruction in physical education. Many teachers feel inadequately prepared to plan creative experiences for children. Yet creative dance is a vital part of the children's physical education experiences. It is the only area in which creativity is a prominent goal. Although the movement-centered curriculum suggested in this book allows the children to develop ideas of their own, the solutions are more often functional rather than creative. Children learn about movement efficiency rather than the use of movement to express ideas and feelings. The creative dance experience for children should be characterized by a spontaneity in response to the movement ideas posed by the teacher, with the children discovering their own right ways to move.

In creative dance the emphasis is placed on helping children develop their expressive abilities by using the body as the instrument in which the ideas become manifest. Like the artist who paints a picture on a canvas, the dancer expresses ideas through body movement. A child may be skillful in performing various locomotor and nonlocomotor movements and may not be able to use these movements effectively in dance. The emphasis in creative dance is to teach the child to use body movements to communicate dance ideas. In creative dance the child is experimenting with movement rather than learning specific skills. At a later time dance technique may be mastered, but in the beginning stages the focus is on the act of moving itself.

Each child brings something unique to the dance experience. Each child varies in ability; some have disabilities. Each child has had different life experiences. These abilities and experiences affect the types of responses each child will make in exploring movement possibilities in dance, resulting in a dance experience unique to each dancer.

Movement in creative dance is a personal expression. As the children move, their attention is directed inward. The result is not only greater awareness of the body but also of the mind and feelings. This increased awareness of the total being is essential to success in the dance experience.

In creating a dance an individual moves with a series of locomotor and nonlocomotor movements, using the movement concepts to present the ideas. Creative dance extends children's understanding of movement. In analyzing a dance one discovers the dancer moving in space and controlling force and time. The use of these concepts is essential to the development of dances that are pleasing to both the performer and the audience.

The goals to be achieved in the creative dance experience are as follows:

1. To enhance the creative potential of each child
2. To develop skillful and controlled use of the body as a means of expression and communication
3. To develop an understanding and appreciation of dance

The creative dance experience should lead to increased self-esteem and confidence in one's ability to move. As a result, children should be able to move more freely in exploring their movement potential.

Although creative dance for young children is mostly an individual activity, children do have an opportunity to share with others in discussion and in performing their dances. The social skills developed focus on acceptance of others and their ideas as well as in later years working with a partner or small group to develop dance ideas. The class must be carefully structured to ensure that each child has an opportunity to contribute to partner and group activities.

Creative dance may also contribute to fitness objects. Many of the activities included in creative dance involve stretching and flexibility. Some activities, as well as the culminating dances, may require vigorous activity.

SUGGESTIONS FOR TEACHING

Creativity can only happen in an environment conducive to creative thinking. To be the model for such behavior, the teacher must do the following:

- Encourage the children to develop their own ideas
- Demonstrate a value for new ideas
- Give assurance to children engaging in the creative process
- Have resources available that encourage the children's search for ideas
- Encourage risk taking in problem solving
- Encourage nontraditional use of the body and objects
- Ask questions that require thinking
- Not leave creativity to chance

Planning the Lesson

The core of each lesson includes activities to enhance the children's awareness of themselves and to develop an understanding of the movement concepts emphasized and provide an opportunity for **improvisation.** The lesson is usually composed of a warm-up activity, the presentation of the movements and/or movement concepts to receive attention, an opportunity to experiment with the lesson material, and finally, the opportunity to use the lesson material in some simple form to create a dance. Continuity results in each part of the lesson building onto the next, flowing smoothly to completion. There should be a feeling of closure at the end of the lesson.

In planning the lesson the teacher must carefully determine the parameters within which the kinds of movements and concept use desired will result. This does not assume that all will move in the same way, but in a variety of ways within the framework provided.

Creative dance lessons need structure. Some teachers may feel that structure in the lesson deprives the children of a truly creative experience. However, the goals must be clearly defined with appropriate activities and questions to help children develop the lesson material. The children need some place to begin if they are to move creatively. It is a difficult task to be creative in too open an atmosphere. Instructions to move as the music tells them to move will be beyond the comprehension of most children.

The planned movement challenges guide each child in developing his or her interpretation of the materials (movements and concepts) used. The teacher determines the types of decisions that will need to be made—decisions determining the movements themselves or the use of the movements in the context of space, time, and force. The children make decisions that relate the conceptual ideas to their own personal movement.

If a theme is to be developed, such as a movement response to a child's poem, the teacher carefully analyzes the movement potential of the poem to be used. The teacher imagines some of the movements and concept use that may be important in the interpretation of the poem. The teacher then develops some movement challenges to explore the essential elements in preparation for the individually designed movements that the children will use in their original interpretations of the poem.

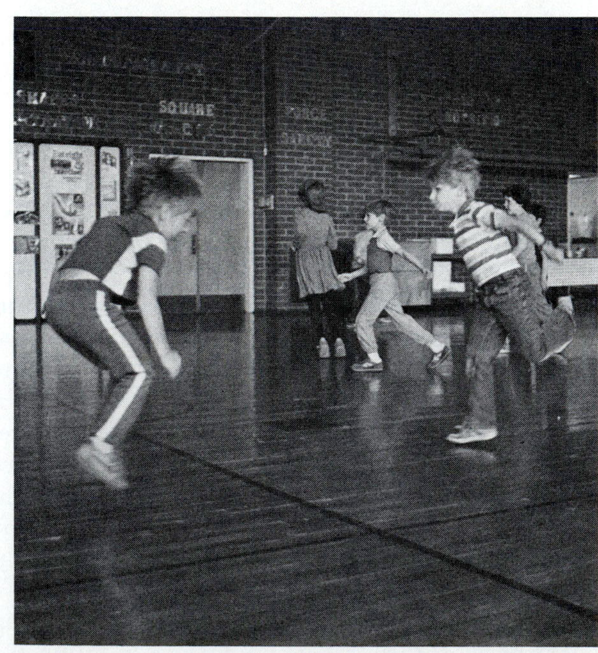

Children need time to explore their movements.

For instance, the poem might suggest certain kinds of locomotor movements, contrasting heavy and light movements and a change in level. After the teacher has explored these possibilities with the children, the poem is introduced to further stimulate the children's individual movements in expressing the ideas generated in the poem.

Lesson material must be carefully selected with consideration for the developmental level and experience of the children. For example, developing the idea of rag dolls may appeal to young children, but an older class may find it too juvenile. Activities within the experience of inner-city children will differ considerably from those for children who live in a rural or suburban setting.

Beginning the Lesson

After defining the area of the space to be used, warm-up activities related to the lesson objectives should get the children moving. Vigorous activities involving a movement or concept will prepare the children not only for physical activity, but also for mental activity.

Organization of the space may include moving alone, in partners, or in small groups, using all the space or moving in groups from one part of the room to another. The atmosphere of the class will greatly affect the responses of the children. The size of the space, physical obstructions, and the distractions of noise and other children will alter possible reactions to lesson material.

After the brief warm-up activities, the children are ready for the *presentation of the lesson material.* Lessons may be organized around a locomotor or nonlocomotor movement, an action of a limb such as extend or swing, or movement in relation to others. Lessons may also be organized around an idea, such as the wind or trees.

The lesson may be presented verbally or with the use of visual aids or props. Care should be taken to keep vocabulary appropriate to the developmental level of the children, with the teacher determining the most meaningful language to use. The suggested actions should be within the children's ability and understanding.

During this presentation phase of the lesson, the teacher conducts some guided experiences to help children become familiar with the material with which they will work. This approach should not limit the children's creativity, but should stimulate their interest to expand the possibilities for movement. The teacher must develop sensitivity to each child, knowing when to help and what questions to ask. The teacher must also be responsive to the group and must be able to judge when the children are ready to move on to the next part of the lesson.

Developing the Lesson

The activity may begin with concentration on one movement or concept and progress to others or combinations of others as the children become ready. For example, the lesson might include exploration of a locomotor or nonlocomotor movement followed by experimentation with the movement in space, varying force or time. There may be exploration of movements in self or general space, moving at different levels, in several directions, varying the degree of force or the time of the movements. Obviously, the first combinations must be simple. For example, the teacher may ask the following: How many different ways can you walk and change direction? This may be a challenge for the inexperienced young dancer. Each lesson should provide a variety of experiences to present a maximum of possibilities for movement. The teacher should ask questions and when necessary stop or restructure the activity to assist in the development of the lesson material.

It is important for the teacher to *avoid those experiences that result in imitation or pantomime.* "Dance is not about something. It is something in itself" (Joyce). Children should be taught to move as humans and not to imitate the movements of animals and other objects. The objective is human movement that takes on characteristics of the idea presented.

Imagery may inhibit creative responses, so *during the exploratory phase the use of imagery should be limited.* Some images may arise out of the activity. After working on galloping, the teacher might ask: What moves like that? If the children were exploring locomotor movements it might be more appropriate to have the children move lightly or heavily, or with big or little steps, rather than having them move like a mouse or an elephant. A more satisfactory approach is to explore the movements or concepts to be developed and then relate them to imagery.

Accompaniment may add considerably to the movement experience. However, it too may stifle creativity if presented at an inappropriate time in the lesson. In the beginning of the lesson, it may distract the children from the task of exploring movement. After some work on the lesson material it may give a new dimension to their creative efforts.

Children need the opportunity to work as individuals, with partners, and in small groups. In the early years, work is almost exclusively individual. As the children mature, work with partners and in small groups should be included. The teacher must carefully plan to ensure that the children have all the social experiences for which they are ready. At times the teacher may allow the children some choice about whether they work alone or with others. The teacher must ensure that children are not excluded from working with others if they so desire.

Conducting the Culminating Activity

After a time of exploration and experimentation, the children are ready for the culminating activity of the lesson, creating a dance that may be presented to the class. All dances should be put into a simple form. Dances should have continuity from beginning to end. They should begin from a definite starting position and should close in a manner that communicates that the dance is completed.

Children enjoy sharing ideas with others.

Once the starting position is assumed, some signal or accompanying music should mark the beginning of the dance. In the upper grades, where a dance may be more complex, the dance should be repeated often enough so that the movements flow continuously. In this way the dance will become a part of the kinesthetic memory rather than requiring conscious effort for each movement.

The dances of young children will be brief and spontaneous. They will be easily forgotten. Dances may be simply the result of the children's exploring the lesson material and then selecting one or two responses they liked best to show to others. Older children may develop some dances over time, such as the entire class period or several classes. In these dances they will begin working with one or two ideas and gradually add other movements or concepts as the dance is developed. The children may be asked to share their work with others at various times throughout the process. Sometimes the process of working on a dance seems to hit a plateau. Students may experience a time of unproductive efforts or a show of frustration as they try to think up and develop new ideas. The teacher may then sense that it is time for individuals or the group to move on to new material. These dances are generally movement sequences the children will remember and will repeat. If the dance is to be developed over several lessons, the children may need time at the close of the lesson to make some notes for next time.

The teacher must know the children well to determine how much direction is needed in developing dances. In the beginning the children will be able to concentrate on only one element at a time, such as exploring a locomotor movement or a space concept. The teacher can combine elements only when the children have had sufficient experience with individual elements to feel comfortable in combining them. Combining too many movements or concepts before the children are ready will only lead to frustration, because too many decisions must be made.

The teacher should plan carefully to allow sufficient time to explore the lesson material and to make up a dance. Even though the same lesson material may be used in several lessons within the unit, some closure on the lesson material should occur each day.

Young children are relatively uninhibited in performing in front of a group. Many children in the fourth, fifth, and sixth grades, however, may feel self-conscious when moving in front of others. Individual work may be presented to the group by having several children or one half the class perform at one time. This approach will help those children who have difficulty in getting up in front of the group, as well as move the presentations along more quickly.

The children should participate in a positive teacher-guided analysis and evaluation of the dances presented. Asking children what they especially liked in each dance performance is a good way to begin. Later, discussion may focus on the ways in which movements and movement concepts were used in the dances to express the dance ideas. Examples of questions that might be asked are the following:

What was the idea the dancer wished to present?
What movements were used?
How were they used to convey the idea of the dance?
What movement concepts were used?

How did they help the dancer present the idea of the dance?

What was your favorite part of the dance?

The teacher might also ask the children for ideas to further develop the idea of the dance. That is, what other ideas do you have that might be added to the dance?

Evaluation of the creative dance experience is essential and perhaps somewhat more difficult than in other activity areas. Because there is no one correct response, process may be more important than product. Evaluation serves two purposes. The first is to give feedback to the dancer. If the evaluation is to be effective, the teacher must know the children, their bodies and their movements, and the extent of their understanding of movement concepts. The teacher must be able to give all children the help they need to accomplish the lesson objectives. The teacher must know when the children need help, how to give it, and when the children need more time for work on their own.

The assessment of the dance experience might take several forms. It might be informal, answering some of the preceding questions to the children. It might be a more formal process. For example, today portfolio assessment is being developed in many curricular areas including dance. Portfolio tools for dance might include improvisation, class critiques of dances, journal writing, videotaping of dances, photographs, sharing ideas with others, costumes, accompaniment, use of props, or writing that becomes material for developing dances.

The second purpose of evaluation is to determine the extent to which lesson and unit objectives are being met. The teacher needs to ask some questions relating to the lesson: Were the class objectives met? Did the children enjoy the activity? Were the children successful in using the lesson material to create some movements of their own? How did the children use the movement content to develop their ideas? What did the children learn about their own ability to move? The teacher must remember that the movements are unique to each child. If the child is to continue to move creatively, the teacher must respect each child's original solutions to the movement ideas.

BUILDING CREATIVE DANCE LESSONS

Emphasis in the creative dance lesson is on the development of controlled, purposeful movement. Because the development of an understanding of the movement concepts in experiences throughout the school year is suggested, this chapter emphasizes the creative development of movement skills with use of the concepts already learned and the introduction of the terminology associated with creative dance. The movement concepts are developed strictly in a way that expands their use as the child begins to use movement to communicate ideas. Creative dance is an area where application of what is known about the movement concepts is used to develop dances unique to each child. The movement content of the creative dance experience is outlined in Figure 20-1.

As the children explore body movement and the use of the movement content, they are encouraged to develop their own interpretations in developing dances. They may begin with the experimentation of a body movement or a movement concept, gradually incorporating additional movements or concepts in their own way. In using body movements as a starting place, the child may quickly review the movement to be used and then explore variations and combinations of variations of the movement. Space or quality of movement concepts are then added to enrich the movement possibilities. Children in the early grades will work with simple combinations. As the children progress through the elementary school years in their dance experiences, the combinations increase in complexity. The result of these experiences should be increased body awareness and control, the development of a movement vocabulary, and the development of a repertoire of personal movement possibilities.

In using the movement content as a theme, exploration of the concept chosen will be followed by adding other concepts or movements that enhance the development of the general theme. For example, children might begin exploring movement in general space. They might then add some change in movement used. Later they might add a change of direction or moving to a particular rhythmic pattern.

One approach used in developing dances is the "movement box," in which children select cards with themes such as space, force, or time. Based on their cards, the children develop their dances individually, with a partner, or in a small group.

In another use of a movement box, the children select cards with movements on them. The children then create dances, putting the movements together in their own order and ways. At a more advanced level they might select a series of movements and movement concepts to use in creating their dances.

In developing the lessons, the teacher may begin with an exploration of movements or concepts related to a movement theme such as the circus or a child's poem. Movement concepts are used to enhance the movement ideas. Accompaniment and props, such as scarves, may also be used. The following activities are only a few of the possibilities for development in creative dance. The teacher may use the activities to develop dances in one area only, i.e., the body moves, or they may wish to incorporate ideas from several areas—body moves, in space, etc., depending on the experience of the students.

Body Movements

Body Shape

The body may assume many different shapes, which may be classified as round, stretched, twisted, or angular. These shapes may be symmetrical or asymmetrical. One

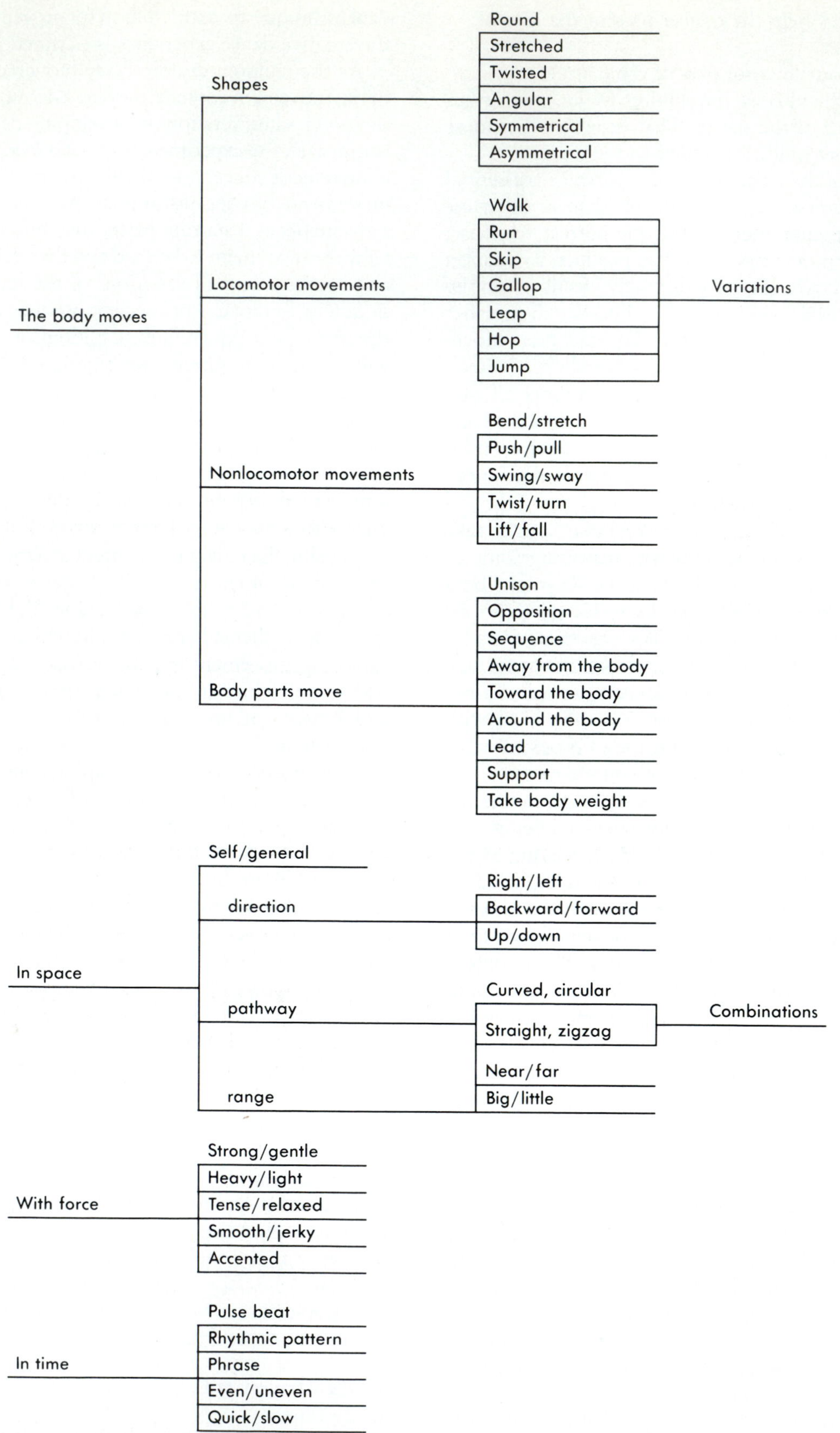
The body moves
Shapes
Round
Stretched
Twisted
Angular
Symmetrical
Asymmetrical
Locomotor movements
Walk
Run
Skip
Gallop
Leap
Hop
Jump
Variations
Nonlocomotor movements
Bend/stretch
Push/pull
Swing/sway
Twist/turn
Lift/fall
Body parts move
Unison
Opposition
Sequence
Away from the body
Toward the body
Around the body
Lead
Support
Take body weight
In space
Self/general
direction
Right/left
Backward/forward
Up/down
pathway
Curved, circular
Straight, zigzag
Combinations
range
Near/far
Big/little
With force
Strong/gentle
Heavy/light
Tense/relaxed
Smooth/jerky
Accented
In time
Pulse beat
Rhythmic pattern
Phrase
Even/uneven
Quick/slow

FIGURE 20-1 Movement content for creative dance.

body segment may assume a particular shape while another segment assumes a different shape. Body control is important in making and changing body shapes. In evaluating the use of body shape, the teacher should look for shapes that challenge the use of the body as children use body shape in their dances.

Body moves:

Explore a variety of different shapes in self space. Shapes may involve the entire body or parts of the body. They may involve shapes supported on different body parts. They may include shapes while standing, sitting, or lying on the floor.

Find a body shape. On the signal assume another shape. (Repeat several more times.) Now begin with a shape you liked, and as I beat the drum slowly change to another shape you enjoyed.

As the music plays, slowly make a shape keeping the movement controlled. Hold momentarily. Slowly and with control continue to change shape, holding each briefly until the music stops. Hold your final shape.

Can you make a dance putting your three favorite shapes together?

Find three different shapes in the room. Make your body into each of the three shapes. Make a dance using the three shapes adding any movement that might be involved.

Integrating with art, take the pictures you drew of shapes and make some of the shapes with your body. Can you combine several of the shapes from your drawings in an interesting dance?

Using props, ribbons, scarves, hoops, and ropes, make various shapes. Combine several of your shapes into a dance.

Make a shape with one body part. Move the shape to another body part. Try other shapes that move from one body part to another.

Make a dance by combining your favorite body parts and their shapes.

In partners, one makes a shape, the other copies it.

In partners, one makes a large shape, the other copies it as a small shape, or stretched and rounded, different bent shapes.

In partners, one makes a shape with a hole in it. The partner makes a shape in the hole.

Make up a dance with a partner using three to five shapes. Each may use the same shapes or different shapes.

Make shapes with a partner face to face, side to side, back to back. Make a dance putting the shapes together and changing shape.

Kaleidoscope shapes. Thinking of the shapes you saw in the kaleidoscope, make a shape with your partner (or a group of three). Make up a dance changing your kaleidoscope shapes.

Using scarves, ribbons, elastics, etc., combine shapes with two other children to make a dance with your equipment.

Make a dance with another child or two using one piece of equipment and using interesting shapes.

In space:

Move in general space and on the signal, make a body shape.

Make a shape while stationary. Now move with the same shape in general space.

Explore a variety of body shapes while moving in general space.

What shapes can you make as you walk? As you skip or gallop? Run? Hop? Jump?

With a partner, choose a shape. One holds the shape in self space while the other moves with the shape in general space. Reverse roles.

Half of the class moves in general space with a shape while the others hold a shape while stationary in self space. On the signal, a moving child assumes the shape of a stationary child near them and the stationary child moves with a new shape in general space.

With a partner, make up a dance using three shapes either stationary and/or moving.

Make a shape at the low level. Medium level. High level.

Move through general space, making shapes and changing levels as you go.

Combine four shapes at different levels into a dance.

Make a stretched shape as you move in a straight pathway. A round shape as you move in a curved pathway. Can you combine a stretched and a round shape as you combine a straight and curved pathway into a dance?

With force:

Make a tight shape. Now a relaxed shape.

Make a shape. On the count of 5, tighten your muscles in various body parts, but do not change your shape.

Make a shape. Tighten your muscles. Now gradually loosen your muscles, ending in the same shape but as relaxed and loose as possible.

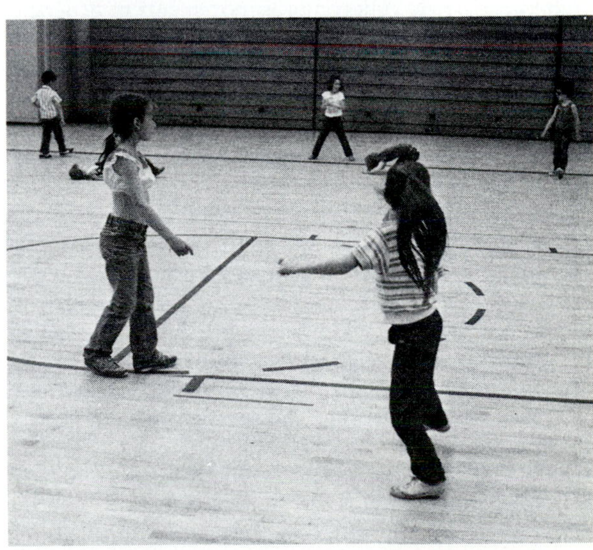

Moving in different ways through space.

Make a shape, gradually loosen your muscles to make a new shape. Now tighten your muscles to create another shape.
Create a dance changing shape by gradually loosening and tightening your muscles.
Change shape in a jerky fashion. Now change shapes as smoothly as you can, moving from one shape to the next without hesitation.
Create a dance in which you change shapes in smooth and jerky fashion.

In time:

Make a body shape. On the count of 4, slowly change to another shape. Hold.
Make a shape as slowly as possible. Make the same shape as quicly as possible.
Change shapes to the beat of the music, taking as many counts as you like.
Change shapes, moving to the rhythmic pattern of the music.
Make up a dance in which you change shapes to the beat and then to the rhythmic pattern of the music.

Locomotor Movements

Most children begin school with mastery of the locomotor movements of running, walking, hopping, and jumping. They may have had less opportunity for skipping, galloping, sliding, and leaping. Control of movement is emphasized as the children explore the use of body parts to perform the skills, modify the movements in a variety of situations, combine them into simple movement sequences, or use them in combination with other body movements. Emphasis in evaluation should be on the use of locomotor movements in a controlled and purposeful way to communicate dance ideas.

The body moves:

Explore a variety of locomotor movements in general space.
As you move through general space, change the locomotor movement on the accented beat of the drum, change in music, etc.
Create a dance combining your two favorite locomotor movements.
Explore variations of locomotor movements by selecting a locomotor movement and seeing how many different ways you can move in general space with that movement. Repeat with other locomotor movements.
Select one locomotor movement and make up a dance, changing the way you move several times.
Using imagery, move as if you are happy, sad, or tired or have a heavy load. The children may suggest other ways to move.
Move as if you were on ice, in mud, on a steep hill, on a sticky surface, etc.
Create a dance that tells a story about moving.
Move in general space in any way you wish with a locomotor movement. Stop. Do a nonlocomotor movement. Move again with a locomotor movement, stopping on the change of phrase in the music to do a nonlocomotor movement.
Make up a dance (ABA) combining a locomotor movement and a nonlocomotor movement beginning and ending with either.
Combine four walks and four hops. Perform the combination to the music. Try moving in different ways as you do the combination.
Make up a dance using the ways you liked best.
Beginning with the preceding combination or some other combination of locomotor skills, such as step, step, step, hop, have the children explore other four-beat combinations.
Choose your favorite combination and repeat it once for eight counts.
Try putting the two combinations together into a dance.

In space:

Explore a variety of locomotor movements, changing the size of your step.
Combine big and little steps as you cross the floor.
Create a dance using two different locomotor movements and varying the size of step.
Explore moving taking high and low steps. Pretend you have something high to cross. Use your dance to show how you would do it.
Explore in general space a variety of locomotor movements while changing direction.
Combine three locomotor skills with at least two changes in direction.
Explore moving with a partner in different ways while holding hands and moving side by side. Now one behind the other. Now facing each other.
Move with your partner, changing relationships on each phrase of the music.
Make up a dance changing relationships three times.
Explore moving in different ways across the room in a curved or straight pathway.
In a group of three, one is the leader and the others follow the path the leader takes. Change leader and pathway on each phrase of the music.
Create a dance in your group, changing pathways four times, once on each change of phrase in the music.

With force:

Explore moving as lightly as you can. Now as heavy as you can.
Listening to the drum, move lightly when the beat is light, heavy when the beat is heavy.
Combine a light and heavy movement into a dance.
Move suddenly. Explode as you begin the move. Try different ways of exploding as you begin to move or are moving.
On the drum beat, move smoothly, keeping the movement going as long as the drum sounds. Listening to a variety of rhythmic instruments, move and continue to move as long as you hear the sound.
Move smoothly and explode on the last beat of the drum.
Make jerky movements as you move in self space. Try jerky movements in general space.

Choose a jerky movement and combine it in general and self space, moving in any way you wish.

Make up a dance using at least two of the kinds of movements—explosive, smooth, or jerky.

In time:

Pick a locomotor movement and move to the music. As the music changes, move in a new way. Use different kinds of music as the children move.

Listen to the beat. Move to the even beat of the drum. Take a step on each beat. Try another movement.

Make up a dance combining even locomotor movements.

Listen to the uneven beat. Move in time to the uneven rhythm.

The drum will now beat even and uneven rhythms. Listen to the drum and move using an even locomotor movement on the even beats and an uneven locomotor movement on the uneven beats.

Make up a dance sequence using uneven locomotor movements.

Make up a dance combining at least two even and uneven locomotor movements.

Move with a partner matching them step for step. Try different movements.

Now in a group of three, each suggests a movement and you all move together.

Create a dance combining at least four different movements.

Make up a movement sequence lasting for eight beats that you can repeat.

Make up a movement sequence to one phrase of the music. Make up a new sequence for the second phrase. Repeat the first sequence on the third phase. (ABA)

Explore moving in different ways to different tempos, moving slowly and then at a faster speed.

Create a dance that includes at least three changes in tempo.

Body Parts and Nonlocomotor Movements

Besides movements that move the body through space, the body may also perform movements while stationary. Body parts may move to lead a movement, to take the body weight momentarily in a movement, or to support the body. Nonlocomotor movements include bending and stretching, pushing and pulling, swinging and swaying, twisting and turning, and lifting and falling. A description of these movements may be found in Chapter 13. These movements may involve body parts moving in unison, in opposition, or in sequence, with one body part beginning to move followed by one or more body parts. Nonlocomotor movements include movements toward the body, away from the body, and around the body. Many variations and combinations are possible. The teacher should look for unique ways of performing these skills.

The body moves:

Explore possible movements of body parts, i.e. bend, stretch, twist, turn, push, pull, swing, sway.

With a partner, facing each other, one moves and the other mirrors the movements. Move a body part. Keep that part moving as you transfer the movement to another part.

Working with a partner do the same movement your partner does. Now the same movement with another body part.

Create a dance with your partner using two different movements suggested by each person.

Move two body parts in the same way. In different ways.

Begin a movement in one body part and gradually move the movement to adjoining body parts so that the movement begins with one body part and moves to others. Try moving in different ways.

Combine movements with a partner.

The teacher raises a question to stimulate thinking.

Create a dance in which the movement flows from one dancer to another.
Explore moving different body parts in unison.
Move body parts in opposition.
Combine a movement in unison with a movement in opposition.
Choose a movement. Create a dance combining unison (or opposition) movements of different body parts.
Put a piece of elastic around two body parts. Initiate a movement with one and have the attached part move with it.
Initiate another movement and have the attached part resist the movement.
Combine two or three movements initiated by the attached body parts moving in sequence or in resistance to the movement.
Working with a partner, attach a piece of yarn loosely to a body part (not around your neck) and to the same body part of your partner. One begins the movement with the attached body part following the movement. Try moving in different ways.
Create a dance with each person initiating a movement in turn, which is followed by the attached body part of the partner.

In space:

Explore moving in self and general space in a variety of ways, identifying the body parts moving in unison, opposition, and in sequence.
Move body parts in unison (or opposition) changing movements on the accented drum beat.
Combine two to four movements (all unison, all opposition, or some of each) to make a dance.
Move two body parts in unison, opposition, or sequence as you change level.
Explore unison, sequence, and opposition movements while moving different directions.
Select two movements in unison and one in opposition and combine with a change of level or direction for your dance.
Working with a partner, choose a couple of movements. One moves in unison, the other in opposition. Dance your movements.

With force:

Explore moving various body parts forcefully.
Swing your arms forcefully and let the momentum of the swing carry the body either forward or backward. Feel the power in your arms. Repeat while swinging some other body part.
Now try swinging different body parts gently.
Combine a forceful swing and a gentle swing.
Create a dance using two forceful movements and three gentle movements ending on a gentle movement.
Move smoothly. Now sharply.
Combine a smooth and a sharp movement.
With a partner, one of you move smoothly and the other attempt similar movements but perform them in a jerky manner.
Make a shaking movement with your hand. Try shaking other parts.
Combine with a partner and make a shaky dance.

In time:

Move to the beat of the drum or music. As the beat changes, change your movement speed to match it. Try a different movement on each phrase.
Create a dance with two different movements, one for each of two phrases, one of which is slow, the other fast.
With various rhythm instruments, move body parts as long as you hear a sound. How did your movements change with a triangle? A wood block?
With a partner, one plays the rhythm instrument, the other dances to the beat or the extended sound. The movement ends as the music fades away.
Move a body part with an accent on the beginning of the movement.
Try accenting the movement in different ways.
Move to the beat of the drum, listening to the drum beat and then accenting your movement on the same beat.
Make up a dance in eight measures (four beats each) with one movement but accenting one of the beats in each measure in a different way. You may include four to eight different ways to accent the beat.

Movement Concepts

The movement concepts of space, force, and time are important to the dance experience. While it is suggested in the previous section that they be treated in relation to the movements of the body, they may also be developed as separate aspects of the creative dance experience.

Space

Effective use of space is extremely important in establishing the mood or feeling of the dance. The use of space may produce a feeling of limited or boundless energy. The amount of space used affects the movement by either limiting or expanding the movement potential of body parts. Changing direction and levels adds interest to the dancers' performance. The effective use of pathways, or floor pattern as it is referred to in dance, can contribute to the audience appeal. The careful consideration of the arrangement and interaction of the dancers also adds to the dance.

As dancers move in space, they define the space to the audience, whether the movements are performed in self space or general space. Children need to develop an awareness of their own personal space and the surrounding space that may be used.

Moving with others increases an understanding of changing relationships with others or objects. Moving in space helps children increase the awareness of their own movement potential through the exploration of self space and general space and the use of direction, level, range, and pathway to express ideas.

Force

Through the study of body movements, children develop their awareness of internal force, which their bodies create, and external force, gravity, to which their bodies must respond. The control of these forces gives quality to the actions of the body. The child moves in a purposeful and controlled manner as the dance movements are performed. Force may vary from the apparent absence of force in complete relaxation to the production of a force, the maximum the body can produce. In each body movement, force in one or more body parts is produced as the body moves through space and in response to the pull of gravity on the body.

Force may be created and used in a variety of ways. It may be smooth, of a sustained nature, in which there is a constant smooth flow of energy. It may be percussive or jerky, in which the force appears to come suddenly, in an explosive manner, or it may be vibratory or shaky and result in a fluttering, staccato, back-and-forth action. As the body moves in dance, it may give the appearance of lightness, weightlessness, heaviness, or strength. The control of these qualities is essential to convey the ideas to the audience.

The activities listed in the previous sections may be taken as a study in themselves or as a part of the developing awareness of the body's movement potential.

Time

Time includes the study of tempo, fast to slow, and the study of the rhythmic elements related to music (see Chapter 18). Because little time is spent on rhythmic elements in other aspects of the program, they should be given attention in the creative dance experience. The children should develop an awareness of the rhythm of their own body actions and also of the movement that is performed with an external or imposed rhythm, such as moving with another person or moving to an accompaniment.

Moving in response to the underlying beat, rhythmic pattern, and phrasing may be further enhanced through the following activities:

Clap time to the underlying beat, move in place, or move in space.
Perform locomotor or nonlocomotor movements to various meters, including 2/4, 3/4, 4/4, and 6/8 time.
Use rhythm instruments to establish the underlying beat for movement.
Clap the rhythmic pattern of your name. A nursery rhyme. A commercial. Repeat with locomotor or nonlocomotor movements.
Clap the underlying beat of a nursery rhyme. Now clap the rhythmic pattern. Clap one and move to the other.
Combine even and uneven rhythms by clapping. Now move to the pattern.
Make up a rhythmic pattern and plan a movement sequence to go with it, adding other concepts as appropriate.
Clap the phrases of a piece of music. Now clap the first, move on the second, clap the third, etc.
Move in general space on one phrase, and move in place on the next.
With a partner, alternate moving. One moves on the first phrase, the other on the second. Continue to alternate moving with each additional phrase.
Contrast movements. On the first phrase take big movements, on the second small movements.
Change level, direction, or pathway on each phrase.
Clap on the accented beat.
Emphasize the step on the accented beat.
Try accenting beat 1, then 2, 3, 4. Accent beats 1 and 3 or 2 and 4.
Move on the accented beat; clap on the others.
Do a nonlocomotor movement on the accent and a locomotor movement on the unaccented beats.
Combine a series of locomotor movements and clap the rhythmic pattern.
Divide into groups assigned whole, half, quarter, and eighth notes, moving to your specified beat as the drum is played. Now try it again as the music plays.
Move in step with a partner with no accompaniment.
In groups, move as if singing a round.

Imagery

The use of imagery may enhance or prevent creative movement. If used too early in the experience, it may limit the movement possibilities for children. But if used after there has been adequate time for exploration of possible movements, it may be a stimulus for creative activity. Joyce suggests the images may (1) lead to a movement, (2) arise from a movement, or (3) be the basis for moving. In the first instance, the teacher may use an image to describe the type of movement desired, such as describing a round shape as being round like a ball. Images that arise from movement may be used to develop an idea. For instance, when the class is working on jumping, the teacher might ask the children, "What do you know that jumps?"

The teacher might use a story, poem, or theme to stimulate creative movement activity. Images may arise from the seasons, the environment, holidays, animals, emotions, geometric lines and figures, moods, words, etc. Possible categories and examples for the use of imagery in developing creative dance lessons are given in the box on p. 382.

If used appropriately, imagery results in increased awareness of elements found in the image and the use of the body to convey the ideas. Images guide the elements being developed and evoke more than imitation. The child dances the element rather than being the image. As

IDEAS FOR DEVELOPING DANCE LESSONS

Holidays
- Halloween
- Columbus Day
- Christmas
- Valentine's Day
- Thanksgiving

Seasons
- Fall
- Spring
- Winter
- Summer

Texture
- Soft
- Scratchy
- Slick
- Smooth
- Sticky
- Rough
- Sharp
- Fuzzy
- Hot
- Cold

Nature
- Trees
- Bugs
- Worms
- Wildflowers
- Squirrels
- Porcupines
- Skunks

Emotions
- Happy
- Sad
- Angry
- Devilish
- Playful
- Jealous
- Anxious
- Afraid
- Lazy

Substances
- Glue
- Ice
- Whip cream
- Hot fudge
- Jello
- Peanut butter
- Lemons
- Cotton candy

Ocean
- Waves
- Surf
- Sand
- Seashells
- Jelly fish
- Crabs
- Fish
- Whales
- Seaweed

Words
- Ooze
- Squirm
- Crash
- Screech
- Tingling
- Swishing
- Flutter
- Creepy

Rhyming words
- Bright, fight, light
- Blue, glue, moo
- Ball, call, fall
- Cool, pool, rule

Cartoon Characters
- Garfield
- Peanuts
- Donald Duck
- Mickey Mouse
- Goofy
- Chip and Dale
- Muppets

Children's stories or rhymes
- Snow White
- Goldilocks and the 3 Bears
- Green Eggs and Ham
- Peter Rabbit
- 3 Blind Mice
- Jack and Jill
- Hickory Dickory Dock

the children explore the image, discussion to identify important elements further develops their concept of the image. Examples of the development of three of these themes may be found in the box on p. 383.

In selecting appropriate images, the age of the children and their immediate experiences must be considered. Poetry, favorite stories, or other writings may be used as themes. Young children enjoy working with nursery rhymes because of their familiarity, their rhyming nature, and also the even meter. Humorous stories or poems are another favorite. Older children may enjoy poetry with an irregular meter, which allows them to establish their own sense of time.

Using Materials to Stimulate Creative Movement

Materials or props may be used to stimulate creative movement. At certain ages, some children may be extremely self-conscious when working on their own. The use of some prop may help them to overcome these feelings. Scarves, ribbons, elastic ropes, feathers, and pompons may be used effectively in dance experiences. An umbrella, a rolling pin, a sponge, or a top are a few of the common objects that might be used to stimulate creative movements. The movement of scarves, ribbons, and other equipment become an extension of the body movement. Children may each work with a piece of equipment or may share one piece of equipment in some way, such as moving it from one to another or each holding the equipment at the same time and moving in some way.

Children may choose from a box of props or be assigned the same or different pieces of equipment. Using the movement box idea, they might draw the equipment they will use. Children might also explore a theme using several different pieces of equipment and then choose one for their final dance. Several children might create a dance with the same props or with different props.

An example for using scarves as a theme may be found in the box on p. 383.

POSSIBLE IDEAS FOR DEVELOPING THEMES

Theme: Winter Snow
Concepts Developed: Symmetrical shapes, gentle and strong forces, pathway, general space, level
Explorations:
Shapes of snowflakes, alone or with a partner
Moving in space—floating softly down, whirling in a snow storm
Covering everything, drifting
Melting
Dance: Make up a snowflake dance combining the above elements

Theme: Outer Space
Concepts Developed: Self and general space, variations in force, ways to travel/land, shapes, possible movements of the body
Explorations:
Moving in the spaceship and in endless space
Floating in space, taking off and landing
Arriving at destination—lack of gravity, different surfaces
Meeting others—aliens and new creatures—shapes, movements, reactions
Dance: In two's or three's make up a story about your space trip and a dance

Theme: Dancing Scarves
Concepts Developed: Pathways, light and heavy force, quick/slow tempo, body movements, levels
Explorations:
Movements of scarves—circles, spirals, serpentine quick/slow, floating/more energy, light/heavy
Body movements—moving the scarf and body in a variety of ways, moving with a partner with a scarf, moving copying the movements of a scarf moved by someone else
Color—words to describe the color ("red makes me feel hot"), movements to describe words
Dance: Dance your color

SUMMARY

Creative dance experiences for children provide further development of movement skills and movement content. Whereas other aspects of the curriculum concentrate on the development of functional movement, creative dance develops movement as a means of personal expression. In creating dances, children use body shape and locomotor and nonlocomotor movements as they move in space, with force, and in time.

Creative dance can be a valuable experience in the physical education program. Because it is the only area of the curriculum dealing with aesthetic education, creative dance makes an important contribution to the development of the total child.

REFERENCES AND RESOURCES

Benzwie T: *A moving experience: dance for lovers of children and the child within,* Tucson, Arizona, 1988, Zephyr Press.

Bucek L: Constructing a child-centered dance curriculum, *JOPERD* 63(9):39, 1992.

Dimondstein G: *Children dance in the classroom,* New York, 1971, Macmillan.

Dimondstein G: Moving in the real and feeling world: rationale for dance in education, *JOPERD* 54(7):42, 1983.

Docherty D: Organizing and developing movement ideas, *JOPERD* 53(3):51, 1982.

Fleming G, editor: *Children's dance,* Reston, Va, 1981, AAHPERD.

Gilbert A: A conceptual approach to studio dance, pre k - 12, *JOPERD* 63(9):43, 1992.

Gilbert A Green: *Creative dance for all ages,* Reston, Va, 1992, American Alliance for Health, Physical Education, Recreation and Dance.

Jensen M: Composing and guiding creative movement, *JOPERD* 54(1):85, 1983.

Joyce M: *First steps in teaching creative dance to children,* ed 3, Mountain View, Calif, 1993, Mayfield Publishing.

Lee MA: Learning through the arts, *JOPERD* 64(5):42, 1993.

Logsdon B et al: *Physical education for children: a focus on the teaching process,* ed 2, Philadelphia, 1984, Lea & Febiger.

McColl S: Dance as aesthetic education, *JOPER* 50(7):44, 1979.

Ritson R: Creative dance: a systematic approach to teaching children, *JOPERD* 57(3):67, 1986.

Russell J: *Creative dance in the primary school,* ed 3, Plymouth, NJ, 1987, Northcote House.

Sandback P: Structuring beginning choreographic experiences, *JOPERD* 57(9):38, 1986.

Smith KL: Dance and imagery—the link between movement and imagination, *JOPERD* 61(2):17, 1990.

Speakman M: Teaching modern educational dance, *JOPER* 49(7):51, 1978.

Stinson S: *Dance for young children: finding the magic in movement,* Reston, Va, 1988, AAHPERD.

Trammell P: Poetry and dance for children, *JOPERD* 53(7):75, 1982.

Winters S: *Creative rhythmic movement for children of elementary school age,* Dubuque, Ia, 1975, Wm C Brown.

Zirulnik A and Young J: Help them "jump for joy," *JOPER* 50(7):43, 1979.

ANNOTATED READINGS

Clements R: Making the most of movement narratives, *JOPERD* 62(9):57, 1991.

Describes steps and examples in using movement narratives such as science fiction movies and comic strips for developing children's creative movement.

Gelbard E: Dance—an aesthetic pie, *JOPERD* 59(5):31, 1988.

Discusses aesthetic theories—imitation, expression, and form.

Hankin T: Presenting creative dance activities to children: guidelines for the nondancer, *JOPERD* 63(2):22, 1992.

Suggestions for guiding the creative experiences of children.

Hottendorf D: Mainstreaming deaf and hearing children in dance classes, *JOPERD* 60(9):54, 1989.
Suggestions for helping children with hearing disabilities get the most from dance classes.

Lloyd M and West B: Where are the boys in dance? *JOPERD* 59(5):47, 1988.
Traces the history of writing about boys in dance since 1925.

Mangelson L: Stimulating the creative process and evaluating the choreographic products, *JOPERD* 58(3):67, 1987.
Discusses the importance of understanding the creative process, learning the craft of choreography, and developing effective systems of evaluation in acquiring a discriminating choreographic eye.

Minton S: Improvisation, *JOPERD* 52(7):74, 1981.
Describes the use of movement exploration or improvisation to discover the body's potential for movement, to enhance creativity, and to work with others.

Purcell T: Children's dance—a place to start, *JOPERD* 60(1):14, 1989.
Offers suggestions for teaching dance.

Purcell T: The use of imagery in children's dance: making it work, *JOPERD* 61(2):22, 1990.
Suggestions for using imagery in teaching children's dance.

Schmitz NB: Children with learning disabilities and the dance/movement classes, *JOPERD* 60(9):59, 1989.
Suggestions for teaching LD children in dance/movement classes.

Stenson S: Evaluate the child: issues for dance educators, *JOPER* 50(7):53, 1979.
Discusses the issue of evaluating dance experiences and its use in the learning process to provide feedback for developing self-awareness.

Wiseman E: Process not product: guidelines for adding creative dance to the elementary school curriculum, *JOPER* 50(7):47, 1979.
Provides steps for developing children's dance lessons, including an introductory activity, body actions, skill focus, and group interactions.

Woodruff J: Improvisation for the inhibited, *JOPERD* 56(1):36, 1985.
Uses improvisation to expand the dance experience and build confidence through contact with others and props.

CHAPTER 21

Singing Games and American and International Folk Dance

OBJECTIVES

After completing this chapter the student will be able to:

1. Define the objectives for singing games and American and international folk dance at the elementary school level
2. Offer suggestions for teaching dance and dance steps and to provide management strategies for dividing the group into partners
3. Analyze dance steps and figures and define dance terminology, formations, and partner relationships
4. Identify the movement concepts important to success in performing dances and suggest activities for their development
5. Describe a progression for the following types of dances to be included at the elementary school level: singing games, American and international folk dances, square and line dances, and dances of Native Americans

The dances included in this section represent the potential for a lifetime of activity. Beyond the school years the opportunity to continue to dance may be found in the many folk dance groups and recreation programs, as well as at weddings and other festive occasions.

SINGING GAMES AND AMERICAN AND INTERNATIONAL FOLK DANCE FOR ELEMENTARY SCHOOL CHILDREN

Dance provides the vigorous activity needed for optimum cardiovascular development. Response to musical accompaniment requires the dancer to maintain a consistent activity level over the duration of the dance. It is not uncommon for dancers to continue until they are virtually ready to drop. Coordination, balance, and agility are other fitness components important for success in these activities.

These dances provide an opportunity to focus on multicultural aspects of the curriculum. Dance experiences have the potential for increasing children's understanding of people of other lands, as well as of their own national heritage. The forms of dance included in this chapter are often integrated with other school subjects such as social studies, language arts, music, and art.

Folk and similar dance activities require partners and small and large groups to work together. Children must be able to adjust their movements to those of other dancers to move effectively with a partner and to maintain appropriate relationships with others while moving in different formations.

The progression of activities provides the opportunity for children to learn increasingly difficult dance steps and figures that must be executed to the imposed rhythm of the accompaniment. Increased body awareness and effective use of space and movement qualities are the results of these dance experiences. Objectives to be emphasized at each level during the elementary school years may be found in the box on p. 386.

Several kinds of dances make up the elementary school dance experience:

Folk dance: A folk dance is a traditional dance of the people, handed down from generation to generation. Folk dances were often associated with the customs, rituals, and occupations of the people but are now mostly performed for social or recreational purposes. Because American culture is relatively young, these dances are primarily dances of other lands.

Singing games: Singing games are activities for young children that are often the result of putting children's poems to music and imitating the actions described in the song.

American dances: American dances are the dances of colonial America in which popular country tunes of the period were used.

Line dance: Line dances are dances of American origin performed in lines or scattered in general space without partners to contemporary music.

Square dance: Square dances are dances of American origin that are executed from a four-couple square set. Because many of the movements are relatively new, they are not considered to be true folk dances. Some of these dances may also be performed in a large circle.

Contra dance: Contra dance is a dance performed by several couples facing each other in two lines.

Native American dance: These dances originated with Native American groups and were performed during ceremonies or at various social occasions.

In addition to the dances included in this chapter, children may create their own dances, using dance formations, steps, and figures they have learned to their own musical selections. Special occasions such as holidays may create an opportunity to make up their own "folk" dances to selections such as Jingle Bells, a Sousa march, etc.

SUGGESTIONS FOR TEACHING

Steps in Teaching a Dance

1. Teach or review the dance steps and/or figures to be used.
2. Give the name and origin of the dance and any other background information.
3. Teach the words to singing games and other dances that have words before beginning instruction in the dance. A poster or other visual aid may be helpful in teaching the words to the song.
4. Before explaining the dance, arrange the children in the formation to be used. This approach enables the children to visualize the partner and group relationships, which will help them in understanding the dance.
5. Break the dance down into logical parts (phrases), and have the children move through the dance. If the dance is long, it may be necessary to work with one part at a time, putting it to music, moving on to the next part, putting it with the first, and so on.
6. Listen to the music, and talk the class through the dance. Everyone listens but does not actually do the dance.
7. Try it with the music, slowing the music down if necessary. Move to the appropriate tempo when the children are ready.

Teaching a Dance Step

1. Select a formation that allows everyone to see.
2. Demonstrate the dance step, and talk through it as you move. Always move in the same path as the students, even if you are facing them. If the step will be done in partners, demonstrate with a partner.

SINGING GAMES AND AMERICAN AND INTERNATIONAL FOLK DANCE OBJECTIVES IN THE ELEMENTARY SCHOOL

OBJECTIVE	LEVEL*			
	I	II	III	IV
To develop locomotor skills (walk, run, hop, skip, gallop, slide)	■	■	⋯	⋯
To develop nonlocomotor skills	■	■	⋯	⋯
To respond to the underlying beat while executing locomotor and nonlocomotor movements	■	■	■	⋯
To respond to musical phrasing	■	■	■	⋯
To combine locomotor and nonlocomotor movements in time to the music		■	■	⋯
To differentiate even and uneven rhythm	■	■	⋯	⋯
To learn and use basic dance steps			■	■
To work with a partner and the group in executing dances	■	■	⋯	⋯
To move in space maintaining relationships with partners and others in the group	■	■	■	⋯
To vary the range of movement as needed		■	■	⋯
To change direction and/or pathway in time to the music	■	■	⋯	⋯
To control force in moving with another person	■	■	⋯	⋯
To change speed smoothly in time to the music		■	■	⋯

*Solid bars represent emphasis of an objective; dotted lines represent continued use of the mastered objective.

3. Have the children first try the step individually and when ready, practice with a partner.
4. It may be necessary to slow down the music in the initial phase of learning. As the children begin to master the dance, the music may be gradually brought up to tempo.
5. Put the steps into a movement sequence.
6. Add a change of direction, speed, and so forth.
7. Dance steps may also be taught through guided discovery, with the students working alone or with partners.

Methods of Selecting and Working with Partners

1. Move the children quickly into formation and into partners.
2. Change partners often so that children have the opportunity to dance with as many other children as possible.
3. Avoid having the children choose their own partners at random, as it may be embarrassing for them; one or two children may be left out, which is a threatening situation for them. It also takes more management time and therefore takes valuable time away from the lesson.
4. Several methods may be used for getting partners.
   a. Have the children form a circle or a line. Usually, they will be next to someone with whom they would like to dance. You may then designate the partners.
   b. Have the class form two lines facing each other. The children across from each other are partners.
   c. Partners may also be selected by forming a double circle, each circle moving in the opposite direction. On the signal to stop, children closest to each other (one from each circle) are partners.
   d. Have the children select a card upon entering. Cards may be pictures, words, opposites, etc. Each child matches a card with another student to determine partners, positions in a square, etc.
5. Below the fifth grade level, do not insist on boy-girl partners. Dance is to be enjoyed, and at some ages students may feel uncomfortable with the opposite sex.
6. Adjust dance positions when necessary. It may be uncomfortable for a short boy to use the varsouvienne position with a tall girl.
7. It is often unnecessary for children to hold hands with partners, especially when moving around the circle. Do not make physical contact mandatory. At some ages this may lead to negative feelings about dance. Holding hands, however, is helpful in maintaining the formation.
8. When boy-girl partners are not used, the use of pinnies, sashes, vests, hats, or scarves will help distinguish partners. This is particularly helpful when teaching figures such as the grand right and left.
9. The closed dance position assumes the ability to lead. Because elementary school children find leading difficult, dances requiring this position would be modified to use a position more within the children's capability.
10. Some dances do not require partners or may be modified to groups of three. These dances work well at the beginning of the lesson or unit.

Effective Teaching

1. Because children are eager to participate, select dances that may be mastered in a reasonable amount of time.
2. Many of the dances for young children can be learned by merely imitating your actions, so formal instruction may not be necessary.
3. Indicate the actions of the dancers by calling on pinnies or non-pinnies rather than by giving directions to boys or girls when boy-girl partners are not required.
4. Teach dances in phrases rather than counting steps. Encourage listening to the music. Teach the children to listen for changes in the music that may indicate changes in steps, directions, and so forth.
5. The beginning of the dance and each sequence should be cued just before the children will begin or change step, direction, and so forth. Give a starting signal, such as, "One, two, ready, go." Use key words to minimize talking.
6. During the learning phase, it is helpful if the teacher moves with the children, either alone or with a child as a partner.
7. Stress good style. Encourage the children to take short and light steps. Some American dances, such as square dances, use a gliding step, with the feet moving close to the ground. Skipping is not appropriate in this form of American dance.
8. Vary the pace of the lesson. Dance is an invigorating activity, and children will require a chance to rest. Ways to accomplish this might be to allow a group to show their dance to the class while the others observe, or for you to review or discuss the background information of the dance.
9. Add the accompaniment as soon as possible.
10. Allow sufficient time to review dances. New dances should be reviewed soon after the initial learning period. Children enjoy doing the dances they have learned in previous lessons.
11. Plan for variety to ensure a well-rounded dance experience. Include dances from different coun-

tries, as well as those with a variety of steps, figures, and formations.

12. Enhance creativity by giving the children an opportunity to make up their own dances or to modify those they have learned.
13. Another way to introduce dances in the upper elementary grades is to let the children read the dance instructions and see how they would interpret the dance.

MOVEMENT CONCEPTS FOR SINGING GAMES AND AMERICAN AND INTERNATIONAL FOLK DANCE

The movement content emphasized in these dance activities is summarized in Figure 21-1. These concepts should be practiced as a part of the learning process for each dance. Special attention should be given to them during the learning phase and before the performance of the dances.

Concepts and Activities

1. To move in relation to a partner while moving apart and together.
   a. Move with a partner in a double circle, performing various locomotor movements or dance steps. (How did you adjust your step to stay together?)
   b. Practice moving in different partner relationships—side-by-side, facing, one behind the other. (What did you do to keep close to your partner? What movements were most difficult? Easiest?)
2. To move in relation to a group while maintaining the formation and appropriate spacing.
   a. Practice moving in various formations with and without a partner. On the signal to stop, check spacing. (How did you adjust your movements to keep the formation?)
3. To respond to even and uneven rhythm.
   a. Using various kinds of music children move in general space in different ways. (How did you know it was even or uneven?)
   b. In partners or small groups, one child using a drum or other rhythm instrument accompanies the others' movements, beating the instrument in time to their movement, uneven for uneven rhythm (skip, gallop, slide, etc.) and even for

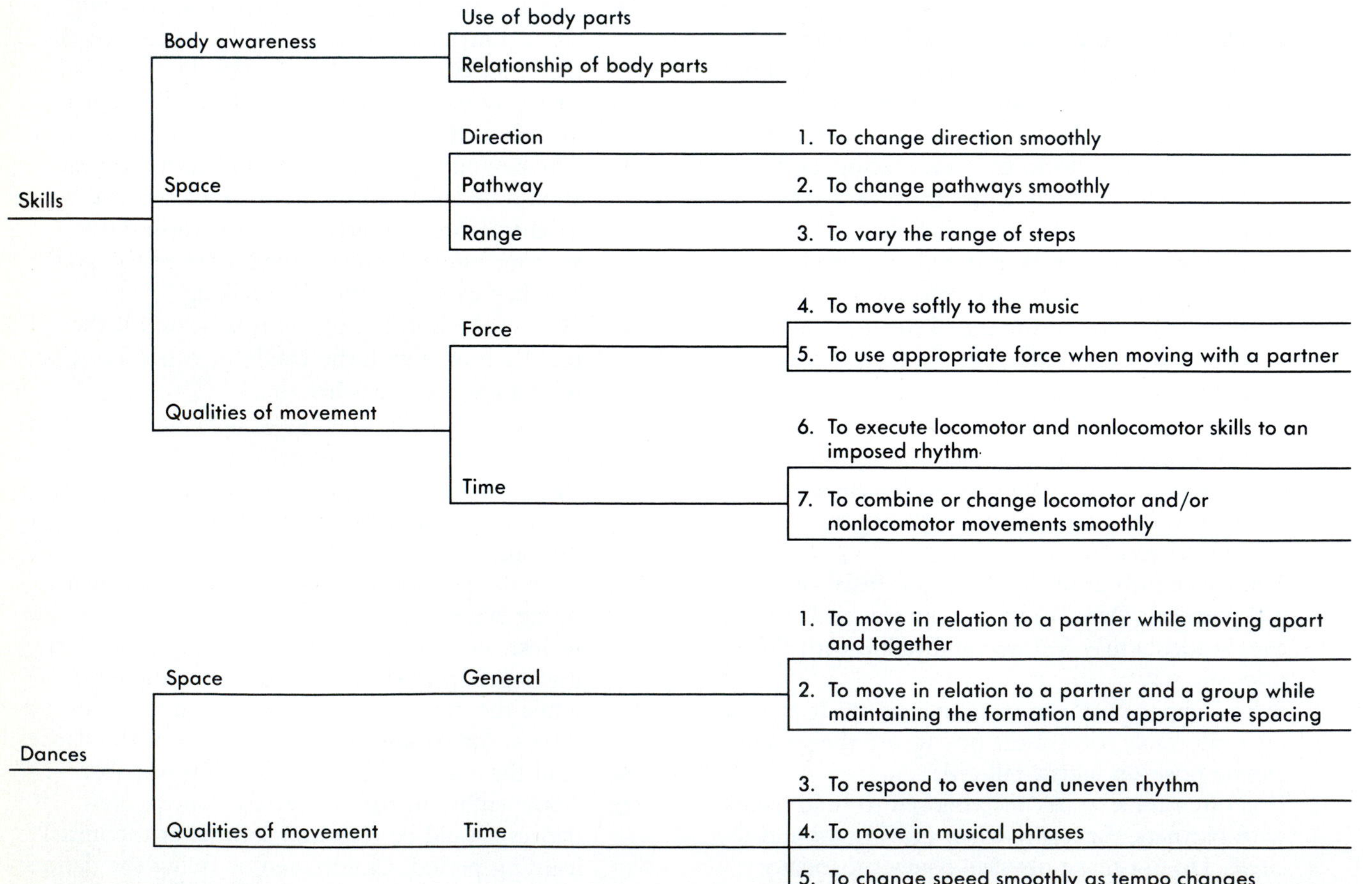

FIGURE 21-1 Movement content for singing games and American and international folk dance.

an even rhythm (such as the step-hop). (Which movements were done in an uneven rhythm? Even?)

4. To move to musical phrases.
   a. In general space the children respond in various ways to phrase such as the following:
      - Clap on first phrase, remain silent on the second.
        Move in place on the first phrase, move in general space on the second.
      - Move using one locomotor movement on the first, another locomotor movement on the second.
      - Perform a nonlocomotor movement on the first, a locomotor movement on the second.
      - Change direction or pathway on each new phrase.
5. To change speed smoothly as the tempo changes.
   a. Moving in general space to a drum or other instrument gradually increase or decrease movements as the instrument increases or decreases speed. (How did you move on the beat as the music went faster? Slower?)

DANCE SKILLS

The locomotor skills used in the dances for children are analyzed in Chapter 13.

Dance Steps

BALANCE

A step forward or backward, followed by a closing step with the opposite foot done in 2/4 or 3/4 rhythm. The weight remains on the stepping foot.

Footwork: Step right forward (count 1). Close left to right (count 2). Hold (count 3).

Footwork: Step back left (count 1). Close right to left (count 2). Hold (count 3).

BLEKING

A light springing step in which children hop on one foot while extending the opposite foot forward, heel touching the floor, and toes up. Repeat hopping on the other foot.

Footwork: Hop right, extend left (count 1). Hop left, extend right (count 2).

GRAPEVINE

A step sideward, alternately crossing the feet in front or in back.

Footwork: Step right to the side (count 1). Cross the left in front of the right (count 2).

Footwork: Step right to the side (count 1). Cross the left behind the right (count 2).

POLKA

A hop, step, close, step, executed in uneven rhythm.

Footwork: Hop left (and). Step right (count 1). Close left to right (and). Step right (count 2).

Footwork: Hop right (and). Step left (count 1). Close right to left (and). Step left (count 2).

The polka is a difficult step for children in the closed dance position. To simplify the polka step for elementary school children, a face-to-face, back-to-back polka may be used. To teach the polka the following sequence is suggested:

1. Children face a partner with one hand joined (right to left). The movement begins toward the unjoined hands.
2. Children take eight slides facing their partners. Continuing to move in the same path, they turn so that partners are back to back and take eight slides. Repeat the face-to-face and back-to-back slides until everyone is comfortable with the changes.
3. Reduce the number of slides to four and repeat as above.
4. Reduce the number of slides to two and repeat. (This is the polka step. The hop is taken on the up beat as the children change direction. The step, close, step follows to the side.)

SCHOTTISHE

Three steps followed by a hop taken on the foot taking the last step, executed in even rhythm.

Footwork: Step right (count 1). Step left (count 2). Step right (count 3). Hop right (count 4).

Footwork: Step left (count 1). Step right (count 2). Step left (count 3). Hop left (count 4).

STEP-HOP

A step on one foot followed by a hop on the same foot, executed in even rhythm. The next step-hop is taken on the opposite foot.

Footwork: Step right (count 1), hop right (count 2). Step left (count 1), hop left (count 2).

The step-hop is difficult for elementary school children to perform. This difficulty may arise because the skip also uses a step-hop combination but in an uneven rhythm, and it is difficult for children to adjust the step-hop back to an even rhythm. It is helpful to have the children practice the step-hop to the beat of a drum or by calling out the even rhythm "Step-hop, Step-hop" as they move.

TWO-STEP

A step, together, step, in uneven rhythm.

Footwork: Step right (count 1). Close left to right (and). Step right (count 2).

Footwork: Step left (count 1). Close right to left (and). Step left (count 2).

The two-step is difficult for children, probably because of its uneven rhythm and the failure to transfer the body weight on the close step. Calling out the steps and rhythm "Step-close-step" while they are moving is helpful in establishing the rhythm.

WALTZ

A series of three steps taken in an uneven rhythm to 3/4 time.

Footwork: Step right forward (count 1). Step left to the side (count 2). Close right to left (count 3).

Footwork: Step left forward (count 1). Step right to the side (count 2). Close left to right (count 3).

Most children have had relatively little experience with 3/4 time. For elementary school children, the waltz step will be easiest to perform in an open dance position. The waltz step may be done as a waltz run, in which the dancer takes three small, even steps forward (without a closing step).

Circle left.

Do-si-do.

Dance Figures

ALLEMANDE LEFT (RIGHT)

Position: In a circle or square set with the boy's partner on his right and his corner lady on his left.

Directions: Face your corner. Take your corner's left hand in your left. Walk forward and around your corner. Drop hands and continue to move back to place.

CIRCLE LEFT (RIGHT)

Position: Group holds hands in a single circle.

Directions: Move clockwise (counterclockwise) in a circle.

DO-SI-DO

Position: Children face their partners.

Directions: Walk forward, passing right shoulders with your partner. Continuing to face forward, move around your partner and back to place, passing left shoulders on the return. This may also be done passing left shoulders first and then right shoulders on the return to position.

ELBOW SWING (RIGHT OR LEFT)

Position: Children face partners, extending appropriate arm.

Directions: Hook elbows and turn in a small circle.

GRAND RIGHT AND LEFT

Position: In a circle or square set.

Directions: Facing your partner, give your right hand to your partner. Walk forward past your partner, giving your left hand to the next person. Continue in this manner, alternately giving the right and left hands to the persons you meet until you meet your partner.

It may be helpful in learning this figure to number the partners 1 and 2, with partners facing. Number 1s extend their right hands to their partners, walking by them to extend the left to the next person. The 2s are stationary, alternately extending their right and left hands to the 1s who pass by. Repeat with the 1s stationary and the 2s moving.

HONOR YOUR PARTNER (CORNER)

Position: Facing partner (corner).

Directions: Acknowledge partner (corner). Boys bow and girls curtsey. (Great variation in this figure exists throughout the United States.)

LADIES CHAIN

Position: In a square or two-couple set, with the boy's partner on his right.

Directions: Facing the opposite couple, girls move forward, giving their right hand to the opposite girls. Moving past each other, girls give their left hand to the opposite boys, who put their right hand on the girls' waist and turn them around to face the opposite couple. Girls repeat the move, giving their right hand to each other and their left to their partners, who then turn them with the boys' right hand on their waist.

PROMENADE

Position: Partners stand side by side with the girl on the boy's right. The boy holds the girl's right hand in his right hand and her left hand in his left.

Directions: Dance is counterclockwise around the set or circle ending in their original position.

RIGHT AND LEFT THROUGH

Position: A square or two-couple set.

Directions: Two couples walk forward with four steps passing through the opposite couple, passing right shoulders with the dancer directly across. Boys take partners' left hand and put right hand at their waist. Both turn to face the other couple. Walk forward again passing through the opposite couple, passing left shoulders with the person directly across. Turn once more with joined left hands and boys' right hands at the girls' waists.

SASHAY

Position: Facing the center of the circle.

Directions: Move once around partner. Boys move sideways to the right and behind the girl. Girls move sideways to the left and in front of the boy.

Honor your partner.

Promenade.

Grand right and left.

Swing your partner.

STAR (RIGHT AND LEFT)

Position: Face the center of the circle or set. Extend right (left) hand into the center joining with the hands of the others. Individuals may hold the wrist of the person in front as they join hands.

Directions: Move clockwise in circle, ending back in place.

GENERAL TERMINOLOGY

Clockwise: A circular movement in the pathway in which the hands of a clock move.

Counterclockwise: A circular movement in the pathway opposite to clockwise.

Line of direction: Counterclockwise.

Reverse line of direction: Clockwise.

FORMATIONS

Single circle, all facing the center: Dancers form a circle, facing the center, with or without partners (Figure 21-2, *A*).

Single circle, all facing counterclockwise (or clockwise): Dancers form a circle and all face counterclockwise (or clockwise) (Figure 21-2, *B*).

Single circle, partners facing: Dancers form a circle facing their partners (Figure 21-2, *C*).

Double circle, partners facing: Dancers form concentric circles facing their partners. The boy is on the inside circle (Figure 21-2, *D*).

Double circle, partners facing clockwise: Dancers form concentric circles with their partners. All face clockwise. Inside hands may be joined. The boy is usually on the inside circle (Figure 21-2, *E*).

Two-couple sets: A double circle of partners alternately facing clockwise and counterclockwise. The boy's partner is on his right (Figure 21-2, *F*).

Longways set: Two parallel lines of dancers (usually no more than six in each line). Each dancer has a partner in the opposite line. The boys are in one line, the girls in the other (Figure 21-2, *G*).

Quadrille or square set: A set of four couples forming a square. The boy has his partner on his right. Two opposing couples are the head couples; the other two couples are the side couples. Couples may be numbered one through four (Figure 21-2, *H*).

PARTNER RELATIONSHIPS

Unless otherwise indicated, the boy always has his partner on his right. Unless otherwise indicated, when couples form a double circle, the boy is in the inside circle.

Promenade position: Partners stand side by side with both hands joined (right to right and left to left), the right hands on top (Figure 21-3, *A*).

Open position: Partners stand side by side with inside hands joined (Figure 21-3, *B*).

Skaters' position: Partners stand side by side facing forward. The boy holds the girl's left hand in his left in front of them, and his right hand is around her waist joined with her right hand at the waist (Figure21-3, *C*).

Groups of three: Groups of three dancers scattered in the area or arranged in a circle all facing the same path. Usually one boy is between two girls (Figure 21-3, *D*).

Shoulder-waist position: Partners face. The boy places both hands at the girl's waist, and the girl places both hands on the boy's shoulders (Figure 21-3, *E*).

Banjo position: Partners face and stand with right hips adjacent. The girl's right hand is in the boy's left and her left hand is on his shoulder. The boy's right hand is at the girl's waist (Figure 21-3, *F*).

Sidecar position: Similar to banjo position, but with left hips adjacent (Figure 21-3, *G*).

Varsouvienne position: Partners stand side by side facing forward. The boy holds the girl's left hand in his left, to the side, and her right in his right, slightly above her shoulder (Figure 21-3, *H*).

A summary of the dances included in the following sections (Table 21-1) may be used to assist the teacher in selecting dances for a particular group. Sources for the records may be found in Appendix 1.

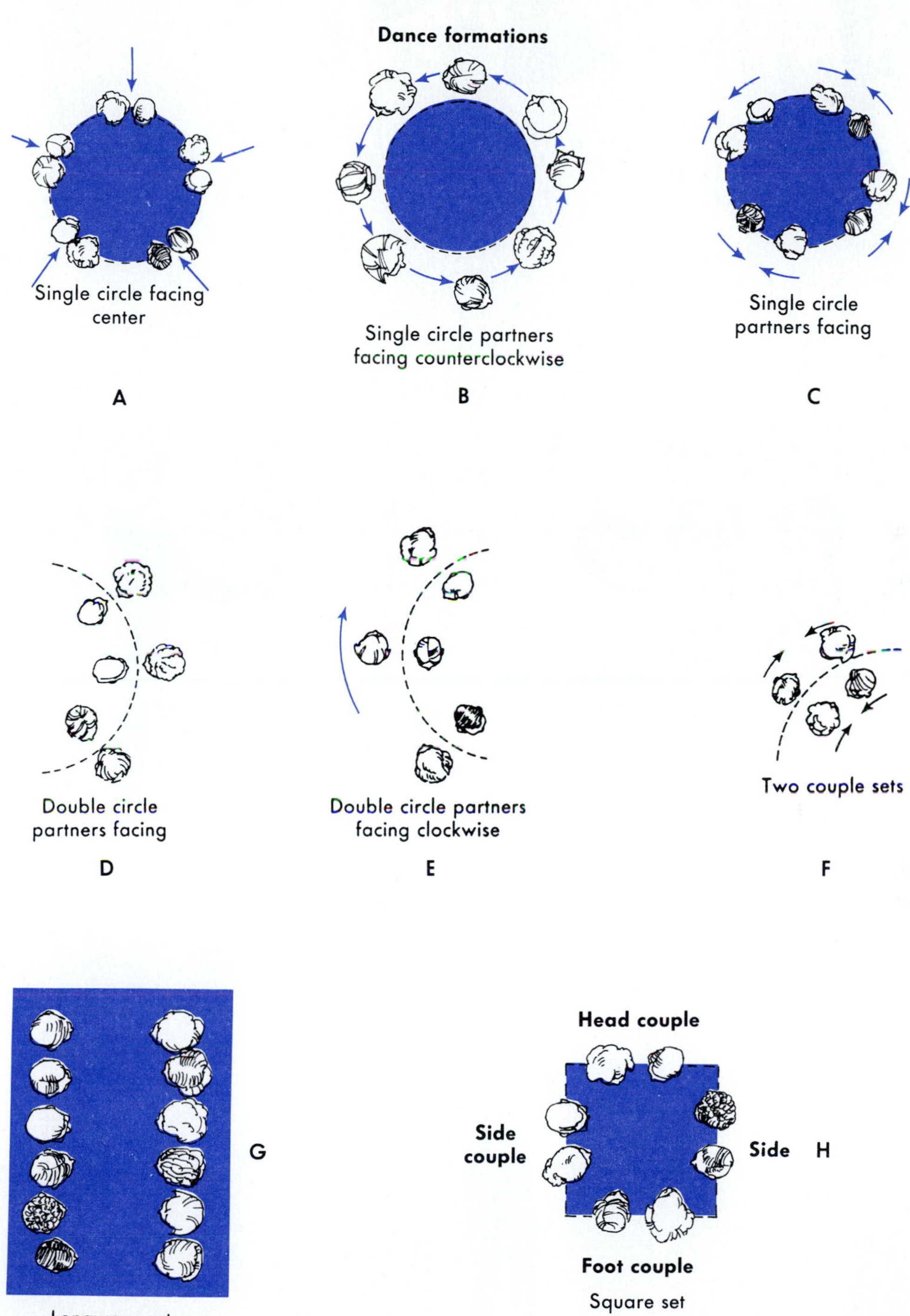

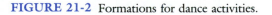

FIGURE 21-2 Formations for dance activities.

Promenade position

A

Open position

B

Skaters position

C

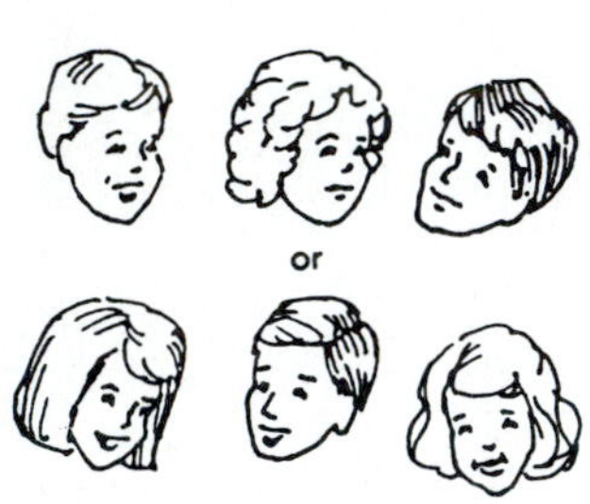

Group of 3

D

Shoulder-waist position

E

Banjo position

F

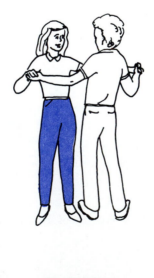

Side-car position

G

Varsouvienne position

H

FIGURE 21-3 Partner relationships for dance activities.

TABLE 21-1 SINGING GAMES

NAME	ORIGIN	FORMATION	BASIC STEPS	SUGGESTIONS/ MODIFICATIONS	PAGE	RECORD	LEVEL
Bluebird	American	Single circle, all facing the center	Walk	Begin with a new bluebird when the chain is made up of three persons	396	Folkcraft: 1180	I
Did You Ever See A Lassie	Scottish	Single circle, all facing the center	Walk	Encourage original movements by imitating animals, varying locomotor and/ or nonlocomotor movements, and so forth	396	Folkcraft: 1183	I
Merry Musicians	French	Single circle, all facing the center	Walk	Have the children suggest other instruments they might imitate	396	Merit Audio Visual: 1041	I
Looby Lou	English	Single circle, all facing the center, hands joined	Skip	Have the children suggest other body parts they could move in the dance	396	Folkcraft: 1102, 1184 Victor: 20214	I
Oats, Peas, Beans, and Barley Grow	American	Single circle, all facing clockwise; one child, the farmer, is in the center	Walk, skip		396	Folkcraft: 1182 Folkdancer: FD34 World of FUN: 2	I
Pease Porridge Hot	English	Double circle, partners facing	Run		397	Folkcraft: 1190	I
A Hunting We Will Go	English	Longways set	Skip, arch	Sets should be of no more than four to six couples so the dance can be completed within the verse and chorus	397	Folkcraft: 1191 Victor: 45-5064, 22759	II
Go Round and Round the Village	English	Single circle, all facing the center, hands joined	Walk, skip		397	Merit Audio Visual: 1041	II
Grand Old Duke of York	English	Longways set	Slide, cast off, arch		398	Folkcraft: 1191	II
Hokey Pokey	English	Single circle, all facing the center; or a single circle of partners	Walk	As a mixer, one person moving clockwise to a new partner on "And you turn yourself about"	398	Capitol: 6026 MacGregor: 669, 6995	II
Jolly Is the Miller	American	Double circle, all facing counterclockwise	March		398	Folkcraft: 1192 Victor: 45-5067, 20214	II
Shoo Fly	American	Single circle of partners all facing the center, hands joined	Walk, skip	If boy-girl partners are not used, designate one person in each pair with a pinnie or colored sash	399	Folkcraft: 1102, 1185	II
The Snail	Unknown	An open circle, all facing the center, hands joined, leader on the right	Walk		399	Folkcraft: 1198	II

SINGING GAMES

BLUEBIRD

Level: I.
Origin: American.
Record: Folkcraft:1180.
Formation: Single circle, hands joined, and facing the center; one child—the bluebird—stands outside the circle.
Skills: Walk.
Song:
Verse: Bluebird, bluebird through my window. Bluebird, bluebird, through my window. Bluebird, bluebird, through my window. Hi diddle, dum dum dee.
Chorus: Take a little boy (girl) and tap him (her) on the shoulder.
Take a little boy (girl) and tap him (her) on the shoulder.
Take a little boy (girl) and tap him (her) on the shoulder.
Hi diddle, dum dum dee.
Action:
During the verse the children in the circle raise their joined hands, forming arches through which the bluebird weaves in and out.
During the chorus, the bluebird taps the circle child lightly on the shoulders with both hands. This child becomes the new bluebird when the verse begins again. The old bluebird remains behind the new bluebird, with hands on the new bluebird's shoulders, forming a train. As the chorus continues, the bluebird train moves in various ways in the center of the circle.
Repeat the dance again, adding a new bluebird to the train.
Teaching suggestions: To avoid a long chain, it may be advisable with young children to begin with a new bluebird once the train has three persons. To maximize activity, begin with several bluebirds.

DID YOU EVER SEE A LASSIE?

Level: I.
Origin: Scottish.
Record: Folkcraft: 1183.
Formation: Single circle, all facing the center, hands joined; one child in the center.
Skills: Walk and other locomotor and nonlocomotor movements.
Song:
Verse: Did you ever see a lassie, a lassie, a lassie?
Did you ever see a lassie go this way and that?
Go this way and that way. Go this way and that way.
Did you ever see a lassie go this way and that?
Action:
Lines 1 and 2: Circle to the left, singing.
Lines 3 and 4: Center child chooses an action to perform, and the children in the circle imitate it.
Teaching suggestions: Alternate the children in the center, substituting "laddie" when a boy is in the center.

MERRY MUSICIANS

Level: I.
Origin: French.
Record: Merit Audio Visual: 1041.
Formation: Single circle, all facing the center.
Skills: Walk and imitate instruments.
Song:
Chorus: I'm a merry musician. From (name of town) I come.
Verse: I can play sweet music upon my little drum. Drrum, dum dum. Drrum, dum dum. Drrum, dum, dum. Drrum, dum, dum. Skipping and playing, Everywhere straying.
Repeat the above chorus and verse.
Repeat the above substituting other instruments, such as:
I can play sweet music upon my violin. Fiddle dee dee. Fiddle dee dee.|.|.|.
I can play sweet music upon my clarinet. Doodle dee doo. Doodle dee do.|.|.|.
I can play sweet music upon my accordion. Squeeze, squeeze, squeeze. Squeeze, squeeze, squeeze.|.|.|.
I can play sweet music upon my fine trumpet. Tootle, doodle, doo. Tootle, doodle doo.|.|.|.
I can play sweet music upon my big bass viol. Brrum fitz, fitz. Brrum fitz, fitz.|.|.|.
For the last verse each of the children imitate the instrument of their choice.
Action:
During the chorus the children walk counterclockwise in a circle. For each of the verses the children stand facing the center of the circle and imitate playing the instrument of the verse.
Teaching suggestions: Have the children suggest other instruments they could imitate.

LOOBY LOU

Level: I.
Origin: English.
Record: Victor: 20214; Folkcraft: 1102, 1184.
Formation: Single circle, all facing the center with hands joined.
Skills: Skip.
Song:
Chorus: Here we go looby lou. Here go we looby light.
Here we go looby lou, All on a Saturday night.
Verse 1: I put my right hand in. I put my right hand out. I give my right hand a shake, shake, shake. And turn myself about.
Verse 2: I put my left hand it. I put my left hand out.|.|.|.
Verse 3: I put my right foot in. I put my right foot out.|.|.|.
Verse 4: I put my left foot in. I put my left foot out.|.|.|.
Verse 5: I put my head in. I put my head out.|.|.|.
Verse 6: I put my whole self in. I put my whole self out.|.|.|.
Action:
Chorus: Children skip around the circle to the left.
Verses: The body parts named are moved as suggested by the words of each verse, turning in place on the last line.
Teaching suggestions: Have the children think of other body parts they could move in the dance.

OATS, PEAS, BEANS, AND BARLEY GROW

Level: I.
Origin: American.
Record: Folkcraft: 1182; World of Fun: 2; Folkdancer: FD 34.

Formation: Single circle, all facing clockwise; one child, the farmer, is in the center of the circle.
Skills: Walk and skip.
Song:
Verse 1: Oats, peas, beans, and barley grow.
Oats, peas, beans, and barley grow.
Do you or I or anyone know?
How oats, peas, beans, and barley grow?
Verse 2: First the farmer sows his/her seed.
Then he/she stands and takes his/her ease.
Stamps his/her foot, and claps his/her hands.
And turns around to view the land.
Verse 3: Waiting for a partner. Waiting for a partner.
So open the ring and take one in. While we all gaily dance and sing.
Verse 4: So now you're married you must obey.
You must be true to all you say.
You must be wise, you must be good.
And help your spouse to chop the wood.
Action:
Verse 1: All sing, clapping hands, while moving to the left. End facing the center.
Verse 2: Pretend to sow the seed. Then stand with arms folded. Stamp your foot, then clap your hands and turn around in place, shading eyes as if viewing the land.
Verse 3: All stand and sing while the farmer walks around in the ring, choosing a partner on the last line.
Verse 4: With hands joined, all skip to the left. The two persons inside the circle join hands in the skaters' position and move around inside the circle in the opposite direction. The person chosen becomes the new farmer, and the original farmer joins the circle as the dance is repeated.

PEASE PORRIDGE HOT

Level: I.
Origin: English.
Record: Folkcraft: 1190.
Formation: Double circle, partners facing.
Skills: Run.
Song:
Verse: Pease porridge hot. Pease porridge cold.
Pease porridge in the pot. Nine days old.
Some like it hot. Some like it cold.
Some like it in the pot. Nine days old.
Action:
The song is sung twice.
First time—Line 1: Clap own hands to thighs; clap own hands together; clap partner's hands. Repeat.
Line 2: Clap hands to thighs; clap own hands together; clap right hand to partner's right; clap own hands together. Clap partner's left hand; clap own hands together; clap both hands to partner's hands.
Lines 3 and 4: Repeat the actions of the first two lines.
Second time—Partners join hands and run around in a small circle to the right for the first two lines. Reverse direction on the last two lines.

A HUNTING WE WILL GO

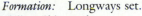

Level: II.
Origin: English.
Record: Folkcraft: 1191, Victor: 45-5064, 22759.

Formation: Longways set.
Skills: Skip, arch.
Song:
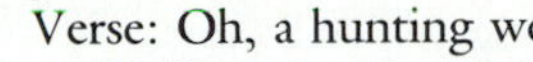
Verse: Oh, a hunting we will go. A hunting we will go. We'll catch a fox and put him in the box. And then we'll let him go.
Chorus: Tra, la, la, la, la, la, la. Tra, la, la, la, la, la.
Tra, la, la, la, la, la, la, la. Tra, la, la, la, la, la.
Action:
Verse: Head couple joins inside hands and skips between the lines to the end of the set. They change hands and return to the head of the set. All other children clap while the head couple is active.
Chorus: The head couple skips around the left side of the set, with all couples following. When the head couple reaches the end of the set, they form an arch by facing each other, joining two hands and holding them high in the air. All other couples proceed through the arch, reforming the set with a new head couple.
Teaching suggestions: The sets should be formed with four to six couples to enable the dancers to stay with the music.

GO ROUND AND ROUND THE VILLAGE

Level: II.
Origin: English.
Record: Merit Audio Visual: 1041.
Formation: Single circle, all facing the center with hands joined; one or more dancers scattered outside the circle.
Skills: Walk, skip.
Song:
Verse 1: Go round and round the village. Go round and round the village. Go round and round the village. As we have done before.
Verse 2: Go in and out the window. Go in and out the window.|.|.|.
Verse 3: Now stand and face your partner. Now stand and face your partner.|.|.|.
Verse 4: Now kneel to show you love (like) her (him). Now kneel to show you love (like) her (him).|.|.|.
Verse 5: Now follow me to London. Now follow me to London.|.|.|.
Verse 6: Shake hands before you leave me. Shake hands before you leave me.|.|.|.
Action:
Verse 1: Circle players walk clockwise, while those on the outside walk counterclockwise.
Verse 2: Circle dancers stand raising joined hands to form arches or windows. Outside players move in and out of the circle passing through the arches, finishing on the inside of the circle.
Verse 3: Dancers in the inside of the circle choose a partner and stand in front of the partner, clapping hands or joining hands.
Verse 4: Inner dancers kneel on one knee and make motions with hands clasped to heart and arms extended to express love.
Verse 5: The chosen dancers follow their partners moving in and outside of the circle, through the arches formed by the remaining circle players, or skip hand in hand on the inside or outside of the circle.
Verse 6: The partners shake hands, with the original dancer joining the circle of dancers, the chosen partner becoming the new dancer moving to the outside of the circle.

GRAND OLD DUKE OF YORK

Level: II.
Origin: English.
Record: Folkcraft: 1191 (A Hunting We Will Go).
Formation: Longways sets of no more than six couples.
Skills: Slide, cast off, arch.
Song:

Oh, the Grand Old Duke of York, he had ten thousand men.
He marched them up to the top of the hill, and he marched them down again.
And when they're up they're up.
And when they're down they're down.
And when they're only half way up they're neither up nor down.
Hail, Britannia, Brittannia rules the waves.
Britons never, never, never, never shall be slaves.

Action:

First couple joins hands in the center and slide eight steps down the set and eight steps back.

First couple turns away from each other and leads his or her line around the outside and down toward the bottom of the set; all follow.

First couple forms an arch by joining hands and holding them high in the air at the bottom of the set. All others meet their partners and move through the arch to form a new set with a new head couple.

Grand Old Duke of York.

Level: II.
Origin: English.
Record: Capitol: 6026; MacGregor: 669, 6995.
Formation: Single circle, all facing the center, or a single circle of partners.
Skills: Walk.
Song:

Verse 1: You put your right foot in.
You put your right foot out.
You put your right foot in.
And you shake it all about.
You do the hokey pokey.
And you turn yourself around.
And that's what it's all about.
Chorus: You do the hokey pokey.
You do the hokey pokey.
You do the hokey pokey.
That's what it's all about.
Verse 2: You put your left foot in.
You put your left foot out. . . .
Verse 3: You put your right hand in.
You put your right hand out. . . .
Verse 4: You put your left hand in.
You put your left hand out. . . .
Verse 5: You put your right elbow in.
You put your right elbow out. . . .
Verse 6: You put your left elbow in.
You put your left elbow out. . . .
Verse 7: You put your head in.
You put your head out. . . .
Verse 8: You put your right hip in.
You put your right hip out. . . .
Verse 9: You put your left hip in.
You put your left hip out. . . .
Verse 10: You put your whole self in.
You put your whole self out. . . .
Verse 11: You put your back side in.
You put your back side out. . . .

Action:

Verse: You put the body part named into the circle. You take it out. You put it back in and shake it toward the center of the circle.

Place palms together above your head and rumba hips. You turn around in place as you shake your hands above your head.

Clap four times.

Chorus: Raise your arms over head and lower arms and head in a bowing motion while shaking your hands from front to back.

Kneel on both knees and raise arms above head and lower arms and head in a bowing motion. Then slap the floor six times.

Teaching suggestions: This dance may be used as a mixer. With partners in a single circle, one person moves clockwise to a new partner, following the turn on "And you turn yourself around."

JOLLY IS THE MILLER

Level: II.
Origin: American.
Record: Victor: 45-5067, 20214; Folkcraft: 1192.
Formation: Double circle, all facing counterclockwise, inside hands joined; one person, the miller, is in the center.
Skills: March.
Song:

Verse: Jolly is the miller who lives by the mill.
The wheel goes around with a right good will.
One hand on the hopper, the other on the sack.
The right steps forward and the left steps back.

Action:

Line 1: All march counterclockwise with inside hands joined.

Lines 2 and 3: The children in the inside circle extend their left arms sideward to form a mill wheel as they continue moving in the circle.

Line 4: The children drop hands and change partners, with the children on the inner circle stepping forward, and the children on the outside circle stepping back. At this time the miller chooses a partner and moves into the circle of couples. The person without a partner becomes the new miller.

SHOO FLY

Level: II.
Origin: American.
Record: Folkcraft: 1102, 1185.
Formation: Single circle of partners, all facing the center, hands joined.
Skills: Walk and skip.
Song:

Shoo fly, don't bother me. Shoo fly, don't bother me.
Shoo fly don't bother me. I belong to company G.
I feel, I feel, I feel, I feel like a morning star.
I feel, I feel, I feel, I feel like a morning star.

Action:

Line 1: Walk four steps toward the center, swinging arms back and forth. Walk four steps back to place, swinging arms.

Line 2: Repeat the action of line 1.

Line 3: Partners face, taking hold of both hands, and turn in a small circle ending in the opposite direction (the partner on the left now has a new partner on their right).

Teaching suggestions: If boy-girl partners are not used, it may be necessary to designate one partner with a pinnie or sash.

THE SNAIL

Level: II.
Origin: Unknown.
Record: Folkcraft: 1198.
Formation: An open circle, all facing the center, hands joined, leader on the right.
Skills: Walk.
Song:

Verse 1: Let's join hands and make a shell. A place for our small snail to dwell.
Round and round we'll creep and sing. Closer, closer, wind each ring.
Here's our house we built it well. Little snail crawl in your shell.
Verse 2: Little snail now turn about. Find a hole and lead us out.
Round and round we'll creep and sing. Winging out of every ring.
Little snail we're out in time. Here we are back in our line.

Action:

Verse 1: The leader winds the group into a close spiral, finishing in the center.

Verse 2: The leader reverses direction and unwinds the spiral, finishing in a large circle.

Repeat with the child on the left leading the group.

AMERICAN AND INTERNATIONAL FOLK DANCE

The dances that follow are summarized in Table 21-2.

DANISH DANCE OF GREETING

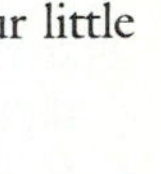

Level: I.
Origin: Danish.
Record: Merit Audio Visual: 1041.
Formation: Single circle of partners all facing the center.
Skills: Run.
Action:

Part I: Clap (your own hands). Clap (again). Bow (to your partner). Clap (your own hands). Clap (again). Bow (to your neighbor). Stamp right foot. Stamp left foot. Individuals turn around in place with four little steps.

Repeat the action of Part I.

Part II: Chorus: Join hands with partner and move to the left for the first phrase (16 steps). Change directions and circle to the right for the second phrase (16 steps).

NIGAREPOLSKA (NIXIE POLKA)

Level: I.
Origin: Swedish.
Record: Merit Audio Visual: 1041.
Formation: Single circle, all facing the center; several children scattered inside the circle.
Skills: Bleking.
Action:

Measures 1 to 4: With hands joined, all spring lightly onto the left foot while extending the right foot forward with the heel on the ground and the toe up (bleking step). Bleking right. Bleking left. Bleking right. (These steps are executed slowly.)

Measures 5 to 8: All clap hands once and shout, "Hey." Center dancers then run around the inside of the circle looking for a partner. They join hands with the partner and run lightly in place to finish the phrase.

The dance is now repeated with the center dancers and their partners holding two hands on measures 1 to 4. On measures 5 to 8, the circle dancers move behind their partners and put their hands on the shoulders of their partners. The two move into line to choose a new partner and the dance continues.

Each time the dance is repeated, the line adds one additional person and reverses so that there is a new leader each time.

SHOEMAKER'S DANCE

Level: I.
Origin: Danish.
Record: Merit Audio Visual: 1042.
Formation: Double circle of partners facing each other.
Skills: Skip.
Action:

Measures 1 to 4: Wind, wind, wind, the bobbin. (Partners execute a winding motion with the hands and arms.) Wind, wind, wind the bobbin. (Reverse winding motion.) Pull. Pull. Tap. Tap. Tap. (Pull hands away from each other to the sides twice and tap one hand on the other three times.)

TABLE 21-2 AMERICAN AND INTERNATIONAL FOLK DANCES

NAME	ORIGIN	FORMATION	BASIC STEPS	SUGGESTIONS/ MODIFICATIONS	PAGE	RECORD	LEVEL
Danish Dance of Greeting	Danish	Single circle of partners all facing the center	Run		399	Merit Audio Visual: 1041	I
Nigarepolska (Nixie Polka)	Swedish	Single circle, all facing the center, several scattered inside the circle	Bleking		399	Merit Audio Visual: 1041	I
Shoemaker's Dance	Danish	Double circle of partners facing one another	Skip		399	Merit Audio Visual: 1042	I
The Thread Follows the Needle	English	Single lines of about seven to eight children, hands joined	Walk		404	Victor: 22760	I
The Wheat	Czechoslovakian	Sets of three in a circle, facing counterclockwise	Walk, elbow swing		404	Merit Audio Visual: 1041	I
Tra La La Ja Saa	Norwegian/ Swedish	Single circle, one person in the center	Walk, elbow swing	More than one child may begin in the center	404	Merit Audio Visual: 1044	I
Ach Ja	German	Double circle, partners facing counterclockwise, inside hands joined	Walk, slide		404	Folk Dancer: 34	II
Bow Belinda	American	Longways set of up to six couples	Right- and left-hand turns, do-si-do, slide		405	Folkcraft: 1189 World of Fun: 2	II
Carrousel	Swedish	Double circle, all facing the center	Slide		405	Merit Audio Visual: 1041	II
Chimes of Dunkirk	French	Double circle, partners facing	Stamp, balance, walk	This dance may be used as a mixer	405	Folkcraft: 1189 World of Fun: 4 Merit Audio Visual: 1042	II
Cshebogar	Hungarian	Single circle of partners all facing the center, hands joined	Slide, walk, skip	This dance may be used as a mixer	405	Merit Audio Visual: 1042 World of Fun: 6	II
Galopede	English	Column of four to six couples, facing forward; couples are numbered from 1 to 6 from the head of the set	Walk, skip, two-hand swing		406	Folkcraft: 1331	II
Greensleeves	English	Double circle of partners all facing counterclockwise, in two-couple sets	Walk, right-hand/left-hand star; arch		406	World of Fun: 1 Merit Audio Visual: 1042	II
Jump Jim Jo	American	Double circle, partners facing	Jump, slide	This dance may be used as a mixer	406	Merit Audio Visual: 1041	II
Kinderpolka	German	Single circle, partners facing with hands joined	Step-draw, walk	This dance may be used as a mixer	406	Merit Audio Visual: 1041	II

TABLE 21-2 AMERICAN AND INTERNATIONAL FOLK DANCES—cont'd

NAME	ORIGIN	FORMATION	BASIC STEPS	SUGGESTIONS/ MODIFICATIONS	PAGE	RECORD	LEVEL
Noriu Miego	Lithuanian	Two couple sets, facing the center (in a square, one person on each side)	Bleking, right-hand/left-hand star		406	Merit Audio Visual: 1042	II
Polly Wolly Doodle	American	Double circle of partners facing one another, hands joined	Slide		407	Merit Audio Visual: 1041	II
Pop Goes the Weasel	American	In sets of three in a circle of sets, all facing counterclockwise	Skip, walk	This dance may be done as a couple and square dances as well	407	Merit Audio Visual: 1043 World of Fun: 2	II
Savila Se Bela Loza	Serbian	Single lines of six to eight dancers	Schottische, run	The schottische may be considered a grapevine, crossing in front of the second step	407	Folkcraft: 1496	II
Skip to My Lou	American	Single circle of partners, all facing the center	Walk, skip, swing, promenade		407	Folk Dancer: FD 34 Folkcraft: 1192	II
Turn the Glasses Over	American	Double circle of partners, all facing counterclockwise, skater's position	Walk		408	Folkcraft: 1181 World of Fun: 2	II
Ace of Diamonds	Danish	Double circle, partners facing	Step-hop, polka		408	World of Fun: 4 Merit Audio Visual: 1044	III
Bingo	American	Double circle of partners, all facing counterclockwise	Walk, slide, grand right and left		408	Folkcraft: 1189 Merit Audio Visual: 1043	III
Buggy Schottische	International	Two-couple sets, one in front of the other, all hands joined	Schottische, step-hop	Variation: rear couple moves forward under the arch formed by the lead couple, "wringing the dish rag"	408	Merit Audio Visual: 1046	III
Cherkassiya	Israeli	Closed or broken circle, hands joined	Grapevine, cherkassiya step, step-hop	Lines of six children may be more appropriate for elementary school children	408	Merit Audio Visual: 1043	III
Christ Church Bells	English	Double circle, partners facing, arranged in two-couple sets	Walk, or run, slide, cast off		409	World of Fun: 5	III
Gustaf's Skoal	Swedish	Square set of four couples	Walk, skip		409	World of Fun: 7 Merit Audio Visual: 1044	III

Continued.

TABLE 21-2 AMERICAN AND INTERNATIONAL FOLK DANCES—cont'd

NAME	ORIGIN	FORMATION	BASIC STEPS	SUGGESTIONS/ MODIFICATIONS	PAGE	RECORD	LEVEL
Hopp Mor Anika	Swedish	Double circle, all facing counter-clockwise	Walk, skip, polka		409	Merit Audio Visual: 1042	III
Horah	Israeli	Single circle, hands on shoulders of persons on either side	Grapevine, hop	Small groups may work best for elementar school children	409	Merit Audio Visual: 1043	III
La Raspa	Mexican	Partners scattered around the room, facing each other, hands joined	Bleking, skip; optional; polka, grand right and left		409	World of Fun: 6 Merit Audio Visual: 1043	III
Moskrosser	Danish	Two-couple sets facing each other, arranged in sets around the circle; couple 1 facing clockwise, couple 2 facing counter-clockwise	Schottische ladies chain, right and left star		410	Merit Audio Visual: 1044	III
Norwegian Mountain March	Norwegian	Sets of three, with the center person in front, and the other two (partners) stand behind; each holds a handkerchief, which is held by another of the set	Waltz or step-hop	The waltz step is preferable, but it may be too difficult for elementary school children	410	Merit Audio Visual: 1044	III
Oh Susanna	American	Single circle of partners, all facing the center	Walk, grand right and left	A partner swing may be substituted for the grand right and left	410	Merit Audio Visual: 1043	III
Seven Jumps	Danish	Single circle, all facing counter-clockwise	Step-hop	This dance may be used with younger children if the skip is substituted for the step-hop	410	Merit Audio Visual: 1043 World of Fun: 4	III
Sicilian Circle	American	Two-couple sets in a circle, alternately facing clockwise and counterclockwise (duple minor set)	Walk, ladies chain, right and left through	A right- and left-hand star may be substituted for the ladies chain and a do-si-do with opposite and partner for the right and left through	411	World of Fun: 1	III
Teton Mountain Stomp	American	Single circle of partners, hands joined	Step-close, walk, two-step or buzz step	The buzz step may be substituted for the two-step to be appropriate for level IV	411	Folkcraft: 1482	III

TABLE 21-2 AMERICAN AND INTERNATIONAL FOLK DANCES—cont'd

NAME	ORIGIN	FORMATION	BASIC STEPS	SUGGESTIONS/ MODIFICATIONS	PAGE	RECORD	LEVEL
Tinikling	Philippine	Groups of three to six with one set of poles	Walk, leap	It may be helpful to have the children practice the steps using parallel lines on the floor before using the sticks	411	Merit Audio Visual: 1047	III
Virginia Reel	American	Longways set of six couples	Walk, do-si-do, reel, slide	Children must be reminded that reeling is always done with the line opposite the one they are in	412	Merit Audio Visual: 1043	III
Black Nag	English	Longways set of three couples, all facing the head of the set	Run, slide, right and left elbow swing, hey		413	World of Fun: 6	IV
Crested Hen	Danish	Sets of three, hands joined to form a circle	Step-hop		413	World of Fun: 4 Merit Audio Visual: 1042	IV
Cumberland Square Eight	English	Square set of four couples	Galop, star, basket	A skipping step may be substituted for the basket	413	World of Fun: 5	IV
Fireman's Dance	American	Two couples in a line facing two couples; sets in a circle as the spokes of a wheel	Slide, gallop, ladies chain, right and left through		414	World of Fun: 1 Folkcraft: 1131	IV
Five Foot Two	American	Double circle, all facing counterclockwise	Two-step, walk, balance		414	Folkcraft: 1420	IV
Gathering Peascods	English	Single circle of partners, all facing the center, hands joined	Slide, walk		414	Merit Audio Visual: 1045	IV
Heel and Toe Polka	American	Couples in the varsouvienne position	Polka, two-step	This may be used as a mixer	415	MacGregor: 5003-B	IV
Highland Fling	Scotch	Individuals scattered in the room	Fling		415	Merit Audio Visual: 1045	IV
Jessie Polka	American	In lines of two or more with hands on waist of person in front	Two-step or polka	This may be used as a mixer	415	Folkcraft: 1093	IV
Maitelitza	Russian-American	Sets of three, inside hands joined, facing counterclockwise	Hop-swing, slide		415	Educational Dance Recordings: FD-2	IV
Mayim	Israeli	Single circle, hands joined and held down	Grapevine, hop, run		416	World of Fun: 6	IV

Continued.

TABLE 21-2 AMERICAN AND INTERNATIONAL FOLK DANCES—cont'd

NAME	ORIGIN	FORMATION	BASIC STEPS	SUGGESTIONS/ MODIFICATIONS	PAGE	RECORD	LEVEL
Miserlou (Kritikos)	Greek	A large broken circle, hands joined; leader at the right end of the line	Grapevine, two-step	Smaller groups may be more successful than one large group	416	Merit Audio Visual: 1046	IV
Road to the Isles	Scotch	Double circle of partners in the varsouvienne position, all facing counterclockwise	Schottische, step-hop, grapevine		416	World of Fun: 3 Merit Audio Visual: 1043	IV
Sicilian Tarantella	Italian	Two-couple sets, men standing side by side, facing their partners	Step-hop, do-si-do, skip, star		416	Merit Audio Visual: 1045 World of Fun: 6	IV

Measures 5 to 8: Repeat the action of measures 1 to 4.
Chorus: Join inside hands with free hand on hips and skip counterclockwise (16 steps).

THE THREAD FOLLOWS THE NEEDLE

Level: I.
Origin: English.
Record: Victor: 22760.
Formation: Single lines of seven or eight children, hands joined; each child is numbered consecutively.
Skills: Walk.
Song:
Verse: The thread follows the needle. The thread follows the needle.
In and out the needle goes. As mother mends the children's clothes.
Action:
The first child (1) is the needle and leads the other children. The needle leads the line under the raised arms of the last two children (7 and 8). When the line has totally passed under the arms, the children turn and face the opposite direction, letting their arms cross in front of them. This forms a stitch.
The leader repeats the action passing under the arms of 6 and 7. This action is repeated until the entire line is sewn, completing the last stitch.
The stitch is then ripped by having all children raise their arms and turn to their original positions.
Repeat the dance with a new leader.

THE WHEAT

Level: I.
Origin: Czechoslovakian.
Record: Merit Audio Visual: 1041.
Formation: Sets of three in a circle, all facing counterclockwise.
Skills: Walk and elbow swing.
Action:
Part I: All walk forward (16 steps).
Part II: Center dancers hook right elbows with their righthand partners and turn twice around (eight steps). Repeat with partner on the left.

TRA LA LA JA SAA

Level: I.
Origin: Norwegian/Swedish.
Record: Merit Audio Visual: 1044.
Formation: Single circle, one person in the center.
Skills: Walk and elbow swing.
Song:
I am waiting, I am hoping that someone will join me in the ring.
Oh won't you come and be my partner. While the others clap and sing.
Tra la, la, la, Ja Saa; Tra la, la, la, Ja Saa.
Won't you come and dance the way I do. Or must I reverse and go with you.
Action:
Line 1: The center person walks counterclockwise inside the circle and sings.
Line 2: The center person chooses a partner who comes into the circle.
Line 3: All turn around in place, stamping on "Ja" and clapping own hands on "Saa." Repeat.
Line 4: The couple in the center hook right elbows and walk around. Reverse with a left elbow swing.
The dance is repeated with each of the center dancers looking for a new partner.
Teaching suggestions: If the group is large, it may be best to begin with several children in the center of the circle.

ACH JA

Level: II.
Origin: German.
Record: Folk Dancer: 34.
Formation: Double circle, partners facing counterclockwise, hands joined.

Skills: Walk and slide.
Action:
Part I—Measures 1 and 2: Partners walk counterclockwise (eight steps).
Measures 3 and 4: Partners drop hands, face each other, and bow. Then turn back to back and bow.
Measures 5 and 8: Repeat measures 1 to 4.
Part II—Measures 1 and 2: Partners join hands and take four slides counterclockwise.
Measures 3 and 4: Partners take four slides clockwise.
Measure 5: Partners drop hands, face each other, and bow.
Measure 6: Child on the inside of the circle walks counterclockwise to a new partner.
Repeat the dance with new partners.

BOW BELINDA

Level: II.
Origin: American.
Record: Folkcraft: 1189; World of Fun: 2.
Formation: Longways set of up to six couples.
Skills: Slide, right- and left-hand turns, and do-si-do.
Song:
Verse I: Bow, bow, O Belinda. Bow, bow, O Belinda.
Bow, bow, O Belinda. Won't you be my partner?
Verse 2: Right hand around, O Belinda.|.|.|.
Verse 3: Left hand around, O Belinda.|.|.|.
Verse 4: Both hands around, O Belinda.|.|.|.
Verse 5: Back to back, O Belinda.|.|.|.
Verse 6: Promenade around, O Belinda.|.|.|.
Verse 7: Through the tunnel, O Belinda.|.|.|.
Action:
Verses 1 to 5: The head boy and foot girl do the action, followed by the head girl and the foot boy.
Verse 1: Move to the center of the set with four running steps, bow, and return to place.
Verse 2: Forward to the center, take right hands, turning once around and then back to place.
Verse 3: Forward to the center, take left hands, turning once and then back to place.
Verse 4: Forward to the center, turn with both hands, and return to place.
Verse 5: Forward to the center, do-si-do, and back to place.
Verse 6: Partners join hands in the skaters' position facing the head of the set. All follow the first couple out to the left, skipping straight down the set, turning sharply at the foot, and promenading up the center of the set back to place.
Verse 7: Couples remain in place, joining hands to form an arch. The head couple goes under the arch to the foot of the set.
The dance is repeated with a new head couple.

CARROUSEL

Level: II.
Origin: Swedish.
Record: Merit Audio Visual: 1041.
Formation: Double circle, all facing the center; inner circle joins hands, outer circle places their hands on the shoulders of the child in front of them.
Skills: Slide.
Song:
Part I: Little children young and gay. Carrousel is running.
It will run til evening. Little ones a nickel.
Big ones a dime.
Hurry up, get a mate or you'll surely be too late.
Part II: Ha, ha, ha. Happy are we. Anderson and Henderson and Peterson and me.
Ha, ha, ha. Happy are we. Anderson and Henderson and Peterson and me.
Action:
Part I: All sing and slide slowly in a clockwise direction.
Part II: Continue in a clockwise direction, sliding in time to music, which increases in tempo.
Change direction and continue sliding.
Repeat the dance with the inner circle changing places with the outer circle.

CHIMES OF DUNKIRK

Level: II.
Origin: French.
Record: Folkcraft: 1189; World of Fun: 4; Merit Audio Visual: 1042.
Formation: Double circle, with partners facing.
Skills: Walk, stamp, and balance.
Action:
Measures 1 and 2: Stamp three times.
Measures 3 and 4: Clap three times.
Measures 5 to 8: Join hands with partner and turn clockwise in place (with eight steps).
Measures 9 and 10: Join right hands and balance (step forward with the right foot, step back on the left).
Measures 11 and 12: Repeat measures 9 and 10.
Measures 13 to 16: With both hands joined, turn clockwise in place (with eight steps).
Repeat the dance.
Teaching suggestions: This dance could become a mixer by having the child on the inside of the circle then circle with partner in measures 13 to 16 and continue walking forward to a new partner.

CSHEBOGAR

Level: II.
Origin: Hungarian.
Record: Merit Audio Visual: 1042; World of Fun: 6.
Formation: Single circle of partners, all facing the center, hands joined.
Skills: Walk, slide, and skip.
Action:
Part I: All slide eight steps to the left, then eight slides to right.
Part II: Three steps forward into the circle. Stamp. Three steps back to place. Stamp. Repeat.
Part III: Partners join hands, arms extended at shoulder height. Take four slow step-draws (step-close) sideways toward the center of the circle, while lowering and raising arms. Repeat returning back to places.
Now take two step-draws into the center, and two out.
Part IV: Partners face, placing right hands around each other's waist (or hooking right elbows). With left hand held high in the air, turn in place with eight running or skipping steps.

Teaching suggestions: This dance may become a mixer by having one of the dancers (the one facing counterclockwise) turn once with his or her partner in Part IV and continue on to the next person, who becomes the new partner.

GALOPEDE

Level: II.
Origin: English.
Record: Folkcraft: 1331.
Formation: Column of four to six couples, facing forward; couples are numbered from one to six from the head of the set; partners facing, hands joined in each line.
Skills: Walk, skip, and two-hand swing.
Action:

A—Measures 1 to 4: All walk three steps forward, bow, and walk back to place with four steps.

Measures 5 to 8: Release hands. Partners change places with eight steps, passing right shoulders and turning to the right to face partners.

Measures 1 to 8: Repeat measures 5 to 8 returning to places.

B—Measures 1 to 8: Partners join hands and do a two-hand swing with skipping steps.

C—Head couple swings down between the two lines to the foot of the set, skipping. All other couples move up one position while clapping.

Repeat the dance with a new head couple.

GREENSLEEVES

Level: II.
Origin: English.
Record: World of Fun: 1; Merit Audio Visual: 1042.
Formation: Double circle of partners, all facing counterclockwise; in two-couple sets.
Skills: Walk, right- and left-hand star, and arch.
Action:

Part I—Measures 1 to 8: Walk forward (16 steps).

Part II—Measures 1 to 8: The couple in front turns to face the couple behind, each turning individually. All four join right hands for a right-hand star and walk (eight steps) clockwise.

Now drop hands and join left hands for a left-hand star, proceeding (eight steps) counterclockwise. On the last count the lead couple faces forward again.

Part III—Measure 1 to 8: Rear couple joins inside hands, forming an arch. The rear couple walks four steps forward, while the lead couple walks back four steps under the arch.

Reverse roles with the new front couple backing under the arch, while the new rear couple walks forward forming the arch.

Repeat turning the sleeves two more times.

JUMP JIM JO

Level: II.
Origin: American.
Record: Merit Audio Visual: 1041.
Formation: Double circle of partners, facing each other; hands joined.
Skills: Jump and slide.
Song:

Jump, jump, oh jump Jim Jo.
Take a little whirl and around you go.
Slide, slide and point your toe.
You're a sprightly little fellow when you jump Jim Jo.

Action:

Line 1: Progressing counterclockwise, take two slow jumps, followed by three quicker jumps.

Line 2: Release hands and turn once in place with four little steps. Finish facing your partner and join hands.

Line 3: Progressing counterclockwise, take two sliding steps. These are followed by tapping the toes of the outside foot three times.

Line 4: Release hands. Take four running steps forward in the line of direction. Face partner, join hands, and end with three jumps sideways, progressing counterclockwise.

Teaching suggestions: This dance may be made into a mixer by having the inside dancer move sideways on the last three jumps, while the outside dancer jumps in place.

KINDERPOLKA (CHILDREN'S POLKA)

Level: II.
Origin: German.
Record: Merit Audio Visual: 1041.
Formation: Single circle, partners facing with hands joined and arms extended sideways, at shoulder level.
Skills: Step-draw and walk.
Action:

Measures 1 and 2: Couples take two step-draws toward the center of the circle (step close, step close) and three steps in place.

Measures 3 and 4: Take two step-draws out and back to place, ending with three steps in place.

Measures 5 to 8: Repeat measures 1 to 4.

Measures 9 and 10: Slap thighs with both hands.Clap own hands. Clap partner's hands three times.

Measures 11 and 12: Repeat measures 9 and 10.

Measures 13 and 14: Place right heel forward and shake right forefinger at partner three times as if scolding. Repeat with the left foot and finger.

Measures 15 and 16: Turn in place with four little steps, ending facing your partner, and stamp three times.

Teaching suggestions: This dance may be used as a mixer by having the child facing counterclockwise move forward to the next dancer, while the inactive dancer stamps during the last measure.

NORIU MIEGO

Level: II.
Origin: Lithuanian.
Record: Merit Audio Visual: 1042.
Formation: Two-couple sets facing the center, in a square, with one person on each side.
Skills: Bleking and right- and left-hand star.
Action:

Part I: All spring onto the left foot, placing the right foot forward, with the heel down and the toes pointing upward (bleking right).

Bleking left.

Four quick bleking steps—right, left, right, left.
Part II: Clap own hands twice and form a right-hand star in the center. Move forward eight steps clockwise.
Clap twice again. Form a left-star and move counterclockwise for eight steps.
Repeat the dance from the beginning.

POLLY WOLLY DOODLE

Level: II.
Origin: American.
Record: Merit Audio Visual: 1041.
Formation: Double circle of partners, facing one another, hands joined.
Skills: Slide.
Song:

Oh, I went down south for to see my Sal.
Sing Polly Wolly Doodle all the day.
My Sal she is a spunky gal.
Sing Polly Wolly Doodle all the day.
Fare thee well. Fare thee well.
Fare thee well, my fairy fay.
For I'm off to Louisiana for to see my Susyanna.
Singing Polly Wolly Doodle all the day.

Action:

Line 1: All slide four steps counterclockwise.
Line 2: Drop hands and turn individually in place with five stamps (slow, slow, quick, quick, quick).
Lines 3 and 4: Repeat the action of lines 1 and 2, but moving clockwise.
Line 5: Both partners bow. Boys have hands on hips; girls hold skirts.
Line 6: Partners move away from each other, moving backward with four walking or skipping steps.
Line 7: Both dancers move diagonally forward to their own left to meet a new partner.
Line 8: Join hands and skip around in place.
Repeat the dance with a new partner.

POP GOES THE WEASEL

Level: II.
Origin: American.
Record: Merit Audio Visual: 1043; World of Fun: 2.
Formation: Several formations may be used, including sets of three children, partners, or as a square dance.
Skills: Skip and walk.
Song:

Round and round the cobbler's bench, the monkey chased the weasel.
In and out and 'round about. Pop goes the weasel.

Action:

In sets of three, spaced in a large circle, inside hands joined; all facing counterclockwise.
Line 1: All walk forward while singing.
Line 2: Join outside hands to make a circle, and circle clockwise. On the words "Pop goes the weasel," the center dancer is "popped" under the joined hands of the outside dancers and moves on to join the twosome in front to form a new group.
In a double circle in two-couple sets, partners join inside hands. Couples numbered: Couples facing clockwise are 1, couples facing counterclockwise are 2.
Line 1: All step forward four steps and back four steps.
Line 2: Couples join hands and circle to the left. On the word "Pop" couple 1 pops under the arch formed by couple 2 and moves forward to join the couple ahead to make a new set.

SAVILA SE BELA LOZA

Level: II.
Origin: Serbian.
Record: Folkcraft: 1496.
Formation: Single line of six to eight dancers.
Skills: Schottische and run.
Action:

Part I—Measures 1 to 10: Face slightly to the right and move right with small running steps (20).
Measures 11 to 20: Immediately turn toward the left and move back to the left with small running steps.
Part II—Measures 1 and 2: Face the center and take one schottische step to the right, beginning with the right foot.
Measures 3 and 4: Repeat the action of measures 1 and 2 but moving to the left, with the first step on the left foot.
Measures 5 to 12: Repeat the pattern of measures 1 to 4, twice more.

Teaching suggestions: Savila Se Bela Loza means "a vine entwined itself." The schottische is almost a grapevine step, with the foot crossing in front (second step).

SKIP TO MY LOU

Level: II.
Origin: American.
Record: Folkdancer, FD34; Folkcraft: 1192.
Formation: A single circle of partners, all facing the center.
Skills: Walk, skip, swing, and promenade.
Song:

Verse 1: Boys to the center. Skip to my Lou.
Boys to the outside. Skip to my Lou.
Boys to the center. Skip to my Lou.
Skip to my Lou, my darling.
Verse 2: Girls to the center. Skip to my Lou.
Girls to the center. Skip to my Lou.
Girls to the center. Skip to my Lou.
Skip to my Lou, my darling.
Verse 3: Swing your partner, skip to my Lou. . . .
Verse 4: I've lost my partner, now what'll I do. . . .
Verse 5: I've got another one, prettier too. . . .

Action:

Verse 1: Boys walk four steps toward the center of the circle. Then take four steps backward to their places. Repeat to the center and back.
Verse 2: Girls repeat the action of the boys in verse 1.
Verse 3: Partners join hands and skip or swing in place.
Verse 4: Partners release hands. Girls walk forward, boys turn and walk in the opposite direction.
Verse 5: Children promenade with their new partners.
Repeat the dance with a new partner.

TURN THE GLASSES OVER

Level: II.
Origin: American.
Record: Folkcraft: 1181; World of Fun: 2.
Formation: Double circle of partners, all facing counterclockwise, in the skater's position.
Skills: Walk.
Song:
Verse: I've been to Harlem. I've been to Dover.
I've traveled the wide world all over.
Over, over, three times over.
Drink all the lemonade, and turn the glasses over.
Chorus: Sailing east, sailing west.
Sailing over the ocean.
You better watch out when the boat begins to rock.
Or you'll lose your girl in the ocean.
Action:
Verse 1: Couples promenade counterclockwise with a walking step. On "Turn the glasses over," they perform a dishrag turn by raising their arms, keeping their hands joined, and turning under their arms, making one complete outward turn.
Chorus: Girls continue walking counterclockwise; boys turn and walk clockwise. Any extra dancers join the children moving in the circle. On the last line, children quickly get a partner. Those without a partner move inside the circle for the repeat of the dance.

ACE OF DIAMONDS

Level: III.
Origin: Danish.
Record: Merit Audio Visual: 1044; World of Fun: 4.
Formation: Double circle, partners facing.
Skills: Step-hop and polka.
Action:
Measures 1 to 4: Clap hands once, hook right elbows with partners, and walk around with partner clockwise (six steps).
Measures 6 to 8: clap hands once, hook left elbows with partners, and walk around with partner counterclockwise (six steps).
Measures 9 to 12: With arms folded high, all take four slow steps-hops toward the center, the boy moving backward and the girl moving forward.
Measures 13 to 16: Take four step-hops back to place.
Measures 17 to 24: Join inside hands and polka counterclockwise around the circle, moving face to face, then back to back.|.|.|.
Variation for measures 9 to 16: A bleking step may be substituted for the step-hop. The rhythm is slow, slow, fast, fast, fast, fast.

BINGO

Level: III.
Origin: American.
Record: Folkcraft: 1189; Merit Audio Visual: 1043.
Formation: Double circle of partners, all facing counterclockwise.
Skills: Walk, slide, and grand right and left.
Song:
A big black dog sat on the back porch and Bingo was his name.
A big black dog sat on the back porch and Bingo was his name.
B I N G O, B I N G O, B I N G O, and Bingo was his name.
B I N G O.
Action:
Lines 1 and 2: In the promenade position, partners walk counterclockwise around the circle (16 steps).
Line 3: As they spell Bingo, they form a single circle by having the dancers in the inside back out. Joining hands, they then slide counterclockwise (12 slides).
Line 4: Partners face each other. Spelling Bingo very slowly they give their right hand to their partners, move past them, and give their left to the next. They continue the grand right and left until they reach a person on "O," who becomes their new partner.
The dance is repeated with a new partner.

BUGGY SCHOTTISCHE

Level: III.
Origin: International.
Record: Merit Audio Visual: 1046.
Formation: Two-couple sets, one couple in front of the other, all hands joined.
Skills: Schottische and step-hop.
Action:
Part I: Take two schottische steps forward, boys beginning on their left, girls on their right.
Take four step-hops forward, swinging free foot forward.
Part II: Take two schottische steps forward.
Take four step-hops, during which the head couple drops their hands but remains holding the hands of the couple behind them. The lead couple casts off, the boy moving left, the girl right, to move in behind the other couple.
The couple in the rear now joins hands and the dance is repeated.
Variation: Instead of casting off the lead couple backs under the arch formed by the rear couple. Without dropping hands they turn as if "wringing the dishrag."
Variation: Instead of casting off, the rear couple moves forward under the arch formed by the lead couple. Without dropping hands they turn as if "wringing the dishrag."

CHERKASSIYA

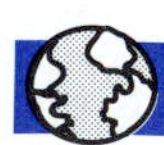

Level: III.
Origin: Israeli.
Record: Merit Audio Visual: 1043.
Formation: Closed or broken circle, hands joined.
Skills: Grapevine (cherkassiya step) and step-hop.
Action:
Chorus: The cherkassiya step, a form of the grapevine, is used. The dancer crosses the right over the left with a stamp, takes the weight on the right and takes a very short step with the left to the left. Next, the right foot crosses behind the left, taking the weight on the right and finishes with another very short step on the left to the left. This step is repeated four times.

The chorus follows each part of the dance.

Part I: Traveling to the right, each dancer steps to the right with the right foot, with the left foot extended to the side.

They then cross the left foot behind the right, taking the weight on the left foot and bending the knees slightly.

This step is done very quickly, almost as a running step (eight times).

Part II: The "horse trot." All face to the right and step-hop, leading with the right foot (eight step-hops).

Part III: The "Susie Q." Keeping both feet together, all lifting the feet, move their heels to the right (eight times).

Part IV: "Scissors forward." Beginning with the right foot, dancers kick their feet alternately forward while remaining in place (right, left, right, left) (16 times).

Part V: "Scissors backward." Repeat the action of Part IV, but kicking the feet backward in place.

Part VI: "The train." All face the right and bending the knees but keeping the trunk erect, walk counterclockwise (14 steps), ending with a high jump on both feet, facing the center.

CHRIST CHURCH BELLS

Level: III.
Origin: English.
Record: World of Fun: 5.
Formation: Double circle, partners facing; arranged in two-couple sets; boys on the inside; couple 1 facing counterclockwise, couple 2 facing clockwise.
Skills: Walk or run, slide, and cast off.
Action:

Part I: Boy 1 turns girl 2 with a right hand round (eight counts), then turns own partner with a left hand turn (eight counts).

Boy 2 turns girl 1 with a right hand round (eight counts), then turns own partner with a left hand turn (eight counts).

Part III: All join hands and slide to the left (eight slides) to finish in original places. Clap own hands, clap right hand of partner, clap own hands, clap partner's left (four counts).

Part III: "Cast off." Couple 1 turns outside away from each other and passes to the outside of couple 2 and couple 2 walks forward. Each couple now faces a new couple.

The dance is repeated from the beginning.

GUSTAF'S SKOAL

Level: III.
Origin: Swedish.
Record: World of Fun: 7; Merit Audio Visual: 1044.
Formation: A square set of four couples, with two head couples (facing and with their backs to the music) and two side couples.
Skills: Walk and skip.
Action:

Measures 1 to 4: Head couples take three steps forward and bow solemnly to each other. Then take three steps back to place and bow to their partners.

Measures 5 to 8: Side couples repeat the action of the head couples.

Measures 1 to 8: Repeat the action of the head and side couples.

Measures 9 to 16: Side couples face and form an arch by joining hands and raising them high in the air. Head couples skip forward.

Boy 1 takes girl 2, and boy 2 takes girl 1 by the hand and turn to face the side couples. The two new couples now skip under the arches they are facing.

After passing under the arch, the couples separate by turning away from each other and skip back to their original places. Everyone swings their partner for the remaining measures.

Repeat the action, with the head couples forming the arches and the side couples active.

HOPP MOR ANIKA

Level: III.
Origin: Swedish.
Record: Merit Audio Visual: 1042.
Formation: Double circle, all facing counterclockwise, inside hands joined.
Skills: Walk, skip, and polka.
Action:

Part I: Swinging hands forward and backward, and free hand on hips, walk forward (16 steps).

Part II: All skip forward (16 steps) and finish facing partner.

Part III: Stamp right foot and clap right hands simultaneously. Clap own hands.

Stamp left and left hands.

Clap right, clap own, clap left, clap own. Repeat.

Clap right, clap own, and stamp three times.

Part IV: Join inside hands, do a face to face, back to back polka counterclockwise (eight polka steps).

At the end, the inside person moves forward to take a new partner and the dance is repeated.

HORAH

Level: III.
Origin: Israeli.
Record: Merit Audio Visual: 1043.
Formation: Single circle, hands on shoulders of persons on either side.
Skills: Grapevine and hop.
Action:

Moving counterclockwise, step right to the side, place left behind right, and step right.

Kick left in front of right while hopping on the right.

Step left to the side, kick right across left while hopping on the left.

Repeat. The music gradually increases in tempo.

Teaching suggestions: Small groups may work best for elementary school children.

LA RASPA

Level: III.
Origin: Mexican.
Record: World of Fun: 6; Merit Audio Visual: 1043.
Formation: Partners scattered around the room, facing each other, hands joined.
Skills: Bleking and skip. Optional: polka and grand right and left.

Action:

Part I—Partners execute one bleking with the right foot forward, one bleking with the left foot forward. Repeat right, left, right. The rhythm is slow, slow, quick, quick, quick. Pause.

Part II—*Variation 1:* Clap hands once, hook right elbows, and skip around with partner (eight skips). Clap again, hook left elbows, and turn again with eight skips.

Variation 2: Join inside hands and do the face to face, back to back polka (16 steps).

Variation 3: In a circle formation, face partner. Give your right hand to your partner, walk forward past your partner, and give your left hand to the next person, doing a grand right and left around the circle.

MOSKROSSER

Level: III.
Origin: Danish.
Record: Merit Audio Visual: 1044.
Formation: Two-couple sets facing each other, arranged around the circle; couple 1 facing clockwise, 2 facing counterclockwise.
Skills: Schottische, ladies chain, right- and left-hand star.
Action:

Couple 1 with inside hands joined take two schottische steps forward, passing between couple 2, who drop hands and walk forward two schottische steps to the outside of couple 1.

All move back to place, with couple 1 dropping hands and passing couple 2 on the outside, couple 2 joining hands and passing between couple 1 (two schottische steps).

Ladies chain with eight schottische steps.

Dancers form a right-hand star by placing right hands in the center and moving around in a circle for four schottische steps. Reverse with a left-hand star for four schottische steps.

Couples face. Holding inside hands and moving counterclockwise, take one schottische step moving away from each other, followed by one schottische step moving toward their partner.

Couples take the shoulder-waist position. They step-hop in the direction they were originally facing, turning as they move around the circle. All couples pass by the couple originally in their set and face a new couple, with whom they will repeat the dance.

NORWEGIAN MOUNTAIN MARCH

Level: III.
Origin: Norwegian.
Record: Merit Audio Visual: 1044.
Formation: Sets of three, with the center person in front, the remaining two behind; each holds a handkerchief between their joined hands.
Skills: Waltz or step-hop.
Action:

Part I—Measures 1 to 8: Take eight step-hops (or waltz) forward beginning with the right foot. The first beat of each step is slightly accented. The lead dancer turns to the right and left, looking at the dancers behind.

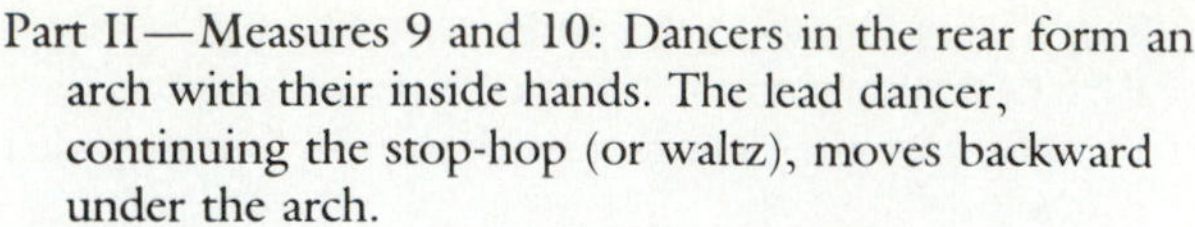

Part II—Measures 9 and 10: Dancers in the rear form an arch with their inside hands. The lead dancer, continuing the stop-hop (or waltz), moves backward under the arch.

Measures 11 and 12: Dancer on the left, moving clockwise, dances across and under the lead dancer's right arm.

Measures 13 and 14: Dancer on the right turns left under the lead dancer's right arm.

Measures 15 and 16: Lead dancer turns right and under own right arm. The group should now be in its original position.

Measures 17 to 24: Repeat measures 9 to 16.

Teaching suggestions: This dance represents a guide leading climbers up and down the mountainside and should be performed with this in mind. Most important is keeping the chain untangled and unbroken. A waltz step is preferable in this dance, but this may be too difficult for many elementary school children.

OH SUSANNA

Level: III.
Origin: American.
Record: Merit Audio Visual: 1043.
Formation: Single circle of partners, all facing the center.
Skills: Walk and grand right and left.
Song:

Measures 1 to 4: Oh, I come from Alabama with a banjo on my knee.

Measures 5 to 8: And I'm goin' to Louisiana for my true love for to see.

Measures 9 to 16: It rained all night the day I left. The weather it was dry.

I cried so hard I broke my heart. Susanna don't you cry.

Chorus: Oh Susanna, Oh don't you cry for me.

For I come from Alabama with a banjo on my knee. Repeat.

Action:

Part I—Measures 1 to 4: Girls walk forward four steps and back four steps as boys clap.

Measures 5 to 8: Boys walk forward four steps and back as girls clap.

Part II—Measures 9 to 16: Partners face each other. All do the grand right and left, giving their right hand to their partner and walking forward to give their left hand to the next. Continue while the chorus "Oh Susanna" is reached (approximately the seventh person).

Measures 17 to 32: At the chorus, join hands with new partner and walk counterclockwise around the circle. (The chorus is repeated.)

Repeat the dance from the beginning with a new partner.

Teaching suggestions: If the children are not ready for the grand right and left, a swing with their partners may be substituted.

SEVEN JUMPS

Level: III.
Origin: Danish.
Record: Merit Audio Visual: 1043; World of Fun: 4.
Formation: Single circle, all facing counterclockwise.
Skills: Step-hop.

Action:

Beginning with the chorus, the children step-hop counterclockwise (eight step-hops). Reverse direction and take eight step-hops clockwise. The chorus is repeated after each figure.

Figure 1: With hands on hips, raise right knee and hold.

Figure 2: With hands on hips, raise right knee and hold. Raise left knee and hold.

Figure 3: Repeat Figure 2 and add kneeling on the right knee and hold.

Figure 4: Repeat Figure 3 and add a kneel on the left knee and hold.

Figure 5: Repeat Figure 4 and add touching the right elbow to the floor. Hold.

Figure 6: Repeat Figure 5 and add touching the left elbow to the floor. Hold.

Figure 7: Repeat Figure 6 and touch your head to the floor. Hold.

Teaching suggestions: Because each hold is for differing amounts of time, encourage the children to listen carefully. If the skip is substituted for the step-hop, the dance becomes suitable for younger children.

SICILIAN CIRCLE

Level: III.

Origin: American.

Record: World of Fun: 1.

Formation: A double circle of two-couple sets, couples alternately facing clockwise and counterclockwise.

Skills: Walk, ladies chain, and right and left through.

Action:

Partners join inside hands and walk forward three steps, bow, and move back to place.

All join hands in the set and circle once around to the left.

Ladies chain across and back to place.

Right and left through across and back to place.

Partners join inside hands and walk forward four steps and then back to place.

Partners walk forward and pass through the opposite couple, passing right shoulders with the opposite person. Each couple now faces a new couple.

Repeat the dance in the new sets.

Teaching suggestions: A right- and left-hand star may be substituted for the ladies chain; a do-si-do with the opposite and then with the partner for the right and left through.

TETON MOUNTAIN STOMP

Level: III.

Origin: American.

Record: Folkcraft: 1482.

Formation: Single circus of partners, facing each other; hands joined.

Skills: Step-close, walk, and two-step or buzz step.

Action:

Measures 1 to 4: Step toward the center of the circle; close the opposite foot to the first. Step once more toward the circle and stamp with the following foot. (Side, close, side, stamp.) Repeat moving away from the circle.

Measures 5 to 8: Step toward the center once again. Stamp the opposite foot close to the stepping foot. Repeat moving away from the center.

Partners shift to a banjo position (right hips adjacent) and walk four steps counterclockwise, the boy moving forward, the girl moving backward.

Measures 9 to 12: Partners shift to a sidecar position (left hips adjacent) by making a half turn to the right. Boy remains on the inside and is now facing clockwise. Boy walks four steps backward while girls walks four steps forward.

Partners shift back to the banjo position by making a half turn to the left. Immediately they release from each other, with the boy moving counterclockwise four steps to meet a new partner.

Measures 13 to 16: New partners join hands and do two two-steps, turning while progressing counterclockwise. Four pivot steps are then taken to the right, so the boy ends up facing the line of direction.

Teaching suggestions: A buzz step may be substituted for the two-steps and pivots. The dancers then take about eight steps while swinging.

TINIKLING

Level: III.

Origin: Philippine.

Record: Merit Audio Visual: 1047.

Formation: Groups of three to six, each group having a set of poles.

Skills: Walk and leap.

Action:

Two long bamboo poles about 9 feet long are needed for each group. These poles may rest on blocks of wood about 2 inches thick and 30 inches long. An individual sits at each end of each pole, holding one in each hand. The sticks should be held with the thumb and fingers

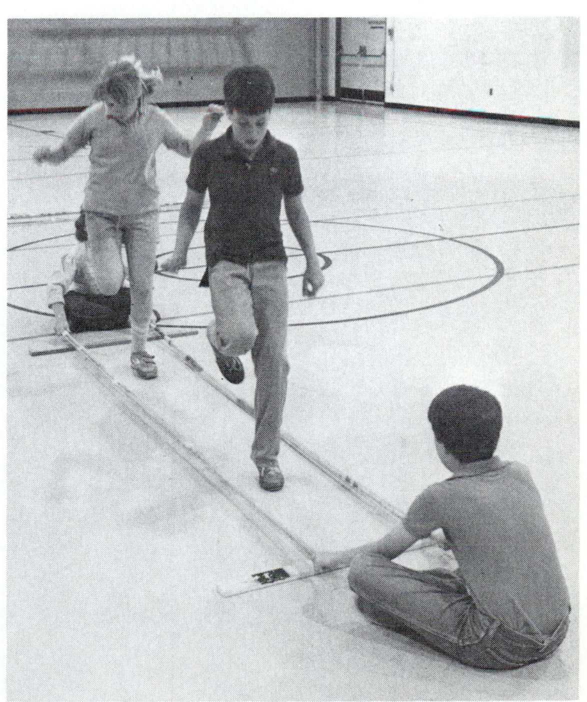

Tinikling.

on the sides of the stick (not underneath). The poles are operated in the following rhythm:

Count 1: Strike sticks together.

Count 2: Strike sticks on the floor or supporting poles about 18 inches apart.

Count 3: Strike sticks apart one more time.

Variation 1: Dancers straddle sticks. On count 1, they jump with both feet apart on either side of the sticks. On counts 2 and 3, they jump with feet close together between the sticks.

Variation 2: Dancers stand with their sides next to and outside the poles.

Count 1: Pause as the poles are struck together.

Count 2: Leap sideways into the poles, touching the floor first with the foot closest to the poles in the starting position.

Count 3: Touch the other foot to the floor between the poles as the first foot is raised slightly from the floor.

Count 1: Continuing in the same direction, step out from between the sticks to the opposite side of the foot closest to the side, while raising the foot taking the step on count 3.

Count 2: Move in between the sticks as in count 2 above but from the opposite side.

Count 3: Repeat count 3 above continuing to move in the new direction.

Continue stepping out from between the sticks on count 1 and stepping with alternating feet on counts 2 and 3.

Variation 3: Dancers move continuously clockwise around and in between the poles.

Counts 1 to 3: Walk parallel to the sticks on the outside as stickhandlers beat together-apart-apart. With the right side toward the sticks, step left, right, left.

Counts 1 to 3: Step right and pivot to face down between the sticks (count 1). Step in between the sticks with the left foot, which is now nearest the sticks (count 2), and with the right (count 3).

Step out with the left on count 1 and repeat the beginning sequence of stepping along and on the outside of the sticks. Four persons at a time may do this by having each one begin at one of the corners, with two moving immediately through the sticks while the other two begin by stepping parallel to the sticks.

Variation 4: Line a series of pairs of sticks parallel to each other. The children proceed down the series of sticks as in variation 2, except that they must cross one foot over the other and into every other set of sticks.

Variation 5: Similar to the variation above, but children turn between each set of sticks, so that the right foot enters first for one set, the left the next.

Variation 6: Arrange two sets of sticks so that they cross in the center. Children proceed as in variation 3, but will step in between a set of sticks for each measure.

Teaching suggestions: It is helpful to have the children practice the steps using parallel lines on the floor before trying them with the moving sticks. There is a tendency for the children operating the sticks to go faster and faster.

The children will need help in maintaining a steady tempo.

VIRGINIA REEL

Level: III.

Origin: American.

Record: Merit Audio Visual: 1043.

Formation: Longways set of no more than six couples.

Skills: Walk, do-si-do, and slide and reeling.

Action:

Part I: Boys join hands in their line, and girls in theirs. All walk forward four steps and then back to place.

Repeat the action above.

All walk forward, join right hands with partners, turning once around clockwise, and then walking back to place.

Repeat the action, joining left hands.

Repeat the action, joining two hands.

Walk forward to meet partner, do-si-do, and walk back to place.

Part II: The first couple joins hands and slides eight slides down the center of the set and eight slides back to place.

Reeling.

First couple begins the reel by hooking right elbows, circling once and a half around, clockwise, so they end facing the opposite line. They then drop elbows and hook left elbows with the next person in the opposite line. They come back to their partners with a right elbow turn and then on to the next in line, proceeding down the set until couple 1 reaches the foot of the set. Couple 1 then joins hands and slides down toward the head of the set.

Part III: Facing toward the head of the set, the first couple casts off, turning away from each other and toward their own line. They then lead their own line to the foot of the set. The first couple then joins hands and forms an arch through while each of the following couples pass. Couple 1 remains at the foot of the set, with couple 2 now becoming active.

The dance is now repeated from the beginning. Couple 2 assumes the original position of couple 1 and will become active in Part II.

Teaching suggestions: It is important for the children to realize that they always reel with their partner and the line opposite from the one in which they are standing.

BLACK NAG

Level: IV.
Origin: English.
Record: World of Fun: 6.
Formation: Longways set of three couples, all facing the head of the set.
Skills: Run, slide, right-left elbow swing, and hey.
Action:

Part I (A)—Measures 1 to 4: "Forward and back a double." Each couple, holding right hands, takes four running steps forward (beginning with the right) and four steps back.

Measures 5 to 8: Repeat the action of measures 1 to 4.

Part I (B)—Measures 1 and 2: Partners face each other, joining both hands at shoulder height. The first couple slips sideways with four sliding steps, toward the head of the set.

Measures 3 and 4: The second couple moves up four slides sideways.

Measures 5 and 6: The third couple takes four slides.

Measures 7 and 8: All "turn single." Releasing hands, dancers turn individually to their right with four steps.

Measures 1 to 8: Repeat the action of measures 1 to 8. The third couple returns to its beginning position. Then the second and finally the first couple. All "turn single."

Part II (A)—Measures 1 to 8: "Siding." Partners pass each other with four steps, passing left shoulders and return, passing right shoulders. Repeat. (On the fourth step, partners turn to face each other so that they face each other on the way back.)

Part II (B)—Measures 1 and 2: The first boy and the last girl (diagonals) change places with four sliding steps, with right shoulders leading and passing back to back.

Measures 3 and 4: The first girl and the last boy (diagonals) do the same, with four sliding steps.

Measures 5 and 6: The second man and lady do the same.

Measures 7 and 8: All "turn single."

Measures 1 to 8: Repeat the action of measures 1 to 8 with all dancers in turn returning to their places. All "turn single."

Part III (A)—Measures 1 to 8: "Arm right" and "arm left." Partners turn each other first with a right elbow swing followed by a left elbow swing, with eight steps for each turn.

Part III (B)—Measures 1 to 8: "Men's hey." Couple 1 faces down the set, couples 2 and 3 facing up the set. The first and second boy start by veering to their left, so that they pass right shoulders with each other, continuing around a large loop into the center. The third boy waits for about two counts, giving the first two boys a chance to pass each other. Boy 3 then begins his "hey" by moving to the right and into the center. Continuing in the figure eight, they end in their original places.

Measures 1 to 8: "Ladies hey." Girls repeat the action of the boys. On the last two measures the boys turn single with four steps.

Teaching suggestions: The name of this dance probably originated in the English tradition of naming taverns with animal names.

CRESTED HEN

Level: IV.
Origin: Danish.
Record: World of Fun: 4; Merit Audio Visual: 1042.
Formation: Sets of three dancers, their hands joined together to form a circle.
Skills: Step-hop.
Action:

Part A—Moving clockwise, step-hop in a circle, take a vigorous stamp on the first beat. Dancers lean away from the circle (eight steps).

Jump bringing feet down sharply on the first beat, step-hop in a circle moving counterclockwise (eight steps).

Part B—Continuing to step-hop, outside dancers drop hands. Placing their free hand on their hips the right-hand dancer step-hops through the arch formed by the center dancer and the dancer on the left.

The center dancer turns under own left arm following the right-hand dancer through the arch, followed almost immediately by the left-hand dancer turning under own right hand so that the dancers do not have to release hands.

Repeat the action by having the left-hand dancer begin the move, moving through the arch formed by the center and the right-hand dancers.

Repeat the sequence once more, beginning with the right-hand dancer and ending with the left-hand dancer.

CUMBERLAND SQUARE EIGHT

Level: IV.
Origin: English.
Record: World of Fun: 5.
Formation: Square set of four couples, designated as head, foot, and side couples.
Skills: Galop, star, and basket.
Action:

Head and foot couples, with partners facing, join hands and galop across set in eight slides, boys passing back to back.

Return to position with eight galops, girls passing back to back.

Repeat the action with the side couples.

Head and foot couples come together in the center of the set, forming a right-hand star (eight counts) and then a left-hand star back to place (eight counts).

Side couples repeat the right- and left-hand stars.

Head and foot couples form a basket (the boys join hands with each other behind the girls' backs; the girls extend their hands behind and under the boys' arms and join hands with each other in front of the boys). Circle to the left and then back to place with two steps (16 steps).

Side couples repeat the action by forming a basket. All join hands and circle to the left (16 counts).

Promenade back to their original position (16 counts).

Teaching suggestions: In place of the basket, the two couples may join hands and skip vigorously to the left in a circle.

FIREMAN'S DANCE

Level: IV.
Origin: American.
Record: World of Fun: 1; Folkcraft: 1131.
Formation: Two couples in a line facing two couples in a line, arranged in a circle as the spokes of a wheel.
Skills: Slide, gallop, ladies chain, and right and left through.
Action:

Part I (A)—Measures 1 to 4: Both boy 1 and the opposite girl 1 (nearest the center of the circle) step forward opposite girl and boy 2 (at the other end of the line) take one step back. The active 1s slide eight steps down the center, between the lines, while the active 2s take eight slides individually behind the lines.

Measures 5 to 8: They return to their places with eight slides, 1s on the inside, 2s on the outside.

Measures 1 to 8: Repeat the action of measures 1 to 8, but with the 2s on the inside and the 1s on the outside.

Part II (B)—Measures 1 to 8: Simultaneously, the 1 couples do a right and left through, while the 2 couples do a ladies chain, all couples ending in their original places.

Measures 1 to 8: Repeat the action but with the 1 couples doing a ladies chain and the 2 couples doing the right and left through.

Part III (C)—With hands joined in lines of four, all advance four steps forward, shouting, "Fire, fire, fire," and walk back four steps shouting, "Water, water, water." They then release hands, walk forward, and pass through the opposite line, passing right shoulders with the opposite dancer, progressing to begin the dance with a new line.

FIVE FOOT TWO

Level: IV.
Origin: American.
Record: Folkcraft: 1420.
Formation: Double circle, all facing counterclockwise in the promenade position.
Skills: Two-step, walk, and balance.
Action:

Part I—Promenade.

Measures 1 and 2: Take two two-steps in the line of direction.

Measures 3 and 4: Walk forward four steps in the line of direction.

Measures 5 and 6: Repeat measures 1 and 2.

Measures 7 and 8: Drop left hands. Boy walks four steps forward, turning to face out of the circle on the last two steps. Girl walks four steps backward, turning to face inside of the circle. All join hands in one large single circle.

Part II—Balance and walk around.

Measures 9 and 10: Balance forward, balance back.

Measures 11 and 12: Drop left hands. Walk four steps around partner, moving clockwise to change places. Girls now face out, boys in. All join hands in a single circle.

Measures 13 and 14: Repeat measures 9 and 10.

Measures 15 and 16: Drop partner's hand. Each boy takes the girl on his left for a new partner and both walk four steps to face in the line of direction in the promenade position.

GATHERING PEASCODS

Level: IV.
Origin: English.
Record: Merit Audio Visual: 1045.
Formation: Single circle of partners, all facing the center, hands joined.
Skills: Slide and walk.
Action:

Part I—All take eight "slips" (slides) to the left. Drop hands and "turn single" (individually turn in place with four small steps).

Repeat, taking eight "slips" to the right and "turn single."

Part II—Boys step forward to form an inner circle, join hands, and take 12 "slips" to the left, returning to their original positions.

Girls form an inner circle and take 12 "slips" to the left, returning to their places.

Part III—Boys "double" (walk) forward three steps and clap.

Girls "double" forward and clap as boys return to their places.

Girls "double" back as boys "double" forward.

All "turn single," the boys returning to their places as they turn.

Repeat Part III.

Part IV: Partners face and "side" (take eight steps forward, passing left shoulders, turn, and pass right shoulders on the return). "Turn single."

Repeat the "siding" and "turn single."

Part V—Repeat Part II, with the girls forming the circle first and then the boys.

Part VI—Repeat Part III, with the girls leading the first "double" and boys leading the repeat.

Part VII—Partners "arm" (elbow swing) with right elbow (eight steps). "Turn single."

Partners "arm" with left elbow (eight steps). "Turn single."

Part VIII—Repeat Part II.

Part IX—Repeat Part III, ending with a final "turn single."

Teaching suggestions: This is one of the many old English dances that were danced in the court of King James I. Later, these dances became popular with the country people, who danced them on the village green for pleasure, not spectacle.

HEEL AND TOE POLKA

Level: IV.
Origin: American.
Record: MacGregor: 5003-B.
Formation: Couples in the varsouvienne position.
Skills: Fling.
Action:

Beginning with the outside foot, touch the heel forward, toe behind, and take a two-step forward (heel, toe, step, close, step).

With the inside foot, touch heel forward, toe behind, and a two-step forward (heel, toe, step, close, step).

Partners take four polka steps.

Teaching suggestions: The polka step may be taken forward or in the face to face, back to back manner. If the polka step is taken in the open position, the children will need some practice in doing the step as they move forward. This dance may be used as a mixer by arranging the dancers in a circle, moving counterclockwise on the polka step. On the last step, the girl takes the step in place, while the boy moves forward to a new partner.

HIGHLAND FLING

Level: IV.
Origin: Scottish.
Record: Merit Audio Visual: 1045.
Formation: Individuals scattered in the room.
Skills: Fling.
Action:

First step—Measures 1 and 2: Spring on the toes; then with the left arm raised overhead and the right hand on the hip, hop on the left foot, bringing the right foot behind the left leg. Hop again on the left foot, bringing right foot in front of left leg. Hop again on the left, bringing the right foot behind again.

Measures 3 and 4: Repeat from the beginning, hopping on the right foot and reversing hands.

Measures 5 and 6: Repeat measures 1 and 2.

Measures 7 and 8: Place both hands on hips and repeat measures 3 and 4, turning once around in place to the right.

Measures 9 to 16: Repeat measures 1 to 8, beginning with the left foot hop, but raising the right arm first.

Second step—Measure 1: Spring on the toes again, landing on both feet.

Measure 2: With left arm raised, hop on the left, touching the right toe forward and to the side. Hop again on the left, bringing the right foot in front of the left leg.

Measures 3 and 4: With both hands on hips and with right-foot hops, turn once around in place to the right (measures 7 and 8 above).

Measures 5 to 8: Repeat measures 1 to 4, beginning with the right-foot hops and raising the right arm. This time turn to the left.

Measures 9 to 16: Repeat measures 1 to 8.

JESSIE POLKA

Level: IV.
Origin: American.
Record: Folkcraft: 1093.
Formation: In lines of two or more with hands on the waist of the person in front.
Skills: Two-step or polka.
Action:

Part I—Heel step.

Measure 1: Beginning left, touch the heel in front, then step left in place.

Measure 2: Touch the right toe behind, then in place, or swing it forward, keeping the weight on the left.

Measure 3: Touch the right heel in front, then step right in place.

Measure 4: Touch the left heel to the left side; sweep the left across in front of the right. Keep the weight on the right.

Part II—Two-step or polka.

Measures 5 to 8: Take four two-steps or polka steps forward in the line of direction.

Teaching suggestions: This dance may become a mixer by having couples, alternating girl, boy in the line. On the last two steps the girl turns out to her right and falls into line behind her partner. The last girl rushes to the head of the line.

MAITELITZA

Level: IV.
Origin: Russian-American.
Record: Educational Dance Recordings: FD-2.
Formation: Sets of three, inside hands joined, facing counterclockwise; in a circle as the spokes of a wheel.
Skills: Hop-swing and slide.
Action:

Part I (A)—Measures 1 to 8: Stamp on the right foot. Hop on the right, swinging on the left foot lightly across in front. Stamp left, swinging the right foot across. Repeat the action three times more. Each group then moves forward for three steps.

Part II (A)—Measures 1 to 8: All turn to face the center (making a quarter turn to the left). Each joins hands with the person on the right and left sides, making three concentric circles. All slide eight steps to the right and then eight steps back to the left.

Part III (B)—Measures 1 to 8: All turn to face counterclockwise and join hands in the original threes. The middle and left persons form an arch by raising their joined hands, and the person on the right walks slowly forward, under the arch, and back to place with eight steps. On the last four steps the middle dancer turns under his or her own arm following the right-hand dancer. The middle dancer then forms an arch with the right-hand dancer and the pattern is repeated with the left-hand dancer going under the arch.

Teaching suggestions: In Part II the circles may slide in opposite directions (inner circle to the left, middle circle to the right, outer circle to the left).

MAYIM

Level: IV.
Origin: Israeli.
Record: World of Fun: 6.
Formation: Single circle, hands joined and held down.
Skills: Grapevine, hop, and run.
Action:

Part I—Grapevine (tscherkessia).

Measures 1 to 4: Moving clockwise, cross the right in front of the left (count 1); step left to the side (count 2); cross right behind left (count 3); step left to the side with a light springing step, accenting the step (count 4). Repeat three or more times.

Part II—Center and back.

Measure 5: Beginning right, take four running steps to the center, leaping slightly and bending the knee on the first step. Lift joined hands gradually above heads as dancers move to the center.

Measure 6: Beginning right, move away from the center with four running steps, lowering arms as they move.

Measures 7 and 8: Repeat measures 5 and 6.

Part III—Run, toe, touch, clap.

Measure 1: Beginning right, move clockwise with three running steps (counts 1 to 3); turn to face the center, weight remaining on the right (count 4).

Measure 2: Hop on the right and touch the left across in front to the right side (count 1). Hop on right and touch left to the side (count 2). Hop right, touching left in front to the right side (count 3). Hop right touching left to the side (count 4).

Measure 3: Repeat measure 2.

Measure 4: Hop on left, touching right in front to the left side and clap hands directly in front at arms length (count 1). Hop on left, touch right to side and swing arms out to the sides at shoulder height (count 2). Hop left, touch right in front to the left side, and clap hands directly in front at arms length (count 3). Hop left, touching the right to the side and swinging arms out to the sides at shoulder height (count 4).

Measure 5: Repeat measure 4.

MISERLOU (KRITIKOS)

Level: IV.
Origin: Greek.
Record: Merit Audio Visual: 1046.
Formation: A large broken circle, hands joined, the leader is at the right end of the line.
Skills: Grapevine and two-step.
Action:

Measure 1: Beginning right, step in place (count 1); hold (count 2); pointing left toe in front of right make a circular out and motion to the left toward the right heel (counts 3 and 4). (Group movement is counterclockwise.)

Measure 2: Step left behind right (count 1); step right to the side (count 2); step left across in front of right (count 3); pivot counterclockwise a half turn on the left to face clockwise (count 4).

Measure 3: Beginning right and moving clockwise take one two-step.

Measure 4: Step back on left (count 1); step right to the side, body facing the center (count 2); step left across in front of right (count 3); hold (count 4).

Teaching suggestions: Smaller groups may be more successful at the elementary school level. A variation for measure 4 is to substitute a two-step moving backward, for the movement described above.

ROAD TO THE ISLES

Level: IV.
Origin: Scottish.
Record: World of Fun: 3; Merit Audio Visual: 1043.
Formation: Double circle of partners in the varsouvienne position, all facing counterclockwise.
Skills: Schottische, step-hop, and grapevine.
Action:

Part I—Point, grapevine.

Measure 1: Point left toe forward to the left.

Measures 2 and 3: Step left behind right (count 1); step right to the right side (count 2); step left in front of right (count 1); hold (count 2).

Measure 4: Point right toe forward to the right.

Measures 5 and 6: Step right behind left (count 1); step left to the left side (count 2); step right in front of left (count 1); hold (count 2).

Measures 7 and 8: Point left toe forward (body leans backward); point left toe back (body leans forward).

Part II—Schottische.

Measures 9 to 12: Beginning left, take two schottische steps in the line of direction. Without releasing hands, turn clockwise on hop (count 2, measure 12) to face the reverse line of direction. The girl is now on the boy's left.

Measures 13 and 14: Beginning left, take one schottische step in the reverse line of direction. Without releasing hands, turn counterclockwise on the hop to face the line of direction. The girl is now back in the original position on the boy's right.

Measures 15 and 16: Stamp in place, right, left, right.

Teaching suggestions: The Scottish style of precise and small footwork should be encouraged. Kicking the heel up on the hop of the schottische step as if to flick the kilt is also characteristic of this dance.

SICILIAN TARANTELLA

Level: IV.
Origin: Italian.
Record: Merit Audio Visual: 1045; World of Fun: 6.
Formation: Two-couple sets, boys standing side by side, facing their partners.
Skills: Step-hop, do-si-do, skip, and star.
Action:

Part I—In place, each person steps on the right foot, hops on it, swinging the left foot forward and at the same time claps own hands (or strikes a tambourine). Repeat the step-hop on the left foot, swinging the right foot forward and clapping.

In place, take four quick running steps, snapping fingers or shaking a tambourine overhead.

Repeat the above three more times.

Part II—Snapping fingers or shaking tambourines, dancers bend forward and take four running steps toward their partners, straighten up, and raise their arms. Take four steps backward, lowering arms and bending forward.
Repeat three more times.
Part III—The head boy and the front girl (diagonally across from one another) clap their own hands, run forward, hook right elbows, turn once, and return to their places.
The foot boy and the head girl repeat the action.
The action is again repeated for both sets but with a left elbow swing.
Part IV—The head boy and the foot girl do a right shoulder do-si-do (pass right shoulders only) and return to places.
The other couple repeats the action.
The do-si-do is repeated for both couples but this time passing left shoulders.
Part V—Dancers face their own right, and with hands on waist, all skip forward counterclockwise for eight steps in the circle. Turning about, they skip clockwise for eight steps.
All four dancers join left hands for a left-hand star and skip counterclockwise for eight steps. They turn, joining hands for a right hand star for eight steps.
They return to their starting positions to begin the dance again.

LINE DANCE

Line dancing, a form of dance that has gained popularity in the United States during the past two decades, has its roots in the contra and free style dances of the past. These activities have often been used as warm-up or introductory activities in dance units and are now becoming an integral part of the dance experience. Line dances provide a fun-filled rhythmic dance activity, combining locomotor and nonlocomotor movements performed without partners or at least without personal contact with a partner.

These dances tend to include movement sequences that are repeated, dancers in lines or scattered in general space moving in the same pathway, and turns after which the sequences are repeated facing a new direction. There is great variation in the dances in different parts of the United States. Most of the dances can be performed to any music with a good 4/4 beat.

The dances included here are all performed in a line or scattered in general space. The line dances are summarized in Table 21-3.

ALLEY CAT

Level: III.
Record: Alley Cat: Atco Records, 45-6226; Bill Justice, Smash Records MCS 27021.
Skills: Touch step.
Action:
Touch right foot forward, touch right foot to the left, touch right foot forward, close right foot to left.
Repeat with left foot.
Touch right foot back, touch right foot to left, touch right foot back, close right foot to left.
Repeat with left foot.
Lift right knee 6 inches above the floor. Touch right to the floor. Lift right knee again and then close right foot to left.
Repeat lifting left knee.
Lift right knee, close right foot to left, lift left knee, close left foot to right.
Clap, pause. Step forward on left as you turn 1/4 turn to the left, touch right foot to left.
Repeat the dance sequences.

This dance originated in the 1960s.

BUS STOP

Level: III.
Record: Ice Ice Baby: Vanilla Ice (slow tempo); Can't Touch This: Hammer (faster tempo).
Skills: Walk, touch step.
Action:
Beginning on the right foot step backward for three steps and clap.
Walk forward three steps and clap.
Repeat backward and forward step sequences.
Turn to the right in a circle with three steps beginning on the right and clap.
Turn to the left in a circle beginning with the left foot for three steps and clap.
Click heels two times as you move your arms in duck fashion twice.
Touch right toe in front two times, then in back two times.
Touch right toe in front once and then touch right toe behind once (two beats each).
Touch right toe to the side once. Lift right knee, and make a 1/4 turn to the left. Pause.
Repeat the dance sequences.

ELECTRIC SLIDE

Level: III.
Record: Electric Boogie, Marcia Griffiths, Tape: Carrousel, 422-842 334-4.
Skills: Slide, walk, touch step.
Action:
Slide to the right three slides, and finish with a clap on 4.
Repeat sliding to the left. Slide, slide, slide, clap.
Starting on the right foot, take three steps back and clap.
Step forward on left, touch right foot to left. Step backward on right foot and touch left to right.
Lift right knee up, take a 1/4 turn to the left.
Repeat entire sequence.

HITCH HIKER

Level: III.
Record: Black and White: Michael Jackson, Epic ET45400; Dancing in the Sheets, Footloose Original Soundtrack.
Skills: Jump, nonlocomotor movements.

TABLE 21-3 LINE DANCES

NAME	BASIC STEPS	SUGGESTIONS	PAGE	RECORD	LEVEL
Alley Cat	Touch step	Practice turn then add sequences before and after	417	Alley Cat: Atco Records 45-6226; Bill Justice, Smash Records MCS 27021	III
Bus Stop	Walk, touch step	Practice turn as above	417	Ice Ice Baby: Vanilla Ice (slow) Can't Touch This: Hammer (faster)	III
Electric Slide	Slide, walk touch step	Practice turn as above	417	Electric Boogie: Carrousel 422-842 334-4	III
Hitch Hiker	Jump, non-locomotor	Practice turn as above	417	Black & White: Michael Jackson, Epic ET 45400	III
Achy Breaky Heart	Grapevine, shuffle, step, stomp	Practice grapevine turn first, add before and after sequences	418	Achy Breaky Heart: Billy Ray Cyrus, Mercury 314-510635-4	IV
Bad Bad Leroy Brown	Grapevine, scissor step, strut	Cue: slow, slow, quick, quick, quick, quick on first 2 sequences	419	Bad Bad Leroy Brown: Jim Croce, Lifesong Records Inc. A135571	IV
L.A. Hustle	Step, grapevine, touch step, slide		419	The Hustle: Van McCoy and Soul City Symphony, Avco Records AV4653	IV
New Yorker	Walk, touch step		419	Disco Inferno: The Tramps, Saturday Night Fever RSO Records RS-2-4001	IV

Action:

Standing with arms down at sides, elbows bent, hands at shoulder level, fingers pointing away from the body and palms facing downward, jab right two times by extending arm to right, fingers pointing to the right. Repeat with two jabs to the left. The head should be turned in the direction of the jabs.

Repeat the action but this time palms face upward, two times to the right, two times to the left.

Thumbs up as if hitch hiking, twice to the right and then to the left.

Roll hands around each other (as if signaling traveling in basketball) to the right, left, out in front and back closer to body.

Cross right hand to left hip, left hand to right hip, place right hand on right gluteus maximus, left hand on left gluteus maximus.

Jump two times forward with hands on gluteus maximus. Jump a 1/4 turn to the left. Pause.

Repeat the dance.

ACHY BREAKY HEART

Level: IV.

Record: Achy Breaky Heart: Billy Ray Cyrus, Mercury, 314-510635-4.

Skills: Grapevine, shuffle, step, stomp.

Action:

Grapevine: Moving to the right, step right, cross left behind right, step right, cross left over right.

Grapevine: Repeat moving to the left.

Grapevine turn: Moving to the right, step right, step left behind right, step right, step left in front of right with a 1/4 turn to the right. Take one grapevine step to the left.

Shuffle: Step forward on an angle to the right, bring left up to right in a slow gallop, repeat three more times.

Shuffle: Repeat moving on an angle to the left, beginning on the left foot.

Step with the right in place. Close the left to the right with a stomp, but keeping weight on the right foot. Step left and stomp with the right. Repeat right and left one more time. Dancers may clap on the stomp as well.

Repeat the dance sequences.

This is a simpler version of the Achy Breaky Heart line dance.

BAD BAD LEROY BROWN

Level: IV.

Record: Bad Bad Leroy Brown: Jim Croce, Lifesong Records Inc., A135571

Skills: Strut, grapevine, scissor step

Action:

Beginning with the right foot take two slow strutting steps forward (two counts each).

Beginning on the right take three steps forward and close left foot to the right (one count each).

Grapevine: Moving to the right step on the right, cross the left behind the right, step right to the right, and kick or swing the left foot in front of the right.

Grapevine: Repeat moving to the left ending with a swing or kick of the right leg in front of the left.

Beginning with the right foot, step backward with two slow strutting steps (two counts each).

Beginning with the right take four steps backward (one count each).

Step sideward to the right with the right foot, and close the left foot to the right. Cross the right foot in front of the left and pause.

Step left to the left side. Close the right foot to the left, cross the left foot in front of the right (scissor) turning 1/4 turn to the right.

Repeat the dance sequences.

The origin of this dance is unknown, but it is a favorite of many authors.

L.A. HUSTLE (Eastern and Midwestern Version)

Level: IV.

Record: The Hustle, Van McCoy and the Soul City Symphony, Avco Records, AV4653.

Skills: Step, grapevine, slide, touch step.

Action:

Beginning with the right foot step backward three steps, and touch left foot to right.

Beginning with the left, step forward three steps and touch right foot to left.

Repeat right and left foot sequences.

Grapevine: Step right to the side, cross left in front of right, step right to the side and touch left foot to the right.

Repeat the grapevine moving to the left, ending by touching the right foot to the left.

Slide forward and pause, slide backward and pause.

Slide forward, slide backward, separate heels and click them together twice.

Touch right foot in front twice, touch right foot in back twice.

Touch right foot in front, in back, to the side, and then kick right foot across in front of left as you turn 1/4 turn to the left.

Repeat the sequences.

This midwestern and eastern version is a modification of the California version written by Rosemary "Red" Hallum.

NEW YORKER

Level: IV.

Record: Disco Inferno: the Tramps Original Soundtrack from Saturday Night Fever, RSO Records, RS-2-4001.

Skills: Walk, touch step.

Action:

Beginning on the right step backward three steps. Touch left foot to right.

Beginning left step forward, touch right foot to left, step right forward, and touch left to right.

Beginning left take one step forward and close right to left. Slide backward two times.

Touch right heel forward, touch right foot in place next to left. Lift right knee and turn 1/4 to left on the left.

Repeat the dance sequences.

This dance was standardized by Ralph Lew of Manhattan, New York, in 1978-1979.

SQUARE DANCE

Square dance calls are of two types: **patter** and **singing** calls. Patter calls are those in which the caller gives the instructions of the dance in a rhythmic manner, with folksy sayings added for color. Patter calls give callers more opportunity to individualize the dance by adding their own sayings. These calls generally rhyme and fit the rhythmic pattern of the music, but the music used varies with the caller. Singing calls are those in which the caller gives instructions to the dancers by singing the call to a familiar tune. There tends to be less variation from caller to caller because these dances are written to particular tunes. A square dance is divided into several parts: the introduction, the main figure, the break, and the closing. The introductory calls get the dancers moving. The break is the actions that are generally called halfway through the main figure. The closing includes the actions that will terminate the dance. In patter calls, the beginning, break, and closing are called at the discretion of the caller. Unlike singing calls they are not standardized in any way. The main figure includes the primary actions from which the dance received its name.

Learning to call square dances takes careful planning, but once the skills are learned a caller may learn to call extemporaneously. Square dance music is generally written in either 4/4 or 2/4 time, both of which can be broken down into series of four even beats. Each four beats constitute a phrase for calling. Calls generally begin on count 1, but in some cases where the call is short, such as allemande left, the next call may begin on count three. Calls never begin on counts 2 or 4 (Babcock).

To practice calling, the caller should write out the calls and attempt to put the counts to the call. Once the calls

TABLE 21-4 SQUARE DANCES

NAME	CALL	FIGURE	SKILLS	PAGE	RECORD	LEVEL
Birdie in the Cage	Patter	Visiting couple	Circle, swing	421	Educational Record: Sq. 3	III
Duck for the Oyster	Patter	Visiting couple	Circle, arch	422	Educational Record: Sq. 2	III
Irish Washerwoman	Singing	Symmetrical	Do-si-do, allemande left, grand right and left, swing, promenade	422	Educational Record: Sq. 2A	III
Just Because	Singing	Symmetrical	Do-si-do, allemande left, grand right and left, swing, promenade, ladies chain	422	Educational Record: Sq. 3	III
Pop Goes the Weasel	Singing	Single visiting	Circle, swing, promenade	423	Educational Record: Sq. 3 World of Fun: 2	III
Red River Valley	Singing	Visiting couple	Allemande left, grand right and left, promenade, circle, swing	423	Educational Record: Sq. 2 World of Fun: I MacGregor: 1204	III
Solomon Levi	Singing	Accumulative	Swing, allemande left, grand right and left, promenade	423	MacGregor: 1204	III
Take a Peek	Patter	Visiting couple	Circle, swing	424	Educational Record: Sq. 4	III
Alabama Jubilee	Singing	Symmetrical	Allemande left, grand right and left, promenade, sashay, swing	424	MacGregor: 638, 640, 1204 Old Timer: 8041, 8043 Windsor: 4414, 4444	IV
Coming Round the Mountain	Singing	Symmetrical	Ladies chain, swing, allemande left and right promenade	424	Educational Record: Sq. 4	IV
Dip and Dive	Patter	Visiting couple	Circle, arch, swing, promenade	424	Educational Record: Sq. 4	IV
Divide the Ring and Tunnel Through	Patter	Split-the-ring	Bow, swing, forward and back, arch, do-si-do	425	Educational Record: Sq. 3	IV
Hot Time in the Old Town	Singing	Accumulative	Circle, allemande left/right, grand right and left, sashay, swing, promenade	425	Folkcraft: 1037 MacGregor: 652, 004-4, 445-4	IV
Hurry, Hurry, Hurry	Patter	Line	Circle, ladies chain	426	Educational Record: Sq. 4	IV
Jessie Polka Square	Singing	Arching	Arch, allemande left, star, promenade, swing, two-step	427	Folkcraft: 1263 MacGregor: 657	IV
Oh Johnny	Singing	Symmetrical	Circle, swing, allemande left, do-si-do, promenade	427	MacGregor: 6525, 1204 Old Timer: 8041 Folkcraft: 1037	IV
Smoke on the Water	Singing	Symmetrical	Allemande left, grand right and left, swing, circle, sashay, star, bow	428	MacGregor: 1204	IV
Texas Star	Patter	Star	Forward and back, right and left star, swing, promenade	428	Educational Record: Sq. 4	IV

Visiting figure.

are determined, the next step is to listen to the music and clap the underlying beats to get an idea where the calls will be made. Once this has been done, the caller may then wish to run through the calls clapping the beats needed for each. In putting the calls to the music, the caller must remember to allow sufficient beats in between the calls to execute the movements called. Obviously, a grand right and left takes more beats than a do-si-do. In actual calling, the caller responds to the dancers, giving them ample time for the figures but keeping them moving along as well. With a little practice, patter calls are fun and provide more variety and challenge to the dancers, who must respond to the changing calls being given.

Square dance figures may be structured in several ways. Some dances use what is known as a **visiting figure.** In these dances, individuals, a couple, or several couples execute the figure with each couple in succession. For example, the visiting person(s) from couple 1 begin by going to couple 2 and executing the figure. They then move on to couple 3 and finally to couple 4 to repeat the main figure two more times. The next visiting person(s) then begins the action, moving from couple to couple. The main figure is concluded when all four couples or individuals have traveled to each of the other couples to repeat the dance.

In some dances all four couples simultaneously perform the actions of the dance. These dances are referred to as **symmetrical figures.** Other dances use the **star, split-the-ring,** or **arching figures.** In the star figure, individuals or couples grasp hands in the center of the set to form a star. In split-the-ring, a couple moves across the set to pass between the two dancers of the opposing couple. In arching figures, one or more couples form an arch by raising joined hands and one or more couples pass under the arch. In many of these dances, the couples alternate forming and passing through the arches.

The next section includes a variety of square dances that may be used at the upper elementary school level. Only the main figure is included for dances that use a patter call because the beginning, break, and closing vary in the records available. A summary of the square dances included may be found in Table 21-4.

BIRDIE IN THE CAGE

Level: III.
Call: Patter.
Figure: Visiting couple.
Record: Educational Recording: Sq.3.
Skills: Circle and swing.
Action:

Main figure.

FIRST COUPLE OUT TO THE COUPLE ON THE RIGHT. CIRCLE FOUR FOR HALF THE NIGHT.

Couples 1 and 2 join hands and circle half a circle so that couple 1 is facing in toward the center of the set; couple 2 is facing toward the outside of the set.

NOW BIRDIE IN THE CAGE, THREE HANDS ROUND.

The girl of couple 1 drops hands and steps into the circle made by the three other dancers. The three dancers circle around the "birdie."

BIRDIE FLY OUT, THE CROW HOP IN.

The girl backs out of the circle to join hands with the other dancers, while her partner steps into the circle. The three dancers circle the "crow."

NOW THE CROW HOP OUT, SWING YOUR OWN, BOTH COUPLES SWING.

The dance is repeated with couple 1 moving to couple 3 and finally to couple 4.

The entire sequence is then repeated for couples 2, 3, and 4.

DUCK FOR THE OYSTER

Level: III.
Call: Patter.
Figure: Visiting couple.
Record: Educational Recordings: Sq.2.
Skills: Circle and arch.
Action:

Main figure:

FIRST COUPLE OUT TO THE COUPLE ON THE RIGHT. CIRCLE FOUR FOR HALF THE NIGHT.

Couple 1 goes to couple 2, the four join hands, and circle to the left halfway around so that couple 1 faces in toward the set and couple 2 faces the outside of the set.

DUCK FOR THE OYSTER, DUCK.

Couple 1 with hands joined moves under the arch formed by couple 2 and backs back to face the set again.

NOW DIVE FOR THE CLAM, DIVE.

Couple 1 forms an arch and couple 2 with hands joined moves under the arch and backs out again.

AND DUCK ON THROUGH AND ON TO THE NEXT.

Couple 2 forms an arch again, couple 1 moves under the arch and on to couple 3 to repeat the action again.

The dance is repeated with couple 1 moving on to do the dance with couples 3 and 4. Following this sequence the dance is repeated, with couples 2, 3, and 4 becoming the visiting couples in turn.

IRISH WASHERWOMAN

Level: III.
Call: Singing.
Figure: Symmetrical.
Record: Educational Recordings: Sq.2A.
Skills: Do-si-do, allemande left, grand right and left, swing, and promenade.
Action:

Introduction:

NOW DO-SI-DO WITH THE CORNERS ALL, BACK TO BACK AROUND THE HALL. DO-SI-DO WITH THE PARTNERS TOO, SQUARE YOUR SET, HERE'S WHAT YOU DO. ALLEMANDE LEFT WITH YOUR LEFT HAND, RIGHT TO YOUR PARTNER, GO RIGHT AND LEFT GRAND. PROMENADE. THE RIGHT FOOT UP, THE LEFT FOOT DOWN, PROMENADE AROUND THE TOWN. SQUARE UP HERE WE GO.

Main figure:

ALL FOUR BOYS YOU LEAD TO THE RIGHT, HONOR THE LADIES SO POLITE.

All boys move to the girl on the right (past partner).

DO-SI-DO, ON HEEL AND TOE. READY NOW AWAY WE GO.

Do-si-do with the right-hand lady.

STEP RIGHT UP AND SWING HER AWHILE, STEP RIGHT BACK AND WATCH HER SMILE.

Boys swing the girl and then take the girl's right hand in their right and step back away from her.

STEP RIGHT UP AND SWING HER AGAIN. STEP RIGHT BACK AND WATCH HER GRIN.

Swing the girl again and promenade her to the boy's home position as his new partner.

The dance is repeated three more times until the boys are back to their original partners.

JUST BECAUSE

Level: III.
Call: Singing.
Figure: Symmetrical.
Record: Educational Recordings: Sq.3.
Skills: Do-si-do, allemande left, grand right and left, swing, promenade, and ladies chain.
Action:

Introduction:

DO-SI-DO YOUR CORNER, SHE'S A DARLING. AND THEN YOU DO-SI-DO YOUR PARTNER, DO THE SAME. ALLEMANDE LEFT TO THE CORNER. GRAND RIGHT AND LEFT, GRAND CHAIN 8 HALF WAY ROUND YOU GO. DO-SI-DO YOUR PARTNER, SHE'S A DARLING. SO SWING THAT PRETTY BABY ROUND AND ROUND. PROMENADE AROUND THAT HALL, JUST WALK AROUND YOU GO. BECAUSE, JUST BECAUSE.

Main figure:

HEAD 2 LADIES CHAIN DOWN THE CENTER OF THE SET. NOW TURN THE LADIES, CHAIN 'EM BACK IN TIME.

Couples 1 and 3 do the ladies chain over and back.

AND NOW THE SIDE 2 LADIES CHAIN DOWN THE MIDDLE OF THAT RING. NOW TURN THE LADIES, CHAIN 'EM BACK IN TIME.

Couples 2 and 4 do the ladies chain over and back.

DO-SI-DO YOUR CORNER, SHE'S A DARLING. DO-SI-DO YOUR PARTNER, DO THE SAME. LET'S TAKE THE CORNER MAID AND WITH HER PROMENADE. BECAUSE, JUST BECAUSE.

The dance is repeated three more times. On the second time through, the head couples begin the chaining first; on the third and fourth times, the side couples begin the ladies chain first.

POP GOES THE WEASEL

Level: III.
Call: Singing.
Figure: Single visiting.
Record: Educational Recordings: Sq.3; World of Fun: 2.
Skills: Circle, swing, promenade.
Action:

Introduction, break, closing:

ALL JOIN HANDS AND CIRCLE LEFT, CIRCLE LEFT, CIRCLE LEFT WITH THE WEASEL. ONCE AROUND TIL YOU COME HOME, SWING WITH THE WEASEL. SWING YOUR PARTNER ONCE AROUND, PROMENADE THE TOWN. PROMENADE EIGHT AND PROMENADE ALL, SQUARE YOUR SETS WITH THE WEASEL.

Main figure:

FIRST GIRL GO OUT TO THE RIGHT, CIRCLE THERE LIKE THUNDER. THREE HANDS AROUND WE GO. POP THE LADY UNDER.

The first lady and couple 2 circle to the left for one half turn. Then couple 2 raises their joined hands and lady 1 moves under the arch and on to couple 3.

GO TO THE NEXT, THE BOY WILL FOLLOW, CIRCLE LEFT LIKE THUNDER. THREE HANDS AROUND WE GO. POP THE COUPLE UNDER.

Repeat the action above, but this time boy 1 waits outside the circle, so when couple 3 makes an arch, he and his partner pop under.

ON TO THE NEXT, THE BOY WILL FOLLOW, CIRCLE THERE LIKE THUNDER. THREE HANDS AROUND WE GO, POP THE COUPLE UNDER. GIRL COME BACK, THE BOY COME ON CIRCLE 4 LIKE THUNDER. FOUR HANDS AROUND WE GO, POP THE COUPLE UNDER.

Come back to couple 4 and repeat the action. This time all four dancers circle.

The dance is repeated with the second, third, and fourth couples becoming active in turn.

RED RIVER VALLEY

Level: III.
Call: Singing.
Figure: Visiting couple.
Record: Educational Recordings: Sq.2; World of Fun: 1; MacGregor, 1204.
Skills: Allemande left, grand right and left, promenade, circle, swing.
Action:

Introduction and closing:

NOW YOU ALLEMANDE LEFT ON THE CORNER. AND THE GRAND RIGHT AND LEFT HALFWAY ROUND. WHEN YOU MEET WITH YOUR PARTNER PROMENADE HER. AND PLACES ALL, LISTEN TO MY CALL.

Main figure:

THE FIRST COUPLE TO THE RIGHT AND CIRCLE. CIRCLE TO THE LEFT, THEN TO THE RIGHT. NOW YOU SWING WITH THE OTHER FELLOW'S PARTNER. NOW YOU SWING WITH YOUR RED RIVER GAL.

Partners swing.

The dance is repeated two more times with couple 1 moving to couples 3 and 4 in turn. Then the entire sequence is repeated with couples 2, 3, and 4 becoming active.

SOLOMON LEVI

Level: III.
Call: Singing.
Figure: Accumulative.
Record: MacGregor: 1204.
Skills: Swing, allemande left, grand right and left, promenade.
Action:

Introduction and closing:

NOW EVERYBODY SWING YOUR HONEY, YOU SWING HER HIGH AND LOW. THE ALLEMANDE LEFT WITH THE OLD LEFT HAND, AROUND THE RING YOU GO. A GRAND OLD RIGHT AND LEFT, WALK ON YOUR HEEL AND TOE. YOU MEET YOUR HONEY AND GIVE HER A TWIRL AND AROUND THE RING YOU GO. SINGING, OH SOLOMON LEVI, TRA LA LA LA LA LA. OH SOLOMON LEVI, TRA LA LA LA LA LA.

Main figure:

NOW THE FIRST OLE COUPLE SEPARATE, GO ROUND THE OUTSIDE TRACK.

Girl and boy 1 go around the set, the girl moving counterclockwise, the boy clockwise.

A KEEP A GOING AROUND THE SET. YOU PASS A COMIN' BACK.

Pass partner at the opposite side of the set and continue moving to your home position.

YOU PASS RIGHT BY YOUR PARTNER, SALUTE YOUR CORNERS ALL. YOU TURN AROUND AND SWING YOUR OWN, AND PROMENADE THE HALL. SINGING OH SOLOMON LEVI, TRA LA LA LA LA LA. OH SOLOMON LEVI, TRA LA LA LA LA LA.

The dance is repeated, with couples 2, 3, and 4 becoming active in turn. Then couples 1 and 3 become active, 2 and 4, and finally all four couples.

TAKE A PEEK

Level: III.
Call: Patter.
Figure: Visiting couple.
Record: Educational Recordings: Sq.4.
Skills: Circle, swing.
Action:

Main figure:

COUPLE NUMBER 1 GO OUT TO THE RIGHT. FACE THE SECOND COUPLE. GO 'ROUND THAT COUPLE AND TAKE A LITTLE PEEK.

Couple 1 separate, lady peeks around the right side of couple 2 and the boy peeks around the left.

BACK TO THE CENTER AND SWING YOUR SWEET. GO 'ROUND THAT COUPLE PEEK ONCE MORE. BACK TO THE CENTER AND SWING ALL FOUR. BOTH COUPLES SWING.

The call is repeated for couples 2, 3, and 4.

ALABAMA JUBILEE

Level: IV.
Call: Singing.
Figure: Symmetrical.
Record: MacGregor: 638, 640, 1204; Old Timer: 8041, 8043; Windsor, 4414, 4444.
Skills: Allemande left, grand right and left, promenade, sashay, and swing.
Action:

Opening and closing:

IT'S THE ALLEMANDE LEFT, GO ALL THE WAY ROUND. RIGHT HAND AROUND THE NEXT GAL AND DON'T YOU FALL DOWN.

Right hand to the partner and grand right and left.

A LEFT HAND AROUND THE NEXT LITTLE GAL, A RIGHT HAND AROUND THE NEXT, SHE'S THE SWEETEST LITTLE PAL. IT'S A LEFT HAND, A RIGHT HAND, NOW DON'T YOU BE SLOW. ALL AROUND THAT LADY IN THE CALICO. MEET YOUR HONEY AND YOU PROMENADE, TAKE A LITTLE WALK WITH THAT SWEET LITTLE MAID, TO THE ALABAMA JUBILEE.

Main figure:

FOUR LITTLE LADIES PROMENADE THE INSIDE OF THE RING. BACK TO YOUR HONEY AND GIVE HIM A SWING. SASHAY AROUND YOUR CORNER GIRL. BOW TO YOUR HONEY BOYS, GIVE HER A WHIRL. NOW FOUR GENTS PROMENADE THE INSIDE OF THE HALL BACK TO YOUR HONEY AND SASHAY ALL. SWING THAT CORNER GAL AROUND, TAKE A LITTLE WALK AROUND THE TOWN, TO THE ALABAMA JUBILEE.

The main figure is repeated three more times until the dancers return to their original partners. On the second and fourth times, the boys begin the action by promenading in the inside of the ring.

COMING ROUND THE MOUNTAIN

Level: IV.
Call: Singing.
Figure: Symmetrical.
Record: Educational Recordings: Sq.4.
Skills: Ladies chain, swing, allemande left and right, and promenade.
Action:

THE HEAD TWO COUPLES CHAIN, SIDE COUPLE SWING. CHAIN THEM AROUND THE MOUNTAIN, CHAIN THEM HOME. THE SIDE TWO COUPLES LADIES CHAIN, HEAD TWO COUPLES SWING AGAIN. CHAIN THEM ROUND THE MOUNTAIN, CHAIN THEM HOME. ALLEMANDE LEFT YOUR CORNERS. ALLEMANDE RIGHT YOUR PARTNERS. COME ALL THE WAY AROUND YOUR PARTNER TO THE NEXT GIRL ON THE RIGHT.

All give their right to their partner, walk around their partner, and continue moving forward to the next person.

SWING THIS LADY UP AND DOWN, SWING HER ROUND AND ROUND AND ROUND. AND PROMENADE THAT PRETTY MOUNTAIN GAL.

Promenade with the new partner to the boy's home position. The dance is repeated until the dancers are with their original partners. The second time the action begins with the head couples chain; the third and fourth times the dance begins with the side couples chain.

DIP AND DIVE

Level: IV.
Call: Patter.
Figure: Visiting couple.
Record: Educational Recordings: Sq.4.
Skills: Circle, arch, swing, and promenade.

Action:
Main figure:

FIRST COUPLE TO THE RIGHT AND CIRCLE FOUR.

Couple 1 goes out to couple 2, they join hands, and all four dancers circle left halfway round, so that couple 1 faces in toward the set and couple 2 faces the outside of the set.

THE INSIDE COUPLE ARCH. IT'S DIP AND DIVE, AND AWAY YOU GO. WITH THE INSIDE HIGH AND THE OUTSIDE LOW. HURRY, HURRY, HURRY, LET'S GO. DUCK OVER AND BE LOW.

Couple 2 makes an arch and couple 1 ducks under it. Couple 1 continues forward, makes an arch. Couple 4 ducks under the arch. Meanwhile, couple 2 turns to face the set, the boy's partner on his right. Couple 4 makes an arch, couple 2 ducks under. This over and under action is repeated until the first couple is back in the center.

NOW DUCK ON THROUGH TO THE OPPOSITE TWO AND CIRCLE FOUR WITH THEM.

On the last move, couple 1 ducks under the arch formed by couple 2 and moves on to couple 3. They circle halfway round with them.

YOU DUCK TO THE NEXT AND CIRCLE FOUR.

Couple 3 forms an arch and couple 1 ducks under to move on to couple 4. Couple 1 circles halfway round with couple 4.

INSIDE COUPLE ARCH. IT'S DIP AND DIVE AND AWAY YOU GO. WITH THE INSIDE HIGH AND THE OUTSIDE LOW. HURRY, HURRY, HURRY, LET'S GO LOW. NOW DUCK ON THROUGH AND HOME YOU GO.

The action is repeated with couples 1, 4, and 2 doing the "dip and dive."

AND EVERYBODY SWING. YOU SWING YOUR PRETTY LITTLE RED WING, AND PROMENADE HER AND SERENADE HER.

The dance is repeated for couples 2, 3, and 4.

DIVIDE THE RING AND TUNNEL THROUGH

Level: IV.
Call: Patter.
Figure: Split-the-ring.
Record: Educational Recordings: Sq.3.
Skills: Bow, swing, forward and back, arch, and do-si-do.

Action:
Main figure:

NOW FIRST COUPLE, NUMBER 1 BOW AND SWING, WE'LL HAVE A LITTLE FUN.
GO DOWN THE CENTER, SPLIT-THE-RING, AND GO ROUND THE SIDES.

Couple 1 walks forward and passes between couple 3, where they separate, the girl turning to her right, the boy to his left. They continue to move around the outside of the set.

JOIN UP WITH THE SIDES, WITH LINES OF THREE.
FORWARD SIX AND BACK.

They end by passing the side couples and standing next to them, the girl next to couple 2, the boy next to couple 4. The two lines of dancers take four steps forward toward each other and then four steps back with hands joined.

NOW FORWARD SIX AND MAKE AN ARCH.

The two lines take four steps forward again. The dancers then join hands with the opposite dancer to form a tunnel.

THIRD COUPLE TUNNEL UNDER AND DON'T YOU BLUNDER, SWING ON THE OTHER SIDE.

Couple 3 passes under the tunnel and swings on the other side (couple 1's home position).

NOW THIRD COUPLE TUNNEL BACK, AND EVERYBODY SWING WITH PARTNER ALL, AND EVERYBODY WHIRL.

Couple 3 moves back to place under the tunnel and everybody swings.

DO-SI-DO YOUR CORNERS ALL AND DO-SI-DO YOUR PARTNERS TOO.

All dancers back in their home positions do the do-si-do first with their corner, and then with their partner. The dance is repeated for couples 2, 3, and 4.

HOT TIME IN THE OLD TOWN

Level: IV.
Call: Singing.
Figure: Accumulative.
Record: Folkcraft: 1037; MacGregor: 652, 004-4, 445-4.
Skills: Circle, allemande left and right, grand right and left, sashay, swing, and promenade.
Action:
Beginning:

ALL JOIN HANDS AND CIRCLE EIGHT AROUND.
BREAK AND TRAIL ALONG THAT LINE.

Drop hands and continue moving left, one after the other in a circle.

WHEN YOU GET HOME, EVERYBODY SWING.
THERE'LL BE A HOT TIME IN THE OLD TOWN TONIGHT.

Main figure:

FIRST COUPLE OUT, AND CIRCLE FOUR AROUND.
PICK UP TWO AND CIRCLE SIX AROUND.

Boy 1 breaks the circle by unclasping left hand and takes the right hand of the couple 3 girl. Couple 3 now joins the group and circles with them to the left.

PICK UP TWO AND CIRCLE EIGHT AROUND.
THERE'LL BE A HOT TIME IN THE OLD TOWN TONIGHT.

Boy 1 breaks the circle again, picking up couple 4 to join the group. All eight circle to the left.

ALLEMANDE LEFT WITH THE LADY ON THE LEFT.
ALLEMANDE RIGHT WITH THE LADY ON THE RIGHT.
ALLEMANDE LEFT WITH THE LADY ON THE LEFT.
AND GRAND RIGHT AND LEFT ALL AROUND.
WHEN YOU MEET YOUR PARTNER, SASHAY ONCE AROUND.
TAKE HER IN YOUR ARMS AND SWING HER ROUND AND ROUND.
PROMENADE AROUND WITH THE PRETTIEST GIRL IN TOWN.
THERE'LL BE A HOT TIME IN THE OLD TOWN TONIGHT.

The dance is repeated, with couples 2, 3, and 4 becoming the visiting couples.

Ending:

ALLEMANDE LEFT WITH THE LADY ON THE LEFT.
ALLEMANDE RIGHT WITH THE LADY ON THE RIGHT.
ALLEMANDE LEFT WITH THE LADY ON THE LEFT.
GRAND RIGHT AND LEFT ALL AROUND.
WHEN YOU MEET YOUR PARTNER, SASHAY ONCE AROUND.
BREAK UP YOUR SETS AND DANCE HER 'ROUND AND 'ROUND.
THERE'LL BE A HOT TIME IN THE OLD TOWN TONIGHT.

HURRY, HURRY, HURRY

Level: IV.
Call: Patter.
Figure: Line.
Record: Educational Recordings: Sq.4.
Skills: Circle and ladies chain.
Action:
Main figure:

THE FIRST COUPLE GO OUT TO THE RIGHT AND CIRCLE FOUR HANDS ROUND. NOW LEAVE THE GIRL, GO ON TO THE NEXT, LET'S MAKE IT THREE HANDS ROUND.

Couple 1 circle with couple 2. Boy 1 goes on to couple 3 and circles to the left with them. Girl 1 stands in a line of three with couple 2.

NOW TAKE THIS COUPLE WITH YOU. LET'S MAKE IT FIVE HANDS ROUND.

Right hand star.

Boy 1 and couple 3 move on to couple 4 and all five circle to the left.

YOU LEAVE THEM THERE AND JOIN THE LINE OF THREE. STAND BY YOUR PARTNER.

Boy 1 leaves couples 3 and 4 standing in a line facing couple 2 and girl 1. He joins partner, to form two lines facing each other.

CHAIN THE LADIES ACROSS THE SET, BUT DON'T YA BE SLOW.

Girls give their right hands to the opposite girl, walk by them, giving their left hands to the opposite boys, who turn them around (a three-quarter turn) to face down the line.

NOW CHAIN THE LADIES DOWN THE LINE, WALK ON YOUR HEEL AND TOE.

Ladies now chain with the couple they are facing (the couple they were standing next to in the line of four). The boys again turn them with a three-quarter turn.

CHAIN THE LADIES ACROSS THE SET, AND KEEP ON MOVING ROUND.

Ladies chain with the couple across the set, once again with a three-quarter turn.

AND TURN AND CHAIN YOUR PARTNER BACK TO PLACE. SQUARE YOUR SET.

Chain once more, ending with the original partners.

The dance is repeated, with couples 2, 3, and 4 taking their turns to lead the figure.

JESSIE POLKA SQUARE

Level: IV.
Call: Singing.
Figure: Arching.
Record: Folkcraft: 1263; MacGregor: 657.
Skills: Arch, allemande left, star promenade, two-step, and swing.
Action:

NOW THE SIDE COUPLES ARCH, HEAD COUPLES DUCK RIGHT UNDER. AND YOU DIP AND YOU DIVE, HOME YOU GO AND DON'T YOU BLUNDER.

Couples 2 and 4 make arches and move clockwise around the square as couples 1 and 3, moving counterclockwise, duck under the arches. Couples 1 and 3 make arches as 2 and 4 duck under. Repeat until they reach their home positions.

NOW YOU ALLEMANDE LEFT, PUT YOUR ARM AROUND YOUR PARTNER IN A STAR PROMENADE. DO THE JESSIE POLKA DANCE.

All give their left hands to their corners and do the allemande left. When the boys return to their partners, put a hand around her waist (girl does a half turn to face the same direction as partner). Boys form a left-hand star and walk forward, counterclockwise. (Star promenade.)

IT'S HEEL AND A TOE, YOU START THE MUSIC JUMPIN'.

Couples do the Jessie Polka: Touch left heel forward (count 1). Step left in place (count 2). Touch right toe back (count 1). Touch right beside left (count 2). Touch right heel forward (count 1). Step right in place (count 2). Touch left heel forward (count 1). Swing left foot across instep of right (count 2).

AS THE LADIES ROLL AWAY, CAN'T YOU SEE THE BUSTLES BUMPIN'.

Couples take four two-steps forward, the girls turn to the right and back to the boys behind them on the last two two-steps.

OH YOU DANCE THROUGH THE NIGHT AS THOUGH IT WERE A MINUTE.

Repeat the Jessie Polka.

YOUR HEARTS ARE REALLY IN IT. THE JESSIE POLKA DANCE.

Couples repeat the two-steps with the girls turning back on the last two two-steps.

NOW WATCH THAT CORNER MAID AND AS SHE COMES AROUND
TAKE HER IN YOUR ARMS AND SWING HER 'ROUND AND 'ROUND.

As the girls roll back the third time, they swing with that boy corner.

THEN YOU PROMENADE HER HOME, KEEP HER FOR YOUR PARTNER.
YOU BALANCE AND YOU SWING 'TIL THE MUSIC STARTS AGAIN.

Keeping their new partners, they promenade to the boy's home position and balance and then swing.

The dance is repeated three times until the dancers are back to their original partners.

OH JOHNNY

Level: IV.
Call: Singing.
Figure: Symmetrical.
Record: MacGregor: 6525, 1204; Old Timer, 8041; Folkcraft, 1037.
Skills: Circle, swing, allemande left, do-si-do, and promenade.

Action:

OH YOU ALL JOIN HANDS AND YOU CIRCLE THE RING.
STOP WHERE YOU ARE AND YOU GIVE HER A SWING.
NOW SWING THAT GIRL BEHIND YOU.
GO BACK HOME, AND SWING YOUR OWN IF YOU HAVE TIME.
ALLEMANDE LEFT WITH THE CORNER GIRL, DO-SI-DO YOUR OWN.
NOW YOU ALL PROMENADE, WITH THAT SWEET CORNER MAID.
SINGING OH JOHNNY, OH JOHNNY, OH.

The call is repeated until the dancers are back to their original partners.

Teaching suggestions: This dance may also be done using a single circle of partners.

SMOKE ON THE WATER

Level: IV.
Call: Singing.
Figure: Symmetrical.
Record: MacGregor: 1204.
Skills: Allemande left, grand right and left, swing, circle, sashay, star, and bow.
Action:

Introduction and closing:

NOW YOU ALLEMANDE LEFT YOUR CORNER AND YOU PASS RIGHT BY YOUR OWN.
RIGHT HAND SWING OLE SALLY GOODIN, A LEFT HAND SWING YOUR OWN.

Sally Goodin is the girl of the couple to the right.

LADIES STAR RIGHT IN THE CENTER, 'TIL YOU MEET YOUR CORNER MAN.
AND YOU ALLEMANDE LEFT YOUR CORNER, PARTNER RIGHT, AND A RIGHT AND LEFT GRAND.
THERE'LL BE SMOKE ON THE WATER, ON THE LAND AND ON THE SEA.
A RIGHT HAND TO YOUR PARTNER, TURN AROUND AND YOU GO BACK THREE.
YOU'LL DO A LEFT, RIGHT, AND A LEFT HAND SWING, GO ALL THE WAY AROUND.
SWING ON THE CORNER, TAKE HER HOME AND SETTLE DOWN.

Main figure:

FOUR GENTS CENTER, MAKE A CIRCLE AND YOU TURN IT ONCE AROUND.
HOME YOU GO, SASHAY YOUR PARTNER, STAR WITH THE RIGHT WHEN YOU COME DOWN.
TURN THAT STAR OUT IN THE CENTER, 'TIL YOU MEET YOUR CORNER GAL.
ALLEMANDE LEFT THE CORNER, RIGHT AND LEFT GO ROUND THE WORLD.
YOU'LL WALK AROUND THAT CIRCLE JUST AS PRETTY AS CAN BE.
A RIGHT HAND TO YOUR PARTNER, TURN AROUND AND YOU GO BACK THREE.
YOU'LL DO A LEFT, RIGHT, A LEFT HAND SWING, GO ALL THE WAY AROUND.
SWING ON THE CORNER, TAKE HER HOME AND SETTLE DOWN.
HEAD GENTS BOW TO YOUR PARTNER AND YOU SWING HER ROUND AND ROUND.
PASS RIGHT THROUGH, RIGHT DOWN THE CENTER, SEPARATE GO ROUND THE TOWN.
WHEN YOU MEET YOUR LITTLE LADY, SASHAY PARTNERS ONE AND ALL.
YOU ALLEMANDE LEFT THE CORNER. RIGHT AND LEFT GO ROUND THE HALL.
THERE'LL BE SMOKE ON THE WATER, ON THE LAND AND ON THE SEA.
A RIGHT HAND TO YOUR PARTNER, TURN AROUND AND YOU GO BACK THREE.
YOU'LL GO LEFT, RIGHT, A LEFT HAND SWING, GO ALL THE WAY AROUND.
SWING ON THE CORNER, TAKE HER HOME AND SETTLE DOWN.

Repeat from:

HEAD GENTS BOW TO YOUR PARTNERS.

But this time the side gents are active.

TEXAS STAR

Level: IV.
Call: Patter.
Figure: Star.
Record: Educational Recordings: Sq.4.
Skills: Forward and back, right and left star, swing, and promenade.
Action:

NOW LADIES TO THE CENTER AND BACK TO THE BAR.
AND GENTS TO THE CENTER WITH A RIGHT-HAND STAR.
TAKE THE RIGHT HAND OUT, PUT THE LEFT HAND IN,
COME BACK AGAIN.

Boys reverse directions, changing to a left-hand star.

NOW MEET YOUR PARTNER, GONNA PASS HER BY.
PICK UP THE NEXT ONE ON THE SLY WITH THE ARM AROUND HER WAIST.
NOW KEEP YOUR ARM AROUND HER WAIST.

Continue moving the star counterclockwise with the girl by the boy's side.

THE MEN BACK OUT AND THE LADIES COME IN WITH A TURN AND A HALF.

AND LADIES STAR WITH A RIGHT-HAND CROSS.
AND EVERYBODY SWING AND EVERYBODY WHIRL.

Boys break the star, couples turn moving counterclockwise one and a half times. The girls form a right-hand star in the center.

SWING WITH THE LADY ROUND YOU GO, AND THE ACE IS HIGH AND THE DEUCE IS LOW.

Girls break the star and swing with their new partners.

PUT HER ON THE RIGHT, LET'S PROMENADE, WALK AROUND THAT HALL.

The dance is repeated until the girls are returned to their original partners.

NATIVE AMERICAN DANCES

Long before European settlers landed on the shores of North America, Native Americans engaged in dance activities. Some of the dances were in celebration of seasonal or other events. Some of the dances, developed to go with songs, told stories of human or animal activities. In some cultures dances were performed to tease individuals or sexes. Some of the dances were individual dances, whereas others were social dances performed at pow wows and other social gatherings. In many of the dances, special costumes and special masks were worn. These dances have been passed down from one generation to the next, usually by watching others perform. Only new dances are taught by the creater. Each of the dances are performed in a particular style. In some of the dances, men and women assume different body postures. The dances included here are summarized in Table 21-5.

Different basic steps are suggested for each dance. These should be practiced to the drum music before putting them into the dances.

CORN GRINDER'S DANCE

Level: III.
Origin: Chippewa.
Music: Kimbo Educational: KLP - 9070 - A.
Formation: Six dancers perform the dance: two dancers representing the corn grinders in the center and "4 winds" take their places just inside the circle's rim at points an equal distance apart. The dancers will move clockwise.
Basic step: Shuffle step: The shuffle step is used throughout the dance: Step forward on the left, slide the right to the left foot, keeping feet flat on the floor. Repeat, with the left foot always stepping and the right foot sliding.
Action:

The "4 winds" dance to the center of the circle. They bow and move backward to their places.

The winds then move clockwise dancing the shuffle step, moving to the next wind's position.

Repeat the action until the dancers are back in their original wind position.

The "4 winds" dance to the center forming a circle around the corn grinders.

The corn grinders give each a handful of corn to scatter to the winds and the earth as they continue to step slide to the left around the corn grinders.

The "4 winds" take their corn to the rim of the circle, lifting it over their heads as if to offer it to the "Great Spirit" and then scatter it around the circle as they move with the shuffle step.

This dance was traditionally performed by women. The women had a giant mortar they had hollowed from a log about 2 feet high and a pestle about 4 feet long. The women ground the corn during the first part of the dance.

RABBIT DANCE

Level: III.
Origin: Plains Indians (Blackfeet)
Music: Pow wow music to a slow beat.
Formation: Couples in a double circle, with boys on the outside. Couples stand side by side with hands clasped behind their backs, right hands joined, left hands joined. Couples face clockwise.
Basic step: Step-close: Beginning with outside feet, take a step forward, slide the inside feet up to close.
Action:

Moving clockwise the dancers take two step-close steps forward, beginning with the outside feet.

They then take a step backward with the outside feet, and with the inside feet step in place.

As the drum beat accentuates the couples turn in unison, turning toward the center of the circle and continuing around to face clockwise once again.

This is a social dance.

RAIN DANCE

Level: III.
Origin: Chippewa.
Music: Kimbo Educational: KLP - 9070 - A.
Formation: Four "braves" represent the "4 winds" as in the corn grinders dance, with the "medicine man" in the center of the circle.
Basic step: Two-heel step: Beginning with the left foot the dancers place the left toe on the floor lifting the heel high. Drop the heel and repeat with the right foot. This step is used throughout the dance.
Action:

The "4 winds" dance to the center of the circle and back out to its rim. They then move on the inside of the circle to the next wind position. As they move they begin, with both arms up overhead moving their arms and fingers to represent the rain coming down. Arms and hands continue to move downward as the winds move to the center until they are down close to the floor. This action is repeated again and again. They may also move in their own circles as they move around the circle.

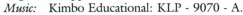

TABLE 21-5 NATIVE AMERICAN DANCES

NAME	ORIGIN	BASIC STEP	MUSIC	PAGE	LEVEL
Corn Grinder's Dance	Chippewa	Shuffle step	Kimbo Educational: KLP9070-A	429	III
Rabbit Dance	Blackfeet	Step-close	Pow wow music	429	III
Rain Dance	Chippewa	Toe-heel step	Kimbo Educational: KLP9070-A	429	III
Oklahoma Two-step	Blackfeet	Step-close	Pow wow music	430	IV
Strawberry Dance	Chippewa	Touch-step	Kimbo Educational: KLP9070-A	430	IV

Continue until the "4 winds" reach their original position.
The medicine man dances in the center throughout the dance.

This is a very vigorous dance. Because rain was important for their survival, the Indians put a lot into this dance. Encourage creative movements as the children dance the dance. How would the braves respond as the "4 winds"? What would the movements of the "medicine man" be like? What type of movements might be used to encourage the rain?

OKLAHOMA TWO-STEP

Level: IV.
Origin: Plains Indians (Blackfeet).
Music: Pow wow music with a medium beat.
Formation: Couples in a line behind a lead couple, with hands joined by crossing the arms in front, right hand to right hand and left to left.
Basic step: Step-close: The dancers step forward with the outside feet and step to close with the inside feet. Repeat with the same foot leading. This step is used throughout the dance.
Action:

The dancers follow the path of the lead couple who may choose to move in:

a. Circles
b. In different directions—forward or backward
c. Moving like a snake
d. Moving in different groupings by picking up other couples and then separating from them
e. Forming an arch with couples moving under the arch and then forming additional arches; the arching continues until the head couple is once again at the head of the line with the following couples back in their original order
f. Splitting with partners, moving in different pathways and then rejoining
g. Moving in a spiral
h. Moving in and out of circles
i. Other ideas created by the leaders

This is a social dance performed at pow wows and other social occasions.

STRAWBERRY DANCE

Level: IV.
Origin: Chippewa
Music: Kimbo Educational: KLP 9070-A.
Formation: Single circle of dancers, some presenting the chief, the medicine man, and the tribe.
Basic step: Touch step: With knees slightly bent take a step forward on the left foot (beat 1). Touch the right foot forward (beat 2), then to the side (beat 3) and then back (beat 4). Repeat stepping on the right foot and touching with the left.
Action:

The chief dances to the center of the circle and places a decorated blanket of the dead warrior on the ground.
The medicine man dances around the blanket to chase away the evil spirits and bless the ground.
The remaining dancers representing the tribe move into the circle one at a time to present their gifts.
They dance to the edge of the circle and continue to move clockwise until all have been to the center.

This dance was probably also performed as a celebration of spring at the height of strawberry season as well as a dance in memory of a fallen warrior as depicted here. The strawberry was also known as the "heart-berry."

SUMMARY

Singing games and American and international folk, line, and square dance, as well as native American dances, are an essential part of the elementary school dance and physical education experience. They not only provide an excellent cardiorespiratory fitness activity, but also contribute to the development of motor and social skills. They also provide an opportunity to develop an understanding of people from various parts of the world as well as the native Americans who lived in our country long before the first European settlers. In addition, they provide an important activity for the application of the movement content as the children work in various partner relationships and formations and perform a variety of locomotor and nonlocomotor skills to many different tempos and rhythms. Teaching these forms of dance requires careful preparation. Dances should be selected that challenge the children, but that can be mastered in a relatively short time. Organization for getting children into partners must be carefully planned to avoid embarrassing situations for upper grade girls and boys. Children should be given many opportunities to repeat the dances they have learned for the enjoyment of moving to the music.

DANCE GLOSSARY

allemande left (right) A dance figure in which the boy gives his left hand to the corner girl and walks around her and back to his partner.

arching figure A square dance figure in which one or more couples pass through an arch formed by one or more couples by raising held hands.

balance A step forward, close, hold; step back, close; hold executed in 2/4 or 3/4 time.

banjo position Partners face with right hips adjacent, girl's right hand in the boy's left, and her left hand on his shoulder; the boy's right hand is at the girl's waist.

bleking A light hop on one foot extending the opposite heel forward, which is repeated several times, alternating feet.

circle left (right) Group forms a single circle facing the center, takes the hands of dancers on either side, and moves in a circle clockwise (counterclockwise).

clockwise Moving to the left in a circle.

counterclockwise Moving to the right in a circle.

do-si-do A dance figure in which couples walk toward each other, passing right shoulders; continuing facing forward, they move back to place passing left shoulders.

elbow swing Face partner, join right or left elbows, and turn with small steps.

grand right and left A dance figure in which the dancers move around the circle, boys moving counterclockwise, girls clockwise, giving first the right hand to their partner and left and right hands to those they meet until once again with their partner.

grapevine A step to the side, alternatively putting the trailing foot across in front of and then behind the other foot.

groups of three Three dancers, usually one boy with a girl on either side.

honor your partner (corner) Face partner, boys bow and girls curtsy.

ladies chain A dance figure in which girls give right hands to each other, their left to the opposite boy as the girls pass, and then turn with boy to face their partner and the opposite girl.

line of direction Counterclockwise.

longways set An arrangement of dancers into two lines with partners facing one another.

open position Partners stand side by side with inside hands joined.

patter call A square dance call in which the caller gives the instructions to the dance in a rhythmical fashion, with folksy sayings added for color.

polka A hop, step, close, step, executed in uneven rhythm.

promenade Partners stand side by side, the girl on the boy's right. Holding each other's right hand and left hand, the two proceed around the set and back to their original place.

quadrille A square set; four couples arranged as the sides of a square.

reverse line of direction Clockwise.

right and left through Two couples facing, walk forward, passing right shoulders with the opposite dancer, turn with partner and pass left shoulders on the way back to place where they turn to face the opposite couple.

sashay Moving around partner, boy moving to the right and then behind the girl, girl moving to the left and then in front of boy.

schottische A step, step, step, hop, in even rhythm.

shoulder-waist position Partners face; boy places both hands at the girl's waist, and the girl places both hands on the boy's shoulders.

sidecar position Partners face, left hips adjacent; girl's right hand in the boy's left, with her left hand on his shoulder; his right hand is at her waist.

singing call A square dance call in which the dance instructions are sung to a familiar tune.

skater's position Partners stand side by side; the boy holds the girl's right hand in his left in front of them, and each puts the remaining hand behind the other's back.

split-the-ring A square dance figure in which a couple moves across the set and passes between the opposite couple.

star A dance figure in which the dancers move to the center of the group, extending right (or left) hands to touch each other, or, with a wrist grasp on the dancer in front of them, they move in a circle.

step-hop A step and a hop on the same foot executed in even rhythm.

symmetrical figure A square dance figure in which all four couples execute the figure at the same time.

two-step A step, together, step, in uneven rhythm.

varsouvienne position Partners stand side by side; the boy holds the girl's left hand in his left to the side, her right in his right slightly above her shoulder.

visiting figure A square dance figure in which the figure is executed by one couple moving to each couple in the set in turn to perform the figure.

waltz A step forward on one foot, a step to the side on the other, and a close executed in 3/4 time.

REFERENCES AND RESOURCES

Babcock A: *Selected games and dances of North American plains Indians,* Regional Games Conference, Hoffstra University, May 1992.

Harris J et al: *Dance a while,* ed 6, New York, 1986, Garden Press Publishers.

Hipps R et al: *World of fun manual of instructions for world of fun records,* Nashville, 1970, Division of Education, Board of Discipleship, The United Methodist Church.

Howard C: *Authentic Indian dances and folklore,* 1971, Long Branch, NJ, Kimbo Educational.

Kraus R: *Folk dancing: a guide for schools, colleges and recreational groups,* New York, 1962, Macmillan.

McLellan J, Sova G, Hocking R: *"Hoop dancing": a native Indian cultural activity,* 1986.

Napier P: Square dancing—Kentucky mountain style, *JOPERD* 55(7):39, 1984.

Ray OM: *Encyclopedia of line dances,* Reston, Va, 1992, AAHPERD Publications.

ANNOTATED READINGS

Cusimano BE and Darst P: Square dance made easy, *The Gym Dandies Quarterly III(2),* Durham, North Carolina, 1989, The Great Activities Publishing Company.

Offers suggestions for developing and teaching a square dance unit in grades 4 through 6.

Forbes J: Early American dance instruction, *JOPERD* 55(7):34, 1984.

Discusses dance forms in early American life.

Kerr KA: Analysis of folk dance with LMA-based tools, *JOPERD* 64(2):38, 1993.

There is more to folk dance than the steps involved. Body positioning, gesture, etc. are an important part of the style of folk dances. Laban notation permits a look at folk dance qualitatively and quantitatively.

O'Brien EF: Teaching dances of other cultures, *JOPERD* 62(2):40, 1991.

Building a dance unit with a focus on authenticity in presenting the dances often involves a collaboration with other teachers, university personnel, local dance groups, etc.

Ramsay J: Folk dancing is for everyone, *JOPERD* 55(7):37, 1984.

Discusses the value of folk dancing in fulfilling the need for cooperative, recreational activity.

Shehan P: Teaching music through Balkan folk dance, *Music Educators Journal* 71(3):47, 1984.

A musical approach to folk dance is discussed; describes four Balkan dances.

Withers A: Teaching clogging in the elementary physical education program, *JOPERD* 55(7):43, 1984.

Discusses the history of clogging and eight basic steps.

CHAPTER 22

Rhythmic Activities with Small Equipment

OBJECTIVES

After completing this chapter the student will be able to:

1. Specify a progression of rhythmic activities using balls, jump ropes, ribbons, rhythm sticks, and hoops
2. Describe rhythmic activities using a parachute
3. Provide suggestions for teaching and organizing rhythmic experiences for elementary school children

Rhythmic activities provide an opportunity for children to use small equipment such as balls, ribbons, ropes, sticks, and hoops and to move themselves and the equipment to an accompaniment. Each individual brings a somewhat different movement background to the physical education experience. As children work to create combinations of skills and creative movement sequences, they have the opportunity to gain understanding of movement and of themselves as movers.

RHYTHMIC ACTIVITIES FOR ELEMENTARY SCHOOL CHILDREN

Children enjoy using small equipment. Rhythmic activities provide the dual challenge of creating interesting ways of using the equipment and using it to the rhythm of the accompaniment.

Body awareness is enhanced as children learn to work within their own abilities and to control objects as the objects are moved. The rhythmic activity experiences should result in learning new ways to use body parts when attempting to control objects.

Space concepts are developed as children learn to control objects. These activities should include opportunities for children to work in their own space as well as in general space and also in relation to other children and the objects they hope to control.

Movement qualities are important aspects of the rhythmic activity experience. Time becomes important as children learn to move themselves and objects within the structure of an imposed rhythm. Children learn not only to respond to the underlying beat, but also to respond to tempo changes, rhythmic patterns, and phrasing. In addition, force, flow, and balance are important movement qualities that must be used effectively for children to be successful in these activities.

Rhythmic activities with equipment such as ribbons and sticks are also a part of cultures other than our own. By introducing children to these multicultural activities, we increase their understanding and respect for early Americans and people of other parts of the world.

Partner and small group activities provide an opportunity for children to work cooperatively in developing rhythmic movement sequences. Activities should be structured so that each child has an opportunity to share at least one idea for the group project. Structuring the activities so that at least one more idea than the number in the group is needed provides an opportunity for children to each contribute one idea and then to share in deciding the remaining parts of the sequence.

Fitness may also be enhanced in sustained vigorous activity as well as in moving with the equipment to stretch and bend various parts of the body.

The objectives to be developed in rhythmic activities may be found in the box on p. 434. To meet these objectives children should be given the opportunity for maximum participation. Creativity must be encouraged, and children should work as individuals, with partners, and in small groups.

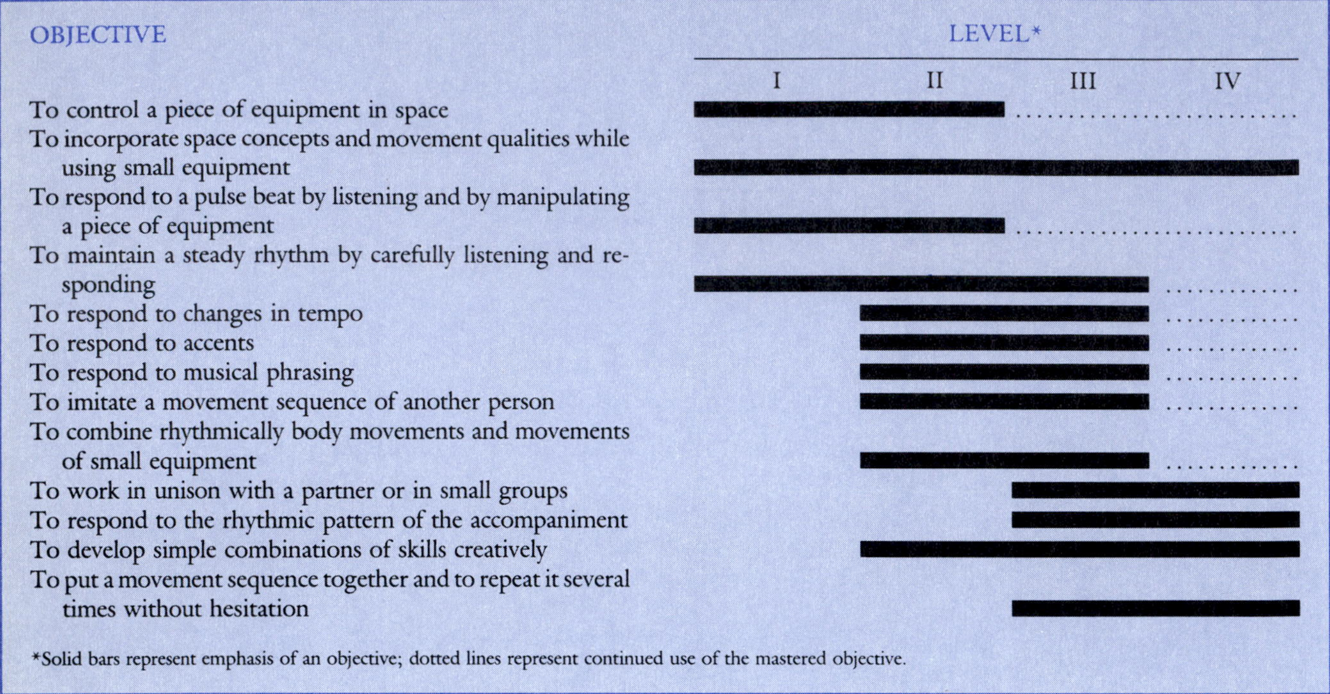

RHYTHMIC ACTIVITY OBJECTIVES IN THE ELEMENTARY SCHOOL

OBJECTIVE — LEVEL* (I, II, III, IV)

To control a piece of equipment in space
To incorporate space concepts and movement qualities while using small equipment
To respond to a pulse beat by listening and by manipulating a piece of equipment
To maintain a steady rhythm by carefully listening and responding
To respond to changes in tempo
To respond to accents
To respond to musical phrasing
To imitate a movement sequence of another person
To combine rhythmically body movements and movements of small equipment
To work in unison with a partner or in small groups
To respond to the rhythmic pattern of the accompaniment
To develop simple combinations of skills creatively
To put a movement sequence together and to repeat it several times without hesitation

*Solid bars represent emphasis of an objective; dotted lines represent continued use of the mastered objective.

TEACHING RHYTHMIC EXPERIENCES

Suggestions for organizing and conducting rhythmic activity experiences for elementary school children may be found in Chapters 8 and 13.

Developing Movement Sequences

A summary of the steps in planning motor sequences and an example for ball skills are given in the box on p. 435.

1. Early activities with a piece of equipment should help children become acquainted with the properties of the object, such as its weight, shape, and how it can be used in space.
2. Encourage the children to find interesting ways to use the equipment and to develop their own movement sequences.
3. Teach in phrases. There are usually eight measures in each phrase, which means 32 beats for 4/4 time, 24 for 3/4 time, and 16 for 2/4 time. Meters of 2/4 or 4/4 are easier for children in their early experiences than are 3/4 rhythms.
4. Cue the beginning so that all children start on the beat, for example, "One, two, ready, go."
5. Begin with using single skills to accompaniment. Move on to simple combinations and finally to more complex combinations when the children are ready. The steps in developing a movement sequence are the following:

   Step 1: To begin, practice single skills without accompaniment. When children have developed some control in their use of skills, add accompaniment.
   Step 2: Combine two skills in a simple sequence. Try several possible combinations. After one or two examples are given, ask the children for additional possibilities.
   Step 3: Give the sequence a time reference. For example, combine two skills into a 4-beat sequence or combine skills to one phrase of the music. This provides a beginning framework for their movement sequences.
   Step 4: Gradually add other elements: space concepts, body movements, change in force, or other movement qualities.

6. In developing movement sequences, it may be helpful to begin by giving the children a combination with which to work, such as the following 4-beat sequence for sticks:

   Standing, beginning the movement from right to left, hit sticks overhead to the right side (1); moving sticks slightly to the left, hit sticks overhead (2); continuing to move to the left, hit sticks overhead slightly to the left (3); and hit sticks overhead to the left (4).

The children all begin with this combination and add one or more 4-beat sequences to it. For example, they might repeat the movement moving from the left to the right, varying the sequence by moving forward or backward, or using some other combination of their choice.

DEVELOPING A MOVEMENT SEQUENCE

Step 1:	*Step 2:*	*Step 3:*	*Step 4:*		
Practice individual skills	Develop movement combinations	Add time reference	Add additional elements		
Practice individual skills without and with accompaniment	Develop several possible combinations; have children give some ideas after a few examples are given	*Examples:* 4 beats; 4 measures of 4 beats; 4 measures of 3 beats	*Locomotor/nonlocomotor* Walk Swing/sway Run Bend/stretch Skip Turn/twist Gallop Push/pull Hop Jump Slide	*Space* Self General Direction Pathway Range Level	*Qualities* Force Balance

EXAMPLE BALL SKILLS

Step 1:	*Step 2:*	*Step 3:*	*Step 4* (Add one at a time):	*Space*	*Qualities*
Bounce (catch)	Bounce, bounce, bounce, catch	4 measures of 4 counts each: Bounce, catch, bounce, catch; Bounce, bounce, bounce, catch (Repeat once)	Locomotor/nonlocomotor Do the sequence from a stationary position first, then walk the second time through	Move forward the first time through Move to the side the second time	Accent the first beat of the measure
Vertical throw (catch)	Throw, catch, bounce, catch	Throw, catch, bounce, catch; Bounce, catch, throw, catch. (Repeat once)			

Refining Tasks

1. Allow sufficient time to have children develop answers to movement challenges. Partner or group work may take longer, because it takes more time to agree with others on movement possibilities.
2. A good beginning and a definite ending are important aspects of a movement sequence.
3. Emphasis should be placed on the smooth transition from one movement to the next and smooth combinations of locomotor and nonlocomotor skills while using the equipment (flow).
4. A variety of accompaniments should be used. Children may be asked to bring in records or tapes of music they like. The teacher should listen to the music ahead of time to determine if it has an appropriate beat and tempo and also to check the appropriateness of the lyrics. The children should be exposed to a variety of meters as well as types and tempos of musical accompaniment.

Some examples of appropriate accompaniment are found in Appendix 1.

RHYTHMIC ACTIVITIES CONCEPTS

The movement concepts applied in rhythmic activities are outlined in Figure 22-1. Suggested activities to apply movement concepts follow. Skill concepts may be found in Chapters 13 and 16.

Activities To Develop Concepts for Rhythmic Activities

1. To control objects while moving in different relationships with others.

   Children work in partners or small groups deciding on the types of movements to be performed or doing a movement sequence the class has learned. They perform the movements, moving together in general space. They may work in different relationships, such as side-by-side, in a line one behind the other, in a circle, etc. (How did you move in relation to others [providing adequate space to perform the movements]?)

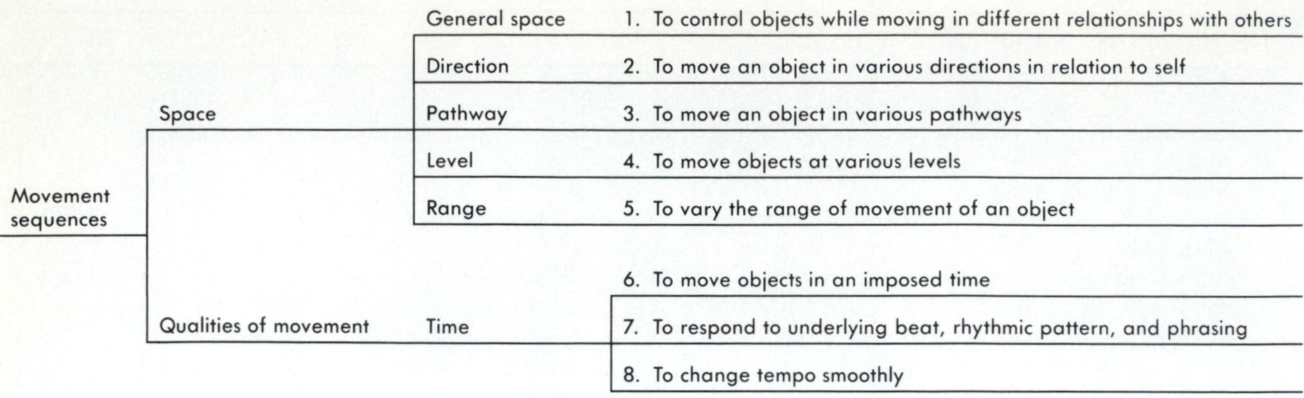
General space
1. To control objects while moving in different relationships with others
Direction
2. To move an object in various directions in relation to self
Space
Pathway
3. To move an object in various pathways
Level
4. To move objects at various levels
Movement sequences
Range
5. To vary the range of movement of an object
6. To move objects in an imposed time
Qualities of movement
Time
7. To respond to underlying beat, rhythmic pattern, and phrasing
8. To change tempo smoothly

FIGURE 22-1 Movement content for rhythmic activities.

2. To move an object in various directions in relation to self.
   a. Students remain stationary while moving an object in front, behind, up, down, to the right or left of the body. Try different ways of moving the object in each direction. Develop a combination of movements in two directions. (Which directions were most challenging?)
   b. Repeat *a* but try the same movements as you move in general space. Now try moving the object in the same or different directions than the direction you are moving in general space. (What ways were most challenging?)
3. To move an object in various pathways.
   a. While remaining stationary, students move the object in various pathways. Now moving in a straight or curved path in general space move the object in a path of its own. (Which paths offered the most variety?)
4. To move objects at various levels.
   a. Students explore moving the object at the level called. (What parts of the body could you use?) Now move the object from one level to another. (How many ways can you do it?)
5. To vary the range of movements of objects.
   a. Students explore using an object and moving it with control away from and toward the body or with large and small movements. (Can you combine three of the movements?)
6. To move objects to an imposed time.
   a. Using a drum or other accompaniment, children respond in moving an object in time to the imposed rhythm. Try different ways of moving the object. Vary the tempo. (What ways were easiest to keep on the beat? How did you change the movement as the beat got slower or faster?)
7. To respond to the underlying beat, rhythmic pattern, or phrasing.
   a. With varying accompaniment the children explore moving an object to 2/4, 3/4, and 4/4 rhythm, moving on the beat. (What different movements did you do to each meter?)
   b. Clap out a rhythmic pattern alone or with an accompaniment. Children attempt to move their object to that rhythm. (How many different ways did you move the object and stay with the rhythmic pattern?)
   c. With an accompaniment, the children move to the phrasing, changing the movements performed as the phrase changes. (How did you know when to get ready to change?)
8. To change tempo smoothly.
   a. Students move with an object, responding to tempo changes of the drum or musical accompaniment. (How did you anticipate the tempo change to change smoothly to the new tempo?)

Activities requiring the application of these concepts are found in each of the following activity sections.

BALLS

Equipment

Children should have an appropriate size ball so that they can easily control it. A variety of balls may be used. The properties of some types of balls may make them difficult for some children to bounce or control. To be successful in rhythmic activities, children must use equipment they can easily control. Seven or eight inch balls work best for most children.

Teaching Suggestions

1. The ball should not be grasped, but should rest on the front part of the palm and fingers.

2. When catching the ball, contact should be made with the finger pads, letting the ball roll into the hand as the arms and body give to absorb forces.
3. The entire body is used when bouncing the ball.
4. The body should follow the path of the ball. As the ball is moved away from the body, it should appear as a natural extension of the body's movement.
5. The children should be encouraged to work with both right and left hands.
6. The action should begin before the beat so the throw or contact on the bounce will be on the beat.
7. Incorporation of movement concepts is a natural part of the activity. Challenges should encourage variety in level, force, self and general space, floor pattern (pathway), direction, and body awareness.
8. Ball rhythms should be introduced early in the teaching of ball skills. Many activities require considerable skill in handling objects and coordinating body parts, and when music is added the difficulty of the activity increases. Therefore, the children must have some opportunity to explore the various ways of controlling the ball using a variety of ball skills before attempting to use the balls in a rhythmic activity. Some prerequisite activities are suggested in Chapter 13.
9. Beginning combinations should be simple (combinations of two to three skills maximum) and should include the repetition of the sequence several times.
10. Beginning combinations may also involve changing hands while executing skills (that is, bouncing the ball twice with the right hand and twice with the left).
11. Accompaniment should have a distinct beat and an appropriate tempo.

Activities

Individual Activities

1. Bounce the ball in front of the body and catch.
   a. Bounce to the side of the body and catch.
   b. Bounce the ball under one leg and catch (O'Leary).
   c. Bounce the ball between the legs from the rear to the front.
2. Toss the ball in the air with a two-hand underhand motion and catch.
3. Bounce, bounce, bounce, catch.
4. Bounce the ball forcefully, run under the ball, then catch it.
5. Bounce the ball, turn around in place, then catch it.
6. Throw the ball vertically in the air, arms stretching upward, and catch it.
7. Throw the ball vertically in the air but slightly forward. Move under it and catch it.
8. Throw the ball vertically in the air, turn around in place, then catch it.

Children should work individually as well as with others.

9. Throw the ball vertically in the air, turn around in place, let it bounce, then catch it.
10. Throw the ball vertically, touch the floor, then catch it.
11. Bounce the ball in a circle around the body.
12. Roll the ball from one hand to the other, side to side.
13. Make a design with the ball as you move it through space.
14. Do a nonlocomotor skill as you work with the ball (bend and stretch).
15. Execute a ball skill in place, stop, do a locomotor movement, stop, repeat.
16. Execute a ball skill as you skip, gallop, hop.
17. Execute a ball skill as you perform a dance step, such as step-hop, schottische, polka.
18. Bounce the ball in front of the body, moving the ball from the left hand to the right hand.
19. Similar to the last activity, but slide to the side as you bounce the ball.
20. Execute ball skills while changing level in space.
21. Execute ball skills while moving in various pathways.
22. Vary the time (fast, slow) of the ball skills but keep in time to the music.
23. Roll the ball down one arm, across the shoulders and down the other arm, and catch it.
24. Move the ball in a figure eight in front of the body, changing supporting hands as you cross the midline of the body.

25. Throw, clap, clap, catch, hold. (Slow, fast, fast, slow, hold.)
26. Throw, catch, throw, catch, throw, clap, catch (two small throws, one high throw).
27. Throw the ball from side to side overhead, from one hand to the other.
28. Respond to various rhythmic patterns.
    a. Slow, slow, quick, quick, slow.
    b. One, two, three. One, two, three.
29. Move the ball while changing direction.
30. Move the ball on the beat.
31. Move the ball on the off-beat.
32. Drop the ball in front of the body, with the arms continuing downward and circling the ball on its downward path, and catch it.
33. Move the ball around the body at different levels.

Individual Ball Combinations

1. Bounce, catch, bounce, catch (1, 2, 3, 4). Bounce, bounce, bounce, catch (1, 2, 3, 4).
2. Vertical throw and catch (1, 2). Bounce and catch (3, 4). Bounce and catch (1, 2). Vertical throw and catch (3, 4).
3. Vertical throw, catch while lowering the ball (1, 2). Vertical throw, catch while lowering the ball (3, 4). Diagonal bounce (left to right), catch (1, 2). Diagonal bounce (right to left), catch (3, 4).
4. Bounce, turn, bounce, catch (1, 2, 3, 4). Bounce, bounce, bounce, catch (to the right side) (1, 2, 3, 4). Bounce, bounce, bounce, catch (to the left side) (1, 2, 3, 4).
5. Diagonal throw overhead left to right, catch (1, 2). Diagonal throw over right to left, catch (3, 4). Diagonal throw overhead left to right, catch (1, 2). Diagonal throw overhead right to left, catch (3, 4). Bounce, bounce, bounce, catch (1, 2, 3, 4). Bounce, bounce, bounce, catch (1, 2, 3, 4).

Combinations of Locomotor and Ball Skills

1. Walk forward four steps, bounce the ball in place four times. Walk backward four steps, bounce the ball in place for four steps.
2. Walk forward two steps, bounce the ball two times, walk forward two steps, toss to self and catch. Repeat.
3. Take two slides to the right, bounce the ball on the right side two times. Take two slides to the left, bounce the ball on the left two times.
4. Take two step-hops forward, toss the ball and catch, toss again and catch. Take two step-hops forward, bounce, bounce, bounce, catch.
5. Take two bounce-catch combinations while standing in place. Take four steps forward bouncing the ball alternating hands (right, left, right) and hold on the fourth step.

Partner Ball Activities

1. Sitting: Roll the ball to a partner, catch, and hold.
2. Sitting: Roll the ball to a partner, stretching the arms and ball high overhead on the catch.
3. Bounce the ball to a partner, catch, and hold.
4. Throw the ball underhand to a partner, catch, and hold.
5. Bounce the ball three times, then throw to a partner.
6. Throw the ball to self three times, bounce to partner.
7. Turn around and roll the ball between the legs to partner.
8. Turn around and throw the ball overhead to partner.
9. Holding the ball overhead, bend from side to side (left, right, left) and then throw to partner.
10. Bounce pass to partner, catch, bounce to self (two times), throw to partner, catch, bounce to self (two times). Repeat reversing the throw and bounce pass.
11. Throw the ball from behind your back to a partner.
12. With each child having a ball and working in pairs, repeat the above skills, with both children throwing in unison.

Group Routines

The preceding skills and combinations may be combined into interesting group routines. By using double lines, square formations, circles, or concentric circles, these skills then become an interesting movement sequence.

HOOPS

Equipment

Hoops vary from 2 feet to more than 3 feet in diameter. They may be constructed of laminated wood or of plastic. The plastic hoops are inexpensive but must be handled with care if they are not to lose their shape.

Teaching Suggestions

Hoops require more individual space than most equipment. Children may need help in identifying their personal space when using hoops so that all have sufficient space within which to work. Hoops may be unfamiliar to most children. Adequate time must be given for exploration in the use of hoops to enable the children to use them effectively. Additional activities may be found in Chapter 16.

Activities

Individual Activities

1. Holding the hoop in two hands, make circles in front of the body by moving the hoop to the side, up, to the other side, and down.
2. Roll the hoop from one side to the other, taking a step to the side as the hoop is rolled.
3. Similar to the last activity but sliding to the side so that you can move the hoop farther in a side direction.
4. Twirl the hoop on one forearm or wrist to one side. Turn it clockwise and counterclockwise.
5. Twirl the hoop on the wrist or forearm in front of the body, changing arms.
6. Step to the side (lunging step) and stretch the hoop overhead to that side. Lunge to the other side and repeat.
7. Holding the hoop in two hands, jump through the hoop as if jumping rope (forward and backward).

Moving hoops in different directions.

8. Step to the side and turn around as the hoop is held high overhead and parallel to the floor.
9. Execute dance steps while moving with a hoop.
10. Execute dance steps in a hoop placed on the floor.
11. Move the hoop overhead from left to right.
12. Move the hoop from side to side, making an arc downward and ending on each side with full extension upward.
13. Move around a stationary hoop with various locomotor movements or dance steps.
14. Move in and out of a stationary hoop with various locomotor or dance steps.

Individual Combinations

1. Circle the hoop in front of the body two times (1, 2, 3, 4, 1, 2, 3, 4). Jump through and turn the hoop as if jumping rope four times (1, 2, 3, 4, 1, 2, 3, 4).
2. Roll the hoop in front of the body to the left as you slide four slides to the left (1, 2, 3, 4). Roll the hoop to the right as you slide four slides to the right (1, 2, 3, 4). Skip forward while rolling the hoop (1, 2, 3, 4). Skip backward while rolling the hoop (1, 2, 3, 4).
3. With the hoop on the floor, move around outside the hoop with four skips (1, 2, 3, 4). Move forward through the hoop with two skips (1, 2). Move backward through the hoop with two skips (3, 4).
4. Stretch the hoop high overhead (1, 2). Stretch to the left (3, 4). Stretch to the right (1, 2). Bring the hoop down in front (3, 4). Walk forward rolling the hoop (1, 2, 3, 4, 1, 2, 3, 4).

Partner Activities

1. Roll the hoop to a partner. Catch.
2. Roll the hoop to a partner. On the catch, stretch the hoop while overhead.
3. One holds the hoop as the partner moves through the hoop.
4. Move in and out of a stationary hoop doing various locomotor movements, with one going in while the other goes out.
5. Walk side by side rolling a hoop between two partners. Alternate rolling the hoop.
6. Walk side by side, each rolling a hoop.
7. Two partners roll a hoop to each other at the same time.

Partner or Group Combinations

Interesting combinations or skills may be developed. The use of various formations and the incorporation of space and other movement concepts add to the challenge of developing a movement sequence that is fun to perform as well as fun to watch.

Native American Hoop Dancing

(McLellan)

Hoop dancing probably originated with the Native Americans living along the Great Lakes. The hoop is a sacred symbol of Native Americans representing the circle of life. As hoops are added in the dance, they represent life's challenges that must be overcome, resulting in a new and beautiful design. The dance uses 20- to 24-inch hoops. It begins with four hoops, but preliminary activities beginning with one hoop develop the progression for adding hoops. The dancers are moving in loose and tight clockwise circles throughout, with a 1-2 step. This step may be two hops on each foot, a toe heel step on each foot, or simultaneous two-beat hops on each foot depending on the movement of the dancer. McLellan et al. suggest the following progression leading to the hoop dance:

1. Beginning with one hoop:
   a. Step through the hoop, bringing it up over the back and then onto the other leg.
   b. Bring the hoop up over the head, step through and on to the other leg.
2. With two hoops:
   a. Put one hoop on the floor and pick up with the toes.
   b. Loop other hoop with other leg, ending in a position with both hoops looped over the same leg, one supporting the other and held in the hand on the same side.
3. With three hoops:
   a. Loop one hoop on each leg, adding the third over the head to be supported by the two-looped hoops.
4. The Hoop Dance begins with four hoops to which others will be added as the dance progresses. To begin, the dancer puts the four hoops over the neck and arms. One hoop is over the neck and arms, one crosses the body over one shoulder and under the opposite arm, a third crosses the opposite way and the fourth hoop goes over the head, around the neck and under the arms. The dancer remains in motion the entire time that the hoops are being positioned. When the hoops are in position, the dancer twirls in a circle. Hoops are supported with the legs and arms. When adding hoops, the hoops are gathered in both hands.

Moving and positioning the hoops takes practice. In the beginning three hoops may be the most the children can master. Children should be encouraged to move with the hoops, moving them around their bodies in interesting ways.

RIBBONS

Equipment

Ribbons may be long streamers, approximately 15 feet long, or rhythmic gymnastics ribbons with handles, as described in Chapter 16.

A number of activities are suggested in Chapter 16 for building movement sequences. They include swinging and circling the ribbons as well as performing figure-eights, spirals, serpentine movements, and tossing and catching ribbons. These movements may be made in front of, to the side, or behind the body at various levels.

Activities

Individual Combinations

1. With a small running step, move in general space, moving the ribbon around in various patterns for eight counts; stop, move the ribbon in the same manner while standing still or holding an interesting balanced position for eight counts.
2. Move backward in space, moving the ribbon in serpentine movements horizontally for four counts; stop, move the ribbon in tight vertical serpents for four counts.
3. While standing, do figure eights in front of the body for eight counts; now while moving, perform figure eights

Ribbons

moving the ribbon on the right side of the body and then the left for eight counts.

4. Move the ribbon in horizontal circles high overhead for four counts; circle the ribbon in front of the body for four counts. Repeat the movements, moving through space for a total of eight more counts.
5. Swing the ribbon overhead while moving in different ways on each eight counts, such as leaping, sliding, performing a scale, etc. ending with a high swing overhead and catching the end in the opposite hand.
6. Swing the ribbon overhead and catch the end; holding one end in each hand, swing the ribbon around the body by first swinging it in front of and then to the left of the body. Continue to move the ribbon around behind the body by arching the trunk backward and then around to the right, finishing in the starting position.

Group Activities

Any of the preceding activities may be combined into partner or small group routines. The group may begin with a known sequence such as those listed earlier and then add their own movements to complete the routine. The children may assume many different positions and relationships in performing the group activities.

BRAIDING THE RIBBONS

In this level III activity, the children are arranged in two lines of three facing each other. Each dancer holds the end of a long streamer, which is also held by the person facing in the opposite line. The dancers are numbered from right to left.

To begin, dancers No. 1 from opposite ends of the lines move to their left passing the ribbon over the dancers in the middle of each line (No. 2). Dancers No. 3 repeat the action, moving to their right and passing the ribbon over the dancers No. 1 who are now in the middle position. Dancers No. 2 are now active. Moving to their right, they pass the ribbon over dancers No. 3 who are now in the center position. The sequence is repeated until the ribbons are braided. The action is then reversed to unbraid the ribbons.

*CHINESE RIBBON DANCE**

A ribbon attached to a stick is used, and each of the patterns is constructed to the 20 beats of the following chant:

Pattern 1: Using the right hand, circle the ribbon overhead and parallel to the floor in a clockwise direction.

Pattern 2: With the right hand, make circles in front of the body and perpendicular to the floor in a clockwise direction.

Pattern 3: With right hand, circle the ribbon on the right side of the body in a clockwise direction.

Pattern 4: Changing the ribbon to the left hand, circle the ribbon on the left side of the body in a counterclockwise direction.

Pattern 5: With the right hand, move the ribbon in a figure eight pathway in front of the body counterclockwise right and clockwise left.

Pattern 6: With the right hand, make a figure eight pattern, moving the ribbon in front of the body and behind the body, counterclockwise in front of the body and clockwise in the back.

Pattern 7: With the right hand, move the ribbon downward in front of the body and upward on the right and then down in front and up on the left in a clockwise manner.

*From Twinson Co., Sunnyvale, Calif: Record (TRDA); Cassette (TRDC); kit (with ribbon sticks) (TRDK).

ROPES

Equipment

The ropes used in rhythmic activities may be long or short. A discussion of the use of ropes, activities, and appropriate lengths for elementary school children may be found in Chapter 16.

Teaching Suggestions

1. Ropes require a large activity area for safe participation. Children may need to be reminded about the amount of space required individually to work safely with their ropes.
2. Rhythmic rope jumping requires considerable skill. Children should have the basic jumping skills well under control before they can expect to be successful when jumping to music. Children at levels III and IV should have the skills necessary to enjoy rhythmic rope jumping.
3. The skills in this chapter are described in more detail in Chapter 16. The box on p. 442 summarizes some possible rope jumping activities.
4. Double-beat or single-beat jumps may be used, although single-beat jumps seem to be preferred.
5. Rope jumping is a strenuous activity, especially for those children who may be having difficulty. Provide a change of pace so that the children can think through possible combinations and have the opportunity to watch each other jump.
6. Provision should be made for a warm-up period at the beginning of the lesson in which children may jump on their own.
7. Some of the skills may be practiced sequentially, beginning without a rope, introducing a long rope (where appropriate), and finally using a short rope.
8. As in ball skills, using music in $^{2}/_{4}$ or $^{4}/_{4}$ meter makes jumping easier for beginners.

ROPE JUMPING SKILLS

Turning the rope	Basic jumps	Special steps
Forward	Single beat	Side to side (skier)
Backward	Double beat	Forward and back (bell)
Single side swing	Rocking step	Side straddle
Double side swing	Running	Forward/backward straddle
Horizontal swing	Shuffle step	Cross feet
Front swing	Skipping	Point your toe to the side
Criss cross		Toe to toe
Double under	**Dance steps**	Heel to heel
Triple under	Step-hop	Heel to toe
	Bleking	Toe touch to rear
Turns	Fling	
Twister	Schottische	
Quarter turn	Step-swing	
Half turn	Grapevine	
Full turn		

Activities

Individual Combinations

1. Combine a single or double side swing with a front swing.
2. Combine a single or double side swing with a criss-cross.
3. Combine a side straddle with a forward/backward straddle.
4. Combine a point your toe to the side with a toe touch to the rear.
5. Combine single- and double-beat jumping.
6. Combine a side to side with a forward and back.
7. Combine the side swing with forward jumping, side swing, backward jumping.
8. Combine single-beat jumping with a double under; jump 1, 2, 3, 4; double under, jump 2, 3, 4.
9. Combine a basic jump or dance step with a turn.
10. Combine a basic jump with a special foot placement. For example, combine four single-beat jumps with four side-to-side jumps.
11. Combine two schottische steps with four step-swings.
12. Combine the schottische and rocking step.

Group Jumping

By using a longer rope, several additional jumpers may stand in front of, to the sides of, or behind the turning child. Many of the individual combinations mentioned previously may be executed by the group with one rope. In addition children should have the opportunity to practice turning the rope to the underlying beat of the accompaniment.

Partner Jumping

The following relationships may be used in partner jumping:

1. Stand face to face: The partner may run in and out of the rope while performing the jumping sequence.
2. Stand one behind the other: The turner may be in front or behind.
3. Partners stand side by side, with one rope; each holds the rope end with the outside hand.
4. Partners stand side by side with two ropes; one rope is held by each child with the left hands, the other rope with the right hands.

Long Rope Jumping

Children may find it easier to perform rope jumping sequences with long ropes than with short ropes. Children may also jump the short rope while standing in the long rope for an added variation.

STICKS

Equipment

Rhythm sticks may be made by cutting 1- to 2-inch dowels, broom handles, or plastic tubing into 1-foot lengths and sanding them lightly to avoid splinters. Rolled magazines or newspapers secured with masking tape can be used when a quieter atmosphere is required. Children also enjoy making and decorating their own sticks. Most of the activities included below require two sticks per child. Long poles or dowels may also be used for some activities.

Teaching Suggestions

1. Children should have a standard position, such as placing the sticks on the floor in front of them, when listening to instructions.

2. The children may be arranged in a circle, scattered in the area, or facing partners. In the upper grades, groups of three or four may be used.
3. The children should be arranged so that all can see the teacher easily.
4. The sticks should be held with the fingers (thumb and fingers on opposite sides of the sticks) and are usually placed on the lower half of the sticks.
5. Action begins before the beat so that the tapping or hitting of sticks is on the beat.
6. Begin with individual activities and progress to partner or group activities as the children are ready.
7. The tips are the upper edges of the sticks, and the ends are the lower edges of the sticks.

Activities

Individual Activities

The following skills assume that each child is using a pair of sticks:

1. Thrust sticks forward.
2. From a standing position, bend and touch sticks to the floor.
3. Stretch high overhead and tap sticks together.
4. Bend from side to side, tapping sticks overhead.
5. Bend forward and backward, tapping sticks.
6. Thrust elbows back twice, bring sticks in front, and tap them together.
7. Hit sticks under and over one knee.
8. Hit sticks in front and behind legs.
9. Hit sticks behind back and then in front of body.
10. Twist body from side to side and hit sticks.
11. Swing arms from the front to back and hit sticks.
12. Swing arms forward and backward alternately (one goes forward as the other goes backward).
13. Swing arms from side to side and hit sticks.
14. Combine hitting sticks with locomotor movements such as walking, running, skipping, or galloping, hitting as you move.
15. Combine hitting sticks with locomotor movements, moving and then hitting while standing still (walk, walk, walk, tap, tap, tap . . . skip, skip, tap, tap . . .).
16. Swing and cross sticks in front of body.
17. Circle arms in front of body.
18. Swing with backward extension.
19. Swing sticks in a figure eight, forward to backward or high to low.
20. Circle sticks above head, each stick making its own circle.
21. Perform the arm action of jumping jacks, hitting sticks overhead.
22. While sitting, tap sticks in front on the floor with either the tips or ends.
23. While sitting, tap sticks right on left, left on right.
24. While sitting, clap sticks together.
25. While sitting, tap the ends to the sides.
26. While sitting, tap sticks together with arms bent in front, arms straight, or arms stretched overhead.
27. Tap sticks on various body parts.
28. While sitting, tap sticks to the floor in front or behind your back.
29. Flip sticks by touching the tips to the floor, turning sticks toward body and regrasp, touching ends to floor.
30. Similar to the last activity, but flip sticks out to the sides.

Rhythm stick activity.

Movement Sequences

1. Have the children perform various tapping movements to the underlying beat of the music, such as tapping in front or to the sides.
2. Have the children tap the rhythmic pattern of the accompaniment.
3. Have the children tap in various rhythms:
   a. Tap, tap, tap, rest. Tap, tap, tap, rest.
   b. Rest, tap, rest, tap. Rest, tap, rest, tap.
   c. Tap . . . , tap. Tap . . . , tap. (Long, short, long, short.)
4. The teacher or a child taps a rhythm. The children then tap the same rhythm.
5. Have the children develop a four-beat pattern that they will repeat several times.

Beginning Stick Combinations

Four-beat combinations:

1. While standing, hit sticks in front of the body two times (1, 2); hit the sticks behind the body (3, 4).
2. Extend arms and sticks to side (1); hit sticks together in front of body (2); hit sticks high overhead (3); hit sticks low in front of body (4).
3. While sitting, hit tips of sticks to the floor at the sides (1); hit tips of sticks to the floor in front (2); hit sticks together (3); hit sticks overhead (4).
4. While sitting, hit ends to the floor in front (1, 2); hit tips to floor in front (3, 4).

Three-beat combinations:

1. Hit both sticks to the right side (1, 2, 3); hit both sticks in front (1, 2, 3); hit both sticks to the left (1, 2, 3); hit both sticks in front (1, 2, 3).
2. While sitting, hit end of sticks to the ground (1); hit sticks together (2, 3).
3. Hit sticks to the sides (1); hit sticks together (2); hit sticks overhead (3).
4. While sitting, hit ends of sticks to the ground (1); hit sticks together (2); exchange sticks (toss right stick to left hand, left stick to right hand) (3).

Stick Routines

The following are 16-count routines:

1. Hit tips to ground in front, hit sticks together; repeat. Hit tips to ground to the side, hit together; repeat. Vertical exchange (right to left, left to right) hold; repeat. Hit tips to ground in front, flip sticks in hands; repeat.
2. Holding sticks in the middle, hit the length of the stick to the floor in front, hit sticks together, hit flat sticks to right side, hit together. Hit flat sticks to the left side, hit together, hit flat sticks in front, flip sticks. Hit flat sticks to the right side, flip, hit flat sticks to the left, flip. Hit flat sticks in front, hit together, cross sticks, and hit to side together.
3. Hit tips to ground in front, hit together, hit tips to ground in front, flip. Hit tips to ground in front, hit together, hit tips to side, flip. Hit tips to ground in front, hit together, hit tips to ground in front. Holding sticks parallel to the ground, switch sticks in hands.
4. Hit tips to ground in front, flip, repeat. Hit tips to ground in front, hit together, hit tips in front, hit tips to the side. Cross sticks and hit to side, uncross and hit to side, hit behind, hit to side. Hit tips to ground in front, hit together, hit tips in front, flip.
5. Hit tips in front, flip, hit tips to the right, flip. Hit tips to left side, flip, hit tips in front, hit together. Hit to side, hit together, hit to side extended, hit together over head. Hit right tip in front and flip right, hit left tip in front and flip left.

Lummi Sticks

This stick game probably originated with a small tribe of Native Americans in northwestern Washington. Sticks, approximately 12 to 14 inches long, were carved, painted, and burned similar to totem poles. Lummi sticks is similar to a stick game played by the Maoris of New Zealand. The sticks are held perpendicular to the floor between the tips of the thumbs and index fingers, with the remaining fingers adding support.

Lummi sticks may be performed in partners seated with legs crossed facing one another or in groups of four forming a square. Each person has two sticks. When working in groups of four, one pair begins the routine, the second pair then begins on the third beat of the first measure to avoid all four hitting sticks in the middle at one time.

When tossing sticks, the sticks should be placed in the air toward the receiver so that they remain perpendicular to the floor. When both sticks are tossed at the same time, one person should toss the sticks close together in the center, while the other separates the sticks and tosses them on the outside.

Several variations are listed below for possible combinations of skills. All are performed to the tune suggested below, which is in ¾ time.

Ma- Ku A, Ko Ta O, A Ku E Ta Na.
Ma- Ku A, Ko Ta O, A Ku E Ta Na.

1. Hit ends to floor, hit own sticks, hit partner's right stick. Hit ends to floor, hit own sticks, hit partner's left stick. Repeat sequence three more times.
2. Hit ends to floor, hit own sticks, hit partner's right stick. Hit partner's left stick. Repeat sequence five more times.
3. Similar to the first sequence, but toss stick to partner rather than hitting partner's stick.

4. Similar to the second sequence, but toss sticks rather than hitting partner's sticks.
5. Hit ends to floor, hit own sticks, toss both sticks to partner. Repeat seven more times.
6. Hit ends of sticks to the ground in front; hit own sticks together; hit partner's right stick; hit partner's left stick; hit partner's right stick; hit partner's left stick. Repeat three more times.
7. Similar to the sixth sequence, but toss sticks, right, left, right, left, instead of hitting partner's sticks.
8. Hit tips to the floor in front; flip sticks toward you; hit end of sticks to the floor; hit own sticks; hit partner's right stick; hit partner's left stick. Repeat three more times.
9. Similar to the eighth sequence, but toss right and left sticks rather than hitting sticks with partner.
10. Hit tips of sticks to the side; flip sticks toward you; hit ends to floor at the side; hit tips to floor in front; flip; hit ends to floor in front; hit partner's right stick; hit partner's left stick; hit ends to floor in front; hit own sticks together; hit partner's right stick; hit partner's left stick. Repeat once more.
11. Hit ends of sticks on the floor; hit own sticks together; pass sticks clockwise by passing the left stick across to partner, transferring the right stick into the left hand. Repeat seven more times.
12. Similar to the eleventh sequence, but complete two passes each time.
13. Similar to the eleventh sequence, but pass until all have their two original sticks.

Activities with Long Poles

The Philippine folk dance Tinikling, with a three-beat pattern, is described in Chapter 21.

Four-beat combinations:

The sticks are moved by two stick handlers, one on each end. The sticks are hit together for the first two beats and apart on the second two beats.

1. Straddling the sticks, jump on the outside the first two beats and between the sticks on beats 3 and 4.
2. Repeat No. 1 with a half turn on beat 4.
3. Straddling the sticks and facing one of the ends jump on the outside and then jump outside turning to face the sticks on the first two beats. Jump with one foot in and the other out on the left on beats 3 and 4. Repeat the sequence now facing the other end and jumping with the foot out on the right on beats 3 and 4.
4. Change the sequence for hitting the sticks to apart on beats 1 and 2 and together on 3 and 4. The jumper faces the sticks and jumps in one foot at a time beginning on the right foot on the first two beats. On beats 3 and 4, the jumper moves along the side of the sticks right and left. On the next four counts, the jumper moves around the end person and then begins the sequence once again.
5. Using the same stick-hitting pattern as in No. 3, jumpers move in a figure-eight pattern, stepping in on beats 1 and 2 and out on 3 and 4, moving toward one of the ends. On the next four beats, the jumper moves around behind one of the ends, then repeats the sequence, this time moving around the other end.
6. The sticks are crossed to form an X. Jumpers move in a circle. The sticks are hit together on beats 1 and 2 and apart on 3 and 4. The jumper steps outside the sticks with the outside foot on beat 1, steps with the inside foot and pivots on beat 2, and steps between the sticks on one end on beats 3 and 4, first with the foot closest to the sticks and then with the other foot. The sequence is repeated moving toward the other end of the sticks.

Activity with Dowels

Limbo

This activity is performed with a dowel stick held by two persons who gradually move the stick closer to the floor each time the dancer passes under it. The person moves forward with a jumping motion under the stick leaning back to move without touching it.

Variation: In Trinidad the limbo is a traditional activity at wakes, but it is performed in reverse from the American version. It begins with the stick as low to the ground as the relatives of the deceased can manage. It is gradually raised to raise the spirit of the person who died.

PANELCHUTES AND PARACHUTES

Equipment

Panelchutes and parachutes are available in various sizes. A size that can be handled easily by the children should be selected. Smaller parachutes and panelchutes enable the children to work in smaller groups and provide more opportunity for individuals to offer suggestions for possible activities or combinations of skills.

Teaching Suggestions

1. Remind the children to keep the parachute fairly taut as they move.
2. Teach in phrases as if you were teaching a folk dance or singing game.
3. Cue the sequences so that the children may change the activity or direction in time to the accompaniment.
4. Rhythmic activities using a parachute provide a challenging opportunity for children to work together. Emphasize the need to coordinate efforts to accomplish the tasks.

Performing La Raspa with a parachute.

Activities

1. Execute locomotor movements while holding the parachute and moving clockwise or counterclockwise.
2. Move in time to the music while moving with the parachute and varying direction (in and out), tempo, and so forth.
3. Do "Ring Around the Rosie" with a parachute.
4. Perform simple singing games and folk dances while moving with the parachute.

Additional activities to use in the development of parachute and panelchute movement sequences may be found in Chapter 16.

SUMMARY

Rhythmic activities provide a creative experience with small equipment. Children apply their rhythmic skills as they develop movement sequences individually, with partners, or in small groups. Some children who feel inadequate in moving alone creatively find confidence in using the equipment as they explore various movement challenges. Because children enjoy working with balls, hoops, ribbons, ropes, sticks, and the parachute, the added dimension of working to an accompaniment adds a new challenge. Suggestions for musical accompaniment may be found in the Appendix.

REFERENCES AND RESOURCES

Carleton N: Chute the works: motivating for fitness and movement, *JOPERD* 60(1):73, 1989.

Geiger J and Popper E: *Musical ball skills,* Freeport, NY, 1969, Educational Activities.

Glass H and Hallum R: *Rhythm stick activities,* Freeport, NY, 1976, Educational Activities.

Keeleric K: *Danish ball rhythms (primary),* Freeport, NY, 1969, Educational Activities.

McLellan J, Sova G, Hocking R: *Hoop dancing a Native Indian cultural activity introduction and hoop formation,* Winnepeg, 1986.

O'Brien EF: Teaching dances of other cultures, *JOPERD* 62(2):40, 1991.

Smith P: *Rope skipping, rhythms, routines, rhymes,* Freeport, NY, 1969, Educational Activities.

Twinson Company: *Chinese ribbon dance,* Los Altos, Calif, 1967, Twinson.

ANNOTATED READINGS

Schmid A: Rhythmic gymnastics: new Olympic sport, *JOPERD* 55(5):70, 1984.

Describes the history of rhythmic gymnastics as an Olympic event and gives a description of the event and scoring.

PART SEVEN

Games for Elementary School Children

If appropriately selected and conducted, games can be a valuable educational experience for elementary school children. Games provide an opportunity for children to use and adapt motor skills, to apply movement concepts in ever-changing games situations, and to develop cooperative and competitive skills in a group setting. They also have the potential to enable children to gain greater understanding of other cultures. Children enjoy games and are challenged by the motor, cognitive, and social opportunities they offer.

OUTLINE

CHAPTER 23

Teaching Children's Games

OBJECTIVES

After completing this chapter the student will be able to:

1. Describe how experience in games and team sports lead-ups is important in meeting the goals of the elementary school physical education program
2. Explain how games analysis is important in identifying the important aspects of games by assisting the teacher in selecting appropriate activities for each group of children
3. Describe the effective planning and conducting of games and team sports lead-ups for the elementary school physical education program
4. Suggest strategies for developing cooperation through the games experience
5. Suggest strategies for encouraging children to modify and create games

Games are a popular form of play for children, especially children between 6 and 12 years of age. Games provide an opportunity for children to demonstrate their skills to other children and to test their ability as they confront others in game play.

In observing children participating in games on the playground or in the neighborhood, one notes several things about their play. Children invent games of many descriptions, some for one person, others for groups varying in number, age, and ability. The games range in complexity according to the ability of the creator, but generally rules are minimal and limited to those needed at that particular moment. Rules are often modified as the game progresses to offer the most favorable opportunity for success for everyone. Occasionally, special rules are applied only on an individual basis as differences in ability are considered by the group.

Children play games without adult supervision, choose teams that provide equal competition (although their methods may be unorthodox), abide by the rules set by the group, and work out most differences of opinion in a reasonable manner. Occasionally, disagreements do end the game or worse.

Scoring may be given little importance, and when the game ends, no real winners are declared. Children's personal satisfaction comes from being physically active and having given their best efforts in the play just completed.

THE VALUE OF GAMES AND TEAM SPORTS LEAD-UPS IN THE ELEMENTARY SCHOOL PHYSICAL EDUCATION PROGRAM

When used effectively, games can make a substantial contribution to the objectives of physical education and consequently to the development of elementary school children. The values of games are not inherent in the games themselves. **Educational games,** used to assist children in developing educational objectives, are those that expand the children's understanding of their own movement and the application of space and quality of movement concepts.

Games provide an opportunity for children to put their motor skills to use in many ways in achieving goals. Not only are a variety of skills used, but also children learn to adapt them and assess their effectiveness in different situations.

Games offer a challenge to accomplish a goal. Game play enhances children's ability to analyze a situation and to plan and to act based on that analysis. It provides for creative thinking as strategy is developed and/or changes are made to make the game better for players of varying abilities or for larger or smaller groups.

Games provide an opportunity to share ideas and to work together to solve challenges in achieving the game

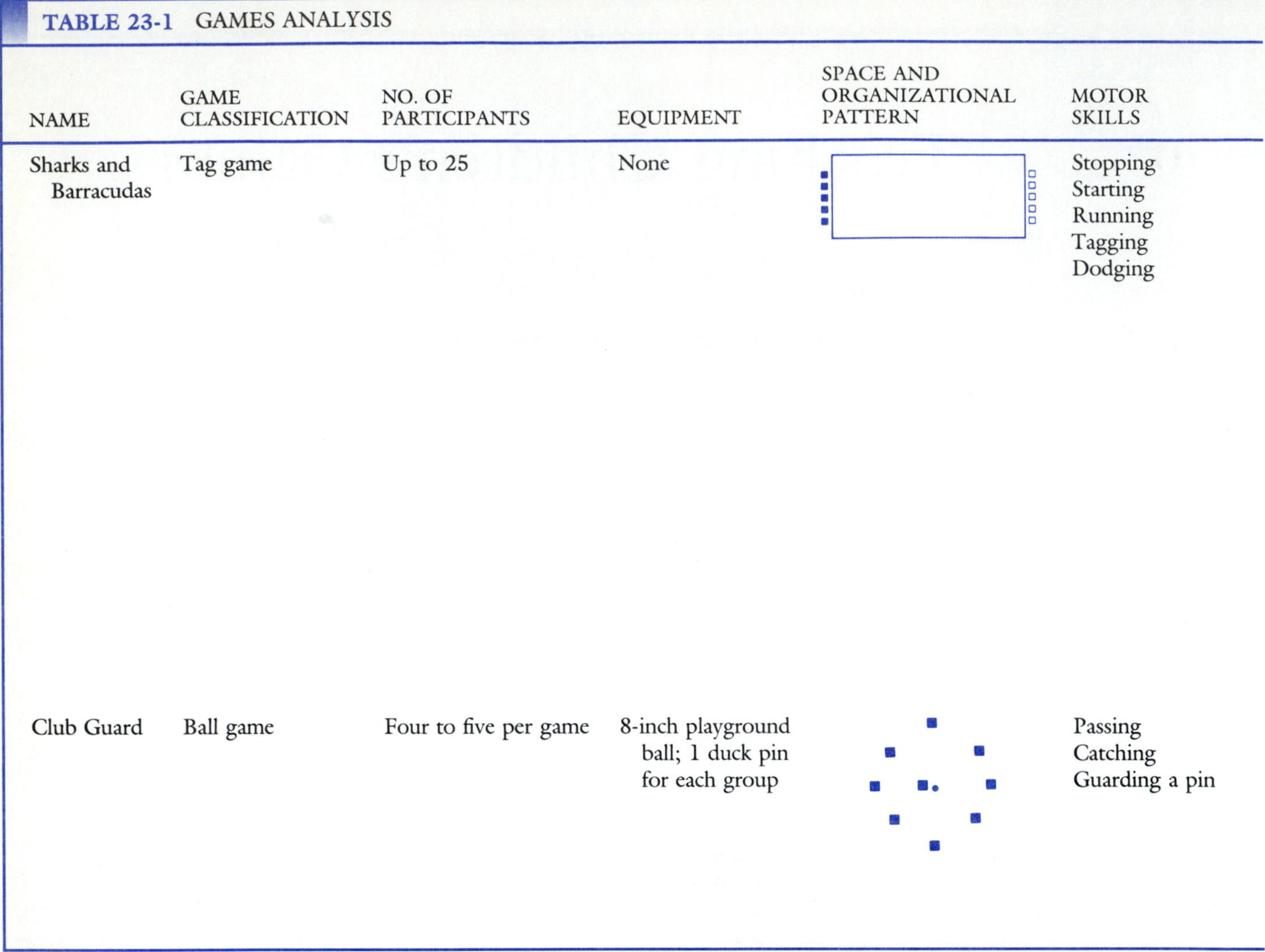

TABLE 23-1 GAMES ANALYSIS

NAME	GAME CLASSIFICATION	NO. OF PARTICIPANTS	EQUIPMENT	SPACE AND ORGANIZATIONAL PATTERN	MOTOR SKILLS
Sharks and Barracudas	Tag game	Up to 25	None		Stopping Starting Running Tagging Dodging
Club Guard	Ball game	Four to five per game	8-inch playground ball; 1 duck pin for each group		Passing Catching Guarding a pin

objectives. They provide chances for children to assume both leader and follower roles.

In the game's environment, children can learn about themselves—their strengths and weaknesses—as they attempt to meet the game's goals. Success in games requires children to find appropriate solutions to game challenges based on their individual skill repertoire. Outside the school environment, recognition of individual differences enables children to modify rules so that players of varying abilities may all find success. Everyone does not necessarily have to play by all the same rules.

Children may take risks in games in a fun way. Games allow the children to move into areas of uncertainty and insecurity without the real threat of failure because the outcome is not an important or life-and-death matter.

> Games are effective as expressive models for gaining experience in the mastery of dangerous emotions very largely because of their miniature scale and their playful context. They are rendered safe by remaining on a plane of unreality in which "reality consequences" do not have to be faced (Devereaux).

Games offer an opportunity for play within the parameters of rules and boundaries. Recognition of the importance of rules for everyone and a willingness to play within the rules require self-discipline of all participants. Assuming responsibility for the enforcement of rules by acting as the leader or official should encourage children's respect for authority in later games.

GAMES ANALYSIS

Because each group of children is unique, it is necessary when selecting games or lead-ups to match game elements to the characteristics of the particular group of children with whom one is working. Morris and Stiehl have suggested a method of analyzing games that has been modified in this text to include the following categories in activity selection: (1) the physical requirements of the game—equipment, space, and organizational pattern; (2) game structure—game classification, number of participants, modifications, and strategy; and (3) personal requirements—motor skills, movement concepts, and social structure. An additional category—level—is added to aid the teacher in matching the game to each group of children. See Table 23-1 and other games chapters for examples of games analysis. In using the game analysis,

MODIFICATIONS	MOVEMENT CONCEPTS	SOCIAL STRUCTURE	STRATEGY	LEVEL
Vary locomotor movements used	Self/general: Moves within the boundaries of the playing area Moves to an open space Moves in relation to others to be avoided Pathways: Changes pathways while moving in space Recognizes and anticipates available pathways within which to move Anticipates the pathways of others to intercept or avoid that path Time/speed: Anticipates the speed of persons moving in space to intercept them	Parallel play II	Wait until opponents get close before giving the signal	I
Could designate a particular type of throw to be used	Self/general: Keeps one's self space between the ball and an object to be guarded Pathways: Recognizes available paths within which to move the ball	Social interaction II	Teamwork is necessary to get the pin; pass quickly to get the ball behind the guard	III

Games allow children to use their skills in challenging ways.

the teacher may be searching for a game in which to use a particular motor skill or movement concept the class is working on or perhaps to reinforce some social behavior. The following considerations are important in selecting games for children:

Physical Requirements

Equipment: Recommendations that consider size and texture of balls and height of baskets or nets for the success and safety of all participants.

Space and organizational pattern: The space and the organization of players in the playing area for the smallest number of participants needed for successful play.

Game Structure

Game classification: Games may be categorized in many different ways, from the type of formation used (circle games, line games, net games), the skills used (running games, ball games, cooperative), to the nature of the game itself (educational, skill, and lead-up).

- **Educational game:** A game used to apply basic motor skills and movement concepts, has few rules, and involves large or small groups, and varying degrees of group cooperation to achieve the game goal.
- **Skill game:** An activity whose primary purpose is the practice of one or a limited number of skills.
- **Lead-up game:** A game that includes some of the skills, rules, and strategies associated with a team sport, such as toss-up basketball.

Number of participants: To maximize the opportunity for all children, the smallest number of participants per team is suggested, assuming several games are being played at the same time.

Modifications: Changes that may be needed to maximize or individualize the game or to emphasize certain skills.

Strategy: Points to be emphasized in the game, which may be brought out indirectly or directly by the leader.

Personal Requirements

Motor skills: Important locomotor and/or ball skills for the use of which the game might be selected.

Movement concepts: Body awareness, space, and/or qualities of movement components essential to game success.

Social structure: The degree to which interaction and cooperation with others is required in the game.

- **Parallel play I:** Children may play in a small or large group, but activity requires little cooperation for an individual's success.
- **Parallel play II:** Similar to I, but each child goes one-on-one with another, usually "It" or a matched opponent.
- **Social interaction I:** Some simple cooperation, such as working together to cover space for tagging; requires little group planning; and marks a beginning group effort (team score).
- **Social interaction II:** Requires group decision on limited offensive and/or defensive strategy (for example, who will carry the ball).
- **Social interaction III:** Requires group planning in developing group offensive and defensive strategy and delegation of responsibilities when activity requires that several jobs be done.

Level: A composite classification according to difficulty indicated by the previous categories.

- **Level I:** Represents activities in which simple motor skills are needed, rules and concepts are few, there is little strategy, and social dependence is absent. These activities are generally associated with the earliest physical education experiences.
- **Level II:** Represents activities of simple combinations of skills, greater understanding of rules and concepts needed, group strategy, and some group decision making and cooperation. These activities are usually appropriate for intermediate grades or when the children are ready to move beyond level I.
- **Level III:** Characterized by increasingly difficult skills and combinations of skills, an increasing number of concepts and rules, and greater dependence on the group for the development of strategy and game success. These activities are usually appropriate for upper elementary school children or when the children are beyond level II.
- **Level IV:** The most advanced level to be achieved during the elementary school years. Children are required to use more complex motor skills and combinations to adjust skills to an ever-changing environment and changing player relationships. The use of movement concepts is more complex, and the development of strategy is more important for success in games. These activities are appropriate for children in the upper grades. Achievement to this level depends on the type and extent of the physical education program.

Experience in physical education determines the level of achievement attained in any activity. The game analysis approach in the selection of games may aid the teacher in more carefully matching games with the characteristics of a particular group of children than will a grade level classification of games. Because there are great variations in exposure to motor skills and movement concepts, in social development, and in actual game experience within a group, as well as from group to group, a closer look at games must be made if the needs of children are to be adequately met.

PLANNING AND CONDUCTING GAMES AND LEAD-UP EXPERIENCES

Adults are often eager to get children involved in adult games, with little consideration of where children are in their games development. Success in games depends on the leader's attention to game analysis. Failure to consider any one of the categories may result in an unfavorable response by the children as they attempt to play the game successfully. The following suggestions should be helpful in adapting games for elementary school children and creating a positive learning experience for all.

An appropriately sized space must be provided. In team sports, children are often asked to play on adult-sized fields with adult-sized goals, although physically they may have only half the size and strength of more mature individuals. If the space is too large, children may not be able to use their skills effectively or to cover the space well on defense. If the space is too small, children may have more success with their skills and space coverage on defense, but may have great difficulty using the space effectively in working with teammates because they tend to be close together. A goal size that enables the defender to cover the space and that provides a space large enough for the offense to have a fair opportunity to score is essential.

Boundary lines must be established far enough from obstacles (4 to 6 feet) to ensure a safe distance for stopping. Children should be encouraged to play within the boundaries and to stop on boundary lines. Some space beyond the boundaries is essential for those children who forget or who misjudge their ability to stop on the line.

Safe play should be stressed at all times. Appropriate footwear is essential to safe participation. Learning to be responsible for one's safety and the safety of others is important. In ball games, especially dodgeball types, rules may need to be established that encourage keeping the ball low. Being under control at all times is an essential trait to be encouraged.

The size, weight, and softness of balls must be considered when selecting appropriate equipment to be used in games. How many times have elementary school children lost interest in playing a game because the ball was too hard when it hit them, when they tried to catch it, or when they attempted to strike it? Selecting equipment that allows all children an opportunity for success without developing fear of it is essential. In small group activities, the availability of balls and other equipment varying in size and weight will enable children some choice in the equipment they wish to use.

A prime reason for selecting games is the opportunity to use specific skills. Because certain skills are used in a game does not ensure their practice during the playing of the game. Therefore, special attention must be given to these skills before the beginning of game play by providing adequate practice activities similar to their use in the game. In addition the game should be structured to provide maximum opportunity for each child to use them throughout the game.

In each game the understanding of movement concepts contributes substantially to successful play. Although often many concepts should be identified, the teacher must emphasize the one or two that are of greatest importance for the students' level of play. Practice of these concepts in the context of their use in the game before game play will help children achieve more successful play.

The games lesson should include practice of the skills and movement concepts, in addition to the games selected to enhance the skills and concepts. Objectives must be continuously emphasized throughout as the games become the means to greater understanding of the objectives. Each activity is chosen for its contribution to the day's objectives, and a variety of experiences should be planned for the development of each objective.

It is important to get the children into the game as quickly as possible to attain maximum activity for the lesson. After the skills and movement concept objectives have been presented, or reviewed, and practiced, the children are ready for the game experience. Whenever possible, the children should be organized into their teams and sitting in formation before the game is introduced. Suggestions for organizing the group may be found in Chapter 8. Children's questions should be answered only after the explanation and demonstration of the game are complete, because most questions will be answered by this time.

Once play is under way, some very important teaching takes place. During play time the teacher guides the children in the game experience. Teachers should take every opportunity to give feedback on the purposes for which the game was chosen. This may include comments to individual children as well as to the group. During this time the teacher may enhance critical thinking and problem solving by raising questions to assist the children in thinking about the game challenges and devising possible solutions.

Developing strategy and establishing the part to be played by each team member are important learning experiences that are a part of games. It often takes a time or two in playing the game before children get beyond understanding the game rules. When they do they are ready to be guided by the teacher in developing game strategies. Children should be encouraged in these efforts through questions posed by the teacher or through brief discussion sessions. Game experience is important in this decision-making process, and the teacher must be patient and give children sufficient experience in the game so that they begin to see possible strategies they might use. At no time should the teacher suggest one or more specific strategies to use.

Emphasis must be on the development of each individual's potential through maximum opportunities for participation. Often games calling for many players do not afford equal opportunity for active involvement by all the children because play can become limited to one area of the playing field or to the most aggressive players on the court. If all children are to have the opportunity to use their skills, efforts must be made to maximize participation by reducing the numbers in the game to the fewest possible needed to achieve the game goals successfully and to equalize participation among the players in each game. Having several small groups playing the game simultaneously in the available space also encourages children to take more responsibility for the game's success and to become more self-directed. Increasing the number of balls used is another way to increase participation in ball games.

Modification of rules may benefit all children. During informal play, children often modify rules of a game for individuals of varying ages and abilities to ensure fair and equal opportunity for success. Adults seldom consider this possibility. In many games, modification of rules for individuals is acceptable to the group and easily administered. All children are encouraged to play by the most challenging rules for their ability, and yet no children are destined to failure by rules that they are unable to meet. If the game is not going as well as anticipated, the teacher may stop play and (1) make changes in the game structure or better yet involve the children in making suggestions on how the game might be modified to improve it for everyone, or (2) after some discussion break the game down into partner or small group activities to focus on the use of motor skills or game concepts needed to enhance meeting the game objectives.

Equal opportunity for successful play should be provided to each participant. The teacher's selection of opponents of comparable ability adds to the challenge and active participation in the game. Each child then has an equal opportunity for successful play. This approach eliminates the fear and intimidation many children feel when opposed by more skillful or aggressive players. In addition, children should have equal opportunity to play various positions in the game, which is guaranteed by a rotation plan worked out by the teacher or students. The teacher also should look for indications that the game structure allows all children the opportunity to use skills and be actively involved in the game play. Changes in organization may sometimes be necessary to ensure the equal opportunity for all children.

Social aspects of games must not be overlooked. Many games require group cooperation, sharing in decision making, and the ability to relate to many players in the playing area. One has only to observe a pick-up game of basketball of elementary school children to recognize the lack of group cooperation in the game. Often the one or two most aggressive and/or well-skilled children dominate play while the others move aimlessly around the court, not knowing where to go and seldom, if ever, receiving a pass or becoming actively involved. Teamwork is not automatic. It must be planned for. Many times rules must be added to ensure team play. For example, there must be three passes before shooting for a goal.

Games provide experience in working with others to achieve game goals.

Games that are highly competitive and those that encourage speed rather than good skill performance should be avoided. Games should provide competition to improve, not to prove. Relays most often result in not only poor quality performance but also winning at the expense of others.

Keeping a score should not be emphasized in physical education. If children are not interested in keeping score, no score should be kept. If a score is kept the teacher should help to make sure an accurate score is kept, and scoring should be kept as simple as possible.

Children should be taught to conduct their games without direct supervision of adults. Children can be given the responsibility of conducting their games if properly prepared. Early games have few rules, and once they are learned children can play the games with decreasing assistance from teachers. Children may begin by being given the opportunity to review the rules of the game for the class. Small group play with indirect supervision by the teacher encourages the children to act more independently. Upper elementary schoolchildren are also capable of serving as referees or umpires for their games, which not only provides an opportunity to make decisions about rules but also teaches respect for officials.

In a game unit, repetition of games is important. Children enjoy playing games they know. From an educational perspective if children are to see possible strategies that could be developed, there must be adequate exposure to a game, not necessarily for long periods but at least for frequent periods of time. In organizing units involving lead-ups to team sports, an even more limited number of games should be included. Perhaps one or two lead-up games should receive the most emphasis to afford children the opportunity to understand the rules, the use of skills and concepts, and the development of offensive and defensive play.

When reviewing games, it is important to have the children as actively involved in the review as possible. The teacher might ask the group to recall the rules verbally or have one child review the game with the group. These are good techniques to help children develop skill in teaching games and increase their ability to organize and verbalize information.

Evaluation of objectives should include not only the children's ability to execute a particular skill or understand a movement concept, but also their ability to use them in a variety of game situations. Objectives should be stated in such a way as to identify the behavior the children can use to achieve them. The teacher can ask the following questions to evaluate the outcomes of games:

1. How well were the specific skills executed?
2. Was each skill used appropriately?
3. Was there evidence that the children understood and applied the important movement concepts in the game?
4. Was there evidence of the children's ability to think in action? Were they able to analyze the situation and plan a course of action?
5. Was there evidence of appropriate social skills? Did they share with others, play by the rules, share in the decision making, and so forth?

Games become educational only when these suggestions are implemented. Games can be a valuable learning experience for children. The teacher must carefully select games and conduct the game experiences so that each child receives the full benefit of the activity, not just some children at the expense of others.

LEAD-UPS TO TEAM SPORTS

To participate successfully in team sports, children must have acquired the following:

Physical skills: The ability to effectively select and execute locomotor and ball-handling skills, which may be used singly or in combination to move the ball individually or to teammates. This includes the development of good technique and the ability to modify skills for their effective use in the game.

Social skills: The ability to recognize the need to work together, to share in the game effort, and to relate to many players in the playing area.

Cognitive skills: The ability to analyze the ever-changing game situation and to make decisions about a course of action, to see position play, to understand and put movement concepts into practice, to comprehend a variety of offensive and defensive strategies, and to understand and play by a complex set of rules.

Since elementary school children do not possess all of the prerequisites for successful play, teachers must plan a progression of experiences that will allow students to participate successfully in the team sports of their choice. Lead-up games are an essential part of the team sports progression because they allow the children to work on single or simple elements of the game at a simple level of understanding. The progression of activities allows for the gradual introduction of the skills, concepts, rules, and strategy that are essential to successful participation in the game.

The lead-up game chosen to match the ability of the children in the group becomes the "official" game for that class. Children do not readily understand the term *lead-up game,* and it should not be used in our discussions with them.

In developing sports skills, both technique and use of the skills must be considered. In evaluating performance, the teacher must decide whether errors are the result of failure to execute the skills correctly or the inability to select and use skills appropriately in the game situation.

A beginning alley basketball game provides one-on-one competition in the three alleys on each half of the court.

Practices are then organized for the correction of errors, emphasizing either the teaching points important to the skill performance (perceiving and refining) or the use of the skills in more gamelike situations (varying). Once the techniques are mastered, emphasis on effective use of the skills through practice and game coaching becomes increasingly important (applying).

Many movement concepts may be identified as essential to a particular team sport. Obviously, it is not feasible to develop all concepts in any one unit. Therefore, the teacher must carefully select the most crucial concepts for development at each stage in the sports progression. After some game play, children may be involved in determining which skills and game concepts need more practice and perhaps even how to practice them.

Rules of games should be adapted and modified to meet the needs of individuals. In many games, rules may be established for individuals to equalize play for all. Modifications for individuals may be found in each sport progression in the chapters that follow.

Lead-ups provide for the gradual increase in complexity of the social environment. Beginning lead-up games requires little social interaction and teamwork, whereas games used later in the progression require greater interdependence of members of the team for successful play.

Children are generally more interested in playing games than practicing their skills. If lead-up activities are organized for maximum participation and at an appropriate level of difficulty, they may play an important role in the development of skills and knowledge important to the team sport. Lead-up games will also help children become aware of the goals toward which they are working.

Cooperative Games

The importance of the development of appropriate social skills has been discussed in both Chapter 1 and 14, with some suggested activities for building group cohesiveness and interdependence included in Chapter 14. Cooperative games are an important tool in developing skills that will enable children to work with others in a variety of settings. Although many games have the potential for developing these important skills, they are often presented in a way that stresses competition and winning by scoring more points than the other team, rather than working together to achieve the same goal. Suggestions for adding a more cooperative dimension to games include the following:

1. Altering the game focus so that each team attempts to improve its own performance rather than merely getting more points than the other team.
   a. For example, in playing the game snowball, the children play the game and then count the number of balls on their side. They play again trying to have fewer balls on their side.
   b. Alternatively, children could set a target (number of balls on their side) and as they play the game try to reach the target they set rather than trying solely to have fewer balls on their side of the court than their opponents. If the target is achieved exactly—no more or no less—they have won. If the target is not achievable after a few tries, they may need to set a new target.
2. Altering scoring.
   a. The team receives a bonus point if the ball is successfully passed before sending it over the net in a net game.
   b. Scoring a point for each pass made before shooting a basket.
3. Require team play before scoring, such as requiring each member of the team to contact the ball before taking a shot on goal.
4. Give children the opportunity to modify a game in some way that requires the active participation of everyone.

The outcomes of cooperative games should be an equal opportunity for active participation of each player, and game success the result of the interdependence of members of the group for achieving the game goal. Cooperative activities and suggestions for encouraging cooperation may be found in the games chapters that follow.

Multicultural Games

Many of the games children play have their origins in Native American culture and other cultures of the world. In teaching these games, we give children the opportunity not only to learn about other people but also to understand and appreciate their contributions to the play experience for all of us. Games activities or modified versions of games from other cultures are included in the games chapters that follow.

Developing New Games

Children should be encouraged to invent their own games and to modify known games to make them more challenging. Creating new games should be an important part of all game experiences. New games may emerge from modifications to games children have learned or from some other parameters set by the teacher or the children themselves. Suggestions for creating new games from known games include the following:

1. Increasing or decreasing the number of players
2. Changing the size or shape of the space used
3. Changing how the space is used
4. Changing the skills used
5. Changing the ways skills are used

6. Using a particular game concept
7. Changing the equipment used
8. Changing one rule of the known game
9. Requiring the cooperation of all players or the players of each team

Many of these suggestions may be used in creating new games. For example the following questions may form the basis for the new game:

1. Can you make up a game for three players?
2. Can you make up a game to play in a circle? a square? a triangle?
3. Can you make up a game in which all players share the same space? Are in adjacent spaces?
4. Can you make up a game that requires underhand striking with the hand?
5. Can you make up a game that requires throwing to targets at different levels?
6. Can you make up a game in which you score by hitting an empty space?
7. Can you make up a game using a ball and a jump rope?
8. Can you make up a game in which you may only throw from a stationary position?
9. Can you make up a game where all must control the ball in a different way before scoring?

SUMMARY

Educational games and team sports lead-up activities are an important element in the elementary school physical education program. They provide an opportunity for children to use motor skills and to apply knowledge learned in physical education to a group activity. They challenge children to use these skills and knowledge in new ways as the games increase in complexity over the elementary school years. Games and lead-ups also provide an environment in which to learn and to use social skills that are essential to successful participation throughout life.

Games may be selected to reinforce the motor skills that the children are learning or to teach concepts. The selection of appropriate games depends on the teacher's ability to analyze games with regard to the motor and social skills and concepts needed for success. The game analysis approach is important if games are to be valuable in meeting the lesson objectives.

The value of games is not inherent in the games themselves; it is the result of careful planning and conducting of the games experiences. Teachers must maximize the opportunity for individual development by organizing games for maximum individual participation, equating competition, modifying game rules to match the players' abilities, encouraging children to work together, providing a safe, nonthreatening environment in which to play, and helping children to see the relationships between the skills and knowledge they have acquired and the games they are playing.

In selecting the game, the teacher looks at the physical requirements of the game, the game structure, and the personal requirements to match the game with the children who will play it.

The progression of lead-up activities for team sports gives children the opportunity to grow in their performance of motor skills and understanding of movement concepts, rules, and strategies over the elementary school years with guaranteed successful participation for all. As skills are refined and more complex understandings are developed, the children gradually move to increasingly complex activities that require the ability to relate to more participants in the playing area and the development of offensive and defense play.

Games that encourage the development of cooperative skills as well as understanding of other cultures are also an important part of the game experience. In addition children should be encouraged to make up their own games as well as to modify those they've learned for new challenges.

REFERENCES AND RESOURCES

Deline J: "Why can't they get along? developing cooperative skills through physical education, *JOPERD* 62(1):21, 1991.

Devereaux E: Backyard versus little league baseball: some observations on the impoverishment of children's games in contemporary America. In Yiannakis A et al, editors: *Sport sociology: contemporary themes,* ed 4, Dubuque, Ia, 1992, Kendall/Hunt Publishing.

Glakas BA: Teaching cooperation skills through games, *JOPERD* 62(5):28, 1991.

Kraft R: Learning through games discovery, *Physical Educator* 44(4):420, 1987.

Kraft RE: Innovative games ideas: let the students create the games, *Strategies* 2(1):27, 1988.

Moore D: The winning alternative: solving the dilemma of the win/lose syndrome, *Childhood Education* 62(3):171, 1986.

Morris G and Stiehl J: *Changing kids games,* ed 2, Champaign, Ill, 1989, Human Kinetics Publishers.

Orlick T: *The second cooperative sports and games book,* 1982, New York, Pantheon Books.

Thorpe R et al: A change in focus for the teaching of games. In Pieron M and Graham G, editors: *Sports pedagogy,* Champaign, Ill, 1986, Human Kinetics.

Werner P: Teaching games, a tactical perspective, *JOPERD* 60(3):97, 1989.

ANNOTATED READINGS

Bean D: Outdoor games teaching: a key to effectiveness, *JOPERD* 54(9):54, 1983.

Relates skills development to their use in games.

Capel S: Games and sports offering social, competitive, and functional purpose, *JOPERD* 57(2):29, 1986.

Discusses movement concepts as an important part of the games experience.

Coulter B: Organizing team sports—think odd, *JOPERD* 57(8):66, 1986.

Describes organizing the class into an odd number of teams, with the extra team working on strategy or skills while the remaining teams play a game.

Gabbard C and Miller G: Intermediate school game curriculum, *JOPERD* 58(6):66, 1987.

Looks at the types of games that make up the intermediate school curriculum and their relative emphases.

Marlow M: Motor experiences through games analysis, *JOPER* 52(1):78, 1981.

Discusses using games analysis for teachers and students to modify games for participants.

Peterson SC: The sequence of instruction in games: implications for developmental appropriateness, *JOPERD* 63(6):36, 1992.

Discusses the selection of games based on children's motor development, individualized for the varying abilities in the class, and based on progression in learning in moving the children gradually to more difficult tasks.

Schwager S: Relay races—are they appropriate for elementary physical education? *JOPERD* 63(6):54, 1992.

Challenges the use of relays in children's physical education in meeting physical education objectives.

Williams NF: The physical education hall of shame, *JOPERD* 63(6):57, 1992.

Discusses activities traditionally a part of children's physical education that are contrary to accepted practice in physical education.

CHAPTER 24

Educational Games

OBJECTIVES

After completing this chapter the student will be able to:

1. Explain the principles that should be considered in planning and conducting educational games experiences
2. Explain the important role movement concepts play in success in educational games
3. Suggest activities to develop movement concepts in the context of educational games
4. Describe running, tag, and ball games as a means to furthering the development of motor skills, social skills, and movement concepts

Educational games—games selected for the practice and use of previously learned motor skills and movement concepts—provide the first group experiences in the physical education of elementary school children. Games offer a challenging opportunity for children to put their motor skills to use as they test their skills against others, first on a one-on-one basis, as in avoiding being tagged, and later in more complex group interactions. As children move through the elementary school grades, the rules, skills, and social structure of their games increase in complexity with their growth in maturity.

EDUCATIONAL GAMES FOR ELEMENTARY SCHOOL CHILDREN

In addition to the suggestions for planning and conducting games described in Chapter 23, the following principles should be kept in mind.

Maximum participation for all should be considered in selecting games. Some running games provide activity for all children all the time. In these games the entire class may play as one group. Other games where only two or three players are active at a time should be organized for many small groups of children to play at the same time. Tag games having more than one person as "It" will also challenge more children as they try to avoid being tagged. Circle games that provide activity for only a few should be avoided.

The elimination of players during the game should be avoided. Games provide equal opportunity for all children to develop and use their skills only when all have equal playing time. Penalties for being tagged, hit with the ball, and the like should not be the elimination of any child from play. Sometimes a change in role, for example, from dodger to thrower, or developing a point system for the number tagged may be all that is necessary to ensure equal playing time for all.

The use of different formations is important in maintaining students' interest. Most motor skills and concepts can be used in a variety of situations. Children not only enjoy using them in different types of games but also need the opportunity to broaden their repertoire of skills and concepts, which a variety of formations provides.

In games where some differentiation of responsibility of players is made, a rotation plan should be in operation that gives each child the opportunity to assume each of the different roles. In some games good strategy might necessitate the division of responsibility into offensive and defensive assignments or in simpler games into the "Its" and those being chased. Within the lesson, all children should have the opportunity to play as many different roles as possible to enable them to use their skills to the fullest.

It is important to get the game off to a good start to maintain enthusiasm. In beginning play, the first group leader or "It" should be someone who will be successful in a short period of time. These beginning moments establish the game goal and set the tone for the activity. Increasing the number of children who are "It" in tag games is another strategy to get the game off in a positive way.

As a rule it is best to change the activity when the interest level is high. The timing of each game is important to the success of the game experience. If the game is played too long, children will not only lose interest at that time, but also may play the game less enthusiastically in subsequent lessons. In the upper grades the game must be played long enough for the children to learn the rules and to develop appropriate strategy. For the development of strategy it may be best to play the game often for short periods rather than occasionally for a long time.

Assisting Children in Games

During the elementary school years, several problems may arise in the conduct of games. If uncontrolled these problems may affect the outcome of the game or the social interaction of the children.

In the beginning stages of game play, some children may have difficulty staying within the boundaries of the playing area. This difficulty may be manifested by running outside of the lines to avoid being tagged, failure to run close to the circle in circle games, or not stopping on the end line. These problems may be the result of the child's need for more space, a lack of control in stopping, or most probably the child's lack of understanding in the use of general space. Movement activities in the exploration of space in which the size of space and the type of movement used are varied will help children develop this concept. Exploring activities in how to keep the body in control, as in stopping or changing direction, may also be helpful. Sometimes a penalty such as considering children tagged if they go out of the playing area or do not stop on the end line may need to be imposed.

Children need to learn the importance of playing by the game rules. In tag games some children may not attempt to avoid being tagged. Others may not admit to being tagged or hit by the ball in dodge ball games. If children appear to want to be tagged, this may be an indication that the game is moving too slowly or is not challenging enough for the children. Children need to be encouraged to play by the rules and to avoid being tagged. Emphasizing being a good dodger by asking, "How many did not get tagged today?" or choosing a new leader from those not tagged are ways children may be encouraged to play by the rules. For the child who will not admit to being tagged or hit with the ball, the teacher will usually see who has been tagged or hit and in a casual, friendly way can indicate that the tag or hit was observed. Game rules need to be enforced in a way that is not intimidating to children and with emphasis on how well the game is being played rather than on declaring a winner.

Sharing in running and ball games should be encouraged. Choosing someone who has not had a turn to be "It" and handing the ball to a child who has not had the opportunity to throw it should be standard procedures in any game to develop a cooperative spirit with concern for others.

Being a good winner or loser may become a problem with some youngsters in the intermediate grades. Keeping winning in perspective is important to a healthy society. Unfortunately, adults and athletes who are models for children sometimes are observed acting inappropriately in a game. Emphasis should be on perfecting the use of skills and concepts and working together in the best effort rather than on winning. Grouping children so that competition is equal for all participants will help. Poor social behavior often is the result of unequal competition in which one team humiliates the other. Match-

Small group play provides more active participation for all.

ing opponents for competition provides everyone an equal opportunity for success and the challenge of giving their best effort.

Social Skills

Games provide an opportunity for developing social skills if carefully planned and conducted. Teachers should encourage supportive behavior and the development of cooperative skills as children learn to play within the rules framework of games. Following the suggestions in Chapter 23 and the beginning of this chapter will help create an environment where appropriate social behavior is more likely to occur, but teachers must actively teach the social behaviors desired and reinforce them throughout play as well as take action when inappropriate behaviors occur.

Modifying games to enhance cooperation and group interdependence as suggested in Chapters 14 and 23 is important. The games experience should include discussion before and after game play regarding the social skills used to achieve game success to increase the children's awareness of the importance of these skills. Additional cooperative games may be found in Chapter 14.

Health-Related Physical Fitness

Cardiorespiratory fitness can be enhanced in games only if maximum vigorous activity is achieved. Following the principles suggested in the beginning of this chapter is essential to achieving fitness goals for all children in games. Games should always be organized so that the maximum number of children are able to move vigorously at all times.

SKILLS

Educational games provide an opportunity for children to use a variety of motor skills that they are learning in the elementary school physical education program. They include locomotor and body control skills as well as a variety of ball skills. Analyses of most of the skills used in educational games and activities to use in their development may be found in Chapter 13.

Before game play, children should have opportunities to develop adequate technique in performing the skill, as well as in varying the technique as the game requires. The children then use or apply the skills during coached game play in which the skills are reinforced further.

Tagging is an additional skill to be taught for use in games. Tagging demands a carefully controlled arm and hand movement that results in a soft touch while running in general space using a lot of force. Thus two different forces must be controlled. Activities to practice tagging and controlling force follow.

1. Duck pins or bowling pins are scattered throughout the space. Children also are scattered in the general space. On the signal the children move in the area, touching the pins gently so that they do not fall over. They try to touch as many pins as possible until the teacher calls them to stop. The children receive one point for every pin they touch that does not fall down. The children repeat this exercise, attempting to improve their personal best. (Do not ask children how many they touched, as this is a competition with self; only ask whether they improved their own mark.)
2. Children are scattered in general space with many duck pins scattered in the area. The children move around the general space using various locomotor movements and speeds indicated by the leader, tagging as many pins without knocking them down as possible before the signal to stop is given. (At what speeds or with what movements was it easy to control the tag without knocking down the pin? Which were the most difficult? What did you have to do to keep from knocking down the pins?)
3. Similar to No. 1, but several children are "It." "Its" try to tag other children, who are safe only when touching (not grasping) a duckpin.
4. Children are scattered in the general space. One third of the group are "It." On signal they attempt to tag others softly, using body parts other than hands, such as forearm or elbow. (Which body parts were easiest to tag with softly? Hardest? Why?)

MOVEMENT CONTENT

The application of movement concepts is an important aspect of game experiences. These concepts are mapped in Figure 24-1. The section that follows identifies the movement content for educational games and some suggestions for practice. Several concepts may be applied in

Some games require different roles for participation.

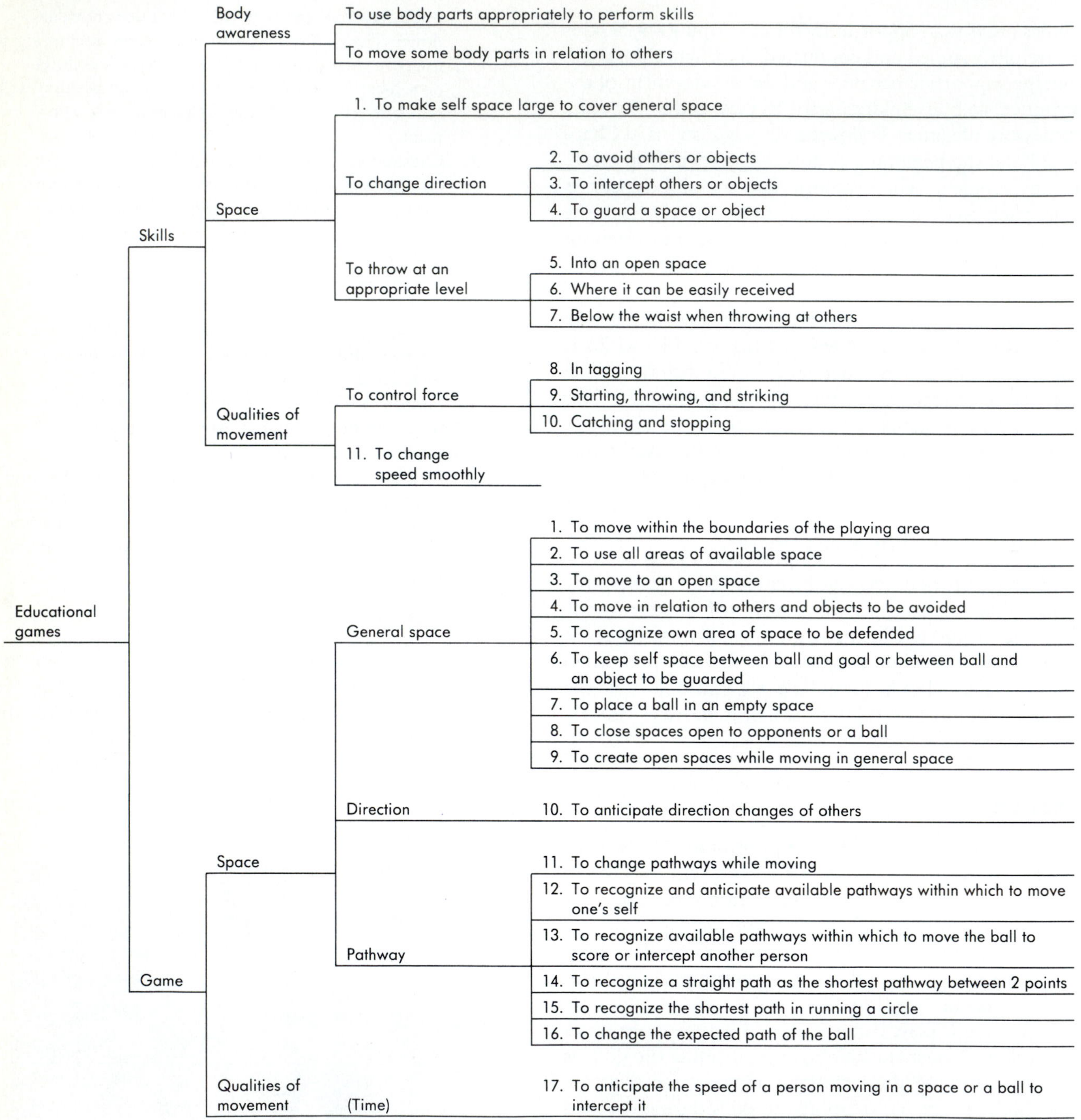

FIGURE 24-1 Concept map for educational games.

each game. The teacher determines the concept needs of the boys and girls in the class. After some work on the concept, the children play the game, during which it is emphasized further. The movement concepts in the games analysis tables found before each games sections in this chapter identify the most important concepts as numbered in the following section.

ACTIVITIES TO DEVELOP CONCEPTS FOR EDUCATIONAL GAMES

1. To move one's self and/or a ball within the boundaries of the playing area.
   a. Children move in the general space in the way suggested by the teacher (locomotor movement, ball skill, direction, pathway, etc.). When they come to a boundary line, they must turn and move along it or toward another boundary. (Which movements were easiest to use to stay in bounds? More difficult?)
2. To use all areas of the available space.
   a. Define boundaries. Children are scattered within the boundaries. On the signal, the children move around in general space, avoiding the self space of others and covering as much of the area as possible. On the signal, the teacher may ask the children to change locomotor movement, direction, or path. (Did you cover all the space? Corners? Sides? Middle? Which locomotor movements enabled you to cover the area fastest?)
3. To move to an open space while moving in general space.
   a. Children are scattered in the general space in which many hoops or ropes tied in circles have been placed. The children move freely in the area, covering as much space as possible. On the signal, they attempt to move into an empty hoop (the open space). Repeat. After a few times, remove hoops and repeat the activity, with the children looking for their own empty space. (Did you all find an empty space? How did you make sure you found one? Did you have to keep looking for an open space as you were moving around? What did you do if someone got there first?)
   b. Children are scattered within the space. On the signal, they move in general space. When they come to another person, they quickly move to a new open space. (How did you move to find a new empty space? How did you anticipate the movements of others to avoid getting into their self space?)
4. To move in general space in relation to others or an object to be avoided.
   a. Assign one third of the class to an area of general space, with the remaining two thirds on either side with balls. The persons on the inside move throughout their space, avoiding balls rolled by the two groups on the outside. (How did you move throughout the space to avoid being hit with the ball?)
   b. Children are scattered in general space. One third are taggers and attempt to tag the rest of the group. Change roles when tagged. (How did you use the space to avoid being tagged?)
5. To recognize one's own area of the general space to be defended.
   a. In partners, one child guards an area of wall space. The other has a ball and attempts to hit the wall within the reach of the guard. Increase the space and try again. Repeat several times. Change positions. (How large an area could you cover? What position enabled you to cover the space best?)
   b. Repeat No. 5a with two persons guarding the space. Continue to add guards and throwers. (What areas were most difficult to defend when you worked with a partner? Others?)
6. To keep one's self space between the ball and the goal or between the ball and an object to be guarded.
   a. Cones are placed in a box formation in several parts of the space, with one child assigned to protect each box. The children outside the boxes attempt to throw beanbags into the boxes, while the child in the box tries to keep them out. (What did you do to protect your box?)
   b. In partners, one child guards a duck pin. The other attempts to throw the ball past the other and knock over the pin. (Use more than one pin if the children have difficulty knocking them down.) Change partners several times so that each child has an opportunity to throw against several different children. Change guards and throwers. (How did you successfully guard your pin?)
7. To place a ball in an empty space in the opponent's playing area or goal.
   a. With a partner, one moves in a limited area, but in all directions. The other attempts to get the ball behind the moving player. (What did you do to get the ball past your partner?)
8. To close spaces open to an opponent or a ball.
   a. Children are scattered in the space. On the signal, they move in general space. On the signal to stop, they attempt to cover as much space as possible by making a large self space. (Where are the open spaces?)
   b. Assign one third of the group an area of general space to cover in the center of the playing area. The remaining two thirds are located on either side of the guarded space, and they attempt to roll balls through the guarded area. Change groups. (What did you do to best protect the area? Throwers, where did you place the ball? What problems arose covering the space? Throwing the balls?)

c. In partners, one attempts to get to a designated line; the other attempts to keep them away. (How did you position yourself to stop your partner?)

9. To create open spaces while moving in general space.

a. In groups of four in designated spaces in the general space, children try to keep as much space between them and the others in their group. Gradually combine the groups. (How did you move in the space to create an open space?)

10. To anticipate directional changes of others.

a. Designate some children as movers, the others as followers. All move freely in the general space changing direction. On the signal, the followers go to the closest person and follow that person, moving in the same direction. On the next signal, all children move freely again. Repeat. (What did you do to anticipate the direction changes of the person you were following?)
b. Using grids or hoops scattered on the floor as safety areas, half of the children move from spot to spot while the others try to tag them. Those tagged change roles with "It." (How did you anticipate the direction they would move? How did you fool "It?")
c. With a partner, one is "It." "It" chases the other partner, following the child's movements and directions. (In which direction was "it" easiest to follow? To avoid "It?" When was a good time to change direction? What cues were there that your partner was going to change direction?)

11. To change pathways while moving in space with or without a ball.

a. Children are arranged in partners on two lines facing each other. On the signal, the partners move toward each other. As they get close together, the teacher gives a signal for one line to be chasers, the other flees. Change the signal again and the partners switch roles. Repeat several times. (What did you do to reverse your pathway quickly?)
b. In partners, one is stationary in a position about half-way between two lines. On the signal, the moving child moves from one line toward the other. Nearing the stationary partner, the moving partner quickly changes pathways to move around the stationary partner and then straight for the other line. Repeat several times. *Variation:* Have the stationary children extend one arm to the side as the partners draw near. (How did you quickly respond to the change in available space?)
c. With a partner scattered in general space, child A, moving in one pathway, tries to tag child B, who is moving in another. On the signal to change, A changes paths and B, in turn, changes to move in a different path to A. The teacher may also call A and B to reverse roles. (How quickly could you respond to the signal? What combinations favored A? B?)

12. To recognize and anticipate pathways within which to move one's self.

a. Three circles at least 10 feet in diameter are placed within the playing area. An "It" stands in each circle. Children move in general space and in and out of the circles. The "Its" try to tag any children moving through their circle. If tagged, "It" changes place with the child tagged. (What did you do to avoid being tagged? To tag? For example, change locomotor movement, directions, speed, or pathway? Could you do anything else? Were you able to anticipate the pathways of the children moving through the space? What clues did you use?)
b. Children are scattered within the boundaries. Half are stationary (one foot must remain in contact with the floor at one spot). The other half move in general space, covering as much space as possible and avoiding the tags of the stationary children. (What did you do to get from one place to another and avoid being tagged? Can you think of another way? What pathways were easiest to find?)
c. Moving in general space, children move in one pathway. Each time they meet a person or a boundary line, they jump out of the way and continue in a new pathway. (Were you able to see the pathways of others? What clues did you use to avoid others?)

13. To recognize available pathways within which to move the ball to score a goal or to intercept a teammate or opponent.

a. Several groups of three children are designated who move in general space. The remaining children, along the boundaries of the area, attempt to throw balls to hit the middle person in each group below the waist. (Throwers, what did you do to successfully hit the moving and guarded target?)
b. In groups of four, two throwers look for available paths to throw the ball and two guards attempt to guard a line. (How did throwers anticipate open paths? Could you create some by working with your partner?)
c. Children are scattered in the general space. Half are taggers; the other half are those being tagged. Designate a locomotor movement and pathway for each child to move. "Its" may only tag those moving in the same pathway as they. Repeat, changing movements and pathway. (What cues did you use to choose those to tag?)
d. In partners, one child has a ball. The child with the ball tries to roll the ball between the legs of the other, who is at first stationary and then sliding from side to side. (What did you have to do to get the ball between your partner's legs? How did you make the path of the ball intercept the path of your partner?)

14. To recognize a straight line as the shortest pathway between two points.

Early games provide one-on-one confrontation.

a. Half the children are "It." Papers with various pathways on them are drawn from a bag by the other children, who must get across the general space along the pathway indicated and without being tagged. They then exchange pathways and try again. Then reverse the roles and repeat. (What did you do to avoid being tagged? In which path was it easiest to tag? To avoid being tagged?)

b. Children choose a pathway to get from point A to point B. The teacher counts out loud as they follow that path. (How long did it take?) Choose another pathway and repeat. Another. (Which path was the shortest?)

15. To recognize the shortest path in running around a circle.

a. Repeat No. 14b, but in a circle formation.

16. To change the expected path of the ball.

a. In groups of four, three throwers and one person in the middle of the three. Throwers pass the ball to each other in any other, the center person attempting to intercept. (How did you change the path of the ball to make it difficult for the center person to get it?)

17. To anticipate the speed of a person moving in space or a ball to intercept them.

a. In partners, one moving in general space, the other with a ball. The thrower throws the ball in the general area but not to the moving player, who must move quickly to intercept the ball. (How did you anticipate the speed of the ball to intercept?)

GAMES ANALYSIS

Table 24-1 (pp. 468-479) includes a games analysis for running and tag games. The games analysis for games using balls and other objects (Table 24-2, pp. 484-489) may be found before that section of games.

The movement concepts refer to the movement concepts numbered in Figure 24-1. Only a few of the most important concepts are suggested.

RUNNING AND TAG GAMES

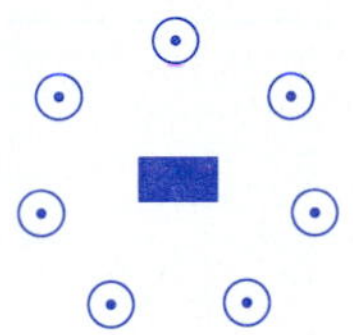

A WIND IS A BLOWIN'

Level: I
Equipment: A hoop for each child arranged in a large circle
Participants: Up to 25
Skills: Locomotor skills, stopping, starting
Description: The leader attempts to get a chair by calling: A wind is a blowin for those who ________ (adding some quality, such as have on blue, birthdays in March, like school, etc.) Those children matching the description attempt to exchange hoops by leaving theirs and moving to another. The person without a hoop gives the new call and hurries to find a hoop.
Teaching suggestions: This game stresses getting to know each other and using that information in the call. The teacher may have to help some children in the beginning to think of something to call, but as the children spend more time together they will have more ideas of what to say. Being "It" should be considered a positive thing, giving the children a chance to be creative in their responses.

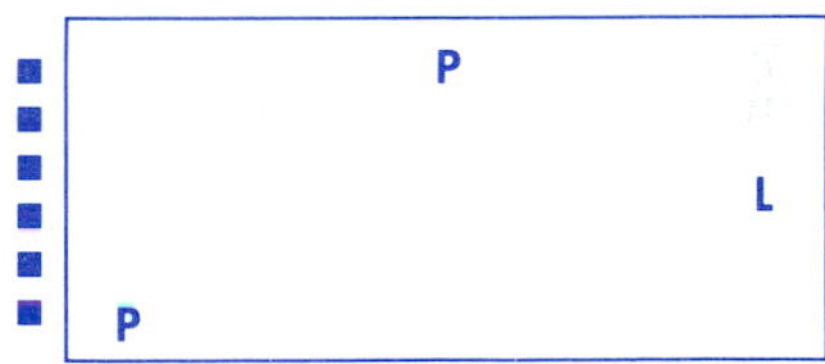

AUTOMOBILES

Level: I
Equipment: None
Participants: Up to 25
Skills: Running, stopping, starting
Description: The children are in a line at one end of the playing area. One leader and one or more traffic police are scattered in the area in front of the line. On the signal from the caller, the automobiles start, their destination is the opposite line. The leader may call for specific locomotor movements, a specific speed, turns to the right or left, reverse, etc. The children respond to the instructions. If a right turn is indicated, they turn to the right and continue in that line until told to change. The first child to the opposite line wins. The police watch to see that all are following the instructions of the leader and help those who are having difficulty following the leader's calls. Modification: The leader may send anyone who is not following their instructions back to the starting line to begin again.

Teaching suggestions: It may be helpful to have all the children moving in general space responding to the leader to get used to the calls before beginning the game. In the first games, the leader may want to call only directional changes. Encourage the children to listen carefully.

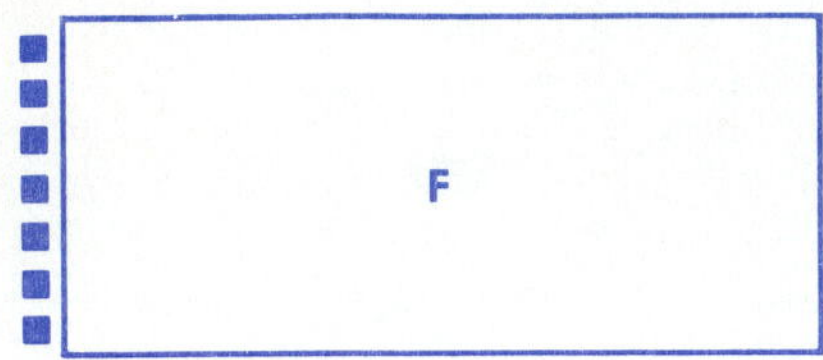

BARNYARD UPSET

Level: I
Equipment: None
Participants: Up to 25
Skills: Running, starting, stopping, dodging, tagging
Description: The children are lined up behind the starting line, with "It," the farmer, facing the group. All children secretly select a farm animal that they will be. The farmer calls the name of a farm animal. Those children who have chosen that animal run to the opposite line, avoiding the farmer, who tries to tag them. If tagged, they must go to the corral. After all children's animals have been called, the game begins again with a new farmer selected from those not tagged. As the game begins again, all children who were tagged rejoin the game. During the game the farmer may call "Barnyard upset," at which time all children whose animal has not been called must run to the opposite line.
Teaching suggestions: Emphasize good starts, controlled stops, and tagging softly. Encourage children to try to avoid being tagged. Asking, "How many did not get tagged today?" may be helpful.

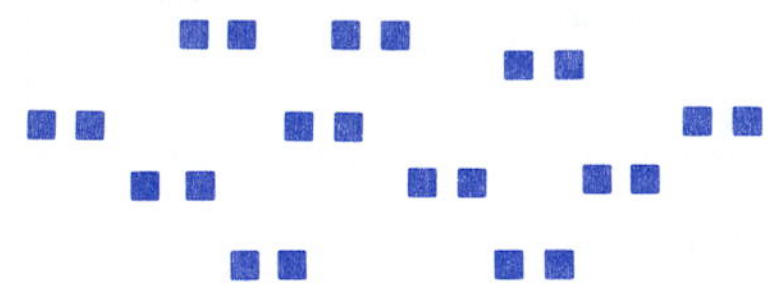

BUSY BEE

Level: I
Equipment: None
Participants: Up to 25
Skills: Stopping
Description: The children are scattered with partners in the playing area, with one extra person who is the leader. The leader calls the name of body parts, such as "Back to back," "Knee to knee," and so forth, and the partners match those parts named. When the leader calls "Busy bee," each person finds a new partner. The one without a partner becomes the new leader.
Teaching suggestions: Emphasize listening carefully to the leader. Encourage the children to think of as many different body parts as possible. The teacher may need to help some children when they are leader with suggestions for body parts.

DOVES AND HAWKS (China)

Level: I
Equipment: None
Participants: Up to 25
Skills: Locomotor skills, stopping, tagging
Description: The children are in groups of three scattered in the space. The children hold hands, with the person on the right of the center person, the "dove", and the person on the left the "hawk." The center person is known as the "Chinese child." On the signal from the leader to "let out the doves," the Chinese children swing the clasped "doves" hands forward releasing them to go wherever they choose in the space. On the signal "release the hawks," the hawks are released and attempt to tag the dove of the same group before they can get back safely to their Chinese children. All three change roles for the next game.
Teaching suggestions: Change the locomotor movements, the directions moved, etc. each time. Encourage soft tags and controlled stops as they make it back to their groups.

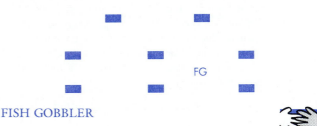

FISH GOBBLER

Level: I
Equipment: None
Participants: Up to 25
Skills: Locomotor and nonlocomotor movements
Description: One person is the leader, the fish gobbler. The others are scattered in the playing area. The fish gobbler calls out commands for the fish to follow together. They may include the following:

You're in the net. (Move to one corner of the space.)
You're on the shore. (Move to the opposite end line.)
Fishnet (Make a circle, hands joined.)
Sardines (All line on the floor.)
Wave (In groups of four, they hold hands and move through the space, swinging their arms up and down.)
Submarines (All form a line, stand on one foot and hold their noses.)

Teaching suggestions:

1. Begin with just a few cues for very young children.
2. Have the children think of different movements and cue words.
3. This activity might be used to group children for some other activity by ending with the arrangement desired.
4. Encourage the children to work together to quickly respond to the signal.

H C C C C C C C

WC

HEN AND WILDCAT (Africa)

Level: I
Equipment: None
Participants: Up to 25
Skills: Locomotor movements, tagging, dodging
Description: One child is designated as the hen and another the wildcat. The remaining children are the chickens. The chickens follow the hen throughout the playing area. The wildcat stands in the playing area and at will decides to chase the chickens (originally the wildcat hid behind a tree and then jumped out). The wildcat attempts to tag as many of the chickens as possible. To avoid a tag, the chickens squat down. Change the hen and wildcat after a few turns.
Teaching suggestions: Encourage the chickens to spread out while following the hen. Encourage the wildcat to make soft tags.

ON THE BANK, IN THE RIVER

Level: I
Area: A space with a line running the length of the space
Equipment: None
Participants: Up to 25
Skills: Jumping
Description: The children stand next to each other on one side of the line, with all facing forward. The side where they are standing is the bank, the other side the river. The leader calls "In the river" and everyone jumps forward to the other side of the line. If "On the bank" is called, they jump backward to the other side of the line. The leader attempts to confuse the group in the calls made. A player who moves to the incorrect side of the line on a call receives a point, or perhaps the first letter of one of the week's spelling words.
Teaching suggestions: Encourage soft landings and carefully sharing the space with those next to them.

JET PILOT

Level: I
Equipment: None
Participants: Up to 25
Skills: Running, stopping, starting
Description: The children are lined up behind the starting line with the leader (the control-tower operator) off to one side. The control-tower operator calls, "Control tower to pilots, control tower to pilots, all planes wearing (color) take off." On the signal, "Off," the children wearing the color called run to the far boundary line and back. The first person with a good stop on the starting line becomes the new control-tower operator (CTO). If desired, the control-tower operator may call. "All planes with all colors," so everyone runs.
Teaching suggestions: Encourage good starting and stopping. Promote good listening for the signal by having the control-tower operator change the speed at which he or she says, "Take off," or hesitating between the two words. If a child is first back and has already had a turn, have the second one back, or first child who has not had a turn become the new control-tower operator, etc.

RED LIGHT

Level: I
Equipment: None
Participants: Up to 25
Skills: Stopping, starting, running
Description: The children are lined up behind the starting line, with the leader in front of the group. The leader facing away from the group calls, "Green light," and counts to 10. The children move forward on the signal, "Green light." The leader then calls, "Red light," turning to face the other children as they stop quickly. After the leader turns around, anyone caught moving once the signal red light is given must go back to the starting line. The first child to reach the opposite line without being seen moving is the new leader.
Teaching suggestions: Encourage a balanced stopping position. For young children the game may be more successful by eliminating the counting or reducing the count. Young children may not see those who are moving out at the sides of the group, so they may need helpers to spot or the teacher's assistance. This game may be more successful if played in small groups.

Text continued on p. 476.

TABLE 24-1 RUNNING AND TAG GAMES ANALYSIS

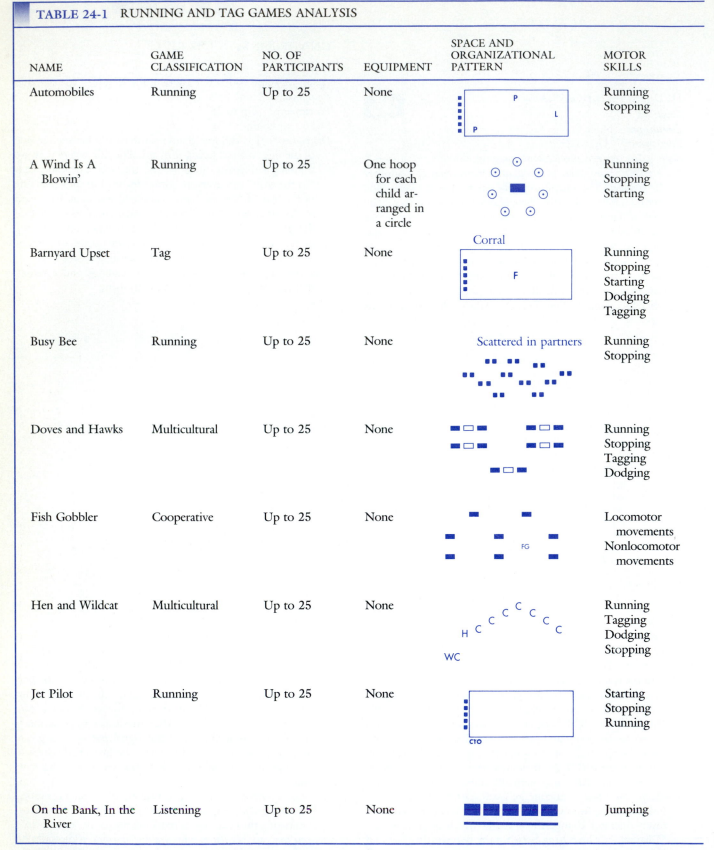

NAME	GAME CLASSIFICATION	NO. OF PARTICIPANTS	EQUIPMENT	SPACE AND ORGANIZATIONAL PATTERN	MOTOR SKILLS
Automobiles	Running	Up to 25	None	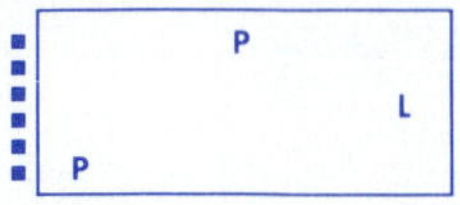 P P L	Running Stopping
A Wind Is A Blowin'	Running	Up to 25	One hoop for each child arranged in a circle	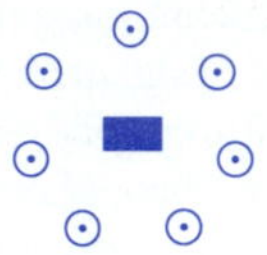	Running Stopping Starting
Barnyard Upset	Tag	Up to 25	None	Corral  F	Running Stopping Starting Dodging Tagging
Busy Bee	Running	Up to 25	None	Scattered in partners 	Running Stopping
Doves and Hawks	Multicultural	Up to 25	None	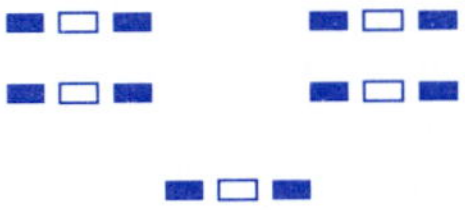	Running Stopping Tagging Dodging
Fish Gobbler	Cooperative	Up to 25	None	 FG	Locomotor movements Nonlocomotor movements
Hen and Wildcat	Multicultural	Up to 25	None	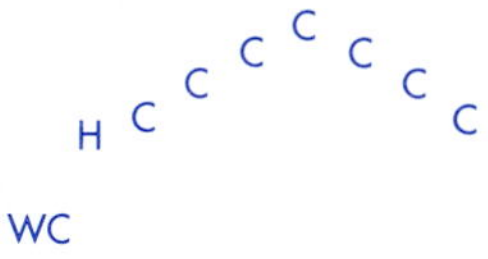 C C C C C C C H WC	Running Tagging Dodging Stopping
Jet Pilot	Running	Up to 25	None	CTO	Starting Stopping Running
On the Bank, In the River	Listening	Up to 25	None		Jumping

*Numbers refer to the movement concepts listed in Figure 24-1 on p. 462.

MODIFICATIONS	MOVEMENT CONCEPTS*	SOCIAL STRUCTURE	STRATEGY	LEVEL
Limit the number of different instructions given	Skills: 9, 10 Game: 1, 10, 11, 14	Parallel play II	Try to move in direction of goal as much as possible	I
Vary the locomotor skills used	Skills: 2, 9, 10 Game: 1, 3, 4, 10-12, 14	Parallel play II	Encourage creative suggestions in getting children to move	I
Vary locomotor movements used; have more than one farmer be "It"	Skills: 2, 3, 8-10 Game: 1, 3, 4, 8, 11, 12, 14, 17	Parallel play II		I
Vary locomotor movements used	Skills: 8, 10 Game: 11	Parallel play II		I
Vary the locomotor skills used Vary the directions in which the children move	Skills: 2, 3, 8-10 Game: 1, 4, 10-12	Parallel play II	Change speed and pathway to avoid being tagged	I
	Skills: 9-11 Game: 4, 10	Social interaction I	Discuss possible movements and give a few examples to get the children started	I
Vary locomotor movements used	Skills: 2, 3, 8-10 Game: 1, 3, 4, 10-12	Parallel play II	The chicks should keep spread out while following the hen to make it more difficult for the wildcat to catch them	I
If the first back has had a turn, let him or her choose someone else (who has not had a turn) to be "It," or take the second back, and so forth; vary locomotor movements used	Skills: 9, 10 Game: 11, 14	Parallel play I	Control tower operator may vary timing on command to "take-off"	I
	Skill: 10 Game: 4	Parallel play I	Listen carefully to the instructions given	I

Continued.

TABLE 24-1 RUNNING AND TAG GAMES ANALYSIS—cont'd

NAME	GAME CLASSIFICATION	NO. OF PARTICIPANTS	EQUIPMENT	SPACE AND ORGANIZATIONAL PATTERN	MOTOR SKILLS
Red Light	Running	Up to 25	None	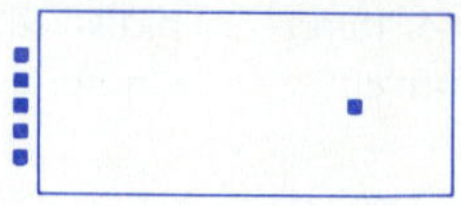	Stopping Starting Running
Sharks and Barracudas	Tag	Up to 25	None		Running Stopping Starting Tagging Dodging
Squirrels in Trees	Running	Up to 25	None	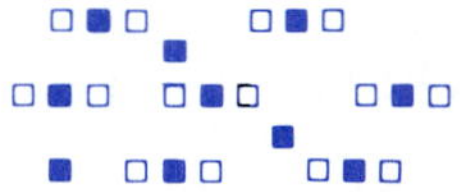	Stopping Starting Running
Bird Catcher	Tag	Up to 25	None	 BC	Starting Stopping Running Tagging Dodging
Circle Race	Tag	Up to 25	None	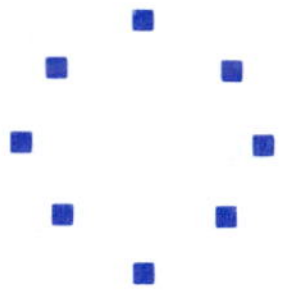	Running Starting Stopping Tagging
Color Tag	Tag	Up to 25	Colored squares in at least three or four colors	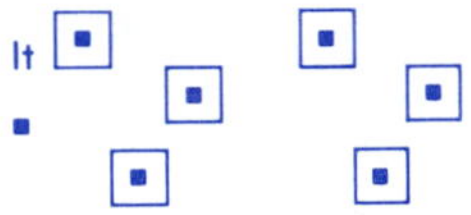 It	Running Stopping Starting Dodging Tagging
Fox and Hound	Tag	Up to 25	None	 H F F F F F F F F F	Running Starting Stopping Tagging Dodging
Gophers in the Garden	Tag	Up to six per game	None	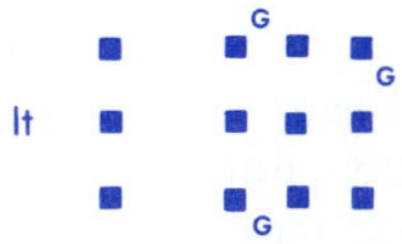 It G G G	Running Tagging Dodging
Great Wall of China	Tag	Up to 25	None	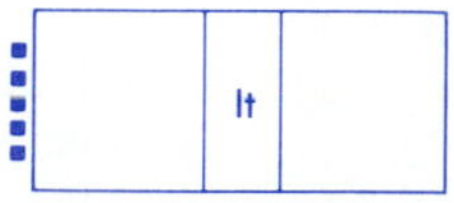 It	Starting Stopping Running Tagging Dodging

MODIFICATIONS	MOVEMENT CONCEPTS*	SOCIAL STRUCTURE	STRATEGY	LEVEL
Eliminate or reduce the numbers counted; have helpers or teacher's assistance in seeing who is moving	Skills: 9, 10, 11, 12 Game: 2	Parallel play II	Can you move when the leader is not watching?	I
Vary locomotor movements used	Skills: 8-10 Game: 1, 11, 12	Parallel play II	Wait until group gets very close before giving the signal	I
Use a variety of locomotor movements; change signal calling for colors they are wearing, birthday months, and so forth	Skills: 2, 9, 10 Game: 2, 3, 11, 12	Parallel play I		I
Vary locomotor movements used	Skills: 2, 3, 8-10 Game: 2, 3, 11, 12	Social interaction I	With helpers how can you cover the space to get more tagged? What must you do now to avoid the tag?	II
Vary locomotor movements used	Skills: 9-11 Game: 1, 4, 15	Parallel play II	Run as close to circle as you can	II
Vary locomotor movements, directions, or pathways used	Skills: 2, 3, 8, 10 Game: 3, 4, 10, 11, 12, 14	Parallel play II		II
Vary locomotor movements used	Skills: 2, 3, 8, 10 Game: 3, 4, 10-12, 14, 17	Parallel play II	Be ready to get into a tree if it gets close	II
Vary locomotor movements used	Skill: 10 Game: 3, 4, 10, 11, 12, 16, 17	Parallel play II	Move in a path difficult for the gardener to follow	II
Vary locomotor movements used	Skills: 1-4, 8, 10 Game: 3, 4, 10-12, 14, 16, 17	Social interaction I	With helpers how can you cover space to get more people tagged?	II

Continued.

TABLE 24-1 RUNNING AND TAG GAMES ANALYSIS—cont'd

NAME	GAME CLASSIFICATION	NO. OF PARTICIPANTS	EQUIPMENT	SPACE AND ORGANIZATIONAL PATTERN	MOTOR SKILLS
Midnight	Multicultural	Up to 25	None	 F	Running Tagging Dodging Stopping
Sharks and Minnows	Tag	Up to 25	None	 S	Running Tagging Dodging Stopping
Steal the Bacon	Multicultural	Six to eight per game	One duck pin/game	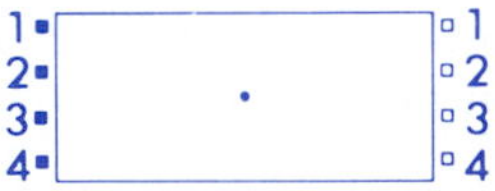 1 2 3 4 / 1 2 3 4	Starting Stopping Tagging Dodging
Stone, Paper, Scissors	Multicultural	Up to 25	None	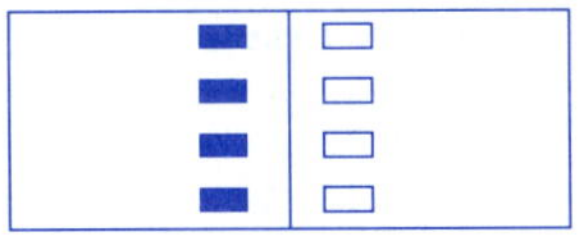	Running Stopping Starting Tagging Dodging
Two Deep	Tag	Six to eight per game	None	 It	Starting Stopping Running Tagging
Uncle Sam	Cooperative	Up to 25	None	 US	Starting Stopping Running Tagging Dodging
Aliens	Tag	Up to 25	None	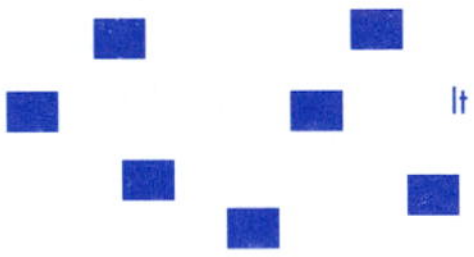 It	Running Starting Stopping Tagging Dodging
Crows and Cranes	Tag	Up to 25	None	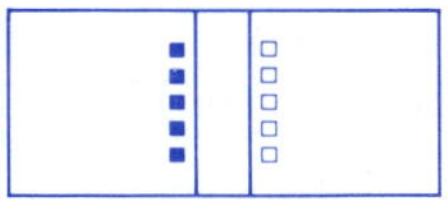	Starting Stopping Reversing pathways Tagging Dodging Running
Cut the Bean Curd	Multicultural	Five per game	None	 It	Locomotor

MODIFICATIONS	MOVEMENT CONCEPTS*	SOCIAL STRUCTURE	STRATEGY	LEVEL
Vary locomotor movements used	Skills: 1-3, 8, 10 Game: 3, 4, 10, 11, 12, 16, 17	Social interaction I	Wait until the group is close and far from end line before calling "Midnight"	II
Vary locomotor movements used	Skills: 2, 3, 8, 10 Game: 2-5, 8, 10-12, 13	Social interaction I	Look for the open spaces to avoid being tagged	II
Could be played on gym scooters; vary scoring: (1) a point for getting pin only or (2) a point for getting pin or tagging	Skills: 2, 3, 8, 10 Game: 4, 10, 11, 12, 16	Social interaction I; social interaction II if second scoring method used	Develop deceptive moves in getting the pin to avoid being tagged	II
	Skills: 2, 8-10 Game: 1, 3, 4, 10-12, 14	Social interaction I		II
Vary locomotor movements used	Skills: 8-11 Game: 1, 4, 15, 17	Parallel play II	Run close to circle	II
Vary locomotor movements used; change the signal to color of hair, birthday, and so forth	Skills: 1, 2, 3, 8-11 Game: 3-5, 8, 10-12, 16, 17	Social interaction I	When Uncle Sam has helpers, how can you cover the space to get more people tagged?	II
Change "it" often	Skills: 2, 8-11 Game: 1-4, 11, 12	Social interaction I		III
Vary locomotor movements used; use long/short vowel sounds as signal; use odd and even numbers or math problems as signals	Skills: 8-10 Game: 11, 12, 14, 16, 17	Parallel play II	Be ready to move in either direction	III
Encourage the children to come up with new commands	Skills: 9, 10 Game: 3, 4, 11, 12	Parallel play II		III

Continued.

TABLE 24-1 RUNNING AND TAG GAMES ANALYSIS—cont'd

NAME	GAME CLASSIFICATION	NO. OF PARTICIPANTS	EQUIPMENT	SPACE AND ORGANIZATIONAL PATTERN	MOTOR SKILLS
Four Door Wind Tag	Multicultural	9-13 for each game	None	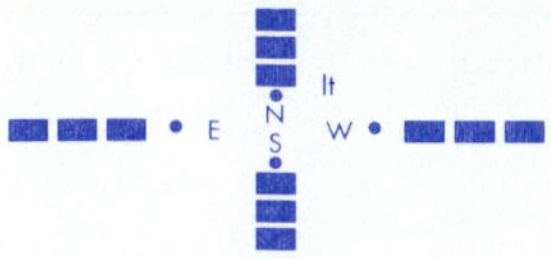	Locomotor Starting
Knock Em Down, Set Em Up	Manipulative	Up to 25	30 cones or bowling pins	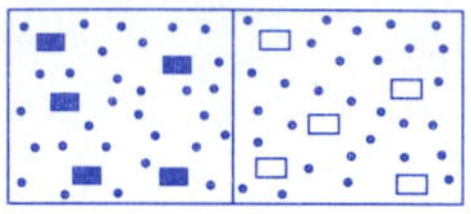	Locomotor
Line Tag	Multicultural	At least 4 in each group	None	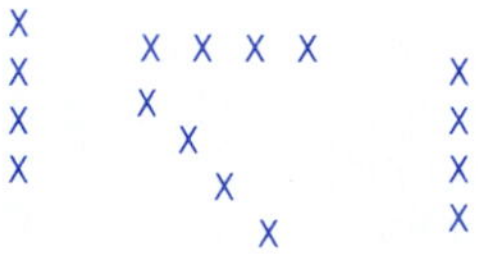	Locomotor Tagging
Monster Tag	Tag	In groups of four	None		Locomotor Tagging
Run for Your Life	Running	Up to 25	Five cones, four form a large square and one is in the middle	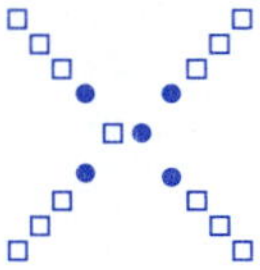	Running Starting Stopping
Steal the Clam	Multicultural	Eight per game	One bean bag per group	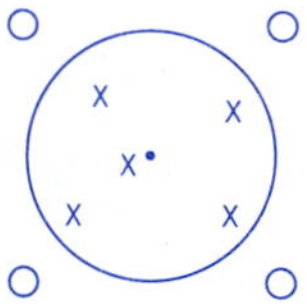	Locomotor skills Tagging Guarding
Touchdown	Tag	Up to 25	One small object that can be concealed in the hand	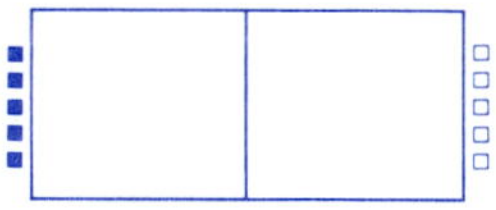	Running Stopping Tagging Dodging
Cross Tag	Cooperative	Up to 25	None		Running Tagging Dodging Stopping
Quattro Cantoni	Multicultural/ Cooperative	Five players per square	None	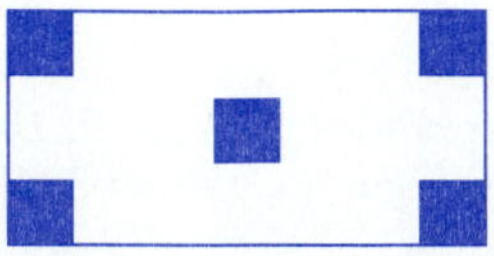	Locomotor

MODIFICATIONS	MOVEMENT CONCEPTS*	SOCIAL STRUCTURE	STRATEGY	LEVEL
	Skill: 9, 10 Game: 1, 4	Parallel play II		III
	Skill: 2, 8-10 Game: 4	Social interactions I and II	The children may plan some strategy for knocking down and setting up the pins	III
Change number of persons in each line	Skill: 2, 8 Game: 4, 10-12	Social interaction I		III
	Skills: 2, 8 Game: 4, 10-12	Social interaction I	Encourage the three children to work together to keep the monster away	III
Vary locomotor skills used	Skill: 9, 10 Game: 1, 3, 14	Parallel play II		III
	Skill: 1, 2, 8 Game: 1, 2, 4, 5, 11, 12	Social interaction I or II	Encourage children to plan strategies for getting the clam	III
Vary locomotor movements used	Skills: 1-4, 8, 10 Game: 2-5, 8-12, 13, 16	Social interaction II	What can you do to create space for ball carrier, close space on defense, or cover each opponent?	III
Vary locomotor movements used	Skill: 2, 8-11 Game: 1-4, 11, 12	Social interaction I	Children might work in partners against it	IV
	Skill: 2, 9, 10 Game: 1, 4	Social interaction II	Think of different ways to communicate to others	IV

Continued.

TABLE 24-1 RUNNING AND TAG GAMES ANALYSIS — cont'd

NAME	GAME CLASSIFICATION	NO. OF PARTICIPANTS	EQUIPMENT	SPACE AND ORGANIZATIONAL PATTERN	MOTOR SKILLS
Stealing Sticks	Tag	Up to 25	Six to eight sticks or duck pins		Running Tagging Dodging
Witches Pot	Tag	Up to 25	None		Running Tagging Dodging

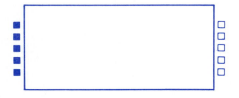

SHARKS AND BARRACUDAS

Level: I
Equipment: None
Participants: Up to 25
Skills: Stopping, starting, running, tagging, dodging
Description: The children are divided into two groups—the sharks and the barracudas. Each group has a leader, who remains facing the opponents. The sharks turn their backs to the barracudas, who sneak up close to the sharks. When the barracudas are close, the head shark gives the signal, "Here come the barracudas," and the sharks turn and chase the barracudas back to their line, trying to tag as many barracudas as possible. Those tagged become sharks. Repeat, reversing roles for sharks and barracudas. When the sharks are close, the head barracuda gives the signal, "Here come the sharks," and the barracudas give chase.
Teaching suggestions: Encourage children to assume a position in which they can reverse their pathway quickly to give chase or to avoid being tagged. Emphasize controlled stops and tagging. Help children to develop the strategy of waiting until opponents are close before giving the signal to run. Change head shark and barracuda after a couple of turns.

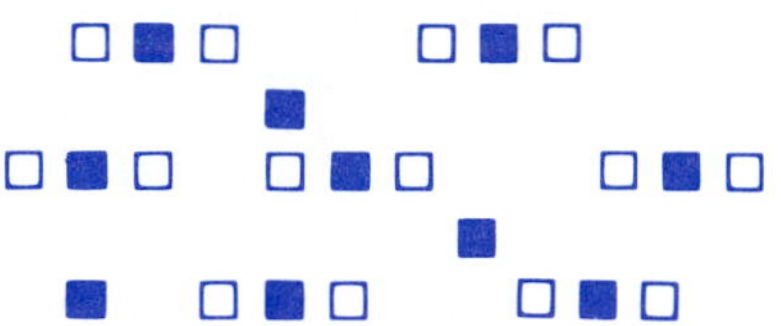

SQUIRRELS IN TREES

Level: I
Equipment: None
Participants: Up to 25, at least two or three squirrels without trees
Skills: Running, stopping, starting
Description: Children are scattered in the playing area in groups of three with one or two extra players. One person is designated as the squirrel in each group and stands between the other two. On the signal, "Change trees," the designated squirrels leave their trees and go to a new one, as do the one or two unassigned squirrels. The object of the game is to always have a tree. After repeating the procedure a few times, children change positions in the group and begin again. Change once more so that all have a chance to be squirrels. Variation: Gradually remove trees adding three more children to search for trees. Children now share trees with others. (How many children can share your tree?)
Teaching suggestions: Encourage good listening and controlled movements. Use other locomotor movements in addition to running. The signal could be changed to calling for squirrels by naming the colors the children are wearing, their birthdays, and so forth to encourage good listening.

MODIFICATIONS	MOVEMENT CONCEPTS*	SOCIAL STRUCTURE	STRATEGY	LEVEL
	Skills: 1-4, 8 Game: 2-5, 8-13	Social interaction II	Work together when planning offense; designate responsibilities for defense	IV
Vary locomotor skills used	Skill: 2, 8 Game: 1-4, 10-12	Parallel play II or Social interaction I	Encourage children to work together as witches and as those avoiding witches	IV

Continued.

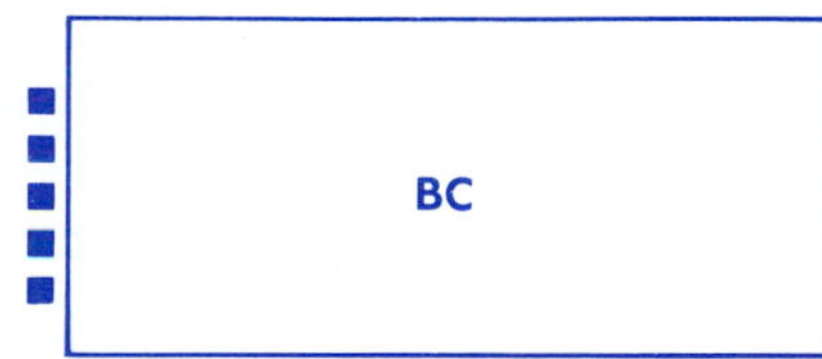

BIRD CATCHER

Level: II
Equipment: None
Participants: Up to 25
Skills: Running, stopping, starting, tagging, dodging
Description: The children are lined up behind one end line with the "bird catcher" out in front. Each child secretly selects a type of bird. The bird catcher calls out the names of birds (robin, sparrow, etc.), and those children who have selected that bird attempt to cross safely to the opposite line without being tagged. Those tagged help the bird catcher. After everyone has crossed to the opposite line, the game is repeated with a new bird catcher selected from those not tagged.
Teaching suggestions: Encourage controlled stops and tags. Raise questions to help children develop strategy to cover the space to tag as many as possible and to avoid being tagged.

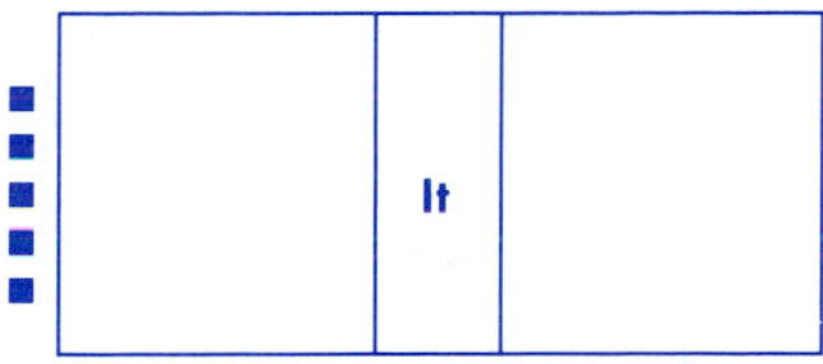

GREAT WALL OF CHINA

Level: II
Equipment: None
Participants: Up to 25, one "It" for every six children
Skills: Running, starting, stopping, dodging, tagging
Description: The children are lined up on the end line facing "It." On the signal, they attempt to cross the wall without being tagged. Those who are tagged then help "It." After four or five have been tagged, a new "It" is chosen to guard the wall from those not tagged.
Teaching suggestions: Emphasize controlled stops and tags. Encourage strategy for guarding the wall and avoiding being tagged.

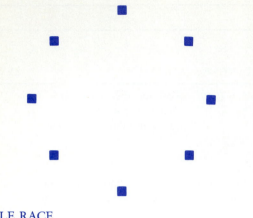

CIRCLE RACE

Level: II
Equipment: None
Participants: Up to 25
Skills: Running in a circle, starting, stopping, tagging
Description: Children are arranged in a circle and numbered off by threes. When the leader calls a number, the children with that number leave their places, run around the circle once and back to place, trying to tag as many children in front of them as possible.
Teaching suggestions: Encourage running as close to the circle as possible and having controlled tags and stops.

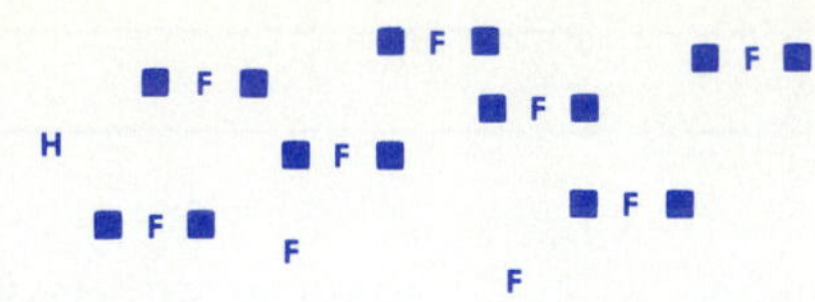

FOX AND HOUND

Level: II
Equipment: None
Participants: Up to 25
Skills: Running, starting, stopping, tagging, dodging
Description: The children are organized in groups of three, with one person designated the fox in each group and the other two the tree. In addition, one or two foxes without trees and an "It," the hound, are needed. The hound attempts to tag the free fox, who may go into a tree to escape. Only one fox may be in a tree at a time, so when the fleeing fox enters the tree, the fox already there must leave. If the hound tags the fox, the two exchange places, with the former fox becoming the hound. After a few tries, have the fox change places with one member of the tree, to ensure that each child has an opportunity to be a fox.
Teaching suggestions: Stress controlled stops and tags. Encourage the use of all space in avoiding the hound and changing direction and pathways. A variety of locomotor movements may be used. There should be several foxes and unassigned hounds to maximize the activity for a large group.

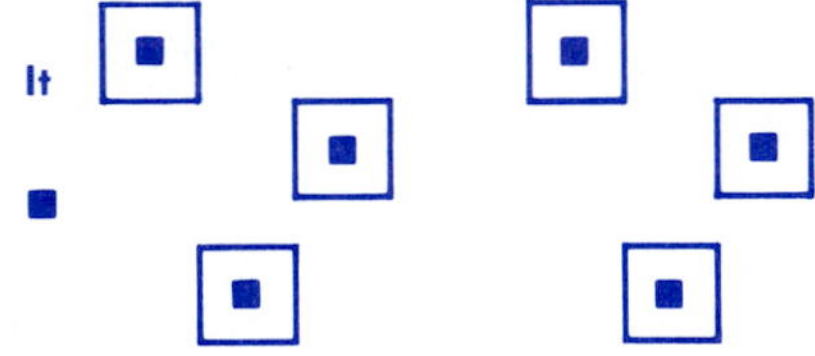

COLOR TAG

Level: II
Equipment: Colored squares or hoops in at least three or four colors
Participants: Up to 25
Skills: Stopping, starting, dodging, tagging, running
Description: The children are divided into color groups of equal size. Colored squares or hoops for each color group are scattered throughout the playing area, numbering one less than the number of children in each group. One person from each group is designated as "It." The children of each color group attempt to move from one square to another while "It" tries to tag them. The children are safe when they are touching the square or are in the hoop of their color only. "It" may tag only those in the same color group. After a few tries, a new "It" is selected for each group, or "It" changes positions with the child tagged.
Teaching suggestions: Emphasize looking out for others as they move throughout the playing area and tagging softly. Color groups may be grouped by ability to provide a challenge for everyone.

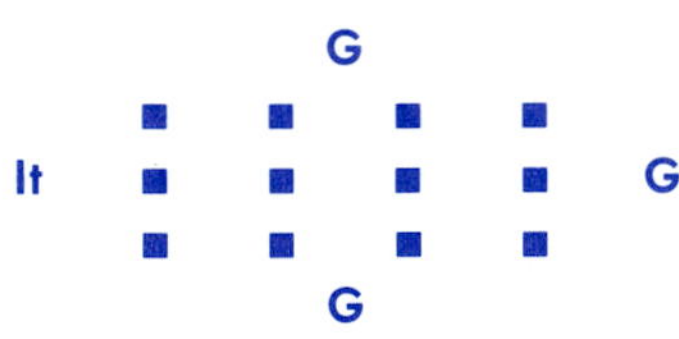

GOPHERS IN THE GARDEN

Level: II
Equipment: Bean bags, duck pins, or bowling pins to mark the garden rows
Participants: Up to six per game
Skills: Running, tagging, dodging
Description: The playing area is organized into gardens, with beanbags, duck pins, bowling pins, etc. marking the rows. Children in each group are scattered in their playing area. On the signal, the gardener ("It") attempts to tag the gophers who run through the garden by chasing the gophers in the same path they took. If the gopher is tagged, the two change places. After a few minutes, a new gardener is chosen.
Teaching suggestions: The leader may call for the gardener to switch places with the gopher that he/she is chasing without a tag being made, which requires listening and a quick response to the signal to change. The gardner will tire quickly, so frequent changes in the group are important. Emphasize making a path difficult to follow and for the gardener to watch the path carefully.

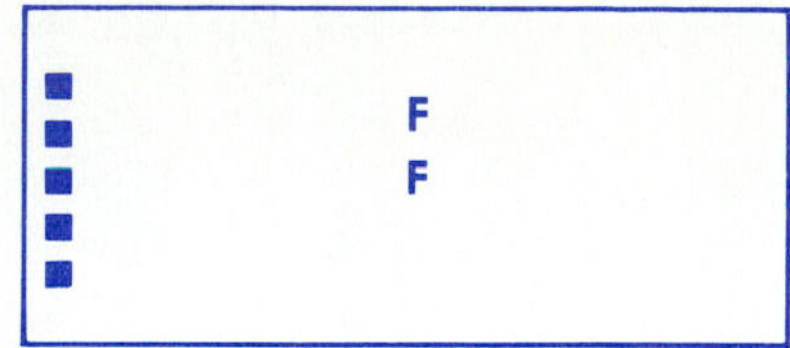

MIDNIGHT

(What is the time, Mr. Wolf? —South Africa)
Level: II
Equipment: None
Participants: Up to 25, with two foxes
Skills: Running, tagging, dodging, stopping, reversing pathways
Description: The children, the chickens, are lined up at one end of the playing area, with "It," the foxes out in front of the group facing away from them. The children move up behind the foxes as the foxes walk toward the opposite side of the playing area. The children ask, "What time is it, Mr. Fox?" to which one of the foxes replies, "2 o'clock," or some other time. The children continue walking and asking the time. When the designated fox replies, "Midnight," the foxes turn and chase the chickens back to the starting line. The game begins again with those tagged helping the fox. After six or so are tagged, a new Mr. Fox should be selected from those not tagged.
Teaching suggestions: Encourage controlled stops at the starting line and soft tags. If children appear to be wanting to be tagged, modify the game so that only those not tagged get to be fox and there are no helpers. Emphasize thinking about what they can do to avoid being tagged and looking for the open spaces (change path, directions, and so forth). "Its" should think about how they can work together to get more tagged. Change the lead fox often.

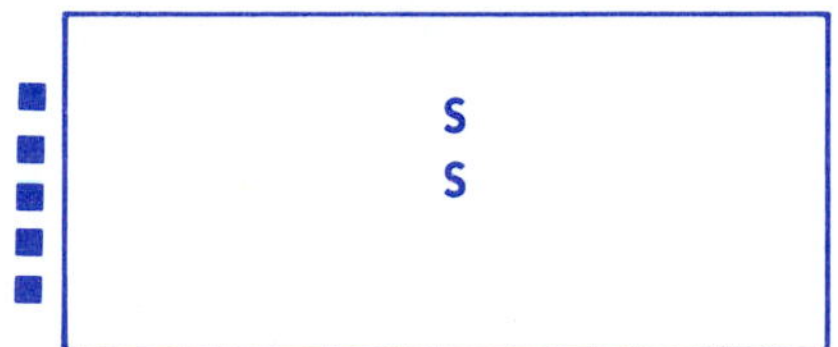

SHARKS AND MINNOWS

Level: II
Equipment: None
Participants: Up to 25, with two sharks
Skills: Running, dodging, tagging, stopping
Description: Children are lined up at one end of the playing area. "It," the shark, calls the minnows to "Cross my sea." Minnows attempt to cross without getting tagged. Those tagged are changed into "seaweed" and stand at the spot where they were tagged. They now help the shark, but must keep one foot stationary at all times. The game continues until all are tagged. The last one tagged is the new shark.
Teaching suggestions: Encourage controlled tags and stops. Emphasize looking for the open spaces and available pathways to avoid being tagged.

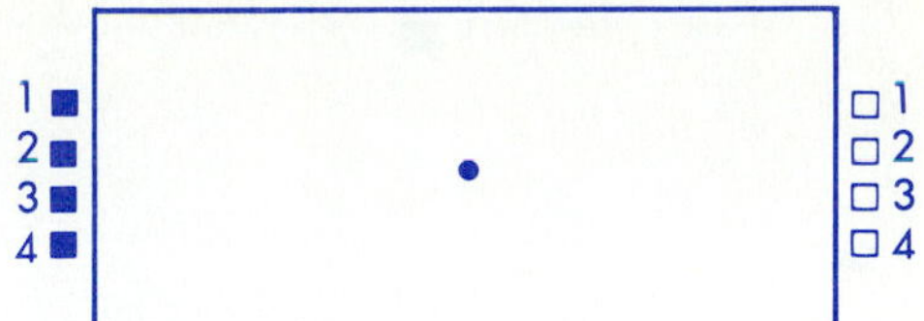

STEAL THE BACON

(The Handkerchief—Nigeria)
(Take Away the Flag—Vietnam)
(Rubabandiera—Italy)
Level: II
Equipment: One duck pin per game
Participants: Six to eight per game
Skills: Tagging, dodging, stopping, starting
Description: The children on each team are numbered consecutively beginning with one and are lined up behind their own boundary line. The leader calls a number, and the players from each team with that number come out and attempt to pick up the pin and bring it back across the line before the player not getting the pin can tag them. If the children desire it, the game may be scored by either (1) receiving a point only when the club is safely over the end line or (2) receiving a point by bringing the club safely over the end line or by tagging the person with the club.
Teaching suggestions: Emphasize controlled tags and stops. Have the children try different ways of getting the pin without getting tagged. What movements worked best? Opponents should be matched for ability to provide a challenge for all. Several small groups may play at the same time, with the leader calling the numbers. For example, all the twos would go after the pins for their games at the same time.

STONE, PAPER, SCISSORS

(Jankenpon—Japan)
Level: II
Equipment: None
Area: Large space with a center dividing line and boundary lines on each end
Participants: Up to 25
Skills: Locomotor movements, tagging, dodging
Description: The group is equally divided approximately three steps from and on either side of the center dividing line with their hands behind their backs. Each group decides on one symbol: stone (make a fist), paper (hold out a flat hand), or scissors (make a cutting motion with first two fingers). On the signal (in Japan it is Jan-ken-pon), each group displays its symbol. The stone beats the scissors (it would dull them), the paper beats the stone (it can wrap up the stone), and the scissors beats the paper (it can cut it). The group with the symbol that wins chases the other group back to its boundary line, tagging as many as possible. Those tagged join the other group.
Teaching suggestions: This is a game for simple, shared decision making. Encourage each group to allow a different person to choose the symbol each time. Encourage gentle tags.

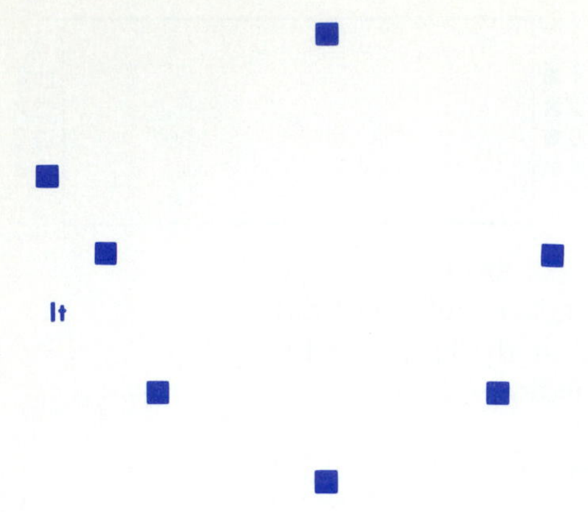

TWO DEEP

Level: II
Equipment: None
Participants: Six to eight per game
Skills: Starting, stopping, running, tagging
Description: The children are organized in a circle, with one player designated as "It" and one other who is being chased. "It" begins the chase. The player being chased may step in front of any player in the circle (two deep) to avoid being tagged. The circle player whose place is taken must then run to avoid being tagged. When the leader calls, "Change," "It" becomes the one being chased and the one formerly chased is now "It."
Teaching suggestions: Encourage running close to the circle and controlling the tag. This is a good transition game following vigorous activity because all are not active at one time.

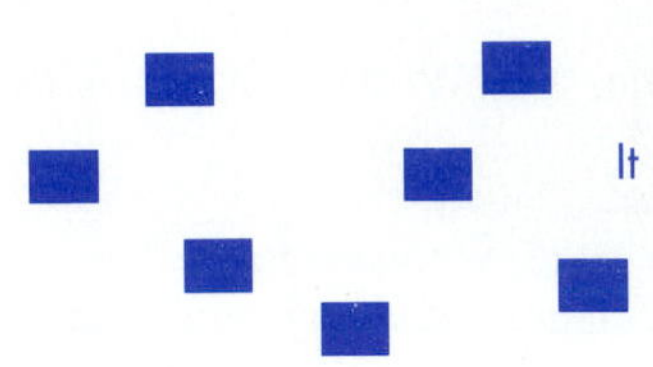

ALIENS

Level: III
Equipment: None
Participants: Up to 25
Skills: Locomotor movements, dodging, tagging
Description: The children are scattered in the playing area. One or two children are "It" and try to tag the other children. The children being chased help each other by crossing the path between "It" and the person being chased. If they cross successfully, "It" must now chase them. If tagged, the children change roles.
Teaching suggestions: This can be a vigorous game for "It," so change roles frequently by calling "Change" at which time the "It" becomes the person being chased.

UNCLE SAM

Level: II
Equipment: None
Participants: Up to 25, one Uncle Sam for every eight children
Skills: Running, starting, stopping, tagging, dodging
Description: The children begin lined up behind the line, with one person designated as "Uncle Sam" facing them. The children call to Uncle Sam, "Uncle Sam, may we cross your river?" to which he replies, "Yes, if you have (color) on." The children wearing the color called attempt to run to the opposite line without being tagged. Those tagged help Uncle Sam as the game progresses. A new Uncle Sam, chosen from those not tagged, should be selected after five to eight people have been tagged.
Teaching suggestions: Encourage controlled stops and tags and avoiding being tagged. Raise questions to help children cover the area on defense so that as many as possible get tagged and also to avoid being tagged.

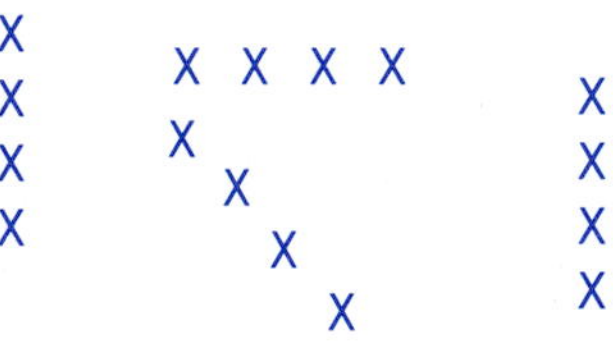

LINE TAG

(Native American)
Level: III
Equipment: None
Partícpants: At least four in each group
Skills: Locomotor skills, tagging
Description: The children form a line holding hands. On a signal from the second person in line, the person at the front of the line attempts to tag the person at the end of the line. The children in the middle twist and turn to keep the head from tagging the tail. If tagged, the tail joins the front of the line as the new head.
Teaching suggestions: Once the children are playing successfully, experiment with different numbers in the lines, thinking about how they communicate as they work together to keep the head from tagging the tail. Another version of this game, Catching the Dragon's Tail, is played in Taiwan, but the children join by having their hands on the shoulders of the person in front of them.

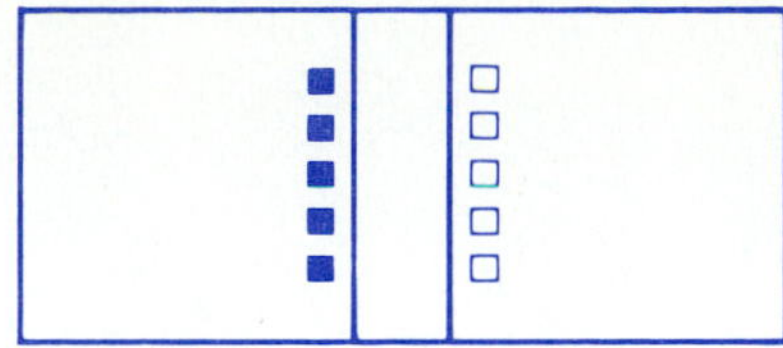

CROWS AND CRANES

Level: III
Equipment: None
Participants: Up to 25
Skills: Stopping, starting, tagging, dodging, running
Description: The group is divided in half, with one group being the crows and the other the cranes. Both teams line up facing each other at the center of the playing area. The leader calls, "Crows," and the crows chase the cranes to their end line, trying to tag as many as possible. If the leader calls, "Cranes," the cranes chase the crows to their end line. Those tagged join the team that tagged them.
Teaching suggestions:

1. At first it may be difficult for the children to keep track of which team they are on and which way to run on the signal. If the leader points in the correct direction, it may be helpful.
2. This game may be modified to work on language arts or math concepts by (1) having one group be long vowel and the other short vowel sounds, with the leader calling words with either sound; (2) having one team be odd numbers and the other even; or (3) with odd and even numbers, having the teacher give math problems (add, subtract, multiply, or divide numbers), the answer determining which group runs and which group chases.
3. Encourage a ready position, which enables the children to quickly move in either pathway. Emphasize controlled tags and stops.

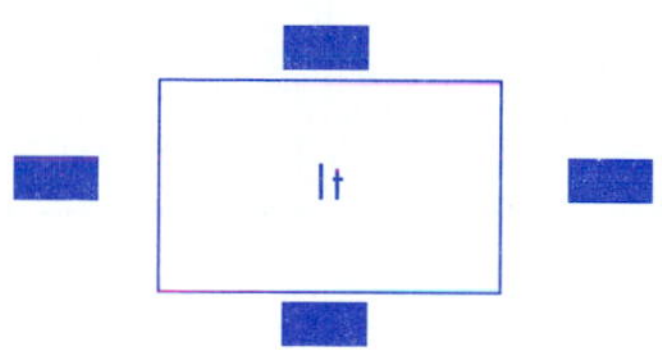

CUT THE BEAN CURD

(China)
Level: III
Equipment: None
Area: An 8-foot square for each game
Participants: Five per game
Skills: Locomotor skills
Description: Four players stand on each of the sides of the square with the fifth player, "It", in the center. "It" calls out commands and players change places with the opposite player: "Cut the curd crosswise" (opposite players change places by moving diagonally across the square); "Cut the curd straight" (opposite players exchange places by moving along the edges of the square); "Carry the water across the river" (opposite players hop on the right foot, pretending to carry a pail); and "Carry the shoe to the shoemaker" on the left foot, pretending to carry a shoe in the right hand). After the command is given, "It" tries to get to one of the sides before the crossing player.

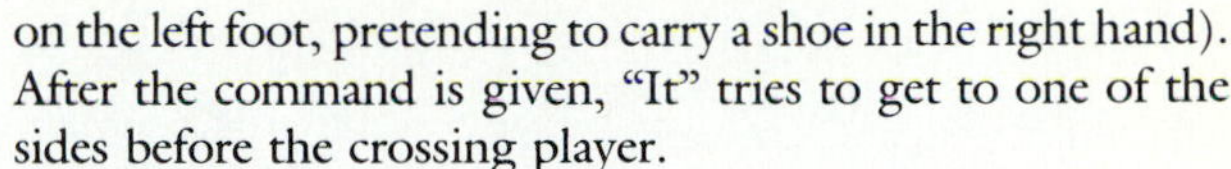

Teaching suggestions: Encourage each group to come up with new commands and new movements.

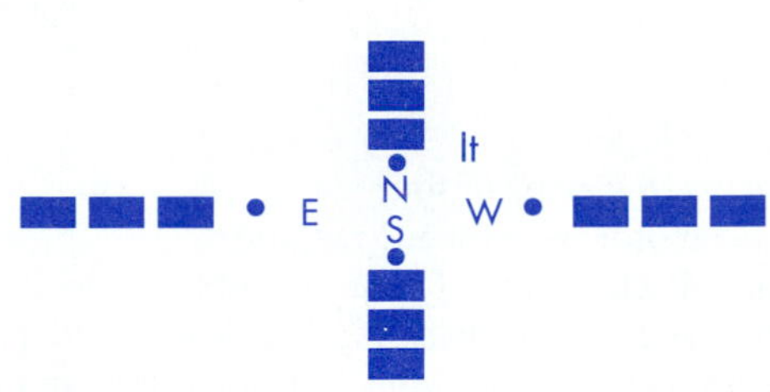

FOUR DOOR WIND TAG

(Islands of the Baltic Sea)
Level: III
Equipment: Four cones to mark positions of teams in the circle
Area: A circle with the four directions (north, south, east, west) marked with cones
Participants: Nine to thirteen for each game
Skills: Locomotor skills, stopping
Description: The group is evenly distributed and in a line behind each of the four cones. One player, the "wind," runs around the outside of the circle, and calls one of the teams. For instance while passing the west, the "wind" calls "East." East and west players attempt to change places, running in the same path as the wind. The wind attempts to get to the east position before the west players, taking one of the positions behind the cone.
Teaching suggestions: Encourage the children to watch for others and move close to the circle.

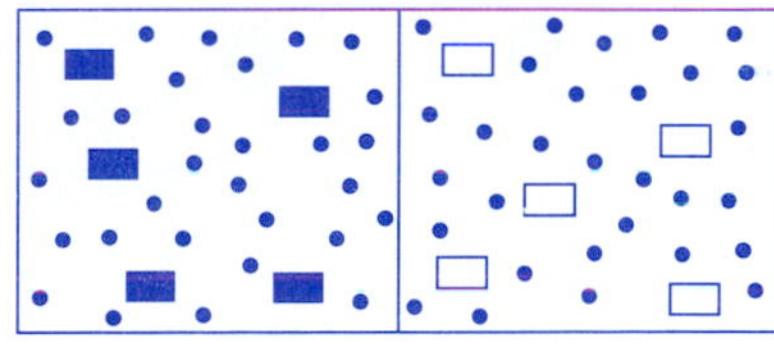

KNOCK EM DOWN, SET EM UP

Level: III
Equipment: 30 cones or bowling pins
Participants: Up to 25
Skills: Locomotor skills
Description: The cones are scattered in the playing area and the children are divided into two teams that occupy opposite sides of the space. On the signal, the children attempt to knock down the other team's cones with their hands while their opponents set them back up. The children are not allowed to guard the cones or to follow the opposite team's players. After a period of time, stop play and see which team has the most pins standing. Variation: This might become a cooperative game, with each team setting targets for the number of pins they wish to knock down and to keep up.
Teaching suggestions: Encourage the groups to work together in designating who will assume the responsibility for knocking down and setting up the cones.

MONSTER TAG

Level: III
Equipment: None
Participants: In groups of four
Skills: Locomotor movements, tagging
Description: Each group of four consists of one leader, one monster, and two protectors. The leader and protectors move together, holding hands to form a circle and trying to keep the monster from tagging the leader from outside the circle. The monster may not reach across the circle of three. The protectors try to keep themselves between the monster and the leader. The players change roles if the hands break or the monster tags the leader.
Teaching suggestions: Encourage the three children to work together to keep the monster away.

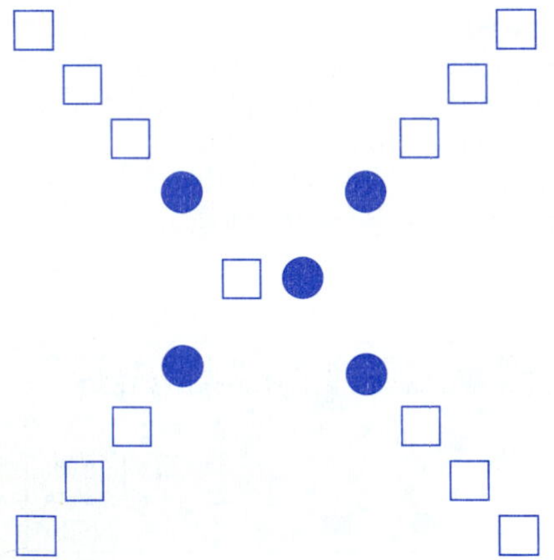

RUN FOR YOUR LIFE

Level: III
Equipment: None
Area: Four cones set up in a square with one cone in the center
Participants: Up to 25
Skills: Locomotor skills, tagging, dodging
Description: One child is "It" and begins at the cone in the center. The others are distributed at the four cones in the square. On the signal "Go" the children at the bases proceed to the next base moving clockwise around the bases. "It" races to one of the cones, trying to beat the other runners to the base. Those who get to the base before "It" are safe; those who do not go to the center cone. On the next signal the game begins again with the new "Its" moving to any of the bases of their choice.
Teaching suggestions: Additional bases may be added if necessary to limit the number at any one base.

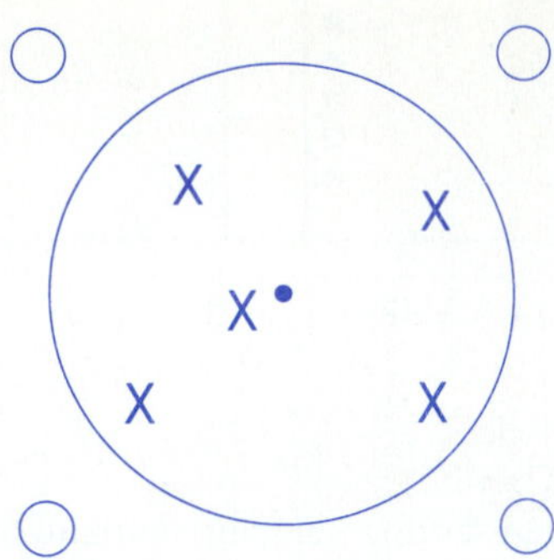

STEAL THE CLAM

(This is a modification of a Native American game in which an individual sat on a clam buried in the sand and others attempted to get it.)

Level: III
Equipment: One beanbag per group
Area: A circle for each group
Participants: Eight per game
Skills: Locomotor skills, tagging, guarding
Description: One person is in the center sitting with a bean bag behind them. Three or four others stand just inside the circle, trying to keep the other three or four from penetrating the circle to get the beanbag. If tagged, the child must try again at another spot on the circle.
Teaching suggestions: Encourage those on the outside of the circle to plan strategies together to get someone inside the circle. Those on the inside must also work together to cover the space.

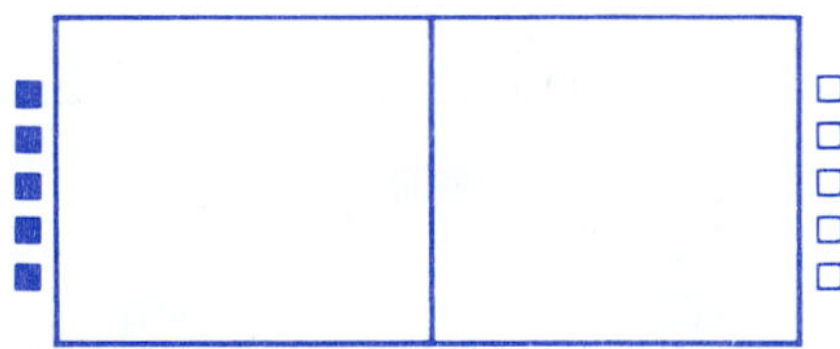

TOUCHDOWN

Level: III
Equipment: A small object that can be concealed in the hand
Participants: Up to 25
Skills: Running, tagging, dodging, stopping
Description: Two teams are gathered on each side of the playing area. One team is given the "football." They huddle and determine the strategy they will use to get the football over the opponents' goal line. The other team plays defense. If the player who has the football is able to get it across the opponents' goal line without being tagged, the team scores 6 points. The football may be concealed from the other team, and tagged players do not have to admit having or not having the football until all are tagged or the football is safely past the line.
Teaching suggestions: In the beginning the children may be more concerned about who will carry the football than with

the group effort to get it safely across the goal line. It may be helpful to have the names of the group on pieces of paper from which they can draw the ball carrier. After one or two times they should begin to see how important it is to work together. On defense it may also take a few times before they will plan strategy. Creating spaces and closing spaces are important aspects of offensive and defensive strategy. This game may be played in smaller groups of six per team. Encourage controlled stops and tags and watching out for others during play. You may wish to begin with a fairly large area and gradually reduce the size of space as children learn to use the space more effectively.

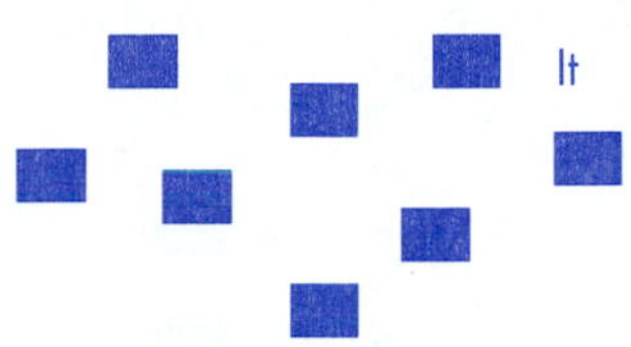

CROSS TAG

Level: IV
Equipment: None
Participants: Up to 25
Skills: Running, tagging, dodging
Description: This game is similar to Aliens with the following exception: all children work together against the children who are "It." Tagged players assist those not being tagged by crossing the path between them and the children being chased providing time for the children being chased to get away. If the path is crossed, "It" must look for another person to chase.
Teaching suggestions: Children need to be in control at all times and to be ready to change pathways as necessary.

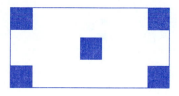

QUATTRO CANTONI

(Means 4 corners and is played in many countries)

Level: IV
Equipment: None
Area: A square space for each group
Participants: 5 children per square
Skills: Locomotor movements
Description: Each child stands in one of the corners of the square with the fifth child in the center. The players in the corners attempt to exchange places with each other using some means of signaling to each other. The center player attempts to get to one of the corners on the exchange.
Teaching suggestions: Encourage the children to think of different ways of communicating to each other.

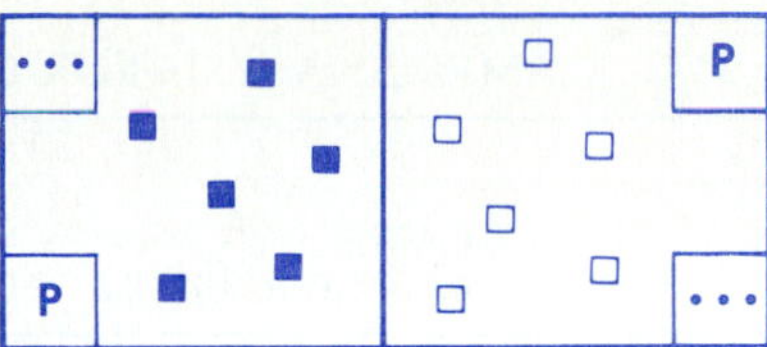

STEALING STICKS

Level: IV
Equipment: Six to eight sticks approximately 12 inches long, bean bags, or duck pins
Participants: Up to 25
Skills: Running, tagging, and dodging
Description: The group is divided into two equal teams, each team scattered in its half of the playing area. Each team attempts to get to its opponents' sticks without being tagged. If a player touches an opponent's stick without being tagged, the stick may be brought back safely to the player's own half of the playing area. Only one stick may be taken at a time. If tagged, players go to their opponents' prison. Prisoners may be rescued by teammates getting to the prison area without being tagged. The first prisoner caught is the first released. Only one prisoner may be released at a time. Once a player has gotten safely to the prison area, both have safe passage back to their half of the playing area. The first team getting all their opponents' sticks wins.
Teaching suggestions: This game may be slow getting started at times because children may hesitate in crossing over into their opponents' territory. Children should be encouraged to work together in trying various offensive and defensive strategies.

WITCHES POT

Level: IV
Equipment: None
Area: A large space with a square marked as the witches spot centered and toward one end and a safety line across the other.
Participants: Up to 25
Skills: Locomotor skills, dodging, tagging
Description: Two or three children are designated as the witches, and they are positioned in the center of the space. On the signal "Tease the witches" the children move out from behind their safety line into the space. The witches try to tag them. If successful the tagged players move to the witches pot. Children now have the option of teasing the witches or rescuing those who are in the witches pot. To do so they must get to the pot and then return to the safety line holding hands and avoiding being tagged as they move to and from the pot. Only one person may be rescued at a time.
Teaching suggestions: Encourage the children to work together either as witches or as those avoiding the witches. Change witches often. Tagging gently is a must.

Text continued on p. 490.

TABLE 24-2 GAMES ANALYSIS FOR GAMES USING BALLS AND OTHER OBJECTS

NAME	GAME CLASSIFICATION	NO. OF PARTICIPANTS	EQUIPMENT	SPACE AND ORGANIZATIONAL PATTERN	MOTOR SKILLS
Falling Stars	Cooperative	Groups of three	Balls varying in size and weight		Throwing Catching
Keep It In, Keep It Out	Beanbag	Four to five per game	Ten to twelve beanbags	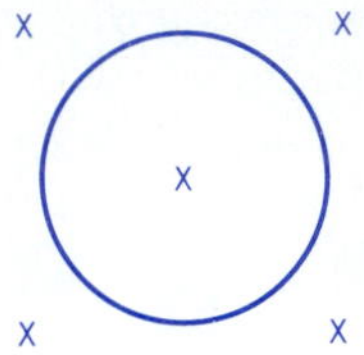	Underhand throw
Nsikwi	Multicultural	Up to 24	A medium size playground or foam ball and a small cone or pin for each child	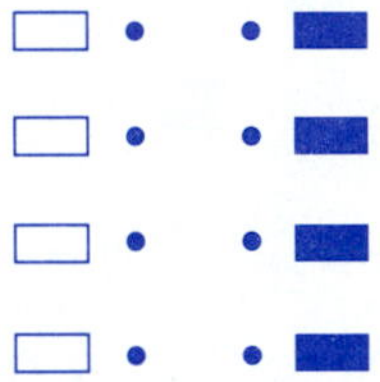	Rolling Catching
Snowball	Ball	Up to 25	A large number of softball-sized fleece or foam balls	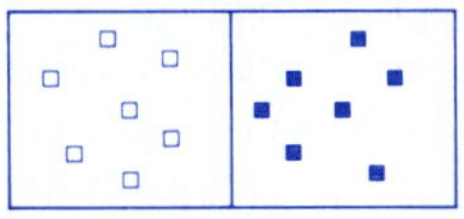	Overhand throw
Stride Ball	Ball	Six to eight per game	One 8-inch ball per group	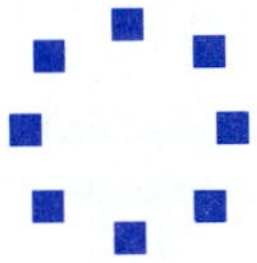	Underhand throw Catching
Volcano	Ball	Eight to ten for each game	12-15 foam or fleece balls of different sizes; large folding mats	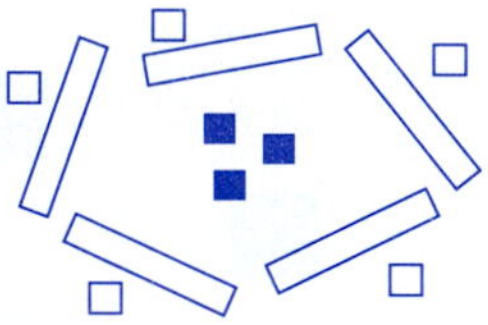	Overhand throw Catching
Boundary Ball	Ball	Up to 25	Six to eight 8-inch balls, preferably foam	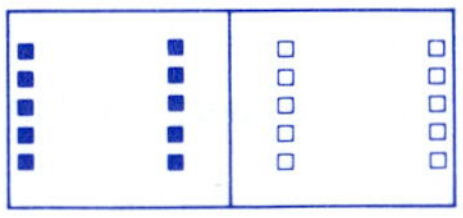	Shoulder or underhand throws Catching
Cleaning House	Net game	Six to eight per team	Six to eight foam balls; one net 6 feet high; standards	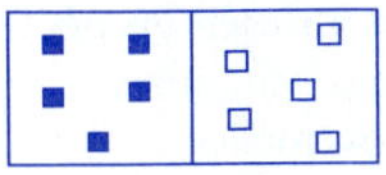	Throwing Catching

*Numbers refer to the movement concepts listed in Figure 24-1 on p. 462.

MODIFICATIONS	MOVEMENT CONCEPTS*	SOCIAL STRUCTURE	STRATEGY	LEVEL
Vary size and weight of balls used; vary throwing skills used	Skills: 6, 9, 10 Game: 17	Social interaction I	Control force of throws so they can be easily received	I
More than one person in the circle	Skill: 9 Game: 7, 13	Parallel play II	Look for the empty spaces to put beanbag	I
Have children stand for a more mature rolling pattern	Skill: 9 Game: 13	Parallel play I	Encourage children to roll the ball carefully	I
	Skills: 1, 3-5, 9 Game: 2, 5, 7, 8, 12, 13	Parallel play I	Look for the empty space in which to put the ball; How can you best cover all space on your side of the playing area?	I
Add another ball to each game	Skills: 7, 9 Game: 7, 8, 12, 13	Parallel play II	Look for unguarded space; look one way and pass another	I
	Skills: 4, 5, 9, 10 Game: 5, 7, 8, 13, 16	Parallel play II	Children in the volcano and out can work together to keep balls out and to get them in	I
	Skills: 1, 3, 4, 5, 7, 9, 10 Game: 5-8, 12, 13	Social interaction I	Designate responsibility for some to guard the line, others to be throwers; How can you best cover the space? Get the ball?	II
1. Use overhead throw for high balls, an underhand throw for low balls	Skills: 3-5, 9, 10 Game: 2, 5, 7, 8, 12, 13	Social interaction I	1. Get rid of ball quickly 2. Look for empty spaces 3. Cover all areas of the court	II

Continued.

TABLE 24-2 GAMES ANALYSIS FOR GAMES USING BALLS AND OTHER OBJECTS — cont'd

NAME	GAME CLASSIFICATION	NO. OF PARTICIPANTS	EQUIPMENT	SPACE AND ORGANIZATIONAL PATTERN	MOTOR SKILLS
Moonball	Cooperative	10 to 15 per game	One cage ball; and at least one ball varying in size for each child	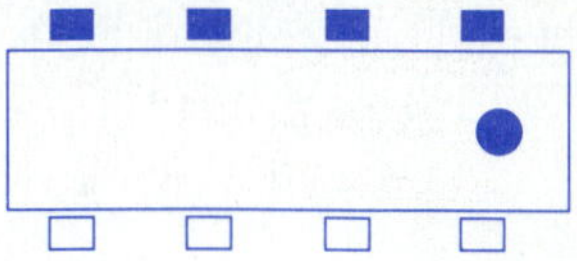	Throwing
Mulambilwa	Multicultural	Eight to ten for each game	One soft or foam ball and a pin for each child	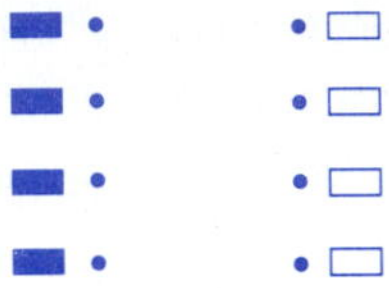	Rolling or throwing Running Tagging Dodging
Newcomb	Net game	Four to six per team	One volleyball or playground ball; net at fingertip height; badminton sized court	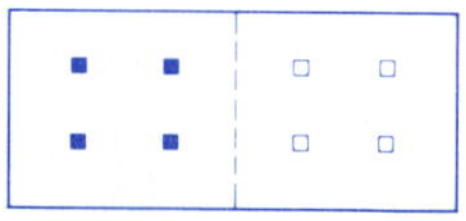	Throwing Catching Passing
Pima-Moving Target	Multicultural	Six to seven per game	A foam ball or other object tied to a rope	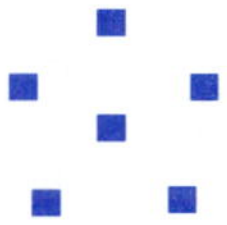	Throwing
Bull in a Ring	Ball	Eight to nine players	One or two foam balls per game	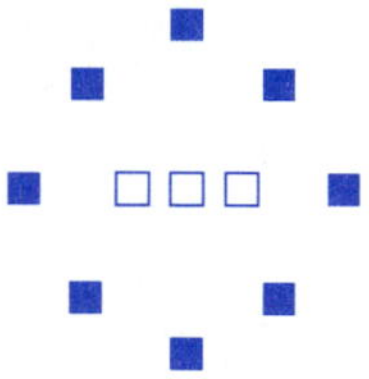	Throwing at a moving target Dodging
Club Guard	Cooperative	Four to six per game	One 8-inch ball and one duck pin per game		Chest pass Underhand throw Catching Guarding a pin
Craters	Ball	Six to eight per game	Balls varying is size, milk crates, boxes, hoops, etc.	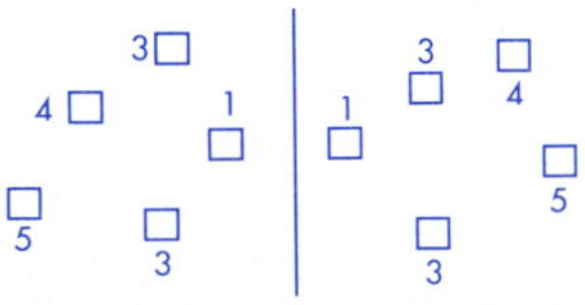 3 4 1 5 3 / 1 3 4 5 3	Throwing
Deck Tennis	Net game	Two to six per team	One deck tennis ring; 4-foot 8-inch net; deck tennis or badminton sized court	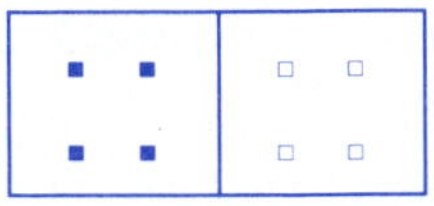	Throwing and catching the deck tennis ring

MODIFICATIONS	MOVEMENT CONCEPTS*	SOCIAL STRUCTURE	STRATEGY	LEVEL
Use other balls as targets rather than a cage ball	Skill: 9 Game: 13, 17	Social interaction II	Explore what happens to the ball when it is hit in different places	II
Children stand in games where there is throwing	Skills: 4, 7, 9 Game: 13	Parallel play II		II
1. Players in back row may not throw ball over the net, but must pass to net players 2. Require two passes per side	Skills: 1-3, 5, 9, 10 Game: 2, 5, 7, 12, 13	Social interaction II	1. Pass to teammates 2. Look for empty spaces 3. Change expected path of ball 4. Vary force in returning ball over the net	II
	Skills: 4, 7, 9	Parallel play II or social interaction I	Work together to hit the ball Throw quickly to a space ahead of the target	II
	Skills: 1, 2, 7, 9 Game: 3, 4, 6, 10, 11, 12, 17	Social interaction II	Leader must move to keep self between balls and tail; pass ball around to keep bull moving	III
	Skills: 1, 4, 7, 9, 10 Game: 4, 6, 7, 12, 13, 16	Social interaction II	Team work is necessary to get to the pin and pass the ball quickly; try to get it behind guard	III
	Skill: 9 Game: 7, 13, 16	Parallel play II or Social interaction I	Have the children determine the values for the targets for each game; have them develop a strategy to beat their own record	III
	Skills: 3-5, 9, 10 Game: 2, 5, 7, 8, 12, 13	Social interaction II	1. In team deck tennis use passing to get the ring into a better position 2. Vary types of throws used 3. Look for empty spaces and change expected ring path	III

Continued.

TABLE 24-2 GAMES ANALYSIS FOR GAMES USING BALLS AND OTHER OBJECTS—cont'd					
NAME	GAME CLASSIFICATION	NO. OF PARTICIPANTS	EQUIPMENT	SPACE AND ORGANIZATIONAL PATTERN	MOTOR SKILLS
Guard the King	Ball	Seven to eight per game	One 8-inch ball per game	 G K	Throwing at a moving target Catching Guarding a moving target Dodging
Kickball	Ball	Two teams of six players	Four bases, one 8-inch playground or soccer ball	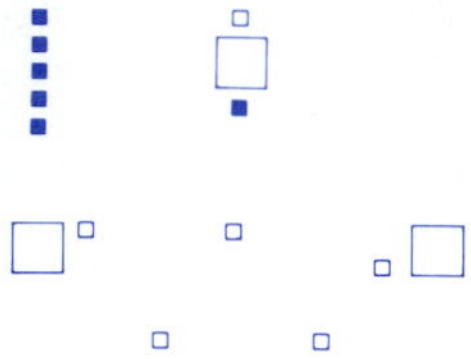	Kicking Catching Throwing Base running
Pin Ball	Ball	Up to 25	One 8-inch ball for each player, four players, up to 12 duck pins	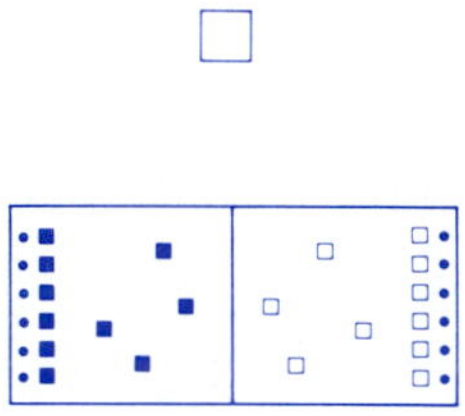	Underhand throw Catching Guarding a pin
Poison Ball	Ball	Two teams of five to six players	Four to six 8-inch playground balls, two different color balls	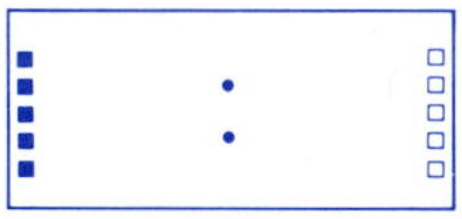	Throwing at a moving target Passing Catching
Keep Away	Multicultural	Three to five per team	One ball per game	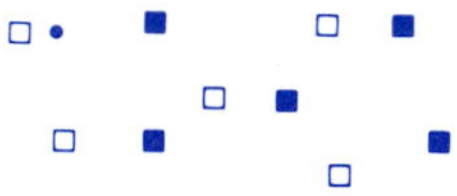	Passing Catching
Muddle	Ball	12 to 24	One medium size playground ball for every two children	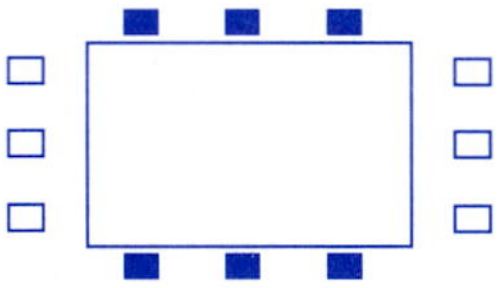	Rolling Catching
Rescue	Ball	Two teams of 10 to 12 players	Six to eight foam balls	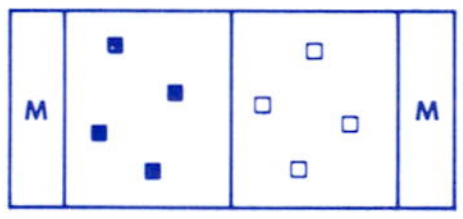 M M	Throwing at a moving target Dodging Catching
Teamball	Ball	Up to six players per team	Volleyball size ball	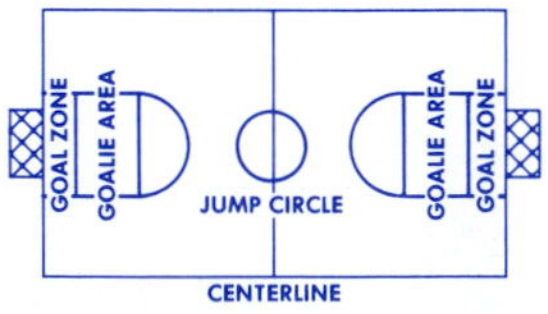 GOAL ZONE, GOALIE AREA, JUMP CIRCLE, GOALIE AREA, GOAL ZONE, CENTERLINE	Chest, bounce and shoulder passing Catching
Team Juggle	Cooperative	Four per group	Four to six small balls per group		Throwing Catching
Modified Ultimate Frisbee	Disc	Three to four players per team	One frisbee or disc		Sidearm and backhand passes

MODIFICATIONS	MOVEMENT CONCEPTS*	SOCIAL STRUCTURE	STRATEGY	LEVEL
Increase number of balls	Skills: 1, 4, 7, 9, 10 Game: 4, 6, 7, 12, 13, 16	Social interaction II	Work together to get king by passing to those in a better position	III
	Skills: 4, 5, 9, 10 Game: 1, 2, 5, 7, 8, 13	Social interaction I	Look for empty spaces in which to place the ball; infielders position yourselves to cover the infield area	III
Could allow rebounds from walls	Skills: 1, 3, 5, 7-9, 10 Game: 5-8, 12, 13	Social interaction I	Designate responsibility for some to guard the pins, others to throw	III
Increase number of poison balls	Skills: 7, 9 Game: 12, 13, 17	Social interaction II	Pass the ball to teammates in a better position to hit the poison ball	III
Dribbling may be allowed	Skills: 3, 4, 6, 9, 10 Game: 2-4, 8-13, 16	Social interaction III	Pass quickly and move to an open space; close spaces on defense	IV
	Skills: 5, 9, 10 Game: 13, 16, 17	Social interaction I	Each team must work together to achieve game goals, timing throws for the most success	IV
If the ball is caught on the fly, the thrower is considered hit	Skills: 2, 7 Game: 4, 10-13, 16, 17	Social interaction III	Protect medic; develop group strategy for getting the medic	IV
	Skills: 1, 3, 4, 9, 10 Game: 1, 2, 3, 4, 6, 7, 8, 9, 11, 12, 13, 16	Social interaction IV	Move to an open space to receive pass; on defense, stay behind opponent's goal	IV
	Skill: 9, 10 Game: 13, 17	Social interaction II	Try to establish a rhythm and speed for throwing	IV
	Skills: 1, 3, 6, 9, 10 Game: 2, 3, 4, 8, 9, 10, 11, 12, 13, 16, 17	Social interaction III	Use all space and move to an open space to receive Frisbee	IV

GAMES USING BALLS AND OTHER OBJECTS

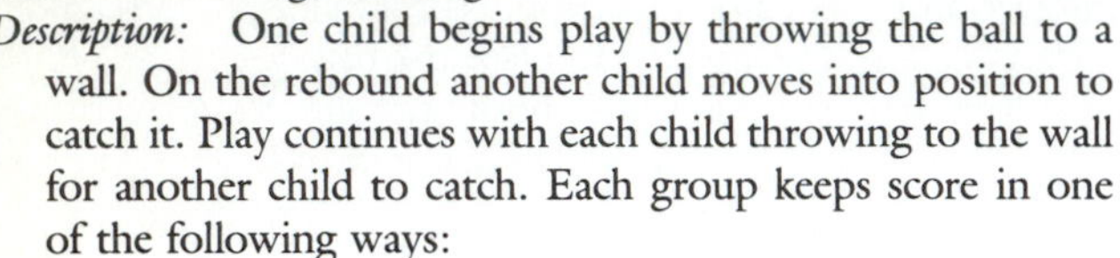

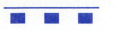

FALLING STARS

Level: I
Equipment: Balls varying in size, weight
Participants: Groups of three
Skills: Throwing, catching
Description: One child begins play by throwing the ball to a wall. On the rebound another child moves into position to catch it. Play continues with each child throwing to the wall for another child to catch. Each group keeps score in one of the following ways:

1. The number of catches made during the game
2. The number of consecutive catches before a miss
3. Achieving a set number of catches decided by the group

The game is repeated with each group attempting to better their score.
Teaching suggestions: This game offers the children an opportunity to play the game based on the needs of the group. Each should be encouraged to make decisions based on the success of each child in the group. Each group of children can be given several choices in meeting the needs of the individual children in the group.

1. What type of throw to use
2. What type of ball to use
3. How high on the wall to throw the ball

Each group will have to compromise so that all can be successful with the one choice made in each category. Additional adjustments that may need to be made include the amount of force used in throwing, which results in balls coming off the wall that are catchable.

Foam balls permit safe play for children with varying abilities.

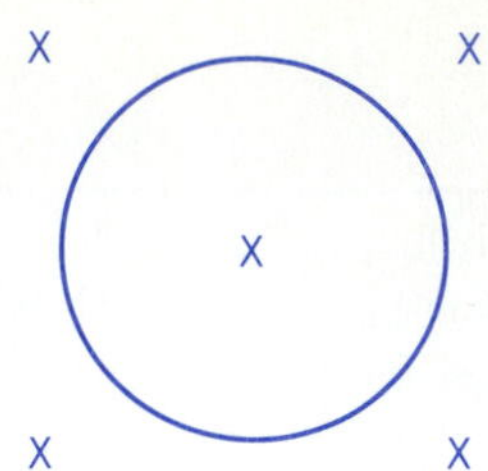

KEEP IT IN, KEEP IT OUT

Level: I
Equipment: 10 to 12 beanbags per game
Participants: Four to five per game
Skills: Underhand throw
Description: The children are arranged outside a circle with one person in the circle. The beanbags are placed in the circle. The circle player attempts to keep the beanbags out of the circle, while the remaining players attempt to keep them in.
Teaching suggestions: The game may be modified to have more than one person in the circle if needed. Encourage the children to look for the empty space to put the beanbags to make it more difficult for the players to keep the beanbags out of their area.

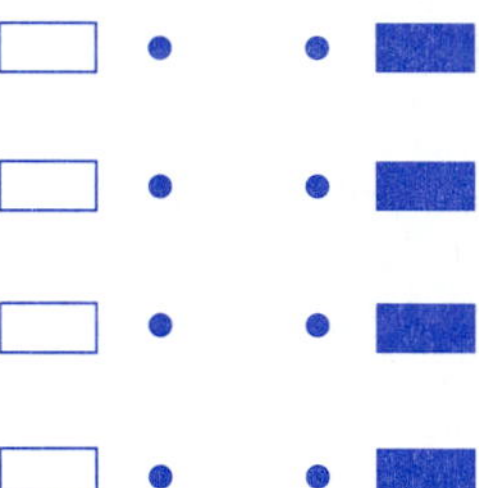

NSIKWI
(Africa)

Level: I
Equipment: A medium size playground or foam ball and a small cone or pin for each child
Participants: Up to 24
Skills: Rolling and catching
Description: The children are divided into two groups and are sitting across from each other about 10 feet apart. Each child has a cone or pin placed in front of them. The children roll the balls across the area trying to knock down one of the pins on the other side. Each cone knocked down scores one point.
Teaching suggestions: Encourage the children to roll the ball carefully to the other side, pointing their fingers where they want the ball to go on the follow-through. The children might try this standing as well, which encourages more mature underhand rolling patterns.

In the African version of this game the children aimed at small pieces of corncob 2 or 3 inches high.

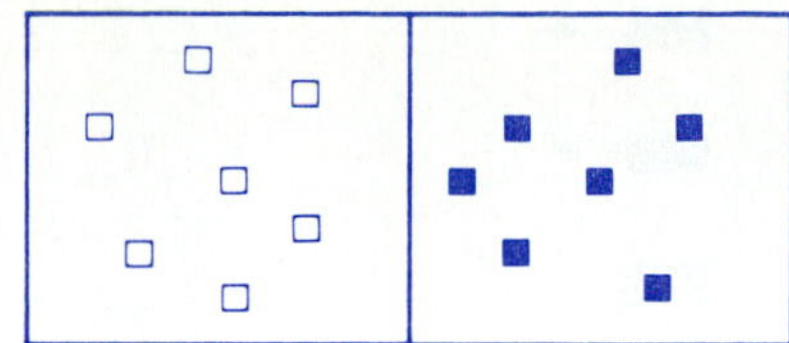

SNOWBALL

Level: I
Equipment: An uneven number of fleece balls, at least one for every two children
Participants: Up to 25
Skills: Overhand throw
Description: Half the children are scattered over each half of the playing area. On the signal to begin, the children throw the fleece balls into the opposite side of the playing area. They continue to field and throw the balls until the signal to stop is given. On the signal to stop, each child with a ball holds it high in the air. Any balls thrown after the signal to stop are returned to the side from which they were thrown. The team with the fewest balls on their side wins. Variation: Children on each team set a goal for having a particular number of balls on their side at game's end. If they do they win their challenge and may wish to set a different one as play continues. (This will necessitate play at a higher level—Level III.)
Teaching suggestions: Emphasize using an overhand throw. A discussion of which are the best areas to throw to may be helpful between games. Emphasis might also be placed on how to cover the space so that all balls may be fielded and thrown quickly. Encourage holding the balls up on the signal where they can be easily counted.

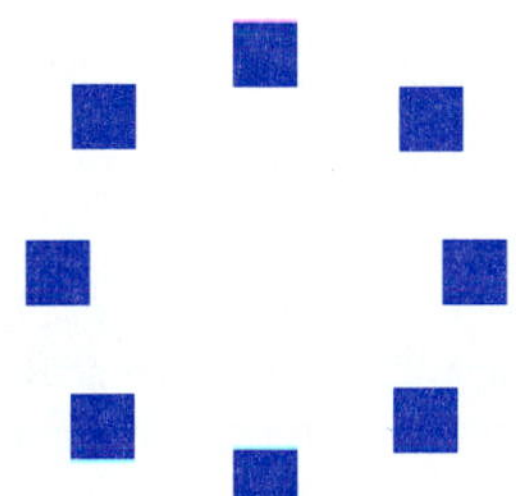

STRIDE BALL

Level: I
Equipment: One 8-inch ball per game
Participants: Six to eight per game
Skills: Underhand throw and catch
Description: The children are arranged in a circle with feet spread to the side, just touching their neighbors' feet and hands on knees. One child has the ball and begins the game by attempting to roll the ball underhand between the feet of a member of the group (but not the children directly next to them on either side). The children may stop the ball only with their hands. If the ball goes through or a player moves to use the feet to stop the ball, a point is scored for the thrower.
Teaching suggestions: Encourage the children to throw quickly and to catch the ball when it comes to them, rather than batting it away. As skill improves, some children may also learn to be more deceptive in their throws by looking one way and throwing another.

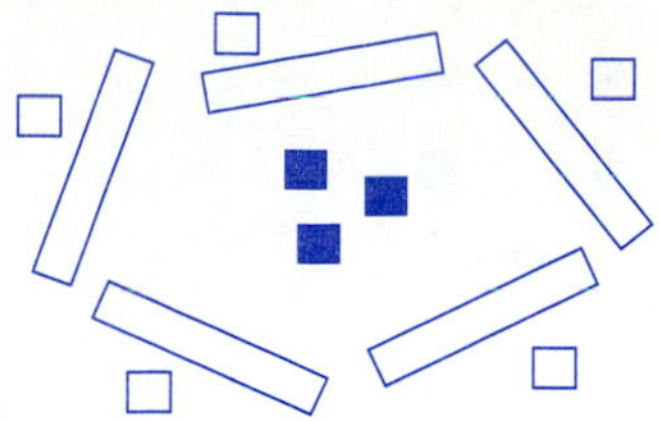

VOLCANO

Level: I
Equipment: 12 to 15 foam or fleece balls in different sizes, large folding mats
Area: Mats are set up on their sides forming a circle
Participants: Eight to ten for each game
Skills: Throwing, catching
Description: Two to three children take a position in the center of the mats with the balls. They throw the balls out of the volcano as the remaining children scattered on the outside of the mats attempt to throw them back in. After a set time period, play is stopped and the balls in the volcano are counted. Positions are exchanged and play resumes.
Teaching suggestions: Encourage them to think of strategies for working together to get rid of the balls. The children in the volcano and those outside may want to set a limit for the number of balls that will be in their area at the end of the game.

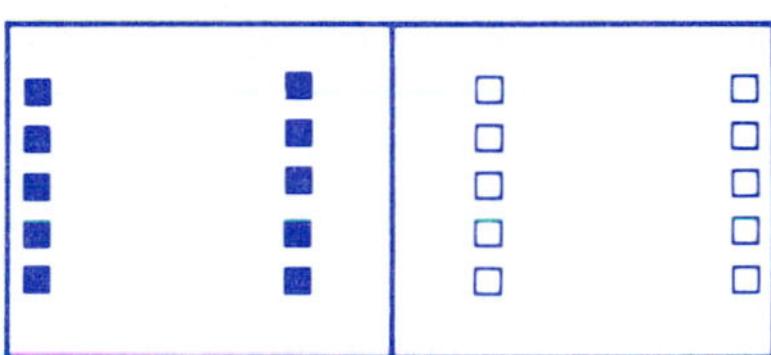

BOUNDARY BALL

Level: II
Equipment: Six to eight 8-inch playground or preferably foam balls
Participants: Up to 25
Skills: Underhand throws and catching
Description: Children are divided into two equal groups, each group scattered within its half of the playing area. Each team begins with three or four balls. One player on each team is designated as scorekeeper to count the balls scored by that side. Each team attempts to throw the balls below the head level of the opposite team and across the opponents' end (boundary) line. One point is scored for each ball crossing the line.
Teaching suggestions: In beginning play, children will try to guard the line and also throw to their opponents' side without much success. After a few minutes of play, a discussion might be conducted to help the children analyze the situation and solve the problems raised. The teacher should lead the children in recognizing that a delegation of responsibility as throwers and guards might be helpful (but do not tell them directly). As responsibilities are delegated, the children should be able to play both as throwers and guards by rotating positions periodically during the game. Encourage the children to control their throws and to throw at an appropriate level (below head height).

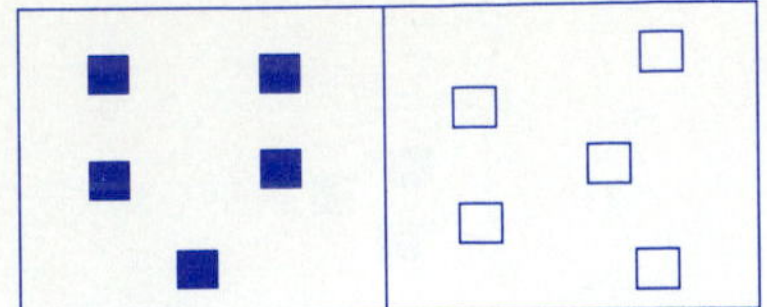

CLEANING HOUSE

Level: II
Equipment: Six to eight foam balls, one net, and two net standards
Participants: Two teams of six to eight players each
Skills: Throwing, catching
Description: Each team is in a scattered formation on its own half of the court. The balls are evenly distributed between the two teams. On the signal, each team throws the balls over the net into the opponents' court. The teams continue to catch and throw until the signal to stop is given. The team with the fewest balls on its side wins.
Teaching suggestions: Encourage the children to look for the empty space to place the ball in the opponents' court and to cover all areas of the court. Move the ball quickly. The teacher must be alert to balls that are in the air as the signal to stop is given and to see that those balls thrown after the signal are recorded for the appropriate team. It may help to have the children put the balls on the floor when the signal to stop is given.

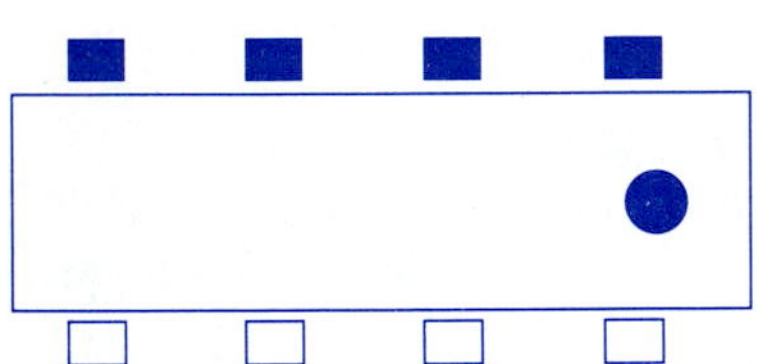

MOONBALL

Level: II
Equipment: A large cage ball and balls ranging in size and weight, at least one for every child
Participants: 10 to 15 per game
Skills: Throwing
Description: The children are arranged on opposite sides of the playing space. A large cage ball is at one end. The children work together to move the cage ball from one end of the space to the other by throwing balls at it.
Teaching suggestions: Encourage the children to remain in their place in line for their throws and to pass balls retrieved to other players in the group. This is a good activity for practicing application of force, having the children observe what happens when the ball is struck at different points. When accommodating several groups, some groups might need to throw at different sized balls and then rotate to the cage ball.

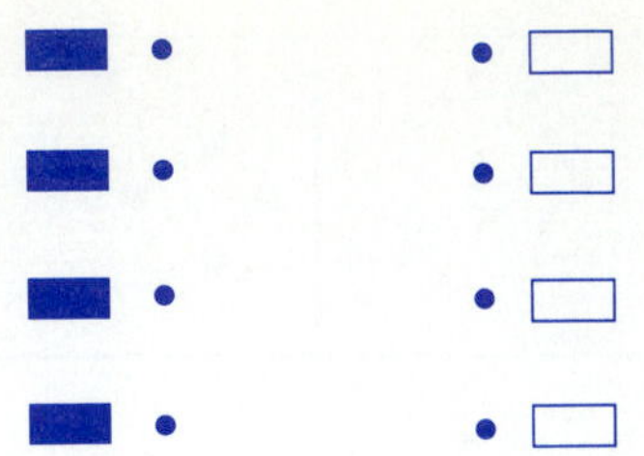

MULAMBILWA
(Africa)

Level: II
Equipment: One soft or foam ball and pin for each child
Participants: Eight to ten for each game
Skills: Rolling or throwing, running, tagging, dodging
Description: The children are divided into two groups and are kneeling 15 to 20 feet apart, facing each other. A pin is placed in front of each player. On the signal to begin, the children throw or roll the balls at the pins of their opponents. When all the pins are knocked down for one team, they get up and run to their goal about 20 to 30 feet away as the other team attempts to tag them. The team receives a point for each player tagged.
Teaching suggestions: The teacher may want to restrict throwing to games where the children stand.

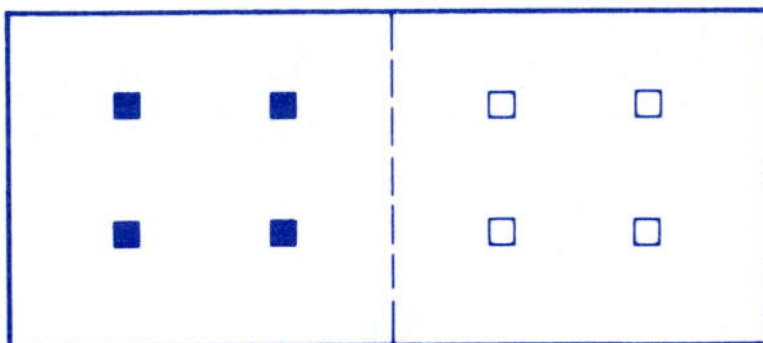

NEWCOMB

Level: II
Equipment: One volleyball-sized foam or playground ball, one net at fingertip height, and two net standards
Participants: Two teams of four to six players
Skills: Throwing and catching
Description: The ball is put into play by one member of the serving team standing in the right back court. The ball is thrown over the net into the opponents' court. The opposing team catches the ball and returns it to the serving team. Play continues, with each team throwing the ball back to the opposing team until one team (1) fails to keep the ball inbounds, (2) fails to throw the ball over the net, or (3) allows the ball to touch the floor in its court. For any of these infractions the opposing team scores. Each team serves three times, and then the service is given to the opponents. Each team rotates positions clockwise before beginning the service.
Teaching suggestions:

1. Encourage the children to get the ball into the best position before sending it over the net and to look for empty spaces in which to put the ball. They should also change the expected path of the ball and vary the force used in placing the ball in their opponents' court.

2. Children will need to be encouraged to pass the ball to teammates and to move the ball quickly. If passing does not occur it may be necessary to require several passes per side before sending the ball over the net or to allow only the net players to throw over the net.

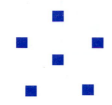

PIMA—MOVING TARGET

(Native American; Pima—Arizona)

Level: II
Equipment: A foam ball or other object tied to a rope
Participants: Six to seven per game
Skills: Throwing
Description: The children form a circle, with one person in the center holding the end of the rope. The children on the edge of the circle throw the ball, trying to hit the moving target as the person in the center moves in the circle while pulling the rope and foam ball. The children receive a point each time they hit the target. The children in the center should attempt to move the rope in a way that makes hitting the target more difficult.
Teaching suggestions: Encourage the children to work together to hit the target by passing to someone in a better position. Throws should also be made quickly and to a space ahead of the moving target.

This is a modification of the Native American game in which the children shot arrows at the moving target (a bundle of rags).

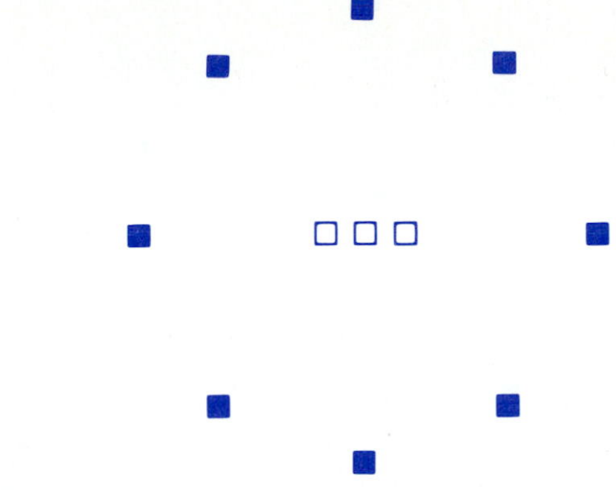

BULL IN A RING

Level: III
Equipment: One to two 8-inch foam balls per game
Participants: Eight to nine players per game
Skills: Throwing at a moving target, dodging
Description: Players are arranged in a circle, with three persons (the head, body, and tail) representing the bull and holding on to each other at the waist. On the signal, circle players attempt to hit the bull's tail by throwing the ball at waist height or below. The head and body attempt to fend off, protecting the tail. All body parts must remain in contact. If the tail is hit, the successful thrower becomes the head; the head, the body; and the body, the new tail. The tail joins the group as a thrower.
Teaching suggestions: Encourage the head player to stay between the balls and the tail, and circle players to pass the ball quickly to others in a better position.

How could this game be changed for maximum activity?

CLUB GUARD

Level: III
Equipment: One 8-inch playground ball and one duck pin per game
Participants: Four to six per game
Skills: Chest pass, underhand throw, catching, guarding a pin
Description: The children are arranged in a circle with one person in the center designated as club guard. The circle players attempt to throw the ball and knock down the duck pin. If the pin is knocked down, the two players change positions. If the guard accidentally knocks down the pin, the guard changes positions with the person who has the ball.
Teaching suggestions: This game requires teamwork. Encourage passing to get the ball behind the club guard.

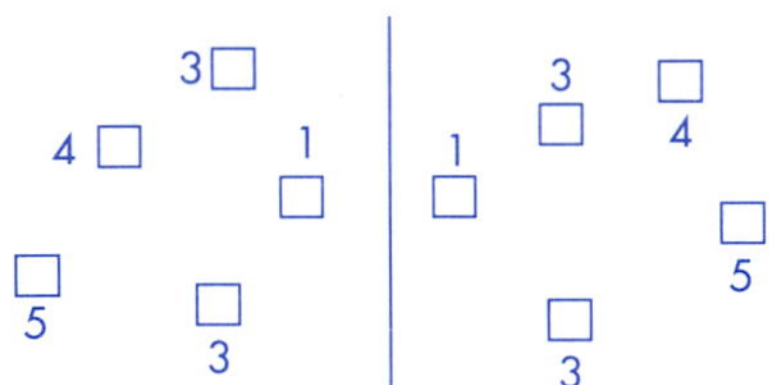

CRATERS

Level: III
Equipment: Balls varying in size; milk crates, boxes, or hoops for targets (at least six for each game)
Participants: Six to eight per game
Skills: Underhand throw
Description: Crates, boxes, hoops, etc. are scattered in the playing area, varying in distance from the center line. Children are divided into two groups located on each side of a center line. On the signal both groups attempt to throw balls so that they land and stay in the target areas on the other half of the playing area. Each target counts for a different score based on the distance from the line (i.e., five for farthest target, three for the next farthest, and one for the closest). Each team retrieves balls that are not in the targets and throws them to the targets on the opposite side. At the end of the game, each group counts up the score for the opposite group. Repeat play trying to beat your own score. Variation: The receiving team may intercept balls once they have touched the ground, but they may not stand directly in front of the targets.
Teaching suggestions: The children can determine the values for the targets for each game. Encourage them to develop a strategy for trying to beat their own record.

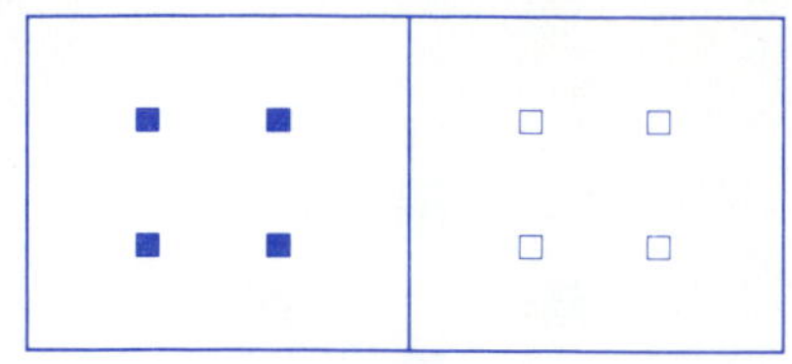

DECK TENNIS

Level: III
Equipment: One deck tennis ring, one net, and two net standards
Area: A court 12 feet wide by 40 feet deep. The net is stretched between the courts at a height of 4 feet 8 inches. The width of the court is increased to 17 feet for four players and 22 feet for six players.
Participants: Teams of two to six players
Skills: Throwing and catching the deck tennis ring
Description: The ring may be legally thrown in two ways: (1) with a backhand or forehand motion so that it moves in an arc parallel to the floor or (2) in an end-over-end manner usually initiated in an underhand motion. It may not be thrown so that it moves perpendicular to the floor. The server begins play by throwing the ring into the opponents' court from a position behind the baseline. If the ring hits the net, it may be played by the receiving team or reserved if it falls within the court boundaries. Points are only scored while serving. When the serving team fails to serve the ring within the boundaries of its opponents' court or fails to return the ring legally over the net on the rally, it loses the serve. Rings landing on boundary lines are considered inbounds. The first team to score 15 points wins. A team must win by two points.
Teaching suggestions:

1. Encourage passing and moving the ring to an advantageous position before throwing it over the net. Look for empty spaces and changing the path of the ring. Vary the throws used.
2. If the game is played by three or more players, a rotation system should be used in which the team winning the serve rotates in a clockwise manner to the next position on the court.
3. A rule requiring a specific number of passes before throwing the ring over the net may be needed to develop teamwork. Encourage the children to get rid of the ring quickly.

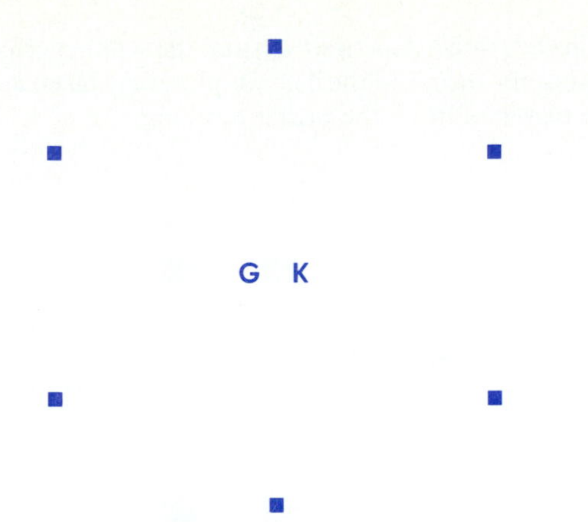

GUARD THE KING

Level: III
Equipment: One 8-inch foam ball per game
Participants: Seven to eight per game
Skills: Throwing at a moving target, catching, guarding a moving target, dodging
Description: The children are arranged in a circle, with one person designated as king and one as guard in the center. The children try to throw the ball so that it hits the king below the waist as the guard attempts to protect the king from such hits. The player who hits the king becomes the guard, and the previous guard becomes the king.
Teaching suggestions: Encourage teamwork in attempting to hit the king by passing the ball to others in a better position, as well as developing strategies to protect the king.

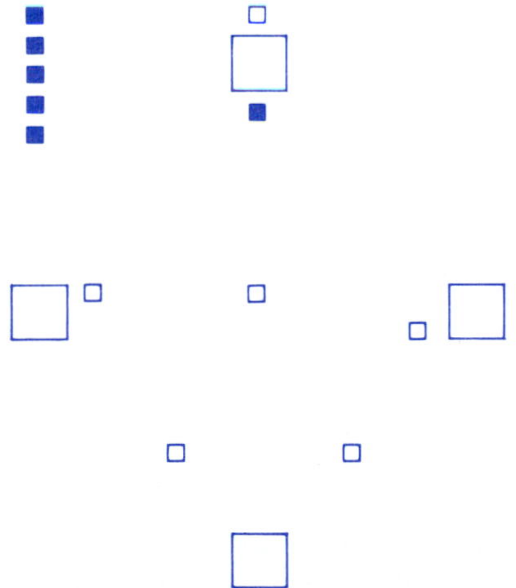

KICKBALL

Level: III
Equipment: One 8-inch playground or soccer ball, four bases
Participants: Two teams of six players
Skills: Kicking, throwing, catching, base running
Description: The pitcher rolls the ball to the batter, who kicks the ball into the playing area (inside the first and third baselines). A fly ball caught is an out. The batter then runs as many bases as possible without having the ball beat the runner to the base. If the ball gets to the base before the runner, the runner is out. All outs are force-outs (the player with the ball touching the base before the runner gets there). The player on base waits to finish the run home until the next batter bats. A run is scored each time a player completes the run around the bases. When each of the six players has had a turn at bat, the fielders and batters change places. Variations: The children can be asked to perform other skills while moving to or at the bases, such as jumping rope, doing sit-ups, performing ball skills, etc.
Teaching suggestions: Encourage looking for empty spaces in which to kick the ball. Players waiting to bat should stand outside the playing area near the first baseline. Fielders should spread out to cover as much of the infield as possible.

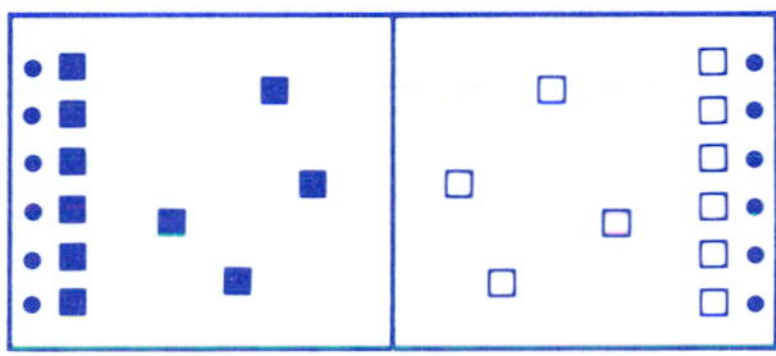

PINBALL

Level: III
Equipment: One 8-inch ball per four players, up to 12 duck pins
Participants: Up to 25
Skills: Underhand throw, catching, guarding a pin
Description: The children are divided into two teams. Each team is scattered on its half of the playing area. The six duck pins for each team are placed on the back boundary line an equal distance apart. Each team begins with one half of the balls in its possession. Each team attempts to throw the balls to knock down the duck pins of the opponents. Once down, a pin remains down until the end of the game. The team with the most pins standing at the end of the playing period wins. If players accidentally knock down pins on their own side, they remain down.
Teaching suggestions: As in Boundary Ball, the children may not at first differentiate between responsibilities of throwers and pin guards. A discussion for group decision making may be necessary after a few minutes of play. ("How can we make the game more effective?") A rotation of positions is important. Encourage controlled throws at an appropriate level. The game may be modified to allow balls rebounding from walls and hitting pins to count. The group may also be divided into smaller games of equal-ability groups to provide better for all abilities.

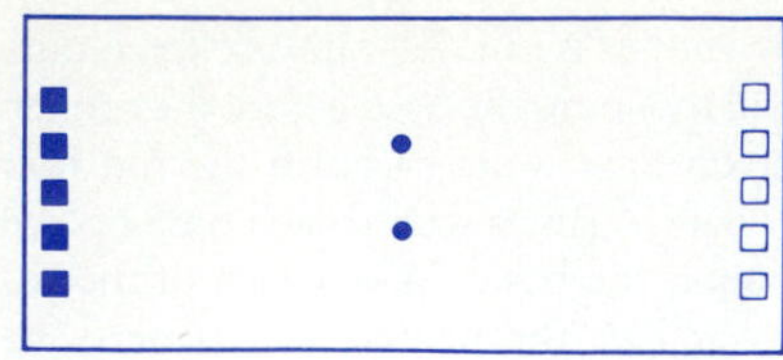

POISON BALL

Level: III
Equipment: Four to six 8-inch playground balls, two poison balls of a different color
Participants: Two teams of five to six players
Skills: Throwing at a moving target, passing, catching
Description: Two teams are lined up behind their respective goal lines. The poison balls are placed in the center of the space between the two teams. On the signal, the teams attempt to throw the playground balls at the poison balls, forcing them over the opponents' goal line. Only the balls may be used to stop the poison balls. A player may hold the ball for no more than 5 seconds before throwing it or passing it to a teammate. A point is scored each time a poison ball crosses the opponents' goal line. Once past the goal line the ball is put back into play by the leader, and play continues.
Teaching suggestions:

1. Encourage teamwork in protecting the goal line by passing the ball to those in a better position.
2. A modification of the game places teams on four sides of a square. Each team then attempts to throw balls at the poison balls to send them over any one of the three other teams' lines.

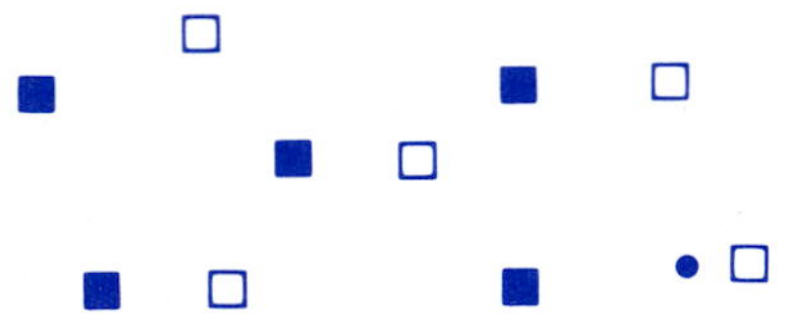

KEEP AWAY
(African Handball—Africa)
(Toss Ball—Native American)

Level: IV
Equipment: One 8-inch playground ball per game
Participants: Two teams of three to five players each
Skills: Passing and catching (possibly dribbling)
Description: One team begins in possession of the ball. They attempt to pass the ball to their teammates, counting the number of passes completed. The other team attempts to intercept a pass and begin its own passing game. If the ball goes out of the playing area, possession is forfeited to the other team. When possession is regained, counting begins again with one. There should be no personal contact or walking with the ball.
Teaching suggestions: Emphasize quick passes and moving to an open space to receive the ball. Encourage the team on defense to experiment with different ways to close available spaces.

In the Native American version, the women often played against the men, and the ball was physically taken away from the players if he or she held it too long.

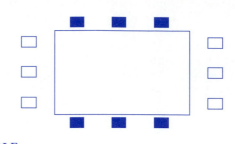

MUDDLE

Level: IV
Equipment: One medium sized ball for every 2 children
Participants: 12 to 24
Skills: Rolling, catching
Description: Children are divided into two teams. Teams are arranged on the sides of a square with teammates facing on opposite lines. One team attempts to roll their balls across to their teammates while the other team attempts to roll balls to hit the rolling balls so that they go to their sides of the square. After a few minutes, count the number of balls on each team, exchange roles, and begin again.
Teaching suggestions: Encourage the children from each team to work together to achieve their goals, timing their throws for the most success.

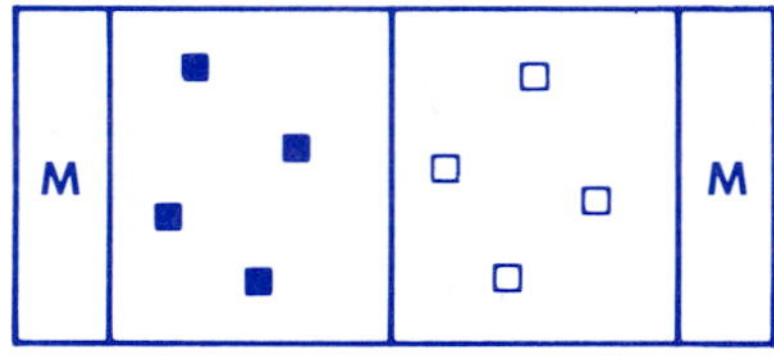

RESCUE

Level: IV
Equipment: Six to eight 8-inch foam balls
Participants: Up to 25
Skills: Throwing at a moving target, dodging, catching
Description: The group is divided into two teams, with each team designating one person as their medic. The area behind the end line is the hospital area, in which the medic is safe. All balls are placed on the center line dividing each team's playing area. On the signal, the players run up to the line, pick up a ball, take it back to their hospital area, and then move out on their half of the playing area. Each player throws the balls, attempting to hit as many opponents as possible below the waist or on the lower arms. Those hit squat down on the spot where they were hit, raise one hand, and call for the medic. The medic then comes out from the hospital area and takes the player by the hand back to the hospital. The hit player may then return to the game. The game proceeds until time is called or until all the players on one team are hit, including the medic.

Teaching suggestions:

This game usually requires several rounds before the children become daring and also begin to develop strategy to protect or hit the medic.

It is probably appropriate not to call the attention of the group to what happens if the medic is hit at first and let that information evolve from game play. From that point, strategy for protecting their medics, as well as strategy to hit the medic, will begin to emerge.

The game may be modified by having the throwers considered hit if the opponents catch the balls thrown at them.

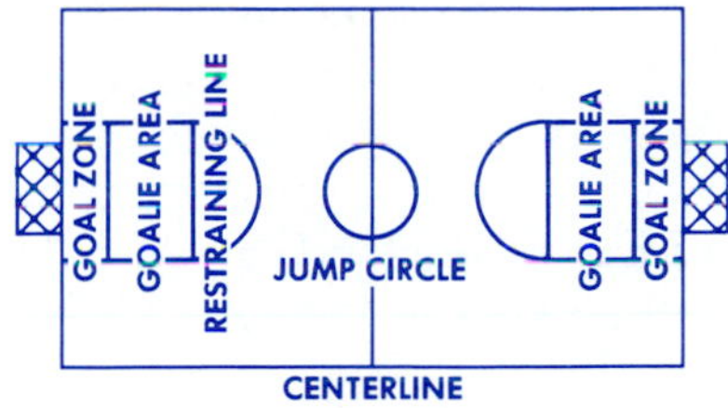

TEAMBALL

Level: IV
Equipment: Two goals with nets and a volleyball-sized ball
Participants: Two teams of four to six players
Skills: Passing: chest, bounce, shoulder
Description: The playing area is divided into two halves, with the offensive players of one team and the defensive players of the other on each half. One of the defensive players of each team assumes a position in the goal area. No players may cross the center line during play. The game begins with a jump ball between two opposing defensive players. The object of the game is to pass the ball to teammates and score by throwing the ball into the goal. No player is allowed past the restraining line. When a goal is scored players of the scoring team change ends so that the defensive players become the offensive players. Players may not move with the ball and may keep possession for only 3 seconds before passing or shooting. After a goal is scored, the team on defense begins play by throwing the ball in from out of bounds at the end line next to the goal where the score occurred. If the player in possession of the ball moves or the ball is thrown out of bounds, the opposing team begins play with a throw-in at the nearest sideline.
Teaching suggestions: Encourage the players to move the ball quickly by passing to teammates who have moved to an advantageous position. Use all the space to make it more difficult for the defense to protect the goal area. The defense should stay between the player they are guarding and the goal.

TEAM JUGGLE

Level: IV
Equipment: Four to six small balls per group
Participants: Four per group
Skills: Throwing, catching
Description: Children form a circle and begin tossing one ball across the group in a predetermined order, keeping the ball going. Other balls are added, with the group trying to keep as many balls going as possible.
Teaching suggestions: Only add balls one at a time. Each group will need to establish a speed and rhythm for throwing and catching. Try it with balls varying in size, beanbags, or other objects.

MODIFIED ULTIMATE FRISBEE

Level: IV
Equipment: One Frisbee or disc
Participants: Two teams of three or four players
Skills: Sidearm and backhand passes
Description: Play begins with each team lined up on their goal line, with one team in possession of the Frisbee. The team with the Frisbee attempts to pass the Frisbee to teammates and to score a goal with a successful pass to a teammate in the opposing teams' end zone. The opposing team attempts to gain possession either by intercepting a pass or by picking up the Frisbee when it touches the ground on an incomplete or dropped pass. Players may not move with the Frisbee in their possession. If a pass is made outside the boundary line at either end of the field, the opposing team takes possession at the sideline at a spot perpendicular to the place at which the Frisbee was thrown. If the Frisbee passes over the sideline, it is returned to the place where it went out of bounds and is thrown in by an opposing player who must have one foot on the line. Each time a goal is scored, the teams switch the direction of attack and the team who was scored upon takes possession. At no time may a player take steps with the Frisbee. If when catching the Frisbee, however, the player takes a couple of steps to stop, play continues. Steps taken at other times require the player to move back to the place where possession was gained to resume play. Pivoting as in basketball is allowed. If the defensive team gains possession in the end zone they may resume play at that point or from a point perpendicular to where the Frisbee was

caught. No physical contact is allowed. The player fouled calls "Foul" and gains possession at the spot of the foul. To score the offensive player must have both feet in the end zone.

Teaching suggestions: Encourage the players to use all the available space and to move to an open space to receive the Frisbee. The defensive team should stay between the offense and the goal.

SUMMARY

Educational games are one of the first group experiences in physical education. They provide children the opportunity to work in large and small groups, promoting interdependence of players as they move through the elementary school grades. Educational games are a favorite activity of elementary school children. If carefully selected and conducted, game playing becomes a valuable learning experience for children. Motor skill and concept development are important outcomes of games if these elements are stressed throughout the games lesson. The class begins with a review of the motor skills to be used and a practice period if needed. Movement challenges emphasizing concept use in the context of the games are introduced to focus the children's attention on the movement content stressed in the lesson. The games are then played, with reinforcement of skill and movement concepts throughout the game play.

The game lesson must be carefully planned and conducted to ensure the safe and equal participation of all children. The teacher must be ever alert to the social environment of games so that all children benefit positively from the game experience. Staying within the boundaries, playing by the rules, sharing equipment with others, and learning to win and lose gracefully are important outcomes of carefully taught games.

REFERENCES AND RESOURCES

Alaskan Department of Education, *Alaskan Games,* Juneau, 1977, Alaska State Museum.

Alexander F, editor: *Games we should play in school,* Byron, Calif, 1985, Front Row Experience.

Babcock A: Selected games and dances of the North American Plains Indians, 1992, Hoffstra Regional Games Conference.

Cole J: Teaching ultimate Frisbee, *Strategies* 1(5):8, 1988.

Council of the National Association for Sport and Physical Education: *Games teaching,* Reston, Va, 1978, AAHPERD.

Fluegelman A, editor: *The new games book,* Garden City, NY, 1976, Dolphin Books, Doubleday.

Harbin E: *Games of many nations,* Nashville, Tenn, 1954, Abingdon Press.

Jernigan SS and Vendien CL: *Playtime: a world recreation handbook,* New York, 1972, McGraw Hill.

McCann P: Breaking away from tradition: a new game for middle school students, *JOPERD* 58(3):76, 1987.

Morris G and Stiehl J: *Changing kid's games,* Champaign, Ill, 1989, Human Kinetics.

Orlick T: *The second cooperative sports and games book,* New York, 1982, Pantheon Books.

Oxendine JB: *American Indian sports heritage,* Champaign, Ill, 1988, Human Kinetics.

Smith MD: Utilizing the games for understanding model at the elementary school level, *Physical Educator* 48(4):192, 1992.

Werner P: *A movement approach to games for children,* St Louis, 1979, Mosby–Year Book.

ANNOTATED READINGS

Benson J: Creating games for learning, *JOPERD* 52(2):22, 1981.

Looks at teacher-created interdisciplinary games using available materials for equipment.

Decker J and Sterne ML: The new way to play: cooperation in physical education, *Strategies* 3(5):13, 1990.

Discusses cooperation in physical education with some suggestions for cooperative games.

Mehrhof JH, Ermler K, Kovar S: Modern day gladiators, *Strategies* 6(3):17, 1992.

Suggests several game such as competitions for fifth and sixth graders.

Werner P: Inderdisciplinary experiences through child-designed games, *JOPERD* 53(7):50, 1982.

Mathematics, art, language arts, and physical education teachers working together to provide interdisciplinary experiences through games created by the students.

Zakrajsek D: Premeditated murder, let's bump-off killer ball, *JOPERD* 57(7):49, 1986.

Discusses elimination and dodge ball games and a suggested alternative.

CHAPTER 25

Basketball

OBJECTIVES

After completing this chapter the student will be able to:

1. Identify modifications in basketball necessary for successful play by elementary school children
2. Analyze basketball skills and their use in basketball and plan activities for their development
3. Identify movement concepts important in the game of basketball and suggest activities to further develop these concepts before their use in basketball lead-ups
4. Describe a series of progressively more difficult lead-up activities used during the upper elementary school years to develop the game of basketball

Basketball, a game that originated in the United States, is a popular game of youth and young adults. Its high recreational appeal stems from the challenge of competing against another person or persons. It can be played in a relatively small area and is easily adapted for as few as two players.

Basketball is a complex game. To be successful, players must have the ability to execute a variety of ball-handling skills, including passing, catching, shooting, and dribbling. They must also be able to run, jump, change direction (pivot), stop, and start in combination with ball-handling skills as defense and offense require and must have the endurance to sustain activity over an extended period of time. The ability to work together and to relate to nine other moving individuals is essential if the player is to be effective.

Cognitively, players must be able to understand and play within the parameters of the game rules, to comprehend and use a variety of offensive and defensive strategies, and to recognize and put into effective use the movement concepts essential to the game.

Multicultural Games

A number of games resembling basketball have been played in different cultures. The ancient Mayans and Aztecs played a court game in which the participants propelled the ball into a goal 15 feet or more from the ground with body parts other than the hands and feet.

Korfball is another basketball type game played in Europe, Africa, Asia, and recently in the United States. Baskets 11.5 feet from the floor are located on each half of the court. The game is usually played with teams of eight—four women and four men—with two players of each sex positioned on each half of the court. A basket scores 1 point. Players may not run with the ball. They pass the ball to move it into position to score. No dribbling is allowed.

BASKETBALL FOR ELEMENTARY SCHOOL CHILDREN

Basketball is a popular game with elementary school children. Their success, however, is often limited unless the game is adapted for them. Basketball lead-up activities may be successfully introduced in the intermediate grades after the children have acquired the fundamental motor skills prerequisite to basketball.

Equipment: Eight-inch utility balls that are not too bouncy or some of the new smaller basketballs should be used in the early years of development, as they can be more successfully handled by intermediate school children. Junior-sized basketballs should be introduced, as children are able to handle them, usually by fifth or sixth grade. Baskets should be lowered to about 7 or 8 feet high or 3 or 4 feet higher than the children to offer more opportunity for success in shooting. Adjustable baskets are available and should be standard equipment in the

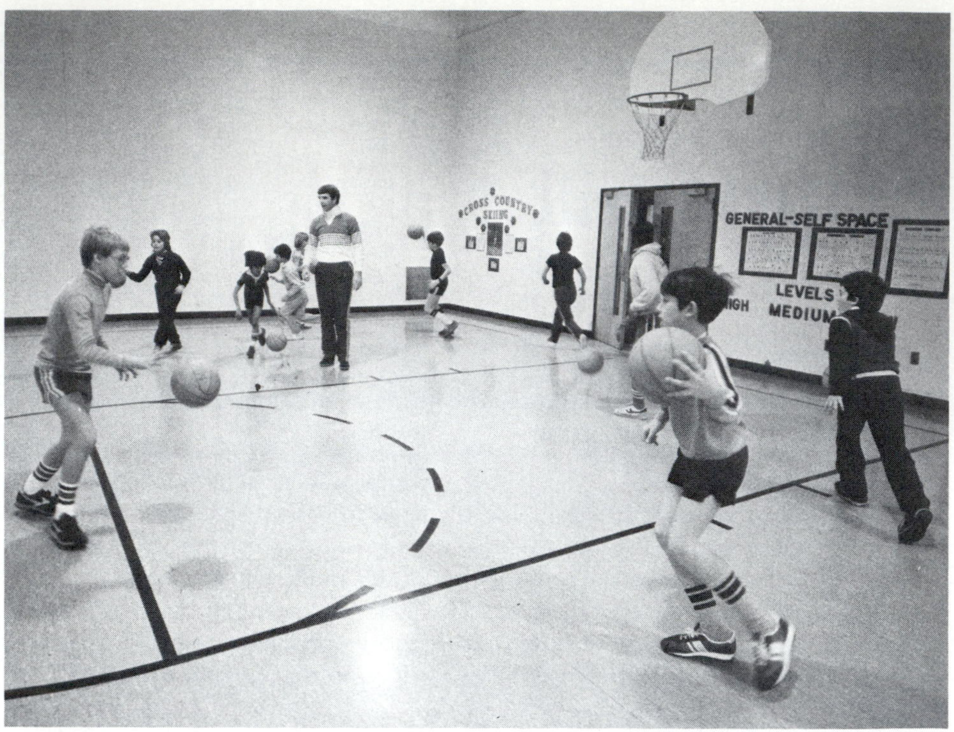

Considerable variability in ball-handling skills may be observed at the elementary school level.

elementary school. Any metal bases should be padded for safety. The free throw line should be moved closer to the basket for young players.

Skills: Basketball requires the use of a variety of ball-handling and locomotor skills. These skills are used in combination, and good body control is important if a player is to avoid traveling and personal contact. Because there is great variability in ball-handling and locomotor skills of elementary school children, it is important to adapt the rules to the needs of individuals. Being under control to avoid personal contact and to use appropriate force in passing should be stressed with everyone. However, **traveling** might be called on an individual basis, with stricter adherence to the rule as children's skills improve. The **double dribble** is another rule with which some children experience difficulty. Games should involve children with like skills, and opponents should be matched according to ability to provide the best opportunity for all.

The game: Basketball requires a great deal of team cooperation. Teamwork takes time to develop, and the basketball progression should be built with a gradually greater dependence on others for success in mind. In beginning games evidence of team play often is rare. A few more aggressive players dominate the game and little passing is observed. Rules must be introduced to ensure that play is evenly distributed among all the players. Modifications to promote involvement are requiring several passes or several individuals handling the ball before a shot is taken or prohibiting players from taking two consecutive shots. Offensive and defensive tactics should be taught.

During these developmental years, the following should be stressed in appropriate lead-up activities.

The role of the offense is to:

1. Maintain possession of the ball.
2. Score points by successfully making baskets.

Offensive tactics that should be stressed include:

1. Moving the ball toward the basket.
2. Passing to a space in front of teammates and in a manner in which the ball can be easily received.
3. Moving to an open space to be free to receive the ball.
4. Remaining spread out to make the work of the defense more difficult.
5. Always being on the move, so that players cannot be guarded easily.

The role of the defense is to:

1. Regain possession of the ball.
2. Prevent the opposing team from scoring.

Children should be encouraged to:

1. Stay between opponents and the basket.
2. Take up as much space as possible when guarding.
3. Continuously shift position in relation to the basket when guarding a player with the ball as opponents and the ball move on the court.

When guarding a player without the ball, stay between the player and the ball.

4. Guard a player who has dribbled more closely than one who has not.
5. Shift quickly to offense when gaining possession of the ball.

These elements of games are best taught through a series of progressively more difficult activities, beginning with those in which children play one on one activities, and gradually increasing the number of active participants to two on two and perhaps for some children three on three.

Social Skills

Basketball offers a wonderful opportunity for children to further develop their social skills, especially those skills needed in working with others to achieve the game goal. As mentioned previously, basketball at this level is not necessarily a team game, and the activities must be carefully planned and conducted to ensure that appropriate skills are developed. Early games may include sharing space on defense. Later they will depend more on each other when passing, moving the ball up the court, or defending the basket area. These skills require discussion if each player is to practice good social skills as well. The teacher should reinforce these skills by giving feedback to children during play as well as by the practice of skills and game concepts.

Health-Related Fitness

Good ball handling skills are essential in basketball, and the warm-up period also may enhance fitness. For example, mass dribbling at the beginning of the class can develop ball handling skills as well as increase heart rate. The teacher may call for changing hands, directions, pathways, speed, etc. to sustain the activity long enough for some cardiorespiratory benefit.

BASKETBALL SKILLS

Movement concepts are an important aspect of skill development. Body awareness and qualities of movement must not be overlooked in the learning process. In learning the skills of basketball, children should be encouraged to develop an awareness and understanding of how body parts are used most effectively in executing various skills. Body awareness should be encouraged by emphasizing the evaluative criteria and teaching points in the presentation, practice, and review of each skill. When time permits, problem solving in the use of body parts should be encouraged. Body control should be stressed, including the use of an appropriate amount of force for the task. Children should be helped to apply principles of balance, laws of motion, and projection in the learning process. These concepts are mapped in Figure 25-1. As skill is developed the children are ready to vary the technique, making the adjustments they will need to use the skills effectively in game play.

Dribbling

Dribbling is used to move the ball on the court while legally maintaining possession of the ball. The ball is pushed to the floor slightly ahead of the moving player with the fingers of one hand so that it rebounds to about hip height, where it may be pushed again and on each successive rebound. This skill is usually introduced in the early years; during basketball play it will be refined, varied, and applied (Figure 25-2).

Common errors:

1. Slapping the ball with the palms rather than pushing with the fingers
2. Failure to look where one is going
3. Bouncing the ball too high
4. Stopping the dribble and then beginning again
5. Bouncing the ball too close to the feet

Activities To Practice Dribbling

Good ball control while moving requires a great deal of practice. Whenever possible, maximum activity should be provided by having as many children dribbling at a time as possible. It may be necessary to use many different kinds of balls when supplies are limited.

1. Each child has a ball. On the signal, children begin dribbling within the defined space. Activities include changing hands and varying the height of the bounce. Stationary obstacles such as cones and hoops may be added to the space around which the children must move. (Emphasis should be on maintaining control of the ball and looking up to see where they are going. The teacher should ask questions regarding the technique.) (refining)
2. Parallel lines are drawn about every 10 to 15 feet. The children begin at line 1 and dribble up to line. They do a **reverse turn** and continue to dribble back to line 1. Then they go to line 3, back to 2, up to line 4, back to 3, and so forth. With each change of pathway, a reverse turn is made. Dribbling should be practiced with one hand and then the other. (What did you do to keep the ball under control as you dribbled and then reversed your pathway?) (refining)

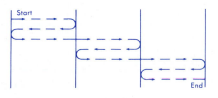

3. Repeat No. 1, changing direction on the signal. (What did you do to shift to the new direction?) (varying)

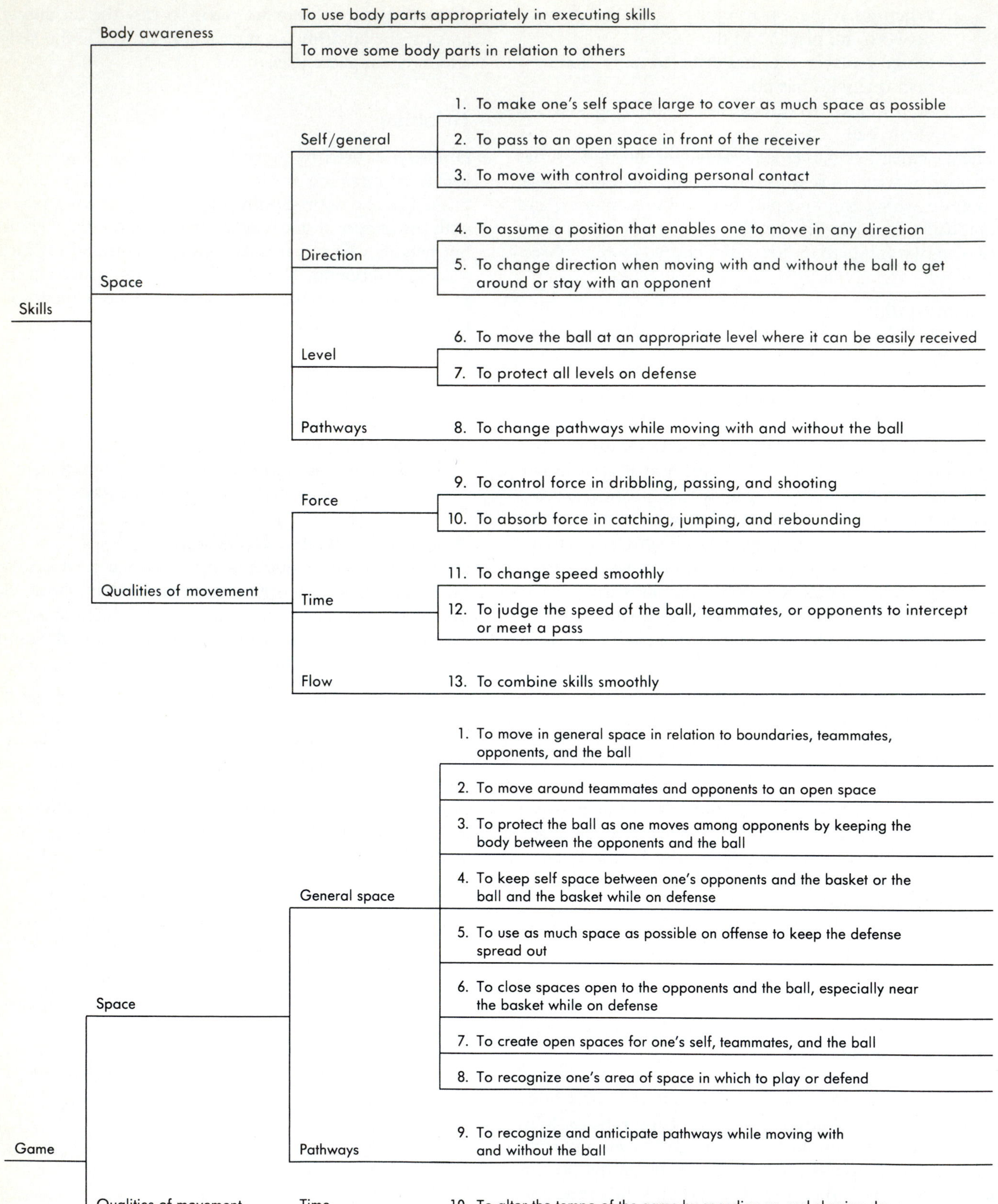

Skills
Body awareness
To use body parts appropriately in executing skills
To move some body parts in relation to others
Space
Self/general
1. To make one's self space large to cover as much space as possible
2. To pass to an open space in front of the receiver
3. To move with control avoiding personal contact
Direction
4. To assume a position that enables one to move in any direction
5. To change direction when moving with and without the ball to get around or stay with an opponent
Level
6. To move the ball at an appropriate level where it can be easily received
7. To protect all levels on defense
Pathways
8. To change pathways while moving with and without the ball
Qualities of movement
Force
9. To control force in dribbling, passing, and shooting
10. To absorb force in catching, jumping, and rebounding
Time
11. To change speed smoothly
12. To judge the speed of the ball, teammates, or opponents to intercept or meet a pass
Flow
13. To combine skills smoothly
Game
Space
General space
1. To move in general space in relation to boundaries, teammates, opponents, and the ball
2. To move around teammates and opponents to an open space
3. To protect the ball as one moves among opponents by keeping the body between the opponents and the ball
4. To keep self space between one's opponents and the basket or the ball and the basket while on defense
5. To use as much space as possible on offense to keep the defense spread out
6. To close spaces open to the opponents and the ball, especially near the basket while on defense
7. To create open spaces for one's self, teammates, and the ball
8. To recognize one's area of space in which to play or defend
Pathways
9. To recognize and anticipate pathways while moving with and without the ball
Qualities of movement
Time
10. To alter the tempo of the game by speeding up and slowing down

FIGURE 25-1 Basketball concepts.

FIGURE 25-2 Evaluative criteria and teaching points for dribbling.
- Pushed with finger pads; body erect, eyes looking forward.
- Ball projected forward.

4. Repeat No. 1, varying speed. (How did you adjust your dribble as you moved more quickly or slowed down?) (varying)
5. Whirl dribble: Cones are scattered in the general space. Each child with a ball dribbles to a cone, pauses with the foot opposite the dribbling hand forward, and pivots on the forward foot to turn away from the cone. The dribbler then fakes one dribble back away from the cone, changes hands, and completes the turn around the cone. (Were you able to keep the dribbling going? Did you complete the dribble around the cone?) (varying)
6. Hot-shot dribbling: Challenge the children by providing opportunities to practice dribbling behind their back or between their legs while stationary or moving. (varying)

Catching

Catching skills are analyzed in Chapter 13. The player should move to the ball, lining up with the oncoming ball, reaching out with two hands, and pulling it in toward the body.

Passing

The *chest pass,* the most frequently used pass in basketball, is a short, quick pass and is particularly advantageous because it allows the receiver to catch the ball and throw it in one continuous movement. To begin, the ball is held just in front of the chest. As the ball is released, there is a snap of the wrists and fingers, which gives power to the throw. The follow-through is in the direction of the throw with arms fully extended toward the receiver's chest (Figure 25-3).

Common errors:

1. Grasping the ball in the hands with thumbs on the side of the ball
2. Extending elbows out from the sides
3. Pushing with one hand more than with the other
4. Not fully extending the arms on follow-through toward the receiver's chest
5. Not controlling the force of the throw by throwing it too hard or not using enough force to reach its destination
6. Releasing the ball too soon or too late

The chest pass requires considerable shoulder girdle strength, often lacking in elementary school children. Children often compensate for this lack of strength by pushing the ball more from one side of the body than the other, which enables them to use trunk rotation to produce additional force. It may be helpful to have them begin the throw from a forward stride position, with a shift of their weight to the rear foot before beginning the throw and then a step forward to transfer weight to the forward foot on the throw to add power. Making a downward circle with the ball before the forward extension of the arms should provide additional power.

The *two-hand bounce pass* is similar to the chest pass in its execution and in its use as a short, quick pass. It is easier for children to catch because the bounce allows more time and expends some of the ball's force. On releasing the ball the arms and hands follow through forward and downward toward the spot on the floor where the ball will land (Figure 25-4).

Common errors:

1. Projecting the ball downward rather than forward and downward
2. Having the ball bounce too close or too far from the receiver
3. Pushing the ball more with one hand than with the other

The *shoulder pass* is generally used for long passes down court, but also may be used for short passes. It is usually a successful pass for elementary school children because more body parts may be used to project the ball than in the chest pass and using two hands affords greater control of the larger ball. The ball is held with both hands on one side of the body at shoulder level. The opposite foot is forward. As the player transfers weight to the forward foot, the arms are extended forward with a wrist snap as the ball is released and hands and arms follow through in the direction of the flight (Figure 25-5).

- Fingers spread, thumbs behind ball.
- Arms at sides, elbows at waist height.

- Step forward.
- Ball pushed forward equally from both arms.

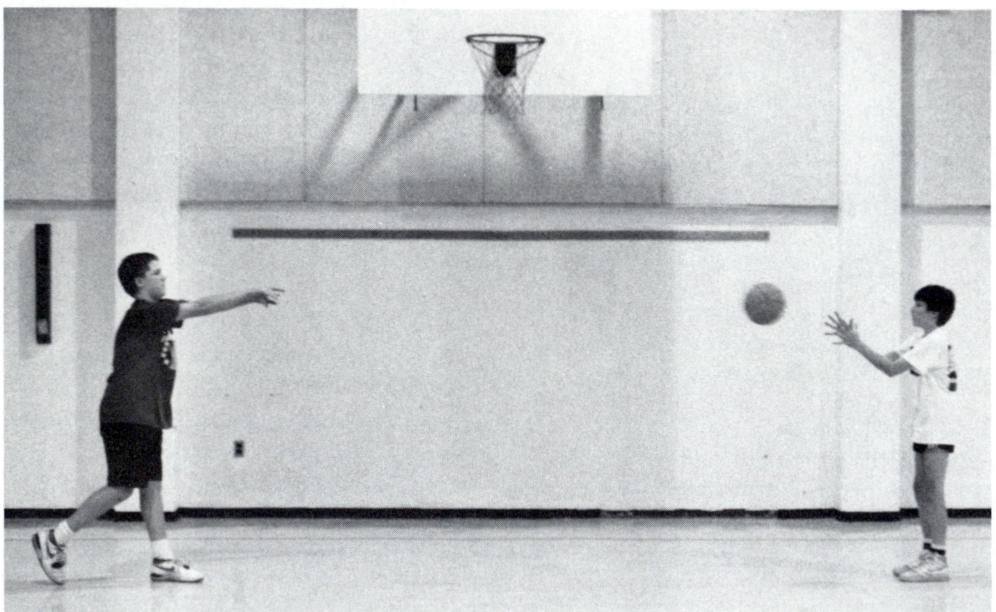

- Arms fully extended, hands rotated inward, thumbs pointing down.
- Ball received at chest level.

FIGURE 25-3 Evaluative criteria and teaching points for chest pass.

- Ball lands three fourths of distance toward receiver.
- Arms fully extended, hands rotated inward, thumbs down.

FIGURE 25-4 Evaluative criteria and teaching points for two-hand bounce pass.

- Ball held with fingers spread on either side of ball.
- Elbows in, arms at sides.
- Step forward on opposite foot.
- Arms extended in direction of flight.
- Ball is received at chest height.

FIGURE 25-5 Evaluative criteria and teaching points for the shoulder pass.

- Hold ball in fingers overhead.
- Step forward as throw is initiated.

- Extend arms with wrist snap.
- Follow through in direction of flight.

FIGURE 25-6 Evaluative criteria and teaching points for two-hand overhead pass.

Common errors:

1. Grasping the ball in the hands
2. Failing to step forward on the opposite foot
3. Not following through in the direction of flight
4. Releasing the ball too soon or too late

Teaching suggestions: As the children are ready and ball size permits, a one-arm overhand throw may be substituted.

The *two-hand overhead pass* is used for short, high passes. The ball is held directly overhead, with one hand positioned on either side of the ball and with elbows bent. As the throw is initiated, there is a step forward as both arms extend forward with a wrist snap on release (Figure 25-6).

Common errors:

1. Pushing with one side of the body more than with the other
2. Using trunk flexion rather than a step forward to impart force
3. Not following through in the direction of the intended throw
4. Releasing the ball too soon or too late

Because children may lack shoulder girdle strength, this throw may be difficult to execute for many elementary school children. Special emphasis may be needed on Nos. 1 and 2.

Activities To Practice Passing

Body control in passing should be stressed, with the responsibility for a successful pass placed primarily on the thrower. In evaluating their success as passers, children should respond to the following questions: Did the ball get to the spot where it was supposed to go? Was the amount of force appropriate so that it could easily be received by the catcher?

Activities that permit the children to experiment with the use of different types of passes at varying distances and forces enhance their ability to select a pass for a particular situation. The following examples illustrate these goals.

1. Each child has a ball and is facing a wall that is about 10 feet away. They practice throwing the ball to the wall so that it rebounds just to themselves or to some designated spot on the floor. Try different passes, moving closer or farther away from the wall. The children could also experiment with different kinds of balls used in the basketball progression. (How did you control the force required for the ball to rebound

in the way you wanted? Which throws were easiest to control? At which distances were you most accurate?) (refining)

2. Half the group is moving in general space, their partners stationary with the ball. When the moving players are open they call "Yes," at which time their partners pass to them. On receiving the ball the players stop, remaining stationary while their partners move to an open space to receive the ball. (Where did you place the ball so that it could be easily received by your partner?) (varying)
3. Select a pass and have a child practice it with a partner a short distance away. Increase the distance between the two children when they have completed five successful passes. Continue increasing the distance until they can no longer complete five throws. (How did you use your body to increase the force needed as the distance became greater? Did this affect your accuracy?) Now try another type of pass and repeat the activity. This may be repeated several times. (Which passes were most effective for short, medium, or long distances? Why were some more difficult? Which were easier for your partner to receive?) Although generalizations can be made about which passes are best in particular situations, there may be individual preferences for certain types of passes. No one pass is best for all, and teachers should encourage children to discover which works best for them. (varying)
4. Galloping Lizzie: Children are arranged in groups of four or five in a circle with an additional person in the center. Circle players attempt to pass the ball quickly to anyone in the circle. The center player attempts to tag the person holding the ball. If "Lizzie" tags a player, the two exchange places. Specific passes may be designated for use. (Where did you want to receive the ball so that you could get rid of it quickly? Which types of throws were easiest to catch and throw again?) (varying)
5. In groups of three or four, one is the passer and the others are spaced in a line for a give and go. The passer throws to the first person in line, who immediately passes back as the passer continues to move, repeating the action with the others in line. When the pass is received from the last player in line, the passer passes the ball to the first player in line and moves to the end of the line. The passer may dribble in between passes depending on the distance to be covered. (Did you receive the ball so you could pass quickly? Where did you place the ball for the moving receiver?) (varying)

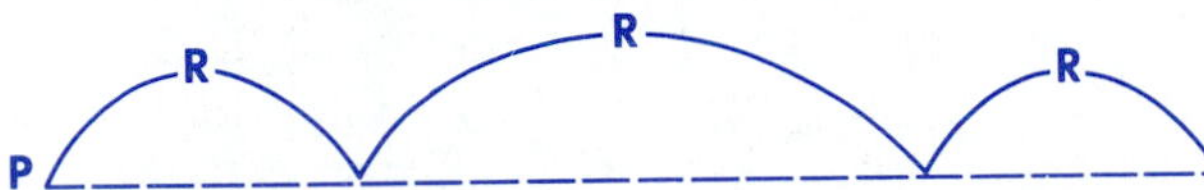

6. In groups of three, two pass the ball back and forth while a stationary guard attempts to intercept the pass. The receiver should establish a target in which he or she would like to receive the ball. (At what level was the ball easiest to receive? What level was most difficult to get the ball past the guard?) (varying)

Once children have an idea of the techniques and controlling force, they should practice passing to moving players. The activities later in this chapter for working on space concepts will also help children work on passing in a gamelike situation.

Shooting

Success in shooting during the elementary school years is limited. The weight of the ball, the height of the basket, and the lack of strength in the arms and shoulders all influence children's shooting abilities. Even with appropriately sized equipment and height of baskets, shooting is difficult.

The *chest shot* (or *two-hand set shot*) is used as a short or long set shot. Because the child can use both hands, more force can be imparted to the ball to get it up to the basket. Although this shot is no longer used at higher levels of basketball, it is one of the most successful shots during the elementary school years. The chest shot is executed as the chest pass but with arm and leg extension upward to give a higher arch to the ball so that it drops down into the basket. It may or may not touch the backboard. However, children should be encouraged to aim for the square on the backboard for a higher percentage shot. If the ball does hit the backboard, it must be a soft contact to avoid rebounding away from the basket (Figure 25-7).

Common errors:

1. Pushing more with one hand than with the other
2. Failing to fully extend the arms upward
3. Not using the legs
4. Not giving enough arch on the ball
5. Contacting the backboard too hard so that the ball rebounds away

The *one-hand set shot* is more difficult to perform than the two-hand set shot because only one hand is used to impart force to the ball. The ball is held with the fingers of both hands opposite the chin and in front of the lead foot. The wrist of the shooting hand is cocked back, and the ball rests on the outspread fingers. The nonshooting hand supports the ball at the side and bottom. (Younger players may need to move the nonshooting hand more to the side to balance the ball in the hands, as shown in Figure 25-8.) The knees are bent and the back is relatively straight. As the movement begins, the legs straighten as the ball is taken in the shooting hand, the arm extending forward and upward and pushing the ball toward the basket. The ball is released with a soft backspin. The lead foot should be on the same side as the shooting hand. The follow-through is forward and upward (Figure 25-8).

Common errors:

1. Resting the ball in the hands
2. Stepping forward on foot opposite shooting hand

- Fingers spread, thumbs behind ball.
- Arms bent, elbows down.

- Ball pushed equally from both hands.
- Arms and legs fully extended upward.
- Arch drops ball into basket.

FIGURE 25-7 Evaluative criteria and teaching points for two-hand set shot.

- Ball is held at chin height with the fingers of the shooting hand behind and slightly under the ball.
- Knees bent, lead foot forward.

- Knees straighten; full extension of shooting arm upward and forward
- Ball arch drops ball into basket.

FIGURE 25-8 Evaluative criteria and teaching points for one-hand set shot.

- Take last step on opposite foot.
- Jump straight up with the shooting knee raised.
- Extend shooting side arm for soft touch on backboard.
- Controlled landing.

FIGURE 25-9 Evaluative criteria and teaching points for lay-up shot.

3. Not fully extending the shooting arm
4. Using too much body action to get the ball up
5. Hitting the backboard forcefully, causing the ball to rebound rather than score

The *lay-up shot* is a fundamental shot. Because the shot is taken while moving, it is more difficult for elementary school children. The last step should be taken by the foot opposite the shooting hand. Raising the knee on the shooting side aids in gaining height on the take-off. The ball is initially held in two hands, and then one hand continues to reach with the ball, being fully extended as the ball is "laid" up softly against the backboard. The ball should be released with the right hand when shooting is from the right and the left when the shot is taken from the left. This technique normally keeps the ball farthest away from the person guarding the player (Figure 25-9).

Common errors:

1. Traveling before releasing the ball
2. Watching the ball rather than the basket on the approach
3. Throwing the ball too hard against the backboard
4. Stopping before shooting
5. Releasing with the incorrect arm or leg
6. Releasing the ball without full extension of the shooting arm

Activities To Practice Shooting

In beginning development of basketball skills, children should be encouraged to develop some of the basic principles of shooting. Not all children will be successful at any particular type of shot. They will need to experiment with various types of shots to determine which is best for them.

How can the children get the ball up to the basket? At this level, emphasis on placing the ball accurately and softly so that it goes into the basket should be stressed, because not all children will be successful at getting the ball up to the basket in the same way. To maximize the activity, no more than six or seven children should work at one basket.

1. *Mass Shooting:* Each child has a ball and all attempt to make as many baskets as they can within the time period. (What type of shot worked best? How did you control the force to get the ball into the basket?) (refining)
2. *Around the World:* Numbers from 1 to 10 are marked randomly on the floor in the basket area. Each child begins at 1 and attempts a shot at the basket. If made, the child moves to 2 and so on. To provide maximum activity children may begin at any number and proceed to the next until they have shot from all 10 numbers. (Which ways did you try that were successful at scoring a basket? Did you use the same type of shot near and far from the baskets, from the side, and in front of the basket?) (varying)
3. *Take a Chance:* Seven numbers are marked randomly on the floor around the basket area. Children are divided into partners or groups of three, with one ball for each group. The first person in each group begins at 1 and shoots for a basket. If made, the player may "take a chance" and attempt to shoot a basket from

the next number. If made, they continue to move up the numbers; if missed, the next person begins, and the players who missed must go back to 1 when it is their turn again. If they choose not to "take a chance," then they begin their next turn at the number to which they advanced. (How did you change your shots as you moved to different locations on the floor? Did you change the type of shot taken? Where did you try to put the ball?) (varying)

Reverse Turn and Pivot

The reverse turn and **pivot** are used to change direction legally while holding the ball. The reverse turn is used to reverse pathways. The feet are in a forward-stride position. Weight is on the balls of the feet as the turn is made toward the rear foot (Figure 25-10).

Common errors:

1. Moving around in a circle rather than turning on the balls of the feet
2. Lifting a foot on the turn

Before beginning the pivot the weight is evenly distributed on both feet, with the ball held firmly in two hands. One foot is designated as the pivot foot. The player may turn in either direction as long as the pivot foot remains on the floor and is not dragged from its original position.

Common errors:

1. Not having the body under control before beginning the pivot
2. Dragging the pivot foot
3. Changing the pivot foot
4. Using the entire foot rather than the ball of the foot

Activities To Practice Reverse Turn and Pivoting

1. Dribbling in general space. On the signal do a reverse turn and proceed in the new pathway. Repeat several times. Change lead foot and repeat. (refining)
2. In groups of two, one person is the pivot person and has a ball. The other takes a position to one side of the player, but not too close. Slowly at first, the pivot player pivots to keep the other from tying up the ball. As skill improves, pick up speed. (How did you move to keep the ball away from your opponent?) (refining)
3. Moving in general space, pivot reversing the pathway to proceed in the same path in which you came; moving again this time stop and pivot to make a right angle turn (moving in an L; moving again this time pivot and move in a V.) (varying)

Guarding

Because one team is trying to gain possession of the ball during basketball, effective *guarding* techniques are a must for each player. The player assumes a slightly crouched position, with feet in a comfortable side stride position slightly larger than the width of the shoulders. One foot may be slightly ahead of the other, and body weight is supported on the balls of the feet. Hands and arms are extended, generally with one hand up forward and the other at shoulder level. Players must be alert to movements of the forwards they are guarding so that feet and arms may be moved to guard the player effectively. The guard plays farther away from a player who has not moved than one who has stopped dribbling. Eyes should focus on players' hips to determine where the move will be made (Figure 25-11).

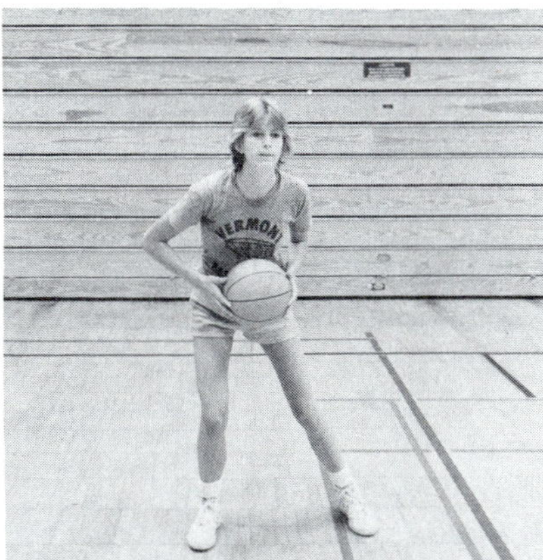

- Reverse turn.
- One foot forward.
- Turn away from forward foot.

- Pivot.
- Pivot foot remains stationary.
- Turn around pivot foot.

FIGURE 25-10 Evaluative criteria and teaching points for reverse turn and point.

Common errors:

1. Body erect with no knee bend
2. Weight supported on the entire foot so it cannot be moved easily
3. Guarding players who have not dribbled too closely so they are able to move around the guard
4. Flailing the arms rather than purposeful movement
5. Running rather than sliding to stay with the opponent

In the early games in the progression, the concern in guarding is to keep the ball out of a particular space by covering the space to block or to intercept throws. Later when children begin to work against an opponent in a one-on-one situation, guarding an individual becomes important.

Activities To Practice Guarding

1. In partners, one thrower and one guard, who attempts to keep the thrower from successfully throwing the ball to a wall. (What did you do to prevent the ball from getting by you? What position seems to work best?) (perceiving)
2. The group faces the leader and assumes a good guarding stance. On the movement by the leader, who moves forward, backward, or to the side, the group responds by moving as if they were trying to contain the leader. (How did you move to stay with the leader? What cues did you use to anticipate which way the leader would move?) (refining)
3. Partners face each other. First without and then with a ball, one attempts to move to some designated area on the floor while the partners or guards attempt to keep them out. Guards may be asked to use feet only at first, with hands behind the back. Later add the use of the arms in guarding. (What did you have to do to keep partners out without using personal contact? Where did you watch so that you could anticipate which way they were going to move?) (refining)
4. In groups of three, two throwers and one guard. The throwers attempt to pass the ball back and forth while the guard attempts to keep the person in possession of the ball from getting the throw away. (What levels were easiest to defend? More difficult?) (varying)

Learning to protect the ball takes much practice.

FIGURE 25-11 Evaluative criteria and teaching points for guarding.

- Body crouched, knees bent.
- Comfortable side stride, one foot slightly ahead.
- Hands up to protect space.
- Can move in all directions.

Movement Skills

The movement skills important to basketball (stopping, jumping and dodging, and sliding) are analyzed in Chapter 13.

BASKETBALL CONCEPTS

Application of the movement content is essential to success in basketball. The concepts mapped in Figure 25-1 begin development at the elementary school level. The importance of the body awareness and quality of movement concepts has already been stressed in the execution and use of basketball skills. These concepts are enhanced further as children adapt skills for use in various game situations. Space concepts are also important as children move on the court in ever-changing relationships with others.

Each lesson should include activities that enhance the application and use of movement concepts in basketball activities. In addition, to emphasize the movement content as it relates to skill development, activities should help children see the relationships between these concepts and play in basketball lead-up games. Specific activities that maximize the activity for all children should be used. These activities may actually be mini aspects of the games themselves. The closer these activities are to the use of the concepts in the games, the greater the chance for transfer to these games as the basketball unit is developed. As the children move on in the lesson to the lead-up activities, the teacher must continue to emphasize the concepts developed in earlier parts of the lesson.

Basketball Concept Activities

1. To move in general space in relation to boundaries, teammates, opponents, and the ball.
   a. The area is divided into the courts to be used in the game selected. Children dribble in the area, covering all the space but staying within the boundaries designated. After a time, rotate the children to other areas of the court. (How did you control the ball in the assigned space?)
   b. Each person dribbles a ball in general space. (Emphasis should be placed on using all space available, avoiding others, and looking for the open spaces.)
   c. Similar to *b,* but now space is alternately increased or decreased. Children continue moving and dribbling, but they modify movement as space changes. (How close can you get together and continue moving without touching? What did you do differently as space increased or decreased to keep the ball under control? What problems did you encounter as the space got smaller?)
2. To move around teammates and opponents to an open space.
   a. Four persons dribble, one behind the other. On the signal, they must break for an open space. On the next signal, they return to file and repeat. (How did you control the ball and look out for others as you moved to the open space?)
   b. In groups of five, one passer, two stationary receivers, and two stationary guards. The passer throws to the first receiver while moving in front of the first guard and slips around behind the guard to receive the pass back, then passes to the next receiver and so on. (How did you time your throw to avoid the defense?) (varying)

   c. Four players are spaced along the foul shooting line. One person has the ball and passes to a person and cuts for the empty space on the lane. (Were you able to keep track of the empty space? Were you always attentive to where the new empty space was?) *Variation:* Number the players so that 1 passes to 2, 2 to 3, and so on.

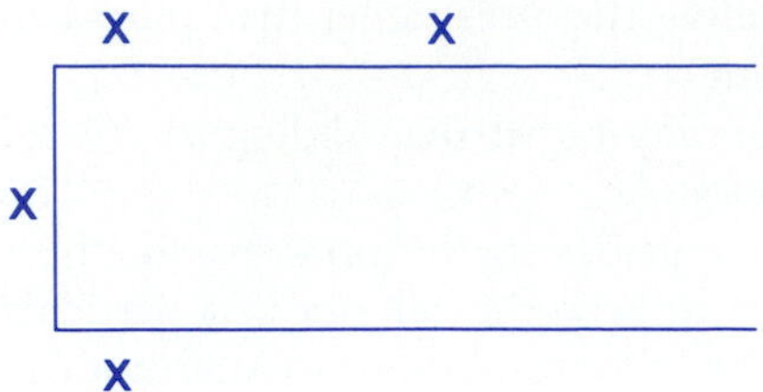

   d. Four players are spaced along the foul shooting lane as in *c.* One person has the ball and passes and moves away from the ball toward another player, who moves to the empty space. Try this slowly at first, then speed it up once the children can perform it. (Were you ready to move so you could quickly change places with the arriving player? Was it easy to find the empty space?)
   e. In groups of three, one person is stationary as if throwing the ball in from out of bounds. One is the receiver and attempts to move to an open space to receive a pass, while the third child attempts to intercept the pass. Change positions after a few attempts. (How did you move to get free of the defender? Were you able to pass to a space in front of the receiver? How did you anticipate where to throw the ball?) Change groups often so players have the opportunity to work against others. *Variation:* Throwing players move in general space while a third attempts to intercept.
3. To protect the ball as one moves among opponents by keeping the body between the opponents and the ball.
   a. Half dribble in space, and the other half is stationary. Players keeping one foot stationary attempt to knock the ball away from the dribblers. No personal contact is allowed. (What must you do to keep the ball from the opponents? How did you protect the ball?)
   b. In small spaces, one dribbles while another moves around in space. The dribblers attempt to keep their bodies between the balls and the other children. (How did you move the ball to protect it from the moving player?)
   c. All are dribbling in general space except for three or four children who attempt to knock the ball away from the dribblers. (How did you protect the ball?)
   d. Four persons with balls are in an area the size of the foul shooting lane. Each dribbles, trying to knock away the balls of others while protecting their own. (What did you do to protect the ball?) No personal contact is allowed. Players should attempt to time knocking the ball away when it is out of the hands.

4. To keep self space between one's opponent and the basket or the ball and the basket while on defense.

   a. One on one, with the offensive player trying to move the ball to a designated area and the defense trying to keep them out. (How did you position yourself to keep the player out of the space you were protecting?)
   b. Two on two: The offense passes to move the ball toward the basket. The defense attempts to stay between the offense and the basket and to maintain the relationship between each other. (What cues did you use to maintain your position in relation to the basket? To each other?)

5. To use as much space as possible on offense to keep the defense spread out.

   a. In small groups moving with balls in general space, try to move without getting tagged by the three or four taggers. Change the size of the space and repeat. (Was it easier to avoid the tag in a large or small space?) Limit space again. (How can you make the space seem as large as possible?)
   b. There are four persons, two on each team, and one ball. Each team attempts to see how many consecutive passes they can complete, while the other team attempts to intercept. No personal contact is allowed. Change size of area. (Which was easier, the smaller or larger space? Why?)

6. To close spaces open to the opponents and the ball, especially near the basket, while on defense.

   a. One on one: Each child has a partner. One has the ball and attempts to move the ball to the basket while the other is the guard and attempts to keep the other from shooting. Personal contact should be avoided. (How did you watch the forwards to anticipate their movements?)

7. To create open spaces for oneself, teammates, and the ball.

   a. Two on one: Two attempt to move the ball toward the goal, while one attempts to intercept a pass. (What did you do to move the guard out of the way to have an unguarded shot for the basket?)
   b. Three attempt to get a ball to a designated area by passing to each other, while two defenders attempt to tag the person with the ball. (How did you work together to create a space for the ball and/or your teammates?)
   c. Two on one: The two offense move the ball toward the basket by passing. As they near the basket, the one with the ball moves in the space, while the other moves in position next to the defensive player (setting a pick). The player with the ball cuts around their partner and in for a shot at the basket. (How did you position yourself to make a space for the player with the ball?)

8. To recognize one's area of space in which to play or defend.

   a. Children have partners, one person guarding a grid about 6 feet square. The player outside the grid tries to dribble the ball through the grid as the partner tries to keep him or her out. (What did you do to protect your space? What did you do to move the person out of the space?)

X 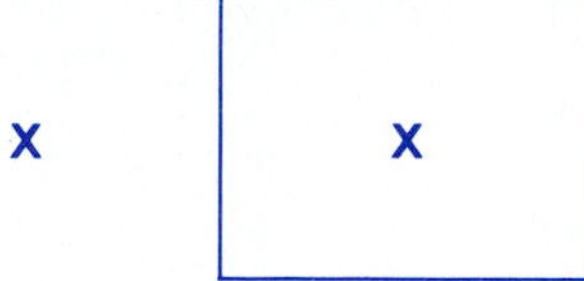

   b. Two on two: Two areas for the defense to guard are marked in front of the basket. The two offense players attempt to pass the ball in such a way as to penetrate the guarded spaces to get a shot for a basket. (How did you move the ball to get the defense out of their areas?)
   c. Two or three stationary guards are in the basket area. Two or three forwards attempt to pass and shoot, avoiding interception by the guards. (How did you work together to keep the forwards from scoring?)

9. To recognize and anticipate pathways while moving with and without the ball.

   a. One third of the group assumes a stationary position and is scattered in the general area. The other children are divided into partners, with one ball for each set of two. The partners move in the available pathways, dribbling and passing to each other as the stationary (defensive) players attempt to intercept. (How did you anticipate the movements of your partner and successfully pass in the available pathways? What cues did you use?)
   b. In groups of three moving in general space, two passing and one trying to intercept a pass. (How did you anticipate the path of the ball so that you would be in position to intercept?)

10. To alter the tempo of the game by speeding up and slowing down.

   a. Children are dribbling in general space against an opponent. On a signal to change speed, they either speed up or slow down. Repeat without signal, allowing individuals to change speed at will. (When was it easiest to change speed? How did you move to get around or get away from your opponent?)
   b. Passing in partners in general space. On the signal, children quicken their pace or slow down. (Were you able to change pace smoothly and keep up with your partner?)

Additional activities for practicing game concepts that may apply to basketball are found in Chapters 26 (hockey) and 29 (soccer).

Text continued on p. 518.

TABLE 25-1 BASKETBALL GAMES ANALYSIS

NAME	GAME CLASSIFICATION	NO. OF PARTICIPANTS	EQUIPMENT	SPACE AND ORGANIZATIONAL PATTERN	MOTOR SKILLS
Endball	Lead-up	Four to six per team	One 8-inch utility ball	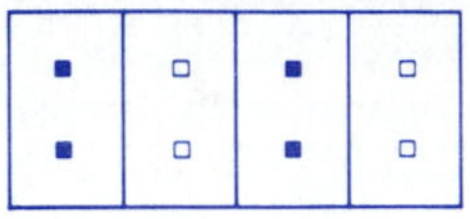	Passing Catching Dribbling Guarding
Basket Endball	Lead-up	Four to six per team	One 8-inch utility ball; two 7- to 8-foot baskets	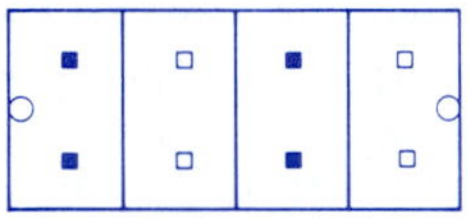	Passing Catching Dribbling Guarding Shooting
Zone Basketball	Lead-up	Four to five per team	One utility ball or junior basketball; two 7- to 8-foot baskets	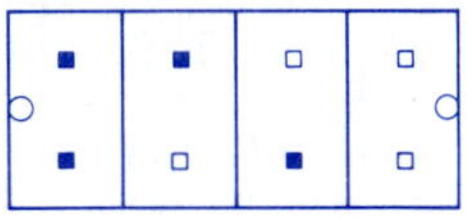	Passing Catching Dribbling Guarding Shooting
Basketball Team Challenge	Skill	Four to six per team	One junior basketball per team; one 7- to 8-foot basket for two teams		Passing Catching Dribbling Shooting

*Numbers refer to the basketball concepts in Figure 25-1 on p. 502

MODIFICATIONS	MOVEMENT CONCEPTS*	SOCIAL STRUCTURE	STRATEGY	LEVEL
1. Rotate players so all have a chance to play all positions 2. Limit types of throws used	Skills: 1, 7, 9, 10 Games: 1, 4, 8, 9	Social interaction I	1. Move the ball quickly 2. Cover the entire area on defense 3. Move to an unguarded area to receive the ball 4. Move the ball to a better throwing position before attempting to throw to teammates in the goal area	III
1. Rotate players so all have a chance to play all positions 2. Limit types of throws used	Skills: 1, 7, 9, 10 Games: 1, 4, 8, 9	Social interaction I	1. Move the ball quickly 2. Cover the entire area on defense 3. Move to an unguarded area to receive the ball 4. Move the ball to a better throwing position before attempting to throw to teammates in the goal area 5. Move close to the basket before taking your shot	III
1. Rotate players so all have a chance to play all positions 2. Limit types of throws used 3. Match opposing players of equal ability in the court areas	Skills: 1-10, 12, 13 Game: 1-4, 6, 9	Social interaction I	1. Move the ball quickly 2. Cover the entire area on defense 3. Move to an unguarded area to receive the ball 4. Move the ball to a better throwing position before attempting to throw to teammates in the goal area 5. Move close to the basket before taking your shot 6. Keep between opponents and goal when on de-fense	III
1. Match opposing players by ability 2. Designate a particular pass to be used	Skills: 2, 6, 9, 10, 13 Game: 1	Social interaction I	1. Pass quickly 2. Begin with pass to player furthest from basket and move ball toward the basket on each throw	III

Continued.

TABLE 25-1 BASKETBALL GAMES ANALYSIS—cont'd

NAME	GAME CLASSIFICATION	NO. OF PARTICIPANTS	EQUIPMENT	SPACE AND ORGANIZATIONAL PATTERN	MOTOR SKILLS
Assist Basketball	Lead-up	Four players per game	One utility or junior basketball per game; 7-8 foot basket	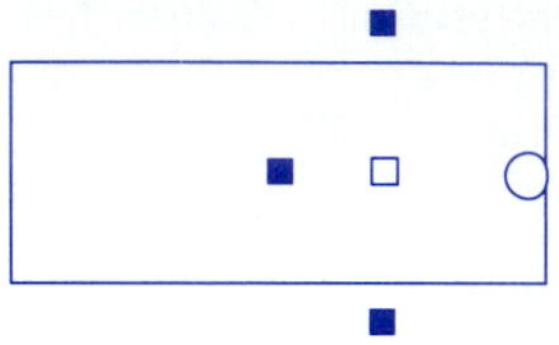	Dribbling Passing Shooting Guarding
Circle Pass Basketball	Lead-up	Two players per team	One junior basketball for each game; 7-8 foot basket	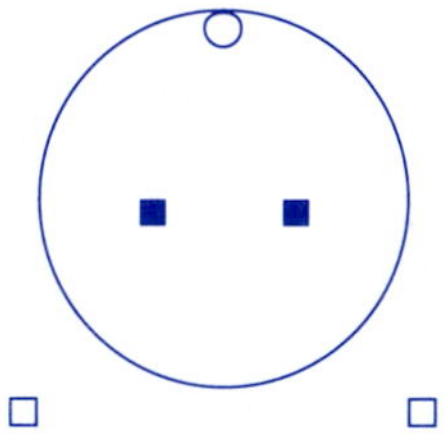	Passing Dribbling Shooting Guarding
Toss-Up Basketball	Lead-up	Four to six per team	One junior basketball; one 7- or 8-foot basket		Passing Catching Dribbling Shooting Guarding
Sideline Basketball	Lead-up	Four to five per team	One junior size basketball; two 8-foot baskets	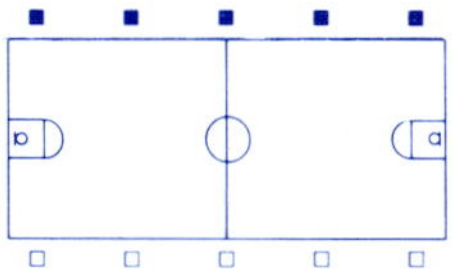	Passing Catching Dribbling Shooting Guarding Pivot, reverse turn Rebounding
Alley Basketball	Lead-up	Five per team	One junior size basketball; two 8-foot baskets	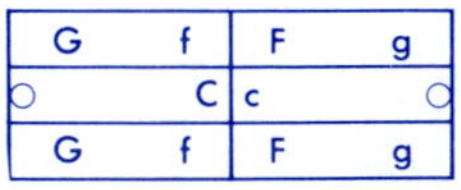	Passing Catching Dribbling Shooting Guarding

MODIFICATIONS	MOVEMENT CONCEPTS*	SOCIAL STRUCTURE	STRATEGY	LEVEL
Require a set number of passes before shooting	Skills: 1-13 Game: 1-10	Social interaction I	1. Use short quick passes 2. Move to an open space to receive a pass 3. Defense stays between forward and the basket 4. Disguise passes to the sideline	III
	Skills: 1-13 Game: 1-10	Social interaction II	1. Use as much space as possible on offense 2. Use short crisp passes and move quickly to an open space to receive the ball 3. Defense must work together to close space near the basket	IV
1. To avoid collisions ball must bounce first before catching it on initial ball toss 2. Distance for free throw adjusted for ability of players 3. It is helpful to call out the number of passes	Skills: 2-13 Game: 1-7, 9	Social interaction I-II (depending on the number of players called)	1. Move ball toward the basket 2. When on defense, stay between opponent and basket (after the two passes are completed) 3. Move to an unguarded area to receive the ball	III
1. Match opponents by ability 2. As individuals become ready, call more than one number at a time 3. When calling more than one number, begin play with a jump ball	Skills: 2-13 Game: 1-7, 9	Social interaction II	1. Move ball toward the basket 2. When on defense, stay between opponent and basket (after the two passes are completed) 3. Move to an unguarded area to receive the ball 4. Use sideline and teammates on court	IV
1. Match opponents by ability	Skills: 2-13 Game: 1-10	Social interaction II	1. Move ball toward the basket 2. When on defense, stay between opponent and basket (after the two passes are completed) 3. Move to an unguarded area to receive the ball	IV

BASKETBALL LEAD-UP GAMES

Table 25-1 includes a game analysis for all the games included here.

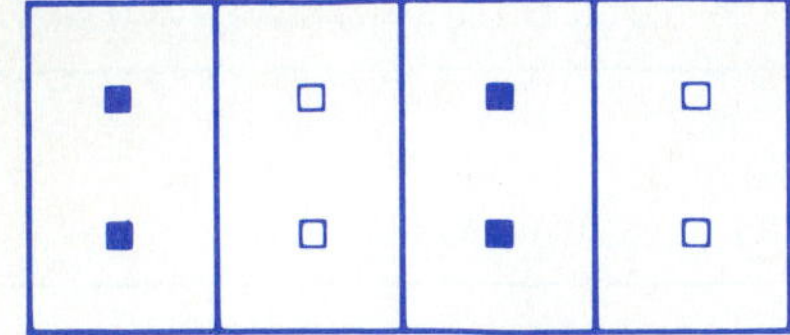

ENDBALL

Level: III

Equipment: One 8-inch utility ball

Area: A rectangular area divided into four courts, the court on each end being the goal area. The size of the playing area depends on the ability of the players.

Participants: Four to six per team

Skills: Passing, catching, dribbling, guarding

Description: Play is begun by giving the ball to a player in one of the inside areas, who attempts to pass the ball to a teammate in the goal area. One point is scored when the ball is thrown to a teammate in the goal area so that it may be caught on a fly or after one bounce. After any score or a missed attempt at scoring, the ball is given to the opposing team in the adjacent court. If the ball is intercepted by the opponents in the scoring effort, they attempt to throw the ball to their players for a score.

Violations: Stepping out of the assigned area, walking with the ball, holding the ball more than 3 seconds, illegal dribble

Penalty: The ball is given to the opponents.

Strategy:

1. Move the ball quickly toward the goal.
2. Move as close as you can to throw the ball to players in the end zone.
3. Cover the entire area on defense.
4. Move to an unguarded area to receive the ball.

Teaching suggestions:

1. Rotate players periodically so that each has an opportunity to play both positions.
2. Emphasize moving the ball to a better throwing position by dribbling or passing to a teammate in the same zone.

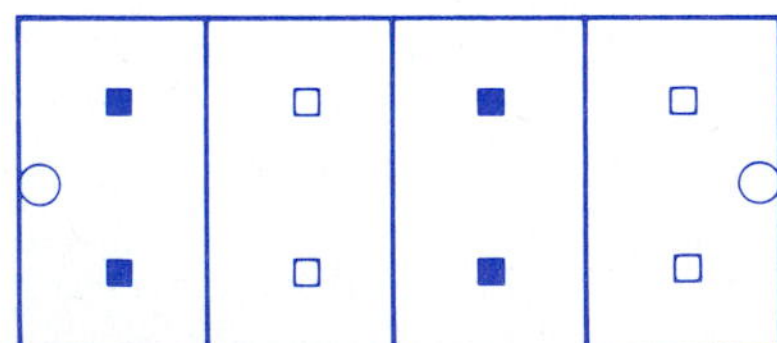

BASKET ENDBALL

Level: III

Equipment: Two 7- to 8-foot baskets and one utility or small basketball

Description: The rules of Endball are used with the addition of one chance to shoot a basket after a successful catch. If the basket is made, two additional points are scored. Encourage children to move close to the basket after receiving the pass to attempt their shots.

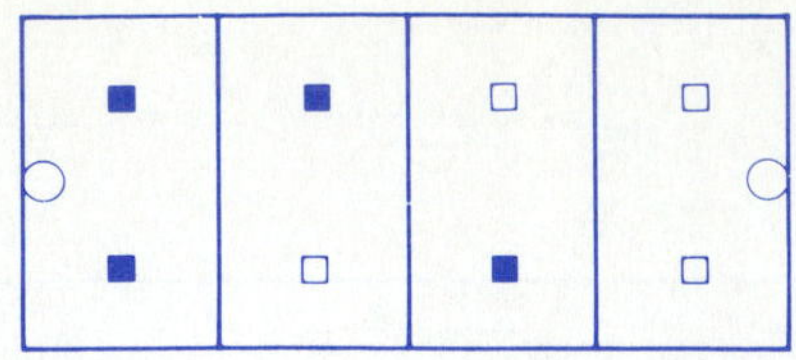

ZONE BASKETBALL

Level: III

Equipment: One 8-inch utility ball, small or junior-size basketball and two 7- to 8-foot baskets per game

Area: A rectangular area divided into four courts as shown in the figure, the size depending on the ability of the players. The end courts are the scoring areas.

Participants: Four to five per team. (The number of courts may be increased to accommodate five players.)

Skills: Passing, catching, dribbling, guarding, shooting

Description: Play is begun by giving the ball to a player of one team in the inside court farthest from the team's goal area. Players attempt to complete a pass to a teammate in the next zone or in the goal area. A point is scored when a player in the goal area catches the ball on a fly or after one bounce. If the ball is caught successfully, one shot for goal may be taken. If made, an additional two points are scored. After a score or attempted score, the ball is given to the opponents in the adjacent court.

Violations: Stepping out of the assigned area, walking with the ball, holding the ball more than 5 seconds, illegal dribble, or personal contact.

Penalty: The ball is given to the opposing team at the nearest sideline.

Fouls: Personal contact

Penalty: One unguarded throw given to the player fouled

Strategy:

1. Move the ball quickly toward the goal.
2. Move as close as you can to throw the ball to players in the end zone.
3. Cover the entire area on defense.
4. Move to an unguarded area to receive the ball.
5. Move close to the basket before attempting to shoot.
6. Keep between opponents and the goal area while on defense.

Teaching suggestions:

1. Rotate positions so that all have an opportunity to play each position.
2. Match players of equal ability in the inside court areas.

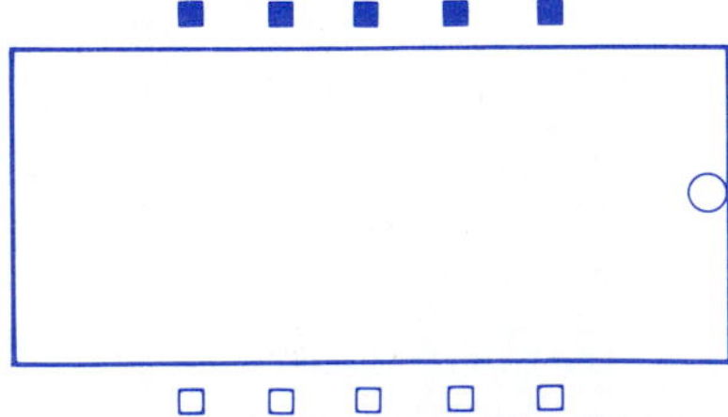

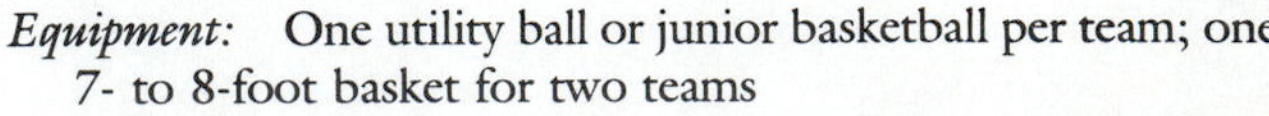

BASKETBALL TEAM CHALLENGE

Level: III

Equipment: One utility ball or junior basketball per team; one 7- to 8-foot basket for two teams

Area: A rectangular playing area with a basket at one end for each game

Participants: Four to six per team

Skills: Passing, catching, dribbling, shooting

Description: Each team is lined up along opposite sides of the court area. The players at the end of the line farthest from the basket begin by running out to the basketballs placed in front of each team, picking them up, and passing them to each member of their team. When the passing is completed, each player shoots for a goal. If the basket is missed two more attempts may be made. When a basket is made or three attempts have been made, players dribble back to their places in line, passing the ball to the player next to them. That player passes the ball back to the end player and then to each player on the team, repeating the action of player one. After all have had a turn, the successful baskets are added. The game is then repeated, with each team attempting to improve its own record.

Strategy:

1. Begin passing with person farthest from the goal and move the ball to the basket.
2. Make short, soft, quick passes.

Teaching suggestions: This is a good activity to use before the introduction of Toss-Up or Sideline Basketball. Match players of similar ability to provide equal competition for each team. Any number of teams may participate at the same time, with no more than two teams per basket.

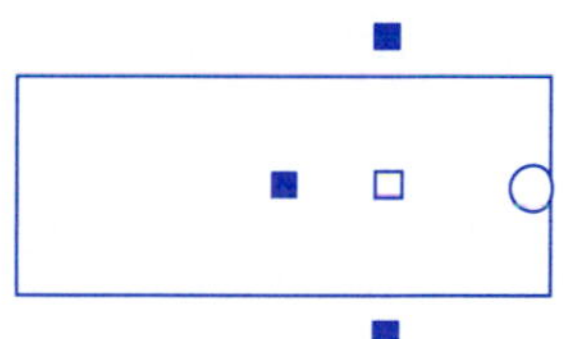

ASSIST BASKETBALL

Level: III

Equipment: One utility or junior basketball and one 7- to 8-foot basket for each game

Area: A small rectangular playing area with a basket at one end

Participants: Four players per game

Skills: Passing, dribbling, catching, guarding

Description: One player, the forward, begins with the ball at the end of the playing area opposite the basket. The forward, with the assistance of two sideline players (located along the side boundary lines), attempts to move the ball toward the basket by passing to either sideline players. The defense player attempts to keep the forward from moving themselves and the ball into a shooting position. If the defensive player intercepts the ball or a basket is scored, play begins again from the starting line, with the defense player changing roles with the forward.

Strategy:

1. Move the ball toward the basket by dribbling and quick short passes.
2. The forward should move to an open space to receive the ball back from the sideline players.
3. Try to disguise your passes to the sideline.

Teaching suggestions: After a time, the active players should change places with the sideline players. It may be a good idea to rotate two of the players to other games to provide the children with an opportunity to play against a variety of players.

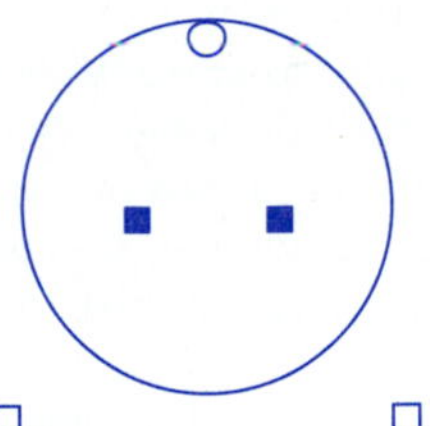

CIRCLE PASS BASKETBALL

Level: IV

Equipment: One junior basketball or utility ball and a 7- to 8-foot basket for each game

Area: A circle area with a basket on one side

Participants: Two players for each team, four per game

Skills: Passing, dribbling, catching, shooting, guarding

Description: The two offensive players begin outside the circle at the side opposite the basket. They attempt to pass the ball, completing at least three passes while penetrating the circle, which is guarded by the other two players. They may move in and out of the circle at will, and the three passes do not have to be consecutive. Once the three passes are complete, they may shoot for a basket from within the circle area while the defenders try to prevent them from getting a successful shot. If the ball is intercepted or a basket is made, the players reverse roles and play begins again.

Strategy:

1. Use as much space as possible to keep the defense spread out.
2. Use short crisp passes and move quickly to an open space to receive the ball.

Teaching suggestions: You may wish to limit the game to passing only, with no dribbling allowed.

TOSS-UP BASKETBALL

Level: III

Equipment: One junior basketball for each game and one 7- to 8-foot basket

Area: A rectangular area half the size of an available basketball court

Participants: Four to six per team

Skills: Passing, catching, dribbling, shooting, guarding

Description: Each team is numbered off and lined up along opposite sidelines. The teacher calls a number and tosses the ball in the air. The players from each team with that number attempt to catch the ball after it has bounced once, complete passes to at least two teammates on the sideline, and attempt one shot at goal. If the shot is made, two points are scored; if missed, play is stopped and a new number is called. The person not getting the ball attempts to gain control by intercepting a pass. If the player is successful, a shot on goal may be attempted after passes to two sideline players. Whenever possession of the ball changes, two passes must be made before a player attempts a shot on goal.

Violations: Stepping outside the playing area, ball going out of bounds, traveling, illegal dribble, or shooting before two passes are completed

Penalty: Ball is put in play by a sideline player of the opposite team

Fouls: Personal contact

Penalty: One free throw awarded. One point is scored if the shot is made. If the shot is missed, play resumes with a new number being called

Strategy:

1. Move toward the basket.
2. When on defense, stay between opponent and basket.
3. Move to an unguarded area to receive the ball.

Teaching suggestions:

1. Distance for free throw should be appropriate for the ability of the players.
2. Children should be matched with others of equal ability.
3. It may be helpful to count orally the number of passes for them as they play the game.

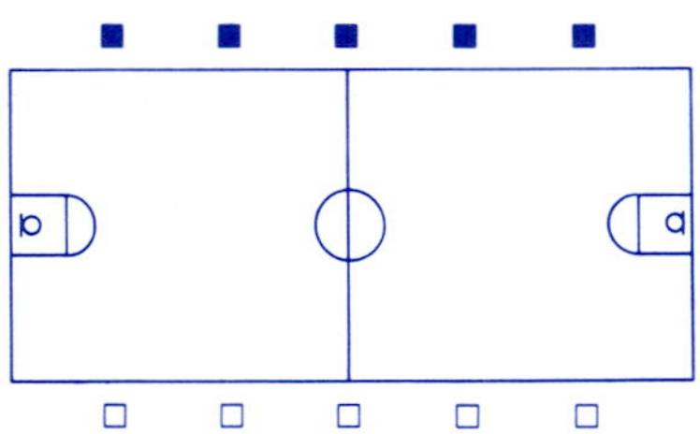

SIDELINE BASKETBALL

Level: IV

Equipment: One junior basketball for each game and two 8-foot baskets

Area: An appropriate sized basketball court for the ability of the players

Participants: Four to six players per team

Skills: Passing, catching, dribbling, shooting, guarding, rebounding, jump ball

Description: Each team is numbered and lined up along opposite sidelines. The leader calls two numbers. Play begins with a jump ball between two opposing players. Passes must be made to two different team members, including the other player on the court and/or sideline players before an attempt for a basket may be made. If the basket is made, play continues with two new numbers being called. If the basket is missed, the ball is in play. If a member of the shooting team receives it, that player may shoot again immediately. If a member of the opposing team receives the ball, that player must complete at least two passes in moving the ball to his or her own basket before shooting.

Violations: Traveling, illegal dribble, moving self or ball out of bounds, shooting before two passes are completed

Penalty: Ball is put in play from the sidelines by the opposite team

Fouls: Personal contact

Penalty: One free throw awarded to the opposite team. If made, one point is scored; if missed, play resumes with new numbers being called.

Strategy:

1. Move the ball quickly toward the goal.
2. Move to an unguarded area to receive a pass.
3. Stay between the opponent and the goal when on defense.
4. Cover as much area on defense as possible.
5. Keep the offense spread out.

Teaching suggestions:

1. This game may be played one on one, two on two, three on three, and so forth as individual players' ability warrants.
2. If available space is limited, the game may be played as a half-court game, with the ball moving to the opposite end (center line) if rebounded by the defensive team.
3. Children should be matched with others of equal ability.
4. It may be helpful to count out orally the number of passes made for them as they play the game.

ALLEY BASKETBALL

Level: IV

Equipment: One junior basketball for each game and two 8-foot baskets

Area: An appropriate sized basketball court for the ability and size of the players divided into three alleys

Participants: Five per team: one center, two forwards, and two guards. The center plays the entire length of the center alley, and the two forwards and two guards play only to the midcourt line.

Skills: Passing, catching, dribbling, guarding, shooting

Description: Play begins with a jump ball between the two opposing centers at midcourt. They attempt to tap the ball to one of their teammates. Play continues with each team attempting to pass and, when in position, to shoot for a basket. If a basket is made, two points are awarded. After a score, play continues with the opposing team passing the ball in from behind the nearest endline.

Violations: Stepping out of the alley, walking with the ball, holding the ball more than 5 seconds, illegal dribble, or center taking possession of the ball on the jump

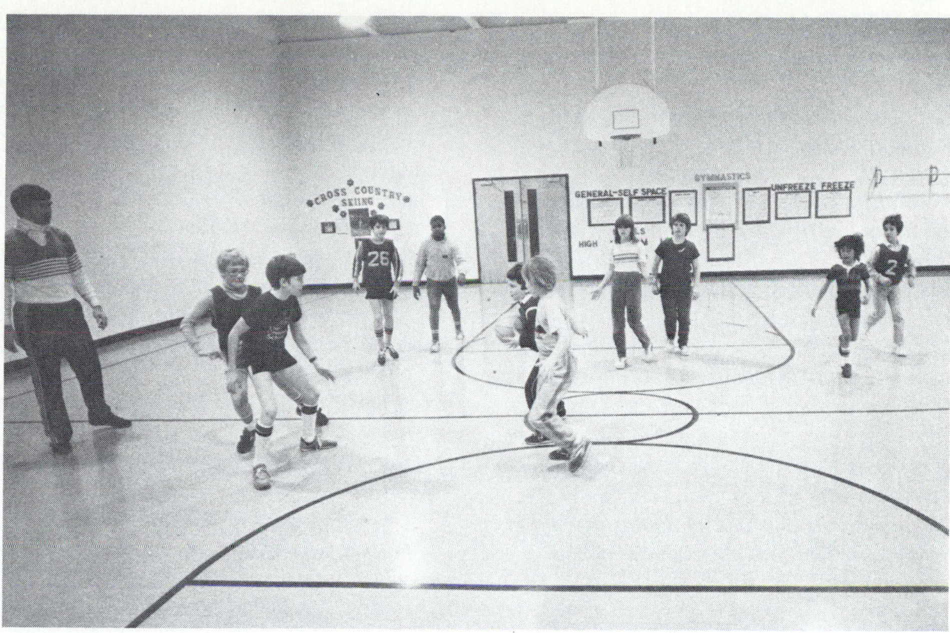

Alley basketball.

Penalty: The ball is given to the opposing team at the nearest sideline

Fouls: Personal contact

Penalty: One free throw awarded the opposing team to be taken by the player fouled (if it is a forward or center). If a guard is fouled, the shot is taken by a forward or center on the team. If the shot is made, one point is awarded and play resumes with the opposing team putting the ball in play from behind the endline.

Strategy:

1. Move the ball quickly toward the goal.
2. Move to an unguarded space to receive a pass.
3. Stay between the opposing forward and the basket while on defense.

Teaching suggestions:

1. It may be necessary to require two or more passes before shooting to encourage teamwork.
2. After a goal is scored, children should rotate positions clockwise or in some other way to ensure matching opponents.
3. Emphasize continually moving in the alley to be free to receive a pass.
4. This game may be modified to allow all five players to move in their alleys the entire length of the court.

SUMMARY

Basketball is a popular activity with children. For elementary school children to be successful, modifications of the playing area, equipment, and game are necessary. A smaller playing area, 7- or 8-foot baskets, and junior basketballs or utility balls are used. Because having 10 players on the court at a time requires an understanding of a complex relationship of teammates and opponents, the numbers are reduced, beginning with a simple one on one and gradually increasing the number of players actively involved. The court may be divided into specific areas of play for individual teams as in Endball or for opposing players as in Zone and Alley Basketball.

The movement content is extremely important for success in basketball activities and should be stressed during skill development and game activities. Activities that emphasize the application of the movement content should be introduced to enhance the children's understanding and use of the movement concepts in basketball games as they practice skills and participate. A progression of lead-up activities is used to assist children in developing the skills and knowledge associated with basketball.

REFERENCES AND RESOURCES

Athletic Institute, editors: *Youth league basketball: coaching and playing,* New York, 1984, Athletic Institute.

Barnes M: *Women's basketball,* ed 2, Newton, Mass, 1980, Allyn & Bacon.

Benham T: Modifications of basketball equipment and children's performance, Paper presented at the National Convention of the American Alliance for Health, Physical Education, Recreation and Dance, Cincinnati, 1986.

Moolenijzer N: United States korfball federation korfball rules, Albuquerque, 1979, University of New Mexico.

Oxendine JB: *American Indian Sports Heritage,* Champaign, Ill, 1988, Human Kinetics.

Scott J: *Step by step basketball fundamentals for the player and coach,* revised ed, Englewood Cliffs, NJ, 1989, Prentice-Hall.

Seidel B et al: *Sports skills: a conceptual approach to meaningful movement,* ed 2, Dubuque, Ia, 1980, Wm C Brown.

Sullivan G: *Better basketball for boys,* New York, 1989, Dodd, Mead & Co.

ANNOTATED READINGS

Adrian M and House G: Sporting miscues, part 2, *Strategies* 1(2):13, 1987.

Discusses miscues given in basketball regarding angle of rebound in shooting and guarding.

Barnes M: Conditioning, *JOPERD* 54(1):30, 1983.

Describes basketball drills to develop strength and endurance, some of which could be used or modified for elementary school children.

Blakemore C et al: Comparison of students taught basketball skills using mastery and nonmastery learning methods, *JTPE* 11(3):235, 1992.

A research study of mastery and nonmastery learning models that demonstrated the importance of mastery learning in skill development.

Farrell J and Weikart P: The forgotten skills: add them to your conditioning program, *JOPERD* 54(1):32, 1983.

Provides activities to develop the body control skills of moving in all directions, changing direction, moving on the diagonal, and changing the support foot.

Frederick J: Lead passes: teaching for success, *Strategies* 1(5):7, 1988.

Emphasizes three major points in successful passing—guarding to the goal, passing in front of receiver, and catching and passing continuously.

Gudger J: The daily dozen, *JOPERD* 54(1):36, 1983.

Describes basketball drills, some of which can be adapted for elementary school children.

Hellison D and Georgiadia N: Teaching values through basketball, *Strategies* 5(4):5, 1992.

Uses basketball to teach the Hellison levels of behavior.

Noone ET: A basketball simulation, *Arithematic Teacher* 38(7):36, 1991.

A model for teaching mathematics through a basketball simulation.

Nutter J: Pass ball: a new game in town, *JOPERD* 56(5):55, 1985.

Describes a lead-up game for basketball that, with some modification, might be played in elementary school.

CHAPTER 26

Field and Floor Hockey

OBJECTIVES

After completing this chapter the student will be able to:

1. Analyze field and floor hockey skills and provide activities and suggestions for their development
2. Apply movement concepts to hockey and identify activities in which these concepts may be developed before their use in lead-ups to the games of field and floor hockey
3. Identify a progression of lead-up activities to be used in the elementary school to introduce the games of field and floor hockey

Field hockey was introduced in the United States in the early 1900s and has become a popular activity for girls and women, particularly on the east coast. Internationally, it is played by both men and women. Originally, its popularity was predominantly in countries where Great Britain was involved in early colonization, such as India and South Africa. It is now popular on the European continent with both men and women, especially in Holland. Men's field hockey first appeared in the Olympic Games in 1932 in Los Angeles, with a men's team from the United States participating at that time. Women's teams made their first appearance in 1980 in Moscow. In 1984 the U.S. men's team participated for a second time and a U.S. women's team played for the first time in the Olympic Games in Los Angeles. The women's team won a bronze medal.

Floor hockey has had a more recent development. Much of its interest today may be the result of the development of plastic elementary school-sized hockey equipment as well as an interest in ice hockey. It is gaining in popularity across the United States as a challenging winter activity.

Success in field hockey depends on the participant's ability to control the ball with one side of the stick while moving it in all directions and pathways. This must be accomplished without **obstructing** the opponent (standing with one's body between an opponent's body and the ball). The player must be able to vary the force, as in a soft pass to a teammate or a hard shot on goal. Using space effectively is also essential to success in field hockey. The participant is continually adjusting to the changing relationships of teammates, opponents, and the ball.

Because field hockey is a large-group activity, with 11 players on each team, complex interactions of players are required. Recently, the game has been adapted to indoor play with six players on a team.

In floor hockey the puck can be handled with both sides of the stick. Skills required are similar to those used in ice hockey. Players learn to shield the puck by keeping their bodies between their opponents and the puck as they move in the playing area, changing direction and pathway. Passing and shooting require the ability to control and vary force. Players must learn to use the space effectively, closing space while on defense and opening space while on the attack.

The game of floor hockey is played with six players per team, and because all but the goalkeeper may move anywhere on the court, a number of different offensive and defensive strategies are possible.

Both games require a team effort; each player has a particular role to play as well as supporting teammates in other positions. In the past two decades, many new styles of play have been introduced that have added to the complexity of the game.

The Native American Game

Native Americans throughout North America have played a game similar to field hockey called Shinny. This game was played primarily by women and girls, but boys and men played it as well. A curved stick much like a field hockey stick is used to drive the ball through the opponent's goal. The ball, ranging in size from a golf ball to a baseball, was made of buckskin, wood, or bone, depending on the location of the team. Teams ranged from 10 to 100 players. Unlike today's game of field hockey, one predominant strategy was to hit the ball over everyone's head to cover as much distance as possible.

HOCKEY FOR ELEMENTARY SCHOOL CHILDREN

Field hockey is well established in some schools, and floor hockey is becoming increasingly popular as an indoor activity throughout the United States. Hockey offers children one of the few opportunities for a group experience in which the ball is moved with an implement—the hockey stick.

Equipment: Teaching field hockey in the elementary school requires the use of light-weight, junior-sized, right-hand sticks. Recently developed plastic field hockey training sticks promote realistic play and performance. A soft 3-inch vinyl ball is used with these new sticks, which are preferable for elementary school children. Junior size wooden sticks and regulation balls also may be used. For indoor play, soft or foam balls allow greater control on a smooth surface.

In floor hockey plastic sticks with a curved or flat blade may be used. The sticks are often longer than those used in field hockey. Wiffle or foam balls or plastic pucks may be used.

Shin guards, worn on the outside or under knee socks, should be required of all players, and goalkeepers must wear protective equipment, including a mask to protect the face. When plastic sticks are used, shin guards may not be needed. In floor hockey all children should wear goggles to protect the eyes. The size of the playing area should be reduced according to the age and ability of the players, with each lead-up game requiring a different size space. The surface should be as smooth as possible, and for field hockey the grass should be cut short. An 8- to 10-foot goal is large enough for elementary school children to defend. A smaller goal, 5 feet, is used for floor hockey.

Skills: At the elementary school level, emphasis in skill development should be placed on stick handling and ball control. Some skills such as Indian dribbling (described later in this chapter) call for great versatility in the use of the stick, and should be introduced at an early age. Floor hockey permits controlling the ball with either side of the stick. Emphasis should also be placed on controlled use of skills. The player should not hit the ball as hard as possible, but only hard enough for the task at hand. Therefore the push pass should be introduced before the hit. In developing skills, it is best to begin work on the techniques with a stationary opponent. Later, as skill is acquired, practice should include working against another person who is actively involved in trying to prevent the skill from being successfully executed. Safety in the use of the stick must also be stressed. Keeping the stick down, holding it correctly, and executing purposeful, controlled movements with the stick should be encouraged throughout the unit to avoid unnecessary injuries. In hitting the ball or puck, the stick should always be kept below shoulder level.

The game: The large number of participants and the large playing area required for field hockey pose problems for elementary school children. The complexity of position play as players interact with one another for both field and floor hockey is difficult for elementary school children to understand. **Marking** (being responsible for an opponent while on defense) must be carefully taught and reinforced throughout the activity. Learning to position and reposition one's self in space in relation to opponents, teammates, the ball, and the goal is not an easy task and takes time to develop. It is best accomplished by breaking down the game into smaller segments in which fewer participants are involved and gradually increasing the number of players and the complexity of the situation as skill and understanding develop.

In both games the responsibilities of the offense are to maintain possession of the ball and to score goals. To accomplish these objectives the team must:

1. Move ball or puck toward the opponent's goal.
2. Control passes to teammates.
3. Move to open spaces to receive passes.
4. Rush each shot on goal.
5. Change the expected path of the ball or puck to keep the defense off guard.
6. Be on the move to adjust one's position in relation to teammates, opponents, and the ball or puck.
7. Keep the ball or puck until a defensive player has become committed to make spaces for the ball or puck and teammates.

The responsibilities of the defense are to prevent the opponents from scoring, regain possession of the ball or puck, and quickly move the ball or puck away from the goal they are defending. To be successful the defense must:

1. Stay between the opponents, ball or puck, and goal.
2. Continually move to reposition oneself to close spaces to opponents.
3. Advance to tackle or harass the opponents.
4. Move the ball or puck quickly away from the goal area.
5. Mark opponents closely in the goal area.
6. Watch closely the opponent being marked and not the ball or puck.
7. Anticipate the movements of opponents, teammates, and the ball or puck.
8. On receiving the ball or puck, pass it quickly to the offense.

Social Skills

The social skills developed in floor and field hockey require children to interact with small and large groups. Not only must teammates share in the game plan, but the children must also control their movements to play safely against one other child or team. Taking the responsibility for one's own play to ensure the safety of others is an important part of any hockey activity.

Health-Related Physical Fitness

Field and floor hockey can be vigorous games that provide an opportunity to develop cardiorespiratory fitness. If maximum activity is provided for each participant through individual practice and partner and small group play and if activity is sustained at an appropriate level, cardiorespiratory fitness may be enhanced. Vigorous warm-up activities for dribbling can get the children off to a good start in the lesson.

HOCKEY SKILLS

Hockey skills demand good body awareness as individuals attempt to control a small ball with a stick while they move in the playing area. Space concepts and qualities of movement also come into play as individuals maintain an appropriate relationship of body, stick, and ball; combine skills smoothly; and vary the force as the situation demands. In teaching hockey skills, control of the stick always must be stressed. Figure 26-1 maps the movement concepts important in hockey.

Dribbling

Dribbling is used to move the ball without the help of teammates when a good pass is not possible. It is also used to draw an opponent out of position or to maneuver around an opponent.

Field Hockey

The left hand controls the movement of the stick, while the right hand acts as support. The dribbler's body leans slightly forward, and the head should be up to watch the ball and the field of play. The ball is controlled 18 to 24 inches diagonally in front of the right foot (Figure 26-2).

Common errors:

1. Facing the back of the left hand in the line of the dribble.
2. Bending left wrist so that it is not in a straight line with the forearm.
3. Holding the stick vertically to the ground or laid back.
4. Pushing the ball with the stick rather than tapping it.
5. Bending the body over the ball, with eyes on the ball only.
6. Dribbling the ball too close or too far away from the body.
7. Placing the right hand too far down the stick.

Indian dribbling allows the ball to be controlled in front of the body rather than to the side. It is used to move the ball around an opponent's stick or to move it to a more favorable position. The ball is tapped alternately with a forehand and then a **reverse stick.** Indian dribbling is a difficult skill and will require considerable practice to develop proficiency. The result is better stick control, and this skill should be introduced as soon as the children are ready.

The stick is gripped so that the back of the left hand points upward toward the right, and the back of the right hand points backward. Contact is made with the ball by first tapping it in the conventional manner toward the left. The next tap is taken with a reverse stick by turning the stick over the ball in a counterclockwise direction with the left hand and with the ball moving forward to the right. The Indian dribble is called the "over-over" dribble, which helps the student remember the stick movement. The right hand grips the stick loosely to allow the stick to turn under it. The stick is then turned back again for a tap on the forehand side, and play continues alternately hitting from the forehand and reverse stick positions. As the ball is tapped diagonally to the right and to the left, it stays within the body's width (Figure 26-3).

Common errors:

1. Facing the back of the hand in the line of the dribble.
2. Placing the right hand too far down the stick.
3. Tapping the ball so that it moves well beyond the width of the body.
4. Watching the ball instead of looking ahead.
5. Rolling the right hand rather than letting the stick move under it for the reverse stick tap.
6. Having the stick angle to the ground too vertical.
7. Turning the stick clockwise rather than counterclockwise when changing to reverse stick. This error is critical because if the stick is turned clockwise it is impossible to execute a reverse stick hit or push correctly.

In teaching this technique, it may help to begin practice by moving the stick to and from the reverse stick position without actually hitting the ball. Have children place a ball directly in front of the body with the stick at a 45-degree angle to the ground and feet shoulder-width apart. Begin turning the stick over the ball without touching it, using only the left hand, and then return it to its original position. Repeat a few times. Now add the right hand as a stabilizer, and let the stick turn under the grip. When ready, players should try dribbling the ball from both positions, controlling it within the width of the body. Indian dribbling is an excellent activity to help develop stick control.

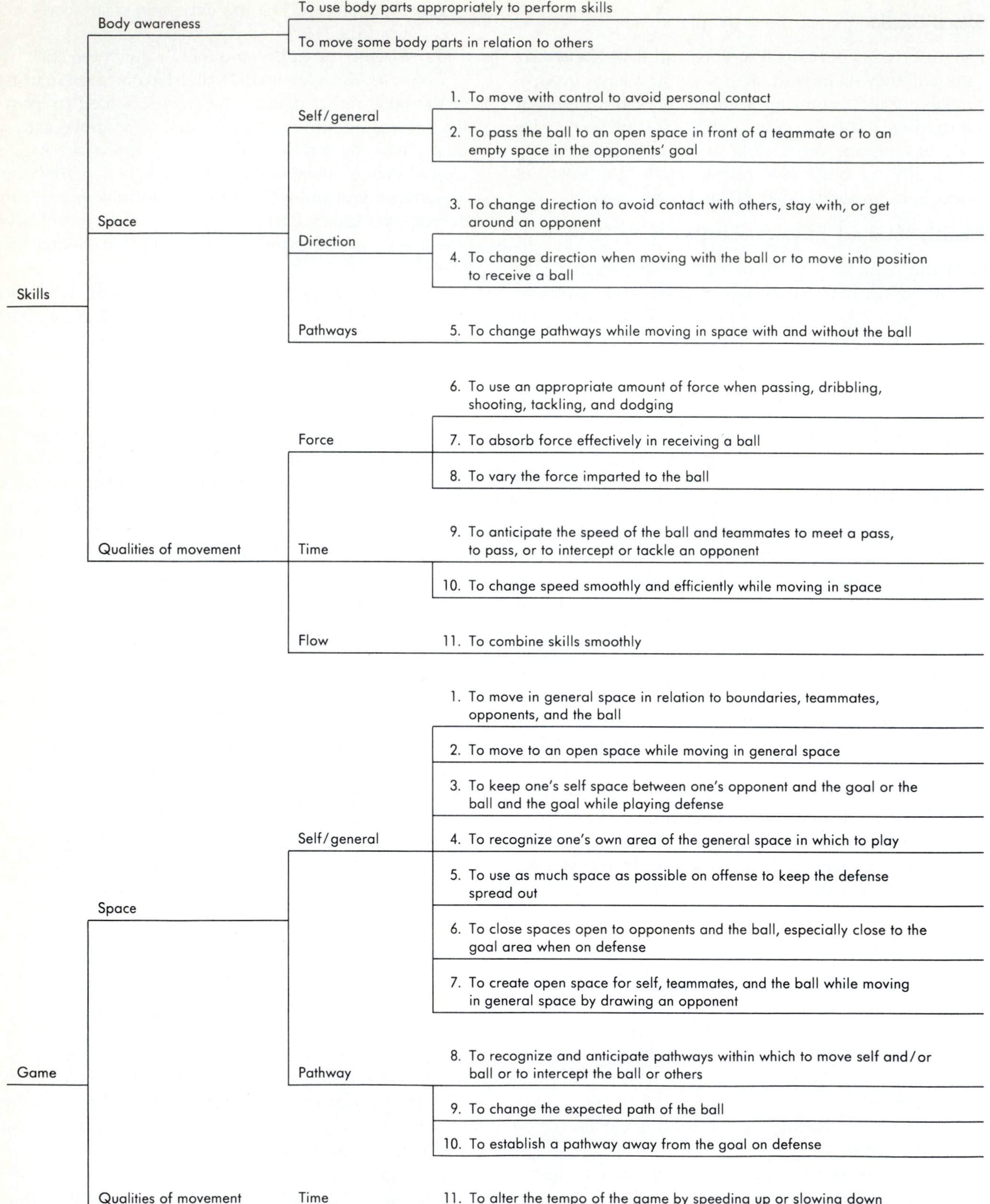
Skills
Body awareness
To use body parts appropriately to perform skills
To move some body parts in relation to others
Space
Self/general
1. To move with control to avoid personal contact
2. To pass the ball to an open space in front of a teammate or to an empty space in the opponents' goal
Direction
3. To change direction to avoid contact with others, stay with, or get around an opponent
4. To change direction when moving with the ball or to move into position to receive a ball
Pathways
5. To change pathways while moving in space with and without the ball
Qualities of movement
Force
6. To use an appropriate amount of force when passing, dribbling, shooting, tackling, and dodging
7. To absorb force effectively in receiving a ball
8. To vary the force imparted to the ball
Time
9. To anticipate the speed of the ball and teammates to meet a pass, to pass, or to intercept or tackle an opponent
10. To change speed smoothly and efficiently while moving in space
Flow
11. To combine skills smoothly
Game
Space
Self/general
1. To move in general space in relation to boundaries, teammates, opponents, and the ball
2. To move to an open space while moving in general space
3. To keep one's self space between one's opponent and the goal or the ball and the goal while playing defense
4. To recognize one's own area of the general space in which to play
5. To use as much space as possible on offense to keep the defense spread out
6. To close spaces open to opponents and the ball, especially close to the goal area when on defense
7. To create open space for self, teammates, and the ball while moving in general space by drawing an opponent
Pathway
8. To recognize and anticipate pathways within which to move self and/or ball or to intercept the ball or others
9. To change the expected path of the ball
10. To establish a pathway away from the goal on defense
Qualities of movement
Time
11. To alter the tempo of the game by speeding up or slowing down

FIGURE 26-1 Hockey concepts.

- Lay stick on ground with flat side down; grasp stick with left hand.

- The right hand is 4 to 8 inches below the left; the left wrist and forearm form a straight line, wrist firm, arm out away from the body.
- The stick is held at a 45-degree angle to the ground, the ball 18 to 24 inches diagonally in front of the right foot.
- The ball is moved by a series of light taps as the player moves down the field; the head is up and body fairly erect.

FIGURE 26-2 Evaluative criteria and teaching points for the dribble.

- Left hand grips stick from above; the right hand is 4 to 8 inches below the left.
- The ball is positioned in front of the player, the stick at a 45-degree angle to the ground.
- The ball is tapped to the left.

- The ball is tapped to the right with the reverse side of the stick.
- Ball stays within the width of the body.

FIGURE 26-3 Evaluative criteria and teaching points for Indian dribble.

- Hands a comfortable distance apart, elbows out, head up.
- Stick blade cupped over the puck at the center of the blade.

- Puck controlled in front of and within the width of the body.

FIGURE 26-4 Evaluative criteria and teaching points for side-to-side dribble.

- Hands apart on the stick, puck kept to the side of the body, head up.
- Stick blade cupped over puck at the center of the blade.

- Puck slightly ahead of forward foot, blade in front cupped in front of puck.

- Stick moved behind puck.

FIGURE 26-5 Evaluative criteria and teaching points for the forward-and-backward dribble.

Floor Hockey

In floor hockey the dribble is executed by alternately contacting the ball with each side of the stick. The hands are farther apart on the stick than in field hockey, 10 to 12 inches to compensate for the longer stick. The stick should be held firmly, but not tightly, for better stick control. As in field hockey, dribbling is controlled by the top hand. The puck should be controlled in the center of the stick blade. A pushing action rather than a tapping action is used. Two types of dribbling are used.

In the *side-to-side dribble,* the puck is kept in front of the body by contact with each side of the stick. The blade is cupped slightly over the puck to keep it from bouncing over the blade and to protect it from opponents. The elbows should be kept well out from the body and the hands and wrists as loose and flexible as possible. The head is up (Figure 26-4).

Common errors:

1. Holding the stick too tightly.
2. Failure to keep the puck within the width of the body.
3. Elbows in.
4. Pushing the puck with the blade perpendicular or laid back.
5. Watching the puck rather than looking up.

In the *forward-and-backward dribble,* the puck is kept at the side of the body rather than out in front. With the puck at the side of the body, the stickhandler alternately brings the puck forward and then controls the puck by placing the blade in front of the puck as he or she progresses in a forward direction. As in the side-to-side dribble, the head is up and the blade is cupped over the puck (Figure 26-5).

Common errors:

1. Holding the stick too tightly.
2. Failure to keep the puck within the body depth.
3. Not looking up.
4. Arms too tight and close to the body.

Activities To Practice Dribbling

1. Each child has a stick and a ball/puck. Dribble in general space. (What must you do to avoid others? How did you use your stick to keep the ball/puck under control as you moved?) (refining)
2. (Floor hockey only) Dribble using the side-to-side dribble. On the signal change to the forward-and-backward dribble. (Where did you move the puck for each dribble?) (refining)
3. All dribble in general space moving clockwise. On the signal, four or five change path by moving counterclockwise. (How did you control the ball/puck as you changed pathway to avoid others?) (varying)
4. Dribble in general space, increasing and decreasing the available space. (What changes did you make in your dribbling as the space got smaller? Larger?) (varying)
5. Dribble in general space. Change speed on a specified signal. (Did your relationship with the ball/puck change as you went faster or slower? What did you have to do to keep the ball/puck under control at all speeds?) (varying)
6. (Field hockey only) Tapping the ball to the left and to the right (Indian dribbling), on the signal combine with regular dribbling. (How did you move your body to stay with the ball? Which side was easier? Why?) (varying)

Striking Techniques

Field Hockey

The *push pass* is used for passing short distances. It should be the second skill introduced and taught immediately after dribbling. During dribbling, the push pass may be executed quickly in any direction.

The passer has both hands on the stick, with the back of the left hand facing forward. The push may be taken from many positions, but the greatest accuracy and power are produced from a forward/backward stride position. The left wrist and forearm are straight. The sweeping action is initiated by both arms and then continues with the right to give added power. Power comes from the strength of the forearms and a whipping action of the wrists. The ball should be pushed along the ground (Figure 26-6).

Common errors:

1. Facing the front of the body, rather than the left shoulder, to the push.
2. Assuming too high a position behind the ball.
3. Placing the stick vertically behind the ball.
4. Using a backswing so that it is a hit rather than a push.
5. Pushing with the ball too far behind or too far in front of the body.

The *hit* is used for long-distance passing and shooting for a goal. In preparation for the hit, the right hand slides up to touch the left. The back of the left hand faces the line of the hit. The ball is a comfortable distance away so that the stick can swing freely. The stick is drawn back in a straight line, the arms not touching the body on the backswing. The wrists are firm and cocked, bringing the stick slightly above the left hand and the toe of the stick pointing upward. The stick speed accelerates as it approaches the ball (Figure 26-7).

Common errors:

1. Positioning the ball too close or too far away for the hit.
2. Not hitting through the ball. (Topping the ball is usually caused by not watching the ball.)
3. Having elbows tucked in.
4. Raising the stick too high on the backswing or follow-through.
5. Placing hands apart on the stick.

At times the hit is misused in hockey. Players often use the hit when a push pass to nearby teammates would be more accurate and much easier to control. The hit should not be introduced until players have learned to control the ball by dribbling and can push pass with ease.

FIGURE 26-6 Evaluative criteria and teaching points for push pass.

- V formed between thumb and fingers on hooked side of stick, with the right hand 6 inches below the left wrist and the forearm straight.
- Feet in a forward/backward stride, shoulder width apart, left foot in front; knees are bent, trunk leaning slightly forward, weight on rear foot.
- The stick is behind the ball at a 35- to 45-degree angle to the ground; ball is midway between the legs, slightly closer to the front foot.
- Left shoulder points in the line of the push; weight shifts to forward foot as arms sweep stick forward.
- Follow-through is long and low in the direction of the hit.

FIGURE 26-7 Evaluative criteria and teaching points for the hit.

- Hands together at the top of the stick.
- Feet shoulder width apart, ball is off left foot for a hit to the left; twist trunk so right shoulder is pulled back, ball diagonally off right for a hit to the right.
- Left shoulder faces the direction of the hit; stick drawn back, left arm straight, right arm relaxed and bent at the elbow; wrists cocked, weight on right foot.
- Stick is pulled to ball, weight shifts to left; wrists straighten and are firm at contact; arm and stick in a straight line; eyes on ball.
- Follow-through is long and low in the direction of the hit.

- Stick laid back under the ball at 45-degree angle to the ground; stick behind the ball.

- Weight shifts forward, stick imparts force to the ball by left arm pull to body as right moves forward and sideways.

- Strong wrist movement turns stick over on long, low follow-through.

FIGURE 26-8 Evaluative criteria and teaching points for the flick, which utilizes the same grip and stance as the push pass.

Bending the elbow on the backswing and reaching forward on the follow-through helps the children keep the stick low on the hit.

The *flick* is an effective shot for goal because the flight of the ball makes it difficult for the receiver to control. It may also be used in passing.

The starting position for the flick is similar to the push pass. The right leg is low to the ground. The left shoulder points in the direction of the flick, and the right shoulder is dipped. The ball is in front and farther from the left foot than in the push pass. The weight shifts to the right leg before the action begins. The stick imparts force to the ball by an explosive lever action of the left arm, which pulls toward the body as the right arm moves forward and sideways. A strong wrist action at the end causes the stick to turn over as final impetus is given to the ball (Figure 26-8).

Common errors:

1. The body facing the flick rather than the left shoulder.
2. Assuming a position too close or too far away from the ball.
3. Placing the stick vertically behind the ball.
4. Not getting low and under the ball.
5. Not using wrist action.

The flick is a difficult field hockey skill that requires considerable practice to be executed effectively. Only a few elementary school children will be ready to try it.

Floor Hockey

The *forehand pass* in floor hockey is the same as the push pass in hockey. As in dribbling, the blade is cupped over the puck as it is pushed across the floor. The stick should remain low and on the floor until the puck has been released (Figure 26-9).

In the *backhand pass,* the stick is swept in a backhand manner, low to the floor. The side is turned in the direction of the pass, and the shoulder of the lower arm remains low throughout the pass to keep the puck on the floor (Figure 26-10).

Common errors:

1. Failure to keep the opposite shoulder low so that the puck rises from the floor.
2. Failure to turn the side in the direction of the pass.
3. Failure to transfer weight to the forward foot.
4. Follow-through too high.

The *drop pass* is used to drop the puck back to a teammate, when a pass to a forward teammate is not possible. As the dribbler moves forward, the stick is placed in front of the puck to stop its forward movement. The dribbler moves on leaving the puck behind for a teammate approaching from behind (Figure 26-11).

Common errors:

1. Pushing the puck backward rather than merely stopping its forward momentum.
2. Failure to move quickly away from the puck.

Receiving

In *receiving* a ball/puck in hockey, the player must be able to get the ball/puck quickly under control by absorbing its force and positioning for the next movement.

In field hockey the stick is held as in dribbling, with the hands apart. The stick should be inclined slightly forward, lined up with the oncoming ball, and on the ground. The stick reaches for the ball and on contact gives sufficiently to keep the ball on the stick. The ball should be received in front of the right foot. This maneuver requires a reverse stick by turning the wrists so

• Hands apart on the stick, blade cupped over the puck.

• Puck is swept forward on the floor, the eyes focused on the target of the pass.

• Follow-through low and in the direction of the pass.

FIGURE 26-9 Evaluative criteria and teaching points for the forehand pass.

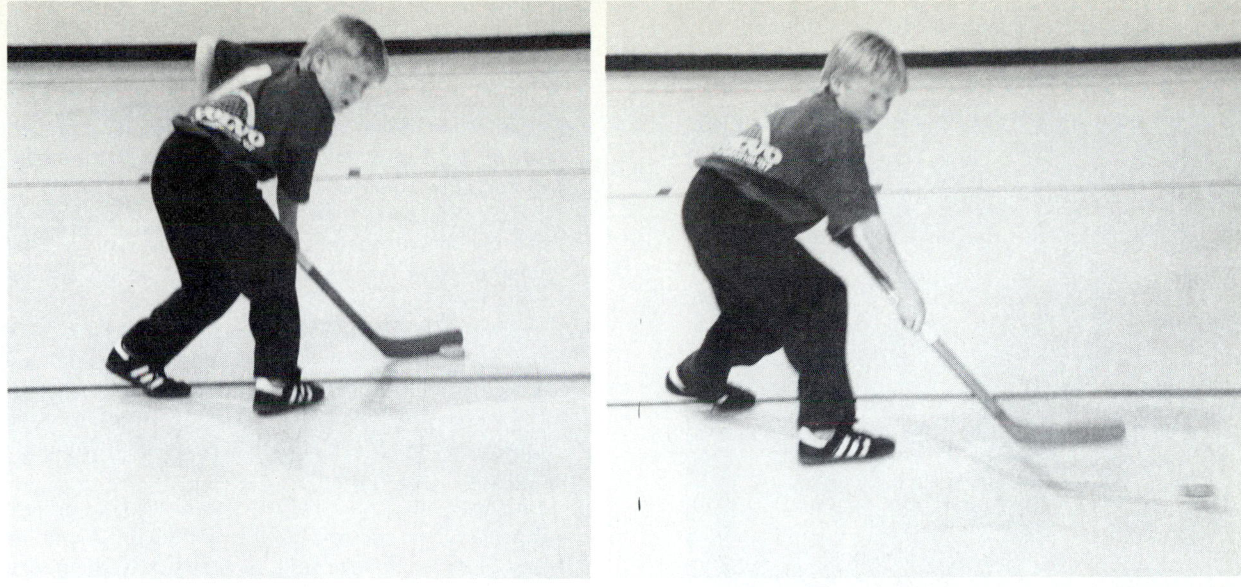

• Side faces the path of the pass, puck to the side.

• Shoulder low, stick swings along the floor.

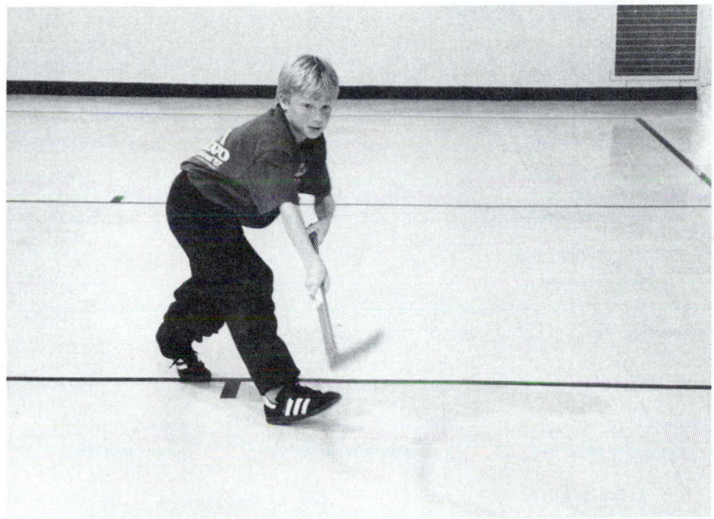

• Follow through low and in the direction of the pass.

FIGURE 26-10 Evaluative criteria and teaching points for the backhand pass.

• Place stick in front of puck to stop forward momentum.

• Leave puck and move forward.

FIGURE 26-11 Evaluative criteria and teaching points for the drop pass.

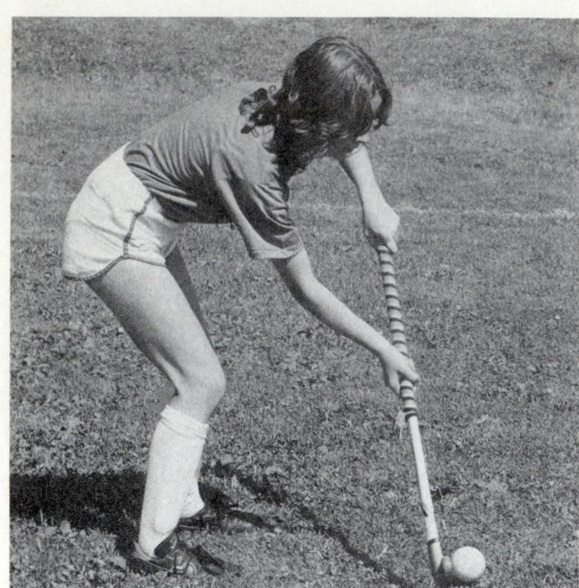

FIGURE 26-12 Evaluative criteria and teaching points for receiving.
- The stick is held with hands apart.
- Player lines the stick up with the oncoming ball, reaching for it, stick on the ground and inclined slightly forward.
- On contact with the ball the stick "gives," thus controlling the ball on the stick.

the blade faces a ball coming from the right. A ball coming from behind is received as it moves in front of the body (Figure 26-12).

In floor hockey the puck is received in much the same way, with one exception. Rather than reaching for the puck, one waits for the puck to make contact with the stick and quickly moves the stick in the path of the puck on contact to absorb its force. The hands should be soft and relaxed on the stick rather than tight.

Common errors:

1. Placing hands too close together or too tightly on the stick.
2. Failing to line the stick up with the ball's path.
3. Having the stick vertical or laid back rather than inclined forward.
4. Not giving sufficiently with the stick on impact, resulting in the ball rebounding from the receiver.

Activities To Practice Striking and Receiving Techniques

1. In partners, push, forehand, or backhand pass while moving in general space. (Were you able to get the ball/puck to your partner each time? Could you find the empty spaces? Where do you want to receive the ball/puck to keep moving?) (refining)
2. Children each have a ball/puck and a wall space. Push, forehand, or backhand pass the ball/puck to the wall so that it rebounds to themselves. (How many passes can you make in 30 seconds? What did you have to do to be able to receive the ball/puck and push it back to the wall quickly?) (refining)
3. Repeat No. 2 but the children dribble around the perimeter of the gym passing to the wall and receiving the rebound. (How did you pass so you could control the rebound as you moved forward?) (refining)
4. In partners scattered in the general space, push pass to each other, increasing and decreasing the space between the partners. (Were you able to get the ball to your partner so it could be received easily each time? How did you change the pass as the distance changed?) (varying)
5. Similar to No. 2, but have two or three lines of varying distances from the wall. Each child begins in one line, pushes the ball to the wall, moves back to the next line, receives the ball, pushes it once again to the wall, and so on. (How did you change your pass as you moved from line to line so it could be received easily?) (varying)
6. In groups of three with one ball/puck, one player is the defense, who stands in a position in front of the other two, who are forwards. One forward begins by dribbling the ball/puck, passes a flat pass to the other forward, who controls the ball/puck and passes a through pass behind the defense to which the first forward cuts to receive the ball/puck. The forwards must watch the defensive player to be sure there is adequate space for the flat pass. Begin at first with an inactive defensive player. After the forwards have successfully executed the drill several times, the defensive players should attempt to position themselves for an interception. The forwards should vary the passes used depending on the position of the defensive player. (varying)
7. Similar to No. 6, but this time a flat pass is followed by a diagonal pass. (varying)
8. (Floor hockey) In partners passing, the first pass is placed ahead of the moving player. The receiver dribbles the puck while the first passer moves into position to receive a drop pass. (varying)

Offensive Skills

Passing is a very important skill and must receive emphasis with beginning players. Elementary school children tend to play as individuals rather than as team players. Often they will keep the ball to themselves rather than pass to teammates (Figure 26-13).

Successful passing requires the cooperative efforts of both the passer and the receiver. An individual should maintain possession of the ball until an opponent begins to move into position to attempt to take the ball away. The passer should look up to see which players are free or who can get free to receive a pass. Theoretically, no passes should be intercepted because only the passer knows where the ball will be directed. Generally, it is the errors of the passer that result in opponents taking the ball. Passers must look for the empty space in which to

place the ball. They must judge the speed of the receiver and use the appropriate amount of force to direct the ball to a spot ahead of the receivers where it can be received easily. The passer may have to hold back slightly while teammates get free to receive the pass. It is important to disguise the pass if possible so that opposing players do not have the opportunity to move into the space through which the ball will travel.
Types of passes:

Upfield pass: A pass at any angle to a teammate who is closer to the goal.
Through pass: A pass parallel to the sidelines in which the passer places the ball straight ahead and the receiver moves forward past the opposing player and cuts for the ball.
Square or flat pass: A pass parallel to the end line used when upfield or through passes are not possible.
Give and go: The passer draws the opponent, passes a square pass to a teammate, moves past the opponent, and receives a return pass.

Figure 26-14 diagrams the preceding passes. In all passes, the receivers should initiate the movement by positioning themselves so that they are free or by starting to cut.
Common errors:
1. Failing to look up and plan the pass.
2. Passing the ball/puck to the player rather than to a space in front of the receiver.
3. Passing the ball/puck so hard that it cannot be received and controlled.
4. Passing the ball/puck too far ahead of the player.
5. Moving in the direction of the pass before passing so that the opponents can cover the pass.

Activities to practice passing are included in the section, Activities to Practice Striking Techniques.

The offensive team must take every opportunity to *shoot* for goal. Any of the techniques included in the section on striking techniques may be used in shooting for goals, although the hit and flick are most frequently used in field hockey.

The first shot at goal should be taken as the ball enters the circle. All forwards have their sticks down in a position where the ball/puck can be played quickly. The ball/puck should be played with as little stick handling as possible before the shot. Forwards should rush the shot to give the goalkeeper little time to control the ball/puck and to increase the possibility of a second attempt if the first one fails. When shooting, forwards should place the ball/puck away from the goalkeeper and preferably into the corners of the goal (Figure 26-15).
Common errors:
1. Directing the ball/puck at the goalkeeper.
2. Too much ball/puck handling close to the goal, so that the opportunity for a shot on goal is lost.

FIGURE 26-13 Evaluative criteria and teaching points for passing.
- Look up to see where the pass might be made.
- Pass ahead of intended receiver.
- Receiver moves to meet the ball.

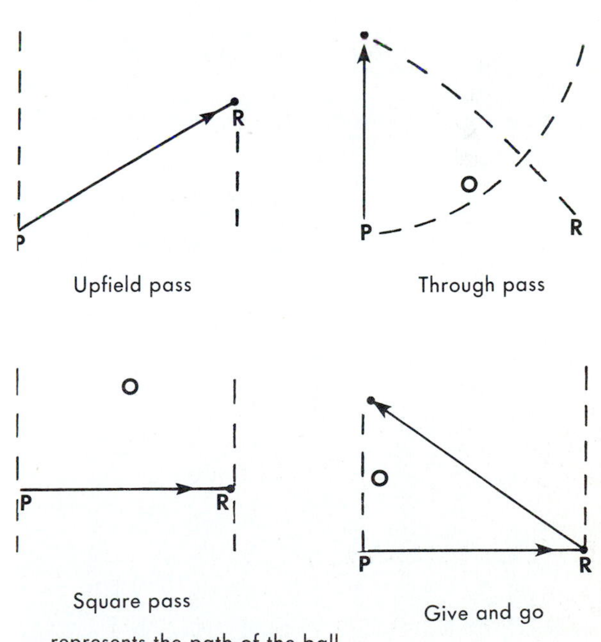

FIGURE 26-14 Field hockey passes.

3. Carrying the stick up in the air rather than near the ground or floor close to the goal.
4. Passing to another player when a shot should be taken.

Success in scoring in hockey requires considerable determination by the attack players. They must play aggressively near the goal, and scoring must be their highest priority.

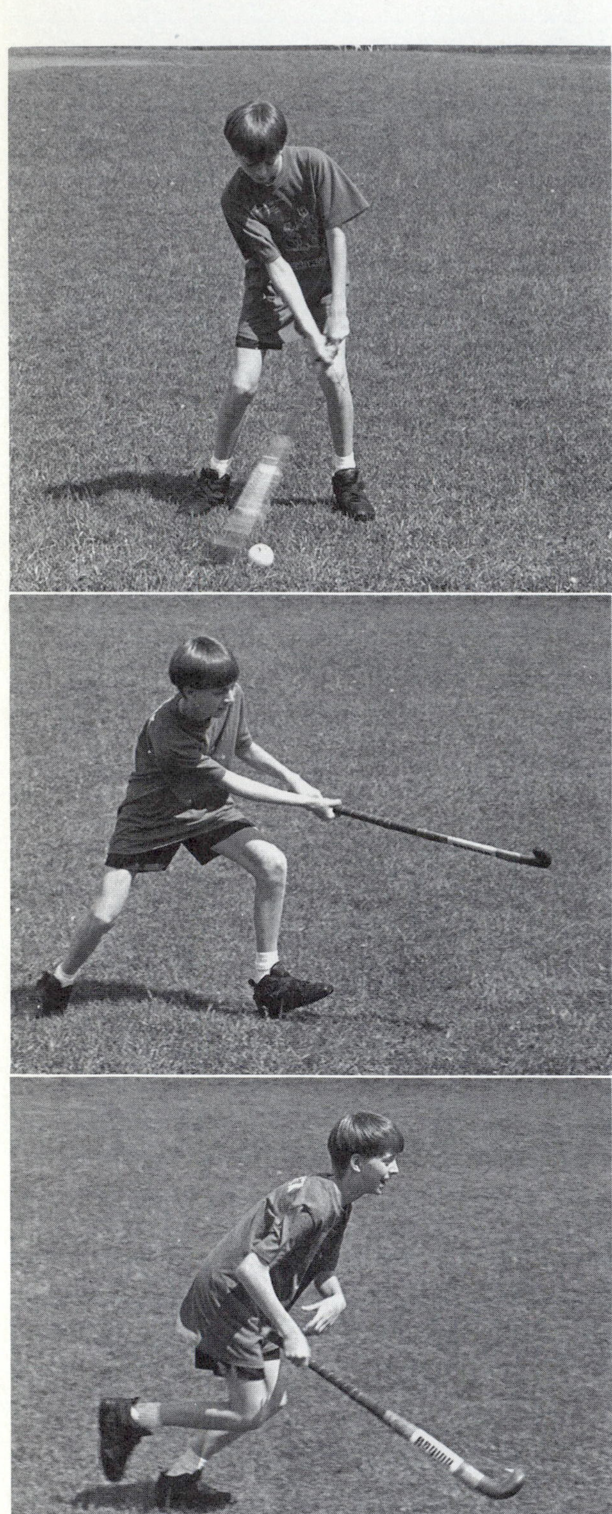

FIGURE 26-15 Evaluative criteria and teaching points for shooting.

- Hands together on stick; weight on foot toward goal as stick is swung to make contact with the ball.
- Stick reaches forward on follow-through below shoulder height.
- Shooter rushes goal after shot is taken.

Activities To Practice Shooting

1. In partners, 10 to 15 feet apart, moving down the field, hit the ball to each other. One partner quickly returns the ball to the other partner as he or she receives it. The one who has the ball at the edge of the circle shoots for a goal. Change sides and repeat. (Where did you try to place the ball to your partner? Where did you want to receive it to get off a quick shot on goal?) (refining)
2. (Field hockey) In groups of three lined up across the field, children move the ball, alternating the use of push passes and hits. When they get to the edge of the circle, they shoot for a goal with all three players rushing the shot. Change positions and repeat at least two more times. (Did you control the force for the push pass and the hit? Did you accurately judge the speed of your teammates so your passes were put accurately into the space ahead of them? Where did you want to receive the ball to get off a quick shot on goal?) (refining)
3. (Floor hockey) Repeat No. 2, alternating forehand, back hand, and drop passes. (refining)
4. (Field hockey) Individuals push pass to the wall, control the rebound, and scoop it to the wall. A goal with a goalkeeper or tires on the goal line may be used instead of the wall. (How quickly were you able to control the ball and scoop for goal? Did you scoop the ball into the empty space past the tires or goalkeeper?) (refining)
5. (Field hockey) Individuals flick into a goal where tires have been placed in the center. (What did you do as you positioned yourself to flick into the corners?) (refining)
6. A player pushes or rolls the puck/ball across the area just outside striking distance of the goal. A forward moves in, receives the ball/puck with one contact to bring it into goal area or the circle, and then immediately shoots for goal. (Where did you want to receive the ball/puck so that you could get the shot off with one contact?) (refining)
7. (Field hockey) Children are in partners, with several balls. One push passes to the other, who receives it and pushes it into a target area (a hoop on the ground). Vary the distance to the target and the relationship (move to one side of the target or the other). (What must you do to get the ball consistently into the target?) (varying)
8. (Field hockey) Individuals flick into a target on a wall, varying the distance from the wall or the orientation to the target (to the left or right of it). (What did you do to flick the ball to the target?) (varying)
9. Several cones are scattered in the goal area at one end of the playing area. Each individual dribbles to the

edge of the circle, dodges the nearest cone, and shoots for a goal through the spaces between the remaining cones. (Were you able to see the open spaces? How did you move to get open for a shot on goal?) (varying)

10. Balls are rolled or pucks pushed across the goal area. An individual rushes into the area with the stick down. The roller calls the placement of the shot into the goal, such as left or right corner. The rushing player attempts to put the ball/puck into the designated area. (Did you plan your placement as you rushed the goal? How did you adjust your position to hit to different areas?) (varying)

Dodging is another important offensive skill. Dodging is the skillful control of the ball/puck around an opponent while dribbling. Sometimes a player wishes to maintain possession of the ball/puck and in doing so must get around an opponent who is blocking the path. To be successful, offensive players must be able to dodge using several different techniques. In dodging, the player may wish to move the ball/puck to the opponent's stick side (forehand) or nonstick side (backhand). Several options for dodging follow.

In the *stick-side (forehand) dodge,* the dribblers draw the ball/puck well to their left and around the opponent's stick. The dribblers pull the balls to their left as they step to the left with the left foot. A second tap is taken, sending the ball/puck straight forward as the right foot steps forward. The ball/puck should be drawn well around the opponent's stick (Figure 26-16).

Common errors:

1. Pulling the ball/puck too forcefully to the left and out of control.
2. Failing to step to the left as the ball/puck is pulled to the left.

In the *nonstick ("Y") dodge,* the ball/puck is pushed to the right just hard enough for the dribbler to move around the opponent. The dribblers push the balls/pucks ahead and to the left of the opposing players. The dribblers accelerate and pass the defenders on their right to regain control of the ball/puck. This maneuver may be reversed for the floor hockey player who holds the stick on the left side of the body (Figure 26-17).

Common errors:

1. Pushing the ball/puck too hard so control is lost.
2. Obstructing (field hockey only) by turning and standing with one's body between the opponent and the ball (the dodger moving to the same side as the ball).

A *direct dodge* (field hockey only) may be executed by dribbling forward, using a quick reverse stick to move the ball to the dribbler's right, and then continuing straight ahead to move around the opponent on the dodger's left side. This dodge may be performed in floor hockey to move around the opponent's backhand side by pushing the puck with one side of the stick.

In the direct dodge, the dribbler uses a quick reverse stick to pull the ball/puck to the right, stepping to the right on the right foot and keeping the shoulders square and facing the opponent. The ball/puck is then tapped straight forward as the move around the opponent is completed, and the dribbler continues by stepping forward with the left foot (Figure 26-18).

Common errors:

1. Pulling the ball/puck too hard so that it travels out of the dribbler's control.
2. Obstructing by turning the left shoulder be-

• Ball pulled to the left as step is taken to the left.

• Ball tapped forward as step is taken forward on the right foot.

FIGURE 26-16 Evaluative criteria and teaching points for stickside dodge.

• Ball is pushed to space to the left of opponent.

• Forward follows ball past opponent.

FIGURE 26-17 Evaluative criteria and teaching points for nonstick dodge.

• Reverse stick tapping ball to the right.
• Step to the right, keeping shoulder square.

• Tap the ball straight ahead, stepping forward on left foot.

FIGURE 26-18 Evaluative criteria and teaching points for direct dodge.

tween the ball and the opponent (field hockey only).

Besides the preceding dodges, a dribbler may choose to dribble the ball/puck toward the opposing player, then sharply change paths to move the ball/puck either to the left or to the right. As the opposing player commits to the new path, the dribbler quickly moves the ball/puck in the opposite direction and around the would-be tackler.

Another type of dodge involves a movement of the stick over the ball/puck as if pulling the ball or puck to the dribbler's left. When the opposing player moves in the direction of the fake, the dribbler moves quickly forward and around the player. In floor hockey, the puck is pulled to the left or right of the opponent because either side of the stick may be used.

Activities To Practice Dodging

1. Each individual has a stick and a ball or puck and is scattered in the playing area. Individuals dribble, pulling the ball or puck to the left or right as designated by the teacher. (Were you able to control the ball/puck? How did you control the ball/puck? How did your legs and stick work together as you moved the ball to the left or right?) (perceiving)
2. Cones or tires are scattered in the playing area. Each participant has a stick and a ball or puck. The leader calls out the particular dodge to be used. Individuals dribble in the area and perform the designated dodge as they approach each cone. (Were you able to dodge without hitting the cone with the ball/puck? How far away from the cone did you begin your dodge to avoid contact?) (refining)
3. In partners, each has a stick and one has a ball or puck. The individuals with the balls or pucks dribble toward their partners, dodging them when they get close. At first the partner should offer little defense against the dodge. As the dodger becomes more skillful in the movements, the partner should become more active in attempting to anticipate the dodge. (How far from your partner did you need to be to begin a successful dodge? Did you use a change of speed to help you get around your opponent? How did you disguise your dodge so that your partner was unsure which way you would go?) (refining)
4. Several players are in a line, one behind the other, and scattered over the length of the playing area. The dribblers begin at one end of the playing area and attempt to dodge each player in turn as they proceed to the other end. Change positions until all have had the opportunity to dodge several times. A different dodge may be executed with each player the dribbler meets if desired. (How far away were you when you began each dodge? Did your opponent anticipate which dodge you would use? How did you disguise the dodge?) (varying)

Defensive Techniques

In playing defense, the team must develop several skills to contain the offensive efforts of their opponents. *Marking* is the skill of positioning oneself (1) to prevent an opponent from getting possession of the ball/puck or, if that is not possible, (2) to be close enough to get to the ball/puck before the opponent can control it. If the ball/puck is under control, marking involves shadowing the player, forcing the opponent to move the ball/puck away from the intended path on the field.

When marking, defensive players maintain a position with their back to the goal and with their body between the goal and the opposing player. The marking player may move slightly to the ball/puck side of a player without the ball/puck to cut off any passes that may be directed to the opponent. Marking players are constantly in motion, adjusting their position to the movements of the opposition and the ball/puck. The stick is down in position for a tackle or interception. The marking player watches the opponent and the ball/puck carefully, attempts to anticipate the movements of each, and is ready to move as needed. In the circle, the defense should mark their opposing forward as closely as possible to intercept or tackle if the marked player receives the ball/puck (Figure 26-19).

FIGURE 26-19 Evaluative criteria and teaching points for marking.
- Maintain relationship with forward between the player and the goal.
- Move with opposing forward with stick down.
- Move to the ball side of a player without the ball.

Common errors:

1. Watching only the ball/puck and not the movements of the opposing player.
2. Failing to stay in a position with the back to the goal and between the ball/puck, the opponent, and the goal.
3. Carrying the stick up, not ready for the interception.

The team who does not have the ball/puck must develop the skill of taking the ball/puck away from the opponents by **tackling.** Although several different tackles have been developed over the years, today the most commonly used tackle is the straight tackle.

The *straight tackle* is used to take the ball/puck from an opponent who is coming directly toward the tackler. The tackler assumes a balanced position, with the feet apart and one foot slightly ahead of the other. The hands grasp the stick as in dribbling, 4 to 6 inches apart, farther apart in floor hockey. It may be necessary to move backward, with the player maintaining a position between the ball/puck and the goal until an opportunity to tackle is available. As the ball/puck is contacted, it is tapped or pushed easily to the side and then controlled by the tackler, who dribbles or passes to a teammate (Figure 26-20).

Common errors:

1. Failing to line up with the opposing player and the ball/puck.
2. Not watching the ball/puck.
3. Hitting the opponent's stick rather than the ball/puck.
4. Contacting the ball/puck too hard so that it cannot be controlled easily by the tackler.

FIGURE 26-20 Evaluative criteria and teaching points for straight tackle.
- Tackler lines up with dribbler.
- Feet are shoulder width apart, knees bent, stick down.
- Ball is contacted when it is off opponent's stick.

Activities To Practice Tackling

1. Working in partners, facing each other, each has a stick and one has a ball/puck. One dribbles toward the partner. The tackler moves up and tackles the dribbler. The dribbler should offer no resistance to the tackle until the tackler has performed the tackle successfully several times. (Where was the ball/puck when you successfully got it away from your partner?) (refining)
2. Children are scattered in the playing area. Each has a stick and half the group have balls or pucks. Those with the balls/pucks dribble within the area. The others attempt to tackle the dribblers and gain control of the balls/pucks. If the tackler is successful, the two individuals change roles. If a ball/puck or dribbler goes out of the playing area, it is considered a successful tackle and the two players change roles. (refining)

Goalkeeping

Goalkeeping ability in field hockey is limited at the elementary school level. Before goalkeepers may be added to the game, protective equipment must be available, including kickers, pads for the legs, a chest protector, a mask that protects the neck as well as the face, and a helmet. Since goalkeeping equipment is not available in small sizes, children will have to be at least at the fifth or sixth grade level before equipment will fit them. If tennis balls are used and striking is limited to push passes, goalkeepers may be added to the game using shin guards and face masks for protection.

In games where goalkeepers will not be used, putting cones or preferably old tires in the goal will help make scoring more challenging. The rules would then prohibit hitting these obstacles on a shot on goal. A rebound off the tire, however, may be converted into a score by hitting the ball into the open space.

In field hockey the goalkeeper assumes a ready position with the stick in the right hand and the flat side forward. The left hand is positioned with the palm forward. The feet are in a comfortable stride position, with the hips, knees, and ankles flexed. The eyes are on the ball, and the goalkeeper shifts position to be always between the ball and the goal as the ball moves on the field.

Goalkeepers should position themselves to cut down the angle for shots at goal. Figure 26-21 demonstrates the goalkeeper's position in relation to the ball and the angle for shooting.

The *double leg stop* is the easiest stop for the goalkeeper. The goalkeeper lines up with the ball stopping it directly in front of the body and padded legs. The legs are bent and the force is absorbed, with the ball resting about one foot in front so that it can be cleared with the single leg clear to the side and away from the goal.

In the *single leg clear* the goalkeeper controls the ball, sending it out to either side of the goal. The kicking leg swings along the ground toward the ball across and in front of the supporting leg. The kicking leg swings through so that the momentum carries the body forward, taking the body weight on to the kicking foot. A ball coming from the left is cleared with the right foot, and a ball coming from the right is cleared with the left foot. This skill is not easy and requires practice to acquire the timing necessary to be successful, as well as the ability to remain in a balanced position ready for the next shot. The single leg clear may be practiced using shin guards only if tennis balls are used and all shots on goal are push passes (Figure 26-22).

In floor hockey the goalkeeper assumes a position in line with the puck with the legs together, the knees flexed, and the body bent forward at the waist. The stick blade is flat on the floor in front of the legs in a backhand manner. A glove is worn on the free hand to catch aerial pucks. The gloved hand is held in an open position at about hip height. The weight is on the balls of the feet. In receiving the puck the goalkeeper attempts to control its force so that it can be pushed away from the goal with the stick or caught in the gloved hand.

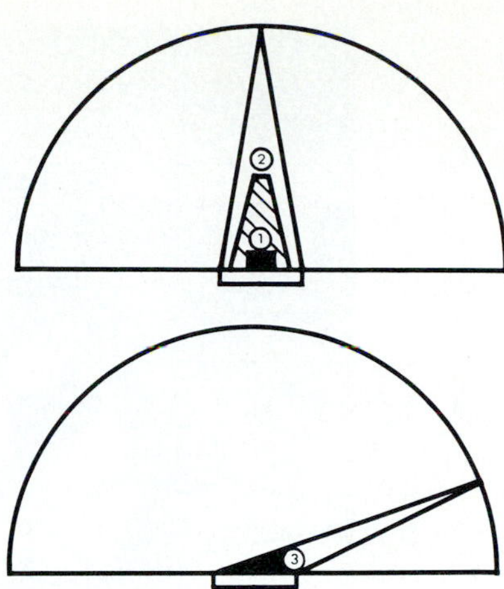

FIGURE 26-21 Shooting angles.

HOCKEY CONCEPTS

Application of the movement concepts outlined in Figure 26-1 is important for success in hockey activities. Activities to help children understand the relationship between movement content and hockey are listed here.

Hockey Concepts and Activities

1. To move in general space in relation to boundaries, teammates, opponents, and the ball.
   a. Two on two in a limited area. The offensive team attempts to move down the field passing. The defensive team attempts to intercept passes and force the offense toward the sidelines. One point is scored for each interception, two points for each time the offense is moved toward the sidelines. (How did you position yourself to limit the space of the offensive team?)
2. To move to an open space while moving in general space.
   a. Three players are arranged as the three sides of a square with one empty corner. Each person is numbered. Number 1 passes to 2, 2 to 3, and 3 to 1. The ball is always placed in the empty corner, and the receiver moves to that space to pick up the ball. (Was the receiver able to get the ball each time? Why? Why not?)
   b. A number of cones or other obstacles are scattered in the field. Groups of two or three players move the ball/puck, passing to each other through the spaces between the obstacles. Receivers should cut to open spaces to receive the ball/puck. (How did you identify the spaces into which you would place the ball/puck?)

FIGURE 26-22 Evaluative criteria and teaching points for single leg clear.
- With support foot turned out, inside of foot is lined up with ball.
- Opposite leg sweeps along the ground.
- Contact with big toe joint.
- Follow-through, taking weight on kicking foot.

Working two against two and a goalkeeper.

3. To keep your self space between your opponent and the goal or the ball/puck and the goal while a playing defense.
   a. In groups of three, the person with the ball passes it across the field so that it passes at the head of the circle. As the pass is made the passer gives the signal, "Go." One player stands behind the end line to play defense, the other is at the 25-yard line. On the signal, both players rush the ball. The forward attempts a shot at goal, and the defensive player attempts to prevent the goal. (On defense, where did you position yourself to prevent the forward a good shot at goal?)
4. To recognize one's own area of the general space in which to play.
   a. Players are arranged in alleys. The offense attempts to pass the ball/puck and move the ball/puck toward the goal. (How did you pass to remain in your own area and for the receivers to control the pass in their area?)

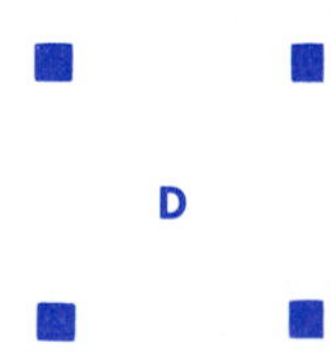

5. To use as much space as possible on offense to keep the defense spread out.
   a. Three on three. The players of each team are numbered, and players with matching numbers are responsible for marking each other. The team who has the ball/puck attempts to complete several consecutive passes, with 1 passing to 2, 2 to 3, and 3 to 1. The opposing team attempts to intercept the passes and gain possession of the ball/puck. (How did you use the space to keep free of your opponent? How did you disguise your passes so that the opponents were not sure where the ball/puck would go?)
6. To close spaces open to opponents and the ball/puck, especially close to the goal area when on defense.
   a. Four players are arranged in a square, with a fifth defending player in the center. The four outside players use flat passes to attempt to move the defense out of position so that a pass may be made across the center of the square (diagonal pass). A point is scored for each successful pass. The defense earns 2 points for each pass intercepted. (How did you control the passes to keep the defense moving? Where did the defensive person try to stay to close the space?)

■ ■

D

■ ■

7. To create open space for self, teammates, and the ball/puck while moving in general space by drawing an opponent.
   a. Three on two. Two forwards attempt to move the ball/puck toward the goal. Before passing, the offense attempts to draw the defensive player out of position to open a space for the ball/puck. (How did you create a space for the ball? How did you move?)

b. Children are arranged in teams of three players, two teams to an area. Teammates attempt to pass to each other and to intercept the passes of the other team. Each team counts the number of consecutive passes. If the ball/puck goes out of the playing area or is touched by the other team, passing must begin again with number 1. (Were you able to find the empty space in which to put the ball/puck?)

8. To recognize and anticipate pathways within which to move self and/or the ball or to intercept the ball or others.
   a. Each player has a ball/puck. Each one attempts to push forehand or backhand pass so that the ball/puck hits the balls/pucks of the other participants as they dribble and push pass in the area. (Were you able to recognize the available pathways in which to move yourself and the ball/puck to avoid others and avoid having your ball/puck hit?)
   b. Partners are scattered in general space. The partner with the puck or ball is stationary while the other moves in the space. On the signal "Yes" from the partner the player passes through the available path to the moving partner, who receives the ball/puck and then stops to become the stationary passer for the next pass. (How did you anticipate the open paths to your partner? Where did you try to place the ball/puck so that it could be easily received?)
   c. Two forwards attempt to move the ball downfield against one defensive player. The forwards dribble and pass, attempting to create pathways in which to put the ball/puck or themselves as they move downfield. The defender tries to cover the space so that the forwards cannot pass successfully. (Where was the best place to position yourself to cover the space? What position prevented a flat pass? A through pass? How did you create spaces for the ball?)
9. To change the expected path of the ball/puck.
   a. Three passing against one defender, who tries to intercept the pass. (How did you decide who was free to receive the pass? How did you disguise your passes?)
10. To establish a pathway away from the goal on defense.
   a. One attack player against two defense players. The attack player shoots for goal. The defender receives the shot and quickly passes the ball/puck to the other defender, who has moved out to the side from the goal area. (How quickly did you get the shot away from the goal?)
11. To alter the tempo of the game by speeding up or slowing down.
   a. Dribblers attempt to move toward a goal while their defending partners attempt to keep them out. Dribblers change speed to get around their opponents. (When did you make your move to pass the defender?)

Additional activities that may be adapted to hockey may be found in Chapters 25 and 29.

HOCKEY LEAD-UP GAMES

An analysis of the games to be included in this section is given in Table 26-1.

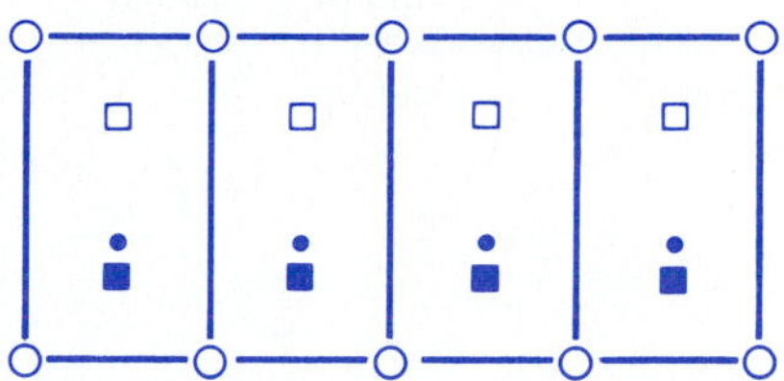

ONE-ON-ONE HOCKEY

Level: III

Equipment: A hockey stick for each player and one ball/puck for each game

Area: The field is divided into small playing areas marked off by four cones

Participants: Two players for each game

Skills: Dribbling

Description: Each two participants have their own area of play. On the signal, the one with the ball/puck tries to dribble over one end line, while the other attempts to intercept the ball/puck and take it to the opposite end line. The ball/puck should only be taken when it is off the opposing player's stick. If the player in possession of the ball/puck or the ball/puck goes out of the playing area, the ball/puck is given to the other participant. A point is scored each time the offense dribbles over the end line.

Fouls: Hitting sticks

Penalty: Loss of possession or free space (3 feet) to move the ball.

Strategy:

1. Use as much of the space as possible on offense.
2. The defense should try to keep their position with their back to the end line and stay between the line and the player with the ball.

Teaching suggestions: Games should be for short periods, one minute or two and then players should rotate to a new area and a new opponent.

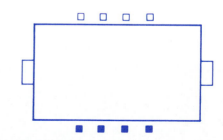

SIDELINE HOCKEY

Level III

Equipment: One stick for each participant, one hockey ball or puck, two hockey goals or four cones to mark the goal areas, and pinnies or vests to designate teams.

Area: A rectangular area 30 by 60 feet with a 5- to 8-foot goal area centered at each end.

Participants: Four to six for each team.

Text continued on p. 548.

TABLE 26-1 FIELD HOCKEY GAMES ANALYSIS

NAME	GAME CLASSIFICATION	NO. OF PARTICIPANTS	EQUIPMENT	SPACE AND ORGANIZATIONAL PATTERN	MOTOR SKILLS
One-On-One Hockey	Lead-up	Two players per game	One ball or puck for every two players; small areas marked off with cones; one stick for each player	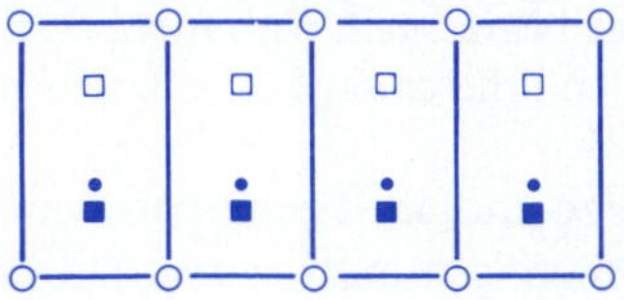	Dribbling
Sideline Hockey	Lead-up	Four to six per team	One stick per participant; one hockey ball; two goals or four cones to mark the goal areas; pinnies or vests		Dribble Push pass Receiving Shooting
Advanced Sideline Hockey	Lead-up	Four to six per team	One stick per participant; one hockey ball; two goals or four cones; four to six tires; pinnies or vests		Dribble Marking Push pass Receiving Shooting Tackling
Circle Hockey	Lead-up	Two players per team	One stick for each player; one ball/puck for each game	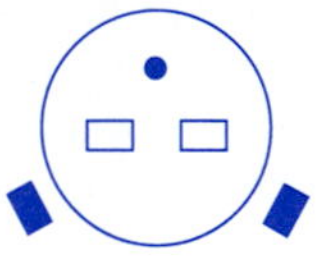	Dribble Push pass Dodging Tackling
Alley Field Hockey	Lead-up	Five per team	One stick per participant; one hockey ball; two goals or four cones; four to six tires; pinnies or vests		Dribble Dodge Hit Marking Push pass Receiving Shooting Tackling

*Numbers refer to the movement concepts listed in Figure 26-1 on p. 526.

MODIFICATIONS	MOVEMENT CONCEPTS*	SOCIAL STRUCTURE	STRATEGY	LEVEL
	Skills: 1, 3-6, 10 Game: 1-3, 4-8	Parallel play II	Use as much space as possible on offense; defense keeps back to goal line and stays between opponent and the goal	III
	Skills: 1-11 Game: 1-3, 6, 8	Social interaction I	1. Move to an open space to receive a pass 2. Stay between your opponent and the goal and the ball and the goal on defense 3. Create a space for the ball by keeping a space between the person with the ball and the receiver	III
	Skills: 1-11 Game: 1-3, 5-8	Social interaction II	1. Move to an open space to receive a pass 2. Stay between your opponent and the goal and the ball and the goal on defense 3. Create a space for the ball by keeping a space between the person with the ball and the receiver 4. Rush your shot on goal	III
Require a number of passes before shooting	Skills: 1-10 Game: 1-3, 5, 6-9	Social interaction II	1. Use short, quick passes 2. The attack must keep moving 3. Defense must work together to close space	III
1. Require a number of passes before a shot for a goal may be taken 2. Increase the number of alleys to five	Skills: 1-11 Game: 1-8, 10	Social interaction II	1. Pass to a space ahead of the receiver 2. Move to an open space to receive a pass 3. Defense should hit the ball away from the goal area 4. Use side alleys to bring the ball downfield, centering it near the goal 5. Mark closely in the area near the goal 6. Offense should maintain possession until defense is drawn to create spaces	III

Continued.

TABLE 26-1 FIELD HOCKEY GAMES ANALYSIS—cont'd

NAME	GAME CLASSIFICATION	NO. OF PARTICIPANTS	EQUIPMENT	SPACE AND ORGANIZATIONAL PATTERN	MOTOR SKILLS
Advanced Alley Field Hockey	Lead-up	Six per team	One stick per participant; two goals or four cones; vests or pinnies; four to six tires (optional); goal keepers equipment (optional)	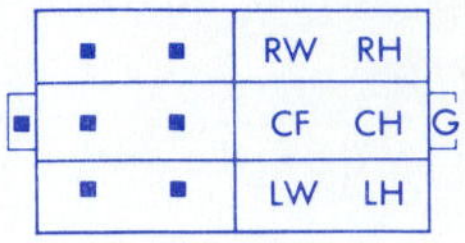 RW RH CF CH G LW LH	Dribble Dodge Hit Marking Push pass Receiving Shooting Tackle Goalkeeping (optional)
Gridlock	Lead-up	Six to eight per game	One hockey stick for each player; one ball/puck for each game; pinnies or vests	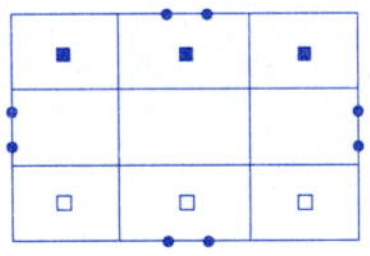	Dribbling Passing Dodging
Modified Field Hockey	Lead-up	Seven per team	One stick per participant; one hockey ball; two goals; vests or pinnies; goalkeepers equipment	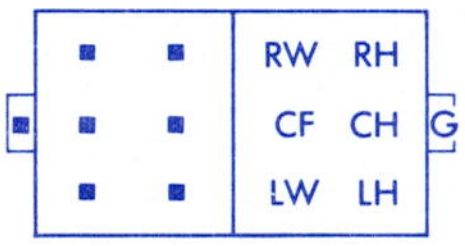 RW RH CF CH G LW LH	Dribble Hit Dodge Push pass Receiving Shooting Tackle Goalkeeping
Floor Hockey	Lead-up	Six per team	One stick per participant; one ball or puck; two goals; vests or pinnies	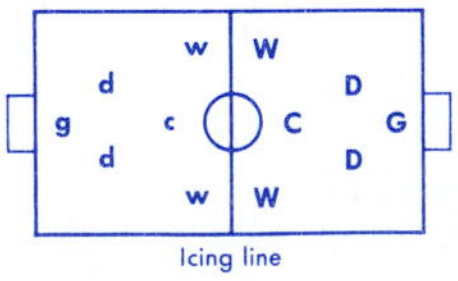 w W d D g c C G d D w W Icing line	Dribble Dodge Pass Receiving Shooting Tackle Goalkeeping

MODIFICATIONS	MOVEMENT CONCEPTS*	SOCIAL STRUCTURE	STRATEGY	LEVEL
1. Add a goalkeeper to each team if equipment is available 2. Require a number of passes before a goal may be attempted	Skills: 1-11 Game: 1-10, 11	Social interaction III	1. Keep a space between you and teammates to create space for the ball. 2. Defense should backup forwards on the attack to give support 3. Forwards should drop back to support defensive efforts	IV
Work with offense first in space, then add defense	Skills: 1-10 Game: 1-11	Social interaction III	Use short quick passes on offense. Look for empty grids in which to move. Offense must stay on the move. Move to support so there is always the option to pass. Defense tries to position themselves between the player with the ball and teammates	IV
	Skills: 1-11 Game: 1-11	Social interaction III	1. Keep a space between you and teammates to create space for the ball 2. Defense should backup forwards on the attack to give support 3. Forwards should drop back to support defensive efforts 4. Use as much space as possible on offense to keep defense spread out	IV
	Skills: 4-13 Game: 1-11	Social interaction III	1. Keep a space between you and teammates to create space for the ball 2. Defense should back up forwards on the attack to give support 3. Forwards should drop back to support defensive efforts 4. Use as much space as possible on offense to keep defense spread out	IV

Skills: Dribble, push, forehand or backhand pass, receive, and shoot.

Description: The participants on each team are numbered. The leader calls a number, and the participants with that number come out. One player is designated to begin with possession of the ball/puck. The team with the ball/puck attempts to complete passes to at least two sideline players before attempting the shot on goal. The opposing player tries to gain possession by intercepting one of the passes or picking up a loose dribble. Tackling or hitting sticks is not allowed. If possession is gained by the opposing player, that team must complete passes to at least two teammates before shooting. When a goal is scored, or time is called, a new number is called. The team not scoring, or if time is called, the one not receiving the ball in the previous play is given possession of the ball/puck when play resumes.

Violations: Hitting the ball/puck over the end line and not into the goal

Fouls: Hitting the ball/puck so that it rises dangerously into the air or at another player, personal contact, tackling, hitting the opponent's stick, obstruction (putting the body between the opponent with the ball and the ball in field hockey only), or dangerously raising the stick (usually above shoulder height).

Penalty: A member of the opposite team's sideline players is given the ball/puck for a free hit (unmarked)

Strategy:

1. Remember to move to an open space to receive a pass.
2. Try to stay between the ball/puck and the goal and the ball/puck and the potential receiver while on defense (goal-side, ball/puck-side).
3. Create spaces for the ball/puck by keeping a space between the person with the ball/puck and the receiver.

Teaching suggestions:

1. Stress passing (a) with appropriate force so that the ball/puck can be controlled easily and (b) to a space ahead of the receiver.
2. The stick should be kept down to be ready to receive or intercept a pass.
3. Emphasize the use of space, either creating space on offense or covering space on defense.
4. Emphasize timing when taking the ball/puck from an opponent so that contact is made when the ball/puck is off the opponent's stick to avoid hitting sticks.
5. Encourage control of the ball/puck and the sticks throughout play.
6. Opposing players should be evenly matched in ability.
7. During indoor play the ball/puck should rise no more than 6 inches from the floor, except on a shot for goal.

ADVANCED SIDELINE HOCKEY

Level: III

Description: Advanced Sideline Hockey is similar to Sideline Hockey, but two or more numbers are called depending on the ability of the players. Passing to two players may now include teammates whose numbers have been called. Two or three tires should be placed on the goal line in the center of each goal. To score, players must now aim for the sides of the goal. The tires provide a surface from which there will be rebounds. Attack players should be encouraged to rush shots on goal so that rebounds may be turned into goals. In floor hockey a goalkeeper may also be used. If two numbers are called, play may begin with a face-off.

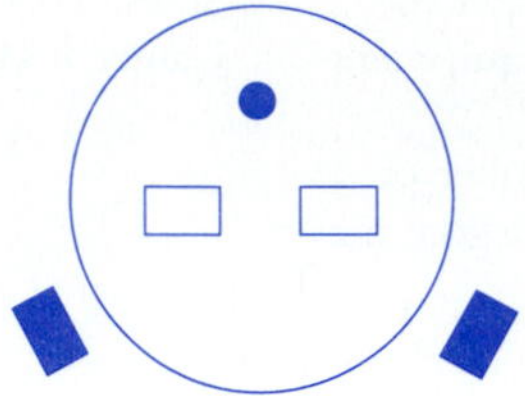

CIRCLE HOCKEY

Level: III

Equipment: One hockey stick for each player and one ball/puck for each game

Area: A circle with a 10-yard radius and a cone for each game

Participants: Two per team

Skills: Dribbling, push passing, dodging, tackling

Description: There are two attack and two defense players in each game. The attack players begin anywhere on the edge of the circle and attempt to dribble, pass, and then shoot for a goal by hitting the cone with the ball/puck. The defense attempts to intercept and push pass the ball/puck out of the circle area. No defense player may be closer than 1 yard from the cone. If the attack hits the cone or the defense pushes the ball/puck out of the circle, one point is scored. After a team scores 3 points, the players reverse roles.

Strategy:

1. Use short, quick passes to open spaces.
2. The attack should always be moving.
3. Defense must work together to close space and keep attack out of scoring area.

Teaching suggestions: It may be necessary to require a particular number of passes before attempting a shot on goal to encourage team play. (Children in each game could decide on the number of passes they will strive for before shooting.)

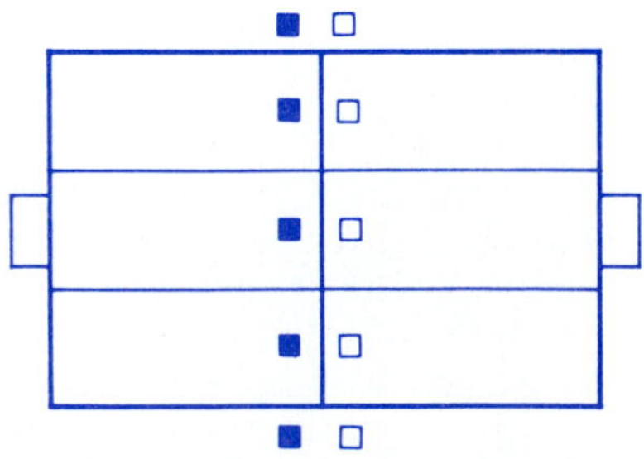

ALLEY FIELD HOCKEY

Level: III

Equipment: One stick for each participant, one hockeyball, two goals, two or three tires placed at the center on each goal line, and pinnies or vests to designate teams

Area: A rectangular playing area 45 by 80 feet, with three alleys 15 feet wide and an 8- to 10-foot goal centered at each end

Participants: Five players for each team, three within the playing area and one sideline guard on each sideline

Skills: Dribble, dodge, hit, mark, push pass, receive, shoot, and tackle

Description: Play begins with a center alley player passing the ball to a teammate. The ball may not cross the center line until it has been touched by someone other than the person taking the hit. The team with the ball attempts to score by moving the ball downfield passing and shooting into the opponent's goal. A shot on goal must be touched by the offensive team in the circle in front of the goal before entering the goal to score. The team on defense attempts to prevent a score by intercepting passes or tackling and then moving offensively to the opposite goal. After a score the ball is awarded to the nonscoring team, and play begins again at the midfield line. After a goal is scored each player rotates one position clockwise.

Out of bounds: If the ball goes out of bounds it is put into play by the nearest sideline guard of the opposing team. A push pass or hit may be used with the nearest player 5 yards away from the spot where the hit is to be taken. The ball may not rise in the air. The penalty for fouls on the hit is a hit awarded to the opposing team.

Fouls: Raising the stick above shoulder height, obstruction, hitting the ball so that it rises dangerously in the air or at another player, personal contact, hitting opponent's stick, or moving outside the alley

Penalty: A free hit is awarded the team fouled against. All other players must be 5 yards away.

Strategy:

1. Remember to pass to a space ahead of the receiver.
2. Remember to move to an open space to receive the ball.
3. The defense should stay between the opponents and the goal and mark closely in the area close to the goal.
4. A forward should maintain possession of the ball by dribbling until an opponent makes a commitment before attempting a tackle.
5. Defense players should hit the ball away from their goal area as quickly as possible.
6. Use all alleys. Use the side alleys to bring the ball downfield and center the ball as you near the goal.

Teaching suggestions:

1. Encourage players to keep spacing and not play too close to their alley lines.
2. To ensure teamwork, it may be necessary to require several passes before attempting a shot on goal.
3. Increase the number of alleys to five.
4. Match opponents by ability to provide an equal opportunity for all.
5. Control of the ball and the stick should be stressed throughout the game.
6. This game also may be adapted for floor hockey.

LH	LW	rw	rh
CH	CF	cf	ch
RH	RW	lw	lh

ADVANCED ALLEY FIELD HOCKEY

Level: IV

Description: Advanced Alley Field Hockey is similar to Alley Field Hockey, with the addition of a defense player in each alley. Players now are named: left halfback, center half back, right halfback, right wing, center, and left wing.

Teaching suggestions:

1. Only two players should play the ball at any one time. Halfbacks mark forwards. At no time should two forwards be playing the ball.
2. When a defense player has the ball, the forwards of the same team should move to a position where they might receive a pass and make a space for the ball.
3. Defense players should play in a position behind their forward line to give support to the attack.
4. Add a goalkeeper to each team if goalkeeping equipment is available or when using a tennis ball and push passes only.
5. Increase the number of alleys to five and add two forwards (inners) and two fullbacks.
6. This game also may be adapted for floor hockey.

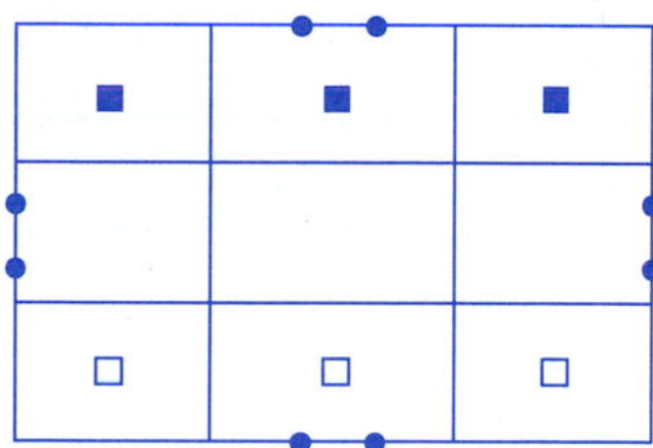

GRIDLOCK

Level: IV

Equipment: A hockey stick for each player and a ball/puck for each game; pinnies or vests to designate each team

Area: A space marked off into nine squares with an (optional) goal centered on each side.

Participants: Six to eight per game

Skills: Dribbling, passing, dodging

Description: Offense attempts to pass the ball and move it to any one of the goal areas. The defense attempts to intercept and prevent them from scoring (tackling is not allowed). As the players move in the space, there may be no more than two players per grid (one offense, one defense). The player with the ball may move within one grid or move to another unoccupied by a teammate. The teammates of the player with the ball attempt to support the player with the ball by moving into the adjacent grids. Scoring may take many forms:

1. One point for each completed pass moving the ball/puck from one grid to another.
2. One point for any pass within one foot of the receivers stick.
3. One point for three consecutive passes from one grid to another.
4. A goal scored at any one of the four goals after at least two completed passes.

Strategy:

1. Use short, quick passes to open spaces.
2. Look for empty grids in which to move.
3. Defense needs to try to position themselves between the player with the ball and teammates.
4. Keep moving to confuse the defense.
5. Move to support so that there are always two options to pass.

Teaching suggestions:

1. Have the attack practice passing without defense players first to learn to support the player with the ball, by moving within one pass of the player with the ball.

MODIFIED FIELD HOCKEY

Level: IV

Description: Modified Field Hockey is similar to Advanced Alley Field Hockey, but the alley lines are removed. Each team consists of seven players: three forwards, three defense, and one goalkeeper. Encourage players to keep their positions and use as much space as possible.

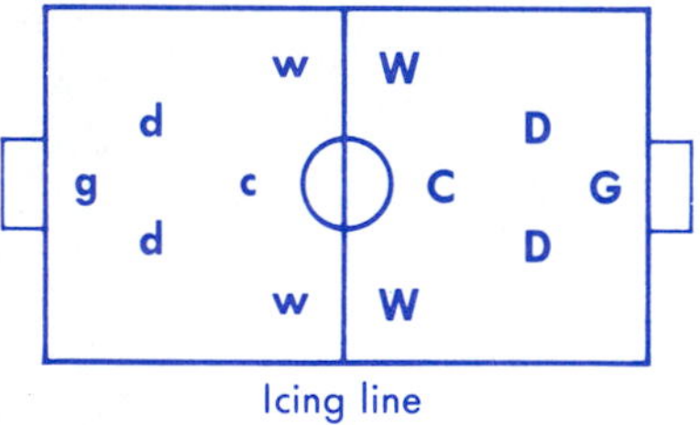

FLOOR HOCKEY

Level: IV

Equipment: One hockey stick for each participant; two 6-foot goals or four cones to mark goal areas; one puck, floor hockey ball, or small foam ball.

Area: A rectangular area 30 by 60 feet with a 5-foot goal centered at each end; a center face-off circle and a midcourt dividing line (the icing line). A goal box extends out from each goal 4 to 5 feet from the goal line and 2 to 3 feet to each side of the goal.

Participants: Six players per team: one center, two wings, two defense players, and one goalkeeper

Skills: Dribble, dodge, hit, forehand, backhand, drop pass, receive, shoot, tackle

Description: Play begins with a face-off in which the official drops the puck between the two centers in the face-off circle. Each center attempts to pass the puck or ball to teammates, moving the ball toward the opponent's goal for a shot on goal. If the walls mark the boundary lines, the puck may be played off the wall as in ice hockey. A goal is 1 point, and play resumes with a face-off in the center after each score. Shots for goal must be made on the opponent's half of the court (past the icing line). Only the goalkeeper may play in the goal box.

Fouls: Personal contact, hitting sticks, raising the stick dangerously, tripping, or raising the puck in the air

Penalty: Players go to a penalty area at one side of the playing area for a designated time or to execute a penalty, such as jumping rope a certain number of times. The team that is penalized plays short until the penalty has been completed. On completion of the penalty, the penalized player rejoins the team.

Strategy:

1. Encourage moving to a space to receive a pass.
2. Stay between the goal and the ball and opponents while on defense.
3. The defense should move the ball quickly to the attack.

Teaching suggestions:

1. Modify the game so that only the center plays the entire area. Wings, defense players, and goalkeeper play in only half the area. This technique may result in better use of the space in beginning play.
2. Require a specified number of passes before shooting for a goal.

SUMMARY

Field and floor hockey offer elementary school children the opportunity for a group experience in which a ball is controlled with an implement. Both games require modification and a progression of activities leading up to modified field hockey or floor hockey in the upper elementary school grades. Control of the stick and ball-handling skills are stressed as the children develop a variety of skills and learn increasingly more complex games. The movement concepts important to success are introduced and stressed in both skill development and game play.

REFERENCES AND RESOURCES

Arrighi M: Spatial concepts of game play: field hockey, *JOPER* 47(7):26, 1976.

Athletic Institute: *Hockey without ice,* North Palm Beach, Fla, The Athletic Institute.

Cadman J and van Heumen W: *Indoor hockey: tactics, technique, training,* London, 1978, Pelham Books.

Castelijn, B: *USA field hockey coaching manual,* ed 2, Colorado Springs, 1988, United States Field Hockey Association.

Falla J: *Hockey: learn to play the modern way,* New York, 1987, Sports Illustrated Winner's Circle Books.

Kostrinsky D: *Field hockey coaching drills,* Ithaca, NY, 1987, Movement Publications.

Oxendine, JB: *American Indian sports heritage,* Champaign, Ill, 1988, Human Kinetics.

USFHA: *Junior field hockey coach's manual,* Colorado Springs, 1985, United States Field Hockey Association.

Wein H: *The science of hockey,* ed 3, London, 1985, Pelham Books.

ANNOTATED READINGS

Anders B: *Beth Anders coaching series, volume 1, Teaching field hockey the bobo way,* Parkerford, Pa, 1988, Longstreth.
Presents a series of drills using bop bags to simulate opposing players.

Anders B: *Beth Anders coaching series, volume 3, On the rebound*—the hit, Parkerford, Pa, 1989, Longstreth.
Presents drills using rebound boards to practice the hit.

Enos M: Goalkeeping: an art and a science, *JOPER* 51(5):30, 1980.
Discusses how to teach positioning to goalkeepers to cut down the angle to the goal.

Fong D: *The coach's collection of field hockey drills,* West Point, 1982, Leisure Press.
An excellent book of drills for developing specific skills and team play.

Gray G: Floor hockey: is it a safe sport for schools? *JOPERD* 60(1):51, 1989.
Discusses the safety factors involved in the game of floor hockey.

Hughes C: *Soccer tactics and teamwork,* Wakefield, 1981, EP Publishing.
A book of soccer strategies that has implications for the teaching of field hockey; includes systems play and suggestions for building the attack and defense.

Tyler S: Building systems play through drills, *Women Coach* 1(3):8, 1975.
Provides drills to develop space and qualities of movement concepts in field hockey.

CHAPTER 27

Flag Football

OBJECTIVES

After completing this chapter the student will be able to:

1. Analyze the skills of flag football and introduce activities to be used in their development in the elementary school
2. Identify the movement concepts important in flag football and describe activities to enhance their development before use in football-type activities
3. Describe a progression of lead-up activities to introduce the skills and concepts of flag football in the elementary school

Football, introduced as an intercollegiate sport in 1852, is one of the most popular sports in the United States. Modified versions enable people of varying ages to play the game. Children and youth find it exciting because it involves the use of a ball that is not round, physical contact, and the use of strategy to move the ball to the goal.

In football, an individual uses specialized skills. The quarterback must be able to pass accurately, to hand the ball to others undetected, and to run with the ball. Some players are ball carriers who move with the ball given to them in the handoff or after receiving a pass. Others are line players who must protect the ball carrier and create a space through which the ball carrier will run. Still others make up the defense who prevent the opponents from scoring. They must not give the offensive team any space in which to run or to receive the ball on a pass. Constant analysis of the situation is important in the game. Football is one of the few games in which the players have the opportunity to plan and organize what they will do on each play or down.

Games of Other Countries

Football-type games are played in many countries including Canada, which closely resembles American football. In Australia, a rugby-type ball is used to kick or hand pass (similar to the underhand serve in volleyball) the ball, moving it into position for a kick to score.

FOOTBALL FOR ELEMENTARY SCHOOL CHILDREN

Football activities on the elementary school level require modification to guarantee the safety of each child and to take into consideration the difficulty of the skills and game fundamentals. At this level, personal contact, as found in blocking and tackling, should be discouraged. A count of 3 (1001, 1002, 1003) may be required in some games before the opposing players may cross the line of scrimmage to give the quarterback time to make the play.

Equipment: The shape and size of an official football make it difficult for elementary school children to control. Junior-sized or small foam footballs should be used. Because blocking and tackling are not used, helmets and protective padding are unnecessary. The size of the field should be reduced to fit the players and the games played. Two flags or pieces of cloth tucked in at the waist are needed for each player for the most advanced game—flag football.

Skills: Football allows play with the ball with both hands and feet. Passing and kicking skills should be developed as well as the ability to center and carry the ball in either hand while running.

Game: A progression of games should be used to develop the skills and knowledge associated with football. The rules are modified for the safety and ability of the players. The most advanced game suggested here is Flag Football. This game is similar to Touch Football; how-

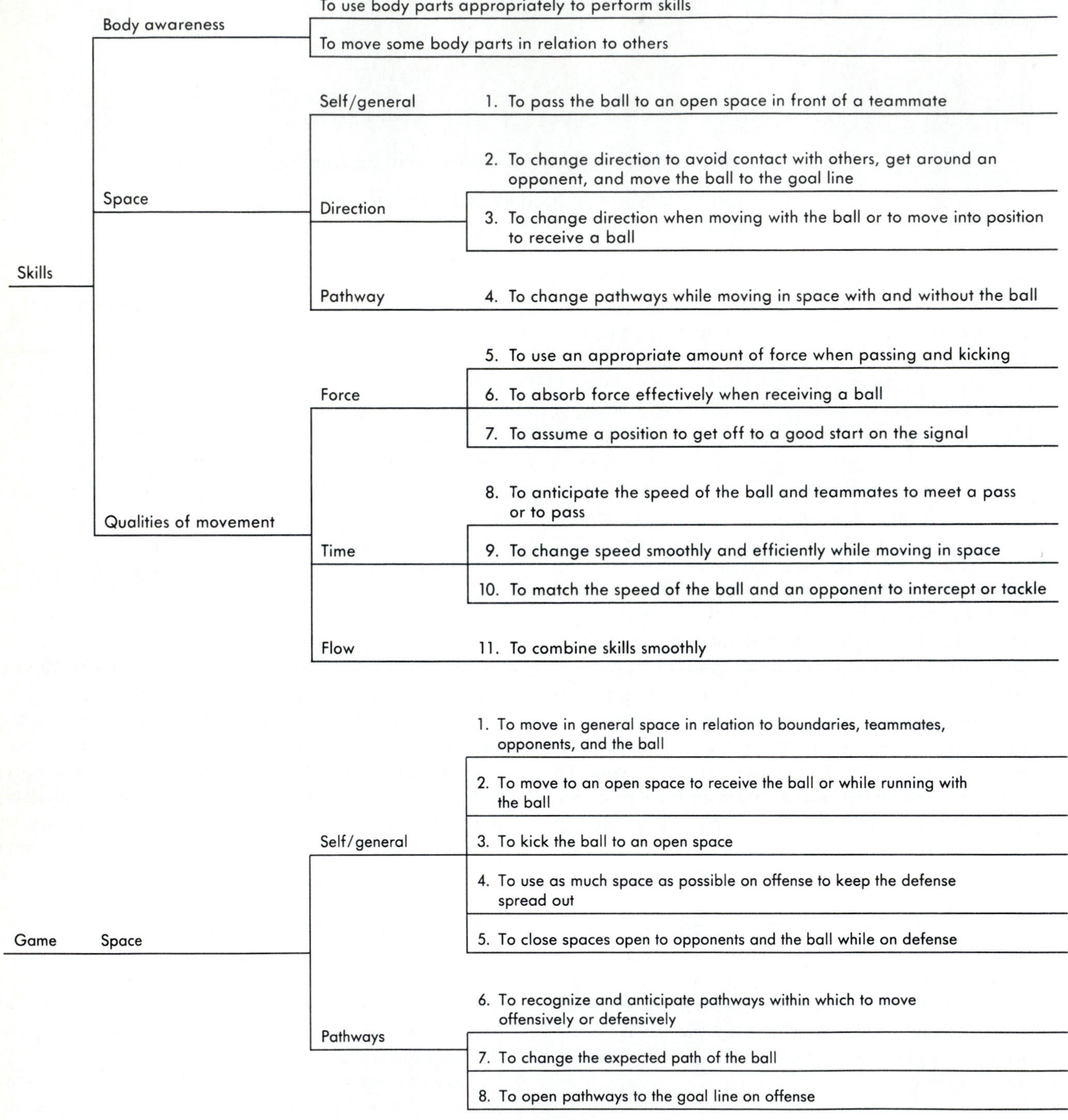
Skills
Body awareness
To use body parts appropriately to perform skills
To move some body parts in relation to others
Space
Self/general
1. To pass the ball to an open space in front of a teammate
Direction
2. To change direction to avoid contact with others, get around an opponent, and move the ball to the goal line
3. To change direction when moving with the ball or to move into position to receive a ball
Pathway
4. To change pathways while moving in space with and without the ball
Qualities of movement
Force
5. To use an appropriate amount of force when passing and kicking
6. To absorb force effectively when receiving a ball
7. To assume a position to get off to a good start on the signal
Time
8. To anticipate the speed of the ball and teammates to meet a pass or to pass
9. To change speed smoothly and efficiently while moving in space
10. To match the speed of the ball and an opponent to intercept or tackle
Flow
11. To combine skills smoothly
Game
Space
Self/general
1. To move in general space in relation to boundaries, teammates, opponents, and the ball
2. To move to an open space to receive the ball or while running with the ball
3. To kick the ball to an open space
4. To use as much space as possible on offense to keep the defense spread out
5. To close spaces open to opponents and the ball while on defense
Pathways
6. To recognize and anticipate pathways within which to move offensively or defensively
7. To change the expected path of the ball
8. To open pathways to the goal line on offense

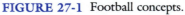

FIGURE 27-1 Football concepts.

ever, the use of the flags leaves no doubt about when a ball carrier has been contacted, and the game permits more twisting and turning as the ball carrier attempts to avoid the tag. Because the game requires a number of different player responsibilities, the class should be structured to ensure that all have the opportunity to play all the positions. All games require learning offensive and defensive skills, which are important in football.

The responsibilities of the offensive team are to maintain possession of the ball and to score touchdowns. Children should be encouraged to:

1. Vary the offensive strategy used to include both passing and running.
2. Move to an open space to receive the ball.
3. Make spaces for the ball carrier.

The defense tries to prevent the opponents from scoring and to regain possession of the ball by intercepting, gaining possession on a fumble, and keeping the offensive team from making the necessary yardage to keep the ball. On defense players should be encouraged to:

1. Close spaces open to opponents.
2. Cover possible ball receivers.
3. Respond quickly to the snap, giving the offense as little time as possible to make their play.

Social Skills

Football lead-ups offer a unique opportunity for children to work together in planning each play offensively and defensively. In beginning games this strategy may be a simple decision about who will be the ball carrier. In more advanced games a number of different roles may be determined. To assist children in these decisions, it may be necessary to help them define the possible roles and decisions to be made. Careful selection of groups is important to make these decisions as effortlessly as possible. Rules that require changing roles on each play of series of downs may be needed to ensure that all have an equal opportunity for play.

Health-Related Physical Fitness

Football games offer vigorous activity when participation is maximized. Small group games offer more opportunities for children to assume more active roles in games and usually allow play to move along at a faster pace.

FOOTBALL SKILLS

The following football skills may be developed at the elementary school level. Important concepts are mapped in Figure 27-1.

Ball-Handling Skills

The *forward pass* is an effective skill for moving the ball downfield and scoring. In football, the pass must be initiated while the passer is behind the **line of scrimmage** (an imaginary line extending across the width of the field that marks the position of the ball). The forward pass uses an overhand throwing motion, with the ball held slightly behind the middle with two or three fingers on the laces. The flight of the ball should be a spiral to lower the air resistance and to make the pass easier to catch (Figure 27-2).

Common errors:

1. Holding the ball in the palm of the hand.
2. Placing the hand too far forward on the ball.
3. Failing to turn the nonthrowing side in the direction of the throw.
4. Failing to use a wrist snap as the ball is released.
5. Failing to release the ball for a spiral flight.
6. Overthrowing or underthrowing the receiver.

Teaching suggestions: Children may be challenged by attempting to increase the distance and accuracy of their passing. The smaller hand, the farther back on the ball the fingers should be to begin the throw. Several different pass patterns may be used in football lead-up games.

Figure 27-3 describes the most common pass patterns. In the down and out pattern the receiver moves forward from the line of scrimmage and then toward the sideline. In the in-cut pattern the receiver moves forward and then to the side nearest the goal posts. In the flag and post patterns, the receiver moves forward and then either to the corner of the field (the flag) or toward the (goal) post. In the streak the receiver moves straight down the field from the line of scrimmage.

When *catching* a forward pass in football activities, the receiver may be facing the passer and the oncoming ball or may be moving away from the passer to the ball, which has been thrown to a space in front of the receiver. Catching a football while facing the passer uses the same body action as described in Chapter 13. Catching a football while moving away from the passer requires timing and watching the ball carefully as it comes into the hands. The arms and hands are reaching diagonally forward and upward in front of the face. As contact is made with the ball, the elbows bend and the hands cradle the ball in toward the body. The ball is quickly moved to the carrying position. When the receiver is facing the passer, the thumbs are together for a high pass; the little fingers are together for a low pass. When the receiver is moving away from the passer, the little fingers are together for a high pass (Figure 27-4).

Common errors:

1. Failing to time the run with the ball so that the ball is overrun or underrun.
2. Not pulling the ball into the body, but carrying it too high and out in front of the body.
3. Failing to keep the eyes on the ball until it is secured.
4. Catching the ball too close to the body so that it rebounds away.

- Ball is held slightly behind the middle with two or three fingers on the laces; the side is turned in the direction of the throw; the ball is brought back with the weight transferring to the rear foot.

- Ball is brought forward in an overhand motion, elbow leading, index finger pointing toward line of flight, weight transferred to forward foot.

- Ball is released with a wrist snap, with thumb turning under and toward the outside; follow-through in direction of flight.

FIGURE 27-2 Evaluative criteria and teaching points for forward pass.

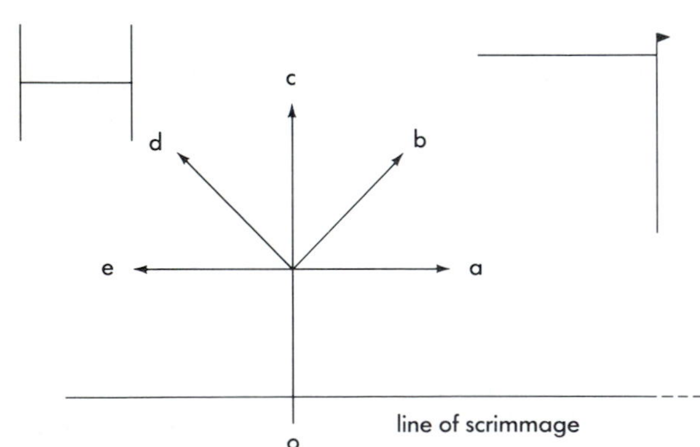

FIGURE 27-3 Pass patterns. *a,* Out cut (down and out). *b,* Flag. *c,* Streak. *d,* Post. *e,* In cut or in curve (down and across).

Teaching suggestions: The hands should be in front of the eyes so that the ball may be seen as it is caught.

The *lateral toss* is used to pass the ball in a slightly backward or sideward motion. The lateral toss may be used from any place on the field. The ball is held in both hands and is brought to the opposite side of the body from the throw in preparation for the throw. An underhand action bringing the ball across the body is used with a release about waist height, the index finger pointing in the line of flight. The weight is transferred in the direction of the throw and the arms follow through in the direction of flight. A spiral flight is desirable (Figure 27-5).

Common errors:

1. Failing to bring the ball to the opposite side before the throw.
2. Releasing the ball too high or too low.
3. Lateraling the ball forward.

Activities To Practice Passing and Catching

1. The children are divided into partners scattered in the general space. One is the passer, the other the receiver. The teacher calls the type of pass to be performed and the children practice the passes from a stationary position. (refining)
2. Once the children have an idea of the skills and the relationship between passer and receiver, the skills are prac

- Looking over the shoulder toward the passer and the ball, arms and hands extended forward and upward in front of the face.

- Watching the ball into the hands, fingers spread, elbows bend.
- Pulling the ball in toward the body.

FIGURE 27-4 Evaluative criteria and teaching points for catching.

- Ball is held in both hands and is brought back to the opposite side from the throw.

- An underhand motion brings the ball across the body.
- Follow-through in the direction of the throw.

FIGURE 27-5 Evaluative criteria and teaching points for lateral toss.

ticed with the receiver moving in the space to receive the ball. Passers and receivers must look out for others as they complete their passes. (refining)

3. In partners, one is the passer, the other the receiver. The passer throws a forward pass to the receiver who moves closer or farther away on each pass. The two change roles on each pass. (varying)
4. The children are in groups of three: the center, the receiver, and the quarterback. On the signal from the quarterback, the ball is snapped by the center, with the receiver moving forward to receive the pass. Vary the distance and path of the throws. (varying)
5. The children are in threes, similar to No. 3. The three determine the pathway the receiver will run, and the quarterback attempts to put the ball into the space to which the receiver is running. (varying)

FIGURE 27-6 Evaluative criteria and teaching points for pitchout.
- Extend arms in direction of pitch.
- Ball moves end over end.

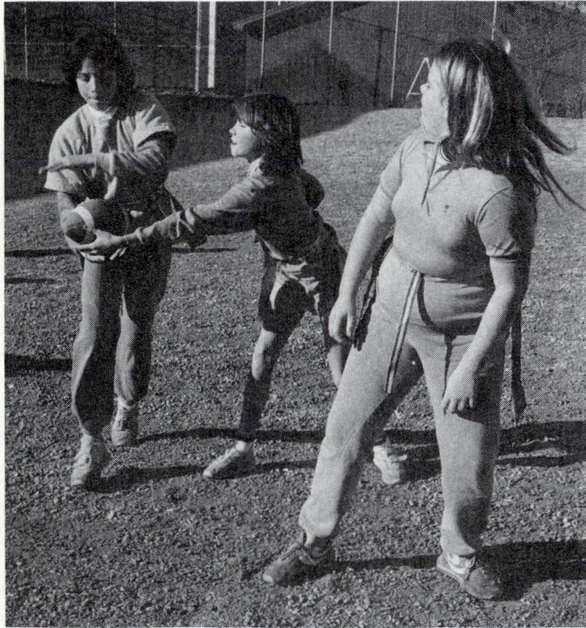

FIGURE 27-7 Evaluative criteria and teaching points for handoff.
- Ball is shifted to one hand, arm extended toward receiver.
- Hands in cradling position, upper thumb against chest, wrist rotated so that palm is out.
- Ball handed to receiver.

The *pitch-out* is a pass either to the side or to a player behind. It is taken behind the line of scrimmage. As the ball is received on the snap, it is brought up to the chest with two to three fingers of the passing hand on the laces and the other hand acting as support. As the pitch-out begins, the arm is extended in the direction of the pitch. On release, the thumb rolls under the ball, with the wrist rotating downward and outward. The flight of the ball is end over end (Figure 27-6).

Common errors:

1. Holding the ball in the palm of the hand.
2. Failing to extend the arm fully in the direction of the pitch.
3. Failing to roll the thumb under the ball, resulting in the flight of the ball not being end over end.

The *handoff* gives the option of giving the ball to a teammate rather than having the quarterback passing or running with the ball. This maneuver should be accomplished in a way that makes it difficult for the opposing team to detect who has the ball. The handoff also may be faked to keep the opponents guessing.

The handoff is initiated by holding the ball in both hands. As the receiver approaches, the ball is shifted to the hand closest to the receiver. The arm is bent at the elbow, and the lower arm is turned out toward the receiver. The ball is handed to the receiver as the two pass. It is not tossed (Figure 27-7).

Common errors:

1. Holding the ball too far away from the body before the handoff.
2. Tossing rather than handing the ball to the receiver.

The receiver forms a box with the hands in which the ball will be placed. The hand away from the quarterback is in the cradling position ready to receive the ball, with the upper-hand thumb against the chest, and the wrist rotated so the palm faces out. As the ball is received, the receiver secures the ball into the carrying position, accelerates, and moves away.

Common errors:

1. Reaching to receive the ball.
2. The receiver failing to secure the ball before moving on.

Teaching suggestions: The children must be encouraged to assume the cradling position before receiving the ball and not reaching for it. Young players may have more success completing the handoff with the use of two hands throughout the handing motion.

When *carrying the ball,* the player must hold it securely to maintain possession of it. The ball is cradled on the inside of the carrying arm and at the inside of the elbow. The ball is held on the right side of the body when running to the right and on the left side when running to the left. In this way the body may be kept between the ball and the defenders (Figure 27-8).

FIGURE 27-8 Evaluative criteria and teaching points for carrying the ball.
- Hand is in cradling position.
- Ball handed to receiver.

Common errors:
1. Failing to hold the football in close to the body.
2. Placing fingers too close together so that the ball is not held securely.

Teaching suggestions: The children should practice carrying the ball on both the right and left sides of the body.

Activities To Practice Ball Carrying

1. Set up an obstacle course of cones or other objects. The ball carriers move through the obstacle course, carrying the ball first on one side and then the other. (refining)

Kicking Skills

Punting in football is similar to the skill used in soccer. At the elementary school level, it is used in a number of lead-up activities. As the ball is received from the snap, it is moved to a position out in front of the body, with the end turned slightly downward and to the inside. A step is taken forward on the right (kicking) foot. The ball is held with the right hand on the side and slightly to the rear. The left hand supports the ball on the opposite side. The kicking leg is then brought forward to contact the ball. The ball is projected forward and upward as the kicking leg follows through in an upward motion (Figure 27-9).

Common errors:
1. Throwing the ball rather than dropping it.
2. Dropping the ball too close to the body so that contact is made on the leg or ankle.
3. Kicking with the toe.
4. Failing to point the toe.
5. Kicking the ball straight up rather than forward and upward.

Teaching suggestions: Practice the drop without kicking the ball first. Emphasize beginning with the weight on the left foot, stepping right, dropping the ball, stepping left, and then kicking with the right foot. Children should practice punting for both distance and accuracy.

The *placekick* is similar to the instep kick in soccer, with the ball held in position by a teammate. This is also called the soccer-style kick or side winder. In the placekick the ball is held by placing one end on the ground, with the laces facing away from the kicker. The kicker approaches the ball, placing the opposite foot to the side and slightly behind the ball. The kicking leg swings forward, contacting the ball, and projecting the ball forward and upward (Figure 27-10).

Common errors:
1. Failing to be on the appropriate step when reaching the ball.
2. Kicking with the toe.
3. Failing to follow through in the intended direction of flight.

Teaching suggestions: Children may practice placekicking for both accuracy and distance.

Activities To Practice Kicking

1. In partners, practice kicking, varying the distance between the two individuals. (varying)
2. In partners, practice kicking the ball away from the receiver, to the right or left. (varying)

Offensive and Defensive Skills

Centering is the means of putting the ball in play after a down. On the signal from the quarterback, the center lifts the ball from the ground and tosses or hands it between his or her legs to the quarterback. At the elementary school level, the **shotgun** is usually used, in which the quarterback is positioned several yards behind the center. As an alternative, a **direct snap,** in which the quarterback is over the center with his or her hands under the center, may be used. In the direct snap the center turns the ball one fourth turn so that it is placed in the quarterback's hands ready to pass.

The center assumes a position behind the line of scrimmage, with the ball on the ground directly in front of the center. The throwing hand is on the ball as it would be for passing, with the other hand on the opposite side of the ball to help guide the ball on the snap. On the signal from the quarterback, the center extends the arms backward between the legs and tosses the ball to the quarterback, who is standing directly behind and (in elementary school games) some distance from the center (Figure 27-11).

Common errors:
1. Lifting the ball off the ground before the signal from the quarterback.
2. Releasing the ball too soon so that it goes too low.

• Ball held in front of and away from the body, the end facing downward; step on kicking foot.

• Ball dropped parallel to the ground; step on left foot.

• Ball contacted on the instep and slightly to the outside of the right foot, with the toe pointed and body leaning away.

• Kicking leg follows through upward and in the direction of the kick.

FIGURE 27-9 Evaluative criteria and teaching points for punting.

3. Having an inappropriate distance between the quarterback and center.
4. Releasing the ball too late so that it goes too high.

The *2-point stance* is the safest stance for elementary school football games. The player stands in a side stride position with feet parallel or one foot slightly in front of the other. The knees are bent and the weight is balanced on the balls of the feet (Figure 27-12).

Common errors:

1. Failing to assume a balanced position.

Blocking at the elementary school level is limited to moving the body into the path of an opposing player, or to intercepting the ball. When blocking, the player moves from the two-point stance to a forward-stride position, the feet a comfortable distance apart and knees bent. The arms are crossed, and the hands grasp the shirt at the shoulders; the elbows are down and in close to the body. The eyes are on the opponent. The head is up as contact is made with the opponent's upper body (Figure 27-13).

Common errors:

1. Placing feet too close together so that the body is not balanced.
2. Keeping legs straight, body too erect.
3. Keeping elbows up or away from the body.
4. Keeping head down.

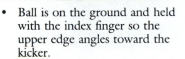

- Ball is on the ground and held with the index finger so the upper edge angles toward the kicker.
- Ball approached, last step on foot opposite the kicking foot.

- Kicking leg swings forward, contacting the ball on the instep.

- Leg follows through in the direction of the kick.

FIGURE 27-10 Evaluative criteria and teaching points for placekick.

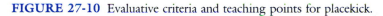

- Assume a stride position with knees bent and body weight forward and over the ball.
- Ball is held in two hands.
- Toes point straight ahead.

- Arms extend back between legs.
- Release ball from fingertips.

FIGURE 27-11 Evaluative criteria and teaching points for centering.

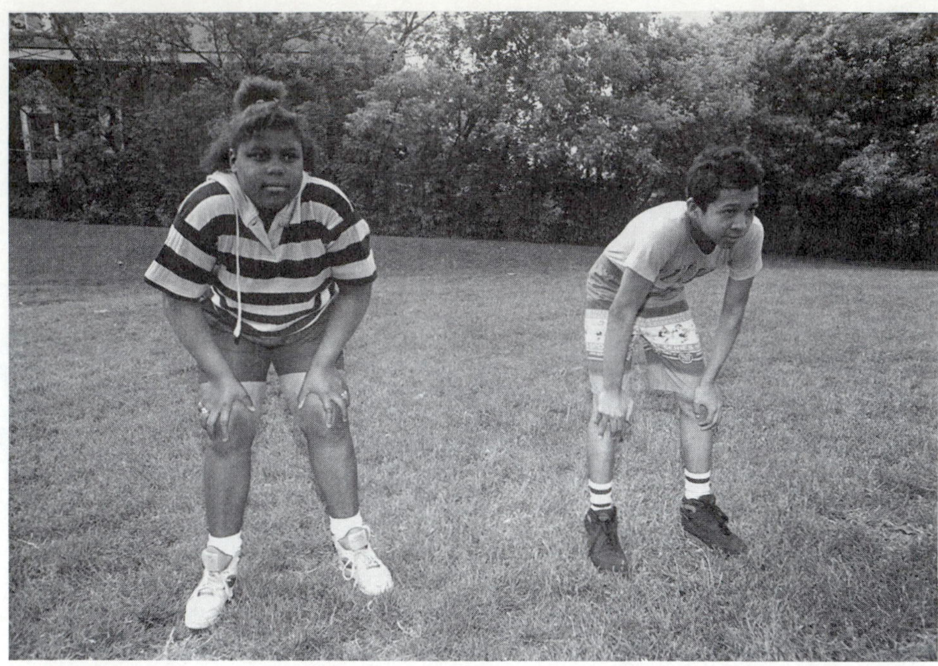

FIGURE 27-12 Evaluative criteria and teaching points for the two-point stance.
- Side stride position.
- Feet parallel or one foot slightly ahead of the other.
- Knees bent, weight balanced on balls of the feet.

FIGURE 27-13 Evaluative criteria and teaching points for blocking.
- Cross arms with hands grabbing shoulders.
- Elbows down and in close to body, head is up.
- Contact made with opponent's upper body.

Teaching suggestions: Have the children practice going from the two-point stance to the blocking position several times before attempting to block another player.

FOOTBALL CONCEPTS

The movement content important for success in football is outlined in Figure 27-1. Activities to develop these concepts should be used in each lesson to help children apply the movement concepts to football activities. A few suggested activities follow.

Football Concepts and Activities

1. To move in general space in relation to boundaries, teammates, opponents, and the ball.
   a. The area is divided into small playing fields for two players. Players use the various passing patterns to move the ball from one end of their field to the other. (Which patterns required careful attention to the space available?)
   b. Repeat *a*, adding a defense player. The offense runs pass or running plays against the defense, who tries to tag the runner. (How did you use the space to avoid your opponent? To Intercept?)
2. To move to an open space to receive the ball or while running with the ball.
   a. The area is marked off into 5-yard squares with cones marking the corners. An offensive and defensive player are located in each square. On the signal from the leader, the offensive player attempts to move around the defensive player. The defensive player tries to move into the intended path of the moving player. Repeat, changing roles. (How did you move to create a space in which to move around your opponent?)
3. To kick the ball to an open space.
   a. In groups of three, a kicker and two receivers. The kicker attempts to place the ball in a space away from the receivers. (What areas were most difficult for the receivers to catch the kick?)
4. To use as much space as possible on offense to keep the defense spread out.
   a. Two moving offensive players attempt to pass the ball back and forth while two defenders try to intercept in a small area. Enlarge the area and repeat. (Which space was easiest to pass without interceptions?) Repeat the activity with the smaller space once more. (How can you make the small space seem like a larger space?)
5. To close spaces open to opponents and the ball while on defense.
   a. Repeat activity No. 2a, but this time use a ball carrier, and require the defense to take the flags. (How did you move to close space to the ball carrier?)
6. To recognize and anticipate pathways within which to move offensively or defensively.
   a. In groups of four, three defensive players and one offensive player. An area is marked off into 10-yard sections, one defensive player in each. The ball carrier attempts to run from one end line to the other through the 10-yard zones without losing flags in his or her belt. (What moves did you make to open a pathway as you ran?)
   b. In groups of five, three stationary defensive players and a quarterback and receiver. The quarterback attempts to hit the receiver with a pass through the available pathways as the stationary defensive players attempt to intercept. (How did you anticipate where the throw must be made?)
   c. Children are in groups of three: a quarterback, a receiver, and a defensive player. The quarterback passes to the moving receiver, while the defender tries to intercept. (What cues helped you to intercept the pass while on defense?)
7. To change the expected path of the ball.
   a. Similar to No. 6c, but there are two receivers. The pass is now made to the receiver who is free. (How did you anticipate where to throw the ball?)
8. To open pathways to the goal while on offense.
   a. In groups of six, three on offense and three on defense. The offense attempts to run the ball to the goal line while three defenders attempt to tag the runner. (How did you open paths for the ball carrier?)

FOOTBALL LEAD-UP GAMES

An analysis of the football lead-up games that follow may be found in Table 27-1.

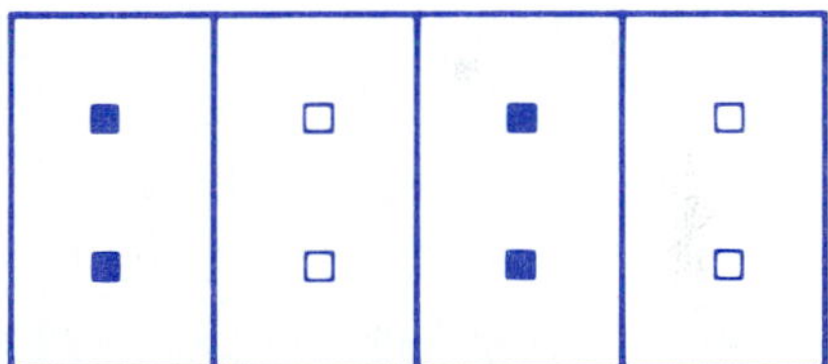

FOOTBALL END BALL

This game is played like End Ball in basketball except that a football is used and running with the ball is not penalized (see Chapter 25).

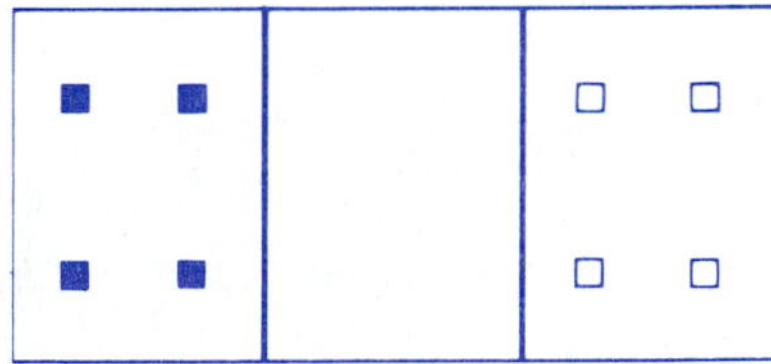

PUNT BALL

Level: III
Equipment: One junior-sized or small foam football
Area: A playing field 35 feet wide by 75 feet long with a neutral area 25 feet wide in the center of the field
Participants: Four to five players per team
Skills: Punting and catching

TABLE 27-1 GAMES ANALYSIS

NAME	GAME CLASSIFICATION	NO. OF PARTICIPANTS	EQUIPMENT	SPACE AND ORGANIZATIONAL PATTERN	MOTOR SKILLS
Football Endball	Lead-up	Three to four per team	One junior or small foam foot-ball	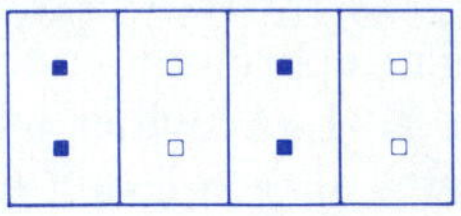	Passing Catching
Punt Ball	Lead-up	Four to five per team	One junior or small football	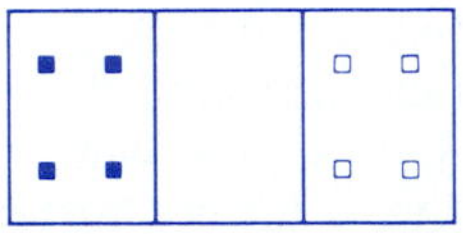	Punting Catching
Zone Football	Lead-up	Six per team	One junior or small foam foot-ball	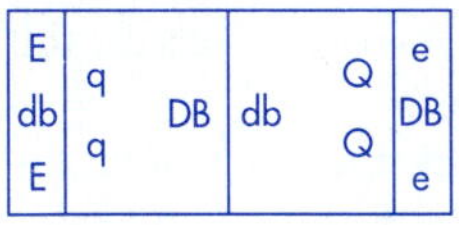 E db E q q DB db Q Q e DB e	Passing Catching
Flickerball	Lead-up	Three to four per team	One foam football, pinnies or vests	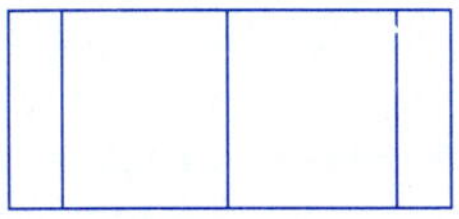	Passing Catching
Pass, Punt, and Kick	Lead-up	Five per team	One junior or small foam foot-ball	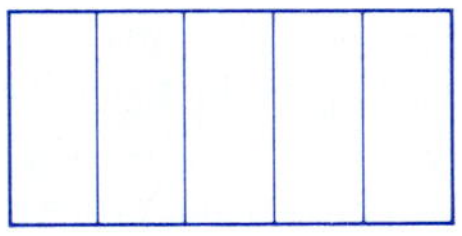	Punt Forward pass Placekick Catch
One Down Football	Lead-up	Five per team	One junior or small foam foot-ball	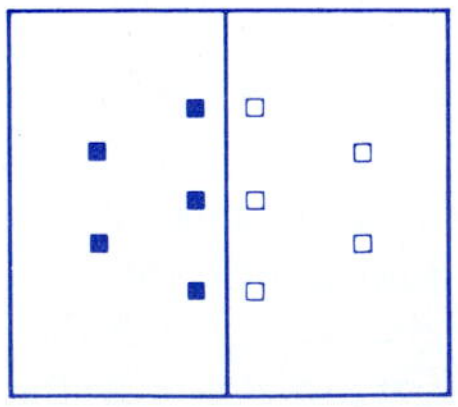	Passing Catching Carrying the ball Tagging
Flag Football	Lead-up	Six per team	One junior or small foam foot-ball	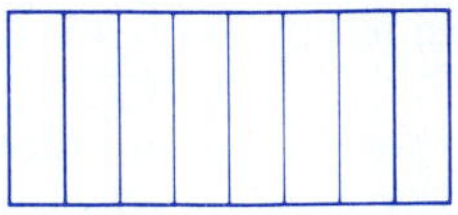	Centering Placekick Punt Forward pass Lateral Handoff Blocking Carrying the ball Pitchout

*Numbers refer to the movement concepts listed in Figure 27-1 on p. 554.

MODIFICATIONS	MOVEMENT CONCEPTS*	SOCIAL STRUCTURE	STRATEGY	LEVEL
1. Rotate players so all have a chance to play all positions	Skills: 1, 3, 5, 6, 8 Game: 1, 2, 5, 7	Social interaction I	1. Move the ball quickly 2. Cover the entire area on defense 3. Move to an unguarded area to receive a pass 4. Move the ball to a better throwing position before attempting to pass to a teammate in the goal area	III
1. Number players (each kicks in turn) 2. Reduce length of field to allow more scoring 3. Modify scoring so receiving team receives points for catching the ball 4. Use placekicking instead of punting	Skills: 5, 6, 10 Game: 1, 3, 5, 7	Social interaction I	1. Receivers stay spread out to cover the entire area 2. When kicking, look for open spaces within which to punt the ball	III
1. Add one defense player to each of middle zones 2. Reduce the size of the playing area	Skills: 1, 3, 5, 6, 8 Game: 1, 2, 5, 7	Social interaction I	1. Offense should stay spread out and moving to get away from defenders	III
	Skills: 1, 3, 6, 8-10 Game: 1, 2, 4-8	Social interaction I	Offense should stay spread out and moving in space	IV
	Skills: 5, 6, 8, 10 Game: 1, 3-8	Social interaction I	1. Move quickly to the ball to receive it as close as possible to the opponent's goal line	III
	Skills: 1-6, 8-11 Game: 1-2, 4-8	Social interaction II	1. Move to an open space to receive a pass 2. Offense keep spread out to increase space defense must cover	IV
	Skills: 1-11 Game: 1-8	Social interaction II	1. Move to an open space to receive a pass 2. Use a variety of skills on offense to keep the defense guessing	IV

Description: One team begins play by kicking the ball to the opponents' end of the field. If the ball goes over the goal line in the air, the kicking team score 3 points. The opposing players attempt to catch the ball, coming into their third of the field between the neutral zone and the goal line. If the ball is caught, they punt the ball back to the other team from the spot where it was caught. If the ball is dropped, the kicking team scores 1 point, and the receiving team kicks the ball from the spot where it first touched the ground.

Fouls:

1. Kicking the ball so that it lands in the neutral zone or out of bounds.
2. Walking with the ball after the catch.

Penalty:

1. Opposing team takes possession of the ball and kicks from anywhere in its area or, if out of bounds, from a spot closest to where the ball went outside the boundaries.
2. Move back to the appropriate spot and kick the ball.

Teaching suggestions:

1. Encourage the receiving team to cover its entire area for possible catches.
2. Encourage the receivers to call for the ball when they attempt to catch it.
3. Number players and have them kick in turn to ensure that all have an equal opportunity.
4. Reduce the length of the field to allow for more field goals to be scored.
5. Modify scoring so that the receiving team scores points for successfully catching the ball.
6. Use placekicking instead of punting.

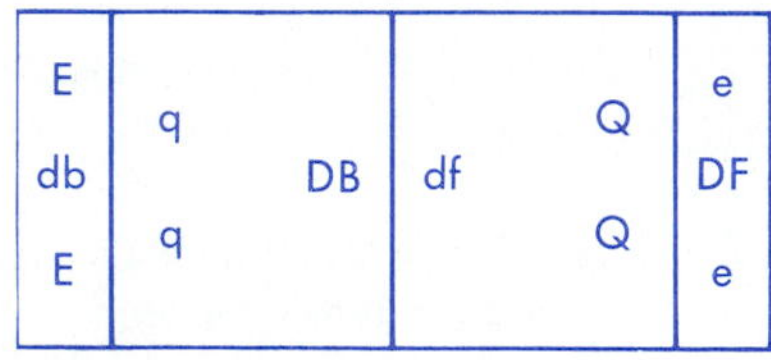

ZONE FOOTBALL

Level: III

Equipment: One junior-sized or small foam football

Area: An area 30 feet wide and 60 feet long divided in the center and 10-foot areas marked off at each end of the playing field

Participants: Six players per team: two ends, two quarterbacks, and two defensive backs

Skills: Passing and catching

Description: One team with the ball begins play. A quarterback attempts to score by throwing the ball to one of the ends. A pass may be completed to the other quarterback on the team if the ends are not free. A point is scored if the ball is successfully caught by an end. After a score the ball is given to a quarterback on the other team to begin play. If the ball is intercepted, the defensive back quickly throws the ball to a quarterback on the same team and play continues. If the ball is dropped, it is given to the opposing team.

Fouls: Personal contact with a member of the opposing team.

Penalty: Ball is awarded to the opposing team's quarterback.

Teaching suggestions:

1. Add an additional defensive player to each of the middle zones.
2. Reduce the size of the playing field.
3. Encourage the children to pass the ball quickly.

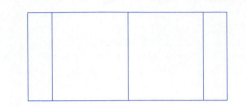

FLICKERBALL

Level: IV

Equipment: One foam football, pinnies or vests

Area: A playing area with a 10-yard line and goal line on each half

Participants: Three to four players per team

Skills: Passing, catching

Description: Players are scattered in the playing area. Play begins at the 10-yard line of one team, who attempt to pass and catch the ball as they move the ball toward the goal line. After catching the ball, players must stop immediately and pass it again within 5 seconds. Defenders may not guard an opponent with the ball, remaining 5 yards away from them. Anytime the ball touches the floor, possession is given to the opposite team. An intercepted pass results in loss of possession for the passing team. A touchdown (1 point) is scored when a pass is caught in the end zone. After a score, play resumes with the opposite team beginning at their 10-yard line.

Fouls:

1. Running with the ball on offense.
2. Defending a passer closer than 5 yards away.

Penalty:

1. Loss of possession.
2. The offense moves three steps closer to the goal to pass.

Teaching suggestions: Encourage the offense to keep moving in the space trying to get open for the pass.

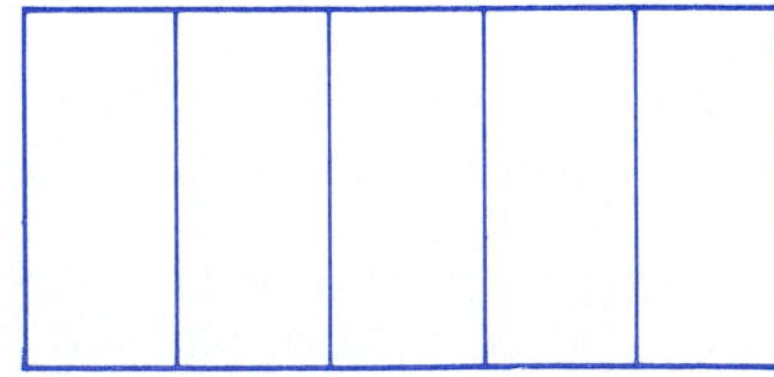

PASS, PUNT, AND KICK

Level: IV

Equipment: One junior-sized or small foam football

Area: A field space 20 yards by 50 yards with 10-yard lines indicated and a goal line at each end

Participants: Five per team, numbered from 1 to 5

Skills: Punt, forward pass, placekick, catch

Description: One team has the ball in its half of the field and attempts to move the ball over the opponents' goal line in the air. Player 1 begins play by punting, passing, or place kicking the ball toward the opponents' goal line from the 10-yard line. If the ball is caught by the opposing team on a fly or after it touches the ground without going over the goal line, play continues, with player 1 on the receiving team using one of the three skills to move the ball toward the other goal line. Players assume responsibility for moving the ball in turn, with the number 2 players coming into action next and so on. If the ball is caught in the air, the team may move three steps forward before passing, punting, or placekicking the ball. A punt over the goal line scores 1 point, a pass 2 points, and a placekick 3 points.

Fouls:

1. Moving forward away from the spot where the ball touched the ground or more than three steps after it was caught.
2. Kicking or passing the ball out of bounds.

Penalty:

1. Move to the appropriate spot and execute one of the skills.
2. The receiving team begins at the spot where the ball went out of bounds.

Teaching suggestions: Encourage the receiving team to move quickly to the ball to get possession as close as possible to the opponents' goal line.

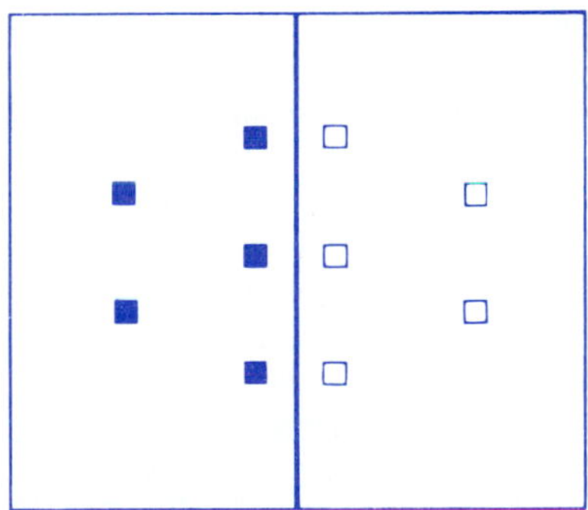

ONE DOWN FOOTBALL

Level: IV

Equipment: One junior-sized or small foam football; two flags for each player.

Area: A playing field 20 yards wide and 25 yards long divided into two equal halves.

Participants: Five per team: three line players, two backs.

Skills: Passing, catching, tagging (taking the flags), carrying the ball.

Description: To begin the game, one team is given the ball at the line of scrimmage. On the signal, "Hike," from one of the backs, players attempt to run or pass any number of times to move the ball to the goal line without being tagged. The defending team attempts to get both flags from the player with the ball or to intercept a pass. If the team is successful in getting the flags or a pass is incomplete, the defensive team takes possession of the ball and play begins at the spot where the last flag was secured or the ball was thrown. If the pass is intercepted, play continues, with the intercepting team attempting to score at the opponents' goal line. If the team does not score, it is given one more play (down) to do so. If a touchdown is scored, play begins once again at the line of scrimmage, with the nonscoring team beginning the play. A touchdown scores 6 points.

Fouls: Pushing; using the hands, hips, or shoulders to block another player

Penalty: On the defense, replay the down if scoring did not result. On the offense, loss of down, opponents take possession where the infraction occurred or where the ball was downed, whichever is closer to the opponents' goal line.

Teaching suggestions:

1. Encourage the offense to stay spread out to create spaces for runners and the ball.
2. The defense should attempt to cover the space but avoid blocking the opponents.
3. Add additional downs to give more opportunities to score.

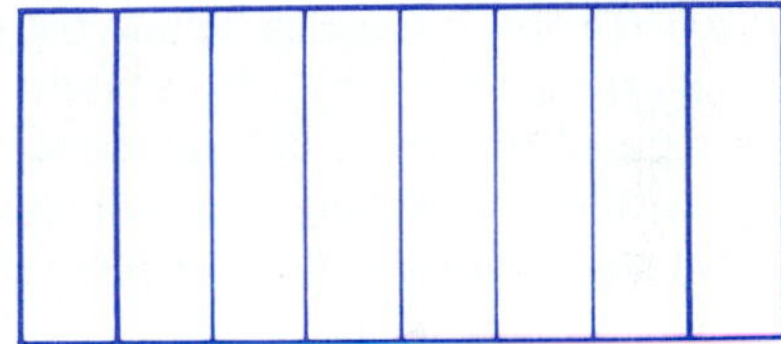

FLAG FOOTBALL

Level: IV

Equipment: One junior-sized or small foam football; two flags for each player

Area: A playing field 30 yards by 60 yards with 10-yard lines indicating the length of the field and two end zones 10 yards wide at either end

Participants: Six players per team; four line players and two backs. Two of the line players are ends and are eligible to receive passes.

Skills: Passing, catching, ball carrying, centering, handoffs, pitchout, placekick, punt, blocking

Description: The game begins with one team kicking off from behind their own goal line with a placekick to the other team. All players on the kicking team must be behind the goal line as the ball is kicked. The receiving team attempts to catch the ball or gain possession of it after it touches the ground and move it to the opposite end zone before both flags are taken. The kicking team attempts to down the ball by taking the flags of the ball carrier. If the ball is fumbled, the team who first touched the loose ball gains possession and play begins at that spot.

Once the ball is downed after the kickoff, the offensive team has four downs to move the ball to the next zone. Each down begins with the ball being centered to one of the backs, who gives the signal, "Hike." The ball may be passed, handed off, or run on each of the downs. If a forward pass is used to move the ball, it must be thrown from behind the line of scrimmage. Each team may "huddle" before each play to decide the strategy it will use. If a team fails to move the ball to the next zone in four tries, the other team takes over and play continues. On the fourth down a team may punt but must indicate their intention to do so before centering

Flag Football.

the ball. Neither team may cross the line of scrimmage until after the ball has been kicked.

Six points are scored for a touchdown. After a touchdown, the scoring team may have one attempt to gain an extra point by taking an additional down from 3 yards out from the goal line. An extra point is earned if the team successfully runs or completes a pass on this play to move the ball past the goal line. If the ball is downed behind the team's own goal line, the opposing team is awarded 2 points. If the kick-off goes into the end zone a player from the receiving team may touch the ball to the ground behind the goal line for a touchback. Play then begins at the receiving team's 20-yard line.

Fouls:

1. The ball going out of bounds on the kick-off.
2. Forward passing on the kick-off return.
3. Failing to indicate the intention to punt.
4. Passing beyond the line of scrimmage.
5. **Off-side:** a player of either team beyond the line of scrimmage before the ball is centered.
6. Pushing or blocking with the hands, hips, or shoulders.

Penalty:

1. Kick the ball again. If it goes out of bounds on the second kick, the receiving team begins play on its 20-yard line.
2. Ball downed. Begin at the point where the ball was caught on the kick-off.
3. Five-yard penalty.
4. Five-yard penalty.
5. Five-yard penalty.
6. Fifteen-yard penalty.

Teaching suggestions:

1. Encourage the children to use a variety of skills (passing, running, and handoffs) to keep the defense guessing.
2. The defense may use a person-to-person or zone coverage.

SUMMARY

Football games offer elementary school children the opportunity to work with a ball that is not round. They are team games in which children have the opportunity to plan a course of action before each play. The skills and knowledge of football are difficult and take time to develop. Football is a very physical game, and care must be taken to provide the safest environment for all by carefully and consistently enforcing the safety rules, particularly concerning physical contact.

Football activities provide another activity in which application to the movement content should be made. Key concepts of space and qualities of movement should be an important part of each lesson. While it is considered to be a sport primarily played by men and boys, girls enjoy the lead-ups as well.

REFERENCES AND RESOURCES

Arnheim D and Pestolesi R: *Elementary physical education: a developmental approach,* ed 2, St Louis, 1978, Mosby–Year Book.

Fuoss D: *Complete handbook of winning football drills,* Newton, Mass, 1984, Allyn & Bacon.

Gustafson M, Wolfe S, King C: *Great games for young people,* Champaign, Ill, 1991, Human Kinetics.

Kirchner G: *Physical education for elementary schoolchildren,* ed 8, Dubuque, Ia, 1993, Wm C Brown.

Schurr E: *Movement experiences for children,* ed 3, Englewood Cliffs, NJ, 1980, Prentice-Hall.

ANNOTATED READINGS

Bahneman C: Pass football, *JOPER* 49(2):53, 1978.
Discusses a game derived from flag football in which several different scoring options are included.

Bowyer G: Australian-rules football in American physical education, *JOPERD* 62(7):24, 1991.
Describes the rules and play for Australian football with suggested activities to develop skills.

Dougherty N: *Principles of safety in physical education and sport,* Reston, Va, 1987, AAHPERD.
Presents a resource of safety considerations for a number of physical education activities, including flag football.

Gustafson J: Razzle dazzle football, *JOPER* 50(6):69, 1979.
Looks at a version of flag football with the option to pass at any time.

Hoppes S: Playing together—values and arrangements of coed sports, *JOPERD* 58(8):65, 1987.
Presents a rationale and guidelines for adapting sports for coed participation, including flag football.

CHAPTER 28

Hand and Paddle Games

OBJECTIVES

After completing this chapter the student will be able to:

1. Analyze the skills used in a variety of hand and paddle games during the elementary school years and introduce activities to be used in their development
2. Identify the movement concepts important in hand and paddle games and describe activities to enhance their development before their use in games
3. Describe a number of different hand and paddle games to be introduced in the elementary school

A number of different types of hand and paddle games may be introduced to elementary school children. Some are games played only at the elementary school level, whereas others are lead-ups to activities enjoyed by older students and adults, such as tennis, racquetball, handball, and badminton.

Success in these activities may require the individual to handle a variety of implements and projectiles. Individuals need to develop some understanding of flight possibilities as they attempt to receive and return different types of balls from and to their opponents. Using space effectively is essential. Participants must not only cover their own space defensively, but also manipulate the space of opponents by varying the placements of balls into their opponent's space. In partner activities they must develop a sense of position play that enables them to share the space defensively as well as work together to develop their offensive strategy.

Games from Other Countries

Racquet and paddle games are popular throughout the world. Some of the games use shuttlecocks, which vary from those used in badminton. Basically, these shuttlecocks consist of a number of feathers attached to a weighted object made and stuffed with various materials. The number of players in these games also may vary from singles and doubles to relatively large group activities. Two Japanese games have been included in the games section of this chapter.

HAND AND PADDLE GAMES FOR ELEMENTARY SCHOOL CHILDREN

Hand and paddle games at the elementary school level provide an opportunity for individual and partner play. As the child moves through the elementary school years, the games require more complex and greater accuracy in striking skills and increasingly complex game strategies.

Equipment: Implements for striking objects vary in size, length, and weight. A variety of racquets and paddles, as well as a range of objects to strike, are now available for children at the elementary school level. In selecting a paddle for children, grip size is an important consideration, because too large a grip will result in the paddle turning in the hand on contact with an object, making the object more difficult to control. As a general rule, the tip of the middle finger should touch between the base and the first joint of the thumb while grasping the racquet. Children begin using the hand in striking, moving to implements with shorter handles and eventually to longer handled implements. A variety of balls may be used that vary in speed of flight. Old tennis balls, wiffle balls, small foam balls, and shuttlecocks are easiest to control. In the beginning, the small foam or Nerf balls give the children greater time to get into position to make contact with the ball. If a variety of balls or shuttlecocks are available, children can choose the type of equipment that they can control for the various activities.

It is important to stress safety in use of the paddles. The use of a paddle increases a person's self space. The children should be sure that they have a large enough space to swing the paddles without hitting other children. As they find a space, they should gently swing the paddle to determine the amount of extra space needed. If they are too close to other children, they must look for a new space. Control of the swing and the object projected must always be stressed. Assuming this responsibility allows the children to work and play safely in limited space.

Skills: Successful participation requires use of a variety of skills. All require an effective serve that puts one's opponents at a disadvantage and effective forehand, backhand, and overhand strokes to win the point. At the elementary school level, the serve in most cases will be a drop and hit rather than an overhand motion as seen in tennis. This will enable the child to better control placement of the ball in the opponent's court. Developing a good ready position from which the player can move easily to cover the court is also important for game success.

Games: The games suggested in this chapter provide a variety of experiences in which the court may include rebounding from walls or merely placement on the floor on the other side of a net or over a line. As children gain experience in the games, they may learn to use ball spin as well as various angles of rebound as a part of their strategy. Court size varies with the space available. Maximum participation for all children in the class results when sufficient smaller courts are provided.

The games may require singles play against one or more opponents or doubles play in which partners share the responsibility for covering the court and winning points.

When on offense the player attempts to:

1. Serve to an open area of the opponent's court.
2. Change the expected path of the ball.
3. Place the ball in an empty space in the opponent's court on all returns.
4. Vary the force used in placing the ball in the opponent's court.

On defense the player attempts to:

1. Close spaces for possible placement of the ball by the opponent.
2. Assume a position on the court in which they can easily move in any direction to play the ball.
3. Move to the offense on receiving the ball, using the offensive strategy suggested earlier.

Figure 28-1 outlines the movement content important in hand and paddle games.

Social Skills

While many of the striking games for elementary school children provide singles play, doubles and group activities should be included in the experiences. In singles play children should be encouraged to play within the rules and to call their own violations. In addition in doubles or group play, children should be encouraged to work together in sharing the space to cover the court and to assist one another when necessary. Emphasis in these games should be on the interdependence of doubles partners and team players in achieving the game's goals.

Health-Related Physical Fitness

Singles and doubles play at an appropriate level of difficulty should provide for some cardiorespiratory fitness. In addition children may be required to strike the object and to move to some other area of the court or to the opposite court for the next hit to provide a vigorous warm-up activity.

STRIKING SKILLS

Striking skills present a challenge for elementary school-aged children. Many will have had little opportunity outside of school to use paddles or racquets; therefore, they will be beginning at the perceiving level for most of the skills. Refining will take time as children learn to move in relation to the ball and to control the racquet or paddle when making contact and directing the ball.

Important movement concepts to be developed include the following:

1. Body awareness: the use and relationship of body parts.
2. Space: the relationship of the hitter, paddle, and ball; maintaining a position that enables the player to move in any direction to play the ball; controlling the level of the object on the hit; and controlling the object's path.
3. Qualities of movement: controlling and varying the force and speed of the object in sending it to the opponent's court (Figure 28-1).

Beginning striking activities may be found in Chapter 13. Most of the skills and activities presented may be used in striking with the hand or a paddle. In addition the following activities challenge children as they attempt to control a ball on a paddle.

Activities To Develop Hand and Paddle Skills

1. Roll the ball around the paddle face. Try it again but this time while standing on one foot.
2. Bounce the ball to the floor.
3. Bounce the ball to the floor, tracing your own shadow.
4. Hit the ball into the air and repeat as many times as possible without losing control. (How did you control the force to keep it going as long as possible?)
5. Similar to the previous activity, but turning the paddle or hand over to alternately hit with a forehand and backhand.
6. Repeat No. 5, but hitting the ball to the floor.
7. Hit a ball suspended from a thin rope, using a forehand, a backhand, or alternating the two strokes. (How

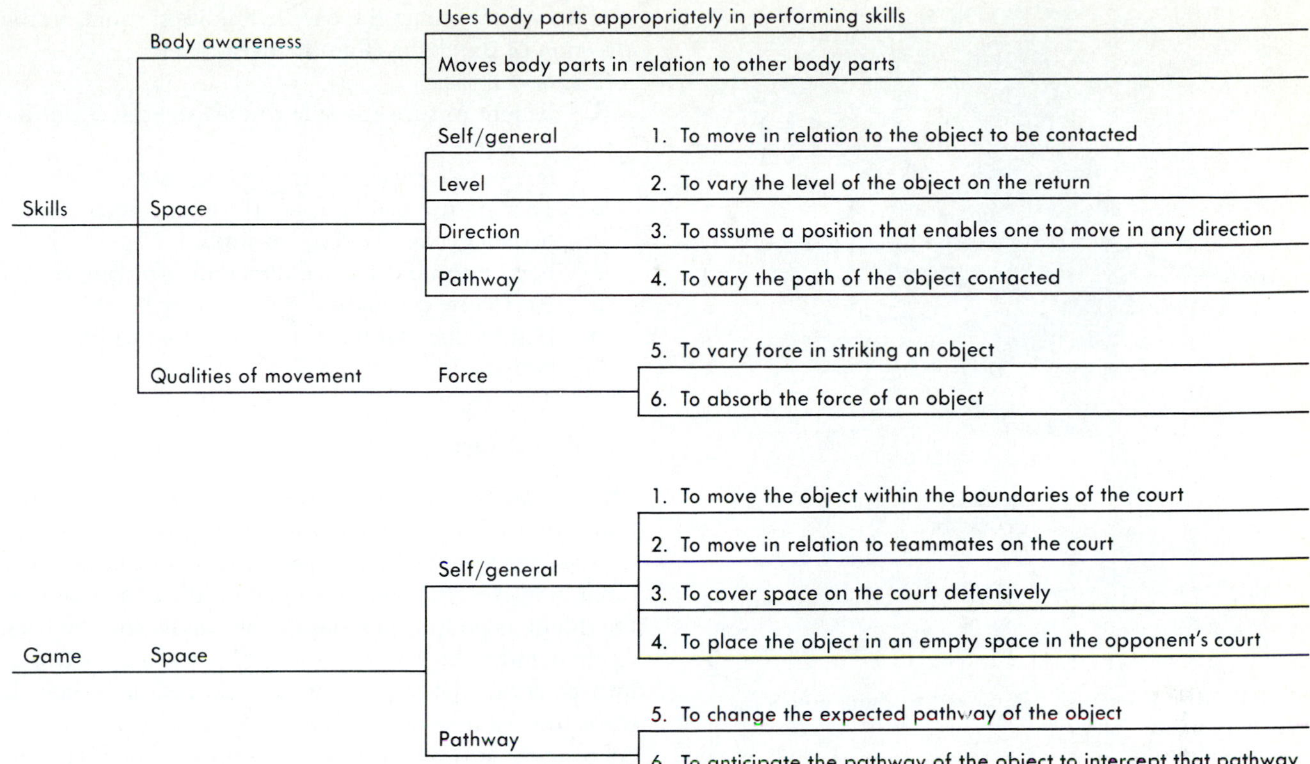

FIGURE 28-1 Concepts for hand and paddle games.

did you control the force to get as many hits as possible?)

8. Begin hitting the ball down to the low level, gradually hitting the ball higher. Hit the ball up to the medium and finally to the high levels. (Can you control the ball at each level, hitting it five consecutive times at each level?) Repeat, but decreasing the consecutive hits at each level on each repetition to end hitting once at each level.
9. Placing the ball on the floor in front of you, draw the racquet toward you over the ball and then scoop the ball up.
10. Place the ball on the floor to the outside of one foot. Squeeze the ball between the paddle and your foot and lift it. Try lifting with the ball on the inside of your foot. At your heel.
11. Hit the ball down with the edge of the paddle.
12. Hit the ball with the edge of the paddle in the following sequence: down, down, up. (Can you repeat the sequence several times?) Make up a sequence of your own.
13. Hit the ball up as in No. 4, but bring the racquet across under the ball to cause it to spin. Repeat, keeping it under control.
14. Now hit for a spin and let the ball rebound from the floor. What was the effect of the spin as the ball bounced on the floor.
15. Repeat No. 13, but alternate the racquet face from forehand to backhand.

Ready Position

Mastering the *ready position* is important for covering the court area and moving into position to play the ball. The player assumes a somewhat crouched position with knees, hips, and ankles slightly bent, slightly to the back and at the center of the playing area. The body is balanced in a side-stride position, with one foot slightly forward of the other. The body weight is carried on the insides and forward part of the feet, with weight evenly distributed until the oncoming ball direction is known. The upper body leans slightly forward. The racquet or paddle is held up in front of the body in the hand of the stroking arm and resting slightly in the other. The eyes are looking ahead toward the oncoming ball. As the ball approaches, the player is then ready to shift position to move to the ball (Figure 28-2).

Common errors:

1. Standing with weight on the entire foot.
2. Failure to position oneself so that the entire court can be covered.
3. Failure to hold the racquet up where it can be shifted to a forehand or backhand position.
4. Not paying attention to the ball.
5. Maintaining an upright position.

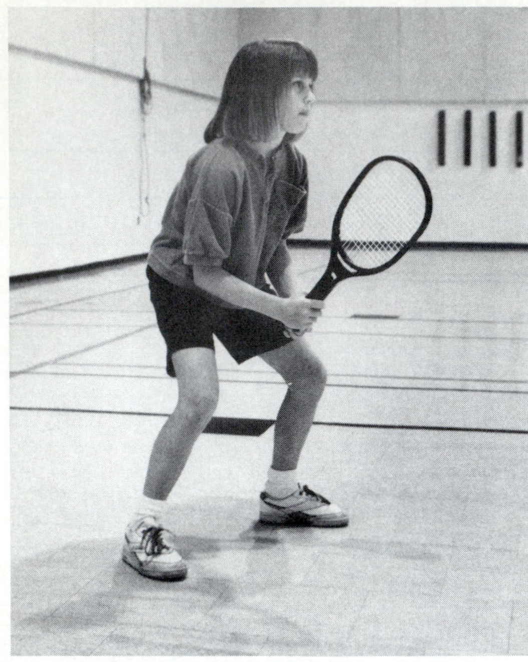

FIGURE 28-2 Evaluative criteria and teaching points for the ready position.
- Leg flexed.
- Weight on inside and forward part of feet.
- Feet in a side stride, one foot slightly ahead of the other.
- Racquet up in front of the body.
- Head up, looking at oncoming ball.

Activities To Practice the Ready Position

1. Students assume a ready position, with the instructor or a partner calling forehand, backhand, up, and back and the player shifting to the position called, hitting an imaginary ball and then returning to the ready position. (perceiving)
2. In partners, one tosses a ball to various positions on the court and the other moves into position to catch the ball at first and then to hit the ball to the tosser. (refining)

Forehand Drive

The *forehand drive* is executed on the side of the body where the paddle is being held. The paddle is grasped as if shaking hands with the paddle. The V formed between the thumb and index finger is on the top as the paddle is held with the paddle face perpendicular to the floor. As the body moves into position to begin the stroke, the side is turned toward the direction of intended flight, with the arm holding the paddle farthest away. The feet are in a comfortable stride position. The paddle arm is brought back, and the body weight is transferred to the back foot. As the paddle swings forward, the weight is taken on the forward foot. Contact with the ball is to the side and slightly ahead of the forward foot. The paddle is held firmly to prevent it from turning in the hand on contact. After contact the paddle follows through in the direction of the flight (Figure 28-3).

Common errors:

1. Failure to turn the side toward the direction of the flight.
2. Stepping forward on the wrong foot.
3. Turning the paddle face up (open) rather than perpendicular (closed) on contact.
4. Failure to hold the paddle family on contact.
5. No follow-through.
6. Hitting the ball when it is too close to the body.

Backhand Drive

The *backhand drive* is taken on the opposite side of the body from where the paddle is being held.

The same grip used in the forehand may be used. Most often, however, the hand is turned on the paddle so that the thumb is on the back side of the paddle and the back of the hand is on top. As the individual moves to get into position, the side on which the paddle is held is turned in the direction of intended flight. As the paddle is brought back, the body weight shifts to the rear foot. The paddle swings forward and the body weight shifts onto the forward foot. The paddle is held firmly, and contact with the ball is in front and to the side of the forward foot. The paddle continues to move forward in the direction of flight on the follow-through (Figure 28-4).

Common errors:

1. Being too close to the ball as it is contacted so that contact is made in front of the body.
2. Stepping toward the ball rather than in the direction of intended flight.
3. Failure to hold the paddle firmly on contact.
4. No follow-through.

Volley

The volley is used to hit a ball before it bounces on the court. The grip taken depends on whether the ball will be stroked on the forehand or backhand side. The action is similar to the forehand or backhand drive; however, there is little backswing before contact. The ball is contacted in front of the body with a punching motion, and there is little follow-through of the paddle after contact (Figure 28-5).

Common errors:

1. Using too much backswing, resulting in too much force.
2. Not holding the paddle firmly on contact.
3. Paddle face is open (angled back) so that the ball is lofted too much.
4. Not planting the feet on the volley, but moving through the ball.

- Shake hands with the paddle.
- The body is turned with the opposite side facing the direction of intended flight.
- The paddle is brought back and weight taken on the rear foot.

- Paddle brought forward, weight transferred to forward foot.
- Contact ball to the side and slightly ahead of forward foot.

- Paddle follows through in direction of flight.

FIGURE 28-3 Evaluative criteria and teaching points for the forehand.

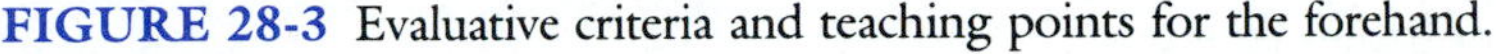

- Hand turned over on the paddle.
- Side turned in direction of hit.
- Paddle back, weight shifted to rear foot.

- Level swing forward as weight shifts to forward foot.
- Contact in front and to the side of forward foot.

- Paddle follows through in direction of flight.

FIGURE 28-4 Evaluative criteria and teaching points for the backhand.

- Forehand or backhand grip.
- Ball contact with a punching action.
- Little follow-through.

FIGURE 28-5 Evaluative criteria and teaching points for the volley.

- A forehand grip is used.
- Side facing forward, knees and hips flexed.
- Ball is dropped, paddle brought back at waist height.
- Ball contact at height of bounce, weight transferred to forward foot.
- Paddle swings forward in direction of flight.

FIGURE 28-6 Evaluative criteria and teaching points for the serve.

Activities To Practice the Forehand and Backhand Drives and the Volley

1. Stand with the arms out in front of the body with the hands together, palms touching. Turn, bring the hands back as if hitting a forehand or backhand drive. Swing the arms forward as if hitting a ball. (perceiving)
2. Starting facing forward as in No. 1, turn, drop the ball, bring the arms back, and then swing the arms forward to catch the ball. (perceiving)
3. Turn, drop the ball, swing, and hit the ball to a wall, catching the rebound. (refining)
4. With a partner who tosses the ball, hit the ball as it rebounds from the floor. (refining)
5. Hit the ball to the wall, hitting it again and again as it rebounds from the wall. (How many consecutive times can you return the ball to the wall?) (refining)
6. Hit the ball so that it bounces to a partner. Continue hitting the ball as many times as possible before losing control. (How did you control the force to keep the ball in play?) (refining)
7. Hit the ball to targets from various distances. (How did your strokes change as you moved closer or farther away?) (varying)
8. Vary the force of the hit so that your partner must move up or back to receive the ball. (How did you vary the force to make your partner move forward or backward?) (varying)
9. Hit the ball to a partner, varying the force of the return as the partner moves closer or farther away. (varying)
10. Hit the ball to targets from various positions, such as from the right, left, or directly in front of the target. Vary the strokes used. (varying)
11. Hit the ball to a space to the right or left of a partner so that the receiver must move to the ball. Use a forehand and a backhand swing. (varying)
12. Hit a ball at the low, medium, and high level. (How did you change your hit to move the ball to the desired level?) (varying)
13. Repeat the type of hit made by a partner. (varying)
14. Hit the ball thrown to the hitter at various levels. (How did you position yourself and the racquet to hit the ball?) (varying)

Serve

The serve is the stroke used to put the ball in play. The paddle is held firmly in a forehand grip. Both feet are behind the baseline, with the nonserving side facing forward. As the ball is dropped, the paddle is brought back at waist height, with the elbow bent and the wrist cocked. The weight is transferred to the rear foot. The paddle swings forward to contact the ball at the height of the bounce, with the paddle face perpendicular to the ground. The body weight is transferred to the forward foot, and the paddle swings forward of the body in the desired direction of flight (Figure 28-6).

Common errors:

1. Failure to hold the paddle firmly on contact.
2. Dropping the ball too close or too far away from the body.
3. Failure to time the swing with the bounce.
4. Opening the paddle face on contact so that the ball goes up in the air.

Activities To Practice the Serve

1. Practice dropping the ball in front of the body to the serving side and catch. (perceiving)
2. Drop the ball, bring the hand back as in preparation for the hit and come through and catch the ball slightly in front of the body on the serving side. (perceiving)
3. Drop the ball and hit it with the hand to a wall. Repeat with a paddle if desired. (Perceiving)
4. Set up relatively large targets on the wall. How many times can you hit the target consecutively with the serve? (refining)
5. Serve across a line or a net to a partner who designates the area to hit. Partner catches the ball on receiving the serve. (refining)
6. Hit to a wall. Can you hit it to the same area five times in a row? Try another spot on the wall. Repeat. (refining)
7. Serving to a partner, hit three to the right of your partner and then three to the left. (varying)
8. Serve to a partner, hitting three short and then three long serves. (varying)
9. Serve the ball into designated areas of the court. (What changes in your stroke did you make to hit the various areas?) (varying)

MOVEMENT CONCEPTS

Children need to practice the use of movement concepts before their application in the games. The following concepts and activities are an important part of game development (see Figure 28-1).

Movement Concepts and Activities

1. To move the object within the boundaries of the court.
   a. In partners, one hitting, one receiving. The receiver moves around the court, and the hitter attempts to hit the ball to the receiver, who catches the ball and throws it back to the hitter. The hitter hits the ball after it rebounds from the floor. (Did you hit it to all areas of the court? Did you keep the ball in bounds?)
   b. In partners, hitting back and forth and trying to hit to all areas of the court. Gradually change the dimensions of the court—shorter, longer, wider, narrower. (How did you hit to all the areas and keep the ball in bounds?)
2. To move in relation to teammates on the court.
   a. In groups of three, one set of doubles partners, one receiver. The partners practice up and back or side by side doubles strategy as the receiver tosses the ball to each part of the court. At first the partners catch the ball; later they attempt to hit it.

3. To cover space on the court defensively.
   a. In partners, one hitter and one thrower. The hitter begins in a covering position and moves to balls thrown to various parts of the court. After hitting the ball, they return to the home position to await the next ball. (Did you remember to move to the home position after each hit? Which area of the court was most difficult to defend?)
4. To place an object in an empty space in the opponent's court.
   a. In partners, one hitter and one receiver. The receiver throws the ball to the hitter and then moves to various positions on the court. The hitter attempts to place the ball in the open spaces away from the receiver. One point is received for each ball landing in the court but not played by the receiver.
5. To change the expected pathway of the object.
   a. In partners, the hitter hits the balls to the left and then to the right of the receiver. Repeat, placing balls in front of or behind the receiver. Repeat once more, varying the placements (right/left, up/back). Add scoring, one point each time the receiver must change position to play the ball.
   b. Repeat No. 5a, but with each person hitting the ball. Each makes up a placement sequence such as right, right up, left back. The opponent attempts to guess the sequence.
   c. Serving in partners, the server calls the area of the court to which the serve will go. Change roles after five serves. Repeat several times trying to improve your record for accurate serves. (How did your serves change to hit the area called?)
   d. In partners rally back and forth. Each person gets a point if the partner has to move to a new position on the court to receive the ball. Count your total points. Repeat trying to improve your record. (How did your hits change as you directed the ball to different parts of the court?)
6. To anticipate the pathway of the object to intercept that pathway.
   a. Repeat the activities in No. 5, but focus on the receiver moving to the ball, anticipating where the ball will go by watching the hitter.
   b. In partners, one hits the ball so that it hits a wall and the other moves into position to get the rebound. (How did you anticipate where the ball would go?)

STRIKING GAMES FOR HANDS AND PADDLES

The following games may be introduced to use the skills and movement concepts. Most may be played using the hand or a paddle for striking. A games analysis may be found in Table 28-1.

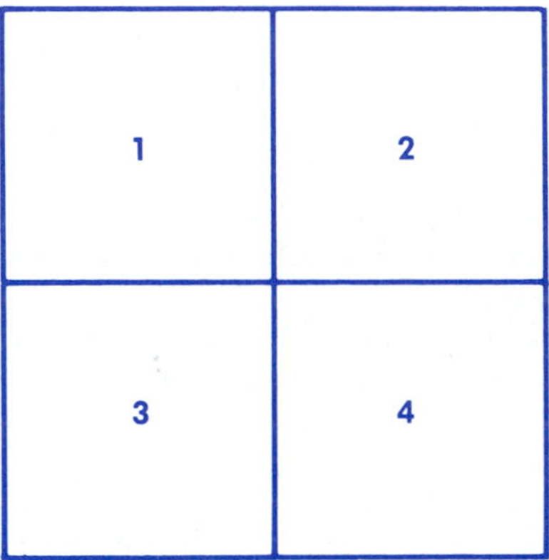

FOUR SQUARE

Level: III
Equipment: One 8-inch playground or four-square ball
Area: Four-square courts of four adjoining 8-foot boxes
Participants: Four per game
Skills: Striking with the hands, underhand and possibly overhand.
Description: One player stands in each of the four playing areas. Player No. 1 begins play by dropping the ball, letting it bounce once and striking it in an underhand motion so that it lands in one of the three other playing areas. The player receiving the ball strikes it in a similar manner so that it

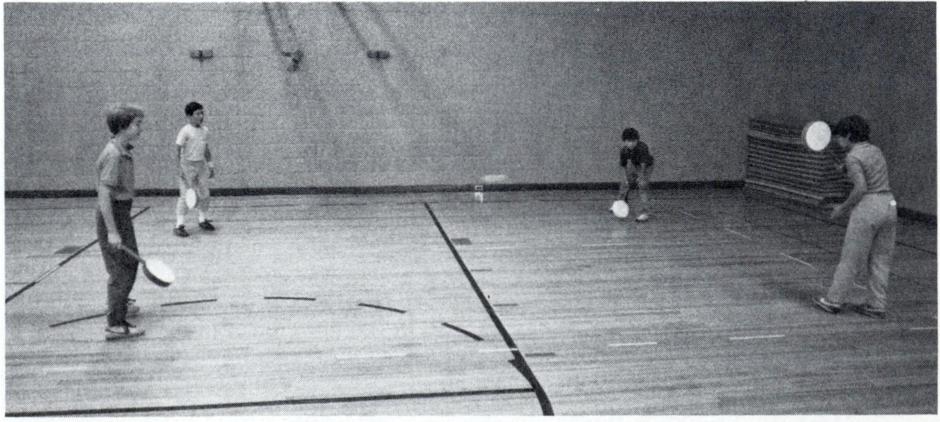

Playing four-square with paddles.

bounces in another playing area. Play continues until it cannot be returned, goes out of bounds, or lands on a line. In each case the player at fault moves to area 4, and the other players move up so that all areas are covered. The object is to get to and remain Player No. 1.

Teaching suggestions: It may be helpful to have students play two square until they have some control of the ball before using four players. Emphasize control and varying the shots with some deceptions to keep others off guard. One or two additional players may be incorporated by having them wait outside the playing area and rotating into court No. 4 in turn when someone makes an error. Modifications include the following:

1. Using an overhand hit or hitting the ball with little force (teeny-weenys)
2. Player in court No. 1 calling out which shots are legal on each serve
3. Using paddle striking skills rather than the hand
4. Requiring serving to a different court each time
5. Playing cooperatively by spelling words (one letter per hit) before beginning a competitive game
6. Allowing one-hand hits only

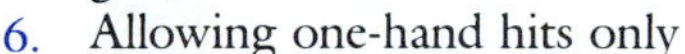

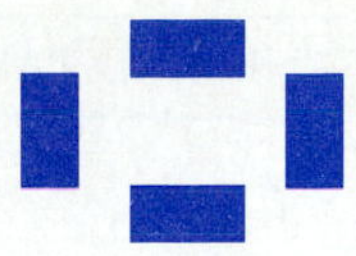

HANETSUKI

(Japan)

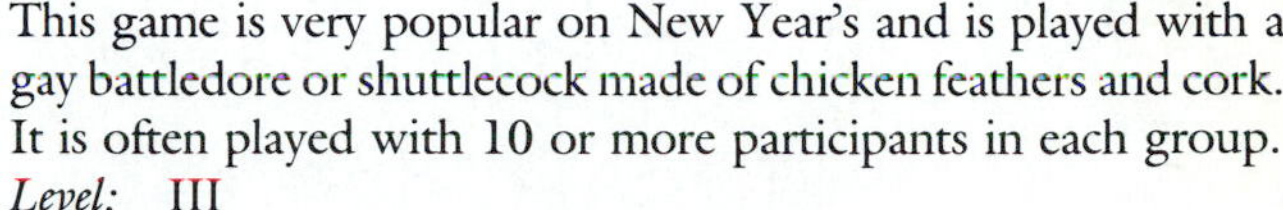

This game is very popular on New Year's and is played with a gay battledore or shuttlecock made of chicken feathers and cork. It is often played with 10 or more participants in each group.

Level: III

Equipment: One shuttlecock per group and a paddle or racquet for each person

Participants: Three to four for each group

Skills: Striking with an underhand stroke.

Description: Each group forms a circle and on the signal to begin, the shuttlecock is hit into the air and the children attempt to keep it in the air as long as possible. At the end of the playing time, the team that kept the shuttlecock in the air the longest gets one point. (Suggested modification: Have each group keep track of their longest number of hits and try to improve their record on each successive play of the game.)

Teaching suggestions: Encourage controlling force and hitting the shuttlecock up in the air to give the receiver the most time to get into position to play it.

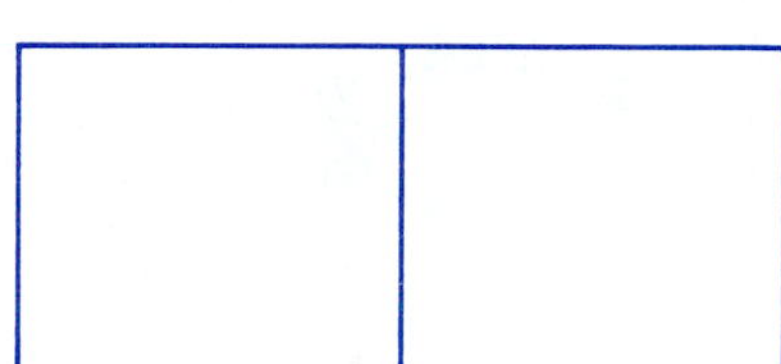

HANDBALL TENNIS

Level: III

Equipment: One small foam or tennis ball

Area: Two courts divided by a center line

Participants: Two to four players per team

Skills: Striking with the hand, underhand, possibly overhand

Description: Play begins when one of the players of the serving team drops the ball and hits it with the hand in an underhand manner from any place on his or her half of court so that it lands across the center line into the other court. Play continues as the receiving team returns the serve, and both teams continue to hit it back and forth until the ball goes out of bounds or someone fails to return it. The ball may bounce more than once before it is returned to the other half of the court. Only the serving team may score. When the service is lost, the other team begins to serve.

Faults:

1. Failure to serve the ball over the center line.
2. Hitting the ball out of bounds.
3. Hitting the ball so that it lands on the center line.

Penalty: For the serving team, a loss of service; for the receiving team, a point for the serving team

Teaching suggestions: Encourage the children to vary the force of their hits and to direct the ball to empty spaces on the opponent's court.

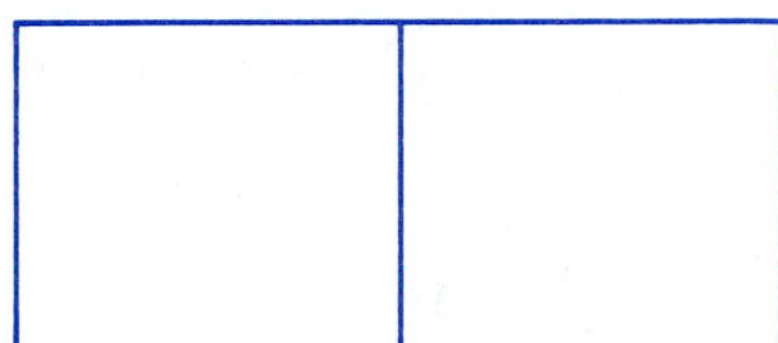

PARTNER PADDLEBALL

Level: III

Equipment: One small foam ball and two paddles

Area: Two courts 8 by 8 feet, divided by a center line

Participants: Two players

Skills: Forehand and backhand drives, volley, and serve

Description: The ball is put into play by one player dropping the ball in the court and serving it with a forehand motion so that it lands in the opponent's court. The receiver hits the ball back to the server's court, and play continues until someone fails to return the ball to the opponent's court. A ball landing on the side or end lines is considered in bounds. The ball may be contacted before it hits the floor. A point is scored when the ball is hit so that the opponent cannot return the ball within the rules of play. A game is completed when one player scores at least 4 points and wins by a 2-point margin.

Faults:

1. Failure to return the ball so that it lands in bounds in the opponent's court.
2. Contacting the ball more than once in returning the ball to the opponent's court.
3. Hitting the ball so that it lands on the center line.

Penalty: A point is scored for the opponent.

Text continued on p. 582.

TABLE 28-1 HAND AND PADDLE GAMES ANALYSIS

NAME	GAME CLASSIFICATION	NO. OF PARTICIPANTS	EQUIPMENT	SPACE AND ORGANIZATIONAL PATTERN	MOTOR SKILLS
Four Square	Striking game	Four	One 8-inch or 4-square ball	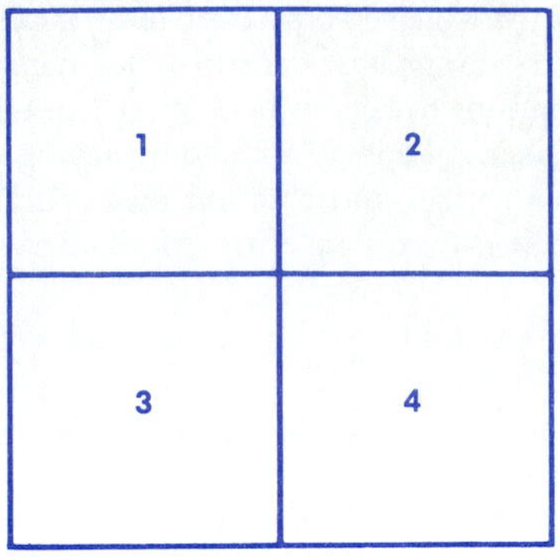 1 2 3 4	Underhand striking with the hands; overhand (optional)
Handball Tennis	Striking game	Two to four players per team	One small foam or tennis ball	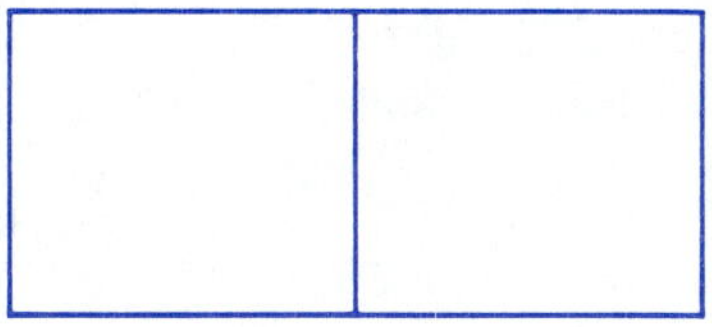	Underhand striking with the hand Possibly overhand striking with hand
Hanetsuki	Multicultural/ Cooperative	Three to four players per group	One shuttlecock per group; a paddle or racquet for each player		Underhand striking
Partner Paddle-ball	Striking game	Two	One small foam ball, two paddles	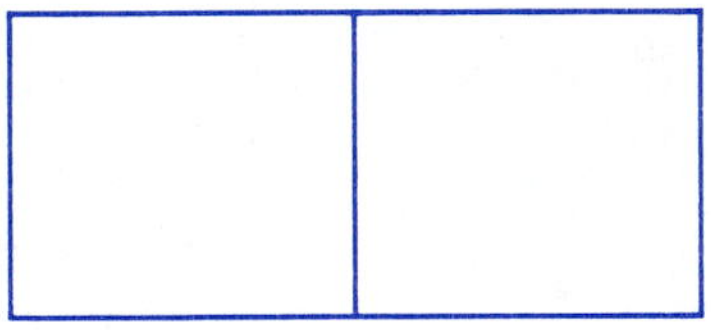	Forehand, backhand drives, volley, serve
Sidewalk Tennis	Striking game	Two to four	One tennis ball	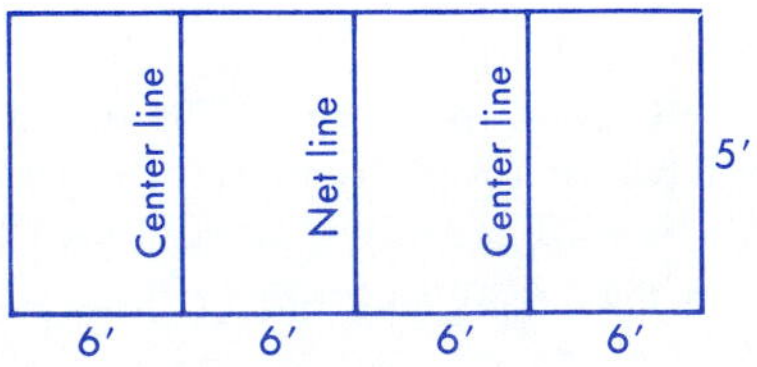 Center line Net line Center line 5′ 6′ 6′ 6′ 6′	Underhand striking with the hand
Yemari	Multicultural/ Cooperative	Three to four players per group	One tennis ball or large rubber ball		Striking with the hand

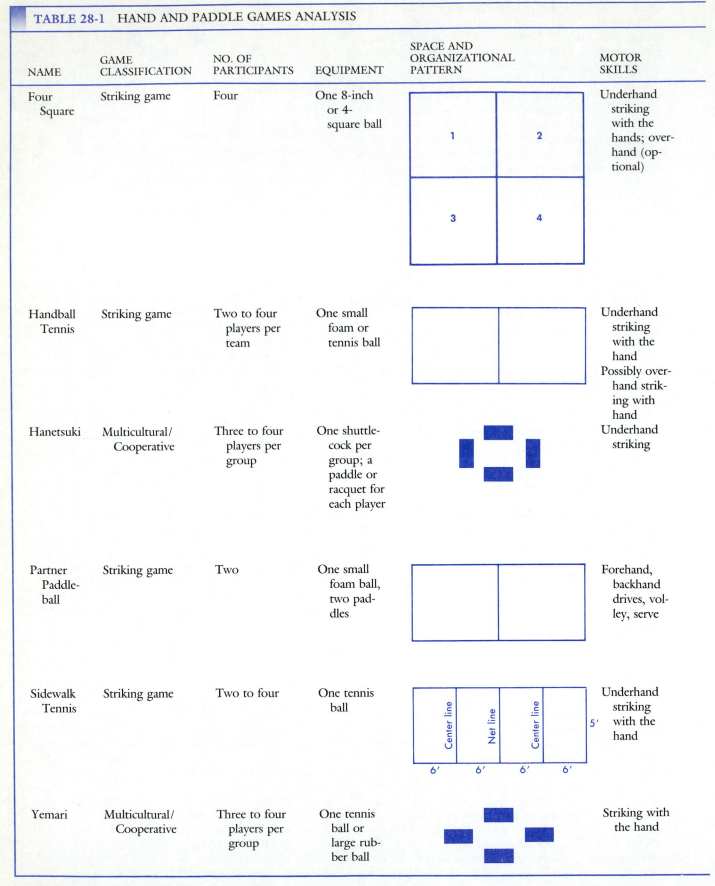

*Numbers refer to the concepts given in Figure 28-1 on p. 571.

MODIFICATIONS	MOVEMENT CONCEPTS*	SOCIAL STRUCTURE	STRATEGY	LEVEL
Play with two players; vary types of hits, use paddles	Skills: 1-6 Game: 1, 3-6	Parallel play II	Hit empty space; vary force	III
Serve to specific player in opposite court	Skills: 1-6 Game: 1-6	Parallel play II or social interaction I	Vary force and direct ball to empty spaces	III
Keep track of consecutive hits and try to improve record	Skills: 1, 3, 6 Game: 1-6	Social interaction I	Encourage controlling force in placing the ball in the air at a high level to assist teammates in receiving the ball	III
	Skills: 1-6 Game: 1, 3-6	Parallel play II	Hit empty space; vary placement of hits; vary force	III
Use paddles	Skills: 1-6 Game: 1-6	Parallel play II or social interaction II	Hit empty space; vary force; vary placement of ball	III
Each child bounces a ball to see who can keep it going the longest	Skill: 1 Game: 1	Parallel play II or social interaction I	Encourage controlling force in hitting the ball downward	III

Continued.

TABLE 28-1 HAND AND PADDLE GAMES ANALYSIS — cont'd

NAME	GAME CLASSIFICATION	NO. OF PARTICIPANTS	EQUIPMENT	SPACE AND ORGANIZATIONAL PATTERN	MOTOR SKILLS
Wall Hand-ball	Striking game	Three	One 8-inch ball or volleyball	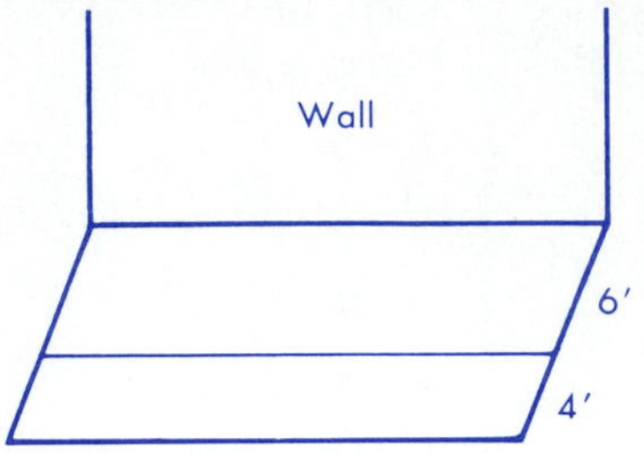 Wall; 6′; 4′	Throwing, catching, overhand striking with the hand (optional)
Wall Paddle Tennis	Striking game	Two to four	One foam or old tennis ball, two to four paddles	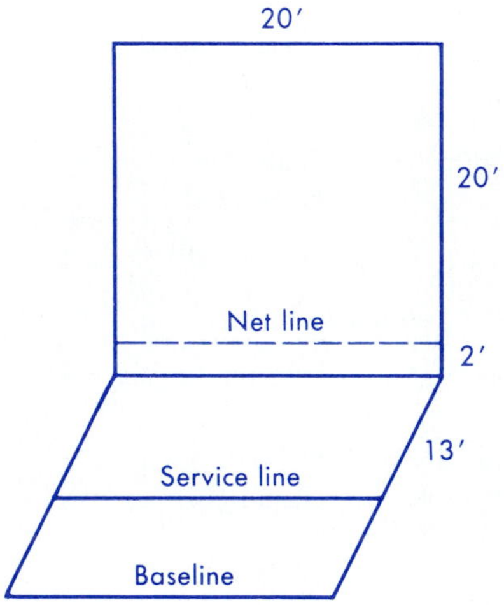 20′; 20′; Net line; 2′; 13′; Service line; Baseline	Forehand, backhand drives, volley, serve
Paddle Tennis	Striking game	Two to four	One foam or tennis ball, two to four paddles	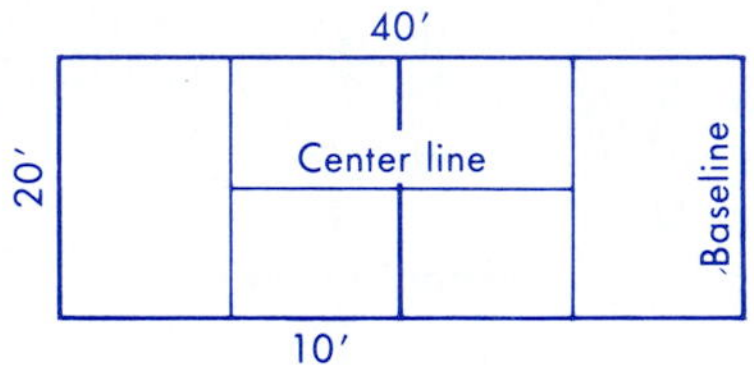 40′; 20′; Center line; Baseline; 10′	Forehand, backhand drives, volley, serve
Pickle Ball (modified)	Striking game	Two to four players per game	One paddle for each player and a plastic wiffle or pickle ball by a center line	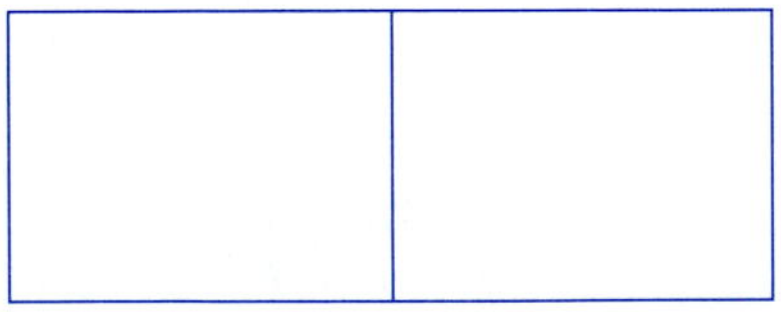	Forehand drive Backhand drive Serve Volley

MODIFICATIONS	MOVEMENT CONCEPTS*	SOCIAL STRUCTURE	STRATEGY	LEVEL
Use overhand striking skills	Skills: 1-6 Game: 1, 3, 5, 6	Parallel play II	Vary force; vary angle of rebound	III or IV
Use hand striking skills	Skills: 1-6 Game: 1-3, 5, 6	Parallel play II or social interaction II	Vary force; vary angle of rebound	IV
	Skills: 1-6 Game: 1-6	Parallel play II or social interaction II	Vary force: hit empty space; vary placement	IV
Allow serve to land anywhere in the court	Skills: 1-6 Game: 1-6	Social interaction II	Encourage varying force in placing the ball in the other court and hitting to empty spaces	IV

Strategy:
1. Vary the force of the hit.
2. Vary the placement of the ball by hitting it just over the center line, to the back of the court, to the right or to the left of the opponent.
3. Hit the ball to an empty space.

Teaching suggestions: Encourage the children to assume a good ready position in the center of the playing area where they can cover the entire court after each hit.

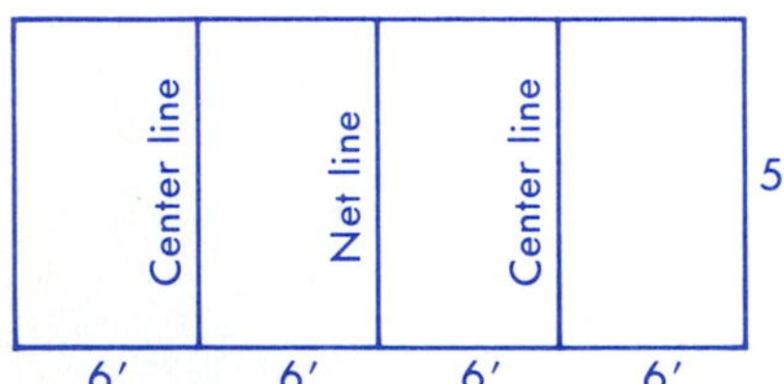

SIDEWALK TENNIS

Level: III
Equipment: One tennis ball
Area: A paved playing surface 24 feet long and 5 feet wide
Participants: Two to four players
Skills: Striking with the hand
Description: To begin play the serving player drops the ball and then hits it with the hand as it rebounds so it passes over the net line into the opponent's court and lands in the area between the net and the center line. The receiving player returns the ball by hitting it back to the server's court. After the serve the ball may be hit on a fly or after a bounce, and the ball may land anywhere within the opponent's court. Play continues until one player fouls. Only the server may score. Service is lost when the serving player fouls. Fifteen points constitute a game. A ball landing on the side or baseline is considered inbounds. A serve landing on the center line is replayed. When playing doubles teammates alternately hit the ball.

Fouls:
1. Stepping over the center line when serving.
2. Hitting the ball out of bounds.
3. Serving the ball outside the service court.
4. Hitting the ball with a body part other than the open hand.

Penalty: Loss of service or point.

Strategy:
1. Vary the placement of hits to keep the opponent moving.
2. Vary the force of hits to use all of the opponent's court.
3. Place the ball in an empty space in the opponent's court.

Teaching suggestions: Encourage the players to assume a ready position after each hit to be ready to move to the returning ball. This game may be played using paddles to strike the ball.

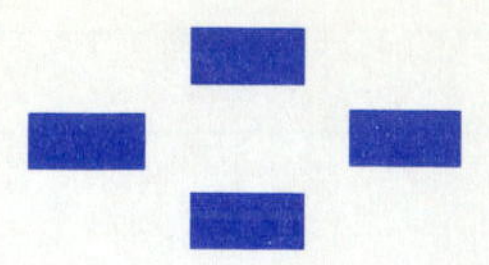

YEMARI

(Japan)
Level: III
Equipment: A tennis ball or a larger rubber ball
Participants: Three or four per group
Skills: Striking the ball with the hand
Description: The children stand in a circle. Play begins when one of the children drops the ball so that it rebounds back to him/her and then hits it downward with an open hand. The child continues to hit the ball downward as long as it rebounds back to them. They may not move to continue to play the ball. As the ball rebounds away, another player continues the bouncing process. Play continues with each player picking up the bouncing action. Play continues until someone fails to hit the ball on the rebound. Variation: Each child bounces a ball to see who can keep the ball going the longest.
Teaching suggestions: Have the children count the number of successive hits, trying to improve their score on each round of the game.

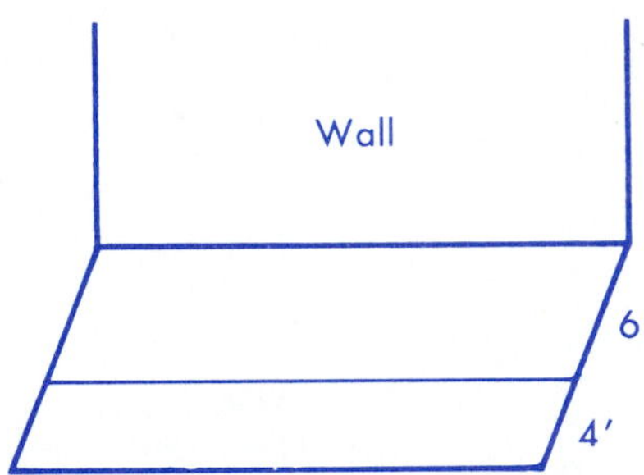

WALL HANDBALL

Level: III or IV
Equipment: One 8-inch utility ball or volleyball
Area: A wall space 10 feet wide with a floor space 12 feet deep
Participants: Three players in a file formation
Skills: Throwing, catching, and overhand striking with the hand (optional)
Description: The first player throws the ball to the ground, causing it to rebound to the wall and then rebound into the court beyond the 6-foot center line. The second player catches the ball after one bounce. If the ball is caught, the game continues, with the second player throwing the ball to the floor and the first player preparing to receive it. If the ball is missed, the third player enters the game and the second player goes out.

Fouls:
1. Failure to catch the ball as it rebounds once from the floor.
2. Failure to throw the ball so that it bounces from the floor to the wall and back to the floor again.
3. Failure to throw the ball so that it rebounds beyond the 6-foot line.

Penalty: Player leaves the game and goes to the waiting line.

Variations: Play begins as above, but after the initial throw the players strike the ball with a downward motion so that it hits the floor and then the wall rather than catching and throwing it. The ball may be played from a bounce or from a direct rebound from the wall.

Strategy:

1. Throw or hit the ball with varying force to keep the opponent guessing.
2. Try to position yourself on the court to be able to cover all possible shots.

Teaching suggestions: Striking the ball with control takes considerable practice. This variation is best suited for children at level IV.

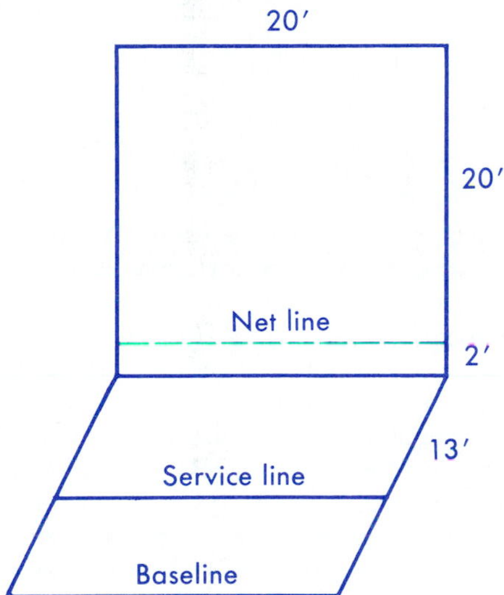

WALL PADDLE TENNIS

Level: IV

Equipment: Two to four paddles and one small foam ball or an old tennis ball

Area: A court 26 by 20 feet and 20 feet high, marked as above. A smaller court may be used where space is limited.

Participants: Two opposing players for singles, two teams of two players for doubles

Skills: Forehand and backhand drive, volley, serve

Description (Singles): Play begins when one player serves from behind the baseline. The ball is bounced and then struck so that it hits the wall above the net line. The ball must rebound off the wall beyond the service line and inbounds. After the ball hits the court, the opponent returns the ball by hitting it to the wall above the net line. The ball may rebound anywhere in the playing area. Play continues with each player alternately hitting the ball. A point is scored when an opponent hits the ball out of bounds or commits a fault. Only the server may score. The service continues until the server commits a fault. The game is completed when one player scores 10 points.

(Doubles): Team members follow the rules for singles, alternately hitting the ball. A server continues to serve until the team commits a fault.

Faults:

1. Failure to serve or hit the ball so that it hits the wall above the net line.
2. Failure to serve the ball so that it rebounds beyond the service line.
3. Hitting the ball so that it rebounds from the wall out of bounds.
4. Failure of the ball to hit the wall before contacting the floor after the hit.

Penalty: Loss of service or point, depending on which player commits the fault.

Strategy:

1. Vary the force of the hit.
2. Vary the placement of the ball on the wall to change the angle of rebound.

Teaching suggestions: In doubles, those not playing the ball should move back and out of the way.

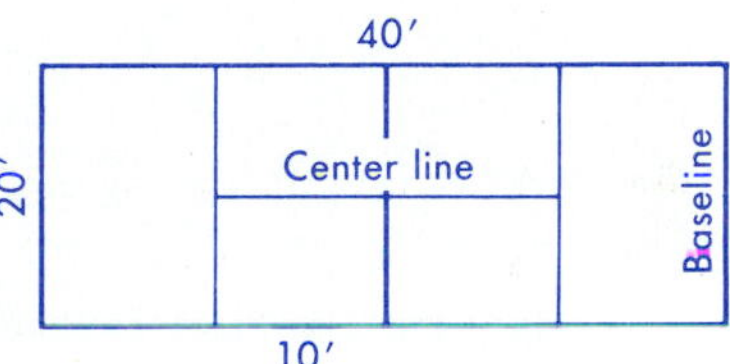

PADDLE TENNIS

Level: IV

Equipment: Two to four paddles and one small foam ball or tennis ball

Area: A 20-foot by 40-foot court with a service line and center line and a net 2.5 feet high.

Participants: Two for singles, four for doubles

Skills: Forehand and backhand drive, volley, serve

Description: Play begins with a serve from the right-hand court to the right-hand court of the opponent. The server is given two chances to hit the ball into the appropriate court. A ball hitting the top of the net and landing in the appropriate service court is a let serve. Another chance for service is awarded. The ball is returned after it bounces once in the opposite service court. After the serve the ball may be returned into any part of the opponent's court within the boundaries. The ball is served alternately from the right and left courts and to the right and left service courts of the opponent. It may be hit before it hits the court or after it has bounced once. Play continues until a fault is made. A point is scored by the opponent each time a fault is committed. A person serves the entire game. The game is completed when one player has scored at least 4 points and wins by a 2-point margin.

Faults:

1. Stepping over the baseline on the service.
2. Failure to serve the ball into the appropriate service court.
3. Failure to hit the ball over the net.
4. Hitting the ball so that it lands out bounds.

Penalty: If a service fault occurs on the first serve for each point, the serve is repeated. If the fault occurs on the repeated serve, a point is scored for the opponent.

Paddle tennis.

Strategy:
1. Look for an empty space to place the ball.
2. Vary the force of the hit.
3. Vary placement of the ball to keep the opponent(s) moving.

Teaching suggestions: Encourage the players to assume a ready position on the court where they can easily cover the court and to assume this position after each hit.

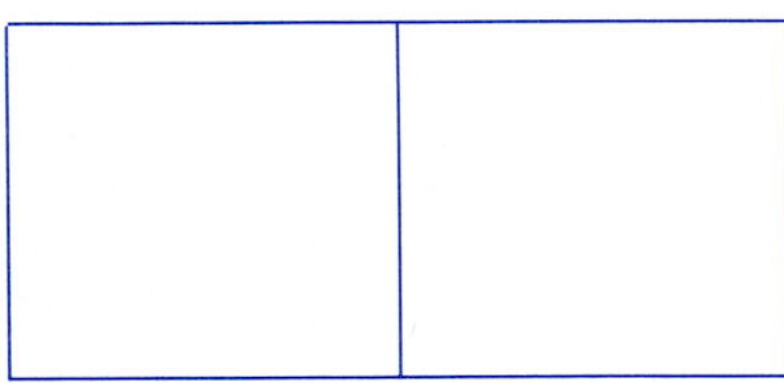

PICKLE-BALL
(Modified)

Level: IV

Equipment: A padde for each player and a plastic wiffle or pickle-ball

Area: A court divided by a net

Participants: Two to four per game

Skills: Serve, forehand drive, backhand drive, volley

Description: Play begins with the server standing with one foot behind the back line. The ball is dropped and hit with an underhand motion on the rebound from the floor. The serve must be hit diagonally so that it lands across the net. On each serve the server changes court to serve to each side of the opposite court. Only one attempt at serve is given unless the ball hits the top of the net when the serve is retaken. A point is scored by the serving team if the receiving team commits a fault. On the first term of service, the serving team is allowed only one fault after which the ball is given to the other team to serve. On all successive terms of service, both players on the team serve before the service is lost. The receiving team must allow the serve to bounce before hitting it, and the serving team must let the return of service bounce before playing it. A game is played for 11 points, with the winning team ahead by 2 points.

Faults:
1. Failure to serve the ball in bounds, or within the appropriate court area
2. Hitting the ball out of bounds
3. Hitting the ball so that it does not clear the net
4. Volleying the ball before it has bounced once on each side of the net
5. Touching the net with the paddle or any part of the body
6. Failure to have one foot behind the back line on the serve

Penalty: Point or loss of service depending on which team faults

Teaching suggestions: Encourage the children to vary their placements by controlling force and looking for empty spaces to put the ball. It may be necessary to allow the serve to land anywhere in the diagonal court for beginning players. In the actual game of pickle-ball, the serve is hit without a bounce and must land between the non-volley zone and the baseline.

SUMMARY

Several striking games may be played at the elementary school level. These games provide children with the opportunity to develop singles or doubles strategy as they play against one or more opponents.

Children practice striking skills using the hand or a paddle as they learn forehand and backhand drives and volley. A modified service is used at the elementary school level.

Movement concepts important to success include varying the placement of balls of different sizes in the empty spaces in the opponent's court by changing the expected path of the ball and varying force.

REFERENCES AND RESOURCES

Arbogast G and Zody J: *Pickle-ball and tennis: the logical combination,* Durham, NC, 1989, The Great Activities Publishing Company.

Curtis J: *Pickle-ball for player and teacher,* Englewood, Colo, 1985, Morton Publishing.

Harbin EO: *Games of many nations,* Nashville, 1954, Abingdon Press.

Maguire J: *Hopscotch, hangman, hot potato, and ha ha ha,* New York, 1990, Simon & Schuster.

Stafford R: *Racquetball: the sport for everyone,* Memphis, Tenn, 1987, The Stafford Co.

Tyson L and Tyson P: *Teaching handball in the elementary schools,* Tucson, Ariz, United States Handball Association.

ANNOTATED READINGS

Corbin D: Inexpensive equipment for learning kicking and striking skills, *JOPER* 51(5):57, 1980.
How to use materials found around the home to improve kicking and striking skills.

Hatfield K: Team paddle tennis, *JOPERD* 56(8):74, 1985.
Discusses a game for large classes with limited courts.

Leath M: Mini-tennis: it works! *Strategies,* 5(7):26, 1992.
Discusses the basics of the game with three checkpoints for the basic strokes.

Moen S: Visual skills: training the eyes for competition—watch the ball? *Strategies* 2(6):20, 1989.
Discusses cues and drills for helping individuals contact the ball on a racquet.

Samuel B: Badminton—the lifetime game of the future, *JOPERD* 62(9):28, 1991.
Discusses badminton in the US and around the world including a history of the sport.

Stewart M and Ahlschwede R: Aerobic tennis, *Strategies* 2(4):5, 1989.
Provides drills to practice tennis skills and develop aerobic efficiency.

Strand B: Seven strategies to extend your racquetball course, *JOPERD* 59(1):19, 1988.
Provides self-testing activities for racquetball, which can also be modified for use with elementary school children.

CHAPTER 29

Soccer

OBJECTIVES

After completing this chapter the student will be able to:

1. Identify modifications necessary to make soccer a successful activity for elementary school children
2. Analyze the skills of soccer to be taught at the elementary school level and describe activities to be used in their development
3. Identify the movement content important in soccer and describe activities to develop movement concepts before their use in soccer activities
4. Describe a series of progressively difficult soccer lead-up games for elementary school children

Soccer, an important international game, is a popular physical education activity in the elementary schools in the United States. This popularity is probably a result of several factors: It provides for large-group participation, requires little equipment, and is an outdoor game commonly played in the fall. In some areas of the country, it is an important interscholastic and collegiate sport as well. Soccer is a complex game. It provides the opportunity for children to use body parts other than the hands to control the ball. It encourages perhaps more creative use of body parts, many of which children have not considered usable in ball games. The skilled player must be able to control the ball received at all levels and vary the force as the situation demands.

Participants must be able to relate to many players, opponents, and teammates moving over a large area and recognize the role each must play for teamwork to be successful. Players must know how to use space, maintaining appropriate relationships with teammates and opponents and moving effectively to open and close spaces as they move offensively and defensively.

Soccer also requires excellent cardiorespiratory conditioning, as it is a game where everyone remains active in moving the ball from one end of the field to the other.

SOCCER IN THE ELEMENTARY SCHOOL

Soccer is an enjoyable game for children and provides an opportunity for progressively larger groups and specialization of responsibility over its development.

Equipment: Soccer is an economical game requiring minimal equipment. Soccer balls are now produced in varying sizes. At the elementary school level, smaller, lighter balls permit better control and use of skills. For indoor play, foam or underinflated utility balls can be more easily controlled on the smooth floor surface. For introducing the skill of heading, foam balls enable the children to master the technique without fear of injury.

Playing areas and goals must also be adjusted to the size of the players. An 8- to 10-foot goal area is large enough for elementary school children to cover. Cones may be used to define the goal area. The size of the field should allow for successful use of skills, permit the development of team play, and provide the opportunity for growth in the use of important movement concepts. Each lead-up game has its own space requirements.

Skills: Soccer requires almost total use of the body in controlling the ball but not the hands. Although the feet are most often used, the child must learn to receive and control the ball with many other body parts, including the head. With an appropriate sized ball most children will master the skills.

In the beginning, children should learn to understand the behavior of the ball under different conditions. Proper execution and timing should be stressed. Passes to teammates should allow for easy reception. Speed should not be stressed. The maximum opportunity for children to develop personal skills should be provided within the limitations of time and space.

Ball control, **collecting,** or *trapping* are terms that refer to a player's ability to receive a ball and to bring it under complete control. Early experiences should emphasize getting the ball under control, and children may first learn to stop the ball. Keeping the ball low is important in beginning level games. Raising the ball is often the result of having the nonkicking (support) foot behind the ball rather than next to it. Later, ball control skills in which the ball is not stopped but merely controlled will become more important in the games.

The game: Soccer offers the complex interaction of a large number of players. Relating to 21 other participants, each with slightly different responsibilities in the game, is confusing to elementary school children. Soccer may also be an inactive game for many at the elmentary school level because children are only beginning to develop team play and to learn to use the large space available. Therefore, it must be broken down into smaller group activities for each child to have an equal opportunity to develop to the fullest. As children progress in the game, a larger space, more players per team, and more advanced rules may be introduced.

The responsibilities of the team on offense are:

1. To score goals.
2. To maintain possession of the ball to prevent the opponents from scoring.

Offensive tactics that should be stressed in the elementary school program include the following:

1. Moving to meet the ball and controlling it before passing or dribbling.
2. Passing ahead to an open space.
3. Controlling soft but quick passes on the ground so that they may be easily received and controlled by a teammate.
4. Supporting a teammate with the ball by keeping within one pass distance to the side or behind.
5. Rushing a shot on goal.
6. Changing the path of the ball to keep defense off guard.
7. Always moving, repositioning in relation to the ball, teammates, and the defense.
8. Maintaining a constant surveillance of teammates, ball position on the field, and its relationship to the goal.
9. Keeping the ball until a defensive player has committed to the player with the ball but before one is about to be tackled.

The responsibilities of the defense are to:

1. Prevent the opposing team from scoring by tackling, intercepting passes, and closing space close to the goal.
2. Get the ball to their offensive teammates as quickly as possible.

Defensive tactics to be stressed include:

1. Staying between opponent and goal.
2. Continually repositioning to close spaces.
3. Advancing to tackle or harass the attack.
4. Clearing the ball away from the goal as quickly as possible.
5. Moving more closely to mark opponents as they near the goal.
6. Anticipating the movement of the ball and opponents.
7. Passing quickly to the attack.
8. Watching the player one is marking, not the ball.

Social Skills

Soccer offers a progression of games in which working together to achieve the game goal becomes more and more important as the interactions of players become more complex. In beginning games it is often necessary to require passing to ensure team play. Later games require children to support one another in play by helping out teammates offensively and defensively. If these experiences are carefully planned and coached, children begin to develop a sense of interdependence important for successful team play.

Health-Related Physical Fitness

Soccer has the potential for enhancing cardiorespiratory endurance in many of the practice and game activities. Beginning soccer warm-up activities such as dribbling in general space should be sustained long enough and at a pace that increases the heart rate. Other fitness components will need to be developed through activities unrelated to soccer.

SOCCER SKILLS

Body awareness concepts are extremely important in the mastery of soccer skills, because more body surfaces may be used to play the ball. Creating and absorbing force with body parts that children have little experience using are challenging for elementary school children (Figure 29-1).

Dribbling

Dribbling is a skill in which an individual player maintains control of the ball while moving the ball downfield. It may be used to move in for a shot on goal, to create a space by drawing a defender, or to allow a teammate time to get free for a pass. The ball is moved down the field with a series of taps with the inside, outside, or instep (top of the foot or on the shoelaces). The ball is kept a comfortable distance from the feet but always within the immediate playing area (Figure 29-2).

Common errors:

1. Looking down at the ball only.
2. Contacting the ball with too much force so that the player must run after it.

- Skills
  - Body awareness
    - To use body parts appropriately to perform skills
    - To move some body parts in relation to others while moving with and without the ball
  - Space
    - Self/general
      1. To move with control to avoid personal contact
      2. To pass the ball to an open space in front of a teammate
      3. To place the ball in an empty space in the opponents' goal
    - Direction
      4. To change direction while moving with and without the ball to avoid contact with others
    - Level
      5. To control a ball received at the high, medium, or low level
    - Pathways
      6. To change pathways while moving in space with and without the ball
  - Qualities of movement
    - Force
      7. To use an appropriate amount of force when passing, dribbling, and shooting
      8. To absorb force effectively with various body parts when receiving a ball
      9. To vary the use of body parts in imparting force to the ball
    - Time
      10. To anticipate the speed of the ball and teammates to meet a pass or to pass
      11. To change speed smoothly and efficiently while moving in space
      12. To match the speed of the ball and an opponent to intercept or tackle
    - Flow
      13. To combine skills smoothly
- Game
  - Space
    - Self/general
      1. To move in general space in relation to boundaries, teammates, opponents, and the ball
      2. To move to an open space while moving in general space
      3. To keep self space between one's opponent and the goal or the ball and the goal while playing defense
      4. To recognize one's own area of the general space in which to play
      5. To use as much space as possible on offense to keep the defense spread out
      6. To close spaces open to opponents and the ball, especially close to the goal area when on defense
      7. To create spaces for self, teammates, and the ball while moving in general space
    - Pathway
      8. To recognize and anticipate pathways within which to move self and/or ball
      9. To change the expected path of the ball
      10. To establish a pathway away from the goal on defense
  - Qualities of movement
    - Time
      11. To alter the tempo of the game by speeding up or slowing down

FIGURE 29-1 Soccer concepts.

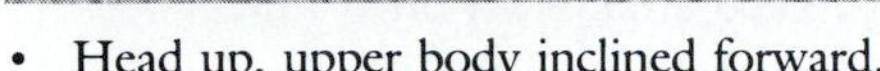

- Head up, upper body inclined forward.
- Run on the balls of the feet.

- Ball is contacted with inside of the foot, outside of foot, or instep.
- Ball is kept within playing distance always.

FIGURE 29-2 Evaluative criteria and teaching points for dribbling.

3. Dribbling too long so that the ball is taken away by an opponent.
4. Dribbling toward the person to whom a pass will be made.
5. Disrupting the rhythm of running while dribbling.

Teaching suggestions: Dribbling is often overused in soccer. It should be used only when good opportunities for passing do not exist because it slows down the offense. Children need coaching during play. They should be encouraged to dribble or pass at the appropriate times. When dribbling around an opponent, players must learn to use body movements to disguise their intent. Maximum ball control is required for these maneuvers.

Activities To Practice Dribbling

1. Each child has a ball and dribbles in general space using as much of the space as possible, controlling the ball, and avoiding contact with others. (How did you keep the ball under control to avoid others?) (perceiving)
2. Dribbling in general space, stop the ball on the signal, and on the next signal begin dribbling again. (What did you do to control the ball?) (refining)
3. In partners, each child has a ball. One follows the other (the leader) as they dribble in general space. Use all the space available. On the signal the follower spurts ahead and becomes the new leader. (What made this activity more difficult than dribbling in space as an individual? What did you do to keep the ball under control and to follow your partner?) (refining)
4. Practice dribbling in general space using one foot only, now the other. Dribble with the inside of the feet only, now the outside of the feet only. (How did you control the ball in each of these dribbles?) (refining)
5. Dribble in general space in which a number of cones or other obstacles have been placed. (How did you move to avoid the obstacles? When was it best to dribble with the inside of the feet? The outside?) (refining)
6. Dribbling in general space, each child pulls the ball to the left, right, or backward on command and then continues dribbling. (What did you do to keep the ball under control as you moved in each direction? How did you change direction? Was any direction change easier? Why?) (varying)
7. Repeat activity No. 2, but after stopping move in a new pathway, initially kicking the ball in the new pathway with the foot behind. (How did you control the ball with the rear foot without looking at it?) (varying)
8. Dribbling in general space, on the signal the student steps over the ball and kicks the ball with the outside of the rear foot to the side. The dribbler then moves in the new pathway and continues dribbling. (How did you control the ball in the new path?) (varying)
9. Dribbling against an opponent who attempts to stay in front of the dribbler, the dribbler attempts to move past the opposing player using the techniques used in activities No. 7 and 8. (Were you able to disguise your movements?) (varying)
10. Each child has a ball and is dribbling in general space. On the signal, the children increase or decrease their speed. (Were you able to control the ball at all speeds? How did your dribble change as you increased or decreased your speed?) (varying)

Passing

Passing is a team skill. It consists of propelling the ball to another player so that the ball can be easily controlled. The pass must be accurate, on the ground, and with just enough force to accomplish the task. In addition, it requires timing and the ability to conceal the intended path of the pass to keep the opponents guessing. The player executing the pass has generally two options: (1) to pass the ball to a space past a defender into which a teammate runs to pick it up or (2) to pass to a teammate who has run into a space behind a defender. To achieve the greatest accuracy, the passer uses as much of the foot as possible when contacting the ball and a long follow-through. The point of contact on the ball determines the height of the trajectory. Accuracy rather than power should be emphasized.

The *inside of the foot pass* (push pass) is used mostly for short, accurate passes along the ground but may be used also for medium-distance passes. Before initiating the pass, the player looks up to see where the pass is to be made, squaring the hips to the target. Contact is made at the center of the ball with the fleshy part of the inside of the foot between the big toes and the heel bone. The lower leg accelerates on contact, and the leg follows through smoothly and firmly in the direction of the pass (Figure 29-3).

Common errors:

1. Failing to look up to see where a pass should be made.
2. Positioning supporting foot too far forward.
3. Failing to focus on the ball at contact.
4. Not squaring the hips to the target.
5. Contacting ball too low or too high.
6. Kicking with the toe.
7. Projecting inappropriate force to the ball.
8. Failing to follow through in direction of pass.
9. Moving downfield toward the intended receiver before passing.

The *outside of the foot pass* (flick pass) is used in diagonal passing, forward and backward, for short or medium distance. The pass is executed quickly, and because it does not disrupt natural running it is difficult for opponents to anticipate. The passer looks up to see where the pass is to be made. The kick originates from the knee rather than the hip with a short back-swing. At contact the eyes are on the ball and there is a quick snap with the kicking leg. The skill ends with a long follow-through in the direction of the pass (Figure 29-4).

Common errors:

1. Failing to look up to see where the pass is to be made.
2. Positioning oneself too close or too far forward or behind the ball.
3. Not keeping foot firm on contact, with toes pointing inward.
4. Not using sufficient force, so that the ball does not reach its destination.
5. Failing to have the eyes focused on the ball at contact.
6. Having a short follow-through not in the direction of the pass.

The *instep drive* uses a kick with the instep in which the ball is raised off the ground, enabling it to cover greater distance. The passer looks up to see where the intended pass should go. Contact is made through the lower one half of the ball with the instep, the toes pointing downward and in the direction of the kick. On contact there is a snap of the lower leg to give added force, and the leg follows through in the direction of the kick (Figure 29-5).

Common errors:

1. Failing to look up to see where the intended pass should be.
2. Placing the supporting foot too far forward or behind the ball.
3. Kicking with the toe rather than the instep.
4. Failing to keep ankle firm on contact.
5. Contacting the ball too high.
6. Failing to follow through in the direction of the pass.

Chipping is used to pass over the head of an opponent and when a long-distance pass is required. The passer looks up to see where the pass is to be made. The ball is approached at an angle, and the last stride is long to permit a long swing of the kicking foot to add power. Contact is made with the instep, the leg straightening as the ball is kicked. The kicking knee is behind the ball more than in the low drive. The eyes are focused on the ball as contact is made, and the follow-through is in the direction of the pass (Figure 29-6).

Common errors:

1. Failing to look up to see where the pass should be made.
2. Assuming a position too far forward or too far behind the ball.
3. Failing to bend the knees.
4. Kicking with the toe.
5. Contacting the ball too high.
6. Failing to watch the ball on contact.
7. Failing to follow through in the direction of the pass.

Activities To Practice Passing

1. Children are in groups of four with one ball. The player with the ball passes the ball to one of the others and then follows the pass as quickly as possible. (What did you do to get the ball directly to the receiver? Were you able to keep the ball moving?) (refining)
2. Children are in groups of three, organized as three corners of a square. A passes to B and moves to the empty corner; B then passes to C and moves to the empty space. C then passes back to A, and the drill begins again. (What did you do to get the ball accurately to the receiver? What kind of a pass did you want to receive?) (refining)

- Supporting foot next to ball with toes turned slightly inward; both knees bent.
- Body and head over ball; eyes on the ball.
- Kicking leg brought back, ankle firm, toes up and leg turned to the side.

- Leg follows through in direction of pass.
- Contact with inside of foot.

FIGURE 29-3 Evaluative criteria and teaching points of inside of the foot pass.

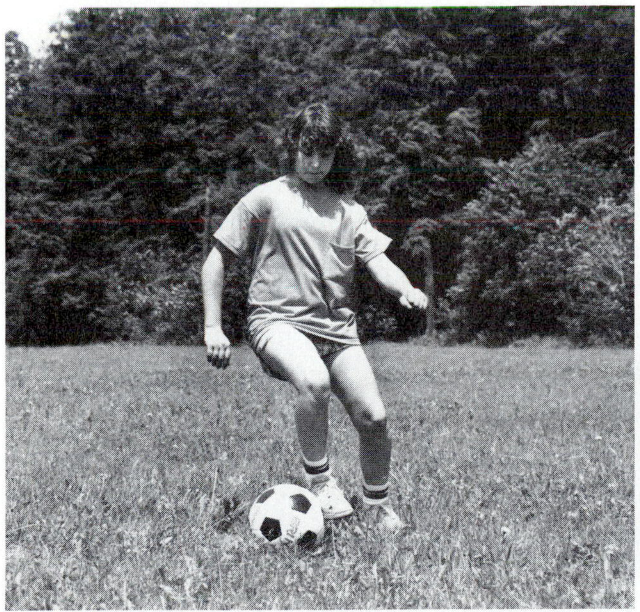

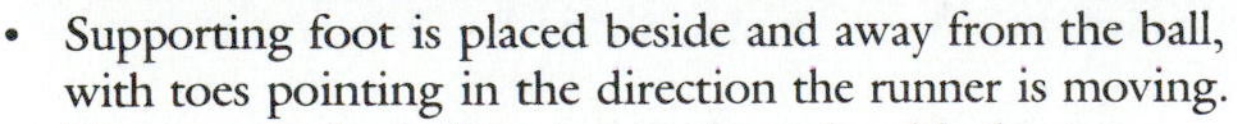

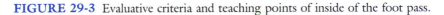

- Supporting foot is placed beside and away from the ball, with toes pointing in the direction the runner is moving.
- Eyes are on the ball as contact is made with the outer edge of the foot, toes pointing inward, ankle flexed and firm.

- Leg follows through in the direction of the pass.

FIGURE 29-4 Evaluative criteria and teaching points for outside of the foot pass.

- Supporting foot is next to ball with both knees bent.
- Eyes are on ball with knee and head over ball.
- Kicking leg is brought back with knee bent and heel close to buttocks.

- Contact is made on laces of shoe with toe down, heel up, and ankle firm.
- Lower leg snaps and leg follows through in direction of kick.

FIGURE 29-5 Evaluative criteria and teaching points for instep drive.

- The ball is approached at an angle, with a long last stride.
- The supporting foot is to the side and slightly behind the lower half of the ball; the knees are bent.

- Contact is made with the instep through the lower half of the ball.
- The kicking knee is slightly behind the ball, with the body leaning back.

- Follow-through is in the direction of the kick.

FIGURE 29-6 Evaluative criteria and teaching points for chipping.

3. Children are in groups of three. The person with the ball passes it to a space and calls out the name of the receiver, who moves to the space to receive the ball. (What are the characteristics of a good pass? Where do you want to receive the ball?) (refining)
4. With a partner, practice passing, using the type of pass indicated by the leader. Beginning 5 yards apart, increase the distance each time a child has successfully completed five passes. Vary the type of passes used. (What changes were necessary in the passes as the distance increased? Were you able to get the ball accurately to your partner?) Variation: Increase and decrease distance on a signal. (Were you able to adjust your passes easily to the changing distances?) (varying)
5. Children are in partners with one ball. Both move down the field in a zigzag fashion, passing back and forth. (Where did you try to place the ball so that your partner could continue moving? How did you change your passes as your partner moved farther away? Closer to you?) (varying)
6. The group is scattered in general space. Half are moving; the others with balls are stationary. Those moving move to an open space and call the passer's name to receive a pass. On receiving the ball they stop and get ready to pass to someone else. (Where did you try to place the ball on the pass? How did you hit the available pathway?) (varying) Variation: Gradually decrease the number of balls to increase the number moving in the space. (varying)

Shooting

Although the kick with the instep is the most frequently used shot for goal, any of the kicks described in the previous section may be used. The major difference between their use as a pass or shot on goal lies in the intent of the kicker. In passing, the objective is to propel the ball so that it can be easily controlled by the receiver, whereas in shooting for goal the intent is to make the kick impossible to stop by the goalkeeper. Both passing and shooting require accuracy. Power is an added ingredient in the attempt to score. Because few goals are scored in soccer, the attack must take as many shots for goal as possible. The attack must quickly react to scoring opportunities and not hesitate to get the shot away. Shots for goal should be directed toward the sides of the goal and preferably the corner farthest from the goalkeeper. Low shots are generally more difficult for the goalkeeper to handle.

Common errors:

1. Missing opportunities to score.
2. Passing off when they should shoot.
3. Using too much power with not enough accuracy.
4. Failing to follow up the shot.
5. Directing kick at the goalkeeper.
6. Failing to look up to see where the shot should be directed.

Teaching suggestions: Shooting practice should involve receiving a moving ball rather than kicking a ball from a stationary position because the ball will not be motionless in the game.

Activities To Practice Shooting

1. In partners, the shooter approaches the goal as the other rolls the ball into the goal area. The shooter receives the ball and then takes a shot for goal. Begin with a gentle roll, and gradually increase the force as skill improves. Begin with shots taken close to the goal and gradually increase the distance. Change the angle at which the shooter approaches the goal. After three attempts change positions. (Were you able to receive the ball and get off an accurate shot at goal? What did you do to be sure the ball was directed into the goal?) (refining)
2. Children are in partners, with two to four cones placed within the goal. (The cones should be placed so that the middle of the goal is covered and the sides and corners open.) Repeat activity No. 1. The shooter must now make a shot for goal and must place the ball in the goal without hitting the cones to score. (What must you do to control the accuracy of your shot?) (refining)
3. In groups of three, repeat activity No. 1, but add a goalkeeper. (What changes in your shooting were necessary with a goalkeeper protecting the goal? Where were the open spaces in the goal?) (refining)
4. Children are in groups of three: two attack and one goalkeeper. The attack brings the ball into the goal area by dribbling and passing. The person with the ball has the opportunity to take a shot for goal and rush the shot or to draw the goal keeper and then make a quick pass to the other attack player, who attempts a quick shot for a score. (What were you able to do to open a space for the ball in the goal?) (varying)

Juggling

Juggling is the skill of keeping the ball in the air in which an individual repeatedly touches the ball with the feet, thigh, or head. It is a skill not used in the game of soccer at the elementary school level, but one that helps players develop "the feel of the ball," concentration, rhythm, control, and confidence in soccer ball-handling skills. At higher levels it may be used during repositioning strategy. While this skill is difficult for young players, it should be introduced during the elementary school years. Juggling provides a very good warm-up activity for everyone.

The ball is contacted with a gentle touch. With contact on the instep, the toes are pointed and the foot firm to avoid backspin, and the ball is touched at knee height. When the thigh is used, the ball is contacted in the middle of the thigh from a position in which the thigh is horizontal to the ground. If the ball is to be juggled with the head, it is contacted with the head tilted back, the forehead parallel to the ground, and the player directly underneath the ball. When the outside of the foot is used, the toes are raised and the knees are bent. A bend at the

- Assume a well-balanced position, slightly crouched, with weight on the balls of the feet.
- Eyes are focused on the ball, which is contacted in a steady rhythm and rebounds no more than 3 inches above part giving impetus.

- With upper thigh, upper leg is horizontal to the ground; contact is in the middle of the thigh.

- With instep, ball is contacted about knee height, the foot is firm.

- With the head back, the forehead is parallel to the ground and contact is on the center of the forehead.

- With the outside of the foot, toes are raised; lean at hip away from the ball to make contact at hip height.

FIGURE 29-7 Evaluative criteria and teaching points for juggling.

hip away from the ball enables contact at hip height. In using the inside of the foot, the toes are raised and the ball is played fairly close to the body. The juggler establishes a steady rhythm, with the ball going no more than about 3 feet in the air above the body part giving impetus (Figure 29-7).

Common errors:

1. Failing to concentrate on the ball.
2. Contacting with too much force so that control is lost.
3. Failing to establish a steady rhythm.
4. Not maintaining a balanced position, with weight on the balls of the feet.

Teaching suggestions: When practicing juggling, it is easiest for children to begin with a toss to themselves. Later they may lift the ball by jumping with it between the ankles or getting a lift by getting the instep under the ball. Sitting on the ground, juggling with the instep is an easy way to get started. It is important that children have an object that they can handle while juggling. Socks stuffed with rags or balls of appropriate size and weight and not too much rebound work best.

Ball Control (Collecting)

Ball control consists of receiving a ball and bringing it under control. It includes trapping when the intent is to stop the ball. Trapping is an important skill for beginning elementary school players who are learning to control the ball with body parts other than their hands. In beginning games, emphasis is on keeping the ball low, which is more easily accomplished by kicking a stationary ball. As skills improve, however, trapping the ball becomes less important than other forms of ball control. Ball control is an essential skill in the game of soccer because the time a player has to dribble, pass, or shoot is determined by efficiency in getting the ball under control on receiving it.

In all ball control skills the player must:

1. Move into the direct line of flight of the ball.
2. Move to meet the ball.
3. Give with the ball using as large a body surface as possible to control the ball.
4. Make a decision about what will be done with the ball before it is received.
5. Relax the part of the body sufficiently so that the ball may be brought under control at the feet or slightly ahead of the body when moving with it.
6. Be in a good balanced position with full attention given to the ball.

Ball control practice requires careful placement of the ball so that it can be received at precisely the level of the body part to be used. It may be difficult for elementary school children to consistently place the ball appropriately to their partners during practice sessions.

The *sole of the foot control* (trap) is used to control ground balls but may also be used to control balls dropping out of the air. The player moves into position in line with the ball's flight, with eyes focused on the ball. The ball is contacted in front of the body with the sole of the foot so that the ball is trapped between the ground and the foot. On impact there is a giving in the ankle, knee, and hip to absorb the force of the ball. If the ball is dropping from the air, the sole of the foot must contact it at the precise moment it touches the ground or it will rebound away (Figure 29-8).

Common errors:

1. Failing to line up with the ball.
2. Not being in a balanced position.
3. Jabbing at the ball rather than placing the foot on top of the ball.
4. Stepping on the ball, resulting in a loss of balance.
5. Failing to watch the ball.

FIGURE 29-8 Evaluative criteria and teaching points for sole of the foot control.

- In line with ball's flight; eyes on the ball.
- Weight on supporting foot, knees bent, and arms out to the side.
- Sole of foot placed squarely on the ball; "give" at the ankle, knee, and hip joints.
- Ball is controlled in front of the body within immediate playing range.

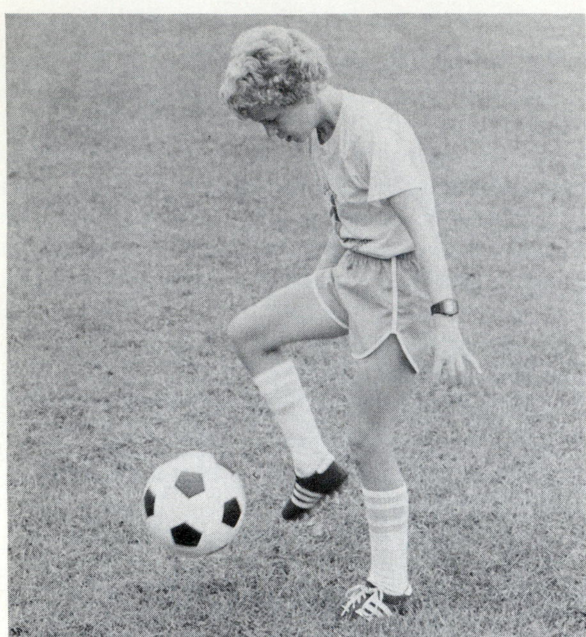

FIGURE 29-9 Evaluative criteria and teaching points for inside of the foot control.
- In line with the ball, eyes on the ball.
- The ball is contacted with inside of foot at its center, weight balanced on supporting foot.
- Foot and leg "give" at impact to control the ball close to the body.
- For a ball in the air, the leg is raised with a slight lean backward.
- The ball is controlled in front of the body and within immediate playing range.

FIGURE 29-10 Evaluative criteria and teaching points for instep control.
- In line with the ball, eyes on the ball, weight on supporting foot.
- Leg is raised to meet oncoming ball, ankle flexed.
- Upon impact, ankle is related and foot is brought to the ground with ball following it.
- Ball is controlled close to body.

The *inside of the foot control* is used primarily to control balls moving along the ground, although it may also be used to control balls dropping through the air. The player assumes a position in line with the ball's flight. The ball is contacted at its center, with the foot giving on impact. The ball is controlled close to the feet in preparation for the next move. A ball being controlled that is in the air is contacted off the ground by raising the controlling leg. A slight backward lean aids in bringing the ball to the ground within playing distance (Figure 29-9).

Common errors:

1. Failing to line up with the ball.
2. Not contacting the center of the ball.
3. Failing to give with foot and leg at impact, resulting in the ball rebounding too far away.
4. Failing to assume a balanced position.

The *instep control* is used to control balls dropping toward the receiver. The receiver assumes a position in line with the oncoming ball. The bottom of the ball is contacted with the instep, and the leg is lowered immediately on impact so that the ball follows the leg to the ground. The foot of the controlling leg must be slightly relaxed on meeting the ball or the ball will rebound up into the air. The ball is controlled slightly in front of the body (Figure 29-10).

Common errors:

1. Failing to position oneself in the ball's line of flight.
2. Contacting the ball as the leg is being raised, which gives it impetus away from the receiver.
3. Failing to relax the ankle so that the ball rebounds off the foot.
4. Failing to control the ball close to the body.

The *thigh control* is used to control balls dropping toward the receiver. The thigh, a large, fleshy surface, is ideal for controlling the ball. The receiver assumes a position in the direct line of the ball's flight. The controlling leg is raised to meet the oncoming ball. On contact with the ball at mid-thigh, the upper leg is approximately parallel to the ground. The thigh gives at impact, cushioning the ball as it drops in front of the body. The arms are spread to aid balance and to avoid contact with the ball. The ball will rise slightly at impact before continuing to the ground. Balls received at lower levels may necessitate raising the leg only partially before contact to control it close to the body. Balls dropping from greater heights

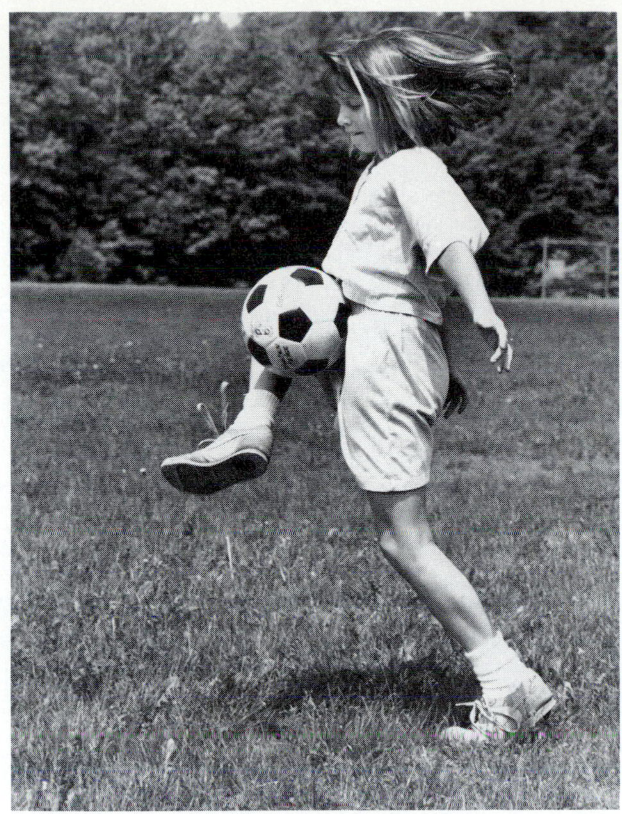

FIGURE 29-11 Evaluative criteria and teaching points for thigh control.
- In line of flight, weight balanced on supporting leg.
- Eyes are on ball as leg is raised to meet the ball.
- Contact at midthigh, slight body lean, arms out and back.
- Leg is dropped to cushion ball and ball drops to the ground.

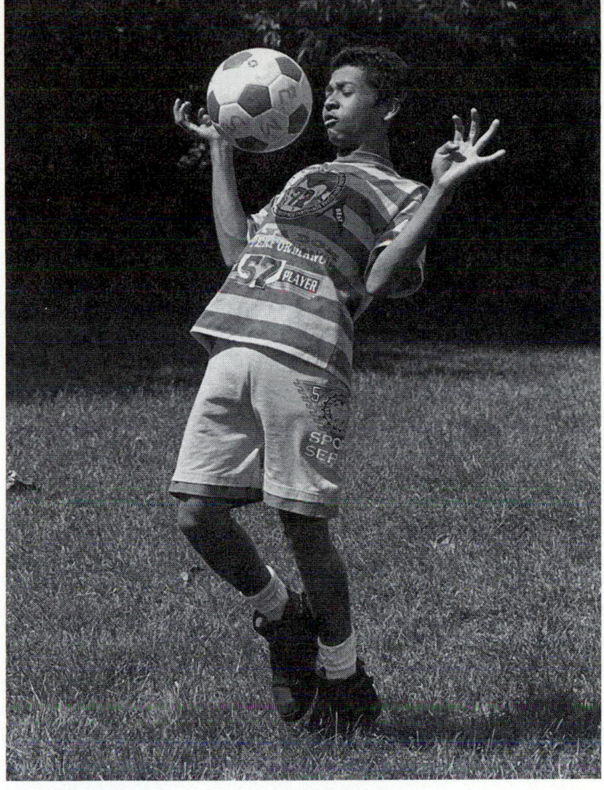

FIGURE 29-12 Evaluative criteria and teaching points for chest control.
- In line with the ball; arms out to the side.
- Ball received high, just below the shoulder.
- Body gives on impact, resulting in slight lean back or forward.
- Weight shifts to rear foot.

also need to be controlled by the feet to put the balls into playing position (Figure 29-11).

Common errors:

1. Failing to line up with the oncoming ball.
2. Contacting the ball with the knee so that the ball rebounds away.
3. Contacting the ball with the hands or arms.
4. Failing to drop the leg immediately on contact with the ball.

The *chest control* is more difficult for children to master, although it involves a much larger surface on which to control the ball. The receiver takes a position in line with the ball's flight, with feet a comfortable distance apart. The arms are out at the sides. The ball is received high, just below the shoulder on either side. On impact the body relaxes, resulting in a slight lean forward or back. As the body gives, much of the body weight may be shifted to the rear foot. The ball must be further controlled by the feet as it drops to the ground to keep it within the immediate playing range (Figure 29-12).

Common errors:

1. Failing to line up with the ball.
2. Failing to give on impact to cushion the ball.
3. Failure to receive the ball high and at the side of the chest.

Activities To Practice Ball Control

1. Juggling individually, children use one or more body parts. They begin sitting, then move to standing and eventually moving. (How many taps can you give the ball before it touches the ground? How many ways can you juggle the ball at the low, medium, and high levels?) (refining)
2. In partners, one throws the ball so that it can be received appropriately for the practice of the ball control skill being developed. Children may need to practice throwing to get it to their partners. If the ball cannot be received at the appropriate level, beginners should not attempt the control. Begin from a stationary position, with the balls thrown directly to the controller.

Have children practice one type of control at a time to give more opportunity to develop timing. (What must you do to receive the ball and get it under control? What body parts were used to absorb the force?) (refining)

3. Repeat activity No. 2, but do not throw the ball directly to your partner. Throw it to the right, left, in front, or behind so that they must adjust their position to receive it. This technique requires control while on the move. (What cues did you use to help you line up with the ball? What did you do differently to control the ball while you were moving?) (varying)
4. Children juggle with a partner. Partners juggle to each other. (How well could you control the ball? How many taps did you give it before it touched the ground?) (varying)

Heading

Soccer is the only sport in which the head is used to play the ball, and consequently children tend to be very timid and even afraid in the beginning stages of learning. Heading is a level IV skill and not used very much at the elementary school level. The forehead provides the best hitting surface because it is large, relatively flat, and allows the ball to be seen on contact. The header moves to a position in line with the ball. As the ball approaches, the weight is shifted to the rear leg and the upper body and head are bent slightly backward. Before contact the weight is shifted to the front leg, and the upper body and head swing forward from the hips to give added power. On contact the neck muscles are tense, the chin is down, and the tongue is behind clenched teeth. The head is projected through the ball as contact is made with the forehead in line with the eyes. If height is an important factor, as when heading the ball away from the goal area, the header assumes a position partially under the ball. Jumping to head a ball requires precise timing of the jump (which should be a one-foot take-off) to the ball (Figure 29-13).

Common errors:

1. The ball is allowed to hit the head, rather than the head hitting the ball.
2. Eyes closed before contact.
3. Poor balance.
4. Jumping too soon or too late.
5. Failure to begin with upper body leaning back and snapping forward at waist on contact.

Teaching suggestions: For introducing heading, soft balls should be used. It may be helpful to have the children hold the ball in both hands and hit the ball to the foreheads lightly at first and then harder to get an idea of where contact should be made and also to realize it will not hurt if executed properly.

Activities To Practice Heading

1. Standing, each child holds a ball out in front of the body, and brings it back while moving the head forward to make contact with the ball at the forehead. (perceiving)
2. Repeat activity No. 1 but head the ball on contact. (perceiving)
3. Each child has a ball. The children toss up the ball, but not too high, and then head it to themselves. (Where do you want to be in relation to the ball on contact? How long can you keep your eyes open?) (refining)
4. Practice juggling with the head individually. (How many times can you hit the ball before it touches the ground? Try using different parts of your head. Which part works best?) (refining)
5. Kneeling on the ground, a partner tosses the ball to the sitting player to head back to the thrower. (How did you use your upper body and head to meet the ball?) (refining)
6. In partners, one puts the ball up into the air, and the other moves to it to head it. (Where did you want to be in relation to the ball? Can you head it back to your partner?) (refining)
7. In partners, practice heading the ball. (How many times can you head the ball before it touches the ground? What must you do to direct the ball to your partner?) (varying)

Tackling

Tackling is the skill of taking the ball away from an opponent. It requires timing, determination, and strength.

The *block tackle* is the most frequently used tackle in soccer and is most effective against a player who is receiving the ball and who does not have it under full control or when an opponent is dribbling the ball. The tackler moves in close to the opposing player. The knees are bent to help absorb the impact and to improve balance. The tackling foot is raised, with the knee turned out, and the ankle firm. Contact with the ball occurs as the ball comes off the opponent's foot. The tackler plays through the ball with the body weight but must be careful not to put all weight on the tackling foot. If the ball becomes blocked between the two players' feet, the tackler must be able to quickly lower the tackling foot to get under the ball to roll it over the opponent's foot. If the ball is successfully contacted while off the opponent's foot, it may be pushed to the side or between the opponent's feet (Figure 29-14).

Common errors:

1. Failing to time the tackle when the ball is off the opponent's foot.
2. Contacting the ball too high.
3. Making body contact with the opponent.
4. Leaning back on contact with the ball.
5. Putting too much weight on the tackling foot so that the tackler cannot move the foot to get under the ball blocked between the opposing player's feet.
6. The tackler lacking determination.
7. Failing to keep a firm ankle.

- Assume a forward/backward stride position, knees bent, weight evenly distributed on balls of feet; weight shifts to rear foot; upper body and head bent back, eyes on ball.

- Weight shifts to front foot; upper body and head swing forward, chin down, neck muscles tense. Keep eyes open and watch ball until contact on forehead. Project head through ball, arms out for balance.

FIGURE 29-13 Evaluative criteria and teaching points for heading.

- The inside of the foot is placed against the center of the ball, ankle firm; the eyes are on the ball, with head and body over the ball.

FIGURE 29-14 Evaluative criteria and teaching points for block tackle.

- The tackler plays through the ball, rolling it over the opponent's foot.

Activities To Practice Tackling

1. In partners, each child begins about two steps from the ball. On the signal, the partners both move in to block the ball between their feet, gently maneuvering the ball to get it away. (What must you do to gain control of the ball? How quickly can you move your foot to get under the ball?) (perceiving)
2. In partners, one loosely dribbles downfield, while the tackler times the tackle to contact the ball when it is off the dribbler's foot. The dribbler offers little resistance. (What cues did you use to make contact when the ball was not in contact by the dribbler?) (refining)
3. Same as activity No. 2, but this time the dribbler attempts to maintain possession of the ball. (What cues did you use to know when to make your move? Did you fool the dribbler?) (refining)

Goalkeeping

Goalkeeping is a specialized position in the game of soccer. A successful goalkeeper must have good hands, agility, patience, sharp reflexes, and courage. The major responsibility of the goalkeeper is to try to prevent the attacker from shooting, and, when that is not possible, to defend the goal. The goalkeeper in soccer is the only player permitted to use the hands as well as the feet in playing the ball. The goalkeeper assumes a ready position, with the feet in a side-stride position. The hands are up with palms facing out, and the arms are close to the body, with elbows bent and fingers spread. The thumbs and index fingers form a W. The eyes are focused on the ball and the players in the immediate area. The goalkeeper always presents as large a target as possible to the attempt at goal, and the body is behind the hands.

The goalkeeper gets into a position where there is the greatest chance to stop the ball. The goalkeeper imagines a triangle, with the goal line as one side and the ball as the apex. By standing directly in front of the goal line, the goalkeeper allows the greatest target area to the shooter. By moving out toward the attacker the target area is greatly reduced and the shooter must rely on greater accuracy to score. This is often called narrowing the angle. Figure 26-22 depicts the angles at various distances from the goal.

The goalkeeper should challenge lone attackers aggressively. By moving toward the attacker, the shooter must look at the goalkeeper as well as the ball. This may result in less concentration on the ball and therefore a greater chance for error. As the goalkeeper moves forward, he or she should assume a position that permits a move to either side (Figure 29-15).

Common errors:

1. Failing to assume a ready position in which the goalkeeper can move in any direction.
2. Not watching the ball.
3. Putting weight on the entire foot.
4. Not keeping hands up and in front of the body.
5. Failing to bring the ball in with two hands.

Activities To Practice Goalkeeping

1. Practice assuming the ready position and moving to meet an imaginary ball. (What body position enabled you to move quickly to meet the ball?) (perceiving)
2. In partners, one rolls the ball to the goalkeeper, who moves into position to field the ball. (How did you move to meet the ball? To bring it in?) (refining)
3. Repeat activity No. 2, but thrower rolls the ball to the right or left of the goalkeeper. (How did you anticipate the path of the ball to move into position to intercept?) (varying)
4. In partners, one dribbles in and shoots for a goal, while the other defends the goal. The shooter attempts to place the ball in the goal to the left or right of the goalkeeper. (What did you do to keep the ball out of the goal? Did the shooter make it obvious where the shot would go? What position enabled you to move quickly to meet the ball?) (varying)

The Throw-In

A *throw-in* is taken when the ball is sent over the sidelines by an opposing player. The thrower assumes either a side or forward/backward stride position. The ball is held in both hands and is brought back behind the head, with the arms bent slightly at the elbows and the trunk arched backward for added force. The arms are brought forward and the ball released when it is overhead or in front of the body, depending on the distance to be thrown. Force is applied equally with both hands. Both feet must be on the ground on release of the ball (Figure 29-16).

Common errors:

1. Having poor balance.
2. Giving impetus to the ball with one hand, rather than equal force with both hands.
3. Lifting one leg on release.
4. Stepping during the execution.
5. Having little follow-through, which reduces the distance and accuracy of the throw.

Teaching suggestions: Throwers should be encouraged to throw the ball as quickly as possible and to find and to throw to an unmarked player.

Activities To Practice the Throw-In

1. Practice throwing to a partner from a kneeling position. (How did you use your body to project the ball?) (perceiving)
2. Practice throwing to a partner, gradually increasing the distance to be thrown. (How did the throw change as the distance became greater? How did you use your body parts to increase the force?) (perceiving)
3. In partners, practice throw-ins. The receiver will control the ball as in soccer. (How did you attempt to control the ball? Where did you want to receive it? Was the throw-in easy to control?) (refining)
4. Repeat activity No. 2, but vary the distance thrown. (How did the throw change as the distance increased?) (varying)

FIGURE 29-15 Evaluative criteria and teaching points for goalkeeping.

- Assume a stride position, knees bent, weight on the balls of the feet; fingers spread, forming a W.
- Upper body leans forward, and eyes on the ball.

- Assume a side or forward/backward stride position, knees bent, the trunk and head arched slightly backward.
- The ball is held in both hands with fingers spread, thumbs close behind the head, arm bent at the elbows.

- The arms are brought forward with the ball; release overhead or in front of body.
- Arms and trunk follow through in direction of throw, and weight is shifted to the balls of the feet or to the front leg as legs extend.
- Both feet are on the ground as the ball is released.

FIGURE 29-16 Evaluative criteria and teaching points for throw-in.

5. Children are in groups of four: one thrower, two attackers, and one defender. The thrower attempts to get the ball to one of the attack players, who tries to control it before the defender can intercept or tackle. (Were you able to get it to the attacker so that it could be easily handled? Could you disguise your throw?) (varying)

SOCCER CONCEPTS

The movement content important to soccer may be found in Figure 29-1. Suggested activities for the development of these movement concepts in soccer activities follow.

Soccer Concepts and Activities

1. To move in general space in relation to the boundaries, teammates, opponents, and the ball.
   a. Dribbling in general space, each child has a ball. Each dribbles avoiding others' self space and their balls, using as much of the available space as possible and staying within the boundaries. The leader indicates an increase or decrease in the available space. (Was it as easy to control the ball in the small space as in the larger space? What did you do as the space got smaller to keep the ball under control, stay within the boundaries, and avoid others? Were you able to cover the large space? The small space? Where did you try to go as you dribbled in both spaces?)
   b. Four or five children without balls are scattered in general space and try to steal the balls from the remainder of the group, all of whom have a ball and dribble in the space. (Were you able to keep control of the ball and avoid the "stealers?" Did you stay inbounds? What did you do to protect the ball?)
   c. Begin with half the class attempting to hit, the other half protecting the balls. (What did you do to avoid your ball being hit? Where you you direct the ball to make contact with another person?)
   d. Each person has a ball. Each dribbles and attempts to pass the ball so that it hits an opponent's ball. There should be no personal contact. (How did you protect your ball as you attempted to hit others?)

2. To move to an open space while moving in general space.
   a. Dribbling in general space, on the signal they move to an empty space and stop. (How close are you to your classmates? Are you really in an empty space?)
   b. Two offense and two defense in two alleys. Offense tries to pass and move to an open space to receive a pass as the defense tries to intercept and close spaces. (What did you do to maneuver around defender to an open space to receive the pass?)

3. To keep your self space between your opponent and the goal or the ball and the goal while playing defense.
   a. Children are in partners. One person attempts to dribble the ball to a spot (the goal), while the other attempts to stay between the dribbler and the spot (goal). (Were you able to stay with your partner? How did you move? What cues enabled you to stay between your partner and the goal?)
   b. In partners, each set marks three spots in the space and a goal area. Players with the balls attempt to dribble to each of the spots while the defenders try to maintain a position between them and the goals. (What cues did you use to maintain the position between the player and the goal?)

4. To recognize one's own area of the general space in which to play.
   a. Players in alleys pass while moving the ball to the goal. (How were you able to pass while staying in your alley?)
   b. Repeat *a,* but add a defensive player in each alley. (Were you able to control the ball offensively or defensively in your alley?)

5. To use as much space as possible on offense to keep the defense spread out.
   a. In a small area there are two teams of two or three players. One team attempts to pass while the other tries to intercept. Increase the space and repeat. (Was it easier to pass successfully in the small or larger space? Why?) Repeat once more in the smaller space. (How can you use the space you have to make it seem as large as possible?)

6. To close spaces open to opponents and the ball, especially close to the goal area when on defense.
   a. Children are in groups of two and have a ball. On the signal they run out. The one getting to the ball first attempts to dribble the ball over the opponent's sideline; the other goes on defense and tries to keep the ball and opponent away from the line. (What did you do to keep the person with the ball away from your sideline?)
   b. A hoop is set up as a goal area with two defenders guarding the space. They may not stand any closer than 5 feet from the hoop. Two offensive players pass the ball trying to score a goal from either side of the hoop. (How did you protect the space closing the goal to the ball?)
   c. Using two alleys, offense tries to pass and move toward the goal, while the defense tries to keep them from the goal side of their alley. (Where did you position yourself to close space toward the goal?)

7. To create open spaces for self, teammates, and the ball while moving in general space.

a. In groups of three, two attempt to pass the ball while the third attempts to intercept. If successful, the person making the errant pass becomes the new defender. (How did you move to create a space for the ball? How did you draw your opponent to create a space?)
b. Repeat No. 6b but emphasize the offense creating spaces for the shot on goal. (How did you work together to create a space for the ball?)
c. Two players pass, moving the ball toward the goal against one defender, who tries to intercept. (How did you open a space for the ball as you moved toward the goal?)
d. Repeat No. 7c, with two passing against two defenders. (Was it more difficult to create an open path? Why?)

8. To recognize and anticipate pathways within which to move self and/or ball.

a. Each child has a ball and dribbles in general space. On a signal from the teacher, they quickly change pathway. (How did you begin the move to a new path? What cues did you use to recognize available paths?)
b. In groups of three or four, one or two persons are in an area between two end players. The end players attempt to kick the ball to one another through the center space, without touching the center players. The center players do not guard the space but move around trying to cover as much of the space as possible. (Were you able to get the ball through the space to your partner? What cues did you use to help identify the available pathways?)
c. With a partner, children move in general space and practice passing. (What did you do to keep the passes under control and avoid others? Were you available to anticipate the open pathways?)
d. In groups of three, one child faces the others, who line up one behind the other and several yards apart. The dribbler moves toward the first person who steps (keeping one foot stationary) to the left or right when the dribbler is within 2 or 3 feet. The dribbler moves to the available pathway and forward again toward the next person. (What cues did you use to anticipate the movements of the other players?)
e. Repeat No. 7a. (How did you position yourself on defense to defend against possible pathways of the ball?)

9. To change the expected pathway of the ball.

a. Repeat No. 8a, but add feinting to the left or right before moving in another pathway.
b. In groups of three, passing in general space. Pretend to pass to one person, but pass to the other instead. (How did you disguise your pass?)
c. Repeat No. 9b, but add a defender. (What cues did you use before deciding the path of the ball?)

10. To establish a pathway away from the goal on defense.

a. In groups of three, one attack player, one goalkeeper, and one defender. The attacker dribbles

Maximizing practice opportunity is essential to skill development.

and shoots for a goal, rushing the goalkeeper after the shot. The goalkeeper fields the ball and quickly passes or kicks the ball to the waiting defender, who has moved out to the side away from the goal. The defender moves the ball upfield and then turns to become the next attack player. (How did you get the ball safely to the waiting defender?)

b. In groups of four, one offensive player rolls or kicks the ball toward the goalkeeper. As the goalkeeper gets the ball, the two defenders scatter to receive the ball from the goalkeeper. (How did you decide which one would get the ball?)

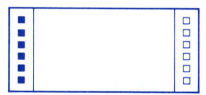

11. To alter the tempo of the game by speeding up and slowing down.

a. One dribbling against one opponent. Speed up and slow down as you move. (Were you able to control the ball at different speeds? Were you able to get past your opponent?)

SOCCER LEAD-UP GAMES

The analysis of the games that follow is given in Table 29-1.

LINE SOCCER

Level: II

Equipment: One soccer ball and pinnies or vests to designate teams

Area: A field approximately 35 by 50 feet with a line 5 feet from and parallel to each goal line

Participants: Six members for each team

Skills: Controlling, dribbling, shooting for goal, tackling

Description: One player from each team comes out from the right end of the team to about 3 feet from the ball. On the signal, each attempts to kick the ball over the opponents' goal line. One point is scored for each goal. After a point is scored, the players move to the end of their lines, and two new players come out on the signal after the ball has been placed in the center of the playing area. A player must control the ball first before shooting for a goal (in other words, they may not simply run out on the signal and immediately kick for goal). Goal line players must control the ball before kicking it to their teammate. Only goal line players may play in the area between the 5-foot lines and goal lines. If the ball is kicked out of bounds, a player from the opposite team's goal line rolls the ball in. Variation: An alternative method for beginning play is to give the ball to one team, with one of the goal line players passing to the active player.

Fouls:

1. Playing the ball with the hands.
2. Kicking for a goal without controlling the ball first.
3. Pushing an opponent.
4. Kicking the ball so that it rises above waist height.
5. Goal line guards failing to attempt to control the ball first before passing to a teammate.
6. An attack player moving within the 5-foot restraining line in front of the goal line.

Penalty: A kick for goal to the team fouled against, where the foul occurred. Only goal line players may guard against an offense kick. No kick may be taken closer than 5 yards from the goal line. In case of a defense (goal line guards) foul, a kick is taken 5 yards from the goal line.

Strategy:

1. Keep feet pointing in the direction of opponent's goal.
2. Field players should move to create a space to receive the pass when goal line guards have the ball.

Teaching suggestions:

1. On the opening play, pull the ball to the side or backward to control it before shooting for a goal.
2. Encourage controlling the ball on offense and defense.
3. Goal line guards may use the sole of the foot for easy control of the ball.
4. Goal line privileges may be introduced.
5. Opponents should be evenly matched by ability to provide equal opportunity for each pair of opponents.
6. Encourage goal line guards to stand in the area between the goal line and the 5-foot line.

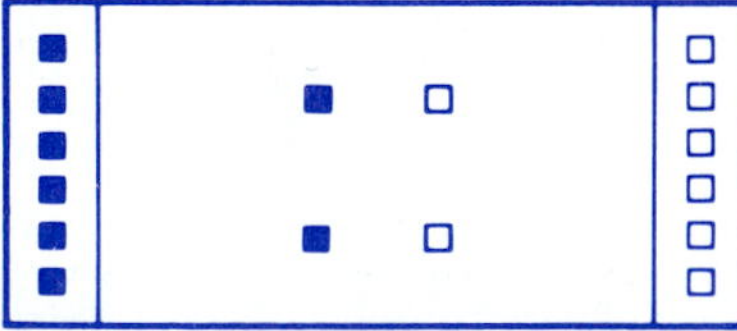

ADVANCED LINE SOCCER

Level: III

Description: The game is identical to Line Soccer except two or more players from each team come out on the signal. The number of players per team may be increased to eight or ten. The skill of passing is added to those already included in Line Soccer.

Teaching suggestions:

1. See those listed for Line Soccer.
2. Encourage passing. A number of passes may be required before shooting for a goal.

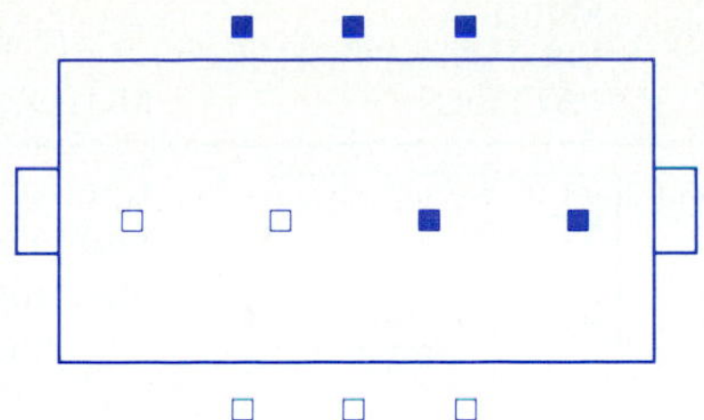

SIDELINE SOCCER

Level: III
Equipment: One soccer ball and pinnies and vests to differentiate teams
Area: A rectangular area approximately 30 by 60 feet with an 8- to 10-foot goal area at each end
Participants: Four to six for each team
Skills: Dribble, pass, shoot, goalkeeping
Description: The participants for each team are numbered. The leader calls a number, and the participants with that number come out. One player is designated to begin with possession of the ball. The team with the ball attempts to complete at least two passes to sideline players before shooting on goal. The opposing team attempts to intercept and keep the team in possession of the ball from scoring. If they intercept, they move the ball toward their own goal by passing at least twice to sideline players before shooting for goal. When a goal is scored or time is called by the leader, a new number is called.
Violations: Hitting the ball out of bounds over the endline.
Fouls: Personal contact with the opposing team.
Penalties: A member of the opposing team's sideline players is given the ball to put in play.
Strategy:

1. Move to an open space to receive a pass.
2. When the passes have been completed, stay between the player and the goal on defense.
3. Create spaces for the ball by moving away from the sideline player with the ball.

Teaching suggestions:

1. Stress passing with appropriate force so that the ball can be easily handled by the receiver.
2. Emphasize the use of space, opening space on offense, and closing space on defense.
3. Opposing players should be evenly matched in ability.

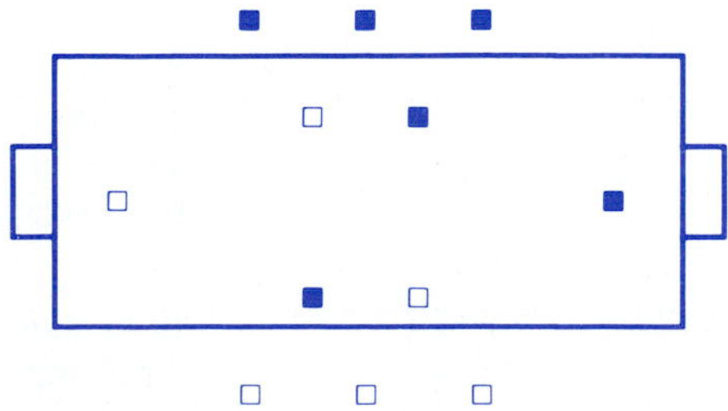

ADVANCED SIDELINE SOCCER

Level: III
Description: Similar to Sideline Soccer except more than one number is called, and passes may be completed to sideline or a teammate in the playing area.

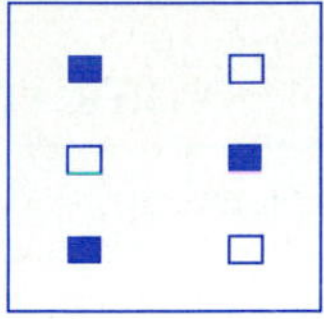

SOCCER PASS BALL

Level: III
Equipment: One soccer ball per game
Area: A field divided into separate spaces for each group
Participants: Three to four per team
Skills: Controlling, passing, tackling
Description: One team begins with possession of the ball and attempts to pass to each of the players on the team. Each time players successfully pass to each of the three to four team members, the team scores a point. The team not in possession attempts to intercept passes and gain control of the ball. Variation: Groups set targets for the number of consecutive passes they will strive for to earn a point.
Teaching suggestions:

1. The offense should continue moving in the space to make it more difficult for the defense to intercept.
2. Short, quick passes to open spaces are most effective.
3. Receivers must anticipate where successful passes might be made and support teammates by staying within one pass of the person with the ball.

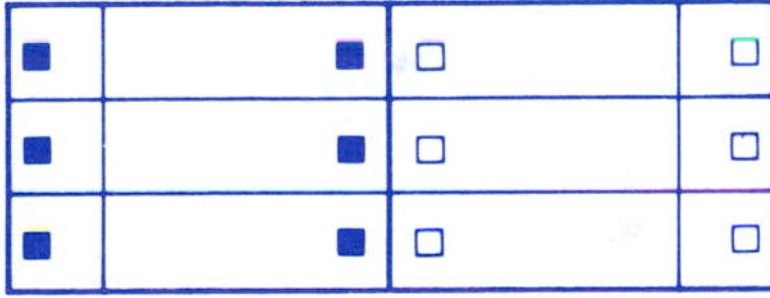

ALLEY SOCCER

Level: III
Equipment: One soccer ball and pinnies or vests to differentiate teams
Area: A field 80 by 100 feet long and alleys each 15 feet wide with a line 5 feet from and parallel to the goal line
Participants: Six per team: a forward and goal line guard for each alley
Skills: Ball control, dribbling, passing, shooting, tackling, throwing
Description: One team is designated as the kickoff team. On the signal, the forward in the center alley takes an unguarded kickoff (opposing forwards must be 5 yards away). On the kickoff, the ball must move at least one revolution in a forward direction across the center line. The player executing the kickoff may not play the ball again until another player has touched it. The forwards continue to advance the ball down the field while the opposing forwards try to tackle or intercept their passes. Forwards of either team may not enter the 5-foot area of the goal line players. On a shot for goal, the goal line guards defend only their alley. Goal line guards have goalkeeper privileges and may play the ball with their

TABLE 29-1 SOCCER GAMES ANALYSIS

NAME	GAME CLASSIFICATION	NO. OF PARTICIPANTS	EQUIPMENT	SPACE/ ORGANIZATIONAL PATTERN	MOTOR SKILLS
Line Soccer	Lead-up	Six per team	One soccer ball; pinnies or vests to designate teams	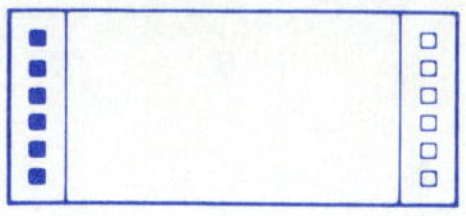	Controlling Dribbling Shooting for goal Tackling
Advanced Line Soccer	Lead-up	Eight to ten per team	One soccer ball per game; pinnies or vests to designate teams	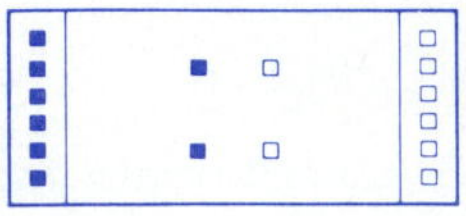	Controlling Dribbling Passing Shooting for goal Tackling
Sideline Soccer	Lead-up	Six per team	One soccer ball; pinnies or vests to designate teams	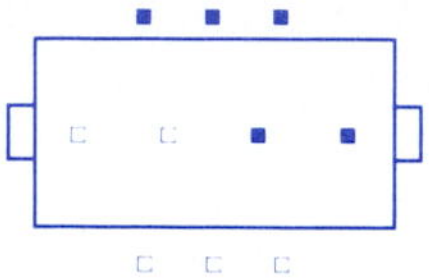	Controlling Dribbling Passing Shooting for goal Tackling Goalkeeping
Advanced Sideline Soccer	Lead-up	Six per team		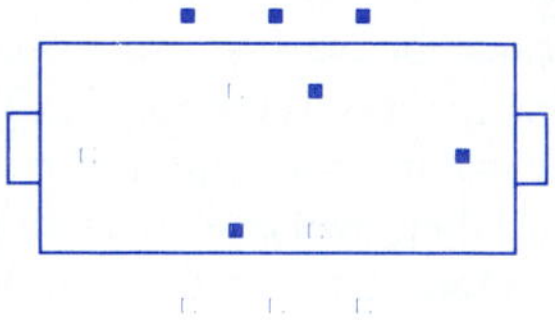	Controlling Dribbling Passing Shooting for goal Tackling Goalkeeping
Soccer Pass Ball	Lead-up	Three or four per team	One soccer ball per team	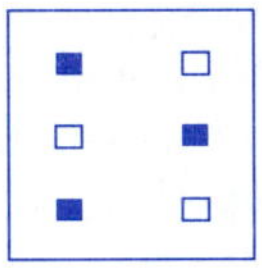	Controlling Passing Tackling
Alley Soccer	Lead-up	Six per team	One soccer ball; pinnies or vests to designate teams	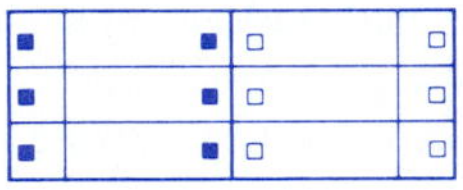	Controlling Dribbling Passing Shooting for goal Tackling
Advanced Alley Soccer	Lead-up	Seven per team	One soccer ball; pinnies or vests to designate team	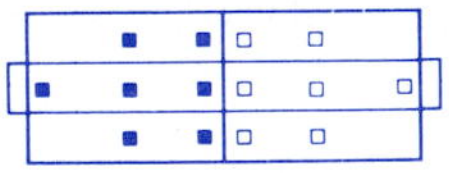	Ball control Dribbling Heading (optional) Passing Shooting for goal Tackling Throw-in Goalkeeping
Modified Soccer	Lead-up	Seven per team	One soccer ball; pinnies or vests to designate teams	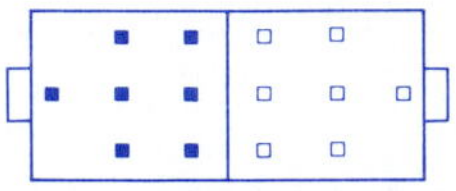	Ball control Dribbling Heading (optional) Passing Shooting for goal Tackling Throw-in Goalkeeping

*Numbers refer to the movement concepts listed in Figure 29-1 on p. 588.

MODIFICATIONS	MOVEMENT CONCEPTS*	SOCIAL STRUCTURE	STRATEGY	LEVEL
	Skills: 1, 3, 4, 5, 7, 8, 13 Game: 1-3, 6, 8, 10	Social interaction I	1. Keep feet pointing in the direction of the opponent's goal 2. Field players should move to create a space to receive the pass when the goal line guards have the ball	II
1. Require a specified number of passes before shooting for a goal	Skills: 1-8, 13 Game: 1-3, 5-8, 10	Social interaction II	1. Keep feet pointing in the direction of the opponent's goal 2. Field players should move to create space to receive a pass	III
1. Require a specific number of passes to the sideline before shooting for goal	Skills: 1, 3, 4, 5, 7, 8, 13 Game: 1-3, 6, 8, 10	Social interaction II	1. Move to an open space to receive a pass 2. Pass to a space in front of a moving receiver	III
1. Require a specific number of passes before shooting for goal 2. Increase number of players active	Skills: 1-8, 13 Game: 1-3, 5-8, 10	Social interaction II	1. Move to an open space to receive a pass 2. Pass to a space in front of the receiver 3. Players should keep spread out to create a space for the ball	III
1. Teams set targets for the number of consecutive passes they will strive for	Skills: 1-7, 9, 10, 12 Game: 1, 2, 5, 7, 8, 9	Social interaction II	1. Offense should keep moving to make it difficult for defense to intercept 2. Use short quick passes 3. Receivers must support teammates by staying within one pass of teammate with the ball	III
1. Increase number of alleys to five 2. Use extra players as sideline guards to throw the ball in on out of bounds violations	Skills: 1-8, 10-13 Game: 1-4, 6, 8-10	Social interaction II	1. Encourage passing to a space in front of a teammate 2. Forwards should maintain possession of the ball until the opposing player makes a commitment to them 3. Goal line guards should quickly move the ball away from the goal area 4. Use side alleys to bring ball down toward the goal and center it near the goal	III
1. Increase alleys to five	Skills: 1-13 Game: 1-13	Social interaction III	1. Encourage passing to a space in front of a teammate 2. Forwards should maintain possession of the ball until the opposing player makes a commitment to them 3. Goalkeeper should quickly move the ball away from the goal area 4. Use side alleys to bring ball down toward the goal and center it near the goal	IV
1. Reduce number of players per team to five	Skills: 1-13 Game: 1-13	Social interaction III	1. Emphasize using all space available and keeping spaced out 2. Encourage position play	IV

Continued.

TABLE 29-1 SOCCER GAMES ANALYSIS—cont'd

NAME	GAME CLASSIFICATION	NO. OF PARTICIPANTS	EQUIPMENT	SPACE/ ORGANIZATIONAL PATTERN	MOTOR SKILLS
Multigoal Soccer	Lead-up	Four players per team	One ball per team; cones to mark goals		Controlling Dribbling Passing Shooting for goal Tackling Heading (optional)
Two-Ball Soccer	Lead-up	Eight players per team	One ball per team		Controlling Dribbling Passing Shooting for goal Tackling Goalkeeping Heading (optional) Throw-in

*Numbers refer to the movement concepts listed in Figure 29-1 on p. 588.

hands. After stopping an attempt for goal, the goal line guard may throw or kick the ball to a teammate. If a goal is scored, 1 point is awarded and the opposing team will kick off. To give each player an opportunity to play all positions, after each goal or designated period of time, players rotate one position clockwise. The ball may be played by the forwards with any body parts except the hands. Balls going out of bounds are thrown into play by the opposing team.

Fouls:

1. Touching the ball with the hands (except goal line guards).
2. Shooting for goal by kicking a ball above the goal line guard's head.
3. Pushing an opponent.
4. Failing to stay in appointed alley.
5. Forwards moving beyond the 5-foot line of the goal area.

Penalty: A free kick is awarded the opponent of the player committing the foul. All other players must be 5 yards away. A goal may not be scored on a free kick. A hit taken for a foul by a goal line player is taken 5 yards opposite the spot where the foul occurred.

Strategy:

1. Encourage passing to an open space in front of a teammate.
2. Forwards should maintain possession of the ball by dribbling until the opposing players make a commitment to them and before the defenders attempt to tackle.
3. Goal line guards should quickly move the ball out of the goal area.
4. Encourage use of all alleys, using the side alleys to bring the ball downfield and centering it as they near the goal.
5. When on defense, forwards should stay between their opponent and the goal.

Teaching suggestions:

1. One or two additional players may be used as sideline guards who will put the ball into play when the ball goes over the sideline. They would move into field positions when the teams rotate.
2. Control of the ball should be stressed throughout the game.

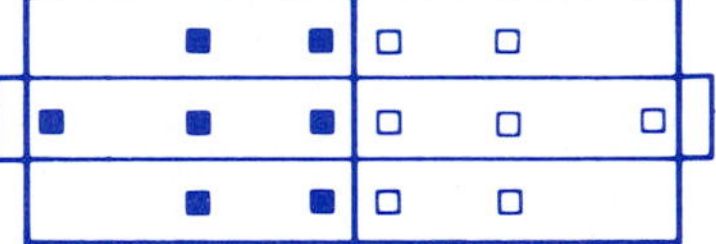

ADVANCED ALLEY SOCCER

Level: IV

Description: Similar to Alley Soccer but with the following changes:

1. There is a restricted goal area at the end of the center alley in which one goalkeeper plays.
2. A defense player is added to each galley: right fullback (RF), center halfback (CH), and left fullback (LF).
3. Each player now covers approximately three fourths of the field. The forward's area extends to the opponent's goal line. The halfback's and fullback's areas begin at their own goal line. One fullback should remain on his or her half of the field.
4. The forward's responsibility is mainly offense. All backs are responsible for taking the ball away from opposing forwards and passing up to the forwards of their team.

MODIFICATIONS	MOVEMENT CONCEPTS*	SOCIAL STRUCTURE	STRATEGY	LEVEL
1. Have teams remain at one goal rotating to another on a signal	Skills: 1-12 Game: 1-11	Social interaction III	1. Offense should use short quick passes 2. Defense should try to stay between goal and offense 3. Offense should use as much space as possible	IV
1. Increase number of players 2. Rotate midfielders often	Skills: 1-12 Game: 1-11	Social interaction III	1. Use short quick passes 2. Defense must maintain position behind offense and also between opponents and goal 3. Offense should use as much space as possible	IV

Teaching suggestions:

1. See those listed for Alley Soccer.
2. No more than two players should attempt to play the ball at any one time. Other alley players should position themselves in open spaces to receive the ball or in a position to back up the play on defense if the offensive player wins the advantage.
3. Increase the number of alleys to five, adding a forward and a defensive player (left halfback and right halfback) to each alley.

Taking a throw-in.

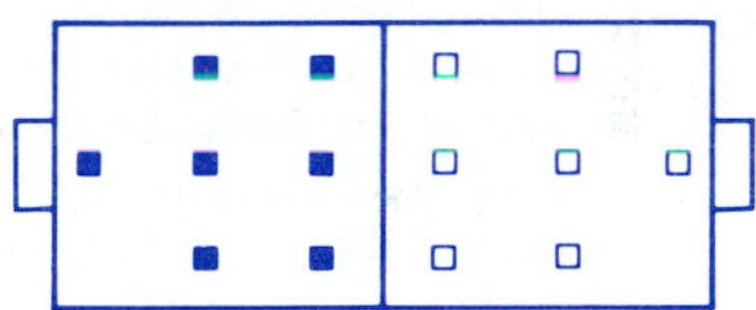

MODIFIED SOCCER

Level: IV

Description: Similar to Advanced Alley Soccer, but alley lines are removed. Each team consists of seven players: three forwards, three backs, and a goalkeeper. Children should be encouraged to use all the space available and stay in their positions.

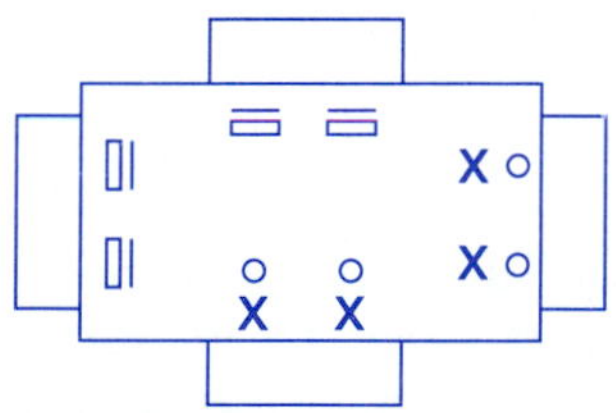

MULTIGOAL SOCCER

Level: IV

Equipment: 1 ball per team, cones to mark each goal area.

Area: Soccer field with four goals set up, one on each end and one centered on each sideline

Participants: Group divided into four-player teams—two defense who remain at one goal area and two forwards who travel to each goal.

Skills: Controlling, dribbling, passing, shooting, tackling, heading (optional)

Description: Each team begins in possession of the ball and attempts to move around the playing area scoring goals at each goal. Goals are scored at the end goals, as in soccer. Goals are scored at the side goals by successfully completing a pass that passes through the goal area. Once a goal is scored, the team may try to score another goal at that area or move to another goal.

Teaching suggestions: In introducing the game, it may be advisable to have each group remain at a goal and then rotate on a signal to the next goal. Additional goals may be used for large classes.

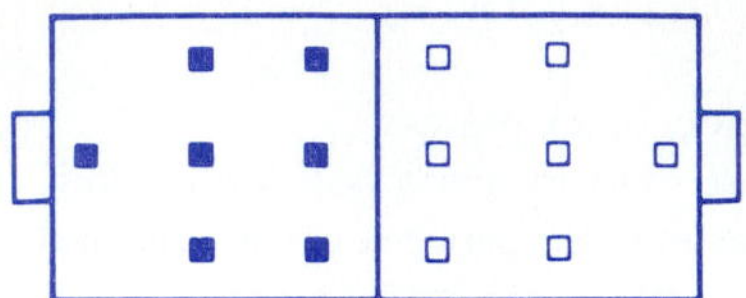

TWO-BALL SOCCER

Level: IV

Equipment: One ball per team

Participants: Eight players for each team—three forwards, two midfielders, two fullbacks, and a goalkeeper

Skills: Controlling, dribbling, passing, shooting, tackling, goalkeeping, heading (optional), throw-in

Description: Play modified soccer but play begins with each team kicking off. Midfielders should be encouraged to be the first line of defense as well as supporting the forwards who are trying to score. If the balls end up on the same end of the field and should go out of bounds, they are put back in play by the appropriate team in the order that they went out.

Teaching suggestions: Rotate players often as midfielders will get quite a workout. The number of players may be increased to 10 per team by increasing the number of forwards and midfielders.

SUMMARY

Soccer provides children with an opportunity to control a ball with most body parts. A variety of skills are used to pass, shoot, and control the ball. Children learn offensive and defensive play in a progression of increasingly complex games in which play requires some differentiation of responsibilities among the players.

Soccer is a large-group activity, although early games provide for a one-on-one experience until children are ready for more advanced play with larger numbers. In the early stages it is important to develop team play in small-group activities to ensure that all children receive ample opportunities to develop and use their skills.

Application of the movement content is important to success in the game. Considerable time must be spent developing these concepts in individual, partner, and small-group activities.

REFERENCES AND RESOURCES

Beim G: *Principles of modern soccer,* Boston, 1977, Houghton-Mifflin.

Canadian Soccer Coaches Association: Manual preliminary coaching level, *Coach* 1(1):12, 1986.

Chyzowch W: *The official soccer book of the U.S. Soccer Foundation,* Chicago, 1985, Rand McNally.

Golfer G: A movement approach for teaching soccer in the elementary school, *JOPER* 50(5):28, 1979.

Herbst D: *Sports Illustrated soccer,* New York, 1984, Harper & Row.

Hopper C et al: *Coaching soccer effectively. The American coaching effectiveness program level I soccer book,* Champaign, Ill, 1988, Human Kinetics Publishers.

Hughes C: *Soccer tactics and teamwork,* Wakefield, Mass, 1981, EP Publishing.

Kline L and Samonisky M: The soccer throw-in, *JOPERD* 52(5):57, 1981.

Laitin K and Laitin S: *Playing soccer,* Manhatten Beach, Calif, 1979, Soccer for Americans.

Moffat B: *The intermediate soccer guide,* Mountain View, Calif, 1982, Anderson World Publishing.

Orlick T: *The second cooperative sports and games book,* New York, 1982, Pantheon Books.

Simon J and Reeves J: *The soccer games book,* West Point, NY, 1982, Leisure Press.

Stewart C: Soccer games that work, *Strategies* 2(5):18, 1989.

Vogelsinger H: *The challenge of soccer: a handbook of skills, techniques and strategy,* La Jolla, Calif, 1982, Inswinger.

ANNOTATED READINGS

Celtnieks V and Lenosky BJ: The soccer circuit a flexible training program, *Strategies* 6(5):16, 1993.
Suggests a circuit to develop soccer skills that can be adapted for elementary schoolchildren.

Olson J: Basic team concepts for beginning level soccer players, *JOPERD* 54(9):51, 1983.
Describes eight-player soccer for young soccer players and player responsibilities.

Ramsay G: Dribbling for young soccer players, *JOPER* 50(7):27, 1979.
Presents activities to help children practice dribbling and to help them know when and where to dribble.

Startzell S: Soccer teamwork: a sport for all, *JOPERD* 52(5):55, 1981.
Describes helping children with special needs to learn soccer.

Sweetland M: A soccer unit for primary grades, *JOPER* 50(7):67, 1979.
Discusses developing kicking and body control soccer skills with primary schoolchildren.

Tant C: A kick is a kick—or is it?, *Strategies* 4(2):19, 1990.
An analysis of an efficient kicking motion.

CHAPTER 30

Softball

OBJECTIVES

After completing this chapter the student will be able to:

1. Describe the modifications needed in softball for successful play by elementary school children
2. Analyze the skills of softball and describe activities for their development
3. Identify the movement concepts important for success in softball and suggest activities for their development before their use in game play
4. Explain a series of progressively more difficult lead-up games used in developing the knowledge and skills of softball at the elementary school level

Softball, a variation of baseball, is a favorite recreational activity of children and adults, whether at family picnics or as simple neighborhood fun. Softball is a difficult game because the rules are complex and the skills must be performed with pinpoint accuracy. Yet it is a game that is readily modified by groups to meet their recreational needs, at times so much so that children begin to believe that the local rules are the official rules.

Although softball requires few skills, control of placement is difficult. A limited number of teammates and opponents are in action at any one time, and each player moves into action from a relatively stationary position. The movements of the offensive team are limited to hitting a ball with an implement and running a narrow base path. To be successful in softball, individuals must have speed in running bases and moving to receive balls in the field, agility, strength in the upper body and legs, and accuracy in placing the ball offensively and defensively.

Space concepts are important in softball as the children attempt to cover all the space in the field and to hit to an open space when at bat. On defense players must visually track balls moving through space, make accurate judgments about the ball's flight, and move quickly into position to field the ball. Creating and absorbing force and time (qualities of movement) are important in the game of softball as children project the ball varying distances and in time to beat the base runner to the base. The team at bat must time the run with the pitch and the fielder's attempts to put them out.

Games From Around the World

Although softball is a popular game in the United States, Canada, and a few other countries, cricket is probably the third most popular game in the world after soccer and basketball. Popular in many countries including many colonized by Great Britain, cricket is played with a flat bat, which is used to hit the hard ball into the field of play, which extends 360 degrees from the batting line. Two lead-up games for cricket are suggested in the games section of this chapter.

Danish rounders, a popular game in Denmark, is also included in the games section. It is similar to softball but involves striking a small ball with the hand.

SOFTBALL IN THE ELEMENTARY SCHOOL

Most children will enjoy softball if it is modified to meet their needs.

Equipment: Soft softballs are a must at the elementary school level to minimize the fear of an oncoming ball. When children are playing or practicing indoors, leather-covered fleece balls or nerf balls should be used to reduce the possibility of some unsuspecting child getting hit with a poorly thrown or batted ball. When possible, children should be taught to use a glove. Lighter, shorter, or plastic bats permit greater control in batting. For safety, catcher's equipment and batting helmets should be required when pitching is used in the game. Base paths

Batting from a batting tee.

The catcher should learn to use safety equipment.

should be reduced to 30 feet for intermediate grades and 35 to 40 feet for upper elementary grades.

Skills: Softball requires few, but difficult, skills. The overhand throwing pattern with a small bat is a difficult skill for children. This pattern not only affects the accuracy of the throw, but also the ability of the player to gather it in when it is poorly placed. Batting also poses problems for children, requiring timing the bat to meet an oncoming ball. Most modifications of the game listed below are needed because of the difficulties the skills impose.

The game: For beginning players softball can become a boring, frustrating, and sedentary game unless some modifications are made to keep the game moving and to enable each team to have an equal opportunity for offense (to be at bat). Because few balls are hit out of the infield at this level, teams of six players will help maximize the activity. To maximize the number of innings played in a class period, the batting teams should be changed after each member has had a turn at bat.

Batting is a problem for many beginning players. Striking out is difficult to accept, especially in front of classmates, and limits a player's opportunity to learn base running. It is better to allow a player to hit off a batting tee, walk, or throw the ball into the infield after three strikes or five pitches so that each child will have an opportunity to learn all offensive aspects of the game.

One reason for difficulty in batting is the lack of accuracy in pitching. This not only results in batting difficulties but also slows down the game because the catcher must often chase the errant pitches. If possible, the teacher or an aide should pitch; if not, the student with the most accurate underhand throw or a batting tee should be used. It may be helpful to have the batting team supply a back-up to help retrieve balls that pass the catcher.

Children should be encouraged to play a different position each inning. However, only those who can accurately throw the ball over the plate should pitch.

When two or more games are played simultaneously, it may be helpful to play all outs on base as **force-outs,** requiring only a step on the base while in possession of the ball to put the runner out. Children are often confused as to when they must tag the runner or merely step on the base. Children have some difficulty with the rule for determining if a ball is fair or **foul.** Because a ball that ends up in foul territory in the infield or a ball that first touches the ground in the outfield is foul, remembering the word SILO (*s*ettles in the *i*nfield, *l*ands in the *o*utfield) may help.

The team in the field must strive to cover all the space adequately in the field as it attempts to put the other team out. Position play must be stressed in softball. It is often difficult to get base players to be infielders and to recognize that they have a space to cover in addition to the base. Emphasis should be on the area of space to be covered by each player and putting oneself in a position where one can move to a ball coming anywhere in that space. Small cones placed on the field provide beginning players an aid to visualize space to be covered and to help them realign themselves after a play. Once they have developed awareness of their positions the cones are removed. It may be helpful to suggest that infielders move toward the batted ball in covering the infield.

When in the field, players must be thinking about what to do with the ball if it comes to their position. Determining where the ball should go only after one has caught it is usually too late to make a successful play. Encouraging the team to think it through and talk about it will help each player be ready to make the correct play. Having the children say out loud what they will do helps them focus on the task.

The team at bat attempts to remain at bat and to score as many runs as possible. Children need coaching in base running and especially running to first base. They must be encouraged constantly to overrun first base, which is difficult to get many young players to do. The following considerations must be made if the game is to be played safely:

1. Members of the team at bat should stand well away from the playing area and preferably behind the backstop or along the first-base side.
2. Batters are responsible for safely putting down the bat after they hit the ball.
3. Fielders should call for balls to avoid collisions.
4. If catcher's equipment is used, its safe use should be taught.
5. Soft softballs or fleece balls should be used indoors.
6. Bases should be secure and, if indoors, not close to walls.
7. Base players and shortstop should be taught to stand where they will not collide with or interfere with the base runners.

Social Skills

Although softball is a team game, it focuses on individual performance. All eyes are on the batters, fielders, and base players when they are actively involved in play. Thus each player experiences a great deal of pressure to do well.

Because softball is a difficult game for children, the teacher needs to encourage supportive behavior. The modifications discussed earlier will help to keep the game moving and somewhat reduce the pressure on players. In addition the teacher may award additional runs to the team that works well together, supporting the play of each member. For some games it might also be helpful to have the team at bat supply the pitcher to enable a teammate to pitch to each member on the team.

Health-Related Physical Fitness

Softball as played by school children does not contribute significantly to fitness. To encourage more cardiorespiratory activity, the teacher can encourage the children to run when moving from the field to bat or vice versa or perhaps have everyone run a complete circuit of the bases beginning at the closest base before changing positions at the end of each inning.

SOFTBALL SKILLS

Movement concepts are important in the learning of softball skills. The child must understand how various body parts come into play in sequencing the actions. The accuracy required in throwing skills is a combination of several concepts, including control of force, judging distance, and throwing the ball to an appropriate level. Time is important in judging the speed of a ball when batting and fielding. Absorbing force is important in catching and in base running. Flow is essential in the continuous movement when a fielder becomes thrower or a batter becomes a base runner. The concepts important for the use of softball skills may be found in Figure 30-1.

Throwing

Points of emphasis for the overhand and underhand throws are found in Chapter 13. They include (1) ball held in the fingers, (2) side facing the target, and (3) weight back transferring to forward foot as the arm is brought forward with the elbow leading. After ball release the arm and hand continue forward following through in the direction of the throw. The learning processes involved with the development of these skills in softball are varying and applying.

Activities To Practice Throwing and Catching

1. Partners throw and catch, increasing and decreasing the distance after each successful specified number of catches. (What did you do to get the ball to your partner as the distance increased or decreased?) (varying)
2. In groups of three or four, two or three fielders stand at varying distances away from a thrower, who is facing them. The thrower throws the ball in turn to each of the fielders, varying the force needed to cover the distance. (What adjustments did you make to get the ball to the fielders as they waited at various distances away?) (varying)

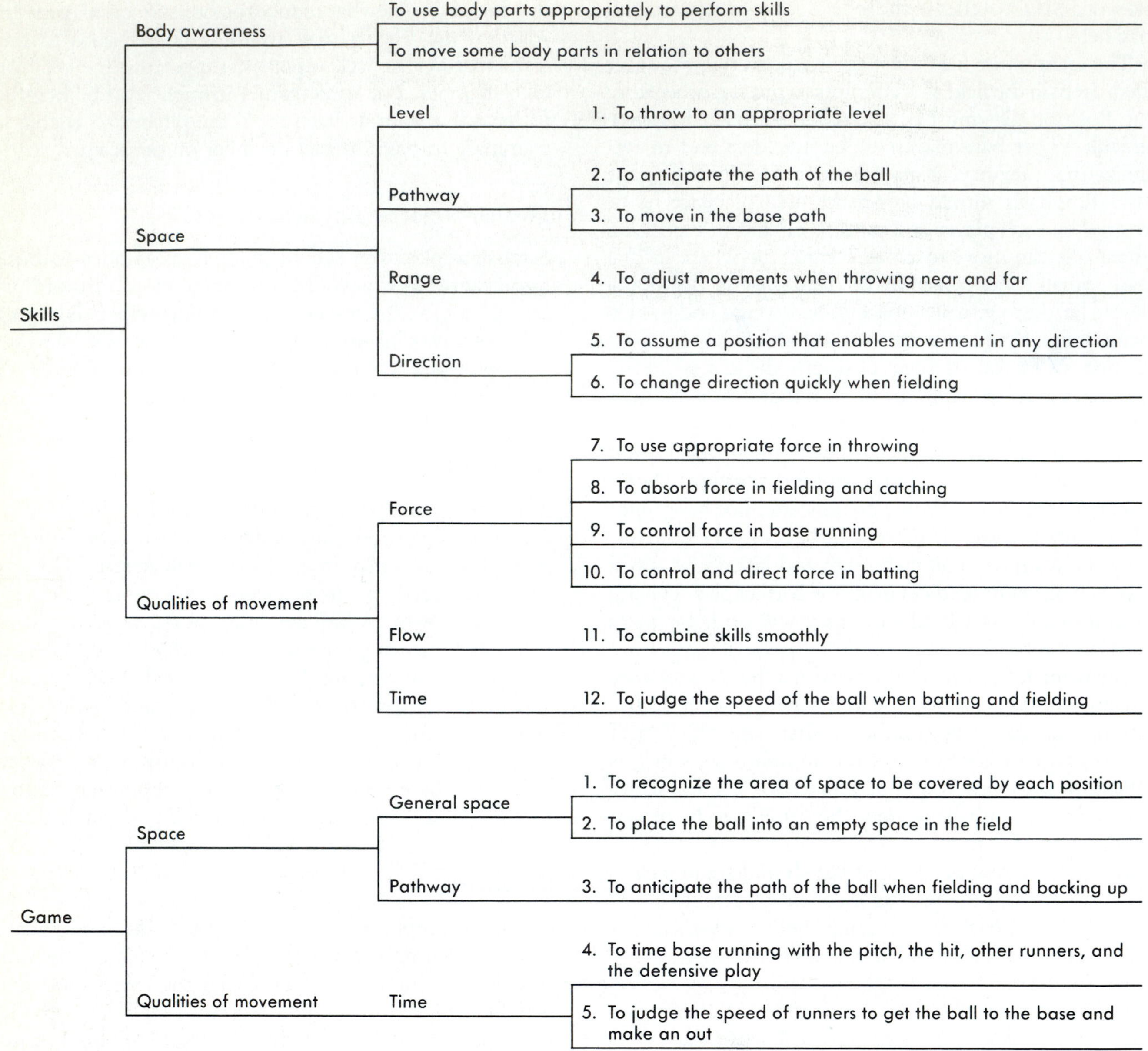

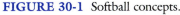

FIGURE 30-1 Softball concepts.

3. Partners who face the same way stand varying distances apart. The lead person throws the ball up, catches it, turns to face a partner who has moved closer or farther away, and then throws the ball to the partner, varying the force needed for the distance to be thrown. (What adjustments did you make to get the ball to your partner so that it could be caught?) (varying)
4. Repeat No. 3 but change the set up to include two bases with base players and a base runner. The thrower now throws to the base to which the runner is moving. (The runner may change bases while the thrower's back is turned.)
5. Children are in groups of four: one catcher-thrower, two base players, and one fielder. The catcher-thrower throws or bats the ball to the fielder, who throws to the base called by the catcher. (How did you adjust the force needed as you threw to the different bases?)
6. Children are in partners, throwing and catching as base players. The receiver calls force or tag, and the thrower throws the ball to the appropriate level to make the play—chest high for a force, low for a tag. The ball should be thrown so that it does not cross a runner's path to the base. (How did you adjust your throw to get it to the appropriate level?) (varying)

The *pitch* is the method of putting the ball in play in which the pitcher, using an underhand motion, throws the ball so that it passes over the home plate within the **strike zone.** The ball is held in the fingers, allowing day-light between the palm and the ball. Both feet are on the

- Ball held with three fingers opposite the thumb.
- Face the plate, eyes on target.

- As the underhand swing is taken, there is a step on the forward foot with the arm fully extended.

- The follow-through is in the direction of the pitch.

FIGURE 30-2 Evaluative criteria and teaching points for pitching.

pitcher's rubber, with the foot opposite the throwing arm slightly forward. As the arm moves forward, a step forward with the opposite foot adds momentum to the throw. The arm swing is smooth, and on release of the ball the arm follows through in the direction of the pitch. The ball crosses the plate at a height between the batter's armpits and knees (Figure 30-2).

Common errors:

1. Gripping the ball with the palm of the hand.
2. Placing incorrect foot forward.
3. Releasing the ball too soon or too late so that it is not within the strike zone.
4. Pitching arm not extended.
5. Not following through in the direction of the plate.

Pitching is a difficult skill for elementary school children. Few will be successful in consistently getting the ball over the plate within the strike zone. Rules for pitching vary slightly in slow- and fast-pitch games. Upper grade children should be introduced to the following rules:

1. Both feet should be in contact with the pitcher's rubber.
2. The ball should be held in two hands for at least 1 second and not more than 20 seconds before delivery.
3. Only one step may be taken toward the batter on delivery.
4. Only one motion toward the batter is legal.
5. The strike zone is directly over the plate at a height between the batter's armpits and knees, or the shoulders and knees if slow-pitch rules are in use.
6. In slow pitch the ball must be thrown so that it arcs 6 to 12 feet about the ground.

Activities To Practice Pitching

1. Practice pitching to wall targets representing the strike zone. (refining)
2. Practice pitching to a catcher who shows with the glove where the pitch should be received. (refining)
3. Practice with a person in the batter's box to visualize the strike zone. (refining)
4. Pitch varying the speed of the ball. (varying)
5. Pitch varying the level of the pitch. (varying)

Catching and Fielding

An analysis of *catching* may be found in Chapter 13. *Fielding* is an essential skill for all players in the infield and outfield. While waiting for the ball to be pitched, the fielder assumes a balanced *ready position* in a comfortable side-stride position, with back straight and at approximately a 45-degree angle to the flexed hips. The fielders are aware of all play options and have tentatively made a decision about what they will do when they receive the ball.

When fielding the batted ball, the player moves to a position in line with the ball. If the ball is hit directly to the fielder, the fielder immediately shifts to a forward-stride position. If the ball is hit to either side, the player steps first with the foot on that side (right foot if to right side) and then uses a cross-over step (that is, left over right if to the right) to reach the ball. If the ball is hit hard and farther to the side, the fielder moves back at a 45-degree angle to the ball. The glove should face the ball. The fielder watches the ball into the glove, and the arms are brought in toward the body and up as contact is made to absorb the force and begin to move the ball into position for the throw.

- Fingers point down for grounders.
- Watch ball into glove, close throwing hand over ball.
- Move quickly to throwing position and throw without hesitation.

- Fingers point up for flies.

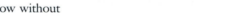

FIGURE 30-3 Evaluative criteria and teaching points for fielding.

In fielding *fly balls,* the fielder's thumbs are together with the hands up. The fielder judges the speed, direction, height, and wind effect and moves quickly to a catching position to wait to receive the ball. In this way the fielder can make the final adjustments necessary while waiting to catch the ball. The ball should be caught at as high a level as possible to allow more time and space to correct for errors. Before catching the ball, the fielder calls for it to avoid collisions with other fielders in the area.

When fielding *grounders,* the fielder's fingers point down with little fingers together. The feet are in a comfortable forward-stride position, with knees and hips flexed so that fingers touch the ground when hanging relaxed. The hands are positioned well out in front of the body. The head is down and the ball is stopped inside the forward foot, allowing the ball to roll into the glove. The fielder should move forward toward slow-moving balls (Figure 30-3).

Common errors:

1. Not assuming a ready position before the pitch.
2. Not moving in line with the ball.
3. Failing to bring the arms in and up on contact.
4. Not watching the ball into the glove.
5. Taking the impact of the ball into the non-gloved hand.
6. Not preplanning what to do with the ball when it is caught.

Teaching suggestions: Fielding is a difficult skill for elementary school children because their judgments of speed and ball path tend to be somewhat inaccurate, and many children are afraid of a batted ball. Proper use of the glove and making a smooth transition from fielder to thrower require much practice. When fielding grounders, some children may find it helpful to put one knee down on the ground so that the body can serve as a backstop if the ball goes through the glove.

Activities To Practice Fielding

1. A leader faces the students, who are spread out in general space and are assuming good fielding positions. The leader fakes a throw to the right, left, in front of, or behind the group. Each moves in the appropriate direction and pretends to field the ball. Players can practice crossovers and slides to the right and left. (Which ways of moving enabled you to move easily in each direction?) (refining)

2. In partners, both with a ball, each quickly rolls a ball to the other, fields, and throws again. (How many pickups can you do in a row? What positions enabled you to pick up the ball quickly and throw again? What did you do as you fielded the ball to get rid of it quickly?) (refining)
3. Partners, about 8 to 10 feet apart, have one ball. One throws to the other, who fields the ball and throws again while moving in a clockwise direction. Reverse and move counterclockwise. Variation: Add another ball. (What footwork enabled you to keep moving and successfully field the ball?) (refining)
4. In partners, about 8 to 10 feet apart. One assumes a fielding ready position, while the other attempts to throw the ball with an underhand motion between the feet of the fielder. (How did you position yourself to close the space?) (refining)
5. Partners face a wall. One person throws a ball so that it rebounds off the wall. The partner attempts to field on the rebound. (What cues did you use to help position yourself for the rebound?) (refining)
6. In partners, the leader has two balls. The leader throws one ball to the right of the partner. The partner fields the ball and throws back to the leader, who throws the second ball to the left of the receiver. (varying)
7. Children are in partners and practice fielding flies and grounders. Vary the path and force of the ball by throwing to the right, left, in front of, or behind the thrower. (What position enabled you to move in any direction to receive the ball? Where did you want to be as you fielded the ball?) (varying)
8. Similar to No. 4 but the ball is thrown so that it hits the floor or ground close to the wall, rebounds against the wall, and then rebounds again into the air. The fielder attempts to judge the flight of the ball for a successful catch. (How did you position yourself to be ready to move to the ball? How did you judge where the ball would go?) (varying)

Batting

Batting, the skill used by the offensive team, requires judgments of speed and height, as well as the coordination of swinging the bat to meet the oncoming ball. The batter stands with the side of the body facing the pitcher, with the knees slightly bent. The distance from home plate is determined by swinging the bat so that the wide part of the hitting surface is over the plate. The hands grip the bat, with the front hand on the bottom and the arms up and away from the body. As the ball is pitched, the batter shifts the body weight to the rear foot and prepares to meet the ball with the bat. The bat is swung smoothly toward the ball, and the body weight shifts to the forward foot. The batter should watch the ball to the bat. The release of the bat is controlled so that it lands near home plate as the batter becomes a base runner (Figure 30-4).

FIGURE 30-4 Evaluative criteria and teaching points for batting.

- Side faces pitcher in comfortable stride position a step away from home plate.
- Hands grip lower bat handle with hands touching each other.
- Bat is held up and off the shoulder.
- Eyes are on the pitcher and the ball.
- Swing is horizontal.
- Bat contacts ball; weight brought to forward foot on contact.
- Follow through in direction of hit and across body with wrists turning over.
- Batter sets bat down.

Common errors:

1. Facing the pitcher.
2. Standing too close to the base.
3. Hands apart on the bat.
4. Holding bat on the shoulder.
5. Not swinging the bat horizontally.
6. Throwing the bat.

Teaching suggestions: At times young batters may need to "choke up" on the bat by gripping the bat farther up on the handle. This technique allows better control when swinging the bat to meet the ball. For those having difficulty in batting, beginning with the bat up but in a horizontal plane may help. A batting tee may also be used to practice the swing and in games for children who are not yet ready to hit a moving ball. Another technique to help those having difficulty hitting a pitched ball is to gently toss the ball up from the side of the batter, which presents the ball to the batter much like fungo hitting described later but with another person tossing the ball.

Bunting is a modification of batting that is used in several offensive situations, for example, to advance a base runner. The batter shifts into position by stepping quickly toward the outside of the batter's box with the front foot and bringing the rear foot up even with it. The toes point toward the pitcher, and the feet are shoulder width apart. As the feet shift, the top hand is slid up the bat. The batter watches the ball and adjusts the body position by flexing the knees and arms to keep the bat above the ball. The hands and arms give on contact (as if catching) to control the ball's force and direction. The ball should be directed down the baselines (Figure 30-5).

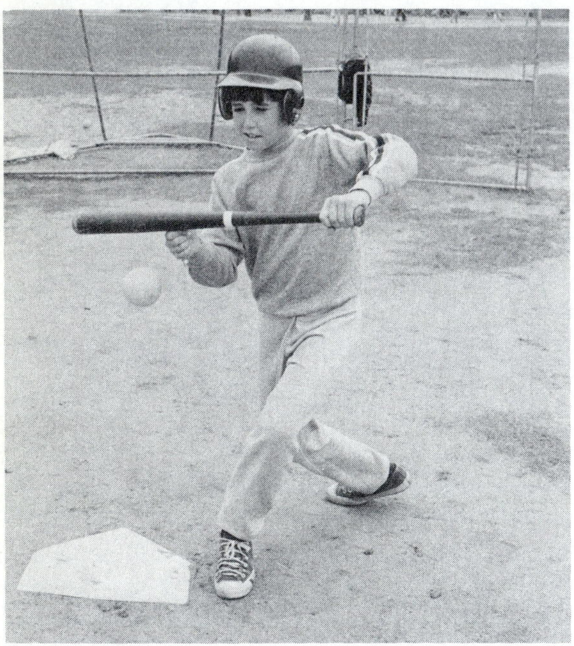

FIGURE 30-5 Evaluative criteria and teaching points for bunting.

- Face the batter before the ball release; keep knees slightly flexed.
- Slide top thumb up toward trademark, fingers underneath, thumb on top.
- Hold bat parallel to ground chest high; elbows slightly away from body.
- Eyes on ball. Adjust body position to keep bat above ball.
- Contact ball out in front of plate, "giving" with hands and arms on contact.
- Ball should hit ground about 4 inches in front of plate on a sacrifice or 7 inches for a base hit and directed down the base lines away from pitcher and catcher.

Fungo hitting is a batting skill for upper grade children. It enables an individual to hit the ball from a self-toss rather than a pitch. The hand that normally is on top in the grip is used to grip the bat, while the lower hand is used to toss the ball about head height for the hit. After the toss, the tossing hand grips the bat in the lower position as the bat is brought back and then forward to strike the ball.

Activities To Practice Batting

1. Working in partners with a batting tee, one bats and the other fields. (Be sure to swing the bat level so that you hit the ball and not the tee.) (perceiving)
2. Children are in groups of four: one catcher, one batter, one fielder, and one pitcher. Players switch positions after each batter has five hits. (What did you look for in a good pitch?) (refining)
3. Similar to activity No. 2, but vary size and weight of balls and bats. (What changes did you make to hit a larger or smaller ball? To use a heavier or lighter bat?) (varying)
4. Similar to activity No. 2, but two cones are placed in the field 5 yards apart. On the pitch, the batter attempts to hit the ball between the cones. Vary the distance between the cones, depending on the ability of the players. (How did you modify your batting to hit the space between the cones?) (varying)

Base Running

The batter becomes a *base runner* when the ball is hit in fair territory. As the ball is hit, the batter pushes off the forward foot and steps on the rear foot toward first base. The runner runs to a spot beyond first base, maintaining speed until touching the base, in running stride. If stopping at first base, the base runner comes back to the base, touching the inside of the base to wait for the next opportunity to run. If running for more than one base, the runner begins the turn by curving slightly outside the baseline and touching the inside corner of the base, as the run to the next base begins.

When waiting on base, with hips, knees, and ankles flexed, the runner leaves the base on the pitch. If the ball is not hit, base runners have the option of returning to the base or stealing if fast-pitch rules are being used. On a fly ball, if desiring to proceed to the next base, the runner must touch the base after the ball is caught before proceeding to the next base (Figures 30-6 and 30-7).

Common errors:

1. Failing to run in a straight line.
2. Slowing down before reaching the base, especially failing to overrun first base.

3. Failing to assume a ready position while waiting on base.
4. Not watching the play to determine what to do (such as running on a fly ball that is caught).

Activities To Practice Base Running

1. Several home plates and first bases are set up, with children in small groups lined up behind each home plate. On the signal the first person in each group runs to first base, overrunning it. (What did you do to run quickly to first base?) (refining)
2. Several diamonds are set up with no more than two or three students on any base. On the signal one person from each base runs the bases. The first person to complete one trip around the bases calls stop. (What path did you take to run completely around the bases?) (refining)
3. Groups of three or four are at each base of a softball diamond. On the signal, "Go," one person from each group runs the bases, beginning at their base. After completing a trip around the bases, they tag the next person in their line, who then begins the run. The first group finishing wins. (What was the quickest way to round the base? Describe your path. Where did you touch the base?) (refining)
4. Children are in partners, two to each base. On the signal, the first runner attempts to run to the next base before being tagged by the partner. The starting distances between the runners should be two strides if running one base, three strides if running two bases, four strides for three bases, and five strides for a round trip. (What was the quickest path? How did you avoid the tag?) (varying)

FIGURE 30-6 Evaluative criteria and teaching points for running to first base.

- Run in a straight line while maintaining speed in reaching the base. (Slow down only after touching the base if stopping at first.)

Position Play

When playing a base and waiting for a throw, the player's foot should be kept on the side of the base so that it will not be stepped on. When executing a force-out, touch the base with the foot and move quickly away to avoid a collision with base runner.

Although all fielders are responsible for a designated area of the field, they also must be ready to assist teammates in situations where they are not directly involved in the play. At times they may be called on to **cover** a base when the base player is involved in fielding a batted ball. In other situations they are needed to **back up** a play by positioning themselves behind a base player in line with a throw to a base or behind a fielder playing the ball so that they can receive the ball in case of an error by the intended receiver (Figure 30-8).

A backup should be available for each play. Outfielders back up balls coming to adjacent areas, as well as the nearest base. Infielders back up balls coming to their adjacent areas. The pitcher backs up throws from the outfield to second and third bases and throws from second to third. The catcher backs up first base unless runners are in a near scoring position (at second or third base).

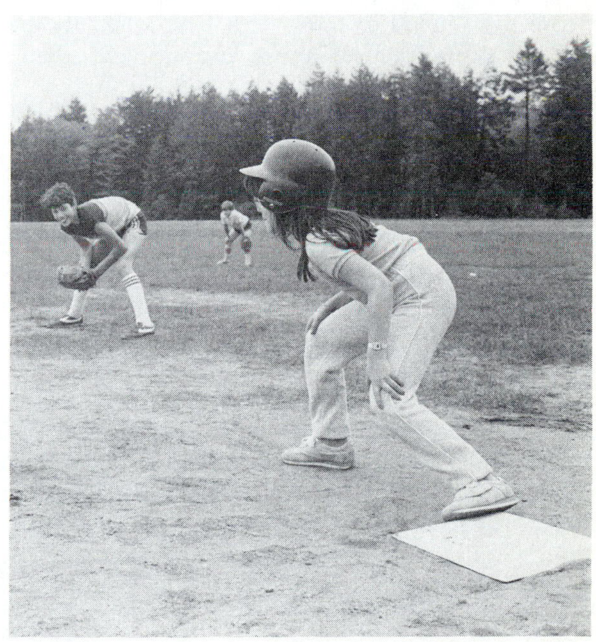

FIGURE 30-7 Evaluative criteria and teaching points for extra bases.

- Facing next base, forward stride with rear foot touching side of base.
- Flex hips, knees, and ankles for good take-off.
- Run in a straight path.

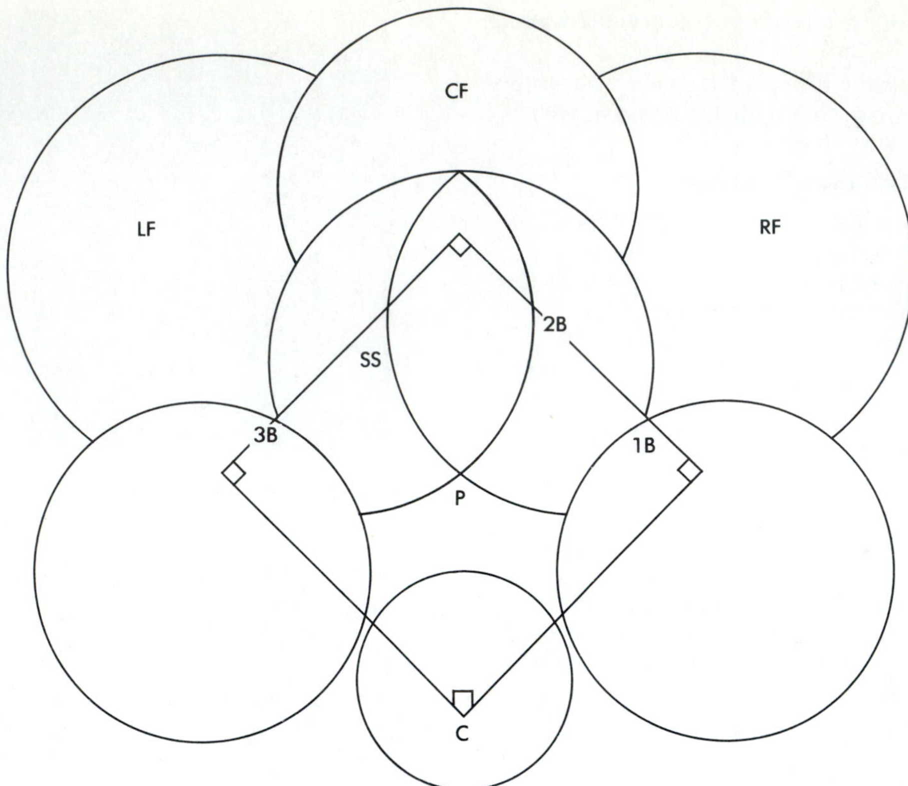

FIGURE 30-8 Areas covered by positions.

Covering is specific to given situations. Generally, someone is assigned to cover each base when the base player or catcher has been drawn away to field a ball.

Additional Activities

1. Organize a pentathlon in which the events are:
   a. Speed run of the bases.
   b. Distance or accuracy throw.
   c. Place hitting.
   d. Sprint to first.
   e. Pitching.

SOFTBALL CONCEPTS

The movement content important in softball is mapped in Figure 30-1. The activities that follow are a few of the possibilities for developing the movement content before their use in games.

Softball Concepts and Activities

1. To recognize the area of space to be covered by each position.
   a. In partners, one stands in an area 5 by 5 feet. The person outside the square attempts to throw the ball so that it touches in the 5-foot area but passes through without contact by the person defending the space. Each successful attempt counts 1 point. After five attempts, change places. (Where did you position yourself to be able to defend the space?)
   b. Children are in groups of three, one batter and two fielders, with one base 15 feet from either fielder. The batter throws or bats the ball and attempts to run to the base before the ball gets there. One fielder attempts to field the ball while the other covers the base. (What areas were most difficult to determine whose position should cover it? How did you work it out?)
   c. In groups of three or four, one person, who is in front of the others, throws the ball up. The fielder who will get it calls for it while another backs up the receiver. (How did you determine who would be the backup and the receiver?)
   d. Using home and second and third bases, with one thrower, two base players, and a shortstop, the thrower at home throws the ball to various places in the shortstop position. The thrower calls the base, and the shortstop throws the ball to the base. (What areas were most difficult to cover in your position? How did you adjust your throws to the base called?)
2. To place the ball in an empty space in the field.
   a. Modify the game so that any ball that the batter throws or hits, which lands in the field, gets through an empty space, and is not fielded, receives an extra point. (What did you look for to find the empty space?)

b. In groups of three, one thrower and two fielders, the thrower throws the ball into an open space, trying to throw the ball past the fielders. The ball must touch the ground in the area in front of the fielders. (What areas were easiest to get the ball through?)

3. To anticipate the path of the ball in fielding and backing up a play.

a. In groups of four, two base players face each other with a player behind each as a backup. Throwers throw to each other, varying throws to the right, left, in front of, and behind the receiver. Backups attempt to stay in line with the ball to retrieve any that the receiver misses. (What position enabled you to move balls quickly to get in line with the path of the ball?)

b. In groups of three, a leader faces two players. The leader throws to one of the two players. As soon as the receiver is determined, the second player moves into position to back up the throw. The backup stays in line with leader, ball, and fielder. (What cues helped you to stay in line with the ball?)

c. In two groups, children are scattered in two halves of a large rectangular playing area. There is at least one soft fleece ball for each two persons. Each team is divided into partners; one is the fielder, the other the backup. On the signal, each team throws the balls to the other team's half of the playing area. Any balls that get by backups score a point. (What position helped you move to cover the area and stay in line with the ball?)

4. To time base running with the pitch, the hit, other runners, and defensive play.

a. Children are in groups of five: one thrower, one base runner, one first base player, and two infielders. The thrower throws the ball in the area of the infielders, who field the ball and throw it to first base before the runner gets there. (How did you determine the force needed to get the ball to the base so that it could be received easily and before the runner arrived? What did you do as base runner to beat the ball to the base?)

b. Children are in groups of five: one pitcher, one catcher, and three base runners. On the pitch, all three leave the base, heading for the next base. The catcher calls fair or foul on receipt of the ball. If fair, runners proceed to the next base; if foul, they must go back. First player to the base wins. (What position enabled you to move forward or back on the call? What cues did you use?)

5. To judge the speed of the runner to get the ball to the base and make an out.

a. Children are in groups of three: two base players and one runner. The runner attempts to run between the bases without getting tagged as the base players throw back and forth. (How did you time your throw to get the runner out?)

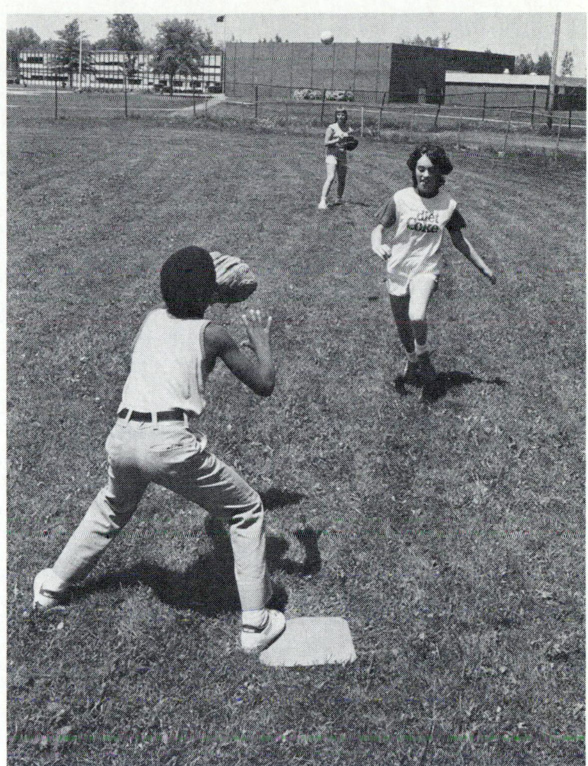

Timing the run and throw.

SOFTBALL GAMES

An analysis of the games that follow may be found in Table 30-1.

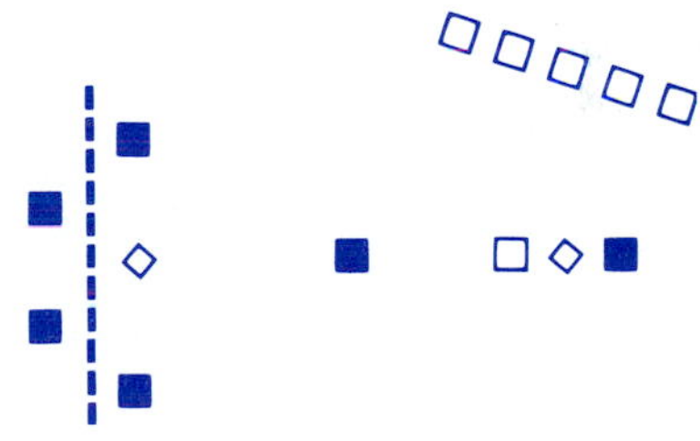

LONG BASE

Level: III

Equipment: Soft softball or leather-covered fleece ball, two bases, batting tee (optional), bats (optional)

Area: A play area with two bases spaced so that batting and fielding teams have an equal opportunity for success

Participants: Six players per team

Skills: Overhand throw and catch, fielding flies and grounders, baserunning, batting (optional).

Description: One team is "at bat," and the other is scattered in the playing area. The first batter throws the ball into the field and attempts to run to the base and back to touch home plate before the fielding team can get the ball to the catcher at home plate. One run is scored if successful. If the catcher gets the ball before the runner makes it home or a fly ball is caught, an out is recorded. After each member of the

TABLE 30-1 SOFTBALL GAMES ANALYSIS

NAME	GAME CLASSIFICATION	NO. OF PARTICIPANTS	EQUIPMENT	SPACE/ ORGANIZATIONAL PATTERN	MOTOR SKILLS
Long Base	Lead-up	Six per team	Soft softball or leather-covered fleece ball, two bases; batting tee and bats (optional)		Overhand throw Catching Fielding flies and grounders Baserunning Batting (optional)
Base on Balls	Lead-up	Six per team	Soft softball or leather-covered fleece ball, four bases; batting tee (optional); bats (optional)	Softball diamond with 30 feet between bases	Overhand throw Catching Fielding flies and grounders Baserunning Batting (optional)
Beat Ball	Lead-up	Six per team	Soft softball; four bases; bats (optional); gloves (optional); batting tee (optional)	Softball diamond with 30 feet between bases	Overhand throw Catching Fielding flies and grounders Baserunning Use of a glove (optional) Batting (optional)
Throw It and Run	Lead-up	Six per team	Soft softball; four bases	Softball diamond with 30 feet between bases	Overhead throw Catching Fielding grounders and flies Baserunning
Danish Rounders	Multicultural	Six per team	Tennis ball; four bases	Square size of half a tennis court; a base in each corner	Striking with the hand Catching Throwing
One Hit Softball	Lead-up	Four per game	Soft softball bat; batting tee (optional); two bases	Field space with two bases 30 feet apart	Batting Pitching Fielding Throwing Catching Baserunning
Work-up	Lead-up	Eight to 12 per game	Soft softball; four bases, bats; gloves; batting tee (optional)	Softball diamond with two to three at bat and remainder assuming positions in the field	Overhand throw Catching Fielding flies and grounders Baserunning Batting Pitching
Modified Softball	Lead-up	Six per team	Soft softball; four bases; bat; gloves; batting tee (optional)	Softball diamond with 30 to 35 feet between bases	Overhand throw Catching Fielding flies and grounders Baserunning Batting Pitching

*Numbers refer to the movement concepts listed in Figure 30-1 on p. 614.

MODIFICATIONS	MOVEMENT CONCEPTS*	SOCIAL STRUCTURE	STRATEGY	LEVEL
1. Add a throwing line beyond the base before which the ball must touch the ground	Skills: 2, 3, 5-8, 12 Game: 1-3	Social interaction I	1. Look for an empty space in which to put the ball when at bat 2. Be sure all areas of the field are covered on defense	III
1. Ball must touch the ground within baselines as it is thrown by the member at bat	Skills: 1-3, 5-9, 12 Game: 1-3	Social interaction I	1. Look for an empty space in which to put the ball when at bat 2. What type of throw will keep the ball in the air longer and thus away from fielders longer? 3. Be sure all areas of the field are covered on defense	III
1. Since there are no strikeouts, when batting is used, the batter should be allowed to throw the ball or hit off batting tee after five pitches 2. Rotate all positions except pitcher each inning	Skills: 1-3, 5-9, 12 Game: 1-3	Social interaction II	1. Try to place the ball into an empty space 2. Each fielder covers a specific area of the playing field	III
1. Three outs or everyone bats (whichever happens first) constitutes half an inning 2. Ball must touch ground in base path 3. No strikeouts	Skills: 1-9, 11, 12 Game: 1-5	Social interaction II	1. Cover your area on defense 2. Place the ball into an empty space and with greatest time in the air 3. Do not slow down before reaching first base	III
1. Change batting team when all have had one turn	Skills: 2-9, 11-12 Game: 1-5		1. Look for an empty space to hit ball when at bat 2. Cover all the space on defense	III
1. Limit number of pitches to each batter to five	Skills: 2, 4-8, 9-12 Game: 1-3		1. Look for an empty space to hit ball when at bat 2. Work together to get the ball to the base 3. Cover all the space on defense	III
1. No strikeouts: walk to first base after five pitches, or throw into infield, or hit from tee 2. Use force-outs only 3. Do not rotate pitchers	Skills: 1-12 Game: 1-5	Social interaction II	1. Cover your area while in the field	IV
1. Rotate positions each inning 2. Best student or teacher pitches 3. Use extra catcher to help retrieve pitches 4. No strikeouts	Skills: 1-12 Game: 1-5	Social interaction III	1. Cover your area on defense 2. Back up teammates when fielding or playing the base 3. Run quickly to first base; do not slow down	IV

Continued

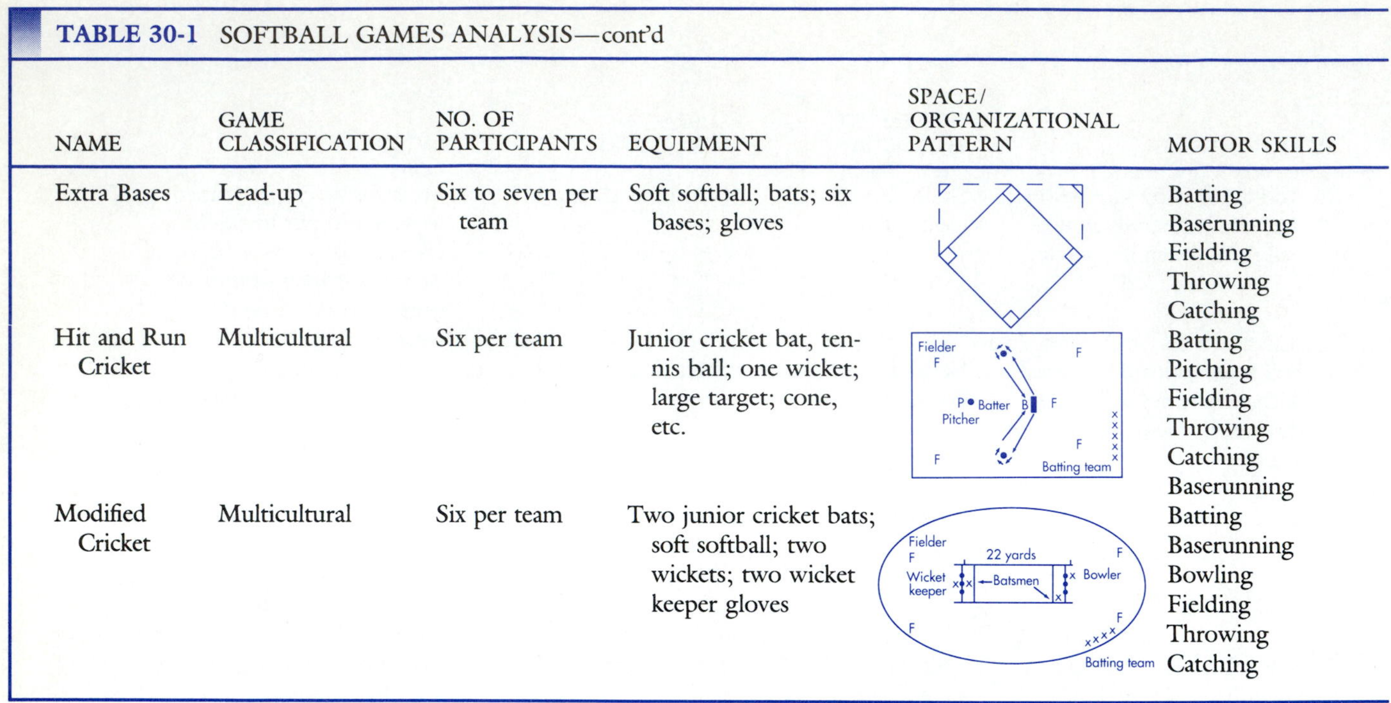

TABLE 30-1 SOFTBALL GAMES ANALYSIS—cont'd

NAME	GAME CLASSIFICATION	NO. OF PARTICIPANTS	EQUIPMENT	SPACE/ ORGANIZATIONAL PATTERN	MOTOR SKILLS
Extra Bases	Lead-up	Six to seven per team	Soft softball; bats; six bases; gloves		Batting Baserunning Fielding Throwing Catching
Hit and Run Cricket	Multicultural	Six per team	Junior cricket bat, tennis ball; one wicket; large target; cone, etc.	Fielder F; F; P • Batter B; Pitcher; F; F; F; Batting team	Batting Pitching Fielding Throwing Catching Baserunning
Modified Cricket	Multicultural	Six per team	Two junior cricket bats; soft softball; two wickets; two wicket keeper gloves	Fielder F; 22 yards; F; Wicket keeper; ←Batsmen; Bowler; F; F; Batting team	Batting Baserunning Bowling Fielding Throwing Catching

Strategy: Place the ball into an empty space far from home plate. Be sure that all areas of the "field" are covered.

Teaching suggestions:

1. It may be necessary to add the following rule: The ball must touch the ground before the throwing line. This will discourage throwing the ball beyond the fielders and wasting playing time retrieving balls well out of the playing area.
2. This game may be modified to use batting from a batting tee in place of throwing the ball into the field.

BASE ON BALLS

Level: III

Equipment: A soft softball or leather-covered fleece ball and batting tee (optional)

Area: A softball diamond with bases no more than 30 feet apart

Participants: Six players per team

Skills: Overhand throw, catching, fielding flies and grounders, base running, and batting from a tee (optional)

Description: One team bats, and the other is scattered within the field, outside the base path. The first batter throws the ball into the field and runs the bases, attempting to get to home plate before the fielding team can get the ball to its catcher. After receiving the ball and stepping on the homeplate, the catcher calls, "Stop." The team counts the number of bases passed before the signal to stop was given, and the base runner then returns to the sidelines with the batting team. After each member of the batting team has a turn, the two teams change positions. A fly ball caught is an out, and no bases are recorded. The team's score is the total number of bases passed by each member.

Strategy: Try to place the ball into an empty space far from home plate. Determine what type of throw will keep the ball away from the fielders longer. Be sure all areas of the playing field are covered on defense.

Teaching suggestions:

1. It may be necessary to add the rule that balls must touch the ground within the infield to keep the game moving.
2. Batting from a batting tee may be substituted for the throw.

BEAT BALL

Level: III

Equipment: Soft softball, four bases, bats (optional), gloves (optional), and batting tee (optional)

Area: Softball diamond with bases spaced to provide equal opportunity for batting and fielding teams and not more than 30 feet apart

Participants: Six players per team

Skills: Overhand throw, catching, fielding flies and grounders, baserunning, batting (optional), use of a glove, pitching (optional)

Description: One team bats. The other team assumes the fielding positions of catcher, first-base player, second-base player, shortstop, third-base player, and pitcher. The pitcher throws the ball underhand to the batter. Each member of the batting team throws or bats the ball in turn into the playing area within the baselines. They then run the bases, attempting to get home before the fielding team can throw the ball to first base and then to the catcher at home plate. If the ball beats the player home or a fly ball is caught, an out is recorded. If the runner is successful, a run is scored. After each member of the batting team has had a turn at bat, the teams change

MODIFICATIONS	MOVEMENT CONCEPTS*	SOCIAL STRUCTURE	STRATEGY	LEVEL
1. Rotate positions each inning 2. Limit pitches to each batter	Skills: 2-12 Game: 1-5	Social interaction III	1. Determine ahead of time if you will try for extra bases 2. Fielders need to think about where to make a play	IV
1. Change batter after three hits unless put out 2. Use batting tee after three pitches	Skills: 2-12 Game: 1-5	Social interaction III	1. Try to place the ball where it is least expected 2. Fielders must work together to cover all the space	IV
Change batter after three hits unless put out	Skills: 2-12 Game: 1-5	Social interaction III	1. Batters need to be ready to run at all times 2. Try to place the ball where it is not expected 3. Fielders throw to nearest base	IV

positions. If the player at bat places the ball outside the baselines, it is a foul ball and the ball is replayed.

Strategy:

Place the ball into an empty space away from first base. All players must cover their part of the playing area.

Teaching suggestions:

1. When batting is used, the teacher, an aide, or the student with the best control should be the pitcher.
2. When batting is used, there are no strikeouts. After five pitches, allow the batter to hit from a batting tee or throw the ball into the infield. This strategy will keep the game moving and reduce the frustration of all players.
3. When the fielding team is able to get the base runners out easily, add another base so that throws must be made to second, to first, and then to home.
4. If batting is used, gloves should be worn (even with a soft softball) because some children are timid in fielding batted balls.
5. Children should rotate positions each inning, except for the pitcher, who must be the one with the most controlled underhand throw.
6. Emphasize position play, especially for base players, who must be responsible for a larger area than just the base.
7. To discourage throwing the bat, call an out if it occurs more than once.

THROW IT AND RUN

Level: III
Equipment: Soft softball, four bases
Area: Softball diamond with bases 30 feet apart
Participants: Six players per team
Skills: Overhand throw, underhand throw (pitch), catching, fielding flies and grounders, baserunning
Description: One team is at bat, and the other team assumes the fielding positions of catcher, pitcher, first-base player, second-base player, shortstop, and third-base player. The pitcher throws the ball to the first "batter," who throws the ball into the field of play. The batter then runs the bases, taking as many as possible before stopping on one of them. The fielding team attempts to put the runner out by getting the ball to the base before the runner gets there (force-outs). A runner not making it to home waits on base until the next batter throws the ball. Each time a runner makes it safely to home plate, one run is scored. If the ball gets to the base ahead of the runner or a fly ball is caught, an out is recorded. After each member of the batting team has had one time at bat, the teams change positions.

Strategy:

Be in position to cover your area when on defense. Run quickly, and do not slow down before reaching first base. Place the ball into an empty space and with as much air time as possible.

Teaching suggestions:

1. Innings may be modified to include three outs or to have everyone bat (whichever happens first).
2. Stress position play, especially for base players, as they tend to stand on the base rather than in a position to cover their area of the field.
3. Have children rotate positions each inning, with the exception of the pitcher.

DANISH ROUNDERS

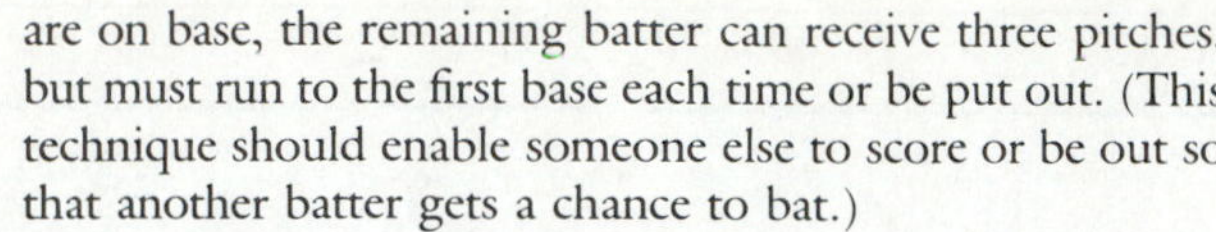

Level: III

Equipment: tennis ball, four bases

Area: A square the size of half a tennis court, with a base in each corner and a designated pitcher's area in the center of the space

Participants: Six players per team

Skills: Striking with the hand, catching, throwing, baserunning

Description: The "out" team, the fielding team, is scattered in the playing area, with one player designated as the pitcher and another as the catcher behind home plate. The pitcher throws the ball above the head of the first hitter on the "in" team, the batting team. The hitter standing on home plate, which is called the hitter's box, strikes the ball with one hand and then runs to the first square. Even if the hitter misses the ball or if the pitch is not good, the hitter runs to the first square. The fielders catch the ball and throw it to the pitcher who grounds the ball in the pitching circle. On grounding the ball the pitcher calls "Down." Runners may proceed to other bases if they can get to the base before the pitcher grounds the ball. Any runners not on a square when "down" is called are out. If the hitter is safe on the base, the next hitter comes up to bat. A run is scored each time runners complete the circuit back to home plate. A fly ball caught is also an out, and any runners not on a base when the ball is caught are out. There is no limit to the number of runners who may be on any base at any one time, and they do not have to run in consecutive order. The game is ordinarily played until there are three outs, but it is best to change batting teams after all team members have had their turn at bat to keep the game moving and provide both an offensive and defensive opportunity for each team. If the game proceeds to three outs, the future batting order is determined by the order in which players returned home. If all players are on base, the remaining batter can receive three pitches, but must run to the first base each time or be put out. (This technique should enable someone else to score or be out so that another batter gets a chance to bat.)

Strategy: Encourage all runners not to stay too long on a base, since runs are scored only by getting to home plate.

Teaching suggestions: Fielders should spread out to cover all the space. The catcher could back up throws to the pitcher.

ONE HIT SOFTBALL

Level: III

Equipment: Soft softball, bat, two bases, batting tee (optional), gloves

Area: Square or rectangular area for each group

Participants: Four players per game

Skills: Batting, pitching, fielding, throwing, catching, baserunning

Description: The players in the game assume the following positions: catcher, batter, pitcher, fielder. Play begins with the batter hitting the ball thrown underhand by the pitcher. After hitting the ball, the batter runs to the base and back to home completing as many circuits as possible. All balls hit in front of the batter toward the pitcher and fielder are fair balls. The batter scores a run for each base passed. The remaining players attempt to get the batter out by fielding the ball and throwing or moving the ball to the base toward which the runner is moving. If the balls beats the runner to the base, the batter is out. If the ball is overthrown at the base, the runner may continue to the next base and then back to the base overthrown if he or she has not been put out, thus scoring two more runs. That ends the batter's turn at bat and players rotate, catcher to batter, pitcher to catcher, fielder to pitcher, and batter to fielder.

Softball game.

Strategy: The pitcher and fielder must carefully position themselves to cover as much space as possible.

Teaching suggestions: It may be helpful to limit the number of pitches to each batter, at the end of which the batter hits off the tee to keep the game moving.

WORK-UP

Level: IV

Equipment: Soft softball, four bases, bats, gloves, batting tee (optional)

Area: Softball diamond with bases spaced 30 feet apart

Participants: Eight to twelve players per game

Skills: Overhand throw, catching, fielding flies and grounders, baserunning, batting, pitching

Description: Three players are at bat, and the remaining players assume field positions. Softball rules are used. Each batter takes a turn at bat, hitting the ball into the field and running the bases. When batting players make an out or after three at bats, they take a position in right field (depending on the number of players), and all other fielders rotate one position as follows: right field to center field to left field to third base to shortstop to second base to first base to pitcher to catcher to batter.

Strategy: Be sure to cover your area while in the field. Run quickly to first base, and step on the base at full speed.

Teaching suggestions:

1. It may be best to have no strikeouts and have the player take first base (walk) after five pitches, hit from the batting tee, or throw the ball so that it lands in the infield.
2. You may not want to rotate everyone to pitcher, as this position requires the most control.
3. Have all outs be force-outs (ball reaches base before runner).

MODIFIED SOFTBALL

Level: IV

Equipment: Soft softball, four bases, bats, gloves, batting tee (optional)

Area: Softball diamond with bases spaced 30 feet apart

Participants: Six players per team

Skills: Overhand throw, catching, fielding flies and grounders, baserunning, batting, pitching

Description: Softball rules are used with the following exceptions:

1. Distance between bases is 30 feet.
2. There are six players per team.
3. All outs are force-outs.
4. There are no strikeouts. After five pitches, the batter walks to first base, hits from the batting tee, or throws the ball into the infield.
5. No stealing is allowed.
6. The teacher, an aide, or the student with the best control pitches.
7. After everyone has had a turn at bat, the batting team changes positions with the fielding team, or the teacher sets a time limit for the batting team to provide equal time for both teams to bat.

Strategy:

1. Cover your area on defense.
2. Run quickly to first base. You should touch first base at full speed.
3. Backup teammates when fielding or playing the bases.

Teaching suggestions:

1. Rotate positions each inning.
2. It may be helpful to have a member of the batting team stand behind the catcher to help retrieve balls, as catching skills may not be well developed yet.
3. Teach backing up throws and fielding for better team defense.

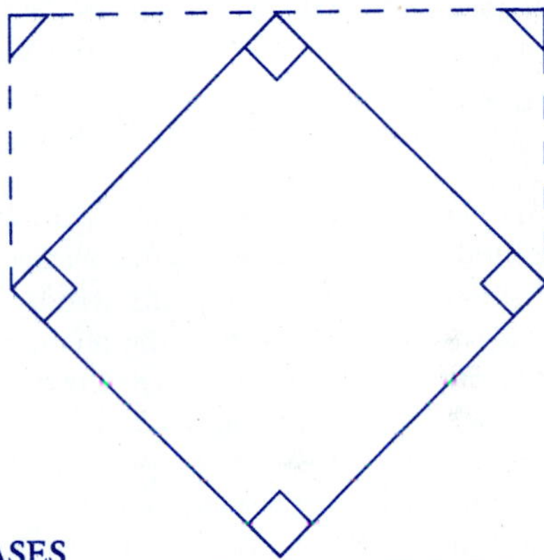

EXTRA BASES

Level: IV

Equipment: Bats, soft softball, six bases, gloves (optional)

Area: A softball diamond with bases placed 30 feet apart, and extra bases placed between first and second, and second and third toward the outfield

Participants: Six to seven players per team

Skills: Batting, baserunning, fielding, throwing, catching

Description: The team at bat catches; the fielding team pitches and provides a base player for each base. The base players assume the positions designated in the accompanying figure. The rules are similar to modified softball with the following exceptions:

1. The score for each runner is determined by the bases passed on route to home plate. Runners left on base after each has had a turn at bat may not count their runs.
2. Runners may choose the long or short route in moving around the bases, either following the traditional soft ball base path or running to the extra bases as well. A complete circuit of the bases counts as either four or six bases.
3. Runners may pass the runner ahead of them if one chooses the long route and one the short route, but no more than one runner may be on any one base at the same time.

Strategy: Encourage the development of team strategy to score the maximum number of runs in each turn at bat. Players should be thinking about where they will try to make a play if the ball comes to them.

Teaching suggestions: Rotate positions after each inning. Encourage backing up throws to the bases.

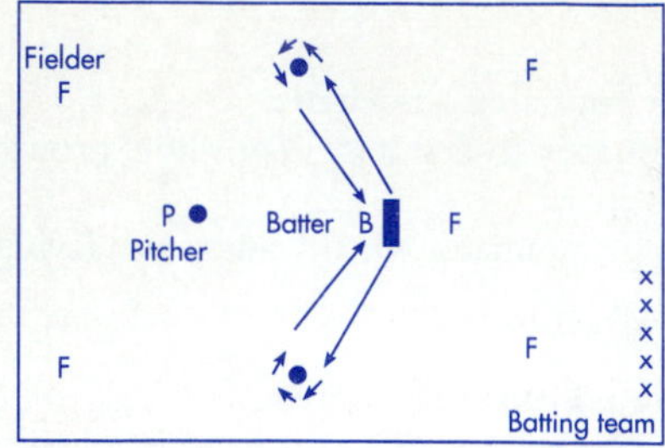

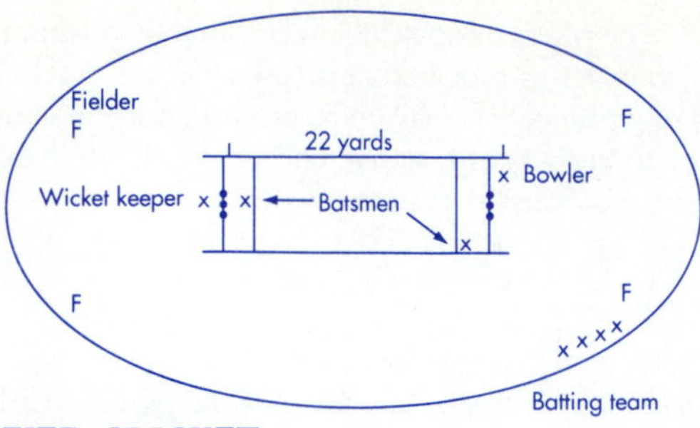

HIT AND RUN CRICKET

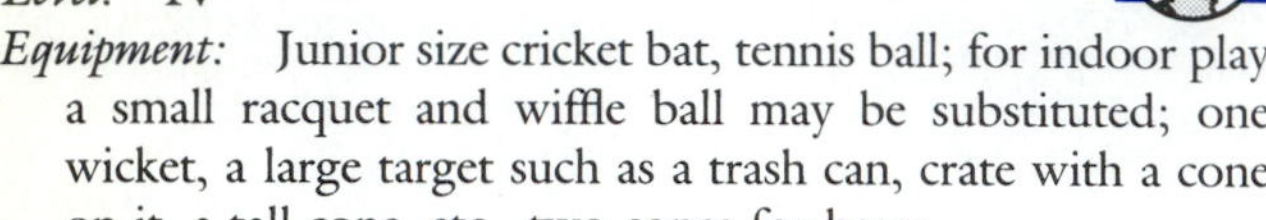

Level: IV

Equipment: Junior size cricket bat, tennis ball; for indoor play a small racquet and wiffle ball may be substituted; one wicket, a large target such as a trash can, crate with a cone on it, a tall cone, etc., two cones for bases

Area: Field area approximately 30 to 40 yards wide

Participants: Six players per team

Skills: Batting, pitching, fielding, baserunning, throwing, catching

Description: The objective of the game is to score as many runs as possible off pitched balls as long as the wicket is protected and a fly ball is not caught. The batter (batsman) attempts to hit the ball thrown overhand by the pitcher (bowler) so that it bounces in front of the batter. If the batter does not hit the ball and the ball hits the wicket, the batter is out. Batters may not use their legs to keep the ball from hitting the wicket. If the ball hits the batter's legs, the umpire may rule the batter out. Unlike softball there is no foul territory, and the ball may be hit in a 360-degree radius from the batting position. When the batter hits the ball, he or she runs to either one of the cones while carrying the bat, circling the cones and returning to the batting position. The fielding team attempts to get the batter out by throwing the ball to the catcher who touches it to the wicket. Sometimes the batter can complete the circuit several times, first to one cone and then to the other, before the ball is thrown to the catcher. Each circuit counts as one run. If the runner is sure to be out, he or she may stop after completing the first run around the cone and return to the batter's position. Runs may be automatically scored by hitting the ball on a fly past the far boundary line (six runs) or past the line on one bounce (four runs). Batters remain at bat until they are out. After all members of the batting team have had turns at bat, players change positions.

Strategy: Batters should try to place the ball where they have the best chance for a run. Fielders should try to cover all the space and be ready for hits to the sides and behind the batter.

Teaching suggestions: Batters should practice hitting the ball to the sides and behind them before game play. It may be advisable to change batters after two or three at-bats to keep the game moving.

MODIFIED CRICKET

Level: IV

Equipment: Two junior cricket bats, soft softball, gloves for wicket keepers, two wickets consisting of three poles 28 inches high placed in a triangle 9 inches wide or one tall cone on which a small beanbag (the bail) has been placed

Area: A large area usually oval in shape at least 30 to 40 yards in diameter, with the wickets placed 16 to 17 yards apart and centered in the space. A safe line is placed 4 feet in front of each wicket.

Participants: Six players per team

Skills: Batting, fielding, baserunning, throwing, catching, bowling

Description: The game begins with one batter (batsman) at each wicket. One of the opposing players from the fielding team stands behind the safe line on one side of the opposite wicket and bowls (pitches) the ball to the batter who is standing between the safe line and the wicket. The batter is safe as long as he or she remains between the safe line and the wicket. If for some reason the player steps out of that area, the wicket keeper may put the player out by hitting the wicket with the ball. The fielding team positions a wicket keeper behind the batter and wicket to serve as the catcher. The pitch or bowl is made using an underhand motion (an modified overhand motion is used in the original game). The batter attempts to protect the wicket and to hit the ball anywhere in the field of play, which extends 360 degrees from the hitting area. Each ball hit is a fair ball. There are no foul balls. Upon hitting the ball, the batter runs to the opposite wicket as the player at the opposite wicket runs to change places with the batter. Players carry their cricket bat with them at all times. The fielding team fields the ball and throws it to the wicket keeper or some other player who hits one of the wickets with the ball, dislodging the bail. The runner is out if he or she is completely outside the safe line when the bail is dislodged. If on hitting the ball, batters recognize that they are unlikely to make it safely to the opposite wicket, they do not have to run and the other runner stays put as well. If they leave or cross the safe line, however, they must run. The batter would then be given another pitch. There are no strike outs in cricket. If the bowl is wild and the wicket keeper is unable to handle it, batters may run. Each time players pass each other in exchanging places and make it to the opposite wicket, one run is scored and the runners may continue to run and score until they decide it is not safe to continue running or are put out by the following: (1) An opposing player touches the ball to a wicket, dislodging the bail; (2) they hit a wicket themselves so that the bail falls off; (3) an opposing player catches a fly ball; or (4) either the hitter or pitcher hits the wicket while batting, dislodging the bail. A ball hit on a fly outside the playing area automatically scores six runs. If the ball goes out of bounds after bouncing once, four runs are scored. The batters remain at bat until they are put out at which time they are replaced by one of their teammates. The fielding team bowls to one wicket six times (this is called an "over"), and then the wicket keeper and pitcher change places, and play continues by bowling to the other wicket.

Strategy: Try to place the ball in areas to the side and behind the batter to catch the opposing team off guard.

Teaching suggestions: With inexperienced batters it may be necessary to have an alternate rule, such as hitting off a batting tee after three pitches, to keep the game moving. To shorten the batting time for each team, batters may be changed after three hits rather than waiting for an out.

SUMMARY

Softball is a popular game with elementary school children, yet it requires the greatest accuracy in the execution of skills and an understanding of a complex set of rules. Game modifications are necessary to ensure the success of everyone. A smaller diamond and a softer ball are needed. Elimination of the strike-out rule and provision for the best possible pitching will help children gain confidence in this team game. The concepts of space, time, and force are very important as children attempt to cover the playing area on defense, to control the force of throws, and to time movements around the bases with other base runners, the pitcher, and the ball. Abilities of children vary greatly in softball at the elementary school level. Modifications should allow for individual differences and keep the game moving.

REFERENCES AND RESOURCES

Jones B and Murray M: *Softball concepts for coaches and teachers,* Dubuque, Ia, 1978, Wm C Brown.

Kneer M and McCord C: *Softball slow and fast pitch,* ed 4, Dubuque, Ia, 1987, Wm C Brown.

Linde K and Hoehn R: *Girls' softball: a complete guide for players and coaches,* West Nyack, NY, 1985, Parker Publishing.

Maguire J: *Hopscotch, hangman, hot potato, and ha ha ha,* New York, 1992, Simon & Schuster.

Melville T: Cricket as a PE sport, *JOPERD* 60(5):74, 1989.

Polk R and Lopiano D: *Baseball-softball playbook,* 1983, Mississippi State University.

Schwager S and Hammond A: *Hit and run cricket,* Materials from Regional Games Conference Hoffstra University, May 1992.

Seidel B et al: *Sports skills: a conceptual approach to meaningful movement,* ed 2, Dubuque, Ia, 1980, Wm C Brown.

Walker J: *Defensive techniques for championship softball,* Waukesha, Wisc, 1989, MacGregor Sports Education.

ANNOTATED READINGS

Adrian M and House G: Sporting miscues, part one, *Strategies* 1(1):11, 1987.
Presents common miscues in teaching skills including batting and pitching in softball.

Arnold L: Exercise, *JOPER* 52(3):31, 1981.
Discusses stretching activities for warming up.

Creehan K: Once around the bases: rotation softball, *Strategies* 5(5):19, 1992.
Suggests a strategy for rotating positions in a softball game.

Lopiano D: Practice, *JOPER* 52(3):28, 1981.
Provides station activities for indoor practice, many of which can be adapted for use with elementary school children.

Peterson S: Softball without strikes, *JOPERD* 52(7):72, 1981.
Presents a progression for teaching and using batting skills during the elementary school years.

Well L and Wright M: Pitching, *JOPER* 52(3):28, 1981.
Discusses how to throw various pitches and an analysis of errors and needed corrections.

Well L and Wright M: Offense, *JOPER* 52(3):34, 1981.
Presents an analysis of batting, including bunting, with an analysis of errors and suggested corrections.

CHAPTER 31

Volleyball

OBJECTIVES

After completing this chapter the student will be able to:

1. List the modifications necessary in teaching volleyball at the elementary school level
2. Describe the progression for skills development in volleyball and suggest activities to practice these skills
3. Explain the application of the movement content in volleyball and suggest specifically designed activities to develop these understandings before their use in games
4. Suggest a series of progressively more difficult lead-up activities for use during the elementary school years

Volleyball, a game developed by William Morgan, is the most popular game played recreationally by adults in the United States, from the beaches of California to the gymnasiums and recreation centers of the East coast. Originating in the United States, volleyball is becoming an important international game and an exciting spectator sport as well. Volleyball is unique among team sports. It is a rebound sport rather than a possession sport. It is a game in which the ball is continually moving, being held stationary only before the service.

Power volleyball requires a high level of difficult skills, yet with modifications of rules, both the novice and the highly skilled player are able to enjoy the game. Skilled players must have a variety of striking skills, including the serve, overhead volley, forearm pass, spike, and block. Participants in volleyball must assume a ready position that enables them to move in relation to the ball so that the needed skill may be executed accurately. They not only know when to use each skill but also are able to vary the skill in force and placement. The volleyball player executes skills using the full range of levels, from a few inches above the floor to high overhead, and must be able to do so from all positions on the court.

The volleyball participant must be a team player. Although each player has the personal responsibility for coverage of a particular area of the court, each must also accept responsibility for the team effort. The fast-moving game requires assisting teammates in their efforts to win the point or service by coming to their aid when a skill has been poorly executed or ill placed. In volleyball there are few one-on-one confrontations, but there is truly a team effort as one team goes against the other.

VOLLEYBALL FOR ELEMENTARY SCHOOL CHILDREN

Volleyball activities are good for children. They provide an opportunity for group cooperation and sharing as well as a progression of activities that gradually demands greater use of striking skills.

Equipment: One difficulty in helping children acquire skills involving striking with the hands has been the availability of a ball of an appropriate size and weight. Children should be exposed to a wide variety of balls while developing striking skills. Balloons and beach balls may be used successfully with young children. Lightweight foam balls may also be used at the elementary school level. One of the difficulties children have in striking the ball is tracking its approaching flight. Development of the volleyball trainer, which is lightweight, brightly colored, larger and slower moving, enables elementary school-aged children to develop good striking skills much faster as well as with fewer injuries to fingers and wrists.

The net height should be adjusted to the level of skill of the children and is usually no higher than fingertip height. The court size best suited for elementary school children is approximately 17 feet wide by 44 feet long, or about the size of a badminton court. The size might need to be further reduced for games in which there are four on a team.

Skills: Elementary school children generally lack experience in striking with the hands, especially in an overhand fashion, but this is the most frequently used pattern in volleyball. Volleyball skills are difficult to master. Many elementary school children lack the upper body development to control even a lightweight ball in this fashion.

Therefore a series of activities and games that gradually introduce striking skills is appropriate if children are to be successful. The progression should allow the modification of rules for individual players because there is a great variation in children's abilities to execute the skills.

Children are usually challenged to attempt the most difficult skill they can master, but they should not be penalized because their skills are under development. It may be necessary to allow some children to catch the ball before executing the skills with a self-toss, overhead volleying, or forearm passing to themselves first before passing to others or hitting the ball over the net, or allowing a bounce or two before striking the ball to ensure success for all. For serving, having several service lines available, some closer to the net, may aid children not only in getting the ball over the net but also in serve placement. These modifications are acceptable to the group because each team wants the best chance for success.

The return of service is one of the most difficult aspects of the game. As the children begin to master the overhead volley and forearm pass, a modification allowing catching and the set to themselves when receiving the serve may still be needed if the game is to be more than a serving battle.

The game: With the modifications already suggested, elementary school children can find success in volleyball. Modifications of skills for individuals help create an atmosphere where individual differences find acceptance, each child is successful, and a climate for sharing and teamwork is enhanced. Teamwork and sharing are not automatic outcomes of games. Children should be encouraged to get the ball to the most advantageous position before sending it over the net by passing to teammates. To ensure teamwork, at times it may be necessary to require several passes on a side or that only net players may hit the ball over the net.

The strategies involved in games take time to develop. Therefore each unit should be limited to one or two different lead-up games. The children will then have time to experiment with various strategies once the rules are learned.

The offensive team tries to keep the serve and score points while the defensive team tries to regain the serve by forcing their opponents to make errors.

The offense attempts to:

1. Serve to an open area in the opponent's court.
2. Move the ball to the most advantageous position on the court before returning it over the net.
3. Change the expected path of the ball.
4. Place the ball in an empty space in the opponent's court on all returns.

The defense attempts to:

1. Cover the area of the court, closing spaces to opponents.
2. Assist each other in controlling the ball as it comes over the net.
3. Move to the offense, incorporating the above offensive strategy to force the serving team to make errors.

Figure 31-1 outlines the movement content important in volleyball.

Social Skills

Because volleyball lead-up games are not fast-moving games for beginners, there is often time for poor social behavior, especially within the team between points. This behavior is often the result of frustration by the better skilled children for the lack of success of their lesser skilled classmates. Modification of skills for individuals usually minimizes these problems. However, points might also be awarded during or at the end of the game for the team that worked the best together, thus encouraging the development of a helpful, cooperative effort by all children.

In addition, activities that emphasize working together to achieve the goal are important. Several cooperative games are included in the games section of this chapter.

Health-Related Physical Fitness

Volleyball for elementary school children does little if anything to enhance their health-related physical fitness and especially cardiorespiratory endurance. A vigorous warm-up activity at the beginning of the lesson may help somewhat to counteract the low cardiorespiratory activity of the volleyball activities.

VOLLEYBALL SKILLS

The nature of volleyball lead-ups provides a unique opportunity for participants. Unlike most team games in which players are moving over a large area, the participant is responsible for a relatively small space. Ths space must be carefully defended, so that players assume a ready position from which they are able to move in any direction and to change level if necessary to get into position to play the ball (Figure 31-2).

Because the children have probably had little prior experience in the type of striking skills important in volleyball, most children will begin at the perceiving level. Skill mastery is difficult, requiring considerable time for refining skills. To initiate children in the use of skills, many skills need to be modified. Modified skills will enable the children to begin varying and then applying movement concepts for use in the early games of the progression.

Volleyball skills are unique. There is more conscientious preparation for the execution of skills because the ball may not rest even momentarily in the hands. This readiness and preparation are vital to ball control. Vol-

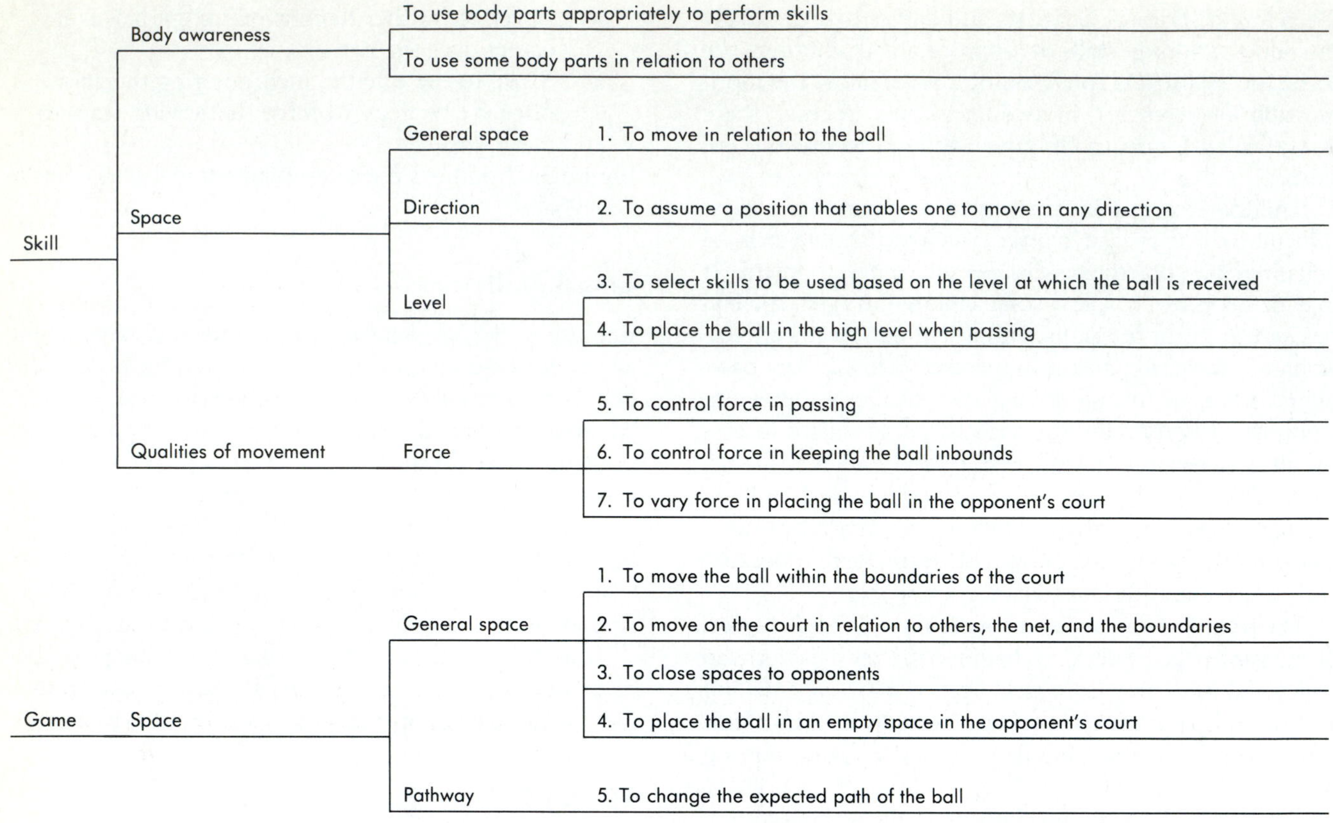

FIGURE 31-1 Volleyball concepts.

leyball skills require the use of the entire body to control and impart force to the ball, with the legs assuming a more important role than in many skills. This role requires greater coordination of body parts in the sequencing of the striking movement for efficient and effective performance. One must not forget that control of flight is the primary focus in skill development.

The important concepts involved in skills development are:

1. Body awareness: including the use and relationship of body parts.
2. Space: the relationship between hitter and the ball, the selection of skills based on the level the ball is received, recognition of the best position for moving in any direction to play the ball, and control of the ball's path.
3. Qualities of movement: controlling the force of the ball in the reception and propulsion of the ball.

Many injuries to fingers and wrists result from the player's failure to prepare those body parts adequately for the skills involved. Even with the lighter-weight balls, children should prepare for the activities with a brief period of warm-ups. Warm-up activities include the following:

1. Opening and closing the fingers.
2. Squeezing a tennis ball.
3. Shaking the wrists quickly forward and backward and from side to side.
4. Rotating the wrists in a figure-eight fashion.
5. With fingers of both hands touching, open and close fingers.

A number of activities for helping children develop beginning striking skills are found in Chapters 13 and 16. Activities to practice each skill presented in this chapter may be found after the explanation and analysis of each. Several groups of children may practice on each court because most of the activities require relatively little space.

The Ready Position

The *ready position* is essential to controlled play on the court and is maintained throughout the game in preparation to receive the ball. The player lowers the center of gravity, assuming a somewhat crouched position. The

FIGURE 31-2 Evaluative criteria and teaching points for ready position.

- Feet in stride position, weight on balls of feet and flexion in hips, knees, and ankles.
- Arms down, elbows bent. Hand position ready for forearm pass.
- Head up and eyes on ball.

body is balanced, the feet in a side-stride position, with one foot slightly forward of the other. The body weight is carried on the insides of the feet, with weight evenly distributed until the exact direction of the oncoming ball is known. The upper body leans slightly forward, with the knees in front of the toes and the shoulders in front of the knees. The hands are held out from the body, with the elbows bent and the hands over the knees. As the ball approaches, the player is ready to move in any direction into position to play the ball (see Figure 31-2).

Common errors:

1. Carrying weight on the entire foot.
2. Maintaining an upright posture.
3. Not paying attention to the ball.
4. Holding arms straight down or in pockets.

Teaching suggestions: Children must be continually reminded about assuming a ready position. When coaching play it is helpful to coach the children to be ready before receiving the serve. When moving to the right or left, a sliding step is used rather than a cross-over step.

Activities To Practice the Ready Position

1. In partners who quickly toss the ball back and forth to each other but not directly to the receiver. What did you have to do to be ready for the next pass? What position helped you to be ready to move in any direction? (perceiving)
2. Students assume a ready position on the court. Teacher calls the direction to move—left, forward, backward, diagonally forward to the right, etc. Players move on the court in relation to each other, moving two to three steps in the direction called. Following the move they then move back to the starting position on the court for the next call. (refining)
3. Repeat the above activity, but this time the teacher calls the direction and also the level at which the ball will be received. Students move in the direction called and also change the hand position to receive the ball at the appropriate level. (varying)
4. In partners, players are on opposite sides of the net. One player, the thrower or hitter, sends the ball over the net in a way that requires the partner to move to receive it. Receiver may catch it or hit it depending on the level of skill. (varying)

The Overhead Volley

The *overhead volley* is the best controlled skill in volleyball because it allows a longer contact period. The ball is contacted at a point above and in front of the forehead with the fingers of both hands simultaneously. The receiver moves into position directly behind and under the ball. The body is in a balanced stride position with one foot slightly ahead of the other. As the ball is contacted, flexion increases and the legs extend, which increases the force projected to the ball. The head is up, watching the path of the oncoming ball. The hands are up, elbows flexed out from the sides with the upper arms parallel to the floor. The hands are below head level before contact. On contact they are above the head. The wrists are flexed slightly backward on contact with the ball. The fingers are relaxed to allow ball contact with the fleshy part of the fingers and not the palms. Wrists spring forward to give additional impetus to the ball. On the follow-through, the body extends in the direction of the line of flight. The equal push of the legs and arms is important in ball control. The ball should be projected several feet above teammates in passing (Figure 31-3).

Common errors:

1. Not getting in line with the ball.
2. Contacting ball too low in front of the chest and pushing it forward rather than upward.
3. Contacting with the palms or slapping the ball.
4. Not flexing and then extending the legs.
5. Stiffening wrists on contact.

Teaching suggestions: The overhead volley is a difficult

- Forward stride, knees bent.
- Fingers spread, elbows bent to sides. Ball contact above and in front of forehead with finger pads.

- Knees and hips extend on contact, wrists spring forward as body extends.
- Follow through up and in direction of flight.

FIGURE 31-3 Evaluative criteria and teaching points for overhead volley.

skill, but modifications can be made for beginning young players. Because children are at different developmental levels, this progression allows children to develop at their own rate in a nonthreatening environment, rather than having the same skill expectations for all children. A progression for learning the skill follows. Emphasis should be on getting into a position in line with and under the ball, using the finger pads for legal contact, flexing and extending the legs in the execution, and putting the ball into the space above the receiver when passing.

1. The individual catches the ball, tosses it up to an appropriate height directly above, gets into position, and then overhead volleys the ball. (The biggest difficulties in volleyball are the return of the serve and, for many children, merely hitting a ball coming toward them. In this manner children have more time to execute the skill and to get into an appropriate relationship with the ball, and they do not have to deal with the oncoming force.)
2. As the children gain confidence in their ability to contact the ball, net players may overhead the ball directly because balls coming just over the net are probably coming more softly. (Note that children should only attempt to overhead volley balls that are received at an appropriate height for the overhead volley until the forearm pass is learned.)
3. Later, back-line players may be given the option of catching first or directly overhead volleying those balls coming to their position.

The Forearm Pass

The *forearm pass* is used to play balls received below chest height. The ball is contacted so that it rebounds off the two forearms simultaneously. This is one of the most difficult skills to control.

The passer assumes a balanced stride position directly in line with the ball. The body is low with the knees bent,

- Forward-backward stride; hips, knees, and ankles flexed.
- Contact on flat surface.

- Waist bent (90 degrees).
- Extension of knees, hips, and ankles.

- Follow through in direction of flight.

FIGURE 31-4 Evaluative criteria and teaching points for forearm pass.

allowing the player to get well under the ball. The hands are held in a manner that presents the forearms evenly to the ball, with attention focused on position of the forearms.

The interlock position is perhaps the best controlled for elementary school children. The arms are held out and away from the body. Wrists and hands are turned down to allow elbow extension and straight arms. Ball contact should be on the fleshy part of the forearms about 2 or 3 inches above the wrists. Body weight shifts forward on contact. Ball contact should be at the midline of the body if possible and about knee level. The arm swing is from the shoulder, with no movement observed at the elbow. On the follow-through, the body action continues in an upward and outward direction in the line of flight. Emphasize keeping arm surface even throughout contact and follow through to the target (Figure 31-4). Activities in which the children continue to hit their own forearm passes help them learn to control the force of the action.

Common errors:

1. Hitting off an uneven surface.
2. Swinging the arms upward and backward (bending the elbows) on contact. (The ball should rebound from arms.)
3. Failing to be in line with the ball.
4. Not getting under the ball in preparation for contact.
5. Keeping the legs straight.
6. Not maintaining a right-angle relationship of arms and body.

Teaching suggestions:

1. A progression similar to that for the overhead volley should be used. Allow the children to catch the ball and then toss and forearm pass first to give them the opportunity to become comfortable with the position and body action. Once this is achieved, they will be ready to get into position for an oncoming ball.
2. This skill may be introduced after the children have experienced some success with the overhead volley and the underhand serve. Some feel this skill should be the first one taught.

Activities To Practice the Overhead Volley or the Forearm Pass

1. The children using a vertical throw toss the ball up, move into position under it and catch it above their heads (overhead) or below their waist (forearm pass). (perceiving)
2. Passing to a partner throw the ball, with a two-hand underhand toss, so that it can be caught above and slightly forward of the head or low when practicing the forearm pass. (perceiving)

3. Children toss the ball up to themselves and then execute an overhead volley or forearm pass, catch it, and repeat the action. (perceiving)
4. Repeat No. 3 but instead of catching the ball continue to volley or forearm pass to yourself. (How many times in a row can you control the ball?) (refining)
5. Individuals toss the ball to the wall and hit it on the rebound. (refining)
6. Passing to a partner, one throws the ball for the appropriate pass, the other moves into position under the ball and hits it. (refining)
7. Pass to a partner. (Can you keep it going?) Children should catch any ball they cannot get into a good position to hit. If using the catch and overhead volley, they should try to catch the ball in the high level. (refining)
8. Place several targets varying in height on the wall for each hitter. Hitter tries to hit each target in turn. (refining)
9. Individual hitting, alternating the overhead volley and the forearm pass. Count the number of continuous hits. If you lose control start again. (Can you improve your score?) (refining)
10. In groups of four, each group has a wall space. Player A volleys the ball to the wall and moves to position D. Other players shift one position clockwise, with B moving to position A to receive the ball. If the ball cannot be received in a high level, catch it and begin again. Count your consecutive successful overhead volleys. (What did you have to do to get into position to receive the ball? Where did you attempt to place the ball so that the next person could receive it? (refining)

B A

C D

11. Follow the leader. One child hits the ball using the overhead volley or forearm pass and the other follows the leader using the same type of hit. (Was it easy to follow the leader? Did you control the force as you hit it for the other person? How many consecutive hits can you make?) (varying)
12. Passing to a partner, vary the distance between partners. (What did you do to get the ball to your partner when the distance increased? Decreased?) (varying)
13. In groups of three, two are on one side of the net, and one is on the other. A volleys the ball over the net to B, who returns it to A. A then hits the ball to C, who returns it to A. Rotate positions periodically. (What did you do differently to pass the ball the longer distance?) Variation: Have C also vary distance by passing back to A directly on first receipt and to B on the second. (varying)

14. Three players are in a line spread across the court. One ball calling the name of the receiver who will receive it at the high level. (How did you move to direct the ball to the named receiver? Were some pathways more difficult? Why?) Variation: Place the leaders on the opposite side of the net so that they must now hit the ball over the net. Vary the distance between receivers and net, changing distance after each successful volley. (varying)

15. Children are numbered in groups of four. Players 1 and 2 are on one side of the net and parallel to the net, and 3 and 4 are on the other side of the net, positioned in a similar manner. Player 1 sets the ball to 2, who hits it over the net to 3. Player 3 sets to 4, who hits it back over the net to 1. Change positions after a few tries. Note that as play continues, the players receiving the ball from over the net will have to select either the overhead volley or the forearm pass, depending on the level the ball is received. (varying)

16. In partners, the receiver calls the level at which the ball is to be received and acts accordingly by moving into the correct position to receive it. Change receivers after five tries. (How did you control the pass so that it could be received at the appropriate level? What position did you assume for balls received in the high level? Low level?) (varying)
17. Children pass to a partner, varying the level at which the ball will be received. (What did you do to get into position for a high pass? Low pass? Which was easiest to control? How did you vary your hits so that they would be received at a low level? High level? What skill did you use for a ball received low? High?) (varying)
18. Three players numbered from 1 to 3 are arranged in a circle. Number one begins play with an overhead volley into the center of the circle, No. 2 moves into position and hits it again for No. 3, who continues play, hitting it for No. 1. Each time, the ball is placed in the space rather than to the receiver. (Were you in position to move to the ball? How many consecutive hits did your group make? Try to beat your own record.)

Serve

The serve is used to put the ball in play. Although generally the floater or overhand serving action is used in power volleyball because of its greater effectiveness, the underhand serve is easiest for most elementary school children to master. The *underhand serve* is the easiest serve for both the server and the receiver to control. The ball

- Opposite foot is forward.
- Ball is held at waist height in front and to the side.
- Contact is made below and behind the ball.

- Weight is transferred to forward foot.

- Follow through in direction of flight.

FIGURE 31-5 Evaluative criteria and teaching points for underhand serve.

is contacted by the hand in an underhand swinging motion.

The server assumes a balanced stride position behind the service line, with the foot opposite the hitting hand forward. This position allows more force to be created through the use of body rotation as well as from the arm and leg action. The ball is held slightly below the waist and may be hit out of the hand or from a low toss after the action is understood. The striking arm is brought back and then forward in an underhand pendulum swinging motion to make contact below and behind the ball at about waist level. Contact with the hand may be made from several hand positions: (1) open hand, contact on the fleshy part of the thumb and hand; (2) with a fist, hand facing upward, contact on fleshy part of the thumb and curled fingers; and (3) a fist, turned sideways so that contact is made on the side of the curled index finger and thumb. The hand and arm continue moving forward and upward in the line of flight (Figure 31-5).

Common errors:

1. Not planning placement.
2. Placing the incorrect foot forward.
3. Holding or moving the ball to a position that is too high for an effective hit.
4. Failing to transfer weight to forward foot.
5. Not following through.

The *floater serve* uses an overhand hitting position and is difficult to return. The server stands behind the service

- Foot in forward-backward stride, weight on rear foot.
- Striking hand raised, elbow high.
- Controlled ball toss.

- Weight transferred to forward foot.
- Contact high and in front of the body.

- Contact with open hand, hitting off heel.
- Follow through up and in direction of flight.

FIGURE 31-6 Evaluative criteria and teaching points for floater serve.

line, with the foot opposite the striking hand forward and weight on the rear foot. The striking hand is raised with the elbow high and arm back so that movement is a forward motion only. The controlled ball toss is just high enough so that the ball can be contacted at full extension. As the arm moves forward the weight shifts to the forward foot. The ball is contacted with an open hand, with impetus given by the heel of the hand. The arm continues its motion, following through upward and in the direction of flight. The point of contact and the direction of the swing determine the ball's flight (Figure 31-6).

Common errors:

1. Not planning placement.
2. Placing the incorrect foot forward.
3. Not making contact at full extension.
4. Not coordinating toss, weight transfer, and contact.
5. Failing to follow through.

Activities To Practice the Serve

1. Servers are on one side of the net, receivers on the other. Servers attempt to hit the ball so that it goes over the net. Receivers roll it back under the net. (You may want to begin closer to the net and gradually increase the distance to the net.) (perceiving and refining)
2. One server faces two players on the opposite side of the net. Opponents call the area, and the server attempts to get the ball into that area. Receivers change their positions on the court on each serve. After three to five serves, change positions. Mats or ropes may be used to designate the areas. *Variation:* Modify the service line if necessary. (What did you do to get the ball into the designated area? Which area was hardest to hit? Why?) (varying)
3. One player is on each side of the net with a limited court area. One person moves to a new position, and the server attempts to place the ball in an open space in the court. Change position and server and repeat. (How did you change your movements to get the ball deep in the court? Left or right? Just over the net?) (varying)

VOLLEYBALL CONCEPTS

Basic strategy development in volleyball requires the application of the movement content. The concepts to be emphasized in the lead-ups included in this book are outlined in Figure 31-1. The activities included here are a part of the applying process of learning. In the following section, the concepts are listed with some suggested activities for their development. Teachers should develop additional activities as they analyze their students' play.

Volleyball Concepts and Activities

A number of movement concepts important for successful play are listed here with suggested activities for their development. Modification of games procedures and scoring may also be used to reinforce the concepts for the game. Questions should be asked to keep the children on task and to require them to describe verbally what they did to demonstrate their understanding. Only a few are suggested in the activities that follow. After practice the concepts should be reinforced in game play.

These concepts should be developed with work in partners or groups of three and four. All require the use of a net. The activities may be played on court areas smaller than the size used for lead-up games to maximize the number of children participating at one time. All require controlling force and using space effectively.

1. To move the ball within the boundaries of the court.
   a. In partners on a relatively large court, one throws the ball to various parts of the partner's court, and the partner moves into position to play the ball. Gradually reduce the size of the court space. (Which lines proved more difficult in keeping the ball in bounds?)
   b. Children work in partners or in groups of four. Each serves and continues serving as long as the ball is kept inbounds on the serve. The ball may be returned directly to the server, who then serves again to some other part of the court, or play may continue until either team fails to return the ball. In either case, the server continues to serve until the ball fails to be served inbounds or over the net.

2. To move on the court in relation to others, the net, and the boundaries.
   a. Children are in position on small courts. On the signal to move in various directions, they move only as far as their position extends in the direction called.
   b. In a group of four arranged on one half of the court, one child begins play by hitting to each of the positions of the others. Repeat three times with each player hitting to each position. (How far does each position extend? Were you able to control the ball in hitting it to each position?)
   c. In groups of four, two on either side of the net, playing side by side. The first player hits or throws (beginners may not be very accurate) the ball over the net to anywhere in the opposite team's court, including the space between players. The receivers attempt to play the ball and return it to the opposite side of the net. The player who receives the ball calls, "Mine." Play may continue or the ball may be caught and play may begin again. Variations: (1) Repeat but change the player relationship to one in front of the other, or (2) repeat with the number of players to be used in the lead-up game.

Requiring the back row to pass to net players enhances team play.

Waiting to receive the ball.

d. In groups of four or six, three or four on each side of the net. The first player throws the ball up as though he or she had lost control of it. Another player moves into the thrower's position to assist, and each passes it to a teammate or over the net. Variation: Repeat, with the thrower calling either a pass or a hit over the net.

3. To close space to opponents.

a. Play in small courts, hitting the ball back and forth. As children cover the space, the court size is gradually enlarged. (What did you do to cover the space as the court size increased?)

b. Begin with four players on each court. The ball is hit back and forth and as play continues the number of players are gradually reduced. (How big a space could you cover? How did you have to work with others to cover the space?)

4. To place the ball in an empty space in the opponent's court.

a. After the serve, the players in the right back court of both teams call the placement of the ball each time it is received across the net. If the ball is accurately placed, 1 bonus point is scored. No player may receive the ball twice in succession. (To what areas of the court was it most difficult to get the ball? What could you do to make it easier?)

b. With a partner each player plays against an opponent on the other side of the net. Scoring occurs only when a ball lands inbounds, not touched by an opponent. Variations: Doubles with two on each team or three or four on a team. (What did you do to get the ball in the empty space? How did you vary your hits? What position helped you cover the court area?)

c. Each team, composed of two or three players, creates a new empty space after each hit. The receiving team must look to see where it is for ball placement. One point is awarded each time a hit is made into the open space. Opponents attempt to get the ball, but may not move into the empty space to cover it. (When did you look for the empty space? How did you get the ball to it?)

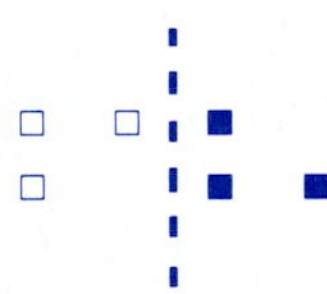

d. Play a game in which points are scored only when the ball hits an empty space.

e. Play a game in which 1 bonus point is awarded when the ball hits an empty space. (When did you plan placement of the ball? How did you change placement to hit the empty space?)

5. To change the expected path of the ball.

a. Teams of four players. Each team is numbered 1 through 4. Number 1 hits to number 1 on the opposite court, who in turn hits to number 2 on the opposite court. Play continues with each player hitting to the appropriate numbered player opposite the net. When the starting player has the ball, each player shifts one position and play begins again. Changes in position on the court will change the pathway needed by each player.

b. In pairs, one on either side of the net. On each hit the players vary the hit to the left or right of the opposite player.
c. The server calls the area of placement in the opposite court (such as right front, left back). If the server gets the ball to the court area named, a bonus point is earned. If the server serves the ball to the same area two times in succession, service is lost. If the serve is received in the appropriate area, it may be returned, and play continues with volleyball scoring. (What did you do to serve the ball in the desired pathway?)

VOLLEYBALL LEAD-UP GAMES

The development of team play requires careful planning. Children need time in the various games to move beyond learning rules to team strategy. A games analysis of the games included in this chapter may be found in Table 31-1. The games represent a progression in developing the game of volleyball. The general rules for all games follow. In some games, the teacher may wish to rotate players from one side of the net to the other when there is a change in serving team to encourage more cooperation among the children as they play. Another modification has the children rotate after each serve to maximize serving opportunity for each child on the team.

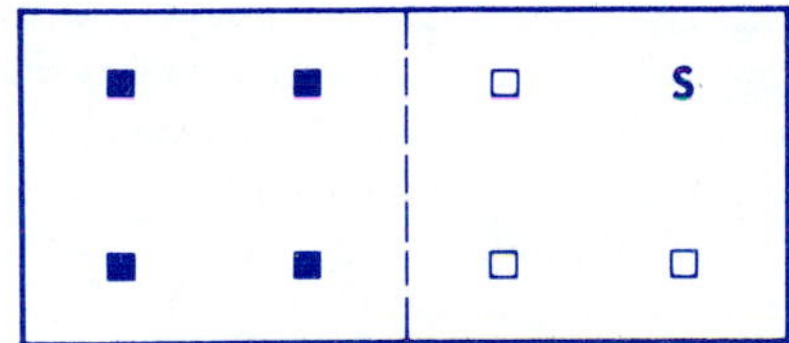

VOLLEYBALL FOR ELEMENTARY SCHOOL CHILDREN (GENERAL RULES)

Equipment: One foam, plastic, or lightweight or trainer volleyball, net at fingertip height

Area: 20 feet wide by 21 feet deep for each team. Games for less than four players per team should be played on proportionately smaller courts.

Participants: Two, three, or four players per team

Description: Play begins with one team serving the ball from the right back service line. A serve is legal if it (1) goes over the net without touching it, (2) lands inbounds (any ball touching a boundary line is inbounds), and (3) is played by any receiving player in or out of the court. Only the serving team may score. One point is awarded the serving team anytime the opposing team fails to return a legal serve. If the serving team fails to make a legal serve, hit the ball out of bounds, or fail to return the ball to the opposite side of the net, the service is lost. The receiving team wins the side-out and then becomes the serving team. When a team wins the side-out after the first term of service in the game, players move clockwise one position, which moves a new player into the service position. Players may not touch the net at any time or step on the line that marks the court boundaries directly under the net.

Teaching suggestions: When necessary, individual children should be permitted to stand closer to the net to get the ball over the net on the serve because they never learn anything about serve placement if they cannot get the ball over the net. Any number of passes should be allowed to encourage team work. Skills and concepts are gradually added to the games as children develop some success in their use.

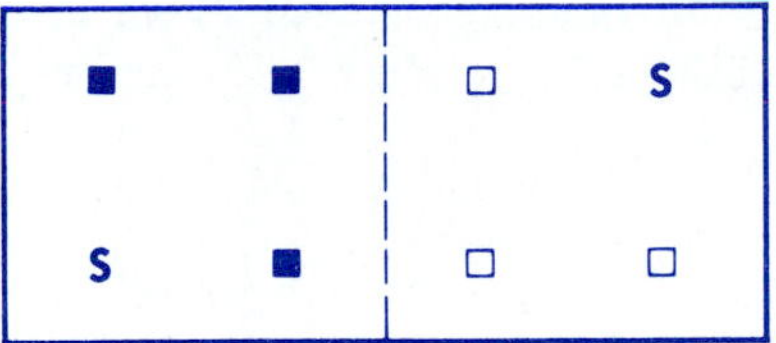

ADVANCED NEWCOMB

Level: III

Skills: Modified overhead volley (catch, toss, and hit).

Description: Using the preceding rules with the following modifications:

1. Children may catch the ball and use the modified overhead volley.
2. Passing is required. A specific number of passes may be required, and only the net players may hit the ball over the net.
3. The modified overhead volley is used when serving, with the server moving closer to the net as needed.

Strategy: Pass to get the ball into the best position before sending it over the net. Look for empty spaces in which to put the ball.

Teaching suggestions: Reinforce passing to teammates. Encourage them to pass the ball quickly. Encourage passing the ball to a space above their teammates. Emphasize a good toss and getting in line with and under the ball for the hit.

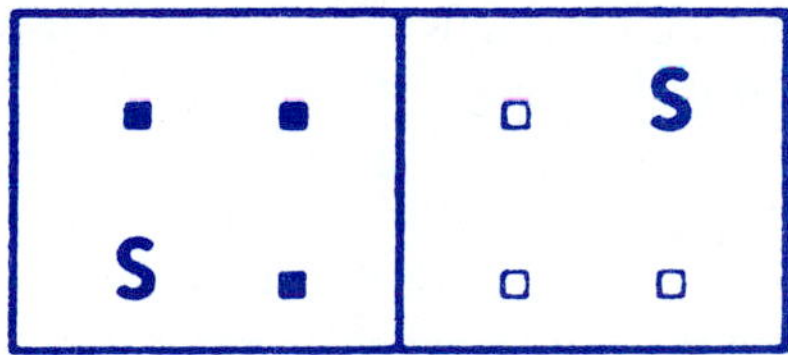

MODIFIED VOLLEYBALL I

Level: III

Skills: Modified overhead volley, regular overhead volley, underhand serve, modified forearm pass, catching

Modifications:

1. Use the modified or overhead volley for all balls received in the high level.
2. Use the modified forearm pass (catch, toss to self, and hit) for balls received in the medium or low levels.
3. The underhand serve is used to begin play and after each point or side-out is called.

Strategy: Pass to get the ball into the best position before sending it over the net. Look for empty spaces in which to put the ball. Vary the force used in placing the ball just over the net or deep into your opponent's court.

TABLE 31-1 NET AND VOLLEYBALL GAMES ANALYSIS

NAME	GAME CLASSIFICATION	NO. OF PARTICIPANTS	EQUIPMENT	SPACE/ ORGANIZATIONAL PATTERN	MOTOR SKILLS
Advanced Newcomb	Lead-up	Four to six per team	One lightweight or trainer volleyball; badminton-sized court; net at fingertip height	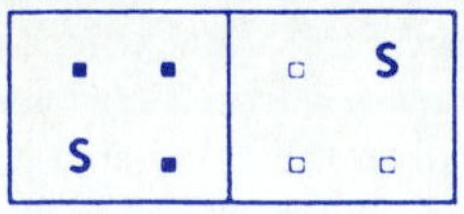 S S	Catching Modified volley Overhead volley
Modified Volleyball I	Lead-up	Four to six per team	Badminton-sized court; net at fingertip height; one lightweight or trainer volleyball	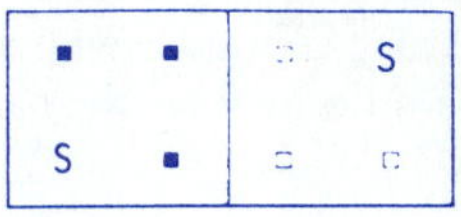 S S	Catching Modified overhead volley Modified forearm pass Underhand serve Overhead volley
All on One Side	Cooperative	Four per game	One balloon per game; badminton size court; net fingertip height	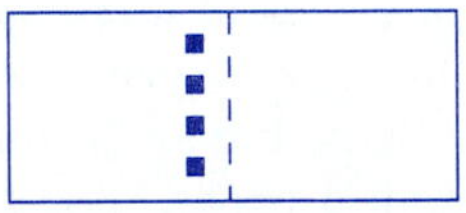	Overhead volley
Queensball	Multicultural	Five to six players per team	One lightweight or trainer volleyball; badminton size court; net fingertip height	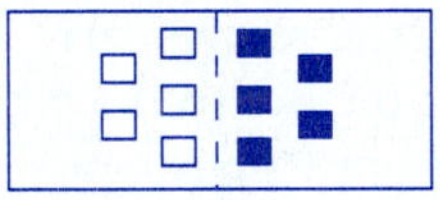	Overhead or modified overhead volley Forearm or modified forearm pass
Towel or Blanket Volleyball	Cooperative	Four per team	One lightweight or trainer volleyball; one beach towel for every two players or one blanket for every four players; badminton size court; net fingertip height	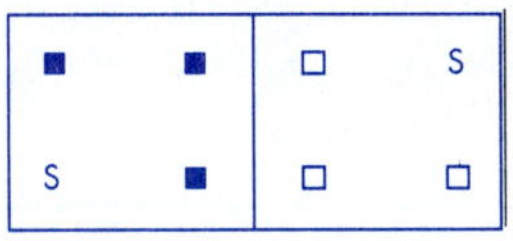 S S	Throwing and catching with a towel or blanket Optional overhead volley and forearm pass
Rotation Volleyball	Cooperative	Four per team	One lightweight trainer volleyball; badminton size court; net fingertip height	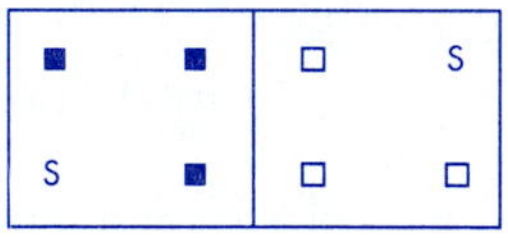 S S	Underhand or floater serve Overhead or modified overhead volley Forearm or modified forearm pass
Team Volley	Cooperative	Six per game	One lightweight or trainer volleyball; badminton size court; net fingertip height	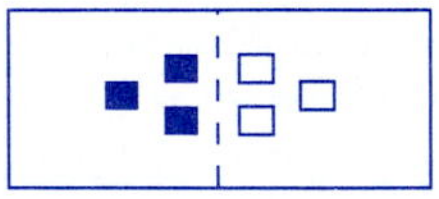	Overhead or modified overhead volley Forearm or modified forearm pass
Modified Volleyball II	Lead-up	Four to six per team	One lightweight or trainer volleyball; badminton-sized court; net fingertip height	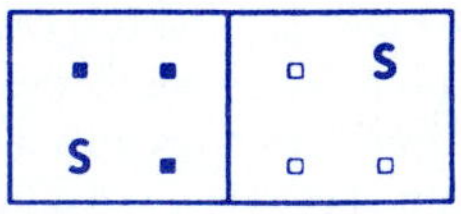 S S	Underhand serve Modified/regular overhead volley Modified/regular forearm pass Optional: floater serve

*Numbers refer to the movement concepts listed in Figure 31-1 on p. 632.

MODIFICATIONS	MOVEMENT CONCEPTS*	SOCIAL STRUCTURE	STRATEGY	LEVEL
1. Allow several service lines, some closer to net	Skills: 1, 2, 4-7 Game: 1-5	Social interaction II	1. Pass to teammates 2. Look for empty spaces 3. Change expected path of ball 4. Vary force in returning ball over the net	III
1. Modified forearm pass and overhead volley may be used 2. Move closer to net to serve 3. Only front line may hit the ball over the net	Skills: 1-7 Game: 1-5	Social interaction III	1. Pass to teammates 2. Look for empty spaces 3. Change expected path of ball 4. Vary force in returning ball over the net	III
1. Vary number of consecutive hits allowed 2. Set group goal for number of times changing courts	Skills: 1, 2, 4, 5 Game: 1, 2	Social interaction I	Keep the balloon high so that it can be easily received	III
Play short games changing roles each time	Skills: 1-7 Game: 1-5	Social interaction II	Keep score a secret until the game ends	III
1. Children in each game work together to see how long they can keep the ball in play 2. Substitute one blanket for four players for the beach towels 3. Play may begin with an overhead volley or forearm pass	Skills: 1, 2, 4-7 Game: 1-5	Social interaction II	Work together to move the ball and in using the beach towel or blanket	III or IV
	Skills: 1-7 Game: 1-5	Social interaction II or III	Look for open spaces to place the ball Work together to cover the space	III or IV
Set a goal for number of hits to achieve	Skills: 1-6 Game: 1, 2	Social interaction I	Control hits and keep ball in the high level so that it can be easily received	IV
1. Use of modified overhead volley or forearm pass 2. Net players must volley balls coming to high level from passes or opponents 3. Several service lines may be used 4. Only designated hitter may return ball over the net	Skills: 1-7 Game: 1-5	Social interaction III	Pass to teammates Look for open spaces to place ball Change expected path Vary force in returning ball over the net	IV

Continued.

TABLE 31-1 NET AND VOLLEYBALL GAMES ANALYSIS—cont'd

NAME	GAME CLASSIFICATION	NO. OF PARTICIPANTS	EQUIPMENT	SPACE/ ORGANIZATIONAL PATTERN	MOTOR SKILLS
Volley Volleyball	Cooperative	Four to six per team	One lightweight or trainer volleyball; badminton size court; net fingertip height		Underhand serve Overhead or modified overhead volley Forearm or modified forearm pass Optional: floater serve
Four Court Volleyball	Lead-up	Two to four per team	One or more lightweight or trainer volleyballs; 2 nets dividing the court into 4 courts		Underhand serve Modified/regular overhead volley Modified/regular forearm pass Optional: floater serve
Blind Volleyball	Novelty	Four to six per team	One lightweight or trainer volleyball; badminton-sized court; net fingertip height		Depending on game used

Teaching suggestions: Encourage passing to a space above teammates and not at them. Rules that require passing should be used as in the previous game. Several service lines, some closer to the net, may be needed to enable everyone to have success on the service.

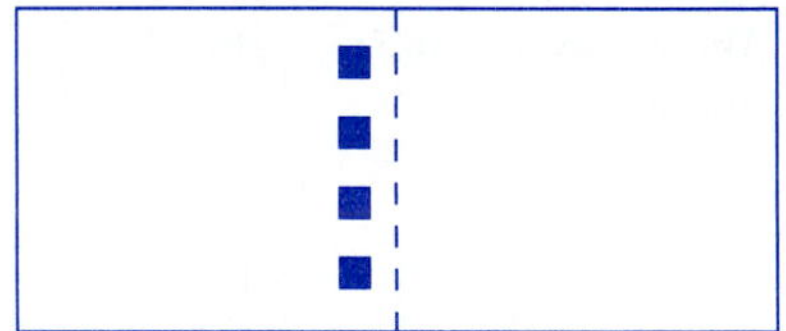

ALL ON ONE SIDE

Level: III
Equipment: One balloon per group
Area: Elementary size volleyball court
Participants: Four per group
Skills: Overhead volley
Description: All players line up on one side of the volleyball court. As play begins, one person hits the balloon to another player and then moves under the net to the other side of the net. Play continues, with each person scooting under the net after hitting the balloon. The last person to receive the balloon hits it over the net and play continues. The object is to see if each group can keep the balloon in the air and move from one side of the court to the other as many times as possible.

Strategy: Try to keep the balloon high so that each person has the maximum time to get into position and to hit it.
Teaching suggestions: Groups might set goals for themselves to achieve regarding the number of consecutive hits or the number of times they can change places.

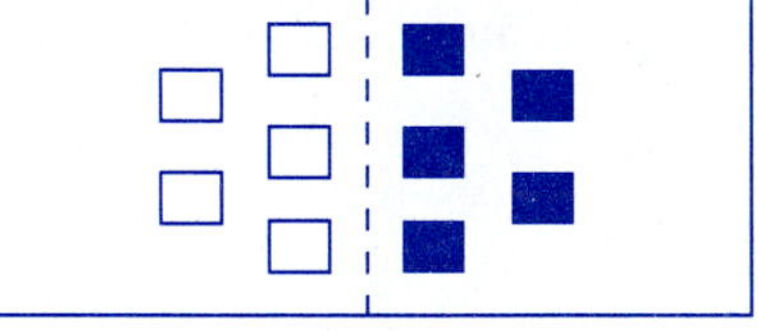
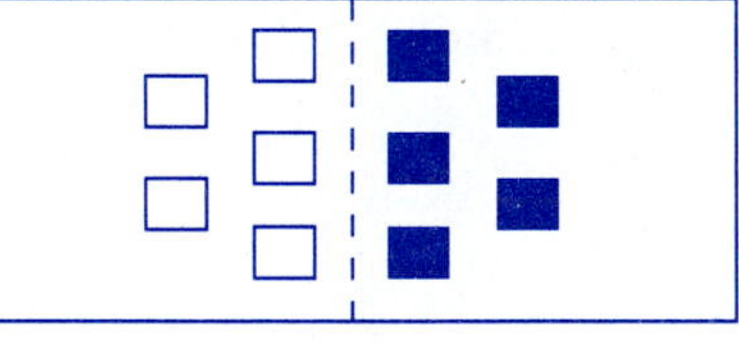

QUEENSBALL

This game is adapted from a throwing and catching game played by children in Austria.
Level: III
Participants: Five to six players, designated as the queen or king, one or two ministers, members of the court, and one scorekeeper
Skills: Overhead volley or modified volley, forearm or modified forearm pass
Description: Each team secretly decides which players will assume which roles. Play begins with one team member hitting the ball over the net to the other team. The game consists of hitting the ball back and forth over the net. Scoring depends on which member of the team hits the ball: The queen or king scores 100 points, the minister 50 points, and the

MODIFICATIONS	MOVEMENT CONCEPTS*	SOCIAL STRUCTURE	STRATEGY	LEVEL
1. Use several service lines 2. Use modified overhead or forearm pass 3. Net players may volley balls received at the high level	Skills: 1-7 Game: 1-5	Social interaction III	Pass to teammates Look for open spaces to place ball Change expected path of the ball Vary force in hitting the ball over the net	IV
1. Use modified overhead volley or forearm pass 2. Several service lines may be used	Skills: 1-7 Game: 1-5	Social interaction III	Pass to teammates Look for open space to place ball Change expected path Vary force in returning ball over the net	IV
Depending on game rules used	Depends on game used	Social interaction II or III	Pass to teammates Vary path of ball Vary force in returning ball over the net	III or IV

members of the court 10 points. The scorekeeper keeps the tally on the sidelines. In each case the ball must be caught inbounds and may not touch the floor first.

Strategy: Keep the score a secret until the game is over to avoid the other team guessing the roles of the various players.

Teaching suggestion: Games should be of short duration with a change in roles for each game.

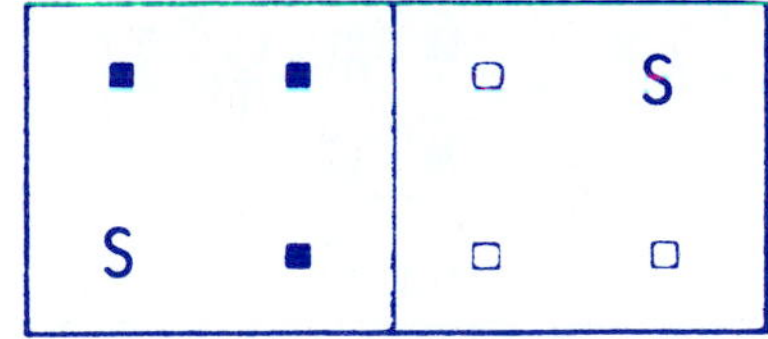

TOWEL OR BLANKET VOLLEYBALL

Level: III or IV

Equipment: A lightweight or trainer volleyball and a large beach towel for every two players, or a small blanket for four players.

Participants: Four per team

Skills: Throwing and catching with a towel or blanket, optional overhead volley or forearm pass

Description: Play begins with one team placing the ball on one of their towels and lifting the towel in such a way as to send the ball over the net. The receiving team attempts to catch the ball with their towel, and play continues until the ball is dropped or goes out of bounds or into the net. Points are scored as in volleyball. Variation: With an odd number of players, towel or blanket players toss the ball up as a set to a net player who hits it over the net.

Teaching suggestions:

1. Children must learn to work together to move and then to control the ball on the towel. When they are ready, a small blanket held by all four teammates may be substituted for the towels.
2. This game may be changed to a cooperative game by having the children on each side of the net work together to see how long they can keep the ball in play.

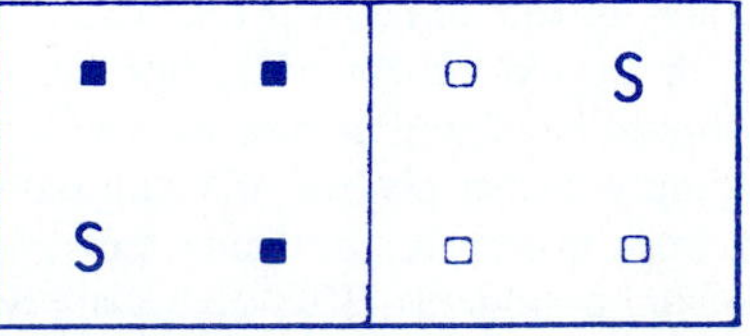

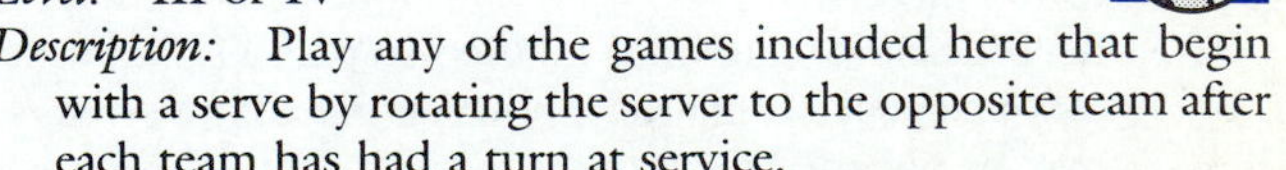

ROTATION VOLLEYBALL

Level: III or IV

Description: Play any of the games included here that begin with a serve by rotating the server to the opposite team after each team has had a turn at service.

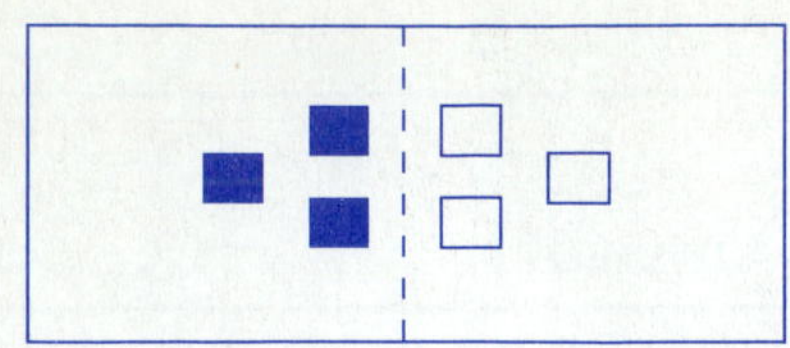

TEAM VOLLEY

Level: IV
Equipment: One lightweight or trainer volleyball for each group
Area: Small volleyball court
Participants: Six per team, three on each side of the net
Skills: Overhead or modified overhead volley, forearm pass or modified forearm pass
Description: The players are arranged with two at the net and one in the back court on each side of the net. Play begins with one back court player volleying the ball to one of the other players on the same side of the net. He or she then hits it to the third player, who hits it over the net high enough so that their teammates on the other side of the net can easily control it for three hits on their side of the net, after which they hit it back over the net once again. Each time the group completes three hits and sends it over the net they score one point. If the ball touches the floor, goes out of bounds, or in some other manner is not able to be returned, play stops and begins again on the side where the ball is. After some time, play is stopped and each group counts their score. Play resumes with each group trying to improve their record.
Strategy: Try to control hits so that they go up above the receiver to give them maximum time to get into position and to play the ball.
Teaching suggestions: Teams may also suggest a number of hits to achieve on the next round.

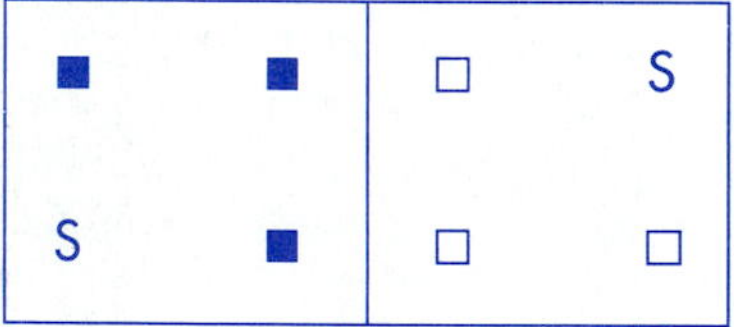

MODIFIED VOLLEYBALL II

Level: IV
Skills: Underhand serve, modified and regular overhead volley, modified and regular forearm pass, floater serve (optional)
Description and modifications:

1. Players may still catch the ball and then use the modified volley or forearm pass if they cannot get into position for a good hit. As skills improve, however, children should be encouraged to use the regular skills, beginning with net players volleying balls received as passes from teammates, and later balls received directly from opponents. The receipt of service is the most difficult to return; balls coming to back-row players are more difficult to return than those coming to net players.
2. Several service lines may be used so that all players can experience some success in serving. Extra points may be awarded for services from the official service line.
3. A new rule to emphasize control is added. Each team has a designated hitter from one position on the front line. Only that person may hit the ball over the net. All passes must end with that player, who hits it to the opposite court. On each rotation, a new player moves into that position.

Strategy: Encourage passing, varying force and pathways of returns, looking for empty spaces, and planned serve placement.
Teaching suggestions: Rules requiring passing will be necessary to ensure that team play is developed. Encourage getting the ball to a space above teammates when passing and a good position in relation to the ball in line and directly under it for forearm pass and volley. Encourage children to catch balls not received appropriately.

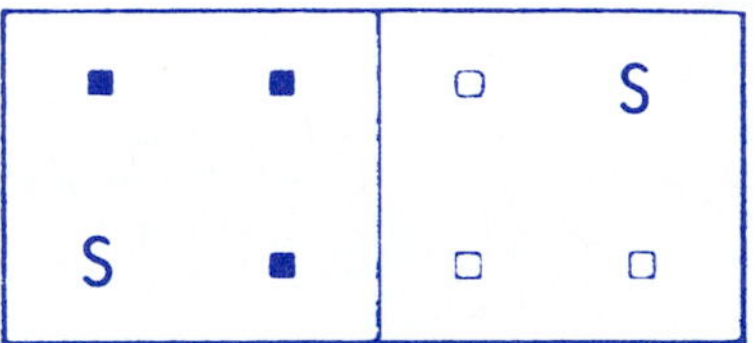

VOLLEY VOLLEYBALL

Level: IV
Description: Play Modified Volleyball II but alter scoring so that each team receives a point for each pass completed on their side before sending the ball over the net.

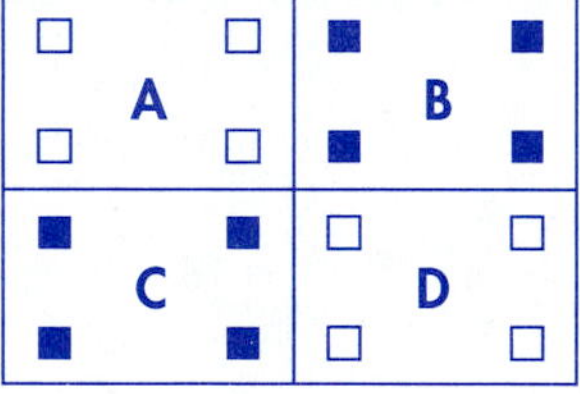

FOUR COURT VOLLEYBALL

Level: IV
Equipment: Two or more foam, plastic, or lightweight volleyballs
Area: A volleyball court divided into four courts by two nets set up to cross in the center of the court at right angles.
Participants: Two to four players per court.
Description: Play begins with a serve from any two diagonal courts. (A and D or B and C.) The serve is placed in the opposite court. (A serves to B, D serves to C, etc.) The receiving teams may then hit the ball to any court after one pass to a teammate. Play continues until one team scores, as in volleyball.
Variations: One or two more balls may be added to the game.
Teaching suggestions: It may be best to begin with one ball and then add another as teams are ready. Service may alternate to each of the three courts on each point.

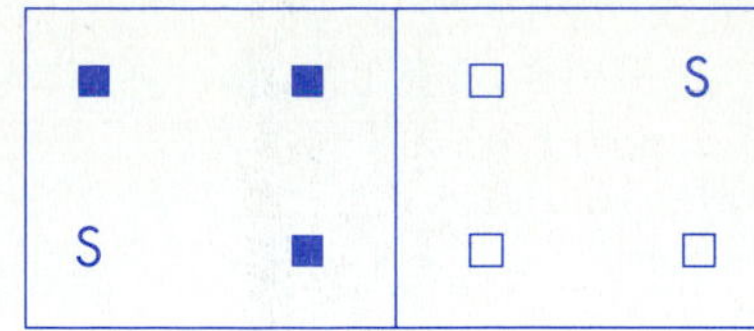

BLIND VOLLEYBALL

Level: III or IV

Description: Use any one of the previously described games, but place sheets over the net so that teams are unable to see the ball until it comes over the net.

Teaching suggestion: Encourage children to be in a good ready position to be able to move quickly into position to play the ball.

SUMMARY

When modified, volleyball lead-ups are popular activities with elementary school children. A lighter ball, a smaller court, and preferably fewer players per team offer children a chance for success. In addition, skills are modified with children selecting skills at a level of difficulty suitable to their ability. Within the game greater variability in skill selection is observed, which serves to help children acquire greater confidence and improves the social environment because all have an opportunity to succeed. Application of the movement content is essential for success, and the beginning games offer children more opportunity to plan the placement of the ball over the net. If children are encouraged in these beginning games and teaching for transfer is planned, the continued use of the movment content should improve the play throughout the development of volleyball in the elementary school.

REFERENCES AND RESOURCES

Angle J: *Modern volleyball drills,* ed 2, Huntington Beach, Calif, 1978, Volleyball Publications.

Dunphy M: *Volleyball,* New York, 1977, Grossett & Dunlap, Inc.

Ferrell J and McPeak C: *Setters, diggers, spikers: youth volleyball coaches manual,* Colorado Springs, Colo, 1983, United States Volleyball Asociation and the YWCA of the USA.

Fluegelman A: *The new games book,* Garden City, New York, 1976 Dolphin Books/Doubleday.

Gozansky S: *Championship volleyball techniques and drills,* West Nyack, NY, 1983, Parker Publishing.

Kessel J: *Coaches guide to beginning volleyball programs,* Colorado Springs, Colo, 1988, The United States Volleyball Association.

Morris G and Stiehl J: *Changing kids' games,* ed 2, Champaign, Ill, 1989, Human Kinetics Publishers.

Peppler M: *Inside volleyball for women,* Chicago, 1977, Henry Regnery.

Seidel B et al: *Sports skills: a conceptual approach to meaningful movement,* ed 2, Dubuque, Ia, 1980, Wm C Brown.

Sterne ML: Cooperative learning, *Strategies* 3(5):15, 1990.

ANNOTATED READINGS

Adrian M and House G: Sporting miscues. Part one, *Strategies* 1(1):11, 1987.

Describes miscues given in teaching volleyball in jumping and in releasing the ball on the overhead volley.

Ashette R and Stocker M: Quadrangular volleyball, *JOPERD* 56(5):19, 1985.

Presents a new four-court game of volleyball.

Barker J: A simplified volleyball skills test for beginning level instruction, *JOPERD* 56(5):20, 1985.

Presents skill tests to use in beginning volleyball, which might be modified as a self-testing activity for children.

Chandler J: Modified volleyball play, *JOPER* 51(5):52, 1980.

Describes a game using three stations to develop volleyball skills.

Dawson L and Polivino G: Bridging the gap in volleyball, *JOPERD* 53(7):25, 1982.

Describes using mini-games to bridge the gap from instruction to game play.

Ellery PJ: Cutting volleyball down to size, *Strategies* 6(6):8, 1993.

Modifications for the game of volleyball for elementary school children.

McBride M: Put some bounce into volleyball, *JOPERD* 52(7):73, 1981.

Looks at using one-bounce volleyball to develop volleyball skills and game play.

Miller D: Two-court volleyball, *JOPERD* 58(9):8, 1987.

Describes a modified game that increases the active participation of all players.

PART EIGHT

Extracurricular Opportunities

In addition to the instructional program of physical education offered in the schools, opportunities for participation outside of class are provided. These activities include intramurals, special interest groups, special events, and demonstrations. Teachers may also be asked to help organize and conduct youth sport activities for children in community-based programs.

OUTLINE

CHAPTER 32

School Activities and Youth Sports

OBJECTIVES

After completing this chapter the student will be able to:

1. Describe the values and list the guidelines for the extra-class program in the elementary school
2. Identify a variety of possible physical activity experiences for the elementary school child that further the goals of the physical education program
3. Describe issues surrounding youth sports today and provide suggestions for physical educators who assume leadership in community-based programs for children

Extra-class programs and special events are an extension of the educational program. As an outgrowth of the regular physical education instructional program, opportunity is provided for further development and use of skills and knowledge introduced in the instructional program, thus supplementing class activities. These activities should provide a positive learning experience for each child through a wide variety of activities designed to meet the needs of all children and to meet the goals of the school physical education program.

The opportunity for all children, not just the gifted, to participate not only promotes positive attitudes toward participation but also exposes children to a variety of recreational or leisure-time activities in which they may engage throughout life. Children need the chance to develop their personal interests in individual as well as in team or group activities.

The conduct of the activities should encourage cooperative behavior and the assumption of responsibility through shared decision making with other children. The teacher is the guide as children are involved in the planning process and the conduct of the activities commensurate with their maturity. The children's responsibility may include selecting the activity, determining whether the activity will be competitive or noncompetitive and formal or informal, establishing the rules to govern the events, setting up tournaments, keeping records and statistics, writing articles for the school paper, publicizing the events, enrolling the participants, and organizing and conducting the event including officiating when needed. As a result, children should develop the skills needed to be more independent of adult supervision in their leisure activities.

Additional outcomes of these programs that are often cited include a more constructive use of leisure time during the school day and better teacher-pupil relations. Children also have the opportunity to participate with children from other classes and in some activities with children varying in age.

Several different kinds of activities are usually included. Intramurals provide a wide variety of experiences, including tournaments and 1-day or short-term events that may be competitive or noncompetitive and that require individual or group participation. Open gym is another way of organizing activities less formally, which allows the children to check out equipment for activities of their own choosing. Special interest groups may also be organized in which children with similar interests meet on a regular basis to develop skills and knowledge in a particular activity. Special events include field or activity days in which the entire school participates, gym shows for parents, or other classes and demonstrations.

GUIDELINES

The following guidelines should be considered in establishing extra-class activities and special events. They should be implemented with local regulations regarding safety and liability in mind.

All children are free to participate. For the program to

be interesting to all children, an attempt should be made to determine their needs and interests. A student survey conducted by the teacher is one approach to obtaining this information. An interest bulletin board is another. A variety of activities are displayed and the children check those they would like to try, as well as list additional activities they would like to see included. Student activity committees might also solicit interests from students in a variety of ways including interviewing individuals, conducting an inquiry on the playground, or leading class discussions.

Equal opportunity is provided for all children to have full participation. All children have the right not just to participate, but to participate fully, with an equal opportunity guaranteed in the scheduling and conduct of the activities and in the use of equipment. The teacher must carefully monitor the activities to be sure the needs of all interested children are met, including equal participation time and the opportunity to play a variety of positions in games.

All participants have parental approval for participation. Many of the activities may be scheduled outside regular school hours. Parental approval is needed, especially if children will be arriving home at some time other than their normal hour or if alternate transportation home will be needed. Because medical approval for participation is recommended for the instructional program, additional medical prescription will probably not be needed.

The activities are supervised by qualified adults who know children and the activities. The activities selected should meet the physical, social, and cognitive needs of all participants. Leaders should select activities appropriate to the maturity level of the children and modify activities when necessary to provide a better experience for all.

The activities are conducted with safety as a prime concern. All safety rules are enforced, and the environment promotes participation without fear of injury. Supervisors are trained in standard first-aid procedures in case of injury. Rest periods are provided when necessary to avoid possible injury caused by fatigue. A warm-up period to prepare students for the activity may be needed.

The activities are organized to allow children to assume responsibility for the safe and efficient conduct of the activities. Students should assume as much responsibility for the conduct of the activities as their maturity allows. They should have input into the development of the program and its conduct. Many of the activities may be conducted with little direct supervision from adults. Children may be organized informally for play. In other activities student officials may be used.

Noncompetitive as well as competitive activities should be included. Children should have many different leisure-time opportunities. They should have the chance to do something just for fun, to self-test their own performance, or to compete with one or more children.

Children need the opportunity to compete as individuals.

In competitive activities each team has an equal opportunity for success. A contest is more satisfying for all if the competitors are of equal ability. An effort must be made to equalize the teams for competition. Emphasis should be placed on the process of participation rather than on winning. When teams have an equal opportunity for success, cooperative behavior within the team is more likely to occur.

Both coeducational activities and activities organized for girls and boys separately should be provided. Children need opportunities to participate with many different children. In some activities and for some events, coeducational grouping may be best. In other activities boys may wish to participate with boys and girls with girls. No child should be excluded from an activity because of gender.

Both informal grouping of children and prearranged grouping of children are used. Children's attendance may be more inconsistent in extra-class activities owing to other commitments and their lack of maturity. Grouping the children as they arrive may facilitate getting activities underway as quickly as possible. Informal grouping also aids in equalizing the teams for play and competition and may result in a less competitive atmosphere than that which may occur when children are prearranged into teams. However, children should have some opportunity for selecting teams and participating with the same group of children on several occasions. This continuity can help children learn to play as a team. Selection of teams, however, should be accomplished under appropriate teacher supervision. Several suggestions for selecting teams may be found in Chapter 8.

Some form of recognition for participation is given. Children may receive a certificate for participation or for their individual achievement in a particular event.

A plan for the systematic evaluation of the program is developed. A plan to evaluate the program ensures that program goals are being met. Children should be involved actively in the evaluation process.

EXTRA-CLASS ACTIVITIES

A number of different types of activities may be included in the extra-class program. When a variety of activities

are offered, it may not be possible or appropriate for the physical education teacher to be responsible for them all. Because the programs are school wide the physical education teacher and the school administration should solicit help from other teachers and interested parents and community members. When doing so, it is important to ensure that they are clear about the program objectives, are familiar with the methods for organizing and conducting the activities, have adequate knowledge of first aid, and have adequate knowledge of children and the level of play to be expected. Special training sessions may be necessary to ensure that the program meets the expectations of the physical education program. Another approach in getting adequate supervision during the activities is to train middle or senior high school students to provide the assistance needed. These students can provide a great deal of help under adult supervision.

The following suggestions for the conduct of intramurals, open gym, and special interest groups will help the physical education teacher plan and conduct appropriate extra-class activities for elementary school children.

Intramurals

Intramural sports are the most prevalent extra-class programs in the elementary school. They are usually available to children beginning in the third or fourth grade. They are most often scheduled at the close of the school day but may be held before school, during the lunch break, or even during recess periods.

A variety of activities may be included in the intramural sports program. Because it is an outgrowth of the instructional program, skills and knowledge necessary to perform the scheduled activities have been introduced in the physical education classes. This extends the opportunity for children to develop and use the skills and knowledge in the less formal atmosphere of intramural play. Obviously, if the children are to benefit from the added opportunity for participation, it is best to schedule these activities shortly after they have been introduced in the physical education class and after the children have had some time to work on the skills and develop sufficient knowledge for successful participation. In games where the children will be responsible for their own officiating, rules should be clarified during the physical education class and some instruction in officiating should be given before it is needed in intramurals.

The availability of intramural activities needs to be well publicized so that students and parents can plan accordingly. It is helpful to establish an intramural bulletin board where children can check the schedule of current activities as well as activities to come.

The intramural sports program may also include activities that the time scheduled for the instructional program does not make feasible. Activities such as swimming, bowling, skating, cross-country skiing, and hiking

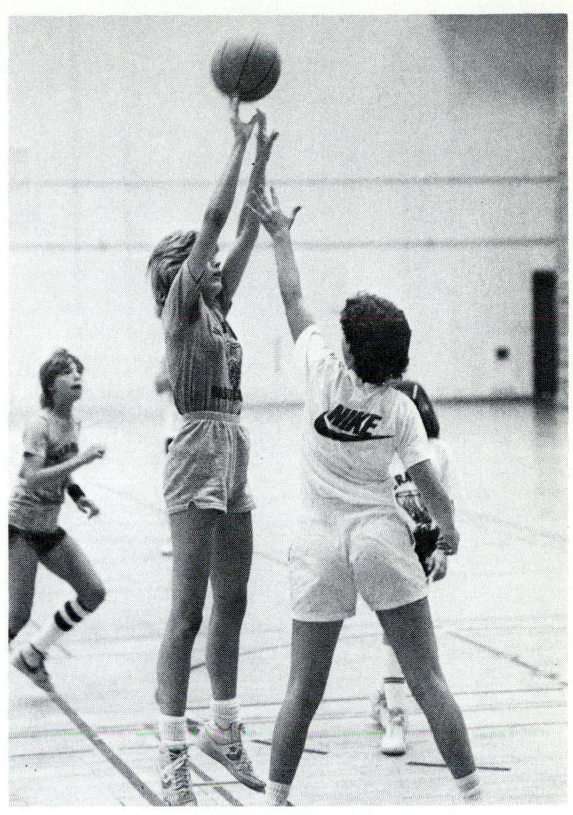

Intramural play provides opportunities beyond classroom experiences.

are a few activities in which community facilities may be used and in which a longer period of time may be needed to provide a worthwhile experience.

Nontraditional activities may also be scheduled. Novelty games and events offer a change of pace from the traditional activities and may appeal to some children who are less interested in the traditional activities.

Individual and team sports should be balanced throughout the school year, with several options available for students during each season. Competitive and noncompetitive activities should be included, as well as coeducational activities for boys and girls.

Activities are usually organized by grade level to provide more easily for the needs of the children varying in age. Activities may be scheduled for 1 day only or for several weeks. The time scheduled for each activity ought to be long enough to maintain enthusiasm but not so long that interest is lost.

Considerations for children with disabilities must be made to allow their participation without jeopardizing the team's effort. Often, special modifications may be needed so that disabled children can participate fully. If disabled students are an active part of the instructional program, other children will accept them as a part of the intramural group. Children are accepting of any additional modifications that need to be made to make children with disabilities equal members of the group.

Activities may be organized informally, with the chil-

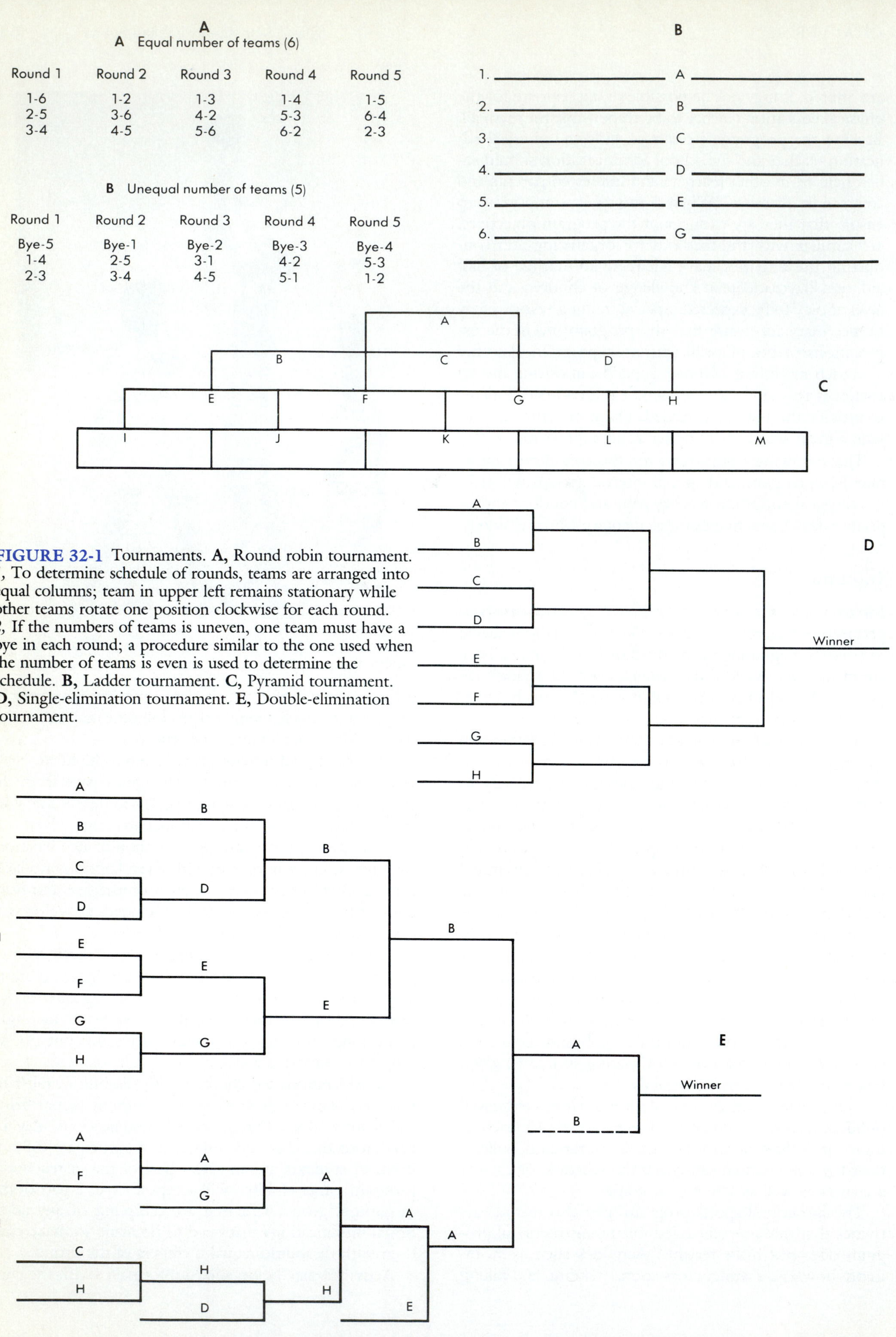

FIGURE 32-1 Tournaments. **A,** Round robin tournament. *1,* To determine schedule of rounds, teams are arranged into equal columns; team in upper left remains stationary while other teams rotate one position clockwise for each round. *2,* If the numbers of teams is uneven, one team must have a bye in each round; a procedure similar to the one used when the number of teams is even is used to determine the schedule. **B,** Ladder tournament. **C,** Pyramid tournament. **D,** Single-elimination tournament. **E,** Double-elimination tournament.

dren divided into teams each day or with preorganized teams. Tournaments may be informally organized each day, or a posted schedule of team play may be used.

Several kinds of tournaments may be used. Some, such as the **round robin** or **ladder tournaments,** guarantee the participation of all throughout the tournament. Others eliminate individuals or teams along the way. The single- and double-elimination tournaments should be scheduled only occasionally at the elementary school level. It is important to plan carefully to ensure that elimination tournaments provide for the participation of all children, including those eliminated from the tournament. Scheduled play should be included for teams or individuals who are no longer in the original tournament. Nontournament play should always be an option for those who do not wish to play in a scheduled tournament. Figure 32-1 illustrates each of the tournament formats.

The round robin tournament provides an opportunity for each participant or team to play all other participants or teams. The round robin tournament is used easily when teams are selected informally and the number of teams is small. Any number of participants may compete in the round robin tournament. When there is an equal number of teams (N), the number of rounds is equal to one less than the number of teams (N – 1). When the team number is unequal, the number of rounds equals the number of teams in the tournament. There is perhaps less emphasis on winning in this tournament format because all participants continue to play the schedule throughout the tournament. Another approach in using this format is to record the number of points each competitor or team scores within a particular time period rather than the number of wins and losses. All matches are for the same period of time in this tournament. This approach motivates the children to try to score as many points as possible rather than being discouraged when they are losing to an opponent. The eventual winner of the tournament is the competitor or team that scores the most points.

The ladder tournament is usually used for individual sports, but also can be used in team competition. The teams are arranged in a vertical line, with the goal of being at the top of the ladder at the end of the tournament. Individuals may challenge players one or two rungs above them on the ladder. When the challenger wins, the two exchange places on the ladder. Some monitoring may be necessary to ensure that all participants have the opportunity to challenge. When many participants are involved, several ladders may be organized.

The **pyramid tournament** is similar to the ladder tournament but permits players more choices in challenging because there are several individuals on the next level of the pyramid. In one variation of this tournament, an individual must challenge and win over one player at the same level before challenging a player on the level above.

In the **single-elimination tournament** each participant remains in the tournament until one match or game is lost. Fewer games must be played to complete the tournament than most tournaments, but consideration should be given to providing continued participation for those players eliminated. The number of participants or teams required is a power of four (4, 8, or 16 teams, and so forth) to complete the tournament without byes.

The **double-elimination tournament** enables competitors to remain in the tournament until two matches or games are lost. As in the single-elimination tournament, the beginning brackets require teams in powers of four. The winners continue to play in bracket I. Those competitors who have lost once play in bracket II. If in the final round the competitor with one previous loss wins, resulting in each having lost once, an additional contest is held to determine the winner of the tournament.

Open Gym

Open gym is a regularly scheduled event in which children are free to check out equipment and to use the facilities for informal play. It may be necessary for the teacher to help organize the available space when several different activities take place simultaneously. This activity may include children varying in age and interests. Safe play must always be stressed, and at times special considerations for the use of space imposed to ensure the safety of all. Open gym may be scheduled before the school day begins, during the lunch break, or after school. This schedule might also provide a good opportunity for a daily fitness session, which might include both teachers and children.

Special Interest Groups

Special interest groups or sports clubs offer an opportunity for children to develop specific interests over time. The goal of these groups is to help children improve their skills for personal enjoyment and/or competition. Each group meets regularly. Special interest groups give children the opportunity to work with others of varying ages who have the same interests. Examples of activities for special interest groups include rope jumping, fitness, gymnastics, square dancing, hiking, or outdoor education.

At the elementary school level it may be helpful to schedule special interest groups seasonally. This approach should encourage children to participate in many different activities throughout the school year rather than specialize in only one.

SPECIAL EVENTS

Special events are usually all-school activities that are held for 1 day or over a short time. They may be competitive but more likely are self-testing in which children strive

PLANNING AND CONDUCTING A FIELD DAY

PLANNING IN ADVANCE OF THE FIELD DAY

Set date and possible rain date(s)
Set time of the field day
Determine participants: specific classes, entire school, school district
Plan for events: what events, space and equipment needed, volunteers needed
Registration for events: forms, maximum number of events per participant, registration dates, when—during class, before or after school, lunchtime
Set schedule of events and rotation plan following registration
Guests—Will spectators be invited? If so, invitations, distribution date
Awards: type given—participation, individual best or school record, form of award—certificates, etc.
Medical supervision: presence of school nurse or physician in case of injury
Volunteers: total needed, how obtained, training needed, set training date, materials needed
Organization: develop a plan for organizing the site
Plan for evaluation
Miscellaneous: refreshments, signs needed, solicit help from teachers, parents, and students; plan what will be needed after the event for clean-up, putting away equipment, etc.

DAY OF THE EVENT

Organize area for events, participants, and guest seating
Put up signs
Designate area for volunteers to pick up materials
Awards and other materials organized
Facility: areas marked or lined as needed
Equipment gathered and organized
Refreshments organized, trash cans in place
Start on time
Keep event as close as possible to schedule
After event supervise clean-up
Plan an evaluation session with others involved, including representation from student participants

to see what they can do. For example, a field day might be held in which the entire school participates in a variety of individual, partner, team, or class activities. There might also be a demonstration such as a gym show or a performance for another class or for parents.

One example of a special event is an all-school field day in which children attempt to improve their own performances in various individual events (rather than to compete against others). Considerations for planning and conducting a field day are found in the box above. Field days may be organized to be cooperative as well. For example, when organized into teams the score of an event may be the combined score of all team members or an event may be over when each team member has completed the task.

Another event might be a fitness run in which classes compete in a run to some destination, such as to the state capital, over a week or two. The distance is broken down into a number of laps run or walked on the school property. Laps are completed before school or during lunch and recess breaks. Individuals record their laps, which are then totaled to determine the class effort. In teacher-student games a team of students competes against a faculty team. Another possible event is the superstars. Children compete with other children of their own age and ability in some unusual events, patterned after the television event. These activities may test courage as well as skill. In addition children might take trips to hiking, skiing, or other outdoor and nature areas as a special event.

Teachers and students may also plan and conduct a demonstration or gym show for another class or for family and friends. For example, they may demonstrate the types of activities, skills, and knowledge taught in the physical education program. It could be a learning project in which the importance of fitness or some other topic is conveyed to a younger group of children. Other special events might include activities in which children participate with their parents. For example, children learning line or square dances might invite their parents to an evening of dancing in which they demonstrate their skills and then teach their parents the dances they have learned. Children may plan a parents' night in which parents participate with children in several sports or dance activities.

YOUTH SPORTS

In the past two decades there has been a marked increase in the availability of sports programs for children. Approximately 20 million school children participate in these community-based activities annually. The majority of these activities are competitive, with children following a set schedule of games or matches within the community or with neighboring communities. Participants may be as young as 5 years of age.

The conduct of these programs should closely follow the guidelines listed previously for extra-class activities and special events. In 1977 a Youth Sports Task Force was organized by the National Association for Sport and Physical Education of the American Alliance for Health, Physical Education, Recreation, and Dance. This group of dedicated professionals formulated the Bill of Rights for Young Athletes listed in the box on p. 657.

Concerns have been raised regarding the actual outcomes of these programs. Although the outcomes are positive for some children, they have been negative for others. Teachers of physical education aware of the potential benefits and hazards as children participate in these

BILL OF RIGHTS FOR YOUNG ATHLETES

1. Right to participate in sports
2. Right to participate at a level commensurate with each child's maturity and ability
3. Right to have qualified leadership
4. Right to play as a child and not as an adult
5. Right of children to share in the leadership and decision making of their sport participation
6. Right to participate in safe and healthy environments
7. Right to proper preparation for participation in sports
8. Right to an equal opportunity to strive for success
9. Right to be treated with dignity
10. Right to have fun in sports

community programs must assume more leadership in helping communities to plan and conduct programs that are in the best interests of all children. Physical educators may help train volunteer coaches and help parents understand the programs from a child's perspective.

A discussion of specific concerns in the areas of physical development, motor skills, social development, and psychological effects follows, with suggestions for minimizing negative outcomes.

Physical Growth

Physical activity stimulates bone and muscle tissue development and increases cardiorespiratory efficiency. Bone size and shape may be altered by external forces, and muscles increase their strength and endurance. Therefore, physical activity is essential for normal human development. Youth sports programs have the potential to provide vigorous physical activity during these developing years.

Studies indicate that training at a moderate intensity accelerates growth in stature and body size in youngsters from ages 11 to 14 years (Seefeldt and Gould). The effects of a heavy training regimen on developing children need further study. Some believe that long-distance running as in training for marathons could result in growth-plate injury owing to the severe strain placed on the articular cartilage (Caine and Lindner). Children appear to be especially vulnerable to growth-plate injury during the pubescent growth spurt (Micheli et al.).

Orthopedists who rarely saw children with sports-related injuries in the past are beginning to see new types of injuries in children. The elbow, shoulder, knee, and ankle joints are most susceptible to growth-plate injury. Stress fractures, tendinitis of the shoulder, bursitis of the hip, and tennis elbow are a few of the injuries that appear to be on the increase for young sports participants. These injuries are believed to be primarily the result of the inappropriate training and overuse of some body segments of young athletes (Micheli et al.). In the past, when children participated in more spontaneous play, they quit when they were hurt and did not return to the activity until the pain went away. Today, in more organized sports, they are often encouraged to play when hurt. Many children are led to believe that only babies refuse to play when hurt or even complain of injuries. Some coaches consider injuries other than fractures of little consequence.

While it is still too soon to tell, some orthopedists (Micheli et al., Seefeldt and Gould) believe the soft tissue injuries in childhood will result in chronic problems in adulthood if not prevented or not properly treated.

Individuals working with children in youth sports programs need to:

1. Understand the process of physical development and recognize the differences in growth patterns in children.
2. Consider using a combination of chronological age, motor ability, and physical maturation in grouping children for physical activity.
3. Avoid gender stereotyping in working with prepubescent boys and girls.
4. Plan appropriate warm-ups and training regimens for the young children in their charge.
5. Modify activities to meet the developmental needs of children, such as decreasing the size of the playing area, shortening the distances to be run, and reducing the number of players per team so that all can have maximum participation.
6. Establish a reasonable amount of practice time to avoid undue stress and fatigue.
7. Watch for fatigue in young players and adjust play accordingly.
8. Know first-aid procedures, the type of injuries common to the activity, and how to prevent and treat these injuries.
9. Treat injuries promptly and see that injuries are cared for reasonably, insisting on medical supervision when deemed necessary.
10. See that all players have a physical exam before participation, including an assessment of body parts used excessively in the activity.
11. Prevent injuries by encouraging participation in lifetime and noncontact sports during the developing years.
12. Set a realistic limit on the number of contests to be played in the season and no more than one per week.
13. Limit the distance to be traveled to contests to ensure proper rest for the participants.

Team activities provide an opportunity for children to work together to accomplish game goals.

Motor Development

Children develop motor skills at varying rates. Although most children are exposed to all the fundamental motor patterns before entering school, they vary considerably in their mastery of these skills. Some of these differences are maturational, whereas others result from experience with the skills. Sports programs for children must take into account these differences in skill mastery. There is some concern that while the physically more mature children may benefit from these programs, children who do not meet the adult expectations for the skill are discouraged, are not given much opportunity to play, or are dropped from the team.

Individuals working with children in youth sports programs need to:

1. Emphasize the improvement in game skills by teaching correct techniques and helping all children overcome performance errors.
2. Modify games and rules to meet the needs of children at various ages and abilities.
3. Emphasize improvement in individual and group play rather than winning.
4. Recognize when children are ready to try new, more advanced techniques or to combine skills efficiently.
5. Give children the opportunity to play various positions to gain a better understanding of the whole game.
6. Encourage participation in a wide variety of activities, resulting in the development of a variety of movement skills.

Social Development

Youth sports greatly influence the social development of children, especially those skills that help individuals behave in socially acceptable ways as they participate. It has often been suggested that youth sports programs further those values we hold dear in our society—to work hard, to play fair, to cooperate with others—when, in fact, what may really be learned is that winning is everything.

Society recognizes certain behaviors as indicative of the true sports person: playing by the rules, being a gracious winner, accepting a loss without blaming others, working with others to accomplish a team goal, and showing respect for teammates, opponents, and officials. These behaviors are learned through the modeling of significant others, the reinforcement of appropriate behavior, and the withdrawal of rewards for socially unacceptable behavior.

Spectators often express socially unacceptable behavior at sports events. Professional athletes may be observed behaving in negative ways as well. Children need to be helped to deal with these inappropriate behaviors. They must learn to recognize them as unacceptable for anyone, regardless of the situation, and to minimize the effects of any of these behaviors that may be directed at them as participants. It may be advisable to hold meetings for participants and their parents to discuss the organization and other matters regarding play, including appropriate behaviors at events.

Individuals working with children in youth sports programs need to:

1. Explain appropriate behavior to the children.

2. Be consistent in actions and words not only by expecting children to behave as good sports persons, but also by demonstrating those desirable behaviors themselves.
3. Reinforce appropriate behavior through encouragement and praise.
4. Withdraw rewards for inappropriate behavior, for example, removal from the game, for all children, including star players who behave inappropriately.
5. Emphasize the fun of the activity and the process of working together rather than winning.
6. Demonstrate respect by encouraging children to compliment opponents and officials at the close of a match or game.

Psychological Development

American society values sports participation. Children who engage in sports activities are esteemed by their peers, parents, and neighbors. Feelings of self-worth are affected by one's choice to participate and by the participation experience itself. Not only must children participate, but they must also participate successfully. One only has to witness a single event to become aware of the psychological pressures that are brought to children by their parents, coaches, and spectators. Parents live vicariously through their children, with their own self-esteem tied up in their children's achievements. Coaches' egos are involved in the team's success or failure. Spectators yell and scream at the players, officials, and coaches. Often the attitudes of these well-meaning adults cause children to feel inadequate about their skills and guilty about their degree of success or even their feelings and commitments to participation in the sport itself.

Children differ in their abilities to handle the pressures of competition. Not only must they please their parents and coaches, but also they must be able to adjust to the crowd and noise, the level of the competition, the reputation of the other team, and their relationships with the individuals on their own team. There may be anxiety over the expectations for winning and the demand for excellence in their endeavors. There may be feelings of apprehension over the role to be played in the game, including whether they will be permitted to participate in the game itself.

Individuals working with children in youth sports need to:

1. Help children set realistic goals for achievement. Help them to challenge themselves but have goals within reach of their efforts.
2. Encourage self-evaluation so that children can first assess what they did well and then look at what they might need to improve.
3. Encourage their best efforts and praise them for the things they do well and for trying their best.
4. Recognize that children make mistakes and help them to be realistic about their errors.
5. Encourage children to think positively and not to dwell on thoughts of possible failure.
6. Recognize that children differ in their emotional maturity and give them all the support they need when they need it.
7. Always end an activity positively. Be sure children leave the practice or game with positive feelings and are looking forward to the next opportunity for participation.
8. Remember that the activity is for children and not for adults.

In summary, sports participation may result in either positive or negative feelings about participation in motor activities. There is evidence that many children drop out of these programs at an early age. Although some may drop out because of changing interests, too many quit because they are discouraged and no longer find the activity fun.

Parents play an important role in their children's success. They must be willing to allow children to decide whether they will participate. Children should be encouraged to be physically active, but the choice of activity is theirs. They may prefer an individual sport over a team sport. They may decide on a more or less competitive environment. They may prefer a lifetime activity in which they test their own powers. Parents must learn to respect these choices. They can encourage their children's participation by helping them learn the skills and by giving them positive feedback. Sometimes it may be helpful to show interest, but only observe the activity from a distance. Whatever children choose, parents should be able to analyze the situation to be sure it is safe, well supervised, and properly equipped and that it provides a good learning experience for the child.

Because physical activity is important in maintaining fitness throughout life, it is important that programs for children encourage rather than discourage them from being physically active. It is up to the adults working in these programs to make the programs the best experience for all children by keeping the needs of children in the forefront and the needs of adults in the background.

SUMMARY

Extra-class activities and special events are an outgrowth of the instructional program of physical education. They provide opportunities for children to develop further and to use the motor skills and knowledge introduced in the physical education classes. They also provide opportunities for children to develop the leadership and organizational skills necessary for leisure time participation without adult direction. In addition, special events give children the chance to perform motor activities in front of others to show parents and friends what they are learning.

Opportunities for elementary school children to participate in youth sports programs have expanded rapidly in the past two decades. Teachers of physical education should involve themselves as advocates for children in helping to plan and conduct these activities. They should assist in training coaches and helping adults involved in such programs (coaches, officials, and parents) to view the activity from the children's perspectives.

Extra-class activities, special events, and youth sports can contribute positively to the development of children. All should be conducted under carefully prescribed guidelines to ensure the safe participation of children. Social, psychological and physical and motor needs of children must be considered for these programs to meet the needs of children and to encourage their participation in physical activity for life.

REFERENCES AND RESOURCES

Barber H: Teaching attitudes and behaviors through youth sports, *JOPERD* 53(3):21, 1982.

Blackwell D: Elementary superstars, *JOPERD* 52(7):28, 1981.

Caine D and Lindner K: Growth plate injury: a threat to young distance runners? *The Physician and Sports Medicine* 12(4):118, 1984.

Calder J and McGregor I: How to succeed in intramurals without really trying, *JOPER* 51(3):48, 1980.

Chambers S: Factors affecting elementary school students' participation in sports, *Elementary School Journal* 91(5):413, 1991.

Feltz D and Weiss M: Developing self-efficacy through sport, *JOPERD* 53(3):24, 1982.

Goldberg B: Injury patterns in youth sports, *The Physician and Sports Medicine* 17(3):174, 1989.

Marston R and Grimm N: Cooperation in special all-school events—field day, *JOPERD* 60(7):67, 1989.

Martens R and Seefeldt V, editors: *Guidelines for children's sports,* Reston, Va, 1979, AAHPERD.

Micheli R et al: Sports in childhood: a round table, *The Physician and Sports Medicine* 11(8):56, 1982.

Ogilvie B: Psychology and the elite young athlete, *The Physician and Sports Medicine* 11(4):195, 1983.

Ryan A: The very young athlete. *The Physician and Sports Medicine* 11(3):45, 1983.

Scanlon T: Motivation and stress in competitive youth sports, *JOPERD* 53(3):27, 1982.

Seefeldt V and Gould D: *Physical and psychological effects of athletic competition on children and youth,* Washington, DC, 1980, ERIC Clearinghouse in Teacher Education.

Smoll F et al: *Children in sport,* ed 3, Champaign, Ill, 1988, Human Kinetics Books.

Tenoschok M: Intramurals, above and beyond, *JOPERD* 52(7):32, 1981.

Thomas J, editor: *Youth sports guide for coaches and parents,* Washington DC, 1978, The Manufacturers Life Insurance Co and NASPE.

Veal ML: A badminton tournament that motivates students, *JOPERD* 62(9):34, 1991.

Weiss M and Gould D, editors: *Sport for children and youths,* Champaign, Ill, 1986, Human Kinetics Publishers.

ANNOTATED READINGS

Boulware C: Special events—the ultimate Rx, *JOPERD* 54(2):27, 1983.

Describes the use of special events in the physical education program to revitalize intramurals. Offer unique nontraditional events, take children away from school, and develop awareness.

Carlton P and Stinson R: Achieving educational goals through intramurals, *JOPERD* 54(2):23, 1983.

Discusses the use of intramurals, clubs, special events, and self-directed activities to meet educational goals.

Ewing M and Seefeldt V: Participation and attrition patterns of American agency-sponsored and interscholastic sports—an executive summary, *NCYS News* 1(3):4, 1988.

Presents a report of a research study on the sports activity participation of youths 10 to 17 years of age.

Feigley D: Intramural and recreational sport program awards, *JOPERD* 58(2):50, 1987.

Discusses an award program that offers awards for other than winning.

Harris J and Almond L: Beyond the badge: award systems in physical education, *Strategies* 5(1):13, 1991.

Suggests guidelines for physical education awards.

Mathias K: Why use student officials? *Strategies* 6(6):21, 1993.

Suggestions for using and training student officials.

Raithel K: Are girls less fit than boys? *The Physician and Sports Medicine* 15(11):156, 1987.

Looks at sex and cultural differences affecting girls' participation.

Remak B: Starting them right: helping parents prepare young children for sports, *Strategies* 2(1):14, 1988.

Provides suggestions for parents as role models for children in fostering abilities and attitudes toward sports.

Smith R et al: *Parents complete guide to youth sports,* Costa Mesa, Calif, 1989, HDL Publishing Co.

Presents a guide for parents including psychological and physical development of children, choosing a program, injuries, and stress.

United States Department of Health and Human Services: *Children and youth in action: physical activities and sports,* Washington, DC, 1980, Superintendent of Documents, United States Printing Office.

Reviews the age characteristics of children, suggestions for parents to help children develop physical fitness and motor skills, and concerns for competitive activities for children and youth.

Weiss M: Is winning everything? *Childhood Education,* 65(4):195, 1989.

Discusses non-school children's sports' activities, highlighting children's reasons for participating and their definition of success.

GLOSSARY

A

abduction Movement of a limb away from the median axis of the body. (p. 167)

academic learning time (ALT-PE) The time a student is engaged with lesson content at an appropriate level of difficulty. (p. 85)

accent Emphasis on a beat, usually, but not always, the first beat of the measure. (p. 366)

activity curriculum model An activity-centered curriculum model in which teaching a variety of activities is the primary focus. (p. 36)

adduction Movement of a limb toward the median axis of the body or closer together (similar parts such as fingers). (p. 167)

adventure model A curriculum model in which goals are focused on building self-esteem, cooperation, trust, challenge, and problem solving. (p. 37)

aerobic efficiency Ability of the body to supply fuel and oxygen to the muscles. (p. 253)

affective development The development of attitudes and values. (p. 8)

aggression Vigorously pursuing a goal. (p. 236)

American dance Dances of colonial America based on popular tunes of the period. (p. 386)

annual plan A schedule that places all units of instruction in the school calendar for a particular year. (p. 66)

anticipatory set The opening of the lesson in which students are prepared for the development of the lesson content. (p. 72)

applying The learning process in which movement concepts and motor skills are used appropriately and efficiently in traditional physical education activities. (p. 42)

atrophy A reduction in size, wasting away, or progressive decline. (p. 10)

augmented feedback Knowledge of results, information about performance given by an observer to an individual. (p. 86)

B

backing up In softball, moving into position behind a fielding player or base player and in line with an oncoming ball to assist if the player misses the ball. (p. 619)

base of support The space covered and limbs utilized in supporting the body in any position. (p. 184)

blind pass A baton pass in pursuit relays in which the receiver is facing away from the baton as it is passed. (p. 351)

block plan A tentative calendar of objectives and activities developed for a unit. (p. 71)

body awareness Understanding of one's own body potential for movement and a sensitivity to one's physical being. (p. 9)

body composition The relationship in percent of body fat to lean body tissue. (p. 10)

body mechanics Efficient use of the body in maintaining good alignment and in performing daily tasks such as lifting, carrying, pushing, and pulling. (p. 242)

bound flow Control or momentary restraint of movement in which the body may be stopped, such as in changing direction of pathway. (p. 189)

bunch start Crouch start; a starting position used in sprints in which the rear knee is placed next to the forward foot. The thumb and index fingers are spread and parallel to the starting line. (p. 350)

C

cardiac output The amount of blood pumped out of the heart each minute. (p. 20)

cardiorespiratory endurance The maximal functional capacity of the heart and lungs to continue activity over a period of time. (p. 10)

center of gravity The weight center of the body; the point around which the body weight is equally distributed. (p. 184)

child self-evaluation An evaluation technique in which the student determines when the criteria for a knowledge or skill taught in physical education have been met. (p. 149)

circuit training A training method in which a number of stations for conditioning different parts of the body or different components of fitness are set up and the participants go to each station for a set period of time. (p. 249)

collecting In soccer, the ability to receive a ball and get it under control using body parts other than the hands. (p. 586)

command A teacher-centered approach to teaching in which the teacher presents the material to be learned directly to the students, who move to the teacher's commands. (p. 92)

competition A contest between individuals or groups. (p. 236)

conflict resolution Skills developed to help individuals resolve disputes in a way in which there are no real winners and losers. (p. 229)

contingency contract A technique in which the child is offered a reward for behaving in a particular manner: "If you will do this, then you may do that." (p. 128)

contra dance Dances done with partners facing in long rows of couples. (p. 386)

cooperation Working together to achieve a goal in which success depends on combined effort. (p. 237)

cooperative learning A process in which children work together to determine the one answer to a learning activity. (p. 227)

cover In softball, to move into position to make a play at a base by someone other than the usual base player. (p. 619)

creating The highest level learning process that results in the creation or invention of movements unique to the individual or new to physical education. (p. 42)

criterion-referenced tests Measures of how a person performs; evaluation against a qualitative standard, such as the evaluative criteria considered for the motor skills in this text. (p. 144)

critical elements Key points of emphasis or evaluative criteria emphasized in teaching the skills, strategies, and movement concepts in physical education. (p. 41)

critical thinking Utilizing the higher thought processes of analysis, problem solving and evaluation. (p. 33)

D

development Changes caused by maturation that lead to more advanced use of particular mechanisms. (p. 2)

developmental physical education Physical education based on the physical, cognitive, social, and affective developmental status of children rather than age or grade. (p. 4)

direct snap Receiving the football from the center when the quarterback assumes a position over the center with the hands under the center. (p. 559)

direction The six ways the body can move in space with different body surfaces leading: forward, backward, right, left, up, and down. (p. 9)

discipline The process for assisting individuals to adjust to their environment; also, the result of failure to adhere to certain standards of behavior. (p. 126)
distributed practice Practice over a period of time in which the time between the practice periods varies. (p. 85)
double dribble In basketball, dribbling the ball, stopping, and beginning to dribble once again or contacting the ball with two hands at any time during dribbling. (p. 500)
double-beat jump The rope jumper jumps as the rope passes under the feet and then again as the rope passes overhead. (p. 291)
double-elimination tournament A tournament that ensures the participation of each team or individual until all but one have lost two matches. (p. 655)
duration recording Recording the amount of time during which an event occurred. (p. 152)
dynamic balance Maintaining balance while moving. (p. 183)

E

educational game A game with few rules, played by small or large groups, that is selected for the practice and use of previously learned motor skills and movement concepts. (p. 449)
epiphysis The part of the bone where growth occurs, found near the end of long bones. (p. 18)
evaluation The act of making judgments about something. (p. 143)
event recording Recording the number of times an event took place. (p. 152)
exploration A child-centered approach to teaching in which the teacher leads the children through a series of very general movement challenges designed to help them learn about their own movement potential or the use of a particular piece of equipment. Many different responses are possible. (p. 36)
extension The act of straightening body parts. (p. 167)

F

feedback Information received while observing one's own performance. (p. 86)
fitness model A curriculum model in physical education that uses activity to enhance fitness. (p. 37)
flexibility The range of motion in a joint. (p. 10)
flexion The act of bending body parts. (p. 107)
floor exercise A combination of stunts, tumbling skills, balances, dance, and locomotor and other movements in which the performer moves on a square mat, using as much space as possible and traveling in several pathways. (p. 312)
flow The ability to combine movements smoothly. (p. 9)
folk dance A traditional dance of the people handed down from one generation to the next. (p. 385)
force out In softball, an out made by getting the ball to the base before the runner and tagging the base. If the player must run to the base the player may be forced out. (p. 612)
formative evaluation Evaluation to determine changing needs throughout the learning process. (p. 143)
foul ball A batted ball that settles outside the baseline or lands outside this extended line in the outfield. (p. 612)
free flow A continuity of movement. (p. 189)
frequency The number of days per week needed to improve fitness.
fundamental motor skill Locomotor, nonlocomotor, and manipulative skills that form the foundation upon which other skills will be learned; examples include walking, running, skipping, pulling, pushing, throwing, and catching. (p. 8)

G

gallop A slide performed in a forward direction. (p. 192)
general space The area that is available for movement, defined by imposed or natural boundaries. (p. 39)
general supervision Supervision provided by a teacher who is in the area of the activity. (p. 111)
give and go An offensive strategy in which the passer draws an opponent, passes a square pass to a teammate, and then receives a return pass after moving around the opposing player. (p. 535)
group sampling Recording at particular intervals throughout the lesson the number of individuals engaged in a particular activity. (p. 153)
growth Change in size. (p. 15)
guided discovery A teaching style in which the teacher leads the children through a series of activities, narrowing their focus at each step of the way until the one or a limited number of solutions to the movement challenges are reached. (p. 24)

H

health-related physical fitness The ability to perform strenuous activity without excessive fatigue and to show evidence of the traits and capacities that limit the risks of developing disease or disorders that limit a person's functional capacity. (p. 10)
hop A locomotor movement in which the performer takes off on one foot and lands on the same foot. (p. 192)
hypertrophy An increase in size of a muscle as a result of appropriate exercise. (p. 10)

I

imagery To use something from a person's experience to convey an idea; i.e., light as a feather. (p. 373)
improvisation Created extemporaneously, without preplanning. (p. 372)
individual education plan (IEP) A plan of long- and short-term goals, activities, and services to meet these goals; it is required for all disabled children by P.L. 94-142. (p. 133)
individualized family plan (IFSP) A plan developed for infants and toddlers with special needs, which includes the assessment of the child's status, family strengths, and needs and services to be given. (p. 134)
inservice Training provided for teachers on various aspects of schooling. (p. 63)
instruction The activities the teacher uses to move the class toward the lesson objectives. (p. 113)
integrated movement curriculum model Includes the study of human movement as an important aspect of each instructional unit. (p. 37)
integration Recognizing and teaching the mutual relationship among subject matter in the schools. (p. 49)
intensity In music, the loudness or softness of an accompaniment; in fitness, the degree of vigor or the amount of effort expended during an activity. (pp. 252, 366)
intersensory integration The ability to use input from several sensory organs at the same time. (p. 20)

interval recording An observation technique in which events are recorded at various time intervals. (p. 153)

intramurals Voluntary recreational activities conducted within the school setting for all children. (p. 4)

intrasensory discrimination The ability to use various sensory stimuli from a single-sense organ. (p. 20)

J

jump A locomotor movement in which the performer takes off on one or both feet and lands on two feet. (p. 192)

K

kinesthetic A sense of the location and place of body parts in body movements. (p. 21)

kyphosis A postural deviation characterized by an increased thoracic curve. (p. 265)

L

ladder tournament A tournament arranged as the rungs of a ladder. Participants may challenge players on one or two rungs above their own position. The winner assumes the higher rung. The individual or team at the top of the ladder at the end of the tournament is the winner. (p. 655)

lead-up game A game with some of the skills, rules, and game elements of a team sport. (p. 452)

lean body weight The weight of the bones, muscles, and internal organs. (p. 255)

leap An extended running step in which the performer takes off on one foot, travels forward through the air, and lands on the opposite foot. (p. 192)

learning A change in behavior brought about as a result of practice. (p. 79)

least restrictive environment In physical education the environment in which a child can participate successfully and safely in as near a normal setting as possible. (p. 133)

legal liability Responsibility for the children in one's care as obligated by the law. (p. 110)

lesson plan The day's plan for meeting unit objectives, including objectives for the day, activities to meet objectives, points of emphasis, and organizational strategies. (p. 72)

level High, medium, and low in relation to the standing position or the location of body parts. (p. 9)

line dance Dances of American origin performed in lines or scattered in general space without partners to contemporary music. (p. 386)

line of gravity An imaginary line that passes through the body from head to foot, passing through the center of gravity and dividing the body into two equal parts from front to back and from side to side. (p. 185)

line of scrimmage In football, the imaginary line running the width of the field that marks the forward progress of the ball. Teams line up on their side of the line to begin play. (p. 555)

locomotor movement A movement through space from one place to another. (p. 192)

lordosis A postural deviation characterized by an increased lumbar curve. (p. 265)

low-intensity exercise An exercise that gets the individual moving but does not increase the heart rate to a fitness-improving level or result in overheating or other discomforts. (p. 253)

M

mainstreaming The placing of disabled persons in the least restrictive learning environment. (p. 133)

management Operations used to move the class through the lesson from one activity to the next. (p. 113)

marking Being responsible for an opponent while playing defense. (p. 524)

massed practice Practice periods scheduled close together. (p. 85)

maximum heart rate The maximum number of heartbeats attained per minute, depending on age and physical condition. (p. 253)

maximum oxygen consumption (MaxVO2) The greatest amount of oxygen a human can consume at the tissue level. (p. 120)

measure Underlying beats grouped together by a unit, the number of which depends on the meter. (p. 366)

medium start A start used in sprints in which the feet are a comfortable distance apart and the hand position is as in the bunch start. (p. 351)

meter The number of beats in a measure, such as 2/4, 3/4, 4/4, or 6/8. The upper number represents the number of beats to a measure, the lower number the type of note to receive one beat. (p. 366)

mixed grip In gymnastics, gripping a bar, with one hand assuming a regular grip, the other a reverse grip. (p. 334)

mood The character of an accompaniment that depicts feelings, such as sadness, gaiety, seriousness, or other emotions. (p. 360)

motivation The process of getting an individual to act in ways that satisfy a need or desire. (p. 82)

motor skills curriculum model Emphasizes the development of motor skills as its primary focus. (p. 37)

movement challenge A movement problem posed that involves problem solving with a focus on the movement content. (p. 9)

movement concepts The elements important in the study of human movement: body awareness, space, and qualities of movement, including force, balance, time, and flow. (p. 9)

movement education A child-centered approach to learning in physical education designed to help children develop greater understanding of themselves as movers, the space in which to move, and the factors affecting efficient movement. (p. 15)

movement model Stresses the movement content as the only legitimate curriculum content; utilizes problem solving and other child-centered approaches for the most part. (p. 37)

muscular endurance The ability of the muscles to sustain effort over time. (p. 10)

muscular strength The amount of force a muscle can exert. (p. 10)

N

Native American dance A dance originating with Native American groups performed during ceremonies or at various social occasions. (p. 386)

nonlocomotor movement A movement executed while the individual remains in one place. (p. 192)

norm setting Applying reality therapy to a group. (p. 128)

norm-referenced tests Measures of quantitative data that serve as a comparison with scores of other children of the same age and sex tested under like conditions, such as the AAHPERD health-related physical fitness test norms. (p. 144)

O

obstruction In field hockey, placing the body between an opponent and the ball. (p. 523)

off-side A player from either team moving across the line of scrimmage before the ball is centered. (p. 568)

ossification The hardening of cartilaginous tissue into bone in the development process. (p. 18)

P

parallel play The play of young children in which they participate alongside other children but do not depend on the others for success or for meeting their play objective. (p. 452)

pathways Lines of movement in space: straight, curved, or combinations of straight and curved. (p. 9)

perceiving The initial phase of learning in which concepts and motor skills are introduced. (p. 41)

perception The ability to use information coming in through the sense organs to make judgments about the environment. (p. 20)

performance A temporary occurrence or action. (p. 79)

phrase A group of measures that constitutes a musical thought. (p. 366)

physical education That aspect of education in the schools designed to develop skillful, fit, and knowledgeable movers through carefully planned and conducted experiences. (p. 4)

pivot A method of changing pathways by rotating the body around one stationary foot, which remains in contact with the floor. (p. 510)

portfolio A method of assesment in which samples of a student's work and evaluations are collected and the results indicate pupil progress and identification of present needs. (p. 150)

practice A teacher-centered teaching style that permits individual practice with teacher supervision. (p. 93)

problem solving A teaching style whereby the teacher leads the children through a series of activities in which the children find an increasing number of possible responses to a movement challenge. (p. 3)

pronation Rotation of the arm to bring the palm downward or backward. (p. 167)

psychomotor Motor activity stimulated by the higher brain centers. (p. 21)

pursuit relay A relay run on an oval in which each member runs a particular distance of the course. (p. 351)

pyramid tournament Participants are arranged in a pyramid. Players challenge others in the level above. The winner assumes the higher position. At the end of the tournament, the player or team at the top is the winner. (p. 655)

Q

qualitative objective A statement that identifies the behavior necessary for success, such as the way body parts are used in performing a motor skill. (p. 68)

qualities of movement Factors affecting efficient movement, such as balance, force, time, and flow. (p. 9)

quantitative objective A statement that measures the result of the behavior, such as the degree of success in a particular situation. (p. 69)

R

range The relation of the body parts to each other or of the body to objects in space. (p. 9)

rating scale An evaluative technique in which values are arranged on a continuum from high to low; on the basis of observation, children's performance is placed along the continuum. (p. 149)

reality therapy A technique used to help persons be responsible for their behavior by identifying undesirable behavior and the consequences of that behavior and developing a plan to meet desired goals. (p. 128)

reciprocal A teaching style that uses peer teaching and feedback. (p. 58)

refining Those phases of learning in which skills are mastered and concepts well understood; ends in habituation of motor skills. (p. 42)

regular grip In gymnastics, gripping a bar with the fingers on top, the thumbs underneath, and the palms facing away from the performer. (p. 334)

reinforcement An event that increases the probability of a behavior occurring again. (p. 87)

retention Degree to which learning is remembered over time. (p. 88)

reverse grip In gymnastics, gripping a bar with the thumbs closest to the performer, the fingers behind the bar, and the palms facing the performer. (p. 334)

reverse stick In field hockey, when the stick is rolled over to hit the ball toward the right. (p. 525)

reverse turn A method of changing pathways from a stride position in which the body runs toward the rear foot as both feet remain in contact with the floor. (p. 501)

rhythmic pattern A combination of notes, even and uneven in time, that constitutes a measure or a phrase. (p. 366)

rotation The turning of a body part about its long axis. (p. 26)

round robin tournament A tournament in which each participant plays every other participant in the tournament, with the winner determined as the one with the best winning record. (p. 655)

S

scoliosis A postural deviation characterized by one or more lateral curvatures of the spine. (p. 265)

self-space The area of space the body occupies and that space within the body's natural extensions. (p. 39)

self-analysis An evaluation technique in which the teacher reflects on the lesson taught, focusing on particular aspects of the lesson the teacher wishes to evaluate. (p. 151)

self-concept Feelings an individual has about herself or himself. (p. 11)

self-esteem The value placed on the perceptions of self. (p. 8)

sequenced model A model for integrating curriculum in which each subject is taught separately so that similar units coincide in several subjects. (p. 49)

shared model A model for integrating curriculum in which two distinct subject areas are brought together into a single focus of overlapping concepts. (p. 49)

shotgun In football, receiving the ball from the center from a position in which the quarterback stands several yards behind the center. (p. 559)

shuttle relay A relay run back and forth between two lines (p. 351)

singing games Activities of young children in which children's poems are put to music and imitative movements are used. (p. 385)

single-beat jump The rope jumper jumps only as the rope passes under the feet. (p. 291)

single-elimination tournament A tournament in which players are eliminated after one loss. A player or team winning all matches is the winner. (p. 655)

skill game A game in which the primary purpose is the practice of a motor skill. (p. 452)

skill test An evaluative technique used to evaluate motor skill performance that usually records a quantitative measure of skill performance. (p. 149)

skinfold caliper An instrument for measuring pecent of body fat. (p. 255)

skip A step-hop combination executed in an uneven rhythm alternating the lead foot. (p. 192)

slide A locomotor movement executed in uneven rhythm in which the performer steps to the side, closes the trailing foot to the lead foot, transfers the weight back to the trailing foot, and repeats the action again. (p. 192)

space concepts Movement concepts including self and general space, direction and pathways, level, and range. (p. 9)

specific supervision Supervision in which the teacher is working directly with the students. (p. 111)

sport elitism Preferential treatment of students who are skilled over those who are less skilled. (p. 231)

sportslike behavior Conduct becoming a sportsperson, including respect for rules and authority, playing fair, working with others in a group effort, being a good competitor, and accepting winning and losing in a socially acceptable manner. (p. 223)

spotting Giving physical assistance to a person performing a motor skill, especially in gymnastics where the possibility of injury is increased in the learning phase. (p. 305)

sprint A dash or short-distance race of 20 to 50 yards for elementary schoolchildren. (p. 349)

square dance Dances of American origin executed in a four-couple set. (p. 386)

square pass In hockey or soccer, a pass parallel to the end line between two players; also called a flat pass. (p. 535)

static balance Balance while stationary. (p. 183)

strike zone In softball, the area between the batter's armpits and the knees. (p. 614)

stroke volume The amount of blood ejected into circulation with each contraction of the heart. (p. 20)

summative evaluation A final evaluation conducted at the end of a unit or program. (p. 143)

supination Rotation of the forearm and hand so that the palm faces downward or upward. (p. 167)

sway A nonlocomotor movement characterized by a pendular movement with the axis below the moving part. (p. 192)

swing A nonlocomotor movement characterized by a pendular movement with the axis above the moving part. (p. 192)

T

tackle A means of taking the ball or puck away from an opponent without personal contact. (p. 540)

tactile The sense of touch. (p. 21)

task A style of teaching in which learning objectives and activities are selected and organized by the teacher but in which students assume responsibility for learning by selecting those objectives and activities on which they need to work. (p. 95)

teacher observation A technique used in the evaluation of students in which the teacher observes the extent to which certain objectives have been met using checklists or rating scales to record observations. (p. 147)

teaching styles Teaching methods and strategies for organizing and presenting learning experiences to children. (p. 91)

tempo The rate of speed from fast to slow. (p. 366)

terminal objectives Statements of the intended final outcomes of the objectives of a unit. (p. 68)

through pass In soccer or hockey, a pass parallel to the sideline in which the passer hits the ball straight ahead and the receiver moves forward past an opposing player and cuts for the ball. (p. 535)

time Duration: the length of fitness activity periods. (p. 252)

time-out Removing a child from activity as a means of controlling inappropriate behavior. (p. 128)

tort A psychological or physical injury resulting from someone's failure to meet their legal responsibility. (p. 110)

transfer The ability to apply what was learned in one situation to new situations. (p. 84)

traveling In basketball, while in possession of the ball, taking more than two steps before dribbling or passing. (p. 500)

U

underlying beat The pulse beat; a steady, even beat found in any piece of music. (p. 365)

unit plan A series of related learning experiences organized around a common theme. (p. 68)

upfield pass In soccer or hockey, a pass on the diagonal, passed at an angle in front of a player who is closer to the goal. (p. 535)

V

varying That phase of learning in which the teacher alters the learning environment, resulting in the need to make adjustments in the use of motor skills and concepts. (p. 42)

vaulting In gymnastics, a movement in which the performer passes over a piece of equipment. (p. 344)

visual pass In track events, a pass of the baton in which the receiver watches the baton into the hand. (p. 351)

W

webbed model A model for integrating curriculum in which a theme is developed that encompasses a variety of subject areas. (p. 49)

wellness A way of life purposely designed to enjoy the highest level of health and well-being possible, including nutrition, weight control, avoiding substance abuse, being physically fit and leading an active life, controlling stress, developing good relationships with others, living with high values and ethics, and attending somewhat to spirituality. (p. 242)

APPENDICES

1. Suggested Equipment and Records
2. Vendors
3. Plans for Homemade Equipment
4. Computer Software
5. Screening Devices, Sources, and IEP Forms
6. Accident and Medical Forms
7. Tools to Assess Teacher Effectiveness

APPENDIX 1

Suggested Equipment and Records

SUGGESTED EQUIPMENT FOR ELEMENTARY SCHOOL PHYSICAL EDUCATION

ITEM	QUANTITY (CLASS SIZE 20-25)	CAN BE IMPROVISED
GENERAL		
Bags to carry balls	6	
Ball inflator	1	
Ball repair kit	1	
Blackboard	1	
Bulletin board	1	
Clipboards	3	
Cones or jug markers	8	X
First aid kit	1	
Line marker	1	
100-foot measuring tape	1	
Pinnies, sashes, or vests (3 colors)	30	X
Record player (with speed control)	1	
Stopwatch	2	
Whistles with rubber mouth guards and lanyards	3	
Wire baskets or racks to store balls		
SMALL EQUIPMENT		
Balance boards	6	X
Beanbags	25	X
Discs (Frisbees)	8	
Duck or bowling pins	24	X
Elastic ropes		
Long	2	
Short	25	
Fleece balls	25	
Hoops	25	X
Horseshoes (rubber)	2 sets	
Jumping ropes		
Long (10 to 15 feet)	8	X
Short (6, 7, and 8 feet)	25	X
Nerf balls (small)	25	
SMALL EQUIPMENT—cont'd		
Paddles	12	X
Rings	25	X
Scooters	6	X
Stilts	6	X
Tennis balls	25	
Wands (dowels or golf tubes)	25	
Wiffle balls	6	
Yarn balls	25	X
DANCE/RHYTHMIC ACTIVITIES		
Dance drum and mallet	1	
Lummi sticks	25 pair	X
Records		
Rhythm instruments	12	X
Wood blocks		
Maracas		
Triangle		
Scarves, ribbons, other props		X
Tambourines	4	
Tinikling poles	12	X
LARGE APPARATUS		
All-purpose climber	1	X
Balance beam (4-inch)		
Low	1	X
Adjustable (30 to 36 inches)	1	X
Climbing ropes	2	X
Horizontal bar	1	
Horizontal ladder	1	
Mats (4 by 8 feet)	8	
Parachute	1	
Parallel bars	1	X
Uneven bars	1	
Vaulting bench or box	1	X

Continued.

SUGGESTED EQUIPMENT FOR ELEMENTARY SCHOOL PHYSICAL EDUCATION—cont'd

ITEM	QUANTITY (CLASS SIZE 20-25)	CAN BE IMPROVISED
GAMES AND SPORTS		
Beach balls	10	
Cage ball or push ball	1	
Nerf balls		
7- or 8-inch	24	
Playground balls		
5-inch	24	
7- or 8-inch	24	
Tether balls	2	
Tether ball poles	2	
Basketballs (junior)	12	
Eight-foot portable baskets	4	
Goals (portable)	2	X
Goalkeeper's equipment	2	
Hockey balls	12	
Hockey pucks	12	
Hockey sticks (junior or plastic)	25	
Old automobile tires	4	X
Shin guards	25	
Flags	2 sets	
Kicking tee	1	
Footballs (junior or Nerf)	12	
Soccer balls (size 4)	25	
Bases		
Indoor	2 sets	
Outdoor	2 sets	
Batting helmets	3	
Batting tee	2	
Chest protector	2	
Gloves	12	
Face mask	2	
Softballs (soft)	12	
Softball bats	6	
Volleyball standards	2 sets	
Volleyball net	2	
Volleyballs		
Leather	4	
Nerf	12	
Batons	4	X
Hurdles	4	X
Shot (4 pound)	2	
High-jump standards	1 set	X
High-jump pit	1	X
Long-jump pit	1	X

SUGGESTED RECORDS

Singing Games, Folk and Square Dance

Appalachian Clog Dancing: Basic single and double clog steps to spirited mountain music.
Source: Educational Activities, Inc.

Young People's Folk Dances: Set of seven records; single records may be purchased. A series of dances increasing in difficulty for children of all ages. Each record has its own simply worded instructions and drawings of formations and dance positions used.
Source: Educational Record Sales

World of Fun: Set of seven records; single records may be purchased. A series of records with a variety of dances including singing games, folk and square dances appropriate for children of all ages. An instruction book is included that describes all dances, dance steps, terminology, positions, and dance formations.
Source: Discipleship Resources, P.O. Box 840, Nashville, TN 37202

Folk Dances from "Round the World": A set of five records, also sold singly. A progression of dances for children and adults with simple directions, historical information, and a dictionary of steps and positions.
Source: Educational Record Sales

Folk Dance Fun: An album of dances for children in grades K-6.
Source: Kimbo Educational

Dances in a Line: No partner, easy dances for upper elementary school children.
Source: Kimbo Educational

Everybody's Square Dances: A set of five records, which may be purchased singly. A variety of square dances varying in complexity including singing and patter calls, visiting, and other square figures. Instructions are included with each record with complete descriptions and illustrations of figures. Music includes all calls.
Source: Educational Record Sales

Get Ready to Square Dance (K-6): An album of eight movement games to teach beginning square dance patterns. An instruction booklet is included.
Source: Kimbo Educational

Rhythmic Activities

Ambrose Brazelton: Clap, Snap and Tap: Finger snapping, rhythmic hand and arm movements, cooperative cross hand patterns, etc. to various types of music.
Body Jive: Identifying body parts, coordination movements, etc.
Source: Educational Activities, Inc.

Musical Ball Skills: Use of bouncing, throwing, rolling, and catching in rhythmic patterns and simple routines.
Source: Educational Activities, Inc.

Ball Gymnastics: Activities utilizing throwing, bouncing, and catching. Ask for Elementary Manual.
Source: Kimbo Educational

Synchronized Ball Skills (K-6): A series of progressively more difficult ball activities for elementary school children.
Source: Educational Activities, Inc.

Lummi Sticks for Kids: Simplified lummi stick activities for preschoolers through 3rd grade.
Source: Kimbo Educational

Rhythm Stick Activities: Music, activities, and instructions for rhythm sticks.
Source: Educational Activities, Inc.

Synchronized Lummi Sticks: Activities for rhythm sticks complete with illustrated manual.
Source: Educational Activities, Inc.

Clubs and Hoops: Skills and routines using hoops and clubs with instructions and illustrations of skills.
Source: Hoctor Dance Records, Inc.

Modern Gymnastics with Ribbons: Ribbon movements including waves, serpents, spirals, and swings.
Source: Kimbo Educational

Rhythmic Rope Jumping: 17 piano tunes. Ask for Elementary Manual.
Source: Kimbo Educational

Jump to the Beat: Aerobic and precision rope jumping routines for beginning and advanced jumpers.
Source: Kimbo Educational

Rope Jumping: Music of various tempos and rhythms for rope jumping. Instruction manual included.
Source: Educational Activities, Inc.

Rhythmic Parachute Play: Using parachute skills while moving to the music.
Source: Kimbo Educational

Playtime Parachute Fun: Developing gross motor skills through parachute routines.
Source: Kimbo Educational

Fitness

Aerobic Dance for Kids: Aerobic exercises including activities to warm up for activity and to cool down. Music with voice cues and music alone are included.
Source: Educational Activities, Inc.

And the Beat Goes On for Physical Education: Exercises for various body parts set to music.
Source: Educational Activities, Inc.

Motor Fitness Rhythm Games: Simple activities to enhance fitness and psychomotor coordination.
Source: Educational Activities, Inc.

A Thriller for Kids: A 20-minute work-out including warm-up, stretches, jogging, and cool-down activities to contemporary tunes.
Source: Kimbo Educational

Movement Activities

Hap Palmer: Getting to Know Myself: Body awareness and activities to enhance the understanding of space relationships.

The Feel of Music: Experiencing the feeling of music—joy, soft and loud, etc.

Learning Basic Skills Through Music, vol. 1: Activities to enhance body awareness and awareness of colors, numbers, and the alphabet.

Movin': Musical moods to explore and creative movement responses.

Walter the Waltzing Worm: Stretching, twisting, and other nonlocomotor movements from slow to fast tempos.
Source: Educational Activities, Inc.
Kimbo Educational

Bean Bag Activities: Games, dances, and other activities to develop coordination.
Source: Kimbo Educational

Individualization in Movement and Music: Action songs, dances, games, and stories to encourage individual responses.
Source: Educational Activities, Inc.

Miscellaneous

Socialization Skills Adaptive Behavior: 16 songs to teach sharing, listening, etc.
Source: Kimbo Educational

CARE AND STORAGE OF EQUIPMENT

1. All equipment should be stored according to manufacturer recommendations.
2. Equipment should be stored in a central location so all physical education teachers have easy access to equipment for their classes.
3. Storage should be organized with areas labeled for storage of particular equipment.
4. Bins, racks, and wire baskets make equipment more easily accessible than bags.
5. Children must be taught to take responsibility for the care of equipment. It should be used only for those activities for which it was manufactured. Children should be encouraged not to sit on the balls (it's very hard on the valves) nor to pull apart foam balls.
6. All equipment should be marked with waterproof markings for easy recognition as equipment belonging to the school.
7. The equipment purchased should be the best the school can afford. Buying inexpensive equipment won't save money in the long run.
8. Equipment used for recess should be stored separately from that used in the physical education classes.
9. Balls should be stored partially deflated and when in use inflated to manufacturer's specifications.
10. Ropes may be color-coded by length by dipping the ends in paint or using colored tape on the ends to specify various lengths. Storing ropes by

folding them and then tying them into a single knot will keep them from being tangled.

11. All equipment should be checked periodically and repairs made before use.
12. Equipment should be kept clean. Children may be recruited for periodic cleaning parties.
13. Empty large ice cream containers provide adequate storage for small items.
14. Equipment should be carefully checked in after use in class, recess, or intramurals.

APPENDIX 2

Vendors

EQUIPMENT, APPARATUS, AND SUPPLY VENDORS

Vendor	Products
Bob Eshelbenner 708 12th St. Terrace Fort Scott, KA 66701	Junior basketball goals.
Brine, Inc. 47 Summer St. Milford, MA 01757	Balls, softcrosses.
BSN Sports P.O. Box 7726 Dallas, TX 75209 (800)527-7510	Balls and sports equipment, small equipment, standards, stop-watches, cones.
Flaghouse 18 W. 18th St. New York, NY 10011 (212)989-9700	Large apparatus, mats, balls, small equipment, parachutes, foam.
Gerstung Manufactors 6310 Blair Hill La. Baltimore, MD 21209	Balls, ropes, hoops, ribbons, and accessories for rhythmic gymnastics.
GSC Athletic Equipment 600 N. Pacific Ave. San Pedro, CA 90733 (213)831-0131	Large apparatus, rhythmic gymnastics, balls, foam, playground apparatus, standards, mats.
Graves-Humphreys 1948 Franklin Road S.W. P.O. Box 13407 Roanoke, VA 24033 (800)336-5998	Balls, sports equipment, large apparatus, playground equipment, mats, parachutes.
Gym Closet 2511 Leach Rd. Rochester Hills, MI 48057	Balls, mats, nets, standards, floor hockey, apparatus, paddles, ropes, parachutes.
Hammett Physical Education Division Hammett Place Box 545 Braintree, MA 02184 (206)336-6666	Balls, mats, foam, small equipment, sports equipment, standards, records.
Mosier Materials 61328 Yakwahtin Ct. Bend, OR 97702	Juggling scarfs, parachutes, cage balls, balance boards, scooters.
North American Sports 1175 State St. New Haven, CT 06511 (800)243-5133	Balls, mats, standards, small equipment, parachutes, stop-watches.
Oriam Sports, Inc. 444 Lincoln Blvd. #403 Venice, CA 90291 (213)399-6602	Buka balls, video, Netsystem

Palos Sports, Inc. P.O. Box 367 12235 S. Harton Ave. Palos Heights, IL 60463	Balls, scooters, ropes, apparatus, paddles, goals, floor hockey.
Passon's Sports 1017 Arch St. Philadelphia, PA 19107 (800)523-1557	Balls, small equipment, large apparatus, mats, standards.
Shield Mfg. 425 Fillmore Ave. Tonawanda, NY 14150 (800)828-7669	Foam and plastic equipment, goals, training hurdles.
Sportime Division Select Service and Supply Co., Inc. 2905-E Anwiler Rd. Atlanta, GA 30360 (800)241-9884	Balls, sports equipment, foam, small equipment, standards, mats, large apparatus.
Sidney Laner and Co. 5315 N. Lincoln Ave. Chicago, IL 60625 (800)526-1300	Small equipment, balls, parachutes, large apparatus, mats.
TAHETA Arts & Culture Group 605 "A" Street Anchorage, AK 99501 (907)272-5829	Eskimo yoyos.
Things From Bell, Inc. 4 Lincoln Ave. P.O. Box 706 Cortland, NY 13045 (607)753-8291	Balls, foam, small equipment, parachutes, large apparatus.
U.S. Games, Inc. Box 360874 Melbourne, FL 32936 (800)521-2832	Balls, playground equipment, parachutes, small equipment, sports equipment, standards.
Wolverine Sports 745 Circle Box 1941 Ann Arbor, MI 48106	Balls, small equipment, large apparatus.

SOURCES FOR RECORDS

Educational Activities, Inc.
P.O. Box 382
Freeport, NY 11520
(800)645-3739

Education Record Center
472 East Paces Ferry Road
Atlanta, GA 30305
(404)233-5935

Educational Recordings of America
P.O. Box 231
Monroe, CT 06468

Educational Record Sales
157 Chambers St.
New York, NY 10007
(212)276-7437

Folk Dancer Record Service
P.O. Box 201
Flushing Long Island, NY 11520

Hoctor Dance Records, Inc.
159 Franklin Turnpike
Post Office Box 38
Waldwick, NJ 07463
(201)652-7767

Kimbo Educational
10 North Third Ave.
Post Office Box 477
Long Branch, NJ 07740
(201)229-4949

Twinson Company
1289 Reamwood Ave. Suite E
Sunnyvale, CA 94089-2234
(408)734-9558

APPENDIX 3

Plans for Homemade Equipment

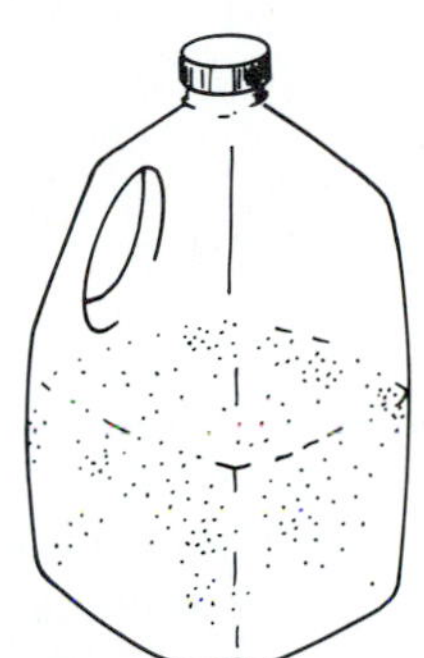

BOUNDARY/GOAL MARKERS

Plastic jugs with handles partially filled with sand and painted or taped in bright colors make adequate boundary markers that can be easily seen and are not easily knocked or blown over.

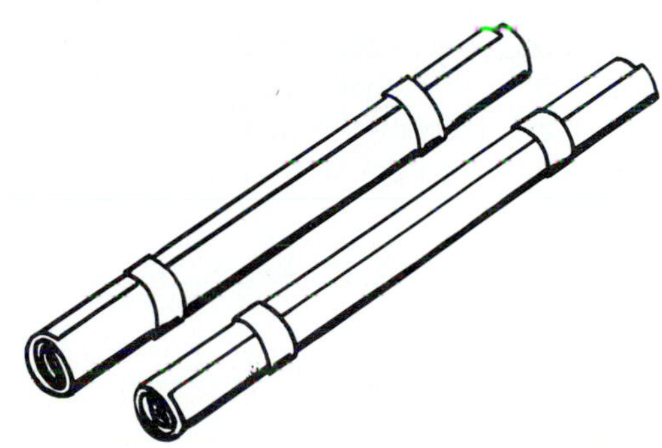

RHYTHM/LUMMI STICKS

1- to 1½-inch dowels cut into 1-foot lengths make good rhythm sticks.

Magazines (*Time* size) or newspapers rolled tightly (1-1½ inches in diameter) and secured with tape make rhythm sticks that are quieter to use.

The sticks may be painted and decorated by the children.

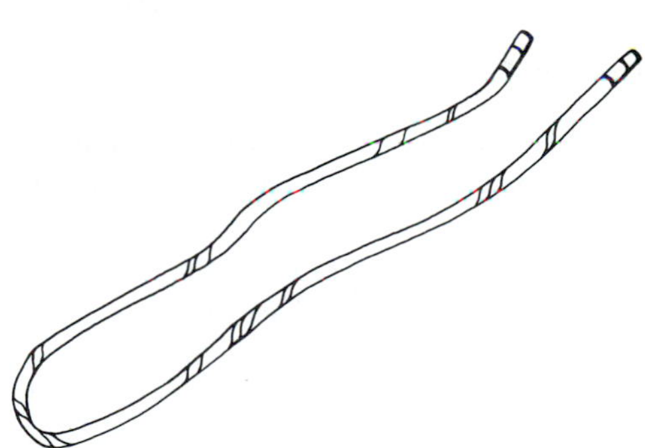

JUMP ROPES

16-pound sash cord or yacht braid (½ inch in diameter) may be cut into 10- to 15-foot lengths for long ropes, and 6-, 7-, and 8-foot lengths for short ropes. Lengths should be color-coded by taping the ends or dipping the ends in paint, which will also prevent fraying.

BEANBAGS

Canvas and denim make ideal covers for beanbags 5 by 6 inches in size filled with small pebbles.

YARN BALLS

Using two cardboard circles (5 inches in diameter) with the center cut out, wrap at least one skein of yarn as shown until the hole in the center is filled. Inserting a scissors between the two circles, carefully cut the yarn around the outer edge of the circle. Secure the yarn by wrapping a light cord between the two circles and tying it tightly. Remove the circles and trim any long ends.

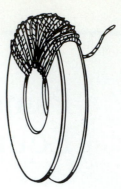

HOOPS/RINGS

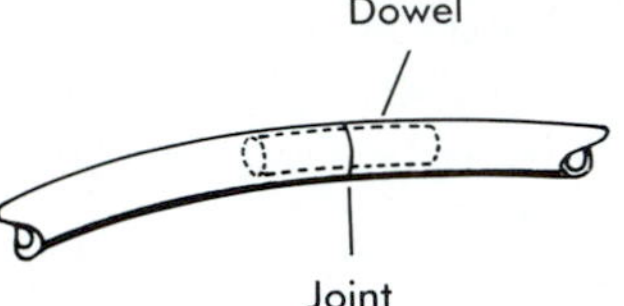

Black plastic water pipe (½ inch) can be used to make hoops of varying sizes. Children may decorate the hoops to make them more pleasing in color. A piece 7 foot 10 inches long makes a hoop approximately 30 inches in diameter. The ends are joined with plastic pipe fittings or a 3-inch piece of ½-inch dowel glued inside the two ends.

One-half inch rubber tubing such as garden hose (18 inches long) will make a smaller ring. The ends are joined by glueing 2-inch pieces of ½-inch dowel into the two ends and covering the joint with colored tape.

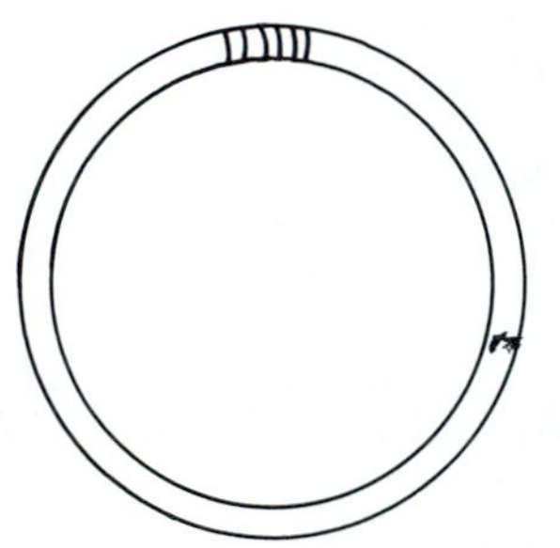

TIN CAN STILTS

Two empty tin cans (No. 10 preferred) may be used to make stilts. Holes are made on opposite sides of each can with a beer can opener. One end of.a piece of rope approximately 60 inches in length is put through the holes and knotted on the outside to form a loop that the children hold while walking on the stilts.

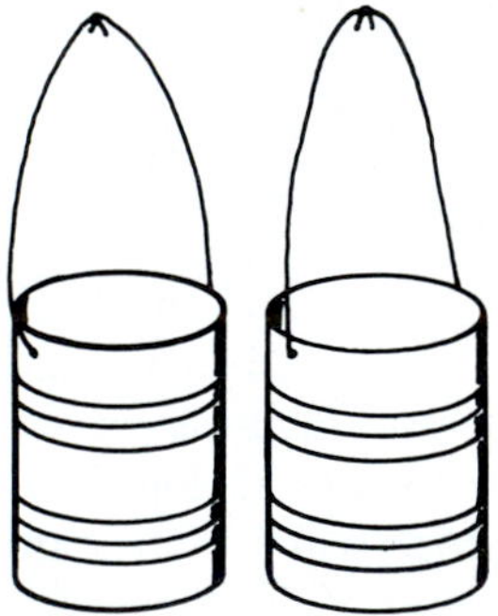

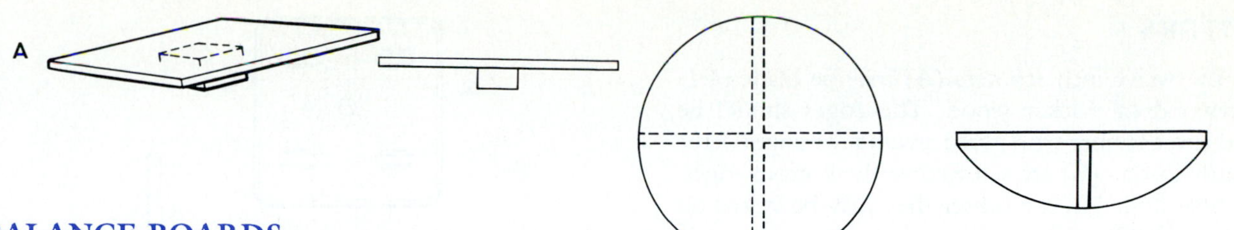

BALANCE BOARDS

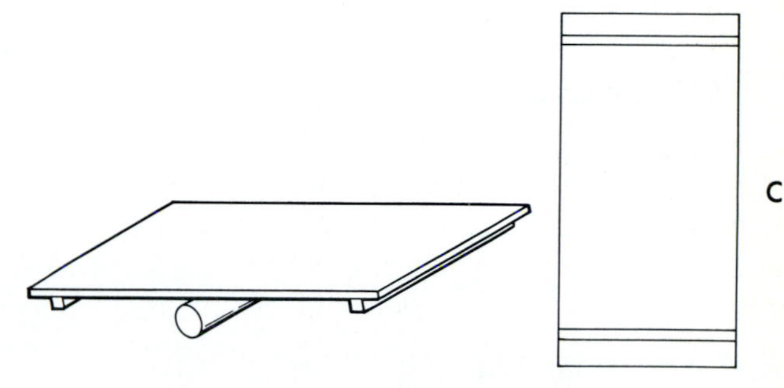

Several different styles of balance boards may be made. A piece of rubber matting should be glued to the top of each to prevent slipping. The boards should be used on mats for safety.

An 18-inch square of ¾-inch plywood **(A)** may be used with several interchangeable bases 6 inches or 3 inches square and 3 inches high.

A round balance board 15 inches in diameter **(B)** with a curved base as shown may also be constructed of ¾-inch plywood.

A rectangular balance board **(C)** may be made using a piece of pole 3 inches in diameter as the base. Strips of 1 by 1 inch wood are glued to the bottom of the board close to the outside edges to prevent the roller from moving outside the board.

PADDLES

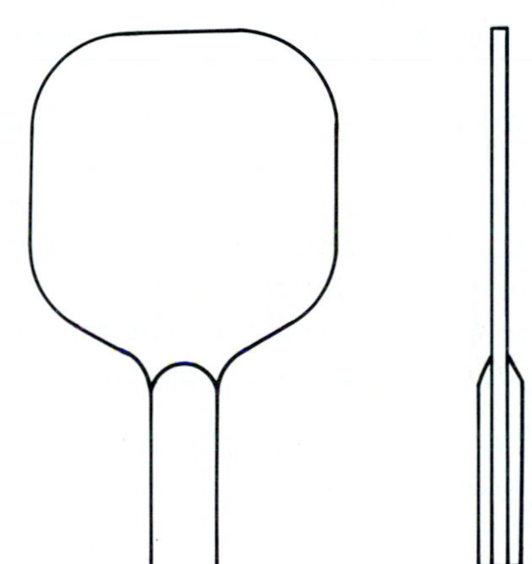

Paddles may be cut from ¼- to ⅜-inch plywood as shown. Each paddle requires a piece of wood 8 × 15 inches in size. The thinner paddle is easiest for young children to handle. The handle should be reinforced by glueing strips ½ inch thick along the handle which are tapered on the paddle end. A hole is drilled at the end of the handle to attach a leather thong.

SCOOPS

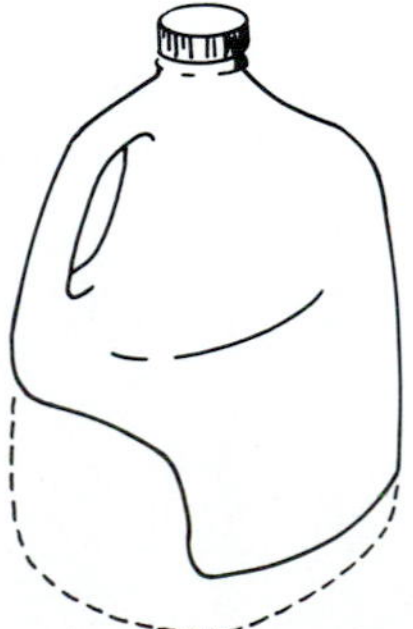

Plastic jugs cut as shown make scoops for catching and throwing small balls.

SCOOTERS

Twelve by twelve inch scooters **(A)** may be made of 1-inch plywood or thicker wood. The edges should be rounded and a rubber strip glued around the edges. Four heavy-duty casters **(B)** are screwed to the bottom edges. With a hole drilled in the center they may be stored on a dowel stand **(C)**.

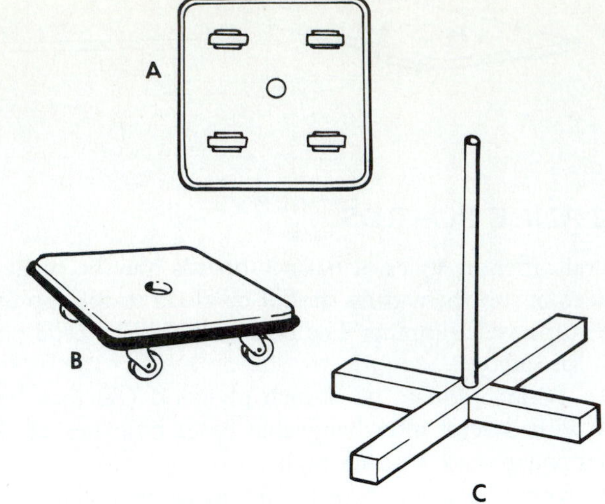

BALANCE BEAM

A low balance beam **(A)** may be made with a hardwood 2 × 4, 10 to 12 feet long supported on a base as illustrated either as a 2- or 4-inch beam. The base may be made of 3 pieces of 1-inch plywood glued together as shown.

An adjustable high beam **(B)** may be made using two 2 × 6s, 12 to 14 feet long glued together with a 1 × 4 piece of hardwood glued to the top and supported as in the diagram on galvanized pipe. Holes are drilled through each section of the base, through which bolts are fastened to regulate the height of the beam. The ends of the base should be taped to prevent scratching the floor.

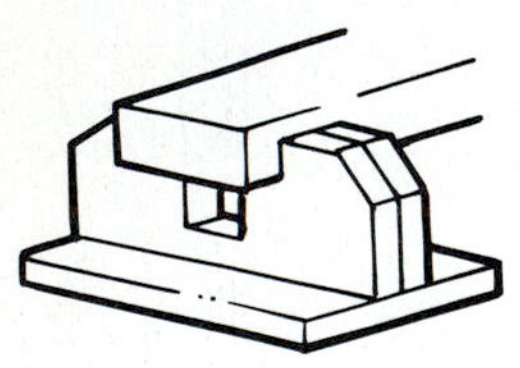

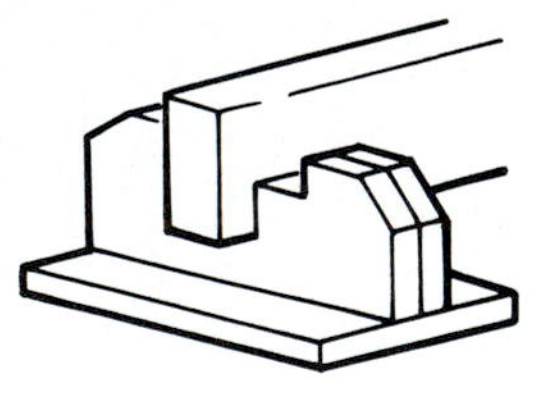

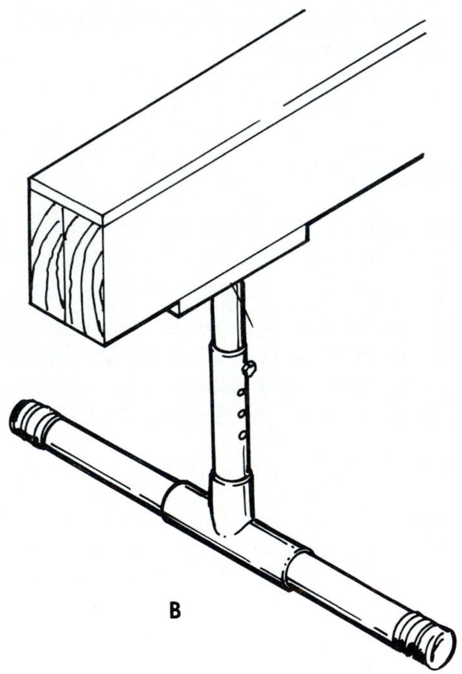

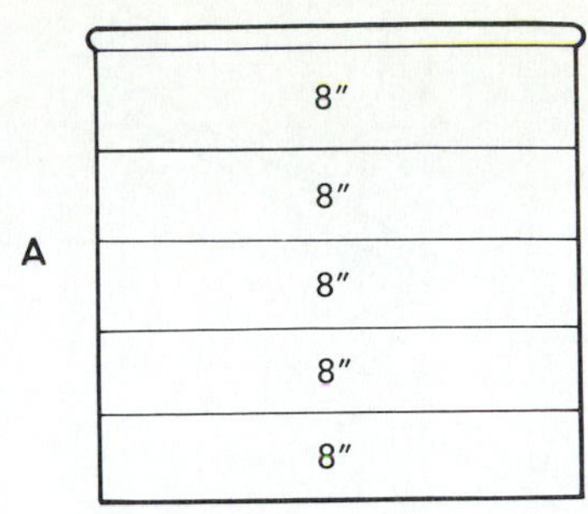

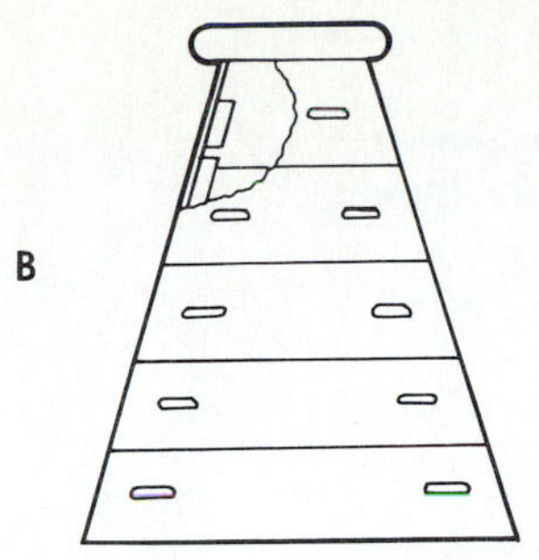

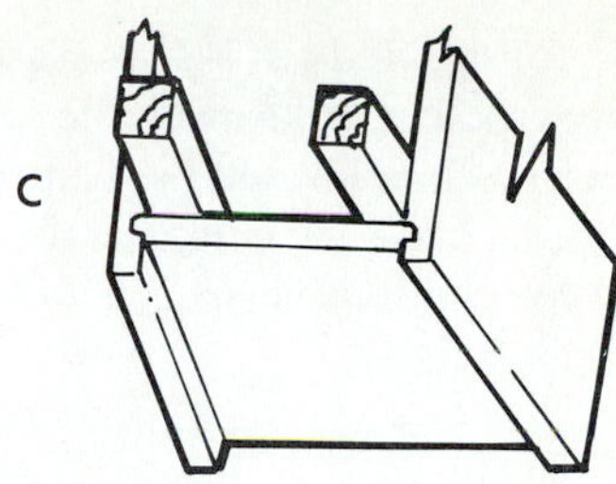

VAULTING BOX

A padded box with 8-inch sections to vary the height as shown provides for children of all sizes. Constructed of ¾-inch plywood, holes in the sides **(B)** make each section easily handled. The top should be padded with foam or sponge rubber with a vinyl or denim cover. Two-by-twos are used on the inside corners and at the center to secure the sections as shown **(C).**

BEAT BOARD

A board to use in vaulting, mounting equipment, or for jumping activities may be made of ¾-inch plywood supported on one end with a 2 × 4 and a 1 × 1 on the other.

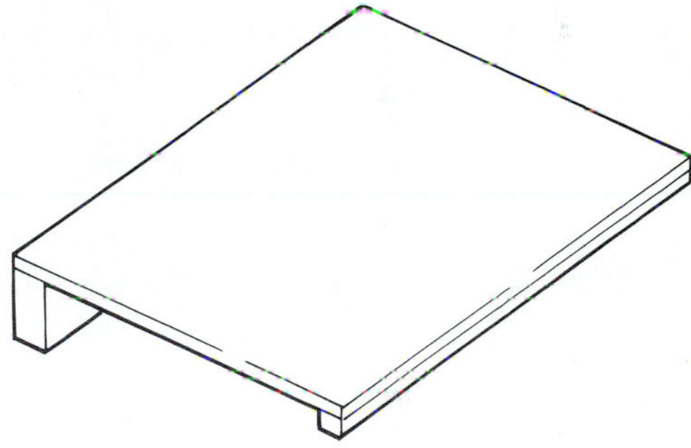

PARALLEL BARS

Parallel bars 4 feet in height may be made of pipe as shown. Adjustments in width between the bars may be made by turning the base, moving one bar slightly forward of the other.

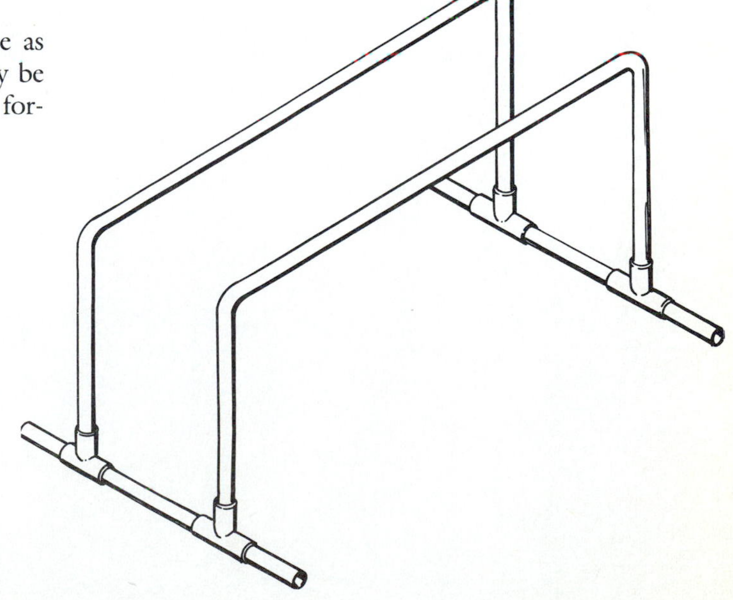

HURDLES

Hurdles constructed of 1-inch plastic pipe with Velcro tear-away crossbars take away the fear of hitting the hurdles. The crossbars should be made of webbing to which Velcro is attached. The height of the hurdles may be easily adjusted for children varying in size and ability.

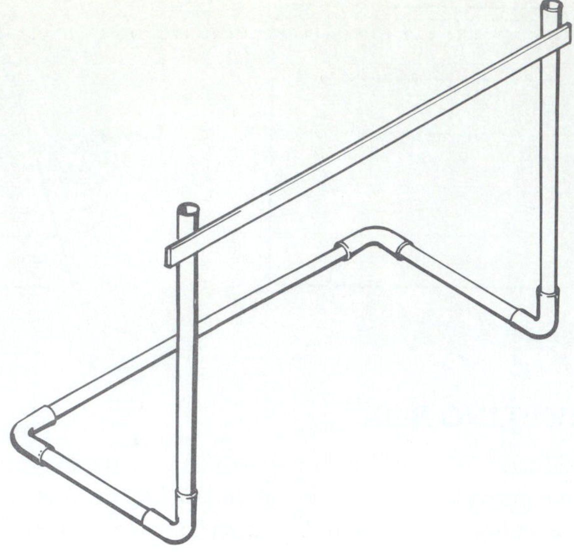

JUMPING PITS

A large net bag filled with foam pieces provides a safe landing surface for the high jump. Several smaller bags laced together may be used to allow for easier storage in the off-season. Inflated innertubes fastened together and covered with a tarp may also provide a safe landing surface.

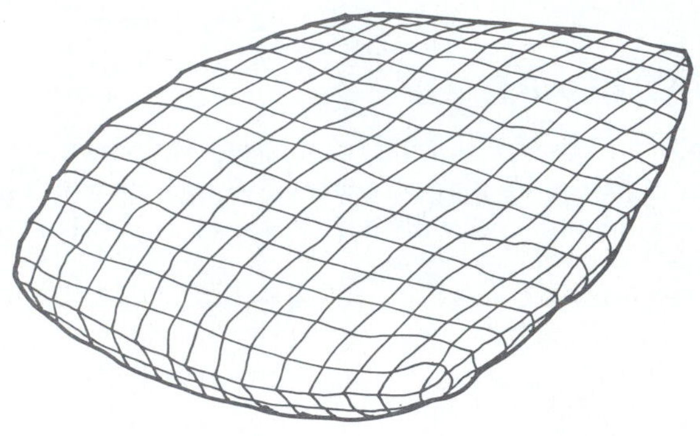

APPENDIX 4

Computer Software

PHYSICAL FITNESS

Physical Best: Program generates individual reports, class records, recommended exercises to improve fitness and an awards tracking program for the physical best fitness test.
Grades K through 6
Apple, IBM
AAHPERD

Personal Body Profile: Determine desirable weight and caloric intake from entry input of age, height, weight, skinfold measures and activity level.
Grade 6
Apple (48K)
CompTech Systems Design

AAHPERD Youth Fitness: Data base management system for administration, management, and analysis of youth fitness test. Several reporting options are available.
Grades 5 and 6
Apple (48K)
CompTech Systems Design

AAPHERD II: Program allows school to enter own norms rather than use 1976 AAHPERD norms. Has some features as AAHPERD youth fitness program above. In addition, student data may be compared to both local and 1976 norms and documentation with step-by-step instructions on how to enter predetermined data tables.
Grades 5 and 6
Apple (48K)
CompTech Systems Design

Health Fitness Profile for Children: Reports raw scores and national norms for AAHPERD Health Related Fitness Test with a graphic presentation of individual fitness profiles.
Grades 1 through 6
Apple II
AAHPERD

Computer Applications of Health Related Physical Fitness Test: Class records management, including viewing, storing, and printing data, locating individual records, determining norms, and producing individual fitness profiles.
Grades 1 through 6
Apple II
AAHPERD

Analysis Health-Related Physical Fitness Test Scores: Displays or prints data for up to 100 students per class, computes percentile norms and class averages, compares pre- and post-test results, and produces individual report cards.
Grades 1 through 6
Apple II
AAHPERD

AAHPERD Youth Fitness Data Base Information Processor: A management system for youth fitness scores of up to 900 students for a period of up to 6 years. Provides percentile norms for student test results and includes fall and spring 3-year reports for individuals and class, and class and individual averages.
Grades 5 and 6
Apple IIe
Networkers

Parkway School District Wellness Profile of Children: Data base management of AAHPERD health-related fitness scores for up to 960 students over a 6-year period. Can produce fall and spring 3-year reports, and compare scores to national and district norms.
Grades 1 through 6
Apple IIe
Parkway School District

Fit America: Physical fitness data base management for the Presidential Challenge Fitness Program, Fitness gram, or AAHPERD Youth Fitness Test.
Grades 4 through 6
Apple, IBM, Macintosh
CompTech Systems Design

Universal Fitness Report: A fitness report generator that allows use of any test battery items and any set of standards desired by the teacher, creating a report of each student's score and a rating and a statement of where improvements need to be made.
Grades K through 6
IBM PC
Persimmon Software

Aerobics: Program allows user to design own exercise program using a variety of exercises and routines. Joystick, Koala Pad, or Paddles necessary to operate this program.
Grade 6
Apple (48K), Atari, Commodore 64
CompTech Systems Design

The Heart: A Mighty Pump: Allows child to follow a red blood cell through the heart and circulatory system. Good prerequisite for Heart and Exercise.
Grades 1 through 6
Apple (48K)
CompTech Systems Design

The Human Pump: The heart and the effects of the food we eat, smoking, and exercise on the heart.
Grades 5 and 6.
Apple II (64K)
Sunburst Communications

Heart and Exercise: Four programs to teach children the heart; role of veins and arteries and effects of exercise; where to find the pulse, and how to take it; and how the heart is affected by participation in various sport activities. Includes a teacher utility program to generate tests and worksheets.
Grade 6
Apple (48K)
CompTech Systems Design

Wellness Pursuit I: Students answer questions on wellness while engaging in a simulated marathon run.
Grades 4 through 6
CompTech Systems Design

PHYSICAL EDUCATION ACTIVITIES

Sports Terminology Series: Program for learning and reinforcing sport vocabulary and definitions. Uses Word Find, Word Game, Spell, and Mix-Up developed by Minnesota Education Computing Consortium. The series may be purchased as a set or as individual disks. Included are: Individual/dual/team sport; Aquatic sports; Swimming and rescue; and Winter sports.
Grades 4 through 6
AppleII/IIe/IIc
CompTech Systems Design

Sports Pursuit Library I: Team sports, introduces sports skill analysis, rules, basic strategies, and terminology; use for class review, pretest or posttest; 50 questions for basketball, baseball/softball, football, ice hockey, soccer, and volleyball.
Grades 4 through 6
Apple (48K)
CompTech Systems Design

Volleyball: Instruction and skill analysis of volleyball skills, strategies, and rules.
Grade 6
Apple (48K)
CompTech Systems Design

MOVEMENT

Right of Way: Introduces and reinforces spatial relationships. Rango the monkey shows children how to know right and left. Activities allow children to use right/left concept in steering cars.
Grades K through 4
Apple (48K)
CompTech Systems Design

MISCELLANEOUS

Round Robin Scheduling: Prints complete schedule of teams, dates and time of game, schedule of facilities, etc.
Apple II (64K)
Good Deal Software

Physical Education Record Keeper: Program to keep records of student progress. Includes biographic and class data, tests and objectives, test scores, indication of objectives still to be met, target goal for each objective, and activity prescription to meet goals not yet attained.
Apple IIe and IIc
Dr. Dick Hurwitz

Physical Skills Manager: Program enables teachers to analyze up to 15 fitness or motor skills of choice, convert raw scores to a range scale (0-10), and chart improvement over time.
CompTech Systems Design

ADDRESSES OF SOURCES

AAHPERD, 1900 Association Drive, Reston, VA 22091, (703)476-3481

CompTech Systems Design, P.O. Box 516, Hastings, MN 55033, (612)437-1350

Dr. Dick Hurwitz, Cleveland State University, Cleveland, OH 44115, (216)687-4878

Good Deal Software, 1721 Skyline Dr., Wenatohee, WA 98801, (509)663-7827

Networkers, 7542 Oxford, Clayton, MO 63105, (314)724-7868

Parkway School District, 455 N. Woods Mill Rd., Chesterfield, MO 63017, (314)851-8100

APPENDIX 5

Screening Devices, Sources, and IEP Forms

AAHPERD Health Related Physical Fitness Test: See Chapter 13.

Bruininks-Oseretsky Motor Development Scale:
Battery of 8 tests to measure gross and fine motor skills including running, speed and agility, balance, bilateral coordination, strength, upper limb coordination, visual-motor response speed, and upper limb speed and dexterity. The complete battery or a short form may be used. Scoring is pass/fail. The score is a composite of all items or a single score if the short form is used.
Source: American Guidance Services, Circle Pines, MN 55014

Denver Developmental Screening Test:
Contains 105 tasks to identify developmental delays in children age zero to 6 in fine motor, gross motor, social, and language skills. The test is administered individually and scored pass/fail, refusal, or no opportunity to respond. Norms indicate the age level when 10, 25, 50, 75, and 90 percent of the children can perform the task.
Source: Frankenberg, W., Dodds, J. & Fandel, A.: Denver Developmental Screening Test manual/workbook for nursing and paramedical personnel, Denver, Colorado, University of Colorado Medical Center.

I CAN: Developed as a program of physical education for the handicapped. The screening tests may be used to determine specific difficulties in technique in a variety of body management, fitness, social, fundamental, and sports skills.
Source: Michigan State University, Lansing, Michigan.

Hyde Motor Development Checklist:
See attached form.
Source: Hyde, B.: A motor development checklist of selected categories for kindergarten children. Unpublished thesis, University of Kansas, 1980.

I Can Physical Education IEP Form

School District/School Central-Westside School

Date Submitted 9/20/77

Student Name or Number Katie - #B123

Date of Planning Meeting 9/1/77

Recommended Total Time in Physical Education 3 Days/Week 30 Minutes/Day

Date(s) of Review (Listed when scheduled)

Current Placement Special Physical Education - TMI

Teachers Ronald Kowalski

	Program goal areas in physical education	Present level(s) of performance	Annual student goals	Short term objectives	Time required (min/day)	Duration dates		Regular education placement	Special designed instruction	Support personnel needed (see back)	Goal attained (date)
						Begin	End				
Area 1	Body management	Body planes-2.a,c	3. a,b,c	2.b/3.a,b,c	10	9/20	10/20	√			
		Forward roll-1.c	3. a,b	1.a,b/2.a,b,c/3.a,b	20	1/4	1/18		√	√	
Area 2	Fundamental skills	Gallop-primary	2.	1./2.	10	9/20	11/4		√		
		Kick-2.a	3. a,b,c	2.b/3.a,b,c	15	4/15	5/15	√			
		Overhand throw-primary	3. a,b,c	1.a,b/2.a,b/3.a,b,c	15	3/15	4/15		√	√	
Area 3	Fitness	Heart/lung endurance-primary	3.	1./2./3.	2	9/20	6/15		√	√	
Area 4	Sport/Leisure	Dribbling-primary	2. a,b	1.a,b,c/2.a,b	15	1/18	2/18		√		
		Batting-2.a,b	3. c,d	3.a,b,c,d	15	5/15	6/15	√			
Area 5	Social skills	Take turns-2.c,d	3. a,b	3.a,b	5	9/20	6/15	√			

Continued.

Short Term Instructional Objectives	Personnel Responsible Including Related Support Personnel Needed (name and title)	Date Services Begin	Date Services End
Forward roll	Physical Therapist	10/5	To be determined at review meeting
Overhand throw	Occupational Therapist	1/4	3/15
Heart/lung endurance	Physical Therapist Regular Physical Education--Intramurals	9/20	6/15

Date of parental acceptance/rejection

Signature

DETROIT PUBLIC SCHOOLS
Individualized Educational Program
Phase II
Local School Planning and Implementation

DATE:________________________________

TO BE COMPLETED:
- Determination of Educational Goals/Instructional Objectives/School Services
- Referrals for Related Services, as Appropriate
- Educational Provisions in the Least Restrictive Environment
- Program Monitoring and Review Provisions

I. Pupil Information

Name ______________ ______________ Birthdate__________

Student Height ______________ Weight__________

D.P.S. Student Membership Number __________

Parent/Guardian/Parent Surrogate __________

Address, Zip Code __________

Telephone (Home) ______________ (Work)__________

School__________

Grade/Program__________

II. Phase II IEP Implementation Team

Position	Name	Signature
Chairperson		
Parent/Guardian		
Parent Surrogate		
Instructional		
Administration		
Student (as Appropriate)		
Other		
Other		

Program Monitoring and Review Provisions

	Date	Date	Date	Date
Local School Administrator				
Special Education Supervisor				
Parent				
General Education Teacher				
Other				

Annual Program Review Meeting
(see attached rec.)

Date:__________

Review Team Member:

Name	Position

III.	Referral Recommendations for Related Services Referral for Evaluation only				To Be Completed by Person Responsible for Delivering Requested Service		
√	Requested Program or Service	Projected Duration of Service From : To	Person Responsible for Initiating Referral	Date Referral Initiated	Date Service Initiated	Person Responsible for Delivering Service	Comments
	Speech Pathology	:					
	Bilingual Instruction	:					
	Occ./Phys. Therapy	:					
	Audiology	:					
	School Social Work	:					
	School Psychology	:					
	Vocational	:					
	Diagnostic/Remedial/ Tutorial Services Available In Region or Local School Type of Service Requested	:					
	Other:	:					

IV. As required in P.L. 94-142 statutes, handicapped children must be provided with a physical education program. John Smith, Adaptive Physical Education Specialist, Special Education Department is available to provide supportive assistance to local school personnel in developing, modifying, adapting or improving physical education programs to meet the needs of handicapped students. Mr. Smith may be reached at 555-5555.

√	Physical Education Program	Projected Duration of Service From : To	Person Responsible for Physical Education Program	Comments
	Regular Physical Education Program	:		
	• Selected Activities in Physical Education Program	:		
	• Self Contained Physical Education Program	:		
	• Supportive reports and documentation must be available to support the decision for the selected physical education program option.			

MOTOR DEVELOPMENT CHECKLIST

Name ____________________ Examiner ____________________
Birthdate __________ Sex _____ Date ____________________

Category	Special Notes and Remarks		
Static balance	__does not attempt tasks	__heel-toe stand, 5 secs balance on preferred foot, arms hung relaxed at sides __ __ __ __ __5 secs __ __ __ __ __10 secs	__heel-toe stand, eyes closed, 5 secs balance on preferred foot, arms hung relaxed at sides, eyes closed __5 secs __ __ __ __ __10 secs
Hopping reflex	__no response __no righting of head, __trunk no step in direction of push __right __left __forward __backward	__head and body right themselves __step or hop in direction of push, __right __left __forward __backward	
Running pattern	__loses balance __almost __twists trunk __leans excessively __jerky, uneven rhythm	__elbows away from body in arm swing __limited arm swing __short strides	__full arm swing in opposition with legs __elbows near body in swing __even flow and rhythm
Jumping pattern	__loses balance on landing __no use of arms __twists or bends sideways	__arms at side for balance __legs bent throughout jump	__arms back as legs bend __arms swing up as legs extend __lands softly with control
Throwing pattern	__pushing or shoving object __loss of balance __almost	__body shifts weight from back to front without stepping	__steps forward with same foot as throwing arm __steps forward with foot opposite throwing arm
Catching pattern	__loses balance __almost __shies away __traps or scoops	__arms stiff in front of body	__arms bent at sides of body __arms "give" as catch __uses hands
Kicking pattern	__misses __off center	__arms at sides or out to sides __uses from knee down to kick	__kicks "through" ball __arm opposition __uses full leg to kick __can kick with either foot

APPENDIX 6

Accident and Medical Forms

SAMPLE FORM FOR ACCIDENT REPORT

ACCIDENT REPORT

Date ______________ School ________________

Name ________________________________ Age _____ Sex F _____ M _____

Parent (guardian) ____________________________ Insurance Yes __ No __

Address ____________________________________ Company ______________

____________________________________ Phone ________________

____

Activity ______________________________ Time of injury ______________

Nature of injury (include type and body parts involved)

Example: Abrasion—right knee, right elbow

____

____

Treatment given ____

____

____

Recommendation for further treatment _____________________________

____

Under what conditions did the accident occur? _______________________

____

____

Where did the accident occur (facility)? ___________________________

Probable cause of injury ____

____

____

Witnessed by ____

____

Signature of person completing report

SAMPLE FORM FOR CLEARANCE FOR PARTICIPATION IN PHYSICAL EDUCATION

PHYSICAL EDUCATION PARTICIPATION EXAMINATION

I have examined ______________________________ on ____________ and

__________ recommend unrestricted participation in vigorous physical education activities.

__________ recommend the following restrictions for participation in physical education activities.

____
Physician's signature

____

____
Physician's address

____
Parent's signature

APPENDIX 7

Tools to Assess Teacher Effectiveness

LESSON EVALUATION

Answer each question, citing examples.

The Objective

Was the objective clear?

Was the objective appropriate (based on the description of class level)?

Did it challenge cognitive as well as motor ability?

The Lesson

How did the teacher establish set?

What was the mode of presentation?

Was the mode of presentation effective?

What questions were used to check understanding and encourage thinking?

Was the activity challenging?

Provide maximum learning?

Encourage correct form?

Individualize learning?

Encourage thinking?

What feedback was given to the group?

To individual children?

Did the teacher monitor the activity? How?

Were any adjustments made?

Was there closure? What was summarized? What needs were identified?

TIME MANAGEMENT STUDY

Management (M): The time taken to get the class ready for instruction, to secure and put away equipment, to move the children into various formations, and to line up at the end of the class.

Instruction (I): The time given to explaining the day's objectives, to going over important teaching points with the whole class, etc.

Activity (A): The time spent working on concepts, practicing skills, using concepts and skills in games, etc.

1. Tape a 30 minute lesson. (If possible have someone call out minute intervals while you are taping.)
2. Play the tape that recorded the aspects outlined above and fill in the form provided below.
3. Analyze the tape and consider the appropriateness of the time spent on each aspect of the lesson.
4. Conclude with any suggestions for changes in management you feel are warranted.

Example:

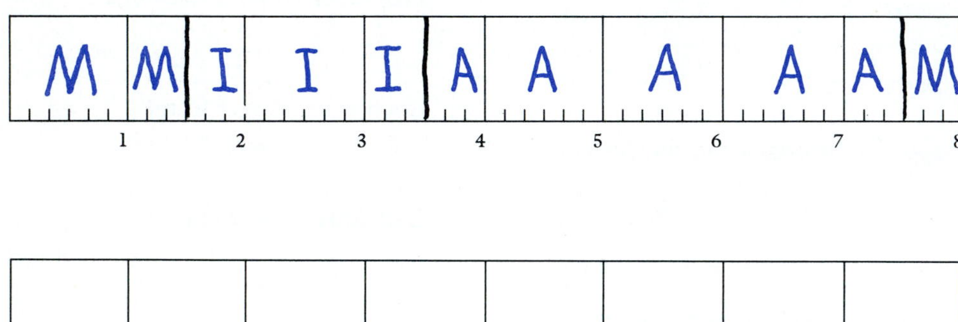

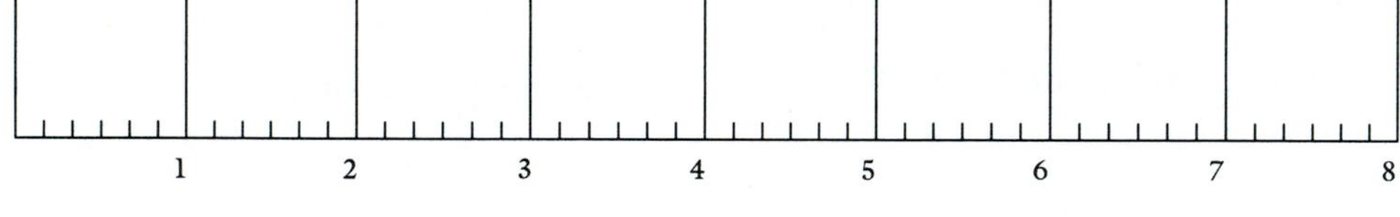

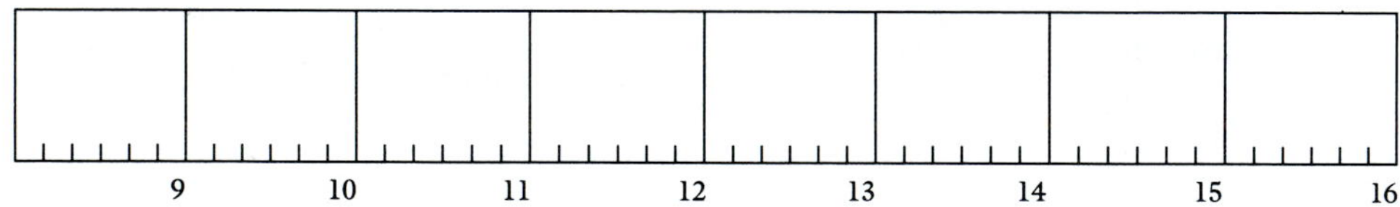

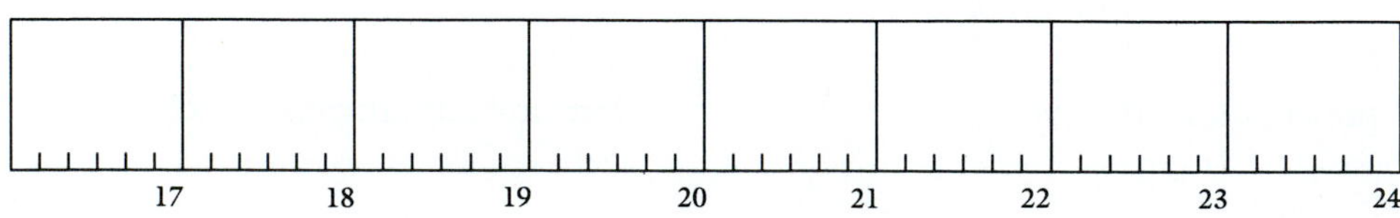

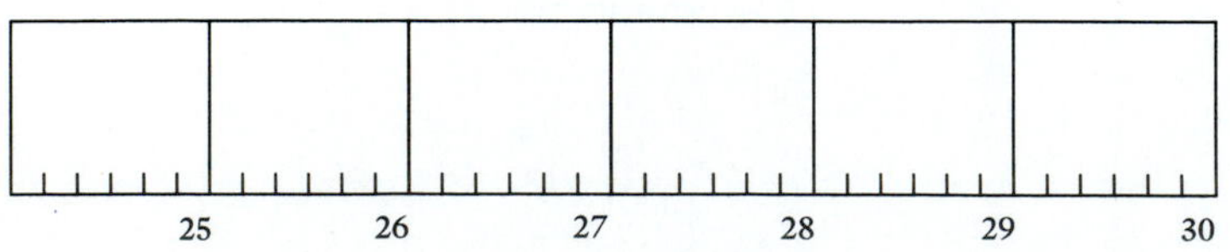

FEEDBACK

Feedback regarding performance is an important aspect of learning in physical education. Knowledge of performance (KP) should provide students with important information needed at their level of skill, which in turn assists students in attending to relevant cues.

Feedback may be *general* (Good job!) or *specific* (I like the way you pointed to the target!). It may be *behavior oriented* (John, are you listening?) or *related to skill or concept* (Step forward as you throw.) It may be *positive* (Good use of the legs in absorbing force, or, I like the way Joe is listening.) or *corrective* (You didn't follow through, or Don't do that!). Obviously, specific, positive feedback is more conducive to learning. Unfortunately, much feedback is of a very general nature.

This observation will be an example of interval and event recording. The events (feedback) will be recorded on the form provided. The intervals used will be 3 minutes long. For example, you will record feedback for 3 minutes, then observe only for 3 minutes, record feedback the next 3 minutes, then observe only the next, etc.

Record feedback as follows:

Column—To whom: Indicate girl or boy and name, number students or indicate what they are wearing to differentiate specific children in the class. (Example: Jim, boy no. 3, girl in green pants)

Column—Regarding: Indicate when feedback is related to the lesson objective (what skill or concept etc.), behavior or something else. Indicate if it was positive with (a) + or corrective (c) or negative (−).

Column—General/Specific: Concisely list the feedback given (Good job!, Grip ball in fingers, etc.).

Discuss the observation findings in detail including:

The total number of responses for each column including positive and negative responses in regarding columns.

Who received the feedback?

What was the nature of the feedback?

Did the feedback provide important information?

Did it help students attend to relevant cues?

Any other comments.

FEEDBACK RECORDING

Class ______________ Activity ____________________ Date ______________

To whom	Regarding			General	Specific
	Objective	Behavior	Other		

TEACHER QUESTIONING/STUDENT RESPONSE

On the form provided record the following:

1. The questions asked by the teacher.
2. The following regarding the questions:
   a. To whom was the question asked? The class? A male student? A female student? (not who answered).
   b. Did the question focus on: student behavior? A skill objective? A concept objective?
   c. What was the nature of the student response? Who responded? a male, female, or the class? What was the nature of their response? Non-verbal, such as nodding? Verbal? A change in behavior, such as improved listening, other social behavior or improved or worse skill performance?
   d. Was the response appropriate or inappropriate?
   e. During which part of the lesson was the question used? the opening, introduction or review of a skill or concept, during the practice session, during transition, in closure.

Answer each of the following questions in as much depth as possible giving specific examples where necessary.

3. What was the general nature of the questions? What does that tell you about the class? The teacher?
4.
   a. If only a few questions were used, what other opportunities were there where the teacher might have used questions?
   b. What other questions could have been given?
5. Add any comments you think might be needed to clarify your responses.

TEACHER QUESTIONS AND OBSERVATION

Question	To whom was the question asked			Regarding			Who responded			Student response					Part of the lesson	Additional comments
	Class	Male	Female	Skill	Concept	Behavior	Class	Male	Female	Verbal	Nonverbal	Change in behavior	No change	Appropriate/ inappropriate		

Index

DANCE ACTIVITIES

American and International Folk Dance

Creative Dance

Dance Figures

Dance Steps

Line Dance

Native American Dances

Rhythmic Activities

Singing Games

Square Dance

GAME ACTIVITIES

Ball Games and Games Using Other Objects

Basketball

Field and Floor Hockey

Flag Football

Hand and Paddle Games

Running and Tag Games

Soccer

Softball

Volleyball

INDIVIDUAL ACTIVITIES
Gymnastics

Small Equipment

Track and Field

COOPERATIVE GAMES

MULTICULTURAL ACTIVITIES

Credits and Acknowledgments

CHAPTER 1 Physical Education in the Elementary School
p. 4 From the Columbus Public Schools: Cedarwood Alternative School and Devonshire Alternative School, Columbus, Ohio; Project Adventure, Inc., Hamilton, Mass. **p. 5** Reproduced with permission from the American Alliance for Health, Physical Education, Recreation, and Dance, Reston, Va.

CHAPTER 2 The Elementary School Child
pp. 16, 17 Courtesy Ross Laboratories. Adapted from Hamill PVV, Drizd TA, Johnson CL, Reed RB, Roche AF, Moore WM: Physical Growth: National Center for Health Statistics percentiles, *Am J Clin Nutr* 32:607-629, 1979. Data from the National Center for Health Statistics (NCHS), Hyattsville, Maryland: HRA25, June 22, 1976, US Department of Health, Education, and Welfare. **p. 18** Art modified from John V. Hagen, for Seeley R, Stephens T, Tate P: *Anatomy & physiology,* ed 2, St. Louis, 1992, Mosby–Year Book. **p. 20** Used with permission from Tuddenham R, Snyder M: Physical growth of California boys and girls from birth to eighteen, Berkeley, Calif, 1954, University of California Press.

CHAPTER 3 The Elementary School Physical Education Program
p. 36 From Logsden B et al: *Physical education for children: a focus on the teaching process,* ed 2, Philadelphia, 1984, Lea & Febiger.

CHAPTER 4 Teaching Across the Elementary School Curriculum
p. 51 From the Westgate Alternative School of Academic and Physical Excellence, Columbus, Ohio.

CHAPTER 8 Safety, Organizational Strategies, and Class Management
pp. 116, 117 From Cooper J et al: *Classroom teaching skills: a handbook,* ed 2, Lexington, Mass, 1982, DC Heath & Co. Adapted from *Classroom management: theory and skill training,* Lois Johnson and Mary Bany, New York, 1970, MacMillan Publishing Co.

CHAPTER 10 Meeting the Special Needs of Children
p. 137 Courtesy United Cerebral Palsy of Vermont: Choosing words with dignity.

CHAPTER 14 Developing Social Skills
p. 226 From Hellison D: *Goals and strategies for teaching physical education,* Champaign, Ill, 1985, Human Kinetics Publishers. **p. 230** From Loridas L: *Culture in the classroom, a cultural enlightenment manual for educators,* 1988, Michigan State Department of Education, Lansing, Wayne County Intermediate School District, Detroit, Michigan.

CHAPTER 15 Fitness, Stress Reduction, and Movement Efficiency
p. 251 *(bottom)* From the Greatest College Football Marches, VSD 29/30, Vanguard Record Society, Inc, 171 West 23rd St, New York, NY 10010. **p. 256** From Seltzer C, Mayer J: A simple criterion of obesity, *Postgraduate Medicine* 38:101A, 1965. **pp. 258** *(top),* **265** Adapted from Kendall H et al: *Posture and pain,* Huntington, NY, 1975, Robert E Krieger Publishing Co, Inc. **p. 261** *(top right)* From AAHPERD: *Health-related physical fitness test manual,* Reston, Va, 1980, AAHPERD. Reprinted by permission of the American Alliance for Health, Physical Education, Recreation and Dance, 1900 Association Drive, Reston, VA, 22091. **p. 263** *(bottom)* From Vermont Modified Pull-Up Test from Vermont Governor's Council on Physical Fitness and Sport: School Fitness Manual, 1982, Montpelier, Vt, State Department of Education. **p. 263** *(top right)* From A new test of upper body strength and endurance, by JK Nelson and KR Nelson, *Teaching Elementary School Physical Education,* 4(1):12-13. With material reprinted with permission from *The Research Quarterly for Exercise and Sport,* 62:4436-4441. *The Research Quarterly for Exercise and Sport* is a publication of the American Alliance for Health, Physical Education, Recreation, and Dance, 1900 Association Drive, Reston, VA 22091. Copyright 1993 by Human Kinetics Publishers. Adapted and reprinted by permission.

CHAPTER 21 Singing Games and American and International Folk Dance
pp. 429, 430 Instructions for Native American dances courtesy of Kimbo Educational, Long Branch, NJ.

CHAPTER 22 Rhythmic Activities with Small Equipment
p. 441 Chinese Ribbon Dance from Twinson Company, 1289-E Reamwood Avenue, Sunnyvale, CA 94089.

CHAPTER 32 School Activities and Youth Sports
p. 659 From Martens R, Seefeldt V, editors: Guidelines for children's sports, Reston, Va, 1979, AAHPERD. Reprinted by permission of the American Alliance for Health, Physical Education, Recreation and Dance, 1900 Association Drive, Reston, Virginia, 22091.

Appendices
pp. 684, 685 From I CAN Physical Education, Janet A. Wessel, Director, copyright 1976 Michigan State University. Reprinted with permission of publisher, Hubbard Scientific Publishing Co, Northbrook, Illinois. **pp. 686, 687** Used with permission from Detroit Public Schools. **p. 688** Courtesy Beverly Hyde.